1995 PGA TOUR

Official Media Guide of the PGA TOUR

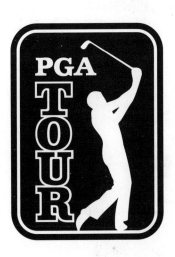

TRIUMPH BOOKS
CHICAGO

TABLE OF CONTENTS

A BRIEF HISTORY OF THE PGA TOUR

It is not always easy to discover the exact beginning of something. So it is with the PGA TOUR. Certainly there were professionals who competed against each other from the earliest days of the game.

In 1895, 10 professional golfers and one amateur played in the first U.S. Open in Newport, RI. Shortly thereafter, tournaments began to pop up across the country. There was the Western Open in 1899. But this was not "tour" golf. The events lacked continuity.

Interest in the game, however, continued to grow. American professionals were rapidly improving. And when John McDermott became the first American-born player to win the U.S. Open, enthusiasm for the game blossomed.

Adding to this growth was a commercially backed exhibition by Englishmen Harry Vardon and Ted Ray. The duo travelled across the country and attracted good crowds wherever they stopped during the warmer months of 1913. A 20-year-old, Francis Ouimet, defeated the pair in a playoff for the United States Open Championship at Brookline, MA. Suddenly golf became front page news and a game for everyone.

In the early '20s, the PGA TOUR saw its first development. Tournaments were held on the West Coast, Texas and Florida. These events were held in the winter, and the golfers played their way east and up to Pinehurst in the spring. By the middle of the decade, the TOUR was doing relatively well--offering $77,000 in total prize money.

The TOUR became more structured following World War II and exploded in the late 1950s and early '60s. Flip through the **Facts and Figures** section of this book and look at such areas as leading money winners and rising tournament purses to witness the continuing growth.

When television became a player in the game, the eyes of the world were on golf. This exposure inspired millions to try the game and, at the same time, TV rights fees sent purses soaring. The bulk of these rights fees, which are distributed by the PGA TOUR to all co-sponsors, have gone back into the purses, accounting for the tripling of prize money in the last decade.

The touring professionals began to gain control of the TOUR in late 1968. Joseph C. Dey was the first Commissioner of what was then called the Tournament Players Division. He served from early 1969 through February 28, 1974, and was succeeded by Deane R. Beman, who took office March 1, 1974.

During Beman's administration, the value of tournament purses escalated at an unprecedented rate: PGA TOUR assets grew from $730,000 in 1974 to over $200 million, and total revenues increased from $3.9 million to $229 million in 1993.

Timothy W. Finchem, previously the TOUR's Deputy Commissioner and Chief Operating Officer, became third Commissioner on June 1, 1994.

Since 1938, PGA TOUR events have donated more than $250 million dollars to charity. Of that total, $109 million has been raised in the 1990s. The 1994 season produced a one-year record $24,701,631 for charity.

The competitive scope of the PGA TOUR also is much broader today. The Senior PGA TOUR is considered by many the sports success story of the 1980s. In 1995, the NIKE TOUR will enjoy its sixth season as a proving ground for professionals, taking golf to 30 additional markets.

Also continuing to grow is the Tournament Players Club Network. When the PGA TOUR opened the Tournament Players Club at Sawgrass in 1980, it introduced the era of Stadium Golf and record-breaking attendance. Owned and operated by the TOUR, the concept means these courses are the only major league sports arenas owned by the players themselves. The TPC Network now includes facilities in Japan, Thailand and China as well as the United States.

CHRONOLOGY OF PGA TOUR

1895 --	First U.S. Open (won by Horace Rawlins) played at Newport (RI) Golf Club
1899 --	Inaugural Western Open (won by Willie Smith) played at Glenview (IL) Golf Club
1900 --	Harry Vardon tour of United States generates widespread interest in game
1913 --	Francis Ouimet captures U.S. Open playoff with Vardon and Ted Ray
1914 --	Walter Hagen wins first of 11 major titles in U.S. Open at Midlothian Country Club outside Chicago
1916 --	PGA of America formed
	Jim Barnes wins first PGA Championship over Jock Hutchison at Siwanoy CC in Bronxville, NY
1922 --	Gene Sarazen (20) becomes youngest ever to win U.S. Open (Skokie Country Club in Glencoe, IL); also wins PGA Championship (Oakmont CC), becoming first to hold both titles at once
1926 --	Los Angeles Open offers $10,000 purse
1927 --	First Ryder Cup matches played, won by United States (Worcester (MA) Country Club)
1930 --	Bob Harlow named manager of PGA Tournament Bureau and broaches idea of year-round tournament circuit; raises annual purse money on the Tour from $77,000 to $130,000 in first year on job; instrumental in creating volunteer system by which TOUR functions to this day; Code of Conduct drawn up

A Brief History of the PGA TOUR, continued

1931 -- Golf Ball and Golf Club Manufacturers Association puts up $5,000 to support sponsors during 1931-32 winter swing

1932 -- "Playing Pros" organization formed, pre-dating by 36 years formation of current PGA TOUR organization

1933 -- Hershey Chocolate Company, at least unofficially, first corporate sponsor on PGA TOUR with Hershey Open

1934 -- Group of players meets to discuss possibilities of year-round tournament circuit

Horton Smith wins first Masters at Augusta National Golf Club

Leading money winner for year Paul Runyan earns $6,767

1937 -- First Bing Crosby Pro-Am/"Clambake" played at San Diego's Rancho Santa Fe CC

Sam Snead becomes nationally recognized figure in golf by winning Oakland Open

1938 -- Palm Beach Invitational makes first TOUR contribution to charity, $10,000

1945 -- Byron Nelson captures 11 consecutive tournaments, seven other official events and one unofficial, a total of 19 wins in one year; voted 1945 Athlete of Year

Tam O'Shanter All-American offers $60,000 purse

1947 -- U.S. Open televised live in St. Louis area

1949 -- Ben Hogan critically injured in head-on collision with Greyhound bus

1950 -- Hogan returns to competitive golf in Los Angeles Open, starting with two-under-par 34 and eventual 280 total tied by Sam Snead; loses playoff ten days later

1953 -- Hogan wins only British Open he ever played

Lew Worsham wins first PGA TOUR event to appear live on national television, Tam O'Shanter World Championship

Golf's "color barrier" broken with PGA constitutional amendment allowing for "Approved Entries," non-members who could play in tournaments if invited by sponsors

1954 -- USGA begins to televise U.S. Open for national audience

"All-Star Golf," first series of matches between pros filmed for television, debuts

1955 -- World Championship of Golf offers first $100,000 purse in PGA TOUR history

1961 -- Caucasians-only clause stricken from PGA constitution; PGA TOUR officially integrated

"Shell's Wonderful World of Golf" begins nine-year run

1965 -- Inaugural Qualifying School held at PGA National Golf Club in Palm Beach Gardens, FL; John Schlee first medalist

1968 -- Association of Professional Golfers (APG), an autonomous tournament players' organization, forms in breakaway from PGA

As compromise, Tournament Players Division of PGA formed under aegis of 10-man policy board late in year

1969 -- Joe Dey becomes first Commissioner of Tournament Players Division

1974 -- Deane Beman succeeds Dey as Commissioner on March 1

Jack Nicklaus captures inaugural Tournament Players Championship (now THE PLAYERS Championship) at Atlanta CC

1977 -- Al Geiberger records first sub-60 round in PGA TOUR history on June 10, a 59 in Danny Thomas Memphis Classic at Colonial CC

1978 -- First "Legends of Golf" played at Onion Creek CC in Austin, TX, precursor of Senior PGA TOUR

1979 -- PGA TOUR Headquarters relocated from Washington, D.C. to Ponte Vedra Beach, Fl

1980 -- Senior PGA TOUR organized with four tournaments

First Tournament Players Club opens, the TPC at Sawgrass in Ponte Vedra, FL

1983 -- All-Exempt TOUR put in place, virtually eliminating Monday qualifying; top 125 players exempt

Tournament Players Series (TPS) begins three-year run

PGA TOUR Pension Program begins

1985 -- PGA TOUR Productions created

1986 -- Panasonic Las Vegas Invitational offers first $1 million purse in PGA TOUR history

1987 -- PGA TOUR surpasses $100 million in charitable contributions

1988 -- 30 players compete at Pebble Beach for $2 million in Nabisco Championships, predecessor of THE TOUR Championship

1990 -- Ben Hogan Tour comes into existence as developmental circuit, succeeded by NIKE TOUR beginning in 1993

1991 -- Chip Beck matches Geiberger's 1977 feat on October 11, carding a 59 at Sunrise Golf Club during Las Vegas Invitational

1992 -- PGA TOUR surpasses $200 million in charitable contributions

1993 -- The PGA TOUR boasts a record five $1 million winners

1994 -- Tim Finchem succeeds Beman as Commissioner on June 1

Inaugural Presidents Cup Match played; U.S. defeats Internationals 20-12

1995 PGA TOUR TOURNAMENT SCHEDULE

Date	Tournament Dir./Media Contact	Location	Official/Total Money	Pro-Am	TV	1994 Winner
Jan. 5-8	**Mercedes Championships** Mike Crosthwaite/Sarah Suggs 619/348-9111 x4612	La Costa Resort & Spa 2100 Costa del Mar Road Carlsbad, CA 92009	$1,000,000/$1,010,000	$10,000	ABC	Phil Mickelson
Jan. 12-15	**United Airlines Hawaiian Open** Chester Kahapea/Bill Bachran 808/526-1232	Waialae Country Club 4997 Kahala Avenue Honolulu, HI 96816	$1,200,000/$1,210,000	$10,000	TBS	Brett Ogle
Jan. 19-22	**Northern Telecom Open** Judy McDermott/Tim Stilb 602/571-0400	Tucson National Golf Resort Starr Pass Golf Club 2727 West Club Drive Tucson, AZ 85741	$1,250,000/$1,265,000	$15,000	ESPN	Andrew Magee
Jan. 26-29	**Phoenix Open** John Lewis/Drew Wathey 602/870-0163	TPC of Scottsdale 17020 N. Hayden Road Scottsdale, AZ 85255	$1,300,000/$1,307,500	$7,500	ESPN	Bill Glasson
Feb. 2-5	**AT&T Pebble Beach National Pro-Am** Louis Russo/Cathy Scherzer 408/649-1533	Pebble Beach Golf Links Spyglass Hill Golf Club Poppy Hills Golf Club 17 Mile Drive Pebble Beach, CA 93953	$1,400,000/$1,470,000	$70,000	CBS	Johnny Miller
Feb. 9-12	**Buick Invitational of California** Tom Wilson/Rick Schloss 619/281-4653	Torrey Pines Golf Courses 11480 Torrey Pines Road La Jolla, CA 92037	$1,200,000/$1,215,000	$15,000	NBC	Craig Stadler
Feb. 15-19	**Bob Hope Chrysler Classic** Edward Heorodt 619/346-8184	Bermuda Dunes Country Club Indian Wells Country Club LaQuinta Country Club Indian Ridge Country Club 42-360 Adams Street Bermuda Dunes, CA 92201	$1,200,000/$1,221,000	$21,000	NBC	Scott Hoch
Feb. 23-26	**Nissan Open** Tom Pulchinski/Toby Zwikel 213/482-1311	Riviera Country Club 1250 Capri Drive Pacific Palisades, CA 90272	$1,200,000/$1,207,500	$7,500	CBS	Corey Pavin
Mar. 2-5	**Doral-Ryder Open** Scott Montgomery/Judy Janofsky 305/477-4653	Doral Country Club (Blue Course) 4400 NW 87th Avenue Miami, FL 33178	$1,500,000/$1,507,500	$7,500	CBS	John Huston
Mar. 9-12	**Honda Classic** Cliff Danley/Gary Ferman 305/384-6000	Weston Hills Country Club 2608 Country Club Way Ft. Lauderdale, FL 33332	$1,200,000/$1,207,500	$7,500	NBC	Nick Price

1995 PGA TOUR TOURNAMENT SCHEDULE *continued*

Date	Tournament Dir./Media Contact	Location	Official/Total Money	Pro-Am	TV	1994 Winner
Mar. 16-19	**The Nestle Invitational** Jim Bell/Bob Fowler 407/876-2888	Bay Hill Club and Lodge 9000 Bay Hill Boulevard Orlando, FL 32819	$1,200,000/$1,207,500	$7,500	NBC	Loren Roberts
Mar. 23-26	**THE PLAYERS Championship** Henry Hughes 904/273-3392	TPC at Sawgrass (Stadium) 110 TPC Boulevard Ponte Vedra Beach, FL 32082	($2,500,000)	--	NBC	Greg Norman
Mar. 30-Apr. 2	**Freeport-McMoRan Classic** Thomas Wulff/Maury MaGill 504/831-4653	English Turn Golf & Country Club One Clubhouse Drive New Orleans, LA 70131	$1,200,000/$1,207,500	$7,500	NBC	Ben Crenshaw
Apr. 6-9	***The Masters** Walton Johnson 706/667-6000	Augusta National Golf Club Augusta, GA 30913	($1,500,000)	—	CBS	Jose Maria Olazabal
Apr. 13-16	**MCI Classic** Michael Stevens/Arnie Burdick 803/671-2448	Harbour Town Golf Links Hilton Head Island, SC 29928	$1,300,000/$1,307,500	$7,500	CBS	Hale Irwin
Apr. 20-23	**Kmart Greater Greensboro Open** Stanhope Johnson/Mo Lantz 910/379-1570	Forest Oaks Country Club 4600 Forest Oaks Drive Greensboro, NC 27406	$1,500,000/$1,507,500	$7,500	CBS	Mike Springer
Apr. 27-30	**Shell Houston Open** Eric Fredricksen/Burt Darden 713/367-7999	TPC at The Woodlands 1730 South Millbend Drive The Woodlands, TX 77380	$1,400,000/$1,407,500	$7,500	ABC	Mike Heinen
May 4-7	**BellSouth Classic** David Kaplan/John Marshall 404/951-8777	Atlanta Country Club 500 Atlanta Country Club Drive Marietta, GA 30067	$1,300,000/$1,307,500	$7,500	CBS	John Daly
May 11-14	**GTE Byron Nelson Classic** Janie Henderson/Charlie Seay 214/742-3896	TPC at Las Colinas Cottonwood Valley Golf Course 4200 North MacArthur Boulevard Irving, TX 75038	$1,300,000/$1,330,000	$30,000	ABC	Neal Lancaster
May 18-21	**Buick Classic** John Cashwell 800/765-4742	Westchester Country Club 99 Biltmore Avenue Rye, NY 10580	$1,200,000/$1,207,500	$7,500	CBS	Lee Janzen
May 25-28	**Colonial** Dennis Roberson/Jerre Todd 817/927-4277	Colonial Country Club 3735 Country Club Circle Ft. Worth, TX 76109	$1,400,000/$1,407,500	$7,500	CBS	Nick Price

( )—1994 Purses

1995 PGA TOUR TOURNAMENT SCHEDULE *continued*

Date	Tournament Dir./Media Contact	Location	Official/Total Money	Pro-Am	TV	()—1994 Purses 1994 Winner
June 1-4	**Memorial Tournament** John Hines 614/889-6700	Muirfield Village Golf Club 5750 Memorial Drive Dublin, OH 43017	$1,700,000/$1,700,000	--	ABC	Tom Lehman
June 8-11	**Kemper Open** Ben Brundred/Charlie Brotman 301/469-3737	TPC at Avenel 10000 Oaklyn Drive Potomac, MD 20854	$1,400,000/$1,407,500	$7,500	CBS	Mark Brooks
June 15-18	***US Open** Elliott Vose 516/259-8000	Shinnecock Hills 190 Tuckahoe Road Southampton, NY 11968	($1,500,000)	--	NBC	Ernie Els
June 22-25	**Canon Greater Hartford Open** Michael Stefano/Mary Engvall 203/522-4171	TPC at River Highlands Golf Club Road Cromwell, CT 06416	$1,200,000/$1,207,500	$7,500	CBS	David Frost
June 29-July 2	**FedEx St. Jude Classic** Dwight Drinkard/Phil Cannon 901/748-0534	TPC at Southwind 3325 Club at Southwind Memphis, TN 38125	$1,250,000/$1,257,500	$7,500	CBS	Dicky Pride
July 6-9	**Motorola Western Open** Greg McLaughlin/Gary Holloway 708/724-4600	Cog Hill Golf & Country Club 12294 Archer Avenue Lemont, IL 60434	$1,200,000/$1,207,500	$7,500	CBS	Nick Price
July 13-16	**Anheuser-Busch Golf Classic** Johnnie Bender 804/253-3985	Kingsmill Golf Club 100 Golf Club Road Williamsburg, VA 23185	$1,100,000/$1,120,000	$20,000	ESPN	Mark McCumber
July 20-23	**Deposit Guaranty Golf Classic** Robert Morgan 601/544-0262	Annandale Golf Club 837 Mannsdale Road Madison, MS 39110	$700,000/$707,500	$7,500	TGC	Brian Henninger
July 20-23	***+British Open** 011-44-344-472112	St. Andrews Fife, Scotland	--	--	ABC	Nick Price
July 27-30	**The New England Classic** Edward Mingolla/Diane Laska-Nixon 508/865-1491	Pleasant Valley Country Club Armsby Road Sutton, MA 01590	$1,000,000/$1,007,500	$7,500	TGC	Kenny Perry
Aug. 3-6	**Buick Open** Rich Brochu/Dave Roman 810/236-3993	Warwick Hills Golf & Country Club G-9057 South Saginaw Road Grand Blanc, MI 48439	$1,200,000/$1,207,500	$7,500	CBS	Fred Couples

Date	Tournament Dir./Media Contact	Location	Official/Total Money	Pro-Am	TV	1994 Winner ( )—1994 Purses
Aug. 10-13	*PGA Championship Jim Magnusson/Julius Mason 310/573-7780	Riviera Country Club 1250 Capri Drive Pacific Palisades, CA 90272	($1,700,000)	--	CBS	Nick Price
Aug. 17-20	The Sprint International Larry Thiel/Buddy Martin 303/660-8000	Castle Pines Golf Club 1000 Humingbird Drive Castle Rock, CO 80104	($1,400,000/$1,410,000)	($10,000)	CBS	Steve Lowery
Aug. 24-27	NEC World Series of Golf Jim Cook 216/644-2299	Firestone Country Club 452 East Warner Road Akron, OH 44319	$2,000,000/$2,010,000	--	CBS	Jose Maria Olazabal
Aug. 31-Sept. 3	Greater Milwaukee Open Tom Strong/Dan Blackman 414/365-4466	Brown Deer Park Golf Course 7835 N. Green Bay Avenue Milwaukee, WI 53209	$1,000,000/$1,007,500	$7,500	ABC	Mike Springer
Sept. 7-10	Bell Canadian Open Bill Paul/Paul Dulmage 905/844-1800	Glen Abbey Golf Club 1333 Dorval Drive R.R.2 Oakville, Ontario Canada L6J 4Z3	($1,300,000/$1,307,500)	($7,500)	ESPN	Nick Price
Sept. 14-17	B.C. Open Alex Alexander/Pat Vavra 607/754-2482	En-Joie Golf Club 722 West Main Street Endicott, NY 13760	$1,000,000/$1,007,500	$7,500	TGC	Mike Sullivan
Sept. 21-24	Quad Cities Open Tony Piazzi/Curt Burnett 309/762-4653	Oakwood Country Club Route 6 Coal Valley, IL 61240	$1,000,000/$1,007,500	$7,500	TGC	Mark McCumber
Sept. 21-24	*+The Ryder Cup	Oak Hill Country Club Rochester, NY	--	--	NBC	
Sept. 28-Oct. 1	Buick Southern Open Robert Berry/Jim Visser 706/324-0411	Callaway Gardens Resort Highway 27 Pine Mountain, GA 31822	$900,000/$907,500	$7,500	ESPN	Steve Elkington
Oct. 5-8	Walt Disney World/ Oldsmobile Classic Michael McPhillips/John Story 407/824-2250	Magnolia, Palm and Eagle Pines Golf Courses Lake Buena Vista, FL 32830	($1,100,000/$1,225,000)	($25,000)	TGC	Rick Fehr

1995 PGA TOUR TOURNAMENT SCHEDULE *continued*

( )—1994 Purses

Date	Tournament Dir./Media Contact	Location	Official/Total Money	Pro-Am	TV	1994 Winner
Oct. 12-15	**Las Vegas Invitational** Jim Cook/Jane Schlosser 702/382-6616	TPC at Summerlin 1700 Village Center Circle Las Vegas, NV 89134	$1,500,000/$1,518,000	$18,000	ESPN	Bruce Lietzke
Oct. 19-22	**Texas Open** Nick Milanovich/Jerry Grotz 210/341-0823	Oak Hills Country Club 5403 Fredericksburg Road San Antonio, TX 78229	$1,000,000/$1,007,500	$7,500	TGC	Bob Estes
Oct. 26-29	**THE TOUR Championship** Marlene Livaudais 918/497-4653	Southern Hills Country Club 2636 East 61st Street Tulsa, OK 74136	($3,000,000/$3,010,000)	($10,000)	ABC	Mark McCumber
Nov. 2-5	**+Lincoln-Mercury Kapalua Int'l.** Margaret A. Santos/Linn Nishikawa 808-669-0244	Kapalua Resort (Plantation & Bay) 2000 Plantation Club Drive Lahaina, Maui, HI 96761	$1,000,000	--	ABC	Fred Couples
Nov. 9-12	**+The World Cup of Golf** Jack Warfield/Tom Place 513/624-2100	ITPC of Mission Hills - Shenzhen Mission Hills Road Guanlan Town Shenzhen, China 518100	$1,200,000	--	NBC	United States (Fred Couples/ Davis Love III)
Nov. 16-19	**+Franklin Funds Shark Shootout** Eric Jonke/Steve Brener 216/436-3440	Sherwood Country Club 2215 West Stafford Road Thousand Oaks, CA 91361	$1,100,000	--	CBS	Fred Couples/ Brad Faxon
Nov. 23-26	**+Skins Game** Chuck Gerber/Steve Brener 310/659-8557	TBA	($540,000)	--	ABC	Tom Watson
Nov. 30-Dec. 3	**+JC Penney Classic** Tom Jewell/Dick Dailey 813/942-5566	Innisbrook Hilton Resort Copperhead Course 36750 US Highway 19 North Palm Harbor, FL 34684	$1,300,000/$1,310,000	$10,000	ABC	Brad/Bryant/ Marta Figueras-Dotti
Dec.	**+Diners Club Matches** Brad Quayle 619/564-1088	PGA West (Nicklaus Course) 55-955 PGA Boulevard La Quinta, CA 92253-4604	$890,000	--	ABC	--
Dec. 30-31	**+Andersen Consulting WCOG**	Grayhawk Golf Club Scottsdale, AZ	$3,650,000	--	ABC	First-year event

* Non-PGA TOUR co-sponsored event   + Unofficial event

9

TOURNAMENT POLICY BOARD

Richard J. Ferris of Northbrook, IL, was elected Chairman of the PGA TOUR's Tournament Policy Board in December 1993, succeeding E.M. (Del) de Windt, who had served in that position for 11 years.

Currently Co-chairman and Chief Executive Officer of the Doubletree Corporation, Ferris previously served as Chairman and Chief Executive Officer of UAL Corporation, which owned United Airlines, Hilton International Hotels, Westin Hotels and Hertz

Ferris, 58, had served two terms on the Senior PGA TOUR Division Advisory Board, including a stint as Chairman, prior to becoming an Independent Director of the PGA TOUR's Tournament Policy Board in 1992.

Richard J. Ferris

Victor F. Ganzi
New York, NY
Independent Director

James F. Nordstrom
Seattle, WA
Independent Director

Harold "Red" Poling
Dearborn, MI
Independent Director

Brad Faxon
Orlando, FL
Player Director

Rick Fehr
Redmond, WA
Player Director

Jay Haas
Greenville, SC
Player Director

Davis Love III
Sea Island, GA
Player Director

Tom Addis III
El Cajon, CA
PGA Director

TOURNAMENT POLICY BOARD

The Tournament Policy Board establishes goals and policies for the operation of the PGA TOUR. The nine-member Board is composed of the following:

Four Player Directors elected by the PGA TOUR membership. A Player Director also serves as Vice President of the PGA of America.

Four Independent Directors, representing the public interest. One serves as Chairman of the Board.

One PGA of America Director, who is a national officer of the PGA of America. A Players Advisory Council consults with the Policy Board.

The Policy Board appoints the Commissioner as chief executive and administrative officer of the PGA TOUR. The tournament staff, serving under the Commissioner, conducts tournament play.

PGA TOUR GOLF COURSE PROPERTIES BOARD

An advisory board of the PGA TOUR Tournament Policy Board, the Golf Course Properties Board makes reports and recommendations relating to the development and operational functions of the Tournament Players Clubs (TPCs) and International Tournament Players Clubs (ITPCs).

Directors of the Golf Course Properties Board are experts in the fields of development, finance, construction, law, international business and other specialties related to property development.

H. James Griggs
Chairman

Edward W. Brown III

James Clark

John L. Steffens

Carl Ware

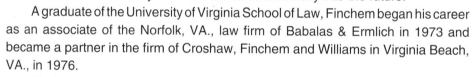

ABOUT THE COMMISSIONER

Timothy W. Finchem
Commissioner

Timothy W. Finchem became the third Commissioner in the 25-year history of the PGA TOUR on June 1, 1994.

Finchem, 47, succeeded Deane R. Beman, who had served as Commissioner for 20 years. The late Joseph C. Dey was the first Commissioner of the PGA TOUR, serving from 1969 until 1974.

A 4-handicapper, Finchem combines a love of the game and a respect for its traditions with a vision that will carry the PGA TOUR successfully into the future.

A graduate of the University of Virginia School of Law, Finchem began his career as an associate of the Norfolk, VA., law firm of Babalas & Ermlich in 1973 and became a partner in the firm of Croshaw, Finchem and Williams in Virginia Beach, VA., in 1976.

Finchem served in the White House as the Deputy Advisor to the President for Economic Affairs in 1978 and 1979, then became National Staff Director of the Carter-Mondale Presidential Campaign in 1980.

In 1981, Finchem became President of Beckel, Finchem, Torricelli and Associates before becoming co-founder of National Strategies and Marketing Group, a Washington, DC., consulting and marketing firm in 1984. He was a consultant to the PGA TOUR while with NSMG.

Finchem joined the TOUR staff as Vice President of Business Affairs in 1987 and became Deputy Commissioner and Chief Operating Officer in 1989.

Born in Ottawa, IL., on April 19, 1947, Finchem was graduated from Princess Anne High School in Virginia Beach. He attended the University of Richmond on a debate scholarship and received his Bachelor of Arts degree from the school in 1969. He received his degree from the University of Virginia Law School in 1973.

Married to the former Holly Bachand, Finchem is the father of four. The Finchems live in Ponte Vedra Beach, FL.

CORPORATE OFFICERS

Helen Atter
Vice President,
Human Resources

John M. Evenson
Vice President,
Broadcasting

Edward L. Moorhouse
Executive Vice President,
Legal & International Affairs

John M. Morris
Vice President,
Communications

Donna Orender
Vice President,
Television & Productions

Stephen C. Rankin
Executive Vice President,
Tournament Affairs &
Sponsor Relations

Michael L. Starks
Vice President,
Corporate Affairs & Planning

Charles L. Zink
Executive Vice President,
Chief Financial Officer

TOURNAMENT AFFAIRS

Steve Rankin
Executive Vice President-
Tournament Affairs/
Sponsor Relations

Duke Butler
Executive Director of
Tournament Administration/
Tournament Director

Gary Becka
Director of
Operations

Arvin Ginn
Assistant Tournament
Director

Ben Nelson
Assistant Tournament
Director

Mike Shea
Senior Director
of Rules

AGRONOMY

Allan MacCurrach
Senior Agronomist

Jeff Haley
Associate Agronomist

Dennis Leger
Associate Agronomist

CHAMPIONSHIP MANAGEMENT

Henry Hughes
Vice President,
Executive Director

Paul Hardwick
Director of Operations

Brian Goin
General Manager

Erica de la Uz
Assistant to the
Vice President

Ron Cross
Tournament Director,
NIKE TOUR
Championship

Marlene Livaudais
Tournament Director,
THE TOUR
Championship

Anne Mullen
Tournament Director,
Senior TOUR
Championship

Greg Wheeler
Tournament Director,
FORD SENIOR
PLAYERS
Championship

PLAYER RELATIONS

Bill Calfee
Vice President
of Player Relations

Sid Wilson
Director of Player Services,
PGA TOUR

COMMUNICATIONS

John Morris
Vice President of
Communications

Dave Lancer
Director
of Information

Denise Taylor
Media Relations
Coordinator

Chuck Adams
PGA TOUR
Media Official

Marty Caffey
PGA TOUR
Media Official

James Cramer
NIKE TOUR
Media Official

Bob Hyde
NIKE TOUR
Media Official

Mark Mitchell
PGA TOUR
Media Official

Lee Patterson
Senior PGA
TOUR Media Official

Wes Seeley
PGA TOUR
Media Official

Phil Stambaugh
Senior PGA
TOUR Media Official

Vicki Page
Administrative
Assistant

Stan Badz
Staff Photographer

Michelle Falcone
Administrative Assistant

Pete Fontaine
Staff Photographer

Sam Greenwood
Staff Photographer

TELEVISION / BROADCASTING

Donna Orender
Vice President,
Televison & Productions

John Evenson
Vice President,
Broadcasting

Roger Stevenson
Vice President,
Operations

Jack Peter
Director
of Production

Terri Montville
Broadcasting
Manager

Jim Pierson
Director of Sales

Tom Alter
Senior
Producer

Al Brito
Senior Producer

Michael O'Connell
Coordinating
Producer

Scott Rinehart
Production
Manager

Scott Goodall
Manager, Field
Operations

Lowell Thaler
Producer

Seth Giambalvo
Feature Producer

Rick Persons
Feature Producer

Glenn Rocha
Associate Producer

Marion Stratford
Associate Producer

RULES OFFICIALS

George Boutell
Tournament Official
Scottsdale, AZ

Jon Brendle
Tournament Official
Orlando, FL

Wade Cagle
Tournament Supervisor
Alpharetta, GA

Frank Kavanaugh
Tournament Official
Pattenburg, NJ

Vaughn Moise
Tournament Official
Kingwood, TX

Mark Russell
Tournament Official
Orlando, FL

Glen Tait
Tournament Official
LaMesa, CA

Slugger White
Tournament Official
Ormond Beach, FL

SCORING AND PROMOTIONS

Jack White
Director of Promotions

Gerald Goodman
Field Manager of Promotions

Larry Strong
Promotions

Don Wallace
Promotions

Rich Pierson
Promotions

Malcolm Turner
Promotions

Nick Price earned his second PGA TOUR Player of the Year Award in 1994, winning five times and topping his own single-season earnings record with $1,499,927.

ALL EXEMPT TOUR PRIORITY RANKINGS

Each PGA TOUR player has earned a position on the priority ranking system that will be used selecting tournament fields. The complete ranking system, in order of priority, is as follows:

I. SPECIAL EXEMPTIONS

1. Winners of PGA Championship or U.S. Open prior to 1970 or in the last 10 calendar years.

Paul Azinger	Doug Ford	Don January	Jack Nicklaus	Sam Snead
Jack Burke	Ed Furgol	Lee Janzen	Andy North	Payne Stewart
Billy Casper	Al Geiberger	Tom Kite	Arnold Palmer	Curtis Strange
John Daly	Wayne Grady	Gene Littler	Gary Player	Lee Trevino
Ernie Els	Hubert Green	Dave Marr	Nick Price	Bob Tway
Dow Finsterwald	Jay Hebert	Orville Moody	Bob Rosburg	Ken Venturi
Jack Fleck	Lionel Hebert	Larry Nelson	Scott Simpson	
Ray Floyd	Hale Irwin	Bobby Nichols	Jeff Sluman	

2. Winners of the THE PLAYERS Championship in the last 10 calendar years.

Steve Elkington	John Mahaffey	Jodie Mudd	Greg Norman	Calvin Peete
Davis Love III	Mark McCumber			

3. Winners of the NEC WORLD SERIES OF GOLF in the last 10 calendar years.

Fulton Allem	Roger Maltbie	Tom Purtzer	Craig Stadler	Denis Watson
David Frost	Dan Pohl	Mike Reid		

4. Winners of The Masters in the last 10 calendar years.

Fred Couples	Nick Faldo	Larry Mize

5. Winners of the British Open in the last 10 calendar years. (1990-present)

Ian Baker-Finch

6. The leader in PGA TOUR official earnings in each of the last five calendar years.

Corey Pavin

7. Winners of PGA TOUR co-sponsored or approved events (except Team events) within the last two calendar years, or during the current year.

Mark Brooks	Mike Heinen	Tom Lehman	Jim McGovern	Loren Roberts
Ben Crenshaw	Nolan Henke	Bruce Lietzke	Rocco Mediate	Vijay Singh
David Edwards	Brian Henninger	Steve Lowery	Phil Mickelson	Mike Springer
Bob Estes	Scott Hoch	Andrew Magee	Johnny Miller	Mike Standly
Rick Fehr	John Huston	Jeff Maggert	Brett Ogle	Mike Sullivan
Jim Gallagher, Jr.	John Inman	Billy Mayfair	Kenny Perry	Howard Twitty
Bill Glasson	Neal Lancaster	Blaine McCallister	Dicky Pride	Grant Waite
Jay Haas				

8. Members of the last-named U.S. Ryder Cup team.

Lanny Wadkins

9. Leaders in official PGA TOUR career earnings, as follows:

a. Players among the Top 50 in career earnings as of the end of the preceding calendar year may elect to use a one-time, one-year exemption for the next year.

b. Players among the Top 25 in career earnings as of the end of the preceding calendar year may elect to use this special exemption for a second year, provided that the player remains among the Top 25 on the career money list.

10. Sponsor exemptions (a maximum of eight, which may include amateurs with handicaps of two or less), on the following basis:

a. Not less than two sponsor invitees shall be PGA TOUR Regular, Life or Past Champion members not otherwise exempt.

b. Not less than two of the top 50 finishers from the last Qualifying Tournament, if not all of them can otherwise be accommodated (Note: PGA TOUR members may receive unlimited number of sponsor invitations. Non-TOUR members may receive maximum of five per year)

11. Two foreign players designated by the Commissioner.

12. The current PGA Club Professional Champion for a maximum of three open events, in addition to any sponsor selections.

Sammy Rachels

13. PGA Section Champion of the Section in which the tournament is played.

14. Four members of the PGA Section in which the tournament is played, who qualify through Sectional qualifying competitions.

15. Four low scorers at Open Qualifying, which shall normally be held on Monday of tournament week.

16. Past champions of the particular event being contested that week, if co-sponsored by the PGA TOUR and the same tournament sponsor (except for Team events), as follows:

Winners prior to July 28, 1970--unlimited exemptions for such events.
Winners after July 28, 1970—ten years of exemptions for such events.

II. TOP 125, PREVIOUS YEAR'S OFFICIAL MONEY LIST—If not exempt under "Special Exemptions" the top 125 PGA TOUR members on the previous year's Official Money List, in order of their positions on the list.

Fuzzy Zoeller	Steve Stricker	Gene Sauers	Bobby Wadkins	Robin Freeman	Ken Green
Brad Bryant	Dave Barr	Ted Tryba	Keith Clearwater	Michael Bradley	John Wilson
Brad Faxon	Gil Morgan	Paul Goydos	Wayne Levi	Dillard Pruitt	Bob Gilder
Hal Sutton	Jay Don Blake	Guy Boros	David Ogrin	Paul Stankowski	Jesper Parnevik
Mark Calcavecchia	Donnie Hammond	Russ Cochran	Mark Carnevale	Yoshinori Mizumaki	Joe Ozaki
John Cook	Steve Pate	Jim Furyk	Jim Thorpe	Ed Humenik	John Morse
Kirk Triplett	Clark Dennis	Bob Lohr	Dave Stockton, Jr.	Brian Claar	Jay Delsing
Lennie Clements	Fred Funk	Gary Hallberg	Scott Verplank	Brandel Chamblee	Dennis Paulson
Robert Gamez	Chip Beck	Mike Hulbert	Brian Kamm	Dan Forsman	Justin Leonard
Glen Day	Greg Kraft	Chris DiMarco	David Feherty	Mark McNulty	Joel Edwards
Craig Parry	Duffy Waldorf	Mark O'Meara	Bob Burns	Steve Rintoul	Curt Byrum
Billy Andrade	D.A. Weibring	Peter Jacobsen	Doug Tewell		

III. SPECIAL MEDICAL EXTENSION—If granted by the Commissioner, if not otherwise eligible, and if needed to fill the field, Special Medical Extension.

					Andy Bean
Steve Jones	Joey Sindelar	Mark Wiebe	Don Pooley	Ed Fiori	Denis Watson

IV. TOP 10 FINISHERS—The top 10 professionals and those tied for 10th in an open tournament whose victory has official status is exempt into the next open tournament whose victory has official status.

V. TOP FIVE MONEY WINNERS ON 1994 NIKE TOUR

Chris Perry	Scott Gump	Pat Bates	Jim Carter	Skip Kendall

VI. QUALIFYING TOURNAMENT—The low 40 scorers and ties from the previous year's PGA TOUR Qualifying Tournament , in order of their finish in the tournament, and players 6-10 on the 1993 NIKE TOUR money list.

Woody Austin	Tommy Armour III*	Charlie Rymer	J.L. Lewis	Kawika Cotner	Bill Britton
Eduardo Romero	Bill Porter	Don Reese	Steve Gotsche	Scott McCarron	Tom Hearn
Tray Tyner	David Duval*	Omar Uresti	Phil Blackmar	Jonathan Kaye	Clark Burroughs
Bruce Fleisher	Ronnie Black	Joey Rassett	Tommy Tolles	Keith Fergus	Jay Williamson
Harry Taylor	Jerry Haas*	Jeff Leonard	Dicky Thompson	Scott Ford	Steve Hart
Dudley Hart	Mike Brisky	Bart Bryant	Kelly Gibson	Tim Loustalot	Michael Allen
Bruce Vaughan*	Emlyn Aubrey*	Lee Rinker	Joe Acosta	Tony Sills	Ryan Howison
Patrick Burke	Doug Martin	Mark Wurtz	J.P. Hayes	Carl Paulson	John Adams
		Marco Dawson	Ray Stewart	Mike Smith	

(* 6-10 1994 NIKE TOUR money list)

VII. NEXT 25 MEMBERS AFTER TOP 125 MEMBERS FROM PREVIOUS YEAR'S OFFICIAL MONEY LIST—If needed to fill the field, the next 25 PGA TOUR members after the top 125 PGA TOUR members from the previous year's Official Money List, in order of their positions on the list.

Dick Mast	David Peoples	Dave Rummells	Jeff Woodland	Steve Brodie	Olin Browne
Peter Jordan	Tim Simpson	Mike Donald	Tom Byrum	Bobby Clampett	Larry Silveira

VIII. SPECIAL MEMBER/MEDICAL

IX. PAST CHAMPION MEMBERS—If not otherwise eligible and if needed to fill the field, Past Champion Members, in order of the total number of co-sponsored or approved events won, excluding Team events. If two or more players are tied, the player who is higher on the PGA TOUR Career Money List shall be eligible.

X. SPECIAL TEMPORARY—If during the course of a PGA TOUR season, a non-member of the PGA TOUR wins an amount of official money (e.g., by playing in PGA TOUR events through sponsor exemptions, Open Qualifying, etc.) equal to the amount won in the preceding year by the 154th/ finisher on the official money winning list will be eligible for the remainder of the year.

XI. TEAM CHAMPIONSHIP WINNERS—If not otherwise eligible and if needed to fill the field, winners of co-sponsored team championships, in order of the total number of team championship tournaments won. If two or more players are tied based on the number of such tournaments won, the player who is higher on the official PGA TOUR career money list shall be eligible.

XII. VETERAN MEMBERS—If not otherwise eligible and if needed to fill the field, Veteran Members (players who have made a minimum of 150 cuts during their career), in order of their standing on the PGA TOUR career money list.

PRONUNCIATION GUIDE

JOE ACOSTA, JR.	uh-COST-uh
BILLY ANDRADE	ANN-drade
EMLYN AUBREY	EHM-lin OB-ree
PAUL AZINGER	AY-zing-r
GUY BOROS	BORE-ohs
MARK CALCAVECCHIA	CAL-kuh-VECK-ee-uh
MARK CARNEVALE	CAR-nuh-VALE
BRANDEL CHAMBLEE	BRAN-dl SHAM-blee
BRIAN CLAAR	CLARE
KAWIKA COTNER	kuh-WEE-kuh
ED DOUGHERTY	DOCK-er-tee
DAVID DUVAL	due-VAHL
ERNIE ELS	Lls
BOB ESTES	ES-tis
DAVID FEHERTY	FAY-er-tee
RICK FEHR	FAIR
KEITH FERGUS	FUR-gus
ED FIORI	fee-OR-ee
BRUCE FLEISHER	FLY-shur
JIM FURYK	FUHR-ic
ROBERT GAMEZ	GAM-ez
STEVE GOTSCHE	GOT-che
PAUL GOYDOS	GOY-dose
JAY/JERRY HAAS	HAWS
DAN HALLDORSON	HALL-duhr-sun
MORRIS HATALSKY	huh-TALL-skee
VANCE HEAFNER	HEF-nur
TOM HEARN	HURN
MIKE HEINEN	HIGH-nen
BRIAN HENNINGER	HEN-ing-uhr
NOLAN HENKE	HENK-e
SCOTT HOCH	HOKE
ED HUMENIK	HEW-men-ick
BARRY JAECKEL	JAY-kl
GARY KOCH	COKE
TOM LEHMAN	LAY-man
WAYNE LEVI	LEV-e
BRUCE LIETZKE	LIT-skee
BOB LOHR	LORE
TIM LOUSTALOT	LOST-a-lot
JEFF MAGGERT	MAG-ert
SCOTT McCARRON	muh-CARE-uhn
ROCCO MEDIATE	MEE-dee-ATE
YOSHI MIZUMAKI	YO-she MIZ-oo-MOCK-ee
BRETT OGLE	OWE-gl
DAVID OGRIN	OWE-grin
MARK O'MEARA	oh-MEER-uh
JOE OZAKI	oh-ZOCK-ee
JESPER PARNEVIK	YES-per PAR-nuh-vic
CRAIG PARRY	PERRY
COREY PAVIN	PAY-vin
DAN POHL	POLE
STEVE RINTOUL	rin-tool
CHARLIE RYMER	RHYME-er
EDUARDO ROMERO	ed-WAHRD-oh row-MARE-oh
TOM SIECKMANN	SEEK-muhn
LARRY SILVEIRA	sil-VARE-uh
VIJAY SINGH	VEE-jay SING
JEFF SLUMAN	SLEW-muhn
STEVE STRICKER	STRICK-uhr
LANCE TEN BROECK	TEN-brook
DOUG TEWELL	TOOL
TOMMY TOLLES	TOLLS
TED TRYBA	TREE-buh
TRAY TYNER	TIE-ner
OMAR URESTI	OWE-mahr u-REST-ee
STAN UTLEY	UT-lee
D.A. WEIBRING	Y-bring
MARK WIEBE	WEE-be
ROBERT WRENN	REN
FUZZY ZOELLER	ZELL-uhr
RICHARD ZOKOL	ZO-kl

FULTON ALLEM

EXEMPT STATUS: Winner, 1993 NEC World Series of Golf

FULL NAME: Fulton Peter Allem

HEIGHT: 5'11"   **WEIGHT:** 215

BIRTH DATE: September 15, 1957

BIRTHPLACE: Kroonstad, South Africa

RESIDENCE: Heathrow, FL

FAMILY: Wife, Colleen; Nadia (7/7/86), Nicholas (1/1/91)

SPECIAL INTERESTS: Riding horses, breeding horses, fishing & hunting

TURNED PROFESSIONAL: 1976

JOINED TOUR: Fall 1987

PLAYER PROFILE

CAREER EARNINGS: $1,977,016

TOUR VICTORIES: **1991** Independent Insurance Agent Open. **1993** Southwestern Bell Colonial,
(TOTAL: 3)   NEC World Series of Golf

MONEY & POSITION:

1987--$ 88,734--105	1990--$ 134,493--116	1993--$851,345-- 9
1988--$163,911-- 73	1991--$ 229,702-- 71	1994--$166,144--109
1989--$134,706--104	1992--$ 209,982-- 74	

BEST 1994 FINISH: T6--Bell Canadian Open

1994 SUMMARY: Tournaments entered--27; in money--16; top ten finishes--1.

1995 PGA TOUR CHARITY TEAM COMPETITION: Nissan Open

NATIONAL TEAMS: Presidents Cup, 1994.

1994 SEASON: Had tough sledding in early going and never did get untracked…after starting season with 16th-place finish in Mercedes Championships, missed four of next five cuts and withdrew from Nestle Invitational after opening with 82…wasn't until 23rd start that posted only top-10, in Bell Canadian Open in September…opened with back-to-back 69s at Glen Abbey to sit two strokes off Robin Freeman's 36-hole lead…closed 71-70 for T6 worth $43,550…only other top-25 came in May, T13 in Shell Houston Open…as direct result, finished with lowest earnings total/money-list position since 1990…also earned $685,201 less than career-year total in 1993…Captain's Choice for International Team in inaugural Presidents Cup Match, played week after Canadian Open…was 1-3 in foursome and four-ball matches, teaming with Mark McNulty to defeat Jim Gallagher, Jr.-John Huston in Saturday Four-Ball…halved Sunday singles match with Phil Mickelson.

CAREER HIGHLIGHTS: Tripled career victory total in 1993 by winning on two of the most storied courses on TOUR, Colonial and Firestone…outdueled Greg Norman for his second TOUR title, that of the Southwestern Bell Colonial…second-round 63 got him into contention, and closing 67 gave a one-stroke decision over Norman…that win got him into NEC World Series of Golf, where a blistering final-round 62 brought him the $360,000 first-place check and 10-year TOUR exemption…in season reminiscent of 1994, struggled much of 1991 campaign– but broke through in final week for first victory in rescheduled Independent Insurance Agent Open…played last two rounds in 11-under-par to edge Billy Ray Brown, Mike Hulbert and Tom Kite by single stroke…had been No. 143 on money list going into IIAO, but with victory came two-year exemption…second-place finish in 1987 World Series brought him TOUR card without having to go to Qualifying Tournament…won 1988 Sun City Million Dollar Challenge…winner of 11 South African events and 15 worldwide.

PERSONAL: Started playing golf at age seven with encouragement from father…countryman Gary Player had large influence on him…had 18 second-place finishes before breaking through with first win on South African Tour.

1994 PGA TOUR STATISTICS

Scoring Average	71.64	(136)
Driving Distance	259.2	(113)
Driving Accuracy	77.5	(11)
Greens in Regulation	62.4	(154T)
Putting	1.819	(142T)
All-Around	843	(136)
Sand Saves	53.8	(57T)
Total Driving	124	(29T)
Eagles	3	(126T)
Birdies	258	(104T)

MISCELLANEOUS STATISTICS

Scoring Avg. (before cut)	71.98	(141T)
Scoring Avg. (3rd round)	71.73	(142T)
Scoring Avg. (4th round)	73.67	(173)
Birdie Conversion	28.0	(96T)
Par Breakers	17.7	(133T)

1994 Low Round: 65: Las Vegas Invitational/2
Career Low Round: 62: 1993 NEC World Series
Career Largest of Golf/4
Paycheck:$360,000/1993 NEC WSOG/1

BILLY ANDRADE

EXEMPT STATUS: 48th on 1994 money list

FULL NAME: William Thomas Andrade

HEIGHT: 5' 8''   **WEIGHT:** 155

BIRTH DATE: January 25, 1964

BIRTHPLACE: Fall River, MA

RESIDENCE: Bristol, RI and Atlanta, GA

FAMILY: Wife, Jody; Cameron James (4/5/94)

COLLEGE: Wake Forest University (1987, Sociology)

SPECIAL INTERESTS: All sports

TURNED PROFESSIONAL: 1987

Q SCHOOL: Fall 1987, 1988

PLAYER PROFILE

CAREER EARNINGS: $2,034,796   **PLAYOFF RECORD:** 1-1

TOUR VICTORIES: 1991 Kemper Open, Buick Classic
(TOTAL: 2)

MONEY AND POSITION:

1988--$ 74,950--134	1991--$615,765 -14	1993--$ 365,759--40
1989--$202,242-- 69	1992--$202,509--76	1994--$ 342,208--48
1990--$231,362-- 64		

BEST 1994 FINISHES: T2--Doral-Ryder Open, T3--Las Vegas Invitational; T5--Buick Classic

1994 SUMMARY: Tournaments entered--26; in money--18, top ten finishes--3.

1995 PGA TOUR CHARITY TEAM COMPETITION: Motorola Western Open

NATIONAL TEAMS: Junior World Cup, 1981 (won team title with Sam Randolph at Portmarnock, Ireland); World Amateur Team Championship, 1986; Walker Cup, 1987.

1994 SEASON: Following an early-season disappointment, finished with third-best earnings total of career and just shy of 1993 figure…held two-stroke lead after three rounds of Doral-Ryder Open, his fifth start of year…closed with 73, three strokes behind John Huston…T2 finish instead of third TOUR title not what he expected…runnerup placing still produced year's biggest check, $123,200…later had T5 in one of his favorite tournaments, Buick Classic, after closing 66-69…final of three top-10s came in his last event, Las Vegas Invitational…ended with three consecutive 67s for 335 total, good for T3…was in contention through three rounds of Phoenix Open, one stroke off 36- and 54-hole leads, before concluding 73 and T18…also had T19 in Bell Canadian Open.

CAREER HIGHLIGHTS: Enjoyed memorable two-week June stretch in 1991, winning Kemper Open and Buick Classic back-to-back…both he and Jeff Sluman carded tournament-record 21-under-par 263s at TPC at Avenel…par was good for victory on first playoff hole…following week edged Brad Bryant by one stroke at Westchester CC…became first to win consecutive events since Hale Irwin (U.S. Open/Buick Classic) the year before…carded final-round 67 at 1993 Buick Southern Open to get into five-man playoff won by John Inman…three-time All-America at Wake Forest, member of 1986 NCAA Championship team…winner 1986 Sunnehanna and North and South Amateurs…recipient of Arnold Palmer Scholarship to Wake Forest…won 1992 JCPenney Classic (with Kris Tschetter).

PERSONAL: Firm believer in power of positive thinking…started playing golf at age five, won first tournament at 11…No. 1 ranked junior player in nation in 1981…named to Rhode Island all-state high school basketball team…born in Fall River, MA, but emphasizes that Bristol, RI is hometown ("Fall River just happened to be where the hospital was my mother had me in.").

1994 PGA TOUR STATISTICS

Scoring Average	70.83	(52)
Driving Distance	258.3	(118)
Driving Accuracy	64.8	(142T)
Greens in Regulation	63.7	(143T)
Putting	1.778	(45T)
All-Around	623	(64)
Sand Saves	59.3	(11)
Total Driving	260	(165)
Eagles	7	(44T)
Birdies	286	(68T)

MISCELLANEOUS STATISTICS

Scoring Avg. (before cut)	71.37	(82T)
Scoring Avg. (3rd round)	70.59	(65T)
Scoring Avg. (4th round)	71.33	(71)
Birdie Conversion	28.7	(66T)
Par Breakers	18.7	(97T)

1994 Low Round: 65: Phoenix Open/2

Career Low Round: 63: 1993 Northern Telecom Open/1

Career Largest Paycheck: **$180,000**/1991 Kemper Open/1
1991 Buick Classic/1

PAUL AZINGER

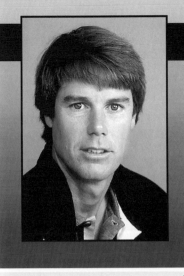

EXEMPT STATUS: Winner, 1993 PGA Championship

FULL NAME: Paul William Azinger

HEIGHT: 6' 2"   **WEIGHT:** 175

BIRTH DATE: January 6, 1960

BIRTHPLACE: Holyoke, MA

RESIDENCE: Bradenton, FL

FAMILY: Wife,Toni; Sarah Jean (12/28/85), Josie Lynn (4/21/89)

COLLEGE: Brevard JC and Florida State University

SPECIAL INTERESTS: Fishing, boating

TURNED PROFESSIONAL: 1981

Q SCHOOL: Fall 1981, 1983, 1984

PLAYER PROFILE

CAREER EARNINGS: $6,774,728   **PLAYOFF RECORD:** 1-2

TOUR VICTORIES: **1987** Phoenix Open, Panasonic-Las Vegas Invitational, Canon-Sammy Davis Jr.-
(TOTAL: 11)   Greater Hartford Open. **1988** Hertz Bay Hill Classic. **1989** Canon Greater Hartford
Open. **1990** MONY Tournament of Champions.**1991** AT&T Pebble Beach National
Pro-Am. **1992** TOUR Championship.**1993** Memorial Tournament, New England
Classic, PGA Championship.

MONEY & POSITION:

1982--$ 10,655--171	1987--$822,481-- 2	1991--$ 685,603-- 9
1984--$ 27,821--144	1988--$594,850-- 11	1992--$ 929,863-- 7
1985--$ 81,179-- 93	1989--$951,649-- 3	1993--$1,458,456-- 2
1986--$254,019-- 29	1990--$944,731-- 4	1994--$ 13,422--242

BEST 1994 FINISH: T19--Buick Southern Open

1994 SUMMARY: Tournaments entered--4; in money--2; top ten finishes--0.

1995 PGA TOUR CHARITY TEAM COMPETITION: B.C. Open

NATIONAL TEAMS: Ryder Cup (3), 1989, 1991, 1993; World Cup, 1989; Co-captain Presidents Cup, 1994

1994 SEASON: Although his consecutive years-with-victory string ended at seven, he scored biggest victory of his life by defeating lymphoma…given clean bill of health following chemotherapy and radiation treatment for cancer diagnosed in Dec. 1993…had benign fatty tumor removed a week before end of radiation program, delaying comeback…after missing defenses of Memorial Tournament (May) and New England Classic (July) titles, returned to TOUR action at Buick Open…missed cut at Warwick Hills and then in defense of PGA Championship, after which experienced rotator cuff discomfort…following another layoff, returned to T19 at Buick Southern Open, followed by T33 at Walt Disney World/Oldsmobile Classic…next setback occurred at Texas Open…back went into spasms on pro-am day, prompting withdrawal there and later from following week's Las Vegas Invitational…that ended his dream of extending victory string to eight years.

CAREER HIGHLIGHTS: Best year of career ended in diagnosis of lymphoma in right shoulder blade…suffered from pain in shoulder for years, had one operation in 1991…captured first major by defeating Greg Norman on second hole of a sudden-death playoff for 1993 PGA Championship at Inverness…earlier won Memorial Tournament in dramatic fashion, holing out from greenside bunker on 72nd hole…third-round 64 put him in position for New England Classic win…10 top-three finishes in '93 the most since Tom Watson in 1980…finished second on money list to Nick Price…also three-time winner in 1987, when again second on money list and won PGA Player of Year honors…runnerup 1987 British Open…1984 Qualifying Tournament medalist…winner 1990-92 BMW Opens (Germany)…winner 1988 (with Bob Tway) and 1991 (with Ben Crenshaw) Fred Meyer Challenges.

PERSONAL: Has dedicated himself to being an inspiration to others ("I have a chance to reach out to thousands of people")…credits much of success to teacher John Redman…started playing golf at five, couldn't break 40 for nine holes as high school senior.

1994 PGA TOUR STATISTICS

Scoring Average	71..27
Driving Distance	269.7
Driving Accuracy	68.2
Greens in Regulation	66.7
Putting	1.788
All-Around	–
Sand Saves	47.4
Total Driving	–
Eagles	0
Birdies	41

MISCELLANEOUS STATISTICS

Scoring Avg. (before cut)	72.00
Scoring Avg. (3rd round)	68.00
Scoring Avg. (4th round)	70.50
Birdie Conversion	31.1
Par Breakers	20.7

1994 Low Round: 68: 2 times
Career Low Round: 62: 2 times, most recent
Career Largest 1989 Texas Open/2
Paycheck: $360,000/1992 TOUR Championship/1

IAN BAKER-FINCH

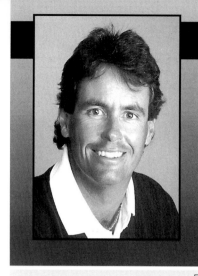

EXEMPT STATUS: Winner, 1991 British Open

FULL NAME: Ian Baker-Finch

HEIGHT: 6'4"   **WEIGHT:** 190

BIRTH DATE: October 24, 1960

BIRTHPLACE: Nambour, Australia

RESIDENCE: Sanctuary Cove, Queensland, Australia; plays out of Sanctuary Cove

FAMILY: Wife, Jennie; Hayley (2/7/89), Laura (10/7/91)

SPECIAL INTERESTS: Water sports, wine, tennis, sports

TURNED PROFESSIONAL: 1979

JOINED TOUR: Fall 1988

PLAYER PROFILE

CAREER EARNINGS: $1,998,077   **PLAYOFF RECORD:** 0-1

TOUR VICTORIES: 1989 Southwestern Bell Colonial
(TOTAL: 1)

MONEY & POSITION: 1988--$ 75,840--133   1991--$649,513--13   1993--$140,621--114
                          1989--$253,309-- 53   1992--$261,817--58   1994--$ 81,326--167
                          1990--$611,492-- 16

BEST 1994 FINISH: T10--The Masters Tournament

1994 SUMMARY: Tournaments entered--20; in money--6; top ten finishes--1.

1995 PGA TOUR CHARITY TEAM COMPETITION: Sprint International

NATIONAL TOUR TEAMS: Four Tours World Championship of Golf (3), 1989, 1990, 1991. Australian World Cup, 1985; Australia/New Zealand Kirin Cup (4), 1985, 1986, 1987, 1988.

1994 SEASON: Experienced a year he would just as soon forget...made but six cuts in 20 starts, earning only $81,326...total lowest since first official TOUR earnings year, 1988...opened '94 campaign with pair of missed cuts, in Honda Classic and Nestle Invitational...then ran off four consecutive events in the money, highlighted by lone top-10 at the Masters...three consecutive rounds of 71 at Augusta National, followed by 74, produced T10 worth $50,000...week later had T64 in MCI Heritage Golf Classic...then began string of 10 consecutive misses, starting with BellSouth Classic and running through PGA Championship...had final two in-the-money appearances in consecutive events, Sprint International (T65) and NEC World Series of Golf (47).

CAREER HIGHLIGHTS: Captured 120th British Open at Royal Birkdale in 1991...closed with rounds of 64-66 to defeat countryman Mike Harwood by two strokes...birdied five of first seven holes Sunday to set stage for victory...win was sweet retribution for 1984, when led British Open through three rounds at St. Andrews before faltering...lone PGA TOUR victory to date came in 1989 Southwestern Bell Colonial...scored four-stroke decision over David Edwards at Colonial...amassed 15 top-10s during 1990-91 TOUR seasons, both of which with earnings over $600,000... qualifed for PGA TOUR card through earnings in 1988 World Series third-place finish at Firestone, along with $75,840 paycheck, meant didn't have to through Qualifying Tournament...was in money in four-of-four events that year, but only World Series counted as official...along with placings in The International and Bank of Boston Classic (latter T15), also had T9 in B.C. Open worth $12,500...1985 appeared in nine events, with best finish T19 in NEC World Series...first stateside money came in 1984 with T16 in Charley Pride Fiesta of Tournament Players Series...winner of numerous events in Australia, Japan and Europe, most notable of which 1988 Australian Masters and most recent 1993 Ford Australian PGA Championship.

PERSONAL: Comes from same "neighborhood" as Greg Norman and Wayne Grady in Queensland, Australia.

1994 PGA TOUR STATISTICS

Scoring Average	72.51
Driving Distance	255.3
Driving Accuracy	59.0
Greens in Regulation	54.0
Putting	1.813
All-Around	–
Sand Saves	55.4
Total Driving	–
Eagles	1
Birdies	131

MISCELLANEOUS STATISTICS

Scoring Avg. (before cut)	73.31
Scoring Avg. (3rd round)	73.20
Scoring Avg. (4th round)	74.20
Birdie Conversion	27.5
Par Breakers	15.0

1994 Low Round: 67: NEC WSOG/1
Career Low Round: 62: 1991 Anheuser-Busch Golf Classic/1
Career Largest Paycheck: $180,000/1989 Southwestern Bell Colonial/1

DAVE BARR

EXEMPT STATUS: 53rd on 1994 money list

FULL NAME: David Allen Barr

HEIGHT: 6' 1" **WEIGHT:** 200

BIRTH DATE: March 1, 1952

BIRTHPLACE: Kelowna, British Columbia

RESIDENCE: Richmond, B.C.; plays out of Swan-E-Set Bay Resort & CC

FAMILY: Wife, Lu Ann; Brent Jason (10/11/80), Teryn Amber (4/13/83)

COLLEGE: Oral Roberts University

SPECIAL INTERESTS: All sports

TURNED PROFESSIONAL: 1974

Q SCHOOL: Fall 1977

PLAYER PROFILE

CAREER EARNINGS: $2,152,105   **PLAYOFF RECORD:** 1-2

TOUR VICTORIES: 1981 Quad Cities Open. **1987** Georgia-Pacific Atlanta Golf Classic. (TOTAL: 2)

MONEY & POSITION:

1978--$11,897--133	1984--$113,336--62	1990--$197,979-- 80
1979--$13,022--142	1985--$126,177--65	1991--$144,389--108
1980--$14,664--141	1986--$122,181--70	1992--$118,859--119
1981--$46,214-- 90	1987--$202,241--54	1993--$179,264-- 96
1982--$12,474--166	1988--$291,244--33	1994--$314,885-- 53
1983--$52,800-- 96	1989--$190,480--75	

BEST 1994 FINISHES: T3--Canon Greater Hartford Open; T5--FedEx St. Jude Classic; T7--Greater Milwaukee Open; T10--Shell Houston Open

1994 SUMMARY: Tournaments entered--28; in money--19; top ten finishes--4.

1995 PGA TOUR CHARITY TEAM COMPETITION: Bob Hope Chrysler Classic

NATIONAL TEAMS: World Cup (13), 1977, 1978, 1982, 1983, 1984, 1985, 1987, 1988, 1989, 1990, 1991, 1993, 1994 (won individual title in 1983 and team title with Dan Halldorson in 1985). Canadian World Amateur Cup, 1972. Dunhill Cup (7), 1986, 1987, 1988, 1989, 1990, 1993, 1994.

1994 SEASON: Hard-working Canadian veteran enjoyed best season of 17-year career...finest moment came away from TOUR, when captained Canadian team (which included Rick Gibson and Ray Stewart) to Dunhill Cup victory over United States...had four top-10 finishes, best of which–T3 in Canon Greater Hartford Open–crafted through closing 65 at TPC at River Highlands...first top-10 came after opening 66, one stroke off early lead, in Shell Houston Open (T10)...during summer had two top-10s in four starts, at FedEx St. Jude Classic and Greater Milwaukee Open...finished T5, two strokes out of Dicky Pride-Gene Sauers-Hal Sutton playoff in Memphis...second-round 64, his lowest of season, had him two strokes out of midpoint lead in GMO, where finished T7...season earnings of $314,885, best ever for a Canadian.

CAREER HIGHLIGHTS: T2 in 1993 Nissan Los Angeles Open produced biggest payday--$66,000--since winning 1987 Georgia-Pacific Atlanta Golf Classic...went off back-side at Riviera CC on Sunday of rain-shortened event and carded 66, day's best round...'87 performance in Atlanta produced 23-under-par 265 winning total...came from five strokes back last day of 1981 Quad Cities Open to tie Dan Halldorson, Victor Regalado, Frank Conner and Woody Blackburn...ensuing playoff lasted eight holes, second longest in TOUR history...winner of 12 tournaments on Canadian Tour...four-time winner Canadian Order of Merit: 1977-85-86-88...13-time member Canadian World Cup team...captured World Cup individual title in 1983, teamed with Dan Halldorson to win team title in 1985...eight-time member Canadian Dunhill Cup team, captain 1994...winner of numerous SCORE awards as Canada's top player.

PERSONAL: Employs baseball grip instead of overlapping or interlocking...an avid hockey fan, who played the sport as youngster.

1994 PGA TOUR STATISTICS

Scoring Average	70.62	(43)
Driving Distance	259.6	(108)
Driving Accuracy	72.8	(49T)
Greens in Regulation	70.9	(6T)
Putting	1.802	(111T)
All-Around	513	(33)
Sand Saves	47.2	(142)
Total Driving	157	(57)
Eagles	8	(28T)
Birdies	319	(26T)

MISCELLANEOUS STATISTICS

Scoring Avg. (before cut)	70.95	(46T)
Scoring Avg. (3rd round)	70.06	(22)
Scoring Avg. (4th round)	70.67	(32)
Birdie Conversion	26.8	(130T)
Par Breakers	19.5	(61T)

1994 Low Round: 64: Greater Milwaukee Open/2
Career Low Round: 63: 1988 Canon Sammy Davis Jr. Greater Hartford Open/4
Career Largest Paycheck: $108,000/1987 Georgia-Pacific Atlanta Golf Classic/1

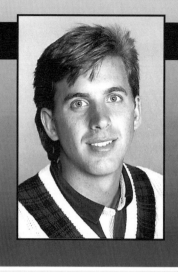

PAT BATES

EXEMPT STATUS: 3rd on 1994 NIKE TOUR money list

FULL NAME: Patrick Alfred Bates

HEIGHT: 6' 3"　　　　**WEIGHT:** 190

BIRTH DATE: July 26, 1969

BIRTHPLACE: St. Louis, MO

RESIDENCE: Boca Raton, FL

FAMILY: Single

COLLEGE: University of Florida

SPECIAL INTERESTS: Bible study, all sports

TURNED PROFESSIONAL: 1991

JOINED TOUR: 1995

| PLAYER PROFILE |

NIKE TOUR PLAYER RECORD

CAREER EARNINGS: $156,140　　　　**PLAYOFF RECORD:** 0-1

NIKE TOUR VICTORIES: 1994 NIKE Dakota Dunes Open

MONEY & POSITION: 1991--$ 671--278　　　　1994--$155,469--3

BEST 1994 FINISH: 1 - NIKE Dakota Dunes Open

1994 SUMMARY: Tournaments entered--23, in money--16; top ten finishes--8

1995 PGA TOUR CHARITY TEAM COMPETITION: MCI Classic

1994 SEASON: Was constantly flirting with victory on last year's NIKE TOUR…in addition to winning the NIKE Dakota Dunes Open, posted three second-place finishes and two thirds…lost to Omar Uresti at Shreveport Open on the sixth playoff hole…also runnerup at NIKE South Carolina Classic and NIKE Carolina Classic…finished T3 at NIKE Pensacola Classic and NIKE Ozarks Open…showed ability to play well under pressure with final-round scoring average of 69.59 (fourth best on NIKE TOUR)…in 78 rounds of play, ranked third in par breakers at 23.6%, seventh in overall scoring at 70.35, 11th among eagle leaders with nine and 15th among birdie leaders with 323…finished year strong with 10 in-money finishes in final 12 events…played those 12 events 79-under par, an average of 6.58 under per tournament with all 10 of the in-money finishes in the top-25…one of longer hitters on '94 NIKE TOUR…missed cut in only '94 PGA TOUR event (New England Classic).

CAREER HIGHLIGHTS: Played four 1993 PGA TOUR events (Kmart GGO, Kemper Open, New England Classic and Canadian Open), missed cut in each…three-time All-America selection at Florida and three-time first-team All-SEC, won three college tournaments…college highlight was winning 1990 Golf Digest Invitational at TPC at The Woodlands…Florida teammates were Jeff Barlow, Chris DiMarco and Dudley Hart…played Canadian Tour in 1992-93, finishing 19th on '92 Order of Merit.

PERSONAL: Very active in FCA and TOUR's Bible study group…after taking two-shot penalty for hitting wrong ball in '93 Canadian Tour event, has taken to marking his golf ball with a Bible verse…says he's more than casual sports fan: "I played all sports growing up and played baseball and basketball until I gave them all up in high school to concentrate on golf."

1994 PGA TOUR STATISTICS	
Scoring Average	N/A
Driving Distance	N/A
Driving Accuracy	N/A
Greens in Regulation	N/A
Putting	N/A
All-Around	N/A
Sand Saves	N/A
Total Driving	N/A
Eagles	N/A
Birdies	N/A

MISCELLANEOUS STATISTICS	
Scoring Avg. (before cut)	N/A
Scoring Avg. (3rd round)	N/A
Scoring Avg. (4th round)	N/A
Birdie Conversion	N/A
Par Breakers	N/A

1994 Low Round: N/A

Career Low Round: N/A

Career Largest

Paycheck: N/A

CHIP BECK

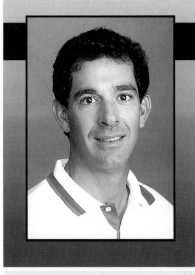

EXEMPT STATUS: 68th on 1994 money list

FULL NAME: Charles Henry Beck

HEIGHT: 5' 10" **WEIGHT:** 170

BIRTH DATE: September 12, 1956

BIRTHPLACE: Fayetteville, NC

RESIDENCE: Lake Forest, IL; plays out of Royal Melbourne, Long Grove, IL

FAMILY: Wife, Karen Marie; Charles (11/12/83), Elizabeth Tuttle (3/16/87), Mary Catherine (7/7/90), Anne Marie (5/28/92)

COLLEGE: University of Georgia (1978, Journalism)

SPECIAL INTERESTS: Tennis, landscaping, water skiing

TURNED PROFESSIONAL: 1978

Q SCHOOL: Fall 1978

PLAYER PROFILE

CAREER EARNINGS: $5,585,763   **PLAYOFF RECORD:** 0-2

TOUR VICTORIES: **1988** Los Angeles Open, USF&G Classic. **1990** Buick Open.
(TOTAL: 4)   **1992** Freeport-McMoRan Classic.

MONEY & POSITION:

1979--$ 4,166--194	1985--$ 76,038--97	1991--$578,535--16
1980--$ 17,109--131	1986--$215,140--39	1992--$689,704--17
1981--$ 30,034--110	1987--$523,003-- 9	1993--$603,376--25
1982--$ 57,608-- 76	1988--$916,818-- 2	1994--$281,131--68
1983--$149,909-- 33	1989--$694,087-- 9	
1984--$177,289-- 34	1990--$571,816--17	

BEST 1994 FINISH: 3--Nissan Los Angeles Open

1993 SUMMARY: Tournaments entered--27; in money--19; top ten finishes--1.

1995 PGA TOUR CHARITY TEAM COMPETITION: Motorola Western Open

NATIONAL TEAMS: Ryder Cup (3), 1989,1991, 1993; Kirin Cup, 1988; Asahi Glass Four Tours World Championship of Golf, 1989.

1994 SEASON: Less-than-satisfying campaign for one of TOUR's most "up" players, attributable at least in part to some lower back tightness…ended seven-year run during which made Top 30 each year…earnings lowest since 1986, with $215,140…money-list placing worst since 1985 (No. 97)…still nothing could put damper on his sunny disposition…followed T12 at AT&T Pebble Beach National Pro-Am with only top-10, Nissan Los Angeles Open T3 in fourth start of year…opened with 66, two off Tom Purtzer's early lead, closed with 68 good for $68,000…biggest check rest of way $34,000 for T15 in Masters…had pair of back-to-back T14s, in GTE Byron Nelson Classic and Memorial Tournament…posted second-round 63, his lowest of year, in final round of weather-shortened Byron Nelson…best finish over last three months Buick Open T17 in early August…had nothing better than T40 in September-October, missed last two cuts of year.

CAREER HIGHLIGHTS: Recorded 59 October 11, 1991, during third round of Las Vegas Invitational at Sunrise GC…made 13 birdies during bogey-free round, sinking three-foot putt on 18th hole to join Al Geiberger as only sub-60 shooters in TOUR history… received $500,000 from Hilton Hotels for historic feat, with another $500,000 designated for charity…set up Chip Beck Scholarship Fund for distribution of monies…best year on TOUR 1988, when won L.A. Open and USF&G Classic…repeated as New Orleans winner in 1992…had two runnerup finishes in 1993, at Masters and in Anheuser-Busch Golf Classic…A-B finish enabled him to make third Ryder Cup team…singles victory over Barry Lane at The Belfry gave United States second consecutive victory …winner 1988 Vardon Trophy…victor 1989-92 Merrill Lynch Shoot-Out Championships.

PERSONAL: First started playing golf during summer of 10th year, won Pee Wee division by end of that summer…three-time All-American at Georgia, where majored in journalism…named Athlete of Year as senior.

1994 PGA TOUR STATISTICS

Scoring Average	70.60	(39T)
Driving Distance	260.3	(103T)
Driving Accuracy	72.5	(52)
Greens in Regulation	63.8	(140T)
Putting	1.766	(19T)
All-Around	613	(62)
Sand Saves	48.7	(125T)
Total Driving	155	(55)
Eagles	5	(87T)
Birdies	300	(48T)

MISCELLANEOUS STATISTICS

Scoring Avg. (before cut)	71.02	(52T)
Scoring Avg. (3rd round)	70.59	(65T)
Scoring Avg. (4th round)	71.71	(108T)
Birdie Conversion	30.4	(22T)
Par Breakers	19.7	(55T)

1994 Low Round: 63: GTE Byron Nelson Classic.2
Career Low Round: 59: 1991 Las Vegas Invitational/3
Career Largest Paycheck: $216,000/1987 Nabisco Championships of Golf/2

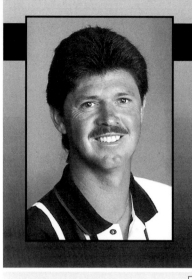

JAY DON BLAKE

EXEMPT STATUS: 55th on 1994 money list

FULL NAME: Jay Don Blake

HEIGHT: 6' 2" **WEIGHT:** 180

BIRTH DATE: October 28, 1958

BIRTHPLACE: St. George, UT

RESIDENCE: St. George, UT

FAMILY: Jamie Dawn (10/1/79), Bridgette (4/11/83)

COLLEGE: Utah State

SPECIAL INTERESTS: Fishing, hunting, all sports

TURNED PROFESSIONAL: 1981

Q SCHOOL: Fall 1986

PLAYER PROFILE

CAREER EARNINGS: $1,943,438

TOUR VICTORIES: 1991 Shearson Lehman Brothers Open
(TOTAL: 1)

MONEY & POSITION:

1987--$ 87,634--106	1990--$148,384--106	1993--$202,482--86
1988--$131,937-- 90	1991--$563,854-- 21	1994--$309,351--55
1989--$200,499-- 71	1992--$299,298-- 51	

BEST 1994 FINISHES: T2--Northern Telecom Open; T4--Bell Canadian Open

1994 SUMMARY: Tournaments entered--25; in money--20, top ten finishes--2.

1995 PGA TOUR CHARITY TEAM COMPETITION: Kemper Open

1994 SEASON: Enjoyed second-best season of eight-year career, surpassing $300,000 for first time since 1991...had just two top-10 finishes but nine in top-25 as crafted $309,351 earnings composite...opened year with T14 in United Airlines Hawaiian Open, featuring second-round 65...first top-10 came the following week, T2 in Northern Telecom Open...was just one stroke off 54-hole lead after rounds of 68-69-67...finished two strokes behind Andrew Magee, tied with Loren Roberts, Vijay Singh and Steve Stricker...final top-10 virtually at opposite end of campaign...posted T4 in Bell Canadian Open in third-to-last event of year...was up and down in Canada, carding career-low 63 in Round 2 following opening 74, then closing with 68 after third-round 73...63 over demanding Glen Abbey layout featured 11 threes...had three top-25s (including Canadian Open) in final four starts.

CAREER HIGHLIGHTS: Best year of career came in 1991, when captured only tournament title, Shearson Lehman Brothers Open...closed with consecutive 67s at Torrey Pines to edge Bill Sander by two strokes...had five other top-10 finishes during that campaign, which produced earnings of $563,854 and only Top-30 money list placing to date (No. 21)...went over $200,000 in earnings for first time in 1989, with best finish T3 in BellSouth Atlanta Classic...had pair of Buick-sponsored T4s in 1993, in Buick Invitational of California and at Buick Open, his top finishes that year...posted solo second in 1991 BellSouth Classic, three strokes behind Tom Kite...led TOUR in putting in 1991, averaging 1.733 putts per green in regulation...finished in top-10 in putting the next year, as well...winner 1988 Utah State Open.

PERSONAL: Has experienced back trouble for four years, all of which he attributes to appendix removal...returned to action prematurely following appendectomy, causing damage to lower back muscles...winner of 1980 NCAA Championship during junior year at Utah State, runnerup in 1981...named College Player of Year in 1981...knew by age 12 wanted to be professional golfer.

1994 PGA TOUR STATISTICS

Scoring Average	70.50	(36)
Driving Distance	260.4	(102)
Driving Accuracy	69.9	(78)
Greens in Regulation	69.2	(22T)
Putting	1.761	(13)
All-Around	504	(32)
Sand Saves	45.6	(153)
Total Driving	180	(93T)
Eagles	5	(87T)
Birdies	339	(13)

MISCELLANEOUS STATISTICS

Scoring Avg. (before cut)	70.31	(13T)
Scoring Avg. (3rd round)	70.17	(28)
Scoring Avg. (4th round)	71.17	(58T)
Birdie Conversion	31.3	(9T)
Par Breakers	22.0	(7)

1994 Low Round: 63: Bell Canadian/2
Career Low Round: 63: 1994 Bell Canadian/2
Career Largest Paycheck: $180,000/1991 Shearson Lehman Brothers Open/1

GUY BOROS

EXEMPT STATUS: 76th on 1994 money list

FULL NAME: Guy Donald Boros

HEIGHT: 6'1"   **WEIGHT:** 240

BIRTH DATE: September 4, 1964

BIRTHPLACE: Ft. Lauderdale, FL

RESIDENCE: Ft. Lauderdale, FL

FAMILY: Single

COLLEGE: University of Iowa

SPECIAL INTERESTS: Hunting, fishing

TURNED PROFESSIONAL: 1986

Q SCHOOL: 1993

PLAYER PROFILE

CAREER EARNINGS: $240,775

BEST-EVER FINISH: T3--1994 Deposit Guaranty Golf Classic

MONEY & POSITION: 1994--$240,775--76

BEST 1994 FINISHES: T3--Deposit Guaranty Golf Classic; T6--Bob Hope Chrysler Classic; T8--Las Vegas Invitational; T9--New England Classic

1994 SUMMARY: Tournaments entered--36; in money--19, top ten finishes--4

1995 PGA TOUR CHARITY TEAM COMPETITION: Kmart Greater Greensboro Open

1994 SEASON: Son of one of the greats of the game, lost his father, two-time U.S. Open champion Julius Boros, in May, while Guy was playing in Southwestern Bell Colonial…finished well up on list of rookie money winners, trailing just Ernie Els, Mike Heinen, Glen Day, Steve Stricker and Dicky Pride…posted first of four top-10s in fourth start, T6 in Bob Hope Chrysler Classic…rounds of 66-67-68-69-69 worth $36,850, largest check of campaign until claimed T8 in Las Vegas Invitational…that one worth $42,000, which put him over $200,000 for year…LVI featured second-round 63, matching his low of year (Round 2 of Southwestern Bell Colonial)…enjoyed successful two-week stretch in July, finishing T3 in Deposit Guaranty Golf Classic and T9 in New England Classic…went 69-67 in weather-abbreviated Deposit Guaranty…two-week run put $54,713 in bank.

CAREER HIGHLIGHTS: Not exactly a first-year player, since played Canadian Tour for four years and also Australasian Tour in 1991-92…qualified for PGA TOUR by finishing T18 in 1993 Qualifying Tournament…led 1991 Canadian Tour Order of Merit…finished 13th on 1993 NIKE TOUR money list with $75,104.

PERSONAL: All-Big Ten player 1984-85-86 at University of Iowa.

1994 PGA TOUR STATISTICS

Scoring Average	71.00	(68T)
Driving Distance	270.7	(28)
Driving Accuracy	67.3	(116)
Greens in Regulation	67.2	(51T)
Putting	1.779	(50T)
All-Around	374	(14)
Sand Saves	55.4	(41)
Total Driving	144	(46)
Eagles	14	(3)
Birdies	333	(17)

MISCELLANEOUS STATISTICS

Scoring Avg. (before cut)	70.84	(42)
Scoring Avg. (3rd round)	71.50	(130T)
Scoring Avg. (4th round)	71.25	(65T)
Birdie Conversion	29.6	(40T)
Par Breakers	20.7	(23T)

1994 Low Round: 63: 2 times
Career Low Round: 63: 2 times, most recently
Career Largest 1994 Las Vegas Invitational/2
Paycheck: $42,000/1994 Las Vegas Invitational/T8

MICHAEL BRADLEY

EXEMPT STATUS: 104th on 1994 money list

FULL NAME: Michael John Bradley

HEIGHT: 6'   **WEIGHT:** 180

BIRTH DATE: July 17, 1966

BIRTHPLACE: Largo, FL

RESIDENCE: Valrico, FL; plays out of Bloomingdale Golfers' Club, Brandon, FL

FAMILY: Wife, Jennifer

COLLEGE: Oklahoma State

SPECIAL INTERESTS: Sports

TURNED PROFESSIONAL: 1988

Q SCHOOL: 1992

PLAYER PROFILE

CAREER EARNINGS: $301,296

BEST-EVER FINISH: T3--1993 Kemper Open

MONEY & POSITION: 1993--$126,160--121   1994--$175,137--104

BEST 1994 FINISHES: T4--Anheuser-Busch Golf Classic; T10--Kemper Open; T10--Hardee's Golf Classic

1994 SUMMARY: Tournaments entered--29; in money--15; top ten finishes--3.

1995 PGA TOUR CHARITY TEAM COMPETITION: BellSouth Classic

1994 SEASON: With three top-10s, improved over rookie season by nearly $55,000…missed 11 cuts in first 19 starts, still had earnings of $83,418 through first half of season…included in that stretch T10 at Kemper Open, which is rapidly becoming his favorite tournament…posted best finish of year in second start of July, T4 in Anheuser-Busch Golf Classic…$45,467 payday, his best of year, came with rounds of 68-69-69-67…273 total six strokes behind Mark McCumber…season almost went out window following Buick Open, when injured elbow in pickup basketball game…missed five weeks, then returned to missed cut at B.C. Open…following week third-round 62, low of his career, helped propel him to T10 in Hardee's Golf Classic.

CAREER HIGHLIGHTS: Top finish of first two years on TOUR T3 in 1993 Kemper Open…closed with rounds of 69-68 at TPC at Avenel, tying Scott Hoch for third…277 total was two strokes behind winner Grant Waite…check for $74,500 largest of career…next best finish of rookie season T18 in Freeport-McMoRan Classic…after 7-under-par 64, held first-round lead of 1993 FedEx St. Jude Classic, one stroke ahead of defending champion Jay Haas and Davis Love III…winner of two Canadian Tour events…also played Australasian Tour, finishing 52nd on Order of Merit in 1992.

PERSONAL: In what might be considered especially appropriate for a golfer, has a special interest in agronomy…1987-88 All-American at Oklahoma State.

1994 PGA TOUR STATISTICS

Scoring Average	70.98	(65T)
Driving Distance	271.2	(26T)
Driving Accuracy	60.7	(170)
Greens in Regulation	65.5	(98T)
Putting	1.786	(68T)
All-Around	534	(40T)
Sand Saves	59.2	(12)
Total Driving	196	(119)
Eagles	6	(64T)
Birdies	313	(31)

MISCELLANEOUS STATISTICS

Scoring Avg. (before cut)	71.48	(96)
Scoring Avg. (3rd round)	69.64	(10)
Scoring Avg. (4th round)	70.29	(16T)
Birdie Conversion	29.8	(34T)
Par Breakers	19.9	(48T)

1994 Low Round: 62: 1994 Hardee's/3
Career Low Round: 62: 1994 Hardee's/3
Career Largest
Paycheck: $74,500/Kemper Open/T3

MARK BROOKS

EXEMPT STATUS: 1994 tournament winner

FULL NAME: Mark David Brooks

HEIGHT: 5' 9"   **WEIGHT:** 150

BIRTH DATE: March 25, 1961

BIRTHPLACE: Fort Worth, TX

RESIDENCE: Fort Worth, TX

FAMILY: Wife, Cynthia; Lyndsay (1/24/86), Hollie (9/21/89)

COLLEGE: University of Texas

SPECIAL INTERESTS: All sports, cooking

TURNED PROFESSIONAL: 1983

Q SCHOOL: Fall 1983, 1984, 1985, 1987

PLAYER PROFILE

CAREER EARNINGS: $2,885,016   **PLAYOFF RECORD:** 2-2

TOUR VICTORIES: **1988** Canon Sammy Davis, Jr-Greater Hartford Open. **1991** Kmart Greater
(TOTAL: 4)   Greensboro Open, Greater Milwaukee Open. **1994** Kemper Open

MONEY & POSITION:

1984--$ 40,438--122	1988--$280,636-- 36	1992--$629,754--21
1985--$ 32,094--141	1989--$112,834--115	1993--$249,696--66
1986--$ 47,264--140	1990--$307,948-- 45	1994--$474,985--31
1987--$ 42,100--165	1991--$667,263-- 11	

BEST 1994 FINISHES: 1--Kemper Open; T7--Memorial Tournament; T8--GTE Byron Nelson Classic;
T8--Buick Classic.

1994 SUMMARY: Tournaments entered--32; in money--22; top ten finishes--4.

1995 PGA TOUR CHARITY TEAM COMPETITION: Colonial Tournament

1994 SEASON: Finally won a non-"Greater" tournament, capturing Kemper Open in June…first three titles came in "Greater" events: Hartford, Greensboro and Milwaukee…first- and second-round leader at TPC at Avenel, relinquished lead to Bobby Wadkins (by two) after 54 holes…closing 69 produced three-stroke final edge over Wadkins and D.A. Weibring…Kemper win part of five-event stretch in which posted four top-10 finishes…went back-to-back in GTE Byron Nelson Classic (T8) and Memorial (T7), then followed Kemper victory with T8 in Buick Classic…proceeded to miss cut in seven of next 10 starts…righted self in time to make stretch drive for TOUR Championship…was in money in final five events, climaxed by closing 65 in Las Vegas Invitational which gave him T14…that placing worth $27,750 and final berth (by just $154 over Craig Stadler) in season-ending tournament… played in 33 events, just one shy of season-high 34 posted by Ted Tryba and John Inman.

CAREER HIGHLIGHTS: Best season to date–1991–featured pair of victories, in Kmart Greater Greensboro Open and Greater Milwaukee Open…fired 8-under-par 64 on final day to catch Gene Sauers, then defeated him with par on third extra hole for GGO title… later edged Robert Gamez by one stroke after opening with 9-under-par 63 in GMO…first TOUR victory, in 1988 Canon Sammy Davis, Jr.-Greater Hartford Open, came in playoff with Joey Sindelar and Dave Barr…sank 10-foot birdie putt on second extra hole for the win…posted 11 top-10 finishes in 1992, going over $600,000 mark for second time in career…was part of five-man playoff won by John Inman at 1993 Buick Southern Open…took part in Qualifying Tournament four times before finally making it through in 1987.

PERSONAL: Two-time All-American at University of Texas…was introduced to golf by his grandfather at age of eight.

1994 PGA TOUR STATISTICS

Scoring Average	70.81	(49)
Driving Distance	258.8	(114T)
Driving Accuracy	67.7	(110)
Greens in Regulation	63.9	(138T)
Putting	1.769	(28)
All-Around	534	(40T)
Sand Saves	51.6	(90)
Total Driving	224	(143T)
Eagles	15	(2)
Birdies	372	(3)

MISCELLANEOUS STATISTICS

Scoring Avg. (before cut)	70.78	(38)
Scoring Avg. (3rd round)	71.33	(113T)
Scoring Avg. (4th round)	71.23	(64)
Birdie Conversion	28.9	(61T)
Par Breakers	19.2	(73T)

1994 Low Round: 64: 2 times

Career Low Round: 61: 1990 Shearson Lehman Hutton Open/2

Career Largest Paycheck: $225,000/1991 Kmart Greater Greensboro Open/1

BRAD BRYANT

EXEMPT STATUS: 18th on 1994 money list

FULL NAME: Bradley Dub Bryant

HEIGHT: 5' 10"   **WEIGHT:** 170

BIRTH DATE: December 11, 1954

BIRTHPLACE: Amarillo, TX

RESIDENCE: Winter Garden, FL

FAMILY: Wife, Sue; William Jamieson (1/27/91);
Jonathan David (4/26/93)

COLLEGE: University of New Mexico

SPECIAL INTERESTS: Bass fishing, hunting

TURNED PROFESSIONAL: 1976

Q SCHOOL: Fall 1978, 1987, 1988

PLAYER PROFILE

CAREER EARNINGS: $1,935,399   **PLAYOFF RECORD:** 0-1

BEST-EVER FINISHES: 2--1991 Buick Classic; T2--1982 Tournament Players Championship; T2--1982 Quad Cities Open;T2--1983 Byron Nelson Golf Classic. T2-1993 Buick Southern Open (lost playoff to John Inman); T2--1994 Doral-Ryder Open; T2--1994 Kmart Greater Greensboro Open.

MONEY & POSITION:

1978--$ 4,350--173	1984--$ 36,805--127	1990--$189,795-- 86
1979--$ 63,013-- 67	1985--$ 1,683--232	1991--$152,202-- 99
1980--$ 56,115-- 68	1986--$ 11,290--202	1992--$227,529-- 69
1981--$ 52,070-- 80	1987--$ 17,090--191	1993--$230,139-- 74
1982--$ 99,576-- 37	1988--$ 62,614--141	1994--$687,803-- 18
1983--$ 93,021-- 61	1989--$174,393-- 84	

BEST 1994 FINISHES: T2--Doral-Ryder Open, Kmart Greater Greensboro Open; 3--Buick Southern Open, THE TOUR Championship; 7--GTE Byron Nelson Classic; T8--Texas Open

1994 SUMMARY: Tournaments entered--32; in money--25; top ten finishes--6.

1995 PGA TOUR CHARITY TEAM COMPETITION: United Airlines Hawaiian Open

1994 SEASON: "Close but no cigar," a term applied periodically throughout his winless 17-year career, had further relevance in '94…finished second twice more (for career total of seven), but that's only part of story…as only non-winner in TOUR Championship field, came close to tasting victory for first time but finished one stroke out of Mark McCumber-Fuzzy Zoeller playoff…solo third still worth $207,000, largest check of career…had two T2s in five starts, at Doral-Ryder Open and Kmart Greater Greensboro Open…at the time, Doral paycheck for $123,200 was all-time best…six top-10s (also GTE Byron Nelson Classic and Texas Open) helped produce career year with earnings of $687,803 (next best $230,139 in 1993)…led TOUR in birdies with 397…In December won the unofficial JCPenney Classic with Marta Figueras-Dotti.

CAREER HIGHLIGHTS: Before spectacular 1994 season, money-won total (with exception of 1991) increased steadily each year following shoulder surgery in 1985…was part of five-man 1993 Buick Southern Open playoff won by John Inman…marked first time ever as tied for lead after 72 holes…finished with 67 at Callaway Gardens to gain playoff, but Inman closed with birdie on second extra hole…feels had best shot at winning three weeks earlier in Bell Canadian Open, where held one-stroke lead entering final round but closed with 74 to finish third behind David Frost…other runnerup finishes came in 1991 Buick Classic (one stroke behind Billy Andrade), 1983 Byron Nelson, 1982 Tournament Players Championship (inaugural at TPC at Sawgrass won by Jerry Pate) and 1982 Quad Cities.

PERSONAL: Played hurt from 1983 until undergoing shoulder surgery in 1985…took until 1988 for full recovery, since which has been solid performer…an avid fisherman…nickname "Dr. Dirt" bestowed by Gary McCord.

1994 PGA TOUR STATISTICS

Scoring Average	70.72	(46)
Driving Distance	264.4	(67)
Driving Accuracy	66.9	(121T)
Greens in Regulation	70.2	(17)
Putting	1.774	(36T)
All-Around	393	(17T)
Sand Saves	53.7	(61T)
Total Driving	188	(107T)
Eagles	7	(44T)
Birdies	397	(1)

MISCELLANEOUS STATISTICS

Scoring Avg. (before cut)	70.67	(34)
Scoring Avg. (3rd round)	71.14	(98T)
Scoring Avg. (4th round)	70.48	(24)
Birdie Conversion	28.8	(63T)
Par Breakers	20.6	(25T)

1994 Low Round: 64: WDW/Oldsmobile Classic/1
Career Low Round: 64: 9 times, most recent 1994
Career Largest   WDW/Oldsmobile Classic/1
Paycheck: $207,000/1994 TOUR Championship/3

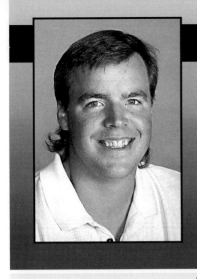

BOB BURNS

EXEMPT STATUS: 101st on 1994 money list

FULL NAME: Robert David Burns

HEIGHT: 5' 8" **WEIGHT:** 150

BIRTH DATE: May 5, 1968

BIRTHPLACE: Mission Hills, CA

RESIDENCE: Granada Hills, CA

FAMILY: Single

COLLEGE: California State University-Northridge

SPECIAL INTERESTS: Backpacking

TURNED PROFESSIONAL: 1991

Q SCHOOL: 1993

PLAYER PROFILE

CAREER EARNINGS: $178,168

BEST-EVER FINISH: T5--1994 Buick Classic

MONEY & POSITION: 1994--$178,168 --101

BEST 1994 FINISHES: T5--Buick Classic; T8--Texas Open; T9--Northern Telecom Open.

1994 SUMMARY: Tournaments entered--24; in money--12; top ten finishes--3

1995 PGA TOUR CHARITY TEAM COMPETITION: Phoenix Open

1994 SEASON: Having weathered Northridge earthquake in January, first TOUR season had to be viewed as a piece of cake…home was (and still is) near epicenter of massive trembler…shortly after earthquake struck, closed with 65 in second start of season, good for T9 in Northern Telecom Open…following week posted T13 in Phoenix Open, giving him $44,240 after three events…biggest payday of rookie campaign came in June, when final-round 68 lifted him to T5 at Buick Classic…Westchester finish interrupted what later became string of seven missed cuts…more importantly, $43,800 check raised earnings total to $137,140, putting him on solid footing at season's midpoint to retain playing privileges for 1995…later had to withdraw during second round of Bell Canadian Open with ligament damage to right wrist…returned to action at Texas Open and played without brace for first time since injury, fashioning opening-round 65 and eventual T8 worth $25,000…posted yet another 65 the following week, during Round 3 of Las Vegas Invitational, where finished season with T26.

CAREER HIGHLIGHTS: Qualified for TOUR by placing T11 in 1993 Qualifying Tournament…finished 31st on 1992 Ben Hogan Tour money list…lost '92 Hogan South Texas Open to Brian Henninger on first playoff hole…also finished 31st on 1993 NIKE TOUR money list.

PERSONAL: Mentor is fellow Californian Duffy Waldorf…winner 1990 Division II Championship…NCAA All-American.

1994 PGA TOUR STATISTICS

Scoring Average	71.40	(112T)
Driving Distance	259.3	(111T)
Driving Accuracy	72.2	(54)
Greens in Regulation	67.1	(56)
Putting	1.792	(87T)
All-Around	792	(122T)
Sand Saves	46.6	(145)
Total Driving	165	(66T)
Eagles	4	(104T)
Birdies	234	(123T)

MISCELLANEOUS STATISTICS

Scoring Avg. (before cut)	71.96	(140)
Scoring Avg. (3rd round)	70.50	(57T)
Scoring Avg. (4th round)	70.80	(38T)
Birdie Conversion	28.4	(82)
Par Breakers	19.4	(64T)

1994 Low Round: 65: 3 times

Career Low Round: 65: 3 times, most recent

Career Largest — 1994 Las Vegas Invitational/3

Paycheck: $43,800/1994 Buick Classic/T5

CURT BYRUM

EXEMPT STATUS: 128th on 1994 money list

FULL NAME: Curt Allen Byrum

HEIGHT: 6' 2" **WEIGHT:** 190

BIRTH DATE: December 29,1958

BIRTHPLACE: Onida, SD

RESIDENCE: Scottsdale, AZ; plays out of Desert Mountain GC

FAMILY: Wife, Cyndi; Christina Suzanne (10/13/90), Jake (6/11/92)

COLLEGE: University of New Mexico

SPECIAL INTERESTS: All sports

TURNED PROFESSIONAL: 1982

Q SCHOOL: 1982

PLAYER PROFILE

CAREER EARNINGS: $1,152,905

TOUR VICTORIES: 1989 Hardee's Golf Classic
(TOTAL: 1)

MONEY & POSITION:

1983--$30,772--130	1987--$ 212,450 -- 46	1991--$ 78,725--148
1984--$27,836--143	1988--$ 208,853 -- 55	1992--$ 31,450--194
1985--$ 6,943--193	1989--$ 221,702 -- 64	1993--$ --
1986--$79,454--108	1990--$ 117,134 --129	1994--$137,587--128

BEST 1994 FINISHES: T5--B.C. Open; T6--Hardee's Golf Classic

1994 SUMMARY: Tournaments entered--28; in money--13, top ten finishes--2.

1995 PGA TOUR CHARITY TEAM COMPETITION: GTE Byron Nelson Classic

1994 SEASON: After writing one of great comeback stories last half of campaign, almost saw everything go out window at Las Vegas Invitational…seemingly on verge of regaining playing privileges for first time since 1991, inadvertently played wrong ball on 16th hole of final round and was disqualified…when Jose Maria Olazabal decided not to join TOUR for 1995, 128th place (because of non-members Olazabal and Colin Montgomerie, and most of Mark McNulty's earnings coming from NEC World Series of Golf) became final slot in Top 125…missed cut in 12 of first 16 starts, earning just $15,352 through Anheuser-Busch Golf Classic…T11 in Deposit Guaranty Golf Classic produced biggest payday, $14,840, since T16 in 1992 Northern Telecom Open ($15,431)…from that point forward was in money in seven of next nine starts, earning $107,394…that stretch saw back-to-back top-10s in B.C. Open (T5) and Hardee's Golf Classic (T6), best finishes since T8 in 1991 USF&G Classic…missed cut in next-to-last start, Texas Open, before Las Vegas "drama" unfolded.

CAREER HIGHLIGHTS: Was at top of game in 1989, when went over $200,000 for third consecutive year and captured Hardee's Golf Classic title in July…that victory, coupled with brother Tom's Kemper Open win seven weeks earlier, made Byrums first brothers to win in same year since Dave and Mike Hill in 1972…fell first to No. 129 and then 148 during two seasons under victory exemption…plunge continued in 1992, with elbow trouble finally leading to Dec. surgery…opted for NIKE TOUR route to regain playing privileges, which did with No. 10 finish in 1993…Hardee's tournament provided sponsors exemption in 1986, after loss of TOUR membership previous year…held two-stroke lead over Mark Wiebe entering final round…although finished second to Wiebe, accompanying $43,200 paycheck earned special membership and full exemption for 1987…went over $200,000 for first time in '87…teamed with Bobby Nichols to win 1986 Showdown Classic at Jeremy Ranch, a PGA TOUR/Senior PGA TOUR event.

PERSONAL: Exceptional high school athlete, all-state in both football and basketball…named South Dakota Athlete of Year in 1977…winner 1979 Pacific Coast Amateur…four-time winner South Dakota State Juniors, five-time winner South Dakota State Amateur…1980 All-American at New Mexico.

1994 PGA TOUR STATISTICS

Scoring Average	71.18	(82)
Driving Distance	272.6	(21)
Driving Accuracy	63.6	(153)
Greens in Regulation	68.3	(37T)
Putting	1.802	(111T)
All-Around	695	(87)
Sand Saves	44.6	(156)
Total Driving	174	(83T)
Eagles	6	(64T)
Birdies	285	(71T)

MISCELLANEOUS STATISTICS

Scoring Avg. (before cut)	71.28	(73)
Scoring Avg. (3rd round)	70.36	(46)
Scoring Avg. (4th round)	71.25	(65T)
Birdie Conversion	28.6	(74T)
Par Breakers	20.0	(45T)

1994 Low Round: 64: 3 times
Career Low Round: 63: '83 Miller High
Career Largest Life Quad Cities Open/1
Paycheck: $126,000: '89 Hardee's Classic/1

MARK CALCAVECCHIA

EXEMPT STATUS: 30th on 1994 money list

FULL NAME: Mark John Calcavecchia

HEIGHT: 6'   **WEIGHT:** 200

BIRTH DATE: June 12, 1960

BIRTHPLACE: Laurel, NE

RESIDENCE: West Palm Beach, FL

FAMILY: Wife, Sheryl; Brittney Jo (8/8/89), Eric Jordan (1/1/94)

COLLEGE: University of Florida

SPECIAL INTERESTS: Bowling, music

TURNED PROFESSIONAL: 1981

Q SCHOOL: Spring 1981; Fall 1982, 1983

PLAYER PROFILE

CAREER EARNINGS: $4,489,962   **PLAYOFF RECORD:** 0-3

TOUR VICTORIES: **1986** Southwest Golf Classic. **1987** Honda Classic. **1988** Bank of Boston Classic.
(TOTAL: 6)   **1989** Phoenix Open, Nissan Los Angeles Open. **1992** Phoenix Open.

MONEY & POSITION:

1981--$ 404--253	1986--$155,012-- 58	1991--$323,621--50
1982--$25,064--134	1987--$522,423-- 10	1992--$377,234--39
1983--$16,313--161	1988--$751,912-- 6	1993--$630,366--21
1984--$29,660--140	1989--$807,741-- 5	1994--$533,201--30
1985--$15,957--162	1990--$834,281-- 7	

BEST 1994 FINISHES: 2--Bell Canadian Open; T3--Motorola Western Open, Greater Milwaukee Open; T8--Sprint International; T9--Buick Invitational of California; T10--Hardee's Golf Classic.

1994 SUMMARY: Tournaments entered--27; in money--18; top ten finishes--6.

1995 PGA TOUR CHARITY TEAM COMPETITION: Bell Canadian Open

NATIONAL TEAMS: Ryder Cup (3), 1987, 1989, 1991; Kirin Cup 1987; Asahi Glass Four Tours World Championship of Golf (2), 1989, 1990; Dunhill Cup (2), 1989, 1990.

1994 SEASON: Injured knee in December 1993 skiing accident, Arizona resident still played in Northern Telecom and Phoenix Opens…underwent arthroscopic surgery week after Phoenix, where finished T18…surgery repaired torn anterior cruciate ligament and cartilage damage…suffered no apparent after-effects, posting T9 in first start back, Buick Invitational of California, where closed with 65…finished year in Top 30 for second consecutive season, sixth time in last eight years…earnings total fifth-best of 14-year career…had eight-tournament stretch July through September where finished in top-10 five times…began string with T3 in Motorola Western Open, two weeks later closed 67-68 for T11 in British Open…after missing cut at PGA Championship, ran off four consecutive top-10s: Sprint International (8), Greater Milwaukee Open (T3), Bell Canadian Open (2), Hardee's Golf Classic (T10)…third-round 64 at GMO had him one stroke out of 54-hole lead…following week finished second to Mark McCumber in Canada.

CAREER HIGHLIGHTS: Captured 1989 British Open at Troon, last American winner of British championship…defeated Wayne Grady and Greg Norman under Royal and Ancient's multi-hole playoff system…hit 5-iron to seven feet from 190 yards on fourth and final playoff hole to finish with flourish…earlier that year won twice during TOUR's West Coast swing, Phoenix (for first time) and Nissan Los Angeles Open…seven-stroke winner at TPC at Scottsdale, where won by five strokes in 1992…battled Sandy Lyle down stretch to take L.A. Open…had four-year victory string, 1986-89…streak began with first TOUR title in 1986 Southwest Golf Classic…playoff loser to close friend Billy Mayfair in 1993 Greater Milwaukee Open when Mayfair chipped in from 20 feet on fourth extra hole…winner 1988 Australian Open.

PERSONAL: Winner 1976 Florida State Junior Championship and Orange Bowl Championship…first-team All-SEC in 1979…thrilled when family moved from Nebraska to Florida when he was 13, because he could play golf every day.

1994 PGA TOUR STATISTICS

Scoring Average	70.25	(25T)
Driving Distance	273.1	(17T)
Driving Accuracy	64.8	(142T)
Greens in Regulation	67.0	(57T)
Putting	1.764	(16)
All-Around	364	(11)
Sand Saves	53.6	(64T)
Total Driving	159	(58T)
Eagles	10	(11T)
Birdies	312	(32T)

MISCELLANEOUS STATISTICS

Scoring Avg. (before cut)	71.08	(56T)
Scoring Avg. (3rd round)	69.44	(7)
Scoring Avg. (4th round)	69.88	(7T)
Birdie Conversion	30.8	(17)
Par Breakers	21.3	(14T)

1994 Low Round: 64: Greater Milwaukee Open/3

Career Low Round: 63: 5 times, most recent '92 NEC World Series of Golf/3

Career Largest Paycheck: $180,000 /1989 Nissan Los AngelesOpen/1
1992 Phoenix Open/1

MARK CARNEVALE

EXEMPT STATUS: 93rd on 1994 money list

FULL NAME: Mark Kevin Carnevale

HEIGHT: 6'2"   **WEIGHT:** 238

BIRTH DATE: May 21, 1960

BIRTHPLACE: Annapolis, MD

RESIDENCE: Williamsburg, VA

FAMILY: Single

COLLEGE: James Madison University

SPECIAL INTERESTS: Jazz, travel, sailing, skiing

TURNED PROFESSIONAL: 1983

Q SCHOOL: 1991

PLAYER PROFILE

CAREER EARNINGS: $513,621   **PLAYOFF RECORD:** 0-1

TOUR VICTORIES: 1992 Chattanooga Classic.
(TOTAL: 1)

MONEY & POSITION: 1992--$220,921--70   1993--$100,046--145   1994--$192,653--93

BEST 1994 FINISHES: T2--GTE Byron Nelson Classic; 5--Buick Invitational of California

1994 SUMMARY: Tournaments entered--31; in money--14; top ten finishes--2.

1995 PGA TOUR CHARITY TEAM COMPETITION: GTE Byron Nelson Classic

1994 SEASON: Two top-10 finishes cornerstone to campaign which saw him miss 17 cuts, including 10 of last 12...high point of year T2 at GTE Byron Nelson Classic, where took part in TOUR-record six-man playoff won by Neal Lancaster...opening 65 (low round of season) put him in second place, one stroke behind David Ogrin...closed with 67 for 36-hole total of 132 and playoff slot...five-way runnerup worth $72,000 each...Nelson payday second-largest check of career...earlier in year posted final-round 67 for fifth in Buick Invitational of California ...that placing worth $44,000...also had pair of top-25s, T18 in Kemper Open three weeks after Byron Nelson and 24th in Sprint International, last cut made.

CAREER HIGHLIGHTS: Chosen PGA TOUR Rookie of Year by his peers for outstanding first-year campaign in 1992...season highlight two-stroke victory over Ed Dougherty and Dan Forsman in Chattanooga Classic...trailed by five strokes after three rounds, posted final-round 8-under-par 64 for win...final-round comeback matched David Edwards and Lanny Wadkins for best-come-from-behind-for-victory in '92...Chattanooga win his only top-10 that season...best finish of 1993 T13 in Buick Southern Open...also had T14 at Kemper Open worth $24,050...finished 19th in 1991 Qualifying Tournament...winner 1990 Utah Open and 1984 Virginia Open.

PERSONAL: Quit game for brief period during late 1980s to go to work for brokerage firm...father Ben Carnevale longtime basketball coach at Navy, also coached University of North Carolina to first national championship basketball game in 1945.

1994 PGA TOUR STATISTICS

Scoring Average	71.85	(149)
Driving Distance	256.8	(130)
Driving Accuracy	76.0	(19)
Greens in Regulation	66.7	(65T)
Putting	1.832	(162)
All-Around	831	(132)
Sand Saves	41.4	(174)
Total Driving	149	(49)
Eagles	8	(28T)
Birdies	258	(104T)

MISCELLANEOUS STATISTICS

Scoring Avg. (before cut)	72.45	(163)
Scoring Avg. (3rd round)	71.36	(117)
Scoring Avg. (4th round)	71.36	(72T)
Birdie Conversion	25.0	(159T)
Par Breakers	17.2	(146T)

1994 Low Round: 65: GTE Byron Nelson Classic/1
Career Low Round: 64: 1992 Chattanooga Classic/4
Career Largest Paycheck: $144,000/1992 Chattanooga Classic/1

JIM CARTER

EXEMPT STATUS: 4th on 1994 NIKE TOUR money list
FULL NAME: Jim Laver Carter
HEIGHT: 6'0"   **WEIGHT:** 170
BIRTH DATE: June 24, 1961
BIRTHPLACE: Spring Lake, NC
RESIDENCE: Scottsdale, AZ
FAMILY: Wife, Cyndi; Shane (10/5/91)
COLLEGE: Arizona State (1984, Business)
SPECIAL INTERESTS: Music, sports
TURNED PROFESSIONAL: 1985
Q SCHOOL: Fall 1985, 1986

PLAYER PROFILE

CAREER EARNINGS: $628,700

BEST-EVER FINISH: T3--1989 AT&T Pebble Beach National Pro-Am

MONEY & POSITION: 1987--$ 60,102--134   1989--$319,719-- 33   1991--$ 2,450--278
1988--$191,489-- 60   1990--$ 54,392--172   1993--$ 2,753--289

1995 PGA TOUR CHARITY TEAM COMPETITION: Phoenix Open

1995 NIKE TOUR SUMMARY: Tournaments entered--20; in money--17; top ten finishes--8

1994 SEASON: Win at NIKE New Mexico Charity Classic (Sept.4 at Albuquerque) highlight of season that also saw him finish second three times (NIKE Miami Valley Open, NIKE Dominion Open and T2 at NIKE Gateway Classic)...missed cut in only two of 19 NIKE TOUR events entered last year, added fourth-place finish at NIKE Utah Classic and T4 at NIKE Tri-Cities Open to total six finishes of fourth or better out of 17 cuts made...low tournament was 17-under-par at NIKE Dominion Open, finished 16-under in New Mexico win...finished third in scoring average with 70.14, and his average of 69.93 before cut ranked first...ranked 18th among eagle leaders with eight, 25th among par breakers with 21.1% and 34th among birdie leaders with 266...missed cut at Northern Telecom Open in only '94 PGA TOUR event.

CAREER HIGHLIGHTS: Finished 33rd on PGA TOUR money list in 1989, a year that saw him record his best-ever finish and also compile a total of six top-10 finishes...his 11-under-par 61 during second round of 1989 Centel Classic (Tallahassee, FL) was tournament record in last year of that event...enjoyed brilliant collegiate career at Arizona State, capped by winning NCAA Championship in 1983...named university's Athlete -of-the-Year in 1984...two-time winner of Arizona State Amateur and the Southwest Amateur championships.

PERSONAL: Began golfing at age 13 and soon was traveling around state with his father, competing in junior tournaments.

1994 PGA TOUR STATISTICS

Scoring Average	N/A
Driving Distance	N/A
Driving Accuracy	N/A
Greens in Regulation	N/A
Putting	N/A
All-Around	N/A
Sand Saves	N/A
Total Driving	N/A
Eagles	N/A
Birdies	N/A

MISCELLANEOUS STATISTICS

Scoring Avg. (before cut)	N/A
Scoring Avg. (3rd round)	N/A
Scoring Avg. (4th round)	N/A
Birdie Conversion	N/A
Par Breakers	N/A

1994 Low Round: N/A
Career Low Round: 61: 1989 Centel Classic/2
Career Largest Paycheck: $52,000/1989 Pebble Beach/3

BRANDEL CHAMBLEE

EXEMPT STATUS: 111th on 1994 money list

FULL NAME: Brandel Eugene Chamblee

HEIGHT: 5' 10"   **WEIGHT:** 155

BIRTH DATE: July 2, 1962

BIRTHPLACE: St. Louis, MO

RESIDENCE: Scottsdale, AZ

FAMILY: Wife, Karen

COLLEGE: University of Texas

SPECIAL INTERESTS: Tennis, horses

TURNED PROFESSIONAL: 1985

Q SCHOOL: 1987, 1990, 1991, 1992

PLAYER PROFILE

CAREER EARNINGS: $483,638

BEST-EVER FINISH: 3--1994 Honda Classic

MONEY & POSITION: 1988--$33,618--166   1992--$ 97,921--133   1994--$161,018--111
                          1991--$64,141--161   1993--$126,940--119

BEST 1994 FINISH: 3--Honda Classic

1994 SUMMARY: Tournaments entered--27; in money--20; top ten finishes--1.

1995 PGA TOUR CHARITY TEAM COMPETITION: Greater Milwaukee Open

1994 SEASON: Continued steady climb up earnings chart, finishing with best year of five on TOUR...money-won total has increased each of last four seasons...had career-best third-place finish in Honda Classic worth $74,800, also largest check...shared lead first two rounds at Weston Hills CC after opening 67-68...held solo 54-hole lead, two strokes in front of Davis Love III...closing 71 left him two strokes behind Nick Price, who finished with 66 for first win of season...two weeks before, final 68 lifted him to T24 in Buick Invitational of California...had only other top-25 in weather-shortened Deposit Guaranty Golf Classic, T11...consistency key to season and $161,018 final earnings total...was in money in 20 of 27 starts...closed out campaign with seven cuts made.

CAREER HIGHLIGHTS: Persistence paid off in 1993, when retained playing privileges for first time in four years on TOUR...secured his card in next-to-last tournament of campaign, Texas Open, where T27 was worth $7,100...best finish of year came in AT&T Pebble Beach National Pro-Am, where registered T9...posted third-best score recorded on final day at Pebble, 2-under-par 70...had second and last top-10 that year in Canadian Open, T10...had T5 in 1991 Deposit Guaranty Golf Classic...member of Ben Hogan Tour in inaugural season of 1990...posted one victory, winning New England Classic at Woodlands CC in Falmouth, ME...at conclusion of 54-hole event was only golfer under par, at 1-under 215...finished seventh on money list with $73,251...winner 1986 TPA Sun City Classic.

PERSONAL: Enjoyed excellent collegiate career...winner 1982 Bluebonnet Tournament and 1983 Rice Planters Championship...winner 1983 Southwest Conference Championship and 1984 Morris Williams Tournament...selected first-team All-American in 1983, second-team 1982 and 1984.

1994 PGA TOUR STATISTICS

Scoring Average	71.57	(127T)
Driving Distance	256.4	(132)
Driving Accuracy	67.4	(113T)
Greens in Regulation	63.5	(147)
Putting	1.793	(91T)
All-Around	957	(150)
Sand Saves	48.4	(130)
Total Driving	245	(156)
Eagles	3	(126T)
Birdies	271	(91T)

MISCELLANEOUS STATISTICS

Scoring Avg. (before cut)	71.15	(63T)
Scoring Avg. (3rd round)	72.81	(170)
Scoring Avg. (4th round)	72.24	(145)
Birdie Conversion	27.6	(112T)
Par Breakers	17.7	(133T)

1994 Low Round: **66:** 4 times

Career Low Round: **64:** 2 times most recent '93

Career Largest Paycheck: **$74,800**/ Honda Classic/3

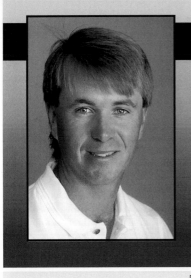

BRIAN CLAAR

EXEMPT STATUS: 110th on 1994 money list

FULL NAME: Brian James Claar

HEIGHT: 5' 8"   **WEIGHT:** 145

BIRTH DATE: July 29, 1959

BIRTHPLACE: Santa Monica, CA

RESIDENCE: Palm Harbor, FL; plays out of East Lake Woodlands CC

FAMILY: Wife, Tracy; Zackary (7/15/90)

COLLEGE: University of Tampa (1981)

SPECIAL INTERESTS: Fishing, Tampa Bay Bucs

TURNED PROFESSIONAL: 1981

Q SCHOOL: Fall 1985, 1989.

PLAYER PROFILE

CAREER EARNINGS: $1,221,389

BEST-EVER FINISH: T2--1991 AT&T Pebble Beach National Pro-Am

MONEY & POSITION:

1986--$117,355-- 75	1989--$ 88,010--133	1992--$192,255-- 78
1987--$ 43,111--162	1990--$161,356-- 98	1993--$202,624-- 85
1988--$ 30,276--172	1991--$251,309-- 67	1994--$165,370--110

BEST 1994 FINISHES: T3--B.C. Open; T10--FedEx St. Jude Classic

1994 SUMMARY: Tournaments entered--31; in money--19; top ten finishes--2

1995 PGA TOUR CHARITY TEAM COMPETITION: Walt Disney World/Oldsmobile Golf Classic

1994 SEASON: Posted fifth consecutive year with earnings over $160,000…had pair of top-10 finishes, both of which came in second half of season…best placing until final week of July was T27…had pair of T27s to that point, in Nissan Los Angeles Open and Buick Classic…at FedEx St. Jude Classic recorded first top-10 since 1993 BellSouth Classic…went 69-67-68-67 at TPC at Southwind, good for T10…after missing cuts in next three starts, posted T3 in B.C. Open…third-round 65 (low of season) moved to within three strokes of lead, but closed with 71…B.C. Open finish his finest since career-best T2 in 1991 AT&T Pebble Beach National Pro-Am…two weeks later carded T11 at Buick Southern Open, only other top-25 of campaign.

CAREER HIGHLIGHTS: Arrived on TOUR in 1986 with No.7 5 money-list finish, which translated into Rookie of Year honors…fell back markedly in terms of earnings next three campaigns…showed flash of brilliance with T5 in 1989 U.S. Open at Oak Hill…finished with rounds of 68-69, two lowest of weekend…regained playing privileges again at 1989 Qualifying Tournament…tied Corey Pavin for second at 1991 AT&T, four strokes behind Paul Azinger…finish contributed to best year to date…top 1993 placing T7 in BellSouth Classic…had four other top-25 finishes that year…finished T8 in 1992 Bob Hope Chrsyler Classic, where second-round LaQuinta course-record-tying (at that time) 63 had him one stroke off midpoint lead…led Asian Tour Order of Merit in 1989, when won Hong Kong and Thailand Opens.

PERSONAL: Once gave reason for shaving mustache as "aerodynamics" ("Now the wind can't blow me around as much")…knew wanted to play TOUR by junior year of college…introduced to game by neighbor, who watched him hitting golf balls with baseball bat.

1994 PGA TOUR STATISTICS

Scoring Average	71.21	(86T)
Driving Distance	254.0	(154)
Driving Accuracy	72.8	(49T)
Greens in Regulation	68.7	(32T)
Putting	1.805	(119T)
All-Around	720	(97)
Sand Saves	49.4	(119)
Total Driving	203	(124T)
Eagles	3	(126T)
Birdies	311	(35T)

MISCELLANEOUS STATISTICS

Scoring Avg. (before cut)	71.32	(76T)
Scoring Avg. (3rd round)	71.61	(135)
Scoring Avg. (4th round)	70.95	(45T)
Birdie Conversion	25.4	(150T)
Par Breakers	17.6	(139T)

1994 Low Round: 64: B.C. Open/3

Career Low Round: 62: 1991 Anheuser-Busch Golf Classic/3

Career Largest Paycheck: $96,800/1991 AT&T Pebble Beach National Pro-Am/T2

KEITH CLEARWATER

EXEMPT STATUS: 90th on 1994 money list

FULL NAME: Keith Allen Clearwater

HEIGHT: 6' **WEIGHT:** 180

BIRTH DATE: September 1, 1959

BIRTHPLACE: Long Beach, CA

RESIDENCE: Orem, UT

FAMILY: Wife, Sue; Jennifer (3/9/85), Melissa (6/30/88)

COLLEGE: Brigham Young University

SPECIAL INTERESTS: Family and church activities, home building, all sports, water sports

TURNED PROFESSIONAL: 1982

Q SCHOOL: Fall 1986

PLAYER PROFILE

CAREER EARNINGS: $2,021,787

TOUR VICTORIES: 1987 Colonial National Invitation, Centel Classic.
(TOTAL: 2)

MONEY & POSITION:

1987--$320,007-- 31	1990--$130,103--118	1993--$348,763--44
1988--$ 82,876--127	1991--$239,727-- 69	1994--$203,549--90
1989--$ 87,490--136	1992--$609,273-- 22	

BEST 1994 FINISHES: T6--Bob Hope Chrysler Classic, Buick Open; T7--AT&T Pebble Beach National Pro-Am.

1994 SUMMARY: Tournaments entered--27; in money--18; top ten finishes--3.

1995 PGA TOUR CHARITY TEAM COMPETITION: Quad Cities Open

1994 SEASON: Money-won total fourth-lowest of eight-year career…dropped off for second consecutive season from career high in 1992…earnings figure of $203,549 lowest since 1990…missed cut in three of first six events, but at same time was posting two of three top-10s…finished T7 at AT&T Pebble Beach National Pro-Am in fourth start of season, then two weeks later had T6 at Bob Hope Chrysler Classic…second-round 64 (season low) at Indian Wells left him second to Scott Hoch, three strokes behind the eventual winner…third and final top-10 came at Buick Open, where carded middle rounds of 67-69…two weeks later had T18 at Sprint International.

CAREER HIGHLIGHTS: Came out of chute in spectacular fashion in 1987, earning two victories and MasterCard Rookie of Year honors…money-won total that season his best until career-year of 1992…fired consecutive 64s last two rounds of Colonial National Invitation to equal tournament record…finished with winning 266 total after playing 36 holes on final day…later that year caught national attention with 64 in third round of U.S. Open at Olympic Club…closed out season with second victory in Centel Classic…had three top-10s during first nine outings in 1992, best of which was T2 in Doral-Ryder Open…finished stroke out of Corey Pavin-Fred Couples playoff at Honda Classic…solo fourth in '92 TOUR Championship, carding final-round 67 at Pinehurst No. 2…winner 1985 Alaska State Open.

PERSONAL: Through regimen of exercise and vitamins, has become one of strongest players on TOUR…winner 1982 North and South Amateur…member 1981 National Championship team at Brigham Young…teammates at BYU included Rick Fehr, Richard Zokol and Bobby Clampett.

1994 PGA TOUR STATISTICS

Scoring Average	71.24	(91T)
Driving Distance	257.1	(127T)
Driving Accuracy	67.4	(113T)
Greens in Regulation	65.4	(100T)
Putting	1.773	(34T)
All-Around	671	(79T)
Sand Saves	52.7	(76T)
Total Driving	240	(153T)
Eagles	4	(104T)
Birdies	319	(26T)

MISCELLANEOUS STATISTICS

Scoring Avg. (before cut)	71.09	(58T)
Scoring Avg. (3rd round)	71.29	(109T)
Scoring Avg. (4th round)	72.12	(138)
Birdie Conversion	30.4	(22T)
Par Breakers	20.2	(34T)

1994 Low Round:	64: Bob Hope Chrysler Classic/2
Career Low Round:	61: 1993 Southwestern Bell Colonial/2
Career Largest Paycheck:	$123,200/1992 Doral Ryder Open/T2

LENNIE CLEMENTS

EXEMPT STATUS: 39th on 1994 money list

FULL NAME: Leonard Clyde Clements

HEIGHT: 5' 8"   **WEIGHT:** 160

BIRTH DATE: January 20, 1957

BIRTHPLACE: Cherry Point, NC

RESIDENCE: San Diego, CA

FAMILY: Wife, Jan; Elizabeth (11/19/83), Christopher (7/16/86)

COLLEGE: San Diego State University

SPECIAL INTERESTS: Family activities, all sports

TURNED PROFESSIONAL: 1980

JOINED TOUR: 1981   **Q SCHOOL:** 1992

PLAYER PROFILE

CAREER EARNINGS: $1,296,925

BEST-EVER FINISH: T2--1994 Bob Hope Chrysler Classic

MONEY & POSITION:

1981--$ 7,766-- 178	1986--$112,642-- 79	1991--$ 62,827--163
1982--$44,796-- 97	1987--$124,989-- 83	1992--$ 30,121--198
1983--$44,455-- 110	1988--$ 86,332--120	1993--$141,526--113
1984--$25,712-- 146	1989--$ 69,399--147	1994--$416,880-- 39
1985--$49,383-- 120	1990--$ 80,095--146	

BEST 1994 FINISHES: T2--Bob Hope Chrysler Classic; T4-Doral Ryder Open; T6--BellSouth Classic; T8--United Airlines Hawaiian Open, Nissan Los Angeles Open; T9--Buick Invitational of California

1994 SUMMARY: Tournaments entered--22; in money--21; top ten finishes--6.

1995 PGA TOUR CHARITY TEAM COMPETITION: New England Classic

1994 SEASON: Had by-far the finest season of 14-year career, with much of reason for that coming early in campaign...posted five top-10 finishes in first seven starts, total of six overall...only missed cut came in last event of season, Las Vegas Invitational...after going over $100,000 ($141,526) for first time in six years in 1993, tripled that figure in '94...after first seven tournaments already had earned $234,560...during that early stretch had career-best T2 in Bob Hope Chrysler Classic worth $82,133...third-round course-record 61 at LaQuinta gave him one-stroke lead over eventual winner Scott Hoch...Hope paycheck biggest of career...also had T4 in first Florida start, Doral-Ryder Open...$57,867 payday second-largest of season...final top-10 T6 in BellSouth Classic...best finish over last five months T16 at New England Classic.

CAREER HIGHLIGHTS: Many of career highlights concentrated in 1994 season...played well during mid-1980s, retaining playing privileges four consecutive years 1985-88...experienced tough times from that point forward until rediscovered game in 1993...best '93 finish T8 in Northern Telecom Open...later that season had T8 in Anheuser-Busch Golf Classic...previous best finish T3 in 1983 Miller High Life Quad Cities Open...vaulted into contention through third-round 65 at Oakwood CC...missed Danny Edwards-Morris Hatalsky play-off by one stroke...winner 1982 Timex Open (France) and 1983 Sahara Nevada Open...winner 1988 Spalding Invitational on Monterey Peninsula.

PERSONAL: Had success early in career, winning 1975 California State High School Championship...medalist 1979 California State Amateur...winner 1979 Southwestern Amateur...two-time All-American at San Diego State.

1994 PGA TOUR STATISTICS

Scoring Average	69.98	(16)
Driving Distance	254.7	(148T)
Driving Accuracy	75.6	(21T)
Greens in Regulation	70.6	(9T)
Putting	1.763	(14T)
All-Around	332	(7)
Sand Saves	54.3	(53)
Total Driving	169	(72T)
Eagles	8	(28T)
Birdies	304	(43T)

MISCELLANEOUS STATISTICS

Scoring Avg. (before cut)	69.77	(5)
Scoring Avg. (3rd round)	70.30	(41)
Scoring Avg. (4th round)	71.20	(62T)
Birdie Conversion	28.5	(76T)
Par Breakers	20.6	(25T)

1994 Low Round: 61: Bob Hope Chrysler Classic/3

Career Low Round: 61: 1994 Bob Hope Chrysler Classic/3

Career Largest Paycheck: $82,133/'94 Bob HopeChrysler Classic/T2

RUSS COCHRAN

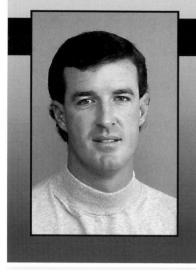

EXEMPT STATUS: 77th on 1994 money list

FULL NAME: Russell Earl Cochran

HEIGHT: 6'   **WEIGHT:** 160

BIRTH DATE: October 31, 1958

BIRTHPLACE: Paducah, KY

RESIDENCE: Paducah, KY

FAMILY: Wife, Jackie; Ryan (9/4/83), Reed (9/28/85), Case (4/5/89), Kelly Marie (2/21/92)

COLLEGE: University of Kentucky

SPECIAL INTERESTS: Basketball

TURNED PROFESSIONAL: 1979

Q SCHOOL: Fall 1982

PLAYER PROFILE

CAREER EARNINGS: $2,523,319   **PLAYOFF RECORD:** 0-1

TOUR VICTORIES: 1991 Centel Western Open. (TOTAL: 1)

MONEY & POSITION:

1983--$ 7,968--188	1987--$148,110-- 74	1991--$684,851 --10
1984--$133,342-- 51	1988--$148,960-- 80	1992--$326,290 --46
1985--$ 87,331-- 87	1989--$132,678--107	1993--$293,868 --59
1986--$ 89,817-- 92	1990--$230,278-- 65	1994--$239,827 --77

BEST 1994 FINISHES: 5--Hardee's Golf Classic; T5--Federal Express St. Jude Classic; T6--BellSouth Classic; T7--MCI Heritage Classic.

1994 SUMMARY: Tournaments entered--28; in money--20; top ten finishes--4.

1995 PGA TOUR CHARITY TEAM COMPETITION: FedEx St. Jude Classic

1994 SEASON: Steady lefthander has been on bit of downward trend of late, dropping off three years running from career year in 1991...troubled during latter part of '94 by wrist problem, which contributed to several missed cuts and withdrawal from Greater Milwaukee Open...following WD from GMO, returned three weeks later to solo fifth in Hardee's Golf Classic...opened 67-65 at Oakwood CC, then closed with 65...had pair of top-10s during four-week April-May stretch, T7 at MCI Heritage Classic followed three weeks later by T6 in BellSouth Classic...finished T5 in FedEx St. Jude Classic, where third-round 65 produced three-way tie with Gil Morgan and eventual winner Dicky Pride for 54-hole lead...closed with 69 at TPC of Southwind, finishing two strokes out of Pride-Gene Sauers-Hal Sutton playoff...missed five cuts (plus one withdrawal) over final 11 starts, with wrist troubling during part of that stretch...still managed pair of fifth-place finishes.

CAREER HIGHLIGHTS: Broke into winner's circle for first time at 1991 Centel Western Open...trailed Greg Norman by five strokes with eight holes to play...won by two after posting final 68 and Norman struggled down stretch...came close on two other occasions that year, losing playoffs to Craig Stadler (TOUR Championship) and Larry Silveira (Deposit Guaranty Golf Classic)...with beloved Kentucky Wildcats in NCAA Final Four at New Orleans Superdome, still able to finish T2 in 1993 Freeport-McMoRan Classic, one stroke behind Mike Standly...winner of two Tournament Players Series events in 1983, Magnolia Classic and Greater Baltimore Open...playing in eight events, finished as leading money winner in TPS...received TOUR exemption for 1984.

PERSONAL: Ardent University of Kentucky basketball fan...son Ryan scored hole-in-one at age six, one of youngest ever to record ace...started playing with ladies set because couldn't find any other lefthanded clubs...won 1975 Kentucky State High School Championship.

1994 PGA TOUR STATISTICS

Scoring Average	71.24	(91T)
Driving Distance	261.6	(91T)
Driving Accuracy	69.2	(90)
Greens in Regulation	66.2	(81T)
Putting	1.799	(105T)
All-Around	632	(67)
Sand Saves	52.0	(87)
Total Driving	181	(97T)
Eagles	7	(44T)
Birdies	304	(43T)

MISCELLANEOUS STATISTICS

Scoring Avg. (before cut)	71.24	(70)
Scoring Avg. (3rd round)	71.00	(84T)
Scoring Avg. (4th round)	71.50	(91T)
Birdie Conversion	27.2	(121T)
Par Breakers	18.4	(110T)

1994 Low Round: 65: 2 times

Career Low Round: 63: 1991 Deposit Guaranty Golf Classic/4

Career Largest Paycheck: $216,000/1991 THE TOUR Championship/2

44

JOHN COOK

EXEMPT STATUS: 37th on 1994 money list

FULL NAME: John Neuman Cook

HEIGHT: 6' **WEIGHT:** 175

BIRTH DATE: October 2, 1957

BIRTHPLACE: Toledo, OH

RESIDENCE: Rancho Mirage, CA

FAMILY: Wife, Jan; Kristin (7/20/81), Courtney (4/11/84), Jason (1/10/86)

COLLEGE: Ohio State University

SPECIAL INTERESTS: Auto racing, skiing, all sports

TURNED PROFESSIONAL: 1979

Q SCHOOL: Fall 1979

PLAYER PROFILE

CAREER EARNINGS: $4,274,977   **PLAYOFF RECORD:** 3-3

TOUR VICTORIES: **1981** Bing Crosby National Pro-Am. **1983** Canadian Open. **1987** The International.
(TOTAL: 6)   **1992** Bob Hope Chrysler Classic, United Airlines Hawaiian Open, Las Vegas Invitational

MONEY & POSITION:

1980--$ 43,316-- 78	1985--$ 63,573--106	1990--$ 448,112-- 28
1981--$127,608-- 25	1986--$255,126-- 27	1991--$ 546,984-- 26
1982--$ 57,483-- 77	1987--$333,184-- 29	1992--$1,165,606-- 3
1983--$216,868-- 16	1988--$139,916-- 84	1993--$ 342,321-- 45
1984--$ 65,710-- 89	1989--$ 39,445--172	1994--$ 429,725-- 37

BEST 1994 FINISHES: 3--Memorial Tournament; T4--PGA Championship; 5--U.S. Open; T9--Southwestern Bell Colonial, Canon Greater Hartford Open; T10--FedEx St. Jude Classic.

1993 SUMMARY: Tournaments entered--24; in money--16; top ten finishes--6.

1995 PGA TOUR CHARITY TEAM COMPETITION: Walt Disney World/Oldsmobile Golf Classic

NATIONAL TEAMS: World Cup, 1983; World Amateur Team Championship, 1979; Ryder Cup, 1993.

1994 SEASON: Rebounded from "down" season of 1993, campaign that anytime else would have been considered solid--except for career year in 1992...improved eight places on money list, edging closer to regaining Top 30 slot occupied 1990-92, as well as earlier in career...opened year on less-than-positive note, missing first four cuts...rallied for six top-10 finishes in seven-event span May to August...one-time Ohio State Buckeye began spurt, appropriately, in Columbus, OH...ran second each of first three rounds of Memorial Tournament, carded 71 for third-place finish...proceeded to place in top-10 each of next three starts, with U.S. Open solo fifth (second-round 65) in between pair of T9s (Southwestern Bell Colonial and Canon Greater Hartford Open)...had third-round 64 at GHO, low of campaign...followed T10 in Federal Express St. Jude Classic with T4 in PGA Championship, giving him pair of top-10 finishes in majors...won Fred Meyer Challenge in August (with Mark O'Meara).

CAREER HIGHLIGHTS: Has had string of solid finishes in recent majors...1994: U.S. Open (5), PGA Championship (T4); 1993: PGA Championship (T6); 1992: British Open (2), PGA Championship (T2)...surpassed $1 million in earnings in 1992, when won three times...captured five-man playoff at Bob Hope Chrysler Classic, outlasting Gene Sauers with three birdies and an eagle over four holes...posted two-stroke victories in United Airlines Hawaiian Open and Las Vegas Invitational...first victory came in 1981 Bing Crosby, winning another five-man playoff...defeated Johnny Miller at 1983 Canadian Open on the sixth playoff hole...other title was in 1987 International...winner of numerous amateur titles, principal among which 1978 U.S. Amateur...winner 1982 Sao Paulo-Brazilian Open...teamed with Rex Caldwell to win 1983 World Cup.

PERSONAL: Although born in Ohio, grew up in Southern California....convinced by Jack Nicklaus and Tom Weiskopf to attend Ohio State, where was three-time All-American (1977-79)...member 1979 Ohio State NCAA Championship Team.

1994 PGA TOUR STATISTICS

Scoring Average	70.30	(27)
Driving Distance	258.8	(114T)
Driving Accuracy	75.6	(21T)
Greens in Regulation	70.1	(18)
Putting	1.790	(80T)
All-Around	546	(45)
Sand Saves	56.2	(38)
Total Driving	135	(36)
Eagles	2	(146T)
Birdies	262	(102T)

MISCELLANEOUS STATISTICS

Scoring Avg. (before cut)	70.92	(44T)
Scoring Avg. (3rd round)	69.81	(17)
Scoring Avg. (4th round)	70.50	(25T)
Birdie Conversion	26.0	(144)
Par Breakers	18.3	(115T)

1994 Low Round: 64: Canon Greater Hartford Open/3
Career Low Round: 62: 1992 Las Vegas Invitational/3
Career Largest Paycheck: $234,000/1992 Las Vegas Invitational/1

FRED COUPLES

EXEMPT STATUS: Winner, 1992 Masters Tournament

FULL NAME: Frederick Stephen Couples

HEIGHT: 5' 11"   **WEIGHT:** 185

BIRTH DATE: October 3, 1959

BIRTHPLACE: Seattle, WA

RESIDENCE: Dallas, TX

FAMILY: Single

COLLEGE: University of Houston

SPECIAL INTERESTS: All sports, tennis, antiques, bicycling, vintage cars

TURNED PROFESSIONAL: 1980

Q SCHOOL: Fall 1980

PLAYER PROFILE

CAREER EARNINGS: $6,889.149   **PLAYOFF RECORD:** 4-4

TOUR VICTORIES: **1983** Kemper Open. **1984** Tournament Players Championship. **1987** Byron
(TOTAL: 11)   Nelson Golf Classic. **1990** Nissan Los Angeles Open. **1991** Federal Express St.
Jude Classic, B.C. Open. **1992** Nissan Los Angeles Open, Nestle Invitational,
Masters. **1993** Honda Classic. **1994** Buick Open

MONEY & POSITION:

1981--$ 78,939--53	1986--$116,065--76	1991--$ 791,749-- 3
1982--$ 77,606--53	1987--$441,025--19	1992--$1,344,188-- 1
1983--$209,733--19	1988--$489,822--21	1993--$ 796,579--10
1984--$334,573-- 7	1989--$693,944--11	1994--$ 625,654--23
1985--$171,272--38	1990--$757,999-- 9	

BEST 1994 FINISHES: 1--Buick Open; 2--Mercedes Championships, Nissan Los Angeles Open; T8--NEC World Series of Golf

1994 SUMMARY: Tournaments entered--15; in money--15; top ten finishes--4.

1995 PGA TOUR CHARITY TEAM COMPETITION: Las Vegas Invitational

NATIONAL TEAMS: U.S.A. vs. Japan, 1984; Ryder Cup (3), 1989, 1991, 1993; Asahi Glass Four Tours World Championship of Golf (2), 1990, 1991; Dunhill Cup (3), 1992,1993,1994; World Cup (3), 1992,1993,1994; Presidents Cup, 1994.

1994 SEASON: Campaign that began in solid fashion (playoff loss to Phil Mickelson in Mercedes Championships, battle to wire with Corey Pavin at Nissan Los Angeles Open) turned decidedly sour at Doral-Ryder Open…back went into spasms before final round (diagnosis: tear in outer layer of disc in lower back)…unable to defend Honda Classic title following week…after missing three months, returned with T27 at Buick Classic, followed by T16 at U.S. Open…two starts later had 11th TOUR title, two-stroke victory over Pavin in Buick Open…Warwick Hills outing featured pair of middle round 65s…had final top-10 of season in NEC World Series of Golf, T8 featuring third-round 65…playing in just 15 events, still won more than $625,000…week after TOUR Championship won second consecutive Lincoln-Mercury Kapalua International, final round of which featured first career hole-in-one…week after Kapalua produced record third consecutive World Cup of Golf title with Davis Love III…also captured first World Cup individual title…won Shark Shootout with Brad Faxon following week.

CAREER HIGHLIGHTS: Owns longest existing consecutive-years-with-victory string on TOUR, five…career year 1992, when won three events (including Masters) and over $1.3 million…named PGA TOUR Player of Year for second year in row…second-extra-hole winner over Robert Gamez at 1993 Honda Classic…holed out from bunker on No. 17 to force eventual playoff…first TOUR win came in five-man playoff at 1983 Kemper Open…captured Tournament Players Championship in 1984, carding TPC at Sawgrass course-record 64 in process…lowered mark to 63 in 1992 PLAYERS Championship…claimed first of two Nissan Los Angeles Open titles in 1990…multiple winner for first time in 1991…won 1991 Johnnie Walker World Championship of Golf in Jamaica…teamed with Raymond Floyd to win 1990 RMCC Invitational hosted by Greg Norman…winner (with Mike Donald) of 1990 Sazale Classic.

PERSONAL: Teammate of Blaine McCallister and CBS-TV broadcaster Jim Nantz at University of Houston…three have teamed for annual Three Amigos Celebrity Tournament…his charity Millie Medin Violet Sobich Couples Fund, in memory of mother…introduced to golf by father, who worked in Seattle Parks and Recreation Department.

1994 PGA TOUR STATISTICS

Scoring Average	69.28	(2)
Driving Distance	279.9	(3)
Driving Accuracy	60.1	(172)
Greens in Regulation	70.5	(12)
Putting	1.787	(73T)
All-Around	551	(46)
Sand Saves	53.8	(57T)
Total Driving	175	(85T)
Eagles	6	(64T)
Birdies	182	(168T)

MISCELLANEOUS STATISTICS

Scoring Avg. (before cut)	69.73	(4)
Scoring Avg. (3rd round)	70.00	(18T)
Scoring Avg. (4th round)	70.58	(29T)
Birdie Conversion	28.1	(91T)
Par Breakers	20.5	(29T)

1994 Low Round: **65:** 3 times

Career Low Round: **62:** 1990 Nissan Los Angeles Open/3

Career Largest Paycheck: **$270,000**/1992 Masters/1

BEN CRENSHAW

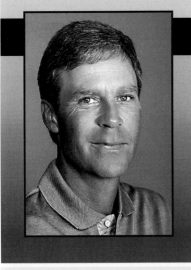

EXEMPT STATUS: 1994 tournament winner

FULL NAME: Ben Daniel Crenshaw

HEIGHT: 5' 9"   **WEIGHT:** 170

BIRTH DATE: January 11, 1952

BIRTHPLACE: Austin, TX

RESIDENCE: Austin, TX; plays out of Barton Creek Club in Austin

FAMILY: Wife, Julie; Katherine Vail (10/6/87), Claire Susan (4/23/92)

COLLEGE: University of Texas

SPECIAL INTERESTS: Fishing, bird watching, golf artifacts, golf course architecture, country music

TURNED PROFESSIONAL: 1973

JOINED TOUR: Fall 1973

PLAYER PROFILE

CAREER EARNINGS: $5,448,507   **PLAYOFF RECORD:** 0-8

TOUR VICTORIES: **1973** San Antonio-Texas Open. **1976** Bing Crosby National Pro-Am, Hawaiian
(TOTAL: 18)   Open, Ohio Kings Island Open. **1977** Colonial National Invitation. **1979** Phoenix
Open, Walt Disney World Team Championship (with George Burns). **1980**
Anheuser-Busch Classic. **1983** Byron Nelson Classic. **1984** Masters Tournament. **1986** Buick Open,
Vantage Championship. **1987** USF&G Classic. **1988** Doral Ryder Open. **1990** Southwestern Bell
Colonial. **1992** Centel Western Open. **1993** Nestle Invitational.**1994** Freeport-McMoRan Classic.

MONEY & POSITION:

1973--$ 76,749-- 34	1981--$151,038-- 20	1989--$433,095-- 21
1974--$ 71,065-- 31	1982--$ 54,277-- 83	1990--$351,193-- 33
1975--$ 63,528-- 32	1983--$275,474-- 7	1991--$224,563-- 75
1976--$257,759-- 2	1984--$270,989-- 16	1992--$439,071-- 31
1977--$123,841-- 16	1985--$ 25,814-149	1993--$318,605-- 51
1978--$108,305-- 21	1986--$388,169-- 8	1994--$659,252-- 21
1979--$236,769-- 5	1987--$638,194-- 3	
1980--$237,727-- 5	1988--$696,895-- 8	

BEST 1994 FINISHES: 1--Freeport-McMoRan Classic; T6-Buick Open; T7--Memorial Tournament;
T8--GTE Byron Nelson Classic, Texas Open; T9--PGA Championship.

1994 SUMMARY: Tournaments entered--24; in money--20; top ten finishes--6.

1995 PGA TOUR CHARITY TEAM COMPETITION: Freeport-McMoran Classic

NATIONAL TEAMS: Ryder Cup (3), 1981, 1983, 1987; World
Cup (2), 1987, 1988 (won individual title in 1988); U.S. vs. Japan,
1983; Kirin Cup, 1988.

1994 PGA TOUR STATISTICS

Scoring Average	70.46	(33T)
Driving Distance	258.0	(120T)
Driving Accuracy	64.5	(146T)
Greens in Regulation	62.7	(153)
Putting	1.739	(2)
All-Around	605	(59T)
Sand Saves	63.1	(2)
Total Driving	266	(166)
Eagles	4	(104T)
Birdies	303	(45)

1994 SEASON: With April victory in Freeport-McMoRan Classic came unusual
statistic: each of last three top-10 finishes had been win (including 1993 Nestle
Invitational and 1992 Centel Western Open)…brought that streak to close with
five other top-10s in '94, first of which was T8 in GTE Byron Nelson
Classic…enjoyed nonwinning top-10 so much, turned around and did again
very next week (T7 in Memorial Tournament)…later had another pair of back-
to-back top-10s, T6 in Buick Open, T9 PGA Championship…final T8 came in
Texas Open, crafted by closing 65 at Oak Hills CC…aside from best earnings
year since 1988, $659,252 total produced first Top-30 finish (and TOUR
Championship appearance) since 1989…Freeport-McMoRan payday of
$216,000 biggest check of 22-year career.

CAREER HIGHLIGHTS: Has produced win-a-year since turning 40…prior to
Freeport-McMoRan Classic, fortysomething titles 1991 Western Open and
1992 Nestle…biggest victory came at 1984 Masters, where final-round 68 and
277 total gave him two-stroke decision over Tom Watson…first triumph came
in first start as official member of PGA TOUR, 1973 San Antonio-Texas
Open…winner of two events at Colonial CC 13 years apart, 1977 Colonial
National Invitation and 1990 Southwestern Bell Colonial…most recent of three
multiple victory seasons 1986, when claimed Buick Open and Vantage Championship, precursor of TOUR Championship…winner of 1983 Byron Nelson
Classic…winner 1976 Irish Open…won 1973 Qualifying Tournament by then-
record 12 strokes…runnerup to Davis Love III 1993 Merrill Lynch Shoot-Out
Championship.

MISCELLANEOUS STATISTICS

Scoring Avg. (before cut)	70.50	(25)
Scoring Avg. (3rd round)	71.30	(111)
Scoring Avg. (4th round)	71.20	(62T)
Birdie Conversion	31.2	(13)
Par Breakers	19.8	(52T)

1994 Low Round: 65: Texas Open/4

Career Low Round: 61: 1979 Phoenix Open/2

Career Largest Paycheck: $216,000/1994 Freeport McMoRan Classic/1

PERSONAL: Noted golf historian…enjoys golf course architecture and is
building Sand Hills GC in Nebraska…fought winning battle against Graves
disease in mid-1980s…winner 1971-72-73 NCAA Championships, co-winner
with Tom Kite 1972…winner of Fred Haskins Award as nation's outstanding
collegiate golfer each of those years.

JOHN DALY

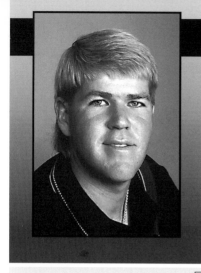

EXEMPT STATUS: Winner, 1991 PGA Championship

HEIGHT: 5' 11" **WEIGHT:** 175

BIRTH DATE: April 28,1966

BIRTHPLACE: Sacramento, CA

RESIDENCE: Germantown, TN

COLLEGE: University of Arkansas

FAMILY: Shynah Hale (6/10/92)

SPECIAL INTERESTS: Most sports

TURNED PROFESSIONAL: 1987

Q SCHOOL: Fall 1990

PLAYER PROFILE

CAREER EARNINGS: $1,527,863

TOUR VICTORIES: 1991 PGA Championship. **1992** B.C. Open. **1994** BellSouth Classic (TOTAL: 3)

MONEY & POSITION: 1991--$574,783--17   1993--$225,591--76   1994--$340,034--49
1992--$387,455--37

BEST 1994 FINISHES: 1--BellSouth Classic; T4--Honda Classic; T7--Shell Houston Open.

1994 SUMMARY: Tournaments entered--17; in money--9; top ten finishes--3

1995 PGA TOUR CHARITY TEAM COMPETITION: Shell Houston Open

1994 SEASON: One of golf's brightest young talents returned to action in March on positive note, T4 at Honda Classic...carded final-round 68 at Weston Hills to finish T4 behind Nick Price...missed cut three of next four starts, then followed with T7 at Shell Houston Open, where closed with 67...produced shining moment of '94 in very next outing...with second-round 64, took lead at BellSouth Classic and held on tight, chalking up third victory in fourth TOUR season as first Nolan Henke and then Brian Henninger fell short...having opened year under TOUR suspension, gave hope that finally back on track...playing performances erratic over remainder of his season...during mid-year suffered pain from swollen muscle tissue in lower back...following parking lot scuffle at NEC World Series of Golf, decision was made that he would voluntarily withdraw from any further competition in 1994 in order to get himself ready both physically and mentally for 1995...return to TOUR action was set for Mercedes Championships...fell one round short of earning fourth consecutive driving distance title.

CAREER HIGHLIGHTS: A crowd-pleaser each time takes driver out of bag, delighted golf world with surprising victory at 1991 PGA Championship at Crooked Stick...as last alternate in field, saw Crooked Stick for first time during Round 1...opening 69 left him two strokes out of lead...added rounds of 67-69-71 for three-stroke win over Bruce Lietzke...completed rookie season with third-place finish in TOUR Championship at Pinehurst No. 2...subsequently recognized by peers with selection as PGA TOUR Rookie of Year...removed any doubt that PGA Championship win a fluke by dominating field and winning 1992 B.C. Open by six strokes...played Ben Hogan Tour in 1990 after winning only Hogan Tour Qualifying Tournament...later in inaugural season won Ben Hogan Tour Utah Classic...finished ninth on money list with over $64,000...won several events on South African Tour...winner 1987 Missouri Open.

PERSONAL: Served as non-paid assistant coach for University of Arkansas golf team during hiatus between 1994-95 TOUR seasons...started playing as youngster after father gave him full-sized set of clubs.

1994 PGA TOUR STATISTICS

Scoring Average	71.77
Driving Distance	290.2
Driving Accuracy	59.6
Greens in Regulation	60.2
Putting	1.778
All-Around	N/R
Sand Saves	43.2
Total Driving	N/R
Eagles	3
Birdies	176

MISCELLANEOUS STATISTICS

Scoring Avg. (before cut)	73.16
Scoring Avg. (3rd round)	71.11
Scoring Avg. (4th round)	73.22
Birdie Conversion	33.1
Par Breakers	20.3

1994 Low Round: 64: BellSouth Classic/2
Career Low Round: 63: 1991 Las Vegas Invitational/2
Career Largest Paycheck: $230,000/1991 PGA Championship/1

GLEN DAY

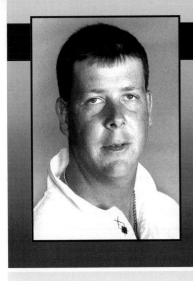

EXEMPT STATUS: 45th on 1994 money list

FULL NAME: Glen Edward Day

HEIGHT: 5' 10"   **WEIGHT:** 170

BIRTH DATE: November 16, 1965

BIRTHPLACE: Mobile, AL

RESIDENCE: Little Rock, AR

FAMILY: Wife, Jennifer Ralston-Day

COLLEGE: University of Oklahoma

SPECIAL INTERESTS: Hunting

TURNED PROFESSIONAL: 1988

Q SCHOOL: 1993

PLAYER PROFILE

CAREER EARNINGS: $357,236

BEST-EVER FINISH: 2--1994 Anheuser-Busch Golf Classic

MONEY & POSITION: 1994--357,236--45

BEST 1994 FINISHES: 2--Anheuser-Busch Golf Classic; T7--Walt Disney World/Oldsmobile Classic; T9--Canon Greater Hartford Open; T10--Nestle Invitational.

1994 SUMMARY: Tournaments entered--30; in money--18; top ten finishes--4

1995 PGA TOUR CHARITY TEAM COMPETITION: THE TOUR Championship

1994 SEASON: Rookie of Year candidate after finishing third on money list among first-year players…trailed just Ernie Els and Mike Heinen with $357,236…went over $100,000 for season in early April by cashing in seven consecutive events, following missed cut in first start, United Airlines Hawaiian Open…biggest check during that stretch $30,000 for first of four top-10 finishes, T10 at Nestle Invitational…also had pair of $25,000-plus paydays during that skein, for T11 in Bob Hope Chrysler Classic and T12 at Freeport-McMoRan Classic…put himself over top in June--in terms of money needed to retain playing privileges--with T9 at Canon Greater Hartford Open, where also recorded pair of holes-in-one in the second round…after opening with season-low 64, stood three strokes off lead from start to finish in Anheuser-Busch Golf Classic…second-place finish behind Mark McCumber was worth $118,800…also opened with 64 at B.C. Open, single stroke off early lead, but finished T22…parlayed first-round 65 at Walt Disney World/Oldsmobile Classic into closing T7.

CAREER HIGHLIGHTS: Earned TOUR playing privilges with T11 in 1993 Qualifying Tournament…winner 1989 Malaysian Open.

PERSONAL: 1987-88 All-American at University of Oklahoma.

1994 PGA TOUR STATISTICS

Scoring Average	70.78	(48)
Driving Distance	262.5	(83)
Driving Accuracy	68.7	(97)
Greens in Regulation	65.1	(110T)
Putting	1.770	(29T)
All-Around	425	(22)
Sand Saves	56.5	(33T)
Total Driving	180	(93T)
Eagles	11	(7T)
Birdies	329	(18)

MISCELLANEOUS STATISTICS

Scoring Avg. (before cut)	70.68	(35)
Scoring Avg. (3rd round)	71.29	(109T)
Scoring Avg. (4th round)	71.78	(112T)
Birdie Conversion	29.9	(32T)
Par Breakers	20.1	(40T)

1994 Low Round: 64: 2 times

Career Low Round: 64: 2 times, most recent 1994 B.C. Open/1

Career Largest Paycheck: $118,000/1994 Anheuser-Busch/2

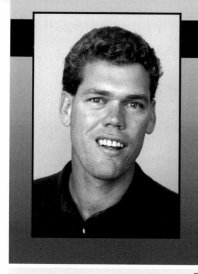

JAY DELSING

EXEMPT STATUS: 124th on 1994 money list

FULL NAME: James Patrick Delsing

HEIGHT: 6' 5 1/2"   **WEIGHT:** 185

BIRTH DATE: October 17, 1960

BIRTHPLACE: St. Louis, MO

RESIDENCE: St. Louis, MO; plays out of CC of St. Albans, MO

FAMILY: Wife, Kathy; Mackenzie (5/31/89), Gemma (12/9/91)

COLLEGE: UCLA (1983, Economics)

SPECIAL INTERESTS: Fishing, all sports

TURNED PROFESSIONAL: 1984

Q SCHOOL: Fall 1984, 1988, 1989

PLAYER PROFILE

CAREER EARNINGS: $1,274,532

BEST-EVER FINISH: T2--1993 New England Classic

MONEY & POSITION:

1985--$ 46,480--125	1989--$ 26,565--187	1993--$233,484-- 71
1986--$ 65,407--123	1990--$207,740-- 74	1994--$143,738--124
1987--$ 58,657--136	1991--$149,775--100	
1988--$ 45,504--152	1992--$296,740-- 52	

BEST 1994 FINISHES: T7--AT&T Pebble Beach National Pro-Am; T8--Nissan Los Angeles Open.

1994 SUMMARY: Tournaments entered--27; in money--16; top ten finishes--2.

1995 PGA TOUR CHARITY TEAM COMPETITION: Buick Open

1994 SEASON: Suffered through worst season since 1989, when earned just $26,565 before running off four solid campaigns...held on--but barely--to playing privileges...wound up No. 124...wasn't confident of prospects when finished out of money in final seven starts (missed cut in six/disqualified in another)...had largest measure of success through first four months, earning $123,373 in 11 events...only missed cut during that stretch Doral-Ryder Open...posted consecutive top-10s in AT&T Pebble Beach National Pro-Am (T7) and Nissan Los Angeles Open (T8)...strong opening rounds keys in each case: 66 at Pebble, 67 at Los Angeles...over course of rest of campaign missed cut in 10 of 15 starts, plus the DQ at the B.C. Open...highest May-October finish T26 at Canon Greater Hartford Open.

CAREER HIGHLIGHTS: Went over $200,000 three of four years 1990-1993 (exception 1991)...best placing of 10-year career came at '93 New England Classic, where finished T2, four strokes behind Paul Azinger...climbed hill steadily, but was unable to overcome 10-stroke deficit he faced after Round 1...closing 67 brought him $88,000 payday, largest of career...very next week carded course-record 10-under-par 61 in final round at TPC at Southwind, vaulting into T8...earned $121,000 for those two weeks...posted four top-10 finishes, including T4s Phoenix and Canadian Opens, solo fourth Hardee's Golf Classic, during 1992 campaign, his best to date...co-holds course record at En-Joie GC, home of B.C. Open, with 9-under-par 62 in 1985.

PERSONAL: Father, who played for New York Yankees, Chicago White Sox, St. Louis Browns and Kansas City A's, part of the answer to a baseball trivia question: Who was the midget who batted for the Browns in 1951? (Eddie Gaedel) Who pinchran for Eddie Gaedel? (Jim Delsing)...teammates at UCLA included Corey Pavin, Steve Pate and Duffy Waldorf...Missouri Amateur medalist.

1994 PGA TOUR STATISTICS

Scoring Average	71.13	(78)
Driving Distance	269.6	(32)
Driving Accuracy	61.4	(163T)
Greens in Regulation	65.7	(92T)
Putting	1.782	(62T)
All-Around	526	(36)
Sand Saves	54.5	(51T)
Total Driving	195	(115T)
Eagles	11	(7T)
Birdies	305	(41T)

MISCELLANEOUS STATISTICS

Scoring Avg. (before cut)	71.11	(60T)
Scoring Avg. (3rd round)	71.27	(107)
Scoring Avg. (4th round)	72.06	(131T)
Birdie Conversion	29.3	(49T)
Par Breakers	19.9	(48T)

1994 Low Round:	**65:** 2 times
Career Low Round:	**61:** 1993 FedEx St. Jude/4
Career Largest Paycheck:	**$88,000**/1993 New England Classic/T2

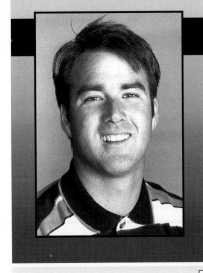

CLARK DENNIS

EXEMPT STATUS: 65th on 1994 money list

FULL NAME: Clark Sherwood Dennis

HEIGHT: 5' 11" **WEIGHT:** 180

BIRTH DATE: February 14, 1966

BIRTHPLACE: Houston, TX

RESIDENCE: Ft. Worth, TX; plays out of Mira Vista CC

FAMILY: Wife, Vickie

COLLEGE: University of Arkansas

SPECIAL INTERESTS: Fishing

TURNED PROFESSIONAL: 1986

Q SCHOOL: 1990, 1991, 1993

PLAYER PROFILE

CAREER EARNINGS: $450,506

BEST EVER FINISH: T3--1990 Hawaiian Open

MONEY & POSITION:

1988--$ 1,027--309	1991--$ 57,760--170	1994--$289,065--65
1989--$ 1,040--288	1992--$ 12,935--227	
1990--$103,721--136	1993--$ 6,050--259	

BEST 1994 FINISHES: T6--U.S. Open; T9--Canon Greater Hartford Open; 10--BellSouth Classic

1994 SUMMARY: Tournaments entered--30; in money--22; top ten finishes--3.

1995 PGA TOUR CHARITY TEAM COMPETITION: NEC World Series of Golf

1994 SEASON: Enjoyed finest TOUR season with earnings of $289,065, which—most importantly—enabled retention of playing privileges for first time in five tries...had card for 1995 by end of May, when finished T15 in Southwestern Bell Colonial...$23,800 paycheck raised season's total to $143,689...was in money nine of next ten events, top finish among which T6 in U.S. Open, where collected $49,485 for biggest payday of season...posted 1-under-par 283 total at Oakmont CC...following week finished T9 in Canon Greater Hartford Open, where opening-round 65 had him in four-way tie for lead...also had solo 10th in May at BellSouth Classic...posted second-round 66, final-round 69...top finish over final 12 starts after GHO T11 at Walt Disney World/Oldsmobile Classic.

CAREER HIGHLIGHTS: Best previous effort came in first year on TOUR, in 1990...finished No. 136 on money list with earnings of $103,721...had top finish to date that year, T3 in United Airlines Hawaiian Open worth $52,000 (also biggest paycheck through 1994)...returned to TOUR for 1994 by finishing T8 at 1993 Qualifying Tournament...finished No. 22 on 1993 NIKE TOUR money list with $64,779...won 1993 NIKE Bakersfield Open...winner 1992-93 Newport Classics...winner 1988 Nevada State Open.

PERSONAL: 1983 Texas State Junior Champion.

1994 PGA TOUR STATISTICS

Scoring Average	70.82	(50T)
Driving Distance	261.8	(89)
Driving Accuracy	76.9	(15T)
Greens in Regulation	70.6	(9T)
Putting	1.794	(95T)
All-Around	439	(23)
Sand Saves	49.7	(110T)
Total Driving	104	(21)
Eagles	6	(64T)
Birdies	357	(7)

MISCELLANEOUS STATISTICS

Scoring Avg. (before cut)	70.82	(41)
Scoring Avg. (3rd round)	71.37	(118)
Scoring Avg. (4th round)	71.16	(56T)
Birdie Conversion	28.7	(66T)
Par Breakers	20.6	(25T)

1994 Low Round: 65: 2 times

Career Low Round: 65: 5 times, most recently '94 Canon GGO/1

Career Largest Paycheck: $52,000/1990 Hawaiian Open/T4

CHRIS DiMARCO

EXEMPT STATUS: 85th on 1994 money list

FULL NAME: Christian Dean DiMarco

HEIGHT: 6' **WEIGHT:** 180

BIRTH DATE: August 23, 1968

BIRTHPLACE: Huntington, NY

RESIDENCE: Apopka, FL; plays out of The CC at Heathrow

COLLEGE: University of Florida

FAMILY: Wife, Amy

SPECIAL INTERESTS: Fishing, tennis

TURNED PROFESSIONAL: 1990

JOINED TOUR: 1994

PLAYER PROFILE

CAREER EARNINGS: $216,839

BEST-EVER FINISH: T3--1994 Deposit Guaranty Classic

MONEY & POSITION: 1994--$216,839--85

BEST 1994 FINISHES: T3--Deposit Guaranty Classic; 4--New England Classic; T6--Sprint International; T7--Freeport McMoRan Classic

1994 SUMMARY: Tournaments entered--29; in money--16; top ten finishes--4.

1995 PGA TOUR CHARITY TEAM COMPETITION: JCPenney Classic

1994 SEASON: Parlayed ninth-place finish on 1993 NIKE TOUR into fine first-year season on PGA TOUR…with earnings of $216,839, finished eighth among rookies…pair of back-to-back top-10s among keys to his season…finished T3 in weather-shortened Deposit Guaranty Golf Classic, followed by solo fourth in New England Classic…those two weeks combined worth $79,570 at the bank…first of four top-10s came in April, T7 at Freeport-McMoRan Classic, where finished 66-69…New Orleans outing came during stretch where missed nine of first 17 cuts…consecutive top-10s among eight of final 12 events in the money…also had T6 at The Sprint International…Castle Pines check for $48,650 largest of campaign, topping New England Classic payday by $650.

CAREER HIGHLIGHTS: Ninth on 1993 NIKE TOUR money list with $90,687…won Canadian Tour Order of Merit in 1992…also led Canadian Tour in stroke average in '92…NIKE TOUR member in 1991, finishing No. 53 with $23,333…best previous finish in PGA TOUR event T43 in 1989 Beatrice Western Open (as amateur).

PERSONAL: Wife Amy caddies for him on occasion…NCAA All-American in 1990…SEC Player of Year 1990…All-SEC 1989-90…winner 1989 SEC Championship.

1994 PGA TOUR STATISTICS

Scoring Average	71.51	(119T)
Driving Distance	265.4	(59)
Driving Accuracy	64.0	(150T)
Greens in Regulation	66.6	(75)
Putting	1.808	(122T)
All-Around	704	(91)
Sand Saves	54.9	(45T)
Total Driving	209	(131)
Eagles	5	(87T)
Birdies	301	(47)

MISCELLANEOUS STATISTICS

Scoring Avg. (before cut)	71.59	(107)
Scoring Avg. (3rd round)	70.93	(82T)
Scoring Avg. (4th round)	71.79	(114T)
Birdie Conversion	29.2	(54T)
Par Breakers	19.8	(52T)

1994 Low Round: 65: Federal Express St. Jude Classic/3
Career Low Round: 65: 1994 Federal Express St. Jude Classic/3
Career Largest Paycheck: $48,650: 1994 Sprint International/T6

DAVID EDWARDS

EXEMPT STATUS: 1993 tournament winner

FULL NAME: David Wayne Edwards

HEIGHT: 5' 8" **WEIGHT:** 155

BIRTH DATE: April 18, 1956

BIRTHPLACE: Neosho, MO

RESIDENCE: Edmond, OK; plays out of Karsten Creek GC

FAMILY: Wife, Jonnie; Rachel Leigh (12/21/85), Abby Grace (11/22/93)

COLLEGE: Oklahoma State University

SPECIAL INTERESTS: Automobiles, motorcycles, radio controlled miniature cars, flying own plane

TURNED PROFESSIONAL: 1978

Q SCHOOL: Fall 1978

PLAYER PROFILE

CAREER EARNINGS: $3,420,417 **PLAYOFF RECORD:** 1-1

TOUR VICTORIES: 1980 Walt Disney World National Team Championship (with Danny Edwards), **1984** Los Angeles Open. **1992** Memorial Tournament. **1993** MCI Heritage Classic.
(TOTAL: 4)

MONEY & POSITION:

1979--$ 44,456-- 88	1985--$ 21,506--157	1991--$396,695-- 38
1980--$ 35,810-- 93	1986--$122,079-- 71	1992--$515,070-- 27
1981--$ 68,211-- 65	1987--$148,217-- 73	1993--$653,086-- 20
1982--$ 49,896-- 91	1988--$151,513-- 76	1994--$458,845-- 34
1983--$114,037-- 48	1989--$239,908-- 57	
1984--$236,061-- 23	1990--$166,028-- 95	

BEST 1994 FINISHES: T2--GTE Byron Nelson Classic; T4--MCI Heritage Classic; 5--Memorial; 8--Honda Classic; T8--Mercedes Championships, Kmart Greater Greensboro Open.

1994 SUMMARY: Tournaments entered--23; in money--20; top ten finishes--6.

1995 PGA TOUR CHARITY TEAM COMPETITION: THE TOUR Championship

1994 SEASON: Continued solid play of last four campaigns with third-best earnings year of career…had made $407,864 through U.S. Open, but earned just $50,981 over last four months, when best finish was T13 in B.C. Open…as result, finished No. 34 on money list…opened year with T8 in Mercedes Championships, then had a second eighth-place finish at Honda Classic…one month later began four-tournament top-10 string with T4 in defense of MCI Heritage Classic title…closed 65-64 at Harbour Town, but was too little too late as finished four strokes behind winner Hale Irwin…following week posted T8 at Kmart GGO…two weeks later had season high, T2 as part of six-man playoff at GTE Byron Nelson Classic won by Neal Lancaster…concluded four-event run with solo fifth in another tournament has won, Memorial, where opened 69-67 and was tied for second after 36 holes…had T18 at Masters, T15 in Southwestern Bell Colonial immediately before and after Heritage-Memorial skein.

CAREER HIGHLIGHTS: After having not won on TOUR for eight years, collected pair of victories in 11 months: 1992 Memorial and 1993 MCI Heritage Classic…shared 36- and 54-hole leads in Heritage, where closing 69 on 37th birthday provided two-stroke win over David Frost…broke victory drought by winning Memorial in darkness, defeating Rick Fehr on second playoff hole…second-round 65 at Muirfield Village vaulted into contention, closing 67 left tied with Fehr…final-round 65 at Texas Open, good for T3 and $46,800 in final full-field event of season, bumped Ben Crenshaw for 30th and final spot in 1992 TOUR Championship…teamed with brother Danny in 1980 Walt Disney World National Team Championship…four years later won Los Angeles Open by three strokes over Jack Renner.

PERSONAL: Member of PGA TOUR "Air Force," flies own plane to most tournament stops…winner 1978 NCAA Championship…All-American selection 1977-78…winner 1973 Oklahoma State Junior title…started tagging along with older brother Danny to golf course when about 12 years old.

1994 PGA TOUR STATISTICS

Scoring Average	70.23	(24)
Driving Distance	253.1	(155T)
Driving Accuracy	81.6	(1)
Greens in Regulation	69.1	(27)
Putting	1.799	(105T)
All-Around	595	(55)
Sand Saves	52.6	(79T)
Total Driving	156	(56)
Eagles	3	(126T)
Birdies	281	(78)

MISCELLANEOUS STATISTICS

Scoring Avg. (before cut)	70.39	(20)
Scoring Avg. (3rd round)	70.72	(70)
Scoring Avg. (4th round)	71.72	(110)
Birdie Conversion	27.5	(115T)
Par Breakers	19.2	(73T)

1994 Low Round: 64: MCI Heritage Classic/4
Career Low Round: 61: 1987 Bob Hope Chrysler Classic/1
Career Largest Paycheck: $234,000/1992 Memorial Tournament/1

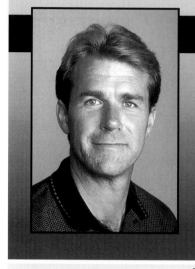

JOEL EDWARDS

EXEMPT STATUS: 127th on 1994 money list

FULL NAME: Joel Ashley Edwards

HEIGHT: 6'   **WEIGHT:** 165

BIRTH DATE: November 22, 1961

BIRTHPLACE: Dallas, TX

RESIDENCE: Irving, TX

FAMILY: Wife, Rhonda

COLLEGE: North Texas State

SPECIAL INTERESTS: Music, movies

TURNED PROFESSIONAL: 1984

Q SCHOOL: 1988, 1989, 1990

PLAYER PROFILE

CAREER EARNINGS: $660,508

BEST EVER FINISH: T2--1992 B.C. Open

MONEY & POSITION:
1989--$ 46,851-- 167   1991--$106,820-- 131   1993--$150,623--106
1990--$109,808-- 132   1992--$107,264-- 126   1994--$139,141--127

BEST 1994 FINISHES: 6--Kemper Open; T8--Kmart Greater Greensboro Open.

1994 SUMMARY: Tournaments entered--28; in money--13; top ten finishes--2.

1995 PGA TOUR CHARITY TEAM COMPETITION: B.C. Open

1994 SEASON: Ended year as he began, with string of missed cuts, six at outset and four at end of season…in between, pulled together second-best earnings campaign of career, good enough–by two spots–to retain playing privileges…what put him over top was T49 at Hardee's Golf Classic, final in-money event, worth $2,495 and final total of $139,141 (No. 127)…best finish solo sixth at Kemper Open, where closed 68-69 and collected check for $46,800…opened with back-to-back 69s in Kmart Greater Greensboro Open, finishing with T8 worth $42,000…total of $88,800 for two top-10s cornerstone of earnings year…only other top-25, T22 at B.C. Open, came after opening 64, one stroke off Jeff Sluman's early lead…during Freeport-McMoRan Classic saw English Turn course-record 64 (established in 1991) broken not once but twice on successive days: by Jose Maria Olazabal (63 in Round 1) and Dennis Paulson (62 in Round 2).

CAREER HIGHLIGHTS: Played as fully exempt player for first time in 1993, finishing in top-25 five times…best finish T11 at THE PLAYERS Championship…opened with 6-under-par 66 at TPC at Sawgrass, followed with 69 to stand three strokes off 36-hole lead…was one-over-par on weekend but collected check for $53,000, largest of career…produced best earnings year of six on TOUR…put together rounds of 69-66-69-68 to finish T2 in 1992 B.C. Open, six strokes behind John Daly…finish and accompanying check for $52,800 enabled him to retain playing privileges for first time…best finish prior to B.C. Open T5 in 1991 USF&G Classic, where posted English Turn course record which stood until Olazabal and Paulson came along three years later…winner 1988 North Dakota Open.

PERSONAL: Commented after 1992 B.C. Open T2: "Andy Warhol promised me this (15 minutes of fame), so I'm just going to enjoy it"… American Junior Golf Association All-American…named to All-Southland Conference Team at North Texas State.

1994 PGA TOUR STATISTICS

Scoring Average	71.94	(155)
Driving Distance	255.3	(143)
Driving Accuracy	67.4	(113T)
Greens in Regulation	64.5	(125T)
Putting	1.824	(153)
All-Around	1,032	(162)
Sand Saves	52.1	(83T)
Total Driving	256	(163T)
Eagles	2	(146T)
Birdies	248	(114)

MISCELLANEOUS STATISTICS

Scoring Avg. (before cut)	72.64	(169)
Scoring Avg. (3rd round)	71.38	(119T)
Scoring Avg. (4th round)	71.00	(49T)
Birdie Conversion	25.1	(155T)
Par Breakers	16.3	(161)

1994 Low Round: 64: B.C. Open/1
Career Low Round: 64: 4 times, most recent 1994 B.C. Open/1
Career Largest Paycheck: $53,000/1993 PLAYERS Championship/T11

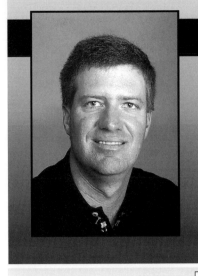

STEVE ELKINGTON

EXEMPT STATUS: Winner, 1991 THE PLAYERS Championship

FULL NAME: Stephen John Elkington

HEIGHT: 6' 2"   **WEIGHT:** 190

BIRTH DATE: December 8, 1962

BIRTHPLACE: Inverell, Australia

RESIDENCE: Sydney, Australia and Houston, TX; plays out of Champions GC

FAMILY: Wife, Lisa

COLLEGE: University of Houston (1985, Recreation)

SPECIAL INTERESTS: Character drawing, fishing, hunting

TURNED PROFESSIONAL: 1985

Q SCHOOL: Fall 1986

PLAYER PROFILE

CAREER EARNINGS: $3,271,135   **PLAYOFF RECORD:** 1-3

TOUR VICTORIES: **1990** Kmart Greater Greensboro Open. **1991** THE PLAYERS Championship.
(TOTAL: 4)   **1992** Infiniti Tournament of Champions. **1994** Buick Southern Open.

MONEY & POSITION:

1987--$ 75,738--118	1990--$548,564--18	1993--$675,383--17
1988--$149,972-- 79	1991--$549,120--25	1994--$294,943--62
1989--$231,062-- 61	1992--$746,352--12	

BEST 1994 FINISHES: 1--Buick Southern Open; T7--PGA Championship.

1994 SUMMARY: Tournaments entered--20; in money--15; top ten finishes--2.

1995 PGA TOUR CHARITY TEAM COMPETITION: Bob Hope Chrysler Classic

NATIONAL TEAMS: Presidents Cup, 1994

1994 SEASON: Although earnings total lowest since 1989, shortfall easily explained...early-season medical problems hampered play signficantly...was hospitalized in January, spent early part of year recuperating from serious virus...while in hospital had malignant growth removed from shoulder...in May underwent sinus surgery, which helped alleviate longtime breathing problem...finally, in August, posted first top-25 finish...middle rounds of 68-69 helped produce Buick Open T11, which was followed next week by T7 in PGA Championship...third-round 66 was followed by closing 69 at Southern Hills...comeback from early-season medical problems was completed in Buick Southern Open...ran to five-stroke lead after three rounds at Callaway Gardens, then was awarded fourth TOUR title when weather created 54-hole event...member International Team in inaugural Presidents Cup Match.

CAREER HIGHLIGHTS: First TOUR victory came in 1990 Kmart Greater Greensboro Open, where final-day 66 brought him from seven strokes back for win...scored biggest triumph by outdueling Fuzzy Zoeller to win THE PLAYERS Championship in 1991...collected $288,000 paycheck and 10-year TOUR exemption...won 1992 Infiniti Tournament of Champions in playoff with Brad Faxon...late in year lost H-E-B Texas Open playoff to Nick Price...made all 23 cuts in 1993, when best performance was playoff loss to Rocco Mediate in Kmart GGO...runnerup finish witnessed by parents, visiting from Australia...also finished T3 in '93 Masters...winner 1993 Fred Meyer Challenge (with Tom Purtzer)...winner 1992 Australian Open...runnerup 1986 Qualifying Tournament.

PERSONAL: Idol growing up in Outback fellow Aussie Bruce Devlin...winner 1980 Australia-New Zealand Amateur...winner 1981 Australian Amateur and Doug Sanders Junior World Championship...spotted at latter by Houston coach Dave Williams, who gave him scholarship...two-time All-American at Houston, where teammates included Billy Ray Brown...two-time Southwest Conference Champion...member 1984-85 NCAA Championship teams.

1994 PGA TOUR STATISTICS

Scoring Average	71.10	(76)
Driving Distance	271.2	(26T)
Driving Accuracy	65.5	(134T)
Greens in Regulation	66.0	(85)
Putting	1.787	(73T)
All-Around	721	(98)
Sand Saves	56.5	(33T)
Total Driving	160	(60T)
Eagles	2	(146T)
Birdies	213	(148)

MISCELLANEOUS STATISTICS

Scoring Avg. (before cut)	71.46	(94)
Scoring Avg. (3rd round)	71.33	(113T)
Scoring Avg. (4th round)	71.38	(76T)
Birdie Conversion	28.9	(61T)
Par Breakers	19.3	(67T)

1994 Low Round: 66: 6 times

Career Low Round: 62: 3 times, most recent '91 Southwestern Bell Colonial/3

Career Largest Paycheck: $288,000/1991 THE PLAYERS Championship/1

ERNIE ELS

EXEMPT STATUS: Winner, 1994 United States Open

FULL NAME: Theodore Ernest Els

HEIGHT: 6' 3" **WEIGHT:** 210

BIRTH DATE: October 17, 1969

BIRTHPLACE: Johannesburg, South Africa

RESIDENCE: Orlando, FL

FAMILY: Single

SPECIAL INTERESTS: Movies, reading, sports

TURNED PROFESSIONAL: 1989

JOINED TOUR: 1994

PLAYER PROFILE

CAREER EARNINGS: $684,440   **PLAYOFF RECORD:** 1-0

TOUR VICTORIES: **1994** U.S. Open
(TOTAL:1)

MONEY & POSITION: 1991--$ 2,647--274   1993--$ 38,185--190
                         1992--$ 18,420--213   1994--$684,440-- 19

BEST 1994 FINISHES: 1--U.S. Open; 2--Buick Classic; 4--Sprint International; T8--Masters Tournament

1994 SUMMARY: Tournaments entered--11; in money--10; top ten finishes--4.

1995 PGA TOUR CHARITY TEAM COMPETITION: Nissan Open

NATIONAL TEAMS: Dunhill Cup (2) 1992, 1993; World Cup (2) 1992, 1993

1994 SEASON: Although not unknown to American golf public, certainly took country by storm with playoff victory over Loren Roberts and Colin Montgomerie in U.S. Open...on basis of Oakmont CC win, which came on 20th hole of continuing playoff with Roberts, made decision to join PGA TOUR in August...Open triumph came week after runnerup finish to Lee Janzen in Buick Classic...held midpoint lead at Westchester CC...also was third-round leader at Oakmont...had T8 finish in the Masters, later in season solo fourth in Sprint International...as TOUR member, participated in first TOUR Championship and stood one stroke off Bill Glasson 36-hole lead...combined earnings for 11 TOUR events placed No. 19 overall, far and away No. 1 among first-year players...subsequently named PGA TOUR Rookie of Year for 1994...in January won Dubai Desert Classic on PGA European Tour, in February runnerup at Australian Masters...defeated Colin Montgomerie for World Match Play Championship in October, eliminating Seve Ballesteros and Jose Maria Olazabal to get to Montgomerie.

CAREER HIGHLIGHTS: Prior to 1994, top finish in TOUR event T7 at 1993 U.S. Open...played in six TOUR events in 1993, three in 1992...top '92 finish T31 at International...also competed in 1991 International, 1990 Buick Southern Open...participated in nine Ben Hogan Tour events in 1991, with top finish T9 in Tulsa Open...placed T6 in 1993 British Open, T5 in 1992...winner six 1992 tournaments in Africa, including South African Open, South African PGA Championship, South African Masters...winner 1993 Dunlop Phoenix (Japan).

PERSONAL: Started playing golf at age 9...also was an accomplished junior tennis player, but turned sole focus to golf at 14.

1994 PGA TOUR STATISTICS

Scoring Average	69.77
Driving Distance	279.2
Driving Accuracy	63.3
Greens in Regulation	63.5
Putting	1.760
All-Around	--
Sand Saves	56.5
Total Driving	--
Eagles	3
Birdies	139

MISCELLANEOUS STATISTICS

Scoring Avg. (before cut)	70.20
Scoring Avg. (3rd round)	70.00
Scoring Avg. (4th round)	73.22
Birdie Conversion	32.0
Par Breakers	20.8

1994 Low Round: 66: 3 times

Career Low Round: 66: 3 times, most recently
Career Largest   1994 NEC WSOG/2
Paycheck: $320,000/1994 U.S. Open/1

BOB ESTES

EXEMPT STATUS: 1994 tournament winner

FULL NAME: Bob Alan Estes

HEIGHT: 6' 1"   **WEIGHT:** 175

BIRTH DATE: February 2, 1966

BIRTHPLACE: Graham, TX

RESIDENCE: Austin, TX; plays out of The Hills of Lakeway, near Austin

FAMILY: Single

COLLEGE: University of Texas

SPECIAL INTERESTS: Music, hunting

TURNED PROFESSIONAL: 1988

Q SCHOOL: Fall 1988

PLAYER PROFILE

CAREER EARNINGS: $1,898,408   **PLAYOFF RECORD:** 0-2

TOUR VICTORIES: 1994 Texas Open.
(TOTAL: 1)

MONEY & POSITION:

1988--$ 5,968--237	1991--$147,364--105	1993--$447,187--32
1989--$135,628--102	1992--$190,778-- 80	1994--$765,360--14
1990--$212,090-- 69		

BEST 1994 FINISHES: 1--Texas Open; 2--Phoenix Open; T3--Greater Milwaukee Open; T4--BellSouth Classic; T6--Buick Invitational of California; T7--MCI Heritage Classic; T9--Bob Hope Chrysler Classic; T10--Bell Canadian Open

1994 SUMMARY: Tournaments entered--27; in money--23; top ten finishes--8.

1995 PGA TOUR CHARITY TEAM COMPETITION: Lincoln-Mercury Kapalua International

1994 SEASON: Much anticipated first TOUR victory came in home state of Texas...at Texas Open, became third wire-to-wire winner of TOUR season...others: Greg Norman, PLAYERS; Mike Springer, Kmart GGO...opened with nine-under-par 62, matching par-71 Oak Hills CC record...led Bob Tway first two rounds, Gil Morgan and Don Pooley through three, held on for one-stroke win over Morgan...victory eighth top-10 of season, all of which contrib-uted to career-best earnings of $765,360 and first Top-30 finish...had three top-10s in first five starts, with solo second at Phoenix best of trio...one stroke off lead each of first three rounds at TPC of Scottsdale...in February posted T9 Bob Hope Chrysler Classic, T6 Buick Invitational back-to-back...co-first-round leader at MCI Heritage Classic after opening 65 (finished seventh), held 54-hole lead at Greater Milwaukee Open after rounds of 67-66-65...closed with 72 at Brown Deer Park GC for T3...followed GMO with T10 at Bell Canadian Open for second back-to-back pair...other top-10 BellSouth Classic (T4) in May...All-Around category leader.

CAREER HIGHLIGHTS: Had early close call with winning in Rookie-of-Year season of 1989...lost B.C. Open playoff to Mike Hulbert on first extra hole...participant in five-man playoff at 1993 Buick Southern Open won by John Inman...two weeks later, third-round 64 helped to solo fourth in Texas Open...with T3 at Las Vegas Invitational, missed final berth in 1993 TOUR Championship by just $1,135...one stroke out of lead after 54 holes of '93 PGA Championship, held lead during final round, only to finish with 73 and T6...won first professional event, Bogey Hills Invitational in St. Charles, MO in 1988.

PERSONAL: First played golf at four, set sights on TOUR career at 12...high school teammate of Mike Standly (Standly senior during his sophomore year)...won numerous amateur events, including 1983 Texas High School Championship, 1985 Trans-Mississippi Amateur, 1988 Texas State Amateur...named Fred Haskins and Jack Nicklaus Award winners as 1988 College Player of Year.

1994 PGA TOUR STATISTICS

Scoring Average	69.78	(10)
Driving Distance	263.2	(78)
Driving Accuracy	73.3	(43T)
Greens in Regulation	70.9	(6T)
Putting	1.771	(31T)
All-Around	227	(1)
Sand Saves	60.4	(6T)
Total Driving	121	(25T)
Eagles	7	(44T)
Birdies	352	(9)

MISCELLANEOUS STATISTICS

Scoring Avg. (before cut)	69.80	(6)
Scoring Avg. (3rd round)	69.15	(5)
Scoring Avg. (4th round)	70.33	(19)
Birdie Conversion	29.0	(57T)
Par Breakers	21.0	(19T)

1994 Low Round: **62:** Texas Open/1	
Career Low Round: 61: 1991 Chattanooga	
Career Largest Classic/2	
Paycheck: $180,000: 1994 Texas Open/1	

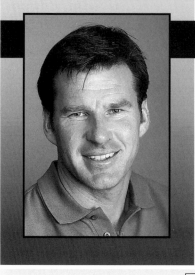

NICK FALDO

EXEMPT STATUS: Winner, 1992 British Open

FULL NAME: Nicholas Alexander Faldo

HEIGHT: 6' 3" **WEIGHT:** 195

BIRTH DATE: July 18, 1957

BIRTHPLACE: Welwyn Garden City, England

RESIDENCE: Orlando, FL and Windlesham, England

FAMILY: Wife, Gill; Natalie (9/18/86), Matthew (3/17/89), Georgia (3/20/93)

SPECIAL INTERESTS: Fly fishing, flying helicopters

TURNED PROFESSIONAL: 1976

JOINED TOUR: 1981, 1995

PLAYER PROFILE

CAREER EARNINGS: $1,186,236 **PLAYOFF RECORD:** 2-1

TOUR VICTORIES: **1984** Sea Pines Heritage Classic; **1989** Masters Tournament; **1990** Masters
(TOTAL: 3) Tournament

MONEY & POSITION:

1981--$ 23,320--119	1986--$ 52,965--135	1991--$127,156--117
1982--$ 56,667-- 79	1987--$ 36,281--169	1992--$345,168-- 41
1983--$ 67,851-- 79	1988--$179.120-- 64	1993--$188,886-- 91
1984--$116,845-- 38	1989--$327,981-- 31	1994--$221,146-- 83
1985--$ 54,060--117	1990--$345,262-- 37	

BEST 1994 FINISHES: T4--PGA Championship; 5--THE PLAYERS Championship

1994 SUMMARY: Tournaments entered--9; in money--6; top ten finishes--2.

1995 PGA TOUR CHARITY TEAM COMPETITION: Deposit Guaranty Golf Classic

NATIONAL TEAMS: Ryder Cup (9) 1977, 1979, 1981, 1983, 1985, 1987, 1989, 1991, 1993. Dunhill Cup (6) 1985, 1986, 1987, 1991, 1993. World Cup (2) 1977, 1991. Nissan Cup, 1986. Kirin Cup, 1987. Asahi Glass Four Tours, 1990. Hennessy Cognac Cup (4) 1978, 1980, 1982, 1984. Double Diamond, 1977.

1994 SEASON: Rejoined TOUR in September as fulltime member for 1995...played in nine TOUR events in '94, posting top-10 finishes in two: PLAYERS Championship and PGA Championship...opened with rounds of 67-69-68 at PLAYERS, closed with 73 for solo fifth...carded final-round 66 at Southern Hills for T4...with closing 64, also had T8 in British Open, event has won three times...captured 30th PGA European Tour tournament title in June, winning Dunhill Open (Belgium) in playoff...supplanted by Greg Norman in February atop Sony World Rankings after record 81-week reign.

CAREER HIGHLIGHTS: One of game's finest technicians, has earned five major titles: 1987-90-92 British Opens, 1989-90 Masters...in addition to two Masters, has one other PGA TOUR victory, in 1984 Sea Pines Heritage Classic...first became member of PGA TOUR in March 1981...finished second to Greg Norman in 1993 British Open, third to Paul Azinger in '93 PGA Championship...held second-round lead at Royal St. George's, then shared 54-lead with Corey Pavin before finishing two strokes behind Norman...trailed third-round leader Norman by two strokes at Inverness, finished one stroke out of Azinger-Norman playoff after closing with 68...first foreigner to win PGA Player of Year Award in 1990...playoff loser to Curtis Strange in 1988 U.S. Open...led European Tour Order of Merit (money list) in 1983 and 1992...1977 European Tour Rookie of Year...1977 Ryder Cup victory over Tom Watson at Royal Lytham highlight of start of career...winner British PGA Championship 1978-80-81...had 11 top-10 finishes in 16 European Tour starts in 1983, compiling 69.03 stroke average...finished eighth on European Order of Merit in 1994...awarded MBE (Member of British Empire) in 1987.

PERSONAL: Decided to give golf a try at age 14, after watching Jack Nicklaus on television...rebuilt swing completely under watchful eye of David Leadbetter...won 1975 British Youths Amateur and English Amateur Championships.

1994 PGA TOUR STATISTICS

Scoring Average	70.32
Driving Distance	262.7
Driving Accuracy	75.0
Greens in Regulation	67.0
Putting	1.831
All-Around	–
Sand Saves	50.0
Total Driving	–
Eagles	0
Birdies	88

MISCELLANEOUS STATISTICS

Scoring Avg. (before cut)	71.78
Scoring Avg. (3rd round)	71.33
Scoring Avg. (4th round)	72.00
Birdie Conversion	24.3
Par Breakers	16.3

1994 Low Round: **66:** PGA Championship/4
Career Low Round:62: 1981 Hawaiian Open/2
Career Largest
Paycheck: $225,000/ 1990 Masters/1

BRAD FAXON

EXEMPT STATUS: 24th on 1994 money list

FULL NAME: Bradford John Faxon Jr.

HEIGHT: 6' 1"　　　**WEIGHT:** 170

BIRTH DATE: August 1, 1961

BIRTHPLACE: Oceanport, NJ

RESIDENCE: Barrington, RI

FAMILY: Wife, Bonnie, Melanie (1/3/89), Emily (5/13/91)

COLLEGE: Furman University (1983, Economics)

SPECIAL INTERESTS: Racquet sports, sports psychology

TURNED PROFESSIONAL: 1983

Q SCHOOL: Fall 1983

PLAYER PROFILE

CAREER EARNINGS: $3,065,652　　　　　**PLAYOFF RECORD:** 1-2

TOUR VICTORIES: 1986 Provident Classic. **1991** Buick Open. **1992** New England Classic, (TOTAL: 4)　　The International.

MONEY & POSITION:

1984--$ 71,688-- 82	1988--$162,656-- 74	1992--$812,093-- 8
1985--$ 46,813--124	1989--$222,076-- 63	1993--$312,023-- 55
1986--$ 92,716-- 90	1990--$197,118-- 81	1994--$612,847-- 24
1987--$113,534-- 90	1991--$422,088-- 34	

BEST 1994 FINISHES: T3--Buick Classic, NEC World Series of Golf; 4--Nissan Los Angeles Open; T5--Southwestern Bell Colonial; T6--THE PLAYERS Championship; T9--Memorial Tournament

1994 SUMMARY: Tournaments entered--25; in money--23; top ten finishes--6.

1995 PGA TOUR CHARITY TEAM COMPETITION: New England Classic

NATIONAL TEAMS: Walker Cup, 1983

1994 SEASON: Returned to pre-January 1993 skiing injury form with earnings second only to career year of 1992, when posted pair of victories…had six top-10 finishes, best of which pair of T3s at Buick Classic and NEC World Series of Golf…top performance came at British Open, where was one stroke off midpoint lead and shared third-round lead with Fuzzy Zoeller…final-round 73 meant seventh-place finish at Turnberry…posted closing 66 in Buick Classic, third-round 65 in NEC World Series, three strokes off 54-hole lead…first top-10 came in third start of year, 4th in Nissan Los Angeles Open…opened with consecutive 68s in PLAYERS Championship, where placed T6…had back-to-back top-10s in May, T9 at Memorial Tournament followed by T5 in Southwestern Bell Colonial…model of consistency, missed but two cuts in 25 starts…won Franklin Funds Shark Shootout (with Fred Couples) in November.

CAREER HIGHLIGHTS: Rib cage skiing injury hampered early in 1993…didn't return to form until middle of season…as result, earnings fell more than $500,000 from 1992 campaign…captured pair of titles that year, winning on home turf in New England Classic and at International…won by two strokes at Pleasant Valley, had 14-point performance on Sunday to capture International…also lost 1992 playoffs at Tournament of Champions and Buick Open…first TOUR win came at 1986 Provident Classic, powered by final-round 63…scored playoff win over Chip Beck at 1991 Buick Open…won 1993 Heineken Australian Open.

PERSONAL: As youngster, played golf with father on course grandmother owned on Cape Cod…winner 1983 Fred Haskins, *Golf Magazine* and NCAA Coaches Awards as nation's outstanding collegiate player…member 1983 Walker Cup team…1982-83 All-American selection…winner 1980-81 New England Amateur…winner 1979-80 Rhode Island Amateur.

1994 PGA TOUR STATISTICS

Scoring Average	70.15	(21)
Driving Distance	263.6	(74T)
Driving Accuracy	68.3	(101T)
Greens in Regulation	64.7	(117T)
Putting	1.775	(38T)
All-Around	540	(43T)
Sand Saves	53.5	(66T)
Total Driving	175	(85T)
Eagles	4	(104T)
Birdies	327	(19T)

MISCELLANEOUS STATISTICS

Scoring Avg. (before cut)	70.56	(26)
Scoring Avg. (3rd round)	71.45	(127T)
Scoring Avg. (4th round)	70.73	(36)
Birdie Conversion	30.5	(20T)
Par Breakers	20.0	(45T)

1994 Low Round: 65: 2 times
Career Low Round: 62: 1986 Provident Classic/2
Career Largest
Paycheck: $216,000/1992 The International/1

DAVID FEHERTY

EXEMPT STATUS: 100th on 1994 money list

FULL NAME: David William Feherty

HEIGHT: 5' 11"   **WEIGHT:** 175

BIRTH DATE: August 13, 1958

BIRTHPLACE: Bangor, Northern Ireland

RESIDENCE: Crawfordsburn, Northern Ireland, and Dallas, TX

FAMILY: Wife, Caroline; Shey (7/2/88), Rory (4/29/92)

SPECIAL INTERESTS: Music, cars

TURNED PROFESSIONAL: 1976

Q SCHOOL: 1993

PLAYER PROFILE

CAREER EARNINGS: $178,501

BEST-EVER FINISH: 2--1994 New England Classic.

MONEY & POSITION: 1991--$ 38,000--187   1992--$ 11,668--231   1994--$178,501--100

BEST 1994 FINISHES: 2--New England Classic; T9--Northern Telecom Open.

1994 SUMMARY: Tournaments entered--22; in money--13; top ten finishes--2.

1995 PGA TOUR CHARITY TEAM COMPETITION: Kmart Greater Greensboro Open

NATIONAL TEAMS: Ryder Cup, 1991. Dunhill Cup (3) 1985, 1986, 1990, 1991. World Cup, 1990. Asahi Glass Four Tours (2) 1990, 1991.

1994 SEASON: First TOUR campaign somewhat of an up-and-down experience...as Qualifying Tournament graduate, found playing opportunities somewhat limited early...made most of second one, posting T9 in Northern Telecom Open ...that came as part of stretch during which missed five cuts and withdrew once in 11 first-half starts...had just one other top-10 finish, but it assured playing privileges for 1995...opened with 65 at New England Classic, was in hunt throughout before placing second, one stroke behind Kenny Perry...Pleasant Valley runnerup, worth $108,000, put him over top in earnings with $153,136 to that juncture...New England experience part of positive two-week trans-Atlantic sojourn, since returned to U.S. straight from Turnberry and T4 in British Open...had one other top-25 finish, T20 in Buick Open which came two weeks after New England Classic.

CAREER HIGHLIGHTS: Qualified for PGA TOUR by placing T11 in 1993 Qualifying Tournament...prior to 1994, best finish in TOUR event T7 in 1991 PGA Championship...made ten TOUR starts before '94...busiest year 1992, with seven starts (best finish T28 in B.C. Open)...PGA Championship only U.S. appearance in 1991...played stateside for first time in 1988, when missed cut at International, then next week finished 33rd in NEC World Series of Golf...winner of five PGA European Tour events: 1986 Italian and Scottish Opens, 1989 BMW International Open, 1991 Credit Lyonnais Cannes Open, 1992 Iberia Madrid Open...member 1991 European Ryder Cup team...represented Ireland in 1985-86-90-91 Dunhill Cups and 1990 World Cup.

PERSONAL: Learned game while caddying for travel agent father...trained as an opera singer, sang for 5-6 years in school and church choirs before deciding "the world doesn't need another bad Irish tenor"...first played in U.S. in early 1980s, when London businessman sponsored him and several others on Florida mini-tour...worked on Disney World golf staff for year.

1994 PGA TOUR STATISTICS

Scoring Average	71.83	(147)
Driving Distance	257.9	(123T)
Driving Accuracy	71.1	(61T)
Greens in Regulation	65.6	(96T)
Putting	1.818	(138T)
All-Around	879	(144)
Sand Saves	52.5	(81T)
Total Driving	184	(103T)
Eagles	5	(87T)
Birdies	215	(146)

MISCELLANEOUS STATISTICS

Scoring Avg. (before cut)	71.81	(128T)
Scoring Avg. (3rd round)	71.31	(112)
Scoring Avg. (4th round)	72.23	(143T)
Birdie Conversion	27.1	(123T)
Par Breakers	18.2	(119T)

1994 Low Round: 65: New England Classic/1
Career Low Round: 65; 1994 New England Classic/1
Career Largest Paycheck: $108,000/1994 New England Classic/2

RICK FEHR

EXEMPT STATUS: 1994 tournament winner

FULL NAME: Richard Elliott Fehr

HEIGHT: 5' 11" **WEIGHT:** 170

BIRTH DATE: August 28, 1962

BIRTHPLACE: Seattle, WA

RESIDENCE: Redmond, WA; plays out of Desert Canyon Golf Resort, Orondo, WA

FAMILY: Wife, Terri; J.D. (1/26/91), Mitchell (10/26/93)

COLLEGE: Brigham Young University (1984, Finance)

INTERESTS: Family, gardening, basketball, Christianity

TURNED PROFESSIONAL: 1984

Q SCHOOL: Fall 1985.

PLAYER PROFILE

CAREER EARNINGS: $2,472,430 **PLAYOFF RECORD:** 0-3

TOUR VICTORIES: 1986 B.C. Open. **1994** Walt Disney World/Oldsmobile Classic (TOTAL: 2)

MONEY & POSITION:

1985--$ 40,101--133	1989--$ 93,142--131	1992--$433,003-- 33
1986--$151,162-- 61	1990--$149,867--105	1993--$556,322-- 28
1987--$106,808-- 94	1991--$288,983-- 55	1994--$573,963-- 27
1988--$ 79,080--130		

BEST 1994 FINISHES: 1--Walt Disney World/Oldsmobile Classic; 2--Sprint International; T6--Phoenix Open; T9--Northern Telecom Open.

1994 SUMMARY: Tournaments entered--25; in money--16; top ten finishes--4.

1995 PGA TOUR CHARITY TEAM COMPETITION: THE PLAYERS Championship

NATIONAL TEAMS: Walker Cup, 1983

1994 SEASON: Had planned to have hernia surgery week of Walt Disney World/ Oldsmobile Classic, but decided to delay operation–and fortunately so...because of transportation mixup, arrived just 15 minutes before Sunday tee time, but still wound up with second career title...opened with 63 to share first-round lead with Bob Lohr, trailed by one stroke after two rounds, then co-held 54-hole lead with Craig Stadler...final-round 68 gave him two-stroke win over Stadler and Fuzzy Zoeller, as well as berth in TOUR Championship for second year in row...opened year with back-to-back top-10s at Northern Telecom Open (T9) and Phoenix Open (T6)...had $123,382 and string of five consecutive missed cuts through PGA Championship...following week posted solo second at Sprint International worth $151,200, then came $198,000 Disney payday...hernia surgery was performed November 9.

CAREER HIGHLIGHTS: Earnings total has risen progressively for six years...first victory came at 1986 B.C. Open, where began play simply hoping to retain card and finished with two-stroke win over Larry Mize...with '94 second at Sprint International, has seven runnerup finishes since 1991...1991: Federal Express St. Jude Classic, Canon Greater Hartford Open (playoff loss to Billy Ray Brown); 1992: Bob Hope Chrysler Classic (five-man playoff won by John Cook), Memorial Tournament (playoff loss to David Edwards); 1993: Bob Hope (with fourth-round 62 at Indian Wells) and Federal Express St. Jude Classic...low amateur 1984 Masters and 1984 U.S. Open.

PERSONAL: Member PGA TOUR Policy Board from 1992-present...winner 1979 Washington State Junior and PGA National Junior Championships...winner 1982 Western Amateur...two-time All-American at Brigham Young.

1994 PGA TOUR STATISTICS

Scoring Average	70.99	(67)
Driving Distance	263.6	(74T)
Driving Accuracy	67.1	(117T)
Greens in Regulation	65.4	(100T)
Putting	1.771	(31T)
All-Around	685	(84)
Sand Saves	50.0	(105T)
Total Driving	191	(111T)
Eagles	4	(104T)
Birdies	276	(87T)

MISCELLANEOUS STATISTICS

Scoring Avg. (before cut)	71.34	(79T)
Scoring Avg. (3rd round)	70.15	(26)
Scoring Avg. (4th round)	71.00	(49T)
Birdie Conversion	30.4	(22T)
Par Breakers	20.2	(34T)

1994 Low Round: 63: Walt Disney World/Olds Golf Classic/1

Career Low Round: 62: 1993 Bob Hope Chrysler Classic/4

Career Largest Paycheck: $198,000/1994 Walt Disney World/Olds Golf Classic/1

ED FIORI

EXEMPT STATUS: Special Medical Extension

FULL NAME: Edward Ray Fiori

HEIGHT: 5' 7"   **WEIGHT:** 190

BIRTH DATE: April 21, 1953

BIRTHPLACE: Lynwood, CA

RESIDENCE: Sugarland, TX

FAMILY: Wife, Debbie; Kelly Ann (1/29/82), Michael Ray (10/22/84)

COLLEGE: University of Houston

SPECIAL INTERESTS: Fishing, bird hunting

TURNED PROFESSIONAL: 1977

Q SCHOOL: Fall 1977

PLAYER PROFILE

CAREER EARNINGS: $1,831,823   **PLAYOFF RECORD:** 2-0

TOUR VICTORIES: 1979 Southern Open. **1981** Western Open. **1982** Bob Hope Desert Classic. (TOTAL: 3)

MONEY & POSITION:

1978--$ 19,846-- 109	1984--$ 41,582--119	1990--$108,816--133
1979--$ 64,428-- 65	1985--$116,002-- 71	1991--$120,722--123
1980--$ 79,488-- 52	1986--$ 70,828--119	1992--$124,537--115
1981--$105,510-- 48	1987--$104,570-- 95	1993--$117,617--127
1982--$ 91,599-- 45	1988--$193,765-- 58	1994--$108,259--150
1983--$175,619-- 26	1989--$188,637-- 77	

BEST 1994 FINISH: 3--New England Classic

1994 SUMMARY: Tournaments entered-15; in money--8; top ten finishes--1.

1994 SEASON: Hampered by early-season foot problems…T27 at PLAYERS Championship, best finish over first three months, also last start until July following foot surgery in May…had successful start in second appearance after return, solo third at New England Classic…opened with pair of 66s at Pleasant Valley to take second-round lead…shared 54-hole lead with David Feherty after carding 70, also final-round score…272 total four strokes behind winner Kenny Perry…made just one start in August (T46 at Buick Open), then missed last three cuts after T40 in Buick Open…playing under special medical extension, has 15 events to meet money requirement.

CAREER HIGHLIGHTS: All three victories came in four-year span near start of career…registered first triumph in second season, playoff win over Tom Weiskopf at 1979 Southern Open…finished 67-69-67 to score four-stroke victory in 1981 Western Open… following year defeated Tom Kite in playoff to claim Bob Hope Desert Classic…top two 1993 finishes T10s at Freeport-McMoRan Classic and Kemper Open…best money-list finish No. 25 in 1983, when made $175,619…two highest earnings years came in back-to-back campaigns, 1988 ($193,765) and 1989 ($188,637)…has gone over $100,000 each of past eight seasons…medalist at 1977 Fall Qualifying Tournament at Pinehurst CC.

PERSONAL: Nickname "The Grip" for unusual way in which holds club …attended Wharton JC for semester, then went to Houston, where was important member of 1977 National Championship Team…All-American selection in 1977…while growing up, used to sneak onto nine-hole course near home.

1994 PGA TOUR STATISTICS

Scoring Average	71.63
Driving Distance	240.4
Driving Accuracy	76.6
Greens in Regulation	66.7
Putting	1.797
All-Around	---
Sand Saves	59.3
Total Driving	---
Eagles	2
Birdies	149

MISCELLANEOUS STATISTICS

Scoring Avg. (before cut)	71.39
Scoring Avg. (3rd round)	72.00
Scoring Avg. (4th round)	71.13
Birdie Conversion	26.7
Par Breakers	18.0

1994 Low Round:	66: 2 times
Career Low Round:	63: 2 times, most recent 1992 Phoenix Open/2
Career Largest Paycheck:	$68,000/1989 Kmart Greater Greensboro Open/3

RAYMOND FLOYD

EXEMPT STATUS: Winner, 1969 PGA Championship

FULL NAME: Raymond Loran Floyd

HEIGHT: 6' 1" **WEIGHT:** 200

BIRTH DATE: Sept. 4, 1942

BIRTHPLACE: Fort Bragg, NC

RESIDENCE: Miami, FL; plays out of The Bahama Club, Great Exuma, Bahamas

FAMILY: Wife, Maria; Raymond Jr. (9/20/74), Robert Loran (1/23/76), Christina Loran (8/29/79)

COLLEGE: University of North Carolina

TURNED PROFESSIONAL: 1961

JOINED TOUR: 1963

PLAYER PROFILE

CAREER EARNINGS: $5,129,013 **PLAYOFF RECORD:** 5-10

TOUR VICTORIES: **1963** St. Petersburg Open. **1965** St. Paul Open. **1969** Jacksonville Open, American **(TOTAL: 22)** Golf Classic, PGA Championship. **1975** Kemper Open. **1976** Masters, World Open. **1977** Byron Nelson Classic, Pleasant Valley Classic. **1979** Greensboro Open. **1980** Doral-Eastern Open. **1981** Doral-Eastern Open, Tournament Players Championship, Manufacturers Hanover-Westchester Classic. **1982** Memorial Tournament, Danny Thomas-Memphis Classic, PGA Championship. **1985** Houston Open. **1986** U.S. Open, Walt Disney/Oldsmobile Classic. **1992** Doral Ryder Open.

MONEY & POSITION:

1963--$ 10,529-- 58	1974--$119,385-- 18	1985--$378,989-- 5
1964--$ 21,407-- 30	1975--$103,627-- 13	1986--$380,508-- 9
1965--$ 36,692-- 25	1976--$178,318-- 7	1987--$122,880-- 86
1966--$ 29,712-- 32	1977--$163,261-- 7	1988--$169,549-- 69
1967--$ 25,254-- 47	1978--$ 77,595-- 30	1989--$ 74,699-- 145
1968--$ 63,002- -24	1979--$122,872-- 26	1990--$264,078-- 55
1969--$109,957-- 8	1980--$192,993-- 10	1991--$284,897-- 56
1970--$ 47,632-- 24	1981--$359,360-- 2	1992--$741,918-- 13
1971--$ 70,607-- 32	1982--$386,809-- 2	1993--$126,516-- 120
1972--$ 35,624-- 70	1983--$208,353-- 20	1994--$ 95,017-- 158
1973--$ 39,646-- 77	1984--$102,813-- 68	

BEST 1994 FINISHES: T10--The Masters Tournament

1994 SUMMARY: Tournaments entered--4; in money--4; top ten finishes--1.

1995 PGA TOUR CHARITY TEAM COMPETITION: Memorial Tournament

NATIONAL TEAMS: Ryder Cup (8), 1969, 1975, 1977, 1981, 1983, 1985,1991, 1993. Captain of 1989 Ryder Cup team. U.S. vs. Japan, 1982. Nissan Cup, 1985.

1994 SEASON: Made fewest appearances ever in PGA TOUR events–four–while playing in 20 Senior TOUR tournaments…was in money in all four…best finish T10 at Masters, event he won in 1976…next-best finish T13 at Doral-Ryder Open, which he has claimed three times (1980-81, 1992)…also had top-25 at AT&T Pebble Beach National Pro-Am (T19), where played with son Raymond, Jr…son Robert played (and won) with Dudley Hart team portion of event…also had T61 in PGA Championship played at Southern Hills, where he won second major title in1982.

CAREER HIGHLIGHTS: Last PGA TOUR victory 1992 Doral-Ryder Open, which he won at 49…later that year, after turning 50 and becoming eligible for Senior TOUR events, captured GTE North Classic…two victories made him first to win on PGA TOUR and Senior PGA TOUR in same year…joined Sam Snead as only players to win TOUR events in four different decades…1986 U.S. Open victory made him oldest in the U.S. Open, distinction taken away in 1990 by Hale Irwin…first major title came at 1976 Masters…also won 1981 Tournament Players Championship…winner 1983 Vardon Trophy…1989 Ryder Cup captain…winner 1985 Chrysler Team Championship (with Hal Sutton)…winner 1988 Skins Game…winner 1990 RMCC Invitational (with Fred Couples), winner 1993 Franklin Funds Shark Shootout (with Steve Elkington).

PERSONAL: Son of career Army man, grew up in Fort Bragg, NC… devoted Chicago Cubs fan, chose golf over possible career in professional base-ball…1992 Doral-Ryder Open victory saga made even more stirring by fact win came two weeks after Miami home burned…Robert plays golf at University of Florida, Raymond Jr. at Wake Forest.

1994 PGA TOUR STATISTICS

Scoring Average	69.98
Driving Distance	264.7
Driving Accuracy	76.2
Greens in Regulation	62.2
Putting	1.782
All-Around	–
Sand Saves	50.0
Total Driving	–
Eagles	2
Birdies	48

MISCELLANEOUS STATISTICS

Scoring Avg. (before cut)	71.75
Scoring Avg. (3rd round)	70.75
Scoring Avg. (4th round)	72.25
Birdie Conversion	26.8
Par Breakers	17.4

1994 Low Round: 65: Doral Ryder Open/1	
Career Low Round: 63: 2 times, most recent	
Career Largest	1992 MCI Heritage Classic/2
Paycheck: $252,000/1992 Doral Ryder Open/1	

DAN FORSMAN

EXEMPT STATUS: 112th on 1994 money list

FULL NAME: Daniel Bruce Forsman

HEIGHT: 6' 4"   **WEIGHT:** 195

BIRTH DATE: July 15, 1958

BIRTHPLACE: Rhinelander, WI

RESIDENCE: Provo, UT; plays out of Riverside CC

FAMILY: Wife, Trudy; Ricky (1/18/85), Thomas (12/15/89)

COLLEGE: Arizona State University

SPECIAL INTERESTS: Snow skiing, reading

TURNED PROFESSIONAL: 1982

Q SCHOOL: Fall 1982

PLAYER PROFILE

CAREER EARNINGS: $2,845,611   **PLAYOFF RECORD:** 1-0

TOUR VICTORIES: 1985 Lite Quad Cities Open. **1986** Hertz Bay Hill Classic. **1990** Shearson Lehman
(TOTAL: 4)   Hutton Open. **1992** Buick Open.

MONEY & POSITION:	1983--$ 37,859--118	1987--$157,727-- 63	1991--$214,175-- 78
	1984--$ 52,152--105	1988--$269,440-- 40	1992--$763,190-- 10
	1985--$150,334-- 53	1989--$141,174-- 99	1993--$410,150-- 36
	1986--$169,445-- 54	1990--$319,160-- 43	1994--$160,805--112

BEST 1994 FINISH: T12--AT&T Pebble Beach National Pro-Am

1994 SUMMARY: Tournaments entered--23; in money--13; top ten finishes--0.

1995 PGA TOUR TEAM CHARITY COMPETITION: Greater Milwaukee Open

1994 SEASON: Least-productive season since 1989 best can be explained by battles with illness and injury...T16 at Las Vegas Invitational put stamp on retention of playing privileges for 1995...went without top-10 finish for first time in 12-year career...money-list finish lowest since first year on TOUR...looked for a time at Las Vegas that LVI might become fifth TOUR victory...second-round 64 brought to within two of lead...part of three-way tie for lead after third-round 68...closed 70-71 for final placing, worth $21,750...opened year with back-to-back top-25s, T13 at Phoenix Open, followed by T12 at AT&T Pebble Beach National Pro-Am (where overcame first-round 77)...held share of first- and third-round leads at Phoenix...missed three consecutive cuts after Pebble, then rebounded with T21 at Nestle Invitational...had consecutive 14th-place finishes at Masters and MCI Heritage Classic, latter with closing 64...missed seven of final 14 cuts.

CAREER HIGHLIGHTS: Best season and No. 10 spot on money list came in 1992, when captured Buick Open and finished second in three other events...fired final-round 67 at Warwick Hills to enter three-man playoff with Steve Elkington and Brad Faxon...par on second playoff hole gave him fourth TOUR title...runnerup finishes came in Federal Express St. Jude Classic, Chattanooga Classic and Canon Greater Hartford Open...missed but one cut in 29 starts...first TOUR victory came in 1985 Lite Quad Cities Open...the next year captured rain-shortened Hertz Bay Hill Classic...became three-time winner at 1990 Shearson Lehman Hutton Open...had another Canon GHO runnerup in 1993, when carded final-round 65 to finish one stroke behind Nick Price...earlier that year finished T7 in Masters after being tied for second (with Chip Beck) after three rounds...winner 1987 MCI Long Distance Driving Competition...1987-88 birdies leader.

PERSONAL: Two-time All-American at Arizona State...grew up in San Francisco Bay Area, where amateur golf competitors included Bobby Clampett.

1994 PGA TOUR STATISTICS

Scoring Average	71.30	(97T)
Driving Distance	266.3	(49T)
Driving Accuracy	75.4	(26T)
Greens in Regulation	71.2	(5)
Putting	1.821	(146T)
All-Around	694	(85T)
Sand Saves	43.2	(167)
Total Driving	75	(7)
Eagles	6	(64T)
Birdies	220	(140T)

MISCELLANEOUS STATISTICS

Scoring Avg. (before cut)	71.22	(68T)
Scoring Avg. (3rd round)	71.91	(153)
Scoring Avg. (4th round)	71.92	(122)
Birdie Conversion	25.3	(153)
Par Breakers	18.5	(106T)

1994 Low Round: 64: 2 times

Career Low Round: 62: 1988 Bob Hope

Career Largest Paycheck: $180,000/1992 Buick Open/1 — Chrysler Classic/2

ROBIN FREEMAN

EXEMPT STATUS: 103rd on 1994 money list

FULL NAME: Robin Lee Freeman

HEIGHT: 6'   **WEIGHT:** 185

BIRTH DATE: May 7, 1959

BIRTHPLACE: St. Charles, MO

RESIDENCE: Rancho Mirage, CA; plays out of
PGA West, La Quinta, CA

FAMILY: Single

COLLEGE: University of Central Oklahoma

SPECIAL INTERESTS: All sports

TURNED PROFESSIONAL: 1982

Q SCHOOL: 1988, 1991, 1992, 1993

PLAYER PROFILE

CAREER EARNINGS: $397,299

BEST-EVER FINISH: T3--1993 Northern Telecom Open

MONEY & POSITION: 1989--$ 26,517--188   1993--$ 92,069--148   1994--$177,044--103
1992--$101,642--128

BEST 1994 FINISHES: T6--Buick Invitational of California; T8--Buick Classic; T10--B.C. Open.

1994 SUMMARY: Tournaments entered--29; in money--20; top ten finishes--3.

1995 PGA TOUR CHARITY TEAM COMPETITION: Bell Canadian Open

1994 SEASON: After failing in three previous tries, former club pro finally succeeded in retaining playing privileges…got first of three top-10 finishes with T6 at Buick Invitational of California, giving him $75,493 after first six starts…proceeded to miss five of next six cuts, then only one rest of way until final two weeks…opened with three consecutive 69s, then closed with 70 for T8 at Buick Classic…final top-10 came after learning experience week before…after back-to-back 68s, held one stroke lead at midpoint of Bell Canadian Open…stumbled home 75-79 to finish T53 at Glen Abbey…although closed with 73 in next week's B.C. Open, was still good for T10 following opening rounds of 68-65-69…began season with low round of year, opening 63 at United Airlines Hawaiian Open which matched career-low posted in Round 1 of 1992 GTE Byron Nelson Classic.

CAREER HIGHLIGHTS: Only two-time medalist in PGA TOUR Qualifying Tournament history…co-medalist with Ty Armstrong and Dave Stockton, Jr. in 1993 Qualifying Tournament…medalist for first time in 1988 Q-Tournament…best TOUR finish came in 1993 Northern Telecom Open, where final-round 66 lifted him to T3 with Jim Gallagher, Jr., and Michael Allen, three strokes behind winner Larry Mize (only other time over $100,000)…had first top-10 in '92, T4 at Buick Open after closing 69-66-68…top 1989 finish T24 in GTE Byron Nelson Classic.

PERSONAL: Got into golf at 14 after fracturing a leg (had been involved in all sports)…worked as club pro for five years at Oak Tree and PGA West…First-Team NAIA All-American 1981-82.

1994 PGA TOUR STATISTICS

Scoring Average	71.05	(73T)
Driving Distance	265.3	(60)
Driving Accuracy	65.9	(131)
Greens in Regulation	64.2	(133)
Putting	1.779	(50T)
All-Around	529	(38)
Sand Saves	54.2	(54)
Total Driving	191	(111T)
Eagles	13	(4T)
Birdies	323	(24)

MISCELLANEOUS STATISTICS

Scoring Avg. (before cut)	70.79	(39)
Scoring Avg. (3rd round)	71.76	(146)
Scoring Avg. (4th round)	71.47	(89T)
Birdie Conversion	30.7	(18)
Par Breakers	20.5	(29T)

1994 Low Round: **63:** United Airlines Hawaiian Open/1
Career Low Round: **63:** 2 times, most recently
Career Largest United Airlines Hawaiian Open/1
Paycheck: $52,800/1993 Northern Telecom Open/T3

DAVID FROST

EXEMPT STATUS: Winner, 1989 NEC World Series of Golf

FULL NAME: David Laurence Frost

HEIGHT: 5' 11"   **WEIGHT:** 172

BIRTH DATE: Sept. 11, 1959

BIRTHPLACE: Cape Town, South Africa

RESIDENCE: Dallas, TX; plays out of Preston Trail GC

FAMILY: Sean (2/24/88), Noelle (1/15/90)

SPECIAL INTERESTS: All sports, rugby

TURNED PROFESSIONAL: 1981

Q SCHOOL: Fall 1984

PLAYER PROFILE

CAREER EARNINGS: $4,428,831   **PLAYOFF RECORD:** 2-2

TOUR VICTORIES: **1988** Southern Open, Northern Telecom Tucson Open. **1989** NEC World Series
(TOTAL: 9)   of Golf. **1990** USF&G Classic. **1992** Buick Classic, Hardee's Golf Classic. **1993**
Canadian Open, Hardee's Golf Classic. **1994** Canon Greater Hartford Open.

MONEY & POSITION:

1985--$118,537--70	1989--$620,430-- 11	1992--$ 717,883-- 15
1986--$187,944--46	1990--$372,485-- 32	1993--$1,030,717-- 5
1987--$518,072--11	1991--$171,262-- 93	1994--$ 671,683--20
1988--$691,500-- 9		

BEST 1994 FINISHES: 1--Canon Greater Hartford Open; T3--Hardee's Golf Classic; T4--MCI Heritage
Classic, THE TOUR Championship; 5--Nissan Los Angeles Open; T8--Motorola Western Open.

1994 SUMMARY: Tournaments entered--23; in money--20; top ten finishes--6.

1995 PGA TOUR CHARITY TEAM COMPETITION: Buick Classic

NATIONAL TEAMS: Presidents Cup, 1994

1994 SEASON: Posted third top-30 campaign in a row (sixth of 10 years on TOUR), highlighted by ninth victory at Canon Greater Hartford Open...Canon GHO triumph gave him wins in three consecutive seasons...shared first- and third-round leads, was one stroke behind Dave Stockton, Jr. at midpoint...held off Greg Norman down stretch for one-stroke win...followed GHO with another top-10 following week, T8 in Motorola Western Open...had solo fifth in second start of campaign, at Nissan Los Angeles Open, where opened and closed with 67s...course-record second-round 61 provided 36-hole lead in MCI Heritage Classic, where finished T4...ended campaign with top-10s in final two starts...finished T3 at Hardee's Golf Classic, where was seeking to be first since Tom Watson in 1980 (1978-79-80 Byron Nelson Classics) to win same tournament three years running...final-round 66 brought TOUR Championship T4 on Halloween...won South African PGA Championship in January, Hong Kong Open in March...member of International Team for inaugural Presidents Cup Match.

CAREER HIGHLIGHTS: Enjoyed finest season of career in 1993, when collected two wins, two runnersup and one third--and surpassed $1 million in earnings for first time...recorded back-to-back victories at Canadian Open and in Hardee's Golf Classic...by so doing, became first since Johnny Miller (1975) to successfully defend title week after winning another tournament...259 Hardee's total two strokes off TOUR record for 72 holes...two-time winner for second time in 1992, when claimed Buick Classic and Hardee's Classic...holed out from bunker on 72nd hole of 1990 USF&G Classic to beat Greg Norman...scored biggest win of career at 1989 NEC World Series of Golf...second-hole playoff victory over Ben Crenshaw provided 10-year TOUR exemption...won twice in 1988, Southern Open (beat Bob Tway in playoff) and Northern Telecom Open...carded career-low 60 in Round 2 of 1990 Northern Telecom...winner 1987 Merrill Lynch Shoot-Out Finals...winner Sun City Million Challenge 1989-1990.

PERSONAL: Was bearded winner of 1992 Hardee's Golf Classic...shaved trademark mustache in Feb. 1993...first played in U.S. (with little success) in 1981, returning in 1985.

1994 PGA TOUR STATISTICS

Scoring Average	69.85	(11T)
Driving Distance	256.7	(131)
Driving Accuracy	73.6	(37T)
Greens in Regulation	64.3	(131T)
Putting	1.742	(3)
All-Around	579	(53)
Sand Saves	52.5	(81T)
Total Driving	168	(69T)
Eagles	4	(104T)
Birdies	279	(81T)

MISCELLANEOUS STATISTICS

Scoring Avg. (before cut)	70.26	(11)
Scoring Avg. (3rd round)	71.28	(108)
Scoring Avg. (4th round)	70.72	(35)
Birdie Conversion	30.9	(14T)
Par Breakers	20.2	(34T)

1994 Low Round: 61: MCI Heritage Classic/2
Career Low Round: 60: 1990 Tucson Open/2
Career Largest
Paycheck: $216,000/ 1994 Canon GHO/1

FRED FUNK

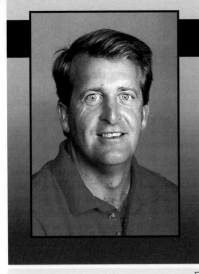

EXEMPT STATUS: 67th on 1994 money list

FULL NAME: Frederick Funk

HEIGHT: 5'8"   **WEIGHT:** 165

BIRTH DATE: June 14, 1956

BIRTHPLACE: Takoma Park, MD

RESIDENCE: Ponte Vedra Beach, FL

FAMILY: Wife, Sharon; Eric (8/2/91)

COLLEGE: University of Maryland
(1980, Law Enforcement)

SPECIAL INTERESTS: Water, snow skiing

Q SCHOOL: Fall 1988, 1989.

PLAYER PROFILE

CAREER EARNINGS: $1,474,226

TOUR VICTORIES: 1992 Shell Houston Open.
(TOTAL:1)

MONEY & POSITION:

1989--$ 59,695--157	1991--$226,915--73	1993--$309,435--56
1990--$179,346-- 91	1992--$416,930--34	1994--$281,905--67

BEST 1994 FINISHES:T6--New England Classic; T8--Phoenix Open, Buick Open; T10--Shell Houston Open

1994 SUMMARY: Tournaments entered--30; in money--23; top ten finishes--4.

1995 PGA TOUR CHARITY TEAM COMPETITION: Buick Invitational of California

1994 SEASON: With four top-10 finishes, had third-best campaign of six on TOUR…one of those top-10s came at Shell Houston Open, event which won in 1992…wrapped three 71s around second-round 67 for T10…posted T8 in third start of season, Phoenix Open, where closed with 66…biggest check of year ($33,500) came with best finish, T6 at New England Classic…was two strokes off midpoint lead after opening 68-66…stumbled with third-round 75, then righted himself with final 66…two weeks later put final top-10 of year on board, T8 at Buick Open…first-round 65, matching his low for year, gave him early lead…but 70-71-72 finish took him out of strong contention…earlier had opening 65 at MCI Heritage Classic, where shared lead with Bob Estes before eventual T12 finish.

CAREER HIGHLIGHTS: Course-record 62 in Round 3, followed by closing 70, gave him victory in 1992 Shell Houston Open…held off Kirk Triplett by two strokes at TPC at The Woodlands…best previous finishes had been T3s in 1990 Chattanooga Classic and (unofficial) 1989 Deposit Guaranty Golf Classic…earned exempt status for first time after fine 1990 campaign…posted all five of his 1993 top-10s in seven starts from mid-June to early August…best finishes came in back-to-back weeks, T6s at Federal Express St. Jude Classic and Buick Open…also recorded T7 at '93 U.S. Open…co-TOUR high with 34 starts in 1993…won 1984 Foot-Joy National Assistant Pro Championship…shot 59 on Desert Course at TPC of Scottsdale during separate pro-am at 1992 Phoenix Open…winner 1993 Mexican Open.

PERSONAL: Golf coach at University of Maryland for eight years before joining TOUR…majored in Law Enforcement at Maryland…the "Other Fred" on TOUR, "Poof Poof" to Fred Couples' "Boom Boom."

1994 PGA TOUR STATISTICS

Scoring Average	70.90	(57T)
Driving Distance	251.4	(160)
Driving Accuracy	80.1	(2)
Greens in Regulation	67.6	(46T)
Putting	1.809	(125T)
All-Around	523	(34)
Sand Saves	53.8	(57T)
Total Driving	162	(64T)
Eagles	6	(64T)
Birdies	343	(12)

MISCELLANEOUS STATISTICS

Scoring Avg. (before cut)	70.80	(40)
Scoring Avg. (3rd round)	71.68	(141)
Scoring Avg. (4th round)	71.68	(104)
Birdie Conversion	26.8	(130T)
Par Breakers	18.5	(106T)

1994 Low Round: 65: 2 times

Career Low Round: 62: 2 times, most recent

Career Largest   1992 Shell Houston Open/3

Paycheck: $216,000/1992 Shell Houston Open/1

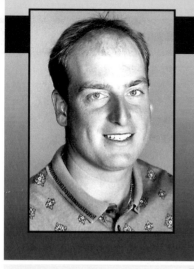

JIM FURYK

EXEMPT STATUS: 78th on 1994 money list

FULL NAME: James Michael Furyk

HEIGHT: 6' 2"   **WEIGHT:** 200

BIRTH DATE: May 12, 1970

BIRTHPLACE: West Chester, PA

RESIDENCE: Manheim, PA

FAMILY: Single

COLLEGE: University of Arizona

SPECIAL INTERESTS: All sports

TURNED PROFESSIONAL: 1992

Q SCHOOL: 1993

PLAYER PROFILE

CAREER EARNINGS: $236,603

BEST-EVER FINISH: T5--1994 Las Vegas Invitational

MONEY & POSITION: 1994--$236,603--78

BEST 1994 FINISHES T5--Las Vegas Invitational; T7--Northern Telecom Open; T10--Anheuser-Busch Classic.

1994 SUMMARY: Tournaments entered--31; in money--17; top ten finishes--3.

1995 PGA TOUR CHARITY TEAM COMPETITION: Northern Telecom Open

1994 SEASON: With swing described as "one only a mother could love," finished seventh in rookie earnings and almost won final event of season…posted one early and two second-half top-10s, with best finish coming in last start, T5 at Las Vegas Invitational…recorded T7 in second outing, at Northern Telecom Open…opened 68-67-67, last of which gave him share of third-round lead…closed with 71, worth $35,475…in money next three starts, then missed cut in 10 of following 14…did have solo 11th during that stretch, worth $30,000, at Freeport-McMoRan Classic…next top-10 came at Anheuser-Busch Golf Classic…closed 66-69 for T10…had T15 in Texas Open week before Las Vegas…273 finish at Oak Hills produced paycheck for $15,500 which, combined with following week's $54,750, gave him earnings of $70,250 for final two week's work…held lead after 72 holes of Las Vegas Invitational which, unfortunately for him, is a 90-hole event…career-low second-round 64 brought him to within two strokes of 36-hole lead, fourth-round 66 gave him sole possession after four rounds…fifth-round 70 led to final placing.

CAREER HIGHLIGHTS: Qualified for PGA TOUR with T37 in 1993 Qualifying Tournament…finished No. 26 on 1993 NIKE TOUR money list with $58,240…won NIKE Mississippi Gulf Coast Classic, defeating Robert Friend on first playoff hole…lost NIKE Bakersfield Classic in playoff with Clark Dennis.

PERSONAL: Northern Telecom top-10 came on familiar turf, since parents have place adjoining Tucson National Resort…played course often while at University of Arizona…two-time All-American selection…twice named to First-Team All-PAC-10.

1994 PGA TOUR STATISTICS

Scoring Average	70.98	(65T)
Driving Distance	254.3	(150T)
Driving Accuracy	71.7	(56)
Greens in Regulation	65.4	(100T)
Putting	1.781	(59T)
All-Around	642	(70T)
Sand Saves	52.7	(76T)
Total Driving	206	(128T)
Eagles	4	(104T)
Birdies	312	(32T)

MISCELLANEOUS STATISTICS

Scoring Avg. (before cut)	71.33	(78)
Scoring Avg. (3rd round)	70.24	(35T)
Scoring Avg. (4th round)	71.41	(79)
Birdie Conversion	27.9	(102T)
Par Breakers	18.5	(106T)

1994 Low Round: 64: Las Vegas Invitational/2

Career Low Round: 64: Las Vegas Invitational/2

Career Largest Paycheck: $54,750/1994 Las Vegas Invitational/T5

JIM GALLAGHER, JR.

EXEMPT STATUS: 1993 tournament winner

FULL NAME: James Thomas Gallagher, Jr.

HEIGHT: 6' **WEIGHT:** 180

BIRTH DATE: March 24, 1961

BIRTHPLACE: Johnstown, PA

RESIDENCE: Greenwood, MS; plays out of Brickyard Crossing, Indianapolis, IN

FAMILY: Wife, Cissye; Mary Langdon (1/13/92), James Thomas III (12/1/93)

COLLEGE: University of Tennessee (1983, Marketing)

SPECIAL INTERESTS: Music, duck hunting, following family golf careers

TURNED PROFESSIONAL: 1983

Q SCHOOL: Fall 1983, 1984

PLAYER PROFILE

CAREER EARNINGS: $3,526,698   **PLAYOFF RECORD:** 1-1

TOUR VICTORIES: 1990 Greater Milwaukee Open. **1993** Anheuser-Busch Golf Classic, THE TOUR (TOTAL: 3)   Championship

MONEY & POSITION:

1984--$ 22,249--148	1988--$ 83,766--124	1992--$ 638,314--19
1985--$ 19,061--159	1989--$265,809-- 50	1993--$1,078,870-- 4
1986--$ 79,967--107	1990--$476,706-- 25	1994--$ 325,976--51
1987--$ 39,402--166	1991--$570,627-- 18	

BEST 1994 FINISHES: T2--Bob Hope Chrysler Classic; T8--Motorola Western Open; T9--Honda Classic; T10--FedEx St. Jude Classic.

1994 SUMMARY: Tournaments entered--27; in money--16; top ten finishes--4.

1995 PGA TOUR TEAM CHARITY COMPETITION: Greater Milwaukee Open

NATIONAL TEAMS: Four Tours World Championship of Golf, 1991; Ryder Cup, 1993; Presidents Cup, 1994

1994 SEASON: A career year, particularly one with earnings over $1 million, frequently is a difficult thing to follow...money won went down for first time since 1987, but still stood as fifth best total of 11-year career...No. 51 finish meant was not able to defend TOUR Championship title...played last four weeks in all-out effort to requalify, but fell short...final stretch produced T11 at Walt Disney World/Oldsmobile Classic, where stood one behind midpoint lead after opening 65-68, and T12 in Las Vegas Invitational, where fourth-round 64 had him four strokes off 72-hole lead...missed cut in four of final eight starts...had no top-10s after July, when finished T10 in FedEx St. Jude Classic...opened 66-67 and closed 62-68 in Bob Hope Chrysler Classic, where third-round 74 proved undoing in T2 finish, three strokes behind Scott Hoch...two starts later posted T9 in Honda Classic...first week of July registered T8 at Motorola Western Open, where carded consecutive 68s in Rounds 2 and 3...member of U.S. Team in inaugural Presidents Cup Match.

CAREER HIGHLIGHTS: 1993 season one to be remembered...captured Anheuser-Busch Golf Classic (second TOUR title) and then TOUR Championship...latter's first prize of $540,000 (largest ever on TOUR) pushed past million-dollar plateau...also had stalwart Ryder Cup...all this came after nursing pinched nerve during middle of campaign...final-day 65 at A-B Classic provided two-stroke win over Chip Beck and enough points for first Ryder Cup berth...finished off U.S. victory with 3-and-2 defeat of Seve Ballesteros in singles...opened TOUR Championship with Olympic Club course-record 63...edged Greg Norman and David Frost by one stroke...first victory came in 1990 Greater Milwaukee Open, tournament which has special place in his heart...was given sponsor's exemption into 1988 GMO, where finished second...two years later defeated Ed Dougherty and Billy Mayfair on first playoff hole at Tuckaway CC...leading money winner on TPS in 1985.

PERSONAL: Member of golfing family...father Jim, PGA Professional in Marion, IN, started him in game at age two... wife Cissye, former LSU golfer, also was member of LPGA...sister Jackie Gallagher-Smith is LPGA member...brother Jeff NIKE TOUR member since 1990.

1994 PGA TOUR STATISTICS

Scoring Average	70.82	(50T)
Driving Distance	274.5	(12T)
Driving Accuracy	67.0	(120)
Greens in Regulation	68.8	(30T)
Putting	1.779	(50T)
All-Around	503	(30T)
Sand Saves	49.1	(122)
Total Driving	132	(34)
Eagles	6	(64T)
Birdies	296	(55T)

MISCELLANEOUS STATISTICS

Scoring Avg. (before cut)	71.39	(85)
Scoring Avg. (3rd round)	70.43	(50T)
Scoring Avg. (4th round)	70.47	(21T)
Birdie Conversion	28.8	(63T)
Par Breakers	20.2	(34T)

1994 Low Round: 62: Bob Hope Chrysler Classic/4
Career Low Round: 61: 1991 Las Vegas Invitational/4
Career Largest Paycheck: $540,000/1993 TOUR Championship/1

ROBERT GAMEZ

EXEMPT STATUS: 44th on 1994 money list

FULL NAME: Robert Anthony Gamez

HEIGHT: 5'9"   **WEIGHT:** 170

BIRTH DATE: July 21, 1968

BIRTHPLACE: Las Vegas, NV

RESIDENCE: Las Vegas, NV; plays out of Ko Olina GC, Ewa Beach, Oahu, HI

FAMILY: Single

COLLEGE: University of Arizona

SPECIAL INTERESTS: Music, movies

TURNED PROFESSIONAL: 1989

Q SCHOOL: Fall 1989

PLAYER PROFILE

CAREER EARNINGS: $1,574,214   **PLAYOFF RECORD:** 0-1

TOUR VICTORIES: 1990 Northern Telecom Tucson Open, Nestle Invitational. (TOTAL: 2)

MONEY & POSITION: 1989--$ 4,827--237   1991--$280,349--59   1993--$236,458--70
1990--$461,407-- 27   1992--$215,648--72   1994--$350,353--44

BEST 1994 FINISHES: 2--Las Vegas Invitational; 6--Memorial Tournament, Walt Disney World/Oldsmobile Classic; T7--Northern Telecom Open; T10--Kemper Open.

1994 SUMMARY: Tournaments entered--23; in money--15; top ten finishes--5.

1995 PGA TOUR CHARITY TEAM COMPETITION: Doral-Ryder Open

NATIONAL TEAMS: Walker Cup, 1989

1994 SEASON: Earnings rose for second year in row as posted second-best campaign of career...ended season with solo second in hometown Las Vegas Invitational and $162,000 paycheck, matching those earned for pair of wins in 1990...overcame second-round 70 with pair of 64s, in third and final rounds, to finish one stroke behind Bruce Lietzke...two weeks earlier finished sixth at Walt Disney World/Oldsmobile Classic, giving him $201,600 for last two starts...opened and closed with 66s in second start of season, Northern Telecom Open, to finish T7...later had solo sixth at Memorial Tournament, where opened with 77 but finished with rounds of 69-66-67...$54,000 payday for Muirfield Village performance second largest of season...followed two weeks later with T10 in Kemper Open...winner of Pebble Beach Invitational and Casio World Open in off-season.

CAREER HIGHLIGHTS: Won first official start on PGA TOUR, capturing Northern Telecom Open by four strokes over Mark Calcavecchia in 1990 debut...two months later electrified golf world by holing 7-iron from 176 yards for eagle on 18th hole at Bay Hill/72nd hole of Nestle Invitational, giving him one-stroke victory over Greg Norman...two victories and first-year earnings of $461,407 led to PGA TOUR Rookie of the Year honors...playoff loser to Fred Couples in wind-shortened 1993 Honda Classic...blistered Tuckaway CC with opening-round 61 en route to runnerup finish in 1991 Greater Milwaukee Open...also had solo second in 1991 Buick Southern Open and T2 in 1992 Federal Express St. Jude Classic.

PERSONAL: Hosts annual charity tournament each February in Las Vegas...event benefits Robert Gamez Foundation, managed by brother Randy, still his occasional caddie who carried bag in both wins...1989 Fred Haskins and Jack Nicklaus Award winners as outstanding collegiate player of year...winner 1989 Porter Cup...member 1989 Walker Cup team...prefers Robert (not Bob or Bobby).

1994 PGA TOUR STATISTICS

Scoring Average	71.60	(133)
Driving Distance	278.4	(5)
Driving Accuracy	69.5	(82T)
Greens in Regulation	69.2	(22T)
Putting	1.809	(125T)
All-Around	624	(65)
Sand Saves	41.0	(176T)
Total Driving	87	(12)
Eagles	12	(6)
Birdies	282	(75T)

MISCELLANEOUS STATISTICS

Scoring Avg. (before cut)	71.81	(128T)
Scoring Avg. (3rd round)	71.00	(84T)
Scoring Avg. (4th round)	71.57	(98T)
Birdie Conversion	30.0	(31)
Par Breakers	21.6	(12)

1994 Low Round: 64: 2 times

Career Low Round: 61: 1991 Greater Milwaukee Open/1

Career Largest Paycheck: $162,000/1990 Tucson Open/1
1990 Nestle Invitational/1

BOB GILDER

EXEMPT STATUS: 118th on 1993 money list

FULL NAME: Robert Bryan Gilder

HEIGHT: 5' 9"   **WEIGHT:** 165

BIRTH DATE: Dec. 31, 1950 **BIRTHPLACE:** Corvallis, OR

RESIDENCE: Corvallis, OR

FAMILY: Wife, Peggy; Bryan (3/24/75); Cammy Lynn (6/10/77); Brent (3/3/81)

COLLEGE: Arizona State (1973, Business Administration)

SPECIAL INTERESTS: All sports, car racing

TURNED PROFESSIONAL: 1973

Q SCHOOL: Fall 1975

PLAYER PROFILE

CAREER EARNINGS: $2,497,111   **PLAYOFF RECORD:** 1-0

TOUR VICTORIES: **1976** Phoenix Open. **1980** Canadian Open. **1982** Byron Nelson Classic, Manufacturers
(TOTAL: 6)   Hanover Westchester Classic, Bank of Boston Classic. **1983** Phoenix Open.

MONEY & POSITION:

1976--$101,262-- 24	1983--$139,125-- 39	1990--$154,934--102
1977--$ 36,844-- 72	1984--$ 23,313--147	1991--$251,683-- 66
1978--$ 72,515-- 36	1985--$ 47,152--123	1992--$170,761-- 91
1979--$134,428-- 22	1986--$ 98,181-- 85	1993--$148,496--108
1980--$152,597-- 19	1987--$ 94,310--100	1994--$154,868--118
1981--$ 74,756-- 59	1988--$144,523-- 82	
1982--$308,648-- 6	1989--$187,910-- 78	

BEST 1994 FINISHES: T5--Shell Houston Open; T8--GTE Byron Nelson Classic.

1994 SUMMARY: Tournaments entered--28; in money--16; top ten finishes--2.

1995 PGA TOUR CHARITY TEAM COMPETITION: United Airlines Hawaiian Open

NATIONAL TEAMS: Ryder Cup, 1983; World Cup, 1982; U.S. vs. Japan, 1982.

1994 SEASON: Produced seventh consecutive season with earnings of over $154,000...has now been over $100,000 in 12 of 19 years on TOUR...month of May key to campaign, with pair of top-10 finishes in three weeks...opened with 66 at Shell Houston Open, then closed 69-67 for best finish of year, T5...two weeks later recorded pair of 67s for T8 in rain-shortened GTE Byron Nelson Classic...two Texas events produced $80,600 of final total of $154,868...also had three other top-25s, best among which Bob Hope Chrysler Classic...went 69-69-66-69 before final 71 put him at T18...Hope finish came after season-opening stretch which saw him miss five cuts in first five starts...only non-miss during that early period T24 at AT&T Pebble Beach National Pro-Am...held third-round lead at (unofficial) Lincoln-Mercury Kapalua International...final 73 dropped to second, two strokes behind Fred Couples.

CAREER HIGHLIGHTS: First victory came in 1976 Phoenix Open, where overtook Roger Maltbie to win by two strokes...win came in second TOUR start (missed cut at Tucson week before)...won at Phoenix again in 1983, this time in playoff with Johnny Miller, Rex Caldwell and Mark O'Meara...'83 Phoenix Open title his last on TOUR...best year 1982, when won three times: Byron Nelson Classic, Manufacturers Hanover-Westchester Classic, Bank of Boston Classic...Nelson 266 lowest total of tournament's 16 years at Preston Trail...posted 19-under-par 261 to win at Westchester...highlight of that performance third-round double-eagle on 509-yard 18th hole...fairway marker commemorates feat and marks spot from where hit 3-wood...playoff winner over Jack Newton and Bob Charles in 1974 New Zealand Open...two-stroke winner over John Mahaffey in 1988 Isuzu Kapalua International...winner of three events in Japan: 1982 Bridgestone International, 1988 Acom Team title (with Doug Tewell), 1990 Acom P.T.

PERSONAL: Teammate of Tom Purtzer and Howard Twitty at Arizona State.

1994 PGA TOUR STATISTICS

Scoring Average	71.28	(95T)
Driving Distance	255.9	(137)
Driving Accuracy	71.0	(66T)
Greens in Regulation	64.8	(115T)
Putting	1.795	(99T)
All-Around	769	(117)
Sand Saves	56.6	(32)
Total Driving	203	(124T)
Eagles	2	(146T)
Birdies	280	(79T)

MISCELLANEOUS STATISTICS

Scoring Avg. (before cut)	71.41	(87)
Scoring Avg. (3rd round)	70.75	(71T)
Scoring Avg. (4th round)	71.50	(91T)
Birdie Conversion	29.3	(49T)
Par Breakers	19.1	(79T)

1994 Low Round: 66: 6 times
Career Low Round: 62: 1979 New Orleans Open/3
Career Largest
Paycheck: $72,000/1982 Westchester Classic/1

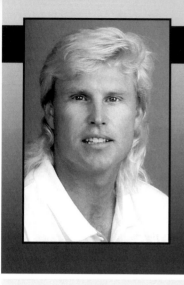

BILL GLASSON

EXEMPT STATUS: 1994 tournament winner

FULL NAME: William Lee Glasson, Jr.

HEIGHT: 5' 11"   **WEIGHT:** 165

BIRTH DATE: April 29, 1960   **BIRTHPLACE:** Fresno, CA

RESIDENCE: Stillwater, OK

FAMILY: Wife, Courtney; Maxwell Alexander (9/30/88); Dakota Jade (2/26/92)

COLLEGE: Oral Roberts University (1982, Business)

SPECIAL INTERESTS: Flying own plane

TURNED PROFESSIONAL: 1983

Q SCHOOL: Fall 1983, 1984

PLAYER PROFILE

CAREER EARNINGS: $ 2,818,133

TOUR VICTORIES: **1985** Kemper Open. **1988** B.C. Open, Centel Classic. **1989** Doral-Ryder Open.
(TOTAL: 6)   **1992** Kemper Open. **1994** Phoenix Open

MONEY & POSITION:

1984--$ 17,845--162	1988--$380,651-- 30	1992--$283,765-- 54
1985--$195,449-- 29	1989--$474,511-- 19	1993--$299,799--57
1986--$121,516-- 72	1990--$156,791--100	1994--$689,110--17
1987--$151,701-- 69	1991--$ 46,995--178	

BEST 1994 FINISHES: 1--Phoenix Open; T3--Motorola Western Open; T4--THE TOUR Championship; T5--Las Vegas Invitational; T7--B.C. Open; T9--New England Classic; T10--Nestle Invitational

1994 SUMMARY: Tournaments entered--21; in money--16; top ten finishes--7.

1995 PGA TOUR CHARITY TEAM COMPETITION: Northern Telecom Open

1994 SEASON: Enjoyed relatively healthy season–and it showed …had finest year of 11 on TOUR with earnings of $689,110 and near-victory in TOUR Championship…however, still found time for more surgery (elbow this time)…got year off on positive foot with sixth TOUR title in second start, Phoenix Open…opened with three 68s at TPC of Scottsdale to sit two strokes off 54-hole lead…closed with 64 for three-stroke victory and $216,000 payday, second largest of career…had next-best finish in Motorola Western Open, T3 that began with first-round 66…three weeks later opened with consecutive 68s and closed with 69 for T9 in New England Classic…T10 at Nestle Invitational produced by final-round 68, T7 at B.C. Open featured second-round 65…closed 65-66 at Las Vegas Invitational, good for T5…following week opened 66-68 at Olympic Club, held second- and third-round leads before finishing T4 in TOUR Championship.

CAREER HIGHLIGHTS: Possesses one of most impressive medical histories on TOUR…along with '94 elbow surgery, has had four sinus operations (deviated septum), four knee surgeries, lip surgery (skin cancer)…sat out most of 1991 season due to lower back problems…almost filed for permanent disability, but trouble corrected via injections…started 1992 under special medical extension, later that season ended 38-month winless skein by capturing second Kemper Open title…first TOUR victory/first Kemper came in 1985, when 40-foot birdie putt on final hole provided win…two-time winner in 1988, collecting titles at B.C. Open and Centel Classic…one-stroke victory over Fred Couples in 1989 Doral-Ryder Open produced biggest paycheck, $234,000…led TOUR in Driving Distance (276.5 yards per drive) in rookie season.

PERSONAL: Flies own plane to many TOUR stops…teacher Ken Cayce is head pro at Congressional, site of first Kemper win…two-time All-American selection at Oral Roberts.

1994 PGA TOUR STATISTICS

Scoring Average	69.93	(14)
Driving Distance	277.1	(8T)
Driving Accuracy	73.4	(40T)
Greens in Regulation	73.0	(1)
Putting	1.787	(73T)
All-Around	257	(3)
Sand Saves	56.5	(33T)
Total Driving	48	(2)
Eagles	8	(28T)
Birdies	293	(60)

MISCELLANEOUS STATISTICS

Scoring Avg. (before cut)	70.32	(15)
Scoring Avg. (3rd round)	69.67	(11)
Scoring Avg. (4th round)	70.00	(11)
Birdie Conversion	29.7	(38T)
Par Breakers	22.3	(5)

1994 Low Round: 64: 2 times
Career Low Round: 62: 1985 Panasonic Las Vegas Invitational/1
Career Largest Paycheck: $234,000/1989 Doral Ryder Open/1

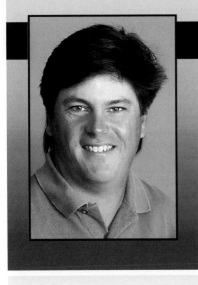

PAUL GOYDOS

EXEMPT STATUS: 75th on 1994 money list

FULL NAME: Paul David Goydos

HEIGHT: 5' 9"   **WEIGHT:** 190

BIRTH DATE: June 20, 1964

BIRTHPLACE: Long Beach, CA

RESIDENCE: Long Beach, CA; plays out of Virginia CC, Long Beach, GA

FAMILY: Wife, Wendy; Chelsea Marie (8/21/90), Courtney (9/8/92)

COLLEGE: Long Beach State University

SPECIAL INTERESTS: Sports

TURNED PROFESSIONAL: 1989

Q SCHOOL: 1992, 1993

PLAYER PROFILE

CAREER EARNINGS: $328,910

BEST-EVER FINISH: T7--1994 B.C. Open

MONEY & POSITION: 1993--$ 87,803--152   1994--$241,107--75

BEST 1994 FINISHES: T7--B.C. Open; T8--United Airlines Hawaiian Open; T9--Buick Invitational of California.

1994 SUMMARY: Tournaments entered--31; in money--22; top ten finishes--3.

1995 PGA TOUR TEAM CHARITY COMPETITION: Quad Cities Open

1994 SEASON: Virtually tripled money-won total of rookie campaign in retaining playing privileges for 1995…took first step in that direction right off the bat, with T8 in first start, United Airlines Hawaiian Open…closed 69-67 for first top-10 of career…enjoyed experience so much, five starts later finished T9 in Buick Invitational of California, again with closing 67…later in season, after missing four cuts in previous five starts, posted third top-10…opened with rounds of 68-68-67 at B.C. Open…closing 71 gave him T7 finish at En-Joie GC…had six other top-25 finishes, best of which T11 at BellSouth Classic…low round of season 66 in second round of weather-shortened GTE Byron Nelson Classic.

CAREER HIGHLIGHTS: Finished T13 in 1993 Qualifying Tournament…best finish of rookie season also T13, in 1993 Buick Open…in another Buick event that year, Buick Open, was two strokes off Larry Mize's first-round lead after opening 66…No. 17 on 1992 Ben Hogan Tour money list with $61,104…winner 1992 Ben Hogan Yuma Open…finished 39th on1991 Hogan list with $30,237…winner 1990 Long Beach Open.

PERSONAL: Frequent visitor to TOUR press rooms…simply likes to hang out (also wouldn't shy away from occasional interview opportunity)…Pacific Coast Athletic Association All-Conference 1985-86…former school teacher in Long Beach, CA.

1994 PGA TOUR STATISTICS

Scoring Average	71.20	(84T)
Driving Distance	258.0	(120T)
Driving Accuracy	74.1	(33T)
Greens in Regulation	63.8	(140T)
Putting	1.786	(68T)
All-Around	605	(59T)
Sand Saves	57.4	(24)
Total Driving	153	(52T)
Eagles	3	(126T)
Birdies	346	(10)

MISCELLANEOUS STATISTICS

Scoring Avg. (before cut)	71.35	(81)
Scoring Avg. (3rd round)	71.10	(97)
Scoring Avg. (4th round)	72.05	(130)
Birdie Conversion	29.0	(57T)
Par Breakers	18.6	(102T)

1994 Low Round: 66: GTE Byron Nelson/2

Career Low Round: 64: 1993 Deposit Guaranty/3

Career Largest Paycheck: $31,200/1994 United Airlines Hawaiian Open/T8

WAYNE GRADY

EXEMPT STATUS: Winner, 1990 PGA Championship

FULL NAME: Wayne Desmond Grady

HEIGHT: 5' 9"   **WEIGHT:** 160

BIRTH DATE: July 26, 1957

BIRTHPLACE: Brisbane, Australia

RESIDENCE: Queensland, Australia; plays out of Royal Pines Resort

FAMILY: Wife, Lyn; Samantha (11/23/86)

SPECIAL INTERESTS: Cricket, fishing, all sports

TURNED PROFESSIONAL: 1978

Q SCHOOL: Fall 1984

PLAYER PROFILE

CAREER EARNINGS: $1,808,421   **PLAYOFF RECORD:** 1-0

TOUR VICTORIES: 1989 Manufacturers Hanover Westchester Classic. **1990** PGA Championship. (TOTAL: 2)

MONEY & POSITION:

1985--$167,497-- 41	1989--$402,364-- 27	1992--$183,361-- 83
1986--$ 49,417--137	1990--$527,185-- 21	1993--$ 45,959--187
1987--$ 73,552--122	1991--$126,650--118	1994--$120,901--140
1988--$111,536--102		

BEST 1994 FINISH: T5--FedEx St. Jude Classic.

1994 SUMMARY: Tournaments entered--19; in money--10; top ten finishes--1.

1995 PGA TOUR CHARITY TEAM COMPETITION: Colonial Tournament

NATIONAL TEAMS: Australian World Cup (3) 1978, 1983, 1989; Australian Nissan Cup, 1985; Australian Four Tours World Championship of Golf (2), 1989, 1990. Dunhill Cup (2), 1989,1990.

1994 SEASON: Rebounded from dismal 1993 with seventh earnings season over $100,000...still has considerable distance to go to get back to peak performance levels of 1989-90...recorded first top-10 finish since 1992...finished with rounds of 66-67-66 at FedEx St. Jude Classic, good for T5 and check for $45,625...FESJC payday virtually equaled entire 1993 total of $45,959...had three other top-25s, with best being T13 in Nestle Invitational...rounds of 71-70-71-70 produced 282 total...low 18 was second-round 65 in Southwestern Bell Colonial, where finished T25...also registered T22 in second start of season at Northern Telecom Open.

CAREER HIGHLIGHTS: Biggest victory of career came in 1990 PGA Championship at Shoal Creek...was never headed after second-round 67...closed 72-71 for 282 total and three-stroke win over Fred Couples...first TOUR victory came in 1989 Manufacturers Hanover-Westchester Classic...finished at 7-under-par 277, then defeated Ronnie Black with birdie on first hole of their playoff...playoff loser (along with Greg Norman) to Mark Calcavecchia in 1989 British Open... first played Asian Tour with limited success, then started playing in Europe in 1983...won 1984 German Open...qualified for PGA TOUR by finishing sixth in 1984 Qualifying Tournament...winner 1988 and 1991 Australian PGA Championships...member of 1978-83-89 Australian World Cup teams...played for Australia in 1989-90 Dunhill Cups and Four Tours World Championships of Golf.

PERSONAL: As youngster, dreamed about someday becoming pilot in Australian Air Force...first turned professional at 16, then regained amateur status...turned pro again at 21...worked for several years under Charley Earp at Royal Queensland (Earp also worked with Greg Norman).

1994 PGA TOUR STATISTICS

Scoring Average	71.00	(68T)
Driving Distance	257.1	(127T)
Driving Accuracy	70.0	(77)
Greens in Regulation	63.3	(148T)
Putting	1.765	(17T)
All-Around	768	(116)
Sand Saves	52.6	(79T)
Total Driving	204	(127)
Eagles	5	(87T)
Birdies	183	(165T)

MISCELLANEOUS STATISTICS

Scoring Avg. (before cut)	71.58	(106)
Scoring Avg. (3rd round)	71.00	(84T)
Scoring Avg. (4th round)	72.50	(153)
Birdie Conversion	28.7	(66T)
Par Breakers	18.7	(97T)

1994 Low Round: 65: Southwestern Bell Colonial/2

Career Low Round: 63: 1991 Hardee's Golf Classic/2

Career Largest Paycheck: $225,000/1990 PGA Championship/1

HUBERT GREEN

EXEMPT STATUS: Winner, 1985 PGA Championship

FULL NAME: Hubert Myatt Green

HEIGHT: 6' 1"   **WEIGHT:** 175

BIRTH DATE: Dec. 28, 1946

BIRTHPLACE: Birmingham, AL

RESIDENCE: Birmingham, AL

FAMILY: Wife, Karen; Hubert Myatt, Jr. (8/18/75); Patrick (10/17/78); J.T. (2/11/84)

COLLEGE: Florida State University (1968)

SPECIAL INTERESTS: Fishing, gardening

TURNED PROFESSIONAL: 1970

Q SCHOOL: Fall 1970

PLAYER PROFILE

CAREER EARNINGS: $2,580,463   **PLAYOFF RECORD:** 2-3

TOUR VICTORIES: **1971** Houston Champions International. **1973** Tallahassee Open, B.C. Open. **1974** Bob Hope Classic, Greater Jacksonville Open, Philadelphia Classic, Walt Disney **(TOTAL: 19)** World National Team Play (with Mac McLendon). **1975** Southern Open. **1976** Doral-Eastern Open, Jacksonville Open, Sea Pines Heritage Classic. **1977** U.S. Open. **1978** Hawaiian Open, Sea Pines Heritage Classic. **1979** Hawaiian Open, New Orleans Open. **1981** Sammy Davis, Jr.-Greater Hartford Open. **1984** Southern Open. **1985** PGA Championship.

MONEY & POSITION:

1970--$	1,690--218	1979--$183,111--	13	1988--$	52,268--147		
1971--$	73,439--	29	1980--$ 83,307--	50	1989--$161,190--	86	
1972--$	44,113--	58	1981--$110,133--	32	1990--$ 65,948--165		
1973--$114,397--	11	1982--$ 77,448--	54	1991--$ 18,031--212			
1974--$211,709--	3	1983--$ 29,171--135	1992--$ 23,602--204				
1975--$113,569--	12	1984--$181,585--	33	1993--$ 29,786--199			
1976--$228,031--	4	1985--$233,527--	16	1994--$ 4,854--277			
1977--$140,255--	9	1986--$120,051--	73				
1978--$247,406--	5	1987--$ 63,349--129					

BEST 1994 FINISH: T65--GTE Byron Nelson Classic

1994 SUMMARY: Tournaments entered--15; in money--2; top ten finishes--0.

NATIONAL TEAMS: Ryder Cup (3), 1977, 1979, 1985.

1994 SEASON: With just two cuts made in 15 starts, had lowest earnings total since (partial) first TOUR season back in 1970… after qualifying at Fall 1970 Q-School, made $1,690 in two starts: T13 Sea Pines Open Invitation ($540) and T23 Bahama Islands Open ($1,150)…best '94 finish T65 at weather-shortened GTE Byron Nelson Classic ($2,304)…only other placing 68th at MCI Heritage Classic ($2,550)… missed final nine cuts, from Kemper Open through Las Vegas Invitational.

CAREER HIGHLIGHTS: Becomes eligible for Senior PGA TOUR in 1996…a 19-time winner during 25 years on TOUR…16 of those wins came during the 1970s, when was one of outstanding players in world …claimed first of two major titles in 1977 U.S. Open at Southern Hills in Tulsa…last victory was in 1985 PGA Championship …outdueled Lee Trevino down the stretch at Cherry Hills for that win in Denver… captured first win in 1971 Houston Champions International…has won four events twice: Greater Jacksonville Open, Southern Open, Heritage Classic, Hawaiian Open …won three consecutive events in 1976: Doral Eastern Open, Greater Jacksonville Open, Sea Pines Heritage Classic…1971 Rookie of Year…winner 1975 Dunlop Phoenix (Japan), 1977 Irish Open…member 1977-79-85 Ryder Cup teams.

PERSONAL: Swing unorthodox but effective…active in golf course design…worked with Fuzzy Zoeller on TPC at Southwind…won two Southern Amateurs.

1994 PGA TOUR STATISTICS

Scoring Average	73.82
Driving Distance	239.1
Driving Accuracy	77.2
Greens in Regulation	53.9
Putting	1.845
All-Around	–
Sand Saves	64.3
Total Driving	–
Eagles	0
Birdies	73

MISCELLANEOUS STATISTICS

Scoring Avg. (before cut)	73.80
Scoring Avg. (3rd round)	71.50
Scoring Avg. (4th round)	75.50
Birdie Conversion	22.1
Par Breakers	11.9

1994 Low Round: 67: Las Vegas Invitational/1
Career Low Round: 62: 1978 San Antonio Texas Open/1
Career Largest Paycheck: $125,000: 1985 PGA Championship/1

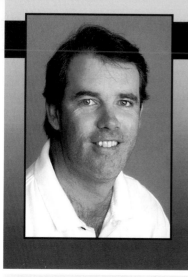

KEN GREEN

EXEMPT STATUS: 116th on 1994 money list

FULL NAME: Kenneth J. Green

HEIGHT: 5' 10''   **WEIGHT:** 175

BIRTH DATE: July 23, 1958   **BIRTHPLACE:** Danbury, CT

RESIDENCE: West Palm Beach, FL; plays out of Breakers West

FAMILY: Kenny (12/19/81), Brad (6/26/83), Brooke (7/17/85), Hunter (9/30/88)

COLLEGE: Palm Beach JC

SPECIAL INTERESTS: Bowling, platform tennis

TURNED PROFESSIONAL: 1979

Q SCHOOL: Fall 1981, 1982, 1984

PLAYER PROFILE

CAREER EARNINGS: $3,174,225   **PLAYOFF RECORD:** 0-2

TOUR VICTORIES: **1985** Buick Open. **1986** The International. **1988** Canadian Open, Greater Milwaukee
(TOTAL: 5)   Open. **1989** Kmart Greater Greensboro Open.

MONEY & POSITION:

1982--$ 11,899--167	1987--$237,271-- 36	1992--$360,397-- 41
1983--$ 40,263--114	1988--$779,181-- 4	1993--$229,750-- 75
1984--$ 20,160--156	1989--$304,754-- 37	1994--$155,156--116
1985--$151,355-- 52	1990--$267,172-- 54	
1986--$317,835-- 16	1991--$263,034-- 65	

BEST 1994 FINISHES: T9--Canon Greater Hartford Open, New England Classic.

1994 SUMMARY: Tournaments entered--28; in money--18; top ten finishes--2.

1995 PGA TOUR CHARITY TEAM COMPETITION: Anheuser-Busch Golf Classic

NATIONAL TEAMS: Ryder Cup, 1989; Four Tours World Championship of Golf, 1989

1994 SEASON: With just two top-10 finishes (both T9s), posted lowest money-won total since 1985, when began string of 10 consecutive seasons with earnings over $150,000…first T9 for Connecticut native came in Canon Greater Hartford Open, where closed with back-to-back 68s and picked up biggest paycheck of season, $28,800…GHO finish part of four-tournament stretch during which earned better than $23,000 three times…two weeks later had T12 in Anheuser-Busch Golf Classic worth $24,200…two weeks after that had T9 in New England Classic, where collected $23,143…also finished with consecutive 68s at Pleasant Valley…posted low 18 of season in sixth round of 1994, 8-under-par 63 in Round 2 of Phoenix Open…No. 116 money-list placing lowest since 1984.

CAREER HIGHLIGHTS: Has captured five titles since joining TOUR in 1982…first victory came in 1985 Buick Open, where posted 20-under-par 268 to win by four strokes…repeated at inaugural International in 1986…turned discouraging 1988 campaign around by winning Canadian Open and Greater Milwaukee Open back-to-back…second-day 65 helped set up Glen Abbey win, while used third-round Tuckaway CC course-record 61 as springboard to easy GMO victory…earlier in '88 campaign three-putted final hole to drop into playoff with Sandy Lyle in Kmart Greater Greensboro Open, which he lost…made up for that loss by winning 1989 Kmart GGO…lost (along with Greg Norman and David Frost) playoff to Seve Ballesteros in '89 Manufacturers Hanover-Westchester Classic…three-putted final hole in 1989 Pensacola Classic to finish second…winner 1985 and 1992 Connecticut Opens…winner 1988 Dunlop Phoenix (Japan) and 1990 Hong Kong Open…member 1989 Ryder Cup team.

PERSONAL: Started playing golf at age 12 in Honduras, where father was principal of the American School–and only sports choices were golf or soccer.

1994 PGA TOUR STATISTICS

Scoring Average	71.34	(103T)
Driving Distance	257.9	(123T)
Driving Accuracy	69.0	(92T)
Greens in Regulation	65.2	(108T)
Putting	1.792	(87T)
All-Around	701	(90)
Sand Saves	57.1	(26)
Total Driving	215	(136T)
Eagles	5	(87T)
Birdies	282	(75T)

MISCELLANEOUS STATISTICS

Scoring Avg. (before cut)	71.52	(99T)
Scoring Avg. (3rd round)	71.50	(130T)
Scoring Avg. (4th round)	71.56	(95T)
Birdie Conversion	28.1	(91T)
Par Breakers	18.6	(102T)

1994 Low Round: 63: Phoenix Open/2

Career Low Round: 61: 1988 Greater Milwaukee Open/3

Career Largest Paycheck: $180,000/1986 The International/1
1989 Kmart GGO/1

SCOTT GUMP

EXEMPT STATUS: 2nd on 1994 NIKE TOUR money list

FULL NAME: Scott Edward Gump

HEIGHT: 6'2"   **WEIGHT:** 165

BIRTH DATE: December 17, 1965

BIRTHPLACE: Rockledge, FL

RESIDENCE: Orlando, FL

FAMILY: Wife, Chris

COLLEGE: University of Miami

SPECIAL INTERESTS: Whitewater rafting

TURNED PROFESSIONAL: 1988

Q SCHOOL: 1990

PLAYER PROFILE

CAREER EARNINGS: $457,507

BEST EVER FINISH: T2 --1991 International

MONEY & POSITION: 1991--$207,809-- 80   1993--$ 96,822--147
  1992--$148,696--102   1994--$ 4,181--286

BEST 1994 FINISH: T52--Buick Southern Open

1994 SUMMARY: Tournaments entered--3; in money--2; top ten finishes--0.

1995 PGA TOUR CHARITY TEAM COMPETITION: Doral-Ryder Open

1994 SEASON: Exempt status for 1994 PGA TOUR was 126-150 after finishing 147 on 1993 money list…year began with questions about how many PGA TOUR events he could play, causing him to take look at NIKE TOUR schedule…after playing in two early-season PGA TOUR events, won second event of the NIKE TOUR season, NIKE Monterrey (Mexico) Open, by a single stroke over Brian Henninger…became NIKE TOUR's first two-time winner of 1994 with victory at the NIKE Greater Greenville Classic, posting one-shot win over Tim Conley…finished T2 at NIKE Cleveland Open and T3 at NIKE Boise Open in other top NIKE TOUR finishes…NIKE TOUR summary for 1994: tournaments entered–24; in money–20; top 10 finishes–9; top 25 finishes–16…statistics for 87 rounds on 1994 NIKE TOUR: second among secoring leaders with 69.93, fifth among birdie leaders with 347, eighth among par breakers with 22.5% and 36th among eagle leaders with six…showed ability to finish tournaments strong, as evidenced by final-round scoring average of 69.57, which ranked second to Chris Perry…returned to PGA TOUR for one event late in season, finishing T52 at the Buick Southern Open.

CAREER HIGHLIGHTS: Enjoyed best PGA TOUR finish at 1991 International…posted five birdies and three bogeys on final day, earned seven points and tie for second behind Jose Maria Olazabal…that finish produced biggest paycheck of PGA TOUR career, $82,133…top finish on PGA TOUR money list was 80th in 1991, when he earned $207,809…first-year member of NIKE TOUR in 1990, earning $20,863 to finish 50th on that money list…that finish earned exemption into second stage of Q-School, where earned first PGA TOUR card for 1991.

PERSONAL: Received a lot of good-natured ribbing from fellow players last year with new nickname, "Forrest"…during break in 1994 NIKE TOUR schedule tried to open-qualify for British Open, but fell just short.

1994 PGA TOUR STATISTICS

Scoring Average	72.44
Driving Distance	263.0
Driving Accuracy	78.4
Greens in Regulation	71.2
Putting	1.865
All-Around	–
Sand Saves	61.1
Total Driving	–
Eagles	1
Birdies	36

MISCELLANEOUS STATISTICS

Scoring Avg. (before cut)	71.17
Scoring Avg. (3rd round)	71.00
Scoring Avg. (4th round)	73.33
Birdie Conversion	25.5
Par Breakers	18.7

1994 Low Round: 69: Bob Hope Chrysler Classic/3
Career Low Round: 64: 1992 Federal Express
Career Largest   St. Jude/3
Paycheck: $82,133/1991 International/T2

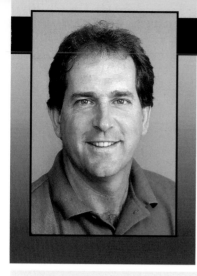

JAY HAAS

EXEMPT STATUS: 1993 tournament winner

FULL NAME: Jay Dean Haas

HEIGHT: 5' 10" **WEIGHT:** 170

BIRTH DATE: December 2, 1953

BIRTHPLACE: St. Louis, MO

RESIDENCE: Greenville, SC; plays out of Thornblade GC

FAMILY: Wife, Janice; Jay, Jr. (3/8/81), William Harlan (5/24/82), Haley (1/18/84); Emily Frances (9/25/87), Georgia Ann (3/12/92)

COLLEGE: Wake Forest University

SPECIAL INTERESTS: All sports

TURNED PROFESSIONAL: 1976

Q SCHOOL: Fall 1976

PLAYER PROFILE

CAREER EARNINGS: $4,604,562   **PLAYOFF RECORD:** 3-0

TOUR VICTORIES: **1978** Andy Williams-San Diego Open. **1981** Greater Milwaukee Open, B.C. Open.
(TOTAL: 9)   **1982** Hall of Fame Classic, Texas Open. **1987** Big "I" Houston Open. **1988** Bob Hope Chrysler Classic. **1992** Federal Express St. Jude Classic. **1993** H-E-B Texas Open.

MONEY & POSITION:

1977--$ 32,326--77	1983--$191,735--23	1989--$248,830--54
1978--$ 77,176--31	1984--$146,514--45	1990--$180,023--89
1979--$102,515--34	1985--$121,488--69	1991--$200,637--84
1980--$114,102--35	1986--$189,204--45	1992--$632,628--20
1981--$181,894--15	1987--$270,347--37	1993--$601,603--26
1982--$229,746--13	1988--$490,409--20	1994--$593,386--25

BEST 1994 FINISHES: T3--Buick Classic; T4--Mercedes Championships; T5--Masters Tournament; 6--TOUR Championship; T7--Anheuser-Busch Golf Classic.

1994 SUMMARY: Tournaments entered--30; in money--25; top ten finishes--5.

1995 PGA TOUR CHARITY TEAM COMPETITION: Honda Classic

NATIONAL TEAMS: Ryder Cup, 1983; Walker Cup, 1975; Presidents Cup, 1994.

1994 SEASON: Although didn't win for first time in three seasons, did enjoy campaign comparable to previous two with earnings of almost $600,000…stretch of six top-25 finishes in seven starts, beginning with T7 at Anheuser-Busch Golf Classic and concluding in T11 at Greater Milwaukee Open, assured third consecutive trip to TOUR Championship…those seven events produced $171,197, lifting him to $474,976 heading into inaugural Presidents Cup Match, where was Captain's Choice for U.S. Team…had profitable week in San Francisco, where final-round 66 produced TOUR Championship sixth worth $108,000…began year with T4 in Mercedes Championships, closing with consecutive 69s…had T5 at Masters, carding final-round 69…among contenders at PGA Championship, where middle rounds of 66-68 had him tied for second after 36 holes and solo second after 54…T7 in A-B Classic came with closing rounds of 65-67…highest placing T3 at Buick Classic.

CAREER HIGHLIGHTS: Defeated Bob Lohr with birdie on second extra hole to win playoff and capture 1993 H-E-B Texas Open, his ninth TOUR title…closed with consecutive 64s on the weekend to win 1992 FedEx St. Jude Classic, edging Robert Gamez and Dan Forsman by one stroke…opened with 63 en route to victory in 1988 Bob Hope Chrysler Classic…tied Buddy Gardner in 1987 Big "I" Houston Open by making 70-foot putt on 72nd hole…defeated Gardner on first playoff hole…first-time winner at 1978 Andy Williams-San Diego Open…won twice in 1981 and 1982, capturing first Texas Open in 1982…winner 1976 Southwestern and Missouri Opens…winner 1991 Mexican Open…member 1983 Ryder Cup team.

PERSONAL: Uncle, former Masters champion Bob Goalby, got him started in golf…won first trophy at National Pee Wee Championship in Orlando, FL at age seven…brother Jerry qualified for 1995 PGA TOUR by finishing ninth on 1994 NIKE TOUR money list…brother-in-law is TOUR member Dillard Pruitt…won 1975 NCAA Championship while attending Wake Forest…winner 1975 Fred Haskins Award as outstanding collegiate player…1975-76 All-American selection.

1994 PGA TOUR STATISTICS

Scoring Average	70.32	(28)
Driving Distance	264.2	(71T)
Driving Accuracy	72.6	(51)
Greens in Regulation	68.7	(32T)
Putting	1.776	(42T)
All-Around	345	(8)
Sand Saves	54.1	(55T)
Total Driving	122	(27)
Eagles	6	(64T)
Birdies	374	(2)

MISCELLANEOUS STATISTICS

Scoring Avg. (before cut)	70.28	(12)
Scoring Avg. (3rd round)	71.00	(84T)
Scoring Avg. (4th round)	69.95	(10)
Birdie Conversion	29.7	(38T)
Par Breakers	20.7	(23T)

1994 Low Round: 64:	NEC World Series of Golf/2
Career Low Round: 63:	3 times, most recent 1990 Nissan Los Angeles Open/3
Career Largest Paycheck:	**$198,000**/1992 Federal Express St. Jude Classic/1

GARY HALLBERG

EXEMPT STATUS: 82nd on 1994 money list

FULL NAME: Gary George Hallberg

HEIGHT: 5' 10"   **WEIGHT:** 155

BIRTH DATE: May 31, 1958

BIRTHPLACE: Berwyn, IL

RESIDENCE: Castle Rock, CO

FAMILY: Wife, Shirley; Christina (8/19/92), Eric Anders (1/10/94)

COLLEGE: Wake Forest University

SPECIAL INTERESTS: Family, sports, TOUR Bible study

TURNED PROFESSIONAL: July 2, 1980

JOINED TOUR: July, 1980

PLAYER PROFILE

CAREER EARNINGS: $2,028,975

PLAYOFF RECORD: 0-2

TOUR VICTORIES: **1983** Isuzu-Andy Williams San Diego Open. **1987** Greater Milwaukee Open. **1992** (TOTAL: 3)   Buick Southern Open.

MONEY & POSITION:

1980--$ 64,244-- 63	1985--$108,872-- 75	1990--$128,954--121
1981--$ 45,793-- 91	1986--$ 68,479--121	1991--$273,546-- 62
1982--$ 36,192--111	1987--$210,786-- 48	1992--$236,629-- 67
1983--$120,140-- 45	1988--$ 28,551--179	1993--$147,706--111
1984--$187,260-- 30	1989--$146,833-- 95	1994--$224,965-- 82

BEST 1994 FINISHES: T5--Southern Bell Colonial; T9--THE PLAYERS Championship.

1994 SUMMARY: Tournaments entered--27; in money--14; top ten finishes--2.

1995 PGA TOUR CHARITY TEAM COMPETITION: Honda Classic

1994 SEASON: Quiet performer went over $200,000 for fourth time in 15-year career and third season in last four, despite missing almost half his cuts...from U.S. Open on did not complete nine of last 11 starts, so most of his production came during first half of campaign...T9 at PLAYERS Championship brought largest check of year, $65,000...opened with three rounds in 60s (68-69-69) before closing with 73 at TPC at Sawgrass...had T14 in Honda Classic two weeks before PLAYERS...in May followed T11 in Memorial Tournament with T5 at Southwestern Bell Colonial...opened with pair of 67s at Colonial CC before carding 65 in Round 3, low 18 of season...had final-round 72...back-to-back weeks combined for earnings of $85,600.

CAREER HIGHLIGHTS: A three-time winner during career, most recent of which came at 1992 Buick Southern Open...posted rounds of 68-69-69 at weather-shortened Callaway Gardens event to edge Jim Gallagher, Jr., by one stroke...recorded best earnings campaign in 1991, when had three top-10 finishes, including playoff loss to Blaine McCallister in H-E-B Texas Open...1987 Greater Milwaukee Open victory keyed by 50-foot birdie chip-in on 17th hole...win came Monday after weather interrupted final round the day before...margin was two strokes over Robert Wrenn and Wayne Levi...posted final-round 66 to come from four strokes off Tom Kite lead and win 1983 Isuzu-Andy Williams San Diego Open...lost playoff to Gary Koch in 1984 Andy Williams event...in 1980 became first TOUR player to earn $8,000 needed at time (won $64,244 in 11 events) to obtain playing privileges without going through Qualifying Tournament...winner 1981 Lille Open (France), 1982 Chunichi Crowns Invitational (Japan)...winner 1986 Chrysler Team Championship (with Scott Hoch).

PERSONAL: An impressive winner throughout amateur career, was first four-time first-team All-America selection (accomplishment later matched by Phil Mickelson and David Duval)...winner 1979 NCAA Championship...winner 1978-79 North and South Amateurs.

1994 PGA TOUR STATISTICS

Scoring Average	71.74	(143)
Driving Distance	266.6	(47)
Driving Accuracy	63.8	(152)
Greens in Regulation	60.4	(173T)
Putting	1.781	(59T)
All-Around	752	(108)
Sand Saves	52.7	(76T)
Total Driving	199	(122)
Eagles	10	(11T)
Birdies	271	(91T)

MISCELLANEOUS STATISTICS

Scoring Avg. (before cut)	72.67	(171T)
Scoring Avg. (3rd round)	70.23	(34)
Scoring Avg. (4th round)	72.62	(156)
Birdie Conversion	32.1	(5)
Par Breakers	20.1	(40T)

1994 Low Round: 65: Southwestern Bell Colonial/3
Career Low Round: 63: 4 times, most recent '91 Fed. Ex. St. Jude Classic/2
Career Largest Paycheck: $126,000/1992 Buick Southern Open/1

DONNIE HAMMOND

EXEMPT STATUS: 61st on 1994 money list

FULL NAME: Donald William Hammond

HEIGHT: 5'10"   **WEIGHT:** 170

BIRTH DATE: April 1, 1957

BIRTHPLACE: Frederick, MD

RESIDENCE: Winter Park, FL; plays out of Marriott Ownership Resorts

FAMILY: Matthew William (10/22/86); Brittany Marie (3/8/89)

COLLEGE: Jacksonville University (1979, Psychology)

SPECIAL INTERESTS: Sports, cars, gardening, tennis, flying

TURNED PROFESSIONAL: 1979

Q SCHOOL: Fall 1982, 1991

PLAYER PROFILE

CAREER EARNINGS: $2,426,578   **PLAYOFF RECORD:** 1-0

TOUR VICTORIES: 1986 Bob Hope Chrysler Classic. **1989** Texas Open presented by Nabisco. (TOTAL: 2)

MONEY & POSITION:

1983--$ 41,336--112	1987--$157,480-- 64	1991--$102,668--135
1984--$ 67,874-- 86	1988--$256,010-- 44	1992--$197,085-- 77
1985--$102,719-- 77	1989--$458,741-- 20	1993--$340,432-- 47
1986--$254,987-- 28	1990--$151,811--104	1994--$295,436-- 61

BEST 1994 FINISHES: 4--Memorial Tournament; T6--Kmart Greater Greensboro Open; T7--Walt Disney World/Oldsmoble Classic.

1994 SUMMARY: Tournaments entered--25; in money--19; top ten finishes--3.

1995 PGA TOUR CHARITY TEAM COMPETITION: Nissan Open

1994 SEASON: Made just under $300,000 in posting third-best earnings campaign of 12-year career with $295,436…amassed $124,125 for pair of top-10s which came during five-week April-May stretch…had T6 at Kmart Greater Greensboro Open, where carded third-round 69 and collected check for $52,125…three starts later had best finish and payday of season, solo fourth at Memorial Tournament…three 60s plus third-round 70 for 11-under-par 277 total was worth $72,000…late in campaign followed T11 at Buick Southern Open with final top-10, T7 at Walt Disney World/Oldsmobile Classic…recorded 67 in final round of weather-shortened Buick Southern…had first-round 68 at Disney, then closed with pair of 67s for 14-under 274…those two finishes followed string of three missed cuts and helped get final month of campaign off on positive note.

CAREER HIGHLIGHTS: Winner of two TOUR events, last of which came at 1989 Texas Open presented by Nabisco…turned in superlative performance over four days, posting 22-under-par 258 total… cumulative score second lowest in TOUR history, one shy of all-time record (257)…individual rounds at Oak Hills CC were 65-64-65-64…finished second to Tim Simpson in next start, at Walt Disney World/ Oldsmobile Classic…followed with fifth in season-ending Nabisco Championships, giving him top-10s in final three starts and best earnings year with $458,741…first victory came in 1986 Bob Hope Chrysler Classic…defeated John Cook with birdie on first playoff hole…medalist in 1982 Qualifying Tournament…broke Ben Crenshaw record in winning Q-Tournament by 14 strokes…carded then-course-record 65 during Round 4 of six-round event at TPC at Sawgrass…winner 1982 Florida Open.

PERSONAL: Got start in golf through Baltimore Colts…yes, the Baltimore Colts…grew up in Frederick, MD near Colts' training camp at Westminster College…would go with father to watch Colts practice, then play nine-hole course there…charter member of Jacksonville (FL) University Sports Hall of Fame.

1994 PGA TOUR STATISTICS

Scoring Average	70.42	(31)
Driving Distance	266.0	(53T)
Driving Accuracy	72.9	(47T)
Greens in Regulation	70.3	(15T)
Putting	1.775	(38T)
All-Around	351	(9)
Sand Saves	53.1	(71)
Total Driving	100	(17T)
Eagles	9	(17T)
Birdies	280	(79T)

MISCELLANEOUS STATISTICS

Scoring Avg. (before cut)	70.38	(19)
Scoring Avg. (3rd round)	70.56	(63T)
Scoring Avg. (4th round)	70.53	(27)
Birdie Conversion	26.6	(138T)
Par Breakers	19.3	(67T)

1994 Low Round: 65: Bob Hope Chyrsler Classic/1	
Career Low Round: 63: 2 times, most recent	
Career Largest	1992 H-E-B Texas Open/2
Paycheck:	$108,000/1986 Bob Hope Classic/1 1989 Texas Open /1

MIKE HEINEN

EXEMPT STATUS: 1994 tournament winner

FULL NAME: William Michael Heinen, Jr.

HEIGHT: 6' 1"   **WEIGHT:** 195

BIRTH DATE: January 17, 1967

BIRTHPLACE: Rayne, LA

RESIDENCE: Lake Charles, LA

FAMILY: Wife, Kathy

COLLEGE: University of Southwestern Louisiana

SPECIAL INTERESTS: Hunting, fishing

TURNED PROFESSIONAL: 1989

Q SCHOOL: 1993

PLAYER PROFILE

CAREER EARNINGS: $390,963

TOUR VICTORIES: 1994 Shell Houston Open
(TOTAL: 1)

MONEY & POSITION: 1994--$390,963--40

BEST 1994 FINISHES: 1--Shell Houston Open; 7--NEC World Series of Golf; T10--B.C. Open

1994 SUMMARY: Tournaments entered--27; in money--12; top ten finishes--3.

1995 PGA TOUR CHARITY TEAM COMPETITION: Freeport-McMoRan Classic

1994 SEASON: After missing six of first nine cuts, made start No. 10 of first TOUR season one to remember…opened Shell Houston Open with 5-under-par 67, then carded second-round 68 to trail Tom Kite by one stroke at midpoint…shared 54-hole lead with Kite and Jeff Maggert following a 69…closing 68 carried to three-stroke win over Kite, Maggert and fellow Louisianan Hal Sutton…in addition to first TOUR win, victory also provided $234,000 cornerstone to first-year earnings of $390,963, second among rookies only to Ernie Els…still missed more cuts (nine) than made (eight) rest of way, but two more top-10s were included in "made" column…had solo seventh in NEC World Series of Golf, for which qualified through Houston win…posted middle rounds of 67-65 over Firestone CC's North Course…three weeks later opened with 65 in B.C. Open, eventually finishing T10…closed rookie year with three cuts made, longest streak of season, final of which T14 in Las Vegas Invitational…opened LVI with pair of 66s, then wrapped two 68s around fourth-round 71.

CAREER HIGHLIGHTS: Finished T26 in 1993 Qualifying Tournament…placed 16th on 1993 NIKE TOUR money list with $71,706…finished second to Dave Stockton, Jr. in NIKE Hawkeye Open.

PERSONAL: Hal Sutton his golf idol while growing up in Louisiana…two-time NCAA Division I All-American at Southwestern Louisiana.

1994 PGA TOUR STATISTICS

Scoring Average	71.32	(100T)
Driving Distance	275.3	(10)
Driving Accuracy	70.7	(70T)
Greens in Regulation	66.7	(65T)
Putting	1.791	(83T)
All-Around	555	(47)
Sand Saves	50.3	(102T)
Total Driving	80	(9T)
Eagles	7	(44T)
Birdies	279	(81T)

MISCELLANEOUS STATISTICS

Scoring Avg. (before cut)	71.80	(127)
Scoring Avg. (3rd round)	69.75	(15)
Scoring Avg. (4th round)	71.17	(58T)
Birdie Conversion	29.4	(47T)
Par Breakers	20.1	(40T)

1994 Low Round: **64:** Walt Disney World/Olds Golf Classic/3

Career Low Round: 64: Walt Disney World/Olds Golf Classic/3

Career Largest Paycheck: **$234,000**/1994 Shell Houston Open/1

NOLAN HENKE

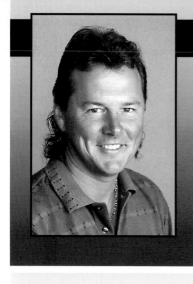

EXEMPT STATUS: 1993 tournament winner

FULL NAME: Nolan Jay Henke

HEIGHT: 6'   **WEIGHT:** 165

BIRTH DATE: November 25, 1964

BIRTHPLACE: Battle Creek, MI

RESIDENCE: Fort Myers, FL; plays out of Vines CC

FAMILY: Wife, Marcy

COLLEGE: Florida State University

SPECIAL INTERESTS: Jet ski, tennis

TURNED PROFESSIONAL: 1987

Q SCHOOL: Fall 1988, 1989.

PLAYER PROFILE

CAREER EARNINGS: $1,978,048

TOUR VICTORIES: 1990 B.C. Open. **1991** Phoenix Open. **1993** BellSouth Classic. (TOTAL: 3)

MONEY & POSITION:

1989--$ 59,465--159	1991--$518,811--28	1993--$502,375--31
1990--$294,592-- 48	1992--$326,387--45	1994--$278,419--70

BEST 1994 FINISHES: T2--BellSouth Classic; T4--MCI Heritage Classic; T9--THE PLAYERS Championship

1994 SUMMARY: Tournaments entered--26; in money--12; top ten finishes--3.

1995 PGA TOUR CHARITY TEAM COMPETITION: Lincoln-Mercury Kapalua International

1994 SEASON: Although money-won total was fifth lowest of six-year career, came close to fourth TOUR win in defense of BellSouth Classic title...was clubhouse leader after closing with 69 and posting 13-under-par 275 at Atlanta CC...was denied when third-round leader John Daly, who finished with 72, birdied 72nd hole for one-stroke win...Brian Henninger also eagled final hole for second-place tie worth $105,600 apiece...Atlanta performance third top-10 in five starts...first was T9 in PLAYERS Championship, where registered final three rounds of 69-69-68 at TPC at Sawgrass...three weeks later, opened with pair of 69s and closed with pair of 66s for T4 at MCI Heritage Classic...began year with T17 in Mercedes Championships, where opened with 69...only other top-25 finish T21 in Texas Open, where middle rounds were 67-66...missed cut in seven of final 12 starts, 14 of 26 overall.

CAREER HIGHLIGHTS: Final-round 67 brought victory in 1993 BellSouth Classic, a two-stroke win over Nick Price, Tom Sieckmann and Mark Calcavecchia...entered final round four strokes behind Price, left it with biggest check ($216,000) of career...had pair of solid performances in '93 majors, T7 in U.S. Open and T6 at PGA Championship...was 7-under-par for the weekend at Inverness...first TOUR win came in 1990 B.C. Open, where defeated Mark Wiebe by three strokes...second-round 64 keyed En-Joie GC win...enjoyed winning experience so much, staged repeat at 1991 Phoenix Open...although led by four strokes at start of Sunday's round, had to make 18-foot birdie putt on 72nd hole to clinch victory over formidable trio of Tom Watson, Curtis Strange and Gil Morgan at TPC of Scottsdale.

PERSONAL: Outstanding collegiate golfer who won seven tournaments while at Florida State...First-Team All-American in 1987...runnerup 1987 NCAA Championship...winner 1986 Porter Cup, 1987 American Amateur, 1987 Monroe Invitational.

1994 PGA TOUR STATISTICS

Scoring Average	71.16	(81)
Driving Distance	259.3	(111T)
Driving Accuracy	70.1	(76)
Greens in Regulation	62.9	(151)
Putting	1.777	(44)
All-Around	642	(70T)
Sand Saves	53.7	(61T)
Total Driving	187	(106)
Eagles	10	(11T)
Birdies	257	(107T)

MISCELLANEOUS STATISTICS

Scoring Avg. (before cut)	71.53	(101)
Scoring Avg. (3rd round)	70.83	(77)
Scoring Avg. (4th round)	70.92	(44)
Birdie Conversion	28.7	(66T)
Par Breakers	18.8	(92T)

1994 Low Round: 65: Las Vegas Invitational/1

Career Low Round: 63: 1992 Las Vegas Invitational/4

Career Largest Paycheck: $216,000/1993 BellSouth Classic/1

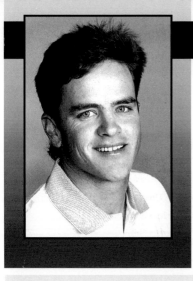

BRIAN HENNINGER

EXEMPT STATUS: 1994 tournament winner

FULL NAME: Brian Hatfield Henninger

HEIGHT: 5' 8"   **WEIGHT:** 155

BIRTH DATE: October 19, 1963

BIRTHPLACE: Sacramento, CA

RESIDENCE: Lake Oswego, OR; plays out of The Oregon GC

FAMILY: Wife, Catherine

COLLEGE: University of Southern California

SPECIAL INTERESTS: Hunting, fishing, and horses

TURNED PROFESSIONAL: 1987

JOINED TOUR: 1993

PLAYER PROFILE

CAREER EARNINGS: $406,886   **PLAYOFF RECORD:** 1-0

TOUR VICTORIES: 1994 Deposit Guaranty Golf Classic
(TOTAL: 1)

MONEY & POSITION: 1993--$112,811--130   1994--$294,075-- 63

BEST 1994 FINISHES: 1--Deposit Guaranty Golf Classic; T2--BellSouth Classic.

1994 SUMMARY: Tournaments entered--21; in money--16; top ten finishes--2.

1995 PGA TOUR CHARITY TEAM COMPETITION: Deposit Guaranty Golf Classic

1994 SEASON: After falling just short of Top 125 in 1993 (No. 130), took care of business early…gutsy second shot over water and onto green on 72nd hole of BellSouth Classic set up eagle putt worth $105,600…that putt produced second-place tie with Nolan Henke, one stroke behind playing partner John Daly, at Atlanta CC…had earned virtually enough ($129,688) by time got to Annandale GC in July to assure playing privileges for 1995…resolved any further uncertainties with first TOUR win in Deposit Guaranty Golf Classic, worth $126,000…birdied first hole of Sunday playoff with Mike Sullivan after weather caused event to be shortened to 36 holes, which he played 67-68…had no other top-10 finishes (nor any top-25s, for that matter), but Atlanta and Annandale proved enough…next-best finish T26 at Hardee's Golf Classic, where closed 67-67-69 after opening 71…recorded low round of season/career at New England Classic, first-round 64…also registered second-round 65 to just make cut in PGA Championship after opening with 77 at Southern Hills.

CAREER HIGHLIGHTS: Top finish of rookie season T4 in 1993 Sprint Western Open…two weeks later posted only other top-25 of first-year campaign, T19 at New England Classic…missed Top 125 by just two positions, since 125 actually went to 128 because of non-members and other factors…finished second to John Flannery on 1992 Ben Hogan Tour money list to earn PGA TOUR playing privileges for 1993…won $128,301 and three '92 Hogan Tour events: Texas Open, Macon Open, Knoxville Open…one of seven players to win three times in season on NIKE/Hogan Tour…89th on 1991 Hogan Tour money list with $10,877…posted record 25-under-par 263 in second stage of 1991 Qualifying Tournament.

PERSONAL: Outstanding prep tennis player who switched to golf as high school junior… first on 1989 Golden State Order of Merit …made college golf team as walk-on.

1994 PGA TOUR STATISTICS

Scoring Average	71.05	(73T)
Driving Distance	268.5	(37T)
Driving Accuracy	66.8	(123T)
Greens in Regulation	61.8	(159T)
Putting	1.766	(19T)
All-Around	598	(56)
Sand Saves	58.1	(15T)
Total Driving	160	(60T)
Eagles	7	(44T)
Birdies	232	(128T)

MISCELLANEOUS STATISTICS

Scoring Avg. (before cut)	70.63	(30)
Scoring Avg. (3rd round)	71.14	(98T)
Scoring Avg. (4th round)	73.21	(169)
Birdie Conversion	30.2	(27T)
Par Breakers	19.2	(73T)

1994 Low Round: 64:	New England Classic/1
Career Low Round: 64:	1994 New England Classic/1
Career Largest Paycheck:	**$126,000**/1994 Deposit Guaranty Golf Classic/1

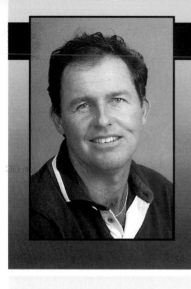

SCOTT HOCH

EXEMPT STATUS: 1994 tournament winner

FULL NAME: Scott Mabon Hoch

HEIGHT: 5' 11" **WEIGHT:** 160

BIRTH DATE: November 24, 1955

BIRTHPLACE: Raleigh, NC

RESIDENCE: Orlando, FL

FAMILY: Wife, Sally; Cameron (5/1/84), Katie (5/16/86)

COLLEGE: Wake Forest University
(1978, BA in Communications)

SPECIAL INTERESTS: All sports

TURNED PROFESSIONAL: 1979

Q SCHOOL: Fall 1979

PLAYER PROFILE

CAREER EARNINGS: $4,673,255 **PLAYOFF RECORD:** 0-1

TOUR VICTORIES: **1980** Quad Cities Open. **1982** USF&G Classic. **1984** Lite Quad Cities Open. **1989**
(TOTAL: 5) Las Vegas Invitational. **1994** Bob Hope Chrysler Classic

MONEY & POSITION:

1980--$ 45,600--75	1985--$186,020--35	1990--$333,978-- 40
1981--$ 49,606--85	1986--$222,077--36	1991--$520,038-- 27
1982--$193,862--16	1987--$391,747--20	1992--$ 84,798--146
1983--$144,605--37	1988--$397,599--26	1993--$403,742-- 37
1984--$224,345--27	1989--$670,680--10	1994--$804,559-- 11

BEST 1994 FINISHES: 1--Bob Hope Chrysler Classic; 2--NEC World Series of Golf; T3--Motorola Western Open, Deposit Guaranty Classic; T8--Phoenix Open, Las Vegas Invitational; T10--Kemper Open.

1994 SUMMARY: Tournaments entered--28; in money--21; top ten finishes--7.

1995 PGA TOUR CHARITY TEAM COMPETITION: Nestle Invitational

NATIONAL TEAMS: World Amateur Team Championship, 1978; Walker Cup, 1979; Presidents Cup, 1994.

1994 SEASON: Proved beyond shadow of doubt comeback from 1992 shoulder surgery is complete with victory in Bob Hope Chrysler Classic…was inspired to Hope victory, fifth of career but first since 1989, by heroic Winter Olympics performance of speedskater Dan Jansen…seven top-10 performances, including runnerup in NEC World Series of Golf, helped produce best earnings year ($804,559) and berth on U.S. Team in inaugural Presidents Cup Match…second-round 62 moved into Hope lead, which assumed for good with fourth-round 66…after middle rounds of 64-65, was one stroke behind Steve Lowery after three rounds of NEC World Series of Golf…final 70 left him one stroke behind Jose Maria Olazabal, who closed with 67…had pair of T3s in three-week July span, at Motorola Western Open and Deposit Guaranty Golf Classic…had T8s in second (Phoenix Open) and next-to-last (Las Vegas Invitational) starts, with LVI featuring second-round 63…other top-10 T10 in Kemper Open.

CAREER HIGHLIGHTS: Had arthroscopic surgery in Feb. 1992 to correct shoulder impingement…start of season delayed until May, after which earned just under $85,000 (lowest total since first two years on TOUR)…enjoyed top money-list finish in 1989, when placed No. 10…year included fourth win and career-best $225,000 first-place check from Las Vegas Invitational…Las Vegas triumph came in playoff with Robert Wrenn, just three weeks after Masters playoff loss to Nick Faldo…first win came in first year on TOUR, 1980 Quad Cities Open…won in Quad Cities for second time four years later, two years after capturing 1982 USF&G Classic…won 1986 Vardon Trophy…winner 1982 Pacific Masters, 1982-86 Casio World Opens (Japan), 1990-91 Korea Opens…winner 1986 Chrysler Team Championship (with Gary Hallberg).

PERSONAL: Donated $100,000 of Las Vegas Invitational winner's share to Arnold Palmer Children's Hospital in Orlando…son Cameron successfully treated there for rare bone infection in right leg…runnerup 1978 U.S. Amateur…1977-78 All-America selection…member 1975 NCAA Championship team…winner 1977-78 ACC Tournament…winner 1977 Northeast Amateur, 1976-79 North Carolina Amateurs…brother Buddy a professional golfer, father won All-ACC honors in baseball at Wake Forest.

1994 PGA TOUR STATISTICS

Scoring Average	70.10	(19)
Driving Distance	259.9	(106)
Driving Accuracy	70.8	(68T)
Greens in Regulation	70.0	(19)
Putting	1.791	(83T)
All-Around	366	(12)
Sand Saves	60.3	(8T)
Total Driving	174	(83T)
Eagles	7	(44T)
Birdies	327	(19T)

MISCELLANEOUS STATISTICS

Scoring Avg. (before cut)	70.59	(27)
Scoring Avg. (3rd round)	69.68	(12)
Scoring Avg. (4th round)	70.58	(29T)
Birdie Conversion	27.6	(112T)
Par Breakers	19.7	(55T)

1994 Low Round:	62: 1994 Bob Hope/2
Career Low Round:	62: 1994 Bob Hope/2
Career Largest Paycheck:	$198,000/1994 Bob Hope Chrysler Classic/1

MIKE HULBERT

EXEMPT STATUS: 84th on 1994 money list

FULL NAME: Michael Patrick Hulbert

HEIGHT: 6'   **WEIGHT:** 175

BIRTH DATE: April 14, 1958   **BIRTHPLACE:** Elmira, NY

RESIDENCE: Orlando, FL; plays out of Bay Hill and Lake Nona

FAMILY: Wife, Teresa; Justin Michael (7/25/93)

COLLEGE: East Tennessee State
(1980, Business Management)

SPECIAL INTERESTS: Fishing, running

TURNED PROFESSIONAL: 1981

Q SCHOOL: Fall 1984; 1985

PLAYER PROFILE

CAREER EARNINGS: $2,566,972   **PLAYOFF RECORD:** 2-0

TOUR VICTORIES: **1986** Federal Express-St. Jude Classic. **1989** B.C. Open. **1991** Anheuser-Busch
(TOTAL: 3)   Golf Classic.

MONEY & POSITION:

1985--$ 18,368--161	1989--$477,621-- 16	1993--$ 193,833--89
1986--$276,687-- 21	1990--$216,002-- 67	1994--$ 221,007--84
1987--$204,375-- 49	1991--$551,750-- 24	
1988--$127,752-- 94	1992--$279,577-- 55	

BEST 1994 FINISHES: T3--B.C. Open; T10--Doral-Ryder Open.

1994 SUMMARY: Tournaments entered--31; in money--21; top ten finishes--2.

1995 PGA TOUR CHARITY TEAM COMPETITION: MCI Classic

1994 SEASON: Reversed trend that had seen earnings drop each of two previous seasons...posted fifth-highest money-won total of 10-year career...best finish T3 in B.C. Open, home-area event which won in 1989...closed with 70 at En-Joie GC after posting rounds of 67-67-68...check for $52,200 lifted him over $200,000 plateau once again...only other top-10 was in sixth start of year, T10 in Doral-Ryder Open...carded final-round 66 to earn $35,000...Doral finish came three weeks after third-best placing of campaign back on West Coast, T12 in Nissan Los Angeles Open...matched that finish with another in July at Anheuser-Busch Golf Classic...two weeks after A-B Classic registered final top-25 with T24 at FedEx St. Jude Classic, both events he has won...with 31 playing appearances, extended ironman string that has seen him play in at least 31 events each year since 1987.

CAREER HIGHLIGHTS: Last of three TOUR victories came in 1991 Anheuser-Busch Golf Classic...two-putted for par from 40 feet on first playoff hole to defeat Kenny Knox in near darkness...first win came in very first season, one-stroke victory over childhood friend Joey Sindelar in 1986 Federal Express St. Jude Classic... early that season, in third career start, finished T3 in Shearson Lehman Brothers Andy Williams Open...triumph in 1989 B.C. Open was special, since grew up less than an hour from En-Joie GC in Horseheads, NY...playoff victory over Bob Estes one of seven top-10 finishes in career year, which also included Canadian Open runnerup and earnings of $477,621...winner 1987 Chrysler Team Championship (with Bob Tway)...also won 1991 Ping Kapalua International in playoff with Davis Love III.

PERSONAL: Avid fisherman who, when son Justin was born weighing 8 lb., 3 oz. in 1993, said he was "just perfect for mounting"... 1980 All-American selection.

1994 PGA TOUR STATISTICS

Scoring Average	70.88	(56)
Driving Distance	255.4	(141T)
Driving Accuracy	69.3	(87T)
Greens in Regulation	68.8	(30T)
Putting	1.799	(105T)
All-Around	469	(26)
Sand Saves	57.8	(17T)
Total Driving	228	(147)
Eagles	10	(11T)
Birdies	326	(22T)

MISCELLANEOUS STATISTICS

Scoring Avg. (before cut)	71.05	(54T)
Scoring Avg. (3rd round)	70.20	(31T)
Scoring Avg. (4th round)	72.14	(139T)
Birdie Conversion	25.6	(147T)
Par Breakers	18.1	(123T)

1994 Low Round:	**65:** Federal Express St. Jude Classic/2
Career Low Round:	**63:** 2 times, most recent 1993 SW Bell Colonial/4
Career Largest Paycheck:	**$180,000**/1991 Anheuser-Busch Golf Classic/1

ED HUMENIK

EXEMPT STATUS: 108th on 1994 money list

FULL NAME: Edward Francis Humenik

HEIGHT: 5'11"   **WEIGHT:** 210

BIRTH DATE: June 29, 1959

BIRTHPLACE: Detroit, MI

RESIDENCE: Hobe Sound, FL

FAMILY: Wife, Lori; Nancy (9/24/84), Ed, Jr. (5/12/89)

COLLEGE: Michigan (1983)

SPECIAL INTERESTS: Basketball, fishing

TURNED PROFESSIONAL: 1984

Q SCHOOL: Fall 1988

PLAYER PROFILE

CAREER EARNINGS: $ 641,112

BEST EVER FINISH: T2--1994 Kmart Greater Greensboro Open

MONEY & POSITION:
1989--$ 46,384--168	1992--$149,337--100	1994--$168,332--108
1991--$124,497--121	1993--$152,562--105	

BEST 1994 FINISH: T2--Kmart Greater Greensboro Open.

1994 SUMMARY: Tournaments entered--31; in money--14; top ten finishes--1.

1995 PGA TOUR CHARITY TEAM COMPETITION: United Airlines Hawaiian Open

1994 SEASON: Took season that began badly (seven consecutive missed cuts, nine of first 11) and turned it into best earnings campaign of five years on TOUR...catalyst to turnaround occurred three weeks after ninth missed cut, when finished T2 in Kmart Greater Greensboro Open...best finish to that point (of three cuts made) T18 in Honda Classic, where fired closing 67...as season developed, Honda finish his only other top-25...followed GGO-opening 72 with second-round 65...slid back in Round 3 with 73, but put $112,000 in bank with final-round 68 that tied Hale Irwin and Brad Bryant at 10-under-par 278, three behind winner Mike Springer...runnerup finish and Kmart GGO payday both career highs for University of Michigan grad...Greensboro win came during stretch in which made money in eight of nine events...concluded year with seven missed cuts in final 11 tournaments.

CAREER HIGHLIGHTS: Has steadily increased earnings total each year on TOUR...prior to Kmart GGO T2, best finish had been T4 in 1992 Buick Southern Open...opened with 5-under-par 67 highlighted by pair of eagles...finished four strokes behind winner Gary Hallberg in rain-shortened event...posted pair of top-10s early in 1993, T-10 at Doral-Ryder Open and solo fifth in Nestle Invitational...top 1991 finish T7 at Las Vegas Invitational...finished fifth on Ben Hogan Tour money list in 1990, earning PGA TOUR exempt status for 1991...after Monday qualifying, won Hogan Macon Open and then Santa Rosa Open...led TOUR in driving distance in 1989 with average of 280.9 yards per drive, but failed to keep card...named Michigan Player of Year in 1988, when won Michigan Open and Michigan Match Play.

PERSONAL: 1982 U.S. Amateur quarterfinalist.

1994 PGA TOUR STATISTICS

Scoring Average	71.84	(148)
Driving Distance	271.8	(24)
Driving Accuracy	71.5	(58T)
Greens in Regulation	64.5	(125T)
Putting	1.820	(144T)
All-Around	865	(140T)
Sand Saves	44.4	(157)
Total Driving	82	(11)
Eagles	2	(146T)
Birdies	290	(63)

MISCELLANEOUS STATISTICS

Scoring Avg. (before cut)	72.32	(156T)
Scoring Avg. (3rd round)	73.08	(174)
Scoring Avg. (4th round)	71.43	(80T)
Birdie Conversion	28.0	(96T)
Par Breakers	18.2	(119T)

1994 Low Round: 65: 2 times
Career Low Round: 63: 1991 United Airlines Hawaiian Open/1
Career Largest Paycheck: $112,000/1994 Kmart GGO/T2

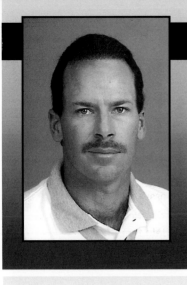

JOHN HUSTON

EXEMPT STATUS: 1994 tournament winner

FULL NAME: Johnny Ray Huston

HEIGHT: 5' 10"   **WEIGHT:** 155

BIRTH DATE: June 1, 1961

BIRTHPLACE: Mt. Vernon, IL

RESIDENCE: Palm Harbor, FL; plays out of Innisbrook Hilton Golf Resort

FAMILY: Wife, Suzanne; Jessica (11/9/87)

COLLEGE: Auburn University

SPECIAL INTERESTS: All sports

TURNED PROFESSIONAL: 1983

Q SCHOOL: Fall 1987

PLAYER PROFILE

CAREER EARNINGS: $3,113,443   **PLAYOFF:** 0-1

TOUR VICTORIES: 1990 Honda Classic.**1992** Walt Disney World/Oldsmobile Classic. **1994** Doral-Ryder Open
(TOTAL: 3)

MONEY & POSITION:

1988--$150,301--78	1991--$395,853--40	1994--$731,499--16
1989--$203,207--68	1992--$515,453--26	
1990--$435,690--30	1993--$681,441--15	

BEST 1994 FINISHES: 1--Doral Ryder Open; 3--United Airlines Hawaiian Open; T5--NEC World Series of Golf; T6--Hardee's Golf Classic; T9--Northern Telecom Open, Bob Hope Chrysler Classic; T10--Masters Tournament, TOUR Championship.

1994 SUMMARY: Tournaments entered-25; in money--19; top ten finishes--8.

1995 PGA TOUR CHARITY TEAM COMPETITION: Doral-Ryder Open

NATIONAL TEAMS: Presidents Cup, 1994

1994 SEASON: Earned biggest paycheck of career in March, winning Doral-Ryder Open and $252,000...Doral victory, third in seven years on TOUR, capped early stretch of four top-10 finishes in six starts (missed cut in two non-top-10s)...began year with solo third in United Airlines Hawaiian Open, where closed with back-to-back 67s...followed with T9 in Northern Telecom Open, again closing with 67...missed cuts in Phoenix Open and Nissan Los Angeles Open were followed by T9 in Bob Hope Chrysler Classic...Doral first stop in Florida, where final-round 66 gave him three-stroke edge over Billy Andrade and Brad Bryant...closing 69 produced T10 in Masters...went three months without another top-10, then put together season-closing stretch like one at beginning...finished year with three top-10s (plus one T11) in final five starts, including T10 in TOUR Championship, where made third consecutive appearance...had back-to-back top-10s, although four weeks apart, in NEC World Series of Golf (T5) and Hardee's Golf Classic (T6)...appearance for U.S. Team in inaugural Presidents Cup Match came in between.

CAREER HIGHLIGHTS: Certainly no surprise all victories have been in Florida...as young player, enjoyed great success on Florida mini-tours, winning 10 events...first TOUR win came in wind-swept 1990 Honda Classic, where held off strong Mark Calcavecchia challenge to win by two strokes...fired closing 62 to pass Mark O'Meara to win 1992 Walt Disney World/Oldsmobile Classic...Disney-winning 26-under-par 262 one stroke off all-time TOUR record for most strokes under par...lost playoff to Jim McGovern at 1993 Shell Houston Open...finished '93 campaign with TOUR Championship T2, knotting Greg Norman, Scott Simpson and David Frost, one stroke behind Jim Gallagher, Jr...won 1988 JCPenney Classic (with Amy Benz)...medalist in 1987 Qualifying Tournament...won 1985 Florida Open.

PERSONAL: Says would be mini-tour professional if not a member of PGA TOUR...father first put golf club in his hands at age seven.

1994 PGA TOUR STATISTICS

Scoring Average	70.17	(22)
Driving Distance	275.0	(11)
Driving Accuracy	69.3	(87T)
Greens in Regulation	69.2	(22T)
Putting	1.757	(11)
All-Around	250	(2)
Sand Saves	55.2	(42T)
Total Driving	98	(15)
Eagles	7	(44T)
Birdies	345	(11)

MISCELLANEOUS STATISTICS

Scoring Avg. (before cut)	70.69	(36T)
Scoring Avg. (3rd round)	70.22	(33)
Scoring Avg. (4th round)	69.67	(2)
Birdie Conversion	33.0	(2)
Par Breakers	23.3	(1)

1994 Low Round: 64: 2 times
Career Low Round: 62: 1992 Walt Disney
Career Largest   World/Oldsmobile Classic/4
Paycheck: $252,000/ 94 Doral-Ryder Open/1

JOHN INMAN

EXEMPT STATUS: 1993 tournament winner

FULL NAME: John Samuel Inman

HEIGHT: 5' 10"   **WEIGHT:** 155

BIRTH DATE: November 26, 1962

BIRTHPLACE: Greensboro, NC

RESIDENCE: Roswell, GA

FAMILY: Wife, Patti

COLLEGE: University of North Carolina

SPECIAL INTERESTS: Fishing, music

TURNED PROFESSIONAL: 1985

Q SCHOOL: Fall 1986, 1990

PLAYER PROFILE

CAREER EARNINGS: $1,017,182   **PLAYOFF RECORD:** 1-0

TOUR VICTORIES: 1987 Provident Classic. **1993** Buick Southern Open.
(TOTAL: 2)

MONEY & POSITION:

1987--$148,386-- 72	1990--$ 85,289--143	1993--$ 242,140-- 69
1988--$ 66,305--137	1991--$ 84,501--167	1994--$ 117,356--144
1989--$ 99,378--178	1992--$173,828-- 87	

BEST 1994 FINISH: T13--Greater Milwaukee Open

1994 SUMMARY: Tournaments entered--34; in money--15; top ten finishes--0.

1995 PGA TOUR CHARITY TEAM COMPETITION: Greater Milwaukee Open

1994 SEASON: Coming off year in which won second TOUR title, struggled much of campaign...over one stretch beginning late January missed 16 of 21 cuts, including six in a row...finally got back on track late July...opened year with pair of top-25 finishes, solo 23rd in Mercedes Championships and T23 in United Airlines Hawaiian Open...Mercedes Championships produced biggest check of year, $19,000...top placing came during season-best string of six consecutive cuts made, T13 in Greater Milwaukee Open...opened with 68 at Brown Deer Park GC, then lowered score one stroke each successive round until posted third-round 66...at 12-under-par 201 stood three shots off 54-hole lead, but closed GMO with 73...had T15 at Texas Open, where opened 66-69-68 but finished with 70...played in 34 events, matching Ted Tryba for most starts in 1994.

CAREER HIGHLIGHTS: First TOUR victory came in 1987 Provident Classic, where rounds of 65-67-67-66 produced 15-under-par 265 and one-stroke win over Rocco Mediate and Bill Glasson...second victory at 1993 Buick Southern Open contributed to best campaign of eight on TOUR, when made $242,140...victory came via five-man playoff with Bob Estes, Billy Andrade, Mark Brooks and Brad Bryant...birdie on second extra hole defeated Estes...trailed Estes, 54-hole leader, by two strokes following course-record 64 during Round 3 on Callaway Gardens Mountain View Course...finished regulation play with 2-under-par 70, which put him in first playoff...also posted T10 in 1993 Kemper Open...had pair of top-10s in 1992, T6 at Freeport-McMoRan Classic and T7 in Chattanooga Classic (former Provident Classic).

PERSONAL: Had fifth career hole-in-one, fourth on TOUR, during Round 2 of 1994 BellSouth Classic...all five aces have come via 4-iron ...wife Patti is President of TOUR Wives Association...older brother Joe, former TOUR member who won 1976 Kemper Open, helped prepare him for TOUR life...winner 1984 NCAA Championship...winner 1984 Fred Haskins Award as nation's outstanding collegiate player.

1994 PGA TOUR STATISTICS

Scoring Average	72.00	(156)
Driving Distance	245.4	(177)
Driving Accuracy	75.8	(20)
Greens in Regulation	62.2	(157)
Putting	1.827	(156T)
All-Around	867	(142T)
Sand Saves	59.9	(10)
Total Driving	197	(120)
Eagles	5	(87T)
Birdies	258	(104T)

MISCELLANEOUS STATISTICS

Scoring Avg. (before cut)	72.38	(160)
Scoring Avg. (3rd round)	71.07	(92T)
Scoring Avg. (4th round)	72.27	(146)
Birdie Conversion	22.8	(174)
Par Breakers	14.5	(175T)

1994 Low Round:	**64:** MCI Heritage Classic/2
Career Low Round:	**64:** 2 times, most recent 1994 MCI Heritage Classic/2
Career Largest Paycheck:	**$126,000**/1993 Buick Southern Open/1

HALE IRWIN

EXEMPT STATUS: Winner, 1990 United States Open

FULL NAME: Hale S. Irwin

HEIGHT: 6'   **WEIGHT:** 175

BIRTH DATE: June 3, 1945

BIRTHPLACE: Joplin, MO

RESIDENCE: Frontenac, MO; plays out of Kapalua, Maui, HI

FAMILY: Wife, Sally Stahlhuth; Becky (12/15/71), Steven (8/6/74)

COLLEGE: University of Colorado (1968, Marketing)

SPECIAL INTERESTS: Fishing, hunting, photography

TURNED PROFESSIONAL: 1968

Q SCHOOL: Spring 1968

CAREER EARNINGS: $5,654,063 | **PLAYER PROFILE** | **PLAYOFF RECORD:** 4-5

TOUR VICTORIES: **1971** Heritage Classic. **1973** Heritage Classic. **1974** U. S. Open. **1975** Western Open, Atlanta
(TOTAL: 20) Classic. **1976** Glen Campbell Los Angeles Open, Florida Citrus Open. **1977** Atlanta Classic, Hall of
Fame Classic, San Antonio-Texas Open. **1979** U. S. Open. **1981** Hawaiian Open, Buick Open. **1982**
Honda-Inverrary Classic. **1983** Memorial Tournament. **1984** Bing Crosby Pro-Am. **1985** Memorial
Tournament. **1990** U.S. Open, Buick Classic. **1994** MCI Heritage Classic.

MONEY & POSITION:

1968--$ 9,093--117	1977--$221,456-- 4	1986--$ 59,983--128
1969--$ 18,571-- 88	1978--$191,666-- 7	1987--$100,825-- 96
1970--$ 46,870-- 49	1979--$154,168-- 19	1988--$164,996-- 72
1971--$ 99,473-- 13	1980--$109,810-- 38	1989--$150,977-- 93
1972--$111,539-- 13	1981--$276,499-- 7	1990--$838,249-- 6
1973--$130,388-- 7	1982--$173,719-- 19	1991--$422,652-- 33
1974--$152,529-- 7	1983--$232,567-- 13	1992--$ 98,208--131
1975--$205,380-- 4	1984--$183,384-- 31	1993--$252,686-- 65
1976--$252,718-- 3	1985--$195,007-- 31	1994--$814,436-- 10

BEST 1994 FINISHES: 1--MCI Heritage Classic; T2--Kmart Greater Greensboro Open; 3--Southwestern Bell Colonial; 4--
THE PLAYERS Championship; T8--Buick Classic; T10--NEC World Series of Golf.
1994 SUMMARY: Tournaments entered--22; in money--19; top ten finishes--6.
1995 PGA TOUR CHARITY TEAM COMPETITION: Memorial Tournament
NATIONAL TEAMS: World Cup (2), 1974, 1979 (won individual title in 1979); Ryder Cup (5), 1975, 1977, 1979, 1981, 1991;
U.S. vs. Japan, 1983; Presidents Cup (playing captain), 1994.

1994 SEASON: Posted two of six top-10s after turning 49 in June, then went on to complete second-best of 27 years on TOUR with earnings of $814,436…had added responsibility over course of season as U.S. Team Captain for inaugural Presidents Cup Match, which United States won 20-12…highlighted campaign with third victory in MCI Heritage Classic in April, two-stroke victory over Greg Norman worth $225,000, largest check of career…wrapped opening and closing 68s around pair of 65s for 20th title…recorded tournament record 18-under-par 266, two strokes better than Payne Stewart's 1989 mark…contended for win No. 21 very next week at Kmart Greater Greensboro Open, where finished in three-way tie for second…first top-10 finish, solo fourth at PLAYERS Championship, produced second-biggest check of year, $120,000…opened with 64 and closed with 65 for third in Southwestern Bell Colonial, then put back-to-back top-10s on board for second time with T8 two weeks later at Buick Classic.

CAREER HIGHLIGHTS: Owns three U.S. Open titles, last of which came in grueling 19-hole playoff with Mike Donald at Medinah in 1990…sank 60-foot putt on final hole to force playoff…by ending playoff with 10-foot birdie putt became, at age 45, oldest to win Open…followed that victory with another very next week at Buick Classic…two wins combined to help produce career-best $838,249…other two Open victories came at Winged Foot in 1974 and Inverness in 1979…first of 20 career wins (and first of three at Harbour Town) came in 1971 Heritage Classic…repeated there two years later…also two-time winner of Atlanta Classic (1975-77) and Memorial Tournament (1983-85)…from early 1975 through 1978 played 86 tournaments without missing cut, third best streak in TOUR history…1974-75 Picadilly World Match Play Champion…winner 1978 Australian PGA, 1979 South African PGA, 1981 Bridgestone Classic (Japan), 1982 Brazilian Open, 1986 Bahamas Classic, 1987 Fila Classic.

PERSONAL: Unusual two-sport participant at University of Colorado: 1967 NCAA Champion in golf, also two-time All-Big Eight selection as football defensive back.

1994 PGA TOUR STATISTICS

Scoring Average	69.72	(9)
Driving Distance	254.7	(148T)
Driving Accuracy	78.0	(6)
Greens in Regulation	68.5	(35)
Putting	1.759	(12)
All-Around	567	(50)
Sand Saves	46.4	(146T)
Total Driving	154	(54)
Eagles	3	(126T)
Birdies	278	(85T)

MISCELLANEOUS STATISTICS

Scoring Avg. (before cut)	70.40	(21)
Scoring Avg. (3rd round)	70.47	(55T)
Scoring Avg. (4th round)	70.71	(34)
Birdie Conversion	30.5	(20T)
Par Breakers	21.1	(17T)

1994 Low Round: 64:	Southwestern Bell Colonial/1
Career Low Round: 61:	1982 Southern Open/4
Career Largest Paycheck: $225,000/	1994 Heritage/1

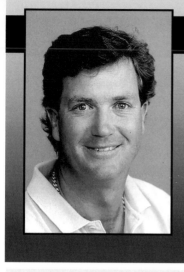

PETER JACOBSEN

EXEMPT STATUS: 88th on 1994 money list

FULL NAME: Peter Erling Jacobsen

HEIGHT: 6' 3"　　**WEIGHT:** 200

BIRTH DATE: March 4, 1954

BIRTHPLACE: Portland, OR

RESIDENCE: Portland, OR; plays out of Waikoloa Resort, HI

FAMILY:　Wife, Jan; Amy (7/19/80), Kristen (2/23/82), Mickey (10/12/84)

COLLEGE: University of Oregon

SPECIAL INTERESTS: Music, antique car collection

TURNED PROFESSIONAL: 1976

Q-SCHOOL: Fall 1976

PLAYER PROFILE

CAREER EARNINGS: $3,472,507　　　**PLAYOFF RECORD:** 1-3

TOUR VICTORIES: **1980** Buick-Goodwrench Open. **1984** Colonial National Invitation, Sammy Davis,
(TOTAL: 4)　　　Jr.-Greater Hartford Open. **1990** Bob Hope Chrysler Classic.

MONEY & POSITION:

1977--$ 12,608--129	1983--$158,765-- 29	1989--$267,241-- 48
1978--$ 34,188-- 82	1984--$295,025-- 10	1990--$547,279-- 19
1979--$ 49,439-- 44	1985--$214,959-- 23	1991--$263,180-- 64
1980--$138,562-- 8	1986--$112,964-- 78	1992--$106,100--127
1981--$ 85,624-- 44	1987--$ 79,924--111	1993--$222,291-- 77
1982--$145,832-- 25	1988--$526,765-- 16	1994--$211,762-- 88

BEST 1994 FINISHES: T6--Nissan Los Angeles Open; T7--Shell Houston Open; T9--Canon Greater Hartford Open.

1994 SUMMARY: Tournaments entered--19; in money--15; top ten finishes--3.

1995 PGA TOUR CHARITY TEAM COMPETITION: Las Vegas Invitational

1994 SEASON: Despite several physical problems, still managed to produce second consecutive season with earnings over $200,000 and eighth overall…began year on "disabled list" after surgery, having cut two fingers on right hand to tendon while playing with children Dec. 20…made first start at Phoenix Open late January, finishing T49…bothered by pulled rib muscles May into June…posted best finish with T6 at Nissan Los Angeles Open…later collected biggest check of year with T7 at Shell Houston Open worth $40,517…closed with back-to-back 69s at TPC at The Woodlands…three weeks later pulled rib muscles at Memorial Tournament…layoff didn't seem to hurt, as returned to action with T9 at Canon Greater Hartford Open…opened with pair of 68s at TPC at River Highlands, then closed 70-69 for final top-10 of season…next-best finish T12 in MCI Heritage Classic.

CAREER HIGHLIGHTS: Bothered by sinus trouble throughout 1992, lost exempt status by finishing No. 127…regained playing privileges in 1993 with three top-10 finishes, best of which pair of T6s at Nissan Los Angeles Open and New England Classic…followed back surgery in 1987 with second-best earnings year in 1988…last TOUR victory, one-stroke win over Scott Simpson in 1990 Bob Hope Chrysler Classic, helped key best year with earnings of $547,279…earned pair of titles in 1984, when finished Top 10 on money list for second time…defeated Payne Stewart in playoff for Colonial title, which dedicated to father, who had just undergone very serious surgery…later captured Sammy Davis, Jr. Greater Hartford Open…came from six strokes back on final day to claim first win, 1980 Buick-Goodwrench Open…won Oregon Open and Northern California Open after turning professional in 1976…winner 1979 Western Australia Open, 1981-82 Johnnie Walker Cups (Spain)…winner 1986 Fred Meyer Challenge (with Curtis Strange).

PERSONAL: Has own television production company, Peter Jacobsen Productions…founded "Jake Trout and the Flounders," musical group which used to perform at TOUR events…three-time All-American 1974-76…winner 1974 PAC-8 Conference title…Player Director TOUR Policy Board 1983-85, again 1990-92.

1994 PGA TOUR STATISTICS

Scoring Average	70.67	(44)
Driving Distance	263.1	(79)
Driving Accuracy	75.6	(21T)
Greens in Regulation	70.4	(13T)
Putting	1.787	(73T)
All-Around	563	(49)
Sand Saves	51.4	(92)
Total Driving	100	(17T)
Eagles	3	(126T)
Birdies	247	(115)

MISCELLANEOUS STATISTICS

Scoring Avg. (before cut)	70.92	(44T)
Scoring Avg. (3rd round)	70.33	(44)
Scoring Avg. (4th round)	70.47	(21T)
Birdie Conversion	28.7	(66T)
Par Breakers	20.4	(32)

1994 Low Round:	66: Las Vegas Invitational/3
Career Low Round:	62: 1982 Manufacturers Hanover Westchester Classic/2
Career Largest Paycheck:	$180,000/1990 Bob Hope Chrysler Classic/1

LEE JANZEN

EXEMPT STATUS: Winner, 1993 U.S. Open

FULL NAME: Lee MacLeod Janzen

HEIGHT: 6'   **WEIGHT:** 175

BIRTH DATE: August 28, 1964

BIRTHPLACE: Austin, MN

RESIDENCE: Kissimmee, FL; plays out of Bloomingdale Golfers' Club, Brandon, FL

FAMILY: Wife, Beverly; Connor MacLeod (10/20/93)

SPECIAL INTERESTS: Music, movies, snow skiing, all sports

COLLEGE: Florida Southern (1986, Marketing)

TURNED PROFESSIONAL: 1986

JOINED TOUR: Fall 1989.

PLAYER PROFILE

CAREER EARNINGS: $2,531,430

TOUR VICTORIES: 1992 Northern Telecom Open. **1993** Phoenix Open, U.S. Open. **1994** Buick Classic. (TOTAL: 4)

MONEY & POSITION: 1990--$ 132,986--115   1992--$795,279--9   1994--$442,588--35
1991--$ 228,242-- 72   1993--$932,335--7

BEST 1994 FINISHES: 1--Buick Classic; T4--Kemper Open.

1994 SUMMARY: Tournaments entered--26; in money--19; top ten finishes--2.

1995 PGA TOUR CHARITY TEAM COMPETITION: Canon Greater Hartford Open

NATIONAL TEAMS: Ryder Cup, 1993

1994 SEASON: Fell off from career year of 1993, due in large part to fact was bothered by hernia from February until had July surgery to repair…still managed to post fourth career victory in June, giving him wins in last three seasons…tuned up for defense of U.S. Open title by winning Buick Classic by three strokes over Ernie Els who, of course, went on to win Open the following week…third-round 64 gave him lead at Westchester CC, one stroke in front of Els…closed with 66 to take home $216,000, second biggest check of five-year career…Buick Classic win came week after only other top-10 of season, T4 at Kemper Open…missed cuts at U.S. Open and Canon Greater Hartford Open, then withdrew from FedEx St. Jude Classic after hernia surgery July 20…operation performed week after finished T35 in British Open, where closed with rounds of 69-69-67…returned to action at Buick Open, where also missed cut…best finish in final eight starts T13 at B.C. Open.

CAREER HIGHLIGHTS: Earned biggest victory of career in head-to-head battle with Payne Stewart at 1993 U.S. Open…posted four rounds in 60s, good for two-stroke win over Stewart at Baltusrol…272 total tied Jack Nicklaus for lowest cumulative score in Open history…triumph provided $290,000 payday and 10-year TOUR exemption…fourth start that season produced second TOUR win, two-stroke Phoenix Open victory over Andrew Magee…earned first title at 1992 Northern Telecom Open, where was 17-under-par over last three rounds, which included final-round 65…also in 1992 was runnerup to Brad Faxon at The International and to Paul Azinger (tied with Corey Pavin) at TOUR Championship…best finish prior to Northern Telecom win fifth during rookie season at 1990 Deposit Guaranty Golf Classic…leading money winner on U.S. Golf (mini) Tour in 1989.

PERSONAL: Started to take golf seriously at age 14 after family moved to Florida from Maryland, where played Little League baseball…won first tournament at 15 as member of Greater Tampa Junior Golf Association…still avid baseball fan…winner 1986 Division II National Championship…selected First-Team All-American in 1985-86.

1994 PGA TOUR STATISTICS

Scoring Average	70.87	(55)
Driving Distance	262.7	(81)
Driving Accuracy	71.5	(58T)
Greens in Regulation	68.1	(40T)
Putting	1.796	(101T)
All-Around	666	(76)
Sand Saves	43.8	(162)
Total Driving	139	(39)
Eagles	4	(104T)
Birdies	288	(65T)

MISCELLANEOUS STATISTICS

Scoring Avg. (before cut)	71.42	(88T)
Scoring Avg. (3rd round)	71.00	(84T)
Scoring Avg. (4th round)	71.17	(58T)
Birdie Conversion	26.7	(134T)
Par Breakers	18.4	(110T)

1994 Low Round: **64:** Buick Classic/3
Career Low Round: 61: 1993 Colonial/4
Career Largest
Paycheck: $290,000/1993 U.S. Open/1

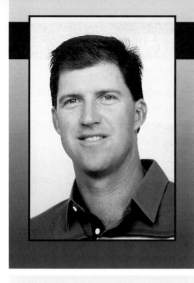

STEVE JONES

EXEMPT STATUS: Special Medical Extension

FULL NAME: Steven Glen Jones

HEIGHT: 6' 4"   **WEIGHT:** 185

BIRTH DATE: December 27, 1958

BIRTHPLACE: Artesia, NM

RESIDENCE: Phoenix, AZ; plays out of Desert Mountain GC

FAMILY: Wife, Bonnie; Cy Edmond (2/27/91)

COLLEGE: University of Colorado

SPECIAL INTERESTS: Snow skiing, basketball

TURNED PROFESSIONAL: 1981

Q SCHOOL: Fall 1981, 1984, 1986

PLAYER PROFILE

CAREER EARNINGS: $1,894,679

TOUR VICTORIES: 1988 AT&T Pebble Beach National Pro-Am; **1989** MONY Tournament of Champions, (TOTAL: 4)   Bob Hope Chrysler Classic, Canadian Open.

MONEY & POSITION:

1982--$ 1,986--229	1987--$157,918-- 66	1991--$294,961-- 54
1984--$ 788--264	1988--$241,877-- 45	1992--Did not play
1985--$ 43,379--129	1989--$745,578-- 8	1993--Did not play
1986--$ 51,473--136	1990--$350,982-- 34	1994--$ 8,740--254

BEST 1994 FINISH: T31--Hardee's Golf Classic.

1994 SUMMARY: Tournaments entered--2; in money--2; top ten finishes--0.

1995 PGA TOUR CHARITY TEAM COMPETITION: Freeport-McMoRan Classic

1994 SEASON: At B.C. Open saw first PGA TOUR action since 1991 Independent Insurance Agent Open…dirt bike accident Nov. 25, 1991 sidelined him for almost three full seasons…shot 67-70-70-74, good for 3-under-par 281 and T40…made second (and final) 1994 start at Hardee's Golf Classic, where placed T31 with rounds of 69-70-67-69…left ankle and shoulder injured in accident three days before Thanksgiving, but longer-term ligament and joint damage to left ring finger (and inability to grip club properly) what kept him away from TOUR…went 17 months without swinging club, then reinjured finger twice, once while swinging and once doing yard work…began preparations for '94 return by playing two NIKE TOUR events, in some state opens, and finally three European tournaments in August…finished T10 in NIKE Carolina Classic in June (opened with 68), T26 Wichita Open in July…will play 1995 season under special medical extension.

CAREER HIGHLIGHTS: Had finest season of first eight on TOUR in 1989, with three victories and earnings of $745,578…opened year with back-to-back wins in MONY Tournament of Champions and Bob Hope Chrysler Classic…tied Paul Azinger and Sandy Lyle at end of regulation, then birdied first playoff hole for win…captured Canadian Open for third title of year…has been in two other playoffs, defeating Bob Tway for 1988 AT&T Pebble Beach National Pro-Am title and losing to Payne Stewart at 1990 MCI Heritage Classic…also finished T3 in 1990 PLAYERS Championship…had four top-10 finishes in 1991, including third in Greater Milwaukee Open…GMO finish one of seven consecutive top-25s to end final season until 1994…winner 1987 JCPenney Classic (with Jane Crafter)…medalist 1986 Qualifying Tournament.

PERSONAL: Played golf and ran track in high school, where also earned all-state honors in basketball before concentrating on golf alone at University of Colorado…Second-Team All-American…semifinalist 1976 USGA Junior Championship.

1994 PGA TOUR STATISTICS

Scoring Average	69.2
Driving Distance	249.9
Driving Accuracy	67.6
Greens in Regulation	61.1
Putting	1.716
All-Around	–
Sand Saves	33.3
Total Driving	–
Eagles	1
Birdies	28

MISCELLANEOUS STATISTICS

Scoring Avg. (before cut)	69.00
Scoring Avg. (3rd round)	68.50
Scoring Avg. (4th round)	71.50
Birdie Conversion	31.8
Par Breakers	20.1

1994 Low Round: 67: 2 times	
Career Low Round: 63: 4 times, most recently '91	
Career Largest	Las Vegas Invitational/3
Paycheck: $180,000/1989 Bob Hope Chrysler Classic/1	

BRIAN KAMM

EXEMPT STATUS: 98th on 1994 money list

FULL NAME: Brian Thomas Kamm

HEIGHT: 5'6"　　**WEIGHT:** 160

BIRTH DATE: September 3, 1961

BIRTHPLACE: Rochester, NY

RESIDENCE: Tampa, FL

FAMILY: Wife, Yvette; Brandy (11/7/84), Michael (5/3/87)

COLLEGE: Florida State University

SPECIAL INTEREST: All sports

TURNED PROFESSIONAL: 1985

Q-SCHOOL: Fall 1989, 1990

PLAYER PROFILE

CAREER EARNINGS: $475,796

BEST EVER FINISH: T6--1994 Bell Canadian Open

MONEY & POSITION:

1990--$ 8,775--237	1992--$ 20,020--211	1994--$181,884--98
1991--$ 81,932--146	1993--$183,185-- 94	

BEST 1994 FINISHES: T6--Bell Canadian Open; T7--Walt Disney World/Oldsmobile Classic; T10--Kemper Open

1994 SUMMARY: Tournaments entered--32; in money--16; top ten finishes--3.

1995 PGA TOUR CHARITY TEAM COMPETITION: Kemper Open

1994 SEASON: Parlayed pair of late-season top-10s into retention of playing privileges for 1995…had missed 15 of 25 cuts by time arrived at Bell Canadian Open in September…posted closing rounds of 69-68 at Glen Abbey, good for T6 and largest career payday of $43,550…still was shy of money needed to keep card when got to Walt Disney World/Oldsmobile Classic in October…began with pair of 69s, then followed with pair of 68s for 14-under-par 274 total…T7 finish was worth $33,138, which put him over…opened with 65 following week at Texas Open, then went 67-68 before final 73 gave him T15…fired season-low and career-best-matching 64 to begin Las Vegas Invitational, where closed with back-to-back 72s…had first top-10 of year in Kemper Open, where finished T10…only other top-25 finish came in BellSouth Classic, where closing 68 gave him T18.

CAREER HIGHLIGHTS: Prior to 1994, best TOUR finish T7 in 1993 Canon Greater Hartford Open…closed with 6-under-par 64 at TPC at River Highlands to finish six strokes behind winner Nick Price…had two other top-10s in '93, when fashioned solid season and retained playing privileges with No. 94 money-list finish…three consecutive 69s, followed by 67, provided T8 at Greater Milwaukee Open…closing 68 gave him T10 and $35,000 payday at Las Vegas Invitational, his largest check until '94 Canadian Open…had moment in sun at 1991 U.S. Open, where first-round 69 had him just two strokes off early lead (ultimately finished T31)…finished seventh on 1992 Ben Hogan Tour money list with $88,608 to earn TOUR exemption for 1993…had nine top-10 finishes, including win in fifth Hogan start…final-round 69 good for one-stroke victory over Jeff Gallagher in Ben Hogan Panama City Beach Classic…winner 1987 North Dakota Open.

PERSONAL: Won two collegiate tournaments at Florida State.

1994 PGA TOUR STATISTICS

Scoring Average	71.34	(103T)
Driving Distance	264.7	(64)
Driving Accuracy	67.9	(106T)
Greens in Regulation	65.4	(100T)
Putting	1.808	(122T)
All-Around	602	(57)
Sand Saves	61.4	(5)
Total Driving	170	(74T)
Eagles	6	(64T)
Birdies	308	(38T)

MISCELLANEOUS STATISTICS

Scoring Avg. (before cut)	71.51	(97T)
Scoring Avg. (3rd round)	71.93	(155T)
Scoring Avg. (4th round)	71.88	(121)
Birdie Conversion	27.8	(105T)
Par Breakers	18.6	(102T)

1994 Low Round: 64:: 1994 Las Vegas Invitational/1
Career Low Round: 64: 5 times, most recent 1994 Las Vegas Invitational/1
Career Largest Paycheck: $43,550/94 Bell Canadian Open/T6

SKIP KENDALL

EXEMPT STATUS: 5th on 1994 NIKE TOUR money list

FULL NAME: Jules I. Kendall

HEIGHT: 5'8" **WEIGHT:** 145

BIRTH DATE: September 9, 1964

BIRTHPLACE: Milwaukee, WI

RESIDENCE: Palm Harbor, FL

FAMILY: Wife, Beth

COLLEGE: University of Nevada-Las Vegas

SPECIAL INTERESTS: Sports, movies

TURNED PROFESSIONAL: 1987

Q SCHOOL: 1992

PLAYER PROFILE

CAREER EARNINGS: $123,581

BEST-EVER FINISH: 8--1993 The International

MONEY & POSITION: 1990--$2,118--275   1993--$115,189--129   1994--$ 8,392--257

BEST 1994 FINISH: T32--United Airlines Hawaiian Open

1994 SUMMARY: Tournaments entered--4; in money--2; top ten finishes--0.

1995 PGA TOUR CHARITY TEAM COMPETITION: THE PLAYERS Championship

1994 SEASON: Entered initial NIKE TOUR event of 1994 (NIKE Inland Empire Open in Moreno Valley, CA) and was onsite when decided not to go to AT&T Pebble Beach National Pro-Am as second alternate…decision a good one as led NIKE event wire-to-wire winning by six strokes…quickly decided to spend year on NIKE TOUR and aim for a fully exempt spot awarded to top-five finishers…again made right choice, as finished fifth on NIKE TOUR money list and is fully exempt on PGA TOUR in 1995…after winning opening event, strung together 11 consecutive in-money finishes on NIKE TOUR and eight top-25 finishes in first 12 events before missing first cut of year June 12 at Cleveland…set record for consecutive weeks leading NIKE TOUR money list beginning a season (11)…two weeks after missing first cut, won second NIKE TOUR event, NIKE Carolina Classic…1994 NIKE TOUR tournament summary: events entered–26; in-money–19; top 10 finishes–5; top-25 finishes–13…NIKE TOUR statistics for 87 rounds in 1994: eighth among birdie leaders with 339, ninth among scoring leaders with 70.40, 11th among par breakers with 21.9% and 53rd among eagle leaders with four.

CAREER HIGHLIGHTS: Co-medalist at 1993 Qualifying Tournament at TPC at The Woodlands…in only full season on PGA TOUR (1993), earned $115,189 to finish 129th on money list…played one PGA TOUR event in 1990, Greater Milwaukee Open, and earned $2,118…also played NIKE TOUR events in 1991-93, with top year prior to 1994 coming in 1992, when finished 23rd on money list with $54,175 in 23 events…finished 65th on NIKE TOUR money list in 1991 and 86th in 1993 when not competing on PGA TOUR.

PERSONAL: Winner 1988-89 Wisconsin State Opens…wife Beth was his caddy throughout 1994 NIKE TOUR season…became first NIKE TOUR player to serve as host of "Inside the PGA TOUR."

1994 PGA TOUR STATISTICS

Scoring Average	72.23
Driving Distance	250.7
Driving Accuracy	62.5
Greens in Regulation	65.7
Putting	1.803
All-Around	–
Sand Saves	42.9
Total Driving	–
Eagles	1
Birdies	38

MISCELLANEOUS STATISTICS

Scoring Avg. (before cut)	72.13
Scoring Avg. (3rd round)	71.00
Scoring Avg. (4th round)	71.50
Birdie Conversion	26.8
Par Breakers	18.1

1994 Low Round:	**66:** United Airlines Hawaiian Open/2
Career Low Round:	**65:** 1993 Walt Disney World/ Oldsmobile Classic/1
Career Largest Paycheck:	**$40,300**/ 1993 International/8

TOM KITE

EXEMPT STATUS: Winner, 1992 U.S. Open

FULL NAME: Thomas O. Kite, Jr.

HEIGHT: 5' 8"　　**WEIGHT:** 155

BIRTH DATE: December 9, 1949

BIRTHPLACE: Austin, TX

RESIDENCE: Austin, TX

FAMILY: Wife, Christy; Stephanie Lee (10/7/81), David Thomas and Paul Christopher (twins) (9/1/84)

COLLEGE: University of Texas

SPECIAL INTERESTS: Landscaping

TURNED PROFESSIONAL: 1972

Q SCHOOL: Fall 1972

PLAYER PROFILE

CAREER EARNINGS: $9,159,419　　　　**PLAYOFF RECORD:** 6-4

TOUR VICTORIES: **1976** IVB-Bicentennial Golf Classic. **1978** B.C. Open. **1981** American Motors-
(TOTAL: 19)　　Inverrary Classic. **1982** Bay Hill Classic. **1983** Bing Crosby National Pro-Am. **1984**
Doral-Eastern Open, Georgia-Pacific Atlanta Classic. **1985** MONY Tournament of
Champions. **1986** Western Open. **1987** Kemper Open. **1989** Nestle Invitational, THE PLAYERS Championship, Nabisco Championships. **1990** Federal Express St. Jude Classic. **1991** Infiniti Tournament of
Champions. **1992** BellSouth Classic, U.S. Open. **1993** Bob Hope Chrysler Classic, Nissan Los Angeles
Open

MONEY & POSITION:

1972--$	2,582--233	1980--$ 152,490-- 20	1988--$ 760,405-- 5
1973--$	54,270-- 56	1981--$ 375,699-- 1	1989--$1,395,278-- 1
1974--$	82,055-- 26	1982--$ 341,081-- 3	1990--$ 658,202-- 15
1975--$	87,045-- 18	1983--$ 257,066-- 9	1991--$ 396,580-- 39
1976--$	116,180-- 21	1984--$ 348,640-- 5	1992--$ 957,445-- 6
1977--$	125,204-- 14	1985--$ 258,793-- 14	1993--$ 887,811-- 8
1978--$	161,370-- 11	1986--$ 394,164-- 7	1994--$ 658,689-- 22
1979--$	166,878-- 17	1987--$ 525,516-- 8	

BEST 1994 FINISHES: T2--Shell Houston Open; 3--Mercedes Championships; 4--Masters Tournament;
5--Sprint International; T6--BellSouth Classic; T9--Honda Classic, THE PLAYERS Championship,
PGA Championship.

1994 SUMMARY: Tournaments entered--23; in money--18; top ten finishes--8

1995 PGA TOUR CHARITY TEAM COMPETITION: Texas Open

1994 SEASON: Took status as TOUR's all-time leading money winner to new plateau in August…became first to surpass $9 million with $22,500 paycheck for T11 at Buick Open…years-with-victory streak ended at five with best finish T2 at Shell Houston Open…held midpoint lead after opening 68-65 at TPC at The Woodlands, but finished in three-way tie with Jeff Maggert and Hal Sutton, three strokes behind surprise winner Mike Heinen…very next week started BellSouth Classic with 6-under-par 66, good for share of early lead with Sutton, but ultimately finished T6…opened year with third-place finish in Mercedes Championships, where closed 68-69-68…ran off three top-10s in a row March into April, starting with T9s in Honda Classic and PLAYERS Championship, where began with 65…capped that skein with fourth at Masters, posting rounds of 69-72-71-71…also had top-10s in British Open and PGA Championship, T8 at Turnberry and T9 at Southern Hills…followed PGA performance with fifth in Sprint International.

CAREER HIGHLIGHTS: Greatest victory came in 1992 U.S. Open at Pebble Beach, where even-par 72 in tough Sunday conditions gave him two-stroke win over Jeff Sluman…win earlier that year in BellSouth Classic ended 16-month victory drought…got off to blazing start in 1993, posting two wins, a second and eighth in five starts before March back injury slowed him down…was untouchable in '93 Bob Hope Chrysler Classic, closing with rounds of 64-65-62 to set TOUR record for most-strokes-under-par in 90-hole event…finished at 35-under 325, which also was good for six-stroke win over Rick Fehr…in next start, Nissan Los Angeles Open, even weather couldn't stop him…4-under-par 67 on final day of rain-shortened event produced 19th career victory…owns two Arnold Palmer Awards, for 1981 and 1989…1981 GWAA Player of Year…winner 1979 Bob Jones Award…Rookie of Year for 1973…winner 1981-82 Vardon Trophies…winner 1980 European Open.

PERSONAL: Three recent victories came on holidays: BellSouth Classic/Mother's Day, U.S. Open/Father's Day, Bob Hope Chrysler Classic/Valentine's Day…co-winner with Ben Crenshaw of 1972 NCAA Championship…started playing golf at six, won first tournament at 11.

1994 PGA TOUR STATISTICS

Scoring Average	70.07	(18)
Driving Distance	261.6	(91T)
Driving Accuracy	75.0	(29T)
Greens in Regulation	69.9	(20)
Putting	1.796	(101T)
All-Around	568	(51)
Sand Saves	50.0	(105T)
Total Driving	120	(23T)
Eagles	4	(104T)
Birdies	266	(100T)

MISCELLANEOUS STATISTICS

Scoring Avg. (before cut)	70.45	(23)
Scoring Avg. (3rd round)	70.24	(35T)
Scoring Avg. (4th round)	71.82	(117T)
Birdie Conversion	27.1	(123T)
Par Breakers	19.2	(73T)

1994 Low Round: 64: Buick Classic/3

Career Low Round: 62: 3 times, most recent 1993 Bob Hope Chrysler Classic/5

Career Largest Paycheck: $450,000/1989 Nabisco Championships/1

GREG KRAFT

EXEMPT STATUS: 69th on 1994 money list

FULL NAME: Gregory Thomas Kraft

HEIGHT: 5'11"   **WEIGHT:** 170

BIRTH DATE: April 4, 1964

BIRTHPLACE: Detroit, MI

RESIDENCE: Clearwater, FL

FAMILY: Single

COLLEGE: University of Tampa

SPECIAL INTEREST: Sports

TURNED PROFESSIONAL: 1986

Q-SCHOOL: 1991, 1992

PLAYER PROFILE

CAREER EARNINGS: $659,305

BEST-EVER FINISH: 2--1993 Walt Disney World/Oldsmobile Classic; 2--1994 Motorola Western Open.

MONEY & POSITION: 1992--$88,824--140   1993--$290,581--60   1994--$279,901--69

BEST 1994 FINISHES: 2--Motorola Western Open; T3--Buick Open; T10--Bell Canadian Open.

1994 SUMMARY: Tournaments entered--30; in money--13; top ten finishes--3.

1995 PGA TOUR CHARITY TEAM COMPETITION: Buick Classic

1994 SEASON: Went back to old swing after missing 13 of first 20 cuts…having made $290,581 in 1993, stood with just $34,896 after 20 starts…return to basics produced instant returns on the investment–and almost first official TOUR victory…led through three rounds of Motorola Western Open, but final-round 73 dropped him to second, one stroke behind Nick Price…$129,600 check largest of career, surpassing $118,000 payday for runnerup finish in 1993 Walt Disney World/Oldsmobile Classic…recorded two more top-10s in next six appearances, with best being T3 at Buick Open…closed 67-66 at Warwick Hills to finish tied with Curtis Strange and Steve Pate…four weeks later final-round 69 brought T10 in Bell Canadian Open…only top-25 finish during seven-month down stretch T18 at Kemper Open, where finished with 68…had one other top-25, T15 in next-to-last start of season, at Walt Disney World.

CAREER HIGHLIGHTS: Finished 1993 as third-leading money-winner out of 1992 Qualifying Tournament…rookie season highlighted by (unofficial) victory in Deposit Guaranty Golf Classic, where sank tricky sidehill putt for birdie on 72nd hole to edge Morris Hatalsky and Tad Rhyan by one stroke…prepped for Hattiesburg by finishing T6 in previous week's Freeport-McMoRan Classic…was 54-hole leader at English Turn, standing one stroke ahead of Payne Stewart and Russ Cochran…closed with 3-over-par 75 as Mike Standly claimed first TOUR win…saved best for last, finishing T4 at B.C. Open, then solo second two weeks later at Walt Disney World/Oldsmobile Classic…closed 64-66 in less-than-desireable weather conditions (and rapidly approaching darkness) at Disney to finish three strokes behind Jeff Maggert, another first-time winner…prior to 1993, best finish T6 in 1992 Kemper Open…birdied last two holes to make cut in '92 Qualifying Tournament, then fired 5-under-par 31 on back side at TPC at The Woodlands to qualify for TOUR card…had four top-5 finishes on 1991 Ben Hogan Tour.

PERSONAL: Seven-time winner on mini-tours…not related to Kraft Foods founders.

1994 PGA TOUR STATISTICS

Scoring Average	71.22	(89T)
Driving Distance	255.7	(138)
Driving Accuracy	67.6	(111T)
Greens in Regulation	61.3	(166)
Putting	1.751	(9)
All-Around	711	(92)
Sand Saves	50.3	(102T)
Total Driving	249	(158)
Eagles	8	(28T)
Birdies	286	(68T)

MISCELLANEOUS STATISTICS

Scoring Avg. (before cut)	71.85	(133)
Scoring Avg. (3rd round)	70.69	(69)
Scoring Avg. (4th round)	71.69	(105)
Birdie Conversion	30.1	(29T)
Par Breakers	19.0	(83T)

1994 Low Round: 66: 4 times

Career Low Round: 64: 3 times, most recent 1993

Career Largest   Walt Disney/Olds Classic/3

Paycheck: $129,000/1994 Motorola Western Open/2

NEAL LANCASTER

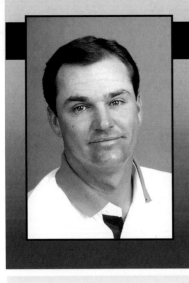

EXEMPT STATUS: 1994 tournament winner

FULL NAME: Grady Neal Lancaster

HEIGHT: 6' **WEIGHT:** 170

BIRTH DATE: September 13,1962

BIRTHPLACE: Smithfield, NC

RESIDENCE: Smithfield, NC; plays out of Johnston City CC

FAMILY: Wife, Lou Ann

SPECIAL INTERESTS: Fishing, movies

TURNED PROFESSIONAL: 1985

Q SCHOOL: 1989, 1990

PLAYER PROFILE

CAREER EARNINGS: $867,091 **PLAYOFF RECORD:** 1-0

TOUR VICTORIES: 1994 GTE Byron Nelson Classic.
(TOTAL:1)

MONEY & POSITION:

1990--$ 85,769--142	1992--$146,967--103	1994--$305,088--58
1991--$180,037-- 90	1993--$149,381--107	

BEST 1994 FINISHES: 1--GTE Byron Nelson Classic.

1994 SUMMARY: Tournaments entered--29; in money--19; top ten finishes--1.

1995 PGA TOUR CHARITY TEAM COMPETITION: JCPenney Classic

1994 SEASON: May victory in GTE Byron Nelson Classic labeled the "Half Nelson," since was turned into 36-hole event by the weather…first TOUR victory resulted from birdie on first hole of six-man playoff with David Ogrin, David Edwards, Mark Carnevale, Tom Byrum and Yoshi Mizumaki at TPC at Las Colinas…actually played three holes Sunday, two to complete second-round 65 (opened with 67) and then one in playoff…birdied all three, last from four feet…$216,000 payday more money than he had earned in any of four previous seasons…best 1994 finish prior to Byron Nelson T35 at PLAYERS Championship…looked for brief period like history might repeat itself at Hardee's Golf Classic…opened with back-to-back 65s at Oakwood CC, good for one-stroke lead after 36 holes…threat of severe weather in Quad Cities area existed for weekend, but final two rounds played without particular difficulty…finished 71-72 for T23, only other top-25 finish of season…did open with four rounds in 60s at Las Vegas Invitational, only to close with 75 and final T45…29 appearances fewest since first year on TOUR (26 in 1990).

CAREER HIGHLIGHTS: Best previous finish T5 in 1991 Greater Milwaukee Open…opened with rounds of 67 and 66 at Tuckaway CC…GMO payday $38,000, almost six times less than made for Byron Nelson win…registered pair of top-10s in 1993…closed with 1-under-par 71 over windswept English Turn, good for T6 in Freeport-McMoRan Classic…final 67 gave him T9 in Buick Open…only 1992 top-10 also Freeport-McMoRan T6…had two other top-10s in 1991, T9 at Northern Telecom Open and T8 in Canadian Open…latter secured playing privileges for first time in career …winner of PineTree Open in Birmingham, AL and Utah State Open in 1989…also mini-tour leading money winner that year.

PERSONAL: Took first golf lesson in 1992, having self-taught through golf magazine pictures until then…that first lesson came from L.B. Floyd, Raymond's father and fellow North Carolina resident.

1994 PGA TOUR STATISTICS

Scoring Average	71.32	(100T)
Driving Distance	273.1	(17T)
Driving Accuracy	62.9	(156T)
Greens in Regulation	63.3	(148T)
Putting	1.803	(115T)
All-Around	672	(81)
Sand Saves	55.2	(42T)
Total Driving	173	(81T)
Eagles	6	(64T)
Birdies	315	(30)

MISCELLANEOUS STATISTICS

Scoring Avg. (before cut)	71.12	(62)
Scoring Avg. (3rd round)	72.00	(157T)
Scoring Avg. (4th round)	72.21	(142)
Birdie Conversion	29.1	(56)
Par Breakers	18.8	(92T)

1994 Low Round:	65: 4 times
Career Low Round:	64: 1992 Southwestern Bell
Career Largest	Colonial/2,4
Paycheck:	$216,000/94 GTE Byron Nelson /1

TOM LEHMAN

EXEMPT STATUS: 1994 tournament winner

FULL NAME: Thomas Edward Lehman

HEIGHT: 6' 2"   **WEIGHT:** 190

BIRTH DATE: March 7, 1959

BIRTHPLACE: Austin, MN

RESIDENCE: Scottsdale, AZ; plays out of Desert Mountain GC

FAMILY: Wife, Melissa; Rachael (5/30/90), Holly (8/13/92)

COLLEGE: University of Minnesota

SPECIAL INTERESTS: Hunting, church activities

TURNED PROFESSIONAL: 1982

PLAYER PROFILE

CAREER EARNINGS: $2,072,026

TOUR VICTORIES: 1994 The Memorial Tournament.
(TOTAL: 1)

MONEY & POSITION:

1983--$9,413--183	1985--$ 20,232--158	1993--$ 422,761--33
1984--$9,382--184	1992--$579,093-- 24	1994--$1,031,144-- 4

BEST 1994 FINISHES: 1--Memorial Tournament; 2--Masters Tournament; 3--Bell Canadian Open; T5--Southwestern Bell Colonial; 6--AT&T Pebble Beach National Pro-Am; T6--Phoenix Open, Nestle Invitational, Hardee's Classic; T8--Buick Open.

1994 SUMMARY: Tournaments entered--23; in money--21; top ten finishes--9.

1995 PGA TOUR CHARITY TEAM COMPETITION: Buick Invitational of California

NATIONAL TEAMS: Presidents Cup, 1994

1994 SEASON: A classic example of perseverance paying off… enjoyed finest year of Part II of PGA TOUR career, winning first TOUR title (Memorial Tournament) and $1,031,144 (No. 4)…five-stroke victory over Greg Norman fashioned through four consecutive 67s, producing tournament-record 20-under-par 268…Muirfield Village win came six weeks after Masters runnerup to Jose Maria Olazabal…key to that finish No. 15 on Sunday, when Olazabal eagle putt dropped and his didn't…had opened campaign with three sixth-place finishes in first six starts: Phoenix Open (T6) and AT&T Pebble Beach back-to-back, followed by T6 at Nestle Invitational…at Augusta National was one-stroke out of midpoint lead, held third-round lead by one over Olazabal…followed Columbus performance with T5 at Southwestern Bell Colonial…opened 66-66 at Colonial CC…had three more top-10s in August and September, with best being solo third in Bell Canadian Open…also had T8 at Buick Open, another T6 in Hardee's Golf Classic, where finished 67-65-66…member of U.S. Team in inaugural President's Cup Match.

CAREER HIGHLIGHTS: Following three years of less-than-limited TOUR success (1983-85), decided to pursue other golf opportunities…played, among others, Asian and South African Tours…in building golf portfolio, also collected playing time on various mini-tours…used Ben Hogan/NIKE TOUR as eventual avenue back to PGA TOUR…as last alternate won 1990 Hogan Reflection Ridge Open, then captured three events among 11 top-10 finishes in 1991…named Ben Hogan Tour Player of Year for 1991…returned to PGA TOUR with nine top-10 finishes in 1992, including best-previous T2 at Hardee's Golf Classic…finished tied with fellow first-time 1994 winner Loren Roberts, three strokes behind David Frost…1993 experienced first taste of Masters success, solo third after sharing first-round lead with 67 in first competitive round at Augusta National…winner 1993 Casio World Open (Japan).

PERSONAL: Credits marriage with giving him focus to do well on TOUR…mini-tours experience included PGT, Dakotas, Golden State, South Florida and Carolinas.

1994 PGA TOUR STATISTICS

Scoring Average	69.46	(4)
Driving Distance	269.3	(34T)
Driving Accuracy	70.8	(68T)
Greens in Regulation	70.8	(8)
Putting	1.766	(19T)
All-Around	312	(6)
Sand Saves	47.9	(134)
Total Driving	102	(20)
Eagles	11	(7T)
Birdies	308	(38T)

MISCELLANEOUS STATISTICS

Scoring Avg. (before cut)	69.60	(3)
Scoring Avg. (3rd round)	69.74	(14)
Scoring Avg. (4th round)	70.68	(33)
Birdie Conversion	29.8	(34T)
Par Breakers	21.9	(8T)

1994 Low Round: 64: NEC World Series of Golf/3

Career Low Round:63: 1993 H-E-B Texas Open/2

**Career Largest
Paycheck: $270,000**/94 Memorial/1

JUSTIN LEONARD

EXEMPT STATUS: 126th on 1994 money list

FULL NAME: Justin Charles Garret Leonard

HEIGHT: 5' 9"   **WEIGHT:** 160

BIRTH DATE: June 15, 1972

BIRTHPLACE: Dallas, TX

RESIDENCE: Dallas, TX; plays out of Kiawah Island, SC

FAMILY: Single

COLLEGE: University of Texas (Business, 1994)

SPECIAL INTERESTS: Fishing

TURNED PROFESSIONAL: 1994

JOINED TOUR: 1994

PLAYER PROFILE

CAREER EARNINGS: $140,413

BEST-EVER FINISH: 3--1994 Anheuser-Busch Golf Classic

MONEY & POSITION: 1994--$140,413--126

BEST 1994 FINISHES: 3--Anheuser-Busch Golf Classic; T6--New England Classic.

1994 SUMMARY: Tournaments entered--13; in money-- 5; top ten finishes--2.

1995 PGA TOUR CHARITY TEAM COMPETITION: GTE Byron Nelson Classic

1994 SEASON: Completed University of Texas career in June by winning long-sought first NCAA Championship, then failed to qualify for U.S. Open…made professional debut at Canon Greater Hartford Open…missed cut in that start and eight of 13 TOUR events overall, still avoided Qualifying Tournament by finishing No. 126 on money list…collected $140,413 in five tournaments, best of which solo third at Anheuser-Busch Golf Classic worth $74,800…posted rounds of 67-69-67-69 at Kingsmill GC…A-B Classic third pro start, following T26 at Motorola Western Open… after missed cut in Deposit Guaranty Golf Classic, posted second (and last) top-10 with T6 at New England Classic…Pleasant Valley experience, good for $33,500, achieved special temporary membership…missed next six cuts, then recorded back-to-back top-25s in final two starts of year, T19 at Buick Southern Open followed by T15 in Texas Open…latter worth $15,500, which provided exemption for 1995.

CAREER HIGHLIGHTS: First NCAA Championship on fourth try came in record-tying fashion…17-under-par 271 at Stonebridge CC won by five strokes and equaled NCAA record set by Phil Mickelson in 1992 …NCAA title moved him past Tom Kite into second place on all-time Texas list with 10 wins (Ben Crenshaw No. 1 with 18)…only golfer in Southwest Conference history to win four consecutive conference championships…winner 1992 U.S. Amateur…member 1992 U.S. World Amateur Team, 1993 Walker Cup Team…First-Team All-American 1993-94…winner Texas 5A State Championship 1989-90…1990 AJGA first-team All-America.

PERSONAL: TOUR mentors include all-time University of Texas greats Ben Crenshaw and Tom Kite.

1994 PGA TOUR STATISTICS

Scoring Average	70.58
Driving Distance	252.5
Driving Accuracy	76.4
Greens in Regulation	65.0
Putting	1.733
All-Around	–
Sand Saves	59.5
Total Driving	1,998
Eagles	3
Birdies	111

MISCELLANEOUS STATISTICS

Scoring Avg. (before cut)	71.13
Scoring Avg. (3rd round)	69.75
Scoring Avg. (4th round)	68.80
Birdie Conversion	28.8
Par Breakers	19.2

1994 Low Round:	67: 3 times
Career Low Round:	67: 3 times, most recent
Career Largest	1994 Texas Open/1
Paycheck:	$74,800/94 Anheuser-Busch/3

WAYNE LEVI

EXEMPT STATUS: 91st on 1994 money list

FULL NAME: Wayne John Levi

HEIGHT: 5' 9" **WEIGHT:** 165

BIRTH DATE: February 22, 1952

BIRTHPLACE: Little Falls, NY

RESIDENCE: New Hartford, NY

FAMILY: Wife, Judy; Michelle (7/29/79), Lauren (1/20/83), Christine (12/30/84); Brian (5/1/88)

COLLEGE: Oswego State (NY)

SPECIAL INTERESTS: Financial and stock markets, reading

TURNED PROFESSIONAL: 1973

Q SCHOOL: Spring 1977

PLAYER PROFILE

CAREER EARNINGS: $4,191,292   **PLAYOFF RECORD:** 2-1

TOUR VICTORIES: **1978** Walt Disney World National Team Play (with Bob Mann). **1979** Houston Open.
(TOTAL: 12)   **1980** Pleasant Valley-Jimmy Fund Classic. **1982** Hawaiian Open; LaJet Classic. **1983** Buick Open. **1984** B. C. Open. **1985** Georgia-Pacific Atlanta Classic. **1990** BellSouth Atlanta Classic, Centel Western Open, Canon Greater Hartford Open, Canadian Open.

MONEY & POSITION:

1977--$ 8,136--159	1983--$ 193,252-- 22	1989--$ 499,292-- 16
1978--$ 25,039-- 99	1984--$ 252,921-- 20	1990--$1,024,647-- 2
1979--$ 141,612-- 20	1985--$ 221,425-- 22	1991--$ 195,861-- 87
1980--$ 120,145-- 32	1986--$ 154,777-- 59	1992--$ 237,935-- 65
1981--$ 62,177-- 69	1987--$ 203,322-- 53	1993--$ 179,521-- 95
1982--$ 280,681-- 8	1988--$ 190,073-- 61	1994--$ 200,476-- 91

BEST 1994 FINISHES: T7--Canon Greater Hartford Open; T9--New England Classic; T10--Kemper Open, Hardee's Golf Classic

1994 SUMMARY: Tournaments entered--24; in money--17; top ten finishes--4.

1995 PGA TOUR CHARITY TEAM COMPETITION: AT&T Pebble Beach National Pro-Am

NATIONAL TEAMS: Four Tours World Championship, 1990; Ryder Cup, 1991.

1994 SEASON: Recorded eighth $200,000-plus campaign of 18 on TOUR, returning to that level from (for him) down season in 1993...had four top-10 finishes, all of which came in last half of year... best finish T7 at Canon Greater Hartford Open...opened with rounds of 68-66 at TPC at River Highlands to stand two strokes off Dave Stockton, Jr.'s midpoint lead...closed 71-68 for 7-under-par 273...next-best placing came in next start, four weeks later at New England Classic...began with 5-under-par 66, closed with T9...first top-10 came in Kemper Open, part of pair of T10s over second half...opened with 68 at TPC at Avenel, finished with 3-under-par 281...carded final two rounds of 65-68 at Hardee's Golf Classic for second T10, finishing at 10-under-par 270 at Oakwood CC...next-best finish T16 at Shell Houston Open, where carded middle rounds of 67-69.

CAREER HIGHLIGHTS: Had career year in 1990, for which was accorded selection by peers as first PGA TOUR Player of Year...collected four victories from May to September, opening with BellSouth Atlanta Classic title and closing with Canadian Open...first player since Curtis Strange (1988) to win four times...became fifth to surpass $1 million in single-season earnings...finished second to Greg Norman on money list with $1,024,647...won BellSouth Classic in near darkness after six-hour rain delay... win his second in Atlanta, since also captured 1985 Georgia-Pacific Atlanta Classic...first TOUR victory came with Bob Mann in 1978 Walt Disney World National Team Play...upstate New York native captured 1984 B.C. Open at Endicott, NY...first player to win using colored golf ball (orange), when won 1982 Hawaiian Open... won 1988 Chrysler Team Championship (with George Burns)...member Four Tours World Championship Team in 1990...member victorious 1991 Ryder Cup Team.

PERSONAL: Avid family man who prefers to spend much of time at home...constant follower of stock and financial markets.

1994 PGA TOUR STATISTICS

Scoring Average	71.03 (71)
Driving Distance	258.1 (119)
Driving Accuracy	71.1 (61T)
Greens in Regulation	67.4 (49)
Putting	1.803 (115T)
All-Around	699 (88T)
Sand Saves	44.1 (159)
Total Driving	180 (93T)
Eagles	7 (44T)
Birdies	279 (81T)

MISCELLANEOUS STATISTICS

Scoring Avg. (before cut)	71.02 (52T)
Scoring Avg. (3rd round)	70.00 (18T)
Scoring Avg. (4th round)	73.06 (166)
Birdie Conversion	27.7 (108T)
Par Breakers	19.1 (79T)

1994 Low Round:	**65:** 2 times
Career Low Round:	**62:** 1989 Byron Nelson Golf Classic/1
Career Largest Paycheck:	**$180,000**/4 times, most recent: 1990 Canadian Open/1

BRUCE LIETZKE

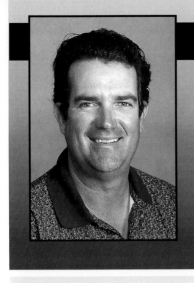

EXEMPT STATUS: 1994 tournament winner

FULL NAME: Bruce Alan Lietzke

HEIGHT: 6' 2"   **WEIGHT:** 185

BIRTH DATE: July 18, 1951

BIRTHPLACE: Kansas City, KS

RESIDENCE: Dallas, TX

FAMILY: Wife, Rosemarie; Stephen Taylor (10/5/83), Christine (10/11/85)

COLLEGE: University of Houston

SPECIAL INTERESTS: Serious fishing, racing cars

TURNED PROFESSIONAL: 1974

Q SCHOOL: Spring 1975

PLAYER PROFILE

CAREER EARNINGS: $5,440,868   **PLAYOFF RECORD:** 6-4

TOUR VICTORIES: **1977** Joe Garagiola-Tucson Open, Hawaiian Open. **1978** Canadian Open. **1979** Joe
(TOTAL: 13)   Garagiola-Tucson Open. **1980** Colonial National Invitation. **1981** Bob Hope Desert
Classic, Wickes-Andy Williams San Diego Open, Byron Nelson Classic. **1982**
Canadian Open. **1984** Honda Classic. **1988** GTE Byron Nelson Classic. **1992** Southwestern Bell Colonial.
1994 Las Vegas Invitational.

MONEY & POSITION:

1975--$ 30,780--74	1982--$217,447--14	1989--$307,987-- 36
1976--$ 69,229--39	1983--$153,255--32	1990--$329,294-- 41
1977--$202,156-- 5	1984--$342,853-- 6	1991--$566,272-- 19
1978--$113,905--18	1985--$136,992--59	1992--$703,805-- 16
1979--$198,439-- 8	1986--$183,761--47	1993--$163,241--101
1980--$163,884--16	1987--$154,383--68	1994--$564,926-- 28
1981--$343,446-- 4	1988--$500,815--19	

BEST 1994 FINISHES: 1--Las Vegas Invitational; 4--Texas Open; T7--Doral-Ryder Open; T10--THE
TOUR Championship.

1994 SUMMARY: Tournaments entered--18; in money--13; in money--4.

1995 PGA TOUR CHARITY TEAM COMPETITION: Colonial

NATIONAL TEAMS: Ryder Cup, 1981; U.S. vs. Japan, 1984.

1994 SEASON: Although no longer one who plays frequently, four-week October stretch to close out campaign proved to be extremely rewarding...collected $399,000, en route to third-best earnings total of 20-year career, over last three weeks of that period (finished T31 at Buick Southern Open in Week 1)...after posting just one top-10 (T7 at Doral-Ryder Open) in first 15 starts, wound up with top-10s in last three appearances--including 13th TOUR title at Las Vegas Invitational...was in contention week before at Texas Open, where carded season-low 64 in Round 3 en route to fourth-place finish worth $48,000...closing 65 in Las Vegas Invitational brought victory and top career paycheck of $270,000...hadn't expected to be in TOUR Championship field, but found himself at Olympic Club fourth week out–so turned trip to San Francisco into T10 worth $81,000...total earnings of $564,926 marked improvement over 1993, when $163,241 lowest since 1987.

CAREER HIGHLIGHTS: Finest season of 20 on TOUR produced earnings of $703,805 in 1992, when won Southwestern Bell Colonial for second time...recorded rounds of 64-66 on the weekend to finish tied with Corey Pavin at 13-under-par 267...birdie on first playoff hole brought first victory since 1988, when captured GTE Byron Nelson Classic...also claimed Nelson Classic in 1981...all told, has won four events twice: Colonial and Nelson, Joe Garagiola-Tucson Open (1977-79), Canadian Open (1978-82)...first victory came in 1977 Tucson Open, where defeated Gene Littler on fourth playoff hole...playoff loser to Greg Norman in 1992 Canadian Open...closed with 67 to miss by one stroke three-man 1993 Greater Milwaukee Open playoff won by Billy Mayfair...member of victorious 1981 Ryder Cup team...played in 1984 U.S. vs. Japan matches.

PERSONAL: Plays limited schedule in order to spend as much time as possible with family...enjoys coaching teams on which his children play...says of role with son's Little League team: "I'm not the head coach. I'm the one who keeps them from climbing on the fence"...holds distinction of being only player in both fields when Al Geiberger (1977) and Chip Beck (1991) shot their 59s...an avid Dallas Cowboys fan.

1994 PGA TOUR STATISTICS

Scoring Average	70.04	(17)
Driving Distance	264.8	(63)
Driving Accuracy	76.7	(17)
Greens in Regulation	70.4	(13T)
Putting	1.766	(19T)
All-Around	528	(37)
Sand Saves	42.0	(172T)
Total Driving	80	(9T)
Eagles	4	(104T)
Birdies	234	(123T)

MISCELLANEOUS STATISTICS

Scoring Avg. (before cut)	70.33	(16T)
Scoring Avg. (3rd round)	68.91	(2)
Scoring Avg. (4th round)	69.75	(4)
Birdie Conversion	31.3	(9T)
Par Breakers	22.4	(4)

1994 Low Round:	64: Texas Open/3
Career Low Round:	63: 5 times, most recent 1992
Career Largest	Anheuser-Busch Golf Classic/2
Paycheck:	$270,000/'94 Las Vegas Invitational/1

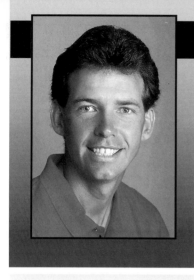

BOB LOHR

EXEMPT STATUS: 80th on 1994 money list

FULL NAME: Robert Harold Lohr

HEIGHT: 6' 1"   **WEIGHT:** 185

BIRTH DATE: November 2, 1960

BIRTHPLACE: Cincinnati, OH

RESIDENCE: Orlando, FL

FAMILY: Wife, Marie; Matthew Robert (7/15/91)

COLLEGE: Miami University, OH (1983, Marketing)

SPECIAL INTERESTS: Hunting, fishing, snow skiing

TURNED PROFESSIONAL: 1983

Q SCHOOL: Fall, 1984

PLAYER PROFILE

CAREER EARNINGS: $1,972,842   **PLAYOFF RECORD:** 1-1

TOUR VICTORIES: 1988 Walt Disney World Oldsmobile Classic.
(TOTAL: 1)

MONEY & POSITION:

1985--$ 93,651-- 81	1989--$144,242-- 98	1993--$314,982-- 54
1986--$ 85,949-- 99	1990--$141,260--109	1994--$225,048-- 80
1987--$137,108-- 80	1991--$386,759-- 41	
1988--$315,536-- 32	1992--$128,307--112	

BEST 1994 FINISHES: 5--Kmart Greater Greensboro Open; T7--Anheuser-Busch Golf Classic.

1994 SUMMARY: Tournaments entered-28; in money--16; top ten finishes--2.

1995 PGA TOUR CHARITY TEAM COMPETITION: Lincoln Mercury-Kapalua International

1994 SEASON: Although started year slowly (missed three of four cuts) and ended in somewhat similar fashion (missed five of last eight), in between assembled fourth-best campaign of 10 on TOUR...pair of top-10s with combined earnings over $94,000 keys to his season...fifth-place finish in Kmart Greensboro Open was worth $60,000...recorded rounds of 69-71-69-70 at Forest Oaks CC...made run at second TOUR title at Anheuser-Busch Golf Classic...opened with career-low 10-under-par 61, course record at 6,797-yard Kingsmill GC, to take three-stroke lead over Glen Day and John Wilson...continued three-stroke advantage through two rounds after 68, fell one stroke back following third-round 73...finished T7 after closing 72...recorded 63, TOUR second-lowest opening round of campaign (to his A-B Classic 61), at Walt DisneyWorld/Oldsmobile Classic...ultimately finished T24 in event claimed for only victory in 1988...next-best finish after top-10s T13 in Nestle Invitational, where wrapped 70s around third-round 72.

CAREER HIGHLIGHTS: Only TOUR victory came via playoff at 1988 Walt Disney World/Oldsmobile Classic...birdied final hole to close regulation play at 25-under-par 263, in deadlock with Chip Beck...birdied fifth extra hole while Beck bogeyed in near darkness...had opened Disney play with 62 on Palm Course...came close to second victory in 1993 H-E-B Texas Open, where lost playoff to Jay Haas...posted second- and fourth-round 64s to finish at 21-under-par 263...Haas won with birdie on second extra hole at Oak Hills CC...also in 1993 had solo third in Sprint Western Open, where closed with 65, and T4 at Bob Hope Chrysler Classic...seven top-10 finishes, including pair of second-place ties (Southwestern Bell Colonial and International), keyed career year with $386,759 in 1991...winner 1990 Mexican Open.

PERSONAL: Golf had stiff competition from baseball when was youngster...outstanding pitcher through high school, golf won out at Miami of Ohio–where both sports played in spring...named All Mid-America Conference three years, Honorable Mention All-American in 1983.

1994 PGA TOUR STATISTICS

Scoring Average	71.14	(79)
Driving Distance	249.7	(165)
Driving Accuracy	76.2	(18)
Greens in Regulation	68.1	(40T)
Putting	1.792	(87T)
All-Around	644	(74)
Sand Saves	52.1	(83T)
Total Driving	183	(100T)
Eagles	4	(104T)
Birdies	286	(68T)

MISCELLANEOUS STATISTICS

Scoring Avg. (before cut)	71.05	(54T)
Scoring Avg. (3rd round)	71.63	(136T)
Scoring Avg. (4th round)	71.18	(61)
Birdie Conversion	26.5	(140)
Par Breakers	18.3	(115T)

1994 Low Round: 61: Anheuser-Busch/1
Career Low Round: 61: '94 Anheuser-Busch/1
Career Largest
Paycheck: $126,000/'88 Walt Disney /1

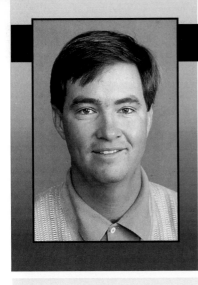

DAVIS LOVE III

EXEMPT STATUS: Winner, 1992 PLAYERS Championship

FULL NAME: Davis Milton Love III

HEIGHT: 6' 3"   **WEIGHT:** 175

BIRTH DATE: April 13, 1964

BIRTHPLACE: Charlotte, NC

RESIDENCE: Sea Island, GA; plays out of Sea Island

FAMILY: Wife, Robin; Alexia (6/5/88), Davis IV (12/4/93)

COLLEGE: University of North Carolina

SPECIAL INTERESTS: Fishing, reading novels, hunting

TURNED PROFESSIONAL: 1985

Q SCHOOL: Fall, 1985

PLAYER PROFILE

CAREER EARNINGS: $4,511,891   **PLAYOFF RECORD:** 0-3

TOUR VICTORIES: **1987** MCI Heritage Classic. **1990** The International. **1991** MCI Heritage Classic. **1992** (TOTAL: 8) THE PLAYERS Championship, MCI Heritage Classic, Kmart Greater Greensboro Open. **1993** Infiniti Tournament of Champions, Las Vegas Invitational.

MONEY & POSITION:

1986--$113,245-- 77	1989--$278,760-- 44	1992--$1,191,630-- 2
1987--$297,378-- 33	1990--$537,172-- 20	1993--$ 777,059--12
1988--$156,068-- 75	1991--$686,361-- 8	1994--$ 474,219--33

BEST 1994 FINISHES: 2--United Airlines Hawaiian Open; T4--Mercedes Championships, Honda Classic; T6--THE PLAYERS Championship.

1994 SUMMARY: Tournaments entered--28; in money--21; top ten finishes--4.

1995 PGA TOUR CHARITY TEAM COMPETITION: MCI Classic

NATIONAL TEAMS: Walker Cup, 1985; Dunhill Cup, 1992; World Cup, (3) 1992,1993,1994; Ryder Cup, 1993; Presidents Cup, 1994.

1994 SEASON: Had four top-10 finishes first three months, none thereafter…best placings from April on, pair of T11s in May (BellSouth Classic) and August (Buick Open)…did finish year on high note, winning–with Fred Couples–World Cup of Golf for record third consecutive time in November…also was member of U.S. Team in inaugural Presidents Cup Match…opened campaign with T4 in Mercedes Championships, event which won to begin 1993 season…had best shot at winning following week, when fired career-low, 12-under-par 60 during Round 2 of United Airlines Hawaiian Open…held both 36- and 54-hole leads, latter by two strokes over Brett Ogle…carded final-round 71 to 68 for Ogle, who claimed one-stroke victory…posted final two top-10s in March in Florida…opened with 68 in Honda Classic, finished T4…two weeks later started with rounds of 68-66 at PLAYERS Championship, closed 70-74 for T6…also had T12 at NEC World Series of Golf…finished No. 33 on money list, missing TOUR Chamionship field by two places…led TOUR in driving distance for second time with 283.8 average (first led in 1986)…led in eagles with 18.

CAREER HIGHLIGHTS: Enjoyed finest season in 1992, when won three times…began with four-stroke victory at PLAYERS Championship…three weeks later successfully defended at MCI Heritage Classic (event also won for first title in 1987), then very next week captured Kmart Greater Greensboro Open…final 62 at Greensboro brought him from three strokes off Rocco Mediate lead for win…started and ended 1993 in winning fashion, beginning with Infiniti Tournament of Champions (one stroke over Tom Kite) and closing with Las Vegas Invitational…captured 1990 International by three points…over three-week period at end of 1992, teamed with Fred Couples to claim first of three World Cups, eagled 72nd hole to win Lincoln-Mercury Kapalua International by two strokes, and joined with Tom Kite to capture Franklin Funds Shark Shootout…member victorious 1993 Ryder Cup team.

PERSONAL: Father, who died in 1990 plane crash, highly regarded teacher…born shortly after Davis Jr. contended in 1964 Masters…enjoys hunting and fishing, North Carolina basketball, Atlanta Braves baseball, stock car racing…winner 1984 North and South Amateur and ACC Championship.

1994 PGA TOUR STATISTICS

Scoring Average	70.73	(47)
Driving Distance	283.8	(1)
Driving Accuracy	61.0	(167T)
Greens in Regulation	66.7	(65T)
Putting	1.780	(57T)
All-Around	451	(25)
Sand Saves	51.5	(91)
Total Driving	168	(69T)
Eagles	18	(1)
Birdies	326	(22T)

MISCELLANEOUS STATISTICS

Scoring Avg. (before cut)	70.65	(32)
Scoring Avg. (3rd round)	71.67	(139T)
Scoring Avg. (4th round)	71.53	(93)
Birdie Conversion	29.8	(34T)
Par Breakers	21.0	(19T)

1994 Low Round: 60: UA Hawaiian Open/2

Career Low Round: 60: '94 UA Hawaiian Open/2

Career Largest Paycheck: $324,000/'92 PLAYERS Championship/1

STEVE LOWERY

EXEMPT STATUS: 1994 tournament winner

FULL NAME: Stephen Brent Lowery

HEIGHT: 6'2"   **WEIGHT:** 210

BIRTH DATE: October 12, 1960

BIRTHPLACE: Birmingham, AL

RESIDENCE: Orlando, FL

FAMILY: Wife, Kathryn

COLLEGE: University of Alabama

SPECIAL INTEREST: Sports

TURNED PROFESSIONAL: 1983

Q SCHOOL: Fall 1987

PLAYER PROFILE

CAREER EARNINGS: $1,205,391   **PLAYOFF RECORD:** 1-0

TOUR VICTORIES: 1994 Sprint International
(TOTAL: 1)

MONEY & POSITION:

1988--$44,327-- 157	1991--$ 87,597-- 143	1994--$794,048--12
1989--$38,699-- 174	1992--$ 22,608-- 207	
1990--$68,524-- 159	1993--$188,287-- 92	

BEST 1994 FINISHES: 1--Sprint International; 2--Buick Invitational of California; T3--NEC World Series of Golf; T6--THE PLAYERS Championship; T8--THE TOUR Championship.

1994 SUMMARY: Tournaments entered--30; in money--20; top ten finishes--5.

1995 PGA TOUR CHARITY TEAM COMPETITION: Buick Southern Open

1994 SEASON: Belief shared by many that just matter of time before he arrived as solid player became reality…after missing first three cuts, almost broke through end of February for first TOUR victory…posted rounds of 67-68-66 at Torrey Pines, good for stroke lead after 54 holes of Buick Invitational of California…carded final 68, but Craig Stadler's 66 meant one-stroke win…next time opportunity knocked, he answered…was second-round leader with 21 points in Sprint International, finished regulation deadlocked with Rick Fehr (35 points)…par good for win on first playoff hole after Fehr found water…win came after missing cuts in previous two starts, withdrawing from one before those…found himself in contention again very next week… after rounds of 67-66-66, held one-stroke lead in NEC World Series of Golf…finished T3 after closing 72…also had top-10s in two of TOUR's richest events, T6 in PLAYERS Championship, T8 in season-ending TOUR Championship…at Olympic Club recorded second hole-in-one in TOUR Championship history… aced No. 8 en route to opening 66 and share of first-round lead.

CAREER HIGHLIGHTS: Played TOUR with limited success each season since 1988, finally made most of first fully exempt year in 1993…earned over $188,000, including more than $60,000 by time TOUR left West Coast…made money in 25 of 32 events, with best finish being T10 in New England Classic…first appeared on TOUR after finishing 12th in 1987 Qualifying Tournament…secured special temporary membership in 1990 and 1991 by earning as much as 150th-place finisher on previous year's money list…best previous finish, T3, came in 1991 Chattanooga Classic…wound up four strokes behind winner Dillard Pruitt…played Ben Hogan Tour in 1992…finished third on Hogan Tour money list with $114,553, good for PGA TOUR membership in 1993…won Ben Hogan Tulsa Open in two-hole playoff with Jeff Coston.

PERSONAL: Alabama Crimson Tide football fan.

1994 PGA TOUR STATISTICS

Scoring Average	70.90	(57T)
Driving Distance	264.9	(61T)
Driving Accuracy	66.2	(129)
Greens in Regulation	65.5	(98T)
Putting	1.768	(25T)
All-Around	533	(39)
Sand Saves	49.5	(116T)
Total Driving	190	(109T)
Eagles	8	(28T)
Birdies	327	(19T)

MISCELLANEOUS STATISTICS

Scoring Avg. (before cut)	71.20	(67)
Scoring Avg. (3rd round)	70.53	(60T)
Scoring Avg. (4th round)	71.71	(108T)
Birdie Conversion	29.5	(43T)
Par Breakers	19.8	(52T)

1994 Low Round: 66: 5 times
Career Low Round: 62: '90 Chattanooga Classic/1
**Career Largest
Paycheck: $252,000**/1994 Sprint International/1

ANDREW MAGEE

EXEMPT STATUS: 1994 tournament winner

FULL NAME: Andrew Donald Magee

HEIGHT: 6'   **WEIGHT:** 180

BIRTH DATE: May 22, 1962

BIRTHPLACE: Paris, France

RESIDENCE: Paradise Valley, AZ

FAMILY: Wife, Susan; Lindsey Ellenberg (6/23/81), Campbell Joseph (11/27/88), Oliver Andrew (9/5/91)

COLLEGE: University of Oklahoma (1984)

SPECIAL INTERESTS: Travel, swimming, fishing, whistling

TURNED PROFESSIONAL: 1984

Q SCHOOL: Fall 1984

PLAYER PROFILE

CAREER EARNINGS: $2,275,955   **PLAYOFF RECORD:** 1-0

TOUR VICTORIES: **1988** Pensacola Open. **1991** Nestle Invitational, Las Vegas Invitational. **1994**
(TOTAL: 4)   Northern Telecom Open.

MONEY & POSITION:

1985--$ 75,593-- 99	1989--$126,770--109	1993--$269,986-- 62
1986--$ 69,478--120	1990--$210,507-- 71	1994--$431,041-- 36
1987--$ 94,598-- 99	1991--$750,082-- 5	
1988--$261,954-- 43	1992--$285,946-- 53	

BEST 1994 FINISHES: 1--Northern Telecom Open; T8--Motorola Western Open; 9--Nestle Invitational

1994 SUMMARY: Tournaments entered--25; in money--20; top ten finishes--3

1995 PGA TOUR CHARITY TEAM COMPETITION: Phoenix Open

1994 SEASON: Captured fourth title of career, first since 1991 Las Vegas Invitational, by claiming Northern Telecom Open in January...tied with Dillard Pruitt and Jim Furyk after 54 holes at 13-under-par 203, closing 67 (last of three consecutive 67s) gave him two-stroke victory over Loren Roberts, Vijay Singh, Jay Don Blake and Steve Stricker...$198,000 first prize second-largest of career behind $270,000 Las Vegas payday...by winning with goatee, became first bearded winner of PGA TOUR event since David Frost (1992 Hardee's Golf Classic)...was in contention after three rounds of Phoenix Open the following week, but closing 73 resulted in T13 finish...held share of 36- and 54-hole leads at TPC of Scottsdale before 2-over-par final round dashed his dream of Arizona Parlay...second top-10 finish (9th) came in March at Nestle Invitational, event he won in 1991...shared midpoint lead, but final-round 74 proved to be his undoing...third (and final) top-10 of year was T8 at Motorola Western Open...earnings total of $431,041 second best to career year of 1991.

CAREER HIGHLIGHTS: First TOUR win came in 1988 Pensacola Open, where he rallied from four strokes back to claim title...climaxed strong early-season run in '91 with second career victory in Nestle Invitational...severe weather ended Bay Hill event after 54 holes...made eagle-3 with 30-foot putt on 16th hole to gain ultimate two-stroke win...later in year posted 31-under-par 329 at Las Vegas Invitational...31-under (matched by D.A. Weibring) set TOUR record for lowest score in 90-hole event, mark since surpassed by Tom Kite's 35-under at 1993 Bob Hope Chrysler Classic ...posted career-low 62 in fourth round at Las Vegas CC... defeated Weibring with par on second extra hole...two '91 wins helped produce best season to date.

PERSONAL: Last year shared with France's Thomas Levet distinction (previously held alone) of being only members of PGA TOUR born in Paris..."Drew" (as Andrew is known to friends) was Paris-born because that's where parents (father was in the oil business) were based at the time...won 1979 Doug Sanders Junior Invitational...three-time All-America at University of Oklahoma.

1994 PGA TOUR STATISTICS

Scoring Average	70.61 (41T)
Driving Distance	270.3 (30T)
Driving Accuracy	69.1 (91)
Greens in Regulation	66.7 (65T)
Putting	1.802 (111T)
All-Around	556 (48)
Sand Saves	55.2 (42T)
Total Driving	121 (25T)
Eagles	3 (126T)
Birdies	299 (50T)

MISCELLANEOUS STATISTICS

Scoring Avg. (before cut)	70.98 (49T)
Scoring Avg. (3rd round)	70.26 (38)
Scoring Avg. (4th round)	71.37 (75)
Birdie Conversion	28.0 (96T)
Par Breakers	18.9 (88T)

1994 Low Round:	65: 2 times
Career Low Round:	62: 1991 Las Vegas /4
Career Largest	
Paycheck:	$270,000/1991 Las Vegas Invitational/1

JEFF MAGGERT

EXEMPT STATUS: 1993 tournament winner

FULL NAME: Jeffrey Allan Maggert

HEIGHT: 5' 9"

WEIGHT: 165

BIRTH DATE: Feb. 20, 1964

BIRTHPLACE: Columbia, MO

RESIDENCE: The Woodlands, TX

FAMILY: Wife, Kelli; Matt (12/10/88), Macy (10/26/90)

COLLEGE: Texas A&M

SPECIAL INTERESTS: Fishing, hunting, camping, sporting events

TURNED PROFESSIONAL: 1986

JOINED TOUR: 1991

PLAYER PROFILE

CAREER MONEY: $2,225,845

TOUR VICTORIES: 1993 Walt Disney World/Oldsmobile Classic.
(TOTAL: 1)

MONEY & POSITION:

1990--$ 2,060--277	1992--$377,408--38	1994--$814,475--9
1991--$240,940-- 68	1993--$793,023--11	

BEST 1994 FINISHES: T2--AT&T Pebble Beach National Pro-Am, Shell Houston Open; 3--THE PLAYERS Championship; T3--Phoenix Open; T4--Mercedes Championships; 7--THE TOUR Championship; T8--United Airlines Hawaiian Open, Buick Classic; T9--Memorial Tournament, U.S. Open, New England Classic.

1994 SUMMARY: Tournaments entered--26; in money--22; top ten finishes--11.

1995 PGA TOUR CHARITY TEAM COMPETITION: Shell Houston Open

NATIONAL TEAMS: Presidents Cup, 1994

1994 SEASON: Quiet, unassuming Texas resident enjoyed finest earnings campaign of four-year career after getting out of blocks with 10 top-10s in first 18 starts…began year with top-10s in first four outings, opening with T4 in Mercedes Championships and closing that streak with T2 at AT&T Pebble Beach National Pro-Am…also had T2 in Shell Houston Open, where shared 54-hole lead with Tom Kite and eventual winner Mike Heinen…closed with 71 to Heinen's 68 to finish three strokes back, deadlocked with Kite and Hal Sutton…first-half successes also included T3 at Phoenix Open, result of final-round 65, and solo third in PLAYERS Championship, which produced best payday ($170,000) of campaign…became third player in Masters history to record double eagle, holing 3-iron from 222 yards on No. 13…led qualifiers for U.S. Presidents Cup Team virtually from outset, finishing more than 40,000 points ahead of runnerup Tom Lehman…was 2-2 in his four matches at Robert Trent Jones GC…missed four cuts, three in final four starts…finished with TOUR co-best 11 top-10s (equaling Greg Norman) after season-ending seventh in TOUR Championship.

CAREER HIGHLIGHTS: Broke through in Oct. 1993 for first win, a floodlight-aided three-stroke triumph over Greg Kraft at Walt Disney World/Oldsmobile Classic…victory came at conclusion of day in which he was forced to play 36 holes because of earlier weather delays…prior to Disney win, achieved best previous career finishes in '93 at Northern Telecom (2) and FedEx St. Jude Classic (T2)…briefly held final-round lead in 1992 PGA Championship…course-record 65 in Round 3 of PGA at Bellerive CC moved him into second-place tie before eventual final-round 74 produced sixth-place finish…led 1991 Independent Insurance Agent Open through three rounds on home course at The Woodlands before faltering…as PGA TOUR rookie in '91, ranked behind only John Daly in earnings with $240,940…T5 in first TOUR start in Northern Telecom Open…1990 Ben Hogan Tour Player of Year with top earnings of $108,644 and victories in Hogan Knoxville and Buffalo Opens.

PERSONAL: Gained international experience in 1989-90…won 1989 Malaysian Open on Asian Tour, 1990 Vines Classic on Australasian Tour…All-America at Texas A&M in 1986 …winner 1980 Texas State Junior, 1988 and 1990 Texas State Opens, 1989 Louisiana Open.

1994 PGA TOUR STATISTICS

Scoring Average	70.25	(25T)
Driving Distance	266.1	(52)
Driving Accuracy	73.4	(40T)
Greens in Regulation	67.2	(51T)
Putting	1.770	(29T)
All-Around	384	(16)
Sand Saves	45.5	(154T)
Total Driving	92	(13)
Eagles	9	(17T)
Birdies	334	(16)

MISCELLANEOUS STATISTICS

Scoring Avg. (before cut)	70.66	(33)
Scoring Avg. (3rd round)	70.00	(18T)
Scoring Avg. (4th round)	71.16	(56T)
Birdie Conversion	31.4	(8)
Par Breakers	21.7	(11)

1994 Low Round: 64: Buick Classic/3

Career Low Round: 64: 3 times, most recent 1994 Buick Classic/3

Career Largest Paycheck: $180,000/1993 Walt Disney World/Oldsmobile Classic/1

JOHN MAHAFFEY

EXEMPT STATUS: Winner, 1986 Tournament Players Championship

FULL NAME: John Drayton Mahaffey

HEIGHT: 5' 9" **WEIGHT:** 160

BIRTH DATE: May 9, 1948

BIRTHPLACE: Kerrville, TX

RESIDENCE: Houston, TX; plays out of The Woodlands Resort

FAMILY: Wife, Denise; John D. Mahaffey III (8/8/88), Meagan (6/12/92)

COLLEGE: University of Houston (1970, Psychology)

SPECIAL INTERESTS: Fishing

TURNED PROFESSIONAL: 1971   **Q SCHOOL:** 1971

PLAYER PROFILE

CAREER EARNINGS: $3,671,400   **PLAYOFF RECORD:** 3-2

TOUR VICTORIES: **1973** Sahara Invitational. **1978** PGA Championship, American Optical Classic. **1979** Bob Hope Desert Classic. **1980** Kemper Open. **1981** Anheuser-Busch Classic. **1984** Bob Hope Classic. **1985** Texas Open. **1986** Tournament Players Championship. **1989** Federal Express St. Jude Classic.
(TOTAL: 10)

MONEY & POSITION:

1971--$ 2,010--230	1979--$ 81,993--45	1987--$193,938-- 57
1972--$ 57,779-- 39	1980--$165,827--15	1988--$266,416-- 41
1973--$112,536-- 12	1981--$128,795--24	1989--$400,467-- 29
1974--$122,189-- 16	1982--$ 77,047--56	1990--$325,115-- 42
1975--$141,471-- 8	1983--$126,915--44	1991--$ 64,403- 159
1976--$ 77,843-- 33	1984--$252,548--21	1992--$101,512--130
1977--$ 9,847--150	1985--$341,595-- 9	1993--$ 36,913--192
1978--$153,520-- 12	1986--$378,172--11	1994--$ 65,380--177

BEST 1994 FINISH: T17--Motorola Western Open.

1994 SUMMARY: Tournaments entered--26; in money--10; top ten finishes--0.

NATIONAL TEAMS: Ryder Cup, 1979; World Cup (2) 1978, 1979 (medalist in 1978).

1994 SEASON: Recent struggles continued as he failed to notch top-10 finish for third time in past four years...most recent top-10s achieved were in 1992: T9 PLAYERS Championship and T7 Chattanooga Classic...produced pair of top-25s, and they came in consecutive weeks in July...carded closing 67 for T17 at Motorola Western Open, then followed with rounds of 69-71-70-69 for T22 at Anheuser-Busch Golf Classic...earlier T27 in THE PLAYERS Championship brought $16,641 paycheck, best of year...PLAYERS also featured third-round 65, his low of campaign...missed cut in nine of first 12 starts, then closed year with seven made over final 14 appearances...has topped $100,000 in earnings only once in last four years.

CAREER HIGHLIGHTS: High point came in 1978 PGA Championship at Oakmont...won in playoff with Tom Watson and Jerry Pate...followed next week with triumph in American Optical Classic at Sutton, MA...earned 10-year exemption with one-stroke victory over Larry Mize in 1986 Tournament Players Championship...fired third-round 7-under-par 65 on Stadium Course at Sawgrass to move into position to win...last victory came in '89 Federal Express St. Jude Classic, where he closed with rounds of 66-65 on new TPC at Southwind course to win by three strokes...member 1979 Ryder Cup team, 1978-79 World Cup squads (medalist in '78)...captured 1990 Merrill Lynch Shoot-Out final and $90,000 at Troon North in Scottsdale, AZ...led TOUR in Greens in Regulation 1985-86.

PERSONAL: Had spendid amateur career, including 1970 NCAA Championship for University of Houston...professional career has been injury-plagued, starting with hyperextended tendon in left elbow suffered in 1976 PGA Championship which made it virtually impossible for him to play in 1977...past player director on Tournament Policy Board.

1994 PGA TOUR STATISTICS

Scoring Average	72.06	(158)
Driving Distance	256.3	(133)
Driving Accuracy	79.0	(3)
Greens in Regulation	67.8	(44)
Putting	1.852	(176)
All-Around	952	(148)
Sand Saves	50.0	(105)
Total Driving	136	(37)
Eagles	1	(167)
Birdies	203	(156)

MISCELLANEOUS STATISTICS

Scoring Avg. (before cut)	72.43	(162)
Scoring Avg. (3rd round)	71.40	(123)
Scoring Avg. (4th round)	72.55	(154)
Birdie Conversion	22.2	(177)
Par Breakers	15.1	(172)

1994 Low Round: **65:** THE PLAYERS/3

Career Low Round: **63:** 2 times, most recent

Career Largest 1985 USF&G Classic/1

Paycheck: $180,000/'89 Fed. Ex. St. Jude Classic/1

ROGER MALTBIE

EXEMPT STATUS: Winner, 1985 NEC World Series of Golf

FULL NAME: Roger Lin Maltbie

HEIGHT: 5' 10"　　**WEIGHT:** 200

BIRTH DATE: June 30, 1951

BIRTHPLACE: Modesto, CA

RESIDENCE: Los Gatos, CA

FAMILY: Wife, Donna; Spencer Davis (3/3/87), Parker Travis (3/12/90)

COLLEGE: San Jose State University

SPECIAL INTERESTS: Music, 49ers football

TURNED PROFESSIONAL: 1973

Q SCHOOL: 1974

PLAYER PROFILE

CAREER EARNINGS: $2,102,415　　　　**PLAYOFF RECORD:** 2-1

TOUR VICTORIES: **1975** Ed McMahon-Quad Cities Open, Pleasant Valley Classic. **1976** Memorial
(TOTAL: 5)　　Tournament. **1985** Manufacturers Hanover Westchester Classic, NEC World
　　Series of Golf.

MONEY & POSITION:

1975--$ 81,035-- 23	1982--$ 77,067-- 55	1989--$134,333--105
1976--$117,736-- 18	1983--$ 75,751-- 70	1990--$ 58,536--169
1977--$ 51,727-- 59	1984--$118,128-- 56	1991--$ 37,962--188
1978--$ 12,440--129	1985--$360,554-- 8	1992--$109,742--125
1979--$ 9,796--155	1986--$213,206-- 40	1993--$155,454--103
1980--$ 38,626-- 84	1987--$157,023-- 65	1994--$ 67,686--174
1981--$ 75,009-- 58	1988--$150,602-- 77	

BEST 1994 FINISHES: T15--Kmart Greater Greensboro Open.

1994 SUMMARY: Tournaments entered--15; in money--8; top ten finishes--0.

1994 SEASON: Increased television commitments helped produce lowest number of events played in his 20-year career…appeared in just 15 tournaments, making cut in eight…due to TV schedule played but one tournament a month January-April…expanded that to three each from May-July…competed in Sprint International in August, then made final appearance of year in Greater Milwaukee Open early September…best placing (only top-25) was in Kmart GGO, where he overcame second-round 75 to finish T15…opened with 69 at Forest Oaks CC, then closed with pair of 70s to earn biggest check of campaign: $22,500…continued solid play in New England by going 68-70-67 in first three rounds of Canon Greater Hartford Open before concluding with 76 and finishing T40.

CAREER HIGHLIGHTS: Had back-to-back wins first year on TOUR in Quad Cities Open and Pleasant Valley Classic, first of several New England success stories he has produced…after latter triumph, left $40,000 winner's check in restaurant near course (new check subsequently issued)…made it three titles in two years on TOUR in '76 with four-hole playoff triumph over Hale Irwin in Memorial Tournament…captured 1985 NEC World Series of Golf and, along with it, 10-year TOUR exemption…earlier that year, won Westchester Classic with birdie on fourth hole of playoff with Raymond Floyd and George Burns…held 36-hole lead and shared 54-hole lead at 1992 New England Classic (eventual T7), then next week among early Canon GHO leaders…was T2 in 1993 GHO, where closing 65 put him one stroke behind Nick Price…that was his best placing since solo second in 1986 Canon GHO…winner 1980 Magnolia Classic in Hattiesburg, MS.

PERSONAL: Member NBC-TV golf coverage team…big San Francisco 49ers fan and possessor of Super Bowl ring given him by team owner Ed DeBartolo, Jr…during playing career has undergone two shoulder surgeries…winner 1972 and 1973 Northern California Amateur, 1974 California State Open…member PGA TOUR Policy Board 1985-87.

1994 PGA TOUR STATISTICS

Scoring Average	71.46
Driving Distance	255.8
Driving Accuracy	69.5
Greens in Regulation	64.0
Putting	1.816
All-Around	–
Sand Saves	40.3
Total Driving	–
Eagles	1
Birdies	129

MISCELLANEOUS STATISTICS

Scoring Avg. (before cut)	72.07
Scoring Avg. (3rd round)	71.86
Scoring Avg. (4th round)	72.14
Birdie Conversion	26.7
Par Breakers	17.2

1994 Low Round:	67: 2 times
Career Low Round:	63: 4 times, most recent
Career Largest	1991 Walt Disney World/ 2
Paycheck:	**$126,000**/'85 NEC World Series of Golf/1

BILLY MAYFAIR

EXEMPT STATUS: 1993 tournament winner

FULL NAME: William Fred Mayfair

HEIGHT: 5' 8"   **WEIGHT:** 175

BIRTH DATE: August 6, 1966

BIRTHPLACE: Phoenix, AZ

RESIDENCE: Scottsdale, AZ; Plays out of Troon North GC

FAMILY: Wife, Tammy

COLLEGE: Arizona State

SPECIAL INTERESTS: All sports

TURNED PROFESSIONAL: 1988

Q SCHOOL: Fall 1988

PLAYER PROFILE

CAREER EARNINGS: $1,854,433   **PLAYOFF RECORD:** 1-2

TOUR VICTORIES: 1993 Greater Milwaukee Open
(TOTAL: 1)

MONEY & POSITION:

1989--$111,998--116	1991--$ 185,668--89	1993--$513,072-- 30
1990--$693,658-- 12	1992--$ 191,878--79	1994--$158,159--113

BEST 1994 FINISH: T9--Northern Telecom Open.

1994 SUMMARY: Tournaments entered--32; in money--18; top ten finishes--1.

1995 PGA TOUR CHARITY TEAM COMPETITION: B.C. Open

NATIONAL TEAMS: Walker Cup, 1987; Four Tours World Championship of Golf, 1991.

1994 SEASON: After solid early start, fell off from success of 1993 to finish with lowest earnings total since rookie year…T13 in season-opening Mercedes Championships (qualified via maiden victory in Greater Milwaukee Open) produced biggest check of campaign, $25,000…had only top-10 in Week 3, T9 in Northern Telecom Open…after T69 following week in hometown Phoenix Open, proceeded to miss seven of next nine cuts, including five in row…during middle of season was in money nine of 12 starts, best finish being T14 at GTE Byron Nelson Classic (tournament which saw T2 in 1993)…'94 Byron Nelson featured May 10 marriage to Tammy McIntire on apron of 18th green at TPC at Las Colinas ("We're going to be spending the rest of our lives on a golf course. We thought we might as well be married on one.")…closed year with four missed cuts in final seven outings, including the GMO.

CAREER HIGHLIGHTS: First tasted victory in 1993 GMO, poetic justice in that one of his two 1990 playoff losses came at Tuckaway CC…defeated good friend Mark Calcavecchia on fourth hole of yet another playoff in '93…won by sinking 20-foot chip…had most financially rewarding second year in PGA TOUR history in 1990, with earnings of $693,658…in 1990 GMO tied for second with Ed Dougherty, both losing to Jim Gallagher, Jr., on first playoff hole…also lost to Jodie Mudd in season-ending Nabisco Championships that year when Mudd birdied first extra hole…had five other top-10 finishes in superlative '90 campaign.

PERSONAL: Celebrated amateur player won 1987 U.S. Amateur and 1986 U.S. Public Links…member 1987 Walker Cup team…1987 Fred Haskins Award recipient as outstanding college player of year… also Arizona player of year in '87…1985-87 Arizona Stroke Play champion…four-time winner Arizona State Juniors…member 1991 Four Tours World Championship of Golf team…close friend of the Phoenix Suns' Dan Majerle.

1994 PGA TOUR STATISTICS

Scoring Average	71.53	(122T)
Driving Distance	259.4	(110)
Driving Accuracy	73.4	(40T)
Greens in Regulation	66.5	(76T)
Putting	1.819	(142T)
All-Around	729	(102T)
Sand Saves	50.9	(97)
Total Driving	150	(50T)
Eagles	5	(87T)
Birdies	296	(55T)

MISCELLANEOUS STATISTICS

Scoring Avg. (before cut)	1.86	(134T)
Scoring Avg. (3rd round)	70.76	(74)
Scoring Avg. (4th round)	71.82	(117T)
Birdie Conversion	25.0	(159T)
Par Breakers	16.9	(156T)

1994 Low Round: 65: Hardee's Classic/3
Career Low Round: 61: 1993 GTE Byron Nelson
Career Largest Classic/2
Paycheck: $270,000/1990 Nabisco Championships/2

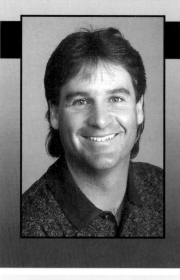

BLAINE McCALLISTER

EXEMPT STATUS: 1993 tournament winner

FULL NAME: Blaine McCallister

HEIGHT: 5' 9"   **WEIGHT:** 175

BIRTH DATE: October 17, 1958

BIRTHPLACE: Ft. Stockton, TX

RESIDENCE: Ponte Vedra, FL; plays out of Ft. Stockton GC

FAMILY: Wife, Claudia

COLLEGE: University of Houston

SPECIAL INTERESTS: Hunting, fishing, tennis, baseball

TURNED PROFESSIONAL: 1981

Q SCHOOL: Fall 1981; 1982; 1985

PLAYER PROFILE

CAREER EARNINGS: $2,439,597   **PLAYOFF RECORD:** 1-1

TOUR VICTORIES: **1988** Hardee's Golf Classic. **1989** Honda Classic, Bank of Boston Classic.
(TOTAL: 5)   **1991** H-E-B. Texas Open. **1993** B.C. Open.

MONEY & POSITION:

1982--$ 7,894--180	1988--$225,660-- 49	1992--$ 261,187--59
1983--$ 5,218--201	1989--$593,891-- 15	1993--$ 290,434--61
1986--$ 88,732-- 94	1990--$152,048--103	1994--$ 351,554--47
1987--$120,005-- 87	1991--$412,974-- 36	

BEST 1994 FINISHES: T3--Phoenix Open; T6--BellSouth Classic; T7--AT&T Pebble Beach National
Pro-Am, B.C. Open, Buick Southern Open; T8--Texas Open; T9--New England Classic.

1994 SUMMARY: Tournaments entered--27; in money--20; top ten finishes--7.

1995 PGA TOUR CHARITY TEAM COMPETITION: THE PLAYERS Championship

1994 SEASON: Enjoyed third-best earnings campaign despite being bothered by illness and physical problems...started and finished strongly, but struggled during middle of season...all seven of his missed cuts occurred over span of 15 tournaments, beginning with PLAYERS Championship and ending with Bell Canadian Open...followed T17 at season-opening Mercedes Championships with T3 at Phoenix Open and T7 in AT&T Pebble Beach National Pro-Am, giving him more than $120,000 after three starts...took six weeks off June into July to recuperate, returning with T9 at New England Classic...closed with three top-10s in final five outings: T7s B.C. Open and Buick Southern Open, T8 Texas Open...third-round 65 put him in contention to defend successfully 1993 B.C. Open title, but final-round 72 ended that...carded pair of 65s (Rounds 2 and 4) two weeks later at Texas Open...season-low round came in Round 2 of PGA Championship at Southern Hills, a 64 one stroke off Raymond Floyd's course record, established in 1982 PGA.

CAREER HIGHLIGHTS: Fashioned pair of victories in best season to date, 1989...with 65-64 finish, captured Honda Classic by four strokes over Payne Stewart...later in '89 fired closing-round 66 to win Bank of Boston Classic by one shot over Brad Faxon; lost 1986 Boston event in playoff with Gene Sauers...became part of TOUR history in winning 1988 Hardee's Golf Classic...middle rounds of 62-63--125 matched Ron Streck's standard established in 1978 Texas Open...battled mononucleosis in early 1990, rebounded with fourth victory in 1991 Texas Open...plagued by illness in 1993 (missed August due to tonsilectomy), came back next month to score one-stroke win over Denis Watson in B.C. Open.

PERSONAL: Wife Claudia suffers from rare eye disease pseudoxanthoma elasticum (PXE)...actively involved with eyesight organizations because of Claudia's affliction... three-time All-America at University of Houston, where roomed with Fred Couples (one year) and CBS-TV sportscaster Jim Nantz (three)...has joined with Couples and Nantz in Three Amigos Celebrity Tournament, first held Oct. 1994...natural lefthander who plays game righthanded but putts southpaw.

1994 PGA TOUR STATISTICS

Scoring Average	70.60	(39T)
Driving Distance	263.3	(77)
Driving Accuracy	72.9	(47T)
Greens in Regulation	66.9	(59T)
Putting	1.750	(8)
All-Around	449	(24)
Sand Saves	47.5	(140)
Total Driving	124	(29T)
Eagles	6	(64T)
Birdies	337	(15)

MISCELLANEOUS STATISTICS

Scoring Avg. (before cut)	70.98	(49T)
Scoring Avg. (3rd round)	70.32	(43)
Scoring Avg. (4th round)	70.65	(31)
Birdie Conversion	29.5	(43T)
Par Breakers	20.1	(40T)

1994 Low Round: 64: PGA Championship/2
Career Low Round: 62: 1988 Hardee's Golf Classic/2
Career Largest Paycheck: $162,000/1991 H-E-B Texas Open/1

MARK McCUMBER

EXEMPT STATUS: Winner, 1988 THE PLAYERS Championship

FULL NAME: Mark Randall McCumber

HEIGHT: 5' 8"   **WEIGHT:** 170

BIRTH DATE: September 7, 1951

BIRTHPLACE: Jacksonville, FL

RESIDENCE: Jacksonville, FL

FAMILY: Wife, Paddy; Addison (1/28/76), Megan (6/14/80), Mark Tyler (4/4/91)

SPECIAL INTERESTS: Family activities, golf course architecture

TURNED PROFESSIONAL: 1974

Q SCHOOL: Spring 1978

PLAYER PROFILE

CAREER EARNINGS: $4,423,778

PLAYOFF RECORD: 1-0

TOUR VICTORIES: **1979** Doral-Eastern Open. **1983** Western Open, Pensacola Open **1985** Doral-Eastern Open. **1987** Anheuser-Busch Classic. **1988** THE PLAYERS Championship. **1989** Beatrice Western Open. **1994** Anheuser-Busch Classic, Hardee's Golf Classic, The TOUR Championship.
(TOTAL: 10)

MONEY & POSITION:

1978--$ 6,948--160	1984--$133,445--50	1990--$ 163,413-- 97
1979--$ 67,886-- 60	1985--$192,752--32	1991--$ 173,852-- 92
1980--$ 36,985-- 88	1986--$110,442--80	1992--$ 136,653--106
1981--$ 33,363--103	1987--$390,885--22	1993--$ 363,269-- 41
1982--$ 31,684--119	1988--$559,111--13	1994--$1,208,209-- 3
1983--$268,294-- 8	1989--$546,587--14	

BEST 1994 FINISHES: 1--Anheuser-Busch Golf Classic, Hardee's Golf Classic, THE TOUR Championship; T4--Bell Canadian Open; T9--Southwestern Bell Colonial; T10--Doral-Ryder Open.

1994 SUMMARY: Tournaments entered--20; in money--18; top ten finishes--6.

1995 PGA TOUR CHARITY TEAM COMPETITION: Quad Cities Open

NATIONAL TEAMS: World Cup (2), 1988, 1989; Ryder Cup 1989.

1994 SEASON: With three victories, including season-ending TOUR Championship, enjoyed finest campaign of 17-year career…$540,000 first prize for Olympic Club playoff win over Fuzzy Zoeller boosted him to No. 3 on money list, behind only Nick Price and Greg Norman…bogeyed 72nd hole of $3 million event to necessitate playoff, which he won with 40-foot birdie putt on first extra hole…$1,208,209 total more than double best previous season…notched first win in five years in July, three-stroke decision over Glen Day in Anheuser-Busch Golf Classic…won for second time in September (first time as multiple winner since 1983) with one-stroke victory over Kenny Perry in Hardee's Golf Classic…named PGA TOUR Player of Month for September and October, one of only two players (Price the other) to be honored with two selections…finished year with top-10s (two wins) in three of last four starts, three wins in final nine appearances.

CAREER HIGHLIGHTS: Jacksonville, FL native and resident achieved popular hometown victory in 1988 by winning THE PLAYERS Championship…final-hole reception at TPC at Sawgrass one of most memorable in tournament history…captured first win, 1979 Doral-Eastern Open, in second year on TOUR, but in only his 12th tournament…hit stride in 1983 with pair of victories in Western and Pensacola Opens…repeat victor in Doral-Eastern Open (1985) and Beatrice Western Open (1989), latter in playoff with Peter Jacobsen…1994 victory in A-B Classic gave him pair of titles in three different events, since also won at Williamsburg in 1987…with increased involvement in golf course design projects affecting his game, made decision in 1993 to put full focus on golf when playing tournaments…that call produced immediate results, including best money-list finish since 1989…one of 14 players to win tournaments in 1970s, '80s, and '90s.

PERSONAL: Member 1989 Ryder Cup team, 1988-89 World Cup squads (victors in '88)…making impact in golf course design with Mark McCumber and Associates, design arm of McCumber Golf, company he helps operate with his brothers…nephew Josh McCumber up-and-coming golfer at the University of Florida…member American Society of Golf Course Architects.

1994 PGA TOUR STATISTICS

Scoring Average	69.56	(5)
Driving Distance	264.6	(65T)
Driving Accuracy	75.3	(28)
Greens in Regulation	71.3	(4)
Putting	1.791	(83T)
All-Around	480	(27)
Sand Saves	56.5	(33T)
Total Driving	93	(14)
Eagles	1	(167T)
Birdies	269	(95T)

MISCELLANEOUS STATISTICS

Scoring Avg. (before cut)	69.90	(7)
Scoring Avg. (3rd round)	69.78	(16)
Scoring Avg. (4th round)	69.83	(5T)
Birdie Conversion	27.6	(112T)
Par Breakers	19.7	(55T)

1994 Low Round: **65:** 2 times
Career Low Round: **63:** 1980 Texas Open/2
Career Largest Paycheck: **$540,000/** 1994 TOUR Championship/1

JIM McGOVERN

EXEMPT STATUS: 1993 tournament winner

FULL NAME: James David McGovern

HEIGHT: 6'2"   **WEIGHT:** 195

BIRTH DATE: February 5, 1965

BIRTHPLACE: Teaneck, NJ

RESIDENCE: River Edge, NJ; plays out of Hackensack GC

FAMILY: Wife, Lauren

COLLEGE: Old Dominion

SPECIAL INTERESTS: All sports

TURNED PROFESSIONAL: 1988

Q SCHOOL: 1991

PLAYER PROFILE

CAREER EARNINGS: $1,074,015   **PLAYOFF RECORD:** 1-0

TOUR VICTORIES: 1993 Shell Houston Open.
(TOTAL: 1)

MONEY & POSITION: 1991--$ 88,869--141   1993--$587,495--27   1994--$224,764--79
                          1992--$169,889-- 92

BEST 1994 FINISH: T5--Masters Tournament

1994 SUMMARY: Tournaments entered--30; in money--18; top ten finishes--1.

1995 PGA TOUR CHARITY TEAM COMPETITION: BellSouth Classic

1994 SEASON: Played in 30 tournaments, lowest total of four years on TOUR...acquired "Ironman" label for competing in 101 events first three seasons (34-33-34)...bothered early by ribcage problem first encountered in 1993 at Walt Disney World/Oldsmobile Classic...still had second-best earnings season...had lone top-10 at Masters, T5 for first visit to Augusta National which ensured return engagement this year... followed Masters performance with 11th in MCI Heritage Classic...two weeks combined for more than $104,000 of final total...began campaign by missing three cuts in first five starts, later missed five in row from PGA Championship through B.C. Open...had but 16 sub-70 rounds of 95 played, including none in first five starts...next-to-last event of year, Texas Open, produced first tournament with three rounds in 60s.

CAREER HIGHLIGHTS: "Jersey Kid" captured initial PGA TOUR victory with birdie on second playoff hole of weather-shortened 1993 Shell Houston Open to defeat John Huston...after back-to-back bogeys in final round, hit fairway driver to within three feet for eagle on No. 15, then sank eight-footer for par on final hole to tie Huston...prior to Houston victory, top TOUR finish had been solo fourth in 1992 Federal Express St. Jude Classic...Memphis appearance featured TPC at Southwind record-tying 62 in second round...qualified for first year on TOUR in '91 by finishing second on 1990 Ben Hogan Tour money list...road to Hogan Tour not easy, since failed to earn card at PGA TOUR Qualifying Tournament and gained only alternate spot in Hogan Tour Q-Tournament...victory in Hogan Lake City Classic provided not only first-place check of $20,000 but also exemption into remaining tournaments...played 29 of 30 Hogan Tour events in '90, also winning Texarkana and New Haven Opens...led Hogan Tour in birdies with 292 in 1990.

PERSONAL: First exposed to game when parents bought house adjacent to Hackensack (NJ) Golf Club...because of minimum age restriction, couldn't gain admittance to club until tree knocked down connecting fence during storm, then with brothers hit balls on course until late at night...brother Rob played linebacker in NFL...wife Lauren an attorney.

1994 PGA TOUR STATISTICS

Statistic	Value	Rank
Scoring Average	71.36	(106T)
Driving Distance	265.8	(55T)
Driving Accuracy	69.3	(87T)
Greens in Regulation	66.9	(59T)
Putting	1.826	(154T)
All-Around	603	(58)
Sand Saves	56.3	(37)
Total Driving	142	(41T)
Eagles	7	(44T)
Birdies	292	(61)

MISCELLANEOUS STATISTICS

Statistic	Value	Rank
Scoring Avg. (before cut)	71.62	(110T)
Scoring Avg. (3rd round)	72.47	(168)
Scoring Avg. (4th round)	71.44	(84T)
Birdie Conversion	25.5	(149)
Par Breakers	17.5	(141T)

1994 Low Round: 65: MCI Heritage Classic/2
Career Low Round: 62: 1992 Fed. Ex. St. Jude Classic/2
Career Largest Paycheck: $234,000/1993 Shell Houston Open/1

MARK McNULTY

EXEMPT STATUS: 114th on 1994 money list

FULL NAME: Mark William McNulty

HEIGHT: 5'10"　　　　**WEIGHT:** 158

BIRTH DATE: October 25, 1953

BIRTHPLACE: Bindwa, Zimbabwe

RESIDENCE: Sunningdale, England

FAMILY: Wife, Sue; Matthew, Catharine

SPECIAL INTERESTS: Piano, fine arts, Koi fish, snooker, cars

TURNED PROFESSIONAL: 1977

JOINED TOUR: June 1982, 1994

PLAYER PROFILE

CAREER EARNINGS: $253,465

BEST-EVER FINISH: 4--1982 Danny Thomas Memphis Classic; T4--1982 Sammy Davis Jr. Greater Hartford Open

MONEY & POSITION:

1982--$ 50,322-- 90	1986--$ 6,170--225	1991--$ 34,321--194
1983--$ 40,062--115	1987--$ 4,165--243	1992--$ 46,171--181
1984--$ 5,382--198	1988--$ 39,481--159	1994--$157,700--114
1985--$ 3,600--217	1990--$ 34,375--188	

BEST 1994 FINISHES: T5--NEC World Series of Golf, Texas Open

1994 SUMMARY: Tournaments entered--6; in money--5; top ten finishes--1.

1995 PGA TOUR CHARITY TEAM COMPETITION: B.C. Open

NATIONAL TEAMS: Presidents Cup, 1994; Dunhill Cup, 1993; World Cup, 1993

1994 SEASON: Became special temporary member after finishing T5 in NEC World Series of Golf, worth $76,000…joined TOUR as exempt player by finishing 114th on 1994 money list, position that was cemented by T5 at Texas Open…member of International Team in inaugural Presidents Cup…won (with Fulton Allem) only four-ball match Saturday, halved Friday and lost in Saturday foursomes, lost to Jay Haas in Sunday singles, 4 and 3…missed PLAYERS cut in first U.S. start of '94…in August finished T15 in PGA Championship, 20th next week in Sprint International…World Series placing fashioned in large part by third-round 65 over Firestone CC North Course…World Series earnings counted toward his position among Top 125, but not in terms of establishing final list…captured PGA European Tour's BMW International Open in August, firing course-record 65 on final day to win…was runnerup to Vijay Singh in Scandinavian Masters…finished 13th on PGA European Tour Order of Merit.

CAREER HIGHLIGHTS: Through last season, top PGA TOUR finishes continued to be pair of "celebrity" fourths in 1982, solo in Danny Thomas Memphis Classic and T4 Sammy Davis Jr. Greater Hartford Open…has won 38 events worldwide, including 12 on the European Tour…best European season was 1990, when he won twice and finished second in five starts…two-time runnerup on PGA European Tour Order of Merit (1987 and 1990)…runnerup with Nick Price, representing Zimbabwe, in 1993 World Cup of Golf…Price teammate in annual Dunhill Cup competition.

PERSONAL: Considered one of top short-game players in world…sports trademark Ben Hogan-style cap on course…based in England…grew up playing junior golf with Nick Price…gimpy knee allows him to forecast the weather.

1994 PGA TOUR STATISTICS

Scoring Average	68.82
Driving Distance	270.7
Driving Accuracy	78.1
Greens in Regulation	68.7
Putting	1.751
All-Around	N/R
Sand Saves	65.0
Total Driving	N/R
Eagles	0
Birdies	46

MISCELLANEOUS STATISTICS

Scoring Avg. (before cut)	69.88
Scoring Avg. (3rd round)	67.33
Scoring Avg. (4th round)	70.00
Birdie Conversion	26.6
Par Breakers	18.3

1994 Low Round: 65: 2 times
Career Low Round: 65: 2 times, most recent 1994
Career Largest Texas Open/2
Paycheck: $76,000/1994 NEC World Series of Golf/T5

ROCCO MEDIATE

EXEMPT STATUS: 1993 tournament winner

FULL NAME: Rocco Anthony Mediate

HEIGHT: 6' 1"   **WEIGHT:** 200

BIRTH DATE: December 17, 1962

BIRTHPLACE: Greensburg, PA

RESIDENCE: Ponte Vedra, FL

FAMILY: Wife, Linda; Rocco Vincent (9/19/90), Nicco Anthony (1/29/93)

COLLEGE: Florida Southern

SPECIAL INTERESTS: Photography, music, collecting trading cards

TURNED PROFESSIONAL: 1985

Q SCHOOL: Fall 1985, 1986

PLAYER PROFILE

CAREER EARNINGS: $2,261,620   **PLAYOFF RECORD:** 2-0

TOUR VICTORIES: 1991 Doral-Ryder Open. **1993** Kmart Greater Greensboro Open. (TOTAL: 2)

MONEY & POSITION:

1986--$ 20,670--174	1989--$132,501--108	1992--$301,896-- 49
1987--$112,099-- 91	1990--$240,625-- 62	1993--$680,623-- 16
1988--$129,829-- 92	1991--$597,438-- 15	1994--$ 45,940--193

BEST 1994 FINISH: T9--Northern Telecom Open

1994 SUMMARY: Tournaments entered--6; in money--3; top ten finishes--1.

1995 PGA TOUR CHARITY TEAM COMPETITION: Sprint International

1994 SEASON: Season account reads more like medical chart than playing slate...back trouble flared late in '93 campaign, forcing withdrawal from Las Vegas Invitational and almost causing him to miss TOUR Championship...problem, diagnosed as two herniated discs in lower back, reared ugly head again in January...after 24th at season-opening Mercedes Championships and T9 in Northern Telecom (featuring final-round 65), was forced to withdraw from Phoenix Open...tried again next week, pulling out after two rounds of AT&T Pebble Beach National Pro-Am...began aggressive rehab program...subsequently diagnosed in April with fragmented disc...persisted in efforts to play, finishing T38 in Buick Classic, then withdrawing after three rounds of U.S. Open...underwent surgery for removal of fragmented disc on July 12...returned to aggressive rehab, was swinging club again by late October, and returned to action at JCPenney Classic.

CAREER HIGHLIGHTS: Captured second TOUR title in April 1993, birdieing fourth playoff hole to defeat Steve Elkington and win Kmart Greater Greensboro Open... both career victories earned via playoff route...GGO triumph climaxed five-tournament string that featured four top-10 finishes...had finished ninth at Forest Oaks CC in 1992...earned first TOUR title in sixth season...Doral-Ryder Open victory on Blue Monster course came in playoff with Curtis Strange...caught Strange with birdies on 17th and 18th holes...sank 10-footers on each green...captured playoff and $252,000 winner's check by making five-foot birdie putt on first extra hole after Curtis missed 15-foot attempt...got out of blocks in spectacular fashion in '91, posting six top-10 finishes in first seven starts...winner 1992 Perrier French Open.

PERSONAL: Was using long putter before back problems began...in fact, was first to win PGA TOUR event using elongated putter... has said he's well ahead of game in terms of getting ready for Senior TOUR...grew up in Greensburg, PA, not far from Latrobe home of Arnold Palmer...played golf with Palmer for first time at age 19...attended California (PA) State College before transferring to Florida Southern.

1994 PGA TOUR STATISTICS

Scoring Average	71.64
Driving Distance	263.4
Driving Accuracy	67.5
Greens in Regulation	67.6
Putting	1.831
All-Around	–
Sand Saves	41.4
Total Driving	–
Eagles	1
Birdies	62

MISCELLANEOUS STATISTICS

Scoring Avg. (before cut)	71.73
Scoring Avg. (3rd round)	73.00
Scoring Avg. (4th round)	69.33
Birdie Conversion	28.3
Par Breakers	19.4

1994 Low Round: 65: Northern Telecom Open/4
Career Low Round: 63: 2 times, most recent 1991
Career Largest Paycheck: $270,000/1993 Kmart GG Open/1

PHIL MICKELSON

EXEMPT STATUS: 1994 tournament winner

FULL NAME: Phil A. Mickelson

HEIGHT: 6' 2"   **WEIGHT:** 190

BIRTH DATE: June 16, 1970

BIRTHPLACE: San Diego, CA

RESIDENCE: Scottsdale, AZ; plays out of Grayhawk GC

FAMILY: Single

COLLEGE: Arizona State University

SPECIAL INTERESTS: Snow and water skiing

JOINED TOUR: June 1992

PLAYER PROFILE

CAREER MONEY: $ 1,548,764   **PLAYOFF RECORD:** 1-0

TOUR VICTORIES: **1991** Northern Telecom Open. **1993** Buick Invitational of California,
(TOTAL: 4)   The International. **1994** Mercedes Championships

MONEY & POSITION: 1992--$171,713 --90   1993--$628,735--22   1994--$748,316--15

BEST 1994 FINISHES: 1--Mercedes Championships; 3--Buick Invitational of California, PGA Championship; T3--Las Vegas Invitational; T4--Kemper Open; 8--Southwestern Bell Colonial; T8--Phoenix Open; T9--Northern Telecom Open; T10--Sprint International.

1994 SUMMARY: Tournaments entered--18; in money--17; top ten finishes--9.

1995 PGA TOUR CHARITY TEAM COMPETITION: Sprint International

NATIONAL TEAMS: Walker Cup, 1989,1991; Presidents Cup, 1994.

1994 SEASON: Was well on way to spectacular season before March skiing accident.. .suffered fractured left femur and hairline fracture of right ankle March 3 at Arizona Snow Bowl...expected to carry rod in femur for 18 months...had four top-10s in six starts prior to ski slope spill, including fourth TOUR title with playoff victory over Fred Couples in season-opening Mercedes Championships...had third-place finish in hometown Buick Invitational of California, featuring final-round 64, week prior to accident...returned to action end of May, much earlier than expected...finished eighth in Southwestern Bell Colonial (final-round 65) and T4 very next week in Kemper Open...recorded first TOUR hole-in-one at Kemper...had back-to-back top-10s in August, 3rd PGA Championship and 10th Sprint International...Captain's Choice for U.S. Team in inaugural Presidents Cup...final-round 63, matching career low, boosted him to T3 in Las Vegas Invitational.

CAREER HIGHLIGHTS: Earned second and third titles in just second year as TOUR member in 1993...wins also his initial two as professional, since first came as amateur in 1991...playing before home crowd, captured Buick Invitational of California after opening with 75 (highest first round for winner in '93)...closed with 65, good for four-shot win over Dave Rummells...followed T6 in PGA Championship with second victory of campaign, an eight-point win over Mark Calcavecchia worth $234,000 (largest check of career)...turned professional at 1992 U.S. Open...finished second in third professional start at New England Classic worth $108,000...while still playing for Arizona State, captured 1991 Northern Telecom Open by one stroke over Bob Tway and Tom Purtzer...winner 1989-90-92 NCAA Championships for ASU...won 1990 U.S. Amateur, only lefthander to do so...became only player other than Jack Nicklaus to win NCAA and U.S. Amateur titles in same year...one of four collegians (Ben Crenshaw, Curtis Strange, Billy Ray Brown) to win NCAA title in freshman year.

PERSONAL: Four-time first-team All-America 1989-92 (only Gary Hallberg and David Duval have achieved same status)...winner 1990-92 Fred Haskins and Jack Nicklaus Awards as collegiate player of year...1991 Golf World Amateur Player of Year...1989, '91 Walker Cupper...low amateur 1990-91 U.S. Opens, 1991 Masters...Golf Magazine Junior Player of Year 1986-88...righthanded in everything but golf (when father started him in game, became mirror-image process).

1994 PGA TOUR STATISTICS

Scoring Average	69.66	(8)
Driving Distance	273.7	(15)
Driving Accuracy	63.0	(155)
Greens in Regulation	68.1	(40T)
Putting	1.744	(4T)
All-Around	397	(19)
Sand Saves	54.9	(45T)
Total Driving	170	(74T)
Eagles	8	(28T)
Birdies	262	(102T)

MISCELLANEOUS STATISTICS

Scoring Avg. (before cut)	69.48	(2)
Scoring Avg. (3rd round)	70.81	(75)
Scoring Avg. (4th round)	69.69	(3)
Birdie Conversion	32.9	(3)
Par Breakers	23.1	(2)

1994 Low Round: 63: Las Vegas Invitational/5
Career Low Round: 63: 2 times, most recent
Career Largest 1994 Las Vegas Invitational/5
Paycheck: $234,000/1993 International/1

JOHNNY MILLER

EXEMPT STATUS: 1994 tournament winner

FULL NAME: John Laurence Miller

HEIGHT: 6'2"   **WEIGHT:** 180

BIRTH DATE: April 29, 1947

BIRTHPLACE: San Francisco, CA

RESIDENCE: Napa, CA

FAMILY: Wife, Linda Strauss; John S. (6/2/70), Kelly (12/26/72), Casy (7/30/74), Scott (5/12/76), Brent (2/3/78), Todd (1/22/80)

COLLEGE: Brigham Young (Physical Education, 1969)

SPECIAL INTERESTS: Fishing, church activities, course architecture, golf club design, television work

TURNED PROFESSIONAL: 1969 **JOINED TOUR:** Spring 1969

PLAYER PROFILE

CAREER EARNINGS: $2,746,424   **PLAYOFF RECORD:** 1-5

TOUR VICTORIES: **1971** Southern Open. **1972** Heritage Classic. **1973** U.S. Open. **1974** Bing Crosby Pro-
(TOTAL: 24) Am, Phoenix Open, Dean Martin-Tucson Open, Heritage Classic, Tournament of Champions, Westchester Classic, World Open, Kaiser International. **1975** Phoenix Open, Dean Martin Tucson Open, Bob Hope Desert Classic, Kaiser International. **1976** NBC Tucson Open, Bob Hope Desert Classic. **1980** Jackie Gleason Inverarry Classic. **1981** Joe Garagiola Tucson Open, Glen Campbell Los Angeles Open. **1982** Wickes Andy Williams San Diego Open. **1983** Honda Inverrary Classic. **1987** AT&T Pebble Beach National Pro-Am. **1994** AT&T Pebble Beach National Pro-Am.

MONEY & POSITION:

1969--$ 8,364--135	1978--$ 17,740--111	1987--$139,398-- 78
1970--$ 52,391-- 40	1979--$ --	1988--$ 31,989--169
1971--$ 91,081-- 18	1980--$127,117-- 30	1989--$ 66,171--150
1972--$ 99,348-- 17	1981--$193,167-- 12	1990--$ 8,900--235
1973--$127,833-- 9	1982--$169,065-- 20	1991--$ 2,864--269
1974--$353,021-- 1	1983--$230,186-- 14	1992--$ 4,321--269
1975--$226,118-- 2	1984--$139,422-- 47	1993--$ --
1976--$135,887-- 14	1985--$126,616-- 64	1994--$225,000-- 81
1977--$ 61,025-- 48	1986--$ 71,444--118	

BEST 1994 FINISH: 1--AT&T Pebble Beach National Pro-Am.

1994 SUMMARY: Tournaments entered--4; in money--1; top ten finishes--1.

NATIONAL TEAMS: Ryder Cup (2), 1975, 1981; World Cup (3), 1973, 1975, 1980, (individual winner in 1973 and 1975).

1994 SEASON: One of the real cinderella stories of '94…made first start since 1993 AT&T Pebble Beach National Pro-Am a winning one at Pebble…moved into contention with third-round 67, one stroke behind leader Dudley Hart at 9-under-par 207, then held on in face of his own closing 74 to win for first time since 1987 AT&T…battle to wire almost flashback to another era, with Tom Watson one of main contenders…victory produced largest golf payday of career…with four starts in '94, marked first time since 1989 he had appeared more than twice in year…last time appeared in double figures 1989 (11), just 13 in 1988…since 1990 had played in just six events total over four-year span prior to '94…bad knees and television commitments caused drastic cutback in number of appearances over that period, all of which served to make Pebble Beach win that much more incredible…previous cut made came in 1992 Northern Telecom Open (T67)…withdrew from Doral-Ryder Open after first round and missed cuts at Masters and U.S. Open in three other starts.

CAREER HIGHLIGHTS: 1994 AT&T Pebble Beach National Pro-Am marked 24th PGA TOUR title…also captured 1976 British Open crown, one of two majors…claimed 1973 U.S. Open at Oakmont, winning by five strokes over John Schlee, after a final-round 63…enjoyed lion's share of success on West Coast, winning 13 events in California and Arizona, including four times (1974-76 and 1981) in Tucson…last year's Pebble Beach win came 20 years after his first there; in between was 1987 Pebble victory, his last career triumph prior to '94…first TOUR victory was in 1971 Southern Open…ranks fifth on all-time list with eight victories in single season (1974)…with winning defense of 1975 Tucson Open title, was last to successfully defend title after winning (Phoenix Open) week before until David Frost did so at 1993 Hardee's Golf Classic week after capturing Canadian Open…winner 1983 Chrysler Team Championship (with Jack Nicklaus)…winner 1974 Dunlop Phoenix (Japan) and 1979 Lancome Trophy…member 1975 and 1981 Ryder Cup teams, 1973-75-80 World Cup teams (individual winner 1973 and 1975)…1974 PGA Player of Year.

PERSONAL: NBC-TV golf analyst …known for sharp insight and candor…winner 1964 U.S. Junior.

1994 PGA TOUR STATISTICS

Scoring Average	72.17
Driving Distance	248.6
Driving Accuracy	64.8
Greens in Regulation	59.9
Putting	1.876
All-Around	N/R
Sand Saves	23.1
Total Driving	N/R
Eagles	0
Birdies	23

MISCELLANEOUS STATISTICS

Scoring Avg. (before cut)	75.71
Scoring Avg. (3rd round)	67.00
Scoring Avg. (4th round)	74.00
Birdie Conversion	23.7
Par Breakers	14.2

1994 Low Round: 67: AT&T Pebble Beach/3
Career Low Round: 61: 2 times, most recent 1975 Tucson Open/4
Career Largest Paycheck: $225,000/1994 AT&T Pebble Beach/1

116

LARRY MIZE

EXEMPT STATUS: Winner 1987 Masters Tournament

FULL NAME: Larry Hogan Mize

HEIGHT: 6'   **WEIGHT:** 165

BIRTH DATE: Sept. 23, 1958

BIRTHPLACE: Augusta, GA

RESIDENCE: Columbus, GA

FAMILY: Wife, Bonnie; David (4/17/86), Patrick (2/12/89), Robert (4/2/93)

COLLEGE: Georgia Tech

SPECIAL INTERESTS: Fishing, all sports

TURNED PROFESSIONAL: 1980

Q SCHOOL: Fall 1981

PLAYER PROFILE

CAREER EARNINGS: $4,294,710   **PLAYOFF RECORD:** 1-2

TOUR VICTORIES: 1983 Danny Thomas-Memphis Classic. **1987** Masters. **1993** Northern Telecom Open, (TOTAL: 4)   Buick Open

MONEY & POSITION:

1982--$ 28,787--124	1987--$561,407-- 6	1992--$316,428--47
1983--$146,325-- 35	1988--$187,823--62	1993--$724,660--13
1984--$172,513-- 36	1989--$278,388--45	1994--$386,029--42
1985--$231,041-- 17	1990--$668,198--14	
1986--$314,051-- 17	1991--$279,061--60	

BEST 1994 FINISHES: 3--Masters; 5--Nestle Invitational; T7--Buick Southern open; T9--MCI Heritage Classic.

1994 SUMMARY: Tournaments entered--22; in money--17; top ten finishes--4.

1995 PGA TOUR CHARITY TEAM COMPETITION: Phoenix Open

NATIONAL TEAMS: Ryder Cup, 1987.

1994 SEASON: Fell off somewhat from career year in 1993, still finished with fourth-best earnings campaign of 13 on TOUR...withdrew from season-opening Mercedes Championship, missed cut in defense of Northern Telecom Open title two weeks later, then finished no better than T40 in next three starts...underwent arthroscopic surgery March 8 for left knee pain first encountered at 1993 Walt Disney World/Oldsmobile Classic...was back in action one week later, finishing surprising fifth at Nestle Invitational...top finish solo third at Masters, site of greatest victory in 1987...returned to TOUR next week with T9 in MCI Heritage Classic, fashioned by final-round 65...although missed cut in U.S. Open, enjoyed success in all other majors: T11 British Open, T15 PGA Championship...final of four top-10s came in Buick Southern Open (T7), near hometown of Columbus, GA.

CAREER HIGHLIGHTS: Captured two titles in season for first time in 1993, winning Northern Telecom and Buick Opens...those victories his first since 1987 Masters...gained final-round lead at Tucson National when 54-hole co-leaders Dudley Hart and Phil Mickelson faltered, then held off Jeff Maggert for third career win...came from four strokes off Fuzzy Zoeller's third-round lead to claim Buick Open...played just three tournaments in two months preceding Buick event, missing cut in each and taking July away from TOUR entirely...probably best known for "impossible" shot which captured Masters...finished regulation tied with Greg Norman and Seve Ballesteros after birdieing final hole...after Ballesteros went out on first playoff hole, used sand wedge to sink 140-foot chip from right of green on second extra hole...first victory was in 1983 Danny Thomas-Memphis Classic, where sank 25-foot birdie putt to edge Zoeller, Sammy Rachels and Chip Beck... lost playoff to Norman in 1986 Kemper Open, Payne Stewart in 1990 MCI Heritage Classic...winner 1993 Johnnie Walker World Championships (and $550,000) as last alternate in field of Jamaica event...winner 1988 Casio World Open, 1989-90 Dunlop Phoenix (Japan)...member 1987 Ryder Cup team.

PERSONAL: Plays somewhat limited schedule each year, preferring to keep large measure of focus on young family...Player Director, PGA TOUR Policy Board 1988-90...winner Atlanta Amateur Championship ...played No. 1 three years at Georgia Tech, captain for two.

1994 PGA TOUR STATISTICS

Scoring Average	70.49	(35)
Driving Distance	256.9	(129)
Driving Accuracy	78.8	(5)
Greens in Regulation	65.9	(86T)
Putting	1.766	(19T)
All-Around	651	(75)
Sand Saves	49.3	(120)
Total Driving	134	(35)
Eagles	1	(167T)
Birdies	272	(90)

MISCELLANEOUS STATISTICS

Scoring Avg. (before cut)	70.61	(29)
Scoring Avg. (3rd round)	71.33	(113T)
Scoring Avg. (4th round)	71.44	(84T)
Birdie Conversion	30.6	(19)
Par Breakers	20.2	(34T)

1994 Low Round:	65: 2 times
Career Low Round:	64: 7 times, most recent 1993 Buick Open/1
Career Largest Paycheck:	$198,000/1993 Northern Telecom Open/1

YOSHI MIZUMAKI

EXEMPT STATUS: 107th on 1994 money list

FULL NAME: Yoshinori Mizumaki

HEIGHT: 5'11"   **WEIGHT:** 170

BIRTH DATE: August 27, 1958

BIRTHPLACE: Tokyo, Japan

RESIDENCE: Tokyo, Japan

FAMILY: Wife, Jumko; Kento

COLLEGE: Hosel University (Japan)

TURNED PROFESSIONAL: 1985

Q SCHOOL: 1993

PLAYER PROFILE

CAREER EARNINGS: $168,450   **PLAYOFF RECORD:** 0-1

BEST-EVER FINISH: T2--1994 GTE Byron Nelson Classic

MONEY & POSITION: 1993--$1,718--321   1994--$168,450--107

BEST 1994 FINISHES: T2--GTE Byron Nelson Classic; T10--Anheuser-Busch Golf Classic

1994 SUMMARY: Tournaments entered--18; in money--13; top ten finishes--2.

1995 PGA TOUR CHARITY TEAM COMPETITION: BellSouth Classic

1994 SEASON: Although did not play any TOUR events after Aug. 21, still managed to earn enough in 18 tournaments to retain playing privileges…main contributor to cause was GTE Byron Nelson, where consecutive 66s in weather-shortened event got him into six-man playoff won by Neal Lancaster…had a chance to win on last hole, but missed birdie putt…five-way tie for second worth $72,000…made $18,180 following week for T19 at The Memorial…second and last top-10, T10 at Anheuser-Busch Golf Classic, helped push him over top in terms of retaining card…began first full TOUR season by making cut in three of first four starts, then missing three in row…didn't miss again, earning money in 10 consecutive events, until final start of '94 at the Sprint International…pair of 66s at Byron Nelson matched low round of season, a final-round 66 at Nissan Los Angeles Open.

CAREER HIGHLIGHTS: Earned PGA TOUR privileges by finishing T11 in 1993 Qualifying Tournament…played in first TOUR event early that year, posting T83 in Buick Invitational of California… missed cut in only other TOUR event in '93, Nissan Los Angeles Open…placed T27 in 1993 British Open…winner of 1993 JCB Sendai Classic on Japan PGA TOUR…deadlocked at end of regulation with Hajime Meshiai and Tsukasa Watanabe, latter eliminated on 73rd hole…10-foot birdie putt on sixth extra hole brought victory over Meshiai…later in season finished second to Greg Norman in Sumitomo Visa Taiheyo Masters, stroke ahead of third-place trio of David Frost, Barry Lane and Jumbo Ozaki.

1994 PGA TOUR STATISTICS

Statistic	Value	Rank
Scoring Average	70.95	(61)
Driving Distance	252.4	(157)
Driving Accuracy	71.1	(61T)
Greens in Regulation	65.2	(108T)
Putting	1.778	(45T)
All-Around	722	(99)
Sand Saves	53.5	(66T)
Total Driving	218	(139T)
Eagles	6	(64T)
Birdies	196	(160T)

MISCELLANEOUS STATISTICS

Statistic	Value	Rank
Scoring Avg. (before cut)	71.29	(74T)
Scoring Avg. (3rd round)	71.38	(119T)
Scoring Avg. (4th round)	70.54	(28)
Birdie Conversion	27.4	(120)
Par Breakers	18.4	(110T)

1994 Low Round: **66:** 3 times

Career Low Round: 66: 3 times, most recent 1994 GTE Byron Nelson Classic/2

Career Largest Paycheck: $72,000/1994 GTE Byron Nelson/T2

GIL MORGAN

EXEMPT STATUS: 54th on 1994 money list

FULL NAME: Gilmer Bryan Morgan

HEIGHT: 5' 9"   **WEIGHT:** 175

BIRTH DATE: Sept. 25, 1946

BIRTHPLACE: Wewoka, OK

RESIDENCE: Oak Tree Golf Club, Edmond, OK

FAMILY: Wife, Jeanine; Molly (5/18/81), Maggie (8/10/82), Melanie (9/24/84)

COLLEGE: East Central State College (1968, B.S.), Southern College of Optometry (1972, Doctor of Optometry)

SPECIAL INTERESTS: Cars

TURNED PROFESSIONAL: 1972

Q SCHOOL: Fall 1973

PLAYER PROFILE

CAREER EARNINGS: $4,735,868   **PLAYOFF RECORD:** 3-4

TOUR VICTORIES: **1977** B.C. Open. **1978** Glen Campbell-Los Angeles Open, World Series of Golf.
(TOTAL: 7) **1979** Danny Thomas-Memphis Classic. **1983** Joe Garagiola-Tucson Open, Glen Campbell-Los Angeles Open. **1990** Kemper Open.

MONEY & POSITION:

1973--$ 3,800--204	1981--$171,184--18	1989--$300,395--39
1974--$ 23,880-- 94	1982--$139,652--26	1990--$702,629--11
1975--$ 42,772-- 60	1983--$306,133-- 5	1991--$232,913--70
1976--$ 61,372-- 42	1984--$281,948--13	1992--$272,959--56
1977--$104,817-- 24	1985--$133,941--62	1993--$610,312--24
1978--$267,459-- 2	1986--$ 98,770--84	1994--$309,690--54
1979--$115,857-- 29	1987--$133,980--81	
1980--$135,308-- 28	1988--$288,002--34	

BEST 1994 FINISHES: 2--Texas Open; T7--Shell Houston Open; T10--FeEx St. Jude Classic.

1994 SUMMARY: Tournaments entered--18; in money--14; top ten finishes--3.

1995 PGA TOUR CHARITY TEAM COMPETITION: Texas Open

NATIONAL TEAMS: Ryder Cup (2), 1979, 1983.

1994 SEASON: Bothered first half of season by ribcage problem which contributed to four missed cuts and as many missed starts...after being unable to answer starting bell in February, laid off entire month of March and returned with missed cut at Masters...seemingly returned to form with T12 at Kmart Greater Greensboro Open, followed by T7 in Shell Houston Open...problem persisted, causing him to miss two May starts and then three cuts concluding with U.S. Open...from that point forward returned to playing form, collecting two top-10s and four additional top-25s without missing a cut in final nine starts...posted T10 in FedEx St. Jude Classic and solo second in Texas Open...moved into contention at Oak Hills with third-round 65...battled to wire final day with Bob Estes, who began Sunday play with four-stroke lead that ultimately narrowed to one...Texas Open payday, along with T16 in following week's Las Vegas Invitational, pushed him over $300,000 mark for fifth time in 21-year career.

CAREER HIGHLIGHTS: Nine top-10 finishes in 1993 contributed to second-best campaign of career...had leg up on one of great U.S. Opens of all time in 1992...became first to reach 10-under-par in Open early in Round 3, then climbed to 12-under through 43 holes before falling to eventual T13...handled tournament adversity and post-Open followup head-on and with dignity...biggest victory came in 1978 World Series of Golf...defeated Hubert Green in playoff to emerge year's No. 2 money winner behind Tom Watson...had left shoulder rotator cuff surgery in September 1986...after nine-month layoff returned to TOUR in early May 1987 and was near top of game by midsummer...enjoyed most successful year in 1990...captured Kemper Open in early June, first victory since 1983 and seventh career...finished in top eight in seven straight tournaments...won first two events of '83, Joe Garagiola-Tucson Open in playoff with Lanny Wadkins and Glen Campbell-Los Angeles Open.

PERSONAL: Holds Doctor of Optometry Degree (1972) from Southern College of Optometry, but has never practiced...during junior year at East Central State (OK) decided to pursue career in golf, but waited until earned doctor's degree before turning professional...named to NAIA Hall of Fame 1982.

1994 PGA TOUR STATISTICS

Scoring Average	69.96	(15)
Driving Distance	266.0	(53T)
Driving Accuracy	77.2	(14)
Greens in Regulation	70.3	(15T)
Putting	1.763	(14T)
All-Around	423	(21)
Sand Saves	43.3	(165T)
Total Driving	67	(6)
Eagles	9	(17T)
Birdies	231	(130)

MISCELLANEOUS STATISTICS

Scoring Avg. (before cut)	70.41	(22)
Scoring Avg. (3rd round)	69.07	(4)
Scoring Avg. (4th round)	70.29	(16)
Birdie Conversion	28.1	(16T)
Par Breakers	20.5	(29)

1994 Low Round: **63:** FedEx St. Jude/3
Career Low Round: 63: 3 times, most recent
Career Largest 1994 FedEx St. Jude/3
Paycheck: $180,000/1990 Kemper Open/1

JOHN MORSE

EXEMPT STATUS: 122nd on 1994 money list

FULL NAME: John Paul Morse

HEIGHT: 5' 10"   **WEIGHT:** 180

BIRTH DATE: February 16, 1958

BIRTHPLACE: Marshall, MI

RESIDENCE: Casselberry, FL; plays out of Marshall (MI) CC

FAMILY: Wife, Kelly; Christina (7/31/92)

COLLEGE: University of Michigan

SPECIAL INTERESTS: Fishing

TURNED PROFESSIONAL: 1981

JOINED TOUR: 1994

PLAYER PROFILE

CAREER MONEY: $146,137

BEST CAREER FINISH: T6--1994 Kmart Greater Greensboro Open

MONEY & POSITION: 1994--$146,137--122

BEST 1994 FINISH: T6--Kmart Greater Greensboro Open.

1994 SUMMARY: Tournaments entered--26; in money--12; top ten finishes--1

1995 PGA TOUR CHARITY TEAM COMPETITION: Honda Classic

1994 SEASON: Made biggest mark over first five months of campaign, struggled remainder of way...earned virtually enough money Jan.-May to retain playing privileges...had amassed $128,520 through BellSouth Classic (May 8), just $17,617 rest of season...missed 12 cuts his last 16 starts...opened year with T14 United Airlines Hawaiian Open...best stretch Freeport-McMoRan Classic (T12), Kmart Greater Greensboro Open (T6, only top-10 of season), T16 Shell Houston Open...at GGO was in second-place tie after 54 holes, four strokes off lead of eventual winner Mike Springer...carded final-round 73 to earn biggest check of year, $52,125...only one of 12 final rounds, 67 at Northern Telecom Open, was below 70.

CAREER HIGHLIGHTS: Qualified for TOUR in 1994 by finishing fifth on 1993 NIKE TOUR money list...winner of '93 NIKE New England Classic...year also featured pair of consecutive T2 finishes (New Mexico and Wichita), followed by T3 at Texarkana last three weeks of August...also had T3 at Hawkeye Open...played Australasian Tour from 1989-92...returned to Australia following conclusion of '93 NIKE TOUR for select events...winner of 1990 Australian Open in playoff with Craig Parry...that victory provided spot in 1991 NEC World Series of Golf, where T27 brought check for $9,116 (only PGA TOUR payday prior to 1994)...missed cuts in 1984 and 1987 U.S. Opens, as well as four previous PGA TOUR events...winner of 1989 Quebec Open, 1990 Monro Interiors Nedlands Masters, 1991 Air New Zealand Shell Open.

PERSONAL: Very much enjoyed Australian experience, plans to play "down under" whenever possible...decision to play 1993 NIKE TOUR rather than in Australia based on birth of daughter Christina...failed six times to earn playing card at Qualifying Tournament...all-conference high school basketball selection.

1994 PGA TOUR STATISTICS

Scoring Average	71.27	(94)
Driving Distance	250.9	(161T)
Driving Accuracy	75.0	(29T)
Greens in Regulation	66.7	(65T)
Putting	1.811	(130T)
All-Around	787	(121)
Sand Saves	54.5	(51T)
Total Driving	190	(109T)
Eagles	3	(126T)
Birdies	230	(131T)

MISCELLANEOUS STATISTICS

Scoring Avg. (before cut)	71.81	(128T)
Scoring Avg. (3rd round)	70.50	(57T)
Scoring Avg. (4th round)	71.67	(102T)
Birdie Conversion	25.2	(154)
Par Breakers	17.0	(151T)

1994 Low Round: 67: 4 times

Career Low Round: 67: 4 times, most recent

Career Largest   '94 WDW/Oldsmobile/1

Paycheck: $52,125/94 Kmart GGO/T6

JODIE MUDD

EXEMPT STATUS: Winner, 1990 THE PLAYERS Championship

FULL NAME: Joseph Martin Mudd

HEIGHT: 5' 11"   **WEIGHT:** 150

BIRTH DATE: April 23, 1960

BIRTHPLACE: Louisville, KY

RESIDENCE: Louisville, KY

FAMILY: Single

COLLEGE: Georgia Southern University

SPECIAL INTERESTS: Thoroughbred racing, outdoors

TURNED PROFESSIONAL: 1982

JOINED TOUR: April 1982

PLAYER PROFILE

CAREER EARNINGS: $2,763,755   **PLAYOFF RECORD:** 2-2

TOUR VICTORIES: **1988** Federal Express St. Jude Classic. **1989** GTE Byron Nelson Golf Classic. **1990**
(TOTAL: 4)   THE PLAYERS Championship, Nabisco Championships.

MONEY & POSITION:

1982--$ 34,216--114	1987--$203,923-- 51	1992--$ 88,081--141
1983--$ 21,515--145	1988--$422,022-- 23	1993--$ 89,366--150
1984--$ 42,244--114	1989--$404,860-- 26	1994--$ 27,868--214
1985--$186,648-- 34	1990--$911,746-- 5	
1986--$182,812-- 48	1991--$148,453--102	

BEST 1994 FINISH: T32--FedEx St. Jude Classic.

1994 SUMMARY: Tournaments entered--15; in money--7; top ten finishes--0.

1995 PGA TOUR CHARITY TEAM COMPETITION: FedEx St. Jude Classic

NATIONAL TEAMS: World Cup, 1990; Four Tours World Championship of Golf, 1990; Walker Cup, 1981.

1994 SEASON: Continued to be part-time player…made no appearances in June and August, just one in April and May… earnings total lowest since second year on TOUR…money-list placing lowest ever…failed to achieve top-10 finish for first time since 1984…best finish T32 in FedEx St. Jude Classic, where fired final-round 66…after beginning season with three missed cuts, carded pair of 66s to open Bob Hope Chrysler Classic…finished 71-76-73 for T58…carded first-round 69 in THE PLAYERS Championship, event he won in 1990…followed with second-round 78 to miss cut…finished year with rounds of 67-69-70-68-71 in Las Vegas Invitational (T39).

CAREER HIGHLIGHTS: Enjoyed finest season in 1990, when won twice and finished fifth on money list with earnings over $900,000…'90 victories came in THE PLAYERS and Nabisco Championships, TOUR's two richest events…earned 10-year exemption in THE PLAYERS, battling Mark Calcavecchia and making clutch birdie on treacherous 17th at TPC at Sawgrass…in Nabisco Championships birdied last two holes, then birdied first playoff hole to defeat Billy Mayfair and earn $450,000 first-place check…trailed off in '91, collecting three top-10 finishes, including T7 at Masters and T8 in next start at BellSouth Atlanta Classic…joined TOUR week after finishing low amateur in '82 Masters…two weeks later tied for fifth at USF&G Classic, earning over $10,000…member 1981 Walker Cup, 1990 World Cup, 1990 Four Tours World Championship of Golf teams.

PERSONAL: Raises thoroughbreds in Kentucky…three-time All-America at Georgia Southern…U.S. Public Links champion 1980-81…winner 1981 Sunnehanna Amateur.

1994 PGA TOUR STATISTICS

Scoring Average	71.90
Driving Distance	271.8
Driving Accuracy	67.0
Greens in Regulation	64.6
Putting	1.793
All-Around	–
Sand Saves	61.3
Total Driving	–
Eagles	4
Birdies	150

MISCELLANEOUS STATISTICS

Scoring Avg. (before cut)	71.63
Scoring Avg. (3rd round)	71.57
Scoring Avg. (4th round)	71.71
Birdie Conversion	28.0
Par Breakers	18.6

1994 Low Round: 66: 3 times
Career Low Round: 63: 1986 Bob Hope Chrysler Classic/3
Career Largest Paycheck: $450,000/1990 Nabisco Championships/1

LARRY NELSON

EXEMPT STATUS: Winner, 1987 PGA Championship

FULL NAME: Larry Gene Nelson

HEIGHT: 5' 9"   **WEIGHT:** 150

BIRTH DATE: Sept. 10, 1947

BIRTHPLACE: Ft. Payne, AL

RESIDENCE: Marietta, GA; plays out of Centennial

FAMILY: Wife, Gayle; Drew (10/7/76), Josh (9/28/78)

COLLEGE: Kennesaw Junior College (1970)

SPECIAL INTERESTS: Golf course architecture, snow skiing

TURNED PROFESSIONAL: 1971

Q SCHOOL: Fall 1973

PLAYER PROFILE

CAREER EARNINGS: $3,273,248   **PLAYOFF RECORD:** 2-2

TOUR VICTORIES: 1979 Jackie Gleason-Inverrary Classic, Western Open. **1980** Atlanta Classic. **1981**
(TOTAL: 10)   Greater Greensboro Open, PGA Championship. **1983** U.S. Open. **1984** Walt Disney
World Golf Classic. **1987** PGA Championship, Walt Disney World/Oldsmobile Classic.
1988 Georgia-Pacific Atlanta Classic.

MONEY & POSITION:

1974--$ 24,022--93	1981--$193,342--10	1988--$411,284-- 25
1975--$ 39,810--66	1982--$159,134--21	1989--$186,869-- 79
1976--$ 66,482--41	1983--$138,368--40	1990--$124,260--124
1977--$ 99,876--26	1984--$154,689--42	1991--$160,543-- 96
1978--$ 65,686--45	1985--$143,993--54	1992--$ 94,930--135
1979--$281,022-- 2	1986--$124,338--69	1993--$ 54,870--177
1980--$182,715--11	1987--$501,292--14	1994--$ 66,831--175

BEST 1994 FINISH: T10--Doral-Ryder Open

1994 SUMMARY: Tournaments entered--17; in money--8; top ten finishes--1.

NATIONAL TEAMS: Ryder Cup (3) 1979, 1981, 1987.

1994 SEASON: Showed flash of old brilliance in March, when was midpoint leader after second-round 64 in Doral-Ryder Open...137 total good for one-stroke lead over Dick Mast, Billy Andrade and eventual winner John Huston...continued in contention after three rounds, two strokes behind Andrade, before finishing T10 after closing 76...made cuts in next five starts, although no placing higher than T55 over that stretch...closed year by missing cuts in seven of last eight starts, final six in a row...Doral placing first top-10 since T7 at Doral in 1992...continued to play limited schedule, with focus primarily on Southeast...17 starts two more than made in 1993...money-won total lowest since 1978, his fifth year on TOUR, and fifth-lowest of 20-year career.

CAREER HIGHLIGHTS: With exception of 1979 Western Open and 1983 U.S. Open, all career victories achieved in Southeastern U.S.–four in Florida (including 1987 PGA Championship at PGA National), three Georgia (including 1981 PGA at Atlanta Athletic Club) and one North Carolina...finest year on TOUR '87, when won PGA Championship in playoff with Lanny Wadkins at Palm Beach Gardens...later in year captured second Walt Disney World/Oldsmobile Classic en route to earnings of over $500,000 for only time in career...made just 16 starts in 1991, with three top-10 finishes...fired final-round 68 at Hazeltine National to finish T3, just three strokes out of Payne Stewart-Scott Simpson U.S. Open playoff...tied with Robert Gamez for third-round lead at Buick Southern Open, then recorded final-round 72 and T3 finish as David Peoples won by three strokes...member 1979-81-87 Ryder Cup teams...winner 1980 Tokai Classic, 1983 Dunlop International, 1989 Suntory Open, all Japan.

PERSONAL: Former Player Director, PGA TOUR Policy Board...didn't start playing golf until after returning from military service in Japan...broke 100 the first time he ever played.

1994 PGA TOUR STATISTICS

Scoring Average	72.40	(N/R)
Driving Distance	261.0	(N/R)
Driving Accuracy	69.8	(N/R)
Greens in Regulation	64.7	(N/R)
Putting	1.822	(N/R)
All-Around	1,038	(N/R)
Sand Saves	45.9	(N/R)
Total Driving	177	(N/R)
Eagles	4	(N/R)
Birdies	164	(N/R)

MISCELLANEOUS STATISTICS

Scoring Avg. (before cut)	72.32	(N/R)
Scoring Avg. (3rd round)	72.22	(N/R)
Scoring Avg. (4th round)	74.56	(N/R)
Birdie Conversion	25.6	(N/R)
Par Breakers	17.0	(N/R)

1994 Low Round: 64: Doral Ryder Open/2

Career Low Round: 63: 5 times, most recent '89

Career Largest GTE Byron Nelson Classic/1

Paycheck: $150,000/1987 PGA Championship/1

JACK NICKLAUS

EXEMPT STATUS: Winner, 1962 United States Open

FULL NAME: Jack William Nicklaus

HEIGHT: 5' 11"   **WEIGHT:** 190

BIRTH DATE: Jan. 21, 1940

BIRTHPLACE: Columbus, OH

RESIDENCE: North Palm Beach, FL, and Muirfield Village, OH; plays out of Muirfield Village

FAMILY: Wife, Barbara Bash; Jack II (9/23/61), Steven (4/11/63), Nancy Jean (5/5/65), Gary (1/15/69), Michael (7/24/73)

COLLEGE: Ohio State University

SPECIAL INTERESTS: Fishing, hunting, tennis and skiing

TURNED PROFESSIONAL: 1961

JOINED TOUR: 1962

PLAYER PROFILE

CAREER EARNINGS: $5,372,176   **PLAYOFF RECORD:** 13-10

TOUR VICTORIES: **1962** U.S. Open, Seattle World's Fair, Portland. **1963** Palm Springs, Masters, (TOTAL: 70) Tournament of Champions, PGA Championship, Sahara. **1964** Portland, Tournament of Champions, Phoenix, Whitemarsh. **1965** Portland, Masters, Memphis Thunderbird Classic, Philadelphia. **1966** Masters, Sahara. **1967** U.S. Open, Sahara, Bing Crosby, Western, Westchester. **1968** Western, American Golf Classic. **1969** Sahara, Kaiser, San Diego. **1970** Byron Nelson, Four-Ball (with Arnold Palmer). **1971** PGA Championship, Tournament of Champions, Byron Nelson, National Team (with Arnold Palmer), Disney World. **1972** Bing Crosby, Doral-Eastern, Masters, U.S. Open, Westchester, Match Play, Disney. **1973** Bing Crosby, New Orleans, Tournament of Champions, Atlanta, PGA Championship, Ohio Kings Island, Walt Disney. **1974** Hawaii, Tournament Players Championship. **1975** Doral-Eastern Open, Heritage Classic, Masters, PGA Championship, World Open. **1976** Tournament Players Championship, World Series of Golf. **1977** Gleason Inverrary, Tournament of Champions, Memorial. **1978** Gleason Inverrary, Tournament Players Championship, IVB-Philadelphia Classic. **1980** U.S. Open, PGA Championship. **1982** Colonial National Invitation. **1984** Memorial. **1986** Masters.

MONEY & POSITION:

Year	Earnings	Pos.	Year	Earnings	Pos.	Year	Earnings	Pos.
1962	$ 61,869	3	1973	$308,362	1	1984	$272,595	15
1963	$100,040	2	1974	$238,178	2	1985	$165,456	43
1964	$113,285	1	1975	$298,149	1	1986	$226,014	34
1965	$140,752	1	1976	$266,438	1	1987	$ 64,685	127
1966	$111,419	2	1977	$284,509	2	1988	$ 28,845	177
1967	$188,998	1	1978	$256,672	4	1989	$ 96,595	129
1968	$155,286	2	1979	$ 59,434	71	1990	$ 68,054	160
1969	$140,167	3	1980	$172,386	13	1991	$123,797	122
1970	$142,149	4	1981	$178,213	16	1992	$ 14,868	223
1971	$244,490	1	1982	$232,645	12	1993	$ 51,532	182
1972	$320,542	1	1983	$256,158	10	1994	$ 11,514	248

BEST 1994 FINISH: T28--U.S. Open.

1994 SUMMARY: Tournaments entered--8; in money--1; top ten finishes--0.

OTHER ACHIEVEMENTS: PGA Player of the Year five times (1967, 1972, 1973, 1975 and 1976). U.S. Amateur champion in 1959 and 1961. NCAA champion in 1961. Winner of British Open in 1966, 1970 and 1978. Six-time winner Australian Open (1964, 1968, 1971, 1975, 1976 and 1978). Winner 1970 World Match Play. Winner of World Series of Golf (old format) four times (1962, 1963, 1967 and 1970). Named Athlete-of-Decade, 1970-79. Has total of 18 international titles. Member World Golf Hall of Fame. Winner, 1982 Card Walker Award for outstanding contributions to junior golf. Winner 1983 Chrysler Team Invitational (with Johnny Miller). 1988 named "Player-of-the-Century".

NATIONAL TEAMS: Walker Cup (2), 1959, 1961; World Cup (6), 1963, 1964, 1966, 1967, 1971, 1973 (medalist three times); Ryder Cup (6), 1969, 1971, 1973, 1975, 1977, 1981; Ryder Cup Captain (2), 1983, 1987.

SENIOR PGA TOUR SUMMARY

SENIOR PGA TOUR VICTORIES: **1990** Tradition at Desert Mountain, (TOTAL: 6) Mazda Senior Tournament Players Championship. **1991** Tradition at Desert Mountain, PGA Seniors Championship, U.S. Senior Open. **1993** U.S. Senior Open. **1994** Mercedes Championships.

1994 SENIOR PGA TOUR SUMMARY:
Tournaments entered--6; in money--6; top ten finishes--5.

COMBINED CAREER EARNINGS: $6,615,764

1994 PGA TOUR STATISTICS

Scoring Average	72.61
Driving Distance	240.5
Driving Accuracy	65.3
Greens in Regulation	55.3
Putting	1.862
All-Around	–
Sand Saves	58.6
Total Driving	–
Eagles	1
Birdies	37

MISCELLANEOUS STATISTICS

Scoring Avg. (before cut)	74.59
Scoring Avg. (3rd round)	77.00
Scoring Avg. (4th round)	76.00
Birdie Conversion	19.6
Par Breakers	11.1

1994 Low Round:	69: U.S. Open/1
Career Low Round:	62: 2 times, most recent '73 Ohio Kings Island Open
Career Largest Paycheck:	$144,000/1986 Masters/1

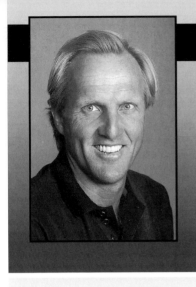

GREG NORMAN

EXEMPT STATUS: Winner, 1993 British Open

FULL NAME: Gregory John Norman

HEIGHT: 6' 1"   **WEIGHT:** 185

BIRTH DATE: February 10, 1955

BIRTHPLACE: Queensland, Australia

RESIDENCE: Hobe Sound, FL; plays out of Medallist

FAMILY: Wife, Laura; Morgan-Leigh (10/5/82), Gregory (9/19/85)

SPECIAL INTERESTS: Fishing, hunting, scuba diving

TURNED PROFESSIONAL: 1976

JOINED TOUR: 1983

PLAYER PROFILE

CAREER EARNINGS: $ 7,937,869   **PLAYOFF RECORD:** 3-7

TOUR VICTORIES: **1984** Kemper Open, Canadian Open. **1986** Panasonic-Las Vegas Invitational, (TOTAL: 12) Kemper Open. **1988** MCI Heritage Classic. **1989** The International, Greater Milwaukee Open, **1990** Doral-Ryder Open, The Memorial Tournament. **1992** Canadian Open.**1993** Doral-Ryder Open. **1994** THE PLAYERS Championship.

MONEY & POSITION:

1983--$ 71,411--74	1987--$ 535,450-- 7	1991--$ 320,196--53
1984--$310,230-- 9	1988--$ 514,854--17	1992--$ 676,443--18
1985--$165,458--42	1989--$ 835,096-- 4	1993--$1,359,653-- 3
1986--$653,296-- 1	1990--$1,165,477-- 1	1994--$1,330,307-- 2

BEST 1994 FINISHES:1--THE PLAYERS Championship; 2--MCI Heritage Classic, Memorial Tournament, Canon Greater Hartford Open; T4--PGA Championship; T6--Nestle Invitational, U.S. Open; T7--Doral-Ryder Open; T8--GTE Byron Nelson Classic, NEC World Series of Golf; 10--Mercedes Championships.
1994 SUMMARY: Tournaments entered--16; in money--16; top ten finishes--11.
1995 PGA TOUR CHARITY TEAM COMPETITION: Mercedes Championships
NATIONAL TEAMS: Australian Nissan Cup (2) 1985, 1986; Australian Kirin Cup, 1987; Australian Dunhill Cup (7) 1985, 1986, 1987, 1988, 1989, 1990, 1992; Australian Four Tours, 1989.

1994 SEASON: Captured 12th title of PGA TOUR career in record-breaking fashion in March, posting 24-under-par 264 total and four-stroke victory over Fuzzy Zoeller in THE PLAYERS Championship...concluded year with third Vardon Trophy, first since 1989-90...had top-10 finishes in seven of first eight starts, including PLAYERS win and pair of seconds in MCI Heritage Classic and The Memorial...later had four consecutive top-10s in U.S. starts, featuring T6 in U.S. Open and T4 at PGA Championship (had T11 in defense of British Open title in July)...made every cut in 16 TOUR starts...a leading Presidents Cup proponent, was forced to withdraw from inaugural matches in September due to illness...after February victory in Johnnie Walker Classic in Thailand, replaced atop Sony Rankings Nick Faldo, who had been there for 81 weeks...supplanted by Nick Price after PGA Championship...won PGA Grand Slam of Golf in November.

CAREER HIGHLIGHTS: Captured second major championship/second British Open title at Royal St. George's in 1993...first British Open win at Turnberry in 1986...had one victory, four seconds and three thirds in 15 1993 TOUR starts...win came in record-setting (23-under 265) style in Doral-Ryder Open...Doral performance also included course-record-tying 62 (his own record) in Round 3...1993 PGA Championship loss to Paul Azinger gave him distinction of losing playoffs in all four majors...winner of 65 tournaments around world...ended 27-month winless drought with playoff victory over Bruce Lietzke in 1992 Canadian Open...in '86 won twice on TOUR and seven times overseas...also held lead going into final round of all four majors that year...suffered back-to-back heartbreaks in 1986-87 Masters, finishing T2 in '86 and losing '87 playoff to Larry Mize's unbelieveable 140-foot chip for birdie...first victory was at West Lakes Classic in Australia in October 1976...had 15-year stretch during which won at least one tournament...has won in 13 countries.

PERSONAL: Well known for charitable involvements, including annual hosting of Franklin Funds Shark Shootout...recipient 1986 and 1990 Arnold Palmer Awards for leading money winner...owns two Dunhill Cup team victories.

1994 PGA TOUR STATISTICS

Scoring Average	68.81	(1)
Driving Distance	277.1	(8T)
Driving Accuracy	73.3	(43T)
Greens in Regulation	69.0	(28T)
Putting	1.747	(6)
All-Around	293	(4)
Sand Saves	57.3	(25)
Total Driving	51	(3)
Eagles	6	(64T)
Birdies	242	(118)

MISCELLANEOUS STATISTICS

Scoring Avg. (before cut)	69.21	(1)
Scoring Avg. (3rd round)	69.00	(3)
Scoring Avg. (4th round)	69.93	(9)
Birdie Conversion	30.9	(14T)
Par Breakers	21.9	(8T)

1994 Low Round: 63: PLAYERS Championship/1
Career Low Round: 62: 4 times, most recent 1993 Doral-Ryder Open/3
Career Largest Paycheck: $450,000/ 1994 PLAYERS Championship/1

ANDY NORTH

EXEMPT STATUS: Winner, 1985 United States Open

FULL NAME: Andrew Stewart North

HEIGHT: 6' 4"   **WEIGHT:** 200

BIRTH DATE: March 9, 1950

BIRTHPLACE: Thorpe, WI

RESIDENCE: Madison, WI; plays out of Beaver Creek, Vail, CO

FAMILY: Wife, Susan; Nichole (11/30/74); Andrea (8/22/78)

COLLEGE: University of Florida (1972)

SPECIAL INTERESTS: All sports

TURNED PROFESSIONAL: 1972

Q SCHOOL: Fall 1972

PLAYER PROFILE

CAREER EARNINGS: $1,364,013

TOUR VICTORIES: **1977** American Express-Westchester Classic. **1978** U.S. Open. **1985** U.S. Open. (TOTAL: 3)

MONEY & POSITION:

1973--$ 48,672--64	1981--$111,401-- 30	1989--$ 13,620--204
1974--$ 58,409--64	1982--$ 82,698-- 49	1990--$ 99,651--137
1975--$ 44,729--53	1983--$ 52,416-- 98	1991--$ 24,653--201
1976--$ 71,267--37	1984--$ 22,131--149	1992--$ 16,360--218
1977--$116,794--18	1985--$212,268-- 24	1993--$ 14,500--230
1978--$150,398--14	1986--$ 41,651--146	1994--$ 3,165--292
1979--$ 73,873--54	1987--$ 42,876--163	
1980--$ 55,212--69	1988--$ 10,759--212	

BEST 1994 FINISH: T64--Memorial Tournament.

1994 SUMMARY: Tournaments entered--6; in money--1; top ten finishes--0.

NATIONAL TEAMS: Ryder Cup, 1985; World Cup, 1978.

1994 SEASON: Medical problems continued to plague man who already has had six knee surgeries, four operations to remove skin cancers from nose and left cheek, right elbow bone spurs, shoulder injury and nagging neck pain...knee trouble persisted, limiting play once again...did appear in two more events than 1993, when off-season knee surgery delayed first appearance to June...only cut came at The Memorial, where finished T64...best round came at Brown Deer Park Golf Course, new Greater Milwaukee Open facility he helped redesign...opened GMO with 77, after which considered not playing next day due to physical limitations...did play and posted 5-under-par 66, one of day's best rounds but three strokes shy of making cut...continued to focus on and expand career as golf reporter for ESPN.

CAREER HIGHLIGHTS: Because of injuries (what else?), made fewest starts of career (four) in 1993...winner of two U.S. Open Championships, one of only 16 golfers with more than one Open win...first came at Cherry Hills in Denver in 1978, second at Oakland Hills in Birmingham, MI in 1985...at Cherry Hills had four-stroke lead with five holes to play...by time reached 18 needed bogey to win, and that's what he got for victory over Dave Stockton and J.C. Snead...at Oakland Hills, 279 total was one stroke better than international runner-up trio of T.C. Chen of Taiwan, Dave Barr of Canada and Denis Watson of Zimbabwe...only other victory in injury-plagued career was 1977 Westchester Classic...winner 1969 Wisconsin State Amateur, 1971 Western Amateur...three-time All-America University of Florida...member 1978 World Cup and 1985 Ryder Cup teams.

PERSONAL: Turned to golf in seventh grade because bone in knee stopped growing and was disintegrating, causing him to give up football and basketball...later returned to basketball, earning all-state honors...spent a few years assisting University of Wisconsin football staff.

1994 PGA TOUR STATISTICS

Scoring Average	73.65	(N/R)
Driving Distance	252.7	(N/R)
Driving Accuracy	52.2	(N/R)
Greens in Regulation	49.1	(N/R)
Putting	1.817	(N/R)
All-Around	–	
Sand Saves	51.1	(N/R)
Total Driving	–	
Eagles	0	(N/R)
Birdies	34	(N/R)

MISCELLANEOUS STATISTICS

Scoring Avg. (before cut)	75.00	(N/R)
Scoring Avg. (3rd round)	72.00	(N/R)
Scoring Avg. (4th round)	76.00	(N/R)
Birdie Conversion	29.6	(N/R)
Par Breakers	14.5	(N/R)

1994 Low Round: 66: Greater Milwaukee Open/2
Career Low Round: 63: 1975 B.C. Open/1
Career Largest
Paycheck: $103,000/1985 U.S. Open/1

BRETT OGLE

EXEMPT STATUS: 1994 tournament winner

FULL NAME: Brett James Ogle

HEIGHT: 6' 2"   **WEIGHT:** 165

BIRTH DATE: July 14, 1964

BIRTHPLACE: Paddington, Australia

RESIDENCE: Melbourne, Australia

FAMILY: Wife, Maggie; Christopher (10/1/90),
Rachel Louise (11/5/93)

SPECIAL INTERESTS: Snooker, tennis, all sports

TURNED PROFESSIONAL: 1985

Q SCHOOL: Fall 1992

PLAYER PROFILE

CAREER EARNINGS: $621,869

TOUR VICTORIES: 1993 AT&T Pebble Beach National Pro-Am. **1994** United Airlines Hawaiian Open. (TOTAL: 2)

MONEY & POSITION: 1993--$337,374--48   1994--$284,495--66

BEST 1994 FINISH: 1--United Airlines Hawaiian Open.

1994 SUMMARY: Tournaments entered--21; in money--10; top ten finishes--1.

1995 PGA TOUR CHARITY TEAM COMPETITION: Memorial Tournament

NATIONAL TEAMS: World Cup, 1992

1994 HIGHLIGHTS: Certainly knows how to hit the big early jackpots …for second year in row, or since gregarious Aussie took PGA TOUR by storm in 1993, early-season winner of a big check…carded back-to-back 66s starting United Airlines Hawaiian Open to trail Davis Love III by four strokes after two rounds (Love had fired course-record 60 in Round 2)…narrowed margin to two after three rounds…closed with 68 to edge Love by one stroke and post second TOUR victory, worth $216,000…had opened season with T11 in Mercedes Championships, worth $28,250…earnings for first two weeks $244,250…after that made just $40,245 for 19 subsequent starts…withdrew due to illness after three rounds of Northern Telecom Open, third event of year…proceeded to miss next five cuts in a row…best later finish T22 at Kmart Greater Greensboro Open, only other top-25 placing of campaign…finished second to Robert Allenby in Australian Open in November.

CAREER HIGHLIGHTS: Had top-10 finishes in two of first four starts of 1993, one of which was three-stroke victory in AT&T Pebble Beach National Pro-Am…win was worth $225,000, largest check of two-year career…began '93 campaign with T4 in United Airlines Hawaiian Open, then three weeks later had first TOUR win…opened with back-to-back 68s at Pebble Beach and Poppy Hills, closed with three-stroke decision over Billy Ray Brown…qualified for TOUR as one of five co-medalists from 1992 Qualifying Tournament…from that group, was only one to retain playing privileges for 1994…qualified for 1991 NEC World Series of Golf by winning 1990 Australian PGA Championship…voiced at that time his strong desire to play PGA TOUR…finished T25 at Firestone CC, earning $10,175.

PERSONAL: Adopted at three weeks, a fact he talks freely about…was introduced to golf at 13-14…his "gift for gab" made him instant favorite among TOUR galleries…trying to overcome putting woes which very nearly drove him from game, has tried every way imaginable: conventional, cross handed, Langer style, long putter…because of his height and rail-thin frame, is a self-described "one iron with ears."

1994 PGA TOUR STATISTICS

Scoring Average	71.78	(145)
Driving Distance	273.9	(14)
Driving Accuracy	67.9	(106T)
Greens in Regulation	66.5	(76T)
Putting	1.811	(130T)
All-Around	833	(133)
Sand Saves	44.3	(158)
Total Driving	120	(23T)
Eagles	7	(44T)
Birdies	196	(160T)

MISCELLANEOUS STATISTICS

Scoring Avg. (before cut)	72.21	(150)
Scoring Avg. (3rd round)	70.43	(50T)
Scoring Avg. (4th round)	71.43	(80T)
Birdie Conversion	28.2	(87T)
Par Breakers	19.4	(64T)

1994 Low Round: 66: 2 times
Career Low Round: 66: 1994 United Airlines
Career Largest   Hawaiian Open/1,2
Paycheck: $225,000/1993 AT&T Pebble
Beach National Pro-Am/1

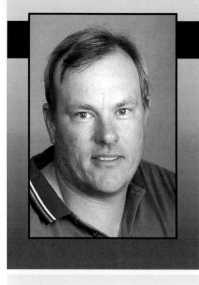

DAVID OGRIN

EXEMPT STATUS: 92nd on 1994 money list

FULL NAME: David Allen Ogrin

HEIGHT: 6'   **WEIGHT:** 220

BIRTH DATE: December 31, 1957

BIRTHPLACE: Waukegan, IL

RESIDENCE: Garden Ridge, TX

FAMILY: Wife, Sharon; Amy (6/20/88), Jessica (9/6/89), Dana (3/6/92), Clark Addison (10/18/93)

COLLEGE: Texas A&M (1980, Economics)

SPECIAL INTERESTS: Christianity, children, Chicago Cubs

TURNED PROFESSIONAL: 1980

Q SCHOOL: Fall 1982, 1992

PLAYER PROFILE

CAREER EARNINGS: $1,146,544   **PLAYOFF RECORD:** 0-2

BEST EVER FINISH: 2--1985 St. Jude Classic (lost playoff to Hal Sutton); 2--1989 Hawaiian Open; T2--1994 GTE Byron Nelson Classic (lost playoff to Neal Lancaster).

MONEY & POSITION:

1983--$ 36,003--121	1987--$ 80,149--110	1991--$ 8,024--235
1984--$ 45,461--113	1988--$138,807-- 86	1992--$ 33,971--193
1985--$ 76,294-- 95	1989--$234,196-- 59	1993--$155,016--104
1986--$ 75,245--113	1990--$ 64,190--167	1994--$199,199-- 92

BEST 1994 FINISHES: T2--GTE Byron Nelson Classic; T8--United Airlines Hawaiian Open.

1994 SUMMARY: Tournaments entered--29; in money--17; top ten finishes--2.

1995 PGA TOUR CHARITY TEAM COMPETITION: Texas Open

1994 SEASON: Having rediscovered his game in 1993, continued the upward trend in '94…earnings total second-best of 12 years on TOUR…missed $200,000 plateau for second time by just $801…best round of year was unofficial, a Texas Open pro-am 60 (his best ever) which featured a front-nine 26 that included a hole-in-one on the ninth hole…best he could do for real at Oak Hills a third-round 65 en route to eventual T15…began year with T8 in United Airlines Hawaiian Open, one of two top-10s…second came in GTE Byron Nelson, where he was part of TOUR record six-man playoff won by Neal Lancaster…opened with 64 in what became known as "Half Nelson," good for one-stroke lead over Mark Carnvevale…second-place finish was third of career…after missing seven cuts in first 12 starts, missed only four in final 17.

CAREER HIGHLIGHTS: Finest season came in 1989, when earned $234,196 and finished second in rain-shortened Hawaiian Open…career seemingly on upswing at that juncture, but failed to keep card after No. 167 money list placing in 1990…rebounded slightly with just $8,024 in 1991…rebounded low ebb with just $8,024 in 1991…route to solid finish in 1993…lost 1985 St. Jude Classic playoff to Hal Sutton birdie on first extra hole…did record unofficial victory in 1987 Deposit Guaranty Golf Classic, edging Nick Faldo by one stroke at Hattiesburg Country Club…money won ($36,000), fashioned by closing 64, was official…made it through Qualifying Tournament on fourth try in 1982, then made it through successfully again 10 years later…winner 1975 Illinois State High School Championship, 1980 Illinois State Open, 1988 Peru Open…winner three collegiate events, including Harvey Penick Invitational…winner 1989 Chrysler Team Championship with Ted Schulz.

PERSONAL: The ultimate Chicago Cubs fan, so much so that named fourth child/first son "Clark Addison" for two streets adjoining Wrigley Field…golf won out over dream of becoming switch-hitting catcher…father put sawed off golf club in his hands at age of two.

1994 PGA TOUR STATISTICS

Scoring Average	71.21	(86T)
Driving Distance	250.0	(163T)
Driving Accuracy	77.9	(7)
Greens in Regulation	66.2	(81T)
Putting	1.810	(129)
All-Around	671	(79T)
Sand Saves	57.0	(27)
Total Driving	170	(74T)
Eagles	4	(104T)
Birdies	283	(74)

MISCELLANEOUS STATISTICS

Scoring Avg. (before cut)	71.69	(118T)
Scoring Avg. (3rd round)	70.14	(25)
Scoring Avg. (4th round)	70.87	(42)
Birdie Conversion	26.4	(141T)
Par Breakers	17.7	(133T)

1994 Low Round: 64: GTE Byron Nelson/1
Career Low Round: 64: 3 times, most recent
Career Largest   '94 GTE Byron Nelson/1
Paycheck: $81,000/1989 Hawaiian Open/2

MARK O'MEARA

EXEMPT STATUS: 86th on 1994 money list

FULL NAME: Mark Francis O'Meara

HEIGHT: 6'   **WEIGHT:** 180

BIRTH DATE: January 13, 1957

BIRTHPLACE: Goldsboro, NC

RESIDENCE: Windermere, FL

FAMILY: Wife, Alicia; Michelle (3/14/87), Shaun Robert (8/29/89)

COLLEGE: Long Beach State (1980, Marketing)

SPECIAL INTERESTS: Golf course consulting, hunting, fishing

TURNED PROFESSIONAL: 1980

Q SCHOOL: Fall 1980

PLAYER PROFILE

CAREER EARNINGS: $5,212,337   **PLAYOFF RECORD:** 1-4

TOUR VICTORIES: **1984** Greater Milwaukee Open. **1985** Bing Crosby Pro-Am, Hawaiian Open. **1989** AT&T
(TOTAL: 8) Pebble Beach National Pro-Am. **1990** AT&T Pebble Beach National Pro-Am, H-E-B. Texas Open. **1991** Walt Disney World/Oldsmobile Classic. **1992** AT&T Pebble Beach National Pro-Am

MONEY & POSITION:		
1981--$ 76,063-- 55	1986--$252,827--30	1991-$563,896--20
1982--$ 31,711--118	1987--$327,250--30	1992-$759,648--11
1983--$ 69,354-- 76	1988--$438,311--22	1993--$349,516--43
1984--$465,873-- 2	1989--$615,804--13	1994--$214,070--86
1985--$340,840-- 10	1990--$707,175--10	

BEST 1994 FINISHES: T8--Texas Open; 9--Bell Canadian Open; T9--Greater Milwaukee Open.

1994 SUMMARY: Tournaments entered--29; in money--17; top ten finishes--3.

1995 PGA TOUR CHARITY TEAM COMPETITION: Walt Disney World/Oldsmobile Golf Classic

NATIONAL TEAMS: Ryder Cup (3), 1985, 1989, 1991; U.S. vs. Japan, 1984; Nissan Cup, 1985.

1994 SEASON: Experienced probably most frustrating of 14 seasons on TOUR...struggles that began midway through 1993 campaign persisted through much of '94...did return to something more akin to Mark O'Meara-like form over last two months, when earned more than half of $214,070 final figure...that total still lowest since third year in 1983...had back-to-back ninth-place finishes in Greater Milwaukee Open (tie) and Bell Canadian Open (solo), followed by T13 in B.C. Open...finished T8 in Texas Open for third and final top-10 of season...earnings from those four placings totaled $107,575, pushing him past $200,000 for 11th consecutive year...began closing charge after missing three consecutive cuts and five in eight weeks...finished T15 in the Masters...won Fred Meyer Challenge with John Cook in August.

CAREER HIGHLIGHTS: Had string of nine consecutive top-30 money-list placings snapped in 1993, when failed to make TOUR Championship for first time...of eight TOUR victories, five have come in pro-am events, including four at Pebble Beach...other pro-am win was 1991 Walt Disney World/Oldsmobile Classic...also lost playoffs at 1990 and '92 pro-am Bob Hope Chrysler Classics...shot final-round 64 to defeat David Peoples by a stroke in Disney Classic...part of five-man playoff in 1992 Hope won by John Cook...in '90 Hope matched Corey Pavin at then-TOUR record 29-under-par for 90 holes...Pavin chipped in for birdie on first extra hole to win...came from four strokes off pace with final-round 63 to capture 1990 Texas Open...member 1985-89-91 Ryder Cup teams...also member 1984 U.S. vs. Japan and 1985 Nissan Cup squads...winner 1979 U.S. Amateur, defeating John Cook...also winner '79 California State and Mexican Amateurs...All-America at Long Beach State...1981 TOUR Rookie of Year...winner 1985 Kapalua International, Fuji Sankei Classic (Japan), 1986 Australian Masters, 1987 Lawrence Batley International (England), 1992 Tokai Classic (Japan).

PERSONAL: Has undertaken fundraising effort for longtime caddie Danny Wanstall, diagnosed with multiple sclerosis at 1994 PLAYERS Championship...numbers among neighbors Orlando Magic center Shaquille O'Neal.

1994 PGA TOUR STATISTICS

Scoring Average	71.11	(77)
Driving Distance	262.6	(82)
Driving Accuracy	66.0	(130)
Greens in Regulation	64.5	(125T)
Putting	1.786	(68T)
All-Around	641	(69)
Sand Saves	51.9	(88T)
Total Driving	212	(134)
Eagles	9	(17T)
Birdies	297	(54)

MISCELLANEOUS STATISTICS

Scoring Avg. (before cut)	71.42	(88T)
Scoring Avg. (3rd round)	71.06	(91)
Scoring Avg. (4th round)	72.19	(141)
Birdie Conversion	28.1	(91T)
Par Breakers	18.7	(97T)

1994 Low Round: **65:** Hardee's Golf Classic/1
Career Low Round: **62:** 1981 Sammy Davis Jr. Greater Hartford Open/2
Career Largest Paycheck: **$198,000**/'92 AT&T Pebble Beach/1

JOE OZAKI

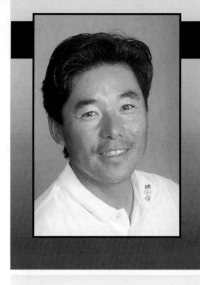

EXEMPT STATUS: 121st on 1994 money list

FULL NAME: Naomichi Ozaki

HEIGHT: 5' 8"   **WEIGHT:** 155

BIRTH DATE: May 18, 1956

BIRTHPLACE: Tekushima, Japan

RESIDENCE: Chiba, Japan

FAMILY: Wife, Yoshie; Takamasa

SPECIAL INTERESTS: Singing, aerobics

TURNED PROFESSIONAL: 1977

JOINED TOUR: Spring 1993

PLAYER PROFILE

CAREER EARNINGS: $441,702

BEST EVER FINISH: T6--1991 NEC World Series of Golf; T6--1992 Federal Express St. Jude Classic; T6--1993 THE PLAYERS Championship

MONEY & POSITION:

1985--$ 880--259	1991--$ 38,850--185	1993--$139,784--115
1989--$ 1,605--274	1992--$ 75,946--151	1994--$147,308--121
1990--$37,330--185		

BEST 1994 FINISH: T8--Buick Classic.

1994 SUMMARY: Tournaments entered--17; in money--15; top ten finishes--1.

1995 PGA TOUR CHARITY TEAM COMPETITION: Franklin Funds Shark Shoot-Out

1994 HIGHLIGHTS: Part of four-way tie for lead (with Mike Springer, Vijay Singh and first-round leader Dillard Pruitt) after two rounds of Northern Telecom Open...opened 66-69, but closed 73-74 for T46 in second start of campaign...had begun season with T20 in United Airlines Hawaiian Open...played consistently if not spectacularly remainder of the way...missed but one cut in 17 starts, at the Nestle Invitational...returned to Japan for season there after Anheuser-Busch Golf Classic in July...opened A-B Classic with 66, matching low round of season...assured retention of playing privileges with only top-10 finish in June, T8 at Buick Classic...$32,400 check for Westchester placing pushed him over $140,000 for year...was two strokes off Ernie Els' 36-hole lead and three behind Lee Janzen after 54 holes before closing with a 72.

CAREER HIGHLIGHTS: Achieved special temporary PGA TOUR membership with T6 finish in 1993 PLAYERS Championship, a placing worth $80,938...PLAYERS finish matched his best-ever in TOUR event, including 1991 NEC World Series of Golf...also had T6 in 1992 FedEx St. Jude Classic...achieved exempt status for 1994 by finishing No. 115 on money list...had 21st place finish in '93 NEC World Series worth $26,550...closed with 69 for T25 in 1993 U.S. Open...winner of 24 events in Japan, including 1988 Japanese Series, 1989 JPGA Match Play Championship and 1990 Gene Sarazen Jun Classic...last three victories in Japan came in 1992, when earnings total of $1,120,862 ranked him 14th on world list...has earned more than $6 million during professional career.

PERSONAL: Youngest of three golfing Ozaki brothers...Masahsi (Jumbo) is 48, Tateo (Jet) is 41...1988 was "Year of the Ozakis" in Japan, when three combined for 12 victories in 35 events (Jumbo six, Joe four, Jet two)...brothers also had nine seconds and four thirds...Jumbo and Joe finished 1-2 on money list, Jet No. 7.

1994 PGA TOUR STATISTICS

Scoring Average	70.84	(53)
Driving Distance	261.1	(97)
Driving Accuracy	67.1	(117T)
Greens in Regulation	67.2	(51T)
Putting	1.775	(38T)
All-Around	786	(120)
Sand Saves	47.7	(137T)
Total Driving	214	(135)
Eagles	2	(146T)
Birdies	214	(147)

MISCELLANEOUS STATISTICS

Scoring Avg. (before cut)	70.33	(16T)
Scoring Avg. (3rd round)	72.07	(162)
Scoring Avg. (4th round)	72.07	(133T)
Birdie Conversion	29.0	(57T)
Par Breakers	19.7	(55T)

1994 Low Round: 66: 2 times
Career Low Round: 65: 1992 Fed Ex St. Jude Classic/1
Career Largest Paycheck: $80,938/1993 PLAYERS Championship/T6

ARNOLD PALMER

EXEMPT STATUS: Winner, 1960 United States Open

FULL NAME: Arnold Daniel Palmer

HEIGHT: 5' 10" **WEIGHT:** 185

BIRTH DATE: September 10, 1929

BIRTHPLACE: Latrobe, PA

RESIDENCES: Latrobe, PA and Bay Hill, FL; plays out of Latrobe CC (PA), Laurel Vally GC (PA), Bay Hill Club (FL)

FAMILY: Wife, Winifred Walzer; Peggy (2/26/56); Amy (8/4/58); five grandchildren

COLLEGE: Wake Forest University

SPECIAL INTERESTS: Flying, business, club-making

TURNED PROFESSIONAL: 1954

JOINED TOUR: 1955

PLAYER PROFILE

CAREER EARNINGS: $1,904,668   **PLAYOFF RECORD:** 14-10

TOUR VICTORIES: **1955** Canadian. **1956** Insurance City, Eastern. **1957** Houston, Azalea, Rubber City, San Diego.
(TOTAL: 60)   **1958** St. Petersburg, Masters, Pepsi Golf. **1959** Thunderbird (Calif.) Invitation, Oklahoma City, West Palm Beach. **1960** Insurance City, Masters, Palm Springs Classic, Baton Rouge, Pensacola, U.S. Open, Mobile Sertoma, Texas Open. **1961** San Diego, Texas, Baton Rouge, Phoenix, Western. **1962** Masters, Palm Springs Classic, Texas, Phoenix, Tournament of Champions, Colonial National, American Golf Classic. **1963** Thunderbird, Pensacola, Phoenix, Western, Los Angeles, Cleveland, Philadelphia. **1964** Oklahoma City, Masters. **1965** Tournament of Champions. **1966** Los Angeles, Tournament of Champions, Houston Champions International. **1967** Los Angeles, Tucson, American Golf Classic, Thunderbird Classic. **1968** Hope Desert Classic, Kemper. **1969** Heritage, Danny Thomas--Diplomat. **1970** Four-Ball (with Jack Nicklaus). **1971** Hope Desert Classic, Citrus, Westchester, National Team (with Jack Nicklaus). **1973** Bob Hope Desert Classic.

MONEY & POSITION:

Year	Earnings	Pos		Year	Earnings	Pos		Year	Earnings	Pos
1955	$ 7,958	32		1969	$105,128	9		1982	$ 6,621	198
1956	$ 16,145	19		1970	$128,853	5		1983	$ 16,904	159
1957	$ 27,803	5		1971	$209,603	3		1984	$ 2,452	217
1958	$ 42,608	1		1972	$ 84,181	25		1985	$ 3,327	214
1959	$ 32,462	5		1973	$ 89,457	27		1986	$ --	--
1960	$ 75,263	1		1974	$ 36,293	72		1987	$ 1,650	269
1961	$ 61,091	2		1975	$ 59,017	36		1988	$ --	--
1962	$ 81,448	1		1976	$ 17,017	115		1989	$ 2,290	253
1963	$128,230	1		1977	$ 21,950	101		1990	$ --	--
1964	$113,203	2		1978	$ 27,073	94		1991	$ 7,738	237
1965	$ 57,770	10		1979	$ 9,276	159		1992	$ --	--
1966	$110,467	3		1980	$ 16,589	133		1993	$ 1,970	316
1967	$184,065	2		1981	$ 4,164	197		1994	$ --	--
1968	$114,602	7								

1994 SUMMARY: Tournaments entered--6; in money--0; top ten finishes--0.

OTHER ACHIEVEMENTS: 1954 U. S. Amateur champion. Winner of 19 foreign titles, including 1961 and 1962 British Open, 1966 Australian Open, 1975 Spanish Open, and 1975 British PGA. 1961, 1963, 1965, 1967, 1971, and 1973 Ryder Cup team. 1960, 1962, 1963, 1964, 1965, 1966, and 1967 World Cup team. Captain, 1986, 1987, 1988 Chrysler Cup Team.

NATIONAL TEAMS: Ryder Cup (6), 1961, 1963, 1965, 1967, 1971, 1973; Ryder Cup Captain (2), 1963, 1975; World Cup (7), 1960, 1962, 1963, 1964, 1965, 1966, 1967; Captain and member of Chrysler Cup team (5), 1986, 1987, 1988, 1989, 1990.

SENIOR PGA TOUR SUMMARY

SENIOR PGA TOUR VICTORIES: **1980** PGA Seniors. **1981** U.S.
(Total: 10)   Senior Open. **1982** Marlboro Classic, Denver Post Champions of Golf. **1983** Boca Grove Senior Classic.
1984 PGA Seniors, Senior Tournament Players Championship, Quadel Senior Classic. **1985** Senior Tournament Players Championship. **1988** Crestar Classic.

1994 SENIOR PGA TOUR SUMMARY:
Tournaments entered--13; in money--12; top ten finishes--0.
COMBINED CAREER EARNINGS: $ 3,439,915

1994 PGA TOUR STATISTICS

Scoring Average	74.36
Driving Distance	249.6
Driving Accuracy	75.5
Greens in Regulation	55.2
Putting	1.919
All-Around	–
Sand Saves	35.5
Total Driving	–
Eagles	0
Birdies	31

MISCELLANEOUS STATISTICS

Scoring Avg. (before cut)	76.38
Scoring Avg. (3rd round)	71.00
Scoring Avg. (4th round)	68.00
Birdie Conversion	20.8
Par Breakers	11.5

1994 Low Round: 68: Bob Hope Chyrsler Classic
Career Low Round: 62: 2 times, most recent
Career Largest   1966 Los Angeles Open/3
Paycheck: $50,000/1971 Westchester Classic/1

JESPER PARNEVIK

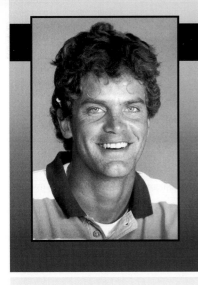

EXEMPT STATUS: 120th on 1994 money list

FULL NAME: Jesper Bo Parnevik

HEIGHT: 6'   **WEIGHT:** 175

BIRTH DATE: March 7, 1965

BIRTHPLACE: Stockholm, Sweden

RESIDENCE: South Palm Beach, FL

FAMILY: Wife, Mia

COLLEGE: Palm Beach Junior College

SPECIAL INTERESTS: Tennis

TURNED PROFESSIONAL: 1986

JOINED TOUR: 1993

PLAYER PROFILE

CAREER EARNINGS: $148,816

BEST-EVER FINISH: 5--1994 United Airlines Hawaiian Open

MONEY & POSITION: 1994---148,816--120

BEST 1994 FINISHES: 5--United Airlines Hawaiian Open; T9--MCI Heritage Classic.

1994 SUMMARY: Tournaments entered--17; in money--12; top ten finishes--2.

1995 PGA TOUR CHARITY TEAM COMPETITION: Bell Canadian Open

NATIONAL TEAMS: World Cup, 1994; Dunhill Cup, 1993.

1994 SEASON: Turned potentially devastating British Open faux pas into semi-profitable experience…capitalized on failure to read Turnberry leaderboards (which led to 18th-hole bogey and subsequent loss to Nick Price) by converting oversight into commercial appearances for hotel chain…held two-stroke lead approaching 72nd hole, having birdied five of seven previous…made bogey through aggressive play, losing by stroke to Price's eagle-birdie-par finish…runnerup finish still worth $142,560 (unofficial)…after T4 in 1993 Qualifying Tournament, finished solo fifth in first PGA TOUR event of '94, crafting closing 63 (his low round of year) in United Airlines Hawaiian Open…$48,000 paycheck largest of initial TOUR campaign…missed cut in second start at Northern Telecom Open, followed by top-25s in AT&T Pebble Beach National Pro-Am (T19) and Nissan Los Angeles Open (T20)…also had top-10 finish (T9) in MCI Heritage Classic, where 272 total was six strokes behind Hale Irwin.

CAREER HIGHLIGHTS: First PGA European Tour win came in 1993 Bell's Scottish Open…lost seven-hole playoff to Seve Ballesteros in 1992 Turespana Open…winner 1988 Odense Open, 1988 Raklosia Open, 1990 Swedish Open…product of Swedish national junior program which turned out, among others, Anders Forsbrand, Joakim Haeggman, Liselotte Neumann and Helen Alfredsson…played at Palm Beach (FL) Junior College from 1984-86 before qualifying for European Tour…winner 1985 Dixie Amateur.

PERSONAL: Father, Bo Parnevik, is Sweden's most famous comedian…wears golf cap in trademark fashion, with bill turned up and brand name stitched on underside…first announced intention of winning British Open at age 13…learned game by hitting floating golf balls into lake behind family home in Osterskar and putting on practice green built in backyard.

1994 PGA TOUR STATISTICS

Scoring Average	70.97	(63T)
Driving Distance	265.8	(55T)
Driving Accuracy	65.6	(133)
Greens in Regulation	65.4	(100T)
Putting	1.794	(95T)
All-Around	804	(124)
Sand Saves	41.0	(176T)
Total Driving	188	(107T)
Eagles	9	(17T)
Birdies	183	(165T)

MISCELLANEOUS STATISTICS

Scoring Avg. (before cut)	71.71	(121)
Scoring Avg. (3rd round)	71.73	(142T)
Scoring Avg. (4th round)	71.55	(94)
Birdie Conversion	27.8	(105T)
Par Breakers	19.0	(83T)

1994 Low Round: 65: GTE Byron Nelson/1
Career Low Round: 65: 1994 GTE Byron Nelson/1
Career Largest Paycheck: $48,000/1994 United Airlines Hawaiian Open/5

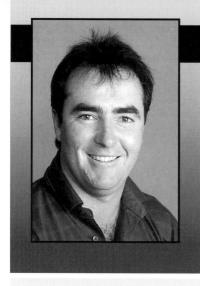

CRAIG PARRY

EXEMPT STATUS: 46th on 1994 money list

FULL NAME: Craig David Parry

HEIGHT: 5'6"   **WEIGHT:** 170

BIRTH DATE: December 1, 1966

BIRTHPLACE: Sunshine, Victoria, Australia

RESIDENCE: Kardinya, Western Australia

FAMILY: Wife, Jenny; April (8/22/92)

SPECIAL INTERESTS: Sailing, water sports, cricket, rugby

TURNED PROFESSIONAL: 1985

JOINED TOUR: April 1992

PLAYER PROFILE

CAREER EARNINGS: $919,570

BEST EVER FINISH: 2--1994 Honda Classic

MONEY & POSITION:

1989--$ 1,650--282	1991--$ 63,767--162	1993--$323,068--50
1990--$43,351--181	1992--$241,901-- 64	1994--$354,602--46

BEST 1994 FINISHES: 2--Honda Classic; T6--United Airlines Hawaiian Open; T7--Kemper Open.

1994 SUMMARY: Tournaments entered--20; in money--15; top ten finishes--3.

1995 PGA TOUR CHARITY TEAM COMPETITION: Franklin Funds Shark Shoot-Out

NATIONAL TEAMS: Kirin Cup, 1988; Four Tours World Championship of Golf (3), 1989, 1990, 1991; Presidents Cup, 1994.

1994 SEASON: Earned best finish and largest check of PGA TOUR career ($118,800) in second start of campaign…final-round 67 left him one stroke behind Nick Price's Honda Classic-winning 276 total…Price closed with 66…had opened season with T6 in United Airlines Hawaiian Open, again finishing with 67…only other top-10 finish, Kemper Open T7…member of International Team in inaugural Presidents Cup Match in September…teamed with Bradley Hughes to defeat Loren Roberts-Tom Lehman in Saturday Four-Ball, then edged Corey Pavin one-up in Sunday singles…winner of Microsoft Australian Masters in February.

CAREER HIGHLIGHTS: Prior to '94 Honda Classic, best TOUR finishes had been pair of T3s…one of those came in 1993 U.S. Open…shared first-round lead after an opening 66, closed 69-68 to finish five shots behind Lee Janzen…also had T3 in 1992 Kmart Greater Greensboro Open…finished solo fifth in '93 Honda Classic…became special temporary member of TOUR in April 1992…was one shot off lead at midpoint of '92 PLAYERS Championship…tied with Ian Woosnam for 36-hole lead in Masters, then held third-round lead outright at 12-under-par 204 before skying to final-round 78 and T13…winner of ten events worldwide, including four on PGA European Tour…pair of European victories came in 1989 playoffs: Wang Four Stars National Pro-Celebrity and German Open…other two European Tour wins registered in '91: Lancia Martini Italian Open and Bell's Scottish Open…in native Australia won 1992 Australian Masters in addition to 1994 victory, 1987-92 New South Wales Opens…also captured Canadian Tournament Players Championship in '87, Bridgestone ASO in Japan in 1989 (his third title that year).

PERSONAL: Nickname is "Popeye" for well-developed forearms…1984-85 State Junior and State Amateur Champion, 1985 State Foursomes Champion in Australia…low amateur 1985 Australian Masters, Tasmanian and SA Opens…1988 co-recipient Epson Shooting Star Award…member 1988-91 Asahi Glass Four Tours, 1988 Kirin Cup, 1991 Dunhill Cup teams.

1994 PGA TOUR STATISTICS

Scoring Average	70.40	(30)
Driving Distance	262.3	(85T)
Driving Accuracy	71.6	(57)
Greens in Regulation	66.8	(63T)
Putting	1.788	(78)
All-Around	611	(61)
Sand Saves	57.5	(23)
Total Driving	142	(41T)
Eagles	3	(126T)
Birdies	211	(149T)

MISCELLANEOUS STATISTICS

Scoring Avg. (before cut)	71.25	(71)
Scoring Avg. (3rd round)	71.23	(103T)
Scoring Avg. (4th round)	71.00	(49T)
Birdie Conversion	28.3	(83T)
Par Breakers	19.2	(73T)

1994 Low Round:	**65:** Federal Express St. Jude Classic/2
Career Low Round:	**65:** 2 times, most recent 1994 Federal Express St. Jude Classic
Career Largest Paycheck:	**$118,000**/1994 Honda Classic/2

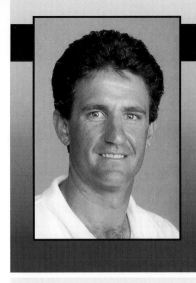

STEVE PATE

EXEMPT STATUS: 64th on 1994 money list

FULL NAME: Stephen Robert Pate

HEIGHT: 6'   **WEIGHT:** 175

BIRTH DATE: May 26, 1961

BIRTHPLACE: Ventura, CA

RESIDENCE: Orlando, FL; plays out of North Ranch CC, Westlake, CA

FAMILY: Wife, Sheri; Nicole (3/12/88), Sarah (10/8/90)

COLLEGE: UCLA (1984, Psychology)

SPECIAL INTERESTS: Fishing

TURNED PROFESSIONAL: 1983

Q SCHOOL: Fall 1984

PLAYER PROFILE

CAREER EARNINGS: $3,571,833   **PLAYOFF RECORD:** 0-2

TOUR VICTORIES: **1987** Southwest Classic. **1988** MONY Tournament of Champions, Shearson Lehman (TOTAL: 5)   Hutton-Andy Williams Open.**1991** Honda Classic. **1992** Buick Invitational of California.

MONEY & POSITION:

1985--$ 89,358--86	1989--$306,554--35	1992--$472,626--30
1986--$176,100--51	1990--$334,505--39	1993--$254,841--64
1987--$335,728--26	1991--$727,997-- 6	1994--$291,651--64
1988--$582,473--12		

BEST 1994 FINISHES: T3--Buick Open; T4--Buick Southern Open; T5--Buick Classic; T8--Phoenix Open; T9--Greater Milwaukee Open.

1994 SUMMARY: Tournaments entered--29; in money--20; top ten finishes--5.

1995 PGA TOUR CHARITY TEAM COMPETITION: Honda Classic

NATIONAL TEAMS: Ryder Cup, 1991, Kirin Cup, 1988.

1994 SEASON: Although money-list position (No. 64) identical to 1993, rebounded slightly from year before in terms of dollars won...had T8 in Phoenix Open in third start of campaign, one of five top-10 placings on year...best finish T3 in Buick Open, followed two starts later by T9 in Greater Milwaukee Open...had earlier Buick success in Buick Classic, where opening 66 at Westchester CC had him one stroke off Mike Reid's first-round lead...carded second-round 66 in U.S. Open at Oakmont, best round of year (64) came three weeks earlier in Round 2 of Southwestern Bell Colonial...second-best finish T4 in Buick Southern Open.

CAREER HIGHLIGHTS: Fifth career victory came in 1992 Buick Invitational of California...tournament shortened to 54 holes by Saturday fog...two-time winner of San Diego event (also 1988)...enjoyed finest season of career in 1991, posting earnings of $727,997...scored three-stroke Honda Classic win over Paul Azinger and Dan Halldorson in '91...high final-day winds at Eagle Trace allowed him to parlay closing 75 into relatively easy victory...later that season lost BellSouth Atlanta Classic playoff to Corey Pavin...first TOUR victory came in 1987 Southwest Classic, then won twice on West Coast to start 1988: MONY Tournament of Champions and Shearson Lehman Hutton-Andy Williams Open...was second at '90 International after making double-eagle two.

PERSONAL: Has earned nickname "Volcano" for sometimes volatile on-course temper...member 1991 Ryder Cup team, but deep hip bruise suffered when three limos collided en route to opening banquet limited play to one team match...member 1988 Kirin Cup squad...made Santa Barbara, CA high school team as freshman, won California Interscholastic Federation title as senior...teammate of Corey Pavin, Duffy Waldorf and Jay Delsing at UCLA...won 1983 PAC-10 Championship, along with four collegiate events...1983 All-America.

1994 PGA TOUR STATISTICS

Scoring Average	70.86	(54)
Driving Distance	261.5	(94)
Driving Accuracy	69.0	(92T)
Greens in Regulation	67.6	(46T)
Putting	1.790	(80T)
All-Around	642	(70T)
Sand Saves	46.4	(146T)
Total Driving	186	(105)
Eagles	4	(104T)
Birdies	319	(26T)

MISCELLANEOUS STATISTICS

Scoring Avg. (before cut)	71.09	(58T)
Scoring Avg. (3rd round)	71.17	(101T)
Scoring Avg. (4th round)	70.95	(45T)
Birdie Conversion	28.2	(87T)
Par Breakers	19.3	(67T)

1994 Low Round: 64: Southwestern Bell Colonial/2

Career Low Round: 62: 1989 Bob Hope Chrysler Classic/3

Career Largest Paycheck: **$180,000**/1991 Honda Classic/1; 1992 Buick Invitational of California/1

DENNIS PAULSON

EXEMPT STATUS: 125th on 1994 money list

FULL NAME: Dennis J. Paulson

HEIGHT: 6'   **WEIGHT:** 195

BIRTH DATE: September 27, 1962

BIRTHPLACE: San Gabriel CA

RESIDENCE: Palm Desert, CA; plays out of The Farms GC of Rancho Santa Fe

FAMILY: Wife, Linda

COLLEGE: San Diego State University

SPECIAL INTERESTS: Bikes, fishing, shooting

TURNED PROFESSIONAL: 1985

Q SCHOOL: 1993

PLAYER PROFILE

CAREER EARNINGS: $142,515

BEST-EVER FINISH: T4--1994 Freeport-McMoRan Classic.

MONEY & POSITION: 1994--$142,515--125

BEST 1994 FINISH: T4--Freeport-McMoRan Classic

1994 SUMMARY: Tournaments entered--27; in money--12; top ten finishes--1.

1995 PGA TOUR CHARITY TEAM COMPETITION: New England Classic

1994 SEASON: Made most of opportunity after finishing 10th in 1993 Qualifying Tournament...assured retention of playing privileges with T18 in Greater Milwaukee Open, worth $12,171, which pushed earnings total to $139,534...made early mark with T4 in Freeport-McMoRan Classic...play at English Turn featured course-record 62 in Round 2, when he was member of last group on course...12-stroke improvement from opening-round 74...posted new standard day after Jose Maria Olazabal had lowered mark to 63...279 total was worth $49,600...after missing pair of cuts to open season, posted T12 in AT&T Pebble Beach National Pro-Am...had second-best finish in Buick Open, T11...missed final four cuts closing out year...second in driving distance to Davis Love III with an average of 283.0.

CAREER HIGHLIGHTS: Played three years on Asian Tour, winning 1990 Philippine Open...winner 1990 California State Open, 1993 Utah State Open...National Long Driving Championship winner.

PERSONAL: Earned playing privileges on ninth visit to Qualifying Tournament in 1993.

1994 PGA TOUR STATISTICS·

Scoring Average	71.31	(99)
Driving Distance	283.0	(2)
Driving Accuracy	57.2	(177T)
Greens in Regulation	66.5	(76T)
Putting	1.787	(73T)
All-Around	679	(83)
Sand Saves	47.7	(137T)
Total Driving	179	(91T)
Eagles	7	(44T)
Birdies	285	(71T)

MISCELLANEOUS STATISTICS

Scoring Avg. (before cut)	71.45	(91T)
Scoring Avg. (3rd round)	70.91	(80T)
Scoring Avg. (4th round)	71.45	(87)
Birdie Conversion	30.9	(14T)
Par Breakers	21.1	(17T)

1994 Low Round: 62: Freeport-McMoRan Classic/2

Career Low Round: 62: 1994 Freeport-McMoRan Classic/2

Career Largest Paycheck: $49,600: 1994 Freeport-McMoRan Classic/T4

COREY PAVIN

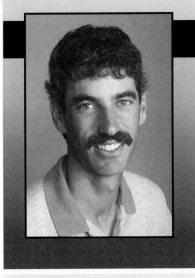

EXEMPT STATUS: 1991 leading money winner

FULL NAME: Corey Pavin

HEIGHT: 5' 9"   **WEIGHT:** 150

BIRTH DATE: November 16, 1959

BIRTHPLACE: Oxnard, CA

RESIDENCE: Orlando, FL

FAMILY: Wife, Shannon; Ryan (5/29/86), Austin James (3/5/93)

COLLEGE: UCLA

TURNED PROFESSIONAL: 1982

Q SCHOOL: Fall 1983

PLAYER PROFILE

CAREER EARNINGS: $5,835,444   **PLAYOFF RECORD:** 5-2

TOUR VICTORIES: (TOTAL: 11) **1984** Houston Coca-Cola Open **1985** Colonial National Invitation **1986** Hawaiian Open, Greater Milwaukee Open. **1987** Bob Hope Chrysler Classic, Hawaiian Open. **1988** Texas Open presented by Nabisco. **1991** Bob Hope Chrysler Classic, BellSouth Atlanta Classic **1992** Honda Classic. **1994** Nissan Los Angeles Open.

MONEY & POSITION:

1984--$260,536--18	1988--$216,768--50	1992--$980,934-- 5
1985--$367,506-- 6	1989--$177,084--82	1993--$675,087--18
1986--$304,558--19	1990--$468,830--26	1994--$906,305-- 8
1987--$498,406--15	1991--$979,430-- 1	

BEST 1994 FINISHES: 1--Nissan Los Angeles Open; 2--Buick Open, PGA Championship; T2--AT&T Pebble Beach National Pro-Am; T3--Canon Greater Hartford Open; 4--United Airlines Hawaiian Open; T8--Masters Tournament; T9--Southwestern Bell Colonial; T10--TOUR Championship.

1994 SUMMARY: Tournaments entered--20; in money--16; top ten finishes--9.

1995 PGA TOUR CHARITY TEAM COMPETITION: NEC World Series of Golf

NATIONAL TEAMS: Ryder Cup (2),1991, 1993; Walker Cup, 1981; Nissan Cup, 1985; Presidents Cup, 1994.

1994 SEASON: Posted third campaign with over $900,000 in earnings, all of which have come in last four years...opened season with three top-10 finishes, climaxed by 11th TOUR title in battle with Fred Couples at Nissan Los Angeles Open...second-round 64 gave him three-stroke lead over Couples at midpoint; Couples was one-up after 54 holes...victory came week after native Californian finished T2 in AT&T Pebble Beach National Pro-Am, one stroke behind Johnny Miller...had solo fourth in United Airlines Hawaiian Open ...missed three cuts following L.A. win, rebounded with T8 in Masters...finished T9 in Southwestern Bell Colonial in May, followed by another three consecutive top-10s from June-August (Canon GHO, Buick Open, PGA Championship)...solo second in PGA his best finish in major...went 2-2-1 in five Presidents Cup matches...concluded season with T10 in TOUR Championship, ninth top-10 finish...won Tokai Classic in Japan in October.

CAREER HIGHLIGHTS: Winner 1993 World Match Play Championship...member 1991-93 Ryder Cup teams, earning "Bulldog" label for role in U.S. win in 1993...holed dramatic 136-yard 8-iron for eagle on final hole of 1992 Honda Classic to force playoff with Fred Couples, then won with birdie on second extra hole...lost playoff to Bruce Lietzke in '92 Colonial...won Arnold Palmer Award as PGA TOUR's Official Money Leader in 1991...also honored as PGA of America's Player of Year...'91 season featured pair of playoff victories: over Mark O'Meara in Bob Hope Chrysler Classic (his second Hope victory) and Steve Pate in BellSouth Atlanta Classic...also lost Canon Greater Hartford Open playoff to Billy Ray Brown...Hope finish was 29-under-par 331, then-TOUR record for 90-hole event...scored victories first five years on TOUR, beginning with Houston Open in 1984...captured 1988 Texas Open with 21-under-par 259, becoming just fifth player in TOUR history to better 260...winner 1983 South African PGA, German Open, Calberson Classic (France)...member 1981 Walker Cup and 1985 Nissan Cup teams.

PERSONAL: At 17, won Junior World title and became youngest winner of Los Angeles City Men's crown...1981 winner North-South Amateur, Southwest Amateur, Maccabiah Games...won 11 college tournaments at UCLA, including 1982 PAC-10 title.

1994 PGA TOUR STATISTICS

Scoring Average	69.63	(7)
Driving Distance	252.3	(158T)
Driving Accuracy	76.9	(15T)
Greens in Regulation	64.5	(125T)
Putting	1.749	(7)
All-Around	540	(43T)
Sand Saves	65.4	(1)
Total Driving	173	(81T)
Eagles	4	(104T)
Birdies	234	(123T)

MISCELLANEOUS STATISTICS

Scoring Avg. (before cut)	70.18	(10)
Scoring Avg. (3rd round)	70.40	(48T)
Scoring Avg. (4th round)	70.47	(21T)
Birdie Conversion	29.6	(40T)
Par Breakers	19.4	(64T)

1994 Low Round: 64: Nissan Los Angeles Open/2

Career Low Round: 62: 1990 H-E-B Texas Open/1

Career Largest Paycheck: **$198,000**/1991 Bob Hope /1 1992 Honda Classic/1

CALVIN PEETE

EXEMPT STATUS: Winner, 1985 Tournament Players Championship

FULL NAME: Calvin Peete

HEIGHT: 5' 10" **WEIGHT:** 165

BIRTH DATE: July 18, 1943

BIRTHPLACE: Detroit, MI

RESIDENCE: Ponte Vedra Beach, FL

FAMILY: Wife, Pepper; Calvin (8/9/68), Dennis (12/4/69), Rickie (12/13/69), Kalvanetta Kristina (5/3/75), Elaine Aisha (11/30/93)

TURNED PROFESSIONAL: 1971

Q SCHOOL: Spring 1975

PLAYER PROFILE

CAREER EARNINGS: $2,302,363   **PLAYOFF RECORD:** 0-1

TOUR VICTORIES: **1979** Greater Milwaukee Open. **1982** Greater Milwaukee Open, Anheuser-Busch Clas-
(TOTAL: 12)   sic, B.C. Open, Pensacola Open. **1983** Georgia-Pacific Atlanta Classic, Anheuser-Busch Classic. **1984** Texas Open. **1985** Phoenix Open, Tournament Players Championship. **1986** MONY Tournament of Champions, USF&G Classic.

MONEY & POSITION:

1976--$ 22,966-- 94	1983--$313,845-- 4	1990--$ 54,379--173
1977--$ 20,525--105	1984--$232,124-- 25	1991--$ 4,978--256
1978--$ 20,459--108	1985--$384,489-- 3	1992--$ --
1979--$122,481-- 27	1986--$374,953-- 12	1993--$ --
1980--$105,716-- 42	1987--$ 56,841--140	1994--4 --
1981--$ 93,243-- 43	1988--$138,310-- 87	
1982--$318,470-- 4	1989--$ 38,584--175	

1994 SUMMARY: Tournaments entered--1; in money--0; top ten finishes--0.

NATIONAL TEAMS: Ryder Cup (2) 1983, 1985; U.S. vs. Japan (2) 1982, 1983; Nissan Cup, 1985

1994 SEASON: Made only PGA TOUR start in THE PLAYERS Championship, withdrawing after one round (85)...earned $175,432 in 19 Senior TOUR events, with best finish and lone top-10 being T5 in Vantage Championship worth $66,000.

CAREER HIGHLIGHTS: "Outstanding" best way to describe play in mid-80s, when won 11 tournaments during five-year span...during that period regarded as one of game's truly great ball-strikers...most prestigious victory came in 1985 Tournament Players Championship, when final-round 66 provided three-stroke edge over D.A. Weibring and 10-year PGA TOUR exemption...first TOUR win came in 1979 Greater Milwaukee Open...repeated GMO success in 1982, when won four times...last triumphs were in 1986: MONY-Tournament of Champions and USF&G Classic...won driving accuracy title 10 straight years (1981-1990)...led TOUR three times in hitting greens in regulation...won Vardon Trophy for low stroke average in 1984...named recipient of Ben Hogan Award, given by Golf Writers Association of America, in 1983...Hogan Award goes to person who overcame physical handicap or illness to play golf...as youngster suffered broken left elbow, and to this day cannot extend arm...member 1983-85 Ryder Cup teams, 1982-83 USA vs. Japan and 1985 Nissan Cup squads.

PERSONAL: Physical problems also have included left shoulder rotator cuff tear and back trouble...took up golf at 23 in 1966 at urging of friends in Rochester, NY...spent most of early life on Florida farm with 18 brothers and sisters–through two marriages by father...dropped out of school at early age, got into business of selling goods to migrant farm workers...travels took him from Florida to upstate New York, which is where start in golf occurred.

1994 PGA TOUR STATISTICS

Scoring Average	N/A
Driving Distance	N/A
Driving Accuracy	N/A
Greens in Regulation	N/A
Putting	N/A
All-Around	N/A
Sand Saves	N/A
Total Driving	N/A
Eagles	N/A
Birdies	N/A

MISCELLANEOUS STATISTICS

Scoring Avg. (before cut)	N/A
Scoring Avg. (3rd round)	N/A
Scoring Avg. (4th round)	N/A
Birdie Conversion	N/A
Par Breakers	N/A

Career Low Round: **63:** 2 times, most recent
Career Largest '82 B.C. Open/2
Paycheck: **$162,000**/'85 PLAYERS Championship/1

CHRIS PERRY

EXEMPT STATUS: 1st on 1994 NIKE TOUR money list

FULL NAME: Christopher J. Perry

HEIGHT: 6'1"   **WEIGHT:** 195

BIRTH DATE: September 27, 1961

BIRTHPLACE: Edenton, NC

RESIDENCE: Powell, OH

FAMILY: Wife, Kathy, Andrew (3/1/93)

COLLEGE: Ohio State (1984, Education)

SPECIAL INTERESTS: Snow skiing, family

TURNED PROFESSIONAL: 1984

Q SCHOOL: Fall, 1984

PLAYER PROFILE

CAREER EARNINGS: $1,095,413

BEST-EVER FINISH: T2--1987 Kemper Open; T2--1990 Canon Greater Hartford Open

MONEY & POSITION:

1985 -- $ 60,801 -- 110	1989 -- $206,932 -- 67	1993 -- $ 25,332 -- 202
1986 -- $ 72,212 -- 114	1990 -- $259,108 -- 58	1994 -- $ 14,840 -- 237
1987 -- $197,593 -- 56	1991 -- $116,105 -- 126	
1988 -- $ 85,546 -- 121	1992 -- $ 53,943 -- 171	

BEST 1994 FINISH: T11--Deposit Guaranty Golf Classic

1994 TOURNAMENT SUMMARY: Tournaments entered--2; in money--1; top ten finishes--0.

1995 PGA TOUR CHARITY TEAM COMPETITION: FedEx St. Jude Classic

1994 SEASON: 1994 NIKE TOUR Player of the Year…set NIKE TOUR record for earnings in season ($167,148)…also established record with 26 consecutive cuts made, finishing in money in 24 events in 1994 and final two events of 1993…collected first-ever professional victory at NIKE Utah Classic in two-hole playoff to John Elliott in NIKE Mississippi Gulf Coast Classic…led NIKE TOUR in scoring average with 69.77 for 91 rounds; third among eagle leaders with 14; sixth among birdie leaders with 344; 11th among par breakers with 21.9%…also ranked first in final-round scoring average with 69.50…1994 NIKE TOUR summary: tournaments entered–24; in money–24; top 10 finishes–10…played two PGA TOUR events in 1994: missed cut at U.S. Open and earned $14,840 with T11 at Deposit Guaranty Golf Classic…captured Mexican Open title.

CAREER HIGHLIGHTS: Member PGA TOUR since 1985…began 1995 season ranked 160th among career money leaders with $1,095,413…top TOUR finishes two T2s (1987 Kemper Open and 1990 Canon Greater Hartford Open)…best year on TOUR saw him earn $259,108 (58th) in 1990…finished higher on money list (56th) in 1987 with earnings of $197,593…lost PGA TOUR card following 1992 season (171 on money list), spent 1993 playing PGA TOUR events when possible and filling in schedule with NIKE TOUR events…earned $13,337 to finish 94th on NIKE TOUR money list…decided to concentrate solely on NIKE TOUR in 1994, a decision that proved wise as he finished first on money list.

PERSONAL: "I became too mechanical with my game, got too many lessons and got away from my natural ability" is how he explains losing PGA TOUR card…joined TOUR after being named 1984 Collegiate Player-of-the-Year at Ohio State…three-time first-team All-America selection (1982-84) who broke Jack Nicklaus' school record for most career victories with 14 and won Big Ten Championship in 1983…was runnerup in 1983 U.S. Amateur to Jay Sigel…also played baseball and hockey as youngster, captain of high school hockey team his senior year…father, Jim Perry, pitched for Cleveland, Minnesota, Detroit and Oakland…uncle, Gaylord Perry, Hall of Fame pitcher…as ninth-grader, had 9-0 pitching record with 0.91 earned run average and batted .325.

1994 PGA TOUR STATISTICS

Scoring Average	N/A
Driving Distance	N/A
Driving Accuracy	N/A
Greens in Regulation	N/A
Putting	N/A
All-Around	N/A
Sand Saves	N/A
Total Driving	N/A
Eagles	N/A
Birdies	N/A

MISCELLANEOUS STATISTICS

Scoring Avg. (before cut)	N/A
Scoring Avg. (3rd round)	N/A
Scoring Avg. (4th round)	N/A
Birdie Conversion	N/A
Par Breakers	N/A

1994 Low Round: 68: Deposit Guaranty Golf Classic

Career Low Round: **63:** 1990 Canon GHO/3

Career Largest Paycheck: **$66,000**/1990 Canon GHO/T2

KENNY PERRY

EXEMPT STATUS: 1994 tournament winner

FULL NAME: James Kenneth Perry

HEIGHT: 6' 1''   **WEIGHT:** 190

BIRTH DATE: August 10, 1960

BIRTHPLACE: Elizabethtown, KY

RESIDENCE: Franklin, KY; plays out of Franklin CC

FAMILY: Wife, Sandy; Lesslye (5/20/84), Justin (11/23/85), Lindsey (4/27/88)

COLLEGE: Western Kentucky University

SPECIAL INTERESTS: Restoring old cars, all sports

TURNED PROFESSIONAL: 1982

Q SCHOOL: Fall 1986

PLAYER PROFILE

CAREER EARNINGS: $2,070,684   **PLAYOFF RECORD:** 1-0

TOUR VICTORIES: **1991** Memorial Tournament. **1994** New England Classic. (TOTAL:2)

MONEY & POSITION:
1987--$107,239--93	1990--$279,881--50	1993--$196,863--88
1988--$139,421--85	1991--$368,784--44	1994--$585,941--26
1989--$202,099--70	1992--$190,455--81	

BEST 1994 FINISHES: 1--New England Classic; 2--Hardee's Golf Classic; T4--Freeport-McMoRan Classic; T7--Kemper Open.

1994 SUMMARY: Tournaments entered-30; in money--22; top ten finishes--4.

1995 PGA TOUR CHARITY TEAM COMPETITION: GTE Byron Nelson Classic

1994 SEASON: Highlight of year, his finest of eight on PGA TOUR, came in July…fired closing-round 65 to take New England Classic by one stroke over David Feherty, who had been co-leader (with Ed Fiori) after 54 holes…was one stroke off both 36- and 54-hole leads…victory was second of career, first since 1991 Memorial…finished in Top 30 on money list for first time, more than $200,000 better than previous best season of '91…finished second by one stroke to Mark McCumber in Hardee's Golf Classic in September after bogeying 72nd hole…was playing with McCumber in final pairing of day…had other top-10s in Freeport-McMoRan Classic in April (T4) and Kemper Open in June (T7)…finished eighth on TOUR in 1994 with 355 birdies.

CAREER HIGHLIGHTS: Claimed first TOUR victory at The Memorial in 1991…Muirfield Village course-record nine-under-par 63 in Round 2 propelled to lead…Hale Irwin caught him on final day, forcing playoff…birdie on first extra hole provided win and $216,000 first-place check. ..Memorial triumph led to best year at that point with earnings of $386,784…'91 season included two other top-10 finishes: T8 Anheuser-Busch Golf Classic, T10 Canon Greater Hartford Open…best finishes prior to Memorial were T2s 1989 MCI Heritage Classic and 1990 AT&T Pebble Beach National Pro-Am…money-won total dropped for first time in career in 1992…rebounded slightly in 1993, but had to play catch-up late in season to save his card…back-to-back September top-10s (T10 Canadian Open, T8 Hardee's Golf Classic) helped put him over top…finished second in Charley Pride Classic on TPS…played collegiately at Western Kentucky.

PERSONAL: Encouraged by his "biggest fan," Kenny Perry, Sr., to start playing golf at age 7…father used to sit for hours teeing golf balls up for him…first competition came at 11…won 1978 Kentucky State High School Championship.

1994 PGA TOUR STATISTICS

Scoring Average	70.46	(33T)
Driving Distance	264.9	(61T)
Driving Accuracy	71.0	(66T)
Greens in Regulation	65.7	(92T)
Putting	1.765	(17T)
All-Around	524	(35)
Sand Saves	43.9	(160T)
Total Driving	127	(32)
Eagles	5	(87T)
Birdies	355	(8)

MISCELLANEOUS STATISTICS

Scoring Avg. (before cut)	70.95	(46T)
Scoring Avg. (3rd round)	70.47	(55T)
Scoring Avg. (4th round)	71.05	(52)
Birdie Conversion	30.3	(26)
Par Breakers	20.2	(34T)

1994 Low Round: 65: 2 times
Career Low Round: 63: 1991 Memorial/2
Career Largest
Paycheck: $216,000/1991 Memorial/1

DAN POHL

EXEMPT STATUS: Winner, 1986 NEC World Series of Golf

FULL NAME: Danny Joe Pohl

HEIGHT: 5' 11"   **WEIGHT:** 175

BIRTH DATE: April 1, 1955

BIRTHPLACE: Mt. Pleasant, MI

RESIDENCE: Mt. Pleasant, MI

FAMILY: Wife, Mitzi; Michelle (2/2/78); Joshua Daniel (9/10/84); Taylor Whitney (9/10/86)

COLLEGE: University of Arizona

SPECIAL INTERESTS: Fishing, hunting

TURNED PROFESSIONAL: 1977

Q SCHOOL: Spring 1978,1979

PLAYER PROFILE

CAREER EARNINGS: $2,742,851   **PLAYOFF RECORD:** 1-2

TOUR VICTORIES: 1986 Colonial National Invitational, NEC World Series of Golf (TOTAL: 2)

MONEY & POSITION:

1978--$ 1,047--224	1984--$182,653-- 32	1990--Did not play
1979--$ 38,393--100	1985--$198,829-- 27	1991--$163,438-- 95
1980--$105,008-- 44	1986--$463,630-- 5	1992--$131,486--110
1981--$ 94,303-- 42	1987--$465,269-- 17	1993--$ 97,830--146
1982--$ 97,213-- 39	1988--$396,400-- 27	1994--$ 21,734--221
1983--$ 89,830-- 62	1989--$195,789-- 74	

BEST 1994 FINISH: T27--Nissan Los Angeles Open.

1994 SUMMARY: Tournaments entered--15; in money--6; top ten finishes--0.

NATIONAL TEAMS: Ryder Cup, 1987

1994 SEASON: His already impressive medical history added new chapters and cut significantly into his playing time…whereas back has been prime problem area for years, knees were main culprit in '94…after earlier surgery on left knee, had subsequent procedure on right…spent 1994 into 1995 off-season rehabbing knees (as well as giving continuing attention to back)…as direct result of physical ailments, played in just 15 events…best finish T27 in Nissan Los Angeles Open, featuring final-round 69…made cut in five of first eight starts, then knee problems kicked in…able to complete just one of final nine events to which had committed.

CAREER HIGHLIGHTS: Made strong early start in 1993 before onset of chronic back trouble sidetracked him…later had to pull out of Kmart Greater Greensboro Open after player on son's baseball team fouled "soft toss" into his mouth, loosening his front teeth and requiring 24 stitches…after enduring back pain for years, finally underwent surgery October 2, 1989…spent entire 1990 season in rehabilitation, returning to TOUR for 1991 campaign…considering circumstances, produced excellent year in '91, finishing 95th on money list…made first four cuts, later finished T8 at Anheuser-Busch Golf Classic and T7 at Canon Greater Hartford Open…at Anheuser-Busch had two-stroke lead after three rounds (64-67-65) before lengthy rain delay made it impossible to stretch out back…finished with 77…won twice in 1986 when captured Colonial National Invitation and NEC World Series of Golf, earning 10-year TOUR exemption…member 1987 Ryder Cup team…winner 1987 Vardon Trophy…winner 1987 All-Around category…winner 1988 EPSON Stats Match…TOUR driving distance leader 1980-81.

PERSONAL: Nickname "Pohl Cat"…pursuing career in golf course architecture…Michigan State Amateur champion 1975, '77…one of leading proponents of and possibly most frequent visitor to Centinela Fitness Trailer, stretching to get loose before every event, then has followup regimen at conclusion of play each day.

1994 PGA TOUR STATISTICS

Scoring Average	72.04
Driving Distance	273.9
Driving Accuracy	69.2
Greens in Regulation	67.7
Putting	1.840
All-Around	–
Sand Saves	51.4
Total Driving	–
Eagles	3
Birdies	122

MISCELLANEOUS STATISTICS

Scoring Avg. (before cut)	71.2
Scoring Avg. (3rd round)	72.50
Scoring Avg. (4th round)	72.50
Birdie Conversion	23.3
Par Breakers	16.1

1994 Low Round: 68: 3 times
Career Low Round: 62: 1989 Honda Classic/2
Career Largest Paycheck: $126,000/'86 NEC World Series of Golf/1

DON POOLEY

EXEMPT STATUS: Special Medical Extension

FULL NAME: Sheldon George Pooley, Jr.

HEIGHT: 6' 3"   **WEIGHT:** 185

BIRTH DATE: August 27, 1951

BIRTHPLACE: Phoenix, AZ

RESIDENCE: Tucson, AZ; plays out of LaPaloma CC, Tucson, AZ

FAMILY: Wife, Margaret; Lynn (1/19/80), Kerri (5/19/82)

COLLEGE: University of Arizona (1973, Business Administration)

SPECIAL INTERESTS: Tennis, basketball

TURNED PROFESSIONAL: 1973

Q SCHOOL: Fall 1975, 1976

PLAYER PROFILE

CAREER EARNINGS: $2,584,319

TOUR VICTORIES: 1980 B.C. Open. **1987** Memorial Tournament.
(TOTAL: 2)

MONEY & POSITION:

1976--$ 2,139--208	1982--$ 87,962--48	1988--$239,534-- 46
1977--$ 24,507-- 94	1983--$145,979--36	1989--$214,662-- 66
1978--$ 31,945-- 84	1984--$120,699--54	1990--$192,570-- 83
1979--$ 6,932--170	1985--$162,094--46	1991--$ 67,549--156
1980--$157,973-- 18	1986--$268,274--22	1992--$135,683--107
1981--$ 75,730-- 57	1987--$450,005--18	1993--$123,105--122
		1994--$ 76,978--171

BEST 1994 FINISH: 3--Texas Open

1994 SUMMARY: Tournaments entered--5; in money--3; top ten finishes--1.

1995 PGA TOUR CHARITY TEAM COMPETITION: Shell Houston Open

1994 SEASON: Season, although abbreviated, nearly produced one of the all-time great comeback stories…after-effects from neck disc surgery 10/15/93 limited play to just two events early, MCI Heritage Classic in April (T30) and BellSouth Classic in May (withdrew after one round)…went from Oct. 1993-April, then again May-September without touching club…wasn't sure whether would ever play again…changed rehab program during summer…credits physical therapist Tom Boers with enabling him to swing again without much pain by September…decided to enter Buick Southern Open, invited Boers to caddy (hastens to point out was to be his "first and last attempt")…finished weather-shortened event, placing T60…decided to enter Texas Open two weeks later…fashioned consecutive middle rounds of 65…was tied with Gil Morgan after 54 holes, four shots behind eventual winner Bob Estes, whose heels he (and Morgan) dogged through final 18…with closing 68 finished solo third, one stroke behind Morgan and two in back of Estes…unable to keep brief success streak going next week at Las Vegas Invitational, where missed cut.

CAREER HIGHLIGHTS: Hampered past four seasons by lower back problems and other ailments…suffered ruptured neck disc while taking practice swing while trying to play way through back problem…back hampered throughout 1991 season, caused him to miss first four months of 1993…received medical extension for 12 tournaments in '92, managed to put together enough playing time in '93 to retain playing privileges for 1994…first victory came in 1980 B.C. Open, where closed with 68 for one-stroke win over Peter Jacobsen…came from four strokes behind final day of 1987 Memorial Tournament to overtake Scott Hoch…scored Million Dollar Hole-in-One at 1987 Bay Hill Classic…192-yard 4-iron hit 17th hole flagstick two feet above cup and dropped in…Arnold Palmer Children's Hospital received $500,000…winner 1989 Ebel Match Play, 1992 Amoco Centel Championship…won 1985 Vardon Trophy, led TOUR in putting average in 1988.

PERSONAL: Made swing change in 1992 to take pressure off lower back.

1994 PGA TOUR STATISTICS

Scoring Average	71.30
Driving Distance	252.5
Driving Accuracy	73.2
Greens in Regulation	61.5
Putting	1.711
All-Around	--
Sand Saves	59.5
Total Driving	--
Eagles	0
Birdies	53

MISCELLANEOUS STATISTICS

Scoring Avg. (before cut)	71.30
Scoring Avg. (3rd round)	69.50
Scoring Avg. (4th round)	70.00
Birdie Conversion	31.9
Par Breakers	19.6

1994 Low Round:	**65:** 2 times
Career Low Round:	**61:** 1986 Phoenix Open/2
Career Largest Paycheck:	**$140,000**/1987 Memorial Tournament/1

NICK PRICE

EXEMPT STATUS: Winner, 1994 PGA Championship

FULL NAME: Nicholas Raymond Leige Price

HEIGHT: 6'   **WEIGHT:** 190

BIRTH DATE: January 28, 1957

BIRTHPLACE: Durban, South Africa

RESIDENCE: Orlando, FL (moving to Jupiter, FL early 1995); plays out of Lake Nona, Orlando

FAMILY: Wife, Sue; Gregory (8/9/91); Robyn Frances (8/5/93)

SPECIAL INTERESTS: Water skiing, tennis, fishing, flying

TURNED PROFESSIONAL: 1977

Q SCHOOL: Fall 1982

PLAYER PROFILE

CAREER EARNINGS: $6,726,418   **PLAYOFF RECORD:** 1-1

TOUR VICTORIES: **1983** World Series of Golf. **1991** GTE Byron Nelson Classic, Canadian Open. **1992** (TOTAL: 14) PGA Championship, H-E-B Texas Open. **1993** The PLAYERS Championship, Canon Greater Hartford Open, Sprint Western Open, Federal Express St. Jude Classic. **1994** Honda Classic, Southwestern Bell Colonial, Western Open, PGA Championship, Bell Canadian Open.

MONEY & POSITION:

1983--$ 49,435--103	1987--$334,169--28	1991--$ 714,389--7
1984--$109,480-- 66	1988--$266,300--42	1992--$1,135,773--4
1985--$ 96,069-- 80	1989--$296,170--42	1993--$1,478,557--1
1986--$225,373-- 35	1990--$520,777--22	1994--$1,499,927--1

BEST 1994 FINISHES: 1--Honda Classic, Southwestern Bell Colonial, Motorola Western Open, PGA Championship, Bell Canadian Open; T2--Nestle Invitational; 4--Federal Express St. Jude Classic; T10--NEC World Series of Golf.

1994 SUMMARY: Tournaments entered--19; in money--14; top ten finishes--8.

1995 PGA TOUR CHARITY TEAM COMPETITION: JCPenney Classic

NATIONAL TEAMS: Zimbabwe Dunhill Cup, 1993; World Cup, 1993; Presidents Cup, 1994.

1994 SEASON: Garnered six more titles, including first British Open crown and second PGA Championship...PGA Championship win moved him to top of Sony Rankings...first to win two majors in year since Nick Faldo (1990)...first to win British Open and PGA back-to-back since Walter Hagen (1924)...winning 269 total at Southern Hills broke Bobby Nichols' PGA Championship record (1964) ...third foreigner to win two PGAs: Jim Barnes 1916-19, Gary Player 1962-72...first since Watson (1980) to win six times in year...10 victories in two years best since Watson won 11 in 1979-80...followed Fred Couples as back-to-back winner of PGA TOUR Player of Year Award...claimed last two PGA Player of Year Awards...first since Curtis Strange in 1987-88 to capture consecutive Arnold Palmer Awards, breaking own money-won record set just last year in process...developed tendinitis in left wrist in February, missing Johnnie Walker Classic in Thailand and two events in Australia, then won Honda Classic in second TOUR start...named Player of Year by GWAA.

CAREER HIGHLIGHTS: From breakthrough victory in 1992 PGA Championship through end of '94 TOUR season, totaled 17 worldwide wins...proved had ability to win consistently with four TOUR victories in 1993...captured '93 PLAYERS Championship in then-record fashion, later won in three consecutive TOUR starts...first PGA TOUR victory came in 1983 NEC World Series of Golf, then waited until 1991 season for next win. ..captured GTE Byron Nelson Classic and Canadian Open in '91...qualified for '83 World Series as leader of South African Order of Merit...prior to 1994 win, was two-time runnerup in British Open (1982 and 1988)...other non-U.S. victories include 1979 Asseng Invitational (South Africa), 1980 Swiss Open, 1981 South African Masters and Italian Open, 1982 Vaal Reefs Open (South Africa), 1985 and 1994 ICL International (South Africa), 1985 Lancome Trophy (Paris), 1989 West End South Australian Open, 1992 Air New Zealand Shell Open, 1993 Sun City Million Dollar Challenge (by 12 strokes).

PERSONAL: Born in South Africa, moved to Rhodesia (now Zimbabwe) at early age...served two years in Rhodesian Air Force...since parents were British citizens, carries British passport...at 17 won Junior World at Torrey Pines in LaJolla, CA...in 1975 played South African and European Tours as amateur...caddy Jeff (Squeeky) Medlen has achieved "celebrity" status.

1994 PGA TOUR STATISTICS

Scoring Average	69.39	(3)
Driving Distance	277.5	(6T)
Driving Accuracy	73.6	(37T)
Greens in Regulation	69.6	(21)
Putting	1.773	(34T)
All-Around	298	(5)
Sand Saves	58.2	(13T)
Total Driving	43	(1)
Eagles	7	(44T)
Birdies	220	(140T)

MISCELLANEOUS STATISTICS

Scoring Avg. (before cut)	70.31	(13T)
Scoring Avg. (3rd round)	69.50	(8)
Scoring Avg. (4th round)	69.83	(5T)
Birdie Conversion	29.3	(49T)
Par Breakers	21.0	(19T)

1994 Low Round: 64: 2 times
Career Low Round: 62: '92 H-E-B Texas Open/2
Career Largest Paycheck: $450,000/1993 PLAYERS Championship/1

DICKY PRIDE

EXEMPT STATUS: 1994 tournament winner

FULL NAME: Richard Fletcher Pride, III

HEIGHT: 6' **WEIGHT:** 175

BIRTH DATE: July 15, 1969

BIRTHPLACE: Tuscaloosa, AL

RESIDENCE: Orlando, FL

FAMILY: Wife, Kim

COLLEGE: University of Alabama

SPECIAL INTERESTS: Basketball, reading

TURNED PROFESSIONAL: 1992

Q SCHOOL: 1993

PLAYER PROFILE

CAREER EARNINGS: $305,769 **PLAYOFF RECORD:** 1-0

TOUR VICTORIES: 1994 Federal Express St. Jude Classic
(TOTAL: 1)

MONEY & POSITION: 1994--$305,769--57

BEST 1994 FINISHES: 1--Federal Express St. Jude Classic; T8--Deposit Guaranty Golf Classic.

1994 SUMMARY: Tournaments entered--27; in money--12; top ten finishes--2.

1995 PGA TOUR CHARITY TEAM COMPETITION: Nestle Invitational

1994 SEASON: Following rather inauspicious beginning (12 missed cuts in first 17 starts), surprised golf world by winning FedEx St. Jude Classic end of July…opened with 66, then followed with three consecutive 67s at TPC at Southwind…sank memorable 20-foot putt on 72nd hole to tie Hal Sutton and Gene Sauers, then made 25-foot birdie putt for win on first playoff hole…was in Memphis field as third alternate…had first top-10 finish two weeks earlier, T8 at weather-shortened Deposit Guaranty Golf Classic…two-round performance at Annandale GC featured final-18 64…$245,300 of total season earnings came during that three-week span…also had T20 finish in another weather-impacted tournament, GTE Byron Nelson Classic…carded 66 in final of two rounds at TPC at Las Colinas.

CAREER HIGHLIGHTS: Qualified for TOUR with T24 finish in 1993 Qualifying Tournament…semifinalist in 1991 U.S. Amateur…two-time All-Southeastern Conference.

PERSONAL: Hole-in-one on 16th hole at Buick Southern Open won Buick of his choice for then-fiancee Kim (they were married in December).

1994 PGA TOUR STATISTICS

Scoring Average	72.40	(170T)
Driving Distance	261.7	(90)
Driving Accuracy	68.0	(105)
Greens in Regulation	62.8	(152)
Putting	1.823	(151T)
All-Around	964	(152T)
Sand Saves	49.5	(116T)
Total Driving	195	(115T)
Eagles	7	(44T)
Birdies	226	(136)

MISCELLANEOUS STATISTICS

Scoring Avg. (before cut)	72.60	(166T)
Scoring Avg. (3rd round)	70.11	(24)
Scoring Avg. (4th round)	73.60	(172)
Birdie Conversion	27.0	(126T)
Par Breakers	17.5	(141T)

1994 Low Round:64: Deposit Guaranty Golf Classic/2
Career Low Round: 64: 1994 Deposit Guaranty Golf Classic/2
Career Largest Paycheck: $225,000/1994 FedEx St. Jude Classic/1

DILLARD PRUITT

EXEMPT STATUS: 105th on 1994 money list

HEIGHT: 5' 11" **WEIGHT:** 180

BIRTH DATE: September 24, 1961

BIRTHPLACE: Greenville, SC

RESIDENCE: Greenville, SC

FAMILY: Wife, Fran

COLLEGE: Clemson

SPECIAL INTERESTS: Music, Harley-Davidson motorcycles

TURNED PROFESSIONAL: 1985

Q SCHOOL: Fall 1988,1989,1990

PLAYER PROFILE

CAREER EARNINGS: $911,625

TOUR VICTORIES: 1991 Chattanooga Classic
(TOTAL: 1)

| **MONEY & POSITION:** | 1988--$33,889--164 | 1991--$271,861--63 | 1993--$168,053-- 98 |
| | 1990--$76,352--150 | 1992--$189,604--82 | 1994--$171,866--105 |

BEST 1994 FINISHES: T8--Texas Open; T9--Northern Telecom Open.

1994 SUMMARY: Tournaments entered--29; in money--18; top ten finishes--2.

1995 PGA TOUR CHARITY TEAM COMPETITION: Anheuser-Busch Golf Classic

1994 SEASON: Had pair of top-10s, each of which came at opposite ends of season spectrum...finished T9 in Northern Telecom Open, his second appearance of campaign...placed T8 in Texas Open, his next-to-last start...opened with 64 at Tucson National to hold early Northern Telecom edge, then shared 36- and 54-hole leads before closing with 73...made $25,000 with Texas Open finish, then earned $21,750 for T16 in final week's Las Vegas Invitational to assure playing privileges for 1995...largest check of season came with T19 in THE PLAYERS Championship, $31,375...began drive for Top 125 with T24 in Walt Disney World/Oldsmobile Classic week before Texas Open...had third-best finish in Buick Classic, T13.

CAREER HIGHLIGHTS: Fired 20-under-par 260 for two-stroke win over Lance Ten Broeck in 1991 Chattanooga Classic...$126,000 winner's share keyed '91 money-won total of $271,861, best of career...other 1991 top-10 finish NEC World Series of Golf...was third-round leader on 30th birthday, but finished with 77 and T6 at 2-over 282...prior to Chattanooga, best previous finish had been T9 in the 1990 International...long-stated dream was to play in Masters, opportunity which Chattanooga victory provided...finished T13 at Augusta National in 1992, allowing return engagement in '93 (missed cut)...T8 in 1993 Anheuser-Busch Golf Classic featured course-record-tying 62 in third round at Kingsmill GC...played European Tour in 1986-87, posting sixth-place finishes in 1987 German Open and Benson & Hedges event in England...winner Sunnehanna Amateur...three-time All-ACC, one-time All-American...winner two collegiate tournaments.

PERSONAL: Used to skip classes at Clemson to attend Masters, finally had chance to play in 1992-93...various family connections to golf: Jay Haas is brother-in-law, Scott Verplank is married to his sister-in-law; Jay and brother Jerry Haas's uncle is Bob Goalby...Jay Haas has had strong influence on development of his game and career...enjoys riding Harley-Davidson motorcycles on roads around Greenville, SC home.

1994 PGA TOUR STATISTICS

Scoring Average	71.26	(93)
Driving Distance	252.3	(158T)
Driving Accuracy	77.3	(12T)
Greens in Regulation	67.7	(45)
Putting	1.803	(115T)
All-Around	580	(54)
Sand Saves	52.8	(73T)
Total Driving	170	(74T)
Eagles	9	(17T)
Birdies	287	(67)

MISCELLANEOUS STATISTICS

Scoring Avg. (before cut)	71.55	(103T)
Scoring Avg. (3rd round)	70.19	(30)
Scoring Avg. (4th round)	71.56	(95T)
Birdie Conversion	26.7	(134T)
Par Breakers	18.7	(97T)

1994 Low Round: **64:** 2 times
Career Low Round: **62:** 2 times, most recent
Career Largest 1993 Anheuser-Busch/3
Paycheck: **$126,000**/1991 Chattanooga Classic/1

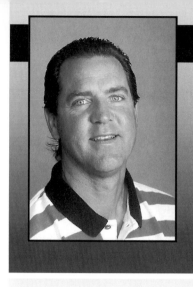

TOM PURTZER

EXEMPT STATUS: Winner, 1991 NEC World Series of Golf

FULL NAME: Thomas Warren Purtzer

HEIGHT: 6'   **WEIGHT:** 180

BIRTH DATE: Dec. 5, 1951

BIRTHPLACE: Des Moines, IA

RESIDENCE: Scottsdale, AZ

FAMILY: Wife, Lori; Laura (7/3/80); Ashley (12/5/83); Eric (11/5/85)

COLLEGE: Arizona State (1973, Business)

SPECIAL INTERESTS: All sports, music, auto racing

TURNED PROFESSIONAL: 1973

Q SCHOOL: Spring 1975

PLAYER PROFILE

CAREER EARNINGS: $3,130,116   **PLAYOFF RECORD:** 2-0

TOUR VICTORIES: **1977** Glen Campbell-Los Angeles Open. **1984** Phoenix Open. **1988** Gatlin Brothers-
(TOTAL: 5)   Southwest Classic. **1991** Southwestern Bell Colonial; NEC World Series of Golf

MONEY & POSITION:

1975--$ 2,093--194	1982--$100,118-- 36	1989--$154,868-- 88
1976--$ 26,682-- 82	1983--$103,261-- 55	1990--$285,176-- 49
1977--$ 79,337-- 37	1984--$164,244-- 39	1991--$750,568-- 4
1978--$ 58,618-- 55	1985--$ 49,979--119	1992--$166,722-- 93
1979--$113,270-- 30	1986--$218,281-- 37	1993--$107,570--136
1980--$118,185-- 34	1987--$123,287-- 85	1994--$187,307-- 94
1981--$122,812-- 27	1988--$197,740-- 57	

BEST 1994 FINISHES: T3--Greater Milwaukee Open; T8--Motorola Western Open.

1994 SUMMARY: Tournaments entered--22; in money--13; top ten finishes--2.

1995 PGA TOUR CHARITY TEAM COMPETITION: Las Vegas Invitational

NATIONAL TEAMS: U.S. vs. Japan, 1979 (medalist); Four Tours Championship, 1991

1994 SEASON: High point of year came at Lincoln-Mercury Kapalua International on Nov. 4, when married Lori Johnson…aside from that, high point of season came in Greater Milwaukee Open, where closing 64 lifted him to T3 worth $48,000…T3 best finish since victory in 1991 NEC World Series of Golf…GMO earnings also helped propel him to best money-won campaign since career year of '91…rebounded strongly from 1993, when had second-lowest money list finish of career…with T8 at Motorola Western Open in July, had more than one top-10 finish in year for first time since 1991…held first-round lead by two strokes in Nissan Los Angeles Open after opening with 64, ultimately finished T12.

CAREER HIGHLIGHTS: Had finest campaign in 1991, winning twice and finishing fourth on money list…victories came in Southwestern Bell Colonial and NEC World Series of Golf…World Series victory came in playoff with Jim Gallagher Jr. and Davis Love III…win at age 39 gave him 10-year TOUR exemption and prompted comment: "Now I can play right on to the Senior TOUR (age 50) without any worries"…victory worth $216,000…in '91 Northern Telecom Open tied with Bob Tway, one stroke behind amateur winner Phil Mickelson…since Mickelson could not accept prize money, runnersup collected $144,000 each…first victory came in 1977 Glen Campbell-Los Angeles Open…next win came on home turf, 1984 Phoenix Open…also captured 1988 Southwest Classic in playoff with Mark Brooks…1972 Arizona State Amateur and Southwest Open champion…winner 1986 JCPenney Mixed Team Classic (with Juli Inkster)…won 1993 Fred Meyer Challenge (with Steve Elkington).

PERSONAL: Often described as having "sweetest" swing on TOUR… played high school football before started to concentrate on golf…went to Arizona State and became one of better collegiate players…brother Paul played TOUR for a while…close friend of future baseball Hall of Famer Robin Yount.

1994 PGA TOUR STATISTICS

Scoring Average	70.70	(45)
Driving Distance	270.3	(30T)
Driving Accuracy	69.5	(82T)
Greens in Regulation	69.2	(22T)
Putting	1.826	(154T)
All-Around	629	(66)
Sand Saves	50.4	(101)
Total Driving	112	(22)
Eagles	6	(64T)
Birdies	230	(131T)

MISCELLANEOUS STATISTICS

Scoring Avg. (before cut)	71.27	(72)
Scoring Avg. (3rd round)	70.50	(57T)
Scoring Avg. (4th round)	70.17	(14)
Birdie Conversion	27.2	(121T)
Par Breakers	19.3	(67T)

1994 Low Round:	**64:** 2 times
Career Low Round:	**63:** 1986 Byron Nelson Golf
Career Largest	Classic/2
Paycheck:	**$216,000/**'91 Southwestern Bell /1
	'91 NEC World Series of Golf/1

MIKE REID

EXEMPT STATUS: Winner, 1988 NEC World Series of Golf

FULL NAME: Michael Daniel Reid

HEIGHT: 5' 11"   **WEIGHT:** 160

BIRTH DATE: July 1, 1954

BIRTHPLACE: Bainbridge, MD

RESIDENCE: Provo, UT

FAMILY: Wife, Randolyn; Brendalyn (2/3/81), Lauren Michelle (8/14/83), Michael Daniel (10/2/86), Clarissa Ann (5/27/90), John William (9/29/93)

COLLEGE: Brigham Young University

SPECIAL INTERESTS: Snow skiing, family activities, fishing

TURNED PROFESSIONAL: 1976

Q SCHOOL: Fall 1976

PLAYER PROFILE

CAREER EARNINGS: $ 3,029,011   **PLAYOFF RECORD:** 1-2

TOUR VICTORIES: 1987 Seiko Tucson Open. **1988** NEC World Series of Golf. (TOTAL: 2)

MONEY & POSITION:

1977--$ 26,314--90	1983--$ 99,135--58	1989--$401,665-- 28
1978--$ 37,420--79	1984--$134,672--49	1990--$249,148-- 60
1979--$ 64,046--66	1985--$169,871--40	1991--$152,678-- 98
1980--$206,097-- 9	1986--$135,143--66	1992--$121,376--117
1981--$ 93,037--44	1987--$365,334--24	1993--$ 5,125--270
1982--$ 80,167--51	1988--$533,343--15	1994--$154,441--119

BEST 1994 FINISHES: T9--Canon Greater Hartford Open; T10--Sprint International

1994 SUMMARY: Tournaments entered--22; in money--13; top ten finishes--2.

1995 PGA TOUR CHARITY TEAM COMPETITION: Colonial

NATIONAL TEAMS: World Cup, 1980; Kirin Cup 1988.

1994 SEASON: Returned successfully from "table tennis wars" to post best money-won campaign since 1990...missed most of 1993 after suffering what was first diagnosed as chip fracture of right wrist sustained while playing table tennis in Japan late 1992...injury subsequently determined to be separated tendon, which was surgically repaired...finished T32 in United Airlines Hawaiian Open, first start since May 1993 in Shell Houston Open...opened with 65 in Buick Classic (low round of year), finished T38...had better luck two weeks later in Canon Greater Hartford Open...was two strokes off midpoint lead after opening 66-68, ultimately finished T9...posted only other top-10 in The Sprint International, T10 worth $36,400 (biggest check of season).

CAREER HIGHLIGHTS: After resting wrist injury early stages of 1993, attempted return to action mid-March...after making just five appearances/one cut through early May, further examination revealed separated tendon...two career victories came in back-to-back years, with first setting up second...after ten winless years on TOUR, finally broke through in 11th season, winning 1987 Seiko Tucson Open...Tucson triumph provided entry into 1988 NEC World Series of Golf, which won in playoff with Tom Watson...par on first extra hole was good for title and 10-year TOUR exemption...another freak injury, this one to his back, curtailed play from late March to early June '91...member 1980 World Cup, 1988 Kirin Cup teams...winner 1983, '85 Utah Opens, 1990 Casio World Open (Japan)...teamed with Bob Goalby to win 1983 Shootout at Jeremy Ranch in Park City, UT (Senior PGA TOUR event).

PERSONAL: One of TOUR's straightest drivers...low amateur 1976 U.S. Open...1976 Western Athletic Conference champion...winner 1976 Pacific Coast Amateur...collegiate All-American 1974-75...brother is TPC at Sawgrass General Manager Bill Reid.

1994 PGA TOUR STATISTICS

Scoring Average	70.96	(62)
Driving Distance	250.0	(163T)
Driving Accuracy	73.8	(35T)
Greens in Regulation	66.7	(65T)
Putting	1.791	(83T)
All-Around	792	(122T)
Sand Saves	45.5	(154T)
Total Driving	198	(121)
Eagles	5	(87T)
Birdies	217	(143)

MISCELLANEOUS STATISTICS

Scoring Avg. (before cut)	71.16	(66)
Scoring Avg. (3rd round)	71.25	(105T)
Scoring Avg. (4th round)	71.25	(65T)
Birdie Conversion	27.0	(126T)
Par Breakers	18.4	(110T)

1994 Low Round: 65: Buick Classic/1
Career Low Round: 64: 7 times, most recent 1991 Anheuser-Busch /4
Career Largest Paycheck: $162,000/'88 NEC World Series of Golf/1

STEVE RINTOUL

EXEMPT STATUS: 115th on 1994 money list

FULL NAME: Steven David Rintoul

HEIGHT: 6' 1" **WEIGHT:** 190

BIRTH DATE: June 7, 1963

BIRTHPLACE: Bowral, Australia

RESIDENCE: Sarasota, FL; plays out of Laurel Oak CC

FAMILY: Wife, Jill

COLLEGE: University of Oregon

SPECIAL INTERESTS: Music, dining out, swimming

TURNED PROFESSIONAL: 1988

Q SCHOOL: 1993

PLAYER PROFILE

CAREER EARNINGS: $157,618

BEST-EVER FINISH: 2--1994 Buick Southern Open

MONEY & POSITION:　1994--$157,618--115

BEST 1994 FINISH: 2--Buick Southern Open.

1994 SUMMARY: Tournaments entered--27; in money--15; top ten finshes--1.

1995 PGA TOUR CHARITY TEAM COMPETITION: Buick Southern Open.

1994 SEASON: Put on stretch drive that would have made a throroughbred proud, earning $118,770 over last five weeks of campaign to retain playing privileges…largest check among final five received was $86,400 payday for second-place finish in Buick Southern Open…was five strokes behind fellow Aussie Steve Elkington when final round scrubbed due to weather…having earned just $38,848 for his first 22 starts, Buick Southern check made it possible for him to even think about playing TOUR again in 1995…what actually put him into Top 125 was Texas Open T21 worth $9,133…began stretch drive off streak of five consecutive missed cuts, from Buick Open through B.C. Open…finished T23 in Hardee's Golf Classic week before Buick Southern…top finish/only top-25 in early going was T24 at Kemper Open in June.

CAREER HIGHLIGHTS: Qualified for TOUR by finishing T11 at 1993 Qualifying Tournament…played NIKE TOUR for three years, with best year being 1993 (No. 17 on money list with $71,579)…winner 1987-88 Oregon Stroke Play Amateur Championship, 1988 Oregon State Amateur, 1991 Northwest Open Champion.

PERSONAL: Member 1982 All-Australian schoolboy team…grew up competing with Steve Elkington, with whom remains close friends to this day.

1994 PGA TOUR STATISTICS

Scoring Average	71.30	(97T)
Driving Distance	267.9	(41)
Driving Accuracy	66.9	(121T)
Greens in Regulation	66.4	(80)
Putting	1.794	(95T)
All-Around	618	(63)
Sand Saves	53.8	(57T)
Total Driving	162	(64T)
Eagles	8	(28T)
Birdies	267	(99)

MISCELLANEOUS STATISTICS

Scoring Avg. (before cut)	71.40	(86)
Scoring Avg. (3rd round)	70.25	(37)
Scoring Avg. (4th round)	70.77	(37)
Birdie Conversion	27.9	(102T)
Par Breakers	19.1	(79T)

1994 Low Round: 65: 4 times

Career Low Round: 65: 4 times, most recent 1994 Texas Open/1

Career Largest Paycheck: $61,200/1985 Tournament Players Championship/3

LOREN ROBERTS

EXEMPT STATUS: 1994 tournament winner

FULL NAME: Loren Lloyd Roberts

HEIGHT: 6'2"   **WEIGHT:** 190

BIRTH DATE: June 24, 1955

BIRTHPLACE: San Luis Obispo, CA

RESIDENCE: Memphis, TN

FAMILY: Wife, Kimberly; Alexandria (10/14/86), Addison (10/15/91)

COLLEGE: Cal Poly San Luis Obispo

SPECIAL INTERESTS: Golf

TURNED PROFESSIONAL: 1975

Q SCHOOL: Fall 1980, 1982, 1983, 1986, 1987

PLAYER PROFILE

CAREER EARNINGS: $3,131,398   **PLAYOFF RECORD:** 0-1

TOUR VICTORIES: 1994 Nestle Invitational
(TOTAL: 1)

MONEY & POSITION:

1981--$ 8,935--172	1987--$57,489--138	1992--$ 338,673--43
1983--$ 7,724--189	1988--$136,890--89	1993--$ 316,506--53
1984--$67,515-- 87	1989--$275,882--46	1994--$1,015,671-- 6
1985--$92,761-- 83	1990--$478,522--24	
1986--$53,655--133	1991--$281,174--58	

BEST 1994 FINISHES: 1--Nestle Invitational; 2--Greater Milwaukee Open, U.S. Open; 3--MCI Heritage Classic; T5--Masters Tournament; T7--Doral-Ryder Open; T8--TOUR Championship; T9--PGA Championship.

1994 SUMMARY: Tournaments entered--22; in money--19; top ten finishes--9.

1995 PGA TOUR CHARITY TEAM COMPETITION: FedEx St. Jude Classic

NATIONAL TEAMS: Presidents Cup, 1994

1994 SEASON: Living evidence that hard work does, in fact, pay off…one of record six members in 1994 Millionaires Club…long-awaited first TOUR victory finally became reality at Nestle Invitational, where edged trio of Fuzzy Zoeller, Nick Price and Vijay Singh by a stroke…by winning, discarded label of biggest money winner without a victory…was three strokes off lead entering Sunday play, which produced final-round 67…had opened his year with T2 in Northern Telecom Open, matching best career finish (T2 in 1992 Hardee's Golf Classic) to that point…preceded Nestle victory with T7 in Doral-Ryder Open…went on to record nine top-10 finishes, including impressive performances in U.S. majors: T5 Masters, T2 U.S. Open and T9 PGA Championship…lost 20-hole Open playoff to Ernie Els after missing chance to win on 72nd hole…with T24 in British Open, had best overall record in '94 majors…finished third in MCI Heritage Classic on basis of closing 62…posted Brown Deer Park GC record 63 on way to yet another runnerup finish in Greater Milwaukee Open…member of U.S. Team in inaugural Presidents Cup Match…his $699,165 prize-money increase from 1993 to 1994 was second-largest in TOUR history…led TOUR in putting…winner of Guadalajara Invitational.

CAREER HIGHLIGHTS: Supplanted Bobby Wadkins as PGA TOUR money leader without a tournament win with T3/$52,800 paycheck at 1993 Walt Disney World/Oldsmobile Classic…prior to 1994, best finish/check had come in 1992 Hardee's Golf Classic…tied with Tom Lehman behind wire-to-wire winner David Frost…was solo third two weeks later at Buick Southern Open, three strokes off Gary Hallberg lead when final round cancelled due to wet conditions…first achieved exempt status in 1984-85, then lost card each of next two seasons…won 1992 Ben Hogan Pebble Beach Invitational.

PERSONAL: Regarded by peers as one of hardest workers on TOUR …said of banner year: "I had three goals [in 1994]: one was to be a consistent money winner, the second was to win a tournament, and the third was to win a major"…winner 1979 Foot-Joy National Assistant Pro Championship.

1994 PGA TOUR STATISTICS

Scoring Average	69.61	(6)
Driving Distance	254.3	(150T)
Driving Accuracy	75.6	(21T)
Greens in Regulation	69.0	(28T)
Putting	1.737	(1)
All-Around	409	(20)
Sand Saves	57.8	(17T)
Total Driving	171	(79)
Eagles	2	(146T)
Birdies	306	(40)

MISCELLANEOUS STATISTICS

Scoring Avg. (before cut)	70.12	(9)
Scoring Avg. (3rd round)	69.29	(6)
Scoring Avg. (4th round)	69.59	(1)
Birdie Conversion	32.0	(6T)
Par Breakers	22.2	(6)

1994 Low Round: 62: MCI Heritage Classic/4
Career Low Round: 62: '94 MCI Heritage Classic/4
Career Largest
Paycheck: $216,000/1994 Nestle Invitational/1

GENE SAUERS

EXEMPT STATUS: 73rd on 1994 money list

FULL NAME: Gene Craig Sauers

HEIGHT: 5' 8" **WEIGHT:** 150

BIRTH DATE: August 22, 1962

BIRTHPLACE: Savannah,GA

RESIDENCE: Savannah, GA; plays out of Haig Point Club, Daufuskie Island, SC

FAMILY: Wife, Tammy; Gene, Jr. (1/23/89), Rhett (7/16/90), Dylan Thomas (8/30/93)

COLLEGE: Georgia Southern

SPECIAL INTERESTS: Snow skiing, hunting, sport fishing

TURNED PROFESSIONAL: 1984

Q SCHOOL: Fall 1983

PLAYER PROFILE

CAREER EARNINGS: $2,690,997 **PLAYOFF RECORD:** 1-3

TOUR VICTORIES: 1986 Bank of Boston Classic. **1989** Hawaiian Open. (TOTAL: 2)

MONEY & POSITION:

1984--$ 36,537--128	1988--$280,719--35	1992--$434,566-- 32
1985--$ 48,526--121	1989--$303,669--38	1993--$117,608--128
1986--$199,044-- 42	1990--$374,485--31	1994--$250,654-- 73
1987--$244,655-- 38	1991--$400,535--37	

BEST 1994 FINISHES: T2--FedEx St. Jude Classic; T4--Buick Southern Open.

1994 SUMMARY: Tournaments entered--26; in money--18; top ten finishes--2.

1995 PGA TOUR CHARITY TEAM COMPETITION: Memorial Tournament

1994 SEASON: Rebounded strongly from "down" 1993 campaign...money-won total only sixth-highest of career, but still got him back on upward track...had increased earnings each successive year 1985 through 1992 before '93 downturn...key to his season T2 in FedEx St. Jude Classic...along with Hal Sutton lost TPC at Southwind playoff to Dicky Pride, after three deadlocked at 17-under-par 267, when Pride birdied first playoff hole...co-runnerup finish worth $110,000, biggest payday since earned $135,000 for solo second in 1991 Kmart Greater Greensboro Open...preceded Memphis with T22 in New England Classic, making almost half of season earnings in consecutive weeks...three weeks after FESJC finished T13 in Sprint International...later in year placed T4 in Buick Southern Open (only other top-10 of campaign), giving him all four top-25s in six starts.

CAREER HIGHLIGHTS: In 1993, for first time in 10th year on TOUR, failed to increase money-won total over previous season...also retained playing privileges for '94 by slimmest of margins...finished 128th on money list, the final position to retain fully exempt status...first time in career failed to achieve at least one top-10...best year of career, 1992, could have been even better...began campaign by birdieing all four holes of Bob Hope Chrysler Classic playoff, yet lost to John Cook...had share of or outright lead first three rounds of PGA Championship...finished second at Nestle Invitational, nine strokes behind Fred Couples...recorded playoff victory over Blaine McCallister in 1986 Bank of Boston Classic...won rain-shortened 1989 Hawaiian Open...captured 1990 (unofficial) Deposit Guaranty Golf Classic...lost three-hole playoff to Mark Brooks in 1991 Kmart Greater Greensboro Open.

PERSONAL: Avid sport fisherman who has won fishing tournaments...winner three Georgia State Opens, one as amateur...winner Trans America Athletic Conference title at Georgia Southern...youngest son, Dylan Thomas, not named for Irish poet.

1994 PGA TOUR STATISTICS

Scoring Average	71.07	(75)
Driving Distance	260.3	(103T)
Driving Accuracy	65.1	(137T)
Greens in Regulation	65.1	(110T)
Putting	1.779	(50T)
All-Around	643	(73)
Sand Saves	57.7	(19T)
Total Driving	240	(153T)
Eagles	6	(64T)
Birdies	278	(85T)

MISCELLANEOUS STATISTICS

Scoring Avg. (before cut)	71.51	(97T)
Scoring Avg. (3rd round)	70.67	(68)
Scoring Avg. (4th round)	70.25	(15)
Birdie Conversion	29.0	(57T)
Par Breakers	19.3	(67T)

1994 Low Round:	**66:** 3 times
Career Low Round:	**62:** 2 times, most recent '90 Southwestern Bell Colonial/4
Career Largest Paycheck:	**$135,000**/'89 Hawaiian Open/1 '91 Kmart/2

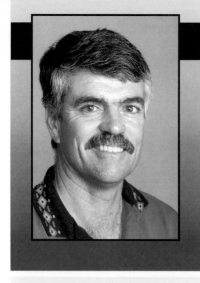

SCOTT SIMPSON

EXEMPT STATUS: Winner, 1987 U.S. Open

FULL NAME: Scott William Simpson

HEIGHT: 6' 2''   **WEIGHT:** 180

BIRTH DATE: Sept. 17, 1955

BIRTHPLACE: San Diego, CA

RESIDENCE: San Diego, CA; Plays out of Makaha Valley, Oahu, HI

FAMILY: Wife, Cheryl; Brea Yoshiko (10/10/82), Sean Tokuzo (10/14/86)

COLLEGE: Univ. of Southern California (1978, Business Administration)

SPECIAL INTERESTS: Ocean sports, Bible study, family activities, jogging

TURNED PROFESSIONAL: 1977   **Q SCHOOL:** Fall 1978

PLAYER PROFILE

CAREER EARNINGS: $3,973,157   **PLAYOFF RECORD:** 1-3

TOUR VICTORIES: **1980** Western Open. **1984** Manufacturers Hanover Westchester Classic. **1987** Greater
(TOTAL: 6)   Greensboro Open, U.S. Open. **1989** BellSouth Atlanta Classic. **1993** GTE Byron Nelson Classic.

MONEY & POSITION:

1979--$ 53,084--74	1985--$171,245-- 39	1991--$322,936--51
1980--$141,323--24	1986--$202,223-- 41	1992--$155,284--97
1981--$108,793--34	1987--$621,032-- 4	1993--$707,166--14
1982--$146,903--24	1988--$108,301--106	1994--$307,884--56
1983--$144,172--38	1989--$298,920-- 40	
1984--$248,581--22	1990--$235,309-- 63	

BEST 1994 FINISHES: 2--Southwestern Bell Colonial; T4--Mercedes Championships.

1994 SUMMARY: Tournaments entered--21; in money--15; top ten finishes--2.

1995 PGA TOUR CHARITY TEAM COMPETITION: AT&T Pebble Beach National Pro-Am

NATIONAL TEAMS: Ryder Cup, 1987; Walker Cup, 1977.

1994 SEASON: Fell off somewhat from career year of 1993, but still managed to earn fourth highest amount of 16-year career...came close to capturing seventh title, but instead wound up playoff loser to Nick Price in Southwestern Bell Colonial...held both second- and third-round leads, latter by four strokes over Gary Hallberg...was tied when Price closed with 64 to his 71...two were among 18 players who, because of weather delays, had to complete fourth round on Monday...Price subsequently birdied first playoff hole for win...opened year with T4 in Mercedes Championships, closing with a 68...following week had T20 in United Airlines Hawaiian Open...preceded Colonial week with T14 in Memorial Tournament...also had back-to-back top-25s, almost month apart, in Buick Invitational of California (T15) and Nestle Invitational (T21).

CAREER HIGHLIGHTS: Enjoyed finest year of career in 1993...captured sixth title by winning GTE Byron Nelson Classic in May...also had T2 in season-ending TOUR Championship at Olympic Club, site of 1987 U.S. Open championship...battled Tom Watson down stretch to win that Open...on final nine made three birdies and saved par three times from off green to win by stroke...has turned Open into own personal showcase since '87 victory...lost Open playoff to Payne Stewart at Hazeltine National in 1991...finished T6 in 1988-89 Opens...defeated Bob Tway in playoff to win 1989 BellSouth Atlanta Classic...claimed first title in second year on TOUR, Western Open in 1980...winner 1984 and 1988 Chunichi Crowns, 1984 Dunlop Phoenix, 1990 Perrier Invitational.

PERSONAL: Winner 1976-77 NCAA Championship, 1976 Porter Cup, 1975 and 1977 PAC-8 Championship...collegiate All-American 1976-77...winner California and San Diego junior titles...winner 1979, 1981 Hawaii State Opens...traditionally takes family time away from TOUR late in season.

1994 PGA TOUR STATISTICS

Scoring Average	70.92	(60)
Driving Distance	260.1	(105)
Driving Accuracy	73.6	(37T)
Greens in Regulation	67.5	(48)
Putting	1.793	(91T)
All-Around	670	(78)
Sand Saves	43.1	(168)
Total Driving	142	(41T)
Eagles	8	(28T)
Birdies	229	(133)

MISCELLANEOUS STATISTICS

Scoring Avg. (before cut)	70.95	(46T)
Scoring Avg. (3rd round)	70.93	(82T)
Scoring Avg. (4th round)	71.79	(114T)
Birdie Conversion	26.9	(128T)
Par Breakers	18.8	(92T)

1994 Low Round: 64: Colonial/3
Career Low Round: 62: 1991 United Airlines Hawaiian Open/1
Career Largest Paycheck: $216,000/'93 GTE Byron Nelson/1

VIJAY SINGH

EXEMPT STATUS: 1993 tournament winner

FULL NAME: Vijay Singh

HEIGHT: 6' 2"   **WEIGHT:** 198

BIRTH DATE: February 22, 1963

BIRTHPLACE: Lautoka, Fiji

RESIDENCE: London, England

FAMILY: Wife, Ardena Seth; Qass Seth (6/19/90)

SPECIAL INTERESTS: Snooker, cricket, rugby, soccer

TURNED PROFESSIONAL: 1982

JOINED TOUR: Spring 1993

PLAYER PROFILE

CAREER EARNINGS: $983,790   **PLAYOFF RECORD:** 1-0

TOUR VICTORIES: 1993 Buick Classic.
(TOTAL: 1)

MONEY & POSITION: 1993--$657,831--19   1994--$325,959--52

BEST 1994 FINISHES: T2--Northern Telecom Open, Nestle Invitational; T5--Shell Houston Open.

1994 SUMMARY: Tournaments entered--21; in money--16; top ten finishes--3.

1995 PGA TOUR CHARITY TEAM COMPETITION: Buick Open

NATIONAL TEAMS: Presidents Cup, 1994

1994 SEASON: Hampered by back problems which began in May…earned only half as much as spectacular Rookie of Year campaign of 1993…forced to withdraw during second round of GTE Byron Nelson Classic, made no money in four subsequent TOUR starts…did return to form, however, on PGA European Tour…captured Scandinavian Masters in July and Lancome Trophy in September… opened with rounds of 65-63--128 in latter, needed birdies on two of final three holes to beat Miguel Angel Jimenez…closing 65 brought T2 in Northern Telecom Open…had subsequent T2 in Nestle Invitational, where held 54-hole lead but closed with 71 to finish tied with Fuzzy Zoeller and Nick Price, one stroke behind Loren Roberts…third top-10 (T5) came in Shell Houston Open, two weeks prior to back injury.

CAREER HIGHLIGHTS: PGA TOUR Rookie of Year for 1993, when won Buick Classic in playoff with Mark Wiebe…came from five strokes back, as did Wiebe, to tie at end of regulation…birdied third extra hole for win…held second-round lead in '93 PGA Championship after Inverness Club record 63…63 equaled lowest 18-hole score in PGA Championship, as well as low 18 in any major…tied PGA 36-hole record of 131 (had opened with 68)…made cut in first eleven PGA TOUR events, first seven of 1993 and four in 1992…gained special temporary membership with T2 finish in '93 Nestle Invitational…winner of 15 events outside U.S., first title came in 1984 Malaysian PGA Championship…joined PGA European Tour in 1989, winning Volvo Open in rookie season…has captured titles in Nigeria, Sweden, Zimbabwe, Spain, Germany, the Ivory Coast and Morocco…led Order of Merit of Safari Tour in Africa in 1988.

PERSONAL: Only world-class golfer produced by Fiji…of Indian ancestry, name means "Victory" in Hindi…Tom Weiskopf was golfing role model…one of TOUR's hardest workers, learned basics of game from father, an airplane technician who also taught golf…left Fiji to pursue dream of becoming professional golfer, tried Australian Tour, later took club job in Malaysia.

1994 PGA TOUR STATISTICS

Scoring Average	71.01	(70)
Driving Distance	274.5	(12T)
Driving Accuracy	64.9	(141)
Greens in Regulation	64.5	(125T)
Putting	1.800	(108T)
All-Around	756	(111)
Sand Saves	46.8	(144)
Total Driving	153	(52T)
Eagles	7	(44T)
Birdies	250	(112)

MISCELLANEOUS STATISTICS

Scoring Avg. (before cut)	71.32	(76T)
Scoring Avg. (3rd round)	71.73	(142T)
Scoring Avg. (4th round)	71.40	(78)
Birdie Conversion	32.4	(4)
Par Breakers	21.5	(13)

1994 Low Round:	65: Northern Telecom Open/4
Career Low Round:	63: 1993 PGA Championship/2
Career Largest Paycheck:	$180,000/1993 Buick Classic/1

JEFF SLUMAN

EXEMPT STATUS: Winner, 1988 PGA Championship

FULL NAME: Jeffrey George Sluman

HEIGHT: 5' 7"   **WEIGHT:** 140

BIRTH DATE: Sept. 11, 1957

BIRTHPLACE: Rochester, NY

RESIDENCE: Chicago, IL

FAMILY: Wife, Linda

COLLEGE: Florida State University (1980, Finance)

SPECIAL INTERESTS: Old cars, stock market, Akitas

TURNED PROFESSIONAL: 1980

Q SCHOOL: Fall 1982, 1984

PLAYER PROFILE

CAREER EARNINGS: $3,296,749   **PLAYOFF RECORD:** 0-3

TOUR VICTORIES: 1988 PGA Championship
(TOTAL: 1)

MONEY & POSITION:

1983--$ 13,643--171	1987--$335,590--27	1991--$552,979--23
1984--$ 603--281	1988--$503,321--18	1992--$729,027--14
1985--$100,523-- 78	1989--$154,507--89	1993--$187,841--93
1986--$154,129-- 60	1990--$264,012--56	1994--$301,178--59

BEST 1994 FINISHES: 2--B.C. Open; T6--Motorola Western Open; T7--Buick Southern Open; T9--U.S. Open.

1994 SUMMARY: Tournaments entered--30; in money--16; top ten finishes-- 4.

1995 PGA TOUR CHARITY TEAM COMPETITION: Canon Greater Hartford Open

1994 SEASON: Came close to elusive second career victory late in campaign, only to fall short once again…held B.C. Open lead through first three rounds, closed with 72 to finish four strokes behind Mike Sullivan…opened with 63 at En-Joie GC, then led Sullivan through Rounds 2 and 3 before stumbling final day… followed Endicott, NY showing with T7 two weeks later in weather-shortened Buick Southern Open…earlier had another pair of top-10s in three weeks, T9 at U.S. Open, T6 in Motorola Western Open…strong finish salvaged up-and-down year…lifted him to over $300,000 and fifth-best earnings campaign …rebounded strongly from 1993, when money-won total worst since 1989.

CAREER HIGHLIGHTS: Recorded one of great finishing rounds in PGA Championship history to win 1988 title…started day three strokes behind Paul Azinger, fired 6-under-par 65 at Oak Tree Golf Club to win by three over Azinger…nearly won twice in 1991, losing playoff to Billy Andrade in Kemper Open and finishing second by stroke to Ted Schulz in Nissan Los Angeles Open…1992 season punctuated by remarkable accomplishments, including final-round 71 and second-place finish in U.S. Open at Pebble Beach (just one of four sub-par rounds that day)…had T4 in Masters, where became first player to ace fourth hole during opening-round 65 that produced tie for lead…first close encounter with victory came in 1987 Tournament Players Championship, where lost three-hole playoff to Sandy Lyle…had unofficial victory in 1985 Tallahassee Open, part of Tournament Players Series.

PERSONAL: Former Player Director, PGA TOUR Policy Board…winner 1980 Metro Conference Championship.

1994 PGA TOUR STATISTICS

Scoring Average	71.04	(72)
Driving Distance	255.4	(141T)
Driving Accuracy	65.1	(137T)
Greens in Regulation	63.9	(138T)
Putting	1.781	(59T)
All-Around	714	(93)
Sand Saves	54.8	(48)
Total Driving	278	(170)
Eagles	6	(64T)
Birdies	296	(55T)

MISCELLANEOUS STATISTICS

Scoring Avg. (before cut)	71.87	(136)
Scoring Avg. (3rd round)	70.53	(60T)
Scoring Avg. (4th round)	71.38	(76T)
Birdie Conversion	28.0	(96T)
Par Breakers	18.2	(119T)

1994 Low Round: 63: B.C. Open/1

Career Low Round: 62: 1992 GTE Byron Nelson Classic/3

Career Largest Paycheck: $160,000/1988 PGA Championship/1

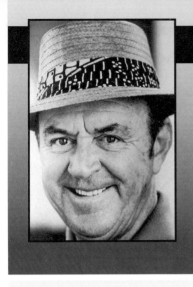

SAM SNEAD

EXEMPT STATUS: Winner, 1942 PGA Championship

FULL NAME: Samuel Jackson Snead

HEIGHT: 5' 11" **WEIGHT:** 190

BIRTH DATE: May 27, 1912

BIRTHPLACE: Hot Springs, VA

RESIDENCE: Hot Springs, VA; represents The Greenbrier, White Sulphur Springs, WV

FAMILY: Sam, Jr. (6/30/44), Ter rance (5/27/52), 2 grandchildren

SPECIAL INTERESTS: Hunting, fishing

TURNED PROFESSIONAL: 1934

JOINED TOUR: 1937

PLAYER PROFILE

CAREER EARNINGS: $620,126 **PLAYOFF RECORD:** 10-8

TOUR VICTORIES: **1936** WestVirginia PGA. **1937** St. Paul Open, Nassau Open, Miami Open, Oakland Open, (TOTAL: 81) Bing Crosby ProAm. **1938** Greensboro Open, Inverness Four-Ball, Goodall Round Robin, Chicago Open, Canadian Open, Westchester 108 Hole Open, White Sulphur Springs Open, Bing Crosby Pro-Am. **1939** Miami Open, St. Petersburg Open, Miami Biltmore Four-Ball. **1940** Inverness Four-Ball, Canadian Open, Anthracite Open. **1941** Canadian Open, St. Petersburg Open, North and South Open, Rochester Times Union Open, Henry Hurst Invitational, Bing Crosby Pro-Am. **1942** St. Petersburg Open, PGA Championship. **1944** Richmond Open, Portland Open. **1945** Los Angeles Open, Gulfport Open, Pensacola Open, Jacksonville Open, Dallas Open, Tulsa Open. **1946** Miami Open, Greensboro Open, Jacksonville Open, Virginia Open, World Championship. **1948** Texas Open. **1949** Greensboro Open, PGA Championship, Masters, Washington Star Open, Dapper Dan Open, Western Open. **1950** Texas Open, MiamiOpen, GreensboroOpen, InvernessFour-Ball, North and South Open, Los Angeles Open, Western Open, Miami Beach Open, Colonial National Inv., Reading Open, Bing Crosby Pro-Am. **1951** Miami Open, PGA Championship. **1952** Inverness Four-Ball, Masters, All American, Eastern Open, Palm Beach Round Robin. **1953** Baton Rouge Open. **1954** Masters, Palm Beach Round Robin. **1955** Miami Open, Greensboro Open, Palm Beach Round Robin, Insurance City Open. **1956** Greensboro Open. **1957** Dallas Open, Palm Beach Round Robin. **1958** Dallas Open. **1960** Greensboro Open, De Soto Open **1961** Tournament of Champions. **1965** Greensboro Open.

MONEY & POSITION:

1937--$10,243-- 3	1952--$19,908-- 4	1967--$ 7,141--104
1938--$19,534-- 1	1953--$14,115-- 15	1968--$43,106-- 39
1939--$ 9,712-- 2	1954--$ 7,889-- 29	1969--$15,439--100
1940--$ 9,206-- 3	1955--$23,464-- 7	1970--$25,103-- 85
1941--$12,848-- 2	1956--$ 8,253-- 36	1971--$22,258-- 94
1942--$ 8,078-- 3	1957--$28,260-- 4	1972--$35,462-- 71
1943--$ --	1958--$15,905-- 18	1973--$38,685-- 78
1944--$ 5,755-- 7	1959--$ 8,221-- 45	1974--$55,562-- 49
1945--$24,436-- 4	1960--$19,405-- 19	1975--$ 8,285--138
1946--$18,341-- 6	1961--$23,906-- 17	1976--$ 2,694--198
1947--$ 9,703-- 12	1962--$ 9,169-- 59	1977--$ 488--256
1948--$ 6,980-- 18	1963--$28,431-- 16	1978--$ 385--265
1949--$31,593-- 1	1964--$ 8,383-- 74	1979--$ 4,671--190
1950--$35,758-- 1	1965--$36,889-- 24	
1951--$15,072-- 6	1966--$12,109-- 72	

SENIOR PGA TOUR SUMMARY

SENIOR VICTORIES: **1964, 1965, 1967, 1970, 1972, 1973** PGA (TOTAL: 13) Seniors. **1964, 1965, 1970, 1972, 1973** World Seniors. **1980** Golf Digest Commemorative Pro-Am; **1982** Legends of Golf (with Don January)

CAREER EARNINGS:
(Regular/Senior TOURS combined): $726,700.

OTHER ACHIEVEMENTS: Credited with 135 victories by independent record keepers. 1949 Player-of-the-Year. 1938, 1949, 1950, 1955 Vardon Trophy winner. 1937, 1939, 1941, 1947, 1949, 1951, 1953 and 1955 Ryder Cup team. Member winning World Cup team in 1956, 1960 and 1961 (won individual title in 1961). Shot age, then bettered it at 1979 Quad Cities (67-66). Member PGA Golf Hall of Fame, World Golf Hall of Fame. Winner, 1946 British Open.

1994 PGA TOUR STATISTICS

Scoring Average	N/A
Driving Distance	N/A
Driving Accuracy	N/A
Greens in Regulation	N/A
Putting	N/A
All-Around	N/A
Sand Saves	N/A
Total Driving	N/A
Eagles	N/A
Birdies	N/A

MISCELLANEOUS STATISTICS

Scoring Avg. (before cut)	N/A
Scoring Avg. (3rd round)	N/A
Scoring Avg. (4th round)	N/A
Birdie Conversion	N/A
Par Breakers	N/A

Career Low Round: 60: 1957 Dallas Open/2
Career Largest
Paycheck: $11,000/1965 Greater Greensboro /1

MIKE SPRINGER

EXEMPT STATUS: 1994 tournament winner

FULL NAME: Michael Paul Springer

HEIGHT: 5'11"   **WEIGHT:** 210

BIRTH DATE: Nov. 3, 1965

BIRTHPLACE: San Francisco, CA

RESIDENCE: Fresno, CA; plays out of Fort Washington CC

FAMILY: Wife, Crystol; Haylee Danielle (5/26/93)

COLLEGE: University of Arizona

SPECIAL INTERESTS: Hunting, skiing

TURNED PROFESSIONAL: 1988

JOINED TOUR: 1991

PLAYER PROFILE

CAREER EARNINGS: $1,308,349

TOUR VICTORIES: 1994 Kmart Greater Greensboro Open, Greater Milwaukee Open. (TOTAL: 2)

MONEY & POSITION: 1991--$178,587-- 91   1993--$214,729--79   1994--$770,717--13
1992--$144,316--104

BEST 1994 FINISHES: 1--Kmart Greater Greensboro Open, Greater Milwaukee Open; T3--Phoenix Open; T4--Freeport-McMoRan Classic; T9--Northern Telecom Open.

1994 SUMMARY: Tournaments entered--24; in money--17; top ten finishes--5.

1995 PGA TOUR CHARITY TEAM COMPETITION: AT&T Pebble Beach National Open

1994 SEASON: Truly had "Greater" season, winning both Kmart Greater Greensboro Open and Greater Milwaukee Open…final earnings total more than first three years combined…GGO win, first on TOUR, a wire-to-wire effort (one of three such in 1994, Greg Norman/PLAYERS Championship, Bob Estes/Texas Open the others)…held four-stroke lead after both 36 and 54 holes, finished three in front of Ed Humenik, Hale Irwin and Brad Bryant…at one juncture Irwin did narrow margin to single stroke, but was unable to climb any closer…win was worth $270,000…GMO victory took different form, since didn't taste lead until late on final day…began Sunday three strokes behind Bob Estes, closed one in front of Loren Roberts after final-round 67…got into position to challenge for lead with third-round 65…year began with back-to-back top-10s in second and third outings, Northern Telecom Open (T9) and Phoenix Open (T3)…later had T4 in Freeport-McMoRan Classic…concluded campaign with T17 in TOUR Championship.

CAREER HIGHLIGHTS: Battled left elbow and wrist problems virtually entire 1993 season, missing 16 cuts and failing to either finish or even start 14 of final 19 tournaments…diagnosis: elbow and wrist out of alignment, for which had periodic chiropractic adjustment…still managed to finish 79th on money list…best placing T3 in Phoenix Open…T2 in 1992 Kemper Open, one shot behind winner Bill Glasson…trailed only John Daly, Jeff Maggert and Scott Gump in 1991 rookie earnings with $178,587…finished third in '91 BellSouth Atlanta Classic, missing eagle putt on final hole to finish stroke out of Corey Pavin-Steve Pate playoff…earned TOUR membership by finishing fourth on 1990 Ben Hogan Tour money list…won first-ever Hogan Tour event at Bakersfield, closed inaugural campaign by winning two of final three tournaments–Reno and El Paso Opens–to finish in top five.

PERSONAL: 1986-88 Second-Team All-America selection at University of Arizona…Arizona teammates included Robert Gamez…winner John Burns Invitational, Fresno State Classic, 1986 California State Amateur.

1994 PGA TOUR STATISTICS

Scoring Average	70.61	(41T)
Driving Distance	273.2	(16)
Driving Accuracy	64.7	(144T)
Greens in Regulation	65.7	(92T)
Putting	1.772	(33)
All-Around	485	(28T)
Sand Saves	49.6	(113T)
Total Driving	160	(60T)
Eagles	10	(11T)
Birdies	311	(35T)

MISCELLANEOUS STATISTICS

Scoring Avg. (before cut)	70.48	(24)
Scoring Avg. (3rd round)	71.67	(139T)
Scoring Avg. (4th round)	71.11	(54T)
Birdie Conversion	31.3	(9T)
Par Breakers	21.2	(16)

1994 Low Round: 64: Kmart GGO/1
Career Low Round: 63: 2 times, most recent
Career Largest   '92 Bob Hope/3
Paycheck: $72,600/1992 Kemper Open/T2

CRAIG STADLER

EXEMPT STATUS: Winner, 1992 NEC World Series of Golf

FULL NAME: Craig Robert Stadler

HEIGHT: 5' 10"   **WEIGHT:** 210

BIRTH DATE: June 2, 1953

BIRTHPLACE: San Diego, CA

RESIDENCE: Denver, CO

FAMILY: Wife, Sue; Kevin (2/5/80), Christopher (11/23/82)

COLLEGE: University of Southern California

SPECIAL INTERESTS: Snow skiing, hunting

TURNED PROFESSIONAL: 1975

Q SCHOOL: Spring 1976

PLAYER PROFILE

CAREER EARNINGS: $5,606,436   **PLAYOFF RECORD:** 2-2

TOUR VICTORIES: **1980** Bob Hope Desert Classic, Greater Greensboro Open. **1981** Kemper Open.
(TOTAL: 11)   **1982** Joe Garagiola-Tucson Open, Masters Tournament, Kemper Open, World
Series of Golf. **1984** Byron Nelson Classic.**1991** THE TOUR Championship. **1992**
NEC World Series of Golf. **1994** Buick Invitational of California

MONEY & POSITION:

1976--$ 2,702--196	1983--$214,496--17	1990--$278,482--52
1977--$ 42,949-- 66	1984--$324,241-- 8	1991--$827,628-- 2
1978--$ 63,486-- 48	1985--$297,926--11	1992--$487,460--28
1979--$ 73,392-- 55	1986--$170,076--53	1993--$553,623--29
1980--$206,291-- 8	1987--$235,831--39	1994--$474,831--32
1981--$218,829-- 8	1988--$278,313--37	
1982--$446,462-- 1	1989--$409,419--25	

BEST 1994 FINISHES: 1--Buick Invitational of California; T2--Walt Disney World/Oldsmobile Classic; T5-
-Texas Open; T8--Nissan Los Angeles Open.

1994 SUMMARY: Tournaments entered--22; in money--15; top ten finishes--4.

1995 PGA TOUR CHARITY TEAM COMPETITION: Buick Open

NATIONAL TEAMS: Ryder Cup (2) 1983, 1985; Walker Cup, 1975; U.S. vs. Japan, 1982.

1994 SEASON: Having used last-minute magic to get into 1993 TOUR Championship, almost succeeded again in '94...T26 at Las Vegas Invitational left him just
$154 behind final qualifier Mark Brooks...stretch-drive effort included T2 in Walt
Disney World/Oldsmobile Classic and T5 Texas Open two prior weeks...shared
third-round Disney lead with eventual winner Rick Fehr, closed with 70...after start
to season which produced T8 in Nissan Los Angeles Open and 11th TOUR victory
in Buick Invitational of California in first five outings, went through stretch where
missed six of eight cuts beginning with PLAYERS Championship...late in campaign
forced to withdraw after opening 75 in Bell Canadian Open...final-round 66
produced one-stroke victory over Steve Lowery in Buick Invitational...trailed
Lowery by one after 54 holes at Torrey Pines.

CAREER HIGHLIGHTS: Went T2-T4-T3-2 in last four starts of 1993 to earn berth
in TOUR Championship field...solo second in Las Vegas Invitational, worth
$151,200, put him over top...in final five events of year, including TOUR Champi-
onship, earned $443,266...captured NEC World Series of Golf in 1992, ten years
after winning same event in 1982...both victories carried ten-year exemptions...start
of 1992 campaign delayed by off-season skiing collision with young girl (Dec.
1991)...accident made it impossible for him to play in Tournament of
Champions...qualified for '92 TofC by winning 1991 TOUR Championship...TOUR
title first victory in seven years...led in earnings in 1982, when won four times,
including Masters and World Series...also captured Kemper Open for second time
in '82, year that began with victory in Joe Garagiola-Tucson Open...named 1982
PGA TOUR Arnold Palmer Award recipient as leading money winner...first title
came in 1980 Bob Hope Chrysler Classic...member 1983-85 Ryder Cup, 1982 U.S.
vs. Japan teams...winner 1978 Magnolia Classic, 1985 European Masters, 1987
Dunlop Phoenix, 1988 Fred Meyer Challenge (with Joey Sindelar), 1990 Scandinavian Open, 1992 Argentine Open.

PERSONAL: One of game's most colorful personalities and gallery
favorites...nickname "Walrus" needs little or no explanation...winner 1971 World
Junior Championship, 1973 U.S. Amateur at Inverness...two-time All-American at
USC (1974-75)...member 1975 Walker Cup team.

1994 PGA TOUR STATISTICS

Scoring Average	70.39	(29)
Driving Distance	273.1	(17T)
Driving Accuracy	69.5	(82T)
Greens in Regulation	69.2	(22T)
Putting	1.776	(42T)
All-Around	377	(15)
Sand Saves	53.6	(64T)
Total Driving	99	(16)
Eagles	10	(11T)
Birdies	254	(110)

MISCELLANEOUS STATISTICS

Scoring Avg. (before cut)	70.88	(43)
Scoring Avg. (3rd round)	69.62	(9)
Scoring Avg. (4th round)	70.46	(20)
Birdie Conversion	29.5	(43T)
Par Breakers	21.3	(14T)

1994 Low Round:	64: NEC World Series/3
Career Low Round:	62: 4 times, most recent '87 Shearson Lehman/2
Career Largest Paycheck:	$360,000/'91 THE TOUR Championship/1

MIKE STANDLY

EXEMPT STATUS: 1993 tournament winner

FULL NAME: Michael Dean Standly

HEIGHT: 6'　　　　**WEIGHT:** 200

BIRTH DATE: May 19, 1964

BIRTHPLACE: Abilene, TX

RESIDENCE: Houston, TX

FAMILY: Wife, Nicole; Charles Allen(11/16/88), Suzanne Augusta (12/11/92)

COLLEGE: University of Houston

SPECIAL INTERESTS: Fishing, hunting

TURNED PROFESSIONAL: 1986

Q-SCHOOL: Fall 1990

PLAYER PROFILE

CAREER EARNINGS: $773,294

TOUR VICTORIES: 1993 Freeport-McMoRan Classic
(TOTAL:1)

MONEY & POSITION:　　1991--$ 55,846--171　　1993--$323,886--49　　1994--$179,850--99
　　　　　　　　　　　　　　1992--$213,712-- 73

BEST 1994 FINISH: T12--AT&T Pebble Beach National Pro-Am

1994 SUMMARY: Tournaments entered--30; in money--19; top ten finishes--0.

1995 PGA TOUR CHARITY TEAM COMPETITION: Deposit Guaranty Golf Classic

1994 SEASON: Struggled primarily during second half of campaign…fell below earnings totals of previous two seasons, and was without a top-10 finish for first time since rookie year of 1991…best placing T12 in AT&T Pebble Beach National Pro-Am in fifth start…opened year with T13 in Mercedes Championships, for which qualified through victory in 1992 Freeport-McMoRan Classic…had back-to-back top-25 finishes twice…March-April: T19 in PLAYERS Championship, T15 in defense of Freeport-McMoRan title; June-July: T15 Canon Greater Hartford Open, T17 Motorola Western Open…largest check ($31,375) came from PLAYERS…carded low round of season (64) in Round 3 of GHO…missed cut six of last 11 starts, four in a row from Deposit Guaranty Golf Classic through Sprint International.

CAREER HIGHLIGHTS: After 1992 New Orleans T2 with Greg Norman, one stroke behind Chip Beck, broke through with one-stroke victory over Russ Cochran and Payne Stewart in 1993 Freeport-McMoRan Classic…carded final-round 67 in coming from two strokes off Greg Kraft 54-hole lead…best finish in nine events leading to English Turn T24 in Honda Classic…win provided berth in following week's Masters, appropriate for someone whose daughter's middle name is "Augusta"…New Orleans triumph came between missed cuts in PLAYERS Championship and at Masters…made cut in 22 of 29 tournaments in 1992…medalist in 1991 Qualifying Tournament…played Ben Hogan Tour in 1990, with earnings of $10,446 in 28 events.

PERSONAL: Runnerup 1986 NCAA Finals…1986 All-American…winner 1984 Boone Links Invitational…wife Nicole joined legion of TOUR skiing-injured in March 1994, breaking wrist.

1994 PGA TOUR STATISTICS

Scoring Average	71.72	(141)
Driving Distance	272.0	(23)
Driving Accuracy	68.3	(101T)
Greens in Regulation	65.9	(86T)
Putting	1.818	(138T)
All-Around	669	(77)
Sand Saves	49.0	(123)
Total Driving	124	(29T)
Eagles	13	(4T)
Birdies	298	(53)

MISCELLANEOUS STATISTICS

Scoring Avg. (before cut)	71.78	(124T)
Scoring Avg. (3rd round)	72.24	(166)
Scoring Avg. (4th round)	71.94	(125)
Birdie Conversion	27.1	(123T)
Par Breakers	18.7	(97T)

1994 Low Round:	64: Canon GHO/3
Career Low Round:	63: 1991 Las Vegas /3
Career Largest Paycheck:	$180,000/'93 Freeport-McMoRan/1

PAUL STANKOWSKI

EXEMPT STATUS: 106th on 1994 money list

FULL NAME: Paul Francis Stankowski

HEIGHT: 6'1"   **WEIGHT:** 175

BIRTH DATE: December 2, 1969

BIRTHPLACE: Oxnard, CA

RESIDENCE: El Paso, TX; plays out of El Paso & Coronado CC

FAMILY: Wife, Regina

COLLEGE: University of Texas-El Paso

SPECIAL INTERESTS: Relaxing, family

TURNED PROFESSIONAL: 1991

Q-SCHOOL: 1993

PLAYER PROFILE

CAREER EARNINGS: $170,393

BEST-EVER FINISH: T5--1994 Las Vegas Inviational

MONEY & POSITION: 1994--$170,393--106

BEST 1994 FINISHES: T5--Las Vegas Invitational; T6--Bob Hope Chrysler Classic; T8--Federal Express St. Jude Classic.

1994 SUMMARY: Tournaments entered--29; in money--10; top ten finishes--3.

1995 PGA TOUR CHARITY TEAM COMPETITION: Doral-Ryder Open

1994 SEASON: The old adage "All good things come to he who waits" certainly applies...couldn't have waited any longer to assure playing privileges for 1995, finishing T5 in final event of year, Las Vegas Invitational...parlayed final-round 65 into that placing and check for $54,750...well-timed payday lifted earnings total to $170,393 and No. 106 on money list...opened Las Vegas play with 70, followed by back-to-back 66s and 69 before closing 65...prior to LVI missed cut in 19 of 28 starts...of cuts made, did have two other top 10s: T6 Bob Hope Chrysler Classic and T8 FedEx St. Jude Classic...Hope start, featuring all five rounds in 60s, was fourth of year, following three missed cuts...made cut in next two events after Hope, longest such streak of season... all four rounds at Memphis also in 60s...FESJC finish followed string of six consecutive missed cuts...had one other top-25, T13 in BellSouth Classic in May.

CAREER HIGHLIGHTS: Qualified for TOUR by placing T26 in 1993 Qualifying Tournament...winner 1992 New Mexico Open.

PERSONAL: Three-time All-American at UTEP...1990 Western Athletic Conference champion.

1994 PGA TOUR STATISTICS

Scoring Average	71.53	(122T)
Driving Distance	262.2	(87)
Driving Accuracy	66.4	(128)
Greens in Regulation	65.8	(90T)
Putting	1.818	(138T)
All-Around	813	(127T)
Sand Saves	49.6	(113T)
Total Driving	215	(136T)
Eagles	8	(28T)
Birdies	257	(107T)

MISCELLANEOUS STATISTICS

Scoring Avg. (before cut)	71.78	(124T)
Scoring Avg. (3rd round)	71.38	(119T)
Scoring Avg. (4th round)	71.11	(54T)
Birdie Conversion	28.2	(87T)
Par Breakers	19.1	(79T)

1994 Low Round: **65:** Las Vegas Invitational/5
Career Low Round: 65: 1994 Las Vegas /5
Career Largest
Paycheck: $54,750/1994 Las Vegas Invitational/T5

PAYNE STEWART

EXEMPT STATUS: Winner, 1991 U.S. Open

FULL NAME: William Payne Stewart

HEIGHT: 6'1"　　**WEIGHT:** 180

BIRTH DATE: Jan. 30, 1957

BIRTHPLACE: Springfield, MO

RESIDENCE: Orlando, FL

FAMILY: Wife, Tracey Ferguson; Chelsea (11/13/85), Aaron (4/2/89)

COLLEGE: Southern Methodist University (1979, Business)

SPECIAL INTERESTS: Hunting, fishing, cooking

TURNED PROFESSIONAL: 1979

Q SCHOOL: Spring 1981

PLAYER PROFILE

CAREER EARNINGS: $6,523,260　　　　　**PLAYOFF RECORD:** 1-5

TOUR VICTORIES: **1982** Quad Cities Open. **1983** Walt Disney World Classic. **1987** Hertz Bay Hill Classic.
(TOTAL: 8)　　　　**1989** MCI Heritage Classic, PGA Championship. **1990** MCI Heritage Classic, GTE
　　　　Byron Nelson Classic. **1991** U.S. Open

MONEY & POSITION:	1981--$ 13,400--157	1986--$ 535,389-- 3	1991--$ 476,971-- 31
	1982--$ 98,686-- 38	1987--$ 511,026--12	1992--$ 334,738-- 44
	1983--$178,809-- 25	1988--$ 553,571--14	1993--$ 982,875-- 6
	1984--$288,795-- 11	1989--$1,201,301-- 2	1994--$ 145,687--123
	1985--$225,729-- 19	1990--$ 976,281-- 3	

BEST 1994 FINISHES: 5--Bob Hope Chrysler Classic; T10--Bell Canadian Open.

1994 SUMMARY: Tournaments entered--23; in money--15; top ten finishes--2.

1995 PGA TOUR CHARITY TEAM COMPETITION: BellSouth Classic

NATIONAL TEAMS: Ryder Cup (4), 1987, 1989, 1991, 1993; Kirin Cup, 1987; Asahi Glass Four Tours World
　　　　Championship of Golf (2), 1989, 1990. World Cup, 1987, 1990. Nissan Cup, 1986.

1994 SEASON: Struggled more with mental side of golf than physical in least productive campaign since second year on TOUR, 1982…money-list finish lowest since rookie season (No. 157)…took long stretches away from game on several occasions…returned from three-week hiatus following PGA Championship to place T10 in Bell Canadian Open, second and final top-10 of year…after three more weeks finished T24 in Walt Disney World/Oldsmobile Classic, fifth and final top-25…in February had solo fifth in Bob Hope Chrysler Classic, followed next week by T19 in Buick Invitational of California…only other top-25 was T15 in FedEx St. Jude Classic in July…Hope final-round 63 lowest of campaign…of seven missed cuts, six occurred over nine-event stretch from PLAYERS Championship through Canon Greater Hartford Open.

CAREER HIGHLIGHTS: Prior to Fuzzy Zoeller in 1994, held TOUR single-season record for most money without tournament win ($982,875 in 1993)…runnerup four times in '93, including head-to-head battle with Lee Janzen in U.S. Open…placed third at Memorial, where Paul Azinger holed out from bunker on 72nd hole to supplant him as tournament leader…owns victories in two majors, 1989 PGA Championship and 1991 U.S. Open…won Open in 18-hole playoff with Scott Simpson at Hazeltine National…was eight strokes off lead after opening 74 at PGA, rebounded to win by stroke…also captured MCI Heritage Classic and lost Nabisco Championship playoff to Tom Kite in '89 to finish second on money list with $1,201,301…won Heritage Classic title in 1990 as well, year in which also won GTE Byron Nelson Classic…missed 10 weeks of 1991 season with nerve problem in neck…winner All-Around Category, 1988 Nabisco Statistics…winner 1981 Indian and Indonesian Opens…third in Asian Tour Order of Merit, 1981…winner 1982 Tweed Head Classic (Australia)…third in Australian Order of Merit, 1982…winner 1982 Magnolia Classic.

PERSONAL: Donated 1987 Bay Hill Classic winner's check to Florida Hospital Circle of Friends in memory of father, who died two years before…met and married Tracey Ferguson of Australia while in Malaysia…1979 Southwest Conference co-champion…1979 All-American…1979 Missouri Amateur champion.

1994 PGA TOUR STATISTICS

Scoring Average	71.33	(102)
Driving Distance	268.8	(36)
Driving Accuracy	64.5	(146T)
Greens in Regulation	64.7	(117T)
Putting	1.805	(119T)
All-Around	763	(114)
Sand Saves	60.4	(6T)
Total Driving	182	(99)
Eagles	3	(126T)
Birdies	252	(111)

MISCELLANEOUS STATISTICS

Scoring Avg. (before cut)	71.11	(60T)
Scoring Avg. (3rd round)	71.73	(142T)
Scoring Avg. (4th round)	72.67	(157T)
Birdie Conversion	28.5	(76T)
Par Breakers	18.6	(102T)

1994 Low Round: 63: WDW/Olds Classic/5
Career Low Round: 61: 1990 Walt Disney World/Oldsmobile Classic/3
Career Largest Paycheck: $270,000/1989 Nabisco/2

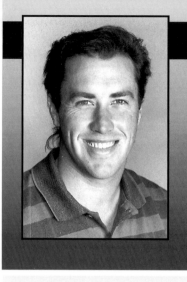

DAVE STOCKTON, JR.

EXEMPT STATUS: 96th on 1994 money list

FULL NAME: David Bradley Stockton, Jr.

HEIGHT: 6'2"　　　　**WEIGHT:** 185

BIRTH DATE: July 31, 1968

BIRTHPLACE: Redlands, CA

RESIDENCE: La Quinta, CA; plays out of Palmilla Hotel & Golf, Los Cabos, Mexico

FAMILY: Single

COLLEGE: University of Southern California

SPECIAL INTERESTS: Hunting, fishing, all sports

TURNED PROFESSIONAL: 1991

Q-SCHOOL: 1993

PLAYER PROFILE

CAREER EARNINGS: $185,205

BEST-EVER FINISH: T3--1994 Canon Greater Hartford Open, Deposit Guaranty Golf Classic

MONEY & POSITION:　　　1994--$185,205--96

BEST 1994 FINISHES: T3--Canon Greater Hartford Open, Deposit Guaranty Golf Classic; T8--Sprint International

1994 SUMMARY: Tournaments entered--31; in money--15; top ten finishes--3.

1995 PGA TOUR CHARITY TEAM COMPETITION: Buick Classic

1994 SEASON: Almost won tournament father won on same weekend father was winning on Senior TOUR...led or near lead for three rounds of Canon Greater Hartford Open while senior Stockton was wrapping up FORD SENIOR PLAYERS Championship...elder Stockton captured 1974 GHO...final-round 72 produced T3, three strokes behind David Frost...opened with back-to-back 66s, was even with Frost going into final round, one stroke in front of Greg Norman, who finished second...Hartford heroics provided check for $57,600, which came after 10 missed cuts in first 16 starts...three weeks later had another T3, in weather-shortened Deposit Guaranty Golf Classic...final top-10 (T8) came at the Sprint International, where check for $42,000 assured playing privileges for 1995...held midpoint lead in Walt Disney World/Oldsmobile Classic after second-round 64, utlimately finished T15...64 featured three eagles, including two on the final two holes at the appropriately named Eagle Pines...added a fourth Disney eagle, doubling his season total (of four coming in) to eight.

CAREER HIGHLIGHTS: Earned playing privileges by finishing as co-medalist (with Ty Armstrong and Robin Freeman) in 1993 Qualifying Tournament...placed 23rd on 1993 NIKE TOUR money list with $64,214...won pair of NIKE TOUR events in '93, Connecticut Open and Hawkeye Open.

PERSONAL: Technically not a Junior, since father's middle name is Knapp and his is Bradley...took Jr. as part of name to show relationship to and pride in father...caddied for his dad on PGA TOUR, as brother Ron does on Senior TOUR...All-American at USC...second in 1989 NCAA Championship.

1994 PGA TOUR STATISTICS

Scoring Average	71.58	(129T)
Driving Distance	269.3	(34T)
Driving Accuracy	65.8	(132)
Greens in Regulation	66.7	(65T)
Putting	1.821	(146T)
All-Around	755	(110)
Sand Saves	42.5	(171)
Total Driving	166	(68)
Eagles	8	(28T)
Birdies	299	(50T)

MISCELLANEOUS STATISTICS

Scoring Avg. (before cut)	71.60	(108)
Scoring Avg. (3rd round)	71.00	(84T)
Scoring Avg. (4th round)	72.14	(139T)
Birdie Conversion	27.7	(108T)
Par Breakers	19.0	(83T)

1994 Low Round: 64: WDW/Olds Classic/2

Career Low Round: 64: 1994 WDW/Olds Classic/2

Career Largest Paycheck: $57,600/'94 Canon GHO/T3

CURTIS STRANGE

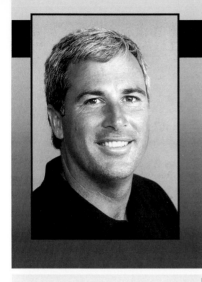

EXEMPT STATUS: Winner, 1988 United States Open

FULL NAME: Curtis Northrop Stange

HEIGHT: 5' 11" **WEIGHT:** 170

BIRTH DATE: January 30, 1955

BIRTHPLACE: Norfolk, VA

RESIDENCE: Kingsmill, VA; plays out of Kingsmill on the James

FAMILY: Wife Sarah; Thomas Wright III (8/25/82), David Clark (4/3/85)

COLLEGE: Wake Forest University

SPECIAL INTERESTS: Hunting and fishing

TURNED PROFESSIONAL: 1976

Q SCHOOL: Spring 1977

PLAYER PROFILE

CAREER EARNINGS: $6,433,442 **PLAYOFF RECORD:** 6-3

TOUR VICTORIES: **1979** Pensacola Open. **1980** Michelob-Houston Open, Manufacturers Hanover Westch-
(TOTAL: 17) ester Classic. **1983** Sammy Davis, Jr.-Greater Hartford Open. **1984** LaJet Classic. **1985** Honda Classic, Panasonic-Las Vegas Invitational, Canadian Open. **1986** Houston Open. **1987** Canadian Open, Federal Express-St. Jude Classic, NEC World Series of Golf. **1988** Independent Insurance Agent Open, Memorial Tournament, U.S. Open, Nabisco Championships. **1989** U.S. Open.

MONEY & POSITION:

1977--$ 28,144--87	1983--$ 200,116--21	1989--$ 752,587-- 7
1978--$ 29,346--88	1984--$ 276,773--14	1990--$ 277,172--53
1979--$138,368--21	1985--$ 542,321-- 1	1991--$ 336,333--48
1980--$271,888-- 3	1986--$ 237,700--32	1992--$ 150,639--99
1981--$201,513-- 9	1987--$ 925,941-- 1	1993--$ 262,697--63
1982--$263,378--10	1988--$1,147,644-- 1	1994--$ 390,881--41

BEST 1994 FINISHES: T3--Buick Open; 4--U.S. Open; T4--Honda Classic; T8--Phoenix Open; T10--Shell Houston Open

1994 SUMMARY: Tournaments entered--23; in money--18; top ten finishes--5.

1995 PGA TOUR CHARITY TEAM COMPETITION: Anheuser-Busch Golf Classic

NATIONAL TEAMS: Ryder Cup (4) 1983, 1985, 1987, 1989; Nissan Cup, 1985; Kirin Cup (2) 1987, 1988; Four Tours Championship, 1989; Dunhill Cup (6), 1987, 1988, 1989, 1990, 1991, 1994; World Amateur Team, 1974; Walker Cup, 1975.

1994 SEASON: Two-time U.S. Open champ missed Ernie Els-Loren Roberts-Colin Montgomerie Open playoff by single stroke...posted four consecutive rounds of one-under-par 70 at Oakmont, where 280 total fell one shy...continued upswing that began in 1993, reaching highest earnings level since 1989...posted fifth-best money-won campaign of 18 on TOUR...money-list finish (No. 41) also best since '89...had pair of top-10s in first five tournaments, T8 at Phoenix Open (with final-round 64) and T4 in Honda Classic...fifth and final top-10 of year T3 at Buick Open.

CAREER HIGHLIGHTS: Earnings rose each of past two seasons after falling below $200,000 in 1992 for first time in 13 years...winner of back-to-back U.S. Opens in 1988 and 1989, first to do so since Ben Hogan (1950-51)...1988 Open victory at The Country Club in Brookline, MA, came in playoff with Nick Faldo...captured '89 crown at Oak Hills in Rochester, NY...three-time recipient of Arnold Palmer Award as TOUR's leading money winner (1985, 1987-88), first to win consecutively since Tom Watson in 1979-80...fourth player to surpass $1 million in yearly earnings in 1988, when won four titles...biggest payday–$360,000–came with playoff victory over Tom Kite in 1988 Nabisco Championships at Pebble Beach...had T2 in 1989 PGA Championship...had seven-year tournament victory streak (1983-89)...earned first victory since 1989 U.S. Open in Greg Norman Holden Classic in Australia in Dec. 1993...holder of Old Course record (62) at St. Andrews, Scotland in 1987 Dunhill Cup...1985-87-88 Golf Writers Player of Year...1988 PGA Player of Year...winner 1986 ABC Cup (Japan).

PERSONAL: Member 1974 World Amateur Cup, 1975 Walker Cup teams...winner 1973 Southeastern Amateur, 1974 NCAA Championship, 1974 Western Amateur, 1975 Eastern Amateur, 1975-76 North and South Amateur, 1975-76 Virginia State Amateur...1974 College Player-of-Year...started playing golf at seven; father owned White Sands CC in Virginia Beach, VA...identical twin brother, Allen, former TOUR member.

1994 PGA TOUR STATISTICS

Scoring Average	70.44	(32)
Driving Distance	257.4	(125)
Driving Accuracy	73.8	(35T)
Greens in Regulation	66.9	(59T)
Putting	1.779	(50T)
All-Around	575	(52)
Sand Saves	54.7	(49)
Total Driving	160	(60T)
Eagles	1	(167T)
Birdies	294	(58T)

MISCELLANEOUS STATISTICS

Scoring Avg. (before cut)	71.34	(79T)
Scoring Avg. (3rd round)	70.28	(40)
Scoring Avg. (4th round)	70.11	(12)
Birdie Conversion	29.4	(47T)
Par Breakers	19.7	(55T)

1994 Low Round: 64: Phoenix Open/4
Career Low Round: 62: 2 times, most recent '83
Career Largest Sammy Davis Jr./2
Paycheck: $360,000/1988 Nabisco/1

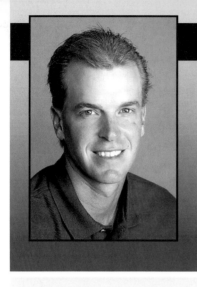

STEVE STRICKER

EXEMPT STATUS: 50th on 1994 money list

FULL NAME: Steven Charles Stricker

HEIGHT: 6'   **WEIGHT:** 185

BIRTH DATE: February 23, 1967

BIRTHPLACE: Edgerton, WI

RESIDENCE: Edgerton, WI; plays out of Cherokee CC

FAMILY: Wife, Nicki

COLLEGE: University of Illinois

SPECIAL INTERESTS: Deer hunting, card collecting

TURNED PROFESSIONAL: 1990

Q-SCHOOL: 1993

PLAYER PROFILE

CAREER EARNINGS: $334,409

BEST-EVER FINISH: T2--1994 Northern Telecom Open

MONEY & POSITION: 1990--$3,973--255   1993--$46,171--186   1994--$334,409--50
1992--$5,550--261

BEST 1994 FINISHES: T2--Northern Telecom Open; T3--Canon Greater Hartford Open; T4--Walt Disney World Oldsmobile Classic; T6--Bell Canadian Open.

1994 SUMMARY: Tournaments entered--26; in money--22; top ten finishes--4.

1995 PGA TOUR CHARITY TEAM COMPETITION: Franklin Funds Shark Shootout

1994 SEASON: After leading first two rounds of 1993 Canadian Open and contending through three, found himself in hunt for first TOUR victory twice more in '94...established credentials early as Rookie of Year candidate...finished in four-way tie for second in Northern Telecom Open, two strokes behind Andrew Magee...$72,600 paycheck largest of year and fledgling career...that followed T14 in United Airlines Hawaiian Open, giving him $92,400 in first two starts...in June wound up in another four-way tie, this time for third, in Canon Greater Hartford Open...had pair of top-10 finishes in last five starts, T6 in Bell Canadian Open and T4 in Walt Disney World/Oldsmobile Classic...was well on way to yet another solid finish in Texas Open, where opened 65-68, then soared to 78 due to illness and had to withdraw after three rounds ...ranked fourth among rookies in earnings, behind only Ernie Els, Mike Heinen and Glen Day.

CAREER HIGHLIGHTS: Finished T18 in 1993 Qualifying Tournament after failing to make finals three years in a row...as non-TOUR member held first- and second-round leads in 1993 Canadian Open, was one stroke behind Brad Bryant after 54 holes...closed with 75 to finish T4, five strokes behind David Frost...matriculated on Canadian Tour, winning 1993 Canadian PGA...placed T10 in 1990 Canadian TPC...winner 1990 Payless/Pepsi Open, Wisconsin Open, second in 1992 Wisconsin Open...Wisconsin native posted final-round 67 in 1992 Greater Milwaukee Open, finishing T31...second in 1990 Ben Hogan Dakota Dunes Open, T5 in 1991 Ben Hogan Shreveport Open.

PERSONAL: Wife Nicki is his caddie...father-in-law Dennis Tiziani, golf coach at University of Wisconsin, also his teacher...Tiziani recruited him for Wisconsin, but opted instead for University of Illinois to get away from home...All-American 1988-89.

1994 PGA TOUR STATISTICS

Scoring Average	70.58	(38)
Driving Distance	268.4	(39T)
Driving Accuracy	69.0	(92T)
Greens in Regulation	68.2	(39)
Putting	1.752	(10)
All-Around	393	(17T)
Sand Saves	47.3	(141)
Total Driving	131	(33)
Eagles	8	(28T)
Birdies	358	(6)

MISCELLANEOUS STATISTICS

Scoring Avg. (before cut)	70.60	(28)
Scoring Avg. (3rd round)	70.20	(31T)
Scoring Avg. (4th round)	70.95	(45T)
Birdie Conversion	31.3	(9T)
Par Breakers	21.9	(8T)

1994 Low Round: **65:** Texas Open/1
Career Low Round: **65:** 1994 Texas Open/1
Career Largest
Paycheck: **$72,600**/'94 Northern Telecom Open/T3

MIKE SULLIVAN

EXEMPT STATUS: 1994 tournament winner

FULL NAME: Michael James Sullivan

HEIGHT: 6'2"   **WEIGHT:** 200

BIRTH DATE: January 1, 1955

BIRTHPLACE: Gary, IN

RESIDENCE: Ocala, FL

FAMILY: Wife, Sandy; Rebecca (6/13/85)

COLLEGE: University of Florida

SPECIAL INTERESTS: Flying, fishing

TURNED PROFESSIONAL: 1975

Q-SCHOOL: Fall, 1976, 1985

PLAYER PROFILE

CAREER EARNINGS: $1,909,914   **PLAYOFF RECORD:** 0-4

TOUR VICTORIES: 1980 Southern Open. **1989** Independent Insurance Agent Open. **1994** B.C. Open. (TOTAL: 3)

MONEY & POSITION:

1977--$ 11,170--142	1983--$ 93,437-- 60	1989--$273,963-- 47
1978--$ 41,184-- 74	1984--$111,415-- 63	1990--$ 80,038--147
1979--$ 38,596-- 97	1985--$ 45,032--127	1991--$106,048--133
1980--$147,759-- 22	1986--$150,407-- 62	1992--$115,441--121
1981--$ 94,844-- 41	1987--$ 79,456--112	1993--$ 68,587--167
1982--$ 37,957--108	1988--$115,994-- 99	1994--$298,586-- 60

BEST 1994 FINISHES: 1--B.C. Open; 2--Deposit Guaranty Golf Classic.

1994 SUMMARY: Tournaments entered--26; in money--11; top ten finishes--2.

1995 PGA TOUR CHARITY TEAM COMPETITION: Bob Hope Chrysler Classic

1994 SEASON: Suffering from stiff neck and with problematic back giving him trouble, having missed 13 cuts in 21 starts and four of previous five, did what one might expect: went out and won the B.C. Open, first tournament victory in five years…dogged for three rounds heels of Jeff Sluman, who had opened with 63…final-round 66 provided four-stroke victory over Sluman…two months (and six tournaments) before, lost playoff to Brian Henninger in weather-shortened Deposit Guaranty Golf Classic…second-place finish his first top-10 since T8 in 1992 Buick Open…also had T13 at Doral-Ryder Open, where carded final-round 66…in terms of money won, two top-10s helped produce finest season of 18 on TOUR, surpassing $273,963 earned in 1989…No. 60 money-list finish also his best since '89.

CAREER HIGHLIGHTS: Because of recurring back problems, has had to struggle last few years to keep or regain playing privileges…captured second career title as early starter in 1989 Independent Insurance Agent Open…barely made cut after opening 76-71, then carded 4-under 68 on third day at TPC at The Woodlands…began final round seven strokes off lead, proceeded to fire 65…8-under 280 total held up for one-stroke victory over Craig Stadler…first win came at 1980 Southern Open, where next year lost playoff to J.C. Snead…also lost 1978 Buick Open playoff to Australian Jack Newton…posted 7-under-par 28 for nine holes in 1988 Texas Open…teamed with Don January to win 1984 Shootout at Jeremy Ranch, then a PGA TOUR/Senior PGA TOUR event.

PERSONAL: Attended University of Florida "briefly"…emphasizes he "survived" rooming with Andy Bean in college.

1994 PGA TOUR STATISTICS

Scoring Average	71.39	(111)
Driving Distance	267.5	(43T)
Driving Accuracy	62.2	(160)
Greens in Regulation	66.8	(63T)
Putting	1.817	(137)
All-Around	773	(118)
Sand Saves	57.6	(21T)
Total Driving	203	(124T)
Eagles	4	(104T)
Birdies	227	(134T)

MISCELLANEOUS STATISTICS

Scoring Avg. (before cut)	71.67	(116T)
Scoring Avg. (3rd round)	71.63	(136T)
Scoring Avg. (4th round)	70.89	(43)
Birdie Conversion	26.6	(138T)
Par Breakers	18.1	(123T)

1994 Low Round:	**65:** B.C. Open/1
Career Low Round:	**62:** 2 times, most recent '92
Career Largest Paycheck:	**$162,000**/'94 B.C. Open/1 Federal Express St. Jude/3

HAL SUTTON

EXEMPT STATUS: 29th on 1994 money list

FULL NAME: Hal Evan Sutton

HEIGHT: 6' 1"   **WEIGHT:** 185

BIRTH DATE: April 28, 1958

BIRTHPLACE: Shreveport, LA

RESIDENCE: Shreveport, LA

FAMILY: Single

COLLEGE: Centenary College (Business)

SPECIAL INTERESTS: Horses, hunting and fishing

TURNED PROFESSIONAL: 1981

Q SCHOOL: Fall 1981

PLAYER PROFILE

CAREER EARNINGS: $3,931,853   **PLAYOFF RECORD:** 3-2

TOUR VICTORIES: **1982** Walt Disney World Golf Classic. **1983** Tournament Players Championship,
(TOTAL: 7)   PGA Championship. **1985** St. Jude Memphis Classic, Southwest Classic. **1986**
          Phoenix Open, Memorial Tournament.

MONEY & POSITION:

1982--$237,434--11	1987--$477,996--16	1992--$ 39,234--185
1983--$426,668-- 1	1988--$137,296--88	1993--$ 74,144--161
1984--$227,949--26	1989--$422,703--23	1994--$540,162-- 29
1985--$365,340-- 7	1990--$207,084--75	
1986--$429,434-- 6	1991--$346,411--47	

BEST 1994 FINISHES: T2--Shell Houston Open, FedEx St. Jude Classic; 4--Buick Invitational of
California; T9--Honda Classic.

1994 SUMMARY: Tournaments entered--29; in money--23; top ten finishes--4.

1995 PGA TOUR CHARITY TEAM COMPETITION: Kemper Open

NATIONAL TEAMS: USA vs. Japan, 1983; Ryder Cup (2), 1985, 1987.

1994 SEASON: Authored one of year's best comeback stories, for which selected
for Hilton Bounceback Award...played on TOUR under one-time exemption for
being Top-50 on all-time money list...returned to Top 30 for first time since 1989,
after having fallen to as low as No. 185 in 1992...had pair of top-10s in three weeks
early in year, 4th at Buick Invitational of California and T9 in Honda Classic...was
two strokes off 54-hole lead at Torrey Pines, eventually falling to four behind Craig
Stadler...also trailed by two strokes after three rounds of Shell Houston
Open...finished T2 with Jeff Maggert and Tom Kite, three behind first-year winner
Mike Heinen...best chance for first victory since 1986 Memorial Tournament came
at FedEx St. Jude Classic...fired final-round 64 to finish in three-way tie with Gene
Sauers and Dicky Pride at 17-under-par 267...$110,000 Memphis payday his best
since second-place finish in 1987 Panasonic Las Vegas Invitational.

CAREER HIGHLIGHTS: After drastic falloff from 1991 ($346,411) to 1992 ($39,234),
rebounded slightly in 1993...had encouraging early start that year with T9 in Buick
Invitational, his best finish since T7 in 1991 Greater Milwaukee Open...enjoyed
finest year in 1983, his second on TOUR...finished atop money list with earnings
of $426,668 and victories in PGA and Tournament Players Championships...wire-
to-wire PGA effort good for one-stroke win over Jack Nicklaus at Riviera
CC...Tournament Players Championship victory came on TPC at Sawgrass course,
just second tournament held at Ponte Vedra layout...outlasted Bob Eastwood down
stretch for win...defeated Bill Britton in four-hole playoff to win first title in final
event of rookie season, 1982 Walt Disney World Classic...notched pair of wins in
both 1985 and 1986...won 1985 Chrysler Team Championship with Raymond
Floyd...1983 PGA and Golf Writers Player of Year.

PERSONAL: Winner 1980 U.S. Amateur...1980 Golf Magazine College Player of
Year... Collegiate All-America...runnerup 1981 NCAA Championship...winner
1974 Louisiana State Juniors.

1994 PGA TOUR STATISTICS

Scoring Average	70.53	(37)
Driving Distance	264.6	(65T)
Driving Accuracy	77.3	(12T)
Greens in Regulation	72.2	(3)
Putting	1.802	(111T)
All-Around	485	(28T)
Sand Saves	43.3	(165T)
Total Driving	77	(8)
Eagles	5	(87T)
Birdies	360	(5)

MISCELLANEOUS STATISTICS

Scoring Avg. (before cut)	70.69	(36T)
Scoring Avg. (3rd round)	70.16	(27)
Scoring Avg. (4th round)	70.95	(45T)
Birdie Conversion	28.6	(74T)
Par Breakers	20.9	(22)

1994 Low Round: **63:** 1993 Bob Hope/1

Career Low Round: 62: 1987 Seiko Tucson/2

Career Largest

Paycheck: $135,000/1987 Panasonic Las Vegas/2

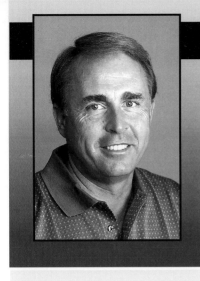

DOUG TEWELL

EXEMPT STATUS: 102nd on 1994 money list

FULL NAME: Douglas Fred Tewell

HEIGHT: 5' 10"   **WEIGHT:** 190

BIRTH DATE: August 27, 1949

BIRTHPLACE: Baton Rouge, LA

RESIDENCE: Edmond, OK; plays out of Oak Tree GC

FAMILY: Wife, Pam; Kristi (9/24/69), Jay (3/31/75)

COLLEGE: Oklahoma State University
(1971, Speech Communications)

SPECIAL INTERESTS: Golf course management & design, family, automobiles

TURNED PROFESSIONAL: 1971

JOINED TOUR: June 1975

PLAYER PROFILE

CAREER EARNINGS: $2,378,598   **PLAYOFF RECORD:** 1-0.

TOUR VICTORIES: 1980 Sea Pines Heritage Classic, IVB-Philadelphia Classic. **1986** Los Angeles Open.
(**TOTAL: 4**)   **1987** Pensacola Open.

MONEY & POSITION:

1975--$ 1,812--201	1982--$ 78,770--52	1989--$174,607-- 83
1976--$ 3,640--185	1983--$112,367--49	1990--$137,795--112
1977--$ 33,162-- 76	1984--$117,988--57	1991--$137,360--111
1978--$ 16,629--113	1985--$137,426--58	1992--$159,856-- 96
1979--$ 84,500-- 43	1986--$310,285--18	1993--$132,478--117
1980--$161,684-- 17	1987--$150,116--71	1994--$177,388--102
1981--$ 41,540-- 94	1988--$209,196--53	

BEST 1994 FINISHES: T7--Walt Disney World/Oldsmobile Classic; T8--Motorola Western Open;
T10--Hardee's Golf Classic.

1994 SUMMARY: Tournaments entered--27; in money--18; top ten finishes--3.

1995 PGA TOUR CHARITY TEAM COMPETITION: THE TOUR Championship

1994 SEASON: Rebounded from shoulder trouble that caused premature shutdown to 1993 campaign to post best money-won year since 1988…opened season slowly, cashing in only two of first eight events…ran off string of 10 placings in row after that, best during streak being T8 in Motorola Western Open…top paycheck and best finish came in next-to-last start of season, T7 in Walt Disney World/Oldsmobile Classic worth $33,138…opened 69-66 at Disney, three strokes off midpoint lead…finished five behind winner Rick Fehr…two weeks prior opened with 65 in Hardee's Golf Classic, two strokes off Robert Wrenn's early lead, wound up T10…65 matched low round of season (Round 3 of Greater Milwaukee Open)…three top-10s most in year since 1988.

CAREER HIGHLIGHTS: Decided to end TOUR season and rest shoulder following 1993 Buick Southern Open…later did compete in Mexican Open…best earnings year 1986, when finished with $310,285 (No. 18)…season featured third career victory, runaway win over Clarence Rose in Los Angeles Open…highest money-list placing No. 17 in 1980, with $161,684…two-time victor in '80, defeating Jerry Pate in Sea Pines Heritage Classic playoff and scoring come-from-behind win over Tom Kite in IVB-Philadelphia Classic…most recent TOUR victory three-stroke 1987 Pensacola Open triumph over Danny Edwards and Phil Blackmar…winner 1988 Acom Team title (Japan) with Bob Gilder…winner 1978 South Central PGA.

PERSONAL: Winner 1971 Tulsa Intercollegiate, 1966 Oklahoma State Junior and Scholastic titles.

1994 PGA TOUR STATISTICS

Scoring Average	71.21	(86T)
Driving Distance	246.8	(174)
Driving Accuracy	79.0	(3T)
Greens in Regulation	68.3	(37T)
Putting	1.793	(91T)
All-Around	735	(104T)
Sand Saves	49.2	(121)
Total Driving	177	(88T)
Eagles	3	(126T)
Birdies	268	(97T)

MISCELLANEOUS STATISTICS

Scoring Avg. (before cut)	71.22	(68T)
Scoring Avg. (3rd round)	70.75	(71T)
Scoring Avg. (4th round)	72.29	(147)
Birdie Conversion	25.9	(145)
Par Breakers	17.9	(129T)

1994 Low Round: 65: 2 times
Career Low Round: 62: 1987 Phoenix Open/3
Career Largest
Paycheck: $81,000/1986 Los Angeles Open/1

JIM THORPE

EXEMPT STATUS: 95th on 1994 money list

FULL NAME: Jimmy Lee Thorpe

HEIGHT: 6'   **WEIGHT:** 200

BIRTH DATE: February 1, 1949

BIRTHPLACE: Roxboro, NC

RESIDENCE: Buffalo, NY

FAMILY: Wife, Carol; Sheronne (3/6/77), Chera (12/3/88)

COLLEGE: Morgan State University

SPECIAL INTERESTS: Football, basketball, hunting

TURNED PROFESSIONAL: 1972

Q SCHOOL: Fall, 1978

PLAYER PROFILE

CAREER EARNINGS: $1,860,930   **PLAYOFF RECORD:** 0-1

TOUR VICTORIES: **1985** Greater Milwaukee Open, Seiko Tucson Match Play Championship. **1986**
(TOTAL: 3)   Seiko Tucson Match Play Championship.

MONEY & POSITION:

1976--$ 2,000--	1985--$379,091-- 4	1992--$ 28,235--200
1979--$ 48,987-- 80	1986--$326,087-- 15	1993--$ 70,375--166
1980--$ 33,671-- 99	1987--$ 57,198--139	1994--$185,714-- 95
1981--$ 43,011-- 93	1988--$ 4,028--252	
1982--$ 66,379-- 63	1989--$104,704--123	
1983--$118,197-- 46	1990--$211,297-- 70	
1984--$135,818-- 48	1991--$ 46,039--179	

BEST 1994 FINISHES: T4--Doral-Ryder Open; T8--Motorola Western Open; T9--Northern Telecom.

1994 SUMMARY: Tournaments entered--26; in money--14; top ten finishes--3.

1995 PGA TOUR CHARITY TEAM COMPETITION: Buick Southern Open

1994 SEASON: Regained playing privileges with finest season since 1990…credits Vijay Singh with reinstilling in him work ethic that led to fourth best earnings campaign of career…got year off on positive early foot with two top-10s in first five starts…posted T9 in second start, Northern Telecom Open, where closed with 67…shared first-round lead in Doral-Ryder Open with Raymond Floyd after opening with 68…finished with 9-under-par 279 total, good for T4 and $57,867…paycheck his best since collecting $97,200 for 1990 Phoenix Open runnerup…after those first five outings, already had earned $102,119, a figure higher than totals in all but six of his 16 previous seasons…with another closing 67, finished T8 in Motorola Western Open, third and final top-10 of season worth $28,000…two final-round 67s among four he posted during year for lowest round.

CAREER HIGHLIGHTS: Last player to win back-to-back match play championships…capped brilliant 1985 season by defeating Jack Renner in final of Seiko-Tucson Match Play event…followed with repeat victory in Tucson in 1986 with defeat of Scott Simpson…each Match Play victory worth $150,000…unable to make it three in a row at Tucson in 1987, when event returned to stroke play…underwent surgery on left wrist/thumb that Sept. 30…missed most of 1988 season due to injury…began to return to form in 1989, when finished T2 in Kemper Open…had another runnerup in 1990 Phoenix Open, second start of year…1985 campaign also featured victory in Greater Milwaukee Open, as well as playoff loss to Scott Verplank in Western Open…co-medalist (with John Fought) in Fall 1978 Qualifying Tournament, finished T2 next year in Joe Garagiola-Tucson Open…first earned card in 1975, but returned home after making just $2,000 in 1976.

PERSONAL: Ninth of 12 children…grew up adjacent to Roxboro (NC) Golf Club, where father was greens superintendent…earned scholarship to Morgan State as football running back…brother Chuck played TOUR in early 1970s.

1994 PGA TOUR STATISTICS

Scoring Average	71.28	(95T)
Driving Distance	262.9	(80)
Driving Accuracy	68.1	(103T)
Greens in Regulation	68.4	(36)
Putting	1.812	(133)
All-Around	717	(96)
Sand Saves	48.2	(131T)
Total Driving	183	(100T)
Eagles	9	(17T)
Birdies	235	(122)

MISCELLANEOUS STATISTICS

Scoring Avg. (before cut)	71.90	(137)
Scoring Avg. (3rd round)	71.08	(94T)
Scoring Avg. (4th round)	70.31	(18)
Birdie Conversion	25.1	(155T)
Par Breakers	17.8	(131T)

1994 Low Round:	67: 4 times
Career Low Round:	63: 2 times, most recently
Career Largest	'90 Greater Milwaukee Open
Paycheck:	$150,000/1985 & 1986 Seiko Tucson/1

KIRK TRIPLETT

EXEMPT STATUS: 38th on 1994 money list

FULL NAME: Kirk Alan Triplett

HEIGHT: 6' 3"   **WEIGHT:** 200

BIRTH DATE: March 29, 1962

BIRTHPLACE: Moses Lake, WA

RESIDENCE: Nashville, TN

FAMILY: Wife, Cathi

COLLEGE: University of Nevada (1985, Civil Engineering)

SPECIAL INTERESTS: Basketball, reading, computers

TURNED PROFESSIONAL: 1985

Q SCHOOL: Fall 1989

PLAYER PROFILE

CAREER EARNINGS: $1,108,222

BEST-EVER FINISH: 2--1992 Shell Houston Open; T2--1994 AT&T Pebble Beach National Pro-Am

MONEY & POSITION: 1990--$183,464-- 88   1992--$175,868--85   1994--$422,171--38
1991--$137,302--112   1993--$189,418--90

BEST 1994 FINISHES: T2--AT&T Pebble Beach National Pro-Am; T6--Buick Invitational of California; T7--Canon Greater Hartford Open; T8--Nissan Los Angeles Open, Las Vegas Invitational; T9--Northern Telecom Open; T10--Kemper Open, Hardee's Golf Classic.

1994 SUMMARY: Tournaments entered--26; in money--19; top ten finishes--8.

1995 PGA TOUR CHARITY TEAM COMPETITION: United Airlines Hawaiian Open

1994 SEASON: Made great advances in terms of establishing himself as quality player…enjoyed finest season of five on TOUR…had four top-10s in first six starts, including T2 in AT&T Pebble Beach National Pro-Am…finished in four-way tie at 6-under-par 282, one stroke behind Johnny Miller…began his year with T9 in Northern Telecom Open…followed Pebble Beach outing with T8 in Nissan Los Angeles Open…two weeks later had T6 in Buick Invitational of California…carded second-round 63, his career low, then after 68 was one stroke off 54-hole lead at Torrey Pines…closed with 72 to finish six strokes behind Craig Stadler…continued steady play rest of way, picking up four more top-10s for career high of eight…closed 67-69 to finish T10 in Kemper Open, then three weeks later fashioned T7 at Greater Hartford Open…in September had T10 at Hardee's Golf Classic…closed out campaign with T8 in Las Vegas Invitational.

CAREER HIGHLIGHTS: Pebble Beach T2 matched career-best finish, solo second behind Fred Funk in 1992 Shell Houston Open…Houston showing produced career paycheck, $129,600…top 1993 placing came in second start, T3 at Phoenix Open…shared first-round 1993 PLAYERS Championship lead with Nick Price after opening 64…placed third in TOUR rookie earnings in 1990 with $183,464, trailing only Robert Gamez ($461,407) and Peter Persons ($218,505)…had solo third in '90 Buick Classic after holding first-round lead with 6-under-par 65…fell back with second-round 74 at Westchester CC before closing 67-66…earlier in 1990 finished fourth in Shearson Lehman Hutton Open…played Australian, Asian and Canadian Tours 1987-89…winner 1988 Alberta Open, Sierra Nevada Open, Ft. McMurray Classic.

PERSONAL: Says of foreign tours play: "I wouldn't trade the experience for anything. I learned so much, not only about golf but about myself. I'll be telling stories about Asia until the day I die"…wife Cathi occasionally caddies for him.

1994 PGA TOUR STATISTICS

Scoring Average	70.12	(20)
Driving Distance	259.5	(109)
Driving Accuracy	74.1	(33T)
Greens in Regulation	68.7	(32T)
Putting	1.768	(25T)
All-Around	359	(10)
Sand Saves	61.6	(4)
Total Driving	142	(41T)
Eagles	4	(104T)
Birdies	312	(32T)

MISCELLANEOUS STATISTICS

Scoring Avg. (before cut)	70.37	(18)
Scoring Avg. (3rd round)	70.05	(21)
Scoring Avg. (4th round)	70.80	(38T)
Birdie Conversion	28.0	(96T)
Par Breakers	19.5	(61T)

1994 Low Round:	**63:** Buick Invt. of CA/ 2
Career Low Round:	**63:** 1994 Buick Invt. of CA/2
Career Largest	
Paycheck:	**$129,600**/1992 Shell Houston Open/2

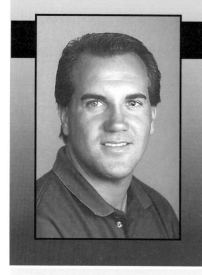

TED TRYBA

EXEMPT STATUS: 74th on 1994 money list

FULL NAME: Ted N. Tryba

HEIGHT: 6' 4"   **WEIGHT:** 205

BIRTH DATE: January 15, 1967

BIRTHPLACE: Wilkes-Barre, PA

RESIDENCE: Orlando, FL

COLLEGE: Ohio State University (1989, Marketing)

SPECIAL INTERESTS: Basketball

TURNED PROFESSIONAL: 1989

Q SCHOOL: Fall 1989

PLAYER PROFILE

CAREER EARNINGS: $393,858

BEST-EVER FINISH: T3--1993 Walt Disney World/Oldsmobile Classic

MONEY & POSITION: 1990--$10,708--226   1993--$136,670--116   1994--$246,481--74

BEST 1994 FINISHES: T6--United Airlines Hawaiian Open; T7--AT&T Pebble Beach National Pro-Am.

1994 SUMMARY: Tournaments entered--34; in money--22; top ten finishes--2.

1995 PGA TOUR CHARITY TEAM COMPETITION: Buick Invitational of Californina

1994 SEASON: Long-striding, 6-foot-4 former Ohio State Buckeye easily recognizable when walking fairways…long-hitter finished fourth on TOUR in birdies with 365…also co-led (with John Inman) in events played, 34…had two top-10 finishes, both of which came in first four starts…T6 in United Airlines Hawaiian Open was followed three weeks later by T7 in AT&T Pebble Beach National Pro-Am…Hawaii finish produced largest check of season, $41,700…opened with three consecutive 70s at Pebble to sit just four strokes off 54-hole lead…stumbled coming in with final-round 74…with those two top-10s wrapped around T20 in Northern Telecom Open and T18 at Phoenix Open, began third TOUR season with earnings of $105,925 after just four outings…biggest payday rest of way $23,800 for T15 in Sprint International.

CAREER HIGHLIGHTS: Finished T3 in 1993 Walt Disney World/ Oldsmobile Classic, his third-to-last event, to retain playing privileges for 1994…carded career-low 64 in Disney opening round, held early lead with Keith Clearwater and Tom Purtzer… $52,800 payday secured place in Top 125…earned TOUR card on first attempt in 1989, lost it after earning just $10,708 in 1990…played Ben Hogan Tour 1990-92…won 1990 Gateway Open, 1991 Utah Classic…became only player to win three consecutive years on Hogan (now NIKE) Tour by capturing 1992 Shreveport Open…earned TOUR card for 1993 by shooting 69 on final day of 1992 season to finish T3 in Fresno Open…finished No. 4 overall with earnings of $105,951…tied for first in Hogan Tour eagles with 12 in 1992.

PERSONAL: Four-time All-Big Ten and three-time NCAA All-American at Ohio State…Pennsylvania State High School Champion.

1994 PGA TOUR STATISTICS

Scoring Average	71.22	(89T)
Driving Distance	260.9	(99)
Driving Accuracy	71.4	(60)
Greens in Regulation	65.8	(90T)
Putting	1.798	(104)
All-Around	503	(30T)
Sand Saves	55.8	(40)
Total Driving	159	(58T)
Eagles	9	(17T)
Birdies	365	(4)

MISCELLANEOUS STATISTICS

Scoring Avg. (before cut)	71.37	(82T)
Scoring Avg. (3rd round)	70.35	(45)
Scoring Avg. (4th round)	71.86	(120)
Birdie Conversion	28.5	(76T)
Par Breakers	19.2	(73T)

1994 Low Round: 66: 3 times
Career Low Round: 64: 1993 WDW/Oldsmobile Classic/1
Career Largest Paycheck: $52,800/'93 WDW/Oldsmobile Classic/T3

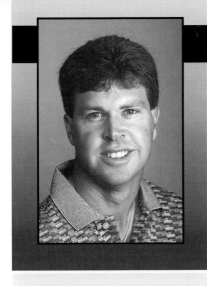

BOB TWAY

EXEMPT STATUS: Winner, 1986 PGA Championship

FULL NAME: Robert Raymond Tway

HEIGHT: 6' 4"   **WEIGHT:** 180

BIRTH DATE: May 4, 1959

BIRTHPLACE: Oklahoma City, OK

RESIDENCE: Edmond, OK; plays out of Oak Tree Golf Club

FAMILY: Wife, Tammie; Kevin (7/23/88),
                    Carly Paige (11/8/93)

COLLEGE: Oklahoma State University

SPECIAL INTERESTS: Snow skiing, fishing, all sports

TURNED PROFESSIONAL: 1981

Q SCHOOL: Fall 1984

PLAYER PROFILE

CAREER EARNINGS: $ 3,028,191   **PLAYOFF RECORD:** 2-3

TOUR VICTORIES: **1986** Shearson Lehman Bros.-Andy Williams Open, Manufacturers Hanover
(TOTAL: 6)   Westchester Classic, Georgia Pacific Atlanta Classic, PGA Championship. **1989**
Memorial Tournament. **1990** Las Vegas Invitational.

MONEY & POSITION:

1985--$164,023--45	1989--$488,340-- 17	1993--$148,120--109
1986--$652,780-- 2	1990--$495,862-- 23	1994--$114,176--146
1987--$212,362--47	1991--$322,931-- 52	
1988--$381,966--29	1992--$ 47,632--179	

BEST 1994 FINISH: T13--Bell Canadian Open.

1994 SUMMARY: Tournaments entered--29; in money--13; top ten finishes--0.

1995 PGA TOUR CHARITY TEAM COMPETITION: Walt Disney World/Oldmobile Classic

NATIONAL TEAMS: World Amateur Cup, 1980; Nissan Cup, 1986.

1994 SEASON: After a promising close to the 1993 season (pair of late top-10s), started slowly in 1994…after T14 in United Airlines Hawaiian Open, missed five cuts in row, then nine of 11…got off to strong start in Bob Hope Chrysler Classic (66-69), only to miss 72-hole cut after pair of 76s…did make ten of final 17 cuts, again offering rays of hope that swing-struggles which began in 1992 may be ending…had confidence-building T13 in Bell Canadian Open, best finish of year…closed campaign with back-to-back top-25s, T21 in Texas Open followed by T16 in Las Vegas Invitational…was second to Bob Estes after two rounds of Texas Open… followed opening 63 with 67 to remain three strokes behind Estes, the eventual wire-to-wire winner…closed with pair of 72s…finished with three consecutive 67s in 90-hole Las Vegas Invitational…made two aces at Memorial, first TOUR player in 30 years to record two holes-in-one in same event…finished as runnerup in 1994 Mexican Open.

CAREER HIGHLIGHTS: Struggled through worst season of 10-year career in 1992…turned things around during late stages of 1993 with pair of top-10 finishes…solo fourth in Hardee's Golf Classic highest finish since T2 behind Phil Mickelson in 1991 Northern Telecom Open…concluded 1993 campaign with T6 in Las Vegas Invitational.…jumped from No. 142 to 109 on money list with that performance…enjoyed dream sophomore season in 1986, collecting four victories, including PGA Championship…won PGA with hole-out from bunker on 72nd hole at Inverness to defeat Greg Norman …named PGA Player of Year and finished No. 2 on money list, just $516 behind Norman…defeated Fuzzy Zoeller by two strokes in 1989 Memorial Tournament, parred first playoff hole to edge John Cook in 1990 Las Vegas Invitational…member 1986 Nissan Cup…winner 1983 Sandpiper-Santa Barbara Open (TPS Series), 1987 Oklahoma State Open…winner 1987 Chrysler Team Championship (with Mike Hulbert), 1988 Fred Meyer Challenge (with Paul Azinger).

PERSONAL: Member 1980 World Amateur Cup team…three-time All-American at Oklahoma State (1979-81)…winner 1981 Fred Haskins Trophy as outstanding collegiate player…member 1978, '80 NCAA Championship teams…winner 1978 Trans-Mississippi Amateur, 1979 Southern Amateur.

1994 PGA TOUR STATISTICS

Scoring Average	71.42	(115)
Driving Distance	266.5	(48)
Driving Accuracy	61.5	(162)
Greens in Regulation	65.3	(106T)
Putting	1.790	(80T)
All-Around	748	(107)
Sand Saves	52.8	(73T)
Total Driving	210	(132T)
Eagles	6	(64T)
Birdies	266	(100T)

MISCELLANEOUS STATISTICS

Scoring Avg. (before cut)	71.61	(109)
Scoring Avg. (3rd round)	71.45	(127T)
Scoring Avg. (4th round)	70.83	(40)
Birdie Conversion	28.3	(83T)
Par Breakers	18.9	(88T)

1994 Low Round: **63:** Texas Open/1
Career Low Round: 61: 1989 Walt Disney /1
Career Largest
Paycheck: $234,000/1990 Las Vegas /1

HOWARD TWITTY

EXEMPT STATUS: 1993 tournament winner

FULL NAME: Howard Allen Twitty

HEIGHT: 6' 5''   **WEIGHT:** 210

BIRTH DATE: Jan. 15, 1949

BIRTHPLACE: Phoenix, AZ

RESIDENCE: Paradise Valley, AZ

FAMILY: Wife, Sheree; Kevin Scott (10/2/76), Jocelyn Noel (11/20/80), Charles Barnes Barris (6/7/89), Mary Caroline Claire (9/11/90), Alicia Anne Marie (1/22/92), William Howard (2/23/94)

COLLEGE: Arizona State University (1972, Business Administration)

SPECIAL INTERESTS: All sports

TURNED PROFESSIONAL: 1974 **Q SCHOOL:** Spring 1975

PLAYER PROFILE

CAREER EARNINGS: $2,524,478   **PLAYOFF RECORD:** 1-0

TOUR VICTORIES: **1979** B. C. Open. **1980** Sammy Davis, Jr.-Greater Hartford Open.
(TOTAL: 3)   **1993** United Airlines Hawaiian Open.

MONEY & POSITION:

1975--$ 8,211--139	1982--$ 57,355-- 78	1989--$ 107,200--119
1976--$ 54,268-- 51	1983--$ 20,000--150	1990--$ 129,444--120
1977--$ 60,091-- 49	1984--$ 51,971--106	1991--$ 226,426-- 74
1978--$ 92,409-- 25	1985--$ 92,958-- 82	1992--$ 264,042-- 57
1979--$179,619-- 15	1986--$156,119-- 57	1993--$ 416,833-- 34
1980--$166,190-- 14	1987--$169,442-- 61	1994--$ 131,408--130
1981--$ 52,183-- 79	1988--$ 87,985--119	

BEST 1994 FINISH: T8--Mercedes Championships.

1994 SUMMARY: Tournaments entered--28; in money--17; top ten finishes--1.

1995 PGA TOUR CHARITY TEAM COMPETITION: Buick Open

1994 SEASON: After five "up" years, his career–kind of like the stock market–suffered a downswing…fell off in earnings for first time since 1988…posted only top-10 in season-opening Mercedes Championships…T8 at LaCosta fashioned by closing rounds of 67-69…7-under-par 281 total produced largest check of season, $34,000…missed next two cuts, including defense of 1993 title in United Airlines Hawaiian Open…struggles then began…withdrew from or unable to start in next four tournaments…after that, had only two top-25s remainder of year…next-best-finish T13 in Kmart Greater Greensboro Open, worth $30,000…opened August with T20 in Buick Open…did make cut in final six tournaments, eight of last nine TOUR starts.

CAREER HIGHLIGHTS: Scored popular victory (third of career) in first start of 1993 season, United Airlines Hawaiian Open…previous victory had come in 1980 Sammy Davis Jr.-Greater Hartford Open…second-round 65 in 1993 Texas Open featured hole-in-one on his final shot of round, enabling him to make cut…best money-list finish No. 14 in 1980…that summer featured run of 13-of-14 rounds in 60s, with cumulative total of 57-under-par…sizzling summer streak featured playoff victory over Jim Simons in GHO, second-place finish at Greater Milwaukee Open, fifth at Hardee's Golf Classic, and opening rounds of 64-66 in IVB-Philadelphia Classic…posted first victory in 1979 B.C. Open, holding off Doug Tewell and Tom Purtzer down stretch…played Asian Tour, winning 1975 Thailand Open.

PERSONAL: Collaborated with Roger Maltbie on well-received course redesign of TPC at River Highlands…Player Director on PGA TOUR Policy Board 1981-82…winner 1970 Sunnehanna and Porter Cup events…1970, '72 All-America at Arizona State.

1994 PGA TOUR STATISTICS

Scoring Average	71.46	(117)
Driving Distance	264.3	(68T)
Driving Accuracy	70.6	(73)
Greens in Regulation	64.3	(131T)
Putting	1.800	(108T)
All-Around	761	(112T)
Sand Saves	48.5	(129)
Total Driving	141	(40)
Eagles	6	(64T)
Birdies	285	(71T)

MISCELLANEOUS STATISTICS

Scoring Avg. (before cut)	71.70	(120)
Scoring Avg. (3rd round)	71.41	(125)
Scoring Avg. (4th round)	72.06	(131T)
Birdie Conversion	28.1	(91T)
Par Breakers	18.4	(110T)

1994 Low Round: 65: Texas Open/2
Career Low Round: 62: 2 times, most recent 1990 Buick Southern Open/1
Career Largest Paycheck: $216,000/1993 United Airlines Hawaiian Open/1

SCOTT VERPLANK

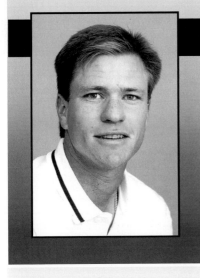

EXEMPT STATUS: 97th on 1994 money list

FULL NAME: Scott Rachal Verplank

HEIGHT: 5'9"   **WEIGHT:** 160

BIRTH DATE: July 9, 1964

BIRTHPLACE: Dallas, TX

RESIDENCE: Edmond, OK

FAMILY: Wife, Kim

COLLEGE: Oklahoma State University

SPECIAL INTERESTS: Hunting, fishing, football

TURNED PROFESSIONAL: 1986

PLAYER PROFILE

CAREER EARNINGS: $993,841

TOUR VICTORIES: 1985 Western Open. 1988 Buick Open.
(TOTAL: 2)

MONEY & POSITION:

1986--$ 19,575--177	1989--$ 82,345--141	1992--$ 1,760--309
1987--$ 34,136--173	1990--$303,589-- 47	1993--$ 0--
1988--$366,045-- 31	1991--$ 3,195--266	1994--$183,015-- 97

BEST 1994 FINISH: T4--Anheuser-Busch Golf Classic

1994 SUMMARY: Tournaments entered--19; in money--14; top ten finishes--1.

1995 PGA TOUR CHARITY TEAM COMPETITION: NEC World Series of Golf

1994 SEASON: Penned inspiring comeback story, having battled back from relatively recent physical adversity and through longterm diabetes...right elbow pain in Nov. 1990 led to Dec. 1991 surgery...missed most of 1991 and 1992 seasons, all of 1993...given special medical extension and 11 tournaments (through U.S. Open) to earn $117,608 in '94, made eight of 11 cuts ...posted T18 in U.S. Open worth $22,478...playing with sponsor's exemptions or as past champion from July on, regained full privileges for 1995...began July with T17 Motorola Western Open, followed by T4 Anheuser-Busch Golf Classic and T20 Deposit Guaranty Golf Classic...those three finishes totaled $67,717, almost exactly as much ($67,529) as made in first 11 starts...final total of $183,015 third best of career...A-B Classic T4 was worth $45,467.

CAREER HIGHLIGHTS: First experienced elbow pain shortly after 1990 season...tried unsuccessfully to play through pain, finally underwent "arthroscopic debridement of the elbow with excision of olecranon spurs" in Dec. 1991...because of diabetic condition, is used to dealing witih adversity...struggled through first two years on TOUR, a victim of high expectations...those expectations stemmed from 1985 Western Open playoff victory (as an amateur) over Jim Thorpe...first amateur to win TOUR event since Gene Littler in 1954...finished well out of Top 125 in 1986 and 1987, had to go to Qualifying Tournament to regain playing privileges for 1988 (finished T6)...took the pressure off by winning 1988 Buick Open...268 total tied second-best score ever at Warwick Hills CC...had been tied with Howard Twitty and Steve Elkington entering final round.

PERSONAL: A highly acclaimed amateur even before 1985 Western Open victory...winner 1984 U.S. Amateur...winner 1986 NCAA Championship...winner 1982-84-85 Texas State Amateur, 1982-83-84-85 LaJet Amateur Classic, 1984 Western Amateur (medalist 1984-85)...winner 1984-85 Sunnehanna Amateur...1984 Big Eight Conference champion...two-time All-American...member 1985 Academic All-America team...1982 AJGA Player of Year...1984 Golf Digest Player of Year.

1994 PGA TOUR STATISTICS

Scoring Average	70.22	(23)
Driving Distance	257.2	(126)
Driving Accuracy	64.4	(148)
Greens in Regulation	64.7	(117T)
Putting	1.767	(24)
All-Around	761	(112T)
Sand Saves	55.9	(39)
Total Driving	274	(167)
Eagles	2	(146T)
Birdies	222	(138T)

MISCELLANEOUS STATISTICS

Scoring Avg. (before cut)	71.45	(91T)
Scoring Avg. (3rd round)	70.31	(42)
Scoring Avg. (4th round)	70.15	(13)
Birdie Conversion	29.9	(32T)
Par Breakers	19.5	(61T)

1994 Low Round:	**65:** Hardee's Golf Classic/4
Career Low Round:	**62:** 1990 Greater Milwaukee Open/2
Career Largest Paycheck:	**$126,000**/1988 Buick Open/1

BOBBY WADKINS

EXEMPT STATUS: 89th on 1994 money list

FULL NAME: Robert Edwin Wadkins

HEIGHT: 6'1"   **WEIGHT:** 195

BIRTH DATE: July 26, 1951

BIRTHPLACE: Richmond, VA

RESIDENCE: Richmond, VA

FAMILY: Wife, Linda; Casey Tanner (2/14/90)

COLLEGE: East Tennessee University (1973, Health & Physical Education)

SPECIAL INTERESTS: Fishing, duck and goose hunting

TURNED PROFESSIONAL: 1973   **Q SCHOOL:** Fall 1974

PLAYER PROFILE

CAREER EARNINGS: $2,281,682   **PLAYOFF RECORD:** 0-2

BEST-EVER FINISH: 2--1979 IVB-Philadelphia Classic, 1985 Sea Pines Heritage Classic. T2--1994 Kemper Open.

MONEY & POSITION:

1975--$ 23,330-- 90	1982--$ 69,400--59	1989--$152,184-- 91
1976--$ 23,510-- 93	1983--$ 56,363-- 92	1990--$190,613-- 85
1977--$ 20,867--103	1984--$108,335-- 67	1991--$206,503-- 81
1978--$ 70,426-- 41	1985--$ 84,542-- 90	1992--$ 30,382--197
1979--$121,373-- 28	1986--$226,079-- 33	1993--$ 39,153--189
1980--$ 56,728-- 67	1987--$342,173-- 25	1994--$208,358-- 89
1981--$ 58,346-- 73	1988--$193,022-- 59	

BEST 1994 FINISHES: T2--Kemper Open; T7--Buick Southern Open

1994 SUMMARY: Tournaments entered--22; in money--14; top ten finishes--2.

1995 PGA TOUR CHARITY TEAM COMPETITION: Buick Southern Open

1994 SEASON: Although undone by final-round 74, came close to winning Kemper Open, which would have been first victory in 20th year on TOUR...playing under sponsor's exemption, ran second to Mark Brooks through first two rounds at TPC at Avenel, then took lead by two strokes over Brooks with third-round 65...lost ball and triple-bogey eight on sixth hole of final 18 led to his undoing...closing-round disappointment left him tied with D.A. Weibring for second at 10-under-par 274, three behind Brooks...$114,400 payday lifted earnings total to $136,780, virtually assuring playing privileges for 1995...final total of $208,358 best campaign since career year of 1987... continues as TOUR's all-time leader in earnings without win...relinqushed that distinction to Loren Roberts in Oct. 1993, but then Roberts won Nestle Invitational in March '94...commented after Kemper loss that while runnerup paycheck was nice, would have given it all back for win...later had T7 at Buick Southern Open, first of three top-25 finishes to complete season...also had top-25 (T20) in weather-shortened Deposit Guaranty Golf Classic.

CAREER HIGHLIGHTS: 1994 Kemper T2 matched career bests in 1979 IVB-Philadelphia Classic and 1985 Sea Pines Heritage Classic...playoff loser in each instance, to Lou Graham in '79 and Bernhard Langer in '85...Kemper finish also helped prove has come back from April 1992 neck surgery (herniated disc), which limited play that year to just 15 events, none from May to August...surgery occurred Tuesday after '92 Kmart Greater Greensboro Open, last cut made that year...returned to action for Canadian Open, missing cuts in final five starts...played under special medical extension for 1993, when on-going rehab delayed start until May...best finish that year T25 in Memorial...although has not won on TOUR, has three victories overseas: 1978 European Open in Surrey, England and two Dunlop Phoenix titles in Japan (1979 and '86)...prior to 1992 had streak of 14 consecutive years (1978-91) among top 100 money winners.

PERSONAL: Winner 1971 Virginia State Amateur, 1981-82 Virginia State Open...1972-73 NCAA All-America at East Tennessee State...attended University of Houston for year...along with older brother Lanny kept Richmond, VA city junior title in family six straight years (Lanny 4, Bobby 2).

1994 PGA TOUR STATISTICS

Scoring Average	70.97	(63T)
Driving Distance	263.4	(76)
Driving Accuracy	69.0	(92T)
Greens in Regulation	67.2	(51T)
Putting	1.778	(45T)
All-Around	694	(85T)
Sand Saves	48.7	(125T)
Total Driving	168	(69T)
Eagles	3	(126T)
Birdies	245	(116T)

MISCELLANEOUS STATISTICS

Scoring Avg. (before cut)	71.00	(51)
Scoring Avg. (3rd round)	70.18	(29)
Scoring Avg. (4th round)	71.58	(100T)
Birdie Conversion	30.2	(27T)
Par Breakers	20.6	(25T)

1994 Low Round:	**65:** 2 times
Career Low Round:	**64:** 8 times, most recently 1991 Texas Open/2
Career Largest Paycheck:	**$114,000**/'94 Kemper Open/T2

LANNY WADKINS

EXEMPT STATUS: Member, 1993 Ryder Cup team

FULL NAME: Jerry Lanston Wadkins

HEIGHT: 5' 9"   **WEIGHT:** 170

BIRTH DATE: Dec. 5, 1949

BIRTHPLACE: Richmond, VA

RESIDENCE: Dallas, TX; plays out of The Homestead

FAMILY: Wife, Penelope; Jessica (10/14/73), Travis (8/25/87), Tucker (8/19/92)

COLLEGE: Wake Forest University

SPECIAL INTERESTS: Fishing, hunting, snow skiing, scuba-diving

TURNED PROFESSIONAL: 1971

Q SCHOOL: Fall 1971

PLAYER PROFILE

CAREER EARNINGS: $5,931,370   **PLAYOFF RECORD:** 3-2

TOUR VICTORIES: **1972** Sahara Invitational. **1973** Byron Nelson Classic, USI Classic. **1977** PGA Champion-
(TOTAL: 21)   ship, World Series of Golf. **1979** Glen Campbell Los Angeles Open, Tournament Players
Championship. **1982** Phoenix Open, MONY--Tournament of Champions, Buick Open.
1983 Greater Greensboro Open, MONY--Tournament of Champions. **1985** Bob Hope Classic, Los Angeles Open,
Walt Disney World/Oldsmobile Classic. **1987** Doral-Ryder Open. **1988** Hawaiian Open, Colonial National
Invitation. **1990** Anheuser-Busch Golf Classic. **1991** United Hawaiian Open. **1992** Canon Greater Hartford Open.

MONEY & POSITION:

1971--$ 15,291--111	1979--$195,710--10	1987--$501,727-- 13
1972--$116,616-- 10	1980--$ 67,778--58	1988--$616,596-- 10
1973--$200,455-- 5	1981--$ 51,704--81	1989--$233,363-- 60
1974--$ 51,124-- 54	1982--$306,827-- 7	1990--$673,433-- 13
1975--$ 23,582-- 88	1983--$319,271-- 3	1991--$651,495-- 12
1976--$ 42,849-- 64	1984--$198,996--29	1992--$366,837-- 40
1977--$244,882-- 3	1985--$446,893-- 2	1993--$244,544-- 68
1978--$ 53,811-- 61	1986--$264,931--23	1994--$ 54,114--185

BEST 1994 FINISH: T18--The Masters tournament.

1994 SUMMARY: Tournaments entered--25; in money--9; top ten finishes--0.

1995 PGA TOUR CHARITY TEAM COMPETITION: Shell Houston Open

NATIONAL TEAMS: Ryder Cup (8), 1977, 1979, 1983,1985, 1987, 1989, 1991; 1993 World Cup (3), 1977,
1984, 1985; Walker Cup (2) 1969, 1971; World Amateur Cup, 1970; U.S. vs. Japan (2), 1982, 1983; Nissan
Cup, 1985; Kirin Cup 1987.

1994 SEASON: In terms of money-list ranking, suffered through worst campaign of
24-year career...No. 185 position partially explainable by increasing demands made
on him as U.S. team captain for 31st Ryder Cup...large portion of time taken up with
planning for Sept. 22-24 competition at Oak Hill CC in Rochester, NY... had but two
top-25 finishes, T18 in Masters and T23 in Hardee's Golf Classic, where closed with
66...Masters finish produced biggest check of year, $24,343, almost half of final
total...eight of his rounds in 60s came during last six starts, three in Hardee's
tournament (opened 69-68 before closing 66)...first time in career with no top-10
finishes...also missed more cuts than made for first time.

CAREER HIGHLIGHTS: Battled system infection part of 1993, injured back following
'93 PGA Championship...latter jeopardized his chances for making eighth Ryder
Cup team, but was Captain's Choice of Tom Watson...captured 21st title in 22nd
year on TOUR, winning 1992 Canon Greater Hartford Open...playing 75 minutes
ahead of leaders, came from three strokes off lead with final-round 65 to put 274 on
board, then watched from CBS-TV tower as all contenders fell short...one of game's
fiercest competitors...has won twice in season five times and three times twice
(1982, 1985)...named PGA Player of Year in '85...had highest money list finish that
year, No. 2...in 1977 won PGA Championship in playoff with Gene Littler, then World
Series of Golf title at Firestone CC...claimed 1979 Tournament Players Championship in fierce winds on Sawgrass course, scoring five-stroke victory over Tom
Watson...winner 1978 Canadian PGA, 1978 Garden State PGA (Australia), 1979
Bridgestone Open (Japan), 1984 World Nissan Championship (Japan)...winner
1990 Fred Meyer Challenge (with Bobby Wadkins).

PERSONAL: Inspirational leader to younger players in recent Ryder Cups, factor
which entered into 1995 Captain selection...winner 1963-64 National Pee Wee,
1970 U.S. Amateur, 1970 Western Amateur, 1968 and '70 Southern Amateur, 1969
Eastern Amateur...1970-71 Collegiate All-America...member 1969-71 Walker Cup,
1970 World Amateur Cup teams.

1994 PGA TOUR STATISTICS

Scoring Average	72.37
Driving Distance	247.3
Driving Accuracy	68.1
Greens in Regulation	60.5
Putting	1.779
All-Around	1,007
Sand Saves	42.0
Total Driving	276
Eagles	5
Birdies	208

MISCELLANEOUS STATISTICS

Scoring Avg. (before cut)	72.84
Scoring Avg. (3rd round)	70.89
Scoring Avg. (4th round)	73.44
Birdie Conversion	28.5
Par Breakers	17.7

1994 Low Round:	**66:** Hardee's Golf Classic/4
Career Low Round:	**62:** 1989 Texas Open
Career Largest	Presented by Nabisco/1
Paycheck:	**$198,000**/'91 Hawaiian Open/1

GRANT WAITE

EXEMPT STATUS: 1993 tournament winner

FULL NAME: Grant Osten Waite

HEIGHT: 6'   **WEIGHT:** 185

BIRTH DATE: August 11, 1964

BIRTHPLACE: Palmerston, New Zealand

RESIDENCE: Palmerston North, New Zealand

FAMILY: Wife, Lea; Osten Holland (6/1/94)

COLLEGE: University of Oklahoma

SPECIAL INTERESTS: Wind surfing,reading, skiing,fitness

TURNED PROFESSIONAL: 1987

Q SCHOOL: Fall 1989, 1992

PLAYER PROFILE

CAREER EARNINGS: $533,176

TOUR VICTORIES: 1993 Kemper Open.
(TOTAL: 1)

MONEY & POSITION: 1990--$50,076--177   1993--$411,405--35   1994--$71,695--172

BEST 1994 FINISH: T18--Phoenix Open.

1994 SUMMARY: Tournaments entered--25; in money--13; top ten finishes--0.

1995 PGA TOUR CHARITY TEAM COMPETITION: Motorola Western Open

1994 SEASON: Had anticipated high point of season would be defense of Kemper Open title…Kemper week still high point of season, but for different reason…after checking in at TPC at Avenel, wound up withdrawing to be with wife Lea in Arizona as she delivered their first child, son Osten Holland born June 1…from performance standpoint, first month was high point of campaign in which wound up missing almost 50 percent of cuts…had no top-10 finishes after four in 1993, just two top-25s…both top-25s occurred in January…opened year with T20 in Mercedes Championships…three weeks later closed 67-69 for T18 in Phoenix Open…missed next three cuts, sign of things to come…from that point forward, best finish T29 in Nestle Invitational… Kemper withdrawal came in middle of string of four misses…ended year on down note, as well, missing final three cuts and four of last five…final total of $71,695 was $339,710 less than money won in 1993.

CAREER HIGHLIGHTS: After playing TOUR with limited success in 1990, made successful return in 1993 after finishing T20 in 1992 Qualifying Tournament… captured first TOUR title in head-to-head battle with Tom Kite in Kemper Open… held first- and second-round leads after going 66-67, then gave way to Kite at 54-hole juncture…held steady in face of pressure from TOUR's all-time money leader, carding final-round 70 for one-stroke win…posted T7 in AT&T Pebble Beach National Pro-Am for first of four top-10s…was Deposit Guaranty Golf Classic clubhouse leader following final-round 63, his career low…ultimately finished T4 in Hattiesburg, MS event…final top-10 of '93 came in NEC World Series of Golf, where made 10-stroke improvement over third-round score with closing 65…prior to 1993, best finish had been T6 in 1990 Hawaiian Open…finished three strokes behind winner David Ishii…finished 25th in 1989 Qualifying Tournament…winner 1992 New Zealand Open.

PERSONAL: Selected by CBS Sports as "New Breed Player of Year" for 1993…three-time All-American at Oklahoma…two-time Australian Junior Champion.

1994 PGA TOUR STATISTICS

Scoring Average	72.34	(167)
Driving Distance	258.8	(114)
Driving Accuracy	74.5	(31)
Greens in Regulation	64.0	(136)
Putting	1.839	(171)
All-Around	1,016	(160)
Sand Saves	51.1	(94)
Total Driving	145	(47)
Eagles	2	(146)
Birdies	202	(157)

MISCELLANEOUS STATISTICS

Scoring Avg. (before cut)	72.28	(154)
Scoring Avg. (3rd round)	74.10	(178)
Scoring Avg. (4th round)	71.70	(106)
Birdie Conversion	25.1	(155)
Par Breakers	16.2	(162)

1994 Low Round:	**65**: FedEx St. Jude C;assoc/2
Career Low Round: 63: 2 times, most recent	1993 Deposit Guaranty/ 4
Career Largest	
Paycheck: $234,000/1993 Kemper Open/1	

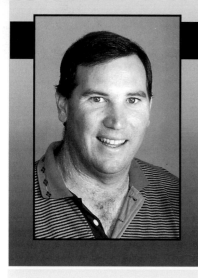

DUFFY WALDORF

EXEMPT STATUS: 71st on 1994 money list

HEIGHT: 5' 11" **WEIGHT:** 225

BIRTH DATE: August 20, 1962

BIRTHPLACE: Los Angeles, CA

RESIDENCE: Valencia, CA

FAMILY: Wife, Vicky; Tyler Lane (7/16/90),
Shea Duffy (4/23/92), Kelli Ann (1/14/94)

COLLEGE: UCLA (1985, Psychology)

SPECIAL INTERESTS: Colorful hats & clothes,
wine collecting, football, music

TURNED PROFESSIONAL: 1985

Q SCHOOL: Fall 1986, 1987, 1988, 1990

PLAYER PROFILE

CAREER EARNINGS: $1,587,825

BEST EVER FINISH: 2--1992 Phoenix Open, 2--1992 Buick Classic

MONEY & POSITION:
1987--$ 53,175--148	1990--$ 71,673--157	1993--$202,638--84
1988--$ 55,221--143	1991--$196,081-- 86	1994--$274,971--71
1989--$149,945-- 94	1992--$582,120-- 23	

BEST 1994 FINISHES: 3--Sprint International; T8--Buick Open; T9--U.S. Open; T10--FedEx St. Jude Classic

1994 SUMMARY: Tournaments entered--26; in money--14; top ten finishes--4.

1995 PGA TOUR CHARITY TEAM COMPETITION: Mercedes Championships

1994 SEASON: Turned potentially disastrous season into second-best of career with some late-year heroics…through most of first seven months and 18 starts, had missed 12 cuts…earnings total at that juncture $70,642, $37,180 of which came for T9 in U.S. Open at Oakmont…also had stretch of four consecutive cuts made April (T15 Freeport-McMoRan Classic) through early May…Open finish came in middle of six misses…after final miss in that string, New England Classic, began positive streak that turned season around…ran off three straight top-10s, part of season-ending skein of eight consecutive events in money…opened with T10 in FedEx St. Jude Classic, where closed with back-to-back 67s…followed with T8 in Buick Open, then posted solo third in Sprint International worth $95,200…total for those three events $155,580, raising season figure to $226,492 en route to final tally of $274,971…produced three top-25s in final five starts, concluding with T16 in Las Vegas Invitational…64 in Round 4 of LVI his season low.

CAREER HIGHLIGHTS: Best shot at winning in 1993 came in Buick Classic, where had share of second- and third-round leads…final 75 dropped him to T10, four strokes out of Vijay Singh-Mark Wiebe playoff…held midpoint lead in 1992 Centel Western Open, where finished T3…had rain-delayed 54-hole lead at Kemper Open, but dropped off to T13…also had pair of career-best second-place finishes in 1992, at Phoenix Open and in Buick Classic…finished five shots behind Phoenix winner Mark Calcavecchia after closing with three 67s…held or shared second place for last three rounds of Buick Classic, which David Frost won by eight strokes…finished two strokes behind Fulton Allem in 1991 Independent Insurance Agent Open…tied for third-round lead at Kmart Greater Greensboro Open after 63, but finished four strokes behind Mark Brooks…Qualifying Tournament medalist fourth time through in 1990.

PERSONAL: An avid wine collector and connoisseur…colorful shirt and cap combinations make him easy to spot on course…winner 1984 California State Amateur, 1984 Broadmoor Invitational, 1985 Rice Planters (Charleston, SC)…1985 College Player of Year…1985 All-American.

1994 PGA TOUR STATISTICS

Scoring Average	71.34	(103T)
Driving Distance	271.4	(25)
Driving Accuracy	68.6	(98)
Greens in Regulation	66.7	(65T)
Putting	1.789	(79)
All-Around	635	(68)
Sand Saves	46.4	(146T)
Total Driving	123	(28)
Eagles	7	(44T)
Birdies	282	(75T)

MISCELLANEOUS STATISTICS

Scoring Avg. (before cut)	71.54	(102)
Scoring Avg. (3rd round)	71.50	(130T)
Scoring Avg. (4th round)	71.36	(72T)
Birdie Conversion	29.3	(49T)
Par Breakers	20.1	(40T)

1994 Low Round:	**64:** Las Vegas Invitational/4
Career Low Round:	**63:** 3 times, most recent '91 Kmart Greater Greensboro /3
Career Largest Paycheck:	**$108,000**/1992 Phoenix Open/2 1992 Buick Classic/2

TOM WATSON

EXEMPT STATUS: 43rd on 1994 money list

FULL NAME: Thomas Sturges Watson

HEIGHT: 5' 9"　　　　**WEIGHT:** 160

BIRTH DATE: Sept. 4, 1949

BIRTHPLACE: Kansas City, MO

RESIDENCE: Mission Hills, KS

FAMILY: Wife, Linda; Meg (9/13/79), Michael Barrett (12/15/82)

COLLEGE: Stanford University (1971, Psychology)

SPECIAL INTERESTS: Hunting, fishing, guitar

TURNED PROFESSIONAL: 1971

Q SCHOOL: Fall 1971

PLAYER PROFILE

CAREER EARNINGS: $6,751,328　　　　**PLAYOFF RECORD:** 8-4

TOUR VICTORIES: **1974** Western Open. **1975** Byron Nelson Golf Classic. **1977** Bing Crosby National Pro-Am, Wickes-Andy Williams San Diego Open, Masters, Western Open. **1978** Joe Garagiola-Tucson Open, Bing Crosby National Pro-Am, Byron Nelson Golf Classic, Colgate Hall of Fame Classic, Anheuser-Busch Classic. **1979** Sea Pines Heritage Classic, Tournament of Champions, Byron Nelson Golf Classic, Memorial Tournament, Colgate Hall of Fame Classic. **1980** Andy Williams-San Diego Open, Glen Campbell-Los Angeles Open, MONY-Tournament of Champions, New Orleans Open, Byron Nelson Classic, World Series of Golf. **1981** Masters, USF&G-New Orleans Open, Atlanta Classic. **1982** Glen Campbell-Los Angeles Open, Sea Pines Heritage Classic, U.S. Open. **1984** Seiko-Tucson Match Play, MONY-Tournament of Champions, Western Open. **1987** Nabisco Championships of Golf.
(TOTAL: 32)

MONEY & POSITION:

1971--$ 2,185--224	1979--$462,636-- 1	1987--$616,351-- 5
1972--$ 31,081-- 79	1980--$530,808-- 1	1988--$273,216--39
1973--$ 74,973-- 35	1981--$347,660-- 3	1989--$185,398--80
1974--$135,474-- 10	1982--$316,483-- 5	1990--$213,988--68
1975--$153,795-- 7	1983--$237,519--12	1991--$354,877--45
1976--$138,202-- 12	1984--$476,260-- 1	1992--$299,818--50
1977--$310,653-- 1	1985--$226,778--18	1993--$342,023--46
1978--$362,429-- 1	1986--$278,338--20	1994--$380,378--43

BEST 1994 FINISHES: T2--AT&T Pebble Beach National Pro-Am; T6--Nissan Los Angeles Open, U.S. Open; 8--Nestle Invitational; T9--PGA Championship.

1994 SUMMARY: Tournaments entered--15; in money--14; top ten finishes--5.

1994 PGA TOUR CHARITY TEAM COMPETITION: Anheuser-Busch Golf Classic

NATIONAL TEAMS: Ryder Cup (4), 1977, 1981, 1983, 1989; U.S. vs. Japan (2) 1982, 1984.

1994 SEASON: Had excellent early-season opportunity to win for first time since 1987 Nabisco Championships, but putter failed him during final round of AT&T Pebble Beach National Pro-Am... finished in four-way T2, one stroke behind Johnny Miller, who won in spite of his own putting woes...despite playing normal limited schedule, posted best earnings total since 1987 (when finished No. 5 with $616,351)...money list finish also best since 1988...Pebble Beach T2 one of three top-10 finishes in first five starts...followed with T6 in Nissan Los Angeles Open very next week, then earned solo eighth in Nestle Invitational...once again found himself in contention at Bay Hill...after 54 holes was tied with Nick Price and Andrew Magee, one stroke behind Vijay Singh... putter contributed to final-round 73...later had pair of top-10s in majors, T6 in U.S. Open and T9 PGA Championship...also played well in Masters (13) and British Open (T11)...low final round of the four was 71 in PGA Championship; posted closing 74 in each of other three...only missed cut came in GTE Byron Nelson Classic, event he won three times in succession (1978-80) and four times overall...winner of Skins Game and $210,000 with playoff birdie.

CAREER HIGHLIGHTS: Holds record for consecutive seasons with earnings over $100,000 (21)...captained United States to victory in 1993 Ryder Cup at The Belfry...also had top-10 finishes in 1993 U.S. Open (T5) and PGA Championship (5)... numbers five British Opens (1975-77-80-82-83), two Masters and 1982 U.S. Open among his 32 career titles...of majors, only PGA Championship has escaped him...leading money winner on TOUR five times, including 1977-80 consecutively... became first player to earn $500,000 in season in 1980, when won six TOUR events, plus third British Open...winner 1977-79 Vardon Trophies...winner 1980 Dunlop Phoenix (Japan)...six-time PGA Player of Year (1977-78-79-80-82-84).

PERSONAL: Big fan of hometown Kansas City Royals...elected to PGA World Golf Hall of Fame 1988.

1994 PGA TOUR STATISTICS

Scoring Average	69.85	(11T)
Driving Distance	268.5	(37T)
Driving Accuracy	75.4	(26T)
Greens in Regulation	68.0	(43)
Putting	1.809	(125T)
All-Around	535	(42)
Sand Saves	53.7	(61T)
Total Driving	63	(5)
Eagles	6	(64T)
Birdies	182	(168T)

MISCELLANEOUS STATISTICS

Scoring Avg. (before cut)	70.64	(31)
Scoring Avg. (3rd round)	70.54	(62)
Scoring Avg. (4th round)	71.46	(88)
Birdie Conversion	27.5	(115T)
Par Breakers	19.3	(67T)

1994 Low Round: 67: 4 times

Career Low Round: 62: 1973 World Open/5

Career Largest Paycheck: $360,000/'87 Nabisco Championships/1

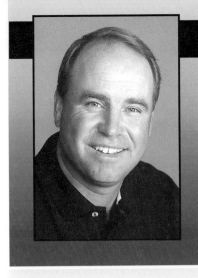

D. A. WEIBRING

EXEMPT STATUS: 72nd on 1994 money list

FULL NAME: Donald Albert Weibring, Jr.

HEIGHT: 6' 1"   **WEIGHT:** 190

BIRTH DATE: May 25, 1953

BIRTHPLACE: Quincy, IL

RESIDENCE: Plano, TX

FAMILY: Wife, Kristy; Matt (12/4/79), Katey (12/29/82), Allison Paige (10/3/87)

COLLEGE: Illinois State University

TURNED PROFESSIONAL: 1975

Q SCHOOL: Spring 1977

PLAYER PROFILE

CAREER EARNINGS: $3,095,307   **PLAYOFF RECORD:** 0-2

TOUR VICTORIES: 1979 Quad Cities Open. **1987** Beatrice Western Open. **1991** Hardee's Golf Classic. (TOTAL: 3)

MONEY & POSITION:

1977--$ 1,681--215	1983--$ 61,631--84	1989--$ 98,686--127
1978--$ 41,052-- 75	1984--$110,325--65	1990--$156,235--101
1979--$ 71,343-- 57	1985--$153,079--50	1991--$ 558,648-- 22
1980--$ 78,611-- 53	1986--$167,602--55	1992--$ 253,018-- 62
1981--$ 92,365-- 45	1987--$391,363--21	1993--$ 299,293-- 58
1982--$117,941-- 31	1988--$186,677- 63	1994--$ 255,757-- 72

BEST 1994 FINISHES: T2--Kemper Open; T4--Doral Ryder Open; T10--Nestle Invitational.

1994 SUMMARY: Tournaments entered--20; in money--14; top ten finishes--3.

1995 PGA TOUR CHARITY TEAM COMPETITION: Mercedes Championship

1994 SEASON: Hand injured late in season contributed to missed cuts in three of last four starts...still wound up with fourth-best earnings total of 18-year career...because of pain almost withdrew from Hardee's Golf Classic, event he has won twice... did play, but missed Quad Cities cut by single stroke...began year with back-to-back top-10s in third and fourth starts: T4 in Doral-Ryder Open, followed by T10 in Nestle Invitational...middle rounds of 69-65 got him into contention at Doral, where finished five strokes behind winner John Huston...closed with three consecutive 68s at Kemper Open, good for second-place tie with Bobby Wadkins, three strokes in back of Mark Brooks...held first- and second-round leads in Greater Milwaukee Open after rounds of 65-66...was four behind Bob Estes after three rounds, but closed with 74 to finish T25.

CAREER HIGHLIGHTS: Illinois native whose victories constitute "Illinois Slam"...all three wins have come in Illinois...finest season came in 1991, when captured Hardee's Golf Classic for second time and lost playoff to Andrew Magee in Las Vegas Invitational...finished Hardee's with sizzling 64 to win by stroke over Paul Azinger and Peter Jacobsen...in Las Vegas, tied Magee at 31-under-par 329, at that time TOUR record for low 90-hole total...won 1987 Western Open at Butler National GC by stroke over Larry Nelson and Greg Norman...captured 1979 Quad Cities Open, precursor of Hardee's Golf Classic...finished T2 twice in 1993, at GTE Byron Nelson and in Hardee's tournament...other high career finishes include second in 1985 Tournament Players Championship, fourth in 1986 PGA Championship, T3s 1987 PGA and 1988 U.S. Open...winner 1985 Polaroid Cup (Japan), 1985 Shell-Air New Zealand Open, 1989 Family House Invitational in Pittsburgh...lost Morocco Open playoff to Payne Stewart.

PERSONAL: Involved in golf course architecture...responsible for "fine tuning" of several holes at TPC at Las Colinas...co-winner 1991 Hilton Bounceback Award, product of successful rebound from right wrist surgery in November 1989.

1994 PGA TOUR STATISTICS

Scoring Average	70.90	(57T)
Driving Distance	253.1	(155T)
Driving Accuracy	77.6	(10)
Greens in Regulation	66.1	(83T)
Putting	1.780	(57T)
All-Around	678	(82)
Sand Saves	56.7	(30T)
Total Driving	165	(66T)
Eagles	2	(146T)
Birdies	220	(140T)

MISCELLANEOUS STATISTICS

Scoring Avg. (before cut)	71.15	(63T)
Scoring Avg. (3rd round)	70.08	(23)
Scoring Avg. (4th round)	72.42	(152)
Birdie Conversion	29.3	(49T)
Par Breakers	19.6	(60)

1994 Low Round: 65: 2 times

Career Low Round: 64: 8 times, most recent '91

Career Largest Paycheck: $180,000/1991 Hardee's Golf Classic/1 Las Vegas /2&4

MARK WIEBE

EXEMPT STATUS: Special Medical Extension

FULL NAME: Mark Charles Wiebe

HEIGHT: 6' 2"   **WEIGHT:** 210

BIRTH DATE: September 13, 1957

BIRTHPLACE: Seaside, OR

RESIDENCE: Denver, CO

FAMILY: Wife, Cathy; Taylor Lynn (9/9/86), Gunner (1/1/89), Collier (4/17/92)

COLLEGE: San Jose State

SPECIAL INTERESTS: Fishing, skiing

TURNED PROFESSIONAL: 1980

Q SCHOOL: Fall 1983, 1984

PLAYER PROFILE

CAREER EARNINGS: $2,136,907   **PLAYOFF RECORD:** 1-1

TOUR VICTORIES: 1985 Anheuser-Busch Classic. **1986** Hardee's Golf Classic. (TOTAL: 2)

MONEY & POSITION:

1984--$ 16,257--166	1988--$392,166-- 28	1992--$174,763-- 86
1985--$181,894-- 36	1989--$296,269-- 41	1993--$360,213-- 42
1986--$260,180-- 25	1990--$210,435-- 72	1994--$ 16,032--233
1987--$128,651-- 82	1991--$100,046--136	

BEST 1994 FINISH: T33--Texas Open

1994 SUMMARY: Tournaments entered-- 9; in money--5; top ten finishes--0.

1995 PGA TOUR CHARITY TEAM COMPETITION: Buick Classic

1994 SEASON: Rapidly acquiring reputation as "The Comeback Kid," one which would just as soon not have…no sooner had completed successful comeback from right shoulder (bicep tendon) problem encountered in 1992 than suffered broken and dislocated shoulder March 7 in Colorado skiing accident…year had begun poorly enough, anyway…missed cut in four of first five events…returned in August for Sprint International, held in own (Denver) backyard at Castle Pines…finished 70th but did record hole-in-one…made cut in all four tournaments played following return…best finish T33 in Texas Open, where opened with pair of 68s and concluded 70-70 for 276 total…due to skiing accident, is playing under special medical extension this year…has 20 tournaments to meet money requirement.

CAREER HIGHLIGHTS: Waged strong comeback in 1993 from previous shoulder trouble…season earnings of $360,213 second-best of career…came close to winning third title in Buick Classic…closing rounds of 67-66 at Westchester CC produced tie with Vijay Singh at 280…Singh went on to capture first TOUR title with birdie on third playoff hole…had four other top-10 finishes in 1993, with best being Western Open T4…wound up with top money-list ranking since 1989…had to rely on sponsor's exemptions to get into many tournament fields in 1992…enjoyed finest earnings season in 1988 with $392,166…lost Anheuser-Busch Classic playoff that year to Tom Sieckmann…A-B Classic provided first TOUR victory in 1985, this time with playoff win over John Mahaffey…captured second tournament title very next year, winning 1986 Hardee's Golf Classic.

PERSONAL: Has emphasized will return to slopes, since skiing is sport his family enjoys…winner 1986 Colorado Open, 1981 "Texas Dolly" Match Play Championship in Las Vegas…Second Team All-American at San Jose State…winner California junior college title at Palomar J.C.

1994 PGA TOUR STATISTICS

Scoring Average	72.29
Driving Distance	257.1
Driving Accuracy	76.5
Greens in Regulation	70.3
Putting	1.848
All-Around	--
Sand Saves	33.3
Total Driving	--
Eagles	2
Birdies	77

MISCELLANEOUS STATISTICS

Scoring Avg. (before cut)	71.94
Scoring Avg. (3rd round)	69.75
Scoring Avg. (4th round)	72.25
Birdie Conversion	23.4
Par Breakers	16.9

1994 Low Round:	67: 2 times
Career Low Round:	61: '88 Northern Telecom/3
Career Largest Paycheck:	$108,000/'93 Buick Classic/2

JOHN WILSON

EXEMPT STATUS: 117th on 1994 money list

FULL NAME: John Arthur Wilson

HEIGHT: 6'1" **WEIGHT:** 165

BIRTH DATE: February 23, 1959

BIRTHPLACE: Ceres, CA

RESIDENCE: Palm Desert, CA; plays out of PGA West

FAMILY: Wife, Kathy; Christopher (2/26/78), Shannon (4/28/79), Spencer (12/10/91)

COLLEGE: College of the Desert

SPECIAL INTERESTS: Fishing, all sports, horticulture

TURNED PROFESSIONAL: 1987

Q SCHOOL: 1990, 1993

PLAYER PROFILE

CAREER EARNINGS: $198,099

BEST-EVER FINISH: T4--1994 Anheuser-Busch Golf Classic

MONEY & POSITION: 1991--$43,041--180 1992--$576--318 1994--$155,058--117

BEST 1994 FINISHES: T4--Anheuser-Busch Golf Classic; T5--Texas Open.

1994 SUMMARY: Tournaments entered--29; in money--14; top ten finishes--2.

1995 PGA TOUR CHARITY TEAM COMPETITION: Franklin Funds Shark Shootout

1994 SEASON: Pair of top-10 finishes, second of which came in penultimate start, were keys to retaining playing privileges for 1995…in fact, T5 in next-to-last start in Texas Open was critical…opening-round 64 at Kingsmill GC left him three strokes behind Bob Lohr's early lead in Anheuser-Busch Golf Classic…closing 67 produced T4 and largest check of season, $45,467…that came four weeks after T13 in Buick Classic, worth $24,000…going into A-B Classic had missed nine cuts in 15 outings, so hefty paycheck there lifted earnings total to $87,641…heading to San Antonio, had made $114,043 and stood No. 141 on money list…opened with three rounds in 60s (66-68-67), capped by one-under-par 70, good for 271 total and, most importantly, paycheck for $36,500 that lifted him to No. 115 (finished 117 after T45 in Las Vegas Invitational)…had T17 finish in B.C. Open in September worth $12,600…made eight of final 13 cuts, with Texas Open finish coming week after withdrawal during Walt Disney World/ Oldsmobile Classic.

CAREER HIGHLIGHTS: Played Australian Tour in 1990…qualified for 1991 PGA TOUR by placing T31 in 1990 Qualifying Tournament…had pair of T19 finishes in '91: Deposit Guaranty Golf Classic and Federal Express St. Jude Classic…T2 in 1991 Ben Hogan Mississippi Gulf Coast Classic.

PERSONAL: Along with Jack Renner, only members of TOUR who attended College of the Desert.

1994 PGA TOUR STATISTICS

Scoring Average	71.20	(84T)
Driving Distance	267.8	(42)
Driving Accuracy	59.9	(174)
Greens in Regulation	65.9	(86T)
Putting	1.782	(62T)
All-Around	715	(94T)
Sand Saves	52.8	(73T)
Total Driving	216	(138)
Eagles	2	(146T)
Birdies	300	(48T)

MISCELLANEOUS STATISTICS

Scoring Avg. (before cut)	71.29	(74T)
Scoring Avg. (3rd round)	70.75	(71T)
Scoring Avg. (4th round)	70.85	(41)
Birdie Conversion	30.1	(29T)
Par Breakers	20.0	(45T)

1994 Low Round:	64: Anheuser-Busch Cl./1
Career Low Round:	64: 1994 Anheuser-Busch Golf Classic/1
Career Largest Paycheck:	$45,467/'94 Anheuser-Busch/T4

FUZZY ZOELLER

EXEMPT STATUS: 5th on 1994 money list

FULL NAME: Frank Urban Zoeller

HEIGHT: 5' 10" **WEIGHT:** 190

BIRTH DATE: Nov. 11, 1951

BIRTHPLACE: New Albany, IN

RESIDENCE: New Albany, IN; plays out of Naples National, Naples, FL

FAMILY: Wife, Diane; Sunnye Noel (5/5/79), Heidi Leigh (8/23/81), Gretchen Marie (3/27/84), Miles Remington (6/1/89)

COLLEGE: Edison Junior College in Ft. Myers, FL, and University of Houston

SPECIAL INTERESTS: All sports, golf course design

TURNED PROFESSIONAL: 1973 **Q SCHOOL:** Fall 1974

PLAYER PROFILE

CAREER EARNINGS: $4,748,065   **PLAYOFF RECORD:** 2-2

TOUR VICTORIES: **1979** Wickes-Andy Williams San Diego Open, Masters. **1981** Colonial National
(TOTAL: 10) Invitation. **1983** Sea Pines Heritage Classic, Las Vegas Pro-Celebrity Classic. **1984** United States Open. **1985** Hertz Bay Hill Classic. **1986** AT&T Pebble Beach National Pro-Am, Sea Pines Heritage Golf Classic, Anheuser-Busch Golf Classic.

MONEY & POSITION:

1975--$ 7,318--146	1982--$126,512--28	1989--$ 217,742-- 65
1976--$ 52,557-- 56	1983--$417,597-- 2	1990--$ 199,629-- 79
1977--$ 76,417-- 40	1984--$157,460--40	1991--$ 385,139-- 42
1978--$109,055-- 20	1985--$244,003--15	1992--$ 125,003--114
1979--$196,951-- 9	1986--$358,115--13	1993--$ 378,175-- 39
1980--$ 95,531-- 46	1987--$222,921--44	1994--$1,016,804-- 5
1981--$151,571-- 19	1988--$209,564--51	

BEST 1994 FINISHES: 2--THE PLAYERS Championship, THE TOUR Championship; T2--Bob Hope Chrysler Classic, Nestle Invitational, Walt Disney World Oldsmobile Golf Classic; T8--Federal Express St. Jude Classic.
1994 SUMMARY: Tournaments entered--19 in money--16; top ten finishes--6.
1995 PGA TOUR CHARITY TEAM COMPETITION: Kmart Greater Greensboro Open
NATIONAL TEAMS: Ryder Cup (3) 1979, 1983, 1985.

1994 SEASON: Established TOUR record by earning $1,016,804 without winning a tournament...his non-winning not for lack of trying, however, since finished second five times...those five runnerup finishes most since Jack Nicklaus and Arnold Palmer recorded six apiece in 1964...previous single-season high without a win: $982,875 by Payne Stewart in 1993...concluded best year of career by losing TOUR Championship playoff to Mark McCumber, finish which produced biggest paycheck of $324,000...ran off three consecutive seconds early, going T2 in Bob Hope Chrysler Classic and Nestle Invitational, followed by solo second to Greg Norman in THE PLAYERS Championship...his 20-under-par 268 total bettered Nick Price's 1993 PLAYERS record by two strokes, but still was four shy of Norman...final-round 66 brought him to within two of Rick Fehr in Walt Disney World/Oldsmobile Classic...held share of 54-hole lead in British Open after third-round 64, closed with 70 for T3...also was in hunt in FedEx St. Jude Classic...in five-way tie for lead after opening 66, held lead alone at midpoint after carding 65...still just one stroke back after third-round 70, finished T8 following closing 69.

CAREER HIGHLIGHTS: Owner of two major titles, 1979 Masters and 1984 U.S. Open...latter came in 18-hole playoff with Greg Norman at Winged Foot...accomplishments have come despite challenges provided by medical history, principally back trouble tracing to high school basketball...back problems became public knowledge prior to '84 PGA Championship...barely could move morning was to play first round at Shoal Creek...was rushed to hospital, where remained for nearly a week...back condition worsened week later in Las Vegas, where was defending Panasonic Invitational title...underwent surgery for ruptured discs, returning to TOUR in February 1985...finished T46 in Doral-Eastern Open, won Hertz Bay Hill Classic two weeks later...first TOUR victory was in 1979 Andy Williams Open...winner 1985-86 Skins Games...winner 1987 Merrill Lynch Shoot-out Championship.

PERSONAL: One of game's all-time personalities and gallery favorites...wears sunglasses while he plays, enjoys "whistling while he works"...golf course design projects include TPC at Summerlin, host course for Las Vegas Invitational...winner 1973 Indiana State Amateur...1972 Florida State Junior College champion.

1994 PGA TOUR STATISTICS

Scoring Average	69.89	(13)
Driving Distance	270.4	(29)
Driving Accuracy	75.5	(25)
Greens in Regulation	72.8	(2)
Putting	1.784	(65)
All-Around	370	(13)
Sand Saves	53.2	(70)
Total Driving	54	(4)
Eagles	4	(104T)
Birdies	291	(62)

MISCELLANEOUS STATISTICS

Scoring Avg. (before cut)	70.07	(8)
Scoring Avg. (3rd round)	70.63	(67)
Scoring Avg. (4th round)	69.88	(7T)
Birdie Conversion	30.4	(22T)
Par Breakers	22.5	(3)

1994 Low Round:	64: Canon GHO/3
Career Low Round:	62: 1982 B.C. Open/2
Career Largest	
Paycheck:	$324,000/1994 TOUR Championship/2

A

ACOSTA, Joe Jr. Birth Date 10/25/73 **Birthplace** San Diego, CA **Residence** Visalia, CA **Height** 6-3 **Weight** 170 **Special Interest** Basketball **Family** Single **College** Fresno State **Turned Professional** 1994 **Q School** 1994 **Other Achievements** Second team All-American 1993, 1994. 1994 WAC Player of the Year and individual champion. Member of 1994 WAC championship team. Left school early to turn professional.
Exempt Status: 27th at 1994 Qualifying Tournament

ADAMS, John Birth Date 5/5/54 **Birthplace** Scottsdale, AZ **Residence** Scottsdale, AZ **Height** 6-3 **Weight** 220 **College** Arizona State **Special Interests** Hunting, fishing **Family** Wife, Jane; Benjamin Craig (6/20/83), Kimberly Jill (10/23/85) **Turned Professional** 1976 **Q School** Spring 1978; Fall 1979; Fall 1985 **Other Achievements** Lost playoff to Jay Haas at 1982 Hall of Fame Classic on famed Pinehurst No. 2. Largest paycheck of career $62,400 at 1992 Las Vegas Invitational, where tied for third. Winner 1975 Arizona State Amateur.
Exempt Status: 46th at 1994 Qualifying Tournament
Best Ever Finish: 2--1982 Hall of Fame Classic

Money and Position:

1978--$2,025-- 196	1984--$ 73,567-- 80	1990--$126,733--122
1979--$1,785-- 224	1985--$ 9,613-- 181	1991--$117,549--125
1980--$19,895--123	1986--$ 64,906--124	1992--$173,069-- 89
1981--$17,898--138	1987--$ 51,976--149	1993--$221,753-- 78
1982--$54,014-- 85	1988--$ 64,341--140	1994--$106,689--151
1983--$59,287-- 87	1989--$104,824--120	

Best 1994 Finish: T6--Sprint International
1994 Summary: Tournaments entered--32; in money--11; top ten finishes--1.
Career Earnings: $1,272,924

ALLEN, Michael Birth Date 1/31/59 **Birthplace** San Mateo, CA **Height** 6-0 **Weight** 190 **Special Interests** Skiing, wine, 49ers football **Family** Wife, Cynthia; Christy (12/8/93) **College** Nevada Las-Vegas **Turned Professional** 1984 **Q School** 1989, 1990, 1991, 1992, 1994 **Other Achievements** Won 1989 Bell's Scottish Open en route to finishing 15th on European Tour Order of Merit for the year. Same year finished second at Scandanavian Open.
Exempt Staus: 44th at 1994 Qualifying Tournament
Best Ever Finish: T3--1993 Northern Telecom Open; T3--1993 Phoenix Open

Money and Position:

1990--$95,319--140	1993--$231,072-- 73
1991--$47,626--177	1994--$ 91,191--162
1992--$11,455--233	

Best 1994 Finish: T13--Greater Milwaukee Open
1994 Summary: Tournaments entered--32 ; in money--17; top ten finishes--0
Career Money: $476,663

ARMOUR III, Tommy Birth Date 10/8/59 **Birthplace** Denver, CO **Residence** Irving, TX **Height** 6-2 **Weight** 205 **Special Interests** Music, sports **Family** Single **College** New Mexico **Turned Professional** 1981 **Q-School** Fall 1981, 1987 **Other Achievements** Winner 1981 New Mexico State Amateur; 1983 Mexican Open; 1981 William Tucker Intercollegiate. Won 1994 NIKE Miami Valley and NIKE Cleveland Opens in consecutive weeks to become first player to win back-to-back NIKE TOUR events. Spent most of 1994 on NIKE TOUR but still finished 147 on PGA TOUR money list. Played in 1994 U.S. Open at Oakmont CC, site of grandfather's 1927 U.S. Open victory.

Exempt Status: 7th on 1994 NIKE TOUR money list
TOUR Victories: 1--1990 Phoenix Open

Money And Position:			
	1982--$ 4,254--208	1989--$185,018-- 81	1992--$ 47,218--180
	1987--$ 970--290	1990--$348,658-- 35	1993--$ 52,011--181
	1988--$175,461-- 66	1991--$ 90,478--140	1994--$112,778--147

Best 1994 Finish: T3--Deposit Guaranty Golf Classic
1994 Summary: Tournaments entered--9; in money--6; top ten finishes--2
Career Money: $1,011,622

AUBREY, Emlyn Birth Date 1/28/64 **Birthplace** Reading, PA **Residence** Princeton, LA **Height** 6-2 **Weight** 185 **Special Interests** Auto racing, hockey **Family** Wife, Cindy **College** LSU **Turned Professional** 1986 **Other Achievements** Played NIKE TOUR full time 1993-94. Earned $72,944 to finish 14th on NIKE money list in 1993 and regained PGA TOUR card by making $113,919 to finish 10th for 1994 NIKE campaign. Finished T62 in 1994 U.S. Open. Winner 1982-84 Pennsylvania State Public Links, 1984 Southeastern Conference title, 1989 Philippines Open and 1994 Indian Open. Wife Cindy serves as caddie.

Exempt Status: 10th on 1994 NIKE TOUR money list

Money and Position:			
	1990--$122,329--126	1991--$91,257--139	1992--$58,087--167

Best Ever Finish: T7--1990 H-E-B Texas Open
Career Earnings: $275,474

AUSTIN, Woody Birth Date 1/27/64 **Birthplace** Tampa, FL **Residence** Tampa, FL **Height** 6-0 **Weight** 170 **Special Interest** Sports **Family** Wife, Shannon **College** Miami **Turned Professional** 1987 **Q School** 1994 **Other Achievements** Finished 23rd on 1994 NIKE TOUR money list with $72,206. Missed cut at '92 Buick Southern Open in only PGA TOUR start. Medalist at 1994 Qualifying Tournament.

Exempt Status: 1st at 1994 Qualifying Tournament

B

BEAN, Andy Birth Date 3/13/53 **Birthplace** Lafayette, GA **Residence** Lakeland, FL **Height** 6-4 **Weight** 225 **Special Interests** Hunting, fishing **Family** Wife, Debbie; Lauren Ashley (4/17/82), Lindsey Ann (8/10/84), Jordan Alise (11/19/85) **College** Florida **Turned Professional** 1975 **Q School** Fall 1975 **Other Achievements** Member, 1987 Ryder Cup team. Low round of career third-round 61 en route to winning 1979 Atlanta Classic. Had outstanding amateur career, winning 1974 Eastern and Falstaff Amateurs and 1975 Dixie and Western Amateurs. All-American at University of Florida.

Exempt Status: Special Medical Extension
TOUR Victories: 11- 1977 Doral-Eastern Open. 1978 Kemper Open, Danny Thomas Memphis Classic, Western Open. 1979 Atlanta Classic. 1980 Hawaiian Open. 1981 Bay Hill Classic. 1982 Doral Eastern Open. 1984 Greater Greensboro Open. 1986 Doral Eastern Open, Byron Nelson Golf Classic.

Money and Position:			
	1976--$ 10,761--139	1983--$181,246-- 24	1990--$129,669--119
	1977--$127,312-- 12	1984--$422,995-- 3	1991--$193,609-- 88
	1978--$268,241-- 3	1985--$190,871-- 33	1992--$ 30,798--195
	1979--$208,253-- 7	1986--$491,938-- 4	1993--$ 37,292--191
	1980--$269,033-- 4	1987--$ 73,808--120	1994--$ 8,810--253
	1981--$105,755-- 35	1988--$ 48,961--149	
	1982--$208,627-- 15	1989--$236,097-- 58	

1994 Best Finish: T44--Bob Hope Chrysler Classic
1994 Summary: Tournaments entered--19; in money--3; top ten finishes--0
Career Money: $3,243,075

Other Prominent Members of the PGA TOUR

BENEPE, Jim Birth Date 10/24/63 **Birthplace** Sheridan, WY **Residence** Jackson Hole, WY
Height 5-7 **Weight** 150 **Special Interests** Hunting, fishing, reading, music **Family** Single
College Northwestern University (1986, Psychology) **Turned Professional** 1986 **Q School**
1990 **Other Achievements** Winner 1982 Wyoming State Amateur (stroke play); 1983
Wyoming State Amateur (medal play). Winner 1982 Western Junior Championship. Winner
1987 Canadian Tour Order of Merit. Named 1987 Canadian Tour Rookie of the Year. Winner
1988 Victorian (Australia) Open. Winner of four collegiate events for Northwestern, including
co-champion 1986 Big Ten title. 1986 Collegiate All-American.

Exempt Status: Past Champion
TOUR Victories: 1--1988 Beatrice Western Open

Money and Position:	1988--$176,055-- 65	1990--$105,087--135	1993--$-- 0--
	1989--$ 38,089--176	1991--$ 62,082--164	

1994 Summary: Tournaments entered --0; in money--0; top ten finishes--0.
Career Earnings: $381,314

BLACK, Ronnie Birth Date 5/26/58 **Birthplace** Hobbs, NM **Residence** Scottsdale, AZ **Height** 6-
1 **Weight** 190 **Special Interests** Hunting, fishing, movies **Family** Wife, Sandra; Justin (12/14/
86), Alex (5/11/88), Anthony (1/26/92) **College** Lamar University **Turned Professional** 1981
Q School 1981, 1982, 1990 **Other Achievements** Won 1983 Southern Open in four-hole
playoff with Sam Torrance. Claimed 1984 Anheuser-Busch Classic with final-round 63, after
opening final day seven strokes off lead. Winner 1976 and 1977 New Mexico State High School
Championship. Winner 1981 Collegiate Conference Championship.

Exempt Status: 9th at 1994 Qualifying Tournament
TOUR Victories: 2--1983 Southern Open. 1984 Anheuser-Busch Classic

Money and Position:	1982--$ 6,329-- 91	1987--$144,158-- 77	1991--$135,865--113
	1983--$ 87,524-- 63	1988--$100,603--112	1992--$129,386--111
	1984--$172,636-- 35	1989--$264,988-- 51	1993--$120,041--125
	1985--$ 61,684--109	1990--$ 34,001--190	1994--$123,404--137
	1986--$166,761-- 56		

Best 1994 Finish: T8--GTE Byron Nelson Classic
1994 Summary: Tournaments entered--27; in money--15; top ten finishes--1
Career Money: $1,547,379

BLACKBURN, Woody Birth Date 7/26/51 **Birthplace** Pikeville, KY **Residence** Orange Park, FL;
plays out of Orange Park CC **Height** 6-2 **Weight** 185 **Special Interests** Fly fishing, all sports
Family Wife, Brenda; Todd (1/7/80), Richard (7/28/83), Brian (7/28/83) **College** Florida **Turned
Professional** 1974 **Other Achievements** Co-medalist 1976 Q-School. All-SEC 1973.

Exempt Status: Past Champion
TOUR Victories: 2--1976 Walt Disney World Team Championship (with Bill Kratzert); 1985
Isuzu Andy Williams San Diego Open.

Money and Position:	1976--$1,859--213	1981--$24,167--118	1985--$139,257-- 57
	1977--$7,600--163	1982--$54,165-- 84	1986--$ 12,901--193
	1978--$5,172--171	1983--$18,105--157	1987--$ 3,453--241
	1979--$1,838--222	1984--$29,074--141	1988--$ 3,323--260
	1980--$9,319--166		

1994 Summary: Tournaments entered--1; in money--0; top ten finishes--0
Career Money: $310,231

BLACKMAR, Phil Birth Date 9/22/57 **Birthplace** San Diego, CA **Residence** Corpus Christi, TX;
plays out of Kings Crossing CC **Height** 6-7 **Weight** 245 **Special Interest** Fishing **Family** Wife,
Carol; Kristin Ashley (3/21/84), Kelli Michelle (9/20/85), Philip James (5/9/88), Mark Fredrik (4/
28/92) **College** Texas **Turned Professional** 1980 **Q School** Fall 1984 **Other Achievements**
Both TOUR victories came in playoffs. Claimed 1985 Sammy Davis, Jr.- Greater Hartford Open
by birdieing first extra hole to defeat Dan Pohl and Jodie Mudd and three years later beat Payne
Stewart at Provident Classic. Earned Rookie of Year honors in 1985. Came in second at 1985
National Long Drive Championship. Winner 1983 Missouri State Open.
Exempt Status: 23rd at 1994 Qualifying Tournament
TOUR Victories: 2- 1985 Canon Sammy Davis, Jr. Greater Hartford Open. 1988 Provident Classic

Money and Position:	1984--$ 3,374--209	1988--$108,403--105	1992--$242,783-- 63
	1985--$198,537-- 28	1989--$140,949--100	1993--$207,310-- 83
	1986--$191,228-- 43	1990--$200,796-- 78	1994--$ 28,159--213
	1987--$ 99,580-- 97	1991--$218,838-- 77	

1994 Best Finish: T11--Buick Southern Open
1994 Summary: Tournaments entered--30; in money--5; top ten finishes--0
Career Money: $1,636,584

BRISKY, Mike Birth Date 5/28/65 **Birthplace** Brownsville, TX **Residence** Orlando, FL **Height** 6-1 **Weight** 185 **Special Interests** Fishing, movies, Bible study **Family** Wife, Judy; Jacob (6/15/94) **College** Pan American University **Turned Professional** 1987 **Q School** 1993, 1994 **Other Achievements** Two-time winner on T.C. Jordan Tour. Played in 1989 U.S. Open. Winner 1994 NIKE Texarkana Open.
Exempt Status: 10th at 1994 Qualifying Tournament
Money and Position: 1994--$38,713--200
Best 1994 Finish: T11--Deposit Guaranty Golf Classic; T11--Buick Southern Open
1994 Summery: Tournaments entered--14; in money--6; top ten finishes--0
Career Money: $38,713

BRITTON, Bill Birth Date 11/13/55 **Birthplace** Staten Island, NY **Residence** Red Bank, NJ; plays out of Shore Oaks GC **Height** 5-7 **Weight** 140 **Special Interest** Chasing his children **Family** Wife, Isabelle; Kevin (1/2/90), Caitlin (2/27/91), Ashley (2/16/94) **College** Florida **Turned Professional** 1979 **Q School** Spring 1980; Fall 1986, 1987, 1994 **Other Achievements** Winner 1979 Metropolitan Open, 1975, 1976 Metropolitan Amateur Championship. Collected 1975 National Junior College Championship. Lost playoff to Hal Sutton at 1982 Walt Disney/ Oldsmobile Classic. Lone TOUR victory came in rain-shortened 1989 Centel Classic. Low round of career a 63, which has posted several times.
Exempt Status: 39th at 1994 Qualifying Tournament
TOUR Victories: 1--1989 Centel Classic
Money and Position:

1980--$ 9,022--171	1985--$ 3,245--215	1991--$282,894-- 57
1981--$39,358-- 97	1987--$ 45,939--158	1992--$391,700-- 36
1982--$75,328-- 57	1988--$110,781--103	1993--$ 74,748--159
1983--$20,492--148	1989--$307,978-- 34	1994--$ 68,033--173
1984--$28,149--142	1990--$278,977-- 51	

1994 Best Finish: T13--Greater Milwaukee Open
1994 Summary: Tournaments entered--22; in money--12; top ten finishes--0
Career Money: $1,736,642

BRODIE, Steve Birth Date 1/24/65 **Birthplace** Compton, CA **Residence** Provo, UT **Height** 5-10 **Weight** 175 **Special Interests** Fishing, Chicago White Sox baseball **Family** Wife, Amy; Alexis (1983), Brooks (1986), Cassidy (1988), Chase (1989) **College** Long Beach State **Turned Professional** 1986 **Other Achievements** Played on 1989 Australian Tour, winner of five mini-tour events. Member 1990, 1991 and 1993 NIKE TOUR. Standout catcher in college until collision with eventual Minnesota Viking linebacker Jack Del Rio resulted in career-ending knee injury. After injury, started playing golf, shot 92 first time out, turned pro less than a year later.
Exempt Status: 149th on 1994 PGA TOUR money list
Best Ever Finish: T7--1994 Freeport-McMoRan Classic
Money and Position: 1994--$112,081--149
Best 1994 Finish: T7--1994 Freeport-McMoRan Classic
1994 Summary: Tournaments entered--28; in money--15; top ten finishes--1
Career Earnings: $112,081

BROWN, Billy Ray Birth Date 4/5/63 **Birthplace** Missouri City, TX **Residence** Missouri City, TX; plays out of Quail Valley CC **Height** 6-3 **Weight** 205 **Special Interests** Hunting, fishing **Family** Wife, Cindy **College** Houston **Turned Professional** 1987 **Other Achievements** Won 1991 Canon Greater Hartford Open in playoff Rick Fehr and Corey Pavin. Other victory came in playoff at rain-shortened 1992 GTE Byron Nelson Classic. Finished T3 in 1990 U.S. Open. Injured wrist at end of 1992 season, causing him to miss 16 weeks in '93. Four-time All-America selection who won 1982 NCAA Championship as freshman. Along with teammate Steve Elkington, member of three NCAA championship teams. Father Charlie was a tackle for Oakland Raiders, brother Chuck played center for St. Louis Cardinals.
Exempt Status: Past Champion
TOUR Victories: 2--1991 Canon Greater Hartford Open. 1992 GTE Byron Nelson Classic
Money and Position:

1988--$ 83,590--125	1991--$348,082--46	1993--$173,662-- 97
1989--$162,964-- 85	1992--$485,151--29	1994--$ 4,254--284
1990--$312,486-- 44		

Best 1994 Finish: T65--GTE Byron Nelson Classic
1994 Summary: Tournaments entered--27; in money--2; top ten finishes--0
Career Money: $1,570,170

BROWNE, Olin Birth Date 5/22/59 **Birthplace** New York, NY **Residence** Jupiter, FL; plays out of Admirals Cove **Height** 5-9 **Weight** 175 **Special Interests** Fly fishing, environment, some politics **Family** Wife, Pam; Olin Jr. (7/9/88), Alexandra Grace (10/24/91) **College** Occidental **Turned Professional** 1984 **Other Achievements** Winner 1991 Ben Hogan Bakersfield Open, Ben Hogan Hawkeye Open; 1993 NIKE Monterrey Open. Recorded double eagle in 1994 Northern Telecom Open.
Exempt Status: 154th on 1994 money list
Best Ever Finish: T4--1992 Northern Telecom Open
Money and Position: 1992--$84,152--147 1993--$2,738--290 1994--$101,580--154
Best 1994 Finish: 6--Northern Telecom Open
1994 Summary: Tournaments entered--31; in money--15; top ten finishes--1
Career Earnings: $188,470

BRYANT, Bart Birth Date 11/18/62 **Birthplace** Gatesville, TX **Residence** Winter Park, FL **Height** 6-0 **Weight** 185 **Special Interests** Fishing, spending time with **Family** Wife, Cathy; Kristin (8/11/88), Michelle (1/11/94) **College** New Mexico State **Turned Professional** 1985 **Q School** 1990, 1994 **Other Achievements** Winner 1984 UCLA Billy Bryant Invitational, 1983, 1984 Sun Country Amateur, 1988 Florida Open. Two-time All-American. PCAA Player of Year in 1984. Older brother Brad is PGA TOUR veteran.

Exempt Status: 17th at 1994 Qualifying Tournament
Best Ever Finish: 7--1991 Honda Classic
Money and Position: 1991--$119,931--124   1992--$52,075--172
Career Money: $172,006

BURKE, Patrick Birth Date 3/17/62 **Birthplace** Hollywood, FL **Residence** Azusa, CA **Height** 5-5 **Weight** 165 **Special Interest** Ice hockey **Family** Wife, Jody; Jaime (10/12/93) **College** Citrus College **Turned Professional** 1986 **Q School** 1989, 1991, 1994 **Other Achievements** Medalist in 1987 Australian Tour Qualifying School. Second team Division II All-American. Winner 1994 Australian TPC and Victoria Open, runnerup Alfred Dunhill Masters. Battled virus during 1994 PGA TOUR season.

Exempt Status: 7th at 1994 Qualifying Tournament
Best Ever Finish: T6--1992 BellSouth Classic
Money and Position: 1990--$ 5,228--247   1993 -- $ 100,717--144   1994--$5,034--276
                              1992--$ 101,513--129

1994 Best Finish: T37--Deposit Guaranty Golf Classic
1994 Summary: Tournaments entered--10; in money--2; top ten finishes--0
Career Money: $212,492

BURNS III, George Birth Date 7/29/49 **Birthplace** Brooklyn, NY **Residence** Boynton Beach, FL **Height** 6-2 **Weight** 200 **Family** Wife, Irene; Kelly (4/2/76), Eileen (8/25/80) **College** University of Maryland **Turned Professional** 1975 **Q School** 1975, 1990 **Other Achievements** Winner 1973 Canadian Amateur and 1974 Porter Cup, North-South Amateur, and New York State Amateur. As professional, won 1975 Scandinavian Open and 1975 Kerrygold (Ireland). 1975 Walker Cup team and 1975 World Amateur Cup team. Winner 1988 Chrysler Team Championship with Wayne Levi.

Exempt Status: Past Champion
TOUR Victories: 4-1979 Walt Disney World Team Championship (with Ben Crenshaw). 1980 Bing Crosby National Pro-Am. 1985 Bank of Boston Classic. 1987 Shearson Lehman Bros.-Andy Williams Open.

Money & Position:			
	1976--$ 85,732--32	1982--$181,864-- 8	1988 --$ 30,130--174
	1977--$102,026-- 2	1983--$ 62,371-- 83	1989 --$ 5,645--230
	1978--$171,498--38	1984--$198,848-- 37	1990 --$ 96,443--139
	1979--$107,830--33	1985--$223,352-- 21	1992 --$ 6,864--254
	1980--$219,928-- 7	1986--$ 77,474--112	1993 --$ 2,550--298
	1981--$105,395--37	1987--$216,257-- 45	

1994 Summary: Tournaments entered --8; in money -- 0; top ten finishes -- 0.
Career Earnings: $1,763,208

BURROUGHS, Clark Birth Date 4/18/63 **Birthplace** Waterloo, IA **Residence** Orlando, FL **Height** 6-3 **Weight** 175 **Special Interests** Children, sports **Family** Single; Connor Clark (3/10/89), Clay Rhodes (5/16/90) **College** Ohio State **Turned Professional** 1985 **Q School** 1991, 1994 **Other Achievements** Winner 1985 NCAA Championship. Member 1985 Walker Cup Team. Played in 1984 Masters.

Exempt Status: 41st at 1994 Qualifying Tournament
Best Ever Finish: T2--1989 Canadian Open
Money and Position: 1987--$ 1,296--279   1989--$124,715--110   1991--$29,377--198
                              1988--$33,670--165   1990--$115,923--130

Career Money: $303,685

BYRUM, Tom Birth Date 9/28/60 **Birthplace** Onida, SD **Residence** Sugarland, TX; plays out of Sweetwater CC **Height** 5-10 **Weight** 175 **Special Interests** Hunting, fishing, all sports **Family** Wife, Dana; Brittni Rene (4/2/88), Corinne (1/21/91) **College** New Mexico State University **Turned Professional** 1984 **Q School** 1985, 1991, 1992 **Other Achievements** Winner 1983 New Mexico State Intercollegiate. Participant in TOUR-record six-man playoff won by Neal Lancaster at 1994 GTE Byron Nelson Classic.

Exempt Staus: 148th on 1994 money list
TOUR Victories: 1--1989 Kemper Open
Money and Postion: 1986--$ 89,739-- 93   1989--$320,939 -- 32   1992--$ 94,399--136
                              1987--$ 146,384-- 76   1990--$136,910 --113   1993--$ 82,354--154
                              1988--$ 174,378-- 67   1991--$ 68,871 --153   1994--$112,259--148
1994 Best Finish: T2--GTE Byron Nelson Classic
1994 Summary: Tournaments entered--12; in money--7; top ten finishes--1
Career Money: $1,226,235

CALDWELL, Rex Birth Date 5/5/50 **Birthplace** Everett, WA **Residence** San Antonio, TX **Height** 6-2 **Weight** 225 **College** San Fernando Valley State **Special Interests** Basketball, jogging **Family** Wife, Jana **Turned Professional** 1972 **Other Achievements** College Division All-American 1971-72. Winner 1978 California State Open. Winner 1983 World Cup team title with John Cook.
Exempt Staus: Past Champion
TOUR Victories: 1--1983 LaJet Classic
Money and Position:

1975--$ 3,094 -- 178	1980--$ 64,859 -- 62	1985--$ 58,689-- 114
1976--$ 24,912 -- 87	1981--$ 33,945 -- 102	1986--$ 39,674-- 149
1977--$ 11,693 -- 137	1982--$ 64,622 -- 68	1987--$ 50,054-- 153
1978--$ 66,451 -- 42	1983--$ 284,434 -- 6	1988--$ 15,896-- 205
1979--$ 96,088 -- 36	1984--$ 126,400 -- 53	1989--$ 55,066-- 161

1994 Summary: Tournaments entered--2; in money--0; top ten finishes--0.
Career Earnings: $1,007,548

CLAMPETT, Bobby Birth Date 4/22/60 **Birthplace** Monterey, CA **Residence** Cary, NC; plays out of Deerfield Greens Resort, Lafollette, TN **Height** 5-10 **Weight** 161 **Special Interests** Bible study, flying, snow skiing **Family** Wife, Ann; Katelyn (10/30/87), Daniel (8/11/89), Michael (12/29/91) **College** Brigham Young University **Turned Professional** 1980 **Q School** 1980, 1990 **Other Achievements** Winner 1978 and 1980 California State Amateur. Low Amateur 1978 U.S. Open. Winner 1978 World Amateur medal. Three-time All-American, 1978-80. Two-time winner Fred Haskins Award, presented to top collegiate player. Active in Children's Flight of Hope program, tied to Children's Hospital at Duke University.
Exempt Status: 152 on 1994 money list
TOUR Victories: 1-1982 Southern Open
Money and Position:

1980-- $ 10,190--163	1985--$ 81,121-- 94	1990--$ 29,268--194
1981-- $ 184,710-- 14	1986--$ 97,178-- 87	1991--$ 127,817--116
1982-- $ 184,600-- 17	1987--$124,872-- 84	1992--$ 29,175--199
1983-- $ 86,575-- 64	1988--$ 88,067-- 118	1993--$ 112,293--131
1984-- $ 41,837--117	1989--$ 68,868-- 148	1994--$ 105,710--152

1994 Best Finish: T7--Freeport-McMoRan Classic
1994 Summary: Tournaments entered--16; in money--8; top ten finishes--2
Career Earnings: $1,372,283

COLE, Bobby Birth Date 5/11/48 **Birthplace** Springs, South Africa **Residence** Orlando, FL **Height** 5-10 **Weight** 165 **Special Interest** Cycling **Family** Wife, Laura; Chelsea (7/23/82), Eric (6/12/88), Haley (4/28/90), Robert (3/13/92), Michael (11/93) **Turned Professional** 1967 **Q School** 1967 **Other Achievements** Winner 1966 British Amateur, 1977 and 1981 South African Open, 1985 Seattle/Everett Open, 1974 World Cup (with Dale Hayes). Member South African World Cup team in 1970, '74, and '76.
Exempt Status: Past Champion
TOUR Victories: 1--1977 Buick Open
Money and Position:

1968--$13,383-- 90	1976--$18,902--107	1985--$ 7,871--187
1969--$17,898-- 90	1977--$41,301-- 68	1986--$88,472-- 95
1970--$ 8,379--140	1978--$32,541-- 83	1987--$46,309--156
1971--$10,585--122	1979--$ 6,525--175	1989--$ 980--284
1972--$19,016--102	1980--$22,202--119	1990--$ 612--310
1973--$28,875-- 89	1981--$13,559--158	1991--$ 1,400--313
1974--$59,617-- 43	1982--$39,060--104	1992--$ --0--
1975--$42,441-- 61	1983--$16,153--162	1993--$ --0--
	1994--$ --0--	

1994 Summary: Tournaments entered--2; in money--0; top ten finishes--0
Career Money: $534,049

CONNER, Frank Birth Date 1/11/46 **Birthplace** Vienna, Austria **Residence** San Antonio, TX **Height** 5-9 **Weight** 190 **Special Interests** Tennis **Family** Wife, Joy; Michelle (5/9/73), Nicole (1/28/75) **College** Trinity University (1969, Business Administration) **Turned Professional** 1971 **Other Achievements** Winner 1982 King Hassan Open. Winner 1988 Deposit Guaranty Classic. Winner 1991 Ben Hogan Knoxville Open and Tulsa Open. One of two men to compete in U.S. Open in both golf and tennis (other: Ellsworth Vines).
Exempt Status: Veteran Member
Best Ever Finish: 2-1982 Sea Pines Heritage Classic; T2--1979 New Orleans Open, 1981 Quad Cities Open, 1984 Bank of Boston Classic.
Money & Position:

1975--$ 4,418-- 165	1982 -- $ 72,181 -- 58	1988 -- $ 44,801 -- 154
1976--$ 9,273-- 147	1983 -- $ 71,320 -- 75	1989 -- $ 3,052 -- 244
1977--$ 15,138-- 122	1984 -- $ 55,405 -- 98	1990 -- $ 3,461 -- 258
1978--$ 11,325-- 136	1985 -- $ 68,804 -- 103	1991 -- $ 18,318 -- 207
1979--$ 46,020-- 87	1986 -- $ 35,729 -- 155	1992 -- $ 74,785 -- 152
1980--$ 37,149-- 87	1987 -- $ 51,475 -- 150	1993 -- $ 34,154 -- 195
1981--$ 85,009-- 51		1994 -- $ 1,435 -- 326

Best 1994 Finish: T62--Deposit Guaranty Golf Classic
1994 Summary: Tournaments entered--2; in money--1; top ten finishes--0.
Career Earnings: $743,253

COTNER, Kawika Birth Date 11/26/66 **Birthplace** Honolulu, HI **Residence** Trophy Club, TX **Height** 5-7 **Weight** 150 **Special Interests** Fishing, cards **Family** Single **College** North Texas State **Turned Professional** 1990 **Q School** 1994 **Other Achievements** Missed cut 1994 United Airlines Hawaiian Open in only PGA TOUR start.
Exempt Status: 30th at Qualifying Tournament

D

DAWSON, Marco Birth Date 11/17/63 **Birthplace** Freising, Germany **Residence** Lakeland, FL **Height** 6-0 **Weight** 195 **College** Florida Southern **Special Interests** Jazz, all sports **Family** Single **Turned Professional** 1986 **Q School** 1990, 1991, 1994 **Other Achievements** Member Ben Hogan Tour in 1990, finished 31st on money list. Fired career-low 63 at 1992 GTE Byron Nelson en route to T5 finish. Was college teammate of Lee Janzen and Rocco Mediate.
Exempt Status: 20th at 1994 Qualifying Tournament
Best Ever Finish: T5--1992 GTE Byron Nelson Classic; T5--1993 H-E-B Texas Open

Money and Position:		
1991--$ 96,756--137	1993--$120,462--124	
1992--$113,464--123	1994--$121,025--139	

Best 1994 Finish: T7--Greater Milwaukee Open
1994 Summary: Tournaments entered--30; in money--13; top ten finishes--0
Career Money: $451,706

DONALD, Mike Birth Date 7/11/55 **Birthplace** Grand Rapids, MI **Residence** Hollywood, FL **Height** 5-11 **Weight** 200 **Family** Single **College** Broward Community College and Georgia Southern University **Turned Professional** 1978 **Q School** Fall 1979 **Other Achievements** Winner 1984 JCPenney Classic with Vicki Alvarez. Winner 1974 National Junior College Championship at Broward Community College and 1973 Florida Junior Championship. Teamed with Fred Couples to win 1990 Sazale Classic. Former Player Director on PGA TOUR Policy Board. Finished second to Hale Irwin in 1990 U.S. Open. Both shot 74 in playoff, and on first sudden-death playoff hole in Open history, Irwin rolled in 10-foot birdie putt for win.
Exempt Status: 141st on 1994 money list   **Playoff Record:** 1-1
TOUR Victories: 1--1989 Anheuser Busch Golf Classic

Money and Position:		
1980--$ 12,365 -- 151	1985--$ 91,888-- 46	1990--$ 348,328 -- 36
1981--$ 50,665 -- 83	1986--$108,772-- 82	1991--$ 88,248 --142
1982--$ 39,967 -- 101	1987--$137,734-- 79	1992--$ 117,252 --120
1983--$ 72,343 -- 73	1988--$118,509-- 96	1993--$ 51,312 --183
1984--$ 146,324 -- 46	1989--$430,232-- 22	1994--$ 119,065 --141

1994 Best Finish: T3--B.C. Open
1994 Summary: Tournaments entered--16; in money--8; top ten finishes--1
Career Earnings: $1,933,004

DOUGHERTY, Ed Birth Date 11/4/47 **Birthplace** Chester, PA **Residence** Linwood, PA **Height** 6-1 **Weight** 215 **Special Interest** Lionel toy trains **Family** Wife, Carolyn **Turned Professional** 1969 **Q School** Fall 1975, 1986, 1989 **Other Achievements** 1985 PGA Club Pro Player of Year, 1985 Club Pro Championship. Lost playoff to Jim Gallagher Jr. in 1990 Greater Milwaukee Open. Visits train stores in most cities PGA TOUR visits. Married high school sweetheart after not seeing her for number of years.
Exempt Status: Veteran Member
Best Ever Finish: T2--1990 Greater Milwaukee Open; 2--1992 Anheuser Busch Classic; 2--1992 Chattanooga Classic

Money and Position:		
1975--$ 9,374--129	1980--$ 9,113--168	1990--$124,505--123
1976--$17,333--113	1982--$27,948--128	1991--$201,958-- 82
1977--$17,606--113	1987--$76,705--115	1992--$237,525-- 66
1978--$ 9,936--141	1988--$22,455--195	1993--$167,651-- 99
1979--$24,802--115	1989--$ 1,800--267	1994--$ 97,137--157

Best 1994 Finish: T15--Freeport-McMoRan Classic
1994 Summary: Tournaments entered--33; in money--18; top ten finishes--0
Career money: $1,075,416

DUVAL, David Birth Date 2/9/71 **Birthplace** Jacksonville, FL **Residence** Ponte Vedra Beach, FL **Height** 6-0 **Weight** 195 **College** Georgia Tech **Special Interests** Mountain bikes, reading **Family** Single **Turned Professional** 1993 **Other Achievements** Four-time first-team All-American, only third Division I golfer to do so (Phil Mickelson and Gary Hallberg). Two-time ACC Player of Year and named national Player of Year as senior by Golf Coaches Association. Winner 1993 NIKE Wichita Open and '93 NIKE TOUR Championship. In '93, played only nine NIKE events but finished 11th on money list. Earned $126,430, $81,076 in last eight tournaments, to finish eighth on NIKE TOUR money list.
Exempt Status: 8th on 1994 NIKE TOUR money list
Best Ever Finish: T8--1994 Motorola Western Open

Money and Position:	
1993--$27,180--201	1994--$44,006--195

1994 Summary: Tournaments entered--6; in money--4; top ten finishes--1
Career Money: $44,006

E

EASTWOOD, Bob Birth Date 4/9/46 **Birthplace** Providence, RI **Residence** Stockton, CA **Height** 5-10 **Weight** 175 **Special Interests** Hunting, fishing **Family** Wife, Connie; Scott (8/19/71),Steven (12/29/73) **College** San Jose State **Turned Professional** 1969 **Q School** Spring 1969 **Other Achievements** Winner 1973 mini-Kemper Open, 1976 Little Bing Crosby (both second Tour); 1965 Sacramento City Amateur, 1966 California State Amateur, 1968 West Coast Athletic Conference, 1981 Morocco Grand Prix. Medalist Spring 1969 Qualifying School.
Exempt Status: Past Champion   **Playoff Record:** 1-0
TOUR Victories: 3--1984 USF&G Classic, Danny Thomas-Memphis Classic. 1985 Byron Nelson Classic.

Money and Position:

Year	Amount	Pos	Year	Amount	Pos	Year	Amount	Pos
1972	$ 9,528		1980	$ 36,751	90	1987	$114,897	88
1973	$ 14,918		1981	$ 66,017	67	1988	$ 94,504	117
1974	$ 18,535	114	1982	$ 91,633	44	1989	$ 84,088	139
1975	$ 16,812	110	1983	$157,640	30	1990	$123,908	125
1976	$ 14,539	123	1984	$232,742	24	1991	$ 65,215	157
1977	$ 19,706	107	1985	$152,839	51	1992	$ 83,818	148
1978	$ 24,681	100	1986	$ 72,449	117	1993	$ 24,289	204
1979	$ 29,630	110				1994	$ 6,737	264

1994 Best Finish: T28--GTE Byron Nelson Classic
1994 Summary: Tournaments entered--6; in money--1; top ten finishes--0
Career Earnings: $1,551,414

EDWARDS, Danny Birth Date 6/14/51 **Birthplace** Ketchikan, AK **Residence** Scottsdale, AZ **Height** 5-11 **Weight** 155 **College** Oklahoma State **Family** Single **Turned Professional** 1973 **Q School** Fall 1974 **Playoff Record** 1-0 **Special Interests** Car collecting and skiing **Other Achievements** Collegiate All-American, 1972 & 1973. Winner 1972 North and South Amateur; member 1973 Walker Cup team; low amateur 1973 British Open. Winner 1972 & 1973 Big Eight Conference, 1972 Southeastern Amateur, 1981 Toshiba Taiheiyo Masters.
Exempt Status: Past Champion
Playoff Record: 1-0
TOUR Victories: 5--1977 Greater Greensboro Open. 1980 Walt Disney World National Team Play (with David Edwards) 1982 Greater Greensboro Open; 1983 Miller High Life-QCO; 1985 Pensacola Open.

Money and Position:

Year	Amount	Pos	Year	Amount	Pos	Year	Amount	Pos
1975	$ 27,301	80	1981	$ 66,567	66	1987	$146,688	75
1976	$ 25,859	85	1982	$124,018	29	1988	$ 36,637	160
1977	$ 96,811	28	1983	$104,942	54	1989	$ 12,917	205
1978	$ 55,343	60	1984	$ 54,472	102	1990	$ 8,343	240
1979	$ 21,238	120	1985	$206,891	25	1991	$ 5,423	253
1980	$ 73,196	57	1986	$126,139	67	1992	$ 10,852	237
						1993	$ 1,557	323

1994 Summary: Tournaments entered--3; in money--0; top ten finishes--0.
Career Earnings: $1,205,194

F

FERGUS, Keith Birth Date 3/3/54 **Birthplace** Temple,TX **Residence** Sugarland, TX **Height** 6-2 **Weight** 200 **College** Houston **Special Interest** Fishing **Family** Wife, Cindy; Steven (9/4/79), Laura (3/5/84) **Turned Professional** 1976 **Q School** Fall, 1976, 1994 **Other Achievements** Runnerup 1975 U.S. Amateur. Winner 1976 Texas State Open. All-American 1974, 1975, 1976. Winner 1971 Texas State Juniors. Head coach University of Houston 1988-94. Won 1994 NIKE Panama City Beach Classic and '94 NIKE Boise Open en route to finishing 13th on money list.
Exempt Status: 33rd at 1994 Qualifying Tournament
TOUR Victories: 3--1981 Memorial; 1982 Georgia-Pacific Atlanta Classic; 1983 Bob Hope Desert Classic

Money and Position:

Year	Amount	Pos	Year	Amount	Pos	Year	Amount	Pos
1977	$ 29,558	84	1982	$122,265	30	1987	$ 4,033	234
1978	$ 55,773	58	1983	$155,922	31	1988	$ 2,002	274
1979	$ 97,045	37	1984	$ 78,758	78	1991	$ 2,532	276
1980	$119,614	33	1985	$136,352	60	1994	$16,749	231
1981	$150,792	21	1986	$ 45,548	142			

Best 1994 Finish: T22--Anheuser-Busch Classic
1994 Summary: Tournaments entered--5; in money--3; top ten finishes--0
Career Money: $1,016,944

FEZLER, Forrest Birth Date 9/23/49 **Birthplace** Hayward, CA **Residence** Hampton, VA **Height** 5-9 **Weight** 165 **Special Interests** Fishing, hunting **Family** Wife, Kathy; five children **College** San Jose Community College **Turned Professional** 1969 **Other Achievements** Winner, 1969 California Amateur; 1969 California Junior College Championship; runnerup 1974 U.S. Open. Named 1969 Junior College Player of the Year.
Exempt Status: Past Champion   **Playoff Record:** 0-1
TOUR Victories: 1--1974 Southern Open

Money & Position

Year	Amount	Pos	Year	Amount	Pos	Year	Amount	Pos
1972	$ 26,542	88	1979	$ 11,427	148	1985	$ 1,400	154
1973	$106,390	12	1980	$ 19,269	127	1986	$ 2,080	244
1974	$ 90,066	24	1981	$ 13,064	158	1987	$ 1,784	258
1975	$ 52,157	43	1982	$ 38,983	105	1988	$ 3,477	207
1976	$ 59,793	44	1983	$ 24,452	143	1989	$ 1,853	152
1977	$ 30,029	82	1984	$ 14,152	150	1993	$ 2,610	295
1978	$ 30,812	85						

1994 Summary: Tournaments entered--3; in money--0; top ten finishes--0.
Career Earnings: $527,996

FLEISHER, Bruce   Birth Date 10/16/48 **Birthplace** Union City, TN   **Residence** Ballen Isles, FL
Height 6-3   **Weight** 205 **College** Miami Dade JC **Family** Wife, Wendy; Jessica (3/23/80)
Special Interests Reading, helping others **Turned Professional** 1970 **Q School** Fall 1971
Other Achievements Lone PGA TOUR victory came at 1991 New England Classic, when
rolled in 50-foot birdie putt on seventh playoff hole to defeat Ian Baker-Finch. Winner 1968 U.S.
Amateur, 1989 Club Pro Championship, 1971 Brazilian Open, 1990 Jamaica, Bahamas and
Brazilian Opens. Low amateur 1969 Masters.
Exempt Status: 4th at 1994 Qualifying Tournament
TOUR Victories: 1--1991 New England Classic
Money and Position:

1972--$ 9,019	1979--$11,420--149	1987--$ 2,405 -- 254
1973--$ 14,610	1980--$13,649--149	1988--$ 2,198 -- 268
1974--$ 33,975 -- 77	1981--$69,221-- 64	1990--$ 10,626 --227
1975--$ 7,773 --141	1982--$36,659--110	1991--$219,335 -- 76
1976--$ 11,295--137	1983--$50,285--102	1992--$236,516 -- 68
1977--$ 9,101 --155	1984--$30,186--138	1993--$214,279 -- 81
1978--$ 8,347 --154	1986--$ 7,866 --213	1994--$ 88,680 -- 163

Best 1994 Finish: T9--Honda Classic
1994 Summary: Tournaments entered--29; in money--13; top ten finishes--1
Career Money: $1,093,056

FORD, Scott   Birth Date 8/19/69 **Birthplace** Germany **Residence** Lake Worth, FL **Height** 5-11
Weight 170 **Special Interests** Baseball, basketball, hockey **Family** Single **College** Rollins
College **Turned Professional** 1991 **Q School** 1994 **Other Achievements** 1989 Florida State
Amateur champion. Named All-American 1990-91. Earned 1990 Wes Berner award as
outstanding Florida golfer. Grandfather is Doug Ford, who won 18 titles on PGA TOUR, including
1955 PGA Championship and 1957 Masters.
Exempt Status: 34th at 1994 Qualifying Tournament

G

GARDNER, Buddy Birth Date 8/24/55 **Birthplace** Montgomery, AL **Residence** Birmingham, AL
Weight 175 **Height** 5-11 **College** Auburn University **Family** Wife, Susan; Brooke Marie (2/1/
87), Payton Webb (12/2/89) **Turned Professional** 1977 **Q School** Fall 1977, 1978, 1982 **Other
Achievements** Winner, 1974, 1975 Alabama Amateur and 1976 Dixie Amateur. Won 1990 Ben
Hogan Panama City Beach Classic. 1977 All-American. Registered back-to-back eagles,
second a hole in one, in round 1 of 1994 Walt Disney/Oldsmobile Classic.
Exempt Status: Veteran Member   **Playoff Record:** 0-2
Best Ever Finish: T2--1979 Tucson Open; 1979 Anheuser-Busch Classic; 2--1984 Houston
Coca-Cola Open. 2--1987 Big I Houston Open.
Money and Position:

1978--$ 5,637 --170	1984--$ 118,945 -- 55	1989--$ 135,488 -- 103
1979--$ 71,468 -- 56	1985--$ 121,809 -- 67	1990--$ 159,737 -- 99
1980--$ 30,907 --102	1986--$ 92,006 -- 91	1991--$ 201,700 -- 83
1981--$ 14,635 --151	1987--$ 173,047 -- 60	1992--$ 113,394 -- 124
1982--$ 6,214 --192	1988--$ 130,589 -- 91	1993--$ 13,721 -- 232
1983--$ 56,529 -- 91		1994--$ 37,609 --201

1994 Best Finish: T4--Buick Southern Open
1994 Summery: Tournaments entered--11; in money--3; top ten finishes--1
Career Earnings: $1,483,705

GIBSON, Kelly Birth Date 5/2/64 **Birthplace** New Orleans, LA **Residence** New Orleans, La **Height**
5-10 **Weight** 180 **Special Interests** New Orleans Saints football **College** Lamar University
Family Single **Turned Professional** 1986 **Q School** 1991, 1994 **Other Achievements** Winner
1991 Ben Hogan Tri-Cities Open en route to finishing 14th on Hogan Tour money list. Placed
third 1991 Canadian Order of Merit.
Exempt Status: 26th at 1994 Qualifying Tournament
Best Ever Finish: T4--1992 Buick Southern Open.
Money and Position: 1992--$137,984--105   1993--$148,003--110   1994--$134,841--129
Best 1994 Finish: T6--Motorola Western Open
1994 Summary: Tournaments entered--33; in money--14; top ten finishes--2
Career Money: $420,828

GONZALEZ, Ernie Birth Date 2/19/61 **Birthplace** San Diego, CA **Residence** Orlando, FL **Height**
5-9 **Weight** 225 **College** United States International University **Special Interests** All sports
Family Wife, Judy; David **Turned Professional** 1983 **Q School** 1984, 1985, 1989 **Other
Achievements** Winner 1981, 1982 San Diego County Amateur Match Play Championship;
1983 San Diego County Open (as amateur); 1984-1985 Queen Mary Open. One of the few
lefthanders on TOUR.
Exempt Status: Past Champion.
TOUR Victories: 1--1986 Pensacola Open.
Money & Position:

1985 -- $ 12,729 --171	1988 -- $ 14,135 -- 207	1991 -- $ 5,550 -- 252
1986 -- $125,548 -- 68	1989 -- $ 13,840 -- 203	1992 -- $ 5,485 -- 262
1987 -- $ 60,234 --154	1990 -- $ 13,540 -- 221	1993 -- $ 2,175 -- 310
		1994 -- $ 16,860 -- 230

1994 Best Finish: T11--Deposit Guaranty Golf Classic
1994 Summary: Tournaments entered--3; in money--2; top ten finishes--0.
Career Earnings: $257,364

GOTSCHE, Steve Birth Date 8/24/61 **Birthplace** Wakeeny, KS **Residence** Great Bend, KS; plays out of Great Petroleum Club **Height** 6-2 **Weight** 200 **College** Nebraska **Special Interests** Fishing **Family** Wife, Linda; Adam (9/23/86), Ryan (7/16/90) **Turned Professional** 1984 **Q School** 1993, 1994 **Other Achievements** 1990 National Assistants Champion. 1990-1993 Midwest Section Player of the Year. Winner, 1990 Kansas Open, 1988 Wyoming Open and 1986 Nebraska Open.
Exempt Status: 22nd at 1994 Qualifying Tournament
Best Ever Finish: 5--1994 New England Classic
Money and Position: 1991--$5,164--255   1993--$ 5,657--264
                                                                    1994--$59,227--182
Best 1994 Finish: 5--New England Classic
1994 Summary: Tournaments entered--21; in money--8; top ten finishes--1
Career Money: $59,227

GRAHAM, David Birth Date 5/23/46 **Birthplace** Windsor, Australia **Residence** Dallas, TX **Height** 5-10 **Weight** 162 **Special Interests** Hunting, golf club design, cars **Family** Wife, Maureen Burdett; Andrew (11/8/74), Michael (10/8/77) **Turned Professional** 1962 **Q School** Fall, 1971 **Other Achievements** Foreign victories include 1970 French Open, 1970 Thailand Open, 1971 Caracas Open, 1971 JAL Open, 1975 Wills Masters, 1976 Chunichi Crowns Invitational (Japan), 1976 Picadilly World Match Play, 1977 Australian Open and South African PGA, 1978 Mexico Cup, 1979 West Lakes Classic (Australia), New Zealand Open, 1980 Mexican Open, Rolex Japan, Brazilian Classic, 1981-1982 Lancome (France), 1985 Queensland Open. **National Teams** Australian World Cup 1970 (won team title with Bruce Devlin), 1970, 1971 1983. Australian Dunhill Cup 1985, 1986, 1988. Captained the International Team in 1994 Presidents Cup.
Exempt Status: Past Champion   **Playoff Record:** 2-1
TOUR Victories: 8-1972 Cleveland Open. 1976 Westchester Classic, American Golf Classic. 1979 PGA Championship. 1980 Memorial Tournament. 1981 Phoenix Open, U.S. Open. 1983 Houston Coca-Cola Open.
Money and Position:

1971 -- $ 10,062 --135	1978 -- $ 66,909 -- 43	1985 -- $ 72,802 -- 101
1972 -- $ 57,827 -- 38	1979 -- $177,683 -- 16	1986 -- $ 95,109 -- 88
1973 -- $ 43,062 -- 71	1980 -- $137,819 -- 27	1987 -- $ 58,860 -- 142
1974 -- $ 61,625 -- 41	1981 -- $188,286 -- 13	1988 -- $ 99,087 -- 113
1975 -- $ 51,642 -- 44	1982 -- $103,616 -- 35	1989 -- $ 22,275 -- 192
1976 -- $176,174 -- 8	1983 -- $244,924 -- 11	1990 -- $ 24,492 -- 204
1977 -- $ 72,086 -- 44	1984 -- $116,627 -- 58	

Career Earnings: $1,874,780

H

HAAS, Jerry   Birth Date 9/16/63 **Birthplace** Belleville, IL **Residence** Belleville, IL **Height** 5-10 **Weight** 170 **Special Interests** Sports **Family** Wife, Elizabeth **College** Wake Forest **Turned Professional** 1986 **Q School** 1989, 1990 **Other Achievements** Finished T31 as amateur at 1985 Masters. Member 1985 Walker Cup Team. Became only second player to win consecutive NIKE TOUR events when he claimed 1994 NIKE Tri-Cities Open and NIKE Sonoma County Open after earlier in year winning NIKE Ozarks Open. Finished ninth on NIKE money list with $116,583. Younger brother of TOUR veteran Jay Haas; nephew of former Masters champion Bob Goalby.
Exempt Status: 9th on 1994 NIKE TOUR money list
Best Ever Finish: T5--1991 Deposit Guaranty Classic
Money and Position: 1990--$72,702--151   1991--$103,104--134   1992--$60,794--163
Career Money: $236,600

HALLDORSON, Dan Birth Date 4/2/52 **Birthplace** Winnipeg, Canada **Residence** Cambridge,IL **Height** 5-10 **Weight** 180 **Special Interests** Sports **Family** Wife, Pat; Angie (4/7/75) **Turned Professional** 1971 **Q School** 1974, 1978, 1990 **Other Achievements** Winner 1986 Deposit Guaranty Golf Classic, unofficial PGA TOUR event. Defeated Paul Azinger by two strokes in Hattiesburg, MS tournament. Member several Canadian World Cup teams. Leader 1983 Canadian Tour Order of Merit.
Exempt Status: Past Champion   **Playoff Record:** 0-1
TOUR Victories: 1--1980 Pensacola Open
Money & Position:

1975 -- $ 619 --243	1984 -- $ 55,215 -- 99	1989 --$ 86,667--137
1979-- $ 24,559 --116	1985 -- $112,102 -- 73	1990 --$ 18,155--215
1980 -- $111,553 -- 36	1986 -- $ 83,876 --101	1991 --$ 158,743-- 97
1981 -- $ 90,064 -- 47	1987 -- $ 69,094 --125	1992 --$ 119,002--118
1982 -- $ 93,705 -- 43	1988 -- $ 96,079 --116	1993 --$ 24,284--205
1983 -- $ 21,458 --146		1994 --$ 7,215--262

1994 Best Finish: T31--Bell Canandian Open
1994 Summary: Tournaments entered--5; in money--1; top ten finishes--0.
Career Earnings: $1,173,133

HART, Dudley Birth Date 8/4/68 **Birthplace** Rochester, NY **Residence** West Palm Beach, FL **Height** 5-10 **Weight** 175 **College** Florida **Family** Single **Special Interests** Sports **Turned Professional** 1990 **Q School** 1990, 1994 **Other Achievements** Four-time All-American. Turned professional in 1990 and won Florida Open and Louisiana Open later in year. Missed 10 weeks of 1994 season due to rib and back problems. Won pro-am portion of 1994 AT&T Pebble Beach National Pro-Am with Raymond Floyd's son Robert.
Exempt Status: 6th at 1994 Qualifying Tournament
Best-Ever Finish: T3--1992 Greater Milwaukee Open; T3--1993 Northern Telecom Open; T3--1993 Kmart Greater Greensboro Open.
Money and Position: 1991--$126,217--120   1993--$316,750--52   1994--$126,313--135
                        1992--$254,903 -- 61
Best 1994 Finish: T7--AT&T Pebble Beach National Pro-Am
1994 Summary: Tournaments entered--31; in money--12; top ten finishes--2
Career Earnings: $824,183

HART, Steve Birth Date 9/13/59 **Birthplace** St. Paul, MN **Residence** Tequesta, FL **Height** 5-8 **Weight** 175 **Special Interests** Deep sea fishing, football **College** Florida State **Turned Professional** 1981 **Q School** 1988, 1991, 1994 **Other Achievements** Winner, 1981 Palm Beach County Amateur Championship. Runnerup, 1981 Florida State Amateur.
Exempt Status: 43rd at 1994 Qualifying Tournament
Money and Position: 1982--$ 2,762--240   1986--$ 1,440--262   1992--$69,124--157
                        1983--$19,314--153   1989--$40,079--171   1993--$ 2,175--310
                        1984--$ 4,060--206   1990--$28,575--196   1994--$ --0--
Career Money: $165,354

HATALSKY, Morris Birth Date 11/10/51 **Birthplace** San Diego, CA **Residence** Ormond Beach, FL **Height** 5-11 **Weight** 165 **Special Interests** Family activities, TOUR Bible study, snow skiing **Family** Wife, Tracy; Daniel (12/11/80), Kenneth (12/11/80) **College** United States International University **Turned Professional** 1973 **Q School** Spring 1976, 1993 **Other Achievements** 1972 NAIA All-American. Captained 1972 U.S. International University team NAIA Championship team. Winner 1968 Mexico National Junior Championship.
Exempt Status: Past Champion   **Playoff Record:** 2-1
TOUR Victories: 4--1981 Hall of Fame Classic. 1983 Greater Milwaukee Open. 1988 Kemper Open. 1990 Bank of Boston Classic.
Money and Position: 1976--$ 249--288   1982--$ 66,128-- 65   1988--$239,019 -- 47
                        1977--$ 32,193-- 79   1983--$102,567-- 56   1989--$ 66,577 -- 149
                        1978--$ 43,062-- 114   1984--$ 50,957--107   1990--$253,639 -- 59
                        1979--$ 61,625-- 69   1985--$ 76,059-- 96   1991--$106,265 -- 132
                        1980--$ 47,107-- 74   1986--$ 105,543-- 83   1992--$ 55,042 -- 170
                        1981--$ 70,186-- 63   1987--$ 150,654-- 70   1993--$111,057 -- 135
                                                                        1994--$ 81,902 -- 166

1994 Best Finish: T22--Northern Telecom Open
1994 Summary: Tournaments entered--25; in money--15; top ten finishes--0
Career Earnings: $1,693,447

HAYES, J.P. Birth Date 8/2/65 **Birthplace** Appleton, WI **Residence** El Paso, TX **Height** 6-0 **Weight:** 170 **Special Interests** Fishing, skiing **Family** Wife, Laura **College** Texas-El Paso **Turned Professional** 1989 **QSchool** 1991, 1994 **Other Achievements** Played NIKE TOUR in 1991, '93 and '94. Member of PGA TOUR in 1992.
Exempt Status: 28th at 1994 Qualifying Tournament
Best-Ever Finish: T6--1992 Anheuser-Busch Golf Classic
Money and Position: 1992--$72,830--155   1993--$6,650--253
Career Money: $79,840

HAYES, Mark Birth Date 7/12/49 **Birthplace** Stillwater, OK **Residence** Edmond, OK; plays out of Oak Tree GC **Height** 5-11 **Weight** 170 **Special Interests** Sports **Family** Wife, Jana; Kelly (12/9/79), Ryan (3/25/83) **College** Oklahoma State **Turned Professional** 1973 **Q School** 1973, 1988, 1989, 1990 **Other Achievements** 1967 and 1971 Oklahoma Amateur Champion. 1970-71 Collegiate All-American.
Exempt Status: Past Champion   **Playoff Record:** 0-2
Tour Victories: 3--1976 Byron Nelson Classic, Pensacola Open. 1977 Tournament Players Championship.
Money and Position: 1973 -- $ 8,637 -- 160   1980 -- $ 66,535 -- 61   1987 -- $ 76,666 -- 116
                        1974 -- $ 40,620 -- 68   1981 -- $ 91,624 -- 46   1988 -- $ 77,072 -- 131
                        1975 -- $ 49,297 -- 47   1982 -- $ 47,777 -- 95   1989 -- $ 87,689 -- 134
                        1976 -- $ 151,699 -- 11   1983 -- $ 63,431 -- 81   1990 -- $ 76,743 -- 149
                        1977 -- $ 115,749 -- 19   1984 -- $ 42,207 -- 115   1991 -- $ 36,370 -- 191
                        1978 -- $ 146,456 -- 15   1985 -- $ 61,988 -- 108   1992 -- $ 50,324 -- 175
                        1979 -- $ 130,878 -- 23   1986 -- $117,837 -- 74   1993 -- $ 6,942 -- 249
                                                                              1994-- $ -- 0 --
1994 Summary: Tournaments entered -- 4; in Money--0; top ten finishes -- 0.
Career Earnings: $1,544,836

HEAFNER, Vance Birth Date 8/11/54 **Birthplace** Charlotte, NC **Residence** Raleigh, NC **Height** 6-0 **Weight** 185 **Special Interests** Fishing, hunting **Family** Wife, Paige; Elizabeth (10/13/85), Allison (10/4/88) **College** North Carolina State **Turned Professional** 1978 **Q School** 1980, 1989 **Other Achievements** All American at North Carolina State 1984, 1985, 1986. Winner 1976-78 Eastern Amateur titles; 1977 Porter Cup. 1977 Walker Cup team. Winner 1977 Azalea Invitational, 1978 American Amateur Classic. Made 150th cut to achieve Veteran Member staus in 1994.

Exempt Status: Past Champion

TOUR Victories: 1-1981 Walt Disney World National Team Championship (w/ Mike Holland)

Money and Position:

1980 -- $ 11,398 -- 156	1984 -- $90,702-- 71	1988 -- $ 2,117-- 170
1981 -- $ 73,244 -- 60	1985 -- $31,964 --142	1989 -- $1,624 -- 273
1982 -- $113,717 -- 33	1986-- $ 28,763 --159	1990 -- $6,525 -- 256
1983 -- $ 68,210 -- 65	1987-- $ 74,489 --119	1994 -- $5,297 -- 271

Best 1994 Finish: T44--Hardee's Golf Classic

1994 Summary: Tournaments entered--2; in money--2; top ten finishes--0

Career Earnings: $526,049

HEARN, Tom Birth Date 8/25/65 **Birthplace** Ft. Pierce, FL **Residence** Ft. Pierce, FL **Height** 6-1 **Weight** 170 **Special Interests** Fishing, snow skiing, travel **Family** Wife, Trish **College** Miami **Turned Professional** 1988 **Q School** 1994 **Other Achievements** 18 mini-tour wins. Leading money winner 1992-93 Space Coast Tour and 1994 Gold Coast Pro Golf Tour Challenge Cup. Brother Ed Hearn caught for New York Mets (1986) and Kansas City Royals (1987-88).

Exempt Status: 40th at 1994 Qualifying Tournament

HINKLE, Lon Birth Date 7/17/49 **Birthplace** Flint, MI **Residence** San Diego, CA; plays out of Eagle Bend GC **Height** 6-2 **Weight** 220 **Special Interests** Reading **Family** Monique (8/10/78), Danielle (3/20/82); Jake (9/6/85) **College** San Diego State University **Turned Professional** 1972 **Q School** 1972, 1991 **Other Achievements** Co-champion 1972 Pacific Coast Athletic Conference. Runnerup 1975 German Open and Sanpo Classic in Japan. Winner 1978 JCPenney Classic with Pat Bradley. Runnerup 1980 European Open. 1981 National Long Drive Champion.

Exempt Status: Past Champion   **Playoff Record:** 1-2

TOUR Victories: 3 --1978 New Orleans Open. 1979 Bing Crosby National Pro-Am, World Series of Golf

Money and Position:

1972 -- $ 7,350 -- 145	1979 -- $ 247,693 -- 3	1986 -- $ 97,610 -- 86
1973 -- $ 7,539 -- 164	1980 -- $ 134,913 -- 29	1987 -- $ 45,751 -- 159
1974 -- $ 6,509 -- 162	1981 -- $ 144,307 -- 22	1989 -- $151,828 -- 92
1975 -- $ 8,420 -- 136	1982 -- $ 55,406 -- 81	1990 -- $ 26,052 -- 201
1976 -- $ 11,058 -- 138	1983 -- $ 116,822 -- 47	1991 -- $ 49,692 -- 174
1977 -- $ 51,494 -- 60	1984 -- $ 89,850 -- 73	1992 -- $ 91,854 -- 139
1978 -- $138,388 -- 16	1985 -- $ 105,499 -- 76	1993 -- $ 8,621 -- 244
		1994 -- $ 4,411 -- 281

1994 Best Finish: T66--AT&T Pebble Beach

1994 Summary: Tournaments entered--7; in money--2 ; top ten finishes--0.

Career Earnings: $ 1,600,247

HOWISON, Ryan Birth Date 12/26/66 **Birthplace** Columbus, OH **Residence** Boynton Beach, FL **Height** 5-10 **Weight** 175 **Special Interests** Baseball, snow skiing, his labrador retriever, hunting **Family** Single **College** North Carolina **Turned Professional** 1990 **Q School** 1994 **Other Achievements** Winner 1994 Benson and Hedges Trinidad & Tobago Open, 1993 Bahamas Lucaya Pro-Am. Played in 1989 College World Series. Won College Scholar Athlete Award.

Exempt Status: 45th at 1994 Qualifying Tournament

I

INMAN, Joe Birth Date 11/29/47 **Birthplace** Indianapolis, IN **Residence** Marietta, GA **Weight** 160 **Height** 5-11 **College** Wake Forest **Family** Wife, Nancy; Craig (4/13/77), Sally (8/9/83), Kate (10/31/86) **Turned Professional** 1972 **Q School** Fall 1973 **Other Achievements** Winner 1969 North and South Amateur. Member 1969 Walker Cup team. Brother John current PGA TOUR member.

Exempt Status: Past Champion

TOUR Victories: 1--1976 Kemper Open

Money and Position:

1973--$ 1,331--227	1979--$75,035-- 52	1985--$62,562-- 107
1974--$46,645-- 61	1980--$35,014-- 95	1986--$23,229-- 170
1975--$53,225-- 41	1981--$51,068-- 82	1987--$ 7,013-- 216
1976--$69,892-- 39	1982--$52,091-- 89	1988--$ 7,400-- 229
1977--$67,064-- 47	1983--$59,913-- 86	1994--$ 1,618--T324
1978--$62,034-- 51	1984--$54,494--101	

Best 1994 Finish: T50--Deposit Guaranty Golf Classic

1994 Summary: Tournaments entered--2; in money--1; top ten finishes--0

Career Money: $729,248

JAECKEL, Barry Birth Date 2/14/49 **Birthplace** Los Angeles, CA **Residence** Palm Desert, CA **Height** 5-11 **Weight** 160 **Special Interests** All sports **Family** Wife, Evelyn **College** Santa Monica J.C. **Turned Professional** 1971 **Q School** Spring 1975 **Other Achievements** 1968 Southern California Amateur champion. Winner 1972 French Open. Father veteran movie character actor Richard Jaeckel.
Exempt Status: Past Champion
TOUR Victories: 1-1978 Tallahassee Open

Money and Position:

1975--$ 8,883--133	1982--$ 62,940-- 70	1988--$ 39,227--173
1976--$ 36,888-- 70	1983--$ 64,473-- 80	1989--$ 64,782--151
1978--$ 72,421-- 37	1984--$ 49,308--110	1990--$ 63,590--168
1979--$ 46,541-- 86	1985--$ 81,765-- 92	1991--$ 59,216--167
1980--$ 25,501--116	1986--$ 80,646--105	1992--$ 13,351--226
1981--$ 87,931-- 48	1987--$ 53,909--144	1993--$ 15,584--226
		1994--$ 15,750--235

1994 Best Finish: T8--MCI Heritage Golf Classic
1994 Summary: Tournaments entered--9; in money--1; top ten finishes--0
Career Earnings: $953,209

JENKINS, Tom Birth Date 12/14/47 **Birthplace** Houston, TX **Residence** Alachua, FL **Height** 5-11 **Weight** 175 **Special Interests** Camping, gardening **Family** Wife, Lynn, one child **College** University of Houston **Turned Professional** 1971 **Joined TOUR** 1972 **Other Achievements** Two-time All-American. Member 1970 NCAA Championship team at Houston.
Exempt Status: Past Champion   **Playoff Record:** 0-1
TOUR Victories: 1--1975 IVB-Philadelphia Classic

Money and Position:

1972 -- $ 1,317 -- 270	1978 -- $ 2,902 -- 186	1984 -- $ 53,200 -- 103
1973 -- $ 38,241 -- 80	1979 -- $ 6,689 -- 171	1985 -- $ 9,347 -- 183
1974 -- $ 30,826 -- 86	1980 -- $ 16,178 -- 137	1986 -- $ 995 -- 275
1975 -- $ 45,267 -- 52	1981 -- $ 78,127 -- 54	1992 -- $ 6,963 -- 253
1976 -- $ 42,740 -- 65	1982 -- $ 64,753 -- 67	1993 -- $ 4,302 -- 277
1977 -- $ 15,780 -- 120	1983 -- $ 52,564 -- 97	

1994 Summary: Tournaments entered--4; in money--0; top ten finishes--0
Career Earnings: $456,669

JORDAN, Pete Birth Date 6/10/64 **Birthplace** Elmhurst, IL **Residence** Valrico, FL **Height** 6-0 **Weight** 180 **Special Interests** Sports, music **Family** Wife, Kelly; Ryan (11/26/91), Peyton Ashley (7/14/94) **College** Texas Christian University **Turned Professional** 1986 **Q School** 1993, 1994 **Other Achievements** 1986 NCAA All-American. Named All-Southwest Conference 1985 and 1986. Member NIKE TOUR 1991-93. Played 1993 U.S. Open.
Exempt Status: 132nd on 1994 PGA TOUR money list
Best-Ever Finish: T4--1994 Southwestern Bell Colonial
Money and Position: 1994--$128,960--132
1994 Summary: Tournaments entered--29; in money--13; top ten finishes--1
Career Money: $128,960

K

KAYE, Jonathan Birth Date 8/2/70 **Birthplace** Denver, CO **Residence** Boulder, CO **Height** 5-10 **Weight** 160 **Special Interests** Skiing, travel **Family** Single **College** Colorado **Turned Professional** 1993 **Q School** 1994 **Other Achievements** Won 1992 Ping Arizona Intercollegiate by beating Phil Mickelson in sudden-death playoff.
Exempt Status: 32nd at 1994 Qualifying Tournament

KNOX, Kenny Birth Date 8/15/56 **Birthplace** Columbus, GA **Residence** Tallahassee, FL **Height** 5-10 **Weight** 175 **Special Interests** Teaching juniors to play golf **Family** Wife, Karen; Michelle (12/24/80) **College** Florida State University (1978 Physical Education) **Turned Professional** 1978 **Q School** Fall 1981, 1983, 1984. **Other Achievements** 1977 and 1978 All-American. Winner 1977 Southeastern Amateur.
Exempt Status: Past champion   **Playoff Record:** 1-1
TOUR Victories: 3-1986 Honda Classic. 1987 Hardee's Golf Classic. 1990 Buick Southern Open.

Money and Position:

1982 -- $ 6,919 -- 186	1987 -- $200,783 -- 55	1991 -- $423,025 -- 32
1984 -- $ 15,606 -- 71	1988 -- $168,099 -- 70	1992 -- $ 24,889 -- 203
1985 -- $ 26,968 -- 41	1989 -- $230,012 -- 62	1993 -- $ 3,630 -- 282
1986 -- $261,608 -- 24	1990 -- $209,679 -- 73	1994-- $ 23,872 -- 218

Best 1994 Finish: T20--Buick Open
1994 Summary: Tournaments entered --15; in money--5; top ten finishes--0.
Career Earnings: $1,595,087

KOCH, Gary **Birth Date** 11/21/52 **Birthplace** Baton Rouge, LA **Residence** Tampa, FL **Height** 5-11 **Weight** 165 **Special Interests** Fishing, reading, music **Family** Wife, Donna; Patricia (4/1/81), Rachel (7/30/83) **College** University of Florida **Turned Professional** 1975 **Q School** Fall 1975 **Other Achievements** Winner 1968, 1969, 1970 Florida State Juniors; 1970 U.S. Juniors; 1969 Orange Bowl Juniors; 1969 Florida State Open; 1973 Trans-Mississippi Amateur; 1973, 1974 Southeastern Conference. First-team All-American 1972, 1973, 1974. Member 1973 NCAA Championship team at Florida. Winner 10 collegiate events. **National Teams** Walker Cup (2), 1973, 1975; U.S. World Amateur Cup Team 1974. Color analyst for ESPN golf coverage. **Exempt Status:** Past Champion   **Playoff Record:** 2-0
TOUR Victories: 6-1976 Tallahassee Open. 1978 Florida Citrus Open. 1983 Doral Eastern Open. 1984 Isuzu-Andy Williams San Diego Open, Bay Hill Classic. 1988 Panasonic-Las Vegas Invitational.

Money and Position:

Year	Money	Pos		Year	Money	Pos		Year	Money	Pos
1976	$ 38,195	69		1982	$ 43,449	98		1988	$ 414,694	24
1977	$ 58,383	52		1983	$ 168,330	27		1989	$ 86,348	138
1978	$ 58,660	54		1984	$ 262,679	17		1990	$ 36,469	186
1979	$ 46,809	84		1985	$ 121,566	68		1991	$ 7,189	243
1980	$ 39,827	82		1986	$ 180,693	50		1992	$ 3,690	274
1981	$ 11,999	162		1987	$ 33,727	175		1993	$ 702	329

1994 Summary: Tournaments entered--2; in money-- 0; top ten finishes--0
Career Money: $1,613,407

KRATZERT, Bill **Birth Date** 6/29/52 **Birthplace** Quantico, VA **Residence** Ft. Wayne, IN **Height** 6-0 **Weight** 190 **Special Interests** Family, all sports **Family** Wife, Janie; Rebecca Brea (9/6/78), Tyler Brennie (12/5/80), Thomas Andrew (4/29/91) **College** Georgia **Turned Professional** 1974 **Q School** Spring 1976 **Other Achievements** Winner 1968 Indiana Amateur and 1969 Indiana Open. 1973 and 1974 All-American. Inducted into Indiana Golf Hall of Fame 1993. **Exempt Status:** Past Champion   **Playoff Record:** 1-1
TOUR Victories: 4--1976 Walt Disney World National Team Play (with Woody Blackburn), 1977 Greater Hartford Open. 1980 Greater Milwaukee Open. 1984 Pensacola Open

Money and Position :

Year	Money	Pos		Year	Money	Pos		Year	Money	Pos
1976	$ 21,253	102		1982	$ 22,779	139		1988	$ 43,519	158
1977	$134,758	10		1983	$ 14,744	166		1989	$ 7,773	220
1978	$183,683	8		1984	$149,827	37		1990	$ 14,630	218
1979	$101,628	35		1985	$180,331	37		1991	$ 19,819	209
1980	$175,771	12		1986	$ 47,421	139		1992	$ 16,439	217
1981	$ 55,513	75		1987	$ 78,232	114		1993	$ 78,992	156
								1994	$ 42,127	196

Best 1994 Finish: T15--Kmart GGO
1994 Summary--Tournaments entered--25; in money--8; top ten finishes--0
Career Money :$1,389,241

L

LEONARD, Jeff **Birth Date** 9/23/64 **Birthplace** Indianapolis, IN **Residence** Tampa, FL **Height** 5-11 **Weight** 165 **Special Interests** Reading, church involvement **Family** Wife, Sara **College** University of Tampa **Turned Professional** 1988 **Q School** 1994 **Other Achievements** Won 1994 Jamiaca Open.
Exempt Status: 16th at 1994 Qualifying Tournament

LEWIS, J.L. **Birth Date** 7/18/60 **Birthplace** Emporia, KS **Residence** Briarcliff, TX **Height** 6-3 **Weight** 195 **Special Interests** Fishing **Family** Wife, Dawn; Cole (5/12/84), Sherry (4/29/87) **College** Southwest Texas **Turned Professional** 1984 **Q School** 1989, 1994 **Other Achievements** Winner 1994 PGA Cup Team. Four-time Player of Year in STPGA. Member two NCAA Division II championship teams. First-team All-American in high school. Named to 1978 All-State basketball team and earned basketball scholarship to Emporia State University.
Exempt Status: 21st at 1994 Qualifying Tournament
Best Ever Finish: T28--1989 Texas Open
Money and Position: 1989--$3,121--214   1993--$5,965--261   1994--$3,299--291
Best 1994 Finish: T47--Shell Houston Open
1994 Summary: Tournaments entered--3; in money--1; top ten finishes--0
Career Money: $12,385

LOUSTALOT, Tim **Birth Date** 4/9/65 **Birthplace** Sacramento, CA **Residence** Fresno, CA **Height** 5-9 **Weight** 155 **Special Interests** Sports, traveling **Family** Wife, Jamie; Ellie Gail (9/21/94) **College** Fresno State **Turned Professional** 1987 **Q School** 1994 **Other Achievements** Won 1992 Ben Hogan Lake City Classic. Played NIKE Tour 1990-94. Winner numerous collegiate tournaments.
Exempt Status: 35th at 1994 Qualifying Tournament

LYE, Mark Birth Date 11/13/52 **Birthplace** Vallejo, CA **Residence** Ft. Myers, FL; plays out of Fiddlesticks, GC **Height** 6-5 **Weight** 175 **Special Interests** Guitar, fishing **Family** Single **College** San Jose State **Turned Professional** 1975 **Q School** Fall 1976 **Other Achievements** Winner 1977 Australian Tour Order of Merit and 1976 Rolex Trophy in Switzerland. Won 1976 Champion of Champions Tournament in Australia. 1975 All-American. Works as commentator for The Golf Channel.
Exempt Status: Special Medical Extension
TOUR Victories: 1--1983 Bank of Boston Classic
Money and Position:

1977--$ 22,034--100	1983--$164,506-- 28	1989--$ 242,884-- 56
1978--$ 13,648--125	1984--$152,356-- 43	1990--$ 201,001-- 77
1979--$ 51,184-- 75	1985--$112,735-- 72	1991--$ 147,530--104
1980--$109,454-- 39	1986--$ 78,960--111	1992--$ 9,921--243
1981--$ 76,044-- 56	1987--$ 73,625--121	1993--$ 106,935--139
1982--$ 67,460-- 61	1988--$106,972--108	1994--$ 63,394--178

1994 Best Finish: T7--Kemper Open
1993 Summary: Tournaments entered--15; in money--7; top ten finishes--1
Career Earnings: $1,800,654

M

MARTIN, Doug Birth Date 12/8/66 **Birthplace** Bluffton, OH **Residence** Edgewood, KY; plays out of Traditions GC **Height** 6-0 **Weight** 200 **Special Interests** Notre Dame football, family **Family** Wife, Gaylynn; Cody Alan (12/24/90), Macy Lynn (12/12/93) **College** Oklahoma **Turned Professional** 1989 **Q School** 1991, 1994 **Other Achievements** Won 1993 NIKE South Texas Open en route to finishing second on NIKE TOUR money list. Member 1989 Walker Cup and NCAA Championship team. Semi-finalist 1989 U.S. Amateur. Three-time All-American. Tremendous fan of Notre Dame football, good friends with Lou Holtz.
Exempt Status: 11th at 1994 Qualifying Tournament
Best Ever Finish: T4--1993 Deposit Guaranty Golf Classic
Money and Position: 1992--$77,204--150   1993--$21,381--212   1994--$81,201--168
Best 1994 Finish: T9--Buick Invitational of California
1994 Summary: Tournaments entered--33; in money--8; top ten finishes--1
Career Money: $179,786

MAST, Dick Birth Date 3/23/51 **Birthplace** Bluffton, OH **Residence** Winter Garden, FL; plays out of Cypress Creek GC **Height** 5-11 **Weight** 180 **Special Interests** TOUR Bible study, fishing, water skiing **College** St. Petersburg Junior College **Family** Wife, Roberta; Richard (4/9/79), Joshua (4/1/83), Caleb (6/11/86), Jonathan (3/14/89), Jacob (12/5/91) **Turned Professional** 1972 **Q School** Fall 1973, 1977, 1978, 1985, 1991. **Other Achievements** Won three Ben Hogan Tour events in 1990--Mississippi Gulf Coast Classic, Pensacola Open and Fort Wayne Open--en route to finishing third on money list. Largest payday $108,000 in 1992 Greater Milwaukee Open. Noted after 1992 GMO, "I've played virtually every tour except the ladies."
Exempt Status: 131st on 1994 money list
Best-Ever Finish: 2--1992 Greater Milwaukee Open
Money and Position:

1974--$7,108--156	1985--$ 2,887--219	1990--$ 4,200--252
1975--$ 280--276	1986--$ 79,389--109	1991--$ 17,274--216
1977--$4,387--182	1987--$ 90,768--103	1992--$150,847-- 98
1979--$5,715--180	1988--$128,568-- 56	1993--$210,125-- 82
	1989--$ 38,955--173	1994--$129,822--131

Best 1994 Finish: T7--Freeport-McMoRan Classic
1994 Summary: Tournaments entered--27; in money--14; top ten finishes--1
Career Money: $866,124

McCARRON, Scott Birth Date 7/10/65 **Birthplace** Sacramento, CA **Residence** Rancho Murietta, CA **Height** 5-10 **Weight** 170 **Special Interests** Flying, playing guitar, skiing, mountain biking, reading, sky diving **Family** Wife, Jennifer **College** UCLA **Turned Professional** 1992 **Q School** 1994 **Other Achievements** Member 1993 Canadian Tour, 1994 Hooters Tour. Played on 1988 UCLA NCAA championship team. Winner 1994 Long Beach Open.
Exempt Status: 31st at 1994 Qualifying Tournament

McCORD, Gary **Birth Date** 5/23/48 **Birthplace** San Gabriel, CA **Residence** Scottsdale, AZ **Height** 6-2 **Weight** 185 **College** University of California-Riverside (1971, Economics) **Special Interest** Enjoys spoofing people **Turned Professional** 1971 **Joined TOUR** Fall 1973; Fall 1982 **Other Achievements** Two-time All-American. 1970 NCAA Division II champion. Player Director on TOUR Policy Board 1983-1986. Color analyst on CBS golf telecasts. Winner 1991 Ben Hogan Gateway Open.
Best-Ever Finish: 2--1975 Greater Milwaukee Open; T2--1977 Greater Milwaukee Open
Exempt Status: Veteran Member
Money and Position:

1973 -- $ 499 --423	1980 -- $ 13,521 -- 146	1987 -- $ 3,689 -- 240
1974 -- $ 33,640 -- 78	1981 -- $ 20,722 -- 130	1988 -- $15,502 -- 204
1975 -- $ 43,028 -- 59	1982 -- $ 27,380 -- 130	1989 -- $29,629 -- 181
1976 -- $ 26,479 -- 84	1983 -- $ 55,756 -- 94	1990 -- $32,249 -- 191
1977 -- $ 46,318 -- 65	1984 -- $ 68,213 -- 85	1991 -- $ 7,365 -- 241
1978 -- $ 15,280 --117	1985 -- $ 32,198 -- 140	1992 -- $59,061 -- 160
1979 -- $ 36,843 --105	1986 -- $ 27,747 -- 160	1993 -- $16,456 -- 225
		1994 -- $25,602 -- 216

1994 Best Finish: T18--Phoenix Open
1994 Summary: Tournaments entered--7; in money--5; top ten finishes--0
Career Earnings: $641,118

McCULLOUGH, Mike **Birth Date** 3/21/45 **Birthplace** Coshocton, OH **Residence** Scottsdale, AZ **Height** 5-9 **Weight** 170 **Special Interests** Flying, outdoor activities **Family** Wife, Marilyn; Jason (4/24/75), Michelle (5/13/86), Mark Andrew (6/7/89) **College** Bowling Green State University (1968, Education) **Turned Professional** 1970 **Joined TOUR** Fall 1972 **Other Achievements** Winner 1970 Ohio State Amateur. Winner 1977 Magnolia Classic, 1974 Mini-Kemper Open.
Exempt Status: Veteran Member
Best-Ever Finish: 2--1977 Tournament Players Championship
Money and Position:

1972 -- $ 227 -- 437	1980 -- $ 19,588 --125	1988 -- $ 27,561 -- 181
1973 -- $ 17,076 --114	1981 -- $ 27,212 --115	1989 -- $ 22,081 -- 193
1974 -- $ 31,961 -- 83	1982 -- $ 43,207 -- 99	1990 -- $ 20,870 -- 210
1975 -- $ 17,706 --109	1983 -- $ 38,660 --116	1991 -- $ 24,600 -- 202
1976 -- $ 29,491 -- 76	1984 -- $ 21,031 --153	1992 -- $ 722 -- 312
1977 -- $ 79,413 --136	1985 -- $ 27,257 --145	1993 -- $ 2,011 -- 314
1978 -- $ 56,066 -- 47	1986 -- $ 60,586 --127	
1979 -- $ 43,664 -- 89	1987 -- $ 75,890 --117	

1994 Summary: Tournaments entered--3; in money--0; top ten finishes 0.
Career Earnings: $681,803

McGOWAN, Pat **Birth Date** 11/27/54 **Birthplace** Grand Forks, ND **Residence** Southern Pines, NC; plays out of Pine Needles Resort **Height** 5-11 **Weight** 170 **College** Brigham Young University **Special Interests** Reading, psycho-cybernetics, bird hunting **Family** Wife, Bonnie **Turned Professional** 1977 **Q School** 1977 **Other Achievements** Winner 1971 Mexican International Junior, 1976 Air Force Academy Invitational, 1977 Pacific Coast Intercollegiate, 1984 Sacramento Classic (TPS). Former member PGA TOUR Tournament Policy Board 1989-92.
Exempt Status: Veteran Member
Best-Ever Finish: 2-1978 Canadian Open, 1986 USF&G Classic; T2-1982 Quad Cities Open.
Money and Position:

1978 -- $ 47,091 -- 67	1984 -- $ 53,008 -- 104	1990 -- $ 66,738 -- 164
1979 -- $ 37,018 --104	1985 -- $ 86,032 -- 89	1991 -- $ 21,098 -- 204
1980 -- $ 28,955 --106	1986 -- $137,665 -- 65	1992 -- $ 4,065 -- 271
1981 -- $ 15,387 --147	1987 -- $ 79,078 -- 113	1993 -- $ 6,650 -- 253
1982 -- $ 58,673 -- 75	1988 -- $ 74,156 -- 135	
1983 -- $100,508 -- 57	1989 -- $ 99,454 -- 125	

1994 Summary: Tournaments entered--1; in money--0; top ten finishes --0.
Career Earnings: $915,577

N

NELFORD, Jim **Birth Date** 6/28/55 **Birthplace** Vancouver, BC **Residence** Scottsdale, AZ **Height** 5-10 **Weight** 155 **College** Brigham Young University **Special Interests** Hockey, tennis, fishing **Family** Wife, Linda; Blake (7/84) **Turned Professional** 1977 **Joined TOUR** 1977, 1987 **Other Achievements** Winner 1975 and 1976 Canadian Amateur, 1977 Western Amateur, 1977 French Nation's Cup, 1978 Cacherel Under 25. Member 1979, 1980 and 1983 Canada World Cup team. Winner of 1980 World Cup team championship with Dan Halldorson. Winner 1983 Essex International Classic (TPS). Commentator on ESPN broadcasts.
Exempt Status: Veteran Member   **Playoff Record:** 0-1
Best-Ever Finish: 2--1983 Sea Pines Heritage Classic, 1984 Bing Crosby National Pro Am
Money and Position:

1978 -- $ 29,959 -- 87	1984 -- $80,470 -- 76	
1979 -- $ 40,174 -- 95	1985 -- $60,276 --112	1990-- $ 4,132 -- 254
1980 -- $ 33,769 -- 98	1986 -- $ 0 --	1991-- $ 3,510 -- 263
1981 -- $ 20,275 --132	1987 -- $24,097 --182	1992-- $ -- 0 --
1982 -- $ 48,088 -- 94	1988 -- $20,209 --200	1993 -- DNP
1983 -- $111,932 -- 50	1989 -- $ 1,225 --289	1994 -- $ 4,435 -- 279

1994 Best Finish: T37--AT&T National Pro-Am
1994 Summary: Tournaments entered--2; in money--1; top ten finishes--0
Career Earnings: $483,251

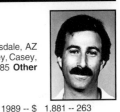

NICOLETTE, Mike   **Birth Date** 12/7/56   **Birthplace** Pittsburgh, PA   **Residence** Scottsdale, AZ **Height** 5-9 **Weight** 155 **Special Interests** Skiing, fishing **Family** Wife, Denise; Mikey, Casey, Kelly **College** Rollins College **Turned Professional** 1978 **Q School** 1979, 1981,1985 **Other Achievements** Three-time Division II All-American
Exempt Status: Past Champion   **Playoff Record:** 1-0
TOUR Victories: 1--1983 Bay Hill Classic

Money and Position:

1979 -- $ 9,140 -- 161	1984 -- $ 61,394 -- 93	1989 -- $ 1,881 -- 263
1980 -- $ 13,196 -- 147	1985 -- $ 41,750 -- 131	1990 -- $ 4,200 -- 252
1981 -- $ 512 -- 248	1986 -- $ 12,197 -- 197	1991 -- $ 33,222 -- 195
1982 -- $ 38,084 -- 106	1987 -- $ 42,407 -- 164	1992 -- $ 22,065 -- 208
1983 -- $127,868 -- 43	1988 -- $ 24,342 -- 199	1993 -- $ 1,556 -- 323

1994 Summary: Tournaments entered--2; in money--0; top ten finishes--0.
Career Earnings: $433,816

NORRIS, Tim Birth Date 11/20/57 **Birthplace** Fresno, CA **Residence** El Paso, TX; plays out of El Paso CC **College** Fresno State **Family** Wife, Shelley **Turned Professional** 1980 **Q School** Fall, 1980 **Other Achievements** Winner 1979 Sun Bowl College All-Star, 1980 Dixie Amateur,1980 California State Open (first start as a professional). Named Fresno State Athlete of Year in 1980. All-American 1979, 1980.
Exempt Status: Past Champion
TOUR Victories: 1-1982 Sammy Davis Jr. Greater Hartford Open

Money and Position:

1981--$32,424--106	1984--$61,189-- 94	1989--$58,124--158
1982--$65,643-- 66	1985--$82,235-- 95	1992--$ 1,624--310
1983--$53,811-- 95	1988--$85,331--122	

Career Money: $544,531

O

O'GRADY, Mac Birth Date 4/26/51 **Birthplace** Minneapolis, MN **Residence** Palm Springs, CA **Height** 6-0 **Weight** 165 **Special Interests** Modern times, sciences, history **Family** Wife, Fumiko Aoyagi **College** Santa Monica Junior College **Turned Professional** 1972 **Q School** 1982

Exempt Status: Past Champion   **Playoff Record:** 1-0
TOUR Victories: 2--1986 Canon-Sammy Davis Jr.-Greater Hartford Open. 1987 MONY Tournament of Champions

Money and Position:

1983 -- $ 50,379 -- 101	1987 --$ 285,109 -- 35	1991 -- $ 14,102 -- 220
1984 -- $ 41,143 -- 120	1988 -- $ 116,153 -- 98	1992 -- $ 2,030 -- 305
1985 -- $223,808 -- 20	1989 -- $ 40,090 --170	1993 -- $ 10,483 -- 240
1986 -- $256,344 -- 26	1990 -- $ -- 0 --	1994 -- $ 2,404 -- 306

1994 Best Finish: T58--Bob Hope Chrysler Classic
1994 Summary: Tournaments entered--1; in money--1; top ten finishes--0
Career Earnings: $1,239,992

P

PATE, Jerry   **Birth Date** 9/16/53 **Birthplace** Macon, GA **Residence** Birmingham, AL **Height** 6-0 **Weight** 175 **Special Interest** Water skiing **Family** Wife, Soozi; Jennifer (10/5/78), Wesley Nelson (9/5/80), James Kendrick (10/12/83) **College** University of Alabama **Turned Professional** 1975 **Q School** Fall 1975. **Other Achievements** Winner 1974 U.S. Amateur; 1974 Florida Amateur; 1976 Pacific Masters; 1977 Mixed Team Championship (with Hollis Stacy).
Exempt Status: Past Champion   **Playoff Record:** 1-2
TOUR Victories: 8-1976 U.S. Open, Canadian Open. 1977 Phoenix Open, Southern Open. 1978 Southern Open. 1981 Danny Thomas-Memphis Classic, Pensacola Open. 1982 Tournament Players Championship.

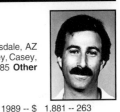

Money and Position:

1976 -- $153,102 -- 10	1982 -- $280,141 -- 9	1988 -- $10,075 -- 265
1977 -- $ 98,152 -- 27	1983 -- $ 28,890 -- 136	1989 -- $ 9,168 -- 213
1978 -- $172,999 -- 10	1984 -- $ 41,746 -- 118	1990 -- $26,953 -- 200
1979 -- $193,707 -- 11	1985 -- $ 7,792 -- 188	1991 -- $ 6,249 -- 248
1980 -- $222,976 -- 6	1986 -- $ 1,445 -- 260	1992 -- $10,971 -- 236
1981 -- $280,627 -- 6	1987 -- $ 2,116 -- 265	1993 -- $ -- 0 --
		1994 -- $ 6,513 -- 268

1994 Best Finish: T55--MCI Heritage Classic
1994 Summary: Tournaments entered—8; in money—3; top ten finishes—0
Career Earnings: $1,556,873

PAULSON, Carl **Birth Date** 12/29/70 **Birthplace** Quantico, VA **Residence** Virginia Beach, VA **Height** 5-9 **Weight** 180 **Special Interest** All sports **Family** Single **College** South Carolina **Turned Professional** 1993 **Q School** 1994 **Other Achievements** SEC Player of Year and All-American in 1993.
Exempt Status: 37th at 1994 Qualifying Tournament

PEOPLES, David Birth Date 1/9/60 **Birthplace** Augusta, ME **Residence** Orlando, FL **Height** 5-9 **Weight** 170 **Special Interests** Fishing, Bible study, hunting **College** Florida **Family** Wife, Melissa; Andrew David (10/20/89), Benjamin Thomas (6/4/92), Matthew Christopher (1/28/94) **Turned Professional** 1981 **Q School** Fall 1982, 1983, 1985, 1986, 1987, 1989 **Other Achievements** Winner 1979 Florida State Amateur. Entered Qualifying Tournament each year 1981-89, earning card six times. Won 1990 Isuzu Kapalua International.
Exempt Status: 133rd on 1994 money list
TOUR Victories: 2--1991 Buick Southern Open; 1992 Anheuser-Busch Golf Classic

Money and Position:

1983--$26,446--137	1988--$65,537--139	1992--$539,531-- 25
1984--$18,124--160	1989--$82,642--140	1993--$105,309--142
1986--$37,668--154	1990--$259,367--57	1994--$126,918--133
1987--$31,234--180	1991--$414,346--35	

1994 Best Finish: T18--Hardee's Golf Classic
1994 Summary: Tournaments entered---28; in money--11; top ten finishes--0
Career Money: $1,609,103

PERSONS, Peter **Birth Date** 9/8/62 **Birthplace** Macon, GA **Residence** Macon, GA **Height** 5-7 **Weight** 155 **Special Interests** Tennis, Georgia football, hunting, reading **Family** Wife, Colyar; Pierce (8/15/91) **College** Georgia **Turned Professional** 1986 **Q School** Fall 1989 **Other Achievements** Runnerup 1985 U.S. Amateur. Three-time All-American, first team 1986. Winner 1985 Southeastern Conference championship, plus five collegiate events. Won 1979 Georgia State Junior and 1985 Georgia State Open.
Exempt Status: Past Champion
TOUR Victories: 1—1990 Chattanooga Classic

Money and Position:

1990 -- $218,505 -- 66	1992 -- $203,625 -- 75	1994--$10,986--249
1991 -- $130,447 --114	1993 -- $ 73,092 --164	

1994 Best Finish: T31--Hardee's Golf Classic
1994 Summary: Tournaments entered—4: in money—2; top ten finishes—0.
Career Earnings: $636,655

PFEIL, Mark **Birth Date** 7/18/51 **Birthplace** Chicago Heights, IL **Residence** La Quinta, CA **Height** 5-11 **Weight** 175 **College** University of Southern California (BS 1974) **Special Interest** Family activities **Family** Wife, Diana; Kimberly Ann (9/19/80), Kathryn (8/23/84) **Turned Professional** 1974 **Joined TOUR** Fall 1975 and Fall 1976 **Other Achievements** Won California Interscholastic Federation; 1973 Walker Cup team; All-American 1973, 1974. Winner Pacific Coast Amateur, 1972, 1974; Southern California Amateur, 1973; PAC-8, 1974. Winner 1983 Anderson-Pacific Classic (TPS). Winner 1991 Concord General Pro-Am.
Exempt Status: Past Champion
TOUR Victories: 1--1980 Tallahassee Open

Money and Position:

1976 -- $ 439 --271	1981 -- $ 62,663 -- 71	1988 -- $ 6,057 -- 235
1977 -- $ 9,924 --149	1982 -- $ 85,477 -- 66	1989 -- $ --0--
1978 -- $ 13,943 --123	1983 -- $101,878 -- 69	1990 -- $ 3,383 -- 260
1979 -- $ 18,963 --125	1985 -- $ 54,098 -- 116	1991 -- $ --0--
1980 -- $ 52,704 -- 72	1986 -- $ 67,488 -- 122	1992 -- $ 2,495 -- 287
1981 -- $ 28,951 --112	1987 -- $ 11,882 -- 203	1993 -- $ 9,100 -- 242
		1994 -- $ 1,435 -- 326

1994 Best Finish: T62--Deposit Guaranty
1994 Summary: Tournaments entered--3: in money--1; top ten finishes--0.
Career Earnings: $530,849

PORTER, Bill Birth Date 9/18/59 **Birthplace** Moses Lake, WA **Residence** Quincy, WA **Height** 6-3 **Weight** 205 **Special Interests** Reading, fishing **Family** Wife, Liz; Billy (5/13/88), Kyle (5/19/91), Gabriel (12/7/92) **Turned Professional** 1980 **Q School** 1994 **Other Achievements** Played NIKE TOUR 1992-94. Best year 1994, when won NIKE Louisiana Open en route to finishing 20th in money. Only PGA TOUR start T73 at 1990 Nissan Los Angeles Open. Winner 1982 Pacific Northwest Assistants Championship, 1985 Dudsdread Open, 1988 Riviera Open, 1990 Eagle Bend Pro-Am.
Exempt Status: 8th at 1994 Qualifying Tournament
Best Ever Finish: T73--1990 Nissan Los Angeles Open

Other Prominent Members of the PGA TOUR

POWERS, Greg Birth Date 3/17/46 **Birthplace** Albany, NY **Residence** Atlanta, GA **Height** 6-0 **Weight** 180 **Special Interests** Fishing, bowling **Family** Single **College** Memphis State **Turned Professional** 1970 **Q School** 1971, 1989 **Other Achievements** Involved in near-fatal car crash in 1992. Returned to TOUR in 1994 after intense rehabilitation on shattered hip. Made 150th cut to earn Veteran Member status early in '92. 1970 All-American.
Exempt Status: Veteran Member
Money and Position:

1976--$ 4,164--180	1983--$29,803--133	1989--$ 1,234--287
1978--$27,499-- 93	1984--$31,845--136	1990--$ 3,806--256
1979--$15,749--136	1985--$10,092--178	1991--$ 6,464--245
1980--$19,939--122	1986--$ 3,329--238	1992--$10,473--241
1981--$82,210-- 52	1987--$58,958--135	
1982--$39,645--102	1988--$30,676--171	

1994 Summary: Tournaments entered--2; in money--0; top ten finishes--0
Career Money: $330,937

R

RANDOLPH, Sam Birth Date 5/13/64 **Birthplace** Santa Barbara, CA **Residence** McKinney, TX **Height** 6-0 **Weight** 175 **Special Interests** All sports, Fishing **Family** Wife, Julie **College** University of Southern California **Turned Professional** 1986 **Q School** 1986, 1990 **Other Achievements** 1985 U.S. Amateur Champion. Winner 1981 Junior World title. California State Amateur. Three-time First-Team All-American. Winner 13 collegiate titles. Awarded 1985 Fred Haskins Trophy as outstanding collegiate player.
Exempt Status: Past Champion
TOUR Victories: 1--1987 Bank of Boston Classic.
Money and Position:

1987--$180,378 -- 58	1990 -- $ 27,529 -- 198	1993-- $ 4,460 --275
1988--$117,132 -- 97	1991 -- $ 68,668 -- 154	1994-- $ 3,513 --290
1989--$ 35,561 -- 178	1992 -- $ 49,085 -- 176	

1994 Best Finish: T39--New England Classic
1994 Summary: Tournaments entered--3; in money--1; top ten finishes--0.
Career Earnings: $486,327

RASSETT, Joey Birth Date 7/5/58 **Birthplace** Turlock, CA **Residence** Plantation, FL **Height** 6-0 **Weight** 190 **Special Interests** Automobiles, golf history, hunting **Family** Wife, Susan; Lauren, J.D. **Q School** 1983, 1984, 1988, 1993 **College** Oral Roberts University **Turned Professional** 1981 **Other Achievements** Low amateur 1981 U.S. Open. Four-time NCAA All-American. Member 1981 Walker Cup team. Broke lateral joints in spine in 1986 car accident, spent eight months in traction. Reinjured back at 1987 Qualifying tounament. Took 3 1/2-year break from golf beginning in 1988. Played 15 Ben Hogan Tour events in 1991, eight in 1992.
Exempt Status: 15th at 1993 Qualifying Tournament
Best Ever Finish: T16—1988 Provident Classic
Money and Position:

1983--$30,792 -- 129	1985--$ 3,450 -- 213	1988 -- $27,554 --182
1984--$11,220 -- 176	1987--$ 2,315 -- 257	

1993 Summary: Tournaments entered--1; in money--0; top ten finishes--0
Career Money: $75,331

RENNER, Jack Birth Date 7/6/56 **Birthplace** Palm Springs, CA **Residence** San Diego, CA **Height** 6-0 **Weight** 150 **College** College of the Desert **Special Interests** Reading, all sports **Family** Wife, Lisa; Jill Marie (6/10/90) **Turned Professional** 1976 **Q School** Spring 1977 **Other Achievements** Winner 1972 World Junior, 1973 U.S Junior.
Exempt Status: Past Champion **Playoff Record:** 1-0
TOUR Victories: 3-1979-Manufacturers Hanover Westchester Classic, 1981-Pleasant Valley-Jimmy Fund Classic, 1984-Hawaiian Open
Money and Position:

1977 -- $ 12,837 -- 128	1982 -- $ 95,589 -- 41	1988 -- $ 82,046 -- 128
1978 -- $ 73,996 -- 33	1983 -- $133,290 -- 41	1989 -- $ --0--
1979 -- $182,808 -- 14	1984 -- $260,153 -- 19	1990 -- $ 7,451 -- 241
1980 -- $ 97,501 -- 45	1985 -- $202,761 -- 26	1991 -- $ 13,612 -- 222
1981 -- $193,292 -- 11	1986 -- $ 84,028 -- 100	1992 -- $ 13,511 -- 225
	1987 -- $ 92,289 -- 102	1993 -- $ -- 0 --
		1994 -- $ 2,819-- 297

1994 Best Finish: T50--United Airlines Hawaiian Open
1994 Summary: Tournaments entered--4; in money--1; top ten finishes--0
Career Earnings: $1,547,984

REESE, Don Birth Date 12/7/53 **Birthplace** O'Conta Falls, WI **Residence** Freeport, FL **Height** 6-0 **Weight** 190 **Special Interests** Hockey, fishing **College** Troy State University **Family** Single **Turned Professional** 1979 **Q School** 1988, 1993 **Other Achievements** Winner 1985 National PGA Match Play Championship; 1985, 1986 Metropolitan PGA Champion. 1976-77 NCAA All-American. All-Gulf South Conference 1976 and 1977. Winner 1991 Ben Hogan Lake City Classic.

Exempt Status: 13th at 1994 Qualifying Tournament
Best-Ever Finish: T5--1989 Hawaiian Open
Money and Position:

1982--$ 4,804--204	1990--$ 6,926--242	1994--$19,760--226
1989--$65,838--155		

Best 1994 Finish: T19--Buick Southern Open
1994 Summary: Tournaments entered--17; in money--5; top ten finishes--0
Career Earnings: $92,329

RINKER, Larry Birth Date 7/20/57 **Birthplace** Stuart, FL **Residence** Winter Park, FL **Weight** 145 **Height** 5-9 **Special Interests** Guitar, jazz, tennis, cooking **Family** Wife, Jan; Devon Lyle (11/15/88), Trevor William (2/12/91), Morgan Elizabeth (6/4/92) **Turned Professional** 1979 **Q School** 1979 **Other Achievements** Won 1985 JCPenney/Mixed Team Classic with sister Laurie, member of LPGA Tour. Brother Lee qualified for PGA TOUR in 1995. Leading money winner on 1980 Space Coast mini-tour and named Player of the Year by Florida Golf Week Magazine the same year. Won 1978 Southeastern Conference Championship. Largest paycheck $61,200 for third at 1985 Tournament Players Championship.

Exempt Status: Veteran Member
Best-Ever Finish: 2--1984 USF&G Classic; T2--1985 Bing Crosby Pro-Am.
Money and Position:

1981--$ 2,729--211	1986--$ 80,635--106	1991--$115,956--127
1982--$ 26,993--132	1987--$ 72,173--123	1992--$163,954-- 94
1983--$ 31,394--128	1988--$125,471-- 95	1993--$130,613--118
1984--$116,494-- 60	1989--$109,305--117	1994--$ 47,435--192
1985--$195,390-- 30	1990--$132,442--117	

Best 1994 Finish: T18--Phoenix Open
1994 Summary: Tournaments entered--28; in money--10; top ten finishes--0
Career Money: $1,350,535

RINKER, Lee Birth Date 11/10/60 **Birthplace** Stuart, FL **Residence** Beavercreek, OH **Height** 6-0 **Weight** 185 **Special Interests** Music, sports **Family** Wife, Molly **College** Alabama **Turned Professional** 1983 **Q School** 1994 **Other Achievements** Finished 12th in money on 1994 NIKE TOUR. Brother Larry is PGA TOUR veteran, while sister Laurie Rinker-Graham has several LPGA victories.

Exempt Status: 18th at 1994 Qualifying Tournament
Best-Ever Finish: T31--1984 Miller High Life Quad Cities Open
Money and Position: 1984--$6,002--196 1985--$3,197--216
Career Money: $9,199

ROMERO, Eduardo Birth Date 7/19/54 **Birthplace** Cordoba, Argentina **Residence** Cordoba, Argentina **Height** 6-2 **Weight** 185 **Special Interests** Parachuting, hunting **Family** Wife, Adriana; Dolly (7/26/81) **Turned Professional** 1980 **Q School** 1985,1994 **Other Achievements** Won numerous events on South American Tour, including 14 in 1985. Winner 1989 Lancome Trophy, Volvo Open de Firenze. Winner 1983, 1984 Argentine PGA Championship, 1984, 1986 Chile Open, 1989 Argentine Open, 1994 Canon European Masters.

Exempt Status: 2nd at 1994 Qualifying Tournament
Best-Ever Finish: T2--1990 International
Money and Position:

1986--$21,749--172	1991--$ 6,179--249
1990--$74,667--152	1992--$18,500--219

Career Earnings: $21,749

ROSBURG, Bob Birth Date 10/21/26 **Birthplace** San Francisco, CA **Residence** Rancho Mirage, CA **Height** 5-11 **Weight** 185 **College** Stanford University (1948) **Special Interest** All sports **Family** Wife, Eleanor; three children **Turned Professional** 1953 **Joined TOUR** 1953 **Other Achievements** 1958 Vardon Trophy winner. Member 1959 Ryder Cup team. Tournament Policy Board Player Director 1972-73. Color commentator ABC golf telecasts.

Exempt Status: Winner, 1959 PGA Championship
TOUR Victories: 7-- 1954 Brawley Open, Miami Open. 1956 Motor City Open, San Diego Open. 1959 PGA Championship. 1961 Bing Crosby Pro-Am. 1972 Bob Hope Desert Classic.
Career Earnings: $436,466

ROSE, Clarence   Birth Date 12/8/57 **Birthplace** Goldsboro, NC **Residence** Goldsboro, NC **Height** 5-8 **Weight** 175 **College** Clemson University **Special Interests** All sports, video games **Family** Wife, Jan; Clark (2/20/89) **Turned Professional** 1981 **Q School** Spring 1981 **Other Achievements** Winner, 1979 North Carolina Amateur. Quarterfinalist 1986 U.S. Amateur. All-American 1980.
Exempt Status: Veteran Member   **Playoff Record:** 0-1
Best-Ever Finish: 2-- 1985 Southern Open; 1986 Los Angeles Open; 1987 Greater Greensboro Open; 1988 GTE Byron Nelson Classic; 1989 The International; T2 -- 1986 Honda Classic.

Money and Position:

1981 -- $	965 -- 233	1986 -- $ 189,387 -- 44		1991 -- $ 9,564 -- 228
1982 -- $	41,075 -- 100	1987 -- $ 173,154 -- 59		1992 -- $10,488 -- 240
1983 -- $	45,271 -- 109	1988 -- $ 228,976 -- 48		1993 -- $ 6,823 -- 251
1984 -- $	62,278 -- 92	1989 -- $ 267,141 -- 49		1994 -- $ 2,992 -- 295
1985 -- $ 133,610 -- 63		1990 -- $ 25,908 -- 202		

1994 Best Finish: T46--Anheuser-Busch Golf Classic
1994 Summary: Tournaments entered--4; in money--1; top ten finishes--0.
Career Earnings: $1,197,633

RUMMELLS, Dave Birth Date 1/26/58 **Birthplace** Cedar Rapids, IA **Residence** West Branch, IA **Height** 6-0 **Weight** 150 **Special Interests** Fishing, bowling, basketball **Family** Wife, Ira; Melissa (12/23/89), Eric (7/1/90) **College** Iowa **Turned Professional** 1981 **Q School** Fall 1985, 1990, 1992 **Other Achievements** Earned $108,000 for second at 1993 Buick Invitational of California, largest paycheck of career. Has carded four 61s in PGA TOUR events. Introduced to golf at age of five by his father.
Exempt Status: 138th on 1994 money list
Best Ever Finish: 2--1993 Buick Invitational of California

Money and Position:

1986--$ 83,227--103	1990--$ 111,539--131	1993--$247,963-- 67
1987--$154,720-- 67	1991--$ 213,627-- 79	1994--$122,872--138
1988--$274,800-- 38	1992--$ 95,203--134	
1989--$419,979-- 24		

Best 1994 Finish: T13--BellSouth Classic
1994 Summary: Tournaments entered--31; in money--21; top ten finishes--0
Career Earnings: $1,723,929

RYMER, Charlie Birth Date 12/18/67 **Birthplace** Cleveland, TN **Residence** Atlanta, GA **Height** 6-4 **Weight** 240 **Special Interests** Fly-fishing, reading, eating **Family** Wife, Carol **College** Georgia Tech **Turned Professional** 1991 **Q School** 1994 **Other Achievements** Won 1994 NIKE South Carolina Classic en route to finishing 21st in money with $75,658. 1985 U.S. Junior Champion
Exempt Status: 12th at 1994 Qualifying Tournament

S

SANDER, Bill   Birth Date 4/16/56 **Birthplace** Seattle,WA **Residence** Tallahassee, FL **Height** 6-2 **Weight** 185 **Special Interests** Fishing, guitar **Family** Wife, Lisa **Turned Professional** 1977 **Q School** Fall 1977, 1984. **Other Achievements** Winner 1976 United States Amateur. Three-time winner Seattle City Amateur.
Exempt Status: Veteran Member
Best-Ever Finish: 2--1991 Shearson Lehman Brothers Open

Money and Position:

1978 -- $ 3,167 -- 183	1983 -- $ 9,416 -- 181	1988 -- $104,324 -- 109
1979 -- $ 9,826 -- 154	1984 -- $ 36,357 -- 131	1989 -- $105,083 -- 122
1980 -- $ 13,644 -- 144	1985 -- $ 54,707 -- 115	1990 -- $172,886 -- 93
1981 -- $ 11,034 -- 165	1986 -- $ 38,564 -- 151	1991 -- $139,444 -- 110
1982 -- $ 7,993 -- 179	1987 -- $ 95,921 -- 101	1992 -- $ 23,248 -- 205
		1993 -- $ 582 -- 336

Career Earnings: $823,428

SCHULZ, Ted Birth Date 10/29/59 **Birthplace** Louisville, KY; plays out of Lake Forest CC **Residence** Louisville, KY **Height** 6-2 **Weight** 190 **Special Interests** All sports, Bible study **Family** Wife, Diane; Samuel Tucker (11/10/91) **College** Louisville **Turned Professional** 1984 **Q School** Fall 1986, 1988 **Other Achievements** Fired 12-under-par 272 to claim one-stroke win over Jeff Sluman in 1991 Nissan Los Angeles Open. Two-time victor in 1989, in Southern Open and in Chrysler Team Championship with David Ogrin. Played Asian Tour after losing card in 1988. Won 1983 Kentucky State Amateur, 1984 and '88 Kentucky State Open.
Exempt Status: Past Champion
TOUR Victories: 2--1989 Southern Open. 1991 Nissan Los Angeles Open

Money and Position:	1987--$ 17,838--190	1991--$508,058--29	1993--$164,260--100
	1989--$391,855-- 30	1992--$259,204--60	1994--$ 37,537--202
	1990--$193,126-- 82		

Best 1994 Finish: T20--Northern Telecom Open
1994 Summary: Tournaments entered--30; in money--8; top ten finishes--0
Career Money: $1,571,878

SIECKMANN, Tom Birth Date 1/14/55 **Birthplace** York, NE **Residence** Omaha, NE **Height** 6-5 **Weight** 210 **Special Interests** Tennis, basketball, reading **Family** Wife, Debbie; Lauren Elizabeth (2/2/94) **College** Oklahoma State **Turned Professional** 1977 **Q School** Fall 1984, 1985, 1987 **Other Achievements** Won 1988 Anheuser-Busch Golf Classic in playoff with Mark Wiebe. Winner 1981 Philippines, Thailand and Brazilian Opens, 1982 Rolex Open (Switzerland), 1984 Singapore Open. Medalist 1985 Qualifying Tournament. Started college at Nebraska before transferring to Oklahoma State, where teammates included Bob Tway and Willie Wood.
Exempt Status: Past Champion
TOUR Victories: 1--1988 Anheuser-Busch Classic

Money and Position:	1985--$ 30,052--143	1989--$ 97,465--128	1992--$173,424-- 88
	1986--$ 63,395--125	1990--$141,241--110	1993--$201,429-- 87
	1987--$ 52,259--146	1991--$278,598-- 61	1994--$ 55,304--184
	1988--$209,151-- 54		

Best 1994 Finish: T13--Greater Milwaukee Open
1994 Summary: Tournaments entered--29; in money--10; top ten finishes--0
Career Money: $1,302,657

SILLS, Tony Birth Date 12/5/55 **Birthplace** Los Angeles, CA **Residence** Bermuda Dunes, CA **Height** 5-10 **Weight** 165 **Special Interests** Running, weights, martial arts **Family** Single **College** University of Southern California **Turned Professional** 1980 **Q School** Fall 1982, 1994 **Other Achievements** Winner 1971 Los Angeles City Junior title, 1976 Southern California Amateur, 1981 Queen Mary Open, 1982 Coors (Kansas) Open.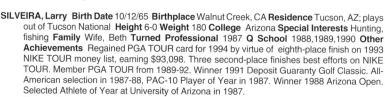
Exempt Status: 36th at 1994 Qualifying Tournament   **Playoff Record**: 1-0
TOUR Victories: 1--1990 Independent Insurance Agent Open

Money and Position:	1983--$ 47,488 --104	1987--$ 107,508 -- 92	1991--$ 13,914 -- 223
	1984--$ 90,055 -- 72	1988--$ 76,689 --132	1992--$ 10,574 -- 238
	1985--$114,895 -- 66	1989--$ 77,181 --143	1993--$ 11,686 -- 233
	1986--$216,881 -- 38	1990--$ 243,350 -- 61	1994--$ 22,807-- 219

1994 Best Finish: T42--Federal Express St. Jude Classic
1994 Summary: Tournaments entered—9; in money—6; top ten finishes—0.
Career Earnings: $1,042,966

SILVEIRA, Larry Birth Date 10/12/65 **Birthplace** Walnut Creek, CA **Residence** Tucson, AZ; plays out of Tucson National **Height** 6-0 **Weight** 180 **College** Arizona **Special Interests** Hunting, fishing **Family** Wife, Beth **Turned Professional** 1987 **Q School** 1988,1989,1990 **Other Achievements** Regained PGA TOUR card for 1994 by virtue of eighth-place finish on 1993 NIKE TOUR money list, earning $93,098. Three second-place finishes best efforts on NIKE TOUR. Member PGA TOUR from 1989-92. Winner 1991 Deposit Guaranty Golf Classic. All-American selection in 1987-88, PAC-10 Player of Year in 1987. Winner 1988 Arizona Open. Selected Athlete of Year at University of Arizona in 1987.
Exempt Status: 155 on 1994 money list

Money and Position:	1989--$ 60,712 --156	1990--$65,696--166	1992--$66,697--159
		1991--$93,893--138	1994--$99,671--155

1994 Best Finish: T8--Motorola Western Open
1994 Summary: Tournaments entered—28; in money—12; top ten finishes—1
Career Earnings: $386,668

SIMPSON, Tim Birth Date 5/6/56 **Birthplace** Atlanta, GA **Residence** Cummings, GA **Height** 5-10 **Weight** 195 **Special Interests** Bow hunting, fishing, Harley Davidsons **Family** Wife, Kathy; Christopher (1/5/84), Katie (9/24/86) **College** University of Georgia **Turned Professional** 1977 **Q School** Spring 1977 **Other Achievements** Winner 1976 Southern Amateur; All-Southeastern Conference and All-American. Winner Georgia and Atlanta Junior Titles; 1981 World Under-25 Championship. Continuing effort to come back from Lyme Disease.
Exempt Status: Special Medical Extension **Playoff Record:** 0-2
TOUR Victories: 4-1985 Southern Open. 1989 USF&G Classic, Walt Disney World/Oldsmobile Classic. 1990 Walt Disney World/Oldsmobile Classic.

Money and Position:

1977 -- $ 2,778 -- 193	1983 -- $ 96,419 -- 59	1989 -- $761,597 -- 6
1978 -- $38,714 -- 78	1984 -- $157,082 -- 41	1990 -- $809,772 -- 8
1979 -- $36,223 -- 106	1985 -- $164,702 -- 44	1991 -- $196,582 -- 85
1980 -- $27,172 -- 112	1986 -- $240,911 -- 31	1992 -- $ 85,314 --144
1981 -- $63,063 -- 70	1987 -- $168,261 -- 62	1993 -- $111,435 --134
1982 -- $62,153 -- 72	1988 -- $200,748 -- 56	1994-- $126,861 --134

1994 Best Finish: T10--Kemper Open
1994 Summary: Tournaments entered--31: in money--16; top ten finishes--1
Career Earnings: $3,348,787

SINDELAR, Joey Birth Date 3/30/58 **Birthplace** Ft. Knox, KY **Residence** Horseheads, NY **Height** 5-10 **Weight** 200 **Special Interests** Fishing, electronics **Family** Wife, Suzanne Lee; Jamison Prescott (2/2/90), Ryan Joseph (5/13/93) **College** Ohio State University **Turned Professional** 1981 **Q School** Fall 1983 **Other Achievements** Member 1988 Kirin Cup and 1990 World Cup teams. Winner 1972 and 1980 New York State Junior. Three-time All-American who claimed 10 collegiate titles. Named 1981 Ohio State Athlete of the Year. Member 1979 NCAA Championship team. 1992 inductee into Ohio State University Athletic Hall of Fame. Withdrew from 1993 PGA Championship with wrist injury which caused him to miss remainder of 1993 season. Underwent Feb. 1994 surgery for removal of hook of hamate bone.
Exempt Status: Special Medical Extension/Past Champion
TOUR Victories: 6--1985 Greater Greensboro Open, B.C. Open. 1987 B.C. Open. 1988 Honda Classic, The International. 1990 Hardee's Golf Classic

Money and Position:

1984--$116,528--59	1989--$196,092--72	1993--$391,649-- 38
1985--$282,762--12	1990--$307,207--46	1994--$114,563--145
1986--$341,231--14	1991--$168,352--94	
1987--$235,033--40	1992--$396,354--35	
1988--$813,732-- 3		

Best 1994 Finish: T3--Greater Milwaukee Open
1994 Summary: Tournaments entered--22; in money--12; top ten finishes--1
Career Money: $3,362,503

SMITH, Mike Birth Date 8/25/50 **Birthplace** Selma, AL **Residence** Titusville, FL **Height** 5-11 **Weight** 175 **Special Interests** Family, hunting, fishing **Family** Wife, Monica; Christopher Michael (6/22/87), Payton (7/5/94) **College** Brevard Junior College **Turned Professional** 1973 **Q School** Spring 1973, Fall 1981, 1983, 1989 **Other Achievements** Winner 1968 Dixie Junior, 1971 National Junior College Tournament.
Exempt Status: 38th at 1994 Qualifying Tournament
Best Ever Finish: 2—1985 Panasonic Invitational

Money and Position:

1980 -- $ 508 --246	1985 -- $158,918 -- 47	1991 -- $149,613 --101
1981 -- $ 19,682 --134	1986 -- $ 19,159 --179	1992 -- $178,964 -- 84
1982 -- $ 13,749 --161	1990 -- $170,034 -- 94	1993 -- $107,375 --137
1984 -- $ 42,045 --116		1994 -- $ 57,850 --183

1994 Best Finish: T8--Kmart GGO
1994 Summary: Tournaments entered--15; in money--5; top ten finishes--12
Career Earnings: $951,531

SNEED, Ed Birth Date 8/6/44 **BirthPlace** Roanoke, VA **Residence** Columbus, OH **Height** 6-2 **Weight** 185 **College** Ohio State University (1967 Marketing) **Special Interests** Bridge, running, reading **Family** Wife, Nancy Kay; Mary Elisa (8/16/74), Erica Kathryn (4/21/77) **Turned Professional** 1967 **Joined TOUR** Fall 1968 **Other Achievements** Winner 1973 New South Wales Open; member 1977 Ryder Cup team; Player Director on Tournament Policy Board, 1977-78 and 1981-82. Winner 1980 Morocco Grand Prix; 1965 Ohio Intercollegiate.
Exempt Status: Past Champion
TOUR Victories: 4-1973 Kaiser International Open; 1974 Greater Milwaukee Open; 1977 Tallahassee Open; 1982 Michelob-Houston Open
Money Summary: Joined TOUR in 1969, winning $4,254 for 170th place. Best year 1982, when won $148,170 for 23rd on money list. Prior to $7,583 earned in 1994, last won money in 1986.
1994 Best Finish: T20--Deposit Guaranty Classic
1994 Summary: Tournaments entered--3; in money--1; top ten finishes--0
Career Money: $853,287

STEWART, Ray Birth Date 12/13/53 **Birthplace** Mission, BC, Canada **Residence** Abbotsford, BC, Canada **Height** 6-0 **Weight** 175 **Special Interest** Life **Family** Wife, Maureen; Brett (11/18/88), Tyler (8/31/93) **College** University of British Columbia **Turned Professional** 1980 **Q School** 1991, 1994 **Other Achievements** Winner 1985 B.C. PGA Championship, 1985 Western North Dakota Open, Cedar Hill Open. Member of victorious 1994 Canadian Dunhill Cup team.
Exempt Status: 29th at Qualifying Tournament
Best Ever Finish: T2--1987 Bank of Boston Classic; T2--1989 Chattanooga Classic

Money and Position:

1983--$ 7,577--192	1989--$133,944--106	1992--$7,151--251
1987--$72,136--124	1990--$139,536--111	1993--$2,670--293
1988--$45,106--153	1991--$ 80,495--147	

Career Money: $488,615

STRECK, Ron Birth Date 6/17/54 **Birthplace** Tulsa, OK **Residence** Tulsa, OK **Height** 6-0 **Weight** 165 **College** Tulsa **Special Interests** Skiing, basketball **Turned Professional** 1976 **Q School** Fall 1976 **Other Achievements** Two-time winner Missouri Valley Conference title. Winner1993 NIKE Yuma Open. Finished 21st on 1993 NIKE TOUR money list with $65,718. Shares PGA TOUR record for low consecutive rounds, 125 (63-62 in final two rounds of 1978 Texas Open).
Exempt Status: Past Champion   **Playoff Record**: 0-1
TOUR Victories: 2--1978 San Antonio-Texas Open; 1981 Michelob-Houston Open

Money and Position:			
1977 -- $ 11,014 --143	1983 -- $ 68,950 -- 77	1989 -- $ 50,444 -- 164
1978 -- $ 46,933 -- 68	1984 -- $ 82,235 -- 81	1990 -- $ 10,356 -- 229
1979 -- $ 39,484 -- 99	1985 -- $142,848 -- 55	1991 -- $ 13,914 -- 221
1980 -- $ 51,728 -- 73	1986 -- $ 21,605 -- 172	1992 -- $ 9,917 -- 244
1981 -- $114,895 -- 29	1987 -- $ 62,289 -- 133	1993 $ 885 -- 328
1982 -- $ 67,962 -- 60	1988 -- $ 31,094 -- 170	1994-- $ 2,189 -- 312

1994 Best Finish: T68--Anheuser-Busch Glof Classic
1994 Summary: Tournaments entered--4; in money--1; top ten finishes--0.
Career Earnings: $817,211

T

TAYLOR, Harry   Birth Date 11/03/54 **Birthplace** Detroit, MI **Residence** Old Hickory, TN **Height** 5-9 **Weight** 170 **Special Interests** Golf club design, classic cars. **Family** Wife, Saundra; Zachary (9/1/83), Brooke (12/19/87) **College** Tennessee (1979, Political Science) **Turned Professional** 1977 **Q School** 1980, 1985, 1986, 1987, 1989, 1992.
Exempt Status: 5th at 1994 Qualifying Tournament
Best-Ever Finish: T5--1990 Chattanooga Classic

Money and Position:			
1986 -- $ 27,017 --166	1988 -- $ 34,132 -- 167	1990 -- $ 45,647 -- 180
1987 -- $ 54,843 --145	1989 -- $ 6,081 -- 229	1993 -- $105,845 -- 140
		1994 -- $ 15,482 -- 236

1994 Best Finish: T19-- Buick Southern Open
1994 Summary: Tournaments entered-—11; in money--4; top ten finishes--0.
Career Earnings: $293,596

TEN BROECK, Lance Birth Date 3/21/56 **Birthplace** Chicago, IL **Residence** Jupiter, FL; plays out of Ballen Isles CC **Height** 6-3 **Weight** 195 **Special Interest** All sports **Family** Wife, Linda; Jonathan (3/13/86) **College** University of Texas **Turned Professional** 1977 **Other Achievements** Winner 1984 Magnolia Classic.
Exempt Status: Veteran Member
Best Ever Finish: 2--1991 Chattanooga Classic

Money and Position:			
1980 -- $ 10,230 --162	1984 -- $ 40,185 -- 123	1988 -- $ 65,987 --138
1981 -- $ 4,464	1985 -- $ 23,591 -- 153	1989 -- $146,568 -- 96
1982 -- $ 25,049 --135	1986 -- $ 18,165 -- 181	1990 -- $ 72,896 --155
1983 -- $ 19,450 --152	1987 -- $ 1,920 -- 266	1993 -- $ 88,262 --151
		1994 -- $ 10,843 --250

1994 Best Finish: T50--Deposit Guaranty Golf Classic
1994 Summary: Tournaments entered—11; in money—5; top ten finishes—0.
Career Earnings: $742,428

THOMPSON, Dicky Birth Date 6/13/57 **Birthplace** Atlanta, GA **Residence** Peachtree City, GA **Height** 5-8 **Weight** 155 **Special Interests** Fishing, reading, computers **Family** Single **College** Georgia **Turned Professional** 1980 **Q School** 1991, 1992, 1994 **Other Achievements** Winner 1990 Ben Hogan Baton Rouge Open and 1990 Ben Hogan Elizabethtown Open. Posted two wins on 1994 Hooters Tour.
Exempt Status: 25th at 1994 Qualifying Tournament
Best-Ever Finish: T9--1991 Las Vegas Invitational
Money and Position: 1991--$86,480--144   1992--$47,770--178
Career Money: $134,250

THOMPSON, Leonard   Birth Date 1/1/47 **Birthplace** Laurinburg, NC **Residence** Myrtle Beach, SC **Height** 6-2 **Weight** 200 **Special Interest** Fishing **Family** Wife, Lesley; Martha (6/7/67), Stephen (4/6/74). **College** Wake Forest **Turned Professional** 1970 **Q School** Fall 1971. **Other Achievements** Winner 1975 Carolinas Open.
Exempt Status: Past Champion
TOUR Victories: 3--1974 Jackie Gleason-Inverrary Classic. 1977 Pensacola Open. 1989 Buick Open.

Money and Position:			
1971 -- $ 6,556 --153	1979 -- $ 90,465 -- 41	1987 -- $ 52,326 -- 147
1972 -- $ 39,882 -- 63	1980 -- $138,826 -- 25	1988 -- $ 84,659 -- 123
1973 -- $ 91,158 -- 15	1981 -- $ 95,517 -- 40	1989 -- $261,397 -- 52
1974 -- $122,349 -- 15	1982 -- $ 60,998 -- 73	1990 -- $ 78,017 -- 148
1975 -- $ 48,748 -- 48	1983 -- $ 76,326 -- 69	1991 -- $114,275 -- 128
1976 -- $ 26,566 -- 83	1984 -- $ 36,920 -- 126	1992 -- $ 30,540 -- 196
1977 -- $107,293 -- 23	1985 -- $ 48,395 -- 122	1993 -- $ 15,152 -- 228
1978 -- $ 52,231 -- 63	1986 -- $ 83,420 -- 102	1994 -- $ 32,992-- 207

1994 Best Finish: T30--Deposit Guaranty Golf Classic
1994 Summary: Tournaments entered--11; in money--7; top ten finishes--0.
Career Earnings: $1,782,683

TOLLES, Tommy Birth Date 10/21/66 **Birthplace** Ft, Myers, FL **Residence** Flat Rock, NC **Height** 6-1 **Weight** 190 **Special Interest** Fishing **Family** Wife, Ilse; Wiekus (3/27/93) **College** Georgia **Turned Professional** 1988 **Q School** 1994 **Other Achievements** Winner 1993 NIKE Ozarks Open and 1994 NIKE Alabama Classic. Four-year NIKE TOUR veteran who had best year in '94 when he finished 16th in money with $98,618. Played in '88 and '91 U.S. Opens.
Exempt Status: 24th at 1994 Qualifying Tournament

TWIGGS, Greg Birth Date 10/31/60 **Birthplace** Los Angeles, CA **Residence** Greensboro, NC **Height** 6-2 **Weight** 225 **Special Interest** Peace of mind **Family** Wife, Teresa; Amber Alexander (10/16/87), Tianna (7/20/90) **College** San Diego State **Turned Professional** 1984 **Q School** Fall 1984, 1986, 1988 **Other Achievements** Lone TOUR victory came in 1989 Shearson Lehman Hutton Open on Torrey Pines GC, a course near home which he had played often. 62 in 1984 Provident Classic lowest score in history of old Tournament Players Series. Lists outstanding achievement in golf as learning to enjoy the game.
Exempt Status: Past Champion
TOUR Victories: 1--1989 Shearson Lehman Hutton Open

Money and Position:

1985--$33,559--139	1989--$154,302-- 90	1992--$ 74,761--153
1986--$41,418--147	1990--$ 49,696--178	1993--$231,823-- 72
1987--$21,443--186	1991--$ 65,080--158	1994--$ 13,676--240
1988--$ 2,999--262		

Best 1994 Finish: T27--Freeport-McMoRan Classic
Best 1994 Summary: Tournaments entered--29; in money--2; top ten finishes--0
Career Money: $685,759

TYNER, Tray Birth Date 9/29/64 **Birthplace** Anchorage, AK **Residence** Humble, TX **Height** 5-10 **Weight** 175 **Special Interests** Hunting, movies, music **Family** Wife, Carrie; Derek (4/1/93) **College** Houston **Turned Professional** 1987 **Q School** 1991, 1994 **Other Achievements** Winner 1988 Malaysian Open and 1989 Texas State Open. Played NIKE TOUR in 1990, '93, and '94.
Exempt Status: 3rd at 1994 Qualifying Tournament
Money and Position: 1992--$44,153--182   1994--$7,193--263
Best 1994 Finish: T32--Shell Houston Open
1994 Summary: Tournaments entered--1; in money--1; top ten finishes--0
Career Money: $51,346

U

URESTI, Omar Birth Date 8/3/68 **Birthplace** Austin, TX **Residence** Austin, TX **Height** 5-6 **Weight** 175 **Special Interests** Billiards, ping pong, going to movies, Stephen King books **Family** Single **College** Texas **Turned Professional** 1991 **Q School** 1994 **Other Achievements** Won 1994 NIKE Shreveport Open en route to finishing 30th on money list for '94 NIKE TOUR campaign. Winner 1994 Hooland Insurance Royal Swiss Sun Classic. 1985 Boys Texas State Junior State champion age 15-17. Biggest thrills in golf nine conscutive birdies during the '94 NIKE Shreveport Open and making hole-in-one at age eight.
Exempt Status: 14th at 1994 Qualifying Tournament

UTLEY, Stan Birth Date 1/16/62 **Birthplace** Thayer, MO; plays out of CC of Missouri **Residence** Columbia, MO **Height** 6-0 **Weight** 175 **Special Interests** Church, basketball, hunting, fishing **Family** Wife, Elayna **College** Missouri **Turned Professional** 1984 **Q School** Fall 1988 **Other Achievements** Won 1993 NIKE Cleveland Open en route to finishing second on NIKE TOUR money list. Three-time All-Big Eight selection and twice All-American. Won 1986 Kansas Open, 1988 & '89 Missouri Opens, 1980 Missouri Junior Championship. His annual "Go For The Gold" Skins Game in Columbia has been benefitting Rainbow House, safe house for children, since 1991.
Exempt Status: Past Champion
TOUR Victories: 1--1988 Chattanooga Classic
Money and Position:

1989--$107,400--118	1991--$127,849--115	1993--$17,371--223
1990--$143,604--108	1992--$ 14,964--222	1994--$63,345--179

Best 1994 Finish: T8--Deposit Guaranty Golf Classic
1994 Summary: Tournaments entered--29; in money--9; top ten finishes--1
Career Money: $474,532

V

VAUGHAN, Bruce Birth Date 9/10/56 **Birthplace** Kankakee, IL **Residence** Hutchinson, KS **Height** 6-3 **Weight** 200 **Special Interests** Hunting, fishing **Family** Wife, Karla **Turned Professional** 1982 **Joined TOUR** 1995 **Other Achievements** Claimed 1994 NIKE Pensacola Open and '94 Permian Basin Open en route to finishing sixth on money list with $129,617. Took up golf at age 20 while he was a fireman. Played in South Africa for six years.
Exempt Status: 6th on 1994 NIKE Tour money list

VENTURI, Ken **Birth Date** 5/15/31 **Birthplace** San Francisco, CA **Residence** Naples, FL **Height** 6-0 **Weight** 175 **College** San Jose State University (1953) **Special Interests** Hunting, fishing, cars. **Family** Wife, Beau; two children. **Turned Professional** 1956 **Joined TOUR** 1957 **Other Achievements** 1964 PGA Player of the Year. 1965 Ryder Cup team member. Color commentator for CBS golf telecasts.
Exempt Status: 1964 U.S. Open winner
TOUR Victories: 14--1957 St. Paul Open, Miller Open; 1958 Thunderbird Invitational, Phoenix Open, Baton Rouge Open, Gleneagles Chicago Open; 1959 Gleneagles Chicago Open, Los Angeles Open; 1960 Bing Crosby Pro-Am, Milwaukee Open; 1964 U.S. Open, Insurance City Open, American Golf Classic; 1966 Lucky International.
Money Summary: Started in 1957 and won $18,781 for 10th place. Best year 1964 with $62,465 for 6th place. Last year won money was 1975.
Career Earnings: $268,293

W

WADSWORTH, Fred **Birth Date** 7/17/62 **Birthplace** Munich, Germany **Residence** Columbus, GA **Height** 6-3 **Weight** 170 **College** University of South Carolina **Special Interests** All sports, fishing **Family** Wife, Juli **Turned Professional** 1984 **Other Achievements** 1984 Eastern Amateur champion. 1984 All-American at South Carolina. Three mini-tour wins. South African Open champion.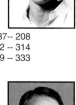
Exempt Status: Past Champion
TOUR Victories: 1 --1986 Southern Open

Money and Position:		
1980--$ 24,129--190	1987--$ 80,585--109	1989--$ 10,587-- 208
1986--$ 75,092--115	1988--$ 24,129--190	1991--$ 1,292 -- 314
		1993--$ 609 -- 333

Career Earnings: $192,977

WATSON, Denis **Birth Date** 10/18/55 **Birthplace** Salisbury, Rhodesia (Zimbabwe) **Residence** Orlando, FL **Height** 6-0 **Weight** 170 **Special Interests** Golf course design, fishing, farming **Family** Wife, Hilary; Kyle (9/23/86), Paige (4/23/89), Ross (7/31/91) **College** Rhodesia (English System) **Turned Professional** 1976 **Q School** 1981 **Other Achievements** Named Rhodesian Sportsman of Year in 1975. Won 1975 World Team title with George Harvey and twice represented South Africa in World Series of Golf (1980 and 1982). Finished T2 in 1985 U.S. Open, one shot behind Andy Bean. Received Special Medical Extension for 11 events in 1995 due to nerve problems in right arm which required surgery in 1994.
Exempt Status: Special Medical Extension
TOUR Victories: 3--1984 New England Classic, NEC World Series of Golf, Panasonic Las Vegas Invitational.

Money and Position:		
1981--$ 49,153--87	1986--$ 59,453--129	1991--$ 17,749--213
1982--$ 59,090--74	1987--$231,074-- 43	1992--$ 16,105--219
1983--$ 59,284--88	1988--$ 51,239--148	1993--$111,977--132
1984--$408,562-- 4	1989--$ 3,595--240	1994--$ 4,250--285
1985--$155,845--48	1990--$ 43,013--182	

Best 1994 Finish: 85--The Players Championship
1994 Summary: Tournaments entered--16; in money--1; top ten finishes--0
Career Money: $1,270,753

WILLIAMSON, Jay **Birth Date** 2/7/67 **Birthplace** St. Louis, MO **Residence** St. Louis, MO **Height** 5-6 **Weight** 180 **Special Interests** Hockey, baseball, politics, stock market **Family** Single **College** Trinity **Turned Professional** 1989 **Q School** 1994 **Other Achievements** Winner 1991 Kansas Open.
Exempt Status: 42nd at 1994 Qualifying Tournament

WOOD, Willie **Birth Date** 10/1/60 **Birthplace** Kingsville, TX **Residence** Edmond, OK; plays out of Desert Mountain **Height** 5-7 **Weight** 150 **Special Interests** Fishing, physical fitness **Family** William King (12/17/86), Kelly Curtis (6/15/88) **College** Oklahoma State **Turned Professional** 1983 **Q School** 1983, 1992 **Other Achievements** Posted all-time low score of 61 at 49ers Club in Tucson, when high school senior. Won 1979 Nevada State Open, 1984 Colorado State Open, 1990 Oklahoma Open. Winner of five major junior titles, including 1977 USGA Junior, 1978 PGA National Junior and 1979 Western Junior. Medalist 1983 U.S. Walker Cup team. Claimed medalist honors at 1983 TOUR Qualifying Tournament. Sister Deanie played LPGA Tour.
Exempt Status: Veteran Member

Money and Position:		
1981--$ 2,729--211	1986--$ 80,635--106	1991--$115,956-- 94
1982--$ 26,993--132	1987--$ 72,173--123	1992--$163,954-- 94
1983--$ 31,394--128	1988--$125,271-- 95	1993--$130,613--118
1984--$116,494-- 60	1989--$109,305--117	1994--$ 87,102--165
1985--$195,390-- 30	1990--$132,442--117	

Best 1994 Finish: T18--Hardee's Golf Classic
1994 Summary: Tournaments entered--26; in money--16; in money--0
Career Money: $1,062,046

WOODLAND, Jeff Birth Date 2/28/57 **Birthplace** Papua, New Guinea **Residence** Queensland, Australia **Height** 6-0 **Weight** 170 **Special Interests** Surfing, sports and wine collecting **Family** Wife, Rita; Troy (2/9/92), Adam (2/19/93) **Turned Professional** 1978 **Other Achievements** Winner 1989 Fiji Open, Harvey Bay Open, Mt. ISA Open on Australian Tour. Won 1991 Ben Hogan Dakota Dunes Open, 1992 Ben Hogan Wichita Charity Classic and 1992 Ben Hogan Utah Open. Holds NIKE TOUR record for low 18 holes with 12-under-par 60 in 1991 Dakota Dunes Open.
Exempt Status: 143 on 1994 money list
Best-Ever Finish: T10—1993 Deposit Guaranty Golf Classic
Money and Position: 1991-- $20,500--207   1993--$73,367--163   1994--$117,627--143
Best 1994 Finish: T8--GTE Byron Nelson Classic
1994 Summary: Tournaments entered--30; in money--14; top ten finishes--1
Career Earnings: $190,994

WRENN, Robert Birth Date 9/11/59 **Birthplace** Richmond, VA **Residence** Richmond, VA **Height** 5-10 **Weight** 170 **Special Interests** Reading, flying, thrill-seeking **Family** Wife, Kathy; Tucker (12/12/92), Jordan (11/9/94) **College** Wake Forest **Turned Professional** 1981 **Q School** Fall 1984, 1985, 1986 **Other Achievements** Winner 1981 Trans-Mississippi Amateur, 1983 Virginia State Open, 1983 Indonesian Open. All-Atlantic Coast Conference 1978-81.
Exempt Status: 143rd on 1993 Money list
TOUR Victories: 1--1987 Buick Open

Money and Position:		
1985--$ 36,396--135	1989--$ 243,638-- 55	1992--$127,729--113
1986--$ 22,869--171	1990--$ 174,308-- 92	1993--$103,928--143
1987--$ 203,557-- 52	1991--$ 141,255--109	1994--$ 77,279--170
1988--$ 209,404-- 52		

1994 Best Finish: T6--Hardee's Golf Classic
1994 Summary: Tournaments entered--17; in money--9; top ten finishes--1
Career Earnings: $1,340,363

WURTZ, MARK Birth Date 10/31/64 **Birthplace** Yakima, WA **Residence** Port Ludlow, WA; plays out of Port Ludlow GC **Height** 5-9 **Weight** 155 **Special Interests** Movies, sports **Family** Single **College** University of New Mexico **Turned Professional** 1986 **Q School** 1993, 1994 **Other Achievements** Winner 1991 Canadian TPC, 1992 California State Open
Exempt Status: 19th at 1994 Qualifying Tournament
Best 1994 Finish: T8--Motorola Western Open
1994 Summary: Tournaments entered--29; in money--14; top ten finishes--1
Career Money: $103,252

Z

ZOKOL, Richard Birth Date 8/21/58 **Birthplace** Kitimat, B.C., Canada **Residence** Richmond, B.C., Canada **Height** 5-9 **Weight** 170 **Special Interests** Hunting **Family** Wife, Joanie; Conor and Garrett (10/14/87), Hayley (6/25/90) **College** Brigham Young University **Turned Professional** 1981 **Q School** Fall 1981, 1982, 1986, 1989, 1991 **Other Achievements** Won 1992 Deposit Guaranty Classic. Member 1980 Canada World Amateur and 1981 Brigham Young University NCAA Championship teams. Winner 1980 International Champions (Morocco), 1981 Canadian Amateur, 1982 British Columbia Open, 1984 Utah Open.
Exempt Status: Veteran Member
TOUR Victories: 1--1992 Greater Milwaukee Open

Money and Position:		
1982--$15,110--156	1987--$114,406--89	1992--$311,909--48
1983--$38,107--117	1988--$142,153--83	1993--$214,419--80
1984--$56,605--102	1989--$51,323--163	1994--$78,074--169
1985--$71,192--152	1990--$191,634--84	
1986--$37,888--102	1991--$78,426--149	

1994 Best Finish: T19--Buick Southern; T19--Anheuser-Busch Golf Classic
1994 Summary: Tournaments entered--26; in money--14; top ten finishes--0
Career Money: $1,401,246

Prominent International Players

Peter Baker

HEIGHT: 5'9" **WEIGHT:** 170 **BIRTH DATE:** October 7, 1967
BIRTHPLACE: Shifnal, England **RESIDENCE:** Wightwick, England
FAMILY: Wife, Helen; Georgina (1992)
SPECIAL INTERESTS: Music, cars, sports, Wolves soccer
TURNED PROFESSIONAL: 1986
BEST-EVER FINISH: T39--1994 U.S. Open
MONEY & POSITION: 1994--$10,598--251
BEST 1994 FINISH: T39--U.S. Open
1994 SUMMARY: Tournaments entered--5; in money--2; top ten finishes--0.
CAREER HIGHLIGHTS: Winner, 1994 Perrier Paris Four-Ball (with David J. Russell),1993 Dunhill British Masters and Scandanavian Masters. Winner, 1990 UAP Under-25 Championship. Winner, 1988 Benson & Hedges International. Placed seventh in 1993 PGA European Tour Order of Merit.
NATIONAL TEAMS: Walker Cup, 1985; Ryder Cup, 1993. Dunhill Cup, 1993.

Seve Ballesteros

HEIGHT: 6' **WEIGHT:** 175 **BIRTH DATE:** April 9, 1957
BIRTHPLACE: Pedrena, Spain **RESIDENCE:** Pedrena, Spain
FAMILY: Wife, Carmen; Baldomero (1990), Miguel (1992)
SPECIAL INTERESTS: Cycling, fishing, hunting
TURNED PROFESSIONAL: 1974 **PLAYOFF RECORD:** 1-2
TOUR VICTORIES: 6 — **1978** Greater Greensboro Open. **1980** Masters Tournament. **1983** Masters Tournament, Manufacturers Hanover Westchester Classic. **1985** USF&G Classic. **1988** Manufacturers Hanover Westchester Classic.

MONEY & POSITION:			
1983--$ 210,933-- 18	1987--$ 305,058-- 32	1991--$ 64,320--160
1984--$ 132,660-- 52	1988--$ 165,202-- 71	1992--$ 39,206--184
1985--$ 206,638-- 26	1989--$ 138,094--101	1993--$ 34,850--193
1986--$ 45,877-- 141	1990--$ 84,584--144	1994--$ 49,245--189

BEST 1994 FINISHES: T18--Masters Tournament, T18--U.S. Open
1994 SUMMARY: Tournaments entered--5; in money--3; top ten finishes--0.
OTHER ACHIEVEMENTS: Winner of three British Opens, 1979, 1984, 1988. Winner of 60 tournaments worldwide including World Match Play, 1981, 1982, 1984, 1985; Lancome Trophy, 1976, 1983, 1986, 1988; Spanish Open, 1981, 1985; French Open, 1977, 1982, 1985, 1986; Dutch Open, 1976, 1980, 1986; Swiss Open, 1977, 1978, 1989; German Open, 1978, 1988; Irish Open, 1983, 1985, 1986; British Masters,1986, 1991; British PGA, 1983; Madrid Open, 1980, 1981, 1989; Japanese Open, 1977, 1978; Australian PGA, 1981; Dunlop Phoenix (Japan), 1977, 1981; Taiheiyo Masters (Japan), 1988; Kenya Open, 1978; Volvo PGA, 1991. Winner, 1992 Dubai Desert Classic and Turespana Open De Baleares. After not winning a tournament in 1993, he won the 1994 Benson & Hedges International and Mercedes German Masters.
NATIONAL TEAMS: European Ryder Cup (7), 1979, 1983, 1985, 1987, 1989, 1991, 1993. World Cup (4), 1975, 1976, 1977, 1992. Dunhill Cup (3), 1985, 1986, 1988.

David Gilford

HEIGHT: 5'10" **WEIGHT:** 160 **BIRTH DATE:** September 14, 1965
BIRTHPLACE: Crewe, England **RESIDENCE:** Crewe, England
BEST-EVER FINISH: T26--1992 Memorial Tournament
MONEY & POSITION: 1992--$ 8,847--249   1993--$ 5,200--272
BEST 1994 FINISH: T44--PGA Championship
1994 SUMMARY: Tournaments entered--1; in money--1; top ten finishes--0.
OTHER ACHIEVEMENTS: Winner, 1994 Turespana Open de Tenerife, 1994 European Open, 1993 Moroccan Open, 1993 Portuguese Open, 1992 Moroccan Open, 1991 English Open. Finished seventh on PGA European Tour Order of Merit in 1994, the best finish of his nine-year career. Led European Tour in Fairways Hit and Greens in Regulation in 1992.
NATIONAL TEAMS: European Ryder Cup, 1991. Dunhill Cup (2) 1992, 1994. World Cup (2) 1992, 1993. Walker Cup, 1985.

Miguel Angel Jimenez

HEIGHT: 5'9" **WEIGHT:** 165   **BIRTH DATE:** January 5, 1964
BIRTHPLACE: Malaga, Spain
RESIDENCE: Malaga, Spain **FAMILY:** Wife, Monserrat
SPECIAL INTERESTS: Cars
TURNED PROFESSIONAL: 1982
OTHER ACHIEVEMENTS: Winner, 1994 Heineken Dutch Open, 1993 PIAGET Open, 1989 Benson & Hedges Trophy (with Xonia Wunsch-Ruiz). Finished fifth on the 1994 PGA European Tour Order of Merit, the best finish of his seven-year career.
NATIONAL TEAMS: Dunhill Cup (4), 1990, 1992, 1993, 1994; World Cup (4) 1990, 1992, 1993, 1994.

Barry Lane

HEIGHT: 5'10" **WEIGHT:** 170   **BIRTH DATE:** June 21, 1960
BIRTHPLACE: Hayes, England **RESIDENCE:** Ascot, England
FAMILY: Wife, Melanie; Benjamin (1990), Emma (1992)
SPECIAL INTERESTS: Cars, chess **TURNED PROFESSIONAL:** 1976
BEST-EVER FINISH: T16-- 1993 U.S. Open
MONEY & POSITION: 1993--$24,088--206   1994--$18,105--229
BEST 1994 FINISH: T25--PGA Championship
1994 SUMMARY: Tournaments entered--4; in money--2; top ten finishes--0.
OTHER ACHIEVEMENTS: Winner of five European Tour Events: 1987 Equity & Law Challenge, 1988 Bell's Scottish Open; 1992 Mercedes German Masters; 1993 Canon European Masters;1994 Iberia Open; 5th on 1992 European Order of Merit, 10th in 1993, 11th in 1994. Winner, 1983 Jamaica Open.
NATIONAL TEAMS: European Ryder Cup, 1993. Dunhill Cup (2),1988, 1994. World Cup (2), 1988, 1994.

Bernhard Langer

HEIGHT: 5'9" **WEIGHT:** 155 **BIRTH DATE:** August 27, 1957
BIRTHPLACE: Anhausen, Germany **RESIDENCE:** Anhausen, Germany
FAMILY: Wife, Vikki; Jackie (1986), Stefan (1990), Christina (1993).
SPECIAL INTERESTS: Snow skiing, soccer, tennis, cycle riding
TURNED PROFESSIONAL: 1976   **PLAYOFF RECORD:** 1-1
TOUR VICTORIES: 3— **1985** Masters, Sea Pines Heritage Classic. **1993** Masters

MONEY & POSITION:		
1984--$ 82,465-- 75	1988--$100,635--111	1992--$ 41,211--181
1985--$271,044-- 13	1989--$195,973-- 73	1993--$ 626,938-- 23
1986--$379,800-- 10	1990--$ 35,150--187	1994--$ 118,241--142
1987--$366,430-- 23	1991--$112,539--129	

BEST 1994 FINISH: T4-- Honda Classic.
1993 SUMMARY: Tournaments entered--6; in money--6; top ten finishes--1.
OTHER ACHIEVEMENTS: Winner of over 30 international tournaments including: 1980 Dunlop Masters, Colombian Open; 1981, 1982, 1985 and 1986 German Open; 1981 Bob Hope British Classic; 1983 Italian Open; 1983 Glasgow Classic; TPC at St. Mellion; 1983 Johnny Walker Tournament; 1983 Casio World (Japan); 1984, 1987, 1994 Murphy's Irish Open; 1984 Dutch Open; 1984 French Open; 1984 Spanish Open; 1985 Australian Masters; 1985 European Open; 1985 Sun City Challenge; Co-winner Lancome Trophy. Winner of seven German National Opens and two German National PGA's (Germans only). Leader in European Order of Merit, 1981 and 1984; 1987 PGA Championship in England, Belgian Classic; 1988 European Epson Match Play; 1989 Peugeot Spanish Open, German Masters; 1990 Madrid Open; 1991 Benson & Hedges Open; 1992 Heineken Dutch Open and Honda Open; 1993 Volvo PGA Championship; 1994 Volvo Masters. Has at least one European Tour victory in each of the last 16 years.
NATIONAL TEAMS: European Ryder Cup (7), 1981, 1983, 1985, 1987, 1989, 1991, 1993; World Cup (9), 1976, 1977, 1978, 1979, 1980, 1990, 1991, 1993, 1994; Dunhill Cup (2), 1992, 1994; Nissan Cup (2), 1985, 1986 (captain both years); Kirin Cup, 1987 (captain in 1987). Four Tours World Championship, 1989 (captain).

Sandy Lyle

HEIGHT: 6'1" **WEIGHT:** 187 **BIRTH DATE:** February 9, 1958
BIRTHPLACE: Shrewsbury, Scotland **RESIDENCE:** Wentworth, England
FAMILY: Wife, Jolande; Stuart (1983), James (1986), Alexandra (1993)
SPECIAL INTERESTS: Motorcycles, cars, airplanes
TURNED PROFESSIONAL: 1977   **PLAYOFF RECORD:** 3-0
TOUR VICTORIES: 5—**1986** Greater Greensboro Open. **1987** Tournament Players Championship. **1988** Phoenix Open, Kmart Greater Greensboro Open, Masters Tournament.

MONEY & POSITION:		
1984--$ 15,532--169	1988--$726,934-- 7	1992--$ 73,459--154
1985--$ 40,452--132	1989--$292,292-- 43	1993--$ 86,121--153
1986--$143,415-- 64	1990--$ 51,280--175	1994--$ 47,538--191
1987--$286,176-- 34	1991--$ 59,794--166	

BEST 1994 FINISH: T9--Honda Classic
1994 SUMMARY: Tournaments entered--7; in money--5; top ten finishes--1.
OTHER ACHIEVEMENTS: Winner, 1985 British Open. Winner of 28 international events including 1978 Nigerian Open; 1979 Scandinavian Open, European Open; 1981 French Open; 1983 Madrid Open; 1984 Italian Open, Lancome Trophy, Kapalua International, Casio World (Japan); 1987 German Masters; 1988 Dunhill Masters, Suntory World Match Play; 1991 BMW International Open; 1992 Lancia Martini Italian Open. Led PGA European Tour Order of Merit in 1979, 1980 and 1985; 61st in 1994.
NATIONAL TEAMS: European Ryder Cup (5), 1979, 1981, 1983, 1985, 1987. Nissan Cup (2), 1985, 1986 (medalist in 1985); Kirin Cup, 1987, 1988. World Cup (3), 1979, 1980, 1987 (medalist in 1980). British Walker Cup, 1977. Dunhill Cup (6), 1985, 1986, 1987, 1988, 1989, 1990.

Colin Montgomerie

HEIGHT: 6'1" **WEIGHT:** 205 **BIRTH DATE:** June 23, 1963
BIRTHPLACE: Glasgow, Scotland **RESIDENCE:** Oxshott, Surrey, England
FAMILY: Wife, Eimear; Olivia (1993)
SPECIAL INTERESTS: Music, cars
TURNED PROFESSIONAL: 1987
BEST-EVER FINISH: T2--1994 U.S. Open

MONEY & POSITION: 1992--$ 98,045--132   1994--$213,828--87   1993--$ 17,992--221

BEST 1994 FINISHES: T2--U.S. Open; T9--THE PLAYERS Championship
1993 SUMMARY: Tournaments entered--5; in money--3; top ten finishes--2.
OTHER ACHIEVEMENTS: Finished first on PGA European Tour Order of Merit in 1993 and 1994. Winner, 1994 Peugeot Open de Espana, Murphy's English Open, Volvo German Open; 1993 Heineken Dutch Open, Volvo Masters. 1989 Portuguese Open; 1991 Scandinavian Masters; 1985 Scottish Stroke Play, 1987 Scottish Amateur Championship. 1988 European Tour Rookie of the Year. Three-time All-American at Houston Baptist.
NATIONAL TEAMS: Walker Cup (2), 1985,1987; Ryder Cup (2), 1991, 1993. Dunhill Cup (4), 1988, 1991, 1992, 1994. World Cup (2), 1988, 1991.

Tommy Nakajima

HEIGHT: 5'11" **WEIGHT:** 180 **BIRTH DATE:** October 24, 1954
BIRTHPLACE: Gunma, Japan **RESIDENCE:** Narita City, Japan
FAMILY: Wife,Ritsuko; Yoshino, Masao **SPECIAL INTERESTS:** Music, skiing
TURNED PROFESSIONAL: 1975
BEST-EVER FINISH: 3--1988 PGA Championship

MONEY & POSITION:			
	1983--$ 46,351--107	1987--$ 82,111--108	
	1984--$ 78,796-- 77	1988--$148,304-- 81	1992--$ 16,951--215
	1985--$ 6,167--198	1989--$ 6,520-- 224	1993--$ 50,578--184
	1986--$ 37,847--153	1991--$ 35,150-- 193	1994--$ 21,200--224

BEST 1994 FINISH: T24--The International
1994 SUMMARY: Tournaments entered--3; in money--2; top ten finishes--0.
OTHER ACHIEVEMENTS: Winner of over 50 events world wide, including the 1993 ANA Open, 1993 Japan Series,1992 Pepsi Ube Kusan, NST Niigata Open and Japan Match Play Championship. Winner of four Japan Opens, three Japan PGA Championships, three Japan Match Play Championships and one Japan Series Championship.

Frank Nobilo

HEIGHT: 5'11" **WEIGHT:** 180 **BIRTH DATE:** May 14, 1960
BIRTHPLACE: Auckland, New Zealand **RESIDENCE:** Auckland, New Zealand
FAMILY: Wife, Gaynor; Bianca **SPECIAL INTERESTS:** Photography, squash
TURNED PROFESSIONAL: 1979
BEST-EVER FINISH: T9--1994 U.S. Open

MONEY & POSITION: 1992--$ 7,000--252   1993--$14,500--230   1994--$ 41,292--198

BEST 1994 FINISH: T9--U.S. Open
1994 SUMMARY: Tournaments entered--3; in money--3; top ten finishes--1.
OTHER ACHIEVEMENTS: Winner of three PGA European Tour events: 1988 PLM Open, 1991 Lancome Trophy, 1993 Turespana Mediterranean Open. Winner, 1985 and 1987 New Zealand PGA. Winner, 1982 New South Wales PGA. Winner, 1978 New Zealand Amateur. Winner, 1994 Indonesian Open.
NATIONAL TEAMS: Presidents Cup, 1994. Dunhill Cup (8), 1985, 1986, 1987, 1989, 1990, 1992, 1993, 1994. World Cup (8), 1982, 1987, 1988, 1990, 1991, 1992, 1993, 1994. World Amateur Team, 1978.

Jose Maria Olazabal

HEIGHT: 5'10"   **WEIGHT:** 160 **BIRTH DATE:** February 5, 1966
BIRTHPLACE: Fuenterrabia, Spain   **RESIDENCE:** Fuenterrabia, Spain
SPECIAL INTERESTS: Music, cinema, hunting, wildlife, ecology
TURNED PROFESSIONAL: 1985
TOUR VICTORIES: 4--**1990** NEC World Series of Golf. **1991** The International. **1994** Masters Tournament, NEC World Series of Golf.

MONEY & POSITION:	1987--$ 7,470--215	1991--$ 382,124-- 43	1993--$ 60,160--174
	1989--$ 56,039--160	1992--$ 63,429--161	1994--$969,900-- 7
	1990--$337,837-- 38		

BEST 1994 FINISHES: 1--Masters Tournament; 1--NEC World Series of Golf; 2--Freeport-McMoRan Classic; T7--PGA Champiosnhip.
1994 SUMMARY: Tournaments entered--8; in money--6; top ten finishes--4.
OTHER ACHIEVEMENTS: Finished fourth on the PGA Europen Tour Order of Merit, the seventh top-10 finish in his nine-year career. Winner of 15 European Tour events -- 1994 Turespana Open Mediterrania, Volvo PGA Championship; 1992 Turespana Open de Tenerife, Open Mediterrania; 1991 Open Catalonia, Epson Grand Prix of Europe; 1990 Benson & Hedges International, Carrolls Irish Open, Lancome Trophy; 1989 Tenerife Open, KLM Dutch Open; 1988 Volvo Belgian Open, German Masters; 1986 Ebel European Masters, Sanyo Open.
NATIONAL TEAMS: European Ryder Cup (4), 1987, 1989, 1991, 1993; Kirin Cup, 1987; Four Tours World Championship (2), 1989, 1990; World Cup, 1989; Dunhill Cup (5), 1986, 1987, 1988, 1989, 1992.

Masashi "Jumbo" Ozaki

HEIGHT: 6' 2" **WEIGHT:** 200 **BIRTH DATE:** January 27, 1947
BIRTHPLACE: Tokushima, Japan
RESIDENCE: Chiba, Japan
TURNED PROFESSIONAL: 1970
BEST-EVER FINISH: T4--1993 Memorial Tournament

MONEY & POSITION:	1987--$21,727--184	1990--$ 31,834--192	1993--$ 66,742--169
	1988--$ 6,321--233	1991--$ 15,765--218	1994--$ 25,557--217
	1989--$47,755--165	1992--$ 13,906--223	

BEST 1994 FINISH: T28--U.S. Open
1994 SUMMARY: Tournaments entered--5; in money--4; top ten finishes--0.
OTHER ACHIEVEMENTS: Winner of over 60 tournaments worldwide, he has won more JPGA Tour events than any other golfer in history. Winner of three events in 1993: Fuji Sankei Classic, Japan PGA Championship and Asahi Beer Golf Digest Tournament. Won six JPGA Tournaments in 1992: Dunlop Open, Chunichi Crowns, Philanthropy Cup, All Nippon Airways Open, Japan Open, Visa Tai heiyo Masters. Has led the JPGA in earnings six times since 1973. Winner, 1990 Yonex Hiroshima Open, Maruman Open and Daiwa KBC Augusta. Winner, seven JPGA events and more than $2 million (first ever) in 1994.

Costantino Rocca

HEIGHT: 5' 8"   **WEIGHT:** 185 **BIRTH DATE:** December 4, 1956
BIRTHPLACE: Bergamo, Italy **RESIDENCE:** Bergamo, Italy
FAMILY: Wife, Antonella; Chiara (1985), Francesco (1991)
SPECIAL INTERESTS: Fishing, soccer
TURNED PROFESSIONAL: 1981
BEST-EVER FINISH: T31--1994 Bob Hope Chrysler Classic
MONEY & POSITION: 1994--$ 16,350--232
BEST 1994 FINISH: T31-- Bob Hope Chrysler Classic
1994 SUMMARY: Tournaments entered--5; in money--3; top ten finishes--0.
OTHER ACHIEVEMENTS: Winner , 1993 Open V33 du Grand Lyons, 1993 Peugeot Open de France. Was first Italian winner on PGA European Tour since 1980. After finishing sixth on PGA European Tour Order of Merit in 1993, he fell to 30th in 1994.
NATIONAL TEAMS: European Ryder Cup, 1993; World Cup (6) 1988, 1990, 1991, 1992, 1993, 1994. Dunhill Cup (4) 1988, 1990, 1991, 1992, 1993. Hennessy Cognac Cup,1984.

Peter Senior

HEIGHT: 5' 6" **WEIGHT:** 170 **BIRTH DATE:** July 31, 1959
BIRTHPLACE: Singapore **RESIDENCE:** Narangba, Queensland, Australia
FAMILY: Wife, June; Krystall, Jasmine
SPECIAL INTERESTS: Fishing, entertaining, reading
TURNED PROFESSIONAL: 1978
BEST-EVER FINISH: T2--1990 International

MONEY & POSITION: 1986--$ 2,498--246   1991--$32,217--197   1993--$3,600--283
                        1988--$ 5,074--245   1992--$ 3,688--275   1994--$ 2,513--304
                        1990--$94,244--141

BEST 1994 FINISH: T71--PGA Championship
1994 SUMMARY: Tournaments entered --3; in money -- 1; top ten finishes --0.
OTHER ACHIEVEMENTS: Led the Australasian Tour Order of Merit in 1987, 1989 and 1993. Winner, 1994 Canon Challenge. Winner, 1993 Heineken Classic, Chunichi Crowns; 1992 Bridgestone ASO Open, Benson & Hedges International; 1991 Pyramid Australian Masters, Johnnie Walker Classic; 1990 European Open; 1989 New South Wales PGA Championship, Australian PGA Championship, Australian Open, Johnnie Walker Classic; 1987 U-Bix Classic, Rich River Classic, PGA Championship of Queensland, Johnnie Walker Monte Carlo Open; 1986 PLM Open; 1984 Stefan Queensland Open, Honeywell Classic; 1979 Dunhill South Australian Open.
NATIONAL TEAMS: Presidents Cup 1994.

Sam Torrance

HEIGHT: 5' 11" **WEIGHT:** 190 **BIRTH DATE:** August 24, 1953
BIRTHPLACE: Largs, Scotland **RESIDENCE:** Wentworth, England
FAMILY: Wife, Suzanne; Daniel (1988), Phoebe (1992)
SPECIAL INTERESTS: Snooker, tennis, cards, family
TURNED PROFESSIONAL: 1970
BEST-EVER FINISH: 2--1983 Southern Open
MONEY & POSITION: 1982--$ 4,550--218   1991--$ --
                        1983--$27,000--138   1992--$123,492--136
                        1984--$ 919--255

BEST 1994 FINISH: 3--Freeport-McMoRan Classic
1994 SUMMARY: Tournaments entered --5; in money -- 5; top ten finishes --1.
OTHER ACHIEVEMENTS: Winner of 18 PGA European Tour events: 1993 Kronenbourg Open, 1993 Heineken Open Catalonia, 1993 Honda Open, 1991 Jersey European Airways Open, 1990 Mercedes German Masters, 1987 Lancia Italian Open, 1985 Johnnie Walker Monte Carlo Open, 1984 Tunisian Open, 1984 Benson&Hedges International, 1984 Sanyo Open, 1983 Scandanavian Enterprise Open, 1983 Potuguese Open, 1981 Carrolls Irish Open, 1976 Piccadilly Medal, 1976 Martini International, 1972 Under-25 Match Play. Winner, 1980 Australian PGA Championship. Finished in top 10 on PGA European Tour Order of Merit nine times; 22nd in 1994. Lost playoff to Ronnie Black 1983 Southern Open.
NATIONAL TEAMS: Ryder Cup (7) 1981, 1983, 1985, 1987, 1989, 1991, 1993. Dunhill Masters (7) 1985, 1986, 1987, 1989, 1990, 1991, 1993. World Cup (10) 1976, 1978, 1982, 1984, 1985, 1987, 1989, 1990, 1991, 1993. Nissan Cup 1985. Asahi Glass Four Tours 1991. Hennessey Cup (5) 1976, 1978, 1980, 1982, 1984. Double Diamond (3) 1973, 1976, 1977.

Ian Woosnam

HEIGHT: 5'4"   **WEIGHT:** 161   **BIRTH DATE:** March 2, 1958
BIRTHPLACE: Oswestry, Wales **RESIDENCE:** Oswestry, Wales
FAMILY: Wife, Glendryth; Daniel, Rebecca
SPECIAL INTERESTS: Fishing, sports, snooker
TURNED PROFESSIONAL: 1976
TOUR VICTORIES: 2—**1991** USF&G Classic, Masters Tournament

MONEY & POSITION: 1986--$ 4,000--233   1989--$146,323-- 97   1992--$52,046--171
                        1987--$ 3,980--236   1990--$ 72,138--156   1993--$55,426--176
                        1988--$ 8,464--219   1991--$485,023-- 23   1993--$51,895--188

BEST 1994 FINISH: T9--PGA Championship
1994 SUMMARY: Tournaments entered--6; in money--4; top ten finishes--1.
OTHER ACHIEVEMENTS: Winner on the PGA European Tour of the 1982 Swiss Open; winner of 1983 Silk Cut Masters; 1984 Scandinavian Enterprise Open; 1986 Lawrence Batley TPC; 1987 Jersey Open, Cespa Madrid Open, Bell's Scottish Open, Lancome Trophy, Suntory World Match Play Championship; 1988 Volvo PGA Championship, Carrolls Irish Open, Panasonic European Open; 1989 Carrolls Irish Open; 1990 Amex Mediterranean Open, Monte Carlo Open, Bell's Scottish Open, Epson Grand Prix, Suntory World Match Play Championship; 1991 Mediterranean Open, Monte Carlo Open; 1992 European Monte Carlo. Also has won the 1979 News of the World under-23 Match-play Championship, 1982 Cacherel under-25 Championship; 1985 Zambian Open; 1986 '555' Kenya Open; 1987 Hong Kong Open and World Cup Individual title; 1992 European Monte Carlo Open; 1993 Murphy's English Open, Lancome Trophy; 1994 Air France Cannes Open, Dunhill British Masters. Finished 12th on the 1994 PGA European Tour Order of Merit.
NATIONAL TEAMS: Ryder Cup (6), 1983, 1985, 1987, 1989, 1991, 1993; World Cup (10), 1980, 1982, 1983, 1984, 1985, 1987, 1990, 1991, 1992, 1993; Dunhill Cup (7), 1985, 1986, 1988, 1989, 1990, 1991, 1993; Nissan Cup (2), 1985, 1986; Kirin Cup, 1987; Four Tours World Championship of Golf (2), 1989, 1990.

Tom Lehman fired four consecutive 5-under-par 67s to earn his first career PGA TOUR victory at the Memorial Tournament.

MERCEDES CHAMPIONSHIPS

La Costa Resort & Spa, Carlsbad, CA
Par: 36-36--72   Yards: 7,022

Purse: $1,000,000
January 6-9, 1994

Mercedes
Championships

LEADERS: First Round--Nolan Henke, Vijay Singh, Brett Ogle and Fred Couples, at 3-under-par 69, led by one over Phil Mickelson, Greg Norman, Scott Simpson and Grant Waite. **Second Round--**Mickelson, at 6-under-par 138, led by one over Couples, Singh and Waite. **Third Round--**Couples and Mickelson, at 8-under-par 208, led by one stroke over David Edwards.

PRO-AM: $10,000. All players received equal shares of $113.64 each in the individual portion of the event. Team--Phil Mickelson, 57, $800.

WEATHER: Near perfect conditions every day.

Winner: **Phil Mickelson**   70-68-70-68   276   **$180,000.00**
(Won playoff with par on second extra Hole)

Fred Couples	2	69-70-69-68	276	$120,000.00
Tom Kite	3	73-68-69-68	278	$80,000.00
Jay Haas	T 4	71-71-69-69	280	$46,625.00
Davis Love III	T 4	71-69-72-68	280	$46,625.00
Jeff Maggert	T 4	72-74-65-69	280	$46,625.00
Scott Simpson	T 4	70-72-70-68	280	$46,625.00
David Edwards	T 8	75-68-66-72	281	$34,000.00
Howard Twitty	T 8	72-73-67-69	281	$34,000.00
Greg Norman	10	70-73-69-70	282	$31,000.00
Ben Crenshaw	T11	71-70-69-73	283	$28,250.00
Brett Ogle	T11	69-72-71-71	283	$28,250.00
Jim Gallagher, Jr.	T13	73-69-73-70	285	$25,000.00
Billy Mayfair	T13	72-68-72-73	285	$25,000.00
Mike Standly	T13	75-72-67-71	285	$25,000.00
Fulton Allem	16	71-76-72-67	286	$23,000.00
Nolan Henke	T17	69-74-71-73	287	$21,500.00
Blaine McCallister	T17	74-74-68-71	287	$21,500.00
Vijay Singh	T17	69-70-76-72	287	$21,500.00
Lee Janzen	T20	71-74-74-70	289	$20,250.00
Grant Waite	T20	70-69-77-73	289	$20,250.00
Jim McGovern	22	73-71-73-73	290	$19,500.00
John Inman	23	71-70-76-74	291	$19,000.00
Rocco Mediate	24	72-71-77-72	292	$18,500.00

UNITED AIRLINES HAWAIIAN OPEN

UNITED AIRLINES

Hawaiian Open

Waialae CC, Honolulu, HI
Par: 36-36--72   Yards: 6,975

Purse: $1,200,000
January 13-16, 1994

LEADERS: First Round--Robin Freeman shot a 9-under-par 63 and led by three strokes over Brett Ogle and Craig Parry. **Second Round--**Davis Love III fired a 12-under-par 60 to move to a 16-under-par 128 total. **Third Round--**Love, at 17-under-par 199, led by two strokes over Ogle.

CUT: 76 players at 3-under-par 141.

PRO-AM: $10,000. Individual--Robert Gamez, 64, $1,000. Team--Jim McGovern, 51, $1,000.

WEATHER: Beautiful with some wind every afternoon.

Winner: Brett Ogle   66-66-69-68   269 $216,000.00

Davis Love III	2	68-60-71-71	270	$129,600.00	Skip Kendall	T32	73-66-68-74	281	$5,840.00
John Huston	3	70-68-67-67	272	$81,600.00	Mike Reid	T32	68-67-75-71	281	$5,840.00
Corey Pavin	4	68-70-70-65	273	$57,600.00	Vijay Singh	T32	74-67-72-68	281	$5,840.00
Jesper Parnevik	5	71-66-74-63	274	$48,000.00	Mike Sullivan	T32	68-69-75-69	281	$5,840.00
Craig Parry	T 6	66-70-72-67	275	$41,700.00	Dave Barr	T44	67-70-70-75	282	$3,628.00
Ted Tryba	T 6	69-71-68-67	275	$41,700.00	Bill Britton	T44	68-73-71-70	282	$3,628.00
Lennie Clements	T 8	69-66-70-71	276	$31,200.00	Brad Lardon	T44	69-69-75-69	282	$3,628.00
Paul Goydos	T 8	67-73-69-67	276	$31,200.00	Wayne Levi	T44	69-70-69-74	282	$3,628.00
David Ishii	T 8	70-67-69-70	276	$31,200.00	Craig Stadler	T44	69-68-76-69	282	$3,628.00
Jeff Maggert	T 8	69-67-68-72	276	$31,200.00	Esteban Toledo	T44	69-72-73-68	282	$3,628.00
David Ogrin	T 8	72-69-68-67	276	$31,200.00	Dudley Hart	T50	71-69-73-70	283	$2,818.67
Seiki Okuda	T 8	71-69-72-64	276	$31,200.00	Yoshi Mizumaki	T50	70-71-73-69	283	$2,818.67
Jay Don Blake	T14	70-65-71-71	277	$19,800.00	Jack Renner	T50	73-68-73-69	283	$2,818.67
Tom Lehman	T14	68-67-68-74	277	$19,800.00	Jeff Sluman	T50	70-71-72-70	283	$2,818.67
John Morse	T14	69-69-69-70	277	$19,800.00	Lanny Wadkins	T50	71-69-73-70	283	$2,818.67
Dave Rummells	T14	69-69-72-67	277	$19,800.00	John Wilson	T50	68-69-75-71	283	$2,818.67
Steve Stricker	T14	68-69-69-71	277	$19,800.00	Russ Cochran	T50	70-70-71-72	283	$2,818.66
Bob Tway	T14	70-71-69-67	277	$19,800.00	Steve Lamontagne	T50	70-69-73-71	283	$2,818.66
Clark Dennis	T20	70-69-71-68	278	$14,480.00	Dave Stockton, Jr	T50	72-68-72-71	283	$2,818.66
Joe Ozaki	T20	71-68-72-67	278	$14,480.00	Brad Bryant	T59	70-71-75-68	284	$2,628.00
Scott Simpson	T20	69-69-71-69	278	$14,480.00	Tom Garner	T59	67-71-73-73	284	$2,628.00
Robin Freeman	T23	63-69-75-72	279	$11,040.00	Sean Murphy	T59	67-69-74-74	284	$2,628.00
John Inman	T23	69-68-70-72	279	$11,040.00	Mike Standly	T59	68-70-74-72	284	$2,628.00
Billy Mayfair	T23	73-68-69-69	279	$11,040.00	Ed Dougherty	T63	73-68-73-71	285	$2,544.00
Hal Sutton	T23	70-69-67-73	279	$11,040.00	Steve Jurgensen	T63	67-74-71-73	285	$2,544.00
Fred Funk	T27	68-73-68-71	280	$8,520.00	Gene Sauers	T63	70-70-73-72	285	$2,544.00
Larry Silveira	T27	70-70-72-68	280	$8,520.00	Chris Dimarco	T66	70-70-69-77	286	$2,448.00
Mike Smith	T27	73-66-74-67	280	$8,520.00	Kelly Gibson	T66	68-70-75-73	286	$2,448.00
Jim Thorpe	T27	70-69-69-72	280	$8,520.00	Brian Henninger	T66	72-66-74-74	286	$2,448.00
Richard Zokol	T27	72-67-72-69	280	$8,520.00	Peter Jordan	T66	71-70-75-70	286	$2,448.00
Steve Brodie	T32	71-67-75-68	281	$5,840.00	David Peoples	T66	68-70-75-73	286	$2,448.00
Mark Brooks	T32	68-72-73-68	281	$5,840.00	John Flannery	71	71-67-74-75	287	$2,376.00
Olin Browne	T32	71-69-70-71	281	$5,840.00	Bill Kratzert	T72	72-68-75-73	288	$2,328.00
David Edwards	T32	70-69-69-73	281	$5,840.00	Dillard Pruitt	T72	71-70-77-70	288	$2,328.00
Wayne Grady	T32	69-70-74-68	281	$5,840.00	David Toms	T72	71-70-76-71	288	$2,328.00
Morris Hatalsky	T32	67-66-75-73	281	$5,840.00	John Mahaffey	75	71-70-77-73	291	$2,280.00
Nolan Henke	T32	69-71-72-69	281	$5,840.00	Ty Armstrong	T76	73-67-81-72	293	$2,244.00
Hale Irwin	T32	67-72-72-70	281	$5,840.00	Rocky Walcher	T76	68-73-76-76	293	$2,244.00

NORTHERN TELECOM OPEN

NORTHERN TELECOM OPEN

Tucson National, Tucson, AZ
Par: 36-36--72   Yards: 7,148
Starr Pass GC, Tucson, AZ
Par: 36-36--72   Yards: 7,010

Purse: $1,100,000
January 20-23, 1994

LEADERS: First Round--Dillard Pruitt, after an 8-under-par 64, held a one-stroke lead over Gary McCord and Larry Nelson. **Second Round**--Mike Springer, Vijay Singh, Joe Ozaki and Pruitt, all at 9-under-par 135, were one stroke ahead of Jay Delsing, Andrew Magee, Jim Furyk and Loren Roberts. **Third Round**--Pruitt, Magee and Furyk were deadlocked at 13-under-par 203, one stroke ahead of Jay Don Blake.

CUT: 72 players at 2-under-par 142.

PRO-AM: Tucson National, $7,500. Individual--Bob Estes, 66, $750. Team--Russ Cochran, Bob Estes, 55, $675 each. Starr Pass, $7,500. Individual--Mike Springer, 63, $750. Team--John Inman, Mike Springer, 53, $675.

WEATHER: Sunny and mild Thursday and Friday. Continued mild Saturday, with wind and clouds increasing throughout the day. Some high overcast and continued mild Sunday. Temperatures in the high 70s all week.

Winner: Andrew Magee   69-67-67-67 270 $198,000.00

Jay Don Blake	T 2	68-69-67-68	272	$72,600.00	Stan Utley	T29	71-69-70-69	279	$6,413.00
Loren Roberts	T 2	68-68-72-64	272	$72,600.00	Willie Wood	T29	70-71-71-67	279	$6,413.00
Vijay Singh	T 2	67-68-72-65	272	$72,600.00	Curt Byrum	T39	71-71-70-68	280	$4,730.00
Steve Stricker	T 2	68-69-68-67	272	$72,600.00	John Morse	T39	70-70-73-67	280	$4,730.00
Olin Browne	6	70-70-66-67	273	$39,600.00	Dave Rummells	T39	70-72-69-69	280	$4,730.00
Jim Furyk	T 7	68-68-67-71	274	$35,475.00	Lennie Clements	T42	70-72-72-67	281	$3,960.00
Robert Gamez	T 7	66-71-71-66	274	$35,475.00	Robin Freeman	T42	70-71-70-70	281	$3,960.00
Bob Burns	T 9	70-72-69-65	276	$22,400.00	Payne Stewart	T42	71-67-71-72	281	$3,960.00
David Feherty	T 9	70-69-67-70	276	$22,400.00	Fuzzy Zoeller	T42	69-71-74-67	281	$3,960.00
Rick Fehr	T 9	73-68-69-66	276	$22,400.00	Ronnie Black	T46	71-69-71-71	282	$2,992.00
John Huston	T 9	68-71-70-67	276	$22,400.00	Guy Boros	T46	69-73-71-69	282	$2,992.00
Billy Mayfair	T 9	69-71-68-68	276	$22,400.00	Glen Day	T46	69-70-70-73	282	$2,992.00
Rocco Mediate	T 9	70-70-71-65	276	$22,400.00	Ken Green	T46	69-73-71-69	282	$2,992.00
Phil Mickelson	T 9	69-70-70-67	276	$22,400.00	Yoshi Mizumaki	T46	71-70-70-71	282	$2,992.00
Dillard Pruitt	T 9	64-71-68-73	276	$22,400.00	Joe Ozaki	T46	66-69-73-74	282	$2,992.00
Mike Springer	T 9	70-65-73-68	276	$22,400.00	Brandel Chamblee	T52	70-68-72-73	283	$2,539.43
Jim Thorpe	T 9	69-70-70-67	276	$22,400.00	Brian Claar	T52	71-71-71-70	283	$2,539.43
Kirk Triplett	T 9	69-69-70-68	276	$22,400.00	John Flannery	T52	68-72-73-70	283	$2,539.43
Ted Schulz	T20	71-71-68-67	277	$13,750.00	Bruce Fleisher	T52	69-70-69-75	283	$2,539.43
Ted Tryba	T20	71-67-71-68	277	$13,750.00	John Inman	T52	71-69-70-73	283	$2,539.43
Mark Brooks	T22	72-68-71-67	278	$9,915.72	Curtis Strange	T52	71-66-71-75	283	$2,539.43
Russ Cochran	T22	71-70-69-68	278	$9,915.72	Brad Bryant	T52	76-65-75-67	283	$2,539.42
Wayne Grady	T22	72-66-73-67	278	$9,915.72	Billy Andrade	T59	71-71-74-68	284	$2,409.00
Morris Hatalsky	T22	69-73-66-70	278	$9,915.71	Bill Britton	T59	71-71-74-68	284	$2,409.00
Mike Heinen	T22	69-70-68-71	278	$9,915.71	Chris Dimarco	T59	68-74-70-72	284	$2,409.00
Gil Morgan	T22	70-69-73-66	278	$9,915.71	Lee Janzen	T59	71-69-73-71	284	$2,409.00
David Toms	T22	70-68-70-70	278	$9,915.71	Peter Jordan	T63	70-72-71-72	285	$2,310.00
Keith Clearwater	T29	71-66-71-71	279	$6,413.00	Bill Kratzert	T63	72-70-72-71	285	$2,310.00
Jay Delsing	T29	68-68-70-73	279	$6,413.00	Bob May	T63	69-71-71-74	285	$2,310.00
Fred Funk	T29	67-71-68-73	279	$6,413.00	Doug Tewell	T63	70-71-70-74	285	$2,310.00
Larry Nelson	T29	65-72-71-71	279	$6,413.00	Jim Woodward	T63	73-68-75-69	285	$2,310.00
Christian Pena	T29	68-73-70-68	279	$6,413.00	Gary McCord	68	65-74-76-71	286	$2,244.00
Gene Sauers	T29	70-70-68-71	279	$6,413.00	Neal Lancaster	69	69-72-71-75	287	$2,222.00
Tom Sieckmann	T29	73-69-71-66	279	$6,413.00	Jim McGovern	70	72-70-75-73	290	$2,200.00
Mike Standly	T29	71-69-69-70	279	$6,413.00	Grant Waite	71	70-71-83-68	292	$2,178.00

PHOENIX OPEN

PHOENIX OPEN

TPC of Scottsdale, Phoenix, AZ **Purse: $1,200,000**
Par: 35-36--71 **Yards: 6,992** **January 27-30, 1994**

LEADERS: First Round--Dan Forsman, Mark Lye and Gary McCord all at 6-under-par 65, were one stroke ahead of Rick Fehr, Bob Estes, Brandel Chamblee and Mike Hurlbert. **Second Round**--Fehr and Andrew Magee, at 9-under-par 133, held a one-shot lead over Estes, Larry Rinker and Billy Andrade. **Third Round**--Forsman, Fehr and Magee, all at 11-under-par 202, were a stroke in front of Andrade, Estes and Bob Burns.

CUT: 73 players (72 professionals and 1 amateur) at 1-under-par 141.

PRO-AM: $7,500. Individual--Rick Fehr, 66, $750. Team--Chip Beck, 51, $750.

WEATHER: Early-morning frost Thursday produced a 40-minute delay; afternoon starting times were delayed 20 minutes. Variable clouds and cool Thursday; Round 1 suspended by darkness at 5:55 p.m. with two groups still on the course. Round 2 began as scheduled at 7:50 a.m. Friday, with resumption of Round 1 getting underway at 8:15 a.m. Cold Friday morning, turning partly sunny and chilly in the afternoon. Sunny and cool with ideal playing conditions Saturday and Sunday.

Winner: Bill Glasson   68-68-68-64   268 $216,000.00

Player		Scores	Total	Money	Player		Scores	Total	Money
Bob Estes	2	66-68-69-68	271	$129,600.00	Willie Wood	T34	70-68-72-70	280	$6,192.00
Jeff Maggert	T 3	70-68-69-65	272	$62,400.00	Chip Beck	T39	69-70-73-69	281	$4,324.80
Blaine McCallister	T 3	67-69-69-67	272	$62,400.00	Jay Don Blake	T39	70-70-71-70	281	$4,324.80
Mike Springer	T 3	68-68-71-65	272	$62,400.00	Brandel Chamblee	T39	66-74-72-69	281	$4,324.80
Rick Fehr	T 6	66-67-69-71	273	$41,700.00	Brad Faxon	T39	74-67-69-71	281	$4,324.80
Tom Lehman	T 6	67-68-73-65	273	$41,700.00	Jim Furyk	T39	68-71-70-72	281	$4,324.80
Fred Funk	T 8	69-69-70-66	274	$32,400.00	Jim Gallagher, Jr.	T39	69-72-71-69	281	$4,324.80
Scott Hoch	T 8	72-66-67-69	274	$32,400.00	Kelly Gibson	T39	70-70-73-68	281	$4,324.80
Phil Mickelson	T 8	67-70-71-66	274	$32,400.00	David Ogrin	T39	68-72-69-72	281	$4,324.80
Steve Pate	T 8	68-69-69-68	274	$32,400.00	Tom Purtzer	T39	68-73-70-70	281	$4,324.80
Curtis Strange	T 8	71-70-69-64	274	$32,400.00	Tom Watson	T39	71-69-72-69	281	$4,324.80
Dave Barr	T13	72-65-69-69	275	$21,840.00	David Feherty	T49	70-70-72-70	282	$2,961.60
Bob Burns	T13	67-69-67-72	275	$21,840.00	Hale Irwin	T49	69-70-75-68	282	$2,961.60
Dan Forsman	T13	65-70-67-73	275	$21,840.00	Peter Jacobsen	T49	71-68-72-71	282	$2,961.60
Bruce Lietzke	T13	69-68-68-70	275	$21,840.00	Greg Kraft	T49	67-73-71-71	282	$2,961.60
Andrew Magee	T13	68-65-69-73	275	$21,840.00	Mark Lye	T49	65-73-73-71	282	$2,961.60
Billy Andrade	T18	69-65-69-73	276	$14,100.00	Michael Bradley	T54	73-68-70-72	283	$2,724.00
Mark Calcavecchia	T18	71-69-69-67	276	$14,100.00	Jay Delsing	T54	71-70-71-71	283	$2,724.00
Gary McCord	T18	65-70-70-71	276	$14,100.00	Bruce Fleisher	T54	70-71-72-70	283	$2,724.00
Larry Rinker	T18	69-65-72-70	276	$14,100.00	Larry Mize	T54	71-70-70-72	283	$2,724.00
Tim Simpson	T18	68-67-70-71	276	$14,100.00	Kenny Perry	T54	69-70-72-72	283	$2,724.00
Vijay Singh	T18	68-69-72-67	276	$14,100.00	Mike Standly	T54	71-69-73-70	283	$2,724.00
Ted Tryba	T18	72-66-68-70	276	$14,100.00	Marco Dawson	T60	69-69-70-76	284	$2,604.00
Grant Waite	T18	70-70-67-69	276	$14,100.00	Ken Green	T60	73-63-75-73	284	$2,604.00
Gil Morgan	T26	68-69-70-70	277	$9,420.00	Joe Ozaki	T60	70-69-72-73	284	$2,604.00
Steve Stricker	T26	70-70-71-66	277	$9,420.00	Mark Wiebe	T60	70-71-70-73	284	$2,604.00
Ed Fiori	T28	69-72-67-70	278	$8,700.00	Todd Demsey	T60	75-66-73-70	284	AMATEUR
Neal Lancaster	T28	71-70-67-70	278	$8,700.00	Mark Carnevale	T65	70-71-77-67	285	$2,508.00
Brian Claar	T30	72-69-70-68	279	$7,620.00	Russ Cochran	T65	71-70-71-73	285	$2,508.00
Mike Hulbert	T30	66-69-74-70	279	$7,620.00	Dan Pohl	T65	70-70-71-74	285	$2,508.00
Lee Janzen	T30	68-69-68-74	279	$7,620.00	Scott Watkins	T65	69-72-69-75	285	$2,508.00
Dillard Pruitt	T30	69-71-70-69	279	$7,620.00	Brad Bryant	T69	68-71-72-75	286	$2,436.00
Clark Dennis	T34	70-70-69-71	280	$6,192.00	Billy Mayfair	T69	71-70-72-73	286	$2,436.00
Trevor Dodds	T34	70-70-68-72	280	$6,192.00	Brian Kamm	T71	72-68-75-73	288	$2,388.00
Robert Gamez	T34	75-66-70-69	280	$6,192.00	Scott Simpson	T71	69-70-73-76	288	$2,388.00
Tom Sieckmann	T34	69-71-69-71	280	$6,192.00	R.W. Eaks	73	70-70-73-76	289	$2,352.00

AT&T PEBBLE BEACH NATIONAL PRO-AM

Pebble Beach GL, Pebble Beach, CA   Purse: $1,250,000
(Host Course)   Par: 72   Yards: 6,799
Spyglass Hill CC   Par: 72   Yards: 6,810   February 3-6, 1994
Poppy Hills CC   Par: 72   Yards: 6,865

LEADERS: First Round--Dudley Hart (PH), with a 7-under-par 65, led by one over Jay Delsing (PB) and Jerry Pate (PH). **Second Round--**Davis Love III (PB) shot a 6-under-par 66 to finish at 9-under-par 135 and lead by one stroke over Tom Watson (PB) and Hart (PB). **Third Round--**Hart (SH), at 10-under-par 206, led by one over Johnny Miller (PB).

CUT: 73 players at 1-over-par 217. Team cut was 25 teams at 18-under-par 198.

WEATHER: Sunny and cool Thursday and Friday. Much cooler and windier on Saturday. Sunday was rainy, windy and cool.

PRO-AM: $70,000. Dudley Hart and Robert Floyd, 257, $7,000.

Winner: Johnny Miller 68-72-67-74 281 $225,000.00

Jeff Maggert	T 2	68-72-72-70	282	$82,500.00	Brad Bryant	T37	74-71-69-75	289	$4,435.00
Corey Pavin	T 2	69-71-71-71	282	$82,500.00	Mark Cato	T37	71-71-72-75	289	$4,435.00
Kirk Triplett	T 2	69-74-67-72	282	$82,500.00	David Duval	T37	69-72-75-73	289	$4,435.00
Tom Watson	T 2	69-67-72-74	282	$82,500.00	David Frost	T37	70-73-73-73	289	$4,435.00
Tom Lehman	6	69-68-73-73	283	$45,000.00	Morris Hatalsky	T37	70-72-74-73	289	$4,435.00
Keith Clearwater	T 7	70-70-71-73	284	$36,375.00	Brian Henninger	T37	72-70-75-72	289	$4,435.00
Jay Delsing	T 7	66-75-70-73	284	$36,375.00	Peter Jacobsen	T37	68-77-71-73	289	$4,435.00
Dudley Hart	T 7	65-71-70-78	284	$36,375.00	Brian Kamm	T37	69-70-77-73	289	$4,435.00
Blaine McCallister	T 7	68-71-72-73	284	$36,375.00	Tom Kite	T37	68-70-72-79	289	$4,435.00
Ted Tryba	T 7	70-70-70-74	284	$36,375.00	Jim Nelford	T37	70-73-71-75	289	$4,435.00
Dan Forsman	T12	77-68-70-70	285	$23,035.72	Mark O'Meara	T37	72-71-71-75	289	$4,435.00
Dennis Paulson	T12	72-67-75-71	285	$23,035.72	Kenny Perry	T37	73-72-72-72	289	$4,435.00
Mike Standly	T12	70-74-71-70	285	$23,035.72	Craig Stadler	T37	72-69-72-76	289	$4,435.00
Chip Beck	T12	74-68-70-73	285	$23,035.71	Phil Tataurangi	T37	67-73-75-74	289	$4,435.00
Clark Dennis	T12	70-70-73-72	285	$23,035.71	Brian Claar	T52	69-75-73-73	290	$2,915.00
Paul Goydos	T12	71-70-70-74	285	$23,035.71	Brad Faxon	T52	73-69-75-73	290	$2,915.00
Larry Silveira	T12	73-69-69-74	285	$23,035.71	Bill Glasson	T52	74-69-73-74	290	$2,915.00
David Edwards	T19	69-70-73-74	286	$15,150.00	Larry Rinker	T52	74-70-71-75	290	$2,915.00
Ray Floyd	T19	70-71-70-75	286	$15,150.00	Willie Wood	T52	75-70-69-76	290	$2,915.00
Bob Lohr	T19	73-71-67-75	286	$15,150.00	Lennie Clements	T57	74-72-70-75	291	$2,800.00
Jesper Parnevik	T19	71-69-73-73	286	$15,150.00	Larry Mize	T57	69-73-73-76	291	$2,800.00
Esteban Toledo	T19	70-74-69-73	286	$15,150.00	Payne Stewart	T57	68-73-73-77	291	$2,800.00
Bob Gilder	T24	67-71-72-77	287	$10,375.00	Ed Dougherty	T60	68-77-72-75	292	$2,712.50
Gary Hallberg	T24	70-72-71-74	287	$10,375.00	Roger Maltbie	T60	69-71-77-75	292	$2,712.50
Davis Love III	T24	69-66-78-74	287	$10,375.00	D.A. Weibring	T60	73-73-71-75	292	$2,712.50
Andrew Magee	T24	70-69-72-76	287	$10,375.00	Mark Wurtz	T60	73-71-73-75	292	$2,712.50
Vijay Singh	T24	70-70-72-75	287	$10,375.00	Steve Lamontagne	T64	72-75-69-77	293	$2,637.50
Bill Britton	T29	70-69-73-76	288	$7,609.38	Jeff Woodland	T64	73-71-71-78	293	$2,637.50
Jim Furyk	T29	67-70-77-74	288	$7,609.38	Robin Freeman	T66	69-74-74-77	294	$2,575.00
Jim Gallagher, Jr.	T29	70-70-73-75	288	$7,609.38	Ted Goin	T66	76-71-70-77	294	$2,575.00
Charles Raulerson	T29	72-68-73-75	288	$7,609.38	Lon Hinkle	T66	68-73-72-81	294	$2,575.00
Jay Haas	T29	69-73-75-71	288	$7,609.37	Glen Day	T69	73-69-75-79	296	$2,512.50
Hale Irwin	T29	76-72-69-71	288	$7,609.37	Tom Garner	T69	71-72-74-79	296	$2,512.50
Mike Reid	T29	68-73-71-76	288	$7,609.37	Fulton Allem	T71	71-69-77-80	297	$2,462.50
Dennis Trixler	T29	71-70-70-77	288	$7,609.37	Ken Green	T71	72-74-71-80	297	$2,462.50
Guy Boros	T37	68-71-76-74	289	$4,435.00					

NISSAN LOS ANGELES OPEN

Riviera CC, Pacific Palisades, CA   **Purse: $1,000,000**
Par: 35-36--71   **Yards: 6,946**   **February 10-13, 1994**

LEADERS: First Round--Tom Purtzer, with a 7-under-par 64, led by two over Corey Pavin and Jesper Parnevik. **Second Round--**Pavin, at 11-under-par 131, led by three over Fred Couples. **Third Round--**Couples, at 11-under-par 202, led by one over Pavin.

CUT: 75 players at 4-over-par 146.

PRO-AM: Individual--Nolan Henke, 66, $750. Team--Craig Stadler and Mark O'Meara, 56, $675.

WEATHER: Beautiful on Thursday. Friday was windy and cool. Saturday was nice with less wind and somewhat warmer. Sunday had perfect conditions.

Winner: Corey Pavin   67-64-72-68 271 $180,000.00

Player	Pos	Scores	Total	Money
Fred Couples	2	67-67-68-71	273	$108,000.00
Chip Beck	3	66-71-72-68	277	$68,000.00
Brad Faxon	4	70-71-68-69	278	$48,000.00
David Frost	5	67-74-71-67	279	$40,000.00
Peter Jacobsen	T6	69-71-68-72	280	$34,750.00
Tom Watson	T6	69-71-71-69	280	$34,750.00
Lennie Clements	T8	68-74-68-71	281	$28,000.00
Jay Delsing	T8	67-72-69-73	281	$28,000.00
Craig Stadler	T8	68-69-71-73	281	$28,000.00
Kirk Triplett	T8	68-76-69-68	281	$28,000.00
Mike Hulbert	T12	70-71-70-71	282	$21,000.00
Tom Purtzer	T12	64-74-74-70	282	$21,000.00
Fuzzy Zoeller	T12	67-73-72-70	282	$21,000.00
Donnie Hammond	T15	69-74-72-68	283	$16,000.00
Tom Lehman	T15	69-73-73-68	283	$16,000.00
Mark O'Meara	T15	69-73-70-71	283	$16,000.00
Jeff Sluman	T15	72-70-71-70	283	$16,000.00
Mike Springer	T15	69-70-74-70	283	$16,000.00
Scott Hoch	T20	69-73-72-70	284	$10,428.58
Robin Freeman	T20	71-68-71-74	284	$10,428.57
Paul Goydos	T20	69-73-69-73	284	$10,428.57
Blaine McCallister	T20	70-76-70-68	284	$10,428.57
Kiyoshi Murota	T20	69-67-73-75	284	$10,428.57
Jesper Parnevik	T20	66-73-72-73	284	$10,428.57
Mike Reid	T20	71-73-68-72	284	$10,428.57
Michael Allen	T27	68-76-71-70	285	$6,245.46
Brian Claar	T27	72-72-71-70	285	$6,245.46
Phil Mickelson	T27	70-73-73-69	285	$6,245.46
Scott Verplank	T27	71-74-70-70	285	$6,245.46
Duffy Waldorf	T27	70-71-74-70	285	$6,245.46
Tom Kite	T27	72-72-71-70	285	$6,245.45
Joe Ozaki	T27	72-71-68-74	285	$6,245.45
Dan Pohl	T27	73-72-71-69	285	$6,245.45
Larry Rinker	T27	70-71-73-71	285	$6,245.45
Hal Sutton	T27	71-68-70-76	285	$6,245.45
Jim Woodward	T27	71-75-71-68	285	$6,245.45
Steve Lowery	T38	73-72-69-72	286	$4,600.00
Vijay Singh	T38	72-71-73-70	286	$4,600.00
Bob Estes	T40	72-72-72-71	287	$3,800.00
Bruce Lietzke	T40	71-75-69-72	287	$3,800.00
Dick Mast	T40	71-73-70-73	287	$3,800.00
Larry Mize	T40	70-74-72-71	287	$3,800.00
Yoshi Mizumaki	T40	72-72-77-66	287	$3,800.00
Richard Zokol	T40	69-75-71-72	287	$3,800.00
Ronnie Black	T46	70-74-72-72	288	$3,000.00
Nolan Henke	T46	67-73-74-74	288	$3,000.00
Jim Furyk	T48	70-76-75-68	289	$2,620.00
Greg Kraft	T48	71-72-75-71	289	$2,620.00
David Peoples	T48	70-76-72-71	289	$2,620.00
Ben Crenshaw	T51	71-73-72-74	290	$2,353.34
Brian Kamm	T51	74-68-75-73	290	$2,353.34
Phil Blackmar	T51	69-73-78-70	290	$2,353.33
Gene Sauers	T51	71-73-74-72	290	$2,353.33
Ted Schulz	T51	70-74-74-72	290	$2,353.33
Jeff Woodland	T51	68-76-75-71	290	$2,353.33
Billy Andrade	T57	71-72-73-75	291	$2,230.00
Bob Burns	T57	73-73-71-74	291	$2,230.00
Gary Hallberg	T57	71-74-72-74	291	$2,230.00
Jim McGovern	T57	69-76-75-71	291	$2,230.00
Neal Lancaster	T61	68-75-74-75	292	$2,140.00
Steve Pate	T61	71-73-75-73	292	$2,140.00
Mike Standly	T61	70-74-78-70	292	$2,140.00
Dave Stockton, Jr	T61	70-75-73-74	292	$2,140.00
Willie Wood	T61	70-74-75-73	292	$2,140.00
Jeff Maggert	T66	72-74-72-75	293	$2,070.00
Payne Stewart	T66	70-74-74-75	293	$2,070.00
Mark Carnevale	T68	74-72-76-72	294	$2,010.00
David Edwards	T68	70-71-73-80	294	$2,010.00
Bruce Fleisher	T68	73-71-76-74	294	$2,010.00
Joey Rassett	T68	69-75-74-76	294	$2,010.00
Brandel Chamblee	72	70-76-75-74	295	$1,960.00
Robert Gamez	T73	70-72-75-81	298	$1,930.00
Tim Simpson	T73	73-73-76-76	298	$1,930.00
Ty Armstrong	75	72-73-76-81	302	$1,900.00

BOB HOPE CHRYSLER CLASSIC

Indian Wells CC (Host Course)
Indian Wells, CA   Par: 72   Yards: 6,478
PGA West/Palmer   Par: 72   Yards: 6,869
Bermuda Dunes CC   Par: 72   Yards: 6,927
LaQuinta CC   Par: 72   Yards: 6,888

Purse: $1,100,000
February 16-20, 1994

LEADERS: First Round--Hal Sutton (IW), with a 9-under-par 63, led by one over Ronnie Black (LQ). **Second Round--**Scott Hoch (PW), at 16-under-par 128, led by three over Keith Clearwater (IW). **Third Round--**Lennie Clements, with a course-record 11-under-par 61 at LaQuinta CC, moved to 19-under-par 197, and led by one over Hoch (LQ). **Fourth Round--**Hoch (BD), at 24-under-par 264, led by four over Bill Glasson (IW) and John Huston (LQ).

CUT: 78 players at 5-under-par 283.

PRO-AM: $5,000. Individual--Bill Glasson, 60, $2,500.

WEATHER: Beautiful on Wednesday, Friday and Saturday. Thursday was overcast with some rain. Sunday was overcast with light rain.

Winner: Scott Hoch   66-62-70-66-70   334   **$198,000.00**

Player	Pos	Scores	Total	Money		Player	Pos	Scores	Total	Money
Fuzzy Zoeller	T 2	70-67-66-68-66	337	$82,133.34		Gene Sauers	T37	68-71-68-74-67	348	$4,730.00
Lennie Clements	T 2	67-69-61-72-68	337	$82,133.33		Tim Simpson	T37	68-69-76-69-66	348	$4,730.00
Jim Gallagher, Jr.	T 2	66-67-74-62-68	337	$82,133.33		Curtis Strange	T37	70-70-73-67-68	348	$4,730.00
Payne Stewart	5	67-69-71-68-63	338	$44,000.00		Andy Bean	T44	69-70-71-70-69	349	$3,179.00
Guy Boros	T 6	66-67-68-69-69	339	$36,850.00		Mark Brooks	T44	72-68-68-72-69	349	$3,179.00
Keith Clearwater	T 6	67-64-70-68-70	339	$36,850.00		Clark Dennis	T44	65-72-69-72-71	349	$3,179.00
Paul Stankowski	T 6	67-66-69-68-69	339	$36,850.00		Brad Fabel	T44	67-68-75-70-69	349	$3,179.00
Bob Estes	T 9	69-69-70-67-68	340	$30,800.00		Peter Jacobsen	T44	69-68-71-68-73	349	$3,179.00
John Huston	T 9	66-68-66-68-72	340	$30,800.00		Doug Martin	T44	67-66-76-71-69	349	$3,179.00
Glen Day	T11	67-67-68-69-70	341	$25,300.00		David Ogrin	T44	68-69-69-74-69	349	$3,179.00
Bruce Lietzke	T11	68-69-65-67-72	341	$25,300.00		Scott Simpson	T44	68-69-69-73-70	349	$3,179.00
Andrew Magee	T11	67-67-71-70-66	341	$25,300.00		Jay Don Blake	T52	73-70-71-64-72	350	$2,579.50
Michael Allen	T14	66-68-70-67-71	342	$19,250.00		Davis Love III	T52	68-70-72-71-69	350	$2,579.50
Bruce Fleisher	T14	68-70-66-70-68	342	$19,250.00		Loren Roberts	T52	69-68-74-72-67	350	$2,579.50
Fred Funk	T14	66-70-68-69-69	342	$19,250.00		Steve Stricker	T52	67-70-72-72-69	350	$2,579.50
Bill Glasson	T14	70-66-66-66-74	342	$19,250.00		Steve Lowery	T56	73-70-69-71-68	351	$2,497.00
Jay Delsing	T18	65-69-66-73-71	344	$15,400.00		Dick Mast	T56	67-72-70-72-70	351	$2,497.00
Robert Gamez	T18	72-67-68-65-72	344	$15,400.00		Jay Haas	T58	69-68-67-77-71	352	$2,409.00
Bob Gilder	T18	69-69-66-69-71	344	$15,400.00		Tommy Moore	T58	67-68-74-72-71	352	$2,409.00
Rick Fehr	T21	73-68-69-68-67	345	$10,638.58		Jodie Mudd	T58	66-66-71-76-73	352	$2,409.00
Dave Barr	T21	69-65-70-72-69	345	$10,638.57		Mac O'Grady	T58	71-72-69-69-71	352	$2,409.00
John Cook	T21	68-72-68-67-70	345	$10,638.57		Joey Rassett	T58	69-72-72-70-69	352	$2,409.00
Robin Freeman	T21	69-73-68-69-66	345	$10,638.57		John Wilson	T58	67-72-73-69-71	352	$2,409.00
David Peoples	T21	68-68-71-71-67	345	$10,638.57		Brad Bryant	T64	71-72-71-69-70	353	$2,299.00
Hal Sutton	T21	63-70-72-69-71	345	$10,638.57		Ed Dougherty	T64	69-67-73-71-73	353	$2,299.00
Jeff Woodland	T21	68-67-71-71-68	345	$10,638.57		Greg Kraft	T64	71-66-71-73-72	353	$2,299.00
Donnie Hammond	T28	65-69-70-72-70	346	$7,810.00		Mark O'Meara	T64	69-68-70-76-70	353	$2,299.00
Kiyoshi Murota	T28	69-71-71-67-68	346	$7,810.00		Curt Byrum	T68	70-72-69-70-73	354	$2,189.00
Craig Stadler	T28	75-66-71-66-68	346	$7,810.00		Mark Carnevale	T68	70-69-72-69-74	354	$2,189.00
Michael Bradley	T31	72-71-65-68-71	347	$6,380.00		Mike Heinen	T68	71-69-75-68-71	354	$2,189.00
Bob Burns	T31	67-66-72-73-69	347	$6,380.00		Steve Pate	T68	70-71-71-71-71	354	$2,189.00
Paul Goydos	T31	69-69-71-70-68	347	$6,380.00		Steve Rintoul	T68	71-71-70-70-72	354	$2,189.00
Peter Jordan	T31	67-67-74-68-71	347	$6,380.00		Dave Rummells	T68	69-70-72-70-73	354	$2,189.00
Costantino Rocca	T31	69-71-67-69-71	347	$6,380.00		Dennis Paulson	T74	71-73-68-68-75	355	$2,101.00
Jeff Sluman	T31	72-70-64-69-72	347	$6,380.00		Bobby Wadkins	T74	67-72-68-75-73	355	$2,101.00
Russ Cochran	T37	72-69-69-68-70	348	$4,730.00		Todd Barranger	T76	74-69-73-66-75	357	$2,057.00
Marco Dawson	T37	70-67-72-71-68	348	$4,730.00		Dan Pohl	T76	73-68-72-70-74	357	$2,057.00
Trevor Dodds	T37	67-70-70-69-72	348	$4,730.00		Blaine McCallister	78	73-69-68-73-75	358	$2,024.00
Gary McCord	T37	72-74-67-65-70	348	$4,730.00						

BUICK INVITATIONAL
OF CALIFORNIA

Torrey Pines GC, La Jolla, CA **Purse: $1,100,000**
South Course:Par: 36-36--72 **Yards: 7,000**
North Course:Par: 36-36--72 **Yards: 6,592 February 24-27, 1994**

LEADERS: First Round--Ronnie Black (N), Doug Martin (N) and David Toms (S), all at 7-under-par 65, led by one over four players. **Second Round--**Toms, at 14-under-par 130, led by three over Black and Mark Wurtz. **Third Round--**Steve Lowery, at 15-under-par 201, led by one over Craig Stadler, Toms, Black and Kirk Triplett.

CUT: A total of 80 players (79 professionals and 1 amateur) at 3-under-par 141 or better.

PRO-AM: $15,000. South Individual--Steve Lamontagne, 65, $750. South Team--Dan Forsman, 53, $750. North Individual--Mark Wiebe, 66, $750. North Team--Dennis Paulson, 53, $750.

WEATHER: Perfect each day.

Winner: Craig Stadler   67-67-68-66   268 $198,000.00

Steve Lowery	2	67-68-66-68	269	$118,800.00	Brad Faxon	T40	68-66-76-71	281	$4,510.00
Phil Mickelson	3	68-69-69-64	270	$74,800.00	D.A. Russell	T40	69-70-71-71	281	$4,510.00
Hal Sutton	4	68-68-67-69	272	$52,800.00	Mark Wurtz	T40	69-64-71-77	281	$4,510.00
Mark Carnevale	5	67-69-70-67	273	$44,000.00	John Adams	T45	72-69-70-71	282	$3,325.67
Bob Estes	T6	70-67-67-70	274	$36,850.00	Mark Brooks	T45	74-67-70-71	282	$3,325.67
Robin Freeman	T6	68-67-71-68	274	$36,850.00	Steve Lamontagne	T45	68-70-72-72	282	$3,325.67
Kirk Triplett	T6	71-63-68-72	274	$36,850.00	Scott Verplank	T45	66-71-72-73	282	$3,325.67
Mark Calcavecchia	T9	69-72-69-65	275	$28,600.00	Todd Barranger	T45	67-71-70-74	282	$3,325.66
Lennie Clements	T9	66-69-68-72	275	$28,600.00	Steve Brodie	T45	68-69-69-76	282	$3,325.66
Paul Goydos	T9	68-70-70-67	275	$28,600.00	Ed Fiori	T51	69-70-71-73	283	$2,569.60
Doug Martin	T9	65-73-68-69	275	$28,600.00	Fred Funk	T51	67-73-70-73	283	$2,569.60
Ronnie Black	T13	65-68-69-74	276	$22,000.00	Jay Haas	T51	71-68-74-70	283	$2,569.60
Tom Lehman	T13	68-70-67-71	276	$22,000.00	Morris Hatalsky	T51	71-68-72-72	283	$2,569.60
Tom Byrum	T15	70-64-71-72	277	$18,150.00	Gary McCord	T51	70-69-70-74	283	$2,569.60
Bob Lohr	T15	69-67-71-70	277	$18,150.00	Joe Ozaki	T51	69-68-76-70	283	$2,569.60
Scott Simpson	T15	70-70-70-67	277	$18,150.00	David Peoples	T51	68-73-71-71	283	$2,569.60
David Toms	T15	65-65-72-75	277	$18,150.00	Charles Raulerson	T51	70-70-66-77	283	$2,569.60
Russ Cochran	T19	67-72-68-71	278	$13,332.00	Costantino Rocca	T51	69-69-74-71	283	$2,569.60
Glen Day	T19	68-67-72-71	278	$13,332.00	Tim Simpson	T51	72-68-71-72	283	$2,569.60
Ed Dougherty	T19	66-70-73-69	278	$13,332.00	Brad Bryant	T61	70-70-71-73	284	$2,343.00
Payne Stewart	T19	70-66-68-74	278	$13,332.00	Scott Gump	T61	69-70-73-72	284	$2,343.00
Jim Thorpe	T19	72-69-69-68	278	$13,332.00	Mark Lye	T61	69-71-71-73	284	$2,343.00
Brandel Chamblee	T24	67-73-71-68	279	$8,705.72	Billy Mayfair	T61	71-69-69-75	284	$2,343.00
Donnie Hammond	T24	72-66-71-70	279	$8,705.72	Dave Rummells	T61	69-72-71-72	284	$2,343.00
Monte Montgomery	T24	70-71-68-70	279	$8,705.72	Larry Silveira	T61	68-72-74-70	284	$2,343.00
Jay Don Blake	T24	69-66-76-68	279	$8,705.71	Vijay Singh	T61	67-73-72-72	284	$2,343.00
Gary Hallberg	T24	67-70-70-72	279	$8,705.71	Phil Tataurangi	T61	68-68-73-75	284	$2,343.00
Wayne Levi	T24	69-71-68-71	279	$8,705.71	Bruce Fleisher	T69	70-71-72-72	285	$2,200.00
Jeff Woodland	T24	71-69-68-71	279	$8,705.71	Thomas Levet	T69	73-66-73-73	285	$2,200.00
Dave Barr	T31	69-67-75-69	280	$6,105.00	Brad Sherfy	T69	74-67-74-70	285	$2,200.00
Rob Boldt	T31	69-69-72-70	280	$6,105.00	Dave Stockton, Jr	T69	70-71-72-72	285	$2,200.00
Guy Boros	T31	72-66-71-71	280	$6,105.00	Ted Tryba	T69	67-74-71-73	285	$2,200.00
John Cook	T31	71-69-71-69	280	$6,105.00	JC Anderson	T74	71-70-70-75	286	$2,112.00
Steve Pate	T31	71-70-70-69	280	$6,105.00	Roger Gunn	T74	66-70-77-73	286	$2,112.00
Dennis Paulson	T31	68-73-68-71	280	$6,105.00	Mike Smith	T74	67-74-74-71	286	$2,112.00
Paul Stankowski	T31	67-68-75-70	280	$6,105.00	Esteban Toledo	77	73-68-75-71	287	$2,068.00
John Wilson	T31	71-69-70-70	280	$6,105.00	Keith Clearwater	78	68-73-75-74	290	$2,046.00
Todd Demsey	T31	67-74-67-72	280	AMATEUR	Robert Wrenn	79	69-72-77-75	293	$2,024.00
Bobby Clampett	T40	73-68-70-70	281	$4,510.00	Shaun Micheel	80	70-70-77-79	296	$2,002.00
Brad Fabel	T40	69-71-71-70	281	$4,510.00					

DORAL-RYDER OPEN

Doral Resort & CC, Miami, FL **Purse: $1,400,000**
Par: 36-36--72   **Yards: 6,939**   **March 3-6, 1994**

LEADERS: First Round--Jim Thorpe and Ray Floyd, at 4-under-par 68, led by one stroke over Dick Mast. **Second Round--**Larry Nelson, with a 7-under-par 137 total, led by one over Mast, John Huston and Billy Andrade. **Third Round--**Andrade, at 12-under-par 204, led by two over Nelson.

CUT: 77 players at 4-over-par 148.

PRO-AM: An afternoon storm forced the cancellation of the afternoon portion of the event. Equal shares of $144 were paid to all afternoon participants. The morning portion was divided into a front and back-nine event. Front-Nine Individual--Tom Kite, 32, $375. Front-Nine Team--Tom Kite, 38, $375. Back-Nine Individual--Mark Calcavecchia, 33, $375. Back-Nine Team--Vijay Singh, Mark Calcavecchia, Lanny Wadkins, Mark Brooks and Grant Waite, 28, $187.50 each.

WEATHER: Sunny and cool with high winds on Thursday. Friday was sunny with much less wind. Saturday and Sunday were beautiful with almost no wind.

Winner: John Huston   70-68-70-66   274 $252,000.00

Billy Andrade	T 2	70-68-66-73	277	$123,200.00	Mark Carnevale	T39	72-72-72-72	288	$5,600.00
Brad Bryant	T 2	70-69-69-69	277	$123,200.00	Brian Claar	T39	75-69-71-73	288	$5,600.00
Jim Thorpe	T 4	68-72-68-71	279	$57,866.67	Keith Clearwater	T39	75-73-72-68	288	$5,600.00
D.A. Weibring	T 4	74-69-65-71	279	$57,866.67	Tom Purtzer	T39	72-72-70-74	288	$5,600.00
Lennie Clements	T 4	72-70-66-71	279	$57,866.66	Bob Tway	T39	71-73-71-73	288	$5,600.00
Bruce Lietzke	T 7	74-69-71-67	281	$43,633.34	Bruce Fleisher	T45	77-71-68-73	289	$4,214.00
Greg Norman	T 7	71-74-69-67	281	$43,633.33	Ken Green	T45	72-73-73-71	289	$4,214.00
Loren Roberts	T 7	73-70-69-69	281	$43,633.33	Kenny Perry	T45	73-73-71-72	289	$4,214.00
Mike Hulbert	T10	72-74-70-66	282	$35,000.00	Tom Watson	T45	73-74-71-71	289	$4,214.00
Mark McCumber	T10	76-69-68-69	282	$35,000.00	Mark Brooks	T49	73-74-72-71	290	$3,344.45
Larry Nelson	T10	73-64-69-76	282	$35,000.00	Ed Dougherty	T49	76-71-73-70	290	$3,344.45
Curtis Strange	T13	73-72-70-68	283	$27,066.67	Rick Fehr	T49	77-71-72-70	290	$3,344.45
Mike Sullivan	T13	71-75-71-66	283	$27,066.67	Mike Reid	T49	73-75-75-67	290	$3,344.45
Ray Floyd	T13	68-76-69-70	283	$27,066.66	Bob Gilder	T49	74-73-70-73	290	$3,344.44
Bob Burns	T16	70-73-69-72	284	$19,640.00	Paul Goydos	T49	72-74-71-73	290	$3,344.44
Mark Calcavecchia	T16	74-72-68-70	284	$19,640.00	Mark O'Meara	T49	77-71-68-74	290	$3,344.44
Tom Kite	T16	72-73-69-70	284	$19,640.00	Larry Rinker	T49	73-73-72-72	290	$3,344.44
Andrew Magee	T16	75-73-69-67	284	$19,640.00	Ted Tryba	T49	75-73-69-73	290	$3,344.44
Dick Mast	T16	69-69-74-72	284	$19,640.00	Fred Funk	T58	73-71-72-75	291	$3,108.00
Joe Ozaki	T16	75-69-71-69	284	$19,640.00	Neal Lancaster	T58	71-71-77-72	291	$3,108.00
Jeff Sluman	T16	74-71-70-69	284	$19,640.00	John Morse	T58	74-73-74-70	291	$3,108.00
Chip Beck	T23	74-71-68-72	285	$12,880.00	Tom Cleaver	T61	75-71-73-73	292	$2,954.00
Jay Don Blake	T23	74-71-69-71	285	$12,880.00	Steve Elkington	T61	76-70-74-72	292	$2,954.00
David Frost	T23	74-70-69-72	285	$12,880.00	Ed Fiori	T61	75-71-73-73	292	$2,954.00
Craig Stadler	T23	71-73-69-72	285	$12,880.00	Steve Lowery	T61	74-72-72-74	292	$2,954.00
Michael Bradley	T27	75-68-74-69	286	$9,520.00	David Peoples	T61	72-76-73-71	292	$2,954.00
Scott Hoch	T27	72-73-67-74	286	$9,520.00	Steve Stricker	T61	73-69-78-72	292	$2,954.00
Bob Lohr	T27	72-72-73-69	286	$9,520.00	Lanny Wadkins	T61	79-67-71-75	292	$2,954.00
Jim McGovern	T27	75-70-68-73	286	$9,520.00	Jim Woodward	T61	74-73-72-73	292	$2,954.00
Jesper Parnevik	T27	73-72-71-70	286	$9,520.00	Davis Love III	T69	75-68-73-77	293	$2,800.00
Gene Sauers	T27	72-74-69-71	286	$9,520.00	David Toms	T69	72-75-75-71	293	$2,800.00
Hal Sutton	T27	76-71-67-72	286	$9,520.00	Richard Zokol	T69	76-71-74-72	293	$2,800.00
Ben Crenshaw	T34	73-70-73-71	287	$7,224.00	Nick Price	T72	75-73-73-73	294	$2,716.00
David Edwards	T34	70-76-71-70	287	$7,224.00	Dillard Pruitt	T72	73-73-76-72	294	$2,716.00
Jim Furyk	T34	72-73-70-72	287	$7,224.00	Paul Trittler	T72	77-71-72-74	294	$2,716.00
Gary Hallberg	T34	71-73-72-71	287	$7,224.00	Brandel Chamblee	T75	72-75-75-73	295	$2,646.00
Lee Janzen	T34	74-74-68-71	287	$7,224.00	Vijay Singh	T75	72-74-71-78	295	$2,646.00
Dave Barr	T39	78-70-70-70	288	$5,600.00					

HONDA CLASSIC

Weston Hills CC, Ft. Lauderdale, FL   Purse: $1,100,000
Par: 35-36--71   Yards: 6,964   March 10-13, 1994

LEADERS: First Round--Brandel Chamblee and Bernhard Langer, at 4-under-par 67, led by one over 12 other players. **Second Round--**Chamblee and Ed Dougherty at 7-under-par 135 led by one over Bruce Lietzke. **Third Round--**Chamblee, at 6-under-par 207, led by two over Davis Love III.

CUT: 83 players at 5-over-par 147.

PRO-AM: $7,500. Individual--Dudley Hart, 67, $750. Team--Kenny Perry, 53, $750.

WEATHER: Blustery conditions all week long.

Winner: Nick Price   70-67-73-66   276 $198,000.00

Craig Parry	2	68-73-69-67	277	$118,800.00
Brandel Chamblee	3	67-68-72-71	278	$74,800.00
John Daly	T 4	69-70-73-68	280	$43,312.50
Bernhard Langer	T 4	67-72-73-68	280	$43,312.50
Davis Love III	T 4	68-71-70-71	280	$43,312.50
Curtis Strange	T 4	71-67-72-70	280	$43,312.50
David Edwards	8	70-72-69-71	282	$34,100.00
Bruce Fleisher	T 9	68-73-70-72	283	$27,500.00
Jim Gallagher, Jr.	T 9	68-71-74-70	283	$27,500.00
Tom Kite	T 9	71-72-71-69	283	$27,500.00
Sandy Lyle	T 9	71-74-72-66	283	$27,500.00
Hal Sutton	T 9	71-72-70-70	283	$27,500.00
Gary Hallberg	T14	74-70-71-69	284	$19,250.00
Steve Lamontagne	T14	72-75-68-69	284	$19,250.00
Andrew Magee	T14	68-75-73-68	284	$19,250.00
Mark McCumber	T14	68-72-75-69	284	$19,250.00
Fred Funk	T18	70-68-78-69	285	$12,466.67
Ed Humenik	T18	70-71-77-67	285	$12,466.67
Hale Irwin	T18	72-69-75-69	285	$12,466.67
Tom Purtzer	T18	68-74-73-70	285	$12,466.67
Tim Simpson	T18	74-67-75-69	285	$12,466.67
Jeff Woodland	T18	68-75-72-70	285	$12,466.67
Ed Dougherty	T18	70-65-77-73	285	$12,466.66
Paul Goydos	T18	73-71-71-70	285	$12,466.66
Bruce Lietzke	T18	68-68-74-75	285	$12,466.66
Billy Andrade	T27	73-73-71-69	286	$8,140.00
Jim McGovern	T27	70-71-74-71	286	$8,140.00
Vijay Singh	T27	77-67-72-70	286	$8,140.00
Mark Carnevale	T30	75-71-71-70	287	$6,831.00
Brad Fabel	T30	70-73-75-69	287	$6,831.00
Scott Hoch	T30	68-71-75-73	287	$6,831.00
Joe Ozaki	T30	68-76-72-71	287	$6,831.00
Joey Rassett	T30	72-74-71-70	287	$6,831.00
Glen Day	T35	72-72-72-72	288	$5,541.25
John Huston	T35	70-71-79-68	288	$5,541.25
Peter Jordan	T35	70-75-75-68	288	$5,541.25
Scott Verplank	T35	73-74-71-70	288	$5,541.25
Bill Britton	T39	75-72-71-71	289	$3,864.00
Mark Brooks	T39	74-73-71-71	289	$3,864.00
Russ Cochran	T39	70-74-75-70	289	$3,864.00
John Cook	T39	72-72-71-74	289	$3,864.00
Nick Faldo	T39	70-70-73-76	289	$3,864.00
Yoshi Mizumaki	T39	74-72-70-73	289	$3,864.00
Kenny Perry	T39	72-68-75-74	289	$3,864.00
Esteban Toledo	T39	69-74-73-73	289	$3,864.00
Paul Trittler	T39	76-71-73-69	289	$3,864.00
Bob Tway	T39	71-73-76-69	289	$3,864.00
Richard Zokol	T39	72-74-73-70	289	$3,864.00
Jay Delsing	T50	69-76-72-73	290	$2,583.78
Clark Dennis	T50	75-70-70-75	290	$2,583.78
Mike Hulbert	T50	74-72-72-72	290	$2,583.78
Brian Kamm	T50	71-76-70-73	290	$2,583.78
Neal Lancaster	T50	71-72-77-70	290	$2,583.78
Dave Stockton, Jr	T50	74-72-71-73	290	$2,583.78
David Toms	T50	70-74-75-71	290	$2,583.78
Blaine McCallister	T50	73-72-70-75	290	$2,583.77
John Morse	T50	73-74-68-75	290	$2,583.77
Chris Dimarco	T59	71-73-75-72	291	$2,387.00
Mike Donald	T59	71-71-78-71	291	$2,387.00
Wayne Grady	T59	71-75-72-73	291	$2,387.00
Charles Raulerson	T59	72-75-71-73	291	$2,387.00
Paul Stankowski	T59	73-73-73-72	291	$2,387.00
Ian Woosnam	T59	72-71-72-76	291	$2,387.00
Howard Twitty	65	72-75-73-72	292	$2,310.00
Brian Claar	T66	68-77-76-72	293	$2,277.00
Keith Clearwater	T66	72-73-74-74	293	$2,277.00
Joel Edwards	T68	72-75-76-71	294	$2,233.00
Steve Pate	T68	71-74-76-73	294	$2,233.00
Jesper Parnevik	T70	71-75-74-75	295	$2,178.00
Jeff Roth	T70	74-73-72-76	295	$2,178.00
Tom Sieckmann	T70	71-71-79-74	295	$2,178.00
Guy Boros	T73	74-73-76-73	296	$2,123.00
Dan Oschmann	T73	73-72-75-76	296	$2,123.00
Dave Bishop	T75	74-72-78-73	297	$2,057.00
Mike Heinen	T75	75-70-79-73	297	$2,057.00
John Mahaffey	T75	69-74-76-78	297	$2,057.00
David Ogrin	T75	70-77-76-74	297	$2,057.00
Kelly Gibson	79	70-77-78-73	298	$2,002.00
Mark O'Meara	80	72-69-76-82	299	$1,980.00
Gary McCord	81	73-73-84-72	302	$1,958.00

NESTLE INVITATIONAL

Bay Hill Club, Orlando, FL
Par: 36-36--72 Yards: 7,114

Purse: $1,200,000
March 17-20, 1994

LEADERS: First Round--Nick Price, at 6-under-par 66, held a two-stroke lead over Vijay Singh, Greg Norman, Larry Mize, Scott Simpson and Patrick Burke. **Second Round--**Andrew Magee, Mize and Singh, at 7-under-par 137, were one stroke ahead of Price and Glen Day. **Third Round--**Singh, at 11-under-par 205, was a stroke ahead of Tom Watson, Price and Magee.

CUT: 77 players (76 professionals and one amateur) at 3-over-par 147.

PRO-AM: $7,500. Individual--Jim McGovern, 64, $750. Team--Nick Price, 56, $750.

WEATHER: Cloudless Thursday and Friday, partly sunny Saturday and Sunday. Warm throughout. Ideal playing conditions Thursday, some wind early Friday and Saturday.

Winner: Loren Roberts 70-70-68-67 275 $216,000.00

Nick Price	T 2	66-72-68-70	276	$89,600.00	Jumbo Ozaki	T36	74-72-71-69	286	$5,530.00
Vijay Singh	T 2	68-69-68-71	276	$89,600.00	Dan Pohl	T36	70-69-74-73	286	$5,530.00
Fuzzy Zoeller	T 2	72-68-67-69	276	$89,600.00	Billy Andrade	T42	71-72-71-73	287	$4,200.00
Larry Mize	5	68-69-71-69	277	$48,000.00	Brad Bryant	T42	72-72-72-71	287	$4,200.00
Tom Lehman	T 6	72-67-68-71	278	$41,700.00	Mark Calcavecchia	T42	70-74-70-73	287	$4,200.00
Greg Norman	T 6	68-72-71-67	278	$41,700.00	John Cook	T42	72-74-74-67	287	$4,200.00
Tom Watson	8	69-70-67-73	279	$37,200.00	Brad Faxon	T42	74-70-72-71	287	$4,200.00
Andrew Magee	9	70-67-69-74	280	$34,800.00	Peter Jacobsen	T47	72-73-71-72	288	$3,172.80
Glen Day	T10	70-68-72-71	281	$30,000.00	Jeff Maggert	T47	76-71-69-72	288	$3,172.80
Bill Glasson	T10	70-72-71-68	281	$30,000.00	Mark O'Meara	T47	73-72-70-73	288	$3,172.80
D.A. Weibring	T10	71-73-70-67	281	$30,000.00	Craig Parry	T47	73-72-70-73	288	$3,172.80
Bob Estes	T13	72-73-70-67	282	$19,950.00	Dicky Pride	T47	73-72-69-74	288	$3,172.80
Paul Goydos	T13	70-69-70-73	282	$19,950.00	Michael Allen	T52	69-70-73-77	289	$2,798.40
Wayne Grady	T13	71-70-71-70	282	$19,950.00	Steve Lowery	T52	69-76-72-72	289	$2,798.40
Jay Haas	T13	70-74-72-66	282	$19,950.00	Billy Mayfair	T52	75-70-67-77	289	$2,798.40
Donnie Hammond	T13	72-72-68-70	282	$19,950.00	Ted Schulz	T52	71-68-77-73	289	$2,798.40
Bob Lohr	T13	70-70-72-70	282	$19,950.00	Joey Sindelar	T52	74-73-68-74	289	$2,798.40
Blaine McCallister	T13	74-73-69-66	282	$19,950.00	Chris Dimarco	T57	73-73-73-71	290	$2,676.00
Mark McCumber	T13	71-74-67-70	282	$19,950.00	Scott Hoch	T57	72-73-69-76	290	$2,676.00
Jay Don Blake	T21	74-69-70-70	283	$11,265.00	Mike Springer	T57	69-74-73-74	290	$2,676.00
Mark Brooks	T21	72-70-69-72	283	$11,265.00	Leonard Thompson	T57	73-70-76-71	290	$2,676.00
Ben Crenshaw	T21	70-69-73-71	283	$11,265.00	John Harris	T57	77-67-76-70	290	AMATEUR
John Daly	T21	73-72-72-66	283	$11,265.00	Peter Baker	T62	74-72-74-71	291	$2,592.00
Dan Forsman	T21	75-69-68-71	283	$11,265.00	Payne Stewart	T62	73-71-73-74	291	$2,592.00
Bernhard Langer	T21	75-69-65-74	283	$11,265.00	Jim Thorpe	T62	75-72-74-70	291	$2,592.00
Scott Simpson	T21	68-75-69-71	283	$11,265.00	Clark Dennis	T65	74-73-73-72	292	$2,508.00
Kirk Triplett	T21	69-76-67-71	283	$11,265.00	Jodie Mudd	T65	71-73-73-75	292	$2,508.00
Mark Carnevale	T29	70-75-67-72	284	$7,980.00	Steve Stricker	T65	72-73-73-74	292	$2,508.00
John Huston	T29	73-68-68-75	284	$7,980.00	Ian Woosnam	T65	71-72-74-75	292	$2,508.00
Curtis Strange	T29	71-72-70-71	284	$7,980.00	Patrick Burke	T69	68-74-75-76	293	$2,436.00
Grant Waite	T29	69-72-72-71	284	$7,980.00	Jay Delsing	T69	70-75-73-75	293	$2,436.00
David Frost	T33	73-71-70-71	285	$6,780.00	Robin Freeman	T71	72-73-75-74	294	$2,376.00
Jim Gallagher, Jr.	T33	69-74-73-69	285	$6,780.00	Jerry Pate	T71	73-71-77-73	294	$2,376.00
Jesper Parnevik	T33	73-74-66-72	285	$6,780.00	Mike Sullivan	T71	69-75-77-73	294	$2,376.00
Keith Clearwater	T36	77-70-70-69	286	$5,530.00	Larry Nelson	T74	72-73-75-75	295	$2,316.00
Bruce Fleisher	T36	72-72-73-69	286	$5,530.00	Robert Wrenn	T74	74-71-70-80	295	$2,316.00
Ed Humenik	T36	78-69-71-68	286	$5,530.00	John Inman	76	72-75-72-78	297	$2,280.00
Davis Love III	T36	70-73-70-73	286	$5,530.00	David Duval	77	71-74-76-78	299	$2,256.00

THE PLAYERS CHAMPIONSHIP

THE PLAYERS
CHAMPIONSHIP

TPC at Sawgrass, Ponte Vedra Beach, FL **Purse: $2,500,000**
Par: 36-36--72 **Yards: 6,896** **March 24-27, 1994**

LEADERS: First Round--Greg Norman, with a course-record-tying 63, held a two-stroke lead over Colin Montgomerie, Jeff Maggert, Tom Kite and Lee Janzen. **Second Round--**Norman, with a 36-hole tournament record 14-under-par 130, was three strokes in front of Fuzzy Zoeller. **Third Round--**Norman, with a 54-hole tournament record of 19-under-par 197, was four strokes ahead of Zoeller.

CUT: 85 players at even-par 144.

WEATHER: After a 15-minute start delay due to fog, weather conditions were ideal for Thursday play. A 2-hour, 56-minute weather delay, with lightning and heavy rain Friday resulted in a suspension of play for the day at 6:25 p.m.; 72 players were still on the course. Friday, conditions turned sunny and clear in the afternoon, with cloud cover moving in late in the day. The second round was completed Saturday morning under sunny and clear skies; the third round got underway at 11 a.m., with ideal conditions throughout the afternoon. Cloudy skies early Sunday turned mostly sunny later, with winds picking up throughout.

Winner: Greg Norman 63-67-67-67 264 $450,000.00

Player		Scores	Total	Money	Player		Scores	Total	Money
Fuzzy Zoeller	2	66-67-68-67	268	$270,000.00	Ted Tryba	T35	68-73-69-75	285	$11,037.50
Jeff Maggert	3	65-69-69-68	271	$170,000.00	Ernie Els	T45	69-73-72-72	286	$7,150.00
Hale Irwin	4	67-70-70-69	276	$120,000.00	Rick Fehr	T45	70-73-68-75	286	$7,150.00
Nick Faldo	5	67-69-68-73	277	$100,000.00	Wayne Grady	T45	67-73-71-75	286	$7,150.00
Brad Faxon	T6	68-68-70-72	278	$83,750.00	Andrew Magee	T45	72-71-70-73	286	$7,150.00
Davis Love III	T6	68-66-70-74	278	$83,750.00	Joe Ozaki	T45	71-72-70-73	286	$7,150.00
Steve Lowery	T6	68-74-69-67	278	$83,750.00	Kirk Triplett	T45	71-72-70-73	286	$7,150.00
Gary Hallberg	T9	68-69-69-73	279	$65,000.00	David Edwards	T51	69-70-72-76	287	$5,962.50
Nolan Henke	T9	73-69-69-68	279	$65,000.00	Steve Elkington	T51	71-72-75-69	287	$5,962.50
Tom Kite	T9	65-71-70-73	279	$65,000.00	Gene Sauers	T51	73-69-75-70	287	$5,962.50
Colin Montgomerie	T9	65-73-71-70	279	$65,000.00	Grant Waite	T51	74-68-71-74	287	$5,962.50
Mike Springer	13	68-68-72-72	280	$52,500.00	Fulton Allem	T55	70-71-72-75	288	$5,600.00
Dave Barr	T14	68-69-72-72	281	$42,500.00	Brian Claar	T55	68-76-72-72	288	$5,600.00
Jose Maria Olazabal	T14	69-69-73-70	281	$42,500.00	Keith Clearwater	T55	70-72-70-76	288	$5,600.00
Craig Parry	T14	69-66-73-73	281	$42,500.00	Jay Haas	T55	75-69-71-73	288	$5,600.00
Loren Roberts	T14	68-71-71-71	281	$42,500.00	Jim McGovern	T55	72-72-71-73	288	$5,600.00
Tom Watson	T14	71-72-71-67	281	$42,500.00	Larry Nelson	T55	70-67-76-75	288	$5,600.00
Ben Crenshaw	T19	72-72-68-70	282	$31,375.00	Vijay Singh	T55	71-69-69-79	288	$5,600.00
Dillard Pruitt	T19	70-71-68-73	282	$31,375.00	Michael Allen	T62	74-69-73-73	289	$5,250.00
Mike Standly	T19	72-71-68-71	282	$31,375.00	Joel Edwards	T62	68-75-73-73	289	$5,250.00
Hal Sutton	T19	67-68-74-73	282	$31,375.00	Paul Goydos	T62	72-72-71-74	289	$5,250.00
Mark Calcavecchia	T23	70-72-69-72	283	$23,000.00	Mark McCumber	T62	73-71-75-70	289	$5,250.00
John Cook	T23	70-71-72-70	283	$23,000.00	Kenny Perry	T62	69-75-73-72	289	$5,250.00
Tim Simpson	T23	69-71-70-73	283	$23,000.00	Jim Thorpe	T62	73-69-73-74	289	$5,250.00
Steve Stricker	T23	72-70-70-71	283	$23,000.00	Howard Twitty	T62	69-75-72-73	289	$5,250.00
Lennie Clements	T27	68-71-74-71	284	$16,640.63	Ian Baker-Finch	T69	73-69-74-74	290	$4,950.00
Ed Fiori	T27	70-68-74-72	284	$16,640.63	Brandel Chamblee	T69	70-72-72-76	290	$4,950.00
Jim Gallagher, Jr.	T27	76-68-70-70	284	$16,640.63	Russ Cochran	T69	70-73-78-69	290	$4,950.00
Wayne Levi	T27	72-68-72-72	284	$16,640.63	Donnie Hammond	T69	68-73-75-74	290	$4,950.00
Chip Beck	T27	73-71-67-73	284	$16,640.62	D.A. Weibring	T69	75-69-70-76	290	$4,950.00
Jay Delsing	T27	67-73-71-73	284	$16,640.62	Brad Bryant	T74	75-69-75-72	291	$4,725.00
Bernhard Langer	T27	74-68-70-72	284	$16,640.62	Sandy Lyle	T74	71-72-71-77	291	$4,725.00
John Mahaffey	T27	71-73-65-75	284	$16,640.62	Dick Mast	T74	73-70-74-74	291	$4,725.00
Jay Don Blake	T35	70-73-69-73	285	$11,037.50	Tom Sieckmann	T74	73-68-69-81	291	$4,725.00
Bob Estes	T35	70-71-70-74	285	$11,037.50	John Adams	T78	72-70-76-74	292	$4,525.00
Bob Gilder	T35	71-71-70-73	285	$11,037.50	Fred Funk	T78	73-71-73-75	292	$4,525.00
Mike Hulbert	T35	71-71-70-73	285	$11,037.50	Greg Kraft	T78	72-71-72-77	292	$4,525.00
John Huston	T35	68-73-72-72	285	$11,037.50	Corey Pavin	T78	69-73-73-77	292	$4,525.00
Lee Janzen	T35	65-75-70-75	285	$11,037.50	Jumbo Ozaki	82	68-76-75-74	293	$4,400.00
Neal Lancaster	T35	71-68-72-74	285	$11,037.50	Dan Forsman	83	67-77-73-77	294	$4,350.00
Roger Maltbie	T35	71-69-73-72	285	$11,037.50	Robert Gamez	84	70-72-81-72	295	$4,300.00
Joey Sindelar	T35	70-74-70-71	285	$11,037.50	Denis Watson	85	74-69-80-74	297	$4,250.00

FREEPORT-McMoRan CLASSIC

FREEPORT-McMoRan *Golf Classic*

English Turn G&CC, New Orleans, LA　**Purse: $1,200,000**
Par: 36-36--72　　**Yards: 7,106**　　**March 31-April 3, 1994**

LEADERS: First Round--Jose Maria Olazabal, with a course-record 9-under-par 63, held a four-stroke lead over Sam Torrance. **Second Round**--Dennis Paulson, with a course-record 10-under-par 62, eclipsed Olazabal's day-old mark and had a one-stroke advantage over Olazabal and Ben Crenshaw at 8-under-par 136. **Third Round**--Torrance and Crenshaw, at 11-under-par 205, were two strokes in front of Olazabal.

CUT: 73 players at 2-over-par 146.

PRO-AM: $7,500. Individual--Hal Sutton, 66, $750. Team--Hal Sutton, 55, $750.

WEATHER: Sunny, windy and cold Thursday, with temperatures reaching the high 60s later in the day as winds died down. Continued sunny and cool Friday, with little wind. Sunny and clear Saturday, with winds returning. Glorious early Easter Sunday, with cloudy conditions with light rain in the afternoon.

Winner: Ben Crenshaw　　**69-68-68-68　273**　　**$216,000.00**

Jose Maria Olazabal	2	63-74-70-69	276	$129,600.00	Nick Faldo	T35	72-71-70-74	287	$5,665.71
Sam Torrance	3	67-71-67-73	278	$81,600.00	Chris Kite	T35	71-70-72-74	287	$5,665.71
Dennis Paulson	T4	74-62-75-68	279	$49,600.00	Bob Lohr	T35	70-72-71-74	287	$5,665.71
Kenny Perry	T4	69-72-68-70	279	$49,600.00	Joe Ozaki	T35	71-68-74-74	287	$5,665.71
Mike Springer	T4	73-69-69-68	279	$49,600.00	Gary Hallberg	T42	71-69-76-72	288	$4,560.00
Steve Brodie	T7	71-67-72-71	281	$36,150.00	Steve Lamontagne	T42	69-74-70-75	288	$4,560.00
Bobby Clampett	T7	70-68-72-71	281	$36,150.00	Joey Rassett	T44	68-76-73-72	289	$3,541.72
Chris Dimarco	T7	76-70-66-69	281	$36,150.00	Dave Rummells	T44	74-69-75-71	289	$3,541.72
Dick Mast	T7	71-69-74-67	281	$36,150.00	Scott Verplank	T44	76-68-77-68	289	$3,541.72
Jim Furyk	11	70-72-66-74	282	$30,000.00	Mark Brooks	T44	72-67-75-75	289	$3,541.71
Glen Day	T12	72-68-72-71	283	$25,200.00	Mike Hulbert	T44	74-71-70-74	289	$3,541.71
John Flannery	T12	73-72-69-69	283	$25,200.00	Sean Murphy	T44	72-73-71-73	289	$3,541.71
John Morse	T12	72-71-67-73	283	$25,200.00	John Wilson	T44	71-70-73-75	289	$3,541.71
Michael Bradley	T15	72-74-69-69	284	$18,000.00	Jesper Parnevik	T51	73-69-73-75	290	$2,862.00
Bob Burns	T15	71-72-69-72	284	$18,000.00	Tim Simpson	T51	69-70-73-78	290	$2,862.00
Lennie Clements	T15	73-67-73-71	284	$18,000.00	Kirk Triplett	T51	73-72-72-73	290	$2,862.00
Ed Dougherty	T15	74-70-66-74	284	$18,000.00	Richard Zokol	T51	76-70-74-70	290	$2,862.00
Mike Standly	T15	68-71-77-68	284	$18,000.00	Marco Dawson	T55	72-74-70-75	291	$2,736.00
Ted Tryba	T15	72-70-67-75	284	$18,000.00	Edward Kirby	T55	71-74-73-73	291	$2,736.00
Duffy Waldorf	T15	71-72-68-73	284	$18,000.00	Lanny Wadkins	T55	71-70-70-80	291	$2,736.00
Donnie Hammond	T22	73-70-68-74	285	$11,520.00	Clark Dennis	T58	73-70-75-74	292	$2,652.00
Peter Jordan	T22	72-71-67-75	285	$11,520.00	David Frost	T58	74-72-71-75	292	$2,652.00
Doug Martin	T22	75-70-71-69	285	$11,520.00	Tommy Moore	T58	72-73-75-72	292	$2,652.00
Hal Sutton	T22	72-68-73-72	285	$11,520.00	Stan Utley	T58	72-72-74-74	292	$2,652.00
Mark Wurtz	T22	73-71-71-70	285	$11,520.00	Guy Boros	T62	77-69-73-74	293	$2,568.00
Ian Baker-Finch	T27	71-70-72-73	286	$7,987.50	Steve Gotsche	T62	74-72-71-76	293	$2,568.00
Trevor Dodds	T27	75-68-69-74	286	$7,987.50	Dillard Pruitt	T62	73-72-70-78	293	$2,568.00
Joel Edwards	T27	70-75-68-73	286	$7,987.50	Todd Barranger	T65	76-70-70-78	294	$2,496.00
Ernie Els	T27	69-76-69-72	286	$7,987.50	Buddy Gardner	T65	73-73-74-74	294	$2,496.00
Kelly Gibson	T27	72-69-69-76	286	$7,987.50	Brad Lardon	T65	72-71-74-77	294	$2,496.00
Ted Schulz	T27	72-67-73-74	286	$7,987.50	Russell Beiersdorf	68	72-74-73-76	295	$2,448.00
Joey Sindelar	T27	72-69-69-76	286	$7,987.50	Brad King	69	74-72-77-74	297	$2,424.00
Greg Twiggs	T27	76-66-68-76	286	$7,987.50	Lance Ten Broeck	70	72-74-75-77	298	$2,400.00
Russ Cochran	T35	70-71-73-73	287	$5,665.72	Rocky Walcher	71	76-68-78-77	299	$2,376.00
Larry Rinker	T35	70-72-72-73	287	$5,665.72	Payne Stewart	72	72-70-77-81	300	$2,352.00
Gene Sauers	T35	71-75-70-71	287	$5,665.72					

MASTERS TOURNAMENT

Augusta National Golf Club

Augusta National GC, Augusta, GA **Purse: $2,000,000**
Par: 36-36--72   **Yards: 6,925**   **April 7-10, 1994**

LEADERS: First Round--Larry Mize, at 4-under-par 68, led by one stroke over Fulton Allem and Tom Kite. **Second Round--**Mize, at 5-under-par 139, led by one over Tom Lehman, Greg Norman and Dan Forsman. **Third Round--**Lehman, at 7-under-par 209, led by one over Jose Maria Olazabal.

CUT: 51 players at 5-over-par 149 from a starting field of 86. The cut was the low 44 scores and ties and anyone within 10 strokes of the lead.

WEATHER: Thursday was cool with a light breeze. Friday through Sunday were sunny and breezy.

Winner: Jose Maria Olazabal   74-67-69-69 279 $360,000.00

Player		Scores	Total	Money
Tom Lehman	2	70-70-69-72	281	$216,000.00
Larry Mize	3	68-71-72-71	282	$136,000.00
Tom Kite	4	69-72-71-71	283	$96,000.00
Jay Haas	T5	72-72-72-69	285	$73,000.00
Jim McGovern	T5	72-70-71-72	285	$73,000.00
Loren Roberts	T5	75-68-72-70	285	$73,000.00
Ernie Els	T8	74-67-74-71	286	$60,000.00
Corey Pavin	T8	71-72-73-70	286	$60,000.00
Ian Baker-Finch	T10	71-71-71-74	287	$50,000.00
Ray Floyd	T10	70-74-71-72	287	$50,000.00
John Huston	T10	72-72-74-69	287	$50,000.00
Tom Watson	13	70-71-73-74	288	$42,000.00
Dan Forsman	14	74-66-76-73	289	$38,000.00
Chip Beck	T15	71-71-75-74	291	$34,000.00
Brad Faxon	T15	71-73-73-74	291	$34,000.00
Mark O'Meara	T15	75-70-76-70	291	$34,000.00
Seve Ballesteros	T18	70-76-75-71	292	$24,343.00
Ben Crenshaw	T18	74-73-73-72	292	$24,343.00
David Edwards	T18	73-72-73-74	292	$24,343.00
Bill Glasson	T18	72-73-75-72	292	$24,343.00
Hale Irwin	T18	73-68-79-72	292	$24,343.00
Greg Norman	T18	70-70-75-77	292	$24,343.00
Lanny Wadkins	T18	73-74-73-72	292	$24,343.00
Bernhard Langer	T25	74-74-72-73	293	$16,800.00
Jeff Sluman	T25	74-75-71-73	293	$16,800.00
Scott Simpson	T27	74-74-73-73	294	$14,800.00
Vijay Singh	T27	70-75-74-75	294	$14,800.00
Curtis Strange	T27	74-70-75-75	294	$14,800.00
Lee Janzen	T30	75-71-76-73	295	$13,300.00
Craig Parry	T30	75-74-73-73	295	$13,300.00
Nick Faldo	32	76-73-73-74	296	$12,400.00
Russ Cochran	T33	71-74-74-78	297	$11,550.00
Sam Torrance	T33	76-73-74-74	297	$11,550.00
David Frost	T35	74-71-75-78	298	$10,300.00
Nick Price	T35	74-73-74-77	298	$10,300.00
Fuzzy Zoeller	T35	74-72-74-78	298	$10,300.00
Fulton Allem	T38	69-77-76-77	299	$9,000.00
Fred Funk	T38	79-70-75-75	299	$9,000.00
Sandy Lyle	T38	75-73-78-73	299	$9,000.00
Wayne Grady	T41	74-73-73-80	300	$7,400.00
Andrew Magee	T41	74-74-76-76	300	$7,400.00
Hajime Meshiai	T41	71-71-80-78	300	$7,400.00
Costantino Rocca	T41	79-70-78-73	300	$7,400.00
Mike Standly	T41	77-69-79-75	300	$7,400.00
John Cook	T46	77-72-77-75	301	$6,000.00
Ian Woosnam	T46	76-73-77-75	301	$6,000.00
John Daly	T48	76-73-77-78	304	$5,250.00
Howard Twitty	T48	73-76-74-81	304	$5,250.00
Jeff Maggert	T50	75-73-82-75	305	$5,000.00
John Harris	T50	72-76-80-77	305	AMATEUR

MCI HERITAGE CLASSIC

Harbour Town GL, Hilton Head Island, SC
Par: 36-35--71   Yards: 6,916

Purse: $1,250,000
April 14-17, 1994

LEADERS: First Round--Bob Estes and Fred Funk, at 6-under-par 65, led by one stroke over Tom Lehman and Barry Jaeckel. **Second Round--**David Frost, at 11-under-par 131, led by one over Jim McGovern and Larry Mize. Frost posted a course-record 10-under-par 61. **Third Round--**Hale Irwin, at 15-under-par 198, led by two strokes over Greg Norman and Russ Cochran.

CUT: 75 players at 1-over-par 143.

PRO-AM: $7,500. Individual--Bob Estes, 65, $750. Team--Bob Lohr, 53, $750.

WEATHER: Beautiful and breezy all week, with a little fog on Friday afternoon.

Winner: Hale Irwin   68-65-65-68   266 $225,000.00

Player	Pos	Scores	Total	Money		Player	Pos	Scores	Total	Money
Greg Norman	2	67-66-67-68	268	$135,000.00		Tom Purtzer	T38	71-69-73-70	283	$5,500.00
Loren Roberts	3	69-70-68-62	269	$85,000.00		Mike Reid	T38	70-71-70-72	283	$5,500.00
David Edwards	T4	70-71-65-64	270	$51,666.67		Bobby Wadkins	T38	71-72-68-72	283	$5,500.00
David Frost	T4	70-61-72-67	270	$51,666.67		Brian Claar	T42	69-71-73-71	284	$4,021.88
Nolan Henke	T4	69-69-66-66	270	$51,666.66		Keith Clearwater	T42	70-73-70-71	284	$4,021.88
Russ Cochran	T7	67-67-66-71	271	$40,312.50		Ken Green	T42	70-70-75-69	284	$4,021.88
Bob Estes	T7	65-70-68-68	271	$40,312.50		Howard Twitty	T42	68-72-72-72	284	$4,021.88
Larry Mize	T9	67-65-75-65	272	$35,000.00		Ronnie Black	T42	71-71-68-74	284	$4,021.87
Jesper Parnevik	T9	68-68-69-67	272	$35,000.00		Michael Bradley	T42	68-72-71-73	284	$4,021.87
Jim McGovern	11	67-65-73-70	275	$31,250.00		Ed Humenik	T42	69-72-71-72	284	$4,021.87
Fred Funk	T12	65-70-71-70	276	$27,500.00		Blaine McCallister	T42	70-71-70-73	284	$4,021.87
Peter Jacobsen	T12	68-68-71-69	276	$27,500.00		Fulton Allem	T50	75-68-71-71	285	$3,015.00
Dan Forsman	14	72-66-75-64	277	$23,750.00		Bob Gilder	T50	69-73-68-75	285	$3,015.00
Marco Dawson	T15	70-70-66-72	278	$21,250.00		Joey Sindelar	T50	72-67-73-73	285	$3,015.00
Jeff Maggert	T15	67-72-67-72	278	$21,250.00		Mike Springer	T50	72-69-75-69	285	$3,015.00
Vijay Singh	T15	68-75-68-67	278	$21,250.00		Steve Stricker	T50	72-70-72-71	285	$3,015.00
Dave Barr	T18	72-65-71-71	279	$15,750.00		Jay Delsing	T55	74-67-74-71	286	$2,825.00
John Cook	T18	72-70-69-68	279	$15,750.00		John Flannery	T55	72-69-75-70	286	$2,825.00
Barry Jaeckel	T18	66-73-69-71	279	$15,750.00		Andrew Magee	T55	70-73-67-76	286	$2,825.00
Tom Lehman	T18	66-69-73-71	279	$15,750.00		Gil Morgan	T55	70-70-71-75	286	$2,825.00
Tim Simpson	T18	68-72-72-67	279	$15,750.00		Jerry Pate	T55	74-68-70-74	286	$2,825.00
Robert Wrenn	T18	71-69-71-68	279	$15,750.00		Joel Edwards	T60	70-72-73-72	287	$2,712.50
Rick Fehr	T24	69-72-69-70	280	$11,000.00		Scott Hoch	T60	70-73-73-71	287	$2,712.50
John Inman	T24	77-64-73-66	280	$11,000.00		Steve Lowery	T60	69-67-74-77	287	$2,712.50
Wayne Levi	T24	67-70-69-74	280	$11,000.00		Kenny Perry	T60	67-72-73-75	287	$2,712.50
Chip Beck	T27	73-69-70-69	281	$9,250.00		Ian Baker-Finch	T64	70-72-72-74	288	$2,612.50
Mark McCumber	T27	70-70-74-67	281	$9,250.00		Bob Lohr	T64	68-74-77-69	288	$2,612.50
Willie Wood	T27	70-68-70-73	281	$9,250.00		Charles Raulerson	T64	74-69-75-70	288	$2,612.50
Jay Haas	T30	71-69-73-69	282	$7,265.63		Tom Watson	T64	72-70-72-74	288	$2,612.50
Mark Lye	T30	71-69-74-68	282	$7,265.63		Hubert Green	68	68-72-73-76	289	$2,550.00
Don Pooley	T30	70-67-74-71	282	$7,265.63		Dudley Hart	T69	71-67-76-76	290	$2,512.50
Jim Thorpe	T30	71-68-74-69	282	$7,265.63		Dave Rummells	T69	70-72-74-74	290	$2,512.50
Jay Don Blake	T30	73-67-69-73	282	$7,265.62		Neal Lancaster	T71	70-72-73-76	291	$2,462.50
Brad Faxon	T30	69-69-73-71	282	$7,265.62		Larry Nelson	T71	75-66-74-76	291	$2,462.50
Steve Pate	T30	69-70-72-71	282	$7,265.62		Grant Waite	73	71-72-76-73	292	$2,425.00
Mike Standly	T30	71-69-66-76	282	$7,265.62		Brett Ogle	74	72-71-72-78	293	$2,400.00
Dick Mast	T38	72-68-70-73	283	$5,500.00		Doug Tewell	75	72-70-75-81	298	$2,375.00

KMART GREATER GREENSBORO OPEN

Forest Oaks CC, Greensboro, NC   **Purse: $1,500,000**
Par: 36-36--72   Yards: 6,958   **April 21-24, 1994**

LEADERS: First Round--Mike Springer, after an 8-under-par 64, held a one-stroke lead over Hale Irwin. Pete Jordan was in third place with a 66. **Second Round--**Springer, at 11-under-par 133, was four strokes ahead of Ed Humenik. **Third Round--**Springer, at 13-under-par 203, maintained a four-stroke lead over John Morse and Brad Bryant.

CUT: 76 players at one-over-par 145.

PRO-AM: $7,500. Individual--Tom Kite, 67, $750. Team--Michael Allen, 52, $750.

WEATHER: Sunny and clear Thursday with some wind; cool in the morning, with temperatures warming throughout the day. Mostly cloudy, cold and windy Friday, with temperatures getting only to the 50s. Sunny and warm Saturday and Sunday, with cool mornings both days.

Winner: Mike Springer 64-69-70-72 275 $270,000.00

Brad Bryant	T2	68-71-68-71	278	$112,000.00	Kelly Gibson	T37	70-73-73-72	288	$6,450.00
Ed Humenik	T2	72-65-73-68	278	$112,000.00	Ken Green	T37	71-73-70-74	288	$6,450.00
Hale Irwin	T2	65-73-71-69	278	$112,000.00	Steve Stricker	T37	72-73-71-72	288	$6,450.00
Bob Lohr	5	69-71-69-70	279	$60,000.00	Willie Wood	T37	73-72-74-69	288	$6,450.00
Donnie Hammond	T6	70-71-69-70	280	$52,125.00	Billy Andrade	T44	71-73-72-73	289	$4,062.50
John Morse	T6	72-68-67-73	280	$52,125.00	Brandel Chamblee	T44	71-73-74-71	289	$4,062.50
David Edwards	T8	71-74-68-68	281	$42,000.00	Bobby Clampett	T44	74-71-70-74	289	$4,062.50
Joel Edwards	T8	69-69-73-70	281	$42,000.00	Glen Day	T44	69-73-73-74	289	$4,062.50
Dudley Hart	T8	75-69-67-70	281	$42,000.00	Brad Fabel	T44	72-71-75-71	289	$4,062.50
Mike Smith	T8	69-73-69-70	281	$42,000.00	Jim Furyk	T44	70-73-73-73	289	$4,062.50
Gil Morgan	12	68-71-69-74	282	$34,500.00	Mark O'Meara	T44	72-73-74-70	289	$4,062.50
Jay Haas	T13	69-73-71-70	283	$30,000.00	David Peoples	T44	67-75-74-73	289	$4,062.50
Howard Twitty	T13	72-69-71-71	283	$30,000.00	Joey Sindelar	T44	70-75-73-71	289	$4,062.50
Guy Boros	T15	71-73-69-71	284	$22,500.00	Ted Tryba	T44	70-73-73-73	289	$4,062.50
Lennie Clements	T15	71-69-72-72	284	$22,500.00	Duffy Waldorf	T44	69-74-73-73	289	$4,062.50
Marco Dawson	T15	70-74-72-68	284	$22,500.00	Fuzzy Zoeller	T44	74-68-74-73	289	$4,062.50
Brad Faxon	T15	68-73-73-70	284	$22,500.00	John Adams	T56	69-72-76-73	290	$3,330.00
Bill Kratzert	T15	69-72-72-71	284	$22,500.00	Chris Dimarco	T56	69-73-78-70	290	$3,330.00
Steve Lowery	T15	71-72-71-70	284	$22,500.00	Steve Elkington	T56	76-69-71-74	290	$3,330.00
Roger Maltbie	T15	69-75-70-70	284	$22,500.00	David Feherty	T56	70-74-71-75	290	$3,330.00
John Cook	T22	72-72-71-70	285	$13,521.43	Steve Pate	T56	73-72-76-69	290	$3,330.00
Bill Glasson	T22	68-73-72-72	285	$13,521.43	Jeff Sluman	T56	73-72-73-72	290	$3,330.00
John Huston	T22	73-65-75-72	285	$13,521.43	Jeff Woodland	T56	73-69-76-72	290	$3,330.00
Lee Janzen	T22	68-72-73-72	285	$13,521.43	Brian Claar	63	70-71-75-75	291	$3,210.00
Brett Ogle	T22	72-70-71-72	285	$13,521.43	Bob Gilder	T64	73-72-76-71	292	$3,165.00
Mike Reid	T22	70-73-72-70	285	$13,521.43	Vijay Singh	T64	71-73-76-72	292	$3,165.00
Dave Barr	T22	72-71-68-74	285	$13,521.42	Larry Nelson	66	71-72-76-74	293	$3,120.00
Mark Brooks	T29	68-74-69-75	286	$9,975.00	Chris Smith	T67	71-74-78-71	294	$3,075.00
Jay Delsing	T29	69-75-69-73	286	$9,975.00	Kirk Triplett	T67	74-70-76-74	294	$3,075.00
Mike Hulbert	T29	71-72-68-75	286	$9,975.00	Phil Tataurangi	T69	71-74-73-77	295	$3,015.00
Blaine McCallister	T29	70-70-74-72	286	$9,975.00	Bobby Wadkins	T69	75-69-75-76	295	$3,015.00
Mark Calcavecchia	T33	71-70-71-75	287	$8,287.50	Trevor Dodds	T71	69-76-77-74	296	$2,940.00
Peter Jacobsen	T33	72-73-72-70	287	$8,287.50	Peter Jordan	T71	66-77-75-78	296	$2,940.00
Craig Parry	T33	69-71-75-72	287	$8,287.50	Grant Waite	T71	74-71-77-74	296	$2,940.00
Gene Sauers	T33	71-71-74-71	287	$8,287.50	Russ Cochran	74	73-72-79-74	298	$2,880.00
Chip Beck	T37	71-73-71-73	288	$6,450.00	Bob Burns	75	70-74-81-75	300	$2,850.00
Steve Brodie	T37	72-73-74-69	288	$6,450.00	Charles Raulerson	76	74-68-81-78	301	$2,820.00
Robert Gamez	T37	70-74-71-73	288	$6,450.00					

SHELL HOUSTON OPEN

TPC at The Woodlands, The Woodlands, TX   Purse: $1,300,000
Par: 36-36--72   Yards: 7,042   April 28-May 1, 1994

LEADERS: First Round--Andrew Magee, with a 7-under-par 65, led by a stroke over Bob Gilder and Dave Barr. **Second Round--**Tom Kite, at 11-under-par 133, led by one over Mike Heinen. **Third Round-**-Jeff Maggert, Kite and Heinen, at 12-under-par 204, led by two strokes over Hal Sutton.

CUT: 81 players at 1-under-par 143.

PRO-AM: Individual--Fred Funk, 68, $750. Team--Greg Kraft, Jim McGovern and Phil Blackmar, 54, $625 each.

WEATHER: Partly cloudy Thursday, Friday and Sunday. Saturday's round was delayed until 11:33 a.m. due to rain and lightning in the area. Rain, heavy at times, during Saturday's play.

Winner: Mike Heinen   67-68-69-68   272 $234,000.00

Jeff Maggert	T 2	70-66-68-71	275	$97,066.67	Dick Mast	T38	67-76-69-74	286	$5,070.00
Hal Sutton	T 2	68-70-68-69	275	$97,066.67	Jim McGovern	T38	71-72-71-72	286	$5,070.00
Tom Kite	T 2	68-65-71-71	275	$97,066.66	Yoshi Mizumaki	T38	68-72-73-73	286	$5,070.00
Bob Gilder	T 5	66-76-69-67	278	$49,400.00	Steve Rintoul	T38	73-70-70-73	286	$5,070.00
Vijay Singh	T 5	72-67-69-70	278	$49,400.00	Robert Wrenn	T38	70-66-74-76	286	$5,070.00
John Daly	T 7	68-74-70-67	279	$40,516.67	Kelly Gibson	T47	68-74-74-71	287	$3,298.75
Gil Morgan	T 7	70-71-72-66	279	$40,516.67	Mike Hulbert	T47	75-68-72-72	287	$3,298.75
Peter Jacobsen	T 7	68-73-69-69	279	$40,516.66	J.L. Lewis	T47	69-71-76-71	287	$3,298.75
Dave Barr	T10	66-72-71-71	280	$32,500.00	Steve Pate	T47	70-69-73-75	287	$3,298.75
Fred Funk	T10	71-67-71-71	280	$32,500.00	Joey Rassett	T47	68-71-74-74	287	$3,298.75
Curtis Strange	T10	71-72-66-71	280	$32,500.00	Dave Rummells	T47	69-72-72-74	287	$3,298.75
Clark Dennis	T13	69-71-72-69	281	$25,133.34	D.A. Weibring	T47	71-71-71-74	287	$3,298.75
Fulton Allem	T13	72-70-69-70	281	$25,133.33	John Wilson	T47	69-73-71-74	287	$3,298.75
Jeff Woodland	T13	69-72-66-74	281	$25,133.33	Steve Elkington	T55	67-74-72-75	288	$2,925.00
Jay Haas	T16	72-67-73-70	282	$18,237.15	Steve Lamontagne	T55	74-68-72-74	288	$2,925.00
Bob Lohr	T16	70-66-74-72	282	$18,237.15	Neal Lancaster	T55	73-68-74-73	288	$2,925.00
Rick Fehr	T16	71-68-68-75	282	$18,237.14	Shaun Micheel	T55	72-68-74-74	288	$2,925.00
Robert Gamez	T16	69-68-71-74	282	$18,237.14	Larry Rinker	T55	70-72-75-71	288	$2,925.00
Wayne Levi	T16	72-67-69-74	282	$18,237.14	Phil Tataurangi	T55	69-73-73-73	288	$2,925.00
Doug Martin	T16	71-66-70-75	282	$18,237.14	Ronnie Black	T61	71-72-77-69	289	$2,769.00
John Morse	T16	71-70-69-72	282	$18,237.14	Steve Brodie	T61	70-70-70-79	289	$2,769.00
Keith Clearwater	T23	72-67-75-69	283	$12,480.00	Ben Crenshaw	T61	72-70-75-72	289	$2,769.00
Donnie Hammond	T23	70-69-71-73	283	$12,480.00	Keith Fergus	T61	70-72-74-73	289	$2,769.00
Mark McCumber	T23	70-69-70-74	283	$12,480.00	Paul Goydos	T61	68-72-75-74	289	$2,769.00
Peter Jordan	T26	68-71-71-74	284	$9,425.00	Dan Pohl	T61	70-72-74-73	289	$2,769.00
Brian Kamm	T26	70-69-73-72	284	$9,425.00	John Adams	T67	71-71-72-76	290	$2,639.00
Loren Roberts	T26	70-72-69-73	284	$9,425.00	Michael Allen	T67	69-74-73-74	290	$2,639.00
Mike Sullivan	T26	70-71-70-73	284	$9,425.00	Bill Britton	T67	70-70-76-74	290	$2,639.00
Doug Tewell	T26	71-68-71-74	284	$9,425.00	Brad Lardon	T67	72-71-76-71	290	$2,639.00
Stan Utley	T26	71-69-73-71	284	$9,425.00	Russell Beiersdorf	T71	71-70-79-71	291	$2,535.00
Marco Dawson	T32	70-72-74-69	285	$7,193.34	Steve Gotsche	T71	71-71-75-74	291	$2,535.00
Dicky Pride	T32	74-69-73-69	285	$7,193.34	Tim Simpson	T71	73-69-72-77	291	$2,535.00
Lennie Clements	T32	68-71-72-74	285	$7,193.33	Ted Tryba	T71	71-72-71-77	291	$2,535.00
P.H. Horgan III	T32	71-70-74-70	285	$7,193.33	Mark Brooks	75	72-69-75-76	292	$2,470.00
David Toms	T32	71-68-73-73	285	$7,193.33	Mike Brisky	T76	68-75-75-75	293	$2,418.00
Tray Tyner	T32	68-71-72-74	285	$7,193.33	Ed Humenik	T76	69-71-71-82	293	$2,418.00
Curt Byrum	T38	71-72-70-73	286	$5,070.00	Duffy Waldorf	T76	68-69-79-77	293	$2,418.00
Brad Fabel	T38	71-71-71-73	286	$5,070.00	Tom Sieckmann	79	72-70-78-75	295	$2,366.00
Mark Lye	T38	69-74-70-73	286	$5,070.00	Ed Dougherty	80	71-70-82-74	297	$2,340.00
Andrew Magee	T38	65-78-71-72	286	$5,070.00					

BELLSOUTH CLASSIC

Atlanta CC, Marietta, GA   Purse: $1,200,000
Par: 36-36--72   Yards: 7,018   May 5-8, 1994

LEADERS: First Round--Hal Sutton, at 6-under-par 66, led by one stroke over Craig Parry. **Second Round--**John Daly, at 11-under-par 144, led by two over Brian Henninger. **Third Round--**Daly, at 14-under-par 202, led Henninger by two.

CUT: 76 players at even-par 144.

PRO-AM: $7,500. Individual--Jeff Sluman, 66, $750. Team--Fred Funk and Duffy Waldorf, 54, $750.

WEATHER: Partly sunny Thursday and Friday. Saturday was overcast with a few sprinkles, but no delays. Sunday was sunny and cool with some wind.

Winner: John Daly   69-64-69-72   274 $216,000.00

Nolan Henke .... T 2	70-67-69-69	275	$105,600.00
Brian Henninger .... T 2	68-67-69-71	275	$105,600.00
Bob Estes .... T 4	71-69-68-68	276	$52,800.00
David Peoples .... T 4	73-65-68-70	276	$52,800.00
Lennie Clements ... T 6	68-69-72-68	277	$38,850.00
Russ Cochran .... T 6	69-69-69-70	277	$38,850.00
Tom Kite .... T 6	66-72-68-71	277	$38,850.00
Blaine McCallister . T 6	69-68-69-71	277	$38,850.00
Clark Dennis 10	71-66-72-69	278	$32,400.00
Paul Goydos T11	68-72-70-69	279	$28,800.00
Davis Love III T11	70-70-70-69	279	$28,800.00
Olin Browne T13	73-71-65-71	280	$21,840.00
Dave Rummells ... T13	69-67-71-73	280	$21,840.00
Paul Stankowski .. T13	69-69-70-72	280	$21,840.00
Hal Sutton T13	66-71-71-72	280	$21,840.00
Mark Wurtz T13	68-68-72-72	280	$21,840.00
Brian Kamm T18	70-69-74-68	281	$16,800.00
Larry Mize T18	71-71-70-69	281	$16,800.00
Corey Pavin T18	68-71-70-72	281	$16,800.00
Jay Don Blake T21	72-71-68-71	282	$12,480.00
Bill Britton T21	71-70-71-70	282	$12,480.00
Fred Funk T21	72-69-73-68	282	$12,480.00
Mark McCumber .. T21	72-69-68-73	282	$12,480.00
Scott Verplank T21	69-72-68-73	282	$12,480.00
John Adams T26	72-69-70-72	283	$9,060.00
Michael Bradley ... T26	69-75-71-68	283	$9,060.00
Yoshi Mizumaki ... T26	72-72-70-69	283	$9,060.00
Bobby Wadkins T26	71-69-70-73	283	$9,060.00
Billy Andrade T30	70-73-70-71	284	$7,452.00
Hale Irwin T30	71-72-69-72	284	$7,452.00
Wayne Levi T30	68-68-71-77	284	$7,452.00
Joey Sindelar T30	73-69-71-71	284	$7,452.00
Rocky Walcher T30	69-70-71-74	284	$7,452.00
Dave Barr T35	74-70-70-71	285	$5,665.72
Mike Hulbert T35	73-71-70-71	285	$5,665.72
Peter Persons T35	71-70-72-72	285	$5,665.72
Mark Brooks T35	70-69-75-71	285	$5,665.71
Craig Parry T35	67-74-73-71	285	$5,665.71
Steve Stricker T35	73-70-67-75	285	$5,665.71
Esteban Toledo T35	68-72-71-74	285	$5,665.71
Steve Rintoul T42	74-65-73-74	286	$4,560.00
Jeff Woodland T42	70-69-72-75	286	$4,560.00
Russell Beiersdorf T44	70-73-70-74	287	$3,541.72
Ed Humenik T44	71-73-70-73	287	$3,541.72
Doug Tewell T44	71-71-71-74	287	$3,541.72
Joel Edwards T44	74-69-71-73	287	$3,541.71
Greg Kraft T44	73-71-73-70	287	$3,541.71
Neal Lancaster T44	73-70-71-73	287	$3,541.71
David Toms T44	73-69-74-71	287	$3,541.71
Ed Dougherty T51	76-68-68-76	288	$2,888.00
Steve Lowery T51	74-67-73-74	288	$2,888.00
Mark Lye T51	70-69-72-77	288	$2,888.00
John Morse T54	71-72-71-75	289	$2,736.00
Kenny Perry T54	71-70-74-74	289	$2,736.00
Larry Silveira T54	70-74-73-72	289	$2,736.00
Mike Springer T54	76-68-73-72	289	$2,736.00
Duffy Waldorf T54	73-70-73-73	289	$2,736.00
Michael Allen T59	69-73-71-77	290	$2,604.00
Tripp Isenhour T59	72-71-73-74	290	$2,604.00
Billy Mayfair T59	74-69-76-71	290	$2,604.00
Larry Nelson T59	75-69-69-77	290	$2,604.00
Tom Sieckmann ... T59	71-71-76-72	290	$2,604.00
Jeff Sluman T59	72-71-72-75	290	$2,604.00
Ty Armstrong T65	73-70-73-75	291	$2,496.00
Brad Bryant T65	75-69-74-73	291	$2,496.00
Jim McGovern T65	72-71-76-72	291	$2,496.00
David Ogrin T68	72-72-73-75	292	$2,436.00
Willie Wood T68	71-73-76-72	292	$2,436.00
Brandel Chamblee T70	71-69-78-76	294	$2,388.00
David Feherty T70	70-74-73-77	294	$2,388.00
Morris Hatalsky 72	76-68-72-79	295	$2,352.00
Tommy Brannen .. T73	75-67-78-76	296	$2,316.00
Edward Kirby T73	73-69-76-78	296	$2,316.00
Marco Dawson 75	72-72-76-77	297	$2,280.00
Brad King 76	71-72-79-77	299	$2,256.00

GTE BYRON NELSON CLASSIC

TPC at Las Colinas, Irving, TX
Par: 35-35--70   Yards: 6,899
Cottonwood Valley, Irving, TX
Par: 35-36--71   Yards: 6,862

Purse: $1,200,000
May 12-15, 1994

LEADERS: First Round--David Ogrin (CV), with a 7-under-par 64, led by one stroke over Mark Carnevale (TPC).

PRO-AM: $7,500. Individual--Nick Price, 65, $750. Team--Fulton Allem, 52, $750.

WEATHER: Thursday and Friday were cancelled due to soggy course conditions. The event was shortened to 54 holes after Thursday's cancellation. Play started Saturday morning with play on both courses. Play was suspended at 6:40 p.m. due to lightning in the area. Three separate funnel clouds were spotted in the area. Play was postponed until 1 p.m. Sunday, and the decision was made to make the tournament a 36-hole official event on Sunday morning. The field was cut after the completion of 36 holes, with the low 70 scorers and ties being paid.

Winner: Neal Lancaster   67-65   132 $216,000.00
(Won playoff with birdie on first extra hole)

Player	Pos	Rounds	Total	Money	Player	Pos	Rounds	Total	Money
Tom Byrum	T 2	68-64	132	$72,000.00	Chris Dimarco	T42	67-71	138	$3,861.00
Mark Carnevale	T 2	65-67	132	$72,000.00	Dan Forsman	T42	72-66	138	$3,861.00
David Edwards	T 2	67-65	132	$72,000.00	Ken Green	T42	69-69	138	$3,861.00
Yoshi Mizumaki	T 2	66-66	132	$72,000.00	Donnie Hammond	T42	68-70	138	$3,861.00
David Ogrin	T 2	64-68	132	$72,000.00	Larry Mize	T42	67-71	138	$3,861.00
Brad Bryant	7	66-67	133	$40,200.00	Steve Rintoul	T42	67-71	138	$3,861.00
Ronnie Black	T 8	70-64	134	$31,200.00	Bob Tway	T42	70-68	138	$3,861.00
Mark Brooks	T 8	67-67	134	$31,200.00	Todd Barranger	T50	72-67	139	$2,732.80
Ben Crenshaw	T 8	66-68	134	$31,200.00	Trevor Dodds	T50	70-69	139	$2,732.80
Bob Gilder	T 8	67-67	134	$31,200.00	Bob Estes	T50	73-66	139	$2,732.80
Greg Norman	T 8	66-68	134	$31,200.00	Rick Fehr	T50	70-69	139	$2,732.80
Jeff Woodland	T 8	69-65	134	$31,200.00	Robin Freeman	T50	70-69	139	$2,732.80
Tommy Armour	T14	65-70	135	$19,800.00	Robert Gamez	T50	69-70	139	$2,732.80
Chip Beck	T14	72-63	135	$19,800.00	Paul Goydos	T50	73-66	139	$2,732.80
Billy Mayfair	T14	68-67	135	$19,800.00	Jay Haas	T50	71-68	139	$2,732.80
Joe Ozaki	T14	69-66	135	$19,800.00	Jeff Maggert	T50	68-71	139	$2,732.80
Kenny Perry	T14	67-68	135	$19,800.00	Sean Murphy	T50	71-68	139	$2,732.80
Loren Roberts	T14	71-64	135	$19,800.00	Dennis Paulson	T50	73-66	139	$2,732.80
Guy Boros	T20	66-70	136	$12,105.00	Dave Rummells	T50	72-67	139	$2,732.80
Mark Calcavecchia	T20	70-66	136	$12,105.00	D.A. Russell	T50	70-69	139	$2,732.80
Mark O'Meara	T20	69-67	136	$12,105.00	Mike Sullivan	T50	71-68	139	$2,732.80
Nick Price	T20	65-71	136	$12,105.00	Billy Tuten	T50	70-69	139	$2,732.80
Dicky Pride	T20	70-66	136	$12,105.00	Ty Armstrong	T65	68-72	140	$2,304.00
Craig Stadler	T20	69-67	136	$12,105.00	Billy Ray Brown	T65	70-70	140	$2,304.00
Doug Tewell	T20	69-67	136	$12,105.00	Russ Cochran	T65	70-70	140	$2,304.00
Jim Thorpe	T20	68-68	136	$12,105.00	Ed Dougherty	T65	70-70	140	$2,304.00
Jesper Parnevik	T28	65-72	137	$6,737.15	David Frost	T65	72-68	140	$2,304.00
Tim Simpson	T28	67-70	137	$6,737.15	Hubert Green	T65	71-69	140	$2,304.00
Ted Tryba	T28	71-66	137	$6,737.15	Gary Hallberg	T65	69-71	140	$2,304.00
Willie Wood	T28	70-67	137	$6,737.15	Brad King	T65	69-71	140	$2,304.00
Perry Arthur	T28	69-68	137	$6,737.14	Brad Lardon	T65	72-68	140	$2,304.00
Jay Don Blake	T28	68-69	137	$6,737.14	Steve Lowery	T65	69-71	140	$2,304.00
Michael Bradley	T28	67-70	137	$6,737.14	Doug Martin	T65	70-70	140	$2,304.00
Bob Eastwood	T28	71-66	137	$6,737.14	Dillard Pruitt	T65	68-72	140	$2,304.00
Tom Garner	T28	67-70	137	$6,737.14	Joey Rassett	T65	73-67	140	$2,304.00
Morris Hatalsky	T28	73-64	137	$6,737.14	Mike Standly	T65	69-71	140	$2,304.00
Tom Kite	T28	68-69	137	$6,737.14	Hal Sutton	T65	73-67	140	$2,304.00
Corey Pavin	T28	69-68	137	$6,737.14	Bobby Wadkins	T65	72-68	140	$2,304.00
Larry Silveira	T28	68-69	137	$6,737.14	Grant Waite	T65	70-70	140	$2,304.00
D.A. Weibring	T28	68-69	137	$6,737.14	Mark Wurtz	T65	68-72	140	$2,304.00
Brandel Chamblee	T42	68-70	138	$3,861.00	Richard Zokol	T65	72-68	140	$2,304.00

MEMORIAL TOURNAMENT

Muirfield Village GC, Dublin, OH **Purse: $1,500,000**
Par: 36-36--72 **Yards: 7,104** **May 19-22, 1994**

LEADERS: First Round--Mark Brooks, at 8-under-par 64, led by three strokes over Tom Lehman and John Cook. **Second Round--**Lehman, at 10-under-par 134, led by two strokes over Cook and David Edwards. **Third Round--**Lehman, at 15-under-par 201, led by four strokes over Cook.

CUT: 74 players (73 professionals and one amateur) at 4-over-par 148.

WEATHER: Perfect all four days.

Winner: Tom Lehman **67-67-67-67** **268** **$270,000.00**

Player	Pos	Scores	Total	Money
Greg Norman	2	70-69-70-64	273	$162,000.00
John Cook	3	67-69-69-71	276	$102,000.00
Donnie Hammond	4	69-69-70-69	277	$72,000.00
David Edwards	5	69-67-72-70	278	$60,000.00
Robert Gamez	6	77-69-66-67	279	$54,000.00
Mark Brooks	T 7	64-75-70-71	280	$48,375.00
Ben Crenshaw	T 7	72-66-74-68	280	$48,375.00
Brad Faxon	T 9	72-68-72-69	281	$42,000.00
Jeff Maggert	T 9	71-74-66-70	281	$42,000.00
David Frost	T11	69-71-71-71	282	$34,500.00
Gary Hallberg	T11	77-66-68-71	282	$34,500.00
Steve Lowery	T11	71-70-69-72	282	$34,500.00
Chip Beck	T14	72-70-70-71	283	$25,500.00
Scott Hoch	T14	71-73-71-68	283	$25,500.00
Hale Irwin	T14	73-70-70-70	283	$25,500.00
Scott Simpson	T14	68-72-72-71	283	$25,500.00
Curtis Strange	T14	74-69-73-67	283	$25,500.00
Bob Estes	T19	71-68-70-75	284	$18,180.00
Jay Haas	T19	72-70-74-68	284	$18,180.00
Bruce Lietzke	T19	72-71-73-68	284	$18,180.00
Larry Mize	T19	74-67-71-72	284	$18,180.00
Yoshi Mizumaki	T19	72-73-69-70	284	$18,180.00
Kenny Perry	T24	71-73-71-70	285	$13,800.00
Kirk Triplett	T24	72-71-69-73	285	$13,800.00
Billy Andrade	T26	74-71-73-68	286	$11,325.00
Mike Heinen	T26	71-73-76-66	286	$11,325.00
John Huston	T26	73-74-68-71	286	$11,325.00
Loren Roberts	T26	71-74-70-71	286	$11,325.00
Lennie Clements	T30	71-71-72-73	287	$9,315.00
David Duval	T30	73-73-72-69	287	$9,315.00
Hajime Meshiai	T30	73-74-71-69	287	$9,315.00
Larry Nelson	T30	72-74-69-72	287	$9,315.00
Corey Pavin	T30	76-69-70-72	287	$9,315.00
Clark Dennis	T35	72-74-73-69	288	$7,725.00
Jim Thorpe	T35	70-75-72-71	288	$7,725.00
Tom Watson	T35	77-69-70-72	288	$7,725.00
Fulton Allem	T38	74-70-72-73	289	$6,150.00
Peter Jacobsen	T38	72-75-70-72	289	$6,150.00
Bob Lohr	T38	74-74-68-73	289	$6,150.00
Jim McGovern	T38	72-69-74-74	289	$6,150.00
Jesper Parnevik	T38	70-75-72-72	289	$6,150.00
Steve Stricker	T38	72-75-69-73	289	$6,150.00
Bob Tway	T38	71-77-69-72	289	$6,150.00
Steve Elkington	T45	69-72-72-77	290	$4,392.00
Ernie Els	T45	72-74-68-76	290	$4,392.00
Davis Love III	T45	71-70-73-76	290	$4,392.00
Mike Springer	T45	72-71-78-69	290	$4,392.00
Ted Tryba	T45	70-76-76-68	290	$4,392.00
Fred Funk	T50	73-72-74-72	291	$3,652.50
Brian Henninger	T50	74-69-72-76	291	$3,652.50
Ed Humenik	T50	74-74-74-69	291	$3,652.50
Billy Mayfair	T50	69-71-72-79	291	$3,652.50
Mark Calcavecchia	T54	74-74-68-76	292	$3,435.00
Rick Fehr	T54	75-72-71-74	292	$3,435.00
Nolan Henke	T54	72-71-73-76	292	$3,435.00
Mark O'Meara	T54	75-69-74-74	292	$3,435.00
Bradley Hughes	T58	74-73-74-72	293	$3,345.00
Wayne Levi	T58	72-76-68-77	293	$3,345.00
Wayne Grady	T60	73-70-70-81	294	$3,255.00
Lee Janzen	T60	72-75-75-72	294	$3,255.00
John Mahaffey	T60	73-75-72-74	294	$3,255.00
Craig Stadler	T60	71-73-73-77	294	$3,255.00
Paul Goydos	T64	74-72-71-78	295	$3,165.00
Andy North	T64	76-71-72-76	295	$3,165.00
Allen Doyle	T64	75-72-75-73	295	AMATEUR
Keith Clearwater	T67	73-73-72-78	296	$3,105.00
Doug Martin	T67	72-75-75-74	296	$3,105.00
Mike Standly	69	76-72-74-75	297	$3,060.00
Joe Ozaki	70	72-76-75-75	298	$3,030.00
John Daly	71	74-74-73-78	299	$3,000.00
Andy Bean	T72	76-71-70-83	300	$2,955.00
Bill Kratzert	T72	73-74-78-75	300	$2,955.00
Dave Rummells	74	74-71-77-80	302	$2,910.00

SOUTHWESTERN BELL COLONIAL

Colonial CC, Fort Worth, TX   Purse: $1,400,000
Par: 35-35--70   Yards: 7,010   May 26-30, 1994

LEADERS: First Round--Hale Irwin, with a 6-under-par 64, led by one stroke over Nick Price and David Frost. **Second Round--**Scott Simpson, at 9-under-par 131, led by one over Tom Lehman. **Third Round--**Simpson, at 15-under-par 195, led by four over Gary Hallberg.

CUT: 73 players (72 professionals and one amateur) at 2-over-par 142.

WEATHER: $7,500. Due to inclement weather, the pro-am was divided into two separate competitions. Front-Nine Individual--Greg Norman, 28, $450. Front-Nine Team--Phil Mickelson, Fulton Allem, Gil Morgan, Nolan Henke and Mike Standly, 26, $375 each. Back-Nine Individual--Mark McCumber and Scott Simpson, 31, $431.25 each. Back-Nine Team--David Frost and Russ Cochran, 26, $431.25 each.

WEATHER: The first round was suspended at 12:40 a.m. due to rain and lightning in the area. Play was cancelled for the day at 4:30 p.m. Only the morning segment had teed off. Play resumed Friday morning at 9 a.m. with both segments playing. Thursday's afternoon segment played 36 holes on Friday. Thursday's morning segment completed its first round and played its second round Saturday morning. The cut took place on Saturday with the third round starting at 1:45 p.m. The fourth round was delayed from 10:44 a.m. to 1:15 p.m. due to dangerous weather conditions. Play was suspended again at 6:17 p.m. and play was cancelled for the day at 6:55 pm. Play resumed Monday morning at 9 a.m. with 18 players on the course.

Winner: Nick Price   65-70-67-64   266 $252,000.00
(Won playoff with birdie on first extra hole)

Player	Pos	Scores	Total	Money	Player	Pos	Scores	Total	Money
Scott Simpson	2	66-65-64-71	266	$151,200.00	Mike Reid	T30	67-66-71-76	280	$7,478.33
Hale Irwin	3	64-70-68-65	267	$95,200.00	Loren Roberts	T30	70-65-71-74	280	$7,478.33
Peter Jordan	4	68-70-66-66	270	$67,200.00	Dave Stockton, Jr	T30	69-68-68-75	280	$7,478.33
Brad Faxon	T5	70-66-67-68	271	$51,100.00	D.A. Weibring	T30	69-70-68-73	280	$7,478.33
Gary Hallberg	T5	67-67-65-72	271	$51,100.00	Mark Brooks	T42	68-67-72-74	281	$4,900.00
Tom Lehman	T5	66-66-69-70	271	$51,100.00	Davis Love III	T42	72-69-71-69	281	$4,900.00
Phil Mickelson	8	68-68-71-65	272	$43,400.00	Brett Ogle	T42	72-70-67-72	281	$4,900.00
John Cook	T9	66-71-67-70	274	$37,800.00	Joey Sindelar	T42	71-70-72-68	281	$4,900.00
Mark McCumber	T9	68-69-67-70	274	$37,800.00	Steve Stricker	T42	71-67-67-76	281	$4,900.00
Corey Pavin	T9	68-67-69-70	274	$37,800.00	Steve Lowery	T47	71-71-71-69	282	$3,845.34
Mark Calcavecchia	T12	68-69-71-67	275	$29,400.00	Mike Hulbert	T47	70-67-71-74	282	$3,845.33
Ben Crenshaw	T12	69-69-69-68	275	$29,400.00	Dave Stockton	T47	70-68-71-73	282	$3,845.33
Fuzzy Zoeller	T12	68-70-68-69	275	$29,400.00	Tom Byrum	T50	72-69-72-70	283	$3,409.00
Clark Dennis	T15	69-69-67-71	276	$23,800.00	Keith Clearwater	T50	70-68-67-78	283	$3,409.00
David Edwards	T15	72-67-68-69	276	$23,800.00	Donnie Hammond	T50	68-70-69-76	283	$3,409.00
David Frost	T15	65-68-75-68	276	$23,800.00	Jodie Mudd	T50	70-71-72-70	283	$3,409.00
Ken Green	T18	67-66-69-75	277	$18,900.00	John Harris	T50	69-72-71-71	283	AMATEUR
Joe Ozaki	T18	70-69-71-67	277	$18,900.00	Brian Henninger	55	69-71-70-74	284	$3,248.00
Kenny Perry	T18	73-67-69-68	277	$18,900.00	Dave Barr	T56	71-71-69-74	285	$3,136.00
Kirk Triplett	T18	71-68-69-69	277	$18,900.00	Jay Don Blake	T56	69-65-74-77	285	$3,136.00
Guy Boros	T22	70-63-71-74	278	$14,560.00	David Feherty	T56	67-72-68-78	285	$3,136.00
Bob Estes	T22	67-71-71-69	278	$14,560.00	Bruce Fleisher	T56	71-70-71-73	285	$3,136.00
John Huston	T22	70-68-65-75	278	$14,560.00	Jeff Maggert	T56	71-66-75-73	285	$3,136.00
Lennie Clements	T25	70-68-67-74	279	$10,920.00	Greg Norman	T56	70-69-71-75	285	$3,136.00
Wayne Grady	T25	71-65-68-75	279	$10,920.00	Howard Twitty	T56	70-68-73-74	285	$3,136.00
David Ogrin	T25	70-68-68-73	279	$10,920.00	Mark Carnevale	T63	69-73-67-77	286	$2,996.00
Steve Pate	T25	69-64-74-72	279	$10,920.00	Hajime Meshiai	T63	66-74-72-74	286	$2,996.00
Tom Purtzer	T25	71-69-70-69	279	$10,920.00	Jeff Sluman	T63	73-68-74-71	286	$2,996.00
Lee Janzen	T30	70-70-71-69	280	$7,478.34	Fred Funk	T66	68-71-70-78	287	$2,912.00
Andrew Magee	T30	67-73-71-69	280	$7,478.34	John Inman	T66	68-72-74-73	287	$2,912.00
Roger Maltbie	T30	69-67-72-72	280	$7,478.34	Hal Sutton	T66	72-70-70-75	287	$2,912.00
Mike Springer	T30	67-71-73-69	280	$7,478.34	Billy Mayfair	69	71-71-72-74	288	$2,856.00
Glen Day	T30	69-68-71-72	280	$7,478.33	Michael Allen	70	69-73-72-76	290	$2,828.00
Mike Heinen	T30	70-70-68-72	280	$7,478.33	Paul Goydos	T71	70-72-75-74	291	$2,786.00
Scott Hoch	T30	68-70-69-73	280	$7,478.33	Doug Tewell	T71	68-70-75-78	291	$2,786.00
Bruce Lietzke	T30	67-72-69-72	280	$7,478.33	Rick Fehr	73	71-70-77-75	293	$2,744.00

KEMPER OPEN

KEMPER

OPEN

TPC at Avenel, Potomac, MD
Par: 36-35--71   Yards: 7,005

Purse: $1,300,000
June 2-5, 1994

LEADERS: First Round--Mark Brooks, at 6-under-par 65, held a three-stroke lead over Ed Dougherty, Bobby Wadkins and Wayne Levi. **Second Round--**Brooks, at 9-under-par 133, led by two over Wadkins. **Third Round--**Wadkins, at 13-under-par 200, was two strokes ahead of Brooks.

CUT: 76 players at 3-over-par 145.

PRO-AM: $7,500. Individual--Billy Andrade, 65, $750. Team--Andrew Magee, 53, $750.

WEATHER: Partly cloudy and cool early Thursday, becoming sunny and mild with swirling winds. Warming through the day Friday, with sunny skies and little wind. Ideal playing conditions on Saturday. Cloudy and overcast early Sunday, with a brief pre-round shower; partly cloudy, warm and humid the rest of the day.

Winner: Mark Brooks   65-68-69-69   271 $234,000.00

Bobby Wadkins	T 2	68-67-65-74	274	$114,400.00	Brad Fabel	T37	74-69-74-68	285	$5,590.00
D.A. Weibring	T 2	70-68-68-68	274	$114,400.00	Tommy Moore	T37	71-69-72-73	285	$5,590.00
Lee Janzen	T 4	70-71-68-66	275	$57,200.00	Joey Rassett	T37	72-68-72-73	285	$5,590.00
Phil Mickelson	T 4	70-69-67-69	275	$57,200.00	Jeff Sluman	T37	70-73-70-72	285	$5,590.00
Joel Edwards	6	71-70-68-69	278	$46,800.00	Clark Dennis	T44	71-71-69-75	286	$4,040.40
Craig Parry	T 7	69-71-69-70	279	$40,516.67	Brad Faxon	T44	70-69-73-74	286	$4,040.40
Kenny Perry	T 7	72-72-68-67	279	$40,516.67	Steve Lamontagne	T44	77-68-70-71	286	$4,040.40
Mark Lye	T 7	70-70-69-70	279	$40,516.66	Dick Mast	T44	75-69-70-72	286	$4,040.40
Michael Bradley	T10	70-71-67-73	281	$26,975.00	Dillard Pruitt	T44	71-73-67-75	286	$4,040.40
Robert Gamez	T10	72-66-69-74	281	$26,975.00	Russell Beiersdorf	T49	71-68-74-74	287	$3,126.50
Kelly Gibson	T10	75-64-71-71	281	$26,975.00	Marco Dawson	T49	76-67-74-70	287	$3,126.50
Scott Hoch	T10	69-72-67-73	281	$26,975.00	Gary Hallberg	T49	74-69-68-76	287	$3,126.50
Brian Kamm	T10	69-71-68-73	281	$26,975.00	Ed Humenik	T49	73-72-75-67	287	$3,126.50
Wayne Levi	T10	68-70-72-71	281	$26,975.00	Dicky Pride	T49	72-69-71-75	287	$3,126.50
Tim Simpson	T10	71-72-70-68	281	$26,975.00	Paul Stankowski	T49	70-72-70-75	287	$3,126.50
Kirk Triplett	T10	72-73-67-69	281	$26,975.00	Doug Tewell	T49	74-71-70-72	287	$3,126.50
Rob Boldt	T18	70-68-73-71	282	$16,380.00	Esteban Toledo	T49	71-70-73-73	287	$3,126.50
Mark Carnevale	T18	71-69-68-74	282	$16,380.00	John Flannery	T57	72-73-71-72	288	$2,860.00
Bobby Clampett	T18	73-71-65-73	282	$16,380.00	Bradley Hughes	T57	71-73-68-76	288	$2,860.00
Mike Donald	T18	71-70-72-69	282	$16,380.00	John Inman	T57	75-70-70-73	288	$2,860.00
Greg Kraft	T18	74-70-70-68	282	$16,380.00	Roger Maltbie	T57	74-70-74-70	288	$2,860.00
Bob May	T18	71-71-66-74	282	$16,380.00	David Peoples	T57	72-71-70-75	288	$2,860.00
Scott Verplank	T24	72-72-69-70	283	$10,288.58	Payne Stewart	T57	73-68-72-75	288	$2,860.00
Morris Hatalsky	T24	74-69-67-73	283	$10,288.57	Mark Wurtz	T57	74-70-70-74	288	$2,860.00
Andrew Magee	T24	69-72-72-70	283	$10,288.57	Shaun Micheel	64	72-70-75-72	289	$2,756.00
Mark O'Meara	T24	69-68-69-77	283	$10,288.57	Fred Funk	T65	74-71-73-72	290	$2,691.00
Dennis Paulson	T24	72-72-69-70	283	$10,288.57	Neal Lancaster	T65	74-68-74-74	290	$2,691.00
Steve Rintoul	T24	70-73-70-70	283	$10,288.57	Howard Twitty	T65	71-71-74-74	290	$2,691.00
Leonard Thompson	T24	71-70-71-71	283	$10,288.57	Lanny Wadkins	T65	71-74-68-77	290	$2,691.00
Jay Don Blake	T31	71-68-70-75	284	$7,540.00	Gene Sauers	69	74-71-71-75	291	$2,626.00
Brian Claar	T31	75-70-69-70	284	$7,540.00	Willie Wood	70	74-69-73-76	292	$2,600.00
John Daly	T31	73-71-69-71	284	$7,540.00	Billy Mayfair	71	71-72-74-76	293	$2,574.00
Robin Freeman	T31	73-70-69-72	284	$7,540.00	Tom Garner	72	74-70-70-80	294	$2,548.00
Mike Hulbert	T31	71-70-71-72	284	$7,540.00	Olin Browne	T73	73-70-71-81	295	$2,509.00
Dave Rummells	T31	71-70-67-76	284	$7,540.00	Ted Schulz	T73	74-71-76-74	295	$2,509.00
Bill Britton	T37	73-71-71-70	285	$5,590.00	Chris DiMarco	75	70-72-76-78	296	$2,470.00
Keith Clearwater	T37	73-68-71-73	285	$5,590.00	Lance Ten Broeck	76	75-70-81-75	301	$2,444.00
Ed Dougherty	T37	68-74-70-73	285	$5,590.00					

BUICK CLASSIC

Westchester CC, Harrison, NY
Par: 36-35--71   Yards: 6,779

Purse: $1,200,000
June 9-12, 1994

LEADERS: First Round--Mike Reid, with a 6-under-par 65, led by one over Bob Estes, Dillard Pruitt, Steve Brodie, Steve Pate and Wayne Levi. **Second Round--**Ernie Els, at 8-under-par 132, led by one over Reid. **Third Round--**Lee Janzen, at 11-under-par 202, led by one stroke over Els.

CUT: 70 players at 2-over-par 144.

PRO-AM: $7,500. Individual--Tom Watson, 65, $750. Team--Corey Pavin, 52, $750.

WEATHER: Beautiful the first three days. Sunday was overcast with some rain.

Winner: Lee Janzen   69-69-64-66   268 $216,000.00

Player	Pos	Scores	Total	Money	Player	Pos	Scores	Total	Money
Ernie Els	2	68-66-69-68	271	$129,600.00	Brett Ogle	T27	69-70-75-68	282	$7,494.54
Brad Faxon	T 3	70-68-70-66	274	$69,600.00	Fulton Allem	T38	72-69-68-74	283	$5,040.00
Jay Haas	T 3	68-70-69-67	274	$69,600.00	Dave Barr	T38	71-73-69-70	283	$5,040.00
Billy Andrade	T 5	70-71-66-69	276	$43,800.00	Mark Carnevale	T38	72-69-72-70	283	$5,040.00
Bob Burns	T 5	71-67-70-68	276	$43,800.00	Davis Love III	T38	71-71-69-72	283	$5,040.00
Steve Pate	T 5	66-72-69-69	276	$43,800.00	Rocco Mediate	T38	74-67-71-71	283	$5,040.00
Mark Brooks	T 8	71-70-66-70	277	$32,400.00	Mike Reid	T38	65-70-73-75	283	$5,040.00
Robin Freeman	T 8	69-69-69-70	277	$32,400.00	Rob Boldt	T44	73-71-72-68	284	$3,628.00
Hale Irwin	T 8	70-72-65-70	277	$32,400.00	Ben Crenshaw	T44	73-70-68-73	284	$3,628.00
Jeff Maggert	T 8	72-72-64-69	277	$32,400.00	Jay Delsing	T44	74-68-70-72	284	$3,628.00
Joe Ozaki	T 8	69-67-69-72	277	$32,400.00	Blaine McCallister	T44	72-67-73-72	284	$3,628.00
Dillard Pruitt	T13	66-71-68-73	278	$24,000.00	Corey Pavin	T44	72-69-68-75	284	$3,628.00
John Wilson	T13	68-68-69-73	278	$24,000.00	Scott Verplank	T44	71-70-69-74	284	$3,628.00
Tom Kite	15	68-74-64-73	279	$21,600.00	Phil Blackmar	T50	68-72-68-77	285	$2,922.00
Brad Bryant	T16	70-67-73-70	280	$17,400.00	Russ Cochran	T50	69-74-69-73	285	$2,922.00
Bob Estes	T16	66-71-70-73	280	$17,400.00	Wayne Levi	T50	66-74-74-71	285	$2,922.00
Greg Norman	T16	73-67-69-71	280	$17,400.00	Doug Tewell	T50	68-72-73-72	285	$2,922.00
Hal Sutton	T16	71-71-66-72	280	$17,400.00	David Ogrin	T54	73-69-71-73	286	$2,760.00
Phil Tataurangi	T16	71-71-67-71	280	$17,400.00	Steve Rintoul	T54	72-71-75-68	286	$2,760.00
Ted Tryba	T16	71-71-66-72	280	$17,400.00	Bob Tway	T54	71-70-75-70	286	$2,760.00
Gary Hallberg	T22	71-67-72-71	281	$11,520.00	Howard Twitty	57	71-73-72-71	287	$2,712.00
Jim McGovern	T22	73-71-70-67	281	$11,520.00	Steve Brodie	T58	66-76-72-74	288	$2,652.00
Jim Thorpe	T22	71-71-67-72	281	$11,520.00	Dudley Hart	T58	77-67-70-74	288	$2,652.00
Esteban Toledo	T22	71-73-67-70	281	$11,520.00	Mike Hulbert	T58	73-68-73-74	288	$2,652.00
Tom Watson	T22	71-71-70-69	281	$11,520.00	Joey Rassett	T58	75-69-71-73	288	$2,652.00
Ronnie Black	T27	70-71-65-76	282	$7,494.55	Nolan Henke	T62	70-73-73-73	289	$2,568.00
Brian Claar	T27	71-73-68-70	282	$7,494.55	Dave Stockton, Jr	T62	72-70-71-76	289	$2,568.00
David Frost	T27	67-77-71-67	282	$7,494.55	Jeff Woodland	T62	72-71-71-75	289	$2,568.00
John Huston	T27	70-72-75-65	282	$7,494.55	Bob May	T65	72-70-77-71	290	$2,508.00
John Mahaffey	T27	71-73-68-70	282	$7,494.55	Payne Stewart	T65	72-72-72-74	290	$2,508.00
Mark McCumber	T27	69-72-70-71	282	$7,494.55	Todd Barranger	T67	71-73-68-79	291	$2,460.00
Lennie Clements	T27	73-68-72-69	282	$7,494.54	Bill Britton	T67	71-73-76-71	291	$2,460.00
Fred Couples	T27	70-69-70-73	282	$7,494.54	Seve Ballesteros	69	71-73-75-73	292	$2,424.00
John Flannery	T27	72-68-70-72	282	$7,494.54	David Feherty	70	74-70-75-76	295	$2,400.00
Fred Funk	T27	69-70-69-74	282	$7,494.54					

UNITED STATES OPEN

Oakmont CC, Oakmont, PA
Par: 36-35--71   **Yards:**

Purse: $1,700,000
June 16-20, 1994

LEADERS: First Round--Tom Watson shot a 3-under-par 68, one stroke better than Jack Nicklaus, Ernie Els, Frank Nobilo and Hale Irwin. **Second Round--**Colin Montgomerie, after a second-round 65, was at 136, two strokes ahead of Irwin, John Cook and David Edwards. **Third Round--**Els shot a 5-under-par 66 for a 206 total and a two-stroke lead over Nobilo.

CUT: From a field of 159, 65 players (low 60 scores and ties) at 5-over-par 147.

WEATHER: Hazy, hot and humid Thursday with temperatures in the 90s. Play was suspended due to lighting in the area at 8:18 p.m. with 18 players left on the course. The course received one-half inch of rain Thursday night. After morning fog delayed the second round by 10 minutes, Friday was hot and humid. Play again was suspended due to lightning in the area, this time at 7:56 p.m. with 18 players left on the course. More heat and humidity Saturday, Sunday and Monday, but no delays.

Winner: Ernie Els   69-71-66-73 279 $320,000.00
(Els (74-4-4) defeated Roberts (74-4-5) and Montgomerie (78) in an 18-hole playoff)

Player		Scores	Total	Money	Player		Scores	Total	Money
Colin Montgomerie	T 2	71-65-73-70	279	$141,827.50	Ben Crenshaw	T33	71-74-70-78	293	$9,578.34
Loren Roberts	T 2	76-69-64-70	279	$141,827.50	Fulton Allem	T33	73-70-74-76	293	$9,578.33
Curtis Strange	4	70-70-70-70	280	$75,728.00	Brad Faxon	T33	73-69-71-80	293	$9,578.33
John Cook	5	73-65-73-71	282	$61,318.00	Tom Kite	T33	73-71-72-77	293	$9,578.33
Clark Dennis	T 6	71-71-70-71	283	$49,485.34	Tom Lehman	T33	77-68-73-75	293	$9,578.33
Greg Norman	T 6	71-71-69-72	283	$49,485.33	Peter Baker	T39	73-73-73-75	294	$8,005.75
Tom Watson	T 6	68-73-68-74	283	$49,485.33	Gordon J. Brand	T39	73-71-73-77	294	$8,005.75
Jeff Maggert	T 9	71-68-75-70	284	$37,179.75	Bradley Hughes	T39	71-72-77-74	294	$8,005.75
Frank Nobilo	T 9	69-71-68-76	284	$37,179.75	Brandt Jobe	T39	72-74-68-80	294	$8,005.75
Jeff Sluman	T 9	72-69-72-71	284	$37,179.75	Francis Quinn	43	75-72-73-75	295	$7,222.00
Duffy Waldorf	T 9	74-68-73-69	284	$37,179.75	Don Walsworth	T44	71-75-73-77	296	$6,595.34
Scott Hoch	T13	72-72-70-71	285	$29,767.34	Fred Funk	T44	74-71-74-77	296	$6,595.33
David Edwards	T13	73-65-75-72	285	$29,767.33	Paul Goydos	T44	74-72-79-71	296	$6,595.33
Jim McGovern	T13	73-69-74-69	285	$29,767.33	Olin Browne	T47	74-73-77-73	297	$5,105.38
Fred Couples	T16	72-71-69-74	286	$25,899.50	Tim Dunlavey	T47	76-70-78-73	297	$5,105.38
Steve Lowery	T16	71-71-68-76	286	$25,899.50	Mike Emery	T47	74-73-75-75	297	$5,105.38
Seve Ballesteros	T18	72-72-70-73	287	$22,477.67	Barry Lane	T47	77-70-76-74	297	$5,105.38
Scott Verplank	T18	70-72-75-70	287	$22,477.67	David Berganio	T47	73-72-76-76	297	$5,105.37
Hale Irwin	T18	69-69-71-78	287	$22,477.66	Jim Gallagher, Jr.	T47	74-68-77-78	297	$5,105.37
Steve Pate	T21	74-66-71-77	288	$19,464.00	Wayne Levi	T47	76-70-73-78	297	$5,105.37
Sam Torrance	T21	72-71-76-69	288	$19,464.00	Phil Mickelson	T47	75-70-73-79	297	$5,105.37
Bernhard Langer	T23	72-72-73-72	289	$17,223.00	Tommy Armour	T55	73-73-79-73	298	$4,324.67
Kirk Triplett	T23	70-71-71-77	289	$17,223.00	Scott Simpson	T55	74-73-73-78	298	$4,324.67
Chip Beck	T25	73-73-70-74	290	$14,705.67	Hugh Royer	T55	72-71-77-78	298	$4,324.66
Mike Springer	T25	74-72-73-71	290	$14,705.67	Steven Richardson	T58	74-73-76-76	299	$4,105.00
Craig Parry	T25	78-68-71-73	290	$14,705.66	Fuzzy Zoeller	T58	76-70-76-77	299	$4,105.00
Lennie Clements	T28	73-71-73-75	292	$11,514.20	Doug Martin	T60	76-70-74-81	301	$3,967.00
Jim Furyk	T28	69-74-75-74	292	$11,514.20	Dave Rummells	T60	71-74-82-74	301	$3,967.00
Davis Love III	T28	74-72-74-72	292	$11,514.20	Emlyn Aubrey	T62	72-69-81-80	302	$3,802.00
Jack Nicklaus	T28	69-70-77-76	292	$11,514.20	Ed Humenik	T62	74-72-81-75	302	$3,802.00
Jumbo Ozaki	T28	70-73-69-80	292	$11,514.20	Mike Smith	T62	74-73-78-77	302	$3,802.00
Mark Carnevale	T33	75-72-76-70	293	$9,578.34					

CANON GREATER HARTFORD OPEN

TPC at River Highlands, Cromwell, CT   **Purse: $1,200,000**
Par: 35-35--70   Yards: 6,820   June 23-26, 1994

LEADERS: First Round--Clark Dennis, Phil Mickelson, David Frost and Corey Pavin, all at 5-under-par 65, were one stroke in front of six other players. **Second Round**--Dave Stockton, Jr., after a second consecutive 4-under-par 66, was at 8-under-par 132. He led by one over Frost. **Third Round**--Stockton and Frost were tied at 11-under-par 199, one stroke in front of Greg Norman.

CUT: 71 players at 1-over-par 141.

PRO-AM: $7,500. Individual--Peter Jacobsen, Phil Blackmar, Ian Baker-Finch and Fulton Allem, 66, $581.25 each. Team--Brett Ogle, Scott Hoch and Billy Mayfair, 55, $625 each.

WEATHER: Sunny and warm Thursday, with some wind. Cloudy and overcast Friday, with occasional light rain. Foggy and then hazy conditions Saturday morning with some light mist, giving way to ideal playing conditions in the afternoon. Sunny, warm and breezy Sunday.

Winner: David Frost   65-68-66-69   268 $216,000.00

Player	Pos	Scores	Total	Money		Player	Pos	Scores	Total	Money
Greg Norman	2	69-65-66-69	269	$129,600.00		Mark O'Meara	T33	67-72-69-72	280	$6,205.71
Dave Barr	T 3	68-70-68-65	271	$57,600.00		Nick Price	T33	70-70-67-73	280	$6,205.71
Corey Pavin	T 3	65-73-66-67	271	$57,600.00		Mike Springer	T33	73-67-67-73	280	$6,205.71
Dave Stockton, Jr	T 3	66-66-67-72	271	$57,600.00		Roger Maltbie	T40	68-70-67-76	281	$4,440.00
Steve Stricker	T 3	70-67-67-67	271	$57,600.00		Yoshi Mizumaki	T40	70-70-69-72	281	$4,440.00
Wayne Levi	T 7	68-66-71-68	273	$38,700.00		John Morse	T40	69-69-71-72	281	$4,440.00
Kirk Triplett	T 7	71-66-69-67	273	$38,700.00		Dillard Pruitt	T40	70-71-64-76	281	$4,440.00
John Cook	T 9	71-67-64-73	275	$28,800.00		Gene Sauers	T40	73-68-66-74	281	$4,440.00
Glen Day	T 9	72-65-70-68	275	$28,800.00		Scott Simpson	T40	70-68-69-74	281	$4,440.00
Clark Dennis	T 9	65-72-66-72	275	$28,800.00		Jeff Sluman	T40	70-71-71-69	281	$4,440.00
Ken Green	T 9	69-70-68-68	275	$28,800.00		Ed Dougherty	T47	71-70-72-69	282	$3,228.00
Peter Jacobsen	T 9	68-68-70-69	275	$28,800.00		Dudley Hart	T47	69-69-72-72	282	$3,228.00
Mike Reid	T 9	66-68-69-72	275	$28,800.00		Brian Henninger	T47	69-71-72-70	282	$3,228.00
Fred Couples	T15	71-68-71-66	276	$19,200.00		Mike Sullivan	T47	69-68-74-71	282	$3,228.00
Brad Faxon	T15	71-69-64-72	276	$19,200.00		Ty Armstrong	T51	71-70-68-74	283	$2,862.00
Kenny Perry	T15	67-68-69-72	276	$19,200.00		John Elliott	T51	72-69-71-71	283	$2,862.00
Mike Standly	T15	70-71-64-71	276	$19,200.00		Dan Forsman	T51	70-70-71-72	283	$2,862.00
Doug Tewell	T15	67-68-70-71	276	$19,200.00		Morris Hatalsky	T51	69-72-68-74	283	$2,862.00
Steve Lowery	T20	71-66-70-70	277	$15,000.00		Michael Allen	T55	72-69-72-71	284	$2,700.00
Larry Silveira	T20	67-73-71-66	277	$15,000.00		Billy Andrade	T55	71-69-69-75	284	$2,700.00
Tom Byrum	T22	69-68-69-72	278	$12,000.00		Guy Boros	T55	69-71-72-72	284	$2,700.00
Scott Hoch	T22	69-67-68-74	278	$12,000.00		Steve Brodie	T55	73-68-72-71	284	$2,700.00
Ted Tryba	T22	68-66-69-75	278	$12,000.00		Paul Goydos	T55	71-70-67-76	284	$2,700.00
Rocky Walcher	T22	69-69-72-68	278	$12,000.00		David Toms	T55	66-68-74-76	284	$2,700.00
Brandel Chamblee	T26	71-68-66-74	279	$8,520.00		Bill Britton	T61	72-65-70-78	285	$2,604.00
Jay Delsing	T26	74-67-69-69	279	$8,520.00		Olin Browne	T61	74-67-72-72	285	$2,604.00
David Feherty	T26	73-68-69-69	279	$8,520.00		Greg Kraft	63	66-71-73-76	286	$2,568.00
Ed Humenik	T26	69-70-69-71	279	$8,520.00		Steve Elkington	T64	66-73-75-73	287	$2,532.00
Brian Kamm	T26	75-66-69-69	279	$8,520.00		Mark Wurtz	T64	69-69-72-77	287	$2,532.00
Phil Mickelson	T26	65-72-70-72	279	$8,520.00		Chip Beck	T66	70-70-69-79	288	$2,484.00
Fuzzy Zoeller	T26	72-64-73-70	279	$8,520.00		Esteban Toledo	T66	69-70-76-73	288	$2,484.00
Trevor Dodds	T33	71-69-70-70	280	$6,205.72		Joe Ozaki	68	69-70-71-79	289	$2,448.00
Andrew Magee	T33	69-71-69-71	280	$6,205.72		Brad Lardon	69	72-69-71-78	290	$2,424.00
Gil Morgan	T33	68-73-68-71	280	$6,205.72		Chris Kite	70	68-71-74-79	292	$2,400.00
Peter Jordan	T33	66-71-68-75	280	$6,205.71						

MOTOROLA WESTERN OPEN

Cog Hill G&CC (Dubsdread Course), Lemont, IL   Purse: $1,200,000
Par: 36-36--72   Yards: 7,073

June 30-July 1, 1994

LEADERS: First Round--Bob Gilder, Phil Mickelson, John Huston, Bill Glasson and Sean Murphy at 6-under-par 66 led by one stroke over seven other golfers. **Second Round--**Nick Price, at 10-under-par 134, led by one over Phil Mickelson. **Third Round--**Greg Kraft, at 11-under-par 205, led by one stroke over Price and Jeff Sluman.

CUT: 85 players at even-par 144.

PRO-AM: $7,500. Individual--Mark McCumber, Bill Glasson and Marco Dawson, 67, $625 each. Team --Mark McCumber, Tom Watson and Rich Stewart, 54, $625 each.

WEATHER: Sunny and warm on Thursday and Friday. Saturday was much cooler with some sprinkles and wind. Sunday was partly cloudy and warmer.

Winner: Nick Price   67-67-72-71 277 $216,000.00

Player	Pos	Scores	Total	Money		Player	Pos	Scores	Total	Money
Greg Kraft	2	67-70-68-73	278	$129,600.00		Ted Tryba	T36	70-70-72-73	285	$5,166.66
Mark Calcavecchia	T3	67-70-72-70	279	$62,400.00		Olin Browne	T45	70-70-74-72	286	$3,363.43
Bill Glasson	T3	66-70-72-71	279	$62,400.00		Curt Byrum	T45	70-70-71-75	286	$3,363.43
Scott Hoch	T3	67-69-73-70	279	$62,400.00		Bill Kratzert	T45	69-70-71-76	286	$3,363.43
Kelly Gibson	T6	69-72-72-67	280	$41,700.00		Jodie Mudd	T45	71-73-71-71	286	$3,363.43
Jeff Sluman	T6	68-69-69-74	280	$41,700.00		David Ogrin	T45	70-72-70-74	286	$3,363.43
David Duval	T8	73-70-70-68	281	$28,000.00		Scott Simpson	T45	72-70-74-70	286	$3,363.43
David Frost	T8	71-68-74-68	281	$28,000.00		Glen Day	T45	70-67-75-74	286	$3,363.42
Jim Gallagher, Jr.	T8	72-68-68-73	281	$28,000.00		Ed Fiori	T52	71-72-73-71	287	$2,856.00
Andrew Magee	T8	70-71-69-71	281	$28,000.00		Tom Lehman	T52	71-73-71-72	287	$2,856.00
Tom Purtzer	T8	68-72-73-68	281	$28,000.00		Andy Bean	T54	67-71-80-70	288	$2,676.00
Larry Silveira	T8	73-71-68-69	281	$28,000.00		Steve Elkington	T54	69-74-73-72	288	$2,676.00
Doug Tewell	T8	69-72-71-69	281	$28,000.00		Brian Henninger	T54	74-70-68-76	288	$2,676.00
Jim Thorpe	T8	71-72-71-67	281	$28,000.00		Hale Irwin	T54	72-70-73-73	288	$2,676.00
Mark Wurtz	T8	70-70-70-71	281	$28,000.00		Larry Mize	T54	69-67-76-76	288	$2,676.00
Rob Boldt	T17	69-71-72-70	282	$14,666.67		Steve Pate	T54	73-71-72-72	288	$2,676.00
Brad Bryant	T17	70-72-70-70	282	$14,666.67		Steve Rintoul	T54	73-70-77-68	288	$2,676.00
Bob Estes	T17	68-73-70-71	282	$14,666.67		Dave Rummells	T54	67-71-74-76	288	$2,676.00
John Mahaffey	T17	71-72-72-67	282	$14,666.67		Joey Sindelar	T54	72-72-73-71	288	$2,676.00
Mike Standly	T17	70-72-73-67	282	$14,666.67		Curtis Strange	T54	70-74-74-70	288	$2,676.00
Scott Verplank	T17	71-72-72-67	282	$14,666.67		Brian Claar	T64	71-73-74-71	289	$2,520.00
Peter Jacobsen	T17	71-69-71-71	282	$14,666.66		Phil Mickelson	T64	66-69-77-77	289	$2,520.00
Jeff Maggert	T17	70-70-71-71	282	$14,666.66		Steve Stricker	T64	69-75-73-72	289	$2,520.00
Tom Watson	T17	69-68-73-72	282	$14,666.66		Steve Brodie	T67	71-72-77-70	290	$2,400.00
Fred Couples	T26	68-71-69-75	283	$8,880.00		Russ Cochran	T67	71-73-71-75	290	$2,400.00
Morris Hatalsky	T26	72-71-72-68	283	$8,880.00		Ed Dougherty	T67	72-72-76-70	290	$2,400.00
Justin Leonard	T26	70-69-74-70	283	$8,880.00		Joel Edwards	T67	71-72-76-71	290	$2,400.00
Sean Murphy	T26	66-72-74-71	283	$8,880.00		Robin Freeman	T67	73-71-73-73	290	$2,400.00
Craig Stadler	T26	71-73-68-71	283	$8,880.00		Tim Simpson	T67	72-71-79-68	290	$2,400.00
John Flannery	T31	70-73-71-70	284	$7,116.00		Phil Tataurangi	T67	70-74-73-73	290	$2,400.00
Tom Kite	T31	69-70-72-73	284	$7,116.00		Robert Gamez	T74	72-68-75-76	291	$2,268.00
Bob Lohr	T31	69-73-71-71	284	$7,116.00		Tom Garner	T74	74-70-76-71	291	$2,268.00
Mark McCumber	T31	69-71-74-70	284	$7,116.00		John Huston	T74	66-75-74-76	291	$2,268.00
Yoshin Mizumaki	T31	73-69-70-72	284	$7,116.00		Dennis Paulson	T74	71-72-73-75	291	$2,268.00
Michael Allen	T36	69-73-72-71	285	$5,166.67		Dan Forsman	T78	70-69-72-81	292	$2,196.00
Dave Barr	T36	69-74-70-72	285	$5,166.67		D.A. Weibring	T78	69-75-74-74	292	$2,196.00
Ben Crenshaw	T36	68-73-72-72	285	$5,166.67		Peter Jordan	T80	74-69-72-78	293	$2,136.00
Clark Dennis	T36	70-71-72-72	285	$5,166.67		Brian Kamm	T80	72-71-78-72	293	$2,136.00
Mark O'Meara	T36	68-74-71-72	285	$5,166.67		Hal Sutton	T80	71-69-80-73	293	$2,136.00
Joey Rassett	T36	72-72-68-73	285	$5,166.67		Ken Green	83	70-74-71-80	295	$2,088.00
Bob Gilder	T36	66-71-72-76	285	$5,166.66		Jim McGovern	84	73-71-79-73	296	$2,064.00
Steve Lamontagne	T36	67-73-71-74	285	$5,166.66		Paul Goydos	85	70-74-76-77	297	$2,040.00

ANHEUSER-BUSCH GOLF CLASSIC

Kingsmill GC, Williamsburg, VA   **Purse: $1,100,000**
Par: 36-35--72   **Yards: 6,797**   **July 7-10, 1994**

LEADERS: First Round--Bob Lohr, with a course-record 10-under-par 61, led by three strokes over Glen Day and John Wilson. **Second Round--**Lohr, at 13-under-par 129, led by three strokes over Day. **Third Round--**Mark McCumber, at 12-under-par 201, led by one over Lohr.

CUT: 72 players at even-par 142.

PRO-AM: $20,000. Individual--Ted Tryba, 63, $2,000. Team--Brad Bryant, Tom Purtzer, Lanny Wadkins and Jay Don Blake, 53, $1,550 each.

WEATHER: Thursday's round was delayed from 4:04 p.m. to 7:03 p.m. due to a severe thunderstorm. Play was suspended again at 8:27 p.m. due to darkness. The first round resumed Friday at 7:15 a.m. with the second round beginning at 7:45 a.m. The afternoon groups were delayed 15 minutes. Friday and Saturday were hot and breezy. Sunday's round was delayed from 3:39 p.m. until 5:10 p.m. due to a thunderstorm.

Winner: Mark McCumber   **67-69-65-66 267**   **$198,000.00**

Player	Pos	Scores	Total	Money
Glen Day	2	64-68-72-66	270	$118,800.00
Justin Leonard	3	67-69-67-69	272	$74,800.00
Michael Bradley	T4	68-69-69-67	273	$45,466.67
John Wilson	T4	64-70-72-67	273	$45,466.67
Scott Verplank	T4	71-69-66-67	273	$45,466.66
Jay Haas	T7	69-73-65-67	274	$34,283.34
Tommy Armour	T7	69-71-67-67	274	$34,283.33
Bob Lohr	T7	61-68-73-72	274	$34,283.33
Jim Furyk	T10	70-70-66-69	275	$28,600.00
Yoshi Mizumaki	T10	68-70-70-67	275	$28,600.00
Ken Green	T12	67-69-71-69	276	$24,200.00
Mike Hulbert	T12	68-70-67-71	276	$24,200.00
Bobby Clampett	T14	70-70-70-67	277	$18,700.00
Ben Crenshaw	T14	71-67-70-69	277	$18,700.00
Scott Hoch	T14	65-72-70-70	277	$18,700.00
Kenny Perry	T14	70-69-68-70	277	$18,700.00
Tom Purtzer	T14	66-69-70-72	277	$18,700.00
Ty Armstrong	T19	68-70-69-71	278	$14,300.00
Stan Utley	T19	67-71-71-69	278	$14,300.00
Richard Zokol	T19	69-69-69-71	278	$14,300.00
Keith Fergus	T22	69-71-74-65	279	$9,411.12
Ronnie Black	T22	67-69-74-69	279	$9,411.11
Steve Lamontagne	T22	68-69-69-73	279	$9,411.11
John Mahaffey	T22	69-71-70-69	279	$9,411.11
Joey Sindelar	T22	71-70-68-70	279	$9,411.11
Hal Sutton	T22	68-72-70-69	279	$9,411.11
Ted Tryba	T22	74-68-69-68	279	$9,411.11
Robert Wrenn	T22	69-69-71-70	279	$9,411.11
Mark Wurtz	T22	69-73-64-73	279	$9,411.11
Gene Sauers	T31	68-72-71-69	280	$6,238.58
Joe Daley	T31	69-70-69-72	280	$6,238.57
Ed Dougherty	T31	66-75-70-69	280	$6,238.57
Kelly Gibson	T31	74-67-68-71	280	$6,238.57
P.H. Horgan III	T31	71-69-69-71	280	$6,238.57
Charles Raulerson	T31	70-72-69-69	280	$6,238.57
Steve Stricker	T31	68-68-72-72	280	$6,238.57
JC Anderson	T38	69-70-69-73	281	$4,400.00
Russell Beiersdorf	T38	69-68-72-72	281	$4,400.00
Jay Don Blake	T38	70-72-70-69	281	$4,400.00
Bill Britton	T38	69-73-70-69	281	$4,400.00
Jim Gallagher, Jr.	T38	69-71-72-69	281	$4,400.00
Brian Henninger	T38	73-69-68-71	281	$4,400.00
Davis Love III	T38	68-69-74-70	281	$4,400.00
Doug Tewell	T38	71-68-72-70	281	$4,400.00
Todd Barranger	T46	72-67-75-68	282	$2,992.00
Brian Claar	T46	72-70-70-70	282	$2,992.00
Robin Freeman	T46	71-71-69-71	282	$2,992.00
Brad Lardon	T46	72-66-74-70	282	$2,992.00
Dennis Paulson	T46	67-73-72-70	282	$2,992.00
Clarence Rose	T46	67-71-72-72	282	$2,992.00
Rob Boldt	T52	68-72-71-72	283	$2,552.00
Skip Kendall	T52	71-69-74-69	283	$2,552.00
Joe Ozaki	T52	66-71-75-71	283	$2,552.00
Dillard Pruitt	T52	72-67-74-70	283	$2,552.00
Dave Stockton, Jr.	T52	72-69-68-74	283	$2,552.00
Curtis Strange	T52	70-69-76-68	283	$2,552.00
Michael Allen	T58	72-69-71-72	284	$2,431.00
Brandel Chamblee	T58	71-70-73-70	284	$2,431.00
John Flannery	T58	72-70-67-75	284	$2,431.00
Bill Kratzert	T58	72-70-73-69	284	$2,431.00
Steve Gotsche	62	71-70-74-70	285	$2,376.00
Chris Kite	T63	72-70-69-75	286	$2,321.00
Larry Rinker	T63	71-68-79-68	286	$2,321.00
Steve Rintoul	T63	70-72-71-73	286	$2,321.00
Lance Ten Broeck	T63	68-73-71-74	286	$2,321.00
Brad Bryant	T67	73-69-73-72	287	$2,255.00
Don Reese	T67	74-68-73-72	287	$2,255.00
Vance Heafner	T69	73-67-73-75	288	$2,189.00
John Inman	T69	71-70-75-72	288	$2,189.00
Ron Streck	T69	70-72-73-73	288	$2,189.00
Jim Thorpe	T69	69-73-73-73	288	$2,189.00

DEPOSIT GUARANTY GOLF CLASSIC

Annandale GC, Madison, MS   Purse: $700,000
Par: 36-36--72   Yards: 7,157   July 14-17, 1994

LEADERS: First Round--Mike Brisky, Brandel Chamblee, Mike Sullivan, Curt Byrum and John Elliott each posted 6-under-par 66s to lead by one stroke over Brian Henninger, Stan Utley and John Flannery.

CUT: 73 players at even-par 144.

PRO-AM: $7,500. Morning Indivdual--John Adams and Kenny Perry, 68, $431.25. Morning Team--Hubert Green, 54, $450. Afternoon portion was cancelled due to rain. All 26 professionals received equal shares of $144.23.

WEATHER: Thursday's tee times were delayed two hours due to eavy overnight rains. First round play was suspended for the day at 6:50 p.m. due to rain. The first round resumed at 8 a.m. Friday. The second round began at 9 a.m. Second-round play was suspended for the day 3:01 p.m. due to rain. The second round resumed at 10 a.m. Saturday with 74 players remaining on the course. The tournament was shortened to 36 holes after torrential rains flooded the course Saturday night.

Winner: Brian Henninger   67-68   135 $126,000.00
(won playoff with birdie on first extra hole)

Player	Pos	Rounds	Total	Money	Player	Pos	Rounds	Total	Money
Mike Sullivan	2	66-69	135	$75,600.00	Patrick Burke	T37	71-71	142	$2,597.54
Tommy Armour III	T 3	71-65	136	$31,570.00	Tom Byrum	T37	71-71	142	$2,597.54
Guy Boros	T 3	69-67	136	$31,570.00	Clark Dennis	T37	70-72	142	$2,597.54
Chris Dimarco	T 3	70-66	136	$31,570.00	Bob Gilder	T37	70-72	142	$2,597.54
Scott Hoch	T 3	69-67	136	$31,570.00	Donnie Hammond	T37	70-72	142	$2,597.54
Dave Stockton,Jr.	T 3	69-67	136	$31,570.00	Steve Lowery	T37	70-72	142	$2,597.54
Bobby Clampett	T 8	68-69	137	$20,300.00	Dillard Pruitt	T37	74-68	142	$2,597.54
Dicky Pride	T 8	73-64	137	$20,300.00	Tony Sills	T37	71-71	142	$2,597.54
Stan Utley	T 8	67-70	137	$20,300.00	David Toms	T37	74-68	142	$2,597.54
Mike Brisky	T11	66-72	138	$14,840.00	John Wilson	T37	71-71	142	$2,597.54
Curt Byrum	T11	66-72	138	$14,840.00	Brad Lardon	T37	70-72	142	$2,597.53
Brandel Chamblee	T11	66-72	138	$14,840.00	Harry Taylor	T37	72-70	142	$2,597.53
Ernie Gonzalez	T11	68-70	138	$14,840.00	Ty Armstrong	T50	69-74	143	$1,618.17
Chris Perry	T11	68-70	138	$14,840.00	Rob Boldt	T50	72-71	143	$1,618.17
John Flannery	T16	68-71	139	$10,850.00	Olin Browne	T50	69-74	143	$1,618.17
Hal Sutton	T16	70-69	139	$10,850.00	John Elliott	T50	66-77	143	$1,618.17
Leonard Thompson	T16	71-68	139	$10,850.00	Joe Inman	T50	72-71	143	$1,618.17
Esteban Toledo	T16	71-68	139	$10,850.00	Steve Rintoul	T50	74-69	143	$1,618.17
Bobby Wadkins	T20	71-69	140	$7,583.34	Gene Sauers	T50	72-71	143	$1,618.17
Jeff Woodland	T20	68-72	140	$7,583.34	Lance Ten Broeck	T50	73-70	143	$1,618.17
Russell Beiersdorf	T20	70-70	140	$7,583.33	Chad Ginn	T50	72-71	143	$1,618.16
Steve Lamontagne	T20	71-69	140	$7,583.33	P.H. Horgan III	T50	73-70	143	$1,618.16
Ed Sneed	T20	73-67	140	$7,583.33	Kenny Knox	T50	73-70	143	$1,618.16
Scott Verplank	T20	69-71	140	$7,583.33	Rocky Walcher	T50	72-71	143	$1,618.16
David Ogrin	T26	69-72	141	$4,569.10	John Adams	T62	73-71	144	$1,435.00
Phil Blackmar	T26	71-70	141	$4,569.09	Steve Brodie	T62	72-72	144	$1,435.00
Marco Dawson	T26	71-70	141	$4,569.09	Brian Claar	T62	72-72	144	$1,435.00
Brad Fabel	T26	69-72	141	$4,569.09	Russ Cochran	T62	72-72	144	$1,435.00
Keith Fergus	T26	69-72	141	$4,569.09	Frank Conner	T62	72-72	144	$1,435.00
Bruce Fleisher	T26	69-72	141	$4,569.09	Jon Diggetts	T62	73-71	144	$1,435.00
Robin Freeman	T26	72-69	141	$4,569.09	Steve Gotsche	T62	73-71	144	$1,435.00
Shaun Micheel	T26	72-69	141	$4,569.09	Mark Pfeil	T62	70-74	144	$1,435.00
David Peoples	T26	72-69	141	$4,569.09	Dave Rummells	T62	73-71	144	$1,435.00
Kenny Perry	T26	72-69	141	$4,569.09	Grant Waite	T62	75-69	144	$1,435.00
Don Reese	T26	70-71	141	$4,569.09	Jim Woodward	T62	71-73	144	$1,435.00
Todd Barranger	T37	72-70	142	$2,597.54	Richard Zokol	T62	73-71	144	$1,435.00

BRITISH OPEN

Turnberry GC (Ailsa Course), Turnberry, Scotland   **Purse: $1,650,000**
Par: 35-35--70   **Yards: 6,957**   **July 14-17, 1994**

LEADERS: First Round--Greg Turner, at 5-under-par 65, led by one over Jonathan Lomas. **Second Round**--Tom Watson, at 7-under-par 133, led by one over Jesper Parnevik and Brad Faxon. **Third Round**--Fuzzy Zoeller and Faxon, at 9-under-par 201, led by one over Nick Price, Parnevik, Watson and Ronan Rafferty.

CUT: 82 players at 3-over-par 143.

WEATHER: Thursday was sunny in the morning turning windy and rainy in the late afternoon. Friday was cloudy, windy and cold. Saturday and Sunday were mostly sunny and pleasant.

Winner: Nick Price   69-66-67-66   268 $178,200.00

Jesper Parnevik	2	68-66-68-67	269	$142,560.00	Davis Love III	T38	71-67-68-74	280	$9,882.00
Fuzzy Zoeller	3	71-66-64-70	271	$119,880.00	Brian Marchbank	T38	71-70-70-69	280	$9,882.00
David Feherty	T 4	68-69-66-70	273	$82,080.00	Jose Maria Olazabal	T38	72-71-69-68	280	$9,882.00
Anders Forsbrand	T 4	72-71-66-64	273	$82,080.00	Jumbo Ozaki	T38	69-71-66-74	280	$9,882.00
Mark James	T 4	72-67-66-68	273	$82,080.00	Jean Van De Velde	T38	68-70-71-71	280	$9,882.00
Brad Faxon	7	69-65-67-73	274	$58,320.00	David Edwards	T47	68-68-73-72	281	$8,829.00
Nick Faldo	T 8	75-66-70-64	275	$48,600.00	Jim Gallagher, Jr.	T47	73-68-69-71	281	$8,829.00
Tom Kite	T 8	71-69-66-69	275	$48,600.00	Greg Kraft	T47	69-74-66-72	281	$8,829.00
Colin Montgomerie	T 8	72-69-65-69	275	$48,600.00	Howard Twitty	T47	71-72-66-72	281	$8,829.00
Mark Calcavecchia	T11	71-70-67-68	276	$31,320.00	David Frost	T51	70-71-71-70	282	$7,978.00
Russell Claydon	T11	72-71-68-65	276	$31,320.00	Mats Lanner	T51	69-74-69-70	282	$7,978.00
Jonathan Lomas	T11	66-70-72-68	276	$31,320.00	Katsuyoshi Tomori	T51	69-69-73-71	282	$7,978.00
Mark Mcnulty	T11	71-70-68-67	276	$31,320.00	Tsukasa Watanabe	T51	72-71-68-71	282	$7,978.00
Larry Mize	T11	73-69-64-70	276	$31,320.00	Peter Baker	T55	71-72-70-70	283	$7,614.00
Frank Nobilo	T11	69-67-72-68	276	$31,320.00	John Cook	T55	73-67-70-73	283	$7,614.00
Greg Norman	T11	71-67-69-69	276	$31,320.00	Ross Mcfarlane	T55	68-74-67-74	283	$7,614.00
Ronan Rafferty	T11	71-66-65-74	276	$31,320.00	Tommy Nakajima	T55	73-68-69-73	283	$7,614.00
Tom Watson	T11	68-65-69-74	276	$31,320.00	Brian Watts	T55	68-70-71-74	283	$7,614.00
Mark Brooks	T20	74-64-71-68	277	$20,250.00	Robert Allenby	T60	72-69-68-75	284	$7,047.00
Peter Senior	T20	68-71-67-71	277	$20,250.00	Gordon Brand	T60	72-71-73-68	284	$7,047.00
Vijay Singh	T20	70-68-69-70	277	$20,250.00	Wayne Grady	T60	68-74-67-75	284	$7,047.00
Greg Turner	T20	65-71-70-71	277	$20,250.00	Per Johansson	T60	73-69-69-73	284	$7,047.00
Andrew Coltart	T24	71-69-66-72	278	$12,916.00	Bernhard Langer	T60	72-70-70-72	284	$7,047.00
Ernie Els	T24	69-69-69-71	278	$12,916.00	Hajime Meshiai	T60	72-71-71-70	284	$7,047.00
Bob Estes	T24	72-68-72-66	278	$12,916.00	Christy O'Connor	T60	71-69-71-73	284	$7,047.00
Peter Jacobsen	T24	69-70-67-72	278	$12,916.00	Ruben Alvarez	T67	70-72-71-72	285	$6,561.00
Paul Lawrie	T24	71-69-70-68	278	$12,916.00	Lennie Clements	T67	72-71-72-70	285	$6,561.00
Tom Lehman	T24	70-69-70-69	278	$12,916.00	Steve Elkington	T67	71-72-73-69	285	$6,561.00
Jeff Maggert	T24	69-74-67-68	278	$12,916.00	Carl Mason	T67	69-71-73-72	285	$6,561.00
Terry Price	T24	74-65-71-68	278	$12,916.00	Mark Roe	T67	74-68-73-70	285	$6,561.00
Loren Roberts	T24	68-69-69-72	278	$12,916.00	Wayne Riley	T72	77-66-70-73	286	$6,318.00
Mike Springer	T24	72-67-68-71	278	$12,916.00	Warren Bennett	T72	72-67-74-73	286	AMATUER
Craig Stadler	T24	71-69-66-72	278	$12,916.00	Sandy Lyle	74	71-72-72-72	287	$6,237.00
Mark Davis	T35	75-68-69-67	279	$10,854.00	Colin Gillies	T75	71-70-72-75	288	$5,953.00
Gary Evans	T35	69-69-73-68	279	$10,854.00	Craig Ronald	T75	71-72-72-73	288	$5,953.00
Lee Janzen	T35	74-69-69-67	279	$10,854.00	Ben Crenshaw	T77	70-73-73-73	289	$5,751.00
Seve Ballesteros	T38	70-70-71-69	280	$9,882.00	Joakim Haeggman	T77	71-72-69-77	289	$5,751.00
Darren Clarke	T38	73-68-69-70	280	$9,882.00	Craig Parry	T77	72-68-73-76	289	$5,751.00
David Gilford	T38	72-68-72-68	280	$9,882.00	Nic Henning	80	70-73-70-78	291	$5,589.00
Domingo Hospital	T38	72-69-71-68	280	$9,882.00	John Daly	81	68-72-72-80	292	$5,508.00

NEW ENGLAND CLASSIC

new england classic

Pleasnt Valley CC, Sutton, MA **Purse: $1,000,000**
Par: 36-35--71   **Yards: 7,110**   **July 21-24, 1994**

LEADERS: First Round--Brian Henninger and Mark Wurtz, each with 7-under-par 64s, led by one stroke Ronnie Black, Guy Boros and David Feherty. **Second Round--**Ed Fiori, at 10-under-par 132, led by one stroke over Kenny Perry. **Third Round--**Fiori and Feherty, each at 11-under-par 202, led by one over Perry.

CUT: 74 players at 1-under-par 141.

PRO-AM: $7,500. Individual--Roger Maltbie, 62, $750. Team--Jay Haas, 51, $750.

WEATHER: Warm and humid. Friday's round was delayed from 3:05 p.m. to 4 p.m. due to dangerous weather. Saturday's round was delayed from 3:05 p.m. to 5 p.m. due to dangerous weather. Play resumed at 5 p.m. and was again suspended at 5:19 p.m. due to rain and lightning. Play was finally cancelled for the day at 6:17 p.m. with 12 players still on the course. The third round was completed on Sunday morning.

Winner: Kenny Perry   67-66-70-65   268 $180,000.00

Player	Pos	Scores	Total	Money		Player	Pos	Scores	Total	Money
David Feherty	2	65-69-68-67	269	$108,000.00		Brad Bryant	T39	70-71-70-70	281	$3,512.73
Ed Fiori	3	66-66-70-70	272	$68,000.00		Bobby Clampett	T39	71-70-71-69	281	$3,512.73
Chris Dimarco	4	67-68-70-68	273	$48,000.00		Steve Elkington	T39	72-69-73-67	281	$3,512.73
Steve Gotsche	5	68-70-69-67	274	$40,000.00		Bob Gilder	T39	73-68-74-66	281	$3,512.73
Billy Downes	T6	71-68-69-67	275	$33,500.00		Eddie Kirby	T39	70-71-70-70	281	$3,512.73
Fred Funk	T6	68-66-75-66	275	$33,500.00		Kenny Knox	T39	70-71-68-72	281	$3,512.73
Justin Leonard	T6	69-68-70-68	275	$33,500.00		Sean Murphy	T39	71-70-70-70	281	$3,512.73
Bill Glasson	T9	68-68-71-69	276	$23,142.86		Sam Randolph	T39	69-72-69-71	281	$3,512.73
Ken Green	T9	68-72-68-68	276	$23,142.86		Ronnie Black	T39	65-70-72-74	281	$3,512.72
Jeff Maggert	T9	68-69-71-68	276	$23,142.86		Leonard Thompson	T39	67-72-74-68	281	$3,512.72
Blaine McCallister	T9	68-73-69-66	276	$23,142.86		Mark Wurtz	T39	64-73-73-71	281	$3,512.72
Fran Quinn	T9	67-72-66-71	276	$23,142.86		Olin Browne	T50	70-71-72-69	282	$2,348.89
Guy Boros	T9	65-69-70-72	276	$23,142.85		Curt Byrum	T50	66-73-73-70	282	$2,348.89
Wayne Levi	T9	66-71-68-71	276	$23,142.85		Jay Delsing	T50	70-69-73-70	282	$2,348.89
John Adams	T16	71-68-72-66	277	$14,500.00		Joel Edwards	T50	69-72-71-70	282	$2,348.89
Mark Calcavecchia	T16	68-71-69-69	277	$14,500.00		Robin Freeman	T50	69-72-72-69	282	$2,348.89
Lennie Clements	T16	70-69-71-67	277	$14,500.00		Brad Lardon	T50	68-73-67-74	282	$2,348.89
Brad Faxon	T16	70-70-71-66	277	$14,500.00		Mark Lye	T50	69-72-69-72	282	$2,348.89
Donnie Hammond	T16	70-69-71-67	277	$14,500.00		David Toms	T50	72-68-71-71	282	$2,348.89
Dick Mast	T16	66-69-70-72	277	$14,500.00		Jim Thorpe	T50	67-72-75-68	282	$2,348.88
Tommy Armour III	T22	66-69-72-71	278	$9,600.00		Billy Andrade	T59	69-70-71-73	283	$2,200.00
Jim Furyk	T22	71-69-71-67	278	$9,600.00		Larry Rinker	T59	68-71-72-72	283	$2,200.00
Paul Goydos	T22	72-67-70-69	278	$9,600.00		Stan Utley	T59	71-68-71-73	283	$2,200.00
Dave Rummells	T22	71-70-68-69	278	$9,600.00		Mike Donald	T62	70-70-73-71	284	$2,150.00
Gene Sauers	T22	70-69-72-67	278	$9,600.00		Bob Estes	T62	66-75-70-73	284	$2,150.00
Bob Lohr	T27	68-72-68-71	279	$7,400.00		Brian Henninger	T64	64-74-72-75	285	$2,060.00
Tony Sills	T27	67-72-72-68	279	$7,400.00		Mike Hulbert	T64	71-70-71-73	285	$2,060.00
Jeff Sluman	T27	70-71-71-67	279	$7,400.00		Steve Lamontagne	T64	69-70-73-73	285	$2,060.00
Trevor Dodds	T30	71-69-70-70	280	$5,688.89		Billy Mayfair	T64	72-69-72-72	285	$2,060.00
Jay Haas	T30	73-68-70-69	280	$5,688.89		Steve Pate	T64	71-69-74-71	285	$2,060.00
Morris Hatalsky	T30	66-72-73-69	280	$5,688.89		Payne Stewart	T64	70-70-75-70	285	$2,060.00
P.H. Horgan III	T30	68-69-71-72	280	$5,688.89		Lance Ten Broeck	T64	70-68-75-72	285	$2,060.00
John Morse	T30	70-70-69-71	280	$5,688.89		Mike Brisky	T72	71-70-73-72	286	$1,980.00
Dennis Paulson	T30	66-73-71-70	280	$5,688.89		Billy Ray Brown	T72	69-69-77-72	287	$1,950.00
Greg Twiggs	T30	70-71-67-72	280	$5,688.89		Tommy Moore	T72	70-71-70-76	287	$1,950.00
Robert Wrenn	T30	71-70-69-70	280	$5,688.89		Dana Quigley	74	70-71-72-76	289	$1,920.00
Michael Bradley	T30	71-65-73-71	280	$5,688.88						

FEDERAL EXPRESS
ST. JUDE CLASSIC

TPC at Southwind, Memphis, TN
Par: 36-35--71   Yards: 7,006

Purse: $1,250,000
July 28-31, 1994

LEADERS: First Round--Dave Barr, Fuzzy Zoeller, Dicky Pride, Payne Stewart and Ted Schulz with 5-under-par 66, led by a stroke over 14 other players. **Second Round--**Zoeller, at 11-under-par 131, led by one over Gene Sauers, Jay Haas and Pride. **Third Round--**Gil Morgan, Russ Cochran and Pride at 13-under-par 200, led by one over Haas, Zoeller and Sauers.

CUT: 70 players at 2-under-par 140.

PRO-AM: Individual--Jay Haas, Curtis Strange and Fulton Allem, 67, $625. Team--Davis Love III, 51, $750.

WEATHER: Pleasant every day.

Winner   Dicky Pride   66-67-67-67   267 $225,000.00
(Won playoff with birdie on first extra hole)

Player	Pos	Scores	Total	Money	Player	Pos	Scores	Total	Money
Gene Sauers	T2	67-66-68-66	267	$110,000.00	Morris Hatalsky	T35	68-68-73-67	276	$5,901.43
Hal Sutton	T2	67-68-68-64	267	$110,000.00	Loren Roberts	T35	68-71-72-65	276	$5,901.43
Nick Price	4	72-66-66-64	268	$60,000.00	Tony Sills	T35	70-64-72-70	276	$5,901.43
Dave Barr	T5	66-69-67-67	269	$45,625.00	Jim Woodward	T35	67-70-71-68	276	$5,901.43
Russ Cochran	T5	67-68-65-69	269	$45,625.00	Steve Pate	T35	70-68-67-71	276	$5,901.42
Wayne Grady	T5	70-66-67-66	269	$45,625.00	Joel Edwards	T42	69-69-67-72	277	$4,625.00
Paul Stankowski	T8	68-67-69-66	270	$37,500.00	Scott Hoch	T42	71-67-70-69	277	$4,625.00
Fuzzy Zoeller	T8	66-65-70-69	270	$37,500.00	Kirk Triplett	T42	70-69-69-69	277	$4,625.00
Brian Claar	T10	69-67-68-67	271	$28,750.00	Tom Purtzer	T45	69-68-73-68	278	$3,503.58
John Cook	T10	67-70-65-69	271	$28,750.00	Steve Brodie	T45	71-68-66-73	278	$3,503.57
Jim Gallagher, Jr.	T10	71-68-65-67	271	$28,750.00	Jay Delsing	T45	68-67-71-72	278	$3,503.57
Gil Morgan	T10	70-67-63-71	271	$28,750.00	Neal Lancaster	T45	71-65-73-69	278	$3,503.57
Duffy Waldorf	T10	67-70-67-67	271	$28,750.00	Yoshi Mizumaki	T45	71-69-70-68	278	$3,503.57
Chris Dimarco	T15	67-73-65-67	272	$20,625.00	Steve Rintoul	T45	69-70-68-71	278	$3,503.57
Jay Haas	T15	67-66-68-71	272	$20,625.00	Grant Waite	T45	75-65-69-69	278	$3,503.57
Craig Parry	T15	73-65-66-68	272	$20,625.00	Michael Allen	T52	71-69-67-72	279	$2,915.00
Payne Stewart	T15	66-68-69-69	272	$20,625.00	Phil Blackmar	T52	69-71-70-69	279	$2,915.00
John Adams	T19	71-67-65-70	273	$15,150.00	David Feherty	T52	70-68-74-67	279	$2,915.00
Peter Jacobsen	T19	68-70-67-68	273	$15,150.00	Bill Glasson	T52	70-70-68-71	279	$2,915.00
David Ogrin	T19	70-70-66-67	273	$15,150.00	David Peoples	T52	71-68-68-72	279	$2,915.00
Mike Reid	T19	72-67-67-67	273	$15,150.00	Peter Jordan	57	67-72-71-70	280	$2,825.00
Doug Tewell	T19	69-66-68-70	273	$15,150.00	Guy Boros	T58	70-70-71-70	281	$2,775.00
Robin Freeman	T24	71-68-69-66	274	$9,671.88	Michael Bradley	T58	67-70-74-70	281	$2,775.00
Jim Furyk	T24	68-69-70-67	274	$9,671.88	Bob Tway	T58	71-68-71-71	281	$2,775.00
Bob Gilder	T24	69-71-66-68	274	$9,671.88	Tom Sieckmann	T61	72-67-73-70	282	$2,712.50
Ken Green	T24	67-67-75-65	274	$9,671.88	Howard Twitty	T61	69-71-74-68	282	$2,712.50
Lennie Clements	T24	73-66-65-70	274	$9,671.87	John Inman	T63	71-69-73-71	284	$2,625.00
Bob Estes	T24	72-67-63-72	274	$9,671.87	Dan Pohl	T63	68-69-75-72	284	$2,625.00
Mike Hulbert	T24	70-65-70-69	274	$9,671.87	Ted Schulz	T63	66-69-73-76	284	$2,625.00
Mark McCumber	T24	70-66-68-70	274	$9,671.87	Larry Silveira	T63	70-69-73-72	284	$2,625.00
John Huston	T32	67-71-72-65	275	$7,396.67	Stan Utley	T63	72-67-75-70	284	$2,625.00
Jodie Mudd	T32	70-68-71-66	275	$7,396.67	Trevor Dodds	T68	67-73-73-73	286	$2,537.50
Bob Lohr	T32	70-68-70-67	275	$7,396.66	John Mahaffey	T68	73-67-73-73	286	$2,537.50
Billy Andrade	T35	71-69-69-67	276	$5,901.43	Robert Gamez	70	67-73-72-77	289	$2,500.00
Donnie Hammond	T35	69-67-72-68	276	$5,901.43					

BUICK OPEN

Warwick Hills G&CC, Grand Blanc, MI
Par: 36-36--72   Yards: 7,105

Purse: $1,100,000
August 4-7, 1994

LEADERS: First Round--Fred Funk, with a 7-under-par 65, led by one over Corey Pavin. **Second Round--**Pavin, at 13-under-par 131, led by four over Funk. **Third Round--**Pavin, at 15-under-par 201, led by one over Fred Couples.

CUT: 83 players at even-par 144. Due to a 36-hole Sunday, only 65 players played the last two rounds.

PRO-AM: $7,500. Individual--D.A. Weibring and Jeff Sluman, 67, $675 each. Team--Howard Twitty, Billy Andrade and Dave Rummells, 55, $625 each.

WEATHER: Due to heavy rains, Thursday's round was completely postponed until Friday. The cut was made Saturday night, and the contestants played 36 holes on Sunday. Friday, Saturday and Sunday were sunny and mild.

Winner: Fred Couples 72-65-65-68   270 $198,000.00

Player		Scores	Total	Money	Player		Scores	Total	Money
Corey Pavin	2	66-65-70-71	272	$118,800.00	Robin Freeman	T43	70-70-76-69	285	$3,850.00
Greg Kraft	T3	71-72-67-66	276	$57,200.00	Sandy Lyle	T43	70-73-71-71	285	$3,850.00
Steve Pate	T3	71-67-69-69	276	$57,200.00	D.A. Weibring	T43	70-72-71-72	285	$3,850.00
Curtis Strange	T3	71-70-67-68	276	$57,200.00	Dave Barr	T46	69-74-70-73	286	$3,118.50
Keith Clearwater	T6	71-67-69-70	277	$38,225.00	Ed Fiori	T46	71-71-75-69	286	$3,118.50
Ben Crenshaw	T6	72-68-69-68	277	$38,225.00	Eddie Kirby	T46	72-68-76-70	286	$3,118.50
Fred Funk	T8	65-70-71-72	278	$31,900.00	Larry Mize	T46	76-66-70-74	286	$3,118.50
Tom Lehman	T8	71-67-70-70	278	$31,900.00	Billy Mayfair	50	72-71-76-68	287	$2,772.00
Duffy Waldorf	T8	69-67-74-68	278	$31,900.00	Chris Dimarco	T51	75-66-73-74	288	$2,604.80
Steve Elkington	T11	71-68-69-71	279	$22,550.00	Dan Forsman	T51	75-66-76-71	288	$2,604.80
Nick Faldo	T11	70-67-73-69	279	$22,550.00	Wayne Levi	T51	72-70-75-71	288	$2,604.80
Tom Kite	T11	69-68-72-70	279	$22,550.00	Larry Silveira	T51	72-70-74-72	288	$2,604.80
Davis Love III	T11	69-67-72-71	279	$22,550.00	Esteban Toledo	T51	69-70-73-76	288	$2,604.80
Dennis Paulson	T11	70-71-67-71	279	$22,550.00	Olin Browne	T56	71-69-74-75	289	$2,486.00
Tom Purtzer	T11	69-71-65-74	279	$22,550.00	Sean Murphy	T56	70-73-76-70	289	$2,486.00
Chip Beck	T17	70-71-70-69	280	$16,500.00	Richard Zokol	T56	72-70-76-71	289	$2,486.00
Peter Jacobsen	T17	69-71-71-69	280	$16,500.00	Mike Heinen	T59	71-70-70-79	290	$2,420.00
Hal Sutton	T17	70-71-69-70	280	$16,500.00	Sam Torrance	T59	75-68-74-73	290	$2,420.00
David Feherty	T20	71-71-70-69	281	$11,916.67	Rocky Walcher	T59	73-70-73-74	290	$2,420.00
Kenny Knox	T20	71-72-69-69	281	$11,916.67	Jay Delsing	T62	72-71-74-75	292	$2,365.00
David Ogrin	T20	71-71-71-68	281	$11,916.67	Brian Kamm	T62	70-72-72-78	292	$2,365.00
Ted Tryba	T20	71-70-70-70	281	$11,916.67	Grant Waite	64	72-71-76-74	293	$2,332.00
Gil Morgan	T20	73-68-70-70	281	$11,916.66	John Traub	65	72-71-77-78	298	$2,310.00
Howard Twitty	T20	69-70-68-74	281	$11,916.66	Bob Burns	T66	72-72	144	$2,101.00
Joel Edwards	T26	70-73-71-68	282	$8,635.00	Mark Carnevale	T66	70-74	144	$2,101.00
Fuzzy Zoeller	T26	70-71-71-70	282	$8,635.00	Clark Dennis	T66	74-70	144	$2,101.00
Guy Boros	T28	72-68-73-70	283	$7,005.63	Kelly Gibson	T66	70-74	144	$2,101.00
Yoshi Mizumaki	T28	69-69-73-72	283	$7,005.63	Steve Gotsche	T66	70-74	144	$2,101.00
Mike Reid	T28	71-69-73-70	283	$7,005.63	Nolan Henke	T66	72-72	144	$2,101.00
John Wilson	T28	70-68-73-72	283	$7,005.63	Mike Hulbert	T66	72-72	144	$2,101.00
Brad Faxon	T28	72-71-72-68	283	$7,005.62	Ed Humenik	T66	70-74	144	$2,101.00
David Frost	T28	70-71-68-74	283	$7,005.62	John Inman	T66	71-73	144	$2,101.00
Paul Goydos	T28	71-72-71-69	283	$7,005.62	Andrew Magee	T66	71-73	144	$2,101.00
Kenny Perry	T28	72-69-69-73	283	$7,005.62	Dan Olsen	T66	69-75	144	$2,101.00
Jay Don Blake	T36	69-70-73-72	284	$4,957.86	Joey Rassett	T66	72-72	144	$2,101.00
Jim Furyk	T36	71-69-72-72	284	$4,957.86	Dave Rummells	T66	72-72	144	$2,101.00
Craig Parry	T36	69-69-74-72	284	$4,957.86	Tim Simpson	T66	73-71	144	$2,101.00
David Toms	T36	72-71-70-71	284	$4,957.86	Lanny Wadkins	T66	73-71	144	$2,101.00
Bobby Wadkins	T36	73-69-70-72	284	$4,957.86	Willie Wood	T66	73-71	144	$2,101.00
Curt Byrum	T36	73-70-74-67	284	$4,957.85	Jeff Woodland	T66	74-70	144	$2,101.00
Ken Green	T36	72-70-75-67	284	$4,957.85	Mark Wurtz	T66	72-72	144	$2,101.00

PGA CHAMPIONSHIP

Southern Hills CC, Tulsa, OK
Par: 35-35--70   Yards: 6,834

Purse: $1,750,000
Aug. 11-14, 1994

LEADERS: First Round--Nick Price and Colin Montgomerie both fired 3-under-par 67s to lead Fred Couples, Ernie Els, Phil Mickelson and Ian Woosnam by one stroke. **Second Round--**Price, at 8-under-par 132, led Ben Crenshaw, Jay Haas and Corey Pavin by five shots. **Third Round--**Price posted an even-par 70, for an 8-under-par 202 total and a three-stroke lead over Haas.

CUT: 76 players at 5-over-par 145.

WEATHER: Hot all week. Overcast on Sunday.

Winner: Nick Price   67-65-70-67   269 $310,000.00

Corey Pavin	....	2	70-67-69-69	275	$160,000.00	Hale Irwin	.... T39	75-69-68-74	286	$6,030.00
Phil Mickelson	....	3	68-71-67-70	276	$110,000.00	Tom Lehman	.... T39	73-71-68-74	286	$6,030.00
Nick Faldo	.... T 4	73-67-71-66	277	$76,666.67	Billy Mayfair	.... T39	73-72-71-70	286	$6,030.00
Greg Norman	.... T 4	71-69-67-70	277	$76,666.67	Gil Morgan	.... T39	71-68-73-74	286	$6,030.00
John Cook	.... T 4	71-67-69-70	277	$76,666.67	David Edwards	..... T44	72-70-74-71	287	$5,200.00
Steve Elkington	..... T 7	73-70-66-69	278	$57,500.00	David Gilford	..... T44	69-73-73-72	287	$5,200.00
Jose Maria Olazabal T 7	72-66-70-70	278	$57,500.00	Neal Lancaster	..... T44	73-72-72-70	287	$5,200.00
Ben Crenshaw	.... T 9	70-67-70-72	279	$41,000.00	Fulton Allem	.... T47	74-67-74-73	288	$4,112.50
Tom Kite	.... T 9	72-68-69-70	279	$41,000.00	Billy Andrade	.... T47	71-71-78-68	288	$4,112.50
Loren Roberts	.... T 9	69-72-67-71	279	$41,000.00	Bob Estes	.... T47	72-71-72-73	288	$4,112.50
Tom Watson	.... T 9	69-72-67-71	279	$41,000.00	Greg Kraft	.... T47	74-69-70-75	288	$4,112.50
Ian Woosnam	.... T 9	68-72-73-66	279	$41,000.00	Andrew Magee	..... T47	70-74-71-73	288	$4,112.50
Jay Haas	....	14	71-66-68-75	280	$32,000.00	Frank Nobilo	.... T47	72-67-74-75	288	$4,112.50
Glen Day	.... T15	70-69-70-72	281	$27,000.00	Jumbo Ozaki	.... T47	71-69-72-76	288	$4,112.50
Mark Mcnulty	.... T15	72-68-70-71	281	$27,000.00	D.A. Weibring	...... T47	69-73-70-76	288	$4,112.50
Larry Mize	.... T15	72-72-67-70	281	$27,000.00	Kenny Perry	.... T55	78-67-70-74	289	$3,158.34
Kirk Triplett	.... T15	71-69-71-70	281	$27,000.00	Mike Springer	...... T55	77-66-69-77	289	$3,158.34
Bill Glasson	.... T19	71-73-68-70	282	$18,666.67	Tom Dolby	.... T55	73-68-75-73	289	$3,158.33
Mark McCumber	.. T19	73-70-71-68	282	$18,666.67	Fred Funk	.... T55	76-69-72-72	289	$3,158.33
Craig Stadler	.... T19	70-70-74-68	282	$18,666.67	Dudley Hart	.... T55	72-71-75-71	289	$3,158.33
Curtis Strange	...... T19	73-71-68-70	282	$18,666.67	Hal Sutton	.... T55	76-69-72-72	289	$3,158.33
Craig Parry	.... T19	70-69-70-73	282	$18,666.66	Bruce Fleisher	...... T61	75-68-72-75	290	$2,800.00
Fuzzy Zoeller	.... T19	69-71-72-70	282	$18,666.66	Ray Floyd	.... T61	69-76-73-72	290	$2,800.00
Ernie Els	.... T25	68-71-69-75	283	$13,000.00	Ron Mcdougal	..... T61	76-69-72-73	290	$2,800.00
David Frost	.... T25	70-71-69-73	283	$13,000.00	Tommy Nakajima . T61	73-71-74-72	290	$2,800.00
Barry Lane	.... T25	70-73-68-72	283	$13,000.00	Lanny Wadkins	.... T61	69-73-73-75	290	$2,800.00
Bernhard Langer	.. T25	73-71-67-72	283	$13,000.00	Jay Don Blake	..... T66	72-71-74-74	291	$2,600.00
Jeff Sluman	.... T25	70-72-66-75	283	$13,000.00	John Inman	.... T66	70-72-73-76	291	$2,600.00
Brad Faxon	.... T30	72-73-73-66	284	$8,458.34	Lee Janzen	.... T66	73-71-73-74	291	$2,600.00
Richard Zokol	...... T30	77-67-67-73	284	$8,458.34	Todd Smith	.... T66	74-69-71-77	291	$2,600.00
Bob Boyd	.... T30	72-71-70-71	284	$8,458.33	Payne Stewart	...... T66	72-73-72-74	291	$2,600.00
Lennie Clements .. T30	74-70-69-71	284	$8,458.33	Donnie Hammond T71	74-69-76-73	292	$2,512.50
Wayne Grady	...... T30	75-68-71-70	284	$8,458.33	Peter Senior	.... T71	74-71-70-77	292	$2,512.50
Sam Torrance	...... T30	69-75-69-71	284	$8,458.33	Sandy Lyle	.... T73	75-70-76-76	297	$2,462.50
Chip Beck	.... T36	72-70-72-71	285	$7,000.00	Dicky Pride	.... T73	75-69-73-80	297	$2,462.50
Blaine McCallister	T36	74-64-75-72	285	$7,000.00	Brian Henninger ... T75	77-65-78-78	298	$2,412.50
Colin Montgomerie T36	67-76-70-72	285	$7,000.00	Hajime Meshiai T75	74-71-74-79	298	$2,412.50
Fred Couples	.... T39	68-74-75-69	286	$6,030.00				

THE SPRINT INTERNATIONAL

The Sprint SM

INTERNATIONAL

Castle Pines GC, Castle Rock, CO   Purse: $1,400,000
Par: 36-36--72   Yards: 7,559   August 18-21, 1994

FORMAT: Modified Stableford scoring system with points awarded as follows: double-eagle +8; eagle +5; birdie +2; par 0; bogey -1; double-bogey or worse -3.

LEADERS: First Round--Bruce Lietzke, with 16 points, led by two points over Mike Reid. **Second Round--**Steve Lowery, with 21 points, led by one point over Reid and Dave Stockton, Jr. **Third Round--**Keith Clearwater, with 30 points, led by one point over Ernie Els.

CUT: Starting field of 144 players cut to 72 after 36 holes. There was no playoff. After 54 holes, the field was reduced to 24 players with six players playing for five spots. Richard Zokol, Mark Calcavecchia, Mark McNulty, Gene Sauers, Hal Sutton and Jose Maria Olazabal played off, with Zokol being eliminated on the first extra hole. Zokol made a double-bogey, Olazabal made a birdie and everyone else made par.

PRO-AM: $10,000. Individual--Tom Purtzer, 11 points, $1,000. Team--Keith Clearwater, 36 points, $1,000.

WEATHER: Thursday's round was delayed from 12:57 p.m. to 2:17 p.m. due to lightning in the area. There was rain on Friday afternoon, but no delays. Saturday and Sunday were sunny and warm.

Winner Steve Lowery   +35 $252,000.00
(Won playoff with par on first extra hole)

Rick Fehr	2	10-5-9-11	+35	$151,200.00	Mark Wurtz	T32	9-2-5	+16	$7,580.00
Duffy Waldorf	3	7-6-8-13	+34	$95,200.00	Guy Boros	T39	9-2-4	+15	$5,880.00
Ernie Els	4	5-7-17-4	+33	$67,200.00	Hale Irwin	T39	5-10-0	+15	$5,880.00
Tom Kite	5	4-12-10-6	+32	$56,000.00	Bob Tway	T39	7-4-4	+15	$5,380.00
John Adams	T 6	4-2-14-11	+31	$48,650.00	Tom Watson	T39	(-3)-12-6	+15	$5,880.00
Chris Dimarco	T 6	6-6-9-10	+31	$48,650.00	Lennie Clements	T43	(-1)-11-4	+14	$4,900.00
Mark Calcavecchia	T 8	0-8-11-11	+30	$42,000.00	Brad Faxon	T43	2-10-2	+14	$4,900.00
Dave Stockton,Jr	T 8	6-14-5-5	+30	$42,000.00	Joey Sindelar	T43	(-2)-10-6	+14	$4,900.00
Phil Mickelson	T10	0-11-9-9	+29	$36,400.00	Clark Dennis	T46	3-7-3	+13	$3,808.00
Mike Reid	T10	14-6-5-4	+29	$36,400.00	Ken Green	T46	12-1-0	+13	$3,808.00
Jay Haas	12	10-4-8-6	+28	$32,200.00	Brett Ogle	T46	7-3-3	+13	$3,808.00
Tom Lehman	T13	4-13-5-4	+26	$28,000.00	David Peoples	T46	2-3-8	+13	$3,808.00
Gene Sauers	T13	6-9-4-7	+26	$28,000.00	Scott Simpson	T46	1-5-7	+13	$3,808.00
Lee Janzen	T15	5-8-9-3	+25	$23,800.00	Paul Stankowski	T46	2-5-6	+13	$3,808.00
Hal Sutton	T15	11-4-4-6	+25	$23,800.00	Sean Murphy	T52	3-2-6	+11	$3,304.00
Ted Tryba	T15	10-5-5-5	+25	$23,800.00	Craig Parry	T52	5-8-(-2)	+11	$3,304.00
Keith Clearwater	T18	7-12-11-(-6)	+24	$20,300.00	Grant Waite	T52	6-0-5	+11	$3,304.00
Jose Maria Olazabal	T18	4-9-6-5	+24	$20,300.00	Fred Couples	T55	11-(-3)-2	+10	$3,150.00
Mark Mcnulty	20	8-6-5-4	+23	$18,200.00	Robin Freeman	T55	8-2-0	+10	$3,150.00
Bruce Lietzke	21	16-(-2)-9-(-1)	+22	$16,800.00	Davis Love III	T55	3-4-3	+10	$3,150.00
Bradley Hughes	22	8-4-9-0	+21	$15,680.00	Jeff Maggert	T55	1-8-1	+10	$3,150.00
Steve Pate	23	2-6-12-(-1)	+19	$14,560.00	Steve Stricker	T55	0-5-5	+10	$3,150.00
Mark Carnevale	24	8-0-12-(-6)	+14	$13,440.00	David Toms	T55	0-5-5	+10	$3,150.00
Richard Zokol	25	9-5-5	+19	$12,320.00	Bob Burns	61	3-3-3	+9	$3,052.00
Brad Bryant	T26	2-9-7	+18	$10,570.00	Bob Estes	T62	7-0-1	+8	$2,996.00
Steve Elkington	T26	6-6-6	+18	$10,570.00	Craig Stadler	T62	3-4-1	+8	$2,996.00
Dudley Hart	T26	5-3-10	+18	$10,570.00	Willie Wood	T62	6-1-1	+8	$2,996.00
Roger Maltbie	T26	(-3)-12-9	+18	$10,570.00	Ian Baker-Finch	T65	7-(-2)-2	+7	$2,926.00
Morris Hatalsky	T30	7-4-6	+17	$9,310.00	Larry Silveira	T65	2-7-(-2)	+7	$2,926.00
Dicky Pride	T30	3-4-10	+17	$9,310.00	Brian Henninger	67	4-1-1	+6	$2,884.00
Fulton Allem	T32	10-(-3)-9	+16	$7,580.00	Jay Don Blake	T68	(-2)-10-(-4)	+4	$2,842.00
Chip Beck	T32	7-1-8	+16	$7,580.00	Tom Purtzer	T68	(-3)-9-(-2)	+4	$2,842.00
Ronnie Black	T32	7-1-8	+16	$7,580.00	Mark Wiebe	70	5-1-(-3)	+3	$2,800.00
David Edwards	T32	3-8-5	+16	$7,580.00	Brandel Chamblee	T71	8-1-(-8)	+1	$2,758.00
Fred Funk	T32	5-4-7	+16	$7,580.00	Dan Forsman	T71	1-5-(-5)	+1	$2,758.00
D.A. Weibring	T32	(-3)-9-10	+16	$7,580.00					

NEC WORLD SERIES OF GOLF

Firestone CC (North Course), Akron, OH   **Purse: $2,000,000**
Par: 35-35--70   Yards: 6,918   **August 25-28, 1994**

LEADERS: First Round--Loren Roberts and Craig Stadler, at 5-under-par 65, led by one over Jeff Maggert, Mark McCumber and Jose Maria Olazabal. **Second Round--**Steve Lowery, Olazabal and McCumber, at 7-under-par 133, led by one over Nick Price, Ernie Els and Greg Norman.**Third Round-**Lowery, at 11-under-par 199, led by one over Scott Hoch.

PRO-AM: $10,000. Individual--John Inman, Nick Price, 64, $900 each. Team--David Frost, 52, $1,000.

WEATHER: Warm and pleasant on Thursday and Friday. Saturday's round was delayed from 3:39 p.m. to 5:20 p.m. due to lightning in the area. Sunday, tornado watch in effect, some heavy rain at times, but no delays.

Winner: Jose Maria Olazabal   **66-67-69-67**   **269**   **$360,000.00**

Scott Hoch	2	71-64-65-70	270	$216,000.00	Mark Brooks	T26	71-65-69-76	281	$15,110.00
Brad Faxon	T 3	69-68-65-69	271	$116,000.00	Ernie Els	T26	68-66-71-76	281	$15,110.00
Steve Lowery	T 3	67-66-66-72	271	$116,000.00	John Inman	T26	70-67-69-75	281	$15,110.00
John Huston	T 5	73-64-64-71	272	$76,000.00	Phil Mickelson	T26	75-70-68-68	281	$15,110.00
Mark McNulty	T 5	69-68-65-70	272	$76,000.00	Curtis Strange	T26	69-71-68-73	281	$15,110.00
Mike Heinen	7	71-67-65-70	273	$67,000.00	Neal Lancaster	T31	70-73-69-70	282	$14,400.00
Fred Couples	T 8	69-70-65-70	274	$60,000.00	Mark McCumber	T31	66-67-72-77	282	$14,400.00
Greg Norman	T 8	67-67-68-72	274	$60,000.00	Blaine McCallister	33	69-74-67-73	283	$14,250.00
Hale Irwin	T10	70-65-71-70	276	$52,000.00	Andrew Magee	34	71-72-70-71	284	$14,150.00
Nick Price	T10	68-66-69-73	276	$52,000.00	Ben Crenshaw	T35	70-73-70-72	285	$14,000.00
Tom Lehman	T12	72-69-64-72	277	$40,500.00	Lee Janzen	T35	70-71-69-75	285	$14,000.00
Davis Love III	T12	68-72-67-70	277	$40,500.00	Fulton Allem	T37	68-77-68-74	287	$13,800.00
Larry Mize	T12	69-68-68-72	277	$40,500.00	Jeff Roth	T37	74-68-70-75	287	$13,800.00
Loren Roberts	T12	65-70-68-74	277	$40,500.00	David Frost	39	67-71-75-76	289	$13,650.00
Jim Gallagher, Jr.	T16	70-68-70-70	278	$30,000.00	Ikuo Shirahama	40	73-70-77-70	290	$13,550.00
Bill Glasson	T16	71-73-64-70	278	$30,000.00	Mike Springer	41	75-68-69-80	292	$13,450.00
Jeff Maggert	T16	66-74-65-73	278	$30,000.00	Carl Mason	42	72-74-71-76	293	$13,350.00
Corey Pavin	T16	70-70-69-69	278	$30,000.00	Brian Henninger	43	71-73-70-80	294	$13,250.00
Craig Stadler	T16	65-78-64-71	278	$30,000.00	John Daly	44	69-73-70-83	295	$13,150.00
Jay Haas	T21	75-64-70-70	279	$22,400.00	Seiki Okuda	45	70-72-74-80	296	$13,050.00
Billy Mayfair	T21	67-72-69-71	279	$22,400.00	Dicky Pride	46	78-73-70-77	298	$12,950.00
Kenny Perry	T21	69-72-70-68	279	$22,400.00	Ian Baker-Finch	47	67-82-77-76	302	$12,850.00
Tommy Nakajima	T24	69-71-66-74	280	$18,400.00	Hiroshi Goda	48	75-78-73-80	306	$12,750.00
Craig Parry	T24	69-69-71-71	280	$18,400.00					

GREATER MILWAUKEE OPEN

Brown Deer Park GC, Milwaukee, WI
Par: 35-36--71   Yards: 6,716

Purse: $1,000,000
September 1-4, 1994

LEADERS: First Round--D.A. Weibring, at 6-under-par 65, held a one-stroke lead over David Toms, Lon Hinkle, Olin Browne and Michael Allen. **Second Round--**Weibring, at 11-under-par 131, increased his margin to two strokes over Jay Haas, Dave Barr, Bob Estes and Loren Roberts, who fired a course-record 63. **Third Round--**Estes, at 15-under-par 198, had a one-stroke lead over Mark Calcavecchia.

CUT: 73 players at 2-under-par 140.

PRO-AM: $7,500. Individual--Brian Claar, Gary Hallberg, 66, $675. Team--Duffy Waldorf, 54, $750.

WEATHER: Cold early Thursday, with temperatures in the high 40s, turning partly sunny and warming slightly. Overcast and cool Friday, with some wind. Light rain early Saturday, becoming cloudy and overcast with some sun later.

Winner: Mike Springer 69-67-65-67   268 $180,000.00

Loren Roberts	2	70-63-68-68	269	$108,000.00	Curtis Strange	T37	68-71-67-72	278	$4,600.00
Mark Calcavecchia	T3	67-68-64-71	270	$48,000.00	Steve Stricker	T37	71-68-67-72	278	$4,600.00
Bob Estes	T3	67-66-65-72	270	$48,000.00	Jim Thorpe	T37	68-69-69-72	278	$4,600.00
Tom Purtzer	T3	70-69-67-64	270	$48,000.00	Glen Day	T41	68-72-65-74	279	$3,315.56
Joey Sindelar	T3	67-68-66-69	270	$48,000.00	Dave Stockton, Jr	T41	71-69-70-69	279	$3,315.56
Dave Barr	T7	69-64-70-68	271	$32,250.00	Harry Taylor	T41	72-68-70-69	279	$3,315.56
Marco Dawson	T7	68-66-69-68	271	$32,250.00	Bobby Wadkins	T41	68-71-66-74	279	$3,315.56
Mark O'Meara	T9	68-69-67-68	272	$28,000.00	Willie Wood	T41	68-70-70-71	279	$3,315.56
Steve Pate	T9	68-70-65-69	272	$28,000.00	Jim Furyk	T41	68-68-69-74	279	$3,315.55
Jay Don Blake	T11	68-68-66-71	273	$24,000.00	Eddie Kirby	T41	71-69-69-70	279	$3,315.55
Jay Haas	T11	67-66-69-71	273	$24,000.00	Wayne Levi	T41	69-71-65-74	279	$3,315.55
Michael Allen	T13	66-72-69-67	274	$18,200.00	Robert Wrenn	T41	72-68-68-71	279	$3,315.55
Bill Britton	T13	71-64-65-74	274	$18,200.00	John Adams	T50	71-66-68-75	280	$2,362.50
Kelly Gibson	T13	68-68-71-67	274	$18,200.00	Ronnie Black	T50	70-70-71-69	280	$2,362.50
John Inman	T13	68-67-66-73	274	$18,200.00	Lennie Clements	T50	71-67-68-74	280	$2,362.50
Tom Sieckmann	T13	67-72-64-71	274	$18,200.00	Clark Dennis	T50	70-70-68-72	280	$2,362.50
Mark Brooks	T18	69-69-69-68	275	$12,171.43	Bob Gilder	T50	69-71-67-73	280	$2,362.50
Mike Donald	T18	72-68-65-70	275	$12,171.43	Ken Green	T50	69-71-68-72	280	$2,362.50
Bruce Lietzke	T18	71-68-66-70	275	$12,171.43	Tim Simpson	T50	69-71-69-71	280	$2,362.50
Gil Morgan	T18	71-67-68-69	275	$12,171.43	John Wilson	T50	68-71-71-70	280	$2,362.50
Dennis Paulson	T18	68-67-69-71	275	$12,171.43	Tom Garner	T58	71-69-67-74	281	$2,210.00
Joey Rassett	T18	69-68-69-69	275	$12,171.43	P.H. Horgan III	T58	68-71-70-72	281	$2,210.00
David Toms	T18	66-69-67-73	275	$12,171.42	Bill Kratzert	T58	67-73-71-70	281	$2,210.00
John Flannery	T25	69-66-73-68	276	$7,975.00	Leonard Thompson	T58	72-68-70-71	281	$2,210.00
Scott Hoch	T25	69-70-70-67	276	$7,975.00	Steve Brodie	T62	70-68-67-77	282	$2,120.00
Doug Tewell	T25	70-70-65-71	276	$7,975.00	Olin Browne	T62	66-73-74-69	282	$2,120.00
D.A. Weibring	T25	65-66-71-74	276	$7,975.00	Tony Sills	T62	69-71-70-72	282	$2,120.00
Brandel Chamblee	T29	68-70-69-70	277	$6,087.50	Mike Standly	T62	70-69-70-73	282	$2,120.00
David Feherty	T29	69-67-70-71	277	$6,087.50	Ben Walter	T62	71-69-71-71	282	$2,120.00
Bruce Fleisher	T29	69-70-73-65	277	$6,087.50	Sean Murphy	T67	71-69-69-74	283	$2,050.00
Roger Maltbie	T29	69-68-70-70	277	$6,087.50	Dillard Pruitt	T67	72-68-71-72	283	$2,050.00
David Peoples	T29	68-69-67-73	277	$6,087.50	Richard Zokol	69	69-71-70-74	284	$2,020.00
Charles Raulerson	T29	73-67-65-72	277	$6,087.50	Morris Hatalsky	T70	70-70-70-75	285	$1,980.00
Howard Twitty	T29	69-70-71-67	277	$6,087.50	Blaine McCallister	T70	67-71-74-73	285	$1,980.00
Duffy Waldorf	T29	67-68-71-71	277	$6,087.50	Dave Rummells	T70	70-69-72-74	285	$1,980.00
David Ogrin	T37	69-69-68-72	278	$4,600.00	Brook Schmitt	73	72-68-77-81	298	$1,940.00

BELL CANADIAN OPEN

Glen Abbey GC, Oakville, Ontario, Canada
Par: 35-37--72   Yards: 7,112

Purse: $1,300,000
September 8-11, 1994

LEADERS: First Round--Mark O'Meara and Dick Mast, each with 6-under-par 66s, led four players by one stroke. **Second Round--**Robin Freeman, at 8-under-par 136, led Brandel Chamblee, Clark Dennis and Jay Don Blake by one. **Third Round--**Mark McCumber, at 10-under-par 206, led Nick Price by one stroke and Steve Stricker and Tom Lehman by two.

CUT: 78 players at 1-over-par 145.

PRO-AM: $7,500. Individual--Donnie Hammond, 66, $750. Team--Davis Love III, Jim McGovern, Bob Gilder, Hal Sutton, 55, $581.25.

WEATHER: Very nice all week. Sunny with occasionally strong winds.

Winner: Nick Price   67-72-68-68   275 $234,000.00

Player		Scores	Total	Money	Player		Scores	Total	Money
Mark Calcavecchia	2	67-71-71-67	276	$140,400.00	Jim Furyk	T39	69-73-72-73	287	$5,200.00
Tom Lehman	3	69-69-70-69	277	$88,400.00	Steve Lamontagne	T39	70-75-71-71	287	$5,200.00
Jay Don Blake	T 4	74-63-73-68	278	$57,200.00	John Morse	T39	74-68-74-71	287	$5,200.00
Mark McCumber	T 4	74-65-67-72	278	$57,200.00	Mike Sullivan	T39	73-72-69-73	287	$5,200.00
Fulton Allem	T 6	69-69-71-70	279	$43,550.00	Bill Kratzert	T45	75-70-73-70	288	$4,030.00
Brian Kamm	T 6	71-71-69-68	279	$43,550.00	Jesper Parnevik	T45	71-69-75-73	288	$4,030.00
Steve Stricker	T 6	69-70-69-71	279	$43,550.00	Howard Twitty	T45	70-72-73-73	288	$4,030.00
Mark O'Meara	9	66-72-72-70	280	$37,700.00	Chip Beck	T48	72-69-73-75	289	$3,307.20
Bob Estes	T10	72-73-68-68	281	$32,500.00	Steve Lowery	T48	71-71-72-75	289	$3,307.20
Greg Kraft	T10	72-70-70-69	281	$32,500.00	Dillard Pruitt	T48	74-71-71-73	289	$3,307.20
Payne Stewart	T10	68-72-72-69	281	$32,500.00	Larry Silveira	T48	73-70-72-74	289	$3,307.20
Bob Tway	T13	69-73-71-69	282	$26,000.00	Doug Tewell	T48	73-72-70-74	289	$3,307.20
Scott Verplank	T13	75-67-71-69	282	$26,000.00	Ted Schulz	T53	74-71-73-72	290	$2,981.34
Rick Fehr	T15	72-70-67-74	283	$21,450.00	Grant Waite	T53	69-76-73-72	290	$2,981.34
Dick Mast	T15	66-76-74-67	283	$21,450.00	Robin Freeman	T53	68-68-75-79	290	$2,981.33
Curtis Strange	T15	74-68-68-73	283	$21,450.00	P.H. Horgan III	T53	71-74-72-73	290	$2,981.33
Roger Wessels	T15	68-72-72-71	283	$21,450.00	Larry Mize	T53	72-71-70-77	290	$2,981.33
Billy Andrade	T19	71-69-71-73	284	$15,756.00	Dennis Paulson	T53	73-72-72-73	290	$2,981.33
Guy Boros	T19	69-73-73-69	284	$15,756.00	Brandel Chamblee	T59	68-69-78-76	291	$2,782.00
Glen Day	T19	69-71-69-75	284	$15,756.00	Bob Gilder	T59	73-72-76-70	291	$2,782.00
David Edwards	T19	73-69-70-72	284	$15,756.00	Gary Hallberg	T59	67-76-71-77	291	$2,782.00
Bill Glasson	T19	71-72-73-68	284	$15,756.00	Ed Humenik	T59	72-69-76-74	291	$2,782.00
Phil Tataurangi	T24	71-73-73-68	285	$10,288.58	Jeff Maggert	T59	70-70-72-79	291	$2,782.00
Brad Bryant	T24	69-72-75-69	285	$10,288.57	John Mahaffey	T59	71-74-68-78	291	$2,782.00
Steve Elkington	T24	69-76-70-70	285	$10,288.57	Bob May	T59	69-76-75-71	291	$2,782.00
Doug Martin	T24	70-74-69-72	285	$10,288.57	Jodie Mudd	T59	70-75-70-76	291	$2,782.00
Gil Morgan	T24	69-72-69-75	285	$10,288.57	Sean Murphy	T59	71-72-76-72	291	$2,782.00
Rocky Walcher	T24	74-70-70-71	285	$10,288.57	Olin Browne	T68	70-75-74-74	293	$2,639.00
Duffy Waldorf	T24	68-72-72-73	285	$10,288.57	Curt Byrum	T68	71-72-74-76	293	$2,639.00
Keith Clearwater	T31	69-73-72-72	286	$7,215.00	Ronnie Black	T70	71-74-73-77	295	$2,561.00
Clark Dennis	T31	71-66-74-75	286	$7,215.00	Kelly Gibson	T70	73-71-73-78	295	$2,561.00
David Frost	T31	73-69-71-73	286	$7,215.00	Lee Janzen	T70	67-76-76-76	295	$2,561.00
Ken Green	T31	74-70-72-70	286	$7,215.00	Bob Lohr	T70	71-73-75-76	295	$2,561.00
Dan Halldorson	T31	71-70-69-76	286	$7,215.00	David Feherty	74	70-74-76-76	296	$2,496.00
Mike Hulbert	T31	73-69-71-73	286	$7,215.00	Ty Armstrong	T75	71-72-76-78	297	$2,457.00
Davis Love III	T31	71-73-74-68	286	$7,215.00	Brad Faxon	T75	70-75-80-72	297	$2,457.00
Phil Mickelson	T31	69-71-71-75	286	$7,215.00	Paul Stankowski	77	74-71-77-78	300	$2,418.00
Dave Barr	T39	68-77-70-72	287	$5,200.00	Mike Standly	78	70-72-84-80	306	$2,392.00
Fred Couples	T39	70-70-77-70	287	$5,200.00					

B.C. OPEN

En-Joie GC, Endicott, NY
Par: 37-34--71   Yards: 6,966

Purse: $900,000
September 15-18, 1994

LEADERS: First Round--Jeff Sluman, at 8-under-par 63, held a one-stroke lead over Glen Day, Joel Edwards and John Flannery. **Second Round--**Sluman, at 11-under-par 131, was one stroke ahead of Mike Sullivan. **Third Round--**Sluman, at 15-under-par 198, was two strokes in front of Sullivan.

CUT: 77 players at 2-under-par 140.

PRO-AM: $7,500. Individual--Howard Twitty, Joey Sindelar, 64, $675 each. Team--Chip Beck, 50, $750.

WEATHER: Variable cloudiness, unseasonably warm and humid Thursday and Friday. Wind picking up with some intermittment rain Saturday. Partly sunny, windy and cool Sunday.

Winner: Mike Sullivan 65-67-68-66 266 $162,000.00

Jeff Sluman	2	63-68-67-72	270	$97,200.00	Scott Verplank	T32	67-69-68-76	280	$4,770.00
Brian Claar	T3	68-68-65-71	272	$52,200.00	Rob Boldt	T40	70-68-68-75	281	$3,420.00
Mike Hulbert	T3	67-67-68-70	272	$52,200.00	Ed Fiori	T40	69-68-73-71	281	$3,420.00
Russell Beiersdorf	T5	69-66-68-70	273	$34,200.00	Steve Jones	T40	67-70-70-74	281	$3,420.00
Curt Byrum	T5	67-69-66-71	273	$34,200.00	Dick Mast	T40	68-70-73-70	281	$3,420.00
Bill Glasson	T7	70-65-68-71	274	$28,050.00	David Ogrin	T40	70-68-72-71	281	$3,420.00
Paul Goydos	T7	68-68-67-71	274	$28,050.00	Howard Twitty	T40	70-66-71-74	281	$3,420.00
Blaine McCallister	T7	67-70-65-72	274	$28,050.00	Chip Beck	T46	67-71-71-73	282	$2,494.80
Robin Freeman	T10	68-65-69-73	275	$22,500.00	Tom Byrum	T46	65-72-71-74	282	$2,494.80
Mike Heinen	T10	65-70-68-72	275	$22,500.00	Dillard Pruitt	T46	66-73-74-69	282	$2,494.80
P.H. Horgan III	T10	68-67-69-71	275	$22,500.00	Tony Sills	T46	67-72-74-69	282	$2,494.80
Todd Barranger	T13	65-71-69-71	276	$16,875.00	Dave Stockton, Jr	T46	68-69-73-72	282	$2,494.80
David Edwards	T13	66-70-71-69	276	$16,875.00	Michael Allen	T51	67-72-73-71	283	$2,094.75
Lee Janzen	T13	67-67-72-70	276	$16,875.00	Bobby Clampett	T51	66-72-71-74	283	$2,094.75
Mark O'Meara	T13	65-73-67-71	276	$16,875.00	Steve Lowery	T51	69-69-74-71	283	$2,094.75
Brad Bryant	T17	71-65-72-69	277	$12,600.00	Don Reese	T51	71-67-73-72	283	$2,094.75
Sean Murphy	T17	67-68-72-70	277	$12,600.00	Doug Tewell	T51	71-69-71-72	283	$2,094.75
Steve Pate	T17	70-68-70-69	277	$12,600.00	Leonard Thompson	T51	66-73-70-74	283	$2,094.75
Joey Rassett	T17	71-68-67-71	277	$12,600.00	Ted Tryba	T51	68-71-75-69	283	$2,094.75
John Wilson	T17	71-68-69-69	277	$12,600.00	Bobby Wadkins	T51	71-65-77-70	283	$2,094.75
Steve Brodie	T22	67-71-72-68	278	$8,112.86	Olin Browne	T59	72-68-71-73	284	$1,980.00
Joel Edwards	T22	64-72-70-72	278	$8,112.86	Jesper Parnevik	T59	69-71-70-74	284	$1,980.00
Kelly Gibson	T22	71-66-69-72	278	$8,112.86	Esteban Toledo	T59	69-71-72-72	284	$1,980.00
Eddie Kirby	T22	71-68-69-70	278	$8,112.86	Guy Boros	T62	66-74-74-71	285	$1,908.00
Kirk Triplett	T22	70-68-67-73	278	$8,112.86	Peter Jordan	T62	67-70-69-79	285	$1,908.00
Glen Day	T22	64-69-73-72	278	$8,112.85	Tony Saraceno	T62	69-70-76-70	285	$1,908.00
David Peoples	T22	70-65-71-72	278	$8,112.85	Steve Stricker	T62	69-71-70-75	285	$1,908.00
Marco Dawson	T29	65-70-69-75	279	$6,120.00	Willie Wood	T62	70-70-71-74	285	$1,908.00
Bruce Fleisher	T29	67-70-68-74	279	$6,120.00	Lon Hinkle	T67	68-72-72-74	286	$1,836.00
Greg Kraft	T29	70-67-69-73	279	$6,120.00	Larry Silveira	T67	69-71-71-75	286	$1,836.00
Ronnie Black	T32	66-73-69-72	280	$4,770.00	Harry Taylor	T67	71-68-75-72	286	$1,836.00
Keith Clearwater	T32	69-68-72-71	280	$4,770.00	Billy Andrade	T70	70-68-70-79	287	$1,782.00
Chris Dimarco	T32	67-72-67-74	280	$4,770.00	Mike Brisky	T70	69-70-69-79	287	$1,782.00
Mike Donald	T32	70-69-70-71	280	$4,770.00	John Flannery	T70	64-72-74-77	287	$1,782.00
Tom Kite	T32	68-71-68-73	280	$4,770.00	Morris Hatalsky	T73	72-67-72-78	289	$1,737.00
Steve Lamontagne	T32	70-69-65-76	280	$4,770.00	Bob May	T73	70-69-71-79	289	$1,737.00
Neal Lancaster	T32	69-67-72-72	280	$4,770.00	Tom Hearn	75	71-68-70-82	291	$1,710.00

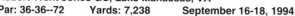

Robert Trent Jones GC, Lake Manassas, VA
Par: 36-36--72   Yards: 7,238   September 16-18, 1994

1994 MATCHES

FIRST DAY

Four-Ball--United States 5, International 0

Corey Pavin/Jeff Maggert (U.S.) def. Steve Elkington/Vijay Singh, 2&1
Jay Haas/Scott Hoch (U.S.) def. Fulton Allem/David Frost, 6&5
Davis Love III/Fred Couples (U.S.) def. Nick Price/Bradley Hughes, 1 up
John Huston/Jim Gallagher, Jr. (U.S.) def. Craig Parry/Robert Allenby, 4&2
Tom Lehman/Phil Mickelson (U.S.) def. Frank Nobilo/Peter Senior, 3&2

Foursomes--United States 2 1/2, International 2 1/2

Hale Irwin/Loren Roberts (U.S.) def. Frost/Allem, 3&1
Haas/Hoch (U.S.) def. Parry/Tsukasa Watanabe, 4&3
Nobilo/Allenby (Int.) def. Pavin/Maggert, 2&1
Elkington/Singh (Int.) def. Mickelson/Lehman, 2&1
Price/Mark McNulty (Int.) halved with Love/Gallagher
Totals: United States 7 1/2, International 2 1/2

SECOND DAY

Four-Ball--International 3 1/2, United States 1 1/2

Allem/McNulty (Int.) def. Gallagher/Huston, 4&3
Watanabe/Singh (Int.) def. Haas/Hoch, 3&1
Parry/Hughes (Int.) def. Roberts/Lehman, 4&3
Couples/Love (U.S.) def. Nobilo/Allenby, 2 up
Price/Elkington (Int.) halved with Mickelson/Pavin
Totals: United States 9, International 6

Foursomes--United States 3, International 2

Frost/Senior (Int.) def. Irwin/Haas, 6&5
Pavin/Roberts (U.S.) def. Parry/Allem, 1 up
Singh/Elkington (Int.) def. Maggert/Huston, 3&2
Love/Gallagher (U.S.) def. Nobilo/Allenby, 7&5
Mickelson/Lehman (U.S.) def. Hughes/McNulty, 3&2
Totals: United States 12, International 8

THIRD DAY

Singles--United States 8, International 4

Irwin (U.S.) def. Allenby, 1 up
Haas (U.S.) def. McNulty, 4&3
Gallagher (U.S.) def. Watanabe, 4&3
Mickelson (U.S.) halved with Allem
Singh (Int.) halved with Lehman
Senior (Int.) def. Huston, 3&2
Hoch (U.S.) halved with Frost
Maggert (U.S.) def. Hughes, 2&1
Nobilo (Int.) halved with Roberts
Couples (U.S.) def. Price, 1 up
Love (U.S.) def. Elkington, 1 up
Parry (Int.) def. Pavin, 1 up
Totals: United States 20, International 12

HARDEE'S CLASSIC

Oakwood CC, Coal Valley, IL　　**Purse: $1,000,000**
Par: 35-35--70　　**Yards: 6,796**　　**September 22-25, 1995**

LEADERS: First Round--Robert Wrenn, after a 7-under-par 63, held a two-stroke lead over Doug Tewell and Neal Lancaster. **Second Round--**Lancaster, after a second successive 65, stood at 10-under-par 130, one stroke in front of Bob Estes. **Third Round--**Kenny Perry and Mark McCumber, at 12-under-par 198, had a one-stroke advantage over Curt Byrum.

CUT: 71 players at even-par 140.

PRO-AM: $7,500. Individual--Wayne Levi, Mark Brooks, Steve Stricker, 64, $625 each. Team--Russ Cochran, 52, $750.

WEATHER: Cold with intermittent rain but little wind Thursday and Friday. Start of the third round (scheduled for 8:40 a.m.) was delayed by wet grounds until 11:52 a.m. Saturday, when two tees were utilized; play completed under cloudy skies and with intermittent rain. Early-morning fog Sunday gave way to cloudy and overcast conditions, allowing round four to get underway as scheduled at 11:22 a.m. Partly cloudy the remainder of the day, with some sun breaking through.

Winner:　Mark McCumber　　66-67-65-67　265　　$180,000.00

Player	Pos	Scores	Total	Money	Player	Pos	Scores	Total	Money
Kenny Perry	2	67-66-65-68	266	$108,000.00	Kenny Knox	T31	69-68-72-66	275	$5,320.00
Mike Donald	T 3	70-66-64-67	267	$58,000.00	Peter Persons	T31	70-68-66-71	275	$5,320.00
David Frost	T 3	68-67-67-65	267	$58,000.00	Dave Rummells	T31	69-70-67-69	275	$5,320.00
Russ Cochran	5	67-66-70-65	268	$40,000.00	Bobby Wadkins	T31	67-70-69-69	275	$5,320.00
Curt Byrum	T 6	69-65-65-70	269	$32,375.00	Ed Dougherty	T41	67-69-69-71	276	$3,900.00
John Huston	T 6	71-66-67-65	269	$32,375.00	Tom Purtzer	T41	70-65-68-73	276	$3,900.00
Tom Lehman	T 6	71-67-65-66	269	$32,375.00	Gene Sauers	T41	71-68-68-69	276	$3,900.00
Robert Wrenn	T 6	63-70-67-69	269	$32,375.00	Todd Barranger	T44	71-69-70-67	277	$3,108.00
Michael Bradley	T10	72-67-62-69	270	$23,000.00	Chip Beck	T44	71-69-70-67	277	$3,108.00
Mark Calcavecchia	T10	66-69-69-66	270	$23,000.00	Vance Heafner	T44	67-68-72-70	277	$3,108.00
Wayne Levi	T10	67-70-65-68	270	$23,000.00	Don Reese	T44	68-69-70-70	277	$3,108.00
Doug Tewell	T10	65-69-69-67	270	$23,000.00	Esteban Toledo	T44	70-69-66-72	277	$3,108.00
Kirk Triplett	T10	67-65-70-68	270	$23,000.00	Fulton Allem	T49	69-68-68-73	278	$2,495.00
Steve Brodie	T15	68-69-71-63	271	$17,000.00	Brian Claar	T49	69-67-75-67	278	$2,495.00
Billy Mayfair	T15	73-66-65-67	271	$17,000.00	Joel Edwards	T49	67-71-71-69	278	$2,495.00
Scott Verplank	T15	69-71-66-65	271	$17,000.00	Steve Lamontagne	T49	72-66-72-68	278	$2,495.00
Tim Conley	T18	68-67-68-69	272	$13,040.00	Mike Brisky	T53	71-67-70-71	279	$2,293.34
Bob Estes	T18	66-65-72-69	272	$13,040.00	Tony Sills	T53	69-68-72-70	279	$2,293.34
Blaine McCallister	T18	69-67-67-69	272	$13,040.00	John Flannery	T53	69-71-68-71	279	$2,293.33
David Peoples	T18	69-68-67-68	272	$13,040.00	Robert Gamez	T53	70-69-71-69	279	$2,293.33
Willie Wood	T18	68-68-66-70	272	$13,040.00	D.A. Russell	T53	71-67-67-74	279	$2,293.33
Neal Lancaster	T23	65-65-71-72	273	$9,600.00	Dave Stockton, Jr	T53	70-65-73-71	279	$2,293.33
Steve Rintoul	T23	71-66-65-71	273	$9,600.00	Mark Brooks	T59	66-70-75-69	280	$2,180.00
Lanny Wadkins	T23	69-68-70-66	273	$9,600.00	Chris Kite	T59	69-68-73-70	280	$2,180.00
Michael Allen	T26	68-67-70-69	274	$7,400.00	Tom Sieckmann	T59	70-67-71-72	280	$2,180.00
Brian Henninger	T26	71-67-67-69	274	$7,400.00	Phil Tataurangi	T59	74-66-72-68	280	$2,180.00
John Inman	T26	72-68-65-69	274	$7,400.00	David Toms	T59	71-68-72-69	280	$2,180.00
Gil Morgan	T26	66-72-67-69	274	$7,400.00	Rob Boldt	T64	70-68-72-71	281	$2,090.00
Steve Stricker	T26	67-68-73-66	274	$7,400.00	Brian Kamm	T64	68-71-71-71	281	$2,090.00
Brad Bryant	T31	72-65-68-70	275	$5,320.00	Charles Raulerson	T64	68-68-71-74	281	$2,090.00
Brandel Chamblee	T31	68-66-70-71	275	$5,320.00	Jeff Woodland	T64	68-70-70-73	281	$2,090.00
Trevor Dodds	T31	68-69-68-70	275	$5,320.00	Robin Freeman	68	72-64-74-72	282	$2,040.00
Nolan Henke	T31	69-68-71-67	275	$5,320.00	Ernie Gonzalez	69	69-71-71-72	283	$2,020.00
Steve Jones	T31	69-70-67-69	275	$5,320.00	Warren Schutte	T70	69-70-76-69	284	$1,990.00
Brad King	T31	68-70-66-71	275	$5,320.00	Jerry Smith	T70	72-68-72-72	284	$1,990.00

BUICK SOUTHERN OPEN

Callaway Gardens Resort, Pine Mountain, GA
Par: 36-36--72   Yards: 7,057

Purse: $800,000
Sept. 29-Oct. 2, 1994

LEADERS: First Round--Todd Barranger, with a 7-under-par 65, led by one over Steve Elkington, Jim McGovern and Steve Lamontagne. **Second Round--**Elkington, at 12-under-par 132, led by three strokes over Steve Rintoul.

CUT: 88 players at even-par 144.

PRO-AM: $7,500. Individual--John Adams, Brian Claar, 67, $675 each. Team--Steve Elkington, Billy Andrade, 56, $675 each.

WEATHER: Play was delayed for 10 minutes at the start of the round on Thursday due to fog. Beautiful for the rest of Thursday, Friday and Saturday. Sunday's round was delayed at 8:27 a.m. and the round was officially cancelled at 10:00 a.m. due to rainy conditions.

Winner: Steve Elkington   66-66-68   200 $144,000.00

Player	Pos	Scores	Total	Money	Player	Pos	Scores	Total	Money
Steve Rintoul	2	70-65-70	205	$86,400.00	Brandel Chamblee	T41	71-72-70	213	$2,532.36
Brad Bryant	3	70-68-69	207	$54,400.00	Marco Dawson	T41	72-70-71	213	$2,532.36
Buddy Gardner	T4	71-69-68	208	$33,066.67	Jim Gallagher, Jr.	T41	72-69-72	213	$2,532.36
Steve Pate	T4	69-71-68	208	$33,066.67	Bob Lohr	T41	72-71-70	213	$2,532.36
Gene Sauers	T4	72-67-69	208	$33,066.66	Doug Tewell	T41	69-72-72	213	$2,532.36
Blaine McCallister	T7	69-71-69	209	$24,100.00	Bob Tway	T41	70-69-74	213	$2,532.36
Larry Mize	T7	69-73-67	209	$24,100.00	Billy Andrade	T52	73-71-70	214	$1,838.00
Jeff Sluman	T7	69-70-70	209	$24,100.00	Olin Browne	T52	69-71-74	214	$1,838.00
Bobby Wadkins	T7	69-72-68	209	$24,100.00	Bob Gilder	T52	69-73-72	214	$1,838.00
Phil Blackmar	T11	71-73-66	210	$15,400.00	Scott Gump	T52	70-72-72	214	$1,838.00
Mike Brisky	T11	67-71-72	210	$15,400.00	Neal Lancaster	T52	72-72-70	214	$1,838.00
Curt Byrum	T11	71-65-74	210	$15,400.00	Sean Murphy	T52	76-66-72	214	$1,838.00
Brian Claar	T11	70-66-74	210	$15,400.00	Mike Standly	T52	72-71-71	214	$1,838.00
Bob Estes	T11	70-70-70	210	$15,400.00	John Wilson	T52	73-69-72	214	$1,838.00
Bill Glasson	T11	68-73-69	210	$15,400.00	John Adams	T60	71-69-75	215	$1,712.00
Donnie Hammond	T11	71-72-67	210	$15,400.00	Michael Allen	T60	70-72-73	215	$1,712.00
Steve Lamontagne	T11	66-69-75	210	$15,400.00	Todd Barranger	T60	65-77-73	215	$1,712.00
Mike Donald	T19	67-74-70	211	$7,733.34	Steve Gotsche	T60	69-73-73	215	$1,712.00
Justin Leonard	T19	69-74-68	211	$7,733.34	Eddie Kirby	T60	69-70-76	215	$1,712.00
Harry Taylor	T19	74-70-67	211	$7,733.34	Davis Love III	T60	72-66-77	215	$1,712.00
David Toms	T19	70-72-69	211	$7,733.34	Don Pooley	T60	72-72-71	215	$1,712.00
Paul Azinger	T19	71-70-70	211	$7,733.33	Russell Beiersdorf	T67	72-72-72	216	$1,608.00
David Ogrin	T19	69-72-70	211	$7,733.33	Tom Byrum	T67	69-74-73	216	$1,608.00
Don Reese	T19	68-69-74	211	$7,733.33	Paul Goydos	T67	71-69-76	216	$1,608.00
Dave Rummells	T19	70-68-73	211	$7,733.33	Ed Humenik	T67	70-73-73	216	$1,608.00
Tom Sieckmann	T19	72-66-73	211	$7,733.33	Paul Stankowski	T67	73-70-73	216	$1,608.00
Kirk Triplett	T19	68-70-73	211	$7,733.33	Mike Sullivan	T67	69-73-74	216	$1,608.00
Willie Wood	T19	70-69-72	211	$7,733.33	Russ Cochran	T73	70-73-74	217	$1,504.00
Richard Zokol	T19	67-70-74	211	$7,733.33	Ed Dougherty	T73	71-72-74	217	$1,504.00
Ronnie Black	T31	68-73-71	212	$4,256.00	P.H. Horgan III	T73	71-70-76	217	$1,504.00
Rick Fehr	T31	69-73-70	212	$4,256.00	Brian Kamm	T73	71-72-74	217	$1,504.00
Mike Hulbert	T31	71-73-68	212	$4,256.00	Kenny Knox	T73	69-73-75	217	$1,504.00
Bruce Lietzke	T31	71-73-68	212	$4,256.00	Charles Raulerson	T73	70-73-74	217	$1,504.00
John Mahaffey	T31	74-69-69	212	$4,256.00	Mark Wurtz	T73	72-72-73	217	$1,504.00
Jim McGovern	T31	66-73-73	212	$4,256.00	Chris Kite	T80	74-70-74	218	$1,416.00
Kenny Perry	T31	67-72-73	212	$4,256.00	Dick Mast	T80	68-76-74	218	$1,416.00
Lee Porter	T31	70-73-69	212	$4,256.00	Mike Smith	T80	73-71-74	218	$1,416.00
Dicky Pride	T31	70-67-75	212	$4,256.00	Ted Tryba	T80	72-72-74	218	$1,416.00
Hal Sutton	T31	70-73-69	212	$4,256.00	Leonard Thompson	T84	73-71-75	219	$1,360.00
Mark Brooks	T41	71-73-69	213	$2,532.37	Stan Utley	T84	67-73-79	219	$1,360.00
Glen Day	T41	70-74-69	213	$2,532.37	Rocky Walcher	T84	71-72-76	219	$1,360.00
Dan Forsman	T41	73-70-70	213	$2,532.37	Robert Wrenn	87	71-73-77	221	$1,328.00
Ted Schulz	T41	71-73-69	213	$2,532.37	Jerry Pate	88	73-71-79	223	$1,312.00
Rob Boldt	T41	72-70-71	213	$2,532.36					

WALT DISNEY WORLD/ OLDSMOBILE CLASSIC

Three Disney Courses

Magnolia (Host Course):	7,190 yards	**Purse: $1,100,000**
Palm:	6,967 yards	**October 6-9, 1994**
Eagle Pines:	6,772 yards	**All Par: 36-36--72**

LEADERS: First Round--Rick Fehr and Bob Lohr, with 9-under-par 63s, led Brad Bryant and Buddy Gardner by a stroke. **Second Round--**Dave Stockton, Jr., at 12-under-par 132, led by one over Jim Gallagher, Jr., Glen Day and Fehr. **Third Round--**Fehr and Craig Stadler, at 15-under-par 201, led by one stroke over John Flannery.

CUT: 77 players at 4-under-par 212, from a field of 132.

WEATHER: Thursday and Friday were partly cloudy and warm. Saturday's round was delayed from 1:45 p.m. to 2:20 p.m. on the Magnolia and Palm courses due to dangerous condtitions. There was no delay at Eagle Pines. Sunday was beautiful.

Winner: Rick Fehr   63-70-68-68   269 $198,000.00

Player		Scores	Total	Money
Craig Stadler	T 2	68-66-67-70	271	$96,800.00
Fuzzy Zoeller	T 2	66-70-69-66	271	$96,800.00
Trevor Dodds	T 4	68-66-70-68	272	$48,400.00
Steve Stricker	T 4	72-67-66-67	272	$48,400.00
Robert Gamez	6	68-69-68-68	273	$39,600.00
Glen Day	T 7	65-68-72-69	274	$33,137.50
Donnie Hammond	T 7	68-72-67-67	274	$33,137.50
Brian Kamm	T 7	69-69-68-68	274	$33,137.50
Doug Tewell	T 7	69-66-71-68	274	$33,137.50
Clark Dennis	T11	67-67-72-70	276	$24,200.00
Jim Gallagher, Jr.	T11	65-68-74-69	276	$24,200.00
John Huston	T11	68-72-70-66	276	$24,200.00
Mark McCumber	T11	69-70-71-66	276	$24,200.00
Steve Brodie	T15	72-67-66-72	277	$15,473.34
Mike Donald	T15	70-70-72-65	277	$15,473.34
Davis Love III	T15	69-69-71-68	277	$15,473.34
Ronnie Black	T15	68-72-69-68	277	$15,473.33
Curt Byrum	T15	67-69-72-69	277	$15,473.33
Greg Kraft	T15	70-68-68-71	277	$15,473.33
Larry Mize	T15	69-70-69-69	277	$15,473.33
Dave Stockton, Jr.	T15	68-64-72-73	277	$15,473.33
Bobby Wadkins	T15	70-71-68-68	277	$15,473.33
Dudley Hart	T24	67-71-71-69	278	$8,323.34
Lee Janzen	T24	72-65-67-74	278	$8,323.34
Duffy Waldorf	T24	68-71-71-68	278	$8,323.34
Bob Lohr	T24	63-71-74-70	278	$8,323.33
Billy Mayfair	T24	68-75-67-68	278	$8,323.33
Dillard Pruitt	T24	70-72-70-66	278	$8,323.33
Mike Reid	T24	69-71-71-67	278	$8,323.33
Joey Sindelar	T24	69-69-70-70	278	$8,323.33
Payne Stewart	T24	69-70-69-70	278	$8,323.33
Gene Sauers	T33	73-69-67-70	279	$5,688.58
Paul Azinger	T33	72-68-68-71	279	$5,688.57
Olin Browne	T33	72-69-71-67	279	$5,688.57
Brad Bryant	T33	64-72-70-73	279	$5,688.57
Fred Funk	T33	70-70-70-69	279	$5,688.57
Larry Rinker	T33	66-69-72-72	279	$5,688.57
Hal Sutton	T33	71-71-68-69	279	$5,688.57
Chip Beck	T40	66-76-69-69	280	$4,070.00
Sean Murphy	T40	74-68-69-69	280	$4,070.00
David Ogrin	T40	71-69-71-69	280	$4,070.00
Bob Tway	T40	69-72-69-70	280	$4,070.00
Howard Twitty	T40	68-72-69-71	280	$4,070.00
Stan Utley	T40	68-71-70-71	280	$4,070.00
Lanny Wadkins	T40	72-69-68-71	280	$4,070.00
Ed Dougherty	T47	66-74-71-70	281	$2,762.23
Wayne Levi	T47	71-70-69-71	281	$2,762.23
Fulton Allem	T47	73-67-70-71	281	$2,762.22
Mark Calcavecchia	T47	71-71-67-72	281	$2,762.22
John Flannery	T47	70-70-62-79	281	$2,762.22
Ed Humenik	T47	71-71-69-70	281	$2,762.22
Bob May	T47	71-72-68-70	281	$2,762.22
Jim McGovern	T47	71-72-68-70	281	$2,762.22
Steve Rintoul	T47	72-71-68-70	281	$2,762.22
Michael Allen	T56	65-75-69-73	282	$2,442.00
Brad Faxon	T56	69-70-72-71	282	$2,442.00
Kelly Gibson	T56	72-70-67-73	282	$2,442.00
Dick Mast	T56	67-72-70-73	282	$2,442.00
Steve Pate	T56	71-71-68-72	282	$2,442.00
Ted Tryba	T56	71-69-71-71	282	$2,442.00
Mark Wiebe	T56	71-73-67-71	282	$2,442.00
Michael Bradley	T63	70-75-66-72	283	$2,288.00
Chris Dimarco	T63	70-73-69-71	283	$2,288.00
Gary Hallberg	T63	70-73-68-72	283	$2,288.00
Mike Hulbert	T63	70-68-69-76	283	$2,288.00
Peter Jacobsen	T63	68-74-70-71	283	$2,288.00
John Morse	T63	67-71-74-71	283	$2,288.00
Mike Standly	T63	70-71-69-73	283	$2,288.00
John Cook	T70	68-73-71-72	284	$2,178.00
Jim Furyk	T70	71-70-69-74	284	$2,178.00
Mike Heinen	T70	73-75-64-72	284	$2,178.00
Jay Haas	73	70-72-70-75	287	$2,134.00
Loren Roberts	T74	74-68-69-77	288	$2,101.00
Scott Simpson	T74	68-72-69-79	288	$2,101.00
David Peoples	76	75-69-68-77	289	$2,068.00
Buddy Gardner	77	64-72-75-79	290	$2,046.00

TEXAS OPEN

Oak Hills CC, San Antonio, TX
Par: 35-36--71   Yards: 6,650

Purse: $1,000,000
October 13-16, 1994

LEADERS: First Round--Bob Estes, with a 9-under-par 62, matching the par-71 course record, held a one-stroke lead over Bob Tway. **Second Round--**Estes, at 15-under-par 127, led by three over Tway. **Third Round--**Estes, at 18-under-par 195, was four strokes in front of Don Pooley and Gil Morgan.

CUT: 76 players at 3-under-par 139.

PRO-AM: $7,500. Individual--David Ogrin, 60, $750. Team--Mark Calcavecchia, 47, $750.

WEATHER: Cool early Thursday, turning warm with increasing humidity throughout the day; sunny with little wind. Mostly cloudy Friday, with some late rain. Because of the anticipated heavy rains overnight Friday, Saturday's start was pushed back to a scheduled 10 a.m. start in threesomes off two tees. Light rain fell most of Saturday, finally giving way to foggy, misty conditions in the late afternoon. Cloudy and overcast early Sunday with some brief rain, becoming partly sunny in the afternoon; muggy throughout. Little wind all four days.

Winner: Bob Estes   62-65-68-70   265 $180,000.00

Gil Morgan	2	66-68-65-67	266	$108,000.00	Sean Murphy	T33	68-65-70-73	276	$5,171.42
Don Pooley	3	69-65-65-68	267	$68,000.00	Guy Boros	T40	71-67-67-72	277	$3,800.00
Bruce Lietzke	4	68-69-64-69	270	$48,000.00	Dudley Hart	T40	68-69-70-70	277	$3,800.00
Mark Mcnulty	T 5	70-65-67-69	271	$36,500.00	P.H. Horgan III	T40	68-70-69-70	277	$3,800.00
Craig Stadler	T 5	68-66-69-68	271	$36,500.00	Neal Lancaster	T40	67-69-69-72	277	$3,800.00
John Wilson	T 5	66-68-67-70	271	$36,500.00	Andrew Magee	T40	66-70-69-72	277	$3,800.00
JC Anderson	T 8	67-64-70-71	272	$25,000.00	Howard Twitty	T40	70-65-72-70	277	$3,800.00
Brad Bryant	T 8	66-67-70-69	272	$25,000.00	Brandel Chamblee	T46	69-68-74-67	278	$2,600.00
Bob Burns	T 8	65-69-68-70	272	$25,000.00	Chris Dimarco	T46	70-67-68-73	278	$2,600.00
Ben Crenshaw	T 8	70-69-68-65	272	$25,000.00	David Edwards	T46	71-66-72-69	278	$2,600.00
Blaine McCallister	T 8	70-65-72-65	272	$25,000.00	Paul Goydos	T46	69-69-70-70	278	$2,600.00
Mark O'Meara	T 8	70-69-67-66	272	$25,000.00	Bob May	T46	69-66-72-71	278	$2,600.00
Dillard Pruitt	T 8	70-68-67-67	272	$25,000.00	Tim Simpson	T46	67-70-71-70	278	$2,600.00
Fred Couples	T15	67-69-68-69	273	$15,500.00	Phil Tataurangi	T46	70-69-67-72	278	$2,600.00
Jim Furyk	T15	70-67-67-69	273	$15,500.00	Ted Tryba	T46	70-69-68-71	278	$2,600.00
John Inman	T15	66-69-68-70	273	$15,500.00	D.A. Weibring	T46	70-67-72-69	278	$2,600.00
Brian Kamm	T15	65-67-68-73	273	$15,500.00	Russ Cochran	T55	67-69-71-72	279	$2,260.00
Justin Leonard	T15	67-69-68-69	273	$15,500.00	Brian Henninger	T55	68-70-71-70	279	$2,260.00
David Ogrin	T15	70-69-65-69	273	$15,500.00	David Peoples	T55	72-65-70-72	279	$2,260.00
Ed Dougherty	T21	67-70-67-70	274	$9,133.34	Scott Simpson	T55	70-68-73-68	279	$2,260.00
Nolan Henke	T21	71-67-66-70	274	$9,133.34	Jeff Woodland	T55	70-68-70-71	279	$2,260.00
Jim McGovern	T21	68-69-67-70	274	$9,133.34	Bill Britton	T60	70-68-68-74	280	$2,150.00
John Cook	T21	69-69-67-69	274	$9,133.33	Steve Brodie	T60	69-70-71-70	280	$2,150.00
Marco Dawson	T21	68-68-68-70	274	$9,133.33	Mike Heinen	T60	69-68-71-72	280	$2,150.00
Lee Janzen	T21	69-69-72-64	274	$9,133.33	Dicky Pride	T60	70-69-69-72	280	$2,150.00
Steve Rintoul	T21	65-68-69-72	274	$9,133.33	Joey Rassett	T60	69-67-72-72	280	$2,150.00
Bob Tway	T21	63-67-72-72	274	$9,133.33	Jim Woodward	T60	69-70-70-71	280	$2,150.00
Bobby Wadkins	T21	69-66-69-70	274	$9,133.33	Billy Mayfair	T66	70-69-72-70	281	$2,070.00
Michael Bradley	T30	66-69-72-68	275	$6,500.00	Curtis Strange	T66	69-69-74-69	281	$2,070.00
Steve Gotsche	T30	69-68-70-68	275	$6,500.00	Larry Rinker	T68	70-68-70-74	282	$2,030.00
Dave Rummells	T30	67-67-69-72	275	$6,500.00	Duffy Waldorf	T68	70-69-70-73	282	$2,030.00
Mark Calcavecchia	T33	70-69-70-67	276	$5,171.43	Rocky Walcher	70	67-71-71-74	283	$2,000.00
Jay Haas	T33	70-69-70-67	276	$5,171.43	Mark Brooks	71	67-70-74-73	284	$1,980.00
Donnie Hammond	T33	67-68-70-71	276	$5,171.43	David Feherty	T72	68-71-74-74	287	$1,950.00
Dick Mast	T33	69-69-69-69	276	$5,171.43	Brad King	T72	68-71-70-78	287	$1,950.00
Mark Wiebe	T33	68-68-70-70	276	$5,171.43	Eddie Kirby	74	68-69-77-76	290	$1,920.00
Richard Zokol	T33	70-67-70-69	276	$5,171.43					

LAS VEGAS INVITATIONAL

LAS VEGAS INVITATIONAL

TPC at Summerlin
Par: 36-36--72   Yards: 7,243
Las Vegas CC
Par: 36-36--72   Yards: 7,164
Las Vegas Hilton CC
Par: 36-35--71   Yards: 6,815

Purse: $1,500,000
October 19-23, 1994

LEADERS: First Round--Brian Kamm (TPC) and Sean Murphy (LVHCC), with 64s, led by one stroke over Dudley Hart (LVCC) and Nolan Henke (LVHCC). **Second Round**--Scott Hoch (LVHCC), with a 129 total, led by two strokes over Hart (LVHCC), Dan Forsman (LVHCC) and Jim Furyk (LVHCC). **Third Round**--Kirk Triplett (LVHCC), Forsman (TPC) and Hoch (TPC) led by one stroke over six players. **Fourth Round**--Furyk, with a 266 total, led by one stroke over Bruce Lietzke and Triplett.

CUT: 76 players at 6-under-par 209.

WEATHER: Gorgeous every day.

Winner: Bruce Lietzke 66-67-68-66-65   332 $270,000.00

Player	Pos	Scores	Total	Money		Player	Pos	Scores	Total	Money
Robert Gamez	2	66-70-64-69-64	333	$162,000.00		Michael Bradley	T39	67-68-69-69-72	345	$6,000.00
Billy Andrade	T 3	66-68-67-67-67	335	$87,000.00		Fred Funk	T39	68-69-67-71-70	345	$6,000.00
Phil Mickelson	T 3	70-66-66-70-63	335	$87,000.00		Lee Janzen	T39	70-65-72-69-69	345	$6,000.00
Jim Furyk	T 5	67-64-69-66-70	336	$54,750.00		Jodie Mudd	T39	67-69-70-68-71	345	$6,000.00
Bill Glasson	T 5	67-68-70-65-66	336	$54,750.00		Mike Standly	T39	66-68-67-72-72	345	$6,000.00
Paul Stankowski	T 5	70-66-66-69-65	336	$54,750.00		Howard Twitty	T39	66-67-73-68-71	345	$6,000.00
Guy Boros	T 8	70-63-67-68-69	337	$42,000.00		Michael Allen	T45	69-70-67-66-74	346	$4,515.00
Scott Hoch	T 8	66-63-70-70-68	337	$42,000.00		Brian Claar	T45	66-69-70-69-72	346	$4,515.00
Sean Murphy	T 8	64-69-67-69-68	337	$42,000.00		Neal Lancaster	T45	66-69-67-69-75	346	$4,515.00
Kirk Triplett	T 8	69-65-65-68-70	337	$42,000.00		John Wilson	T45	67-72-70-70-67	346	$4,515.00
Jay Don Blake	T12	66-69-66-69-68	338	$33,000.00		Keith Clearwater	T49	66-70-69-73-69	347	$3,742.50
Jim Gallagher, Jr.	T12	69-70-67-64-68	338	$33,000.00		Greg Norman	T49	67-69-71-71-69	347	$3,742.50
Mark Brooks	T14	68-69-67-70-65	339	$27,750.00		Dicky Pride	T49	73-67-68-70-69	347	$3,742.50
Mike Heinen	T14	66-66-68-71-68	339	$27,750.00		Tim Simpson	T49	67-69-68-71-72	347	$3,742.50
Steve Elkington	T16	70-67-66-66-71	340	$21,750.00		JC Anderson	T53	71-70-66-71-70	348	$3,510.00
Dan Forsman	T16	67-64-68-70-71	340	$21,750.00		Mike Sullivan	T53	68-68-70-69-73	348	$3,510.00
Gil Morgan	T16	72-67-65-69-67	340	$21,750.00		Ken Green	T55	70-68-64-72-75	349	$3,405.00
Dillard Pruitt	T16	70-66-67-68-69	340	$21,750.00		Donnie Hammond	T55	68-70-71-68-72	349	$3,405.00
Bob Tway	T16	69-70-67-67-67	340	$21,750.00		Morris Hatalsky	T55	68-69-72-72-68	349	$3,405.00
Duffy Waldorf	T16	68-69-72-64-67	340	$21,750.00		Peter Jacobsen	T55	70-71-66-74-68	349	$3,405.00
Brad Bryant	T22	71-67-67-68-68	341	$15,600.00		Nolan Henke	T59	65-73-66-71-75	350	$3,255.00
Clark Dennis	T22	68-67-67-73-66	341	$15,600.00		Mike Hulbert	T59	71-67-69-68-75	350	$3,255.00
John Flannery	T22	68-70-66-69-68	341	$15,600.00		Tom Lehman	T59	69-71-69-72-69	350	$3,255.00
Tommy Armour III	25	71-67-65-69-70	342	$13,200.00		Andrew Magee	T59	68-72-68-71-71	350	$3,255.00
Bob Burns	T26	72-67-65-68-71	343	$10,875.00		Blaine McCallister	T59	72-68-69-70-71	350	$3,255.00
Rick Fehr	T26	68-69-67-69-70	343	$10,875.00		David Toms	T59	74-66-69-72-69	350	$3,255.00
Dudley Hart	T26	65-66-75-70-67	343	$10,875.00		Jay Haas	T65	70-66-70-71-75	352	$3,105.00
Steve Rintoul	T26	71-69-68-67-68	343	$10,875.00		Jim McGovern	T65	69-72-68-73-70	352	$3,105.00
Craig Stadler	T26	71-70-67-68-67	343	$10,875.00		David Peoples	T65	68-70-68-71-75	352	$3,105.00
Willie Wood	T26	70-67-68-68-70	343	$10,875.00		Payne Stewart	T65	70-69-69-71-73	352	$3,105.00
Brian Henninger	T32	67-70-68-70-69	344	$8,121.43		Larry Mize	T69	69-67-71-76-73	356	$3,015.00
Peter Jordan	T32	71-68-68-68-69	344	$8,121.43		Mark Wiebe	T69	71-67-71-72-75	356	$3,015.00
Brian Kamm	T32	64-70-66-72-72	344	$8,121.43		David Edwards	71	72-67-70-72-77	358	$2,970.00
Brett Ogle	T32	68-69-68-68-71	344	$8,121.43		Wayne Levi	72	67-71-71-72-80	361	$2,940.00
Dave Stockton,Jr	T32	70-66-72-66-70	344	$8,121.43		Brandel Chamblee	73	70-69-70-74-79	362	$2,910.00
Fuzzy Zoeller	T32	71-68-68-68-69	344	$8,121.43		Fulton Allem	T74	75-65-69-74-81	364	$2,865.00
Dave Rummells	T32	67-68-69-68-72	344	$8,121.42		Mark Wurtz	T74	68-73-67-72-84	364	$2,865.00

THE TOUR CHAMPIONSHIP

The Olympic Club (Lake Course)   **Purse: $3,000,000**
San Francisco, CA   **October 27-30, 1994**
Par: 35-36--71   Yards: 7,005

THE TOUR
CHAMPIONSHIP

LEADERS: First Round--David Frost, Bill Glasson, Steve Lowery and Mark McCumber at 5-under-par 66 led by one over Rick Fehr. **Second Round--**Glasson, at 8-under-par 134, led by one stroke over Ernie Els, Lowery and Frost. **Third Round--**Glasson, at 8-under-par 205, led by one over Fuzzy Zoeller and McCumber.

PRO-AM: $10,000. Individual--Mike Springer, 67, $1,000. Team--CoreyPavin, Ben Crenshaw, Jay Haas, John Huston, Scott Hoch and Hale Irwin, 57, $666.67.

WEATHER: Foggy all day Thursday. Foggy on Friday morning. Sunny and mild Saturday and Sunday.

Winner: Mark McCumber   66-71-69-68 274 $540,000.00
(won playoff with birdie on first extra hole)

Fuzzy Zoeller	2	71-69-66-68	274	$324,000.00
Brad Bryant	3	72-68-67-68	275	$207,000.00
David Frost	T 4	66-69-75-66	276	$132,000.00
Bill Glasson	T 4	66-68-71-71	276	$132,000.00
Jay Haas	6	69-71-71-66	277	$108,000.00
Jeff Maggert	7	72-66-70-70	278	$102,000.00
Steve Lowery	T 8	66-69-72-72	279	$93,000.00
Loren Roberts	T 8	71-70-68-70	279	$93,000.00
John Huston	T10	74-68-66-72	280	$81,000.00
Bruce Lietzke	T10	69-71-71-69	280	$81,000.00
Corey Pavin	T10	69-69-70-72	280	$81,000.00
Ben Crenshaw	T13	72-70-69-70	281	$71,400.00
Greg Norman	T13	69-75-66-71	281	$71,400.00
Bob Estes	T15	71-70-73-68	282	$64,800.00
Rick Fehr	T15	67-69-77-69	282	$64,800.00
Ernie Els	T17	68-67-72-76	283	$60,000.00
Phil Mickelson	T17	68-71-70-74	283	$60,000.00
Mike Springer	T17	72-67-73-71	283	$60,000.00
Scott Hoch	T20	74-74-68-68	284	$57,000.00
Nick Price	T20	71-74-67-72	284	$57,000.00
Hale Irwin	T22	70-74-67-74	285	$54,600.00
Tom Kite	T22	69-72-72-72	285	$54,600.00
Mark Calcavecchia	T24	73-68-74-71	286	$52,200.00
Hal Sutton	T24	73-70-74-69	286	$52,200.00
Brad Faxon	T26	71-71-73-73	288	$50,100.00
Kenny Perry	T26	75-69-72-72	288	$50,100.00
Tom Lehman	28	73-70-72-74	289	$49,200.00
Mark Brooks	T29	69-72-72-77	290	$48,300.00
Fred Couples	T29	70-72-74-74	290	$48,300.00

LINCOLN-MERCURY
KAPALUA INTERNATIONAL

Lincoln / Mercury
Kapalua International

Plantation Course, Kapalua Resort
Par: 36-37--73   Yards: 7,263
Bay Course, Kapalua Resort
Par: 35-36--71   Yards: 6,600
Kapalua, Maui, Hawaii

Purse: $1,000,000
November 3-6, 1994

LEADERS: First Round--Jim McGovern (PC), Tom Lehman (BC), Fred Couples (BC) and Gary McCord (BC) all fired 66s to lead by two strokes over Sam Torrance, Ed Humenik, Clark Dennis and Kirk Triplett. **Second Round--**Lehman (PC), at 9-under-par 135, led by two strokes over Couples (PC) and Bob Gilder (BC). **Third Round--**Gilder, at 9-under-par 208, led by one stroke over Couples.

WEATHER: Thursday was beautiful with a light breeze. Friday was overcast with sporadic showers. Saturday was extremely windy and sunny. Sunday was slightly overcast with breezy conditions.

Winner: Fred Couples 66-71-72-70   279 $180,000.00

Bob Gilder	2	70-67-71-73	281	$104,000.00	Clark Dennis	T25	68-75-74-75	292	$9,820.00
Tom Lehman	3	66-69-76-72	283	$65,000.00	Paul Goydos	T25	70-73-78-71	292	$9,820.00
Ben Crenshaw	T 4	71-73-70-71	285	$39,925.00	Ted Tryba	T25	71-73-74-74	292	$9,820.00
Bill Glasson	T 4	74-67-73-71	285	$39,925.00	Jay Don Blake	30	73-76-77-67	293	$9,820.00
Peter Jacobsen	6	71-72-72-71	286	$32,000.00	Andy Bean	T31	72-72-77-73	294	$8,850.00
John Cook	T 7	71-69-74-73	287	$25,333.34	Donnie Hammond	T31	72-72-75-75	294	$8,850.00
Keith Clearwater	T 7	72-67-72-76	287	$25,333.33	Jack Nicklaus	T31	69-71-76-78	294	$8,850.00
Barry Lane	T 7	72-67-71-77	287	$25,333.33	Lennie Clements	T34	73-72-76-75	296	$8,600.00
Davis Love III	T10	72-69-73-75	289	$18,500.00	Mike Standly	T34	69-72-81-74	296	$8,600.00
Jim McGovern	T10	66-73-72-78	289	$18,500.00	Mark Brooks	T36	75-72-77-73	297	$8,366.67
David Peoples	T10	76-67-75-71	289	$18,500.00	David Feherty	T36	74-71-74-78	297	$8,366.67
Sam Torrance	T10	68-74-74-73	289	$18,500.00	Justin Leonard	T36	71-76-77-73	297	$8,366.67
Kirk Triplett	T10	68-72-76-73	289	$18,500.00	David Ogrin	39	75-67-80-77	299	$8,250.00
Duffy Waldorf	T10	69-72-75-73	289	$18,500.00	Brad Bryant	T40	72-76-75-77	300	$8,150.00
Steve Pate	T16	72-68-78-72	290	$13,157.15	Hale Irwin	T40	73-73-79-75	300	$8,150.00
Scott Simpson	T16	70-71-77-72	290	$13,157.15	Neal Lancaster	T40	77-75-71-77	300	$8,150.00
Jay Delsing	T16	72-67-74-77	290	$13,157.14	Dave Barr	T43	72-75-75-79	301	$8,025.00
Robert Gamez	T16	70-78-73-69	290	$13,157.14	Nolan Henke	T43	76-73-78-74	301	$8,025.00
Bob Lohr	T16	72-70-74-74	290	$13,157.14	Jim Thorpe	45	70-71-83-78	302	$7,950.00
Gary McCord	T16	66-79-70-75	290	$13,157.14	Chris Dimarco	T46	78-76-77-72	303	$7,875.00
Tom Purtzer	T16	72-73-73-72	290	$13,157.14	Mike Heinen	T46	72-70-85-76	303	$7,875.00
Mike Hulbert	T23	71-74-74-72	291	$11,000.00	Dicky Pride	48	72-76-86-77	311	$7,800.00
Ed Humenik	T23	68-74-75-74	291	$11,000.00	Deane Beman	49	77-74-82-80	313	$7,750.00
Billy Andrade	T25	73-75-72-72	292	$9,820.00	Mark Rolfing	50	82-84-86-86	338	$7,700.00
Glen Day	T25	72-71-73-76	292	$9,820.00					

FRANKLIN FUNDS SHARK SHOOTOUT

Franklin Funds SHARK SHOOTOUT
HOSTED BY GREG NORMAN
SHERWOOD COUNTRY CLUB

Sherwood CC, Thousand Oaks, CA
Par: 36-36--72   Yards: 7,025

Purse: $1,100,000
November 18-20, 1994

LEADERS: First Round--Lanny Wadkins/Andrew Magee fired a 6-under-par 66 in the alternate shot format to lead Fred Couples/Brad Faxon and Chip Beck/Jeff Maggert by two strokes. **Second Round**--Ben Crenshaw/Mark Calcavecchia, after a 10-under-par 62 in the best ball format, were at 13-under-par 131. They led by one stroke over Couples/Faxon and Wadkins/Magee.

WEATHER: Sunny and cool on Friday and Saturday with temperatures in the low-60s. Sunday was sunny and warmer with temperatures reaching the low-70s.

WINNERS: Fred Couples/Brad Faxon		**68-64-58 190**	**$150,000 each**	
Curtis Strange/Mark O'Meara	2	70-64-58	192	85,000
Chip Beck/Jeff Maggert	3	68-65-60	193	57,500
Lanny Wadkins/Andrew Magee	4	66-66-62	194	44,500
Ben Crenshaw/Mark Calcavecchia	5	69-62-64	195	41,500
Arnold Palmer/Peter Jacobsen	6	73-64-59	196	39,000
Greg Norman/Nick Price	T7	72-63-62	197	35,250
Hale Irwin/Bruce Lietzke	T7	70-67-60	197	35,250
David Frost/Fuzzy Zoeller	9	71-67-66	204	32,000
Raymond Floyd/Steve Elkington	10	73-69-63	205	30,000

THE SKINS GAME

Bighorn GC, Palm Desert, CA   Purse: $540,000
Par: 36-36--72 Yards: 6,850   November 26-27, 1994

WEATHER: Saturday was mostly sunny with winds up to 45 m.p.h. and temperatures in the low-60s. Sunday was sunny with light winds and temperatures in the low-60s.

Holes 1-6:	Worth $20,000
Holes 7-12:	Worth $30,000
Holes 13-18:	Worth $40,000

Hole No. 1:	Paul Azinger wins with a birdie/collects $20,000 (one skin)
Hole No. 2:	Azinger, Payne Stewart and Tom Watson halve with a par
Hole No. 3	Azinger, Stewart and Watson halve with a par
Hole No. 4	Azinger wins with a birdie/collects $60,000 (three skins)
Hole No. 5	Watson wins with a par/collects $20,000 (one skin)
Hole No. 6	Fred Couples, Stewart and Watson halve with a par
Hole No. 7	Couples, Stewart and Watson halve with a par
Hole No. 8	Stewart wins with a par/collects $80,000 (three skins)
Hole No. 9	Watson wins with a birdie/collects $30,000 (one skin)
Hole No. 10	All players halve with a par
Hole No. 11	Stewart and Watson halve with a par
Hole No. 12	Azinger, Couples and Watson halve with a par
Hole No. 13	All players halve with a par
Hole No. 14	Couples wins with a birdie/collects $170,000 (five skins)
Hole No. 15	Stewart and Watson halve with a birdie
Hole No. 16	Azinger and Couples halve with a par
Hole No. 17	Azinger, Couples and Watson halve with a par
Hole No. 18	All players halve with a par

PLAYOFF

Hole No. 18	Watson wins with a birdie/collects $160,000 (four skins)

FINAL RESULTS

Tom Watson (six skins)	$210,000
Fred Couples (five skins)	$170,000
Paul Azinger (four skins)	$ 80,000
Payne Stewart (three skins)	$ 80,000

JCPENNEY CLASSIC

Innisbrook Hilton Resort, Tarpon Springs, FL
Par: 36-35--71Yards: 6,394/7,054

Purse: $1,200,000
Dec. 1-4, 1994

LEADERS: First Round--Jane Geddes/Brian Claar, Marta Figueras-Dotti/Brad Bryant and JoAnne Carner/Jim Albus shot 7-under-par 64s to lead eight teams by one stroke. **Second Round--**Helen Alfredsson/Robert Gamez and Beth Daniel/Davis Love III, at 12-under-par 130, led by one stroke over Laura Davies/David Feherty and Amy Alcott/Robin Freeman. **Third Round--**Alfredsson/Gamez, after a 7-under-par 64 for a 19-under-par 194 total, led by one stroke over Alcott/Freeman and Daniel/Love.

PRO-AM: $10,000. Tuesday: Individual--John Huston, 65, $300. Team--Donnie Hammond, 50, $300. Wednesday: Dicky Pride, Davis Love III, 65, $275 each. Team--Brad Bryant, 47, $300.

WEATHER: Beautiful every day. Temperatures reached the high-70s, low 80s each day under cloudless skies.

CHAMPIONS: Marta Figueras-Dotti/Brad Bryant 64-70-62-66--262 $150,000.00 each
(Won playoff with par on fourth extra hole)

2.	Helen Alfredsson/Robert Gamez	66-64-64-68--262	73,000.00
3.	Beth Daniel/Davis Love III	65-65-65-68--263	48,000.00
4.	Amy Alcott/Robin Freeman	65-66-64-69--264	36,500.00
T5.	Kelly Robbins/Dan Pohl	67-66-65-67--265	21,500.00
	Colleen Walker/Lee Janzen	68-67-63-67--265	21,500.00
	Dottie Mochrie/Dave Stockton, Jr.	66-69-62-68--265	21,500.00
	Dana Dormann/Fred Funk	65-68-64-68--265	21,500.00
T9.	Laura Davies/David Feherty	66-65-70-65--266	12,000.00
	Lisa Kiggens/Jim Furyk	67-67-66-66--266	12,000.00
T11.	Deb Richard/Mike Heinen	67-70-64-66--267	9,166.67
	Vicki Goetze/Steve Stricker	65-69-67-66--267	9,166.67
	Martha Nause/Dicky Pride	66-67-66-68--267	9,166.66
T14.	Dale Eggeling/Jim McGovern	66-68-68-66--268	7,500.00
	Pat Bradley/Bill Glasson	69-70-64-65--268	7,500.00
	Elaine Crosby/Ed Humenik	67-69-64-68--268	7,500.00
T17.	Rosie Jones/Mark Carnevale	69-65-68-67--269	5,166.67
	Donna Andrews/Mike Hulbert	66-68-67-68--269	5,166.67
	Barb Mucha/Glen Day	69-65-67-68--269	5,166.67
	Debbie Massey/Mark McCumber	68-67-66-68--269	5,166.67
	Jan Stephenson/Curt Byrum	67-68-66-68--269	5,166.67
	Michele Redman/Guy Boros	67-69-65-68--269	5,166.67
	Betsy King/Rick Fehr	68-72-64-65--269	5,166.66
	Liselotte Neumann/Tony Jacklin	68-64-66-71--269	5,166.66
	Jane Crafter/Steve Jones	68-66-64-71--269	5,166.66
T26.	Brandie Burton/Billy Mayfair	68-69-66-67--270	4,300.00
	Jane Geddes/Brian Claar	64-68-68-70--270	4,300.00
	Chris Johnson/Neal Lancaster	65-68-66-71--270	4,300.00
T29.	Judy Dickinson/Jay Sigel	65-71-67-68--271	4,000.00
	Michelle Estill/Donnie Hammond	72-70-61-68--271	4,000.00
31.	JoAnne Carner/Jim Albus	64-68-70-70--272	3,800.00
T32.	Val Skinner/Mike Standly	71-69-65-68--273	3,600.00
	Carolyn Hill/Michael Bradley	71-71-65-66--273	3,600.00
	Dawn Coe-Jones/Brian Henninger	69-72-67-65--273	3,600.00
T35.	Kris Tschetter/Chris DiMarco	68-67-69-70--274	3,142.86
	Nancy Ramsbottom/Mike Sullivan	65-69-70-70--274	3,142.86
	Laurie Rinker-Graham/Brian Kamm	67-69-69-69--274	3,142.86
	Meg Mallon/Steve Pate	69-68-68-69--274	3,142.86
	Juli Inkster/Tom Purtzer	68-70-68-68--274	3,142.86
	Julie Larsen/Kirk Triplett	70-68-69-67--274	3,142.85
	Missie McGeorge/Jim Thorpe	67-71-70-66--274	3,142.85
T42.	Amy Benz/John Huston	69-68-66-72--275	2,875.00
	Barb Bunkowsky/Ken Green	67-70-68-70--275	2,875.00
T44.	Melissa McNamara/Mike Springer	66-69-67-74--276	2,716.67
	Michelle McGann/Greg Kraft	67-70-67-72--276	2,716.67
	Gail Graham/Dave Barr	65-71-70-70--276	2,716.66
T47.	Alicia Dibos/David Ogrin	67-70-67-73--277	2,575.00
	Nancy Scranton/Tom Wargo	72-67-66-72--277	2,575.00
49.	Alice Ritzman/Jim Dent	68-69-71-70--278	2,500.00
50.	Missie Berteotti/Rocco Mediate	70-71-69-70--280	2,450.00
51.	Tammie Green/Arnold Palmer	72-72-66-71--281	2,300.00
52.	Sherri Steinhauer/Kenny Perry	72-73-70-68--283	2,200.00

1994 PGA TOUR QUALIFYING TOURNAMENT GRADUATES

Grenelefe Resort, Haines City, FL   **Nov. 30-Dec. 5, 1994**
South Course: **Par: 36-35--71**   **Yards: 6,869**
North Course: **Par: 36-36--72**   **Yards: 7,150**

A total of 1,000 applications were excepted with 13 regionals held to reduce the field to 185 players for the final tournament

Woody Austin	1	70-68-72-68-69-67	414
Eduardo Romero	2	71-69-68-71-69-70	418
Tray Tyner	T3	70-70-67-74-72-66	419
Bruce Fleisher	T3	69-70-68-70-73-69	419
Harry Taylor	5	73-67-68-72-70-70	420
Dudley Hart	T6	69-72-70-69-74-67	421
Pat Burke	T6	72-70-67-72-71-69	421
Bill Porter	T8	66-71-69-73-71-72	422
Ronnie Black	T8	67-70-70-71-72-72	422
Doug Martin	T10	72-71-66-71-75-68	423
Mike Brisky	T10	72-72-69-71-71-68	423
Charlie Rymer	T10	71-73-67-68-74-70	423
Omar Uresti	T10	73-74-68-64-72-72	423
Don Reese	T10	70-71-74-68-69-71	423
Jeff Leonard	T15	71-75-67-69-74-68	424
Joey Rassett	T15	68-74-71-70-73-68	424
Bart Bryant	T15	65-67-71-74-77-70	424
Mark Wurtz	T15	69-68-72-73-71-71	424
Lee Rinker	T15	71-76-69-69-68-71	424
Marco Dawson	T15	71-78-69-69-65-72	424
J.L. Lewis	T15	72-69-68-68-75-72	424
Steve Gotsche	T22	70-70-74-71-71-69	425
Phil Blackmar	T22	65-74-66-73-77-70	425
Kelly Gibson	T22	71-72-69-68-74-71	425
Tommy Tolles	T22	71-71-72-71-69-71	425
Dicky Thompson	T22	69-74-67-71-73-71	425
J.P. Hayes	T22	69-70-67-69-78-72	425
Joe Acosta, Jr.	T22	76-71-68-68-70-72	425
Scott McCarron	T29	73-74-74-67-69-69	426
Jonathan Kaye	T29	69-76-74-69-69-69	426
Scott Ford	T29	69-70-70-72-75-70	426
Keith Fergus	T29	74-71-67-74-70-70	426
Ray Stewart	T29	74-70-71-71-72-68	426
Kawika Cotner	T29	70-73-65-75-75-68	426
Tony Sills	T29	69-66-71-70-77-73	426
Tim Loustalot	T29	72-74-73-67-67-73	426
Jay Williamson	T37	70-73-73-70-71-70	427
Tom Hearn	T37	75-70-69-69-74-70	427
Clark Burroughs	T37	73-73-70-70-71-70	427
Bill Britton	T37	68-72-68-72-77-70	427
Michael Allen	T37	72-75-71-66-73-70	427
Mike Smith	T37	72-73-69-70-73-70	427
Ryan Howison	T37	72-73-75-68-69-70	427
Carl Paulson	T37	72-71-71-70-72-71	427
John Adams	T37	74-72-71-68-71-71	427
Steve Hart	T37	69-71-73-72-68-74	427

SUMMARY OF QUALIFYING TOURNAMENTS

DATE	SITE	MEDALIST	CARDS GRANTED	APPLICANTS	FINAL FIELD	FORMAT
1965	PGA National G.C. Palm Beach Gardens, FL	John Schlee	17	49	49	144 holes
1966	PGA National G.C. Palm Beach Gardens, FL	Harry Toscano	32	99	99	144 holes
1967	PGA National G.C. Palm Beach Gardens, FL	Bobby Cole	30	111	111	144 holes
Spring 1968	PGA National G.C. Palm Beach Gardens, FL	Bob Dickson	15	81	81	144 holes
Fall 1968	PGA National G.C. Palm Beach Gardens, FL	Grier Jones	30	79	79	144 holes
Spring 1969	PGA National G.C. Palm Beach Gardens, FL	Bob Eastwood	15	91	91	144 holes
Fall 1969	PGA National G.C. Palm Beach Gardens, FL	Doug Olson	12	182	48	144 holes
1970	Tucson C.C. Tucson, AZ	Robert Barbarossa	18	250	60	72 holes, after nine 54-hole District Qualifiers
1971	PGA National G.C. Palm Beach Gardens, FL	Bob Zender	23	357	75	108 holes, after three 72-hole Regional Qualifiers
1972	Silverado C.C. Napa, CA	Larry Stubblefield John Adams	25	468	81	108 holes, after three 72-hole Regional Qualifiers
1973	Perdido Bay C.C. Pensacola, FL Dunes G.C. N. Myrtle Beach, SC	Ben Crenshaw	23	373	78	144 holes, after three 72-hole Regional Qualifiers
1974	Silverado C.C. Napa CA Canyon C.C. Palm Springs, CA	Fuzzy Zoeller	19	447	78	144 holes, after three 72-hole Regional Qualifiers
Spring 1975	Bay Tree Plantation N. Myrtle Beach, SC	Joey Dills	13	233	233	108 holes
Fall 1975	Walt Disney World Lake Buena Vista, FL	Jerry Pate	25	380	380	108 holes
Spring 1976	Bay Tree Plantation N. Myrtle Beach, SC	Bob Shearer Woody Blackburn	15	276	276	108 holes
Fall 1976	Rancho Viejo C.C. Valley International C.C. Brownsville, TX	Keith Fergus	29	349	349	108 holes

Qualifying Tournament Summary (cont'd.)

DATE	SITE	MEDALIST	CARDS GRANTED	APPLICANTS	FINAL FIELD	FORMAT
Spring 1977	Pinehurst C.C. Pinehurst, NC	Phil Hancock	26	408	408	108 holes
Fall 1977	Pinehurst C.C. Pinehurst, NC	Ed Fiori	34	660	144	72 holes, after Sectional Qualifiers
Spring 1978	U. of New Mexico G.C. Albuquerque, NM	Wren Lum	28	502	150	72 holes, after five 72-hole Regional Qualifiers
Fall 1978	Waterwood National C.C. Huntsville, TX	Jim Thorpe John Fought	27	606	120	72 holes, after five 72-hole Regional Qualifiers
Spring 1979	Pinehurst C.C. Pinehurst, NC	Terry Mauney	25	521	150	72 holes, after five 72-hole Regional Qualifiers
Fall 1979	Waterwood National C.C. Huntsville, TX	Tom Jones	27	652	120	72 holes, after five 72-hole Regional Qualifiers
Spring 1980	Pinehurst C.C. Pinehurst, NC	Jack Spradlin	27	553	150	72 holes, after five 72-hole Regional Qualifiers
Fall 1980	Fort Washington G&CC Fresno, Calif.	Bruce Douglass	27	621	120	72 holes, after five 72-hole Regional Qualifiers
Spring 1981	Walt Disney World Golf Resort Lake Buena Vista, FL	Billy Glisson	25	556	150	72 holes, after five 72-hole Regional Qualifiers
Fall 1981	Waterwood National C.C. Huntsville, TX	Robert Thompson Tim Graham	34	513	120	72 holes, after six 72-hole Regional Qualifiers
1982	Tournament Players Club & Sawgrass Country Club Ponte Vedra, FL	Donnie Hammond	50	696	200	108 holes after eight Regional Qualifiers
1983	Tournament Players Club Ponte Vedra, FL	Willie Wood	57	624	144	108 holes after nine Regional Qualifiers
1984	La Quinta Hotel and G.C. Mission Hills C.C. La Quinta, CA	Paul Azinger	50	800	160	108 holes after ten Regional Qualifiers
1985	Grenelefe Golf and Tennis Club Haines City, FL	Tom Sieckmann	50	825	162	108 holes after 11 Regional Qualifiers
1986	PGA West (Stadium Golf Course) La Quinta Hotel Golf & Tennis Resort (Dunes Course) La Quinta, CA	Steve Jones	53	750	186	108 holes after 14 Regionals

DATE	SITE	MEDALIST	CARDS GRANTED	APPLICANTS	FINAL FIELD	FORMAT
1987	Matanzas Woods GC Pine Lakes CC Palm Coast, FL	John Huston	54	800	183	108 holes after 11 Regionals
1988	La Quinta Hotel (Dunes Course) PGA West Jack Nicklaus Resort Course La Quinta, CA	Robin Freeman	52	750	183	108 holes after 11 Regionals
1989	TPC at The Woodlands The Woodlands Inn & CC The Woodlands, TX	David Peoples	59	825	180	108 holes after 11 Regionals
1990	La Quinta Hotel (Dunes Course) PGA West Jack Nicklaus Resort Course La Quinta, CA	Duffy Waldorf	49	835	182	108 holes after 11 Regionals
1991	Grenelefe Resort & Conference Center Haines City, FL	Mike Standly	48	850	181	108 holes, after 12 regionals
1992	TPC at The Woodlands The Woodlands Inn & CC The Woodlands, TX	Massy Kuramato Skip Kendall Brett Ogle Perry Moss Neale Smith	43	800	186	108 holes, after 13 Regionals
1993	La Quinta Hotel (Dunes Course) PGA West Jack Nicklaus Resort Course La Quinta, CA	Ty Armstrong Dave Stockton, Jr. Robin Freeman	46	800	191	108 holes after 13 Regionals
1994	Grenelefe Resort & Conference Center Haines City, FL	Woody Austin	46	1000	185	108 holes after 13 Regionals

NOTE: The American Professional Golfers also held a School in the fall of 1968, graduating 21. The 144-hole competition was played at Doral C.C. The medalist was Martin Roesink.

Loren Roberts led the PGA TOUR
in putting and collected his first
victory at the 1994 Nestle Invitational.

1994 OFFICIAL PGA TOUR MONEY LIST

	Name	Events	Money		Name	Events	Money
1.	NICK PRICE	19	$1,499,927	67.	FRED FUNK	30	$281,905
2.	GREG NORMAN	16	1,330,307	68.	CHIP BECK	27	281,131
3.	MARK MCCUMBER	20	1,208,209	69.	GREG KRAFT	30	279,901
4.	TOM LEHMAN	23	1,031,144	70.	NOLAN HENKE	26	278,419
5.	FUZZY ZOELLER	19	1,016,804	71.	DUFFY WALDORF	26	274,971
6.	LOREN ROBERTS	22	1,015,671	72.	D.A. WEIBRING	20	255,757
7.	JOSE MARIA OLAZABAL *	8	969,900	73.	GENE SAUERS	26	250,654
8.	COREY PAVIN	20	906,305	74.	TED TRYBA	34	246,481
9.	JEFF MAGGERT	26	814,475	75.	PAUL GOYDOS #	31	241,107
10.	HALE IRWIN	22	814,436	76.	GUY BOROS +	30	240,775
11.	SCOTT HOCH	28	804,559	77.	RUSS COCHRAN	28	239,827
12.	STEVE LOWERY	30	794,048	78.	JIM FURYK +	31	236,603
13.	MIKE SPRINGER	24	770,717	79.	JIM MCGOVERN	30	227,764
14.	BOB ESTES	27	765,360	80.	BOB LOHR	28	225,048
15.	PHIL MICKELSON	18	748,316	81.	JOHNNY MILLER	4	225,000
16.	JOHN HUSTON	25	731,499	82.	GARY HALLBERG	27	224,965
17.	BILL GLASSON	21	689,110	83.	NICK FALDO *	9	221,146
18.	BRAD BRYANT	32	687,803	84.	MIKE HULBERT	31	221,007
19.	ERNIE ELS	11	684,440	85.	CHRIS DIMARCO @	29	216,839
20.	DAVID FROST	23	671,683	86.	MARK O'MEARA	29	214,070
21.	BEN CRENSHAW	24	659,252	87.	COLIN MONTGOMERIE *	5	213,828
22.	TOM KITE	23	658,689	88.	PETER JACOBSEN	19	211,762
23.	FRED COUPLES	15	625,654	89.	BOBBY WADKINS	22	208,358
24.	BRAD FAXON	25	612,847	90.	KEITH CLEARWATER	27	203,549
25.	JAY HAAS	30	593,386	91.	WAYNE LEVI	24	200,476
26.	KENNY PERRY	30	585,941	92.	DAVID OGRIN	29	199,199
27.	RICK FEHR	25	573,963	93.	MARK CARNEVALE	31	192,653
28.	BRUCE LIETZKE	18	564,926	94.	TOM PURTZER	22	187,307
29.	HAL SUTTON	29	540,162	95.	JIM THORPE	26	185,714
30.	MARK CALCAVECCHIA	27	533,201	96.	DAVE STOCKTON,JR +	31	185,209
31.	MARK BROOKS	33	523,285	97.	SCOTT VERPLANK	19	183,015
32.	CRAIG STADLER	22	474,831	98.	BRIAN KAMM	32	181,884
33.	DAVIS LOVE III	28	474,219	99.	MIKE STANDLY	30	179,850
34.	DAVID EDWARDS	23	458,845	100.	DAVID FEHERTY #	22	178,501
35.	LEE JANZEN	26	442,588	101.	BOB BURNS +	24	178,168
36.	ANDREW MAGEE	25	431,041	102.	DOUG TEWELL	27	177,388
37.	JOHN COOK	24	429,725	103.	ROBIN FREEMAN #	29	177,044
38.	KIRK TRIPLETT	26	422,171	104.	MICHAEL BRADLEY	29	175,137
39.	LENNIE CLEMENTS	22	416,880	105.	DILLARD PRUITT	29	171,866
40.	MIKE HEINEN +	27	390,963	106.	PAUL STANKOWSKI #	29	170,393
41.	CURTIS STRANGE	23	390,881	107.	YOSHINORI MIZUMAKI #	18	168,450
42.	LARRY MIZE	22	386,029	108.	ED HUMENIK	31	168,332
43.	TOM WATSON	15	380,378	109.	FULTON ALLEM	28	166,144
44.	ROBERT GAMEZ	23	380,353	110.	BRIAN CLAAR	31	165,370
45.	GLEN DAY +	30	357,236	111.	BRANDEL CHAMBLEE	27	161,018
46.	CRAIG PARRY	20	354,602	112.	DAN FORSMAN	23	160,805
47.	BLAINE MCCALLISTER	27	351,554	113.	BILLY MAYFAIR	32	158,159
48.	BILLY ANDRADE	26	342,208	114.	MARK MCNULTY	6	157,700
49.	JOHN DALY	17	340,034	115.	STEVE RINTOUL +	27	157,618
50.	STEVE STRICKER #	26	334,409	116.	KEN GREEN	28	155,156
51.	JIM GALLAGHER, JR.	27	325,976	117.	JOHN WILSON #	29	155,058
52.	VIJAY SINGH	21	325,959	118.	BOB GILDER	28	154,868
53.	DAVE BARR	28	314,885	119.	MIKE REID	22	154,441
54.	GIL MORGAN	18	309,690	120.	JESPER PARNEVIK #	17	148,816
55.	JAY DON BLAKE	25	309,351	121.	JOE OZAKI	17	147,308
56.	SCOTT SIMPSON	21	307,884	122.	JOHN MORSE @	26	146,137
57.	DICKY PRIDE #	27	305,769	123.	PAYNE STEWART	23	145,687
58.	NEAL LANCASTER	29	305,038	124.	JAY DELSING	27	143,738
59.	JEFF SLUMAN	30	301,178	125.	DENNIS PAULSON #	27	142,515
60.	MIKE SULLIVAN	26	298,586	126.	JUSTIN LEONARD	13	140,413
61.	DONNIE HAMMOND	25	295,436	127.	JOEL EDWARDS	28	139,141
62.	STEVE ELKINGTON	20	294,943	128.	CURT BYRUM @	28	137,587
63.	BRIAN HENNINGER	21	294,075	129.	KELLY GIBSON	33	134,841
64.	STEVE PATE	29	291,651	130.	HOWARD TWITTY	28	131,408
65.	CLARK DENNIS +	30	289,065	131.	DICK MAST	27	129,822
66.	BRETT OGLE	21	284,495	132.	PETER JORDAN +	29	128,960

* Non-PGA TOUR Member   @ 1993 NIKE TOUR Grad   # 1993 Qualifying Tournament Grad
                                                                           + Q-school Grad/NIKE TOUR member

	Name	Events	Money		Name	Events	Money
133.	DAVID PEOPLES	30	$126,918	199.	TODD BARRANGER #	26	$40,356
134.	TIM SIMPSON #	31	126,861	200.	MIKE BRISKY #	14	38,713
135.	DUDLEY HART	31	126,313	201.	BUDDY GARDNER	11	37,609
136.	SAM TORRANCE *	5	123,492	202.	TED SCHULZ	30	37,537
137.	RONNIE BLACK	27	123,404	203.	JC ANDERSON	11	35,022
138.	DAVE RUMMELLS	31	122,872	204.	CHARLES RAULERSON #	24	33,919
139.	MARCO DAWSON	30	121,025	205.	BRAD FABEL *	12	33,812
140.	WAYNE GRADY	19	120,901	206.	BILLY DOWNES *	2	33,500
141.	MIKE DONALD	16	119,065	207.	LEONARD THOMPSON	11	32,992
142.	BERNHARD LANGER *	6	118,241	208.	DAVID ISHII *	1	31,200
143.	JEFF WOODLAND #	30	117,627	209.	BOB MAY @	31	31,079
144.	JOHN INMAN	34	117,356	210.	FRAN QUINN *	4	30,365
145.	JOEY SINDELAR	22	114,563	211.	TY ARMSTRONG +	23	30,181
146.	BOB TWAY	29	114,176	212.	BRADLEY HUGHES *	7	29,891
147.	TOMMY ARMOUR III	9	112,778	213.	PHIL BLACKMAR	30	28,159
148.	TOM BYRUM	12	112,259	214.	JODIE MUDD	15	27,868
149.	STEVE BRODIE +	28	112,081	215.	EDDIE KIRBY *	18	26,744
150.	ED FIORI	15	108,259	216.	GARY MCCORD	7	25,602
151.	JOHN ADAMS	32	106,689	217.	JUMBO OZAKI *	5	25,557
152.	BOBBY CLAMPETT	16	105,710	218.	KENNY KNOX	15	23,872
153.	MARK WURTZ @	29	103,252	219.	TONY SILLS	9	22,807
154.	OLIN BROWNE @	31	101,580	220.	HAJIME MESHIAI *	7	22,124
155.	LARRY SILVEIRA @	28	99,671	221.	DAN POHL	15	21,734
156.	SEAN MURPHY @	31	97,597	222.	ROGER WESSELS *	1	21,450
157.	ED DOUGHERTY	33	96,987	223.	BRAD LARDON +	21	21,429
158.	RAY FLOYD	4	95,017	224.	TOMMY NAKAJIMA *	3	21,200
159.	JOHN FLANNERY	33	94,105	225.	JIM WOODWARD	16	20,996
160.	TREVOR DODDS	29	92,734	226.	DON REESE #	17	19,760
161.	STEVE LAMONTAGNE #	26	91,643	227.	TOM GARNER +	23	18,904
162.	MICHAEL ALLEN	32	91,191	228.	KIYOSHI MUROTA *	4	18,239
163.	BRUCE FLEISHER	29	88,680	229.	BARRY LANE *	4	18,105
164.	DAVID TOMS	32	87,607	230.	ERNIE GONZALEZ	3	16,860
165.	WILLIE WOOD	26	87,102	231.	KEITH FERGUS	5	16,749
166.	MORRIS HATALSKY #	25	81,902	232.	COSTANTINO ROCCA *	5	16,350
167.	IAN BAKER-FINCH	20	81,326	233.	MARK WIEBE	9	16,032
168.	DOUG MARTIN @	33	81,201	234.	JEFF ROTH *	6	15,978
169.	RICHARD ZOKOL	26	78,074	235.	BARRY JAECKEL	9	15,750
170.	ROBERT WRENN	17	77,279	236.	HARRY TAYLOR	11	15,482
171.	DON POOLEY	5	76,978	237.	CHRIS PERRY	2	14,840
172.	GRANT WAITE	25	71,695	238.	BRAD KING #	16	14,254
173.	BILL BRITTON #	22	68,033	239.	CHRIS KITE #	19	13,983
174.	ROGER MALTBIE	15	67,686	240.	GREG TWIGGS	29	13,676
175.	LARRY NELSON	17	66,831	241.	IKUO SHIRAHAMA *	1	13,550
176.	ESTEBAN TOLEDO +	28	66,049	242.	PAUL AZINGER	4	13,422
177.	JOHN MAHAFFEY	26	65,380	243.	CARL MASON *	1	13,350
178.	MARK LYE	15	63,394	244.	TIM CONLEY *	2	13,040
179.	STAN UTLEY @	29	63,345	245.	HIROSHI GODA *	1	12,750
180.	JOEY RASSETT #	24	62,826	246.	TOMMY MOORE @	20	12,601
181.	RUSSELL BEIERSDORF	14	59,443	247.	SHAUN MICHEEL #	19	12,252
182.	STEVE GOTSCHE #	21	59,227	248.	JACK NICKLAUS	8	11,514
183.	MIKE SMITH	15	57,850	249.	PETER PERSONS	4	10,986
184.	TOM SIECKMANN	29	55,304	250.	LANCE TEN BROECK	11	10,843
185.	LANNY WADKINS	25	54,114	251.	PETER BAKER *	5	10,598
186.	P.H. HORGAN III	17	53,734	252.	D.A. RUSSELL #	10	9,536
187.	ROB BOLDT +	20	52,992	253.	ANDY BEAN	19	8,810
188.	IAN WOOSNAM *	6	51,895	254.	STEVE JONES	2	8,740
189.	SEVE BALLESTEROS *	5	49,245	255.	MONTE MONTGOMERY *	1	8,706
190.	PHIL TATAURANGI #	24	47,587	256.	BOB BOYD *	3	8,458
191.	SANDY LYLE *	7	47,538	257.	SKIP KENDALL	4	8,392
192.	LARRY RINKER	28	47,435	258.	GORDON BRAND *	1	8,006
193.	ROCCO MEDIATE	6	45,940	258.	BRANDT JOBE *	1	8,006
194.	SEIKI OKUDA *	3	44,250	260.	DENNIS TRIXLER *	2	7,609
195.	DAVID DUVAL *	6	44,006	261.	ED SNEED	3	7,583
196.	BILL KRATZERT #	25	42,127	262.	DAN HALLDORSON	5	7,215
197.	ROCKY WALCHER #	23	41,759	263.	TRAY TYNER *	1	7,193
198.	FRANK NOBILO *	3	41,292	264.	PERRY ARTHUR *	1	6,737

* Non-PGA TOUR Member   @ 1993 NIKE TOUR Grad   # 1993 Qualifying Tournament Grad
+ Q-school Grad/NIKE TOUR member

Name	Events	Money
264. BOB EASTWOOD	6	$6,737
266. DON WALSWORTH *	1	6,595
267. PAUL TRITTLER *	2	6,580
268. JERRY PATE	8	6,513
269. CHRISTIAN PENA *	1	6,413
270. JOE DALEY *	1	6,239
271. VANCE HEAFNER	2	5,297
272. DAVID GILFORD *	1	5,200
273. DAVID BERGANIO, JR *	4	5,105
273. TIM DUNLAVEY *	1	5,105
273. MIKE EMERY JR. *	1	5,105
276. PATRICK BURKE	10	5,034
277. HUBERT GREEN	15	4,854
278. JOHN ELLIOTT *	2	4,480
279. MARK CATO *	1	4,435
279. JIM NELFORD	2	4,435
281. LON HINKLE	7	4,411
282. HUGH ROYER *	1	4,325
283. LEE PORTER *	1	4,256
284. BILLY RAY BROWN	27	4,254
285. DENIS WATSON	16	4,250
286. SCOTT GUMP	3	4,181
287. STEVEN RICHARDSON *	1	4,105
288. DAVE STOCKTON	2	3,845
289. EMLYN AUBREY *	1	3,802
290. SAM RANDOLPH	3	3,513
291. J.L. LEWIS *	3	3,299
292. ANDY NORTH	6	3,165
293. TOM DOLBY *	1	3,158
294. CHRIS SMITH	2	3,075
295. CLARENCE ROSE	4	2,992
296. TOM CLEAVER *	2	2,954
297. JACK RENNER	4	$2,819
298. RON MCDOUGAL *	1	2,800
299. BILLY TUTEN *	1	2,733
300. TRIPP ISENHOUR *	1	2,604
301. TODD SMITH *	1	2,600
302. TED GOIN *	1	2,575
303. STEVE JURGENSEN *	1	2,544
304. PETER SENIOR *	4	2,513
305. SCOTT WATKINS *	1	2,508
306. MAC O'GRADY	2	2,409
307. R.W. EAKS *	1	2,352
308. TOMMY BRANNEN *	2	2,316
309. JOHN TRAUB *	1	2,310
310. THOMAS LEVET #	10	2,200
310. BRAD SHERFY *	2	2,200
312. RON STRECK	4	2,189
313. DAN OSCHMANN *	1	2,123
314. BEN WALTER *	1	2,120
315. ROGER GUNN *	1	2,112
316. DAN OLSEN *	1	2,101
317. DAVE BISHOP *	1	2,057
318. WARREN SCHUTTE *	2	1,990
318. JERRY SMITH *	1	1,990
320. BROOK SCHMITT *	1	1,940
321. DANA QUIGLEY *	1	1,920
322. TONY SARACENO *	1	1,908
323. TOM HEARN *	1	1,710
324. CHAD GINN *	1	1,618
324. JOE INMAN	2	1,618
326. FRANK CONNER	2	1,435
326. JON DIGGETTS *	1	1,435
326. MARK PFEIL	3	1,435

* Non-PGA TOUR Member   @ 1993 NIKE TOUR Grad   # 1993 Qualifying Tournament Grad
+ Q-school Grad/NIKE TOUR member

1994 PGA TOUR FACTS AND FIGURES

LOW 9: 29 (7-under) — *Davis Love III*, United Airlines Hawaiian Open; *Lennie Clements*, Bob Hope Chrysler Classic; *Ronnie Black*, Buick Invitational; *Larry Nelson*, Doral-Ryder Open; *Dennis Paulson*, Freeport-McMoRan Classic; *Brian Henninger*, New England Classic

29 (6-under) — *Steve Lamontagne*, Honda Classic; *Guy Boros*, Southwestern Bell Colonial

29 (5-under) — *Glen Day*, B.C. Open

LOW 18: 60 (12-under) — *Davis Love III*, United Airlines Hawaiian Open

LOW FIRST 18: 61 (10-under) — *Bob Lohr*, Anheuser-Busch Golf Classic

LOW FIRST 36: 127 (15-under) — *Bob Estes*, Texas Open

128 (16-under) — *Davis Love III*, United Airlines Hawaiian Open; *Scott Hoch*, Bob Hope Chrysler Classic

LOW FIRST 54: 195 (18-under) — *Bob Estes*, Texas Open

197 (19-under) — *Lennie Clements*, Bob Hope Chrysler Classic; *Greg Norman*, THE PLAYERS Championship

LOW FIRST 72: 264 (24-under) — *Scott Hoch*, Bob Hope Chrylser Classic; *Greg Norman*, THE PLAYERS Championship

LOW 90: 332 (27-under) — *Bruce Lietzke*, Las Vegas Invitational

HIGH WINNING SCORE: 281 (7-under) — *Johnny Miller*, AT&T Pebble Beach National Pro-Am

279 (5-under) — *Ernie Els*, US Open

LARGEST WINNING MARGIN: 6 strokes — *Nick Price*, PGA Championship

LOW START BY WINNER: 62 (9-under) — *Bob Estes*, Texas Open

HIGH START BY WINNER: 74 (2-over) — *Jose Maria Olazabal*, Masters

LOW FINISH BY WINNER: 64 (7-under) — *Bill Glasson*, Phoenix Open

64 (6-under) — *Nick Price*, Southwestern Bell Colonial

HIGH FINISH BY WINNER: 74 (2-over) — *Johnny Miller*, AT&T Pebble Beach National Pro-Am

LARGEST 18-HOLE LEAD: 4 strokes — *Jose Maria Olazabal*, Freeport-McMoRan Classic

LARGEST 36-HOLE LEAD: 5 strokes — *Nick Price*, PGA Championship

LARGEST 54-HOLE LEAD: 5 strokes — *Steve Elkington*, Buick Southern Open

LOW 36-HOLE CUT: 141 (3-under) — United Airlines Hawaiian Open, Buick Invitational

140 (even) — Hardee's Golf Classic

139 (3-under) — Texas Open

HIGH 36-HOLE CUT: 148 (4-over) — Doral-Ryder Open

147 (5-over) — Honda Classic, US Open

LOW 54-HOLE CUT: 209 (6-under) — Las Vegas Invitational

HIGH 54-HOLE CUT: 217 (1-over) — AT&T Pebble Beach National Pro-Am

FEWEST TO MAKE 36-HOLE CUT: 70 at Buick Classic, FedEx St. Jude Classic

MOST TO MAKE 36-HOLE CUT: 88 at Buick Southern Open

FEWEST TO MAKE 54-HOLE CUT: 72 at AT&T Pebble Beach National Pro-Am

MOST TO MAKE 54-HOLE CUT: 77 at Walt Disney World/Oldsmobile Golf Classic

MOST CONSECUTIVE EVENTS IN THE MONEY: 25, Fred Couples

CONSECUTIVE YEARS WITH WIN: 5, Fred Couples (1990 through 1994)

TWO EAGLES ONE ROUND: *Davis Love III*, United Airlines Hawaiian Open; *Robert Gamez*, *Ted Tryba*, Northern Telecom Open; *Ted Tryba*, Phoenix Open; *Dudley Hart*, AT&T Pebble Beach National Pro-Am; *Ronnie Black*, Buick Invitational; *Jesper Parnevik*, Nestle Invitational; *Dennis Paulson*, Freeport-McMoRan Classic; *Bob May*, *Scott Hoch*, Kemper Open; *Phil Blackmar*, Buick Classic; *Scott Verplank*, US Open; *Mark O'Meara*, Motorola Western Open; *Steve Lowery*, The Sprint International; *Bill Britton*, *Dave Barr*, *Mark Calcavecchia*, Greater Milwaukee Open; *Phil Mickelson*, Bell Canadian Open; *Curt Byrum*, *Lee Janzen*, B.C. Open; *Jim McGovern*, Buick Southern Open; *Buddy Gardner*, *Dave Stockton, Jr.*, Walt Disney World/Oldsmobile Golf Classic

1994 PGA TOUR FACTS AND FIGURES (cont'd.)

THREE EAGLES ONE ROUND: *Davis Love III*, United Airlines Hawaiian Open (2nd round)
Dave Stockton, Jr., Walt Disney World/Oldsmobile Golf Classic

BACK-TO-BACK EAGLES: *Bill Britton*, Greater Milwaukee Open; *Buddy Gardner*,
Dave Stockton, Jr., Walt Disney World/Olsmobile Golf Classic.

BEST BIRDIE STREAK: 7, *Greg Kraft*, Buick Open

BEST BIRDIE/EAGLE STREAK: *Ken Green*, 2-eagle-3's, 3 birdies, Phoenix Open

BEST COME FROM BEHIND LAST DAY TO WIN: 4 strokes, *John Huston*, Doral-Ryder Open

PLAYOFFS:

Mercedes Championships	*Phil Mickelson* def. *Fred Couples*, par on second extra hole.
GTE Byron Nelson	*Neal Lancaster* def. *Tom Byrum*, *Mark Carnevale*, *David Edwards*, *Yoshi Mizumaki*, *David Ogrin*, birdie on first extra hole.
Southwestern Bell Colonial	*Nick Price* def. *Scott Simpson*, birdie on the first extra hole.
US Open	*Ernie Els* (74-4-4) def. *Loren Roberts* (74-4-5) and *Colin Montgomerie* (78), 20 holes
Deposit Guaranty Golf Classic	*Brian Henninger* def. *Mike Sullivan*, birdie on first extra hole
FedEx St. Jude Classic	*Dicky Pride* def. *Hal Sutton*, *Gene Sauers*, birdie first extra hole
The Sprint International	*Steve Lowery* def. *Rick Fehr*, par first extra hole
THE TOUR Championship	*Mark McCumber* def. *Fuzzy Zoeller*, birdie first extra hole

MOST CONSECUTIVE ROUNDS PAR OR LESS: 19, *Peter Jacobsen* (2 Memorial, 4 Canon GHO, 4 Motorola Western Open, 4 FedEx St. Jude Classic, 4 Buick Open, 1 Hardee's Golf Classic)
19, *Jim Furyk* (4 Anheuser-Busch Golf Classic, 4 New England Classic, 4 FedEx St. Jude Classic, 4 Buick Open, 3 GMO)

HOLES-IN-ONE (44): *Willie Wood*, *Christian Pena*, Northern Telecom Open; *Vijay Singh*, *Olin Browne*, AT&T Pebble Beach National Pro-Am; *Peter Jacobsen*, Nissan LA Open; *Jim Gallagher Jr.*, *Steve Pate*, Bob Hope Chrysler Classic; *Russell Beiersdorf*, Buick Invitational; *Gary Hallberg*, *Russ Cochran*, THE PLAYERS Championship; *Eddie Kirby*, Freeport-McMoRan Classic; *David Edwards*, MCI Heritage Classic; *Steve Lamontagne*, *John Daly*, Shell Houston Open; *John Inman*, *Jeff Sluman*, BellSouth Classic; *Kenny Perry*, GTE Byron Nelson Classic & NEC World Series of Golf; *Bob Tway* (2), Memorial; *Marco Dawson*, *Phil Mickelson*, Kemper Open; *Corey Pavin*, Buick Classic; *Ted Schulz*, Buick Classic & Texas Open; *Glen Day* (2), Canon GHO; *Doug Tewell*, Motorola Western Open; *Morris Hatalsky*, New England Classic; *Mark Wiebe*, Sprint International; *Hale Irwin*, NEC World Series of Golf; *Greg Twiggs*, Greater Milwaukee Open; *Bill Britton*, Kmart GGO & Greater Milwaukee Open; *Wayne Levi*, Bell Canadian Open; *Ernie Gonzalez*, Hardee's Golf Classic; *Dicky Pride*, Buick Southern Open; *John Adams*, *Buddy Gardner*, Walt Disney World/Oldsmobile Golf Classic; *John Flannery*, *Phil Tataurangi*, Texas Open; *Sean Murphy*, Las Vegas Invitational; *Greg Norman*, *Steve Lowery*, THE TOUR Championship

DOUBLE EAGLES: *Olin Browne*, Northern Telecom Open (Tucson National #2, 495 yards, driver/4-iron)
Jeff Maggert, Masters (Augusta National #13, 485 yards, driver/3-iron)
Mike Donald, Texas Open (Oak Hills #15, 527 yards, driver/4-wood)

COURSE RECORDS:
(no ties)
60 (12-under), *Davis Love III*, Waialae CC, United Airlines Hawaiian Open
65 (7-under), *Dudley Hart*, Poppy Hills GC, AT&T Pebble Beach National Pro-Am
61 (11-under), *Lennie Clements*, LaQuinta CC, Bob Hope Chrysler Classic
62 (10-under), *Scott Hoch*, PGA West Palmer Course, Bob Hope Chrysler Classic
63 (9-under), *Jose Maria Olazabal*, English Turn G&CC, Freeport-McMoRan Classic
62 (10-under), *Dennis Paulson*, English Turn G&CC, Freeport-McMoRan Classic
61 (10-under), *David Frost*, Harbour Town GL, MCI Heritage Classic
61 (10-under), *Bob Lohr*, Anheuser-Busch Golf Classic
64 (8-under), *Dicky Pride*, Annandale GC, Deposit Guaranty Golf Classic
63 (8-under), *Loren Roberts*, Brown Deer Park Golf Course, Greater Milwaukee Open

TOURNAMENT RECORDS: *Greg Norman*, 264 (24-under), THE PLAYERS Championship
Hale Irwin, 266 (18-under), MCI Heritage Classic
Tom Lehman, 268 (20-under), Memorial Tournament
Nick Price, 269 (11-under), PGA Championship

WIRE-TO-WIRE WINNERS: *Greg Norman*, THE PLAYERS Championship; *Mike Springer*, Kmart GGO; *Bob Estes*, Texas Open

FEWEST PUTTS, 9 HOLES: 8, *John Inman*, MCI Heritage Classic, fourth round front nine, Harbour Town GL (ties PGA TOUR record)

FIRST-TIME WINNERS: *Loren Roberts*, Nestle Invitational; *Mike Springer*, Kmart GGO; *Mike Heinen*, Shell Houston Open; *Neal Lancaster*, GTE Byron Nelson Classic; *Tom Lehman*, Memorial Tournament; *Ernie Els*, US Open; *Brian Henninger*, Deposit Guaranty Golf Classic; *Dicky Pride*, FedExs St. Jude Classic; *Steve Lowery*, The Sprint International; *Bob Estes*, Texas Open

MULTIPLE WINNERS: *Nick Price* (5), Honda Classic, Southwestern Bell Colonial, Motorola Western Open, PGA Championship, Bell Canadian Open; *Mark McCumber* (3), Anheuser-Busch Golf Classic, Hardee's Golf Classic, THE TOUR Championship; *Jose Maria Olazabal* (2), Masters, NEC World Series of Golf; *Mike Springer* (2), Kmart Greater Greensboro Open, Greater Milwaukee Open

THE LAST TIME

WINNERS:
Last to win back-to-back events .... David Frost, 1993 Canadian Open, Hardee's Golf Classic
Last to win three consecutive events .... Gary Player, 1978 Masters, T of C, Houston Open
Last to win three consecutive starts ...... Nick Price, 1993 Hartford, Western, FedEx St. Jude
Last to defend title .... Nick Price, 1993, 1994 Motorola Western Open
Last lefthander to win .... Phil Mickelson, 1994 Mercedes Championships
Last Monday Open Qualifier to win .... Fred Wadsworth, 1986 Southern Open
Last rookie to win .... Dicky Pride, 1994 Federal Express St. Jude Classic
Last rookie to win twice .... Robert Gamez, 1990 Northern Telecom Tucson Open and
Nestle Invitational
Last amateur to win .... Phil Mickelson, 1991 Northern Telecom Open
Last to win in first-ever TOUR start .... Jim Benepe, 1988 Beatrice Western Open
Last to win in first start as official
member of PGA TOUR .... Robert Gamez, 1990 Northern Telecom Tucson Open
Last wire-to-wire winner (no ties) .... Bob Estes, 1994 Texas Open
Last player to win with over-par score ... Bruce Lietzke, 1981 Byron Nelson Classic, plus-1
Last time player shot 80 and won .... Kenny Knox, 1986 Honda Classic (third round)
Last to repeat as money leader .... Nick Price, 1993, 1994

TOURNAMENT FINISHES
Last 36-hole event .... 1994 Deposit Guaranty Golf Classic
Last 54-hole event .... 1994 Buick Southern Open
Last Monday finish .... 1994 Southwestern Bell Colonial
Last Monday U.S. Open playoff finish ... 1994 Ernie Els defeated Loren Roberts, Colin Montgomerie
Last Tuesday finish .... 1980 Joe Garagiola-Tucson Open
Last 36-hole final day .... 1994 Buick Open
Last time cut made after 18 holes .... 1987 Beatrice Western Open

WEATHER
Last time tournament rained out .... 1991 Independent Insurance Agent Open
Last time it snowed during tournament.. 1987 Greater Greensboro Open

DOUBLE EAGLES, ACES & EAGLES
Last time back-to-back eagles .... Dave Stockton, Jr., 1994 Walt Disney/Oldsmobile Classic
Last time double eagle .... Mike Donald, 1994 Texas Open
Last time three eagles in same round ... Dave Stockton, Jr., 1994 Walt Disney/Oldsmobile Classic
Last time four aces same day,
same hole .... 1989 U.S. Open, Doug Weaver, Mark Wiebe, Jerry Pate,
.... Nick Price on hole No. 6, 160 yards, all used a 7-iron.

PLAYOFF
Last one-hole playoff .... 1994 TOUR Championship (Mark McCumber def. Fuzzy Zoeller)
Last two-hole playoff .... 1994 Mercedes Championships (Phil Mickelson def. Fred
.... Couples)
Last three-hole playoff .... 1993 Buick Classic (Vijay Singh def. Mark Wiebe)
Last four-hole playoff .... 1993 Greater Milwaukee Open (Billy Mayfair def. Mark
Calcavecchia and Ted Schulz)
Last five-hole playoff .... 1989 Las Vegas Invitational (Scott Hoch def. Robert Wrenn)
Last six-hole playoff .... 1986 Kemper Open (Greg Norman def. Larry Mize)
Last seven-hole playoff .... 1991 New England Classic (Bruce Fleisher def. Ian Baker-Finch)
Last eight hole playoff .... 1983 Phoenix Open (Bob Gilder def. Johnny Miller, Mark
O'Meara and Rex Caldwell)
Last 11-hole playoff (TOUR record
for sudden death) .... 1949 Motor City Open (Middlecoff and Mangrum co-winners)
Last 18-hole playoff(plus) .... 1994 U.S. Open (Ernie Els def. Loren Roberts and Colin
.... Montgomerie)
Last playoff won with eagle .... 1992 Bob Hope Chrysler Classic (John Cook defeated Gene
Sauers, Tom Kite, Mark O'Meara and Rick Fehr)
Last playoff won with birdie .... 1994 TOUR Championship (Mark McCumber def. Fuzzy Zoeller)
Last playoff won with bogey .... 1988 Phoenix Open (Sandy Lyle def. Fred Couples, third
extra hole)
Last two-man playoff .... 1994 TOUR Championship (Mark McCumber def. Fuzzy Zoeller)
Last three-man playoff .... 1994 Federal Express St. Jude Classic (Dicky Pride def. Gene
Sauers and Hal Sutton)
Last four-man playoff .... 1990 Doral Ryder Open (Greg Norman def. Paul Azinger,
Mark Calcavecchia and Tim Simpson)
Last five-man playoff .... 1993 Buick Southern Open (John Inman def. Bob Estes, Billy
Andrade, Brad Bryant and Mark Brooks)
Last six-man playoff .... 1994 GTE Byron Nelson Classic (Neal Lancaster def. Tom Byrum,
Mark Carnevale, David Edwards, Yoshinori Mizumaki and
David Ogrin)
Last five-TEAM playoff .... 1985 Chrysler Team Championship

1994 PGA TOUR TOURNAMENT SUMMARY

Denotes first time winner

TOURNAMENT	COURSE	WINNER	SCORE	UNDER PAR	MARGIN	MONEY	RUNNERS-UP
1. Mercedes Championships	LaCosta Resort Carlsbad, CA	Phil Mickelson	276	12	playoff	$180,000	Fred Couples
2. United Airlines Hawaiian Open	Waialae CC Honolulu, HI	Brett Ogle	269	19	1	$216,000	Davis Love III
3. Northern Telecom Open	Tucson National Starr Pass Tucson, AZ	Andrew Magee	270	18	2	$198,000	Loren Roberts Vijay Singh Jay Don Blake Steve Stricker
4. Phoenix Open	TPC of Scottsdale Scottsdale, AZ	Bill Glasson	268	16	3	$216,000	Bob Estes
5. AT&T Pebble Beach National Pro-Am	Pebble Beach GL Spyglass Hill GC Poppy Hills CC Pebble Beach, CA	Johnny Miller	281	7	1	$225,000	Jeff Maggert Kirk Triplett Corey Pavin Tom Watson
6. Nissan Los Angeles Open	Riviera CC Pacific Palisades, CA	Corey Pavin	271	13	2	$180,000	Fred Couples
7. Bob Hope Chrysler Classic	Indian Wells CC LaQuinta CC PGA West/Palmer Bermuda Dunes CC Indian Wells, CA	Scott Hoch	334	26	3	$198,000	Fuzzy Zoeller Jim Gallagher Lennie Clements
8. Buick Invitational	Torrey Pines GCs La Jolla, CA	Craig Stadler	268	20	1	$198,000	Steve Lowery
9. Doral-Ryder Open	Doral Resort & CC Miami, FL	John Huston	274	14	3	$252,000	Billy Andrade Brad Bryant
10. Honda Classic	Weston Hills CC Ft. Lauderdale, FL	Nick Price	277	8	1	$198,000	Craig Parry
11. Nestle Invitational	Bay Hill Club Orlando, FL	*Loren Roberts	275	13	1	$216,000	Vijay Singh Nick Price Fuzzy Zoeller
12. THE PLAYERS Championship	TPC at Sawgrass Ponte Vedra, FL	Greg Norman	264	24	4	$450,000	Fuzzy Zoeller
13. Freeport-McMoRan Golf Classic	English Turn G&CC New Orleans, LA	Ben Crenshaw	273	15	3	$216,000	Jose M.Olazabal
14. The Masters	Augusta National Augusta, GA	Jose Maria Olazabal	279	9	2	$360,000	Tom Lehman
15. MCI Heritage Classic	Harbour Town GL Hilton Head Island, SC	Hale Irwin	266	18	2	$225,000	Greg Norman
16. Kmart Greater Greensboro Open	Forest Oaks CC Greensboro, NC	*Mike Springer	275	13	3	$270,000	Hale Irwin Brad Bryant Ed Humenik
17. Shell Houston Open	TPC @ The Woodlands The Woodlands, TX	*Mike Heinen	272	16	3	$234,000	Hal Sutton Jeff Maggert Tom Kite
18. BellSouth Classic	Atlanta CC Marietta, GA	John Daly	274	14	1	$216,000	Nolan Henke Brian Henninger
19. GTE Byron Nelson Classic	TPC at Las Colinas Irving, TX	*Neal Lancaster	132	9	playoff	$216,000	Yoshi Mizumaki David Ogrin Tom Byrum Mark Carnevale David Edwards
		(event shortened to 36 holes due to adverse weather conditions)					
20. Memorial Tournament	Muirfield Village GC Dublin, OH	*Tom Lehman	268	20	5	$270,000	Greg Norman
21. Southwestern Bell Colonial	Colonial CC Ft. Worth, TX	Nick Price (2)	266	14	playoff	$252,000	Scott Simpson
22. Kemper Open	TPC at Avenel Potomac, MD	Mark Brooks	271	13	3	$234,000	D.A. Weibring Bobby Wadkins
23. Buick Classic	Westchester CC Harrison, NY	Lee Janzen	268	16	3	$216,000	Ernie Els
24. U.S. Open	Oakmont CC Oakmont, PA	*Ernie Els	279	5	playoff	$320,000	Loren Roberts Colin Montgomerie
25. Canon Greater Hartford Open	TPC at River Highlands Cromwell, CT	David Frost	268	12	1	$216,000	Greg Norman
26. Motorola Western Open	Cog Hill Golf & Country Club Dubsdread Course Lemont, IL	Nick Price (3)	277	11	1	$216,000	Greg Kraft

1994 PGA TOUR TOURNAMENT SUMMARY

*Denotes first time winner

	TOURNAMENT	COURSE	WINNER	SCORE	UNDER PAR	MARGIN	MONEY	RUNNERS-UP
27.	Anheuser Busch Golf Classic	Kingsmill Golf Club Williamsburg, VA	Mark McCumber	267	17	3	$198,000	Glen Day
28.	Deposit Guaranty Golf Classic	Annandale Golf Club Madison, MS	Brian Henninger (event shortened to 36 holes due to flooded course)	135	9	playoff	$126,000	Mike Sullivan
29.	New England Classic	Pleasant Valley Country Club Sutton, MA	Kenny Perry	268	16	1	$180,000	David Feherty
30.	Federal Express St. Jude Classic	TPC at Southwind Memphis, TN	*Dicky Pride	267	17	playoff	$225,000	Hal Sutton Gene Sauers
31.	Buick Open	Warwick Hills Country Club Grand Blanc, MI	Fred Couples	270	18	2	$198,000	Corey Pavin
32.	PGA Championship	Southern Hills Country Club Tulsa, OK	Nick Price (4)	269	11	6	$310,000	Corey Pavin
33.	The Sprint International	Castle Pines Golf Club Castle Rock, CO	*Steve Lowery	35 pts	-	playoff	$252,000	Rick Fehr
34.	NEC World Series of Golf	Firestone Country Club North Course Akron, OH	Jose Maria Olazabal (2)	269	11	1	$360,000	Scott Hoch
35.	Greater Milwaukee Open	Brown Deer Park Golf Course Milwaukee, WI	Mike Springer (2)	268	16	1	$180,000	Loren Roberts
36.	Bell Canadian Open	Glen Abbey Golf Club Oakville, Ontario	Nick Price (5)	275	13	1	$234,000	Mark Calcavecchia
37.	B.C. Open	En-Joie Golf Club Endicott, NY	Mike Sullivan	266	18	4	$162,000	Jeff Sluman
38.	Hardee's Golf Classic	Oakwood Country Club Coal Valley, IL	Mark McCumber (2)	265	15	1	$180,000	Kenny Perry
39.	Buick Southern Open	Callaway Gardens Mountain View Course Pine Mountain, GA	Steve Elkington (event shortened to 54 holes due to rain and high winds)	200	16	5	$144,000	Steve Rintoul
40.	Walt Disney World/ Oldsmobile Golf Classic	Magnolia Golf Club Palm Golf Club, Eagle Pines Golf Club Lake Buena Vista, FL	Rick Fehr	269	19	2	$198,000	Craig Stadler Fuzzy Zoeller
41.	Texas Open	Oak Hills Country Club San Antonio, TX	*Bob Estes	265	19	1	$180,000	Gil Morgan
42.	Las Vegas Invitational	Las Vegas Country Club Las Vegas Hilton Country Club TPC at Summerlin Las Vegas, NV	Bruce Lietzke	332	27	1	$270,000	Robert Gamez
43.	THE TOUR Championship	The Olympic Club San Francisco, CA	Mark McCumber (3)	274	10	playoff	$540,000	Fuzzy Zoeller

(END OF OFFICIAL SEASON)

	TOURNAMENT	COURSE	WINNER	SCORE	UNDER PAR	MARGIN	MONEY	RUNNERS-UP
44.	Lincoln-Mercury Kapalua International	Kapalua Resort (Plantation Course, Bay Course) Kapalua, Maui, HI	Fred Couples	279	11	2	$180,000	Bob Gilder
45.	World Cup of Golf	Hyatt Dorado Beach Resort (East Course) Dorado, PR	United States (Fred Couples/ Davis Love III)	536	40	14	$150,000 each	Zimbabwe
46.	Franklin Funds Shark Shootout	Sherwood CC Thousand Oaks, CA	Fred Couples/ Brad Faxon	190	26	2	$150,000 each	Mark O'Meara/ Curtis Strange
47.	The Skins Game	Bighorn GC Palm Desert, CA	Tom Watson	–	–	–	$210,000	Fred Couples
48.	JCPenney Classic	Innisbrook Hilton Resort Tarpon Springs, FL	Brad Bryant/ Marta Figueras-Dotti	262	22	Playoff	$150,000 each	Robert Gamez/ Helen Alfredsson
49.	Diners Club Matches	PGA West Nicklaus Resort Course LaQuinta, CA	Jeff Maggert/ Jim McGovern			(19 holes)	$125,000 each	Lee Janzen/ Rocco Mediate

1994 PGA TOUR STATISTICAL LEADERS

(minimum of 50 rounds)

DRIVING DISTANCE

#	NAME	RDS.	YARDS
1.	DAVIS LOVE III	91	283.8
2.	DENNIS PAULSON	77	283.0
3.	FRED COUPLES	51	279.9
4.	TODD BARRANGER	67	279.1
5.	ROBERT GAMEZ	76	278.4
6.	KELLY GIBSON	93	277.5
6.	NICK PRICE	60	277.5
8.	BILL GLASSON	75	277.1
8.	GREG NORMAN	63	277.1
10.	MIKE HEINEN	79	275.3
11.	JOHN HUSTON	84	275.0
12.	JIM GALLAGHER, JR.	83	274.5
12.	VIJAY SINGH	67	274.5
14.	BRETT OGLE	58	273.9
15.	PHIL MICKELSON	65	273.7
16.	MIKE SPRINGER	84	273.2
17.	MARK CALCAVECCHIA	84	273.1
17.	NEAL LANCASTER	95	273.1
17.	CRAIG STADLER	69	273.1
20.	JOHN ADAMS	82	272.9
21.	CURT BYRUM	81	272.6
22.	STEVE LAMONTAGNE	79	272.3
23.	MIKE STANDLY	93	272.0
24.	ED HUMENIK	89	271.8
25.	DUFFY WALDORF	80	271.4

DRIVING ACCURACY

#	NAME	RDS.	PCT.
1.	DAVID EDWARDS	82	81.6
2.	FRED FUNK	105	80.1
3.	JOHN MAHAFFEY	75	79.0
3.	DOUG TEWELL	84	79.0
5.	LARRY MIZE	75	78.8
6.	HALE IRWIN	74	78.0
7.	DAVID OGRIN	90	77.9
8.	BRUCE FLEISHER	82	77.7
8.	TOM GARNER	56	77.7
10.	D.A. WEIBRING	63	77.6
11.	FULTON ALLEM	82	77.5
12.	DILLARD PRUITT	88	77.3
12.	HAL SUTTON	97	77.3
14.	GIL MORGAN	65	77.2
15.	CLARK DENNIS	98	76.9
15.	COREY PAVIN	68	76.9
17.	BRUCE LIETZKE	59	76.7
18.	BOB LOHR	88	76.2
19.	MARK CARNEVALE	86	76.0
20.	JOHN INMAN	101	75.8
21.	LENNIE CLEMENTS	84	75.6
21.	JOHN COOK	80	75.6
21.	PETER JACOBSEN	68	75.6
21.	LOREN ROBERTS	77	75.6
25.	FUZZY ZOELLER	73	75.5

GREENS IN REGULATION

#	NAME	RDS.	PCT.
1.	BILL GLASSON	75	73.0
2.	FUZZY ZOELLER	73	72.8
3.	HAL SUTTON	97	72.2
4.	MARK MCCUMBER	76	71.3
5.	DAN FORSMAN	68	71.2
6.	DAVE BARR	94	70.9
6.	BOB ESTES	95	70.9
8.	TOM LEHMAN	81	70.8
9.	LENNIE CLEMENTS	84	70.6
9.	CLARK DENNIS	98	70.6
9.	JOEY SINDELAR	65	70.6
12.	FRED COUPLES	51	70.5
13.	PETER JACOBSEN	68	70.4
13.	BRUCE LIETZKE	59	70.4
15.	DONNIE HAMMOND	83	70.3
15.	GIL MORGAN	65	70.3
17.	BRAD BRYANT	109	70.2
18.	JOHN COOK	80	70.1
19.	SCOTT HOCH	94	70.0
20.	TOM KITE	78	69.9
21.	NICK PRICE	60	69.6
22.	5 TIED WITH		69.2

PUTTING LEADERS

#	NAME	RDS.	AVG.
1.	LOREN ROBERTS	77	1.737
2.	BEN CRENSHAW	86	1.739
3.	DAVID FROST	78	1.742
4.	PHIL MICKELSON	65	1.744
4.	MARK WURTZ	81	1.744
6.	GREG NORMAN	63	1.747
7.	COREY PAVIN	68	1.749
8.	BLAINE MCCALLISTER	95	1.750
9.	GREG KRAFT	86	1.751
10.	STEVE STRICKER	93	1.752
11.	JOHN HUSTON	84	1.757
12.	HALE IRWIN	74	1.759
13.	JAY DON BLAKE	87	1.761
14.	LENNIE CLEMENTS	84	1.763
14.	GIL MORGAN	65	1.763
16.	MARK CALCAVECCHIA	84	1.764
17.	WAYNE GRADY	56	1.765
17.	KENNY PERRY	99	1.765
19.	CHIP BECK	86	1.766
19.	BRIAN HENNINGER	69	1.766
19.	TOM LEHMAN	81	1.766
19.	BRUCE LIETZKE	59	1.766
19.	LARRY MIZE	75	1.766
24.	SCOTT VERPLANK	64	1.767
25.	JOHN FLANNERY	94	1.768

1994 PGA TOUR Statistical Leaders *(cont'd.)*

(minimum of 50 rounds)

TOTAL DRIVING

	NAME	TOTAL
1.	NICK PRICE	43
2.	BILL GLASSON	48
3.	GREG NORMAN	51
4.	FUZZY ZOELLER	54
5.	TOM WATSON	63
6.	GIL MORGAN	67
7.	DAN FORSMAN	75
8.	HAL SUTTON	77
9.	MIKE HEINEN	80
9.	BRUCE LIETZKE	80
11.	ED HUMENIK	82
12.	ROBERT GAMEZ	87
13.	JEFF MAGGERT	92
14.	MARK McCUMBER	93
15.	JOHN HUSTON	98
16.	CRAIG STADLER	99
17.	DONNIE HAMMOND	100
17.	PETER JACOBSEN	100
19.	STEVE LAMONTAGNE	101
20.	TOM LEHMAN	102
21.	CLARK DENNIS	104
22.	TOM PURTZER	112
23.	TOM KITE	120
24.	BRETT OGLE	120
25.	2 TIED WITH	121

EAGLE LEADERS

	NAME	RDS.	TOTAL
1.	DAVIS LOVE III	91	18
2.	MARK BROOKS	112	15
3.	GUY BOROS	93	14
4.	ROBIN FREEMAN	91	13
4.	MIKE STANDLY	93	13
6.	ROBERT GAMEZ	76	12
7.	GLEN DAY	94	11
7.	JAY DELSING	88	11
7.	KELLY GIBSON	93	11
7.	TOM LEHMAN	81	11
11.	MARK CALCAVECCHIA	84	10
11.	GARY HALLBERG	78	10
11.	NOLAN HENKE	79	10
11.	MIKE HULBERT	103	10
11.	MIKE SPRINGER	84	10
11.	CRAIG STADLER	69	10
17.	11 TIED WITH		9

BIRDIE LEADERS

	NAME	RDS.	TOTAL
1.	BRAD BRYANT	109	397
2.	JAY HAAS	102	374
3.	MARK BROOKS	112	372
4.	TED TRYBA	108	365
5.	HAL SUTTON	97	360
6.	STEVE STRICKER	93	358
7.	CLARK DENNIS	98	357
8.	KENNY PERRY	99	355
9.	BOB ESTES	95	352
10.	PAUL GOYDOS	104	346
11.	JOHN HUSTON	84	345
12.	FRED FUNK	105	343
13.	JAY DON BLAKE	87	339
14.	DAVE RUMMELLS	100	338
15.	BLAINE MCCALLISTER	95	337
16.	JEFF MAGGERT	88	334
17.	GUY BOROS	93	333
18.	GLEN DAY	94	329
19.	BRAD FAXON	92	327
19.	SCOTT HOCH	94	327
19.	STEVE LOWERY	94	327
22.	MIKE HULBERT	103	326
22.	DAVIS LOVE III	91	326
24.	ROBIN FREEMAN	91	323
25.	KELLY GIBSON	93	322

SAND SAVES

	NAME	RDS.	PCT.
1.	COREY PAVIN	68	65.4
2.	BEN CRENSHAW	86	63.1
3.	STAN UTLEY	73	62.8
4.	KIRK TRIPLETT	90	61.6
5.	BRIAN KAMM	94	61.4
6.	BOB ESTES	95	60.4
6.	PAYNE STEWART	76	60.4
8.	SCOTT HOCH	94	60.3
8.	RICHARD ZOKOL	74	60.3
10.	JOHN INMAN	101	59.9
11.	BILLY ANDRADE	87	59.3
12.	MICHAEL BRADLEY	89	59.2
13.	NICK PRICE	60	58.2
13.	WILLIE WOOD	77	58.2
15.	BRIAN HENNINGER	69	58.1
15.	JOEY SINDELAR	65	58.1
17.	MIKE HULBERT	103	57.8
17.	LOREN ROBERTS	77	57.8
19.	BILL BRITTON	68	57.7
19.	GENE SAUERS	82	57.7
21.	ROB BOLDT	59	57.6
21.	MIKE SULLIVAN	71	57.6
23.	CRAIG PARRY	62	57.5
24.	PAUL GOYDOS	104	57.4
25.	GREG NORMAN	63	57.3

1994 PGA TOUR Statistical Leaders *(cont'd.)*

(minimum of 50 rounds)

SCORING AVERAGE

	NAME	RDS.	AVG.
1.	GREG NORMAN	63	68.81
2.	FRED COUPLES	51	69.28
3.	NICK PRICE	60	69.39
4.	TOM LEHMAN	81	69.46
5.	MARK MCCUMBER	76	69.56
6.	LOREN ROBERTS	77	69.61
7.	COREY PAVIN	68	69.63
8.	PHIL MICKELSON	65	69.66
9.	HALE IRWIN	74	69.72
10.	BOB ESTES	95	69.78
11.	DAVID FROST	78	69.85
11.	TOM WATSON	54	69.85
13.	FUZZY ZOELLER	73	69.89
14.	BILL GLASSON	75	69.93
15.	GIL MORGAN	65	69.96
16.	LENNIE CLEMENTS	84	69.98
17.	BRUCE LIETZKE	59	70.04
18.	TOM KITE	78	70.07
19.	SCOTT HOCH	94	70.10
20.	KIRK TRIPLETT	90	70.12
21.	BRAD FAXON	92	70.15
22.	JOHN HUSTON	84	70.17
23.	SCOTT VERPLANK	64	70.22
24.	DAVID EDWARDS	82	70.23
25.	MARK CALCAVECCHIA	84	70.25

ALL AROUND

	NAME	TOTAL
1.	BOB ESTES	227
2.	JOHN HUSTON	250
3.	BILL GLASSON	257
4.	GREG NORMAN	293
5.	NICK PRICE	298
6.	TOM LEHMAN	312
7.	LENNIE CLEMENTS	332
8.	JAY HAAS	345
9.	DONNIE HAMMOND	351
10.	KIRK TRIPLETT	359
11.	MARK CALCAVECCHIA	364
12.	SCOTT HOCH	366
13.	FUZZY ZOELLER	370
14.	GUY BOROS	374
15.	CRAIG STADLER	377
16.	JEFF MAGGERT	384
17.	BRAD BRYANT	393
17.	STEVE STRICKER	393
19.	PHIL MICKELSON	397
20.	LOREN ROBERTS	409
21.	GIL MORGAN	423
22.	GLEN DAY	425
23.	CLARK DENNIS	439
24.	BLAINE MCCALLISTER	449
25.	DAVIS LOVE III	451

1994 PGA TOUR STATISTICAL HIGH/LOWS

Those with 50 rounds or more based on 179 ranked players.

STATISTICAL CATEGORY	HIGHEST	AVERAGE	LOWEST
Driving Distance	283.8	261.8	237.9
Driving Accuracy	81.6%	69.2%	52.3%
Greens in Regulation	73.0%	65.9%	55.8%
Putting	1.737	1.794	1.891
Par Breakers	23.3%	18.8%	13.4%
Eagles	18	5	0
Birdies	397	269	133
Scoring Average	68.81	71.15	74.31
Sand Saves	65.4%	51.5%	37.1%

YEAR BY YEAR STATISTICAL LEADERS

SCORING AVERAGE
1980	Lee Trevino	69.73
1981	Tom Kite	69.80
1982	Tom Kite	70.21
1983	Raymond Floyd	70.61
1984	Calvin Peete	70.56
1985	Don Pooley	70.36
1986	Scott Hoch	70.08
1987	David Frost	70.09
1988	Greg Norman	69.38
1989	Payne Stewart	*69.485
1990	Greg Norman	69.10
1991	Fred Couples	69.59
1992	Fred Couples	69.38
1993	Greg Norman	68.90
1994	Greg Norman	68.81

DRIVING DISTANCE
1980	Dan Pohl	274.3
1981	Dan Pohl	280.1
1982	Bill Calfee	275.3
1983	John McComish	277.4
1984	Bill Glasson	276.5
1985	Andy Bean	278.2
1986	Davis Love III	285.7
1987	John McComish	283.9
1988	Steve Thomas	284.6
1989	Ed Humenik	280.9
1990	Tom Purtzer	279.6
1991	John Daly	288.9
1992	John Daly	283.4
1993	John Daly	288.9
1994	Davis Love III	283.8

DRIVING ACCURACY
1980	Mike Reid	79.5%
1981	Calvin Peete	81.9
1982	Calvin Peete	84.6
1983	Calvin Peete	81.3
1984	Calvin Peete	77.5
1985	Calvin Peete	80.6
1986	Calvin Peete	81.7
1987	Calvin Peete	83.0
1988	Calvin Peete	82.5
1989	Calvin Peete	82.6
1990	Calvin Peete	83.7
1991	Hale Irwin	78.3
1992	Doug Tewell	82.3
1993	Doug Tewell	82.5
1994	David Edwards	81.6

GREENS IN REGULATION
1980	Jack Nicklaus	72.1%
1981	Calvin Peete	73.1
1982	Calvin Peete	72.4
1983	Calvin Peete	71.4
1984	Andy Bean	72.1
1985	John Mahaffey	71.9
1986	John Mahaffey	72.0
1987	Gil Morgan	73.3
1988	John Adams	73.9
1989	Bruce Lietzke	72.6
1990	Doug Tewell	70.9
1991	Bruce Lietzke	73.3
1992	Tim Simpson	74.0
1993	Fuzzy Zoeller	73.6
1994	Bill Glasson	73.0

PUTTING
1980	Jerry Pate	28.81
1981	Alan Tapie	28.70
1982	Ben Crenshaw	28.65
1983	Morris Hatalsky	27.96
1984	Gary McCord	28.57
1985	Craig Stadler	*28.627
1986	Greg Norman	1.736
1987	Ben Crenshaw	1.743
1988	Don Pooley	1.729
1989	Steve Jones	1.734
1990	Larry Rinker	*1.7467
1991	Jay Don Blake	*1.7326
1992	Mark O'Meara	1.731
1993	David Frost	1.739
1994	Loren Roberts	1.737

ALL-AROUND
1987	Dan Pohl	170
1988	Payne Stewart	170
1989	Paul Azinger	250
1990	Paul Azinger	162
1991	Scott Hoch	283
1992	Fred Couples	256
1993	Gil Morgan	252
1994	Bob Estes	227

SAND SAVES
1980	Bob Eastwood	65.4%
1981	Tom Watson	60.1
1982	Isao Aoki	60.2
1983	Isao Aoki	62.3
1984	Peter Oosterhuis	64.7
1985	Tom Purtzer	60.8
1986	Paul Azinger	63.8
1987	Paul Azinger	63.2
1988	Greg Powers	63.5
1989	Mike Sullivan	66.0
1990	Paul Azinger	67.2
1991	Ben Crenshaw	64.9
1992	Mitch Adcock	66.9
1993	Ken Green	64.4
1994	Corey Pavin	65.4

PAR BREAKERS (category discontinued)
1980	Tom Watson	.213
1981	Bruce Lietzke	.225
1982	Tom Kite	*.2154
1983	Tom Watson	.211
1984	Craig Stadler	.220
1985	Craig Stadler	.218
1986	Greg Norman	.248
1987	Mark Calcavecchia	.221
1988	Ken Green	.236
1989	Greg Norman	.224
1990	Greg Norman	.219

TOTAL DRIVING
1991	Bruce Lietzke	42
1992	Bruce Lietzke	50
1993	Greg Norman	41
1994	Nick Price	43

EAGLES
1980	Dave Eichelberger	16
1981	Bruce Lietzke	12
1982	Tom Weiskopf	10
	J.C. Snead	10
	Andy Bean	10
1983	Chip Beck	15
1984	Gary Hallberg	15
1985	Larry Rinker	14
1986	Joey Sindelar	16
1987	Phil Blackmar	20
1988	Ken Green	21
1989	Lon Hinkle	14
	Duffy Waldorf	14
1990	Paul Azinger	14
1991	Andy Bean	15
	John Huston	15
1992	Dan Forsman	18
1993	Davis Love III	15
1994	Davis Love III	18

BIRDIES
1980	Andy Bean	388
1981	Vance Heafner	388
1982	Andy Bean	392
1983	Hal Sutton	399
1984	Mark O'Meara	419
1985	Joey Sindelar	411
1986	Joey Sindelar	415
1987	Dan Forsman	409
1988	Dan Forsman	465
1989	Ted Schulz	415
1990	Mike Donald	401
1991	Scott Hoch	446
1992	Jeff Sluman	417
1993	John Huston	426
1994	Brad Bryant	397

had to be carried a decimal further to determine winner

RANK	GOLF COURSE	HOLE #	PAR	AVG. SCORE	AVG. OVER PAR	EAGLES	BIRDIES	PARS	BOGEYS	DOUBLE BOGEYS	TRIPLE BOGEY+	TOURNAMENT NAME
1	ARNOLD PALMER COURSE	9	4	4.500	.500		5	76	32	12	3	Bob Hope Chrysler Classic
2	OAKMONT CC	10	4	4.474	.474	3	21	224	156	36	3	U.S. Open
3	WESTCHESTER CC	12	4	4.463	.463	1	22	226	168	27	3	Buick Classic
4	ENGLISH TURN G&CC	18	4	4.440	.440		33	203	164	20	5	Freeport-McMoRan Classic
5	AUGUSTA NATIONAL GC	12	3	3.434	.434		16	157	74	20	5	The Masters
6	OAKMONT CC	1	4	4.433	.433		29	226	157	29	2	U.S. Open
7	PEBBLE BCH GOLF LINKS	9	4	4.426	.426		13	129	98	11		AT&T Pebble Beach National Pro-Am
8	SOUTHERN HILLS CC	2	4	4.423	.423	2	30	233	154	33	2	PGA Championship
9	RIVIERA CC	18	4	4.396	.396		27	227	166	17		Nissan Los Angeles Open
10	TUCSON NAT'L GOLF	10	4	4.389	.389		18	162	102	16		Northern Telecom Open
10	RIVIERA CC	2	4	4.389	.389	1	18	253	142	21	2	Nissan Los Angeles Open
12	AUGUSTA NATIONAL GC	4	3	3.386	.386		9	159	95	8	1	The Masters
13	SOUTHERN HILLS CC	18	4	4.385	.385	1	14	272	147	17	3	PGA Championship
14	OAKMONT CC	16	3	3.372	.372		26	241	161	15		U.S. Open
15	SPYGLASS HILL GC	16	4	4.369	.369		9	109	53	5	3	AT&T Pebble Beach National Pro-Am
16	OAKMONT CC	15	4	4.366	.366		29	249	143	18	4	U.S. Open
17	EN-JOIE GC	15	4	4.365	.365		30	266	142	19	6	B.C. Open
18	ANNANDALE GC	4	4	4.363	.363		16	152	103	7		Deposit Guaranty Classic
19	OAKMONT CC	18	4	4.359	.359		47	218	154	20	4	U.S. Open
20	DORAL RESORT & CC	13	3	3.356	.356		14	261	156	7		Doral-Ryder Open
21	STARR PASS GC	12	4	4.355	.355		20	78	45	7	5	Northern Telecom Open
22	WESTCHESTER CC	15	4	4.349	.349		25	262	142	16	2	Buick Classic
23	RIVIERA CC	4	3	3.343	.343		17	263	149	6	2	Nissan Los Angeles Open
24	TORREY PINES - SOUTH	7	4	4.335	.335		20	185	97	13	1	Buick Invitational of California
25	SPYGLASS HILL GC	8	4	4.330	.330		16	97	58	7	1	AT&T Pebble Beach National Pro-Am
25	FOREST OAKS CC	14	4	4.330	.330	1	37	244	167	12		Kmart Greater Greensboro Open
27	GLEN ABBEY GC	14	4	4.329	.329		34	267	136	25		Canadian Open
28	WESTCHESTER CC	11	4	4.327	.327		21	282	122	21	1	Buick Classic
29	DORAL RESORT & CC	4	3	3.326	.326		23	274	120	17	4	Doral-Ryder Open
30	POPPY HILLS	13	4	4.324	.324		6	122	42	6	3	AT&T Pebble Beach National Pro-Am
31	OAKMONT CC	8	3	3.323	.323		29	256	145	12	1	U.S. Open
32	WESTON HILLS CC	15	4	4.322	.322		40	268	102	30	7	Honda Classic
33	ARNOLD PALMER COURSE	10	4	4.320	.320		9	76	37	5	1	Bob Hope Chrysler Classic
33	TPC AT AVENEL	12	4	4.320	.320		42	266	127	21	6	Kemper Open
33	ANNANDALE GC	14	4	4.320	.320		17	170	79	10	2	Deposit Guaranty Classic
36	SPYGLASS HILL GC	1	5	5.318	.318		10	110	51	8		AT&T Pebble Beach National Pro-Am
36	WESTCHESTER CC	8	4	4.318	.318		36	259	129	20	3	Buick Classic
38	TPC AT AVENEL	15	4	4.314	.314		35	265	145	16	1	Kemper Open
39	MUIRFIELD VILLAGE GC	18	4	4.307	.307		39	204	110	19	2	The Memorial
40	MUIRFIELD VILLAGE GC	2	4	4.302	.302		33	221	99	17	4	The Memorial
41	RIVIERA CC	9	4	4.300	.300	1	36	257	118	24	1	Nissan Los Angeles Open
42	EAGLE PINES	5	4	4.298	.298		8	80	40	2	1	Walt Disney World/Oldsmobile Classic
43	PEBBLE BCH GOLF LINKS	8	4	4.295	.295		22	142	79	7	1	AT&T Pebble Beach National Pro-Am
43	WESTON HILLS CC	5	3	3.295	.295		39	281	95	23	9	Honda Classic
45	FOREST OAKS CC	4	3	3.293	.293		34	273	140	13	1	Kmart Greater Greensboro Open
46	ENGLISH TURN G&CC	14	4	4.292	.292		31	251	132	10	1	Freeport-McMoRan Classic
47	PEBBLE BCH GOLF LINKS	10	4	4.291	.291		17	152	75	6	1	AT&T Pebble Beach National Pro-Am
48	COTTONWOOD VALLEY GC	15	4	4.289	.289		12	86	47	4		GTE Byron Nelson Classic
48	SOUTHERN HILLS CC	14	3	3.289	.289		40	267	125	20	2	PGA Championship
48	FIRESTONE CC (North)	18	4	4.289	.289		22	118	34	17	3	NEC World Series of Golf
51	COG HILL G&CC	18	4	4.286	.286		45	288	120	26	3	Motorola Western Open
51	GLEN ABBEY GC	17	4	4.286	.286		45	264	133	16	4	Canadian Open

Fuzzy Zoeller had five runnerup finishes in 1994, topping his previous best earnings year by nearly $600,000 with a season total of $1,016,804.

ALL-TIME PGA TOUR RECORDS

All information based on official PGA TOUR cosponsored or approved events

SCORING RECORDS

72 holes:

257— (60-68-64-65) by **Mike Souchak**, at Brackenridge Park Golf Course, San Antonio, TX, in 1955 Texas Open (27-under-par).

258— (65-64-65-64) by **Donnie Hammond**, at Oak Hills CC, San Antonio, TX, in 1989 Texas Open Presented by Nabisco (22-under-par).

259— (62-68-63-66) by **Byron Nelson**, at Broadmoor Golf Club. Seattle, WA, in 1945 Seattle Open (21-under-par).

259— (70-63-63-63) by **Chandler Harper,** at Brackenridge Park Golf Course, San Antonio, TX, in 1954 Texas Open (25-under-par).

259— (63-64-66-66) by **Tim Norris**, at Wethersfield CC, Hartford, CT, in 1982 Sammy Davis Greater Hartford Open (25-under-par).

259— (64-63-66-66) by **Corey Pavin**, at Oak Hills CC, San Antonio, TX, in 1988 Texas Open Presented by Nabisco (21-under-par).

259—(68-63-64-64) by **David Frost**, at Oakwood CC, Coal Valley, IL, in 1993 Hardee's Golf Classic (21-under-par).

90 holes:

325— (67-67-64-65-62) by **Tom Kite,** at four courses, Palm Springs, CA, in the 1993 Bob Hope Chrysler Classic (35-under-par).

329— (69-65-67-62-66) by **Andrew Magee**, at three courses, Las Vegas, NV, in the 1991 Las Vegas Invitational (31-under-par).

329— (70-64-65-64-66) by **D.A. Weibring**, at three courses, Las Vegas, NV, in the 1991 Las Vegas Invitational (31-under-par).

Most shots under par:
72 holes:

27— **Mike Souchak** in winning the 1955 Texas Open with 257.

27— **Ben Hogan** in winning the 1945 Portland Invitational with 261.

26— **Gay Brewer** in winning the 1967 Pensacola Open with 262.

26— **Robert Wrenn** in winning the 1987 Buick Open with 262.

26— **Chip Beck** in winning the 1988 USF&G Classic with 262.

26— **John Huston** in winning the 1992 Walt Disney World/Oldsmobile Classic with 262.

90 holes:

35— **Tom Kite** in winning the 1993 Bob Hope Chrysler Classic with 325.

31— **Andrew Magee** in winning the 1991 Las Vegas Invitational with 329.

31— **D.A. Weibring** in finishing second in the 1991 Las Vegas Invitational with 329 (lost playoff).

54 holes:
Opening rounds:

191—(66-64-61) by **Gay Brewer,** at Pensacola CC, Pensacola, FL, in winning 1967 Pensacola Open (25-under-par).

192— (60-68-64) by **Mike Souchak**, at Brackenridge Park Golf Course. San Antonio, TX, in 1955 Texas Open (21-under-par).

192— (64-63-65) by **Bob Gilder**, at Westchester CC, Harrison, NY, in 1982 Manufacturers Hanover Westchester Classic (18-under-par).

Consecutive rounds

189—(63-63-63) by **Chandler Harper** in the last three rounds of the 1954 Texas Open at Brackenridge (24-under-par).

36 holes:
Opening rounds

126— (64-62) by **Tommy Bolt,** at Cavalier Yacht & Country Club, Virginia Beach, VA, in 1954Virginia Beach Open (12-under-par).

126— (64-62) by **Paul Azinger**, at Oak Hills CC, San Antonio, TX, in 1989 Texas Open Presented by Nabisco (14-under-par).

ALL-TIME PGA TOUR RECORDS

All information based on official PGA TOUR cosponsored or approved events.

Consecutive rounds
  125— (64-61) by **Gay Brewer** in the middle rounds of the 1967 Pensacola Open at
    Pensacola CC, Pensacola, FL (19-under-par).
  125— (63-62) by **Ron Streck** in the last two rounds of the 1978 Texas Open at Oak Hills
    Country Club, San Antonio, TX (15-under-par).
  125— (62-63) by **Blaine McCallister** in the middle two rounds of the 1988 Hardee's Golf
    Classic at Oakwood CC, Coal Valley, IL (15-under-par).

18 holes:
  59— by **Al Geiberger**, at Colonial Country Club, Memphis, TN, in second round of 1977
    Memphis Classic (13-under-par).
  59— by **Chip Beck**, at Sunrise Golf Club, Las Vegas, NV, in third round of 1991 Las
    Vegas Invitational (13-under-par).
  60— by **Al Brosch**, at Brackenridge Park Golf Course, San Antonio, TX, in third round of
    1951 Texas Open (11-under-par).
  60— by **Bill Nary**, at El Paso Country Club, El Paso, TX, in third round of 1952 El Paso
    Open (11-under-par).
  60— by **Ted Kroll**, at Brackenridge Park Golf Course, San Antonio, TX, in third round of
    1954 Texas Open (11-under-par).
  60— by **Wally Ulrich**, at Cavalier Yacht and Country Club, Virginia Beach, VA, in second
    round of 1954 Virginia Beach Open (9-under-par).
  60— by **Tommy Bolt**, at Wethersfield Country Club, Hartford, CT, in second round of 1954
    Insurance City Open (11-under-par).
  60— by **Mike Souchak** at Brackenridge Park Golf Course, San Antonio, TX, in first round
    of 1955 Texas Open (11-under-par).
  60— by **Sam Snead**, at Glen Lakes Country Club, Dallas, TX, in second round of 1957
    Dallas Open (11-under-par).
  60— by **David Frost**, at Randolph Park Golf Course, Tucson, AZ, in second round of
    1990 Northern Telecom Tucson Open (12-under-par).
  60— by **Davis Love III**, at Waialae Country Club, Honolulu, HI, in second round of 1994
    United Airlines Hawaiian Open.

9 holes:
  27— by **Mike Souchak**, at Brackenridge Park Golf Course, San Antonio, TX, on par-35
    second nine of first round in 1955 Texas Open.
  27— by **Andy North** at En-Joie Golf Club, Endicott, NY, on par-34 second nine of first
    round in 1975 B.C. Open.

Best Vardon Trophy scoring average:
Non-adjusted:
  69.23—**Sam Snead** in 1950 (6646 strokes, 96 rounds).
  69.30—**Ben Hogan** in 1948 (5267 strokes, 76 rounds).
  69.37—**Sam Snead** in 1949 (5064 strokes, 73 rounds).
Adjusted (since 1988):
  68.81—**Greg Norman** in 1994.
  69.10—**Greg Norman** in 1990.
  69.11—**Nick Price** in 1993.

Most consecutive rounds under 70:
  19— **Byron Nelson** in 1945.

Most birdies in a row:
  8— **Bob Goalby** at Pasadena Golf Club, St. Petersburg FL, during fourth round of 1961
    St. Petersburg Open.
    Fuzzy Zoeller, at Oakwood Country Club, Coal Valley, IL, during first round of 1976
    Quad Cities Open.
    Dewey Arnette, Warwick Hills GC, Grand Blanc, MI, during first round of the 1987
    Buick Open.

Best birdie-eagle streak:
  7— **Al Geiberger**, 6 birdies and 1 eagle, at Colonial Country Club, Memphis, TN,
    during second round of 1977 Danny Thomas Memphis Classic.
    Webb Heintzelman, 5 birdies, eagle and 1 birdie, in 1989 Las Vegas
    Invitational.

ALL-TIME PGA TOUR RECORDS

All information based on official PGA TOUR cosponsored or approved events

Most birdies in a row to win:
   5— by **Jack Nicklaus** to win 1978 Jackie Gleason Inverrary Classic (last 5 holes).

VICTORY RECORDS

Most victories during career (PGA TOUR cosponsored and/or approved tournaments only):
   81— **Sam Snead**
   70— **Jack Nicklaus**
   63— **Ben Hogan**
   60— **Arnold Palmer**
   52— **Byron Nelson**
   51— **Billy Casper**

Most consecutive years winning at least one tournament:
   17— **Jack Nicklaus** (1962-78)
   17— **Arnold Palmer** (1955-71)
   16— **Billy Casper** (1956-71)

Most consecutive victories:
   11— **Byron Nelson**, from Miami Four Ball March 8-11, 1945, through Canadian Open,
        August 2-4, 1945. Tournament, site, dates, score, purse-Miami Four Ball, Miami
        Springs Course, Miami, FL, March 8-11, won 8-6, $1,500; Charlotte Open, Myers
        Park Golf Club, Charlotte, NC, March 16-19, 272, $2000; Greensboro Open,
        Starmount Country Club, Greensboro, NC, March 23-25, 271, $1000; Durham Open,
        Hope Valley Country Club, Durham, NC, March 30-April 1, 276, $1000; Atlanta
        Open, Capital City Course, Atlanta, GA, April 5-8, 263, $2000; Montreal Open,
        Islemere Golf and Country Club, Montreal, Que., June 7-10, 268, $2000; Philadel-
        phia Inquirer Invitational, Llanerch Country Club, Phila., PA, June 14-17, 269, $3000;
        Chicago Victory National Open, Calumet Country Club, Chicago, IL, June 29-July 1,
        275, $2000; PGA Championship, Moraine Country Club, Dayton, OH, July 9-15,4-3,
        $3750; Tam O'Shanter Open, Tam O'Shanter Country Club, Chicago, IL, July 26-29
        269, $10,000; Canadian Open,Thornhill Country Club, Toronto, Ont., August 2-4,
        280, $2000; Winnings for streak $30,250. NOTE: Nelson won a 12th event in Spring
        Lake, NJ which is not accounted as official as its $2,500 purse was below the PGA
        $3000 minimum.
   4— **Jackie Burke, Jr.**, in 1952: From February 14 to March 9-Texas Open, Houston
        Open, Baton Rouge Open, St. Petersburg Open.
   3— **Byron Nelson** in 1944, 1945-46.
        Sam Snead in 1945.
        Ben Hogan in 1946.
        Bobby Locke in 1947.
        Jim Ferrier in 1951.
        Billy Casper in 1960.
        Anold Palmer in 1960, 1962.
        Johnny Miller in 1974.
        Hubert Green in 1976.
        Gary Player in 1978.
        Tom Watson in 1980.
        Nick Price in 1993.

Most victories in a single event:
   8— **Sam Snead**, Greater Greensboro Open: 1938, 1946, 1949, 1950, 1955, 1956, 1960,
        and 1965.
   6— **Sam Snead**, Miami Open: 1937, 1939, 1946, 1950, 1951, and 1955.
   6— **Jack Nicklaus**, Masters: 1963, 1965, 1966, 1972, 1975 and 1986.
   5— **Walter Hagen**, PGA Championship:1921, 1924 1925, 1926, and 1927.
        Ben Hogan Colonial NIT: 1946 1947, 1952, 1953, and 1959.
        Arnold Palmer, Bob Hope Desert Classic: 1960, 1962, 1968, 1971, and 1973.
        Jack Nicklaus Tournament of Champions: 1963, 1964, 1971, 1973, and 1977.
        Jack Nicklaus, PGA Championship: 1963, 1971, 1973, 1975, and 1980.
        Walter Hagen, Western Open: 1916, 1921, 1926, 1927, 1932.

ALL-TIME PGA TOUR RECORDS

All information based on official PGA TOUR cosponsored or approved events.

Most consecutive victories in a single event:
- 4— **Walter Hagen**, PGA Championship, 1924-1927.
- 3— **Willie Anderson**, U.S. Open, 1903-1905.
- 3— **Henry Picard**, Tournament of the Gardens, 1935-1937.
- 3— **Ralph Guldahl**, Western Open, 1936-1938.
- 3— **Gene Littler**, Tournament of Champions, 1955-1957.
- 3— **Billy Casper**, Portland Open, 1959-1961.
- 3— **Arnold Palmer**, Texas Open, 1960-1962, Phoenix Open, 1961-1963.
- 3— **Jack Nicklaus**, Disney World Golf Classic, 1971-1973.
- 3— **Johnny Miller**, Tucson Open, 1974-1976.
- 3— **Tom Watson**, Byron Nelson Classic, 1978-1980.

Most victories in a calendar year:
- 18— **Byron Nelson** (1945)
- 13— **Ben Hogan** (1946)
- 11— **Sam Snead** (1950)
- 10— **Ben Hogan** (1948)
- 8— **Byron Nelson** (1944)
- 8— **Lloyd Mangrum** (1948)
- 8— **Arnold Palmer** (1960)
- 8— **Johnny Miller** (1974)
- 8— **Sam Snead** (1938)
- 7— 11 times

Most first-time winners during one calendar year:
- 14— 1991
- 12— 1979, 1980, 1986
- 11— 1977, 1985, 1988
- 10— 1968, 1969, 1971, 1974, 1983, 1987, 1990, 1994

Most years between victories:
- 12 years, 7 months—**Leonard Thompson** (1977-1989)
- 12 years, 5 months, 21 days— **Howard Twitty** (1980-1993)
- 11 years, 2 months, 27 days— **Bob Murphy** (1975-1986)

Most years from first victory to last:
- 29 years—**Sam Snead** (1936-1965)
- 28 years, 11 months, 22 days—**Ray Floyd** (1963-1992)
- 23 years, 9 months, 26 days—**Jack Nicklaus** (1962-1986)
- 23 years, 3 months, 8 days—**Gene Littler** (1954-1977)
- 21 years, 11 months, 20 days—**Art Wall** (1953-1975)

Youngest winners:
- **Johnny McDermott**, 19 years and 10 months, 1911 U.S. Open.
- **Gene Sarazen**, 20 years and 4 months, 1922, U.S. Open.
- **Horton Smith**, 20 years and 5 months, 1928 Oklahoma City Open.
- **Ray Floyd**, 20 years and 6 months, 1963 St. Petersburg Open.
- **Phil Mickelson**, 20 years and 6 months, 1991 Northern Telecom Open.
- **Seve Ballesteros**, 20 years and 11 months, 1978 Greater Greensboro Open.

Oldest winners:
- **Sam Snead**, 52 years,10 months and eight days, 1965 Greater Greensboro Open.
- **Art Wall**, 51 years , seven months and 10 days, 1975 Greater Milwaukee Open.
- **Jim Barnes**, 51 years three months and seven days, 1937 Long Island Open.
- **John Barnum**, 51 years, one month and five days, 1962 Cajun Classic.
- **Ray Floyd**, 49 years and 6 months, 1992 Doral-Ryder Open.

Widest winning margin: strokes
- 16— **Bobby Locke**, 1948 Chicago Victory National Championship.
- 14— **Ben Hogan**, 1945 Portland Invitational.
- **Johnny Miller**, 1975 Phoenix Open.
- 13— **Byron Nelson,** 1945 Seattle Open.
- **Gene Littler**, 1955 Tournament of Champions.
- 12— **Arnold Palmer**, 1962 Phoenix Open.
- **Jose Maria Olazabal**, 1990 NEC World Series of Golf.

ALL-TIME PGA TOUR RECORDS

All information based on official PGA TOUR cosponsored or approved events

PLAYOFF RECORDS

Longest sudden death playoffs: Holes:
- 11— **Cary Middlecoff** and **Lloyd Mangrum** were declared co-winners by mutual agreement in the 1949 Motor City Open.
- 8— **Dick Hart** defeated **Phil Rodgers** in the 1965 Azalea Open.
- 8— **Lee Elder** defeated **Lee Trevino** in the 1978 Greater Milwaukee Open.
- 8— **Dave Barr** defeated **Woody Blackburn, Dan Halldorson, Frank Conner, Victor Regalado** in the 1981Quad Cities Open.
- 8— **Bob Gilder** defeated **Rex Caldwell, Johnny Miller, Mark O'Meara** in the 1983 Phoenix Open.

Most players in a sudden-death playoff:
- 6— 1994 GTE Byron Nelson Classic—**Neal Lancaster** defeated **Curt Byrum, Mark Carnevale, David Edwards, Yoshinori Mizumaki** and **David Ogrin**.
- 5— Seven times, most recently 1993 Buick Southern Open—**John Inman** defeated **Billy Andrade, Brad Bryant, Mark Brooks** and **Bob Estes**.
- 5— Teams at the 1985 Chrysler Team Championship.

Most playoffs, season:
- 16— 1988, 1991
- 15— 1972

PUTTING RECORDS

Fewest putts, one round:
- 18— **Sam Trahan**, at Whitemarsh Valley Country Club, in final round of 1979 IVB Philadelphia Golf Classic.
- 18— **Mike McGee**, at Colonial CC, in first round of 1987 Federal Express St. Jude Classic.
- 18— **Kenny Knox**, at Harbour Town GL, in first round of 1989 MCI Heritage Classic.
- 18— **Andy North**, at Kingsmill GC, in second round of 1990 Anheuser Busch Golf Classic.
- 18— **Jim McGovern,** at TPC at Southwind, in second round of 1992 Federal Express St. Jude Classic.

Fewest putts, four rounds:
- 93— **Kenny Knox** in 1989 MCI Heritage Classic at Harbour Town Golf Links.
- 94— **Bob Tway** in 1986 MCI Heritage Classic at Harbour Town Golf Links.
- 95— **George Archer** in 1980 Sea Pines Heritage Classic at Harbour Town Golf Links.
- 95— **Lennie Clements** in 1986 PGA Championships at the Inverness Club.
- 95— **Andy Bean** in 1990 MCI Heritage Classic at Harbour Town Golf Links.
- 95— **Mark O'Meara** in 1989 GTE Byron Nelson Classic at the TPC at Las Colinas.

Fewest putts, nine holes:
- 8— **Jim Colbert**, at the Deerwood Club, on front nine of last round in 1967 Greater Jacksonville Open.
- 8— **Sam Trahan**, at Whitemarsh Valley Country Club, on the back nine of the last round in the1979 IVB Philadelphia Golf Classic.
- 8— **Bill Calfee**, at Forest Oaks CC, on the back nine of the third round of the 1980 Greater Greensboro Open.
- 8— **Kenny Knox**, at Harbour Town GL, on the back nine of the first round of the 1989 MCI Heritage Classic.
- 8— **John Inman**, at Harbour Town GL, on the front nine of the fourth round of the 1994 MCI Heritage Classic.

MISCELLANEOUS RECORDS

Most consecutive events without missing cut:
- 113—**Byron Nelson**, during the 1940s.
- 105—**Jack Nicklaus**, from Sahara Open, November 1970, through World Series of Golf, September 1976 (missed cut in 1976 World Open).
- 86— **Hale Irwin**, from Tucson Open, February 1975, through conclusion of 1978 season.
- 72— **Dow Finsterwald**, from Carling Golf Classic, September 1955, through Houston Invitational, February, 1958.

ALL-TIME PGA TOUR RECORDS

All information based on official PGA TOUR cosponsored or approved events.

Youngest pro shooting age:
    66— (4 under), **Sam Snead** (age 67), 1979 Quad Cities Open.

MONEY WINNING RECORDS

Most money won in a single season:
    $1,499,927 by **Nick Price** in 1994
    $1,478,557 by **Nick Price** in 1993
    $1,458,456 by **Paul Azinger** in 1993
    $1,395,278 by **Tom Kite** in 1989
    $1,330,307 by **Greg Norman** in 1994

Most money won by a rookie:
    $684,440 by **Ernie Els** in 1994
    $657,831 by **Vijay Singh** in 1993
    $574,783 by **John Daly** in 1991
    $461,407 by **Robert Gamez** in 1990

Most money won by a second-year player:
    $693,658 by **Billy Mayfair** in 1990
    $652,780 by **Bob Tway** in 1986
    $628,735 by **Phil Mickelson** in 1993

Most money won in first two seasons:
    $983,790 by **Vijay Singh** (1993-1994)
    $962,238 by **John Daly** (1991-1992)
    $816,803 by **Bob Tway** (1985-1986)
    $805,650 by **Billy Mayfair** (1989-1990)

Most consecutive years $100,000 or more:
    21— **Tom Watson** (1974-present)
    19— **Tom Kite** (1976-present)
    18— **Bruce Lietzke** (1977-present)

Most consecutive years $200,000 or more:
    14— **Tom Kite** (1981-present)
    12— **Curtis Strange** (1980-1991)
    12— **Tom Watson** (1977-1988)
    11— **Mark O'Meara** (1984-present)
    10— **Payne Stewart** (1984-1993)

Most consecutive years $500,000 or more:
    7— **Paul Azinger** (1987-1993)
    7— **Chip Beck** (1987-1993)
    6— **Fred Couples** (1989-present)
    5— **Payne Stewart** (1986-1990)
    5— **Greg Norman** (1986-1990)

Most consecutive years $1 million or more:
    3— **Nick Price** (1992-1994)

Most consecutive years Top 10 Money List:
    17— **Jack Nicklaus** (1962-1978)
    15— **Arnold Palmer** (1957-1971)

Most years Top 10 Money List:
    18— **Jack Nicklaus**
    15— **Arnold Palmer**, **Sam Snead**

ALL-TIME PGA TOUR RECORDS

All information based on official PGA TOUR cosponsored or approved events

Most years leading Money List:
    8— **Jack Nicklaus**

Most consecutive years leading Money List:
    4— **Tom Watson** (1977-1980)

Most money won in a single season without a victory:
    $1,016,804 by **Fuzzy Zoeller** in 1994

$1 MILLION IN A SINGLE SEASON

1.	Nick Price	$1,499,927	1994
2.	Nick Price	1,478,557	1993
3.	Paul Azinger	1,458,456	1993
4.	Tom Kite	1,395,278	1989
5.	Greg Norman	1,359,653	1993
6.	Fred Couples	1,344,188	1992
7.	Greg Norman	1,330,307	1994
8.	Mark McCumber	1,208,209	1994
9.	Payne Stewart	1,201,301	1989
10.	Davis Love III	1,191,630	1992
11.	John Cook	1,165,606	1992
12.	Greg Norman	1,165,477	1990
13.	Curtis Strange	1,147,644	1988
14.	Nick Price	1,135,773	1992
15.	Jim Gallagher, Jr.	1,078,870	1993
16.	Tom Lehman	1,031,144	1994
17.	David Frost	1,030,717	1993
18.	Wayne Levi	1,024,647	1990
19.	Fuzzy Zoeller	1,016,804	1994
20.	Loren Roberts	1,015,671	1994

FIRST-YEAR PLAYERS TO EARN $300,000 OR MORE

1.	Ernie Els	$684,440	1994
2.	Vijay Singh	657,831	1993
3.	John Daly	574,783	1991
4.	Robert Gamez	461,407	1990
5.	Mike Heinen	390,963	1994
6.	Glen Day	357,236	1994
7.	Brett Ogle	337,374	1993
8.	Steve Stricker	334,409	1994
9.	Keith Clearwater	320,007	1987
10.	Dicky Pride	305,769	1994

BIGGEST ONE SEASON GAINS

	Season	Money	Season	Money	Gain
1. Mark McCumber	1993	$363,269	1994	$1,208,209	+$844,940
2. Loren Roberts	1993	$316,506	1994	$1,015,671	+$699,165
3. Curtis Strange	1986	$237,700	1987	$ 925,941	+$688,241
4. Hale Irwin	1989	$150,977	1990	$ 838,249	+$687,272
5. Greg Norman	1992	$676,443	1993	$1,359,653	+$683,210
6. Payne Stewart	1988	$553,571	1989	$1,201,301	+$646,720
7. Fulton Allem	1992	$209,982	1993	$ 851,345	+$641,363

Single Tournament Stat Records--PGA TOUR *(1980 thru 1994)*

72-Hole Events

Driving Distance	John Daly	331.4	91 Kemper
Driving Accuracy	Calvin Peete	56 of 56	86 Memorial
	Calvin Peete	56 of 56	87 Memorial
	David Frost	56 of 56	88 Tucson
	Brian Claar	56 of 56	92 Memorial
Greens In Reg.	Jodie Mudd	67 of 72	87 Hawaii
	Dave Rummells	67 of 72	89 Chattanooga
Putts	Kenny Knox	93	89 MCI
Birdies	Chip Beck	29	88 WDW
	Davis Love	29	90 WDW
Eagles	Dave Eichelberger	5	80 Hawaii
	Davis Love	5	94 Hawaii

54-Hole Events

Driving Distance	John Daly	306.3	93 Houston
Driving Accuracy	Keith Fergus	41 of 42	81 AT&T
	Fulton Allem	41 of 42	93 Houston
	John Dowdall	41 of 42	93 Houston
Greens In Reg.	Steve Pate	50 of 54	86 San Diego
	Fulton Allem	50 of 54	89 Hawaii
Putts	Larry Mize	72	93 Houston
Birdies	Hale Irwin	20	81 Houston
	Robert Wrenn	20	92 San Diego
	John Huston	20	93 Houston
	B. McCallister	20	93 Houston
Eagles	Bob Eastwood	3	86 San Diego
	Bill Glasson	3	86 San Diego
	Dan Forsman	3	92 San Diego

90-Hole Events

Driving Distance	Davis Love	304.3	93 Las Vegas
Driving Accuracy	Doug Tewell	64 of 70	92 Las Vegas
Greens In Reg.	John Mahaffey	82 of 90	89 Las Vegas
Putts	Jeff Sluman	129	91 Las Vegas
Birdies	Tom Kite	37	93 Bob Hope
Eagles	Andy Bean	4	86 Las Vegas
	Roger Maltbie	4	86 Las Vegas
	Andy Bean	4	90 Bob Hope
	David Frost	4	90 Las Vegas
	Robert Wrenn	4	90 Las Vegas
	Craig Stadler	4	91 Las Vegas
	Ted Schulz	4	92 Las Vegas
	Fuzzy Zoeller	4	92 Las Vegas
	Davis Love	4	93 Las Vegas

GROWTH OF PGA TOUR PURSES

YEAR	NO.OF EVENTS	TOTAL PURSE	YEAR	NO.OF EVENTS	TOTAL PURSE
1938	38	$158,000	1966	36	3,704,445
1939	28	121,000	1967	37	3,979,162
1940	27	117,000	1968	45	5,077,600
1941	30	169,200	1969	47	5,465,875
1942	21	116,650	1970	55	6,751,523
1943	3	17,000	1971	63	7,116,000
1944	22	150,500	1972	71	7,596,749
1945	36	435,380	1973	75	8,657,225
1946	37	411,533	1974	57	8,165,941
1947	31	352,500	1975	51	7,895,450
1948	34	427,000	1976	49	9,157,522
1949	25	338,200	1977	48	9,688,977
1950	33	459,950	1978	48	10,337,332
1951	30	460,200	1979	46	12,801,200
1952	32	498,016	1980	45	13,371,786
1953	32	562,704	1981	45	14,175,393
1954	26	600,819	1982	46	15,089,576
1955	36	782,010	1983	45	17,588,242
1956	36	847,070	1984	46	21,251,382
1957	32	820,360	1985	47	25,290,526
1958	39	1,005,800	1986	46	25,442,242
1959	43	1,225,205	1987	46	32,106,093
1960	41	1,335,242	1988	47	36,959,307
1961	45	1,461,830	1989	44	41,288,787
1962	49	1,790,320	1990	44	46,251,831
1963	43	2,044,900	1991	44	49,628,203
1964	41	2,301,063	1992	44	49,386,906
1965	36	2,848,515	1993	43	53,203,611
			1994	43	56,416,080

LEADERS IN CAREER MONEY EARNINGS

1.	TOM KITE	$9,159,418
2.	GREG NORMAN	7,937,869
3.	FRED COUPLES	6,889,149
4.	PAUL AZINGER	6,774,728
5.	TOM WATSON	6,751,328
6.	NICK PRICE	6,726,418
7.	PAYNE STEWART	6,523,260
8.	CURTIS STRANGE	6,433,442
9.	BEN CRENSHAW	6,107,759
10.	LANNY WADKINS	5,931,370
11.	COREY PAVIN	5,835,444
12.	HALE IRWIN	5,654,063
13.	CRAIG STADLER	5,606,436
14.	CHIP BECK	5,585,763
15.	BRUCE LIETZKE	5,440,868
16.	JACK NICKLAUS	5,372,176
17.	MARK O'MEARA	5,212,337
18.	RAY FLOYD	5,129,013
19.	DAVID FROST	5,100,514
20.	MARK CALCAVECCHIA	5,023,163
21.	FUZZY ZOELLER	4,748,065
22.	GIL MORGAN	4,735,868
23.	SCOTT HOCH	4,673,254
24.	JAY HAAS	4,604,562
25.	DAVIS LOVE III	4,511,891
26.	MARK MCCUMBER	4,423,778
27.	LARRY MIZE	4,294,710
28.	JOHN COOK	4,274,977
29.	WAYNE LEVI	4,191,292
30.	SCOTT SIMPSON	3,973,157
31.	HAL SUTTON	3,931,853
32.	JOHN MAHAFFEY	3,671,400
33.	STEVE PATE	3,571,833
34.	JIM GALLAGHER, JR.	3,526,698
35.	LEE TREVINO	3,478,449
36.	PETER JACOBSEN	3,472,507
37.	DAVID EDWARDS	3,420,417
38.	JOEY SINDELAR	3,362,503
39.	TIM SIMPSON	3,348,787
40.	JEFF SLUMAN	3,296,749
41.	LARRY NELSON	3,273,248
42.	STEVE ELKINGTON	3,271,135
43.	ANDY BEAN	3,243,075
44.	KEN GREEN	3,174,225
45.	LOREN ROBERTS	3,131,398
46.	TOM PURTZER	3,130,116
47.	JOHN HUSTON	3,113,443
48.	D.A. WEIBRING	3,095,307
49.	BRAD FAXON	3,065,652
50.	MIKE REID	3,029,011
51.	BOB TWAY	$3,028,191
52.	MARK BROOKS	2,933,316
53.	DAN FORSMAN	2,845,611
54.	BILL GLASSON	2,818,132
55.	JODIE MUDD	2,763,755
56.	JOHNNY MILLER	2,746,424
57.	DAN POHL	2,742,851
58.	GENE SAUERS	2,690,997
59.	DON POOLEY	2,584,319
60.	HUBERT GREEN	2,580,463
61.	ANDREW MAGEE	2,575,955
62.	MIKE HULBERT	2,566,972
63.	LEE JANZEN	2,531,430
64.	HOWARD TWITTY	2,524,478
65.	RUSS COCHRAN	2,523,319
66.	BOB GILDER	2,497,111
67.	RICK FEHR	2,472,430
68.	BLAINE MCCALLISTER	2,439,597
69.	DONNIE HAMMOND	2,426,578
70.	DOUG TEWELL	2,378,598
71.	CALVIN PEETE	2,302,363
72.	BOBBY WADKINS	2,281,686
73.	ROCCO MEDIATE	2,261,620
74.	TOM WEISKOPF	2,241,687
75.	JEFF MAGGERT	2,225,845
76.	J.C. SNEAD	2,219,171
77.	DAVE BARR	2,152,105
78.	BRAD BRYANT	2,142,399
79.	MARK WIEBE	2,136,907
80.	ROGER MALTBIE	2,102,415
81.	TOM LEHMAN	2,072,026
82.	KENNY PERRY	2,070,684
83.	BILLY ANDRADE	2,034,796
84.	GARY HALLBERG	2,028,979
85.	KEITH CLEARWATER	2,021,787
86.	IAN BAKER-FINCH	1,998,077
87.	NOLAN HENKE	1,978,048
88.	FULTON ALLEM	1,977,016
89.	BOB LOHR	1,972,842
90.	JAY DON BLAKE	1,943,438
91.	MIKE DONALD	1,933,004
92.	MIKE SULLIVAN	1,909,914
93.	ARNOLD PALMER	1,904,667
94.	BOB ESTES	1,898,407
95.	STEVE JONES	1,894,679
96.	DAVID GRAHAM	1,874,780
97.	JIM THORPE	1,860,830
98.	BILLY MAYFAIR	1,854,433
99.	ED FIORI	1,831,823
100.	GARY PLAYER	1,814,959

PAST LEADING MONEY-WINNERS

1934	Paul Runyan	$6,767.00		1965	Jack Nicklaus	$140,752.14
1935	Johnny Revolta	9,543.00		1966	Billy Casper	121,944.92
1936	Horton Smith	7,682.00		1967	Jack Nicklaus	188,998.08
1937	Harry Cooper	14,138.69		1968	Billy Casper	205,168.67
1938	Sam Snead	19,534.49		1969	Frank Beard	164,707.11
1939	Henry Picard	10,303.00		1970	Lee Trevino	157,037.63
1940	Ben Hogan	10,655.00		1971	Jack Nicklaus	244,490.50
1941	Ben Hogan	18,358.00		1972	Jack Nicklaus	320,542.26
1942	Ben Hogan	13,143.00		1973	Jack Nicklaus	308,362.10
1943	No Statistics Compiled			1974	Johnny Miller	353,021.59
1944	Byron Nelson (War Bonds)	37,967.69		1975	Jack Nicklaus	298,149.17
1945	Byron Nelson (War Bonds)	63,335.66		1976	Jack Nicklaus	266,438.57
1946	Ben Hogan	42,556.16		1977	Tom Watson	310,653.16
1947	Jimmy Demaret	27,936.83		1978	Tom Watson	362,428.93
1948	Ben Hogan	32,112.00		1979	Tom Watson	462,636.00
1949	Sam Snead	31,593.83		1980	Tom Watson	530,808.33
1950	Sam Snead	35,758.83		1981	Tom Kite	375,698.84
1951	Lloyd Mangrum	26,088.83		1982	Craig Stadler	446,462.00
1952	Julius Boros	37,032,97		1983	Hal Sutton	426,668.00
1953	Lew Worsham	34,002.00		1984	Tom Watson	476,260.00
1954	Bob Toski	65,819.81		1985	Curtis Strange	542,321.00
1955	Julius Boros	63,121.55		1986	Greg Norman	653,296.00
1956	Ted Kroll	72,835.83		1987	Curtis Strange	925,941.00
1957	Dick Mayer	65,835.00		1988	Curtis Strange	1,147,644.00
1958	Arnold Palmer	42,607.50		1989	Tom Kite	1,395,278.00
1959	Art Wall	53,167.60		1990	Greg Norman	1,165,477.00
1960	Arnold Palmer	75,262.85		1991	Corey Pavin	979,430.00
1961	Gary Player	64,540.45		1992	Fred Couples	1,344,188.00
1962	Arnold Palmer	81,448.33		1993	Nick Price	1,478,557.00
1963	Arnold Palmer	128,230.00		1994	Nick Price	1,499,927.00
1964	Jack Nicklaus	113,284.50				

*TOTAL MONEY LISTED BEGINNING IN 1968 THROUGH 1974.   ** OFFICIAL MONEY LISTED BEGINNING IN 1975.

ALL-TIME TOUR WINNERS

1.	Sam Snead	81		Craig Wood	21
2.	Jack Nicklaus	70		Lanny Wadkins	21
3.	Ben Hogan	63	T30.	James Barnes	20
4.	Arnold Palmer	60		Hale Irwin	20
5.	Byron Nelson	52		Doug Sanders	20
6.	Billy Casper	51	T33.	Doug Ford	19
T7.	Walter Hagan	40		Hubert Green	19
	Cary Middlecoff	40		Tom Kite	19
9.	Gene Sarazen	38	T36.	Julius Boros	18
10.	Lloyd Mangrum	36		Ben Crenshaw	18
T11.	Horton Smith	32		Jim Ferrier	18
	Tom Watson	32		Johnny Revolta	18
T13.	Harry Cooper	31	T40.	Jack Burke	17
	Jimmy Demaret	31		Bobby Cruickshank	17
15.	Leo Diegel	30		Harold McSpaden	17
T16.	Gene Littler	29		Curtis Strange	17
	Paul Runyan	29	44.	Ralph Guldahl	16
18.	Lee Trevino	27	T45.	Tommy Bolt	15
19.	Henry Picard	26		Ed Dudley	15
T20.	Tommy Armour	24		Denny Shute	15
	Macdonald Smith	24		Mike Souchak	15
	Johnny Miller	24		Tom Weiskopf	15
T23.	Johnny Farrell	22	T50.	Bruce Crampton	14
	Ray Floyd	22		Nick Price	14
T25.	Willie Macfarlane	21		Joe Turnesa	14
	Bill Mehlhorn	21		Ken Venturi	14
	Gary Player	21		Art Wall	14

MOST TOUR WINS YEAR BY YEAR

Year	Player	Wins	Year	Player	Wins
1916	James Barnes	3	1962	Arnold Palmer	7
	Walter Hagen	3	1963	Arnold Palmer	7
1917	James Barnes	2	1964	Jack Nicklaus	4
	Mike Brady	2		Billy Casper	4
1918	Jock Hutchison	1		Tony Lema	4
	Walter Hagen	1	1965	Jack Nicklaus	5
	Patrick Doyle	1	1966	Billy Casper	4
1919	James Barnes	5	1967	Jack Nicklaus	5
1920	Jock Hutchison	4	1968	Billy Casper	6
1921	James Barnes	4	1969	Dave Hill	3
1922	Gene Sarazen	3		Billy Casper	3
	Walter Hagen	3		Jack Nicklaus	3
1923	Walter Hagen	5		Ray Floyd	3
	Joe Kirkwood, Sr	5	1970	Billy Casper	4
1924	Joe Kirkwood, Sr	4	1971	Jack Nicklaus	5
	Walter Hagen	4		Lee Trevino	5
1925	Leo Diegel	5	1972	Jack Nicklaus	7
1926	Bill Mehlhorn	5	1973	Jack Nicklaus	7
	Macdonald Smith	5	1974	Johnny Miller	8
1927	Johnny Farrell	7	1975	Jack Nicklaus	5
1928	Bil Mehlhorn	7	1976	Ben Crenshaw	3
1929	Horton Smith	8		Hubert Green	3
1930	Gene Sarazen	8	1977	Tom Watson	4
1931	Wiffy Cox	4	1978	Tom Watson	5
1932	Craig Wood	3	1979	Tom Watson	5
	Gene Sarazen	3	1980	Tom Watson	6
	Olin Dutra	3	1981	Tom Watson	3
	Mike Turnesa	3		Bruce Lietzke	3
	Tommy Armour	3		Ray Floyd	3
1933	Paul Runyan	9		Bill Rogers.	3
1934	Paul Runyan	7	1982	Craig Stadler	4
1935	Johnny Revolta	5		Calvin Peete	4
	Henry Picard	5	1983	Fuzzy Zoeller	2
1936	Ralph Guldahl	3		Lanny Wadkins	2
	Henry Picard.	3		Calvin Peete	2
	Jimmy Hines	3		Hal Sutton	2
1937	Harry Cooper	8		Gil Morgan	2
1938	Sam Snead	8		Mark McCumber	2
1939	Henry Picard	8		Jim Colbert	2
1940	Jimmy Demaret	6		Seve Ballesteros	2
1941	Sam Snead	7	1984	Tom Watson	3
1942	Ben Hogan	6		Denis Watson	3
1943	Sam Byrd	1	1985	Lanny Wadkins	3
	Harold McSpaden	1		Curtis Strange	3
	Steve Warga	1	1986	Bob Tway	4
1944	Byron Nelson	8	1987	Curtis Strange	3
1945	Byron Nelson	18		Paul Azinger	3
1946	Ben Hogan	13	1988	Curtis Strange	4
1947	Ben Hogan	7	1989	Tom Kite	3
1948	Ben Hogan	10		Steve Jones	3
1949	Cary Middlecoff	7	1990	Wayne Levi	4
1950	Sam Snead	11	1991	Ian Woosnam	2
1951	Cary Middlecoff	6		Corey Pavin	2
1952	Jack Burke, Jr	5		Billy Andrade	2
	Sam Snead	5		Tom Purtzer	2
1953	Ben Hogan	4		Mark Brooks	2
	Lloyd Mangrum	4		Nick Price	2
1954	Bob Toski	4		Fred Couples	2
1955	Cary Middlecoff	6		Andrew Magee	2
1956	Mike Souchak	4	1992	Fred Couples	3
1957	Arnold Palmer	4		Davis Love III	3
1958	Ken Venturi	4		John Cook	3
1959	Gene Littler	5	1993	Nick Price	4
1960	Arnold Palmer	8	1994	Nick Price	5
1961	Arnold Palmer	5			
	Doug Sanders	5			

INDIVIDUAL PLAYOFF RECORDS

AARON, Tommy-- (0-4) 1963: Lost to Tony Lema, Memphis Open; Lost to Arnold Palmer, Cleveland Open. 1972: Lost to George Archer, Glen Campbell Los Angeles Open; Lost to George Archer, Greater Greensboro Open.

ADAMS, John-- (0-1) 1982: Lost to Jay Haas, Hall of Fame Classic.

ALEXANDER, Skip-- (1-0) 1950: Defeated Ky Laffoon, Empire State Open.

ALLIN, Buddy-- (1-0) 1971: Defeated Dave Eichelberger, Rod Funseth, Greater Greensboro Open.

ALLISS, Percy-- (0-1) 1931: Lost to Walter Hagen, Canadian Open.

ANDERSON, Willie-- (2-0) 1901: Defeated Alex Smith, U.S. Open. 1903: Defeated David Brown, U.S. Open.

ANDRADE, Billy-- (1-1) 1991: Defeated Jeff Sluman, Kemper Open. 1993: Lost to John Inman, Buick Southern Open.

ARCHER, George-- (4-3) 1965: Defeated Bob Charles, Lucky International Open. 1969: Lost to Jack Nicklaus, Kaiser International. 1970: Lost to George Knudson, Robinson Open. 1971: Defeated Lou Graham, J.C. Snead, Greater Hartford Open. 1972: Defeated Tommy Aaron, Dave Hill, Glen Campbell Los Angeles Open; Lost to Miller Barber, Bing Crosby National Pro-Am; Defeated Tommy Aaron, Greater Greensboro Open.

ARMOUR, Tommy-- (2-1) 1920: Lost to J. Douglas Edgar, Canadian Open. 1927: Defeated Harry Cooper, U.S. Open. 1930: Defeated Leo Deigel, Canadian Open.

AZINGER, Paul-- (1-2) 1989: Lost to Steve Jones, Bob Hope Chrysler Classic. 1990: Lost to Greg Norman, Doral-Ryder Open. 1993: Defeated Greg Norman, PGA Championship.

BAIRD, Butch-- (1-0) 1976: Defeated Miller Barber, San Antonio Texas Open.

BAKER-FINCH, Ian-- (0-1) 1991: Lost to Bruce Fleisher, New England Classic.

BALDING, Al-- (1-3) 1957: Defeated Al Besselink, Havana Invitational. 1959: Lost to Don Whitt, Memphis Open. 1961: Lost to Arnold Palmer, San Diego Open. 1964: Lost to George Knudson, Fresno Open.

BALLESTEROS, Seve-- (1-1) 1987: Lost to J.C. Snead, Manufacturers Hanover Westchester Classic. 1988: Defeated David Frost, Greg Norman, Ken Green, Manufacturers Hanover Westchester Classic.

BARBER, Jerry-- (1-0) 1961: Defeated Don January, PGA Championship.

BARBER, Miller-- (3-4) 1964: Lost to Gary Player, Pensacola Open. 1967: Defeated Gary Player, Oklahoma City Open. 1970: Defeated Bob Charles, Howie Johnson, Greater New Orleans Open. 1972: Defeated George Archer, Dean Martin Tucson Open. 1973: Lost to Jack Nicklaus, Greater New Orleans Open; Lost to Bert Greene, Ligget and Myers Open. 1976: Lost to Butch Baird, San Antonio Texas Open.

BARNES, James-- (0-3) 1916: Lost to Walter Hagen, Metropolitan Open. 1920: Lost to Walter Hagen, Metropolitan Open. 1923: Lost to Robert MacDonald, Metropolitan Open.

BARR, Dave-- (1-2) 1981: Defeated Woody Blackburn, Frank Conner, Dan Halldorson, Victor Regalado, Quad Cities Open. 1986: Lost to Corey Pavin, Greater Milwaukee Open. 1988: Lost to Mark Brooks, Canon Sammy Davis, Jr.-Greater Hartford Open.

BARRON, Herman-- (1-0) 1946: Defeated Lew Worsham, Philadelphia Inquirer Open.

BAYER, George-- (2-2) 1957: Lost to Doug Ford, Western Open. 1958: Defeated Sam Snead, Havana International. 1960: Defeated Jack Fleck, St. Petersburg Open. 1961: Lost to Eric Monti, Ontario Open.

BEAN, Andy-- (3-3) 1978: Defeated Lee Trevino, Danny Thomas Memphis Classic; Defeated Bill Rogers, Western Open. 1979: Lost to Lon Hinkle, Bing Crosby National Pro-Am. 1984: Lost to Bruce lietzke, Honda Classic; Lost to Jack Nicklaus, Memorial Tournament. 1986: Defeated Hubert Green, Doral-Eastern Open.

BEARD, Frank-- (0-3) 1968: Lost to Jack Nicklaus, American Golf Classic. 1969: Lost to Larry Hinson, Greater New Orleans Open. 1974: Lost to Johnny Miller, World Open.

BECK, Chip-- (0-1) 1991: Lost to Brad Faxon, Buick Open.

BEMAN, Deane-- (1-1) 1968: Lost to Arnold Palmer, Bob Hope Desert Classic. 1969: Defeated Jack McGowan, Texas Open.

BESSELINK, Al-- (1-2) 1957: Lost to Ed Furgol, Caliente Open; Defeated Bob Rosburg, Caracas Open; Lost to Al Balding, Havana Invitational.

BIES, Don-- (1-0) 1975: Defeated Hubert Green, Sammy Davis, Jr.-Greater Hartford Open.

BLACK, Ronnie-- (1-1) 1983: Defeated Sam Torrance, Southern Open. 1989: Lost to Wayne Grady, Manufacturers Hanover Westchester Classic.

BLACKBURN, Woody-- (1-1) 1981: Lost to Dave Barr, Quad Cities Open. 1985: Defeated Ron Streck, Isuzu-Andy Williams-San Diego Open.

BLACKMAR, Phil-- (1-1) 1985: Defeated Jodie Mudd, Dan Pohl, Canon Sammy Davis, Jr.-Greater Hartford Open. 1988: Defeated Payne Stewart, Provident Classic.

BLANCAS, Homero-- (1-1) 1969: Lost to Larry Ziegler, Michigan Golf Classic. 1972: Defeated Lanny Wadkins, Phoenix Open.

BLOCKER, Chris-- (0-1) 1970: Lost to Doug Sanders, Bahama Islands Open.

BOLT, Tommy-- (3-3) 1952: Defeated Jack Burke, Jr., Dutch Harrison, Los Angeles Open; Lost to Jack Burke, Jr., Baton Rouge Open. 1954: Defeated Earl Stewart, Insurance City Open. 1955: Lost to Sam Snead, Miami Beach Open. 1960: Defeated Ben Hogan, Gene Littler, Memphis Open. 1961: Lost to Dave Hill, Home of the Sun Open.

INDIVIDUAL PLAYOFF RECORDS (cont'd.)

BOROS, Julius-- (4-5) 1952: Defeated Cary Middlecoff, World Championship of Golf. 1954: Defeated George Fazio, Carling's World Open. 1958: Lost to Sam Snead, Dallas Open. 1959: Lost to Jack Burke, Jr., Houston Classic. 1963: Defeated Arnold Palmer, Jacky Cupit, U.S. Open; Lost to Arnold Palmer, Western Open. 1964: Defeated Doug Sanders, Greater Greensboro Open. 1969: Lost to Gene Littler, Greater Greensboro Open. 1975: Lost to Gene Littler, Westchester Classic.

BRADLEY, Jackson-- (0-1) 1955: Lost to Henry Ransom, Rubber City Open.

BRADY, Mike-- (1-2) 1911: Lost to John McDermott, U.S. Open. 1916: Defeated Patrick Doyle, Massachusetts Open. 1919: Lost to Walter Hagen, U.S. Open.

BRANCA, Tee-- (0-1) 1938: Lost to Al Zimmerman, Utah Open.

BREWER, Gay-- (2-5) 1959: Lost to Arnold Palmer, West Palm Beach Open. 1965: Defeated Doug Sanders, Greater Seattle Open;Defeated Bob Goalby, Hawaiian Open. 1966: Lost to Jack Nicklaus, Masters Tournament; Lost to Arnold Palmer, Tournament of Champions. 1969: Lost to Dave Hill, IVB-Philadelphia Classic. 1974: Lost to Jim Colbert, American Golf Classic.

BRITTON, Bill-- (0-1) 1982: Lost to Hal Sutton, Walt Disney World Golf Classic.

BROOKS, Mark-- (2-2) 1988: Defeated Dave Barr, Joey Sindelar, Canon Sammy Davis, Jr.-Greater Hartford Open; Lost to Tom Purtzer, Gatlin Brothers Southwest Classic. 1991: Defeated Gene Sauers, Kmart Greater Greensboro Open. 1993: Lost to John Inman, Buick Southern Open.

BROWN, Billy Ray-- (2-0) 1991: Defeated Corey Pavin, Rick Fehr, Canon Greater Hartford Open. 1992: Defeated Ray Floyd, Ben Crenshaw, Bruce Lietzke, GTE Byron Nelson Classic.

BROWN, David-- (0-1) 1903: Lost to Willie Anderson, U.S. Open.

BROWN, Pete-- (1-1) 1964: Lost to Billy Casper, Alamden Open. 1970: Defeated Tony Jacklin, Andy Williams San Diego Open.

BRYANT, Brad-- (0-1) 1993: Lost to John Inman, Buick Southern Open.

BURKE, Billy-- (2-0) 1929: Defeated Bill Mehlhorn, Glens Falls Open. 1931: Defeated George Von Elm, U.S.Open.

BURKE, Jr., Jack-- (4-3) 1950: Defeated Dave Douglas, Sam Snead, Smiley Quick, Bing Crosby Pro-Amateur. 1952: Lost to Tommy Bolt, Los Angeles Open; Defeated Bill Nary, Tommy Bolt, Baton Rouge Open. 1955: Lost to Henry Ransom, Rubber City Open. 1958: Lost to Art Wall, Rubber City Open. 1959: Defeated Julius Boros, Houston Classic. 1961: Defeated Billy Casper, Johnny Pott, Buick Open.

BURNS, George-- (0-2) 1984: Lost to Gary Koch, Bay Hill Classic. 1985: Lost to Roger Maltbie, Manufacturers Hanover Westchester Classic.

BYMAN, Bob-- (1-0) 1979: Defeated John Schroeder, Bay Hill Citrus Classic.

BYRD, Sam-- (1-0) 1945: Defeated Dutch Harrison, Mobile Open.

BYRUM, Tom-- (0-1) 1994: Lost to Neal Lancaster, GTE Byron Nelson Classic.

CADLE, George-- (0-1) 1983: Lost to Morris Hatalsky, Greater Milwaukee Open.

CALCAVECCHIA, Mark-- (0-2) 1990: Lost to Greg Norman, Doral-Ryder Open. 1993: Lost to Billy Mayfair, Greater Milwaukee Open.

CALDWELL, Rex-- (0-2) 1983: Lost to Keith Fergus, Bob Hope Desert Classic; Lost to Bob Gilder, Phoenix Open.

CAMPBELL, Joe-- (1-1) 1961: Lost to Doug Ford, Bing Crosby National Pro-Am. 1966: Defeated Gene Littler, Tucson Open.

CARNEVALE, Mark-- (0-1) 1994: Lost to Neal Lancaster, GTE Byron Nelson Classic.

CASPER, Billy-- (8-8) 1958: Defeated Ken Venturi, Greater New Orleans Open. 1961: Lost to Jack Burke, Jr., Buick Open. 1964: Defeated Pete Brown, Jerry Steelsmith, Almaden Open. 1965: Lost to Wes Ellis, San Diego Open; Defeated Johnny Pott, Insurance City Open. 1966: Defeated Arnold Palmer, U.S. Open. 1967: Defeated Art Wall, Canadian Open; Defeated Al Geiberger, Carling World Open; Lost to Dudley Wysong, Hawaiian Open. 1968: Lost to Johnny Pott, Bing Crosby National Pro-Am. 1969: Lost to Jack Nicklaus, Kaiser International. 1970: Defeated Hale Irwin, Los Angeles Open; Defeated Gene Littler, Masters Tournament. 1971: Lost to Bob Lunn, Glen Campbell Los Angeles Open. 1972: Lost to Chi Chi Rodriguez, Byron Nelson Classic. 1975: Lost to Jack Nicklaus, World Open

CHARLES, Bob-- (0-2) 1965: Lost to George Archer, Lucky International Open. 1970: Lost to Miller Barber, Greater New Orleans Open.

CHEN, Tze-Chung-- (1-1) 1983: Lost to Fred Couples, Kemper Open. 1987: Defeated Ben Crenshaw, Los Angeles Open.

CLAMPETT, Bobby-- (0-2) 1981: Lost to John Cook, Bing Crosby National Pro-Am; Lost to Hale Irwin, Buick Open.

CLARK, Jimmy-- (1-1) 1952: Defeated Jim Turnesa, Ft. Wayne Open. 1955: Lost to Bo Wininger, Baton Rouge Open.

COCHRAN, Russ-- (0-1) 1991: Lost to Craig Stadler, THE TOUR Championship.

COLBERT, Jim-- (2-0) 1974: Defeated Ray Floyd, Gay Brewer, Forrest Fezler, American Golf Classic. 1983: Defeated Fuzzy Zoeller, COlonial National Invitation.

COLLINS, Bill-- (1-3) 1960: Lost to Jack Fleck, Phoenix Open; Defeated Arnold Palmer, Houston Classic; Lost to Arnold Palmer, Insurance City Open. 1962: Lost to Al Johnston, Hot Springs Open.

CONGDON, Charles-- (0-1) 1948: Lost to Ed Oliver, Tacoma Open.

CONNER, Frank-- (0-2) 1981: Lost to Dave Barr, Quad Cities Open. 1982: Lost to Tom Watson, Sea Pines Heritage Classic.

COOK, John-- (3-3) 1981: Defeated Hale Irwin, Ben Crenshaw, Bobby Clampett, Barney Thompson, Bing Crosby National Pro-Am. 1983: Defeated Johnny Miller, Canadian Open. 1986: Lost to Donnie Hammond, Bob Hope Chrysler Classic. 1990: Lost to Tom Kite, Federal Express St. Jude Classic; Lost to Bob Tway, Las Vegas Invitational. 1992: Defeated Gene Sauers, RIck Fehr, Mark O'Meara, Tom Kite, Bob Hope Chrysler Classic.

COOPER, Harry-- (3-2) 1927: Lost to Tommy Armour, U.S. Open. 1935: Defeated Ky Laffoon, Western Open. 1936: Defeated Dick Metz, St. Paul Open. 1937: Defeated Horton Smith, Ralph Guhldahl, St. Petersburg Open. 1938: Lost to Sam Snead, Canadian Open.

COOPER, Pete-- (1-1) 1958: Defeated Wes Ellis, Jr., West Palm Beach Open. 1959: Lost to Arnold Palmer, West Palm Beach Open.

COUPLES, Fred-- (3-4) 1983: Defeated Tze-Chung Chen, Barry Jaeckel, Gil Morgan, Scott Simpson, Kemper Open. 1986: Lost to Tom Kite, Western Open. 1987: Lost to Sandy Lyle, Phoenix Open. 1992: Defeated Davis Love III, Nissan Los Angeles Open; Lost to Corey Pavin, Honda Classic. 1993: Defeated Robert Gamez, Honda Classic. 1994: Lost to Phil Mickelson, Mercedes Championships.

COURTNEY, Chuck-- (0-1) 1972: Lost to DeWitt Weaver, Southern Open.

COX, Wiffy-- (0-1) 1936: Defeated Bill Mehlhorn, Sacramento Open.

CRAMPTON, Bruce-- (0-2) 1970: Lost to Gibby Gilbert, Houston Champions International. 1974: Lost to Richie Karl, B.C. Open.

CRENSHAW, Ben-- (0-8) 1978: Lost to Tom Watson, Bing Crosby National Pro-Am. 1979: Lost to Larry Nelson, Western Open; Lost to David Graham, PGA Championship. 1981: Lost to John Cook, Bing Crosby National Pro-Am; Lost to Bill Rogers, Texas Open. 1987: Lost to Tze-Chung Chen, Los Angeles Open. 1989: Lost to David Frost, NEC World Series of Golf. 1992: Lost to Billy Ray Brown, GTE Byron Nelson Classic.

CRUICKSHANK, Bobby-- (1-3) 1923: Lost to Robert T. Jones, Jr., U.S. Open. 1926: Lost to Johnny Farrell, Florida Open. 1929: Lost to Bill Mehlhorn, South Central Open. 1935: Defeated Johnny Revolta, Orlando Open.

CUPIT, Jacky-- (1-2) 1961: Lost Dave Marr, Greater Seattle Open. 1963: Lost to Julius Boros, U.S. Open. 1966: Defeated Chi Chi Rodriguez, Cajun Classic Open.

DEMARET, Jimmy-- (4-5) 1940: Defeated Toney Penna, Western Open. 1947: Lost to Dave Douglas, Orlando Open. 1948: Lost to Lloyd Mangrum, Lower Rio Grande Open; Defeated Otto Greiner, St. Paul Open. 1949: Lost to Ben Hogan, Long Beach Open; Defeated Ben Hogan, Phoenix Open; Lost to Johnny Palmer, World Championship of Golf. 1957: Defeated Ken Venturi, Mike Souchak, Thunderbird Invitational. 1964: Lost to Tommy Jacobs, Palm Springs Golf Classic.

DEVLIN, Bruce-- (0-3) 1968: Lost to Johnny Pott, Bing Crosby National Pro-Am. 1969: Lost to Bert Yancey, Atlanta Classic. 1972: Lost to David Graham, Cleveland Open.

DICKINSON, Gardner-- (1-2) 1956: Lost to Art Wall, Ft. Wayne Open. 1969: Lost to Raymond Floyd, Greater Jacksonville Open. 1971: Defeated Jack Nicklaus, Atlanta Golf Classic.

DIEGEL, LEO-- (2-2) 1922: Lost to Abe Mitchell, Southern Open. 1924: Defeated Will MacFarlane, Shawnee Open. 1930: Lost to Tommy Armour, Canadian Open; Defeated Gene Sarazen, Oregon Open.

DIEHL, Terry-- (0-1) 1976: Lost to Tom Kite, IVB-Bicentennial Golf Classic.

DODSON, Leonard-- (1-1) 1936: Lost to Ray Mangrum, Wildwood New Jersey Open. 1941: Defeated Dutch Harrison, Ben Hogan, Oakland Open.

DONALD, Mike-- (1-1) 1989: Defeated Tim Simpson, Hal Sutton, Anheuser-Busch Golf Classic. 1990: Lost to Hale Irwin, U.S. Open.

DOUGHERTY, Ed-- (0-1) 1990: Lost to Jim Gallagher, Jr., Greater Milwaukee Open.

DOUGLAS, Dave-- (1-2) 1947: Defeated Jimmy Demaret, Herman Keiser, Orlando Open. 1950: Lost to Jack Burke, Jr., Bing Crosby Pro-Amateur. 1951: Lost to Cary Middlecoff, Kansas City Open.

DOUGLASS, Dale-- (0-3) 1968: Lost to Chi Chi Rodriguez, Sahara Invitational. 1970: Lost to Don January, Greater Jacksonville Open. 1971: Lost to Tom Weiskopf, Kemper Open.

DOYLE, Patrick-- (0-1) 1916: Lost to Mike Brady, Massachusetts Open.

DUTRA, Olin-- (1-0) 1930: Defeated Joe Kirkwood, Sr., Long Beach Open.

EASTWOOD, Bob-- (1-0) 1985: Defeated Payne Stewart, Byron Nelson Classic.

EDGAR, J. Douglass-- (1-0) 1920: Defeated Tommy Armour, Charles Murray, Canadian Open.

EDWARDS, Danny-- (1-0) 1983: Defeated Morris Hatalsky, Miller High Life-Quad Cities Open.

EDWARDS, David-- (1-1) 1992: Defeated Rick Fehr, Memorial Tournament. 1994: Lost to Neal Lancaster, GTE Byron Nelson Classic.

EICHELBERGER, Dave-- (1-1) 1971: Lost to Buddy Allin, Greater Greensboro Open. 1981: Defeated Bob Murphy, Mark O'Meara, Tallahassee Open.

ELDER, Lee-- (2-2) 1968: Lost to Jack Nicklaus, American Golf Classic. 1972: Lost to Lee Trevino, Greater Hartford Open. 1974: Defeated Peter Oosterhuis, Monsanto Open. 1978: Defeated Lee Trevino, Greater Milwaukee Open.

INDIVIDUAL PLAYOFF RECORDS (cont'd.)

ELKINGTON, Steve-- (1-2) 1992: Defeated Brad Faxon, Infiniti Tournament of Champions; Lost to Dan Forsman, Buick Open. 1993: Lost to Rocco Mediate, Kmart Greater Greensboro Open.

ELLIS, Wes-- (1-1) 1958: Lost to Pete Cooper, West Palm Beach Open. 1965: Defeated Billy Casper, San Diego Open.

ELS, Ernie-- (1-0) 1994: Defeated Loren Roberts, Colin Montgomerie, U.S. Open.

ESPINOSA, Al-- (0-1) 1929: Lost to Robert T. Jones, Jr., U.S. Open.

ESPINOZA, Abe-- (0-1) 1924: Lost to Macdonald Smith, Northern California Open.

ESTES, Bob-- (0-2) 1989: Lost to Mike Hulbert, B.C. Open. 1993: Lost to John Inman, Buick Southern Open.

FAIRFIELD, Don-- (0-1) 1959: Lost to Dow Finsterwald, Kansas City Open.

FALDO, Nick-- (2-1) 1988: Lost to Curtis Strange, U.S. Open. 1989: Defeated Scott Hoch, Masters Tournament. 1990: Defeated Ray Floyd, Masters Tournament.

FARRELL, Johnny-- (3-2) 1926: Defeated Bobby Cruickshank, Florida Open. 1928: Lost to Gene Sarazen, Nassau Bahamas Open; Defeated Robert T. Jones, Jr., U.S. Open. 1930: Lost to Willie MacFarlane, Metropolitan Open. 1936: Defeated Vic Ghezzi, New Jersey Open.

FAXON, Brad-- (1-2) 1991: Defeated Chip Beck, Buick Open. 1992: Lost to Steve Elkington, Infiniti Tournament of Champions; Lost to Dan Forsman, Buick Open.

FAZIO, George-- (1-3) 1946: Defeated Dick Metz, Canadian Open. 1948: Lost to Lloyd Mangrum, Utah Open. 1950: Lost to Ben Hogan, U.S. Open. 1954: Lost to Julius Boros, Carling's World Open.

FEHR, Rick-- (0-4) 1991: Lost to Billy Ray Brown, Canon Greater Hartford Open. 1992: Lost to John Cook, Bob Hope Chrysler Classic; Lost to David Edwards, Memorial Tournament. 1994: Lost to Steve Lowery, Sprint International.

FERGUS, Keith-- (2-0) 1982: Defeated Ray Floyd, Georgia-Pacific Atlanta Classic. 1983: Defeated Rex Caldwell, Bob Hope Desert Classic.

FERRIER, Jim-- (1-1) 1947: Defeated Fred Haas, Jr., St. Paul Open. 1950: Defeated Sam Snead, St. Paul Open. 1953: Lost to Cary Middlecoff, Houston Open.

FETCHICK, Mike-- (2-0) 1956: Defeated Lionel Hebert, St. Petersburg Open; Defeated Jay Hebert, Don January, Doug Ford, Western Open.

FEZLER, Forrest-- (0-1) 1974: Lost to Jim Colbert, American Golf Classic.

FINSTERWALD, Dow-- (2-4) 1956: Lost to Doug Sanders, Canadian Open. 1957: Defeated Don Whitt, Tucson Open. 1958: Lost to Art Wall, Rubber City Open. 1959: Lost to Art Wall, Buick Open; Defeated Don Fairfield, Kansas City Open. 1962: Lost to Arnold Palmer, Masters Tournament.

FIORI, Ed-- (2-0) 1979: Defeated Tom Weiskopf, Southern Open. 1982: Defeated Tom Kite, Bob Hope Desert Classic.

FLECK, Jack-- (3-2) 1955: Defeated Ben Hogan, U.S. Open. 1960: Defeated Bill Collins, Phoenix Open; Lost to George Bayer, St. Petersburg Open; Lost to Arnold Palmer, Insurance City Open. 1961: Defeated Bob Rosburg, Bakersfield Open.

FLECKMAN, Marty-- (1-0) 1967: Defeated Jack Montgomery, Cajun Classic Open.

FLEISHER, Bruce-- (1-0) 1991: Defeated Ian Baker-Finch, New England Classic.

FLOYD, Raymond-- (4-11) 1969: Defeated Gardner Dickinson, Greater Jacksonville Open. 1971: Lost to Arnold Palmer, Bob Hope Desert Classic. 1972: Lost to Jack Nicklaus, Bing Crosby National Pro-Am. 1974: Lost to Jim Colbert, American Golf Classic. 1975: Lost to J.C. Snead, Andy Williams San Diego Open. 1976: Defeated Jerry McGee, World Open. 1980: Defeated Jack Nicklaus, Doral-Eastern Open. 1981: Lost to Bruce Lietzke, Wickes Andy Williams-San Diego Open; Defeated Barry Jaeckel, Curtis Strange, Tournament Players Championship. 1982: Lost to Keith Fergus, Georgia-Pacific Atlanta Classic; Lost to Craig Stadler, World Series of Golf. 1985: Lost to Roger Maltbie, Manufacturers Hanover Westchester Classic. 1986: Defeated Mike Sullivan, Lon Hinkle, Walt Disney World/Oldsmobile Classic. 1990: Lost to Nick Faldo, Masters Tournament. 1992: Lost to Billy Ray Brown, GTE Byron Nelson Classic.

FORD, Doug-- (5-7) 1950: Lost to Dutch Harrison, Texas Open. 1951: Lost to Cary Middlecoff, Kansas City Open. 1952: Defeated Sam Snead, Jacksonville Open. 1953: Lost to Earl Stewart, Greensboro Open. 1954: Defeated Ed Furgol, Greater Greensboro Open. 1955: Lost to Henry Ransom, Rubber City Open; Lost to Ted Kroll, Philadelphia Daily News Open. 1956: Lost to Mike Fetchick, Western Open. 1957: Lost to Arnold Palmer, Rubber City Open; Defeated George Bayer, Gene Littler, Billy Maxwell, Western Open. 1961: Defeated Arnold Palmer, "500" Festival Open. 1962: Defeated Joe Campbell, Bing Crosby National Pro-Am.

FORSMAN, Dan-- (1-0) 1992: Defeated Steve Elkington, Brad Faxon, Buick Open.

FOUGHT, John-- (1-0) 1979: Defeated Jim Simons, Buick Goodwrench Open.

FROST, David-- (2-2) 1986: Lost to Tom Kite, Western Open. 1988: Lost to Seve Ballesteros, Manufacturers Hanover Westchester Classic; Defeated Bob Tway, Southern Open. 1989: Defeated Ben Crenshaw, NEC World Series of Golf.

FUNSETH, Rod-- (0-1) 1971: Lost to Buddy Allin, Greater Greensboro Open.

FURGOL, Ed-- (2-2) 1954: Defeated Cary Middlecoff, Phoenix Open; Lost to Doug Ford, Greater Greensboro Open. 1956: Lost to Bob Rosburg, Motor City Open. 1957: Defeated Al Besselink, Caliente Open.

GALLAGHER, Jr., Jim-- (1-1) 1990: Defeated Ed Dougherty, Billy Mayfair, Greater Milwaukee Open. 1991: Lost to Tom Purtzer, NEC World Series of Golf.

GAMEZ, Robert-- (0-1) 1993: Lost to Fred Couples, Honda Classic.

GARDNER, Buddy-- (0-1) 1987: Lost to Jay Haas, Big "I" Houston Open.

GEIBERGER, Al-- (1-1) 1967: Lost to Billy Casper, Carling World Open. 1975: Defeated Gary Player, MONY Tournament of Champions.

GHEZZI, Vic-- (1-4) 1935: Defeated Johnny Revolta, Los Angeles Open. 1936: Lost to Johnny Farrell, New Jersey Open. 1939: Lost to Henry Picard, Metropolitan Open. 1946: Lost to Lloyd Mangrum, U.S. Open. 1948: Lost to Ed Oliver, Tacoma Open.

GILBERT, Gibby-- (1-0) 1970: Defeated Bruce Crampton, Houston Champions International.

GILDER, Bob-- (1-0) 1983: Defeated, Rex Caldwell, Johnny Miller, Mark O'Meara, Phoenix Open.

GOALBY, Bob-- (2-1) 1962: Defeated Art Wall, Insurance City Open. 1965: Lost to Gay Brewer, Hawaiian Open. 1969: Defeated Jim Wiechers, Robinson Open.

GOLDEN, John-- (2-0) 1931: Defeated George Von Elm, Agua Caliente Open. 1932: Defeated Craig Wood, North & South Open.

GRADY, Wayne-- (1-0) 1989: Defeated Ronnie Black, Manufacturers Hanover Westchester Classic.

GRAHAM, David-- (2-1) 1972: Defeated Bruce Devlin, Cleveland Open; Lost to Lou Graham, Liggett and Myers Open. 1979: Defeated Ben Crenshaw, PGA Championship.

GRAHAM, Lou-- (3-1) 1971: Lost to George Archer, Greater Hartford Open. 1972: Defeated Hale Irwin, David Graham, Larry Ziegler, Liggett and Myers Open. 1975: Defeated John Mahaffey, U.S. Open. 1979: Defeated Bobby Wadkins, IVB-Philadelphia Classic.

GREEN, Hubert-- (2-3) 1971: Defeated Don January, Houston Champions International. 1975: Lost to Don Bies, Sammy Davis, Jr.-Greater Hartford Open. 1978: Defeated Bill Kratzert, Hawaiian Open; Lost to Gil Morgan, World Series of Golf. 1986: Lost to Andy Bean, Doral-Eastern Open.

GREEN, Ken-- (0-2) 1988: Lost to Sandy Lyle, Kmart Greater Greensboro Open; Lost to Seve Ballesteros, Manufacturers Hanover Westchester Classic.

GREENE, Bert-- (1-0) 1973: Defeated Miller Barber, Ligget and Myers Open.

GRIENER, Otto-- (0-1) 1948: Lost to Jimmy Demaret, St. Paul Open.

GUHLDAHL, Ralph-- (2-1) 1937: Lost to Harry Cooper, St. Petersburg Open; Defeated Horton Smith, Western Open. 1939: Defeated Denny Shute, Gene Sarazen, Dapper Dan Open.

HAAS, Jr., Fred-- (2-2) 1947: Lost to Jim Ferrier, St. Paul Open. 1948: Lost to Ed Oliver, Tacoma Open; Defeated Ben Hogan, Johnny Palmer, Portland Open. 1949: Defeated Bob Hamilton, Miami Open.

HAAS, Jay-- (3-0) 1982: Defeated John Adams, Hall of Fame Classic. 1987: Defeated Buddy Gardner, Big "I" Houston Open. 1993: Defeated Bob Lohr, H-E-B Texas Open.

HAGEN, Walter-- (5-0) 1916: Defeated James Barnes, Charles Hofner, Metropolitan Open. 1919: Defeated Mike Brady, U.S. Open. 1920: Defeated James Barnes, Metropolitan Open. 1923: Defeated Bill Mehlhorn, Texas Open. 1931: Defeated Percy Alliss, Canadian Open.

HALLBERG, Gary-- (0-2) 1984: Lost to Gary Koch, Isuzu-Andy Williams-San Diego Open. 1991: Lost to Blaine McCallister, H-E-B Texas Open.

HALLDORSON, Dan-- (0-1) 1981: Lost to Dave Barr, Quad Cities Open.

HALLET, Jim-- (0-2) 1990: Lost to Kenny Knox, Buick Southern Open. 1991: Lost to Ian Woosnam, USF&G Classic.

HAMILTON, Bob-- (0-1) 1949: Lost to Fred Haas, Jr., Miami Open.

HAMMOND, Donnie-- (1-0) 1986: Defeated John Cook, Bob Hope Chrysler Classic.

HAMPTON, Harry-- (0-1) 1923: Lost to George McLean, Shawnee Open.

HARBERT, Chick-- (2-1) 1942: Defeated Ben Hogan, Texas Open; Defeated Dutch Harrison, St. Paul Open. 1950: Lost to Henry Ransom, World Championship of Golf.

HARNEY, Paul-- (0-1) 1963: Lost to Arnold Palmer, Thunderbird Classic.

HARPER, Chandler-- (1-1) 1938: Lost to Johnny Revolta, St. Petersburg Open. 1953: Defeated Ted Kroll, El Paso Open.

HARRIS, Jr., Labron-- (1-1) 1968: Lost to Bob Murphy, Philadelphia Golf Classic. 1971: Defeated Bert Yancey, Robinson Open.

HARRISON, Dutch-- (1-8) 1939: Lost to Dick Metz, Oakland Open. 1941: Lost to Leonard Dodson, Oakland Open; Lost to Chick Harbert, St. Paul Open. 1945: Lost to Sam Byrd, Mobile Open. 1946: Lost to Johnny Palmer, Nashville Invitational. 1948: Lost to Ben Hogan, Motor City Open; Lost to Lloyd Mangrum, World's Championship of Golf. 1951: Defeated Doug Ford, Texas Open. 1952: Lost to Tommy Bolt, Los Angeles Open.

HATALSKY, Morris-- (1-2) 1983: Defeated George Cadle, Greater Milwaukee Open; Lost to Danny Edwards, Miller High Life-Quad Cities Open. 1988: Lost to Tom Kite, Kemper Open.

HAWKINS, Fred-- (0-1) 1959: Lost to Ben Hogan, Colonial National Invitation.

HAYES, Mark-- (0-2) 1979: Lost to Lon Hinkle, Bing Crosby National Pro-Am. 1981: Lost to Larry Nelson, Greater Greensboro Open.

HEAFNER, Clayton-- (1-1) 1942: Lost to Byron Nelson, Tam O' Shanter Open. 1947: Defeated Lew Worsham, Jacksonville Open.

INDIVIDUAL PLAYOFF RECORDS (cont'd.)

HEARD, Jerry-- (0-1) 1974: Lost to Bob Menne, Kemper Open.

HEBERT, Jay-- (2-1) 1956: Lost to Mike Fetchick, Western Open. 1961: Defeated Ken Venturi, Houston Classic; Defeated Gary Player, American Golf Classic.

HEBERT, Lionel-- (1-1) 1956: Lost to Mike Fetchick, St. Petersburg Open. 1962: Defeated Gary Player, Gene Littler, Memphis Open.

HENNING, Harold--(0-1) 1969: Lost to Charles Sifford, Los Angeles Open.

HENNINGER, Brian--(1-0) 1994: Defeated Mike Sullivan, Deposit Guaranty Classic.

HILL, Dave-- (4-2) 1961: Defeated Tommy Bolt, Bud Sullivan, Home of the Sun Open. 1963: Defeated Mike Souchak, Hot Springs Open. 1969: Defeated Gay Brewer, Tommy Jacobs, R.H. Sikes, IVB-Philadelphia Classic; Lost to Bob Lunn, Greater Hartford Open. 1972: Lost to George Archer, Glen Campbell Los Angeles Open. 1975: Defeated Rik Massengale, Sahara Invitational.

HINKLE, Lon-- (1-2) 1977: Lost to Ed Sneed, Tallahassee Open. 1979: Defeated Andy Bean, Mark Hayes, Bing Crosby National Pro-Am. 1986: Lost to Ray Floyd, Walt Disney World/Oldsmobile Classic.

HINSON, Larry-- (1-1) 1969: Defeated Frank Beard, Greater New Orleans Open. 1975: Lost to Don January, San Antonion Texas Open.

HISKEY, Babe-- (1-0) 1965: Defeated Dudley Wysong, Cajun Classic.

HOCH, Scott-- (1-1) 1989: Lost to Nick Faldo, Masters Tournament; Defeated Robert Wrenn, Las Vegas Invitational.

HOFNER, Charles-- (0-1) 1916: Lost to Walter Hagen, Metropolitan Open.

HOGAN, Ben-- (8-11) 1941: Lost to Leonard Dodson, Oakland Open. 1942: Defeated Jimmy Thomson, Los Angeles Open; Lost to Chick Harbert, Texas Open; Lost to Byron Nelson, Masters Tournament. 1944: Lost to Harold McSpaden, Chicago Victory Open. 1945: Defeated Harold McSpaden, Montgomery Invitational. 1946: Defeated Herman Keiser, Phoenix Open; Lost to Ray Mangrum, Pensacola Open. 1948: Defeated Dutch Harrison, Motor City Open; Defeated Ed Oliver, Western Open; Lost to Fred Haas, Jr., Portland Open. 1949: Defeated Jimmy Demaret, Long Beach Open; Lost to Jimmy Demaret, Phoenix Open. 1950: Lost to Sam Snead, Los Angeles Open; Defeated Lloyd Mangrum, George Fazio, U.S. Open. 1954: Lost to Sam Snead, Masters Tournament. 1955: Lost to Jack Fleck, U.S. Open. 1959: Defeated Fred Hawkins, Colonial National Invitation. 1960: Lost to Tommy Bolt, Memphis Open.

HOLSCHER, Bud-- (0-1) 1956: Lost to Dick Mayer, Philadelphia Daily News Open.

HULBERT, Mike-- (2-0) 1989: Defeated Bob Estes, B.C. Open. 1991: Defeated Kenny Knox, Anheuser-Busch Golf Classic.

HUNTER, Willie-- (1-0) 1927: Defeated Harold Sampson, California Open.

HUSTON, John-- (0-1) 1993: Lost to Jim McGovern, Shell Houston Open.

INMAN, John-- (1-0) 1993: Defeated Bob Estes, Mark Brooks, Brad Bryant, Billy Andrade, Buick Southern Open.

IRWIN, Hale-- (4-5) 1970: Lost to Billy Casper, Los Angeles Open. 1972: Lost to Lou Graham, Liggett and Myers Open. 1976: Defeated Kermit Zarley, Florida Citrus Open; Lost to Roger Maltbie, Memorial Tournament. 1981: Lost to John Cook, Bing Crosby National Pro-Am; Defeated Bobby Clampett, Peter Jacobsen, Gil Morgan, Buick Open. 1984: Defeated Jim Nelford, Bing Crosby National Pro-Am. 1990: Defeated Mike Donald, U.S. Open. 1991: Lost to Kenny Perry, Memorial Tournament.

JACKLIN, Tony-- (1-1) 1970: Lost to Pete Brown, Andy Williams San Diego Open. 1972: Defeated John Jacobs, Greater Jacksonville Open.

JACOBS, John-- (0-1) 1972: Lost to Tony Jacklin, Greater Jacksonville Open.

JACOBS, Tommy-- (2-2) 1962: Defeated Johnny Pott, San Diego Open. 1964: Defeated Jimmy Demaret, Palm Springs Golf Classic. 1966: Lost to Jack Nicklaus, Masters Tournament. 1969: Lost to Dave Hill, IVB-Philadelphia Classic.

JACOBSEN, Peter-- (1-3) 1981: Lost to Hale Irwin, Buick Open. 1984: Defeated Payne Stewart, Colonial National Invitation. 1985: Lost to Curtis Strange, Honda Classic. 1989: Lost to Mark McCumber, Beatrice Western Open.

JAECKEL, Barry-- (1-2) 1978: Defeated Bruce Lietzke, Tallahassee Open. 1981: Lost to Ray Floyd, Tournament Players Championship. 1983: Lost to Fred Couples, Kemper Open.

JANUARY, Don-- (3-5) 1956: Lost to Mike Fetchick, Western Open. 1961: Lost to Jerry Barber, PGA Championship. 1964: Lost to Chi Chi Rodriguez, Lucky International Open. 1967: Defeated Don Massengale, PGA Championship. 1969: Lost to Jack Nicklaus, Kaiser International. 1970: Defeated Dale Douglass, Greater Jacksonville Open. 1971: Lost to Hubert Green, Houston Champions International. 1975: Defeated Larry Hinson, San Antonio Texas Open.

JENKINS, Tom-- (0-1) 1981: Lost to Bruce Lietzke, Wickes Andy Williams-San Diego Open.

JOHNSON, Howie-- (1-1) 1958: Defeated Arnold Palmer, Azalea Open. 1970: Lost to Miller Barber, Greater New Orleans Open.

JOHNSTON, Al-- (1-0) 1962: Defeated Bill Collins, Hot Springs Open.

JONES, Grier-- (2-0) 1972: Defeated Bob Murphy, Hawaiian Open; Defeated Dave Marad, Robinson's Fall Classic.

JONES, Jr., Robert T.-- (2-2) 1923: Defeated Bobby Cruickshank, U.S. Open. 1925: Lost to Willie MacFarlane, U.S. Open. 1928: Lost to Johnny Farrell, U.S. Open. 1929: Defeated Al Espinosa, U.S. Open.

JONES, Steve-- (2-1) 1988: Defeated Bob Tway, AT&T Pebble Beach National Pro-Am. 1989: Defeated Sandy Lyle, Paul Azinger, Bob Hope Chrysler Classic. 1990: Lost to Payne Stewart, MCI Heritage Classic.

INDIVIDUAL PLAYOFF RECORDS (cont'd.)

KARL, Richie-- (1-0) 1974: Defeated Bruce Crampton, B.C. Open.

KEISER, Herman-- (0-2) 1946: Lost Ben Hogan, Phoenix Open. 1947: Lost to Dave Douglas, Orlando Open.

KIRKWOOD, Sr., Joe-- (1-1) 1923: Defeated Macdonald Smith, California Open. 1930: Lost to Olin Dutra, Long Beach Open.

KITE, Tom-- (6-3) 1976: Defeated Terry Diehl, IVB-Bicentennial Golf Classic. 1982: Lost to Ed Fiori, Bob Hope Desert Classic; Defeated Jack Nicklaus, Denis Watson, Bay Hill Classic. 1986: Defeated Fred Couples, David Frost, Nick Price, Western Open. 1988: Lost to MorrisHatalsky, Kemper Open. 1989: Defeated Davis Love III, Nestle Invitational; Defeated Payne Stewart, Nabisco Championships. 1990: Defeated John Cook, Federal Express St. Jude Classic. 1992: Lost to John Cook, Bob Hope Chrysler Classic.

KLEIN, Willie-- (0-1) 1925: Lost to Willie MacFarlane, Shawnee Open.

KNOX, Kenny-- (1-1) 1990: Defeated Jim Hallet, Buick Southern Open. 1991: Lost to Kenny Knox, Anheuser-Busch Golf Classic.

KNUDSON, George-- (3-0) 1963: Defeated Mason Rudolph, Portland Open. 1964: Defeated Al Balding, Fresno Open. 1970: Defeated George Archer, Robinson Open.

KOCH, Gary-- (2-0) 1984: Defeated Gary Hallberg, Isuzu-Andy Williams-San Diego Open; Defeated George Burns, Bay Hill Classic.

KRATZERT, Bill-- (0-1) 1978: Lost to Hubert Green, Hawaiian Open.

KROLL, Ted-- (1-7) 1952: Lost to Cary Middlecoff, Motor City Open. 1953: Lost to Chandler Harper, El Paso Open; Lost to Cary Middlecoff, Carling's Open. 1954: Lost to Lloyd Mangrum, Western Open. 1955: Defeated Doug Ford, Philadelphia Daily News Open. 1956: Lost to Arnold Palmer, Insurance City Open. 1960: Lost to Johnny Pott, Dallas Open. 1961: Lost to Billy Maxwell, Insurance City Open.

LAFFOON, Ky-- (1-2) 1934: Defeated Paul Runyon, Glens Falls Open. 1935: Lost to Harry Cooper, Western Open. 1950: Lost to Skip Alexander, Empire State Open.

LANCASTER, Neal-- (1-0) 1994: Defeated Tom Byrum, Mark Carnevale, David Edwards, Yoshinori Mizumaki, David Ogrin, GTE Byron Nelson Classic.

LANGER, Bernhard-- (1-1) 1985: Defeated Bobby Wadkins, Sea Pines Heritage Classic. 1986: Lost to Bob Tway, Shearson Lehman Brothers-Andy Williams Open.

LEMA, Tony-- (3-1) 1962: Defeated Bob Rosburg, Orange County Open. 1963: Defeated Tommy Aaron, Memphis Open; Lost to Arnold Palmer, Cleveland Open. 1964: Defeated Arnold Palmer, Cleveland Open.

LEONARD, Stan-- (1-1) 1955: Lost to Gene Littler, Labatt Open. 1960: Defeated Art Wall, Western Open.

LEVI, Wayne-- (2-1) 1980: Defeated Gil Morgan, Pleasant Valley Jimmy Fund Classic. 1984: Lost to Jack Renner, Hawaiian Open. 1985: Defeated Steve Pate, Georgia Pacific Atlanta Classic.

LIETZKE, Bruce-- (6-3) 1977: Defeated Gene Littler, Joe Garagiola-Tucson Open; Lost to Jack Nicklaus, MONY Tournament of Champions. 1978: Lost to Barry Jaeckel, Tallahassee Open. 1981: Defeated Ray Floyd, Tom Jenkins, Wickes Andy Williams-San Diego Open; Defeated Tom Watson, Byron Nelson Classic. 1984: Defeated Andy bean, Honda Classic. 1988: Defeated Clarence Rose, GTE Byron Nelson Classic. 1992: Lost to Billy Ray Brown, GTE Byron Nelson Classic; Defeated Corey Pavin, Southwestern Bell Colonial.

LITTLE, Lawson-- (1-0) 1940: Defeated Gene Sarazen, U.S. Open.

LITTLER, Gene-- (3-8) 1955: Defeated Stan Leonard, Labatt Open. 1956: Lost to Peter Thomson, Texas International Open. 1957: Lost to Doug Ford, Western Open. 1960: Lost to Tommy Bolt, Memphis Open. 1962: Lost to Jay Hebert, Memphis Open. 1966: Lost to Joe Campbell, Tucson Open. 1969: Defeated Orville Moody, Julius Boros, Tom Weiskopf, Greater Greensboro Open. 1970: Lost to Billy Casper, Masters Tournament. 1975: Defeated Julius Boros, Westchester Classic. 1977: Lost to Bruce Lietzke, Joe Garagiola-Tucson Open; Lost to Lanny Wadkins, PGA Championship.

LOCKE, Bobby-- (3-0) 1947: Defeated Ed Oliver, All American Open. 1949: Defeated Frank Stranahan, Cavalier Specialist Tournament. 1950: Defeated Lloyd Mangrum, All American Tournament.

LOHR, Bob-- (0-1) 1993: Lost to Jay Haas, H-E-B Texas Open.

LOVE III, Davis-- (0-3) 1989: Lost to Tom Kite, Nestle Invitational. 1991: Lost to Tom Purtzer, NEC World Series of Golf. 1992: Lost to Fred Couples, Nissan Los Angeles Open.

LOWERY, Steve-- (1-0) 1994: Defeated Rick Fehr, Sprint International.

LUNN, Bob-- (2-0) 1969: Defeated Dave Hill, Greater Hartford Open. 1971: Defeated Billy Casper, Glen Campbell Los Angeles Open.

LYLE, Sandy-- (3-1) 1987: Defeated Jeff Sluman, Tournament Players Championship. 1988: Defeated Fred Couples, Phoenix Open; Defeated Ken Green, Kmart Greater Greensboro Open. 1989: Lost to Steve Jones, Bob Hope Chrysler, Classic.

MacDONALD, Robert-- (1-0) 1923: Defeated James Barnes, Metropolitan Open.

MacFARLANE, Will-- (3-2) 1924: Lost Leo Diegel, Shawnee Open. 1925: Defeated Robert T. Jones, Jr., U.S. Open; Defeated Willie Klein, Shawnee Open. 1930: Defeated Johnny Farrell, Metropolitan Open. 1933: Lost to Denny Shute, Gaspirilla Open.

MAGEE, Andrew-- (1-0) 1991: Defeated D.A. Weibring, Las Vegas Invitational.

MAHAFFEY, John-- (3-2) 1975: Lost to Lou Graham, U.S. Open. 1978: Defeated Jerry Pate, Tom Watson, PGA Championship. 1984: Defeated Jim Simons, Bob Hope Desert Classic. 1985: Lost to Mark Wiebe, Anheuser-Busch Golf Classic; Defeated Jodie Mudd, Texas Open.

MALTBIE, Roger-- (2-1) 1976: Defeated Hale Irwin, Memorial Tournament. 1985: Defeated George Burns, Ray Floyd, Manufacturers Hanover Westchester Classic. 1986: Lost to Mac O'Grady, Canon Sammy Davis, Jr.-Greater Hartford Open.

MANERO, Tony-- (0-1) 1937: Lost to Ray Mangrum, Miami Open.

MANGRUM, Lloyd-- (5-3-1) 1946: Defeated Vic Ghezzi, Byron Nelson, U.S. Open. 1948: Defeated Jimmy Demaret, Lower Rio Grande Open; Defeated Sam Snead, Dutch Harrison, World's Championship of Golf; Defeated George Fazio, Utah Open. 1949: Lost to Sam Snead, Greater Greensboro Open; Tied Cary Middlecoff, Motor City Open. 1950: Lost to Ben Hogan, U.S. Open; Lost to Bobby Locke, All American Tournament.1954: Defeated Ted Kroll, Western Open.

MANGRUM, Ray-- (3-1) 1936: Lost to Henry Picard, North & South Open; Defeated Leonard Dodson, Wildwood New Jersey Open. 1937: Defeated Tony Manero, Miami Open. 1946: Defeated Ben Hogan, Pensacola Open.

MARAD, Dave-- (0-1) 1972: Lost to Grier Jones, Robinson's Fall Classic.

MARR, Dave-- (2-0) 1961: Defeated Bob Rosburg, Jacky Cupit, Greater Seattle Open. 1962: Defeated Jerry Steelsmith, Azalea Open.

MASSENGALE, Don-- (0-1) 1967: Lost to Don January, PGA Championship.

MASSENGALE, Rik-- (0-1) 1975: Lost to Dave Hill, Sahara Invitational.

MAXWELL, Billy-- (1-2) 1955: Lost to Bo Wininger, Baton Rouge Open. 1957: Lost to Doug Ford, Western Open. 1961: Defeated Ted Kroll, Insurance City Open.

MAYFAIR, Billy-- (1-2) 1990: Lost to Jim Gallagher, Jr., Greater Milwaukee Open; Lost to Jodie Mudd, Nabisco Championships. 1993:Defeated Mark Calcavecchia, Ted Schulz, Greater Milwaukee Open.

MAYER, Dick-- (2-0) 1956: Defeated Bud Holscher, Philadelphia Daily News Open. 1957: Defeated Cary Middlecoff, U.S. Open.

MAYFIELD, Shelley-- (1-1) 1953: Lost to Cary Middlecoff, Houston Open. 1955: Defeated Mike Souchak, Thunderbird Invitational.

McCALLISTER, Blaine-- (1-1) 1986: Lost to Gene Sauers, Bank of Boston Classic. 1991: Defeated Gary Hallberg, H-E-B Texas Open.

McCLENDON, Mac-- (1-0) 1978: Defeated Mike Reid, Pensacola Open.

McCUMBER, Mark-- (2-0) 1989: Defeated Peter Jacobsen, Beatrice Western Open. 1994: Defeated Fuzzy Zoeller, THE TOUR Championship.

McDERMOTT, John-- (1-1) 1910: Lost to Alex Smith, U.S. Open. 1911: Defeated Mike Brady, George Simpson, U.S. Open.

McGEE, Jerry-- (0-1) 1976: Lost to Ray Floyd, World Open.

McGOVERN, Jim-- (1-0) 1993: Defeated John Huston, Shell Houston Open.

McGOWAN, Jack-- (0-1) 1969: Lost to Deane Beman, Texas Open.

McLEAN, George-- (1-0) 1923: Defeated Harry Hampton, Shawnee Open.

McCLEOD, Fred-- (1-0) 1908: Defeated Willie Smith, U.S. Open.

McMULLIN, John-- (0-1) 1958: Lost to Sam Snead, Dallas Open.

McSPADEN, Harold-- (3-3) 1940: Lost to Sam Snead, Canadian Open. 1943: Defeated Buck White, All American Open. 1944: Defeated Byron Nelson, Phoenix Open; Defeated Ben Hogan, Chicago Victory Open. 1945: Lost to Byron Nelson, New Orleans Open; Lost to Ben Hogan, Montgomery Invitational.

MEDIATE, Rocco-- (2-0) 1991: Defeated Curtis Strange, Doral-Ryder Open. 1993: Defeated Steve Elkington, Kmart Greater Greensboro Open.

MEHLHORN, Bill-- (1-3) 1923: Lost to Walter Hagen, Texas Open. 1929: Defeated Bobby Cruickshank, Horton Smith, South Central Open; Lost to Billy Burke, Glens Falls Open. 1936: Lost to Wiffy Cox, Sacramento Open.

MENNE, Bob-- (1-1) 1970: Lost to Lee Trevino, National Airlines Open. 1974: Defeated Jerry Heard, Kemper Open.

METZ, Dick-- (1-2) 1936: Lost to Harry Cooper, St. Paul Open. 1939: Defeated Dutch Harrison, Oakland Open. 1946: Lost to George Fazio, Canadian Open.

MICKELSON, Phil-- (1-0) 1994: Defeated Fred Couples, Mercedes Championships.

MIDDLECOFF, Cary-- (6-6-1) 1947: Defeated George Schoux, Charlotte Open. 1948: Lost to Ed Oliver, Tacoma Open. 1949: Tied Lloyd Mangrum, Motor City Open. 1950: Defeated Ed Oliver, St. Louis Open. 1951: Defeated Doug Ford, Dave Douglas, Kansas City Open. 1952: Defeated Ted Kroll, Motor City Open; Lost to Julius Boros, World Championship of Golf. 1953: Defeated Shelley Mayfield, Jim Ferrier, Earl Stewart, Billy Nary, Houston Open; Defeated Ted Kroll, Carling's Open; Lost to Art Wall, Ft. Wayne Open. 1954: Lost to Ed Furgol, Phoenix Open. 1956: Lost to Peter Thomson, Texas International Open. 1957: Lost to Dick Mayer, U.S. Open.

MILLER, Johnny-- (1-5) 1972: Lost to Jack Nicklaus, Bing Crosby National Pro-Am. 1974: Defeated Frank Beard, Bob Murphy, Jack Nicklaus, World Open. 1979: Lost to Tom Watson, Colgate Hall of Fame Classic. 1982: Lost to Tom Watson, Glen Campbell Los Angeles Open. 1983: Lost to Bob Gilder, Phoenix Open; Lost to John Cook, Canadian Open.

INDIVIDUAL PLAYOFF RECORDS (cont'd.)

MILLER, Massie-- (0-1) 1929: Lost to Joe Turnesa, Lannin Memorial Tournament.

MITCHELL, Abe-- (1-0) 1922: Defeated Leo Diegel, Southern Open.

MITCHELL, Bobby-- (1-0) 1972: Defeated Jack Nicklaus, Tournament of Champions.

MIZE, Larry-- (1-2) 1986: Lost to Greg Norman, Kemper Open. 1987: Defeated Greg Norman, Seve Ballesteros, Masters Tournament. 1990: Lost to Payne Stewart, MCI Heritage Classic.

MIZUMAKI, Yoshinori-- (0-1) 1994: Lost to Neal Lancaster, GTE Byron Nelson Classic.

MONTGOMERIE, Colin-- (0-1) 1994: Lost to Ernie Els, U.S. Open.

MONTGOMERY, Jack-- (0-1) 1967: Lost to Marty Fleckman, Cajun Classic Open.

MONTI, Eric-- (1-0) 1961: Defeated George Bayer, Bobby Nichols, Ontario Open.

MOODY, Orville-- (0-2) 1969: Lost to Gene Littler, Greater Greensboro Open. 1973: Lost to Jack Nicklaus, Bing Crosby National Pro-Am.

MORGAN, Gil-- (3-4) 1978: Defeated Hubert Green, World Series of Golf. 1979: Defeated Larry Nelson, Danny Thomas-Memphis Classic. 1980: Lost to Wayne Levi, Pleasant Valley Jimmy Fund Classic. 1981: Lost to Hale Irwin, Buick Open. 1983: Defeated Lanny Wadkins, Curtis Strange, Joe Garagiola-Tucson Open; Lost to Fred Couples, Kemper Open. 1990: Lost to Tony Sills, Independent Insurance Agent Open.

MUDD, Jodie-- (2-2) 1985: Lost to Phil Blackmar, Canon Sammy Davis, Jr.-Greater Hartford Open; Lost to John Mahaffey, Texas Open. 1989: Defeated Larry Nelson, GTE Byron Nelson Classic. 1990: Defeated Billy Mayfair, Nabisco Championships.

MURPHY, Bob-- (1-5) 1968: Defeated Labron Harris, Jr., Phildelphia Golf Classic. 1970: Lost to Bob Murphy, Tucson Open. 1972: Lost to Grier Jones, Hawaiian Open. 1973: Lost to Bobby Nichols, Westchester Classic. 1974: Lost to Johnny Miller, World Open. 1981: Lost to Dave Eichelberger, Tallahassee Open.

MURRAY, Charles-- (0-1) 1920: Lost to J. Douglass Edgar, Canadian Open.

NAGLE, Kel-- (0-1) 1965: Lost to Gary Player, U.S. Open.

NARY, Bill-- (0-2) 1952: Lost to Jack Burke, Jr., Baton Rouge Open. 1953: Lost to Cary Middlecoff, Houston Open.

NELFORD, Jim-- (0-1) 1984: Lost to Hale Irwin, Bing Crosby National Pro-Am.

NELSON, Byron-- (5-4) 1939: Defeated Craig Wood, Denny Shute, U.S. Open. 1941: Lost to Horton Smith, Florida West Coast Open. 1942: Defeated Ben Hogan, Masters Tournament; Defeated Clayton Heafner, Tam O' Shanter Open. 1944: Lost to Harold McSpaden, Phoenix Open. 1945: Defeated Sam Snead, Charlotte Open; Defeated Harold McSpaden, New Orleans Open; Lost to Sam Snead, Gulfport Open. 1946: Lost to Lloyd Mangrum, U.S. Open.

NELSON, Larry-- (3-2) 1979: Lost to Gil Morgan, Danny Thomas-Memphis Classic; Defeated Ben Crenshaw, Western Open. 1981: Defeated Mark Hayes, Greater Greensboro Open. 1987: Defeated Lanny Wadkins, PGA Championship. 1989: Lost to Jodie Mudd, GTE Byron Nelson Classic.

NEWTON, Jack-- (1-0) 1978: Defeated Mike Sullivan, Buick-Goodwrench Open.

NICHOLS, Bobby-- (2-2) 1961: Lost to Eric Monti, Ontario Open. 1962: Defeated Dan Sikes, Jack Nicklaus, Houston Classic. 1973: Defeated Bob Murphy, Westchester Classic. 1975: Lost to J.C. Snead, Andy Williams San Diego Open.

NICKLAUS, Jack-- (13-10) 1962: Lost to Bobby Nichols, Houston Classic; Defeated Arnold Palmer, U.S. Open. 1963: Defeated Gary Player, Palm Springs Golf Classic; Lost to Arnold Palmer, Western Open. 1965: Lost to Doug Sanders, Pensacola Open; Defeated Johnny Pott, Memphis Open. 1966: Defeated Tommy Jacobs, Gay Brewer, Masters Tournament. 1968: Defeated Frank Beard, Lee Elder, American Golf Classic. 1969: Defeated George Archer, Billy Casper, Don January, Kaiser International. 1970: Defeated Arnold Palmer, Byron Nelson Classic. 1971: Lost to Gardner Dickinson, Atlanta Golf Classic; Lost to Lee Trevino, U.S. Open. 1972: Defeated Johnny Miller, Bing Crosby National Pro-Am; Lost to Bobby Mitchell, Tournament of Champions. 1973: Defeated Ray Floyd, Orville Moody, Bing Corsby National Pro-Am; Defeated Miller Barber, Greater New Orleans Open. 1974: Lost to Johnny Miller, World Open. 1975: Lost to Tom Weiskopf, Canadian Open; Defeated Billy Casper, World Open. 1977: Defeated Bruce Lietzke, MONY Tournament of Champions. 1980: Lost to Ray Floyd, Doral-Eastern Open. 1982: Lost to Tom Kite, Bay Hill Classic. 1984: Defeated Andy Bean, Memorial Tournament.

NICOLETTE, Mike-- (1-0) 1983: Defeated Greg Norman, Bay Hill Classic.

NORMAN, Greg-- (3-7) 1983: Lost to Mike Nicolette, Bay Hill Classic. 1984: Lost to Fuzzy Zoeller, U.S. Open; Lost to Tom Watson, Western Open. 1986: Defeated Larry Mize, Kemper Open. 1987: Lost to Larry Mize, Masters Tournament. 1988: Lost to Curtis Strange, Independent Insurance Agent Open; Lost to Seve Ballesteros, Manufacturers Hanover Westchester Classic. 1989: Defeated Paul Azinger, Mark Calcavecchia, Tim Simpson, Doral-Ryder Open. 1993: Lost to Paul Azinger, PGA Championship.

O'GRADY, Mac-- (1-0) 1986: Defeated Roger Maltbie, Canon Sammy Davis, Jr.-Greater Hartford Open.

OGRIN, David-- (0-2) 1985: Lost to Hal Sutton, St. Jude Memphis Classic. 1994: Lost to Neal Lancaster, GTE Byron Nelson Classic.

OLIVER, Ed-- (1-3) 1947: Lost to Bobby Locke, All American Open. 1948: Lost to Ben Hogan, Western Open; Defeated Cary Middlecoff, Fred Haas, Jr., Charles Congdon, Vic Ghezzi, Tacoma Open. 1950: Lost to Cary Middlecoff, St. Louis Open.

INDIVIDUAL PLAYOFF RECORDS (cont'd.)

O'MEARA, Mark-- (1-4) 1981: Lost to Dave Eichelberger, Tallahassee Open. 1983: Lost to Bob Gilder, Phoenix Open. 1991: Lost to Corey Pavin, Bob Hope Chrysler Classic. 1992: Lost to John Cook, Bob Hope Chrysler Classic; Defeated Jeff Sluman, AT&T Pebble Beach National Pro-Am.

OOSTERHUIS, Peter-- (0-1) 1974: Lost to Lee Elder, Monsanto Open.

OUIMET, Francis-- (1-0) 1913: Defeated Harry Vardon, Edward Ray, U.S. Open.

PALMER, Arnold-- (14-10) 1956: Defeated Ted Kroll, Insurance City Open. 1957: Defeated Doug Ford, Rubber City Open. 1958: Lost to Howie Johnson, Azalea Open. 1959: Defeated Gay Brewer, Pete Cooper, West Palm Beach Open. 1960: Lost to Bill Collins, Houston Classic; Defeated Bill Collins, Jack Fleck, Insurance City Open. 1961: Defeated Al Balding, San Diego Open; Defeated Doug Sanders, Phoenix Open; Lost to Doug Ford, "500" Festival Open. 1962: Defeated Gary Player, Dow Finsterwald, Masters Tournament; Defeated Johnny Pott, Colonial National Invitation; Lost to Jack Nicklaus, U.S. Open. 1963: Defeated Paul Harney, Thunderbird Classic; Lost to Julius Boros, U.S. Open; Defeated Tommy Aaron, Tony Lema, Cleveland Open; Defeated Julius Boros, Jack Nicklaus, Western Open. 1964: Lost to Gary Player, Pensacola Open; Lost to Tony Lema, Cleveland Open. 1966: Lost to Doug Sanders, Bob Hope Desert Classic; Defeated Gay Brewer, Tournament of Champions; Lost to Billy Casper, U.S. Open. 1968: Defeated Deane Beman, Bob Hope Desert Classic. 1970: Lost to Jack Nicklaus, Byron Nelson Classic. 1971: Defeated Ray Floyd, Bob Hope Desert Classic.

PALMER, Johnny-- (2-1) 1946: Defeated Dutch Harrison, Nashville Invitational. 1948: Lost to Fred Haas, Jr., Portland Open. 1949: Defeated Jimmy Demaret, World Championship of Golf.

PATE, Jerry-- (1-2) 1977: Defeated Dave Stockton, Phoenix Open. 1978: Lost to John Mahaffey, PGA Championship. 1980: Lost to Doug Tewell, Sea Pines Heritage Classic.

PATE, Steve-- (0-2) 1985: Lost to Wayne Levi, Georgia Pacific Atlanta Classic. 1991: Lost to Corey Pavin, BellSouth Atlanta Classic.

PAVIN, Corey-- (5-2) 1986: Defeated Dave Barr, Greater Milwaukee Open. 1987: Defeated Craig Stadler, Hawaiian Open. 1991: Defeated Mark O'Meara, Bob Hope Chrysler Classic; Defeated Steve Pate, BellSouth Atlanta Classic; Lost to Billy Ray Brown, Canon Greater Hartford Open. 1992: Defeated Fred Couples, Honda Classic; Lost to Bruce Lietzke, Southwestern Bell Colonial.

PEETE, Calvin-- (0-1) 1986: Lost to Curtis Strange, Houston Open.

PENNA, Toney: (0-1) 1940: Lost to Jimmy Demaret, Western Open.

PERRY, Kenny-- (1-0) 1991: Defeated Hale Irwin, Memorial Tournament.

PICARD, Henry-- (2-1) 1936: Defeated Ray Mangrum, North & South Open. 1939: Lost to Sam Snead, St. Petersbrug Open; Defeated Paul Runyon, Vic Ghezzi, Metropolitan Open.

PLAYER, Gary-- (3-9) 1958: Lost to Sam Snead, Dallas Open. 1959: Lost to Don Whitt, Memphis Open. 1961: Lost to Jay Hebert, American Golf Classic. 1962: Lost to Arnold Palmer, Masters Tournament; Lost to Jay Hebert, Memphis Open. 1963: Lost to Jack Nicklaus, Palm Springs Golf Classic. 1964: Defeated Arnold Palmer, Miller Barber, Pensacola Open. 1965: Defeated Kel Nagle, U.S. Open. 1967: Lost to Miller Barber, Oklahoma City Open. 1971: Defeated Hal Underwood, Greater Jacksonville Open; Lost to Tom Weiskopf, Kemper Open. 1975: Lost to Al Geiberger, MONY Tournament of Champions.

POHL, Dan-- (1-2) 1982: Lost to Craig Stadler, Masters Tournament. 1985: Lost to Phil Blackmar, Canon Sammy Davis, Jr.-Greater Hartford Open. 1986: Defeated Payne Stewart, Colonial National Invitation.

POTT, Johnny-- (2-5) 1960: Defeated Bo Wininger, Ted Kroll, Dallas Open. 1961: Lost to Jack Burke, Jr., Buick Open. 1962: Lost to Tommy Jacobs, San Diego Open; Lost to Arnold Palmer, Colonial National Invitation. 1965: Lost to Jack Nicklaus, Memphis Open; Lost to Billy Casper, Insurance City Open. 1968: Defeated Billy Casper, Bruce Devlin, Bing Crosby National Pro-Am.

PRICE, Nick-- (1-1) 1986: Lost to Tom Kite, Western Open. 1994: Defeated Scott Simpson, Southwestern Bell Colonial.

PRIDE, Dicky-- (1-0) 1994: Defeated Gene Sauers, Hal Sutton, Federal Express St. Jude Classic.

PURTZER, Tom-- (2-0) 1988: Defeated Mark Brooks, Gatlin Brothers Southwest Classic. 1991: Defeated Davis Love III, Jim Gallagher, NEC World Series of Golf.

QUICK, Smiley-- (0-1) 1950: Lost to Jack Burke, Jr., Bing Crosby Pro-Amateur.

RAGAN, Jr., Dave-- (1-0) 1962: Defeated Doug Sanders, West Palm Beach Open.

RANSOM, Henry-- (2-0) 1950: Defeated Chick Harbert, World Championship of Golf. 1955: Defeated Jack Burke, Jr., Doug Ford, JacksonBradley, Rubber City Open.

RAY, Edward-- (0-1) 1913: Lost to Francis Ouimet, U.S. Open.

REGALADO, Victor-- (0-1) 1981: Lost to Dave Barr, Quad Cities Open.

REID, Mike-- (1-2) 1978: Lost to Mac McClendon, Pensacola Open. 1985: Lost to Hal Sutton, Southwest Golf Classic. 1988: Defeated Tom Watson, NEC World Series of Golf.

RENNER, Jack-- (1-0) 1984: Defeated Wayne Levi, Hawaiian Open.

REVOLTA, Johnny-- (1-2) 1935: Lost to Vic Ghezzi, Los Angeles Open; Lost to Bobby Cruickshank, Orlando Open. 1938: Defeated Chandler Harper, St. Petersburg Open.

ROBERTS, Loren-- (0-1) 1994: Lost to Ernie Els, U.S. Open.

RODRIGUEZ, Chi Chi-- (3-1) 1964: Defeated Don January, Lucky International Open. 1966: Lost to Jacky Cupit, Cajun Classic Open. 1968: Defeated Dale Douglass, Sahara Invitational. 1972: Defeated Billy Casper, Byron Nelson Classic.

ROGERS, Bill-- (1-2) 1978: Lost to Andy Bean, Western Open. 1979: Lost to Tom Watson, Byron Nelson Classic. 1981: Defeated Bill Rogers, Texas Open.

ROSBURG, Bob-- (1-5) 1956: Defeated Ed Furgol, Motor City Open. 1957: Lost to Al Besselink, Caracas Open. 1958: Lost to Art Wall, Eastern Open. 1961: Lost to Dave Marr, Greater Seattle Open; Lost to Jack Fleck, Bakersfield Open. 1962: Lost to Tony Lema, Orange County Open.

ROSE, Clarence-- (0-1) 1988: Lost to Bruce Lietzke, GTE Byron Nelson Classic.

RUDOLPH, Mason-- (0-1) 1963: Lost to George Knudson, Portland Open.

RUNYON, PAUL-- (0-2) 1934: Lost to Ky Laffoon, Glens Falls Open. 1939: Lost to Henry Picard, Metropolitan Open.

SAMPSON, Harold-- (0-1) 1927: Lost to Willie Hunter, California Open.

SANDERS, Doug-- (5-4) 1956: Defeated Dow Finsterwald, Canadian Open. 1961: Lost to Arnold Palmer, Phoenix Open. 1962: Lost to Dave Ragan, Jr., West Palm Beach Open. 1964: Lost to Julius Boros, Greater Greensboro Open. 1965: Defeated Jack Nicklaus, Pensacola Open; Lost to Gay Brewer, Greater Seattle Open. 1966: Defeated Arnold Palmer, Bob Hope Desert Classic; Defeated Tom Weiskopf, Greater Greensboro Open. 1970: Defeated Chris Blocker, Bahama Islands Open.

SARAZEN, Gene-- (2-5) 1926: Lost to Macdonald Smith, Metropolitan Open. 1927: Lost to Joe Turnesa, Ridgewood CC Open. 1928: Defeated Johnny Farrell, Nassau Bahamas Open. 1930: Lost to Leo Diegel, Oregon Open. 1935: Defeated Craig Wood, Augusta National Invitational. 1939: Lost to Ralph Gulhdahl, Dapper Dan Open. 1940: Lost to Lawson Little, U.S. Open.

SAUERS, Gene-- (1-3) 1986: Defeated Blaine McCallister, Bank of Boston Classic. 1991: Lost to Mark Brooks, Kmart Greater Greensboro Open. 1992: Lost to John Cook, Bob Hope Chrysler Classic. 1994: Lost to Dicky Pride, Federal Express St. Jude Classic.

SCHLEE, John-- (0-1) 1973: Lost to Ed Sneed, Kaiser International

SCHOUX, George-- (0-1) 1947: Lost to Cary Middlecoff, Charlotte Open.

SCHROEDER, John-- (0-1) 1979: Lost to Bob Byman, Bay Hill Citrus Classic.

SCHULZ, Ted-- (0-1) 1993: Lost to Billy Mayfair, Greater Milwaukee Open.

SHEARER, Bob-- (0-1) 1982: Lost to Ed Sneed, Michelob-Houston Open.

SHEPPARD, Charles-- (0-1) 1938: Lost to Al Zimmerman, Utah Open.

SHUTE, Denny-- (2-2) 1933: Defeated Willie MacFarlane, Gaspirilla Open. 1939: Lost to Byron Nelson, U.S. Open; Lost to Ralph Guhldahl, Dapper Dan Open; Defeated Horton Smith, Gelns Falls Open.

SIECKMANN, Tom-- (1-0) 1988: Defeated Mark Wiebe, Anheuser-Busch Golf Classic.

SIFFORD, Charles-- (2-0) 1957: Defeated Eric Monti, Long Beach Open. 1969: Defeated Harold Henning, Los Angeles Open.

SIKES, Dan-- (0-2) 1962: Lost to Bobby Nichols, Houston Classic. 1973: Lost to Lanny Wadkins, Byron Nelson Golf Classic.

SIKES, R.H.-- (0-1) 1969: Lost to Dave Hill, IVB-Philadelpha Classic.

SILLS, Tony-- (1-0) 1990: Defeated Gil Morgan, Independent Insurance Agent Open.

SIMONS, Jim-- (0-3) 1979: Lost to John Fought, Buick Goodwrench Open. 1980: Lost to Howard Twitty, Sammy Davis, Jr.-Greater Hartford Open. 1984: Lost to John Mahaffey, Bob Hope Desert Classic.

SIMPSON, George-- (0-1) 1911: Lost to John McDermott, U.S. Open.

SIMPSON, Scott-- (1-3) 1983: Lost to Fred Couples, Kemper Open. 1989: Defeated Bob Tway, BellSouth Atlanta Golf Classic. 1991: Lost to Payne Stewart, U.S. Open. 1994: Lost to Nick Price, Southwestern Bell Colonial.

SIMPSON, Tim-- (0-2) 1989: Lost to Mike Donald, Anhueser-Busch Golf Classic. 1990: Lost to Greg Norman, Doral-Ryder Open.

SINDELAR, Joey-- (1-1) 1988: Lost to Mark Brooks, Canon Sammy Davis, Jr.-Greater Hartford Open. 1990: Defeated Willie Wood, Hardee's Golf Classic.

SINGH, Vijay-- (1-0) 1993: Defeated Mark Weibe, Buick Classic.

SLUMAN, Jeff-- (0-3) 1987: Lost to Sandy Lyle, Tournament Players Championship. 1991: Lost to Billy Andrade, Kemper Open. 1992: Lost to Mark O'Meara, AT&T Pebble Beach National Pro-Am.

SMITH, Alex-- (1-1) 1901: Lost to Willie Anderson, U.S. Open. 1910: Defeated John McDermott, Macdonald Smtih, U.S. Open.

SMITH, Horton-- (1-4) 1929: Lost to Bill Mehlhorn, South Central Open. 1937: Lost to Harry Cooper, St. Petersburg Open; Lost to Ralph Guhldahl, Western Open. 1939: Lost to Denny Shute, Glens Falls Open. 1941: Defeated Byron Nelson, Florida West Coast Open.

SMITH, Macdonald-- (2-2) 1910: Lost to Alex Smith, U.S. Open. 1923: Lost to Joe Kirkwood, Sr., California Open. 1924: Defeated Abe Espinosa, Northern California Open. 1926: Defeated Gene Sarazen, Metropolitan Open.

SMITH, Willie-- (0-1) 1908: Lost to Fred McLeod, U.S. Open.

INDIVIDUAL PLAYOFF RECORDS (cont'd.)

SNEAD, J.C.-- (3-1) 1971: Lost to George Archer, Greater Hartford Open. 1975: Defeated Ray Floyd, Bobby Nichols, Andy Williams San Diego Open. 1981: Defeated Mike Sullivan, Southern Open. 1987: Defeated Seve Ballesteros, Manufacturers Hanover Westchester Classic.

SNEAD, Sam-- (10-8) 1938: Defeated Harry Cooper, Canadian Open. 1939: Defeated Henry Picard, St. Petersburg Open. 1940: Defeated Harold McSpaden, Canadian Open. 1945: Lost to Byron Nelson, Charlotte Open; Defeated Byron Nelson, Gulfport Open. 1947:Lost to Lew Worsham, U.S. Open. 1948: Lost to Lloyd Mangrum, World's Championship of Golf. 1949: Defeated Lloyd Mangrum, Greater Greensboro Open. 1950: Defeated Ben Hogan, Los Angeles Open; Lost to Jack Burke, Jr., Bing Crosy Pro-Amateur; Lost to Jim Ferrier, St. Paul Open. 1952: Lost to Doug Ford, Jacksonville Open. 1953: Lost to Earl Stewart, Greensboro Open. 1954: Defeated Ben Hogan, Masters Tournament. 1955: Defeated Tommy Bolt, Miami Beach Open. 1956: Defeated Fred Wampler, Greater Greensboro Open. 1958: Defeated Gary Player, Julius Boros, John McMullin, Dallas Open; Lost to George Bayer, Havana International.

SNEED, Ed-- (3-1) 1973: Defeated John Schlee, Kaiser International. 1977: Defeated Lon Hinkle, Tallahassee Open. 1979: Lost to Fuzzy Zoeller, Masters Tournament. 1982: Defeated Bob Shearer, Michelob-Houston Open.

SOUCHAK, Mike-- (0-3) 1955: Lost to Shelly Mayfield, Thunderbird Invitational. 1957: Lost to Jimmy Demaret, Thunderbird Invitational. 1963: Lost to Dave Hill, Hot Springs Open.

STADLER, Craig-- (3-2) 1982: Defeated Dan Pohl, Masters Tournament; Defeated Ray Floyd, World Series of Golf. 1985: Lost to Lanny Wadkins, Bob Hope Desert Classic. 1987: Lost to Corey Pavin, Hawaiian Open. 1991: Defeated Russ Cochran, THE TOUR Championship.

STEELSMITH, Jerry-- (0-2) 1962: Lost to Dave Marr, Azalea Open. 1964: Lost to Billy Casper, Almaden Open.

STEWART, Jr., Earl-- (1-2) 1953: Lost to Cary Middlecoff, Houston Open; Defeated Sam Snead, Doug Ford, Art Wall, Greensboro Open. 1954: Lost to Tommy Bolt, Insurance City Open.

STEWART, Payne-- (2-5) 1984: Lost to Peter Jacobsen, Colonial National Invitation. 1985: Lost to Bob Eastwood, Byron Nelson Classic. 1986: Lost to Dan Pohl, Colonial National Invitation. 1988: Lost to Phil Blackmar, Provident Classic. 1989: Lost to Tom Kite, Nabisco Championships. 1990: Defeated Steve Jones, Larry Mize, MCI Heritage Classic. 1991: Defeated Scott Simpson, U.S. Open.

STILL, Ken-- (1-0) 1970: Defeated Lee Trevino, Bert Yancey, Kaiser International.

STOCKTON, Dave-- (0-1) 1977: Lost to Jerry Pate, Phoenix Open.

STRANAHAN, Frank-- (0-1) 1949: Lost to Bobby Locke, Cavalier Specialist Tournament.

STRANGE, Curtis-- (6-3)1980: Defeated Lee Trevino, Michelob Houston Open. 1981: Lost to Ray Floyd, Tournament Players Championship. 1983: Lost to Gil Morgan, Joe Garagiola-Tucson Open. 1985: Defeated Peter Jacobsen, Honda Classic. 1986: Defeated Calvin Peete, Houston Open. 1988: Defeated Greg Norman, Independent Insurance Agent Open; Defeated Nick Faldo, U.S. Open; Defeated Tom Kite, Nabiscon Championships. 1991: Lost to Rocco Mediate, Doral-Ryder Open.

STRECK, Ron-- (0-1) 1985: Lost to Woody Blackburn, Isuzu-Andy Williams-San Diego Open.

SULLIVAN, Bud-- (0-1) 1961: Lost to Dave Hill, Home of the Sun Open.

SULLIVAN, Mike-- (0-4) 1978: Lost to Jack Newton, Buick-Goodwrench Open. 1981: Lost to J.C. Snead, Southern Open. 1986: Lost to Ray Floyd, Walt Disney World/Oldsmobile Classic. 1994: Lost to Brian Henninger, Deposit Guaranty Golf Classic.

SUTTON, Hal-- (2-2) 1982: Defeated Bill Britton, Walt Disney World Golf Classic. 1985: Defeated David Ogrin, St. Jude Memphis Classic; Defeated Mike Reid, Southwest Golf Classic. 1989: Lost to Mike Donald, Anheuser-Busch Golf Classic. 1994: Lost to Dicky Pride, Federal Express St. Jude Classic.

TEWELL, Doug-- (1-0) 1980: Defeated Jerry Pate, Sea Pines Heritage Classic.

THOMPSON, Barney-- (0-1) 1981: Lost to John Cook, Bing Crosby National Pro-Am.

THOMSON, Jimmy-- (0-1) 1942: Lost to Ben Hogan, Los Angeles Open.

THOMSON, Peter-- (0-1) 1956: Defeated Gene Littler, Cary Middlecoff, Texas International Open.

THORPE, Jim-- (0-1) 1985: Lost to Scott Verplank, Western Open.

TORRANCE, Sam-- (0-1) 1983: Lost to Ronnie Black, Southern Open.

TREVINO, Lee-- (5-5) 1970: Defeated Bob Murphy, Tucson Open; Defeated Bob Menne, National Airlines Open; Lost to Ken Still, Kaiser International. 1971: Defeated Jack Nicklaus, U.S. Open; Lost to Tom Weiskopf, Kemper Open; Defeated Art Wall, Canadian Open. 1972: Defeated Lee Elder, Greater Hartford Open. 1978: Lost to Andy Bean, Danny Thomas-Memphis Classic; Lost to Lee Elder, Greater Milwaukee Open. 1980: Lost to Curtis Strange, Michelob Houston Open.

TROMBLEY, Bill-- (0-1) 1956: Lost to Art Wall, Ft. Wayne Open.

TWAY, Bob-- (2-3) 1986: Defeated Bernhard Langer, Shearson Lehman Brothers-Andy Williams Open. 1988: Lost to Steve Jones, AT&T Pebble Beach National Pro-Am; Lost to David Frost, Southern Open. 1989: Lost to Scott Simpson, BellSouth Atlanta Golf Classic. 1990: Defeated John Cook, Las Vegas Invialional.

TWITTY, Howard-- (1-0) 1980: Defeated Jim Simons, Sammy Davis, Jr.-Greater Hartford Open.

TURNESA, Jim-- (0-1) 1952: Lost to Jimmy Clark, Ft. Wayne Open.

TURNESA, Joe-- (2-0) 1927: Defeated Gene Sarazen, Ridgewood CC Open. 1929: Defeated Massie Miller, Lannin Memorial Tournament.

INDIVIDUAL PLAYOFF RECORDS (cont'd.)

ULOZAS, Tom-- (0-1) 1972: Lost to Bert Yancey, American Golf Classic.

UNDERWOOD, Hal-- (0-1) 1971: Lost to Gary Player, Greater Jacksonville Open.

VALENTINE, Tommy-- (0-1) 1981: Lost to Tom Watson, Atlanta Classic.

VARDON, Harry-- (0-1) 1913: Lost to Francis Ouimet, U.S. Open.

VENTURI, Ken-- (0-3) 1957: Lost to Jimmy Demaret, Thunderbird Invitational. 1958: Lost to Billy Casper, Greater New Orlean Open. 1961: Lost to Jay Hebert, Houston Classic.

VERPLANK, Scott-- (1-0) 1985: Defeated Jim Thorpe, Western Open.

VON ELM, George-- (0-2) 1931: Lost to John Golden, Agua Caliente Open. 1931: Lost to Billy Burke, U.S. Open.

WADKINS, Bobby-- (0-2) 1979: Lost to Lou Graham, IVB-Philadelphia Classic. 1985: Lost to Bernhard Langer, Sea Pines Heritage Classic.

WADKINS, Lanny-- (3-3) 1972: Lost to Homero Blancas, Phoenix Open. 1973: Defeated Dan Sikes, Byron Nelson Golf Classic. 1977: Defeated Gene Littler, PGA Championship. 1983: Lost to Gil Morgan, Joe Garagiola-Tucson Open. 1985: Defeated Craig Stadler, Bob Hope Desert Classic. 1987: Lost to Larry Nelson, PGA Championship.

WALL, Art-- (5-5) 1953: Lost to Earl Stewart, Greensboro Open; Defeated Cary Middlecoff, Ft. Wayne Open. 1956: Defeated Bill Trombley, Gardner Dickinson, Jr., Ft. Wayne Open. 1958: Defeated Dow Finsterwald, Rubber City Open; Defeated Jack Burke, Jr., Bob Rosburg, Eastern Open. 1959: Defeated Dow Finsterwald, Buick Open. 1960: Lost to Stan Leonard, Western Open. 1962: Lost to Bob Goalby, Insurance City Open. 1967: Lost to Billy Casper, Canadian Open. 1971: Lost to Lee Trevino, Canadian Open.

WAMPLER, Fred-- (0-1) 1956: Lost to Sam Snead, Greater Greensboro Open.

WATSON, Denis-- (0-1) 1982: Lost to Tom Kite, Bay Hill Classic.

WATSON, Tom-- (8-4) 1978: Defeated Ben Crenshaw, Bing Crosby National Pro-Am; Lost to John Mahaffey, PGA Championship. 1979: Lost to Fuzzy Zoeller, Masters Tournament; Defeated Bill Rogers, Byron Nelson Classic; Defeated Johnny Miller, Colgate Hall of Fame Classic. 1980: Defeated D.A. Weibring, Andy Williams-San Diego Open. 1981: Lost to Bruce Lietzke, Byron Nelson Classic; Defeated Tommy Valentine, Atlanta Classic. 1982: Defeated Johnny Miller, Glen Campbell Los Angeles Open; Defeated Frank Conner, Sea Pines Heritage Classic. 1984: Defeated Greg Norman, Western Open. 1988: Lost to Mike Reid, NEC World Series of Golf.

WEAVER, DeWitt-- (1-0) 1972: Defeated Chuck Courtney, Southern Open.

WEIBRING, D.A.-- (0-2) 1980: Lost to Tom Watson, Andy Williams-San Diego Open. 1991: Lost to Andrew Magee, Las Vegas Invitational.

WEISKOPF, Tom-- (2-3) 1966: Lost to Doug Sanders, Greater Greensboro Open. 1969: Lost to Gene Littler, Greater Greensboro Open. 1971: Defeated Dale Douglass, Gary Player, Lee Trevino, Kemper Open. 1975: Defeated Jack Nicklaus, Canadian Open. 1979: Lost to Ed Fiori, Southern Open.

WHITE, Buck-- (0-1) 1943: Lost to Harold McSpaden, All American Open.

WHITT, Don-- (1-1) 1957: Lost to Dow Finsterwald, Tucson Open. 1959: Defeated Gary Player, Al Balding, Memphis Open.

WIEBE, Mark-- (1-2) 1985: Defeated John Mahaffey, Anheuser-Busch Golf Classic. 1988: Lost to Tom Sieckmann, Anheuser-Busch Golf Classic. 1993: Lost to Vijay Singh, Buick Classic.

WIECHERS, Jim-- (0-1) 1969: Lost to Bob Goalby, Robinson Open.

WININGER, BO-- (1-1) 1955: Defeated Jimmy Clark, Billy Maxwell, Baton Rouge Open. 1960: Lost to Johnny Pott, Dallas Open.

WOOD, Craig-- (0-3) 1932: Lost to John Golden, North & South Open. 1935: Lost to Gene Sarazen, Augusta National Invitational. 1939: Lost to Byron Nelson, U.S. Open.

WOOD, Willie-- (0-1) 1990: Lost to Joey Sindelar, Hardee's Golf Classic.

WOOSNAM, Ian-- (1-0) 1991: Defeated Jim Hallet, USF&G Classic.

WORSHAM, Lew-- (1-2) 1946: Lost to Herman Barron, Philadelphia Inquirer Open. 1947: Lost to Clayton Heafner, Jacksonville Open. 1947: Defeated Sam Snead, U.S. Open.

WRENN, Robert-- (0-1) 1989: Lost to Scott Hoch, Las Vegas Invitational.

WYSONG, Dudley-- (1-1) 1965: Lost to Babe Hiskey, Cajun Classic. 1967: Defeated Billy Casper, Hawaiian Open.

YANCEY, Bert-- (2-2) 1969: Defeated Bruce Devlin, Atlanta Classic. 1970: Lost to Ken Still, Kaiser International. 1971: Lost to Labron Harris, Jr., Robinson Open. 1972: Defeated Tom Ulozas, American Golf Classic.

ZARLEY, Kermit-- (0-1) 1976: Lost to Hale Irwin, Florida Citrus open.

ZIEGLER, Larry-- (1-1) 1969: Defeated Homero Blancas, Michigan Golf Classic. 1972: Lost to Lou Graham, Liggett and Myers Open.

ZIMMERMAN, Al-- (1-0) 1938: Defeated Tee Branca, Charles Sheppard, Utah Open.

ZOELLER, Fuzzy-- (2-2) 1979: Defeated Ed Sneed, Tom Watson, Masters Tournament. 1983: Lost to Jim Colbert, Colonial National Invitation. 1984: Defeated Greg Norman, U.S. Open. 1994: Lost to Mark McCumber, THE TOUR Championship.

LOW 9:

1994 -- 29 (7 under)   Davis Love III, Hawaiian; Lennie Clements, Bob Hope; Ronnie Black, Buick Invitational; Larry Nelson, Doral-Ryder; Dennis Paulson, Freeport-McMoRan; Brian Henninger, New England.

         29 (6 under)   Steve Lamontagne, Honda; Guy Boros, Southwestern Bell Colonial.

         29 (5 under)   Glen Day, B.C. Open.

1993 -- 28 (7 under)   Keith Clearwater, Wayne Levi, Southwestern Bell Colonial.

         29 (7 under)   Fuzzy Zoeller, Tom Kite, Bob Hope; Greg Norman, Buick Open; Dan Halldorson, Milwaukee.

1992 -- 29 (7 under)   Gil Morgan, Neal Lancaster, Bob Hope; Mark Calcavecchia, Masters; Jim McGovern, Federal Express; John Cook, Las Vegas.

         29 (6 under)   Dillard Pruitt, Phoenix; Robin Freeman, Byron Nelson; David Frost, Hardee's; Donnie Hammond, David Edwards, Texas.

1991 -- 28 (7 under)   Andrew Magee, Los Angeles.

         28 (6 under)   Emlyn Aubrey, Chattanooga.

1990 -- 28 (7 under)   Kenny Knox, Chattanooga.

         29 (7 under)   Tom Kite, Bob Hope.

         29 (6 under)   David Frost, Tucson; Mike Hulbert, Colonial; Kirk Triplett, Buick Classic; Howard Twitty, David Peoples, Southern; Steve Jones, Billy Ray Brown, John Dowdall, Texas.

         29 (5 under)   Chris Perry, Brad Fabel, Canon GHO.

1989 -- 28 (8 under)   Steve Pate, Bob Hope; Webb Heintzelman, Las Vegas.

1988 -- 28 (7 under)   Mike Sullivan, Texas.

         29 (7 under)   Sandy Lyle, Pebble Beach; Dave Eichelberger, Hawaiian; Gil Morgan, Andy Williams; Ken Green, Milwaukee; Mike Donald, Walt Disney; Mark Wiebe, Ken Green, Tucson.

1987 -- 29 (7 under)   Dewey Arnette, Trevor Dodds, Buick.

         30 (7 under)   Joey Sindelar, B.C. Open.

         29 (6 under)   Payne Stewart, Phoenix; David Frost, Andy Williams; Wayne Levi, Hartford; Curtis Strange, Anheuser-Busch; Dave Rummells, Dave Stockton, Hardee's; Robert Thompson, Provident.

1986 -- 29 (7 under)   Hubert Green, Doral; Mike Sullivan, Houston; Charles Bolling, Las Vegas.

         29 (6 under)   Willie Wood, Westchester; Mike Smith, Hardee's; Mike Donald, Southern.

1985 -- 29 (7 under)   Jim Thorpe, Milwaukee.

         29 (6 under)   John Mahaffey, Bob Hope; Larry Mize, Los Angeles; Tom Watson, Colonial; Roger Maltbie, Westchester; Brad Fabel, Quad Cities; Mike Gove, Texas; Ken Brown, Pensacola.

1984 -- 29 (6 under)   George Burns, Colonial; Mike McCullough, Canadian; Mark O'Meara, Hartford.

         30 (6 under)   Gibby Gilbert, Bob Hope; Willie Wood, Phoenix; Greg Norman, Bay Hill; David Graham, T of C; Payne Stewart, Memorial; Tom Kite, Westchester; Tommy Valentine, Mike Donald, Atlanta; Gary Player, PGA; Rod Nuckolls, Steve Brady, Denis Watson, Buick; Lon Hinkle, Scott Simpson, Las Vegas; George Archer, Bank of Boston; Mark Lye, Larry Rinker, Walt Disney.

1983 -- 28 (7 under)   Jeff Sluman, Quad Cities.

         28 (6 under)   Mark O'Meara, B.C. Open.

         29 (7 under)   Hubert Green, Bob Hope; Craig Stadler, Buick.

         29 (6 under)   Jon Chaffee, Rick Pearson, Quad Cities; Gibby Gilbert, PGA; Lanny Wadkins, Anheuser-Busch; George Cadle, Jim Colbert, Texas; Gary Hallberg, Pensacola.

1982 -- 29 (7 under)   George Burns, Hartford.

         29 (6 under)   Scott Hoch, Houston; Gary Koch, Bob Eastwood, Allen Miller, Quad Cities; Fred Couples, PGA; Isao Aoki, Hartford.

1981 -- 29 (6 under)   Mike Holland, Anheuser-Busch; Fuzzy Zoeller, Hartford; Bob Gilder, Southern.

1980 -- 29 (7 under)   Bob Murphy, Tallahassee; Curtis Strange, Houston; John Fought, Buick.

         29 (6 under)   Gary Koch, Byron Nelson.

1979 -- 29 (7 under)   Kermit Zarley, Doral-Eastern; Andy Bean, Atlanta.

         29 (6 under)   Pat McGowan, Phoenix; Brad Bryant, Quad Cities; Allen Miller, Hartford.

1978 -- 29 (7 under)   Gary Koch, Houston.

         29 (6 under)   Rod Funseth, Hartford; Ron Streck, Texas.

         29 (5 under)   Rod Curl, B.C. Open.

1977 -- 29 (7 under)   Graham Marsh, T of C; Bobby Wadkins, Memorial; Al Geiberger, Memphis; Lanny Wadkins, Milwaukee; Rik Massengale, Pleasant Valley; Florentino Molina, Hartford; Leonard Thompson, Hall of Fame.

         29 (6 under)   Fred Marti, Pleasant Valley; Rod Curl, IVB; Bruce Lietzke, Hartford; Tom Weiskopf, World Series.

1976 -- 28 (8 under)   Jim Colbert, Bob Hope; Fuzzy Zoeller, Quad Cities.

1975 -- 27 (7 under)   Andy North, B.C. Open.

         28 (7 under)   Bruce Crampton, Sahara.

         29 (7 under)   Hale Irwin, Phoenix; Tom Weiskopf, Westchester.

         29 (6 under)   Jim Simons, Hartford.

1974 -- 29 (7 under)   Tom Kite, Doral-Eastern; Dan Sikes, New Orleans; Tom Watson, Hartford.

         29 (6 under)   Raymond Floyd, American Classic.

1973 -- 28 (7 under)   Bert Yancey, American Classic.

1972 -- 29 (7 under)   Babe Hiskey, Inverrary; Bert Yancey, Walt Disney.

         29 (7 under)   Dwight Nevil, Southern; Cesar Sanudo, Sahara.

1971 -- 28 (7 under)   Jim Jamieson, Robinson.

1970 -- 29 (6 under)   Dave Hill, Cleveland; George Knudson, Robinson; Wilf Homenuik, Azalea.

         29 (5 under)   Lou Graham, Memphis.

LOW 18:

1994 --	60 (12 under)	Davis Love III, Hawaiian.
1993 --	61 (10 under)	Jay Delsing, Federal Express.
	61 (9 under)	Billy Mayfair, Byron Nelson; Keith Clearwater, Lee Janzen, Colonial.
1992 --	62 (10 under)	David Love III, Kmart GGO; Fred Funk, Houston; John Cook, Las Vegas; Lee Janzen, John Huston, Walt Disney.
	62 (8 under)	David Frost, Hardee's; Nick Price, Texas.
1991 --	59 (13 under)	Chip Beck, Las Vegas.
1990 --	60 (12 under)	David Frost, Tucson.
1989 --	61 (11 under)	Jim Carter, Centel; Bob Tway, Walt Disney.
1988 --	61 (11 under)	Ken Green, Milwaukee; Mark Wiebe, Tucson.
	61 (9 under)	Dave Barr, Southern.
1987 --	61 (11 under)	David Edwards, Bob Hope.
	61 (9 under)	Mike Smith, Hardee's.
1986 --	61 (10 under)	Don Pooley, Phoenix.
	61 (9 under)	Rod Curl, Southern.
	62 (10 under)	George Burns, Las Vegas; Greg Norman, Canadian.
1985 --	62 (10 under)	Jim Thorpe, Milwaukee.
	62 (9 under)	Larry Mize, Los Angeles; Jay Delsing, B.C. Open.
	62 (8 under)	Bill Glasson, Las Vegas; Ron Streck, Quad Cities.
1984 --	61 (11 under)	Mark Lye, Walt Disney.
1983 --	61 (10 under)	George Archer, Los Angeles.
	62 (10 under)	John Fought, Bob Hope; Tom Kite, Bing Crosby.
	62 (9 under)	Andy Bean, Canadian; Curtis Strange, Hartford.
	62 (8 under)	Jon Chaffee, Quad Cities; Craig Stadler, Jim Colbert, Texas.
1982 --	61 (10 under)	Dana Quigley, Hartford.
	61 (9 under)	Hale Irwin, Southern.
	62 (10 under)	Larry Rinker, Tallahassee.
1981 --	62 (10 under)	Nick Faldo, Hale Irwin, Hawaiian.
	62 (9 under)	Andy Bean, Bay Hill; Ron Streck, Houston; Leonard Thompson, Canadian; Mark O'Meara, Hartford.
1980 --	62 (9 under)	Jim Simons, Hartford.
	62 (8 under)	George Burns, Texas.
	63 (9 under)	Andy Bean, Hawaiian; Bob Shearer, Atlanta; Bob Mann, Pensacola.
1979 --	61 (11 under)	Jerry McGee, Kemper; Andy Bean, Atlanta.
	61 (10 under)	Ben Crenshaw, Phoenix.
1978 --	62 (10 under)	Dave Eichelberger, Atlanta.
	62 (9 under)	Joe Inman, Hartford.
	62 (8 under)	Hubert Green, Ron Streck, San Antonio.
1977 --	59 (13 under)	Al Geiberger, Memphis.
1976 --	62 (10 under)	Gary Player, Florida Citrus.
1975 --	61 (11 under)	Johnny Miller, Tucson.
	61 (10 under)	Johnny Miller, Phoenix.
1974 --	61 (11 under)	Bert Yancey, Bob Hope.
1973 --	62 (9 under)	Jack Nicklaus, Ohio Kings Island; Gibby Gilbert, Tom Watson, World.
	62 (8 under)	J.C. Snead, Phoenix.
	63 (9 under)	Dave Stockton, Milwaukee; Hubert Green, Disney.
	63 (8 under)	Johnny Miller, U.S. Open; Hubert Green (twice), Hartford; John Schroeder, Quad Cities.
	63 (7 under)	Dick Rhyan, Southern.
1972 --	61 (10 under)	Homero Blancas, Phoenix.
1971 --	62 (9 under)	Billy Casper, Phoenix; Charles Coody, Cleveland.
	62 (8 under)	Larry Ziegler, Dave Eichelberger, Memphis; Bobby Mitchell, Southern.
1970 --	61 (10 under)	Johnny Miller, Phoenix.

LOW FIRST 18:

1994 --	61 (10 under)	Bob Lohr, Anheuser-Busch.
1993 --	62 (9 under)	Mike Smith, Texas.
	63 (9 under)	Howard Twitty, Hawaiian; Billy Andrade, Northern Telecom.
	63 (8 under)	Jim Gallagher, Jr., TOUR Championship.
	63 (7 under)	Jeff Woodland, Hardee's.
1992 --	62 (10 under)	Lee Janzen, Walt Disney.
	62 (8 under)	David Frost, Hardee's.
1991 --	61 (11 under)	Robert Gamez, Milwaukee.
	61 (9 under)	Marco Dawson, Chattanooga.
1990 --	61 (9 under)	Jose Maria Olazabal, World Series.
	62 (10 under)	Pat McGowan, Tucson.
	62 (9 under)	Larry Silveira, Federal Express.
	62 (8 under)	Howard Twitty, Southern.
1989 --	61 (11 under)	Bob Tway, Walt Disney.
1988 --	62 (10 under)	Bob Lohr, Walt Disney.
1987 --	61 (11 under)	David Edwards, Bob Hope.

LOW FIRST 18 (cont'd.):

1986 --	62 (8 under)	Ernie Gonzalez, Deposit Guaranty.
	63 (9 under)	George Burns, Hawaiian.
	63 (8 under)	Hubert Green, Phoenix.
	63 (7 under)	Bob Lohr, Hardee's.
1985 --	62 (8 under)	Bill Glasson, Las Vegas.
	63 (9 under)	Fred Couples, Honda; John Mahaffey, USF&G.
	63 (8 under)	Lanny Wadkins, Los Angeles; Mac O'Grady, Byron Nelson; John Cook, Pensacola.
1984 --	62 (9 under)	Lon Hinkle, Las Vegas.
1983 --	62 (8 under)	Craig Stadler, Texas.
	63 (9 under)	Craig Stadler, Bob Hope, Fuzzy Zoeller, Las Vegas.
	63 (8 under)	Mark O'Meara, B.C. Open, Mark Lye, Pensacola.
	63 (7 under)	Tom Byrum, Quad Cities.
1982 --	62 (10 under)	Larry Rinker, Tallahassee.
1981 --	63 (8 under)	Lon Nielsen, Hartford.
	63 (7 under)	Dan Halldorson, Tucson; Craig Stadler, Texas.
	64 (8 under)	Skip Dunaway, USF&G.
	64 (7 under)	Tom Watson, Bay Hill; Calvin Peete, B.C. Open.
1980 --	62 (9 under)	Jim Simons, Hartford.
	63 (9 under)	Bob Shearer, Atlanta.
	63 (7 under)	Bruce Lietzke, Colonial; Jack Nicklaus, Tom Weiskopf, U.S. Open; Scott Hoch,Quad Cities.
1979 --	61 (11 under)	Jerry McGee, Greensboro.
1978 --	62 (10 under)	Dave Eichelberger, Atlanta.
	62 (8 under)	Hubert Green, Texas.
1977 --	63 (8 under)	J.C. Snead, Hall of Fame.
	63 (7 under)	Charles Coody, Texas.
	64 (8 under)	Rik Massengale, Bob Hope; George Burns, Buick.
	64 (7 under)	Fred Marti, Pleasant Valley; Lee Elder, Hartford.
	64 (6 under)	Jerry Pate, Southern.
1976 --	63 (9 under)	Johnny Miller, Kaiser International.
	63 (8 under)	Fuzzy Zoeller, Quad Cities; David Graham, Carlton White, Westchester; Buddy Allin, B.C. Open.
	64 (8 under)	Rod Curl, Hawaiian; Ken Still, Milwaukee.
1975 --	63 (8 under)	Andy North, B.C. Open; Miller Barber, Sahara.
	64 (8 under)	Johnny Miller, Bob Hope; Bob Stanton, Inverrary.
	64 (7 under)	Tom Weiskopf, Greensboro; Andy North, Pensacola; Dennis Meyer, Hartford.
1974 --	62 (10 under)	Johnny Miller, Tucson.
1973 --	62 (9 under)	Gibby Gilbert, World.
	62 (8 under)	J.C. Snead, Phoenix.
	63 (8 under)	Hubert Green, Hartford.
	64 (8 under)	Jack Nicklaus, Bob Hope; Gibby Gilbert, Chi Chi Rodriguez, Florida Citrus; Lee Trevino, Doral-Eastern; Tom Weiskopf, Westchester.
1972 --	63 (8 under)	Bert Yancey, Hartford.
	64 (8 under)	DeWitt Weaver, Westchester.
	64 (7 under)	Dave Hill, Monsanto.
	64 (6 under)	Deane Beman, St. Louis.
1971 --	63 (9 under)	Joel Goldstrand, Hartford.
1970 --	63 (7 under)	Dave Hill, Memphis.
	64 (8 under)	Arnold Palmer, Florida Citrus; Bob Menne, National Airlines.
	64 (7 under)	Bert Greene, Phoenix; Arnold Palmer, Tommy Aaron, Greensboro; Tommy Aaron, Sahara.

LOW FIRST 36:

1994 --	127 (15 under)	Bob Estes, Texas.
	128 (16 under)	Davis Love III, Hawaiian; Scott Hoch, Bob Hope.
1993 --	129 (15 under)	Blaine McCallister, Houston.
	129 (11 under)	Dan Forsman, Byron Nelson; Fulton Allem, Colonial.
1992 --	128 (14 under)	Roger Maltbie, Texas.
	130 (10 under)	David Frost, Hardee's.
	130 (12 under)	Davis Love III, Los Angeles; Dan Forsman, Federal Express.
	131 (13 under)	Tom Watson, Brad Faxon, Mike Springer, Buick Invitational.
1991 --	127 (17 under)	Robert Gamez, Milwaukee.
	127 (15 under)	Lennie Clements, Chattanooga.
1990 --	128 (16 under)	Tim Simpson, Walt Disney.
	128 (12 under)	Jose Maria Olazabal, World Series; Peter Persons, Chattanooga; Steve Jones, Texas.
1989 --	126 (14 under)	Paul Azinger, Texas.
	128 (16 under)	Dan Pohl, Honda.
1988 --	127 (13 under)	Corey Pavin, Texas.
	129 (15 under)	Jeff Sluman, Greensboro; Larry Nelson, Atlanta; Bob Lohr, Disney.
1987 --	126 (18 under)	Robert Wrenn, Buick.
	128 (14 under)	Joey Sindelar, B.C. Open.
1986 --	128 (12 under)	Hal Sutton, Phoenix; Ernie Gonzalez, Pensacola.

LOW FIRST 36 (cont'd):

1985 --	128 (12 under)	Tim Simpson, Southern.
1984 --	130 (14 under)	Chip Beck, Walt Disney.
	130 (11 under)	Lon Hinkle, Las Vegas.
	130 (10 under)	Jim Colbert, Texas.
1983 --	128 (12 under)	Jim Colbert, Texas.
	129 (15 under)	Craig Stadler, Bob Hope.
1982 --	127 (15 under)	Tim Norris, Hartford.
	127 (13 under)	Bob Gilder, Westchester.
1981 --	129 (13 under)	Lon Nielsen, Hartford.
1980 --	129 (13 under)	Curtis Strange, Houston.
	129 (11 under)	Scott Hoch, Quad Cities.
	131 (13 under)	Tom Watson, T of C.
	131 (9 under)	Mike Sullivan, Southern.
1979 --	128 (14 under)	Ben Crenshaw, Phoenix.
1978 --	128 (14 under)	Phil Hancock, Hartford.
	128 (12 under)	Ben Crenshaw, Texas.
1977 --	127 (15 under)	Hale Irwin, Hall of Fame.
1976 --	130 (12 under)	Roger Maltbie, Phoenix; Buddy Allin, B.C. Open; Rik Massengale, Hartford.
	131 (13 under)	Raymond Floyd, Masters.
	132 (12 under)	Fuzzy Zoeller, Milwaukee.
1975 --	128 (14 under)	Johnny Miller, Phoenix.
	129 (15 under)	Tom Weiskopf, Westchester.
	129 (13 under)	Jack Nicklaus, Heritage.
1974 --	130 (12 under)	Dave Stockton, Hartford.
	132 (12 under)	Jack Nicklaus, Hawaiian; Hubert Green, Memphis.
1973 --	129 (11 under)	J.C. Snead, Phoenix.
	131 (13 under)	Buddy Allin, Florida Citrus.
	131 (11 under)	Jim Wiechers, Hartford.
	133 (11 under)	John Schlee, Kaiser International.
1972 --	131 (13 under)	Dwight Nevil, Westchester.
	131 (9 under)	Deane Beman, St. Louis.
1971 --	129 (13 under)	Miller Barber, Paul Harney, Gene Littler, Phoenix.
1970 --	130 (12 under)	Bobby Mitchell, Azalea.

LOW FIRST 54 HOLES:

1994 --	195 (18 under)	Bob Estes, Texas.
	197 (19 under)	Lennie Clements, Bob Hope; Greg Norman, PLAYERS.
1993 --	195 (21 under)	Greg Norman, Doral-Ryder.
	195 (15 under)	David Frost, Hardee's.
1992 --	194 (16 under)	David Frost, Hardee's.
	196 (20 under)	Ted Schulz, Mark O'Meara, Walt Disney.
	197 (16 under)	Nick Price, Texas.
1991 --	195 (18 under)	Hal Sutton, Kemper.
	195 (15 under)	Lance Ten Broeck, Chattanooga.
	196 (20 under)	Chip Beck, Bruce Lietzke, Las Vegas.
1990 --	193 (23 under)	Tim Simpson, Walt Disney.
	193 (17 under)	Peter Persons, Chattanooga.
1989 --	194 (16 under)	John Daly, Chattanooga; Donnie Hammond, Texas.
	197 (19 under)	Gene Sauers, Hawaiian.
1988 --	193 (17 under)	Blaine McCallister, Hardee's; Corey Pavin, Texas.
1987 --	195 (21 under)	Robert Wrenn, Buick.
1986 --	196 (17 under)	Hal Sutton, Phoenix.
	196 (14 under)	Ben Crenshaw, Vantage.
	199 (17 under)	Calvin Peete, T of C.
1985 --	197 (13 under)	Jodie Mudd, Texas; Tim Simpson, Southern.
	198 (18 under)	Craig Stadler, Bob Hope; Mark O'Meara, Hawaiian; Woody Blackburn, San Diego.
1984 --	196 (20 under)	Larry Nelson, Walt Disney.
1983 --	194 (16 under)	Jim Colbert, Texas.
	198 (15 under)	Jack Renner, Hartford.
	199 (17 under)	Craig Stadler, Bob Hope.
1982 --	192 (18 under)	Bob Gilder, Westchester.
	193 (20 under)	Tim Norris, Hartford.
1981 --	196 (20 under)	Bruce Lietzke, Bob Hope; Hale Irwin, Hawaiian.
1980 --	195 (18 under)	Curtis Strange, Houston.
	200 (19 under)	Jim Colbert, Tucson.
1979 --	197 (16 under)	Wayne Levi, Houston.
	197 (13 under)	Doug Tewell, Texas.
	198 (18 under)	Hubert Green, Hawaiian; Andy Bean, Atlanta.
1978 --	198 (18 under)	Andy Bean, Houston.
	198 (12 under)	Ben Crenshaw, Texas.

LOW FIRST 54 (cont'd.):

1977 --	196 (17 under)	Bill Kratzert, Hartford; Hale Irwin, Hall of Fame.
1976 --	200 (16 under)	J.C. Snead, San Diego.
	200 (13 under)	Roger Maltbie, Phoenix; Al Geiberger, Greensboro; Rik Massengale, J.C. Snead, Hartford.
	200 (10 under)	Lee Trevino, Colonial.
1975 --	196 (17 under)	Johnny Miller, Phoenix.
1974 --	198 (18 under)	Terry Diehl, Texas.
1973 --	198 (18 under)	Buddy Allin, Florida Citrus.
1972 --	198 (12 under)	Deane Beman, St. Louis.
	201 (15 under)	George Knudson, Kaiser International.
1971 --	194 (19 under)	Paul Harney, Phoenix.
1970 --	198 (15 under)	Bob Murphy, Hartford; Bobby Mitchell, Azalea.
	198 (12 under)	Homero Blancas, Memphis.

LOW FIRST 72:

1994 --	264 (24 under)	Scott Hoch, Bob Hope; Greg Norman, PLAYERS.
1993 --	259 (21 under)	David Frost, Hardee's.
	263 (25 under)	Tom Kite, Bob Hope.
1992 --	262 (26 under)	John Huston, Walt Disney.
1991 --	260 (20 under)	Dillard Pruitt, Chattanooga.
	263 (21 under)	Billy Andrade, Jeff Sluman, Kemper.
	263 (25 under)	Bruce Lietzke, Craig Stadler, D.A. Weibring, Andrew Magee, Las Vegas.
1990 --	260 (20 under)	Peter Persons, Chattanooga.
	264 (24 under)	Bob Tway, Las Vegas; Tim Simpson, Walt Disney.
1989 --	258 (22 under)	Donnie Hammond, Texas.
	266 (22 under)	Blaine McCallister, Honda; Scott Hoch, Las Vegas.
1988 --	259 (21 under)	Corey Pavin, Texas.
	262 (26 under)	Chip Beck, USF&G.
1987 --	262 (26 under)	Robert Wrenn, Buick.
1986 --	267 (21 under)	Calvin Peete, T of C.
	267 (17 under)	Hal Sutton, Phoenix; Rick Fehr, B.C. Open.
1985 --	264 (20 under)	Lanny Wadkins, Los Angeles.
	264 (16 under)	Tim Simpson, Southern.
	267 (21 under)	Mark O'Meara, Hawaiian; Lanny Wadkins, Disney World.
1984 --	265 (15 under)	Hubert Green, Southern.
	266 (22 under)	Larry Nelson, Disney World.
1983 --	261 (19 under)	Jim Colbert, Texas.
	266 (18 under)	Mark McCumber, Pensacola.
	267 (20 under)	Fuzzy Zoeller, Las Vegas.
	268 (20 under)	Isao Aoki, Hawaiian.
1982 --	259 (25 under)	Tim Norris, Hartford.
1981 --	264 (20 under)	Hubert Green, Hartford.
	265 (23 under)	Hale Irwin, Hawaiian.
	265 (15 under)	Johnny Miller, Tucson.
1980 --	265 (15 under)	Lee Trevino, Texas.
	266 (22 under)	Andy Bean, Hawaiian; Bill Kratzert, Milwaukee.
	270 (22 under)	Jim Colbert, Tucson.
	266 (18 under)	Curtis Strange, Lee Trevino, Houston; Howard Twitty, Jim Simons, Hartford.
1979 --	265 (23 under)	Andy Bean, Atlanta.
1978 --	264 (24 under)	Rod Funseth, Hartford.
1977 --	264 (20 under)	Hale Irwin, Hall of Fame.
1976 --	266 (18 under)	Rik Massengale, Hartford.
	268 (16 under)	Bob Gilder, Phoenix; Al Geiberger, Greensboro; John Lister, Quad Cities.
	269 (19 under)	Jack Nicklaus, TPC.
1975 --	260 (24 under)	Johnny Miller, Phoenix.
	263 (25 under)	Johnny Miller, Tucson.
1974 --	267 (21 under)	Lee Trevino, New Orleans.
1973 --	264 (20 under)	Billy Casper, Hartford.
	265 (23 under)	Buddy Allin, Florida Citrus.
1972 --	267 (21 under)	Jack Nicklaus, Walt Disney.
1971 --	261 (23 under)	Miller Barber, Phoenix.
1970 --	267 (17 under)	Bob Murphy, Hartford.
	267 (13 under)	Dave Hill, Memphis.

LOW 90:

1994 --	332 (27 under)	Bruce Lietzke, Las Vegas.
1993 --	325 (35 under)	Tom Kite, Bob Hope.
1992 --	336 (24 under)	John Cook, Gene Sauers, Rick Fehr, Mark O'Meara, Tom Kite, Bob Hope.
1991 --	329 (31 under)	Andrew Magee, D.A. Weibring, Las Vegas.
1990 --	334 (26 under)	Bob Tway, Las Vegas.

LOW 90 (cont'd.):

1989 --	336 (24 under)	Scott Hoch, Robert Wrenn, Las Vegas.
1988 --	338 (22 under)	Jay Haas, Bob Hope.
1987 --	341 (19 under)	Corey Pavin, Bob Hope.
1986 --	333 (27 under)	Greg Norman, Las Vegas.
1985 --	333 (27 under)	Lanny Wadkins, Bob Hope.
1984 --	340 (20 under)	John Mahaffey, Jim Simons, Bob Hope.
1983 --	335 (25 under)	Keith Fergus, Rex Caldwell, Bob Hope.
1982 --	335 (25 under)	Ed Fiori, Bob Hope.
1981 --	335 (25 under)	Bruce Lietzke, Bob Hope.
1980 --	343 (17 under)	Craig Stadler, Bob Hope.
1979 --	343 (17 under)	John Mahaffey, Bob Hope.
1978 --	339 (21 under)	Bill Rogers, Bob Hope.
1977 --	337 (23 under)	Rik Massengale, Bob Hope.
1976 --	344 (16 under)	Johnny Miller, Bob Hope.
1975 --	339 (21 under)	Johnny Miller, Bob Hope.
1974 --	341 (19 under)	Hubert Green, Bob Hope.
1973 --	343 (17 under)	Arnold Palmer, Bob Hope.
1972 --	344 (16 under)	Bob Rosburg, Bob Hope.
1971 --	342 (18 under)	Arnold Palmer, Bob Hope.
1970 --	339 (21 under)	Bruce Devlin, Bob Hope.

HIGHEST WINNING SCORE:

1994 --	281 (7 under)	Johnny Miller, AT&T.
	279 (5 under)	Ernie Els, U.S. Open.
1993 --	281 (7 under)	Mike Standly, Freeport-McMoRan; Rocco Mediate, Kmart GGO.
	280 (4 under)	Vijay Singh, Buick Classic.
1992 --	285 (3 under)	Tom Kite, U.S. Open.
1991 --	282 (6 under)	Payne Stewart, U.S. Open.
	279 (1 under)	Tom Purtzer, World Series.
	279 (5 under)	Craig Stadler, TOUR Championship.
	279 (9 under)	Steve Pate, Honda.
1990 --	282 (6 under)	John Huston, Honda; Steve Elkington, Kmart GGO; Wayne Grady, PGA.
	216 (even)	Greg Norman, Memorial (54 holes).
1989 --	283 (5 under)	Nick Faldo, Masters.
	278 (2 under)	Curtis Strange, U.S. Open.
1988 --	281 (7 under)	Sandy Lyle, Masters.
1987 --	287 (1 under)	Larry Nelson, PGA.
1986 --	287 (1 under)	Kenny Knox, Honda.
	279 (1 under)	Raymond Floyd, U.S. Open.
1985 --	285 (3 under)	Joey Sindelar, Greensboro.
	279 (1 under)	Andy North, U.S. Open.
1984 --	276 (4 under)	Fuzzy Zoeller, U.S. Open.
	280 (8 under)	Bruce Lietzke, Honda; Jack Nicklaus, Memorial; Greg Norman, Kemper; Tom Watson, Western.
1983 --	287 (1 under)	Fred Couples, Kemper.
1982 --	278 (2 under)	Craig Stadler, World Series.
	285 (3 under)	Danny Edwards, Greensboro.
1981 --	281 (1 over)	Bruce Lietzke, Byron Nelson.
1980 --	280 (4 under)	Doug Tewell, Heritage.
1979 --	284 (even)	Hale Irwin, U.S. Open.
1978 --	289 (1 over)	Jack Nicklaus, TPC.
1977 --	289 (1 over)	Mark Hayes, TPC.
1976 --	288 (4 over)	Al Geiberger, Western.
	288 (even)	Roger Maltbie, Memorial.
	281 (1 over)	Dave Stockton, PGA.
1975 --	287 (3 over)	Lou Graham, U.S. Open.
1974 --	287 (7 over)	Hale Irwin, U.S. Open.
	287 (3 over)	Tom Watson, Western.
1973 --	283 (5 under)	Tommy Aaron, Masters; Dave Hill, Memphis.
	277 (3 under)	Lanny Wadkins, Byron Nelson.
1972 --	290 (2 over)	Jack Nicklaus, U.S. Open.
1971 --	283 (3 over)	Gene Littler, Colonial.
1970 --	282 (2 over)	Gibby Gilbert, Houston.

LARGEST WINNING MARGIN:

1994 --	6 strokes	Nick Price, PGA.
1993 --	8 strokes	Davis Love III, Las Vegas.
1992 --	9 strokes	Fred Couples, Nestle.
1991 --	4 strokes	Lanny Wadkins, Hawaiian; Paul Azinger, Pebble Beach.
1990 --	12 strokes	Jose Maria Olazabal, World Series.

LARGEST WINNING MARGIN (cont'd.):

1989 -- 7 strokes   Mark Calcavecchia, Phoenix; Donnie Hammond, Texas.
1988 -- 8 strokes   Corey Pavin, Texas.
1987 -- 7 strokes   Tom Kite, Kemper; Robert Wrenn, Buick; Ken Brown, Southern.
1986 -- 7 strokes   Doug Tewell, Los Angeles; Greg Norman, Las Vegas.
1985 -- 7 strokes   Lanny Wadkins, Los Angeles.
1984 -- 6 strokes   George Archer, Bank of Boston; Hubert Green, Southern.
1983 -- 5 strokes   Gary Koch, Doral; Lanny Wadkins, Greensboro; David Graham, Houston; Jim Colbert, Texas.
1982 -- 7 strokes   Craig Stadler, Tucson; Calvin Peete, B.C. Open; Calvin Peete, Pensacola.
1981 -- 7 strokes   Andy Bean, Bay Hill.
1980 -- 7 strokes   Larry Nelson, Atlanta; Jack Nicklaus, PGA.
1979 -- 8 strokes   Andy Bean, Atlanta.
1978 -- 5 strokes   Andy Bean, Kemper; Tom Kite, B.C. Open.
1977 -- 7 strokes   Jerry Pate, Southern; Rik Massengale, Bob Hope.
1976 -- 8 strokes   Raymond Floyd, Masters.
1975 -- 14 strokes   Johnny Miller, Phoenix.
1974 -- 8 strokes   Lee Trevino, New Orleans; Johnny Miller, Kaiser International.
1973 -- 8 strokes   Buddy Allin, Florida Citrus.
1972 -- 9 strokes   Jack Nicklaus, Walt Disney.
1971 -- 8 strokes   Jack Nicklaus, T of C.
1970 -- 7 strokes   Frank Beard, T of C; Tony Jacklin, U.S. Open.

LOW START BY A WINNER:

1994 -- 62 (9 under)   Bob Estes, Texas.
1993 -- 63 (9 under)   Howard Twitty, Hawaiian.
        63 (8 under)   Jim Gallagher, Jr., TOUR Championship.
1992 -- 62 (8 under)   David Frost, Hardee's.
1991 -- 63 (9 under)   Mark Brooks, Milwaukee.
1990 -- 61 (9 under)   Jose Maria Olazabal, World Series.
1989 -- 64 (8 under)   Greg Norman, Milwaukee.
1988 -- 62 (10 under)   Bob Lohr, Walt Disney.
1987 -- 64 (8 under)   Mike Reid, Tucson.
1986 -- 64 (7 under)   Hal Sutton, Phoenix.
1985 -- 63 (8 under)   Lanny Wadkins, Los Angeles.
        64 (8 under)   Tom Kite, T of C.
1984 -- 64 (6 under)   Peter Jacobsen, Colonial.
1983 -- 63 (9 under)   Fuzzy Zoeller, Las Vegas.
1982 -- 63 (8 under)   Tim Norris, Hartford.
        63 (7 under)   Jay Haas, Texas.
1981 -- 65 (7 under)   Bruce Lietzke, Bob Hope; Hale Irwin, Buick.
        65 (6 under)   David Graham, Phoenix; Morris Hatalsky, Hall of Fame.
1980 -- 63 (7 under)   Bruce Lietzke, Colonial; Jack Nicklaus, U.S. Open; Scott Hoch, Quad Cities.
        65 (7 under)   Tom Watson, T of C.
        66 (7 under)   Jim Colbert, Tucson.
1979 -- 61 (11 under)   Jerry McGee, Kemper.
1978 -- 63 (9 under)   Tom Watson, Tucson.
1977 -- 64 (8 under)   Rik Massengale, Bob Hope.
        64 (6 under)   Jerry Pate, Southern.
        65 (6 under)   Graham Marsh, Heritage; Hale Irwin, Hall of Fame.
        66 (6 under)   Tom Watson, Bing Crosby, San Diego.
1976 -- 63 (8 under)   David Graham, Westchester.
1975 -- 64 (8 under)   Johnny Miller, Bob Hope.
1974 -- 62 (10 under)   Johnny Miller, Tucson.
1973 -- 64 (8 under)   Lee Trevino, Doral-Eastern.
1972 -- 64 (7 under)   Dave Hill, Monsanto.
        65 (7 under)   Grier Jones, Hawaiian.
1971 -- 64 (8 under)   Arnold Palmer, Westchester.
        64 (7 under)   Dave Eichelberger, Milwaukee.
1970 -- 63 (7 under)   Dave Hill, Memphis.

HIGH START BY A WINNER:

1994 -- 74 (2 over)   Jose Maria Olazabal, Masters.
1993 -- 75 (3 over)   Phil Mickelson, Buick Invitational.
1992 -- 73 (1 over)   Greg Norman, Canadian.
1991 -- 73 (1 over)   Ian Woosnam, USF&G.
        72 (2 over)   Tom Purtzer, World Series.
1990 -- 72 (even)   David Ishii, Hawaiian.
1989 -- 76 (4 over)   Steve Jones, Bob Hope; Mike Sullivan, IIAO.
1988 -- 73 (1 over)   Curtis Strange, Memorial.
1987 -- 75 (3 over)   Lanny Wadkins, Doral.
1986 -- 75 (5 over)   Raymond Floyd, U.S. Open.

LOW START BY A WINNER (cont'd.):

1985 --	72 (even)	Bernhard Langer, Masters; Bill Glasson, Kemper.
1984 --	73 (1 over)	Greg Norman, Canadian.
	71 (1 over)	Fuzzy Zoeller, U.S. Open.
1983 --	75 (4 over)	Larry Nelson, U.S. Open.
1982 --	75 (3 over)	Craig Stadler, Masters.
1981 --	74 (2 over)	Ed Fiori, Western.
1980 --	74 (2 over)	Raymond Floyd, Doral-Eastern.
1979 --	76 (4 over)	Fuzzy Zoeller, San Diego.
1978 --	76 (4 over)	Bruce Lietzke, Canadian.
	75 (4 over)	John Mahaffey, PGA.
1977 --	72 (even)	Mark Hayes, TPC; Jack Nicklaus, Memorial; Al Geiberger, Memphis.
1976 --	75 (3 over)	Ben Crenshaw, Pebble Beach.
	73 (3 over)	Lee Trevino, Colonial.
1975 --	74 (3 over)	Lou Graham, U.S. Open.
1974 --	73 (3 over)	Hale Irwin, U.S. Open; Lee Trevino, PGA.
1973 --	73 (2 over)	Rod Funseth, Los Angeles.
1972 --	73 (1 over)	Gary Player, New Orleans.
	72 (1 over)	Deane Beman, Quad Cities.
	71 (1 over)	Gary Player, PGA.
1971 --	75 (7 over)	Buddy Allin, Greensboro.
1970 --	76 (4 over)	Pete Brown, San Diego.

LOW FINISH BY A WINNER:

1994 --	64 (7 under)	Bill Glasson, Phoenix.
	64 (6 under)	Nick Price, Southwestern Bell Colonial.
1993 --	62 (10 under)	Tom Kite, Bob Hope.
	62 (8 under)	Fulton Allem, World Series.
1992 --	62 (10 over)	Davis Love III, Kmart GGO; John Huston, Disney.
1991 --	64 (8 under)	Mark Brooks, Greensboro; Mark O'Meara, Disney.
	64 (6 under)	Tom Purtzer, Colonial; D.A. Weibring, Hardee's.
1990 --	62 (10 under)	Greg Norman, Doral.
1989 --	64 (8 under)	Blaine McCallister, Honda.
	64 (7 under)	Mark Calcavecchia, Phoenix.
	64 (6 under)	Stan Utley, Chattanooga; Donnie Hammond, Texas.
1988 --	64 (8 under)	Tom Purtzer, Southwest.
1987 --	63 (9 under)	Larry Nelson, Walt Disney.
1986 --	62 (9 under)	Mac O'Grady, Hartford.
1985 --	63 (9 under)	Lanny Wadkins, Walt Disney.
1984 --	63 (8 under)	Gary Koch, Bay Hill, Ronnie Black, Anheuser-Busch.
1983 --	63 (9 under)	Calvin Peete, Atlanta.
1982 --	63 (7 under)	Payne Stewart, Quad Cities.
1981 --	62 (9 under)	Ron Streck, Houston.
1980 --	65 (5 under)	Lee Trevino, Texas.
	66 (6 under)	Andy Bean, Hawaiian; Raymond Floyd, Doral-Eastern.
1979 --	64 (7 under)	Lou Graham, IVB.
	65 (7 under)	Calvin Peete, Milwaukee.
1978 --	62 (8 under)	Ron Streck, Texas.
1977 --	64 (6 under)	Mike Hill, Ohio Kings Island.
	65 (7 under)	Miller Barber, Anheuser-Busch.
1976 --	63 (9 under)	Johnny Miller, Bob Hope.
	63 (7 under)	Jerry Pate, Canadian.
	65 (7 under)	Jack Nicklaus, TPC.
1975 --	61 (11 under)	Johnny Miller, Tucson.
1974 --	64 (7 under)	Dave Stockton, Quad Cities.
	65 (7 under)	Hubert Green, Bob Hope; Lee Trevino, New Orleans; Dave Hill, Houston.
1973 --	63 (8 under)	Johnny Miller, U.S. Open.
1972 --	64 (8 under)	Grier Jones, Hawaiian; Jack Nicklaus, Walt Disney.
1971 --	65 (7 under)	George Archer, San Diego.
	65 (6 under)	Miller Barber, Phoenix; Bobby Mitchell, Cleveland.
1970 --	63 (8 under)	George Knudson, Robinson.

HIGH FINISH BY A WINNER:

1994 --	74 (2 over)	Johnny Miller, AT&T.
1993 --	71 (1 over)	Scott Simpson, Byron Nelson.
	71 (1 over)	Brett Ogle, Pebble Beach.
1992 --	72 (even)	Steve Elkington, T of C; Tom Kite, U.S. Open; David Frost, Hardee's.
1991 --	75 (3 over)	Steve Pate, Honda.
1990 --	72 (even)	Mark O'Meara, Pebble Beach; David Ishii, Hawaiian; Dan Forsman, Shearson Lehman.
	71 (even)	Payne Stewart, MCI.
1989 --	72 (1 over)	Wayne Grady, Westchester.
	72 (even)	Bill Glasson, Doral-Ryder.
	70 (even)	Curtis Strange, U.S. Open.

HIGH FINISH BY A WINNER (cont'd):

1988 -- 74 (2 over) Steve Jones, Pebble Beach; Curtis Strange, Nabisco.
1987 -- 72 (1 over) Paul Azinger, Hartford.
71 (1 over) Curtis Strange, World Series.
72 (even) Larry Nelson, PGA.
1986 -- 71 (1 over) Dan Pohl, World Series.
71 (even) Hal Sutton, Phoenix.
71 (1 under) John Mahaffey, TPC; Bob Murphy, Canadian.
1985 -- 74 (2 over) Curtis Strange, Honda; Scott Verplank, Western.
74 (4 over) Andy North, U.S. Open.
1984 -- 73 (1 over) Greg Norman, Kemper.
1983 -- 77 (5 over) Fred Couples, Kemper.
1982 -- 75 (3 over) Danny Edwards, Greensboro.
1981 -- 75 (3 over) Larry Nelson, Greensboro.
1980 -- 74 (3 over) Dave Eichelberger, Bay Hill.
1979 -- 77 (5 over) Lon Hinkle, Bing Crosby.
1978 -- 75 (3 over) Jack Nicklaus, TPC.
1977 -- 74 (2 over) Gene Littler, Houston; Lee Trevino, Canadian.
73 (2 over) Jerry Pate, Phoenix.
1976 -- 76 (4 over) Roger Maltbie, Memorial.
1975 -- 73 (2 over) Lou Graham, U.S. Open.
73 (1 over) Gene Littler, Bing Crosby.
72 (1 over) Tom Jenkins, IVB.
71 (1 over) Jack Nicklaus, PGA.
1974 -- 73 (3 over) Hale Irwin, U.S. Open.
73 (1 over) Allen Miller, Tallahassee.
1973 -- 75 (4 over) Homero Blancas, Monsanto.
1972 -- 74 (2 over) Jack Nicklaus, Masters, U.S. Open; Gary Player, PGA.
73 (3 over) Jerry Heard, Colonial.
1971 -- 74 (4 over) Jerry Heard, American Classic.
1970 -- 72 (1 over) Billy Casper, Los Angeles.
72 (even) Bob Stone, Citrus Open; Ken Still, Kaiser International.

LARGEST 18-HOLE LEAD:

1994 -- 4 strokes Jose Maria Olazabal, Freeport-McMoRan.
1993 -- 5 strokes Jim Gallagher, Jr., TOUR Championship.
1992 -- 3 strokes Billy Ray Brown, PLAYERS.
1991 -- 3 strokes Lanny Wadkins, T of C, Scott Hoch, Buick Open.
1990 -- 4 strokes Fred Couples, Memorial; Jose Maria Olazabal, World Series.
1989 -- 4 strokes Bob Tway, Disney World.
1988 -- 3 strokes Davis Love III, Phoenix; Jeff Sluman, Southern.
1987 -- 4 strokes Mike Sullivan, Honda.
1986 -- 3 strokes Fred Couples, Kemper.
1985 -- 4 strokes Tom Kite, T of C.
1984 -- 3 strokes David Graham, T of C; Ralph Landrum, Pensacola.
1983 -- 4 strokes George Burns, Kemper.
1982 -- 4 strokes Terry Mauney, Los Angeles; Larry Rinker, Tallahassee.
1981 -- 3 strokes Calvin Peete, B.C. Open.
1980 -- 2 strokes Dan Pohl, Bay Hill; Jerry Pate, Heritage; Tom Purtzer, Greensboro; Bob Murphy, Tallahassee; Tom Watson, Byron Nelson, World Series; Bruce Lietzke, Colonial; Bob Shearer, Atlanta; Scott Hoch, Quad Cities; Jim Simons, Hartford; Barry Jaeckel, Hall of Fame.
1979 -- 4 strokes Mark Lye, Atlanta; Dana Quigley, Hall of Fame.
1978 -- 3 strokes Tom Watson, Tucson, Bing Crosby; Jeff Hewes, Canadian.
1977 -- 3 strokes Rik Massengale, Bob Hope; Fred Marti, Pleasant Valley.
1976 -- 3 strokes Mike Reid (amateur), U.S. Open.
1975 -- 3 strokes Bob Stanton, Inverrary; Jack Nicklaus, Heritage; Tom Weiskopf, Greensboro; David Graham, Western.
1974 -- 4 strokes Johnny Miller, Tucson.
1973 -- 5 strokes Gibby Gilbert, World.
1972 -- 3 strokes Jack Nicklaus, Bing Crosby.
1971 -- 3 strokes Charles Coody, Masters.
1970 -- 3 strokes Rod Funseth, San Antonio.

LARGEST 36-HOLE LEAD:

1994 -- 5 strokes Nick Price, PGA.
1993 -- 3 strokes Payne Stewart, Buick Invitational; Steve Stricker, Canadian; Tom Lehman, Buick Southern.
1992 -- 4 strokes Davis Love III, Los Angeles; Chip Beck, Freeport-McMoRan; Bruce Lietzke, Canadian.
1991 -- 4 strokes Blaine McCallister, Texas; Jeff Maggert, IIAO.
1990 -- 9 strokes Jose Maria Olazabal, World Series.

LARGEST 36-HOLE LEAD (cont'd.):

1989 --	5 strokes	Fuzzy Zoeller, Memorial.
1988 --	4 strokes	Paul Azinger, Bay Hill; Larry Nelson, Atlanta.
1987 --	7 strokes	Joey Sindelar, B.C. Open.
1986 --	5 strokes	Sandy Lyle, Greensboro.
1985 --	5 strokes	Calvin Peete, Phoenix.
1984 --	6 strokes	Nick Price, Canadian.
1983 --	6 strokes	Hal Sutton, Anheuser-Busch.
1982 --	6 strokes	Roger Maltbie, Colonial.
1981 --	4 strokes	Jack Nicklaus, Masters; Leonard Thompson, Canadian.
1980 --	5 strokes	Rex Caldwell, Buick.
1979 --	4 strokes	Ben Crenshaw, Phoenix; Tom Watson, Memorial.
1978 --	5 strokes	Mac McLendon, Pensacola.
1977 --	6 strokes	Al Geiberger, Memphis.
1976 --	6 strokes	Bob Dickson, Western.
1975 --	7 strokes	Tom Weiskoipf, Westchester.
1974 --	6 strokes	Johnny Miller, Heritage.
1973 --	4 strokes	Billy Casper, Bing Crosby; Tom Watson, Hawaiian; Lee Trevino, Doral-Eastern; Jack Nicklaus, Atlanta; Forrest Fezler, American Classic.
1972 --	4 strokes	Homero Blancas, Phoenix; Chris Blocker, Florida Citrus; Dave Hill, Monsanto.
1971 --	3 strokes	Jerry Heard, American Classic; Billy Casper, Kaiser International.
1970 --	4 strokes	Grier Jones, Monsanto.

LARGEST 54-HOLE LEAD:

1994 --	5 strokes	Steve Elkington, Buick Southern.
1993 --	6 strokes	Greg Norman, Doral-Ryder.
1992 --	6 strokes	Fred Couples, Nestle.
1991 --	5 strokes	Steve Pate, Honda.
1990 --	8 strokes	Jose Maria Olazabal, World Series.
1989 --	4 strokes	Ian Baker-Finch, Colonial; Greg Norman, Milwaukee; John Daly, Chattanooga.
1988 --	5 strokes	Corey Pavin, Texas.
1987 --	8 strokes	Joey Sindelar, Buick.
1986 --	5 strokes	Fuzzy Zoeller, Pebble Beach; Calvin Peete, USF&G; Mark Calcavecchia, Southwest.
1985 --	5 strokes	Corey Pavin, Colonial.
1984 --	7 strokes	Greg Norman, Kemper.
1983 --	6 strokes	Mike Nicolette, Bay Hill; Hal Sutton, Anheuser-Busch.
1982 --	7 strokes	Craig Stadler, Tucson.
1981 --	5 strokes	Bruce Lietzke, Bob Hope; Hale Irwin, Hawaiian; Jay Haas, Milwaukee.
1980 --	7 strokes	Jim Colbert, Tucson; Seve Ballesteros, Masters.
1979 --	8 strokes	Tom Watson, Heritage.
1978 --	5 strokes	Tom Watson, PGA; Tom Kite, B.C. Open.
1977 --	6 strokes	Lee Trevino, Canadian.
1976 --	8 strokes	Raymond Floyd, Masters.
1975 --	7 strokes	Johnny Miller, Phoenix.
1974 --	6 strokes	Jack Nicklaus, Hawaiian.
1973 --	9 strokes	Jack Nicklaus, Ohio Kings Island.
1972 --	8 strokes	Jim Jamieson, Western.
1971 --	5 strokes	Jack Nicklaus, T of C; Jerry Heard, American Classic.
1970 --	4 strokes	Ron Cerrudo, San Antonio; Bob Stone, Citrus Open; Tony Jacklin, U.S. Open; Bob Murphy, Hartford; Bobby Mitchell, Azalea.

LOW 36-HOLE CUT:

1994 --	139 (3 under)	Texas.
	140 (even)	Hardee's.
	141 (3 under)	Hawaiian, Buick Invitational.
1993 --	140 (4 under)	Shell Houston.
	140 (2 under)	H-E-B Texas.
1992 --	139 (1 under)	Byron Nelson.
	139 (3 under)	Federal Express, Texas.
	140 (4 under)	Buick Invitational.
1991 --	137 (3 under)	Chattanooga.
	140 (4 under)	Milwaukee, Shearson Lehman.
	140 (2 under)	Phoenix, Anheuser-Busch, New England.
1990 --	138 (2 under)	Chattanooga, Texas.
	141 (3 under)	Milwaukee.
1989 --	137 (3 under)	Byron Nelson, Texas.
1988 --	141 (3 under)	Andy Williams, USF&G.
	139 (1 under)	Hardee's, Provident, Texas.
1987 --	140 (4 under)	Andy Williams.
	139 (1 under)	Byron Nelson, Hardee's.
1986 --	141 (3 under)	Buick.
	139 (1 under)	Vantage.

LOW 36-HOLE CUT (cont'd.):

1985 --	139 (5 under)	San Diego.
1984 --	141 (3 under)	San Diego.
	141 (1 under)	Phoenix.
1983 --	139 (3 under)	Hartford.
	139 (1 under)	Texas.
1982 --	139 (3 under)	Hartford.
1981 --	139 (3 under)	Hartford.
1980 --	140 (2 under)	Hartford.
	141 (3 under)	Milwaukee.
1979 --	140 (even)	Tucson.
	141 (1 under)	Phoenix, Houston.
	142 (2 under)	Hawaiian, Pensacola.
1978 --	140 (2 under)	Hartford.
	142 (2 under)	Anheuser-Busch.
	140 (even)	Texas.
1977 --	142 (2 under)	Buick.
1976 --	142 (even)	Phoenix, Hartford.
	143 (1 under)	Hawaiian, San Diego.
	144 (even)	Florida Citrus.
1975 --	142 (even)	Hartford, Sahara.
	144 (even)	Inverrary, Houston, Westchester, Texas, Kaiser International.
1974 --	141 (1 under)	Greensboro, Hartford.
	142 (2 under)	Kemper, Texas.
	143 (1 under)	San Diego.
1973 --	140 (2 under)	Hartford.
1972 --	141 (1 under)	Hartford.
1971 --	137 (5 under)	Phoenix.
1970 --	140 (even)	Memphis.
	141 (1 under)	Azalea.
	141 (1 over)	Magnolia.
	143 (1 under)	Citrus Invitational.

HIGH 36-HOLE CUT:

1994 --	148 (4 over)	Doral-Ryder.
	147 (5 over)	Honda, U.S. Open.
1993 --	152 (8 over)	Freeport-McMoRan.
1992 --	148 (4 over)	Nestle.
	148 (6 over)	PGA.
1991 --	149 (5 over)	USF&G.
1990 --	157 (13 over)	Memorial.
1989 --	150 (6 over)	Memorial.
1988 --	149 (5 over)	Memorial.
1987 --	151 (7 over)	Honda, PGA.
1986 --	150 (10 over)	U.S. Open.
	150 (6 over)	St. Jude Classic.
1985 --	150 (6 over)	Memorial.
1984 --	151 (9 over)	Los Angeles.
	151 (7 over)	Memorial.
1983 --	152 (10 over)	Bay Hill.
1982 --	149 (5 over)	Memorial, Kemper, Western.
	147 (7 over)	Colonial.
1981 --	152 (8 over)	Memorial.
1980 --	150 (6 over)	Memorial, Western.
	149 (9 over)	PGA.
1979 --	157 (13 over)	Memorial.
1978 --	153 (9 over)	TPC.
1977 --	155 (11 over)	TPC.
1976 --	157 (13 over)	Memorial.
1975 --	151 (9 over)	Western.
1974 --	151 (9 over)	Heritage.
	149 (9 over)	PGA.
1973 --	151 (7 over)	Masters.
	149 (9 over)	American Classic.
1972 --	154 (10 over)	U.S. Open.
	150 (10 over)	PGA.
1971 --	152 (10 over)	Heritage.
1970 --	153 (9 over)	U.S. Open.
	151 (9 over)	Heritage.
	151 (7 over)	Masters.
	150 (10 over)	PGA.

FEWEST TO MAKE 36-HOLE CUT:
1994 -- 70 at Buick Classic, Federal Express.
1993 -- 70 at New England.
1992 -- 70 at Texas.
1991 -- 70 at Buick Classic, Chattanooga.
1990 -- 70 at Canadian, Texas.
1989 -- 70 at Doral-Ryder, Memorial, Atlanta, Hardee's, PGA.
1988 -- 70 at Phoenix.
1987 -- 70 at Buick, Centel.
1986 -- 70 at Hawaiian, Heritage, Buick, Anhueser-Busch.
1985 -- 70 at Atlanta, Quad Cities.
1984 -- 70 at Atlanta, PGA, Milwaukee.
1983 -- 70 at Hawaii, Atlanta, Memorial.
1982 -- 70 at Houston, Disney World.
1981 -- 70 at Inverrary.
1980 -- 70 at Doral-Eastern.
1979 -- 70 at Byron Nelson, Pensacola.
1978 -- 70 at Tucson, San Diego, Byron Nelson, American Optical, Westchester.
1977 -- 70 at Hawaiian.
1976 -- 70 at Heritage.
1975 -- 70 at B.C. Open.
1974 -- 70 at Greensboro, American Classic, Sahara.
1973 -- 70 at Jacksonville, IVB, Southern, Kaiser International.
1972 -- 70 at Monsanto, Colonial, Cleveland.
1971 -- 70 at Los Angeles, Tucson, Kaiser International.
1970 -- 70 at San Diego, Canadian, PGA.

FEWEST TO MAKE 54-HOLE CUT:
1994 -- 72 at AT&T Pebble Beach.
1993 -- 73 at Walt Disney World.
1992 -- 72 at Las Vegas Inviational.
1991 -- 73 at AT&T Pebble Beach.
1990 -- 78 at AT&T Pebble Beach.
1989 -- 73 at Las Vegas Invitational.
1988 -- 72 at Las Vegas Invitational.
1987 -- 70 at Las Vegas Invitational.
1986 -- 71 at AT&T Pebble Beach.
1985 -- 70 at Las Vegas Invitational.
1984 -- 73 at Bing Crosby.
1983 -- 75 at Bing Crosby.
1982 -- 70 at Walt Disney World.
1981 -- 77 at Bing Crosby.
1980 -- 75 at Bing Crosby.
1979 -- 78 at Bing Crosby.
1978 -- 70 at Bing Crosby.
1977 -- 73 at Bing Crosby.
1976 -- 76 at Bing Crosby.
1975 -- 75 at Bing Crosby.
1974 -- 71 at Bing Crosby.
1973 -- 71 at Bing Crosby.
1972 -- 70 at Bing Crosby.
1971 -- 80 at Bing Crosby.
1970 -- 71 at Bing Crosby.

MOST TO MAKE 36-HOLE CUT:
1994 -- 88 at Buick Southern Open.
1993 -- 90 at Buick Invitational.
1992 -- 85 at PGA.
1991 -- 84 at Hardee's.
1990 -- 88 at Buick Classic.
1989 -- 85 at Phoenix.
1988 -- 89 at Milwaukee.
1987 -- 87 at USF&G.
1986 -- 86 at Phoenix, Southern.
1985 -- 83 at Buick.
1984 -- 89 at LaJet.
1983 -- 87 at PGA.
1982 -- 90 at Texas.
1981 -- 91 at Hartford.
1980 -- 83 at Phoenix.
1979 -- 88 at Quad Cities.

MOST TO MAKE 36-HOLE CUT (cont'd):
1978 --   85 at New Orleans.
1977 --   86 at Doral-Eastern.
1976 --   85 at Westchester.
1975 --   86 at San Diego.
1974 --   84 at B.C. Open.
1973 --   90 at Phoenix.
1972 --   86 at St. Louis.
1971 --   88 at Hartford.
1970 --   85 at Kaiser International, Sahara.

MOST TO MAKE 54-HOLE CUT:
1994 --   77 at Walt Disney World.
1993 --   82 at AT&T Pebble Beach.
1992 --   82 at AT&T Pebble Beach.
1991 --   80 at Walt Disney World.
1990 --   86 at Las Vegas Invitational.
1989 --   82 at Walt Disney World.
1988 --   76 at AT&T Pebble Beach.
1987 --   82 at AT&T Pebble Beach.
1986 --   81 at Las Vegas Invitational.
1985 --   74 at Walt Disney World.
1984 --   83 at Walt Disney World.
1983 --   80 at Walt Disney World.
1982 --   77 at Bing Crosby.
1981 --   77 at Bing Crosby.
1980 --   75 at Bing Crosby.
1979 --   78 at Bing Crosby.
1978 --   70 at Bing Crosby.
1977 --   73 at Bing Crosby.
1976 --   76 at Bing Crosby.
1975 --   72 at Bing Crosby.
1974 --   71 at Bing Crosby.
1973 --   71 at Bing Crosby.
1972 --   70 at Bing Crosby.
1971 --   80 at Bing Crosby.
1970 --   71 at Bing Crosby.

MOST CONSECUTIVE EVENTS IN THE MONEY (on-going at conclusion of season):
1994 --   25, Fred Couples.
1993 --   25, Steve Elkington.
1992 --   19, Tom Kite.
1991 --   18, Fred Couples.
1990 --   17, Larry Mize.
1989 --   33, Tom Kite.
1988 --   15, Ben Crenshaw.
1987 --   19, Greg Norman.
1986 --   16, Gene Sauers.
1985 --   14, Tom Kite, Scott Hoch.
1984 --   21, Jack Nicklaus.
1983 --   26, Hale Irwin.
1982 --   53, Tom Kite.
1981 --   35, Tom Kite.
1980 --   28, Tom Watson.
1979 --   17, Hubert Green, Bill Rogers.
1978 --   86, Hale Irwin.
1977 --   54, Hale Irwin.
1976 --   105, Jack Nicklaus.
1975 --   91, Jack Nicklaus.
1974 --   74, Jack Nicklaus.
1973 --   56, Jack Nicklaus.
1972 --   37, Jack Nicklaus.

CONSECUTIVE YEARS WITH WIN:
1994 --   5, Fred Couples (1990-94).
1993 --   7, Paul Azinger (1987-93).
1992 --   6, Paul Azinger (1987-92).
1991 --   5, Paul Azinger (1987-91).
1990 --   4, Paul Azinger (1987-90).
1989 --   7, Curtis Strange (1983-89).
1988 --   6, Curtis Strange (1983-88).

CONSECUTIVE YEARS WITH A WIN (cont'd.):

1987 -- 7, Tom Kite (1981-87).
1986 -- 6, Tom Kite (1981-86).
1985 -- 5, Hale Irwin, Tom Kite (1981-85).
1984 -- 4, Hale Irwin, Tom Kite (1981-84).
1983 -- 4, Johnny Miller (1980-83).
1982 -- 6, Bruce Lietzke, Tom Watson (1977-82).
1981 -- 14, Lee Trevino (1968-81).
1980 -- 13, Lee Trevino (1968-80).
1979 -- 12, Lee Trevino (1968-79).
1978 -- 17, Jack Nicklaus (1962-78).
1977 -- 16, Jack Nicklaus (1962-77).
1976 -- 15, Jack Nicklaus (1962-76).
1975 -- 14, Jack Nicklaus (1962-75).
1974 -- 13, Jack Nicklaus (1962-74).
1973 -- 12, Jack Nicklaus (1962-73).
1972 -- 11, Jack Nicklaus (1962-72).
1971 -- 16, Billy Casper (1956-71).
1970 -- 15, Billy Casper (1956-70).

THREE EAGLES IN ONE ROUND:

1994 -- Davis Love, Hawaiian; Dave Stockton, Jr., Walt Disney World.
1992 -- Dan Forsman, Honda; Don Pooley, Texas.
1990 -- David Frost, Las Vegas.
1981 -- Bruce Lietzke, Hawaiian; Howard Twitty, Pensacola.

DOUBLE-EAGLES:

1994 -- Olin Browne, Northern Telecom (Tucson National #2); Jeff Maggert, Masters (Augusta National #13); Mike Donald, Texas (Oak Hills #15).
1993 -- Massy Kuramoto, Deposit Guaranty (Hattiesburg #3); Tom Sieckmann, Kmart GGO (Forest Oaks #9); Bobby Wadkins, Memorial (Muirfield Village #15); Darrell Kestner, PGA (Inverness #13).
1992 -- Mark O'Meara, Bob Hope (Indian Wells #18); Billy Andrade, Las Vegas (LVCC #2).
1991 -- Payne Stewart, Pebble Beach (Spyglass #7); Mark Brooks, Kemper (TPC Avenel #6); Lon Hinkle, Anheuser-Busch (Kingsmill #13); John Daly, Western (Cog Hill #5); Davis Love III, World Series (Firestone #2).
1990 -- Tom Pernice, Phoenix (TPC Scottsdale); Gary Koch, Anheuser-Busch (Kingsmill); Steve Pate, Jim Gallagher, Jr., International (Castle Pines); Greg Bruckner, Southern (Green Island).
1989 -- Bill Britton, Anheuser-Busch (Kingsmill).
1988 -- Mike Reid, Los Angeles (Riviera); Jim Booros, Provident (Valleybrook).
1987 -- David Edwards, Andy Williams (Torry Pines South); Dan Halldorson, Provident (Valleybrook).
1986 -- Mike Hulbert, Pebble Beach (Cypress Point).
1985 -- None.
1984 -- Hal Sutton, Byron Nelson (Las Colinas); John Adams, Canadian (Glen Abbey).
1983 -- None.
1982 -- Bob Gilder, Westchester (Westchester #18); Pat McGowan, Walt Disney (Palm Course #1).
1981 -- Jim Thorpe, LaJet (Fairway Oaks).
1980 -- Bruce Lietzke, Inverrary (Inverrary); Fred Marti, Milwaukee (Tuckaway); Stanton Altgelt, IVB (Whitemarsh Valley).
1979 -- Rik Massengale, Tucson (Randolph North); Bob Murphy, Tallahassee (Killearn).
1978 -- Terry Mauney, Hawaiian (Waialae); George Burns, Colonial (Colonial); Jim Nelford, Tommy Valentine, Atlanta (Atlanta CC).
1977 -- Joe Inman, Bob Hope (La Quinta).
1976 -- Lyn Lott, World (Pinehurst No. 2 #16).
1975 -- Lee Elder, Greensboro (Sedgefield); Miller Barber, Canadian (Royal Montreal).
1974 -- George Knudson, Bob Hope (Indian Wells); Larry Wise, Greensboro (Sedgefield).
1973 -- Jerry Heard, Milwaukee (Tuckaway).
1972 -- Bob Murphy, Bing Crosby (Pebble Beach #2); Roy Pace, Houston (Westwood #13).
1971 -- Rod Curl, Greensboro (Sedgefield); Larry Ziegler, Westchester (Westchester).
1970 -- Rod Curl, Memphis (Colonial); Mike Hill, AVCO (Pleasant Valley).

LONGEST BIRDIE STREAK:

1994 -- 7 Greg Kraft, Buick Open.
1993 -- 7 Keith Clearwater, Colonial.
1992 -- 6 Gil Morgan, Bob Hope; Ed Fiori, Phoenix; Mark Calcavecchia, Masters; Fred Funk, Houston; Tom Kite, BellSouth; Andy Dillard, U.S. Open; Andy Bean, Chattanooga.
1991 -- 6 Mark Lye, Phoenix; Bill Sander, Shearson Lehman; Mark Brooks, Kmart GGO; Karl Kimball, Milwaukee; Chip Beck, Las Vegas.
1990 -- 7 Steve Elkington, Bob Hope; Scott Verplank, Milwaukee.
1989 -- 7 Wayne Grady, Shearson Lehman.
1988 -- 7 Nick Faldo, T of C.

LONGEST BIRDIE STREAK (cont'd):

1987 -- 8 Dewey Arnette, Buick.
1986 -- 6 Doug Tewell, Los Angeles; Don Pooley, USF&G; Dave Rummells, TPC; Jack Nicklaus, Memorial; Kenny Knox, Buick; Mark Calcavecchia, Milwaukee.
1985 -- 7 Hubert Green, Western.
1984 -- 7 Tommy Valentine, Atlanta; Mike McCullough, Canadian; Rod Nuckolls, Buick.
1983 -- 6 Bill Kratzert, Los Angeles; Mike Sullivan, David Graham, Buick.
1982 -- 7 Scott Hoch, Bob Hope.
1981 -- 6 Tom Kite, Pensacola.
1980 -- 7 George Burns, Westchester; John Fought, Buick.
1979 -- 7 John Mahaffey, Bob Hope.
1978 -- 6 Bob Gilder, Doral-Eastern.
1977 -- 7 Bobby Walzel, Pensacola.
1976 -- 8 Fuzzy Zoeller, Quad Cities.
1975 -- 6 Johnny Miller, Masters.
1974 -- 6 Gary McCord, Bing Crosby; Mike McCullough, Bob Hope; Ben Crenshaw, San Diego.
1973 -- 6 Dan Sikes, Westchester; Hale Irwin, World.
1972 -- 7 Bert Yancey, Walt Disney.
1971 -- 6 Gibby Gilbert, Westchester.
1970 -- 6 Frank Beard, T of C; Wilf Homenuik, Azalea.

LONGEST BIRDIE/EAGLE STREAK (5 or more):

1994 -- 5 Ken Green, Phoenix (B,E,B,E,B).
1993 -- 5 Rick Fehr, Bob Hope (B,E,B,B,B).
1992 -- 5 Chris Tucker, Federal Express (B,E,B,B,B); Lee Janzen, Disney, (E,B,B,B,B).
1991 -- 6 Robert Gamez, Milwaukee (B,B,B,E,B,B).
1990 -- 6 David Frost, Tucson (B,B,B,B,B,E).
1989 -- 7 Webb Heintzelman, Las Vegas (B,B,B,B,B,E,B).
1986 -- 5 Raymond Floyd, Bob Hope (E,B,B,B,B); Denis Watson, Hartford (B,E,B,B,B).
1983 -- 6 Craig Stadler, Buick (B,B,E,B,B,B).
1977 -- 7 Al Geiberger, Memphis (B,B,B,B,E,B,B).
1975 -- 5 Bob Mitchell, Memphis (B,B,B,B,E).

BEST COME-FROM-BEHIND, FINAL-ROUND WIN:

1994 -- 4 strokes, John Huston, Doral-Ryder.
1993 -- 5 strokes, Vijay Singh, Buick Classic.
1992 -- 5 strokes, Lanny Wadkins, Canon GHO; David Edwards, Memorial; Mark Carnevale, Chattanooga.
1991 -- 7 strokes, Mark Brooks, Kmart GGO; Fulton Allem, IIAO.
1990 -- 8 strokes, Chip Beck, Buick Open.
1989 -- 7 strokes, Mike Sullivan, IIAO.
1988 -- 7 strokes, Sandy Lyle, Phoenix.
1987 -- 6 strokes, Corey Pavin, Hawaiian; Larry Nelson, Walt Disney.
1986 -- 7 strokes, Tom Kite, Western.
1985 -- 8 strokes, Hal Sutton, Memphis.
1984 -- 7 strokes, Ronnie Black, Anheuser-Busch.
1983 -- 8 strokes, Mark Lye, Bank of Boston.
1982 -- 6 strokes, Tom Kite, Bay Hill.
1981 -- 6 strokes, Raymond Floyd, TPC.
1980 -- 6 strokes, Peter Jacobsen, Buick.
1979 -- 6 strokes, Raymond Floyd, Greensboro; Lou Graham, IVB; Fuzzy Zoeller, Masters.
1978 -- 7 strokes, Gary Player, Masters, T of C; John Mahaffey, T of C.
1977 -- 6 strokes, Lanny Wadkins, PGA; Miller Barber, Anheuser-Busch.
1976 -- 5 strokes, Al Geiberger, Western.
1975 -- 7 strokes, Roger Maltbie, Quad Cities.
1974 -- 6 strokes, Tom Watson, Western.
1973 -- 6 strokes, Johnny Miller, U.S. Open.
1972 -- 5 strokes, Grier Jones, Hawaiian.
1971 -- 5 strokes, Gene Littler, Colonial.
1970 -- 7 strokes, Pete Brown, San Diego.

THREE OR MORE VICTORIES:

1994 -- 5 Nick Price, Honda, Colonial, Western, PGA, Canadian.
3 Mark McCumber, Anheuser-Busch, Hardee's, TOUR Championship.
1993 -- 4 Nick Price, PLAYERS, Canon GHO, Western, Federal Express.
3 Paul Azinger, Memorial, New England, PGA.
1992 -- 3 Fred Couples, Los Angeles, Nestle, Masters; Davis Love III, PLAYERS, MCI, Kmart GGO; John Cook, Bob Hope, Hawaiian, Las Vegas.
1991 -- None.
1990 -- 4 Wayne Levi, Atlanta, Western, Canon GHO, Canadian.
1989 -- 3 Tom Kite, Nestle, PLAYERS, Nabisco.

THREE OR MORE VICTORIES (cont'd):

1988 --	4	Curtis Strange, Houston, Memorial, U.S. Open, Nabisco.
	3	Sandy Lyle, Phoenix, Greensboro, Masters.
1987 --	3	Curtis Strange, Canadian, St. Jude, World Series; Paul Azinger, Phoenix, Las Vegas, Hartford.
1986 --	4	Bob Tway, Andy Williams, Westchester, Atlanta, PGA.
	3	Fuzzy Zoeller, Pebble Beach, Heritage, Anheuser-Busch.
1985 --	3	Curtis Strange, Honda, Las Vegas, Canadian; Lanny Wadkins, Bob Hope, Los Angeles, Disney.
1984 --	3	Tom Watson, Tuscon Match Play, T of C, Western; Denis Watson, Buick, World Series, Las Vegas.
1983 --	None.	
1982 --	4	Calvin Peete, Milwaukee, Anheuser-Busch, B.C. Open, Pensacola; Craig Stadler, Tucson, Masters, Kemper, World Series.
	3	Tom Watson, Los Angeles, Heritage, U.S. Open; Raymond Floyd, Memorial, Memphis, PGA; Lanny Wadkins, Phoenix, T of C, Buick; Bob Gilder, Byron Nelson, Westchester, Bank of Boston.
1981 --	3	Bruce Lietzke, Bob Hope, San Diego, Byron Nelson; Tom Watson, Masters, New Orleans, Atlanta; Raymond Floyd, Doral-Eastern, TPC, Westchester; Bill Rogers, Heritage, World Series, Texas.
1980 --	6	Tom Watson, San Diego, Los Angeles, T of C, New Orleans, Byron Nelson, World Series.
	3	Lee Trevino, TPC, Memphis, Texas.
1979 --	5	Tom Watson, Heritage, T of C, Byron Nelson, Memorial, Hall of Fame.
	3	Lou Graham, IVB, American Optical, Texas.
1978 --	5	Tom Watson, Tucson, Bing Crosby, Byron Nelson, Hall of Fame, Anheuser-Busch.
	3	Gary Player, Masters, T of C, Houston; Andy Bean, Kemper, Memphis, Western; Jack Nicklaus, Inverrary, TPC, IVB.
1977 --	4	Tom Watson, Pebble Beach, San Diego, Masters, Western.
	3	Jack Nicklaus, Inverrary, T of C, Memorial; Hale Irwin, Atlanta, Hall of Fame, Texas.
1976 --	3	Hubert Green, Doral-Eastern, Jacksonville, Heritage; Ben Crenshaw, Pebble Beach, Hawaiian, Ohio Kings Island.
1975 --	5	Jack Nicklaus, Doral-Eastern, Heritage, Masters, PGA, World.
	4	Johnny Miller, Tucson, Phoenix, Bob Hope, Kaiser International.
	3	Gene Littler, Bing Crosby, Memphis, Westchester.
1974 --	8	Johnny Miller, Bing Crosby, Phoenix, Tucson, Heritage, T of C, Westchester, World, Kaiser International.
	3	Hubert Green, Bob Hope, Jacksonville, IVB; Dave Stockton, Los Angeles, Quad Cities, Hartford.
1973 --	7	Jack Nicklaus, Bing Crosby, New Orleans, T of C, Atlanta, PGA, Ohio Kings Island, Walt Disney.
	4	Tom Weiskopf, Colonial, Kemper, IVB, Canadian; Bruce Crampton, Phoenix, Tucson, Houston, American Classic.
1972 --	7	Jack Nicklaus, Bing Crosby, Doral-Eastern, Masters, U.S. Open, Westchester, Match Play, Walt Disney.
	3	Lee Trevino, Memphis, Hartford, St. Louis.
1971 --	5	Lee Trevino, Tallahassee, Memphis, U.S. Open, Canadian, Sahara.
	4	Jack Nicklaus, PGA, T of C, Byron Nelson, Walt Disney.
	3	Arnold Palmer, Bob Hope, Florida Citrus, Westchester.
1970 --	4	Billy Casper, Los Angeles, Masters, IVB, AVCO.

WIRE-TO-WIRE WINNERS (no ties):

1994 --	Greg Norman, PLAYERS; Mike Springer, Kmart GGO; Bob Estes, Texas.
1993 --	Howard Twitty, Hawaiian; Nick Price, Western.
1992 --	Fred Couples, Nestle; David Frost, Hardee's.
1991 --	None.
1990 --	Jose Maria Olazabal, World Series; Tim Simpson, Disney.
1989 --	Ian Baker-Finch, Colonial.
1988 --	Steve Pate, T of C; Larry Nelson, Atlanta; Bob Lohr, Disney; Curtis Strange, Nabisco.
1987 --	Joey Sindelar, B.C. Open; Tom Watson, Nabisco.
1986 --	None.
1985 --	Tom Kite, T of C.
1984 --	Greg Norman, Kemper.
1983 --	Hal Sutton, PGA; Nick Price, World Series.
1982 --	Bob Gilder, Westchester; Ray Floyd, PGA; Tim Norris, Hartford.
1981 --	None.
1980 --	Tom Watson, T of C, Byron Nelson; Bruce Lietzke, Colonial; Scott Hoch, Quad Cities.
1979 --	Bruce Lietzke, Tucson; Tom Watson, Heritage, T of C.
1978 --	Tom Watson, Tucson.
1977 --	Rik Massengale, Bob Hope; Andy Bean, Doral-Eastern; Lee Trevino, Canadian; Jerry Pate, Southern.
1976 --	Raymond Floyd, Masters; Mark Hayes, Byron Nelson.
1975 --	Johnny Miller, Tucson; Tom Weiskopf, Greensboro; Al Geiberger, TPC.
1974 --	Johnny Miller, Tucson, Heritage; Allen Miller, Tallahassee; Ed Sneed, Milwaukee.
1973 --	Lee Trevino, Doral-Eastern; Homero Blancas, Monsanto.
1972 --	Jack Nicklaus, Masters; Dave Hill, Monsanto.
1971 --	Jack Nicklaus, PGA; Arnold Palmer, Westchester.
1970 --	Tony Jacklin, U.S. Open.

Mark McCumber had his first three-victory campaign in 1994, winning the Anheuser-Busch Golf Classic, Hardee's Golf Classic and THE TOUR Championship.

PAST WINNERS OF PGA TOUR EVENTS

MERCEDES CHAMPIONSHIPS

Year	Winner	Score	Location	Par/Yards
TOURNAMENT OF CHAMPIONS				
1953	Al Besselink	280	Desert Inn CC, Las Vegas, NV	72/7209
1954	Art Wall	278	Desert Inn CC, Las Vegas, NV	72/7209
1955	Gene Littler	280	Desert Inn CC, Las Vegas, NV	72/7209
1956	Gene Littler	281	Desert Inn CC, Las Vegas, NV	72/7209
1957	Gene Littler	285	Desert Inn CC, Las Vegas, NV	72/7209
1958	Stan Leonard	275	Desert Inn CC, Las Vegas, NV	72/7209
1959	Mike Souchak	281	Desert Inn CC, Las Vegas, NV	72/7209
1960	Jerry Barber	268	Desert Inn CC, Las Vegas, NV	72/7209
1961	Sam Snead	273	Desert Inn CC, Las Vegas, NV	72/7209
1962	Arnold Palmer	276	Desert Inn CC, Las Vegas, NV	72/7209
1963	Jack Nicklaus	273	Desert Inn CC, Las Vegas, NV	72/7209
1964	Jack Nicklaus	279	Desert Inn CC, Las Vegas, NV	72/7209
1965	Arnold Palmer	277	Desert Inn CC, Las Vegas, NV	72/7209
1966	*Arnold Palmer	283	Desert Inn CC, Las Vegas, NV	72/7209
1967	Frank Beard	278	Stardust CC, Las Vegas, NV	71/6725
1968	Don January	276	Stardust CC, Las Vegas, NV	71/6725
1969	Gary Player	284	LaCosta CC, Carlsbad, CA	72/6911
1970	Frank Beard	273	LaCosta CC, Carlsbad, CA	72/6911
1971	Jack Nicklaus	279	LaCosta CC, Carlsbad, CA	72/6911
1972	*Bobby Mitchell	280	LaCosta CC, Carlsbad, CA	72/6911
1973	Jack Nicklaus	276	LaCosta CC, Carlsbad, CA	72/6911
1974	Johnny Miller	280	LaCosta CC, Carlsbad, CA	72/6911
MONY TOURNAMENT OF CHAMPIONS				
1975	*Al Geiberger	277	LaCosta CC, Carlsbad, CA	72/6911
1976	Don January	277	LaCosta CC, Carlsbad, CA	72/6911
1977	*Jack Nicklaus	281	LaCosta CC, Carlsbad, CA	72/6911
1978	Gary Player	281	LaCosta CC, Carlsbad, CA	72/6911
1979	Tom Watson	275	LaCosta CC, Carlsbad, CA	72/6911
1980	Tom Watson	276	LaCosta CC, Carlsbad, CA	72/6911
1981	Lee Trevino	273	LaCosta CC, Carlsbad, CA	72/6911
1982	Lanny Wadkins	280	LaCosta CC, Carlsbad, CA	72/6911
1983	Lanny Wadkins	280	LaCosta CC, Carlsbad, CA	72/6911
1984	Tom Watson	274	LaCosta CC, Carlsbad, CA	72/7022
1985	Tom Kite	275	LaCosta CC, Carlsbad, CA	72/7022
1986	Calvin Peete	267	LaCosta CC, Carlsbad, CA	72/7022
1987	Mac O'Grady	278	LaCosta CC, Carlsbad, CA	72/7022
1988	~Steve Pate	202	LaCosta CC, Carlsbad, CA	72/7022
1989	Steve Jones	279	LaCosta CC, Carlsbad, CA	72/7022
INFINITI TOURNAMENT OF CHAMPIONS				
1990	Paul Azinger	272	LaCosta CC, Carlsbad, CA	72/7022
1991	Tom Kite	272	LaCosta CC, Carlsbad, CA	72/7022
1992	*Steve Elkington	279	LaCosta CC, Carlsbad, CA	72/7022
1993	Davis Love III	272	LaCosta CC, Carlsbad, CA	72/7022
MERCEDES CHAMPIONSHIP				
1994	*Phil Mickelson	276	LaCosta CC, Carlsbad, CA	72/7022

UNITED AIRLINES HAWAIIAN OPEN

Year	Winner	Score	Location	Par/Yards
HAWAIIAN OPEN				
1965	*Gay Brewer	281	Waialae CC, Honolulu, HI	72/7234
1966	Ted Makalena	271	Waialae CC, Honolulu, HI	72/7234
1967	*Dudley Wysong	284	Waialae CC, Honolulu, HI	72/7234
1968	Lee Trevino	272	Waialae CC, Honolulu, HI	72/7234
1969	Bruce Crampton	274	Waialae CC, Honolulu, HI	72/7234
1970	No Tournament			
1971	Tom Shaw	273	Waialae CC, Honolulu, HI	72/7234
1972	*Grier Jones	274	Waialae CC, Honolulu, HI	72/7234
1973	John Schlee	273	Waialae CC, Honolulu, HI	72/7234

KEY * = Playoff   # = Amateur   ~ = Rain-curtailed

Year	Winner	Score	Location	Par/Yards
1974	Jack Nicklaus	271	Waialae CC, Honolulu, HI	72/7234
1975	Gary Groh	274	Waialae CC, Honolulu, HI	72/7234
1976	Ben Crenshaw	270	Waialae CC, Honolulu, HI	72/7234
1977	Bruce Lietzke	273	Waialae CC, Honolulu, HI	72/7234
1978	*Hubert Green	274	Waialae CC, Honolulu, HI	72/7234
1979	Hubert Green	267	Waialae CC, Honolulu, HI	72/7234
1980	Andy Bean	266	Waialae CC, Honolulu, HI	72/7234
1981	Hale Irwin	265	Waialae CC, Honolulu, HI	72/7234
1982	Wayne Levi	277	Waialae CC, Honolulu, HI	72/7234
1983	Isao Aoki	268	Waialae CC, Honolulu, HI	72/7234
1984	*Jack Renner	271	Waialae CC, Honolulu, HI	72/7234
1985	Mark O'Meara	267	Waialae CC, Honolulu, HI	72/6975
1986	Corey Pavin	272	Waialae CC, Honolulu, HI	72/6975
1987	*Corey Pavin	270	Waialae CC, Honolulu, HI	72/6975
1988	Lanny Wadkins	271	Waialae CC, Honolulu, HI	72/6975
1989	~Gene Sauers	197	Waialae CC, Honolulu, HI	72/6975
1990	David Ishii	279	Waialae CC, Honolulu, HI	72/6975

UNITED HAWAIIAN OPEN

Year	Winner	Score	Location	Par/Yards
1991	Lanny Wadkins	270	Waialae CC, Honolulu, HI	72/6975

UNITED AIRLINES HAWAIIAN OPEN

Year	Winner	Score	Location	Par/Yards
1992	John Cook	265	Waialae CC, Honolulu, HI	72/6975
1993	Howard Twitty	269	Waialae CC, Honolulu, HI	72/6975
1994	Brett Ogle	269	Waialae CC, Honolulu, HI	72/6975

NORTHERN TELECOM OPEN

Year	Winner	Score	Location	Par/Yards

TUCSON OPEN

Year	Winner	Score	Location	Par/Yards
1945	Ray Mangrum	268	El Rio G&CC, Tucson, AZ	70/6418
1946	Jimmy Demaret	268	El Rio G&CC, Tucson, AZ	70/6418
1947	Jimmy Demaret	264	El Rio G&CC, Tucson, AZ	70/6418
1948	Skip Alexander	264	El Rio G&CC, Tucson, AZ	70/6418
1949	Lloyd Mangrum	263	El Rio G&CC, Tucson, AZ	70/6418
1950	Chandler Harper	267	El Rio G&CC, Tucson, AZ	70/6418
1951	Lloyd Mangrum	269	El Rio G&CC, Tucson, AZ	70/6418
1952	Henry Williams	274	El Rio G&CC, Tucson, AZ	70/6418
1953	Tommy Bolt	265	El Rio G&CC, Tucson, AZ	70/6418
1954	No Tournament			
1955	Tommy Bolt	265	El Rio G&CC, Tucson, AZ	70/6418
1956	Ted Kroll	264	El Rio G&CC, Tucson, AZ	70/6418
1957	Dow Finsterwald	269	El Rio G&CC, Tucson, AZ	70/6418
1958	Lionel Hebert	265	El Rio G&CC, Tucson, AZ	70/6418
1959	Gene Littler	266	El Rio G&CC, Tucson, AZ	70/6418
1960	Don January	271	El Rio G&CC, Tucson, AZ	70/6418

HOME OF THE SUN INVITATIONAL

Year	Winner	Score	Location	Par/Yards
1961	*Dave Hill	269	El Rio G&CC, Tucson, AZ	70/6418

TUCSON OPEN

Year	Winner	Score	Location	Par/Yards
1962	Phil Rodgers	263	El Rio G&CC, Tucson, AZ	70/6418
1963	Don January	266	49er CC, Tucson, AZ	72/6722
1964	Jack Cupit	274	49er CC, Tucson, AZ	72/6722
1965	Bob Charles	271	Tucson National GC, Tucson, AZ	72/7305
1966	*Joe Campbell	278	Tucson National GC, Tucson, AZ	72/7305
1967	Arnold Palmer	273	Tucson National GC, Tucson, AZ	72/7305
1968	George Knudson	273	Tucson National GC, Tucson, AZ	72/7305
1969	Lee Trevino	271	Tucson National GC, Tucson, AZ	72/7305
1970	*Lee Trevino	275	Tucson National GC, Tucson, AZ	72/7305
1971	J.C. Snead	273	Tucson National GC, Tucson, AZ	72/7305
1972	Miller Barber	273	Tucson National GC, Tucson, AZ	72/7305

DEAN MARTIN TUCSON OPEN

Year	Winner	Score	Location	Par/Yards
1973	Bruce Crampton	277	Tucson National GC, Tucson, AZ	72/7305
1974	Johnny Miller	272	Tucson National GC, Tucson, AZ	72/7305
1975	Johnny Miller	263	Tucson National GC, Tucson, AZ	72/7305

NBC TUCSON OPEN

Year	Winner	Score	Location	Par/Yards
1976	Johnny Miller	274	Tucson National GC, Tucson, AZ	72/7305

KEY * = Playoff # = Amateur ~ = Rain-curtailed

Year	Winner	Score	Location	Par/Yards
JOE GARAGIOLA TUCSON OPEN				
1977	*Bruce Lietzke	275	Tucson National GC, Tucson, AZ	72/7305
1978	Tom Watson	276	Tucson National GC, Tucson, AZ	72/7305
1979	Bruce Lietzke	265	Randolph Park Muncipal GC, (North), Tucson, AZ	70/6860
1980	Jim Colbert	270	Tucson National GC, Tucson, AZ	72/7305
1981	Johnny Miller	265	Randolph Park Municipal GC, (North), Tucson, AZ	70/6860
1982	Craig Stadler	266	Randolph Park Municipal GC, (North), Tucson, AZ	70/6860
1983	*Gil Morgan	271	Randolph Park Municipal GC, (North), Tucson, AZ	70/6860
SEIKO-TUCSON MATCH PLAY CHAMPIONSHIPS				
1984	Tom Watson	2&1	Randolph Park Municipal GC, (North), Tucson, AZ	70/6860
1985	Jim Thorpe	4&3	Randolph Park Municipal GC, (North), Tucson, AZ	70/6860
1986	Jim Thorpe	67	Randolph Park Municipal GC, (North), Tucson, AZ	70/6860
SEIKO-TUCSON OPEN				
1987	Mike Reid	268	TPC at StarPass, Tucson, AZ	72/7010
NORTHERN TELECOM TUCSON OPEN				
1988	David Frost	266	TPC at StarPass, Tucson, AZ	72/7010
1989	No Tournament held due to the change on schedule from end of year to beginning of year.			
1990	Robert Gamez	270	TPC at StarPass, Tucson, AZ	72/7010
			Randolph Park Municipal GC, Tucson, AZ	72/6902
NORTHERN TELECOM OPEN				
1991	#Phil Mickelson	272	TPC at StarPass, Tucson, AZ	72/7010
			Tucson National GC, Tucson, AZ	72/7305
1992	Lee Janzen	270	TPC at StarPass, Tucson, AZ	72/7010
			Tucson National GC, Tucson, AZ	72/7305
1993	Larry Mize	271	Tucson National GC, Tucson, AZ	72/7148
			Starr Pass GC, Tucson, AZ	72/7010
1994	Andrew Magee	270	Tucson National GC, Tucson, AZ	72/7148
			Starr Pass GC, Tucson, AZ	72/7010

PHOENIX OPEN

Year	Winner	Score	Location	Par/Yards
PHOENIX OPEN INVITATIONAL				
1935	Ky Laffoon	281	Phoenix CC, Phoenix, AZ	71/6726
1936-				
1938	No Tournaments			
1939	Byron Nelson	198	Phoenix CC, Phoenix, AZ	71/6726
1940	Ed Oliver	205	Phoenix CC, Phoenix, AZ	71/6726
1941-				
1943	No Tournaments			
1944	*Harold McSpaden	273	Phoenix CC, Phoenix, AZ	71/6726
1945	Byron Nelson	274	Phoenix CC, Phoenix, AZ	71/6726
1946	*Ben Hogan	273	Phoenix CC, Phoenix, AZ	71/6726
1947	Ben Hogan	270	Phoenix CC, Phoenix, AZ	71/6726
1948	Bobby Locke	268	Phoenix CC, Phoenix, AZ	71/6726
1949	*Jimmy Demaret	278	Phoenix CC, Phoenix, AZ	71/6726
1950	Jimmy Demaret	269	Phoenix CC, Phoenix, AZ	71/6726
1951	Lew Worsham	272	Phoenix CC, Phoenix, AZ	71/6726
1952	Lloyd Mangrum	274	Phoenix CC, Phoenix, AZ	71/6726
1953	Lloyd Mangrum	272	Phoenix CC, Phoenix, AZ	71/6726
1954	*Ed Furgol	272	Phoenix CC, Phoenix, AZ	71/6726
1955	Gene Littler	275	Arizona CC, Phoenix, AZ	70/6216
1956	Cary Middlecoff	276	Phoenix CC, Phoenix, AZ	71/6726
1957	Billy Casper	271	Arizona CC, Phoenix, AZ	70/6216
1958	Ken Venturi	274	Phoenix CC, Phoenix, AZ	71/6726
1959	Gene Littler	268	Arizona CC, Phoenix, AZ	70/6216
1960	*Jack Fleck	273	Phoenix CC, Phoenix, AZ	71/6726
1961	*Arnold Palmer	270	Arizona CC, Phoenix, AZ	70/6216
1962	Arnold Palmer	269	Phoenix CC, Phoenix, AZ	71/6726
1963	Arnold Palmer	273	Arizona CC, Phoenix, AZ	70/6216
1964	Jack Nicklaus	271	Phoenix CC, Phoenix, AZ	71/6726
1965	Rod Funseth	274	Arizona CC, Phoenix, AZ	70/6216
1966	Dudley Wysong	278	Phoenix CC, Phoenix, AZ	71/6726
1967	Julius Boros	272	Arizona CC, Phoenix, AZ	70/6216

KEY * = Playoff # = Amateur ~ = Rain-curtailed

Past Winners of PGA TOUR Events *(cont'd.)*

Year	Winner	Score	Location	Par/Yards
1968	George Knudson	272	Phoenix CC, Phoenix, AZ	71/6726
1969	Gene Littler	263	Arizona CC, Phoenix, AZ	70/6216
1970	Dale Douglass	271	Phoenix CC, Phoenix, AZ	71/6726
1971	Miller Barber	261	Arizona CC, Phoenix, AZ	70/6216
1972	Homero Blancas	273	Phoenix CC, Phoenix, AZ	71/6726
1973	Bruce Crampton	268	Arizona CC, Phoenix, AZ	70/6216
1974	Johnny Miller	271	Phoenix CC, Phoenix, AZ	71/6726
1975	Johnny Miller	260	Phoenix CC, Phoenix, AZ	71/6726
1976	Bob Gilder	268	Phoenix CC, Phoenix, AZ	71/6726
1977	*Jerry Pate	277	Phoenix CC, Phoenix, AZ	71/6726
1978	Miller Barber	272	Phoenix CC, Phoenix, AZ	71/6726
1979	~Ben Crenshaw	199	Phoenix CC, Phoenix, AZ	71/6726
1980	Jeff Mitchell	272	Phoenix CC, Phoenix, AZ	71/6726
1981	David Graham	268	Phoenix CC, Phoenix, AZ	71/6726
1982	Lanny Wadkins	263	Phoenix CC, Phoenix, AZ	71/6726
1983	*Bob Gilder	271	Phoenix CC, Phoenix, AZ	71/6726
1984	Tom Purtzer	268	Phoenix CC, Phoenix, AZ	71/6726
1985	Calvin Peete	270	Phoenix CC, Phoenix, AZ	71/6726
1986	Hal Sutton	267	Phoenix CC, Phoenix, AZ	71/6726
1987	Paul Azinger	268	TPC of Scottsdale, Scottsdale, AZ	71/6992
1988	*Sandy Lyle	269	TPC of Scottsdale, Scottsdale, AZ	71/6992
1989	Mark Calcavecchia	263	TPC of Scottsdale, Scottsdale, AZ	71/6992
1990	Tommy Armour III	267	TPC of Scottsdale, Scottsdale, AZ	71/6992
1991	Nolan Henke	268	TPC of Scottsdale, Scottsdale, AZ	71/6992
1992	Mark Calcavecchia	264	TPC of Scottsdale, Scottsdale, AZ	71/6992
1993	Lee Janzen	273	TPC of Scottsdale, Scottsdale, AZ	71/6992
1994	Bill Glasson	268	TPC of Scottsdale, Scottsdale, AZ	71/6992

AT&T PEBBLE BEACH NATIONAL PRO-AM

Year	Winner	Score	Location	Par/Yards
BING CROSBY PROFESSIONAL-AMATEUR				
1937	Sam Snead	68	Rancho Santa Fe CC, San Diego, CA	73/6769
1938	Sam Snead	139	Rancho Santa Fe CC, San Diego, CA	73/6769
1939	Dutch Harrison	138	Rancho Santa Fe CC, San Diego, CA	73/6769
1940	Ed Oliver	135	Rancho Santa Fe CC, San Diego, CA	73/6769
1941	Sam Snead	136	Rancho Santa Fe CC, San Diego, CA	73/6769
1942	Tie-Lloyd Mangrum			
	Leland Gibson	133	Rancho Santa Fe CC, San Diego, CA	73/6769
1943—1946 No Tournaments				
1947	Tie-Ed Furgol	213	Cypress Point CC, Monterey Peninsula, CA	72/6506
	George Fazio		Monterey Peninsula CC, Monterey Peninsula, CA	71/6356
			Pebble Beach GL, Monterey Peninsula, CA	72/6815
1948	Lloyd Mangrum	205	Cypress Point CC, Monterey Peninsula, CA	72/6506
			Monterey Peninsula CC, Monterey Peninsula, CA	71/6356
			Pebble Beach GL, Monterey Peninsula, CA	72/6815
1949	Ben Hogan	208	Cypress Point CC, Monterey Peninsula, CA	72/6506
			Monterey Peninsula CC, Monterey Peninsula, CA	71/6356
			Pebble Beach GL, Monterey Peninsula, CA	72/6815
1950	Tie-Sam Snead	214	Cypress Point CC, Monterey Peninsula, CA	72/6506
	Jack Burke, Jr		Monterey Peninsula CC, Monterey Peninsula, CA	71/6356
	Smiley Quick		Pebble Beach GL, Monterey Peninsula, CA	72/6815
	Dave Douglas			
1951	Byron Nelson	209	Cypress Point CC, Monterey Peninsula, CA	72/6506
			Monterey Peninsula CC, Monterey Peninsula, CA	71/6356
			Pebble Beach GL, Monterey Peninsula, CA	72/6815
1952	Jimmy Demaret	145	Cypress Point CC, Monterey Peninsula, CA	72/6506
			Monterey Peninsula CC, Monterey Peninsula, CA	71/6356
			Pebble Beach GL, Monterey Peninsula, CA	72/6815
THE BING CROSBY PROFESSIONAL-AMATEUR INVITATIONAL				
1953	Lloyd Mangrum	204	Cypress Point CC, Monterey Peninsula, CA	72/6506
			Pebble Beach GL, Monterey Pennsula, CA	72/6815

KEY * = Playoff # = Amateur ~ = Rain-curtailed

Year	Winner	Score	Location	Par/Yards
1954	Dutch Harrison	210	Cypress Point CC, Monterey Peninsula, CA	72/6506
			Monterey Peninsula CC, Monterey Peninsula, CA	71/6356
			Pebble Beach GL, Monterey Peninsula, CA	72/6815
1955	Cary Middlecoff	209	Cypress Point CC, Monterey Peninsula, CA	72/6506
			Monterey Peninsula CC, Monterey Peninsula, CA	71/6356
			Pebble Beach GL, Monterey Peninsula, CA	72/6815

BING CROSBY NATIONAL PROFESSIONAL-AMATEUR GOLF CHAMPIONSHIP

Year	Winner	Score	Location	Par/Yards
1956	Cary Middlecoff	202	Cypress Point CC, Monterey Peninsula, CA	72/6506
			Monterey Peninsula CC, Monterey Peninsula, CA	71/6356
			Pebble Beach GL, Monterey Peninsula, CA	72/6815
1957	Jay Hebert	213	Cypress Point CC, Monterey Peninsula, CA	72/6506
			Monterey Peninsula CC, Monterey Peninsula, CA	71/6356
			Pebble Beach GL, Monterey Peninsula, CA	72/6815
1958	Billy Casper	277	Cypress Point CC, Monterey Peninsula, CA	72/6506
			Monterey Peninsula CC, Monterey Peninsula, CA	71/6356
			Pebble Beach GL, Monterey Peninsula, CA	72/6815

BING CROSBY NATIONAL

Year	Winner	Score	Location	Par/Yards
1959	Art Wall	279	Cypress Point CC, Monterey Peninsula, CA	72/6506
			Monterey Peninsula CC, Monterey Peninsula, CA	71/6356
			Pebble Beach GL, Monterey Peninsula, CA	72/6815
1960	Ken Venturi	286	Cypress Point CC, Monterey Peninsula, CA	72/6506
			Monterey Peninsula CC, Monterey Peninsula, CA	71/6356
			Pebble Beach GL, Monterey Peninsula, CA	72/6815
1961	Bob Rosburg	282	Cypress Point CC, Monterey Peninsula, CA	72/6506
			Monterey Peninsula CC, Monterey Peninsula, CA	71/6356
			Pebble Beach GL, Monterey Peninsula, CA	72/6815
1962	*Doug Ford	286	Cypress Point CC, Monterey Peninsula, CA	72/6506
			Monterey Peninsula CC, Monterey Peninsula, CA	71/6356
			Pebble Beach GL, Monterey Peninsula, CA	72/6815
1963	Billy Casper	285	Cypress Point CC, Monterey Peninsula, CA	72/6506
			Monterey Peninsula CC, Monterey Peninsula, CA	71/6356
			Pebble Beach GL, Monterey Peninsula, CA	72/6815

BING CROSBY NATIONAL PROFESSIONAL-AMATEUR

Year	Winner	Score	Location	Par/Yards
1964	Tony Lema	284	Cypress Point CC, Monterey Peninsula, CA	72/6506
			Monterey Peninsula CC, Monterey Peninsula, CA	71/6356
			Pebble Beach GL, Monterey Peninsula, CA	72/6815
1965	Bruce Crampton	284	Cypress Point CC, Monterey Peninsula, CA	72/6506
			Monterey Peninsula CC, Monterey Peninsula, CA	71/6356
			Pebble Beach GL, Monterey Peninsula, CA	72/6815
1966	Don Massengale	283	Cypress Point CC, Monterey Peninsula, CA	72/6506
			Monterey Peninsula CC, Monterey Peninsula, CA	71/6356
			Pebble Beach GL, Monterey Peninsula, CA	72/6815
1967	Jack Nicklaus	284	Pebble Beach GL, Monterey Peninsula, CA	72/6815
			Cypress Point CC, Monterey Peninsula, CA	72/6506
			Spyglass Hill GC, Monterey Peninsula, CA	72/6810
1968	*Johnny Pott	285	Pebble Beach GL, Monterey Peninsula, CA	72/6815
			Cypress Point CC, Monterey Peninsula, CA	72/6506
			Spyglass Hill GC, Monterey Peninsula, CA	72/6810
1969	George Archer	283	Pebble Beach GL, Monterey Peninsula, CA	72/6815
			Cypress Point CC, Monterey Peninsula, CA	72/6506
			Spyglass Hill GC, Monterey Peninsula, CA	72/6810
1970	Bert Yancey	278	Pebble Beach GL, Monterey Peninsula, CA	72/6815
			Cypress Point CC, Monterey Peninsula, CA	72/6506
			Spyglass Hill GC, Monterey Peninsula, CA	72/6810
1971	Tom Shaw	278	Pebble Beach GL, Monterey Peninsula, CA	72/6815
			Cypress Point CC, Monterey Peninsula, CA	72/6506
			Spyglass Hill GC, Monterey Peninsula, CA	72/6810
1972	*Jack Nicklaus	284	Pebble Beach GL, Monterey Peninsula, CA	72/6815
			Cypress Point CC, Monterey Peninsula, CA	72/6506
			Spyglass Hill GC, Monterey Peninsula, CA	72/6810
1973	*Jack Nicklaus	282	Pebble Beach GL, Monterey Peninsula, CA	72/6815
			Cypress Point CC, Monterey Peninsula, CA	72/6506
			Spyglass Hill GC, Monterey Peninsula, CA	72/6810

KEY * = Playoff # = Amateur ~ = Rain-curtailed

Past Winners of PGA TOUR Events (cont'd.)

Year	Winner	Score	Location	Par/Yards
1974	~Johnny Miller	208	Pebble Beach GL, Monterey Peninsula, CA	72/6815
			Cypress Point CC, Monterey Peninsula, CA	72/6506
			Spyglass Hill GC, Monterey Peninsula, CA	72/6810
1975	Gene Littler	280	Pebble Beach GL, Monterey Peninsula, CA	72/6815
			Cypress Point CC, Monterey Peninsula, CA	72/6506
			Spyglass Hill GC, Monterey Peninsula, CA	72/6810
1976	Ben Crenshaw	281	Pebble Beach GL, Monterey Peninsula, CA	72/6815
			Cypress Point CC, Monterey Peninsula, CA	72/6506
			Spyglass Hill GC, Monterey Peninsula, CA	72/6810
1977	Tom Watson	273	Pebble Beach GL, Monterey Peninsula, CA	72/6815
			Cypress Point CC, Monterey Peninsula, CA	72/6506
			Monterey Peninsula CC, Monterey Peninsula, CA	71/6400
1978	*Tom Watson	280	Pebble Beach GL, Monterey Peninsula, CA	72/6815
			Cypress Point CC, Monterey Peninsula, CA	72/6506
			Spyglass Hill GC, Monterey Peninsula, CA	72/6810
1979	Lon Hinkle	284	Pebble Beach GL, Monterey Peninsula, CA	72/6815
			Cypress Point CC, Monterey Peninsula, CA	72/6506
			Spyglass Hill GC, Monterey Peninsula, CA	72/6810
1980	George Burns	280	Pebble Beach GL, Monterey Peninsula, CA	72/6815
			Cypress Point CC, Monterey Peninsula, CA	72/6506
			Spyglass Hill GC, Monterey Peninsula, CA	72/6810
1981	~*John Cook	209	Pebble Beach GL, Monterey Peninsula, CA	72/6815
			Cypress Point CC, Monterey Peninsula, CA	72/6506
			Spyglass Hill GC, Monterey Peninsula, CA	72/6810
1982	Jim Simons	274	Pebble Beach GL, Monterey Peninsula, CA	72/6815
			Cypress Point CC, Monterey Peninsula, CA	72/6506
			Spyglass Hill GC, Monterey Peninsula, CA	72/6810
1983	Tom Kite	276	Pebble Beach GL, Monterey Peninsula, CA	72/6815
			Cypress Point CC, Monterey Peninsula, CA	72/6506
			Spyglass Hill GC, Monterey Peninsula CA	72/6810
1984	*Hale Irwin	278	Pebble Beach GL, Monterey Peninsula, CA	72/6815
			Cypress Point CC, Monterey Peninsula, CA	72/6506
			Spyglass Hill GC, Monterey Peninsula, CA	72/6810
1985	Mark O'Meara	283	Pebble Beach GL, Monterey Peninsula, CA	72/6815
			Cypress Point CC, Monterey Peninsula, CA	72/6506
			Spyglass Hill GC, Monterey Peninsula, CA	72/6810

AT&T PEBBLE BEACH NATIONAL PRO-AM

Year	Winner	Score	Location	Par/Yards
1986	~Fuzzy Zoeller	205	Pebble Beach GL, Monterey Peninsula, CA	72/6815
			Cypress Point CC, Monterey Peninsula, CA	72/6506
			Spyglass Hill GC, Monterey Peninsula, CA	72/6810
1987	Johnny Miller	278	Pebble Beach GL, Monterey Peninsula, CA	72/6815
			Cypress Point CC, Monterey Peninsula, CA	72/6506
			Spyglass Hill GC, Monterey Peninsula, CA	72/6810
1988	*Steve Jones	280	Pebble Beach GL, Monterey Peninsula, CA	72/6815
			Cypress Point CC, Monterey Peninsula, CA	72/6506
			Spyglass Hill GC, Monterey Peninsula, CA	72/6810
1989	Mark O'Meara	277	Pebble Beach GL, Monterey Peninsula, CA	72/6815
			Cypress Point CC, Monterey Peninsula, CA	72/6506
			Spyglass Hill GC, Monterey Peninsula, CA	72/6810
1990	Mark O'Meara	281	Pebble Beach GL, Monterey Peninsula, CA	72/6815
			Cypress Point CC, Monterey Peninsula, CA	72/6506
			Spyglass Hill GC, Monterey Peninsula, CA	72/6810
1991	Paul Azinger	274	Pebble Beach GL, Monterey Peninsula, CA	72/6815
			Spyglass Hill GC, Monterey Peninsula, CA	72/6810
			Poppy Hills GC, Monterey Peninsula, CA	72/6865
1992	*Mark O'Meara	275	Pebble Beach GL, Monterey Peninsula, CA	72/6815
			Spyglass Hill GC, Monterey Peninsula, CA	72/6810
			Poppy Hills GC, Monterey Peninsula, CA	72/6865
1993	Brett Ogle	276	Pebble Beach GL, Monterey Peninsula, CA	72/6815
			Spyglass Hill GC, Monterey Peninsula, CA	72/6810
			Poppy Hills GC, Monterey Peninsula, CA	72/6865

KEY * = Playoff   # = Amateur   ~ = Rain-curtailed

1994	Johnny Miller	281	Pebble Beach GL, Monterey Peninsula, CA	72/6815
			Spyglass Hill GC, Monterey Peninsula, CA	72/6810
			Poppy Hills GC, Monterey Peninsula, CA	72/6865

BUICK INVITATIONAL OF CALIFORNIA

Year	Winner	Score	Location	Par/Yards
SAN DIEGO OPEN				
1952	Ted Kroll	276	San Diego CC, San Diego, CA	72/6931
1953	Tommy Bolt	274	San Diego CC, San Diego, CA	72/6931
1954	#Gene Littler	274	Rancho Santa Fe GC, San Diego, CA	72/6797
CONVAIR-SAN DIEGO OPEN				
1955	Tommy Bolt	274	Mission Valley CC, San Diego, CA	72/6619
1956	Bob Rosburg	270	Singing Hills GC, San Diego, CA	72/6573
SAN DIEGO OPEN INVITATIONAL				
1957	Arnold Palmer	271	Mission Valley CC, San Diego, CA	72/6619
1958	No Tournament			
1959	Marty Furgol	274	Mission Valley CC, San Diego, CA	72/6619
1960	Mike Souchak	269	Mission Valley CC, San Diego, CA	72/6619
1961	*Arnold Palmer	271	Mission Valley CC, San Diego, CA	72/6619
1962	*Tommy Jacobs	277	Stardust CC, San Diego, CA	71/6725
1963	Gary Player	270	Stardust CC, San Diego, CA	71/6725
1964	Art Wall	274	Rancho Bernardo CC, San Diego, CA	72/6455
1965	*Wes Ellis	267	Stardust CC, San Diego, CA	71/6725
1966	Billy Casper	268	Stardust CC, San Diego, CA	71/6725
1967	Bob Goalby	269	Stardust CC, San Diego, CA	71/6725
ANDY WILLIAMS-SAN DIEGO OPEN INVITATIONAL				
1968	Tom Weiskopf	273	Torrey Pines GC, San Diego, CA	72/N-6659, S-7021
1969	Jack Nicklaus	284	Torrey Pines GC, San Diego, CA	72/N-6659, S-7021
1970	*Pete Brown	275	Torrey Pines GC, San Diego, CA	72/N-6659, S-7021
1971	George Archer	272	Torrey Pines GC, San Diego, CA	72/N-6659, S-7021
1972	Paul Harney	275	Torrey Pines GC, San Diego, CA	72/N-6659, S-7021
1973	Bob Dickson	278	Torrey Pines GC, San Diego, CA	72/N-6659, S-7021
1974	Bobby Nichols	275	Torrey Pines GC, San Diego, CA	72/N-6659, S-7021
1975	*J. C. Snead	279	Torrey Pines GC, San Diego, CA	72/N-6659, S-7021
1976	J. C. Snead	272	Torrey Pines GC, San Diego, CA	72/N-6659, S-7021
1977	Tom Watson	269	Torrey Pines GC, San Diego, CA	72/N-6659, S-7021
1978	Jay Haas	278	Torrey Pines GC, San Diego, CA	72/N-6659, S-7021
1979	Fuzzy Zoeller	282	Torrey Pines GC, San Diego, CA	72/N-6659, S-7021
1980	*Tom Watson	275	Torrey Pines GC, San Diego, CA	72/N-6659, S-7021
WICKES/ANDY WILLIAMS SAN DIEGO OPEN				
1981	*Bruce Lietzke	278	Torrey Pines GC, San Diego, CA	72/N-6659, S-7021
1982	Johnny Miller	270	Torrey Pines GC, San Diego, CA	72/N-6659, S-7021
ISUZU/ANDY WILLIAMS SAN DIEGO OPEN				
1983	Gary Hallberg	271	Torrey Pines GC, San Diego, CA	72/N-6659, S-7021
1984	*Gary Koch	272	Torrey Pines GC, San Diego, CA	72/N-6659, S-7021
1985	*Woody Blackburn	269	Torrey Pines GC, San Diego, CA	72/N-6659, S-7021
SHEARSON LEHMAN BROTHERS ANDY WILLIAMS OPEN				
1986	~*Bob Tway	204	Torrey Pines GC, San Diego, CA	72/N-6659, S-7021
1987	George Burns	266	Torrey Pines GC, San Diego, CA	72/N-6659, S-7021
SHEARSON LEHMAN HUTTON ANDY WILLIAMS OPEN				
1988	Steve Pate	269	Torrey Pines GC, San Diego, CA	72/N-6659, S-7021
SHEARSON LEHMAN HUTTON OPEN				
1989	Greg Twiggs	271	Torrey Pines GC, San Diego, CA	72/N-6659, S-7021
1990	Dan Forsman	275	Torrey Pines GC, San Diego, CA	72/N-6659, S-7021
SHEARSON LEHMAN BROTHERS OPEN				
1991	Jay Don Blake	268	Torrey Pines GC, San Diego, CA	72/N-6659, S-7021
BUICK INVITATIONAL OF CALIFORNIA				
1992	~Steve Pate	200	Torrey Pines GC, San Diego, CA	72/N-6659, S-7021
1993	Phil Mickelson	278	Torrey Pines GC, San Diego, CA	72/N-6659, S-7021
1994	Craig Stadler	268	Torrey Pines GC, San Diego, CA	72/N-6592, S-7000

KEY * = Playoff   # = Amateur   ~ = Rain-curtailed

BOB HOPE CHRYSLER CLASSIC

Year	Winner	Score	Location	Par/Yards
PALM SPRINGS GOLF CLASSIC				
1960	Arnold Palmer	338	Bermuda Dunes CC, Palm Springs, CA	72/6837
			Indian Wells CC, Indian Wells, CA	72/6478
			Tamarisk CC, Palm Springs, CA	72/6869
			Thunderbird CC, Palm Springs, CA	N/A
1961	Billy Maxwell	345	Bermuda Dunes CC, Palm Springs, CA	72/6837
			Indian Wells CC, Indian Wells, CA	72/6478
			Tamarisk CC, Palm Springs, CA	72/6869
			Thunderbird CC, Palm Springs, CA	N/A
			Eldorado CC, Palm Springs, CA	72/6708
1962	Arnold Palmer	342	Bermuda Dunes CC, Palm Springs, CA	72/6837
			Indian Wells CC, Indian Wells, CA	72/6478
			Tamarisk CC, Palm Springs, CA	72/6869
			Thunderbird CC, Palm Springs, CA	N/A
			Eldorado CC, Palm Springs, CA	72/6708
1963	*Jack Nicklaus	345	Bermuda Dunes CC, Palm Springs, CA	72/6837
			Indian Wells CC, Indian Wells, CA	72/6478
			Tamarisk CC, Palm Springs, CA	72/6869
			Eldorado CC, Palm Springs, CA	72/6708
1964	*Tommy Jacobs	348	Bermuda Dunes CC, Palm Springs, CA	72/6837
			Indian Wells CC, Indian Wells, CA	72/6478
			Eldorado CC, Palm Springs, CA	72/6708
			La Quinta CC, La Quinta, CA	72/6911
BOB HOPE DESERT CLASSIC				
1965	Billy Casper	348	Bermuda Dunes CC, Palm Springs, CA	72/6837
			Indian Wells CC, Indian Wells, CA	72/6478
			Eldorado CC, Palm Springs, CA	72/6708
			La Quinta CC, La Quinta, CA	72/6911
1966	*Doug Sanders	349	Bermuda Dunes CC, Palm Springs, CA	72/6837
			Indian Wells CC, Indian Wells, CA	72/6478
			Eldorado CC, Palm Springs, CA	72/6708
			La Quinta CC, La Quinta. CA	72/6911
1967	Tom Nieporte	349	Bermuda Dunes CC, Palm Springs, CA	72,6837
			Indian Wells CC, Indian Wells, CA	72/6478
			Eldorado CC, Palm Springs, CA	72/6708
			La Quinta CC, La Quinta, CA	72/6911
1968	*Arnold Palmer	348	Bermuda Dunes CC, Palm Springs, CA	72/6837
			Indian Wells CC, Indian Wells, CA	72/6478
			Eldorado CC, Pa!m Springs, CA	72/6708
			La Quinta CC, La Quinta, CA	72/6911
1969	Billy Casper	345	Bermuda Dunes CC, Palm Springs, CA	72/6837
			Indian Wells CC, Indian Wells, CA	72/6478
			Tamarisk CC, Palm Springs, CA	72/6869
			La Quinta CC, La Quinta, CA	72/6911
1970	Bruce Devlin	339	Bermuda Dunes CC, Palm Springs, CA	72/6837
			Indian Wells CC, Indian Wells, CA	72/6478
			Eldorado CC, Palm Springs, CA	72/6708
			La Quinta CC, La Quinta, CA	72/6911
1971	*Arnold Palmer	342	Bermuda Dunes CC, Palm Springs, CA	72/6837
			Indian Wells CC, Indian Wells, CA	72/6478
			Tamarisk CC, Palm Springs, CA	72/6869
			La Quinta CC, La Quinta, CA	72/6911
1972	Bob Rosburg	344	Bermuda Dunes CC, Palm Springs, CA	72/6837
			Indian Wells CC, Indian Wells, CA	72/6478
			Eldorado CC, Palm Springs, CA	72/6708
			La Quinta CC, La Quinta, CA	72/6911
1973	Arnold Palmer	343	Bermuda Dunes CC, Palm Springs, CA	72/6837
			Indian Wells CC, Indian Wells, CA	72/6478
			Tamarisk CC, Palm Springs, CA	72/6869
			La Quinta CC, La Quinta, CA	72/6911

KEY * = Playoff # = Amateur ~ = Rain-curtailed

Year	Winner	Score	Location	Par/Yards
1974	Hubert Green	341	Bermuda Dunes CC, Palm Springs, CA	72/6837
			Indian Wells CC, Indian Wells, CA	72/6478
			Eldorado CC, Palm Springs, CA	72/6708
			La Quinta CC, La Quinta, CA	72/6911
1975	Johnny Miller	339	Bermuda Dunes CC, Palm Springs, CA	72/6837
			Indian Wells CC, Indian Wells, CA	72/6478
			Tamarisk CC, Palm Springs, CA	72/6869
			La Quinta CC, La Quinta, CA	72/6911
1976	Johnny Miller	344	Bermuda Dunes CC, Palm Springs, CA	72/6837
			Indian Wells CC, Indian Wells, CA	72/6478
			Eldorado CC, Palm Springs, CA	72/6708
			La Quinta CC, La Quinta, CA	72/6911
1977	Rik Massengale	337	Bermuda Dunes CC, Palm Springs, CA	72/6837
			Indian Wells CC, Indian Wells, CA	72/6478
			Tamarisk CC, Palm Springs, CA	72/6869
			La Quinta CC, La Quinta, CA	72/6911
1978	Bill Rogers	339	Bermuda Dunes CC, Palm Springs, CA	72/6837
			Indian Wells CC, Indian Wells, CA	72/6478
			Eldorado CC, Palm Springs, CA	72/6708
			La Quinta CC, La Quinta, CA	72/6911
1979	John Mahaffey	343	Bermuda Dunes CC, Palm Springs, CA	72/6837
			Indian Wells CC, Indian Wells, CA	72/6478
			Tamarisk CC, Palm Springs, CA	72/6869
			La Quinta CC, La Quinta, CA	72/6911
1980	Craig Stadler	343	Bermuda Dunes CC, Palm Springs, CA	72/6837
			Indian Wells CC, Indian Wells, CA	72/6478
			Eldorado CC, Palm Springs, CA	72/6708
			La Quinta CC, La Quinta, CA	72/6911
1981	Bruce Lietzke	335	Bermuda Dunes CC, Palm Springs, CA	72/6837
			Indian Wells CC, Indian Wells, CA	72/6478
			Tamarisk CC, Palm Springs, CA	72/6869
			La Quinta CC, La Quinta, CA	72/6911
1982	*Ed Fiori	335	Bermuda Dunes CC, Palm Springs, CA	72/6837
			Indian Wells CC, Indian Wells, CA	72/6478
			Eldorado CC, Palm Springs, CA	72/6708
			La Quinta CC, La Quinta, CA	72/6911
1983	*Keith Fergus	335	Bermuda Dunes CC, Palm Springs, CA	72/6837
			Indian Wells CC, Indian Wells, CA	72/6478
			Tamarisk CC, Palm Springs, CA	72/6869
			La Quinta CC, La Quinta, CA	72/6911

BOB HOPE CLASSIC

Year	Winner	Score	Location	Par/Yards
1984	*John Mahaffey	340	Bermuda Dunes CC, Palm Springs, CA	72/6837
			Indian Wells CC, Indian Wells, CA	72/6478
			Eldorado CC, Palm Springs, CA	72/6708
			La Quinta CC, La Quinta, CA	72/6911
1985	*Lanny Wadkins	333	Bermuda Dunes CC, Palm Springs, CA	72/6837
			Indian Wells CC, Indian Wells, CA	72/6478
			Tamarisk CC, Palm Springs, CA	72/6869
			La Quinta CC, La Quinta, CA	72/6911

BOB HOPE CHRYSLER CLASSIC

Year	Winner	Score	Location	Par/Yards
1986	*Donnie Hammond	335	Bermuda Dunes CC, Palm Springs, CA	72/6837
			Indian Wells CC, Indian Wells, CA	72/6478
			Eldorado CC, Palm Springs, CA	72/6708
			La Quinta CC, La Quinta, CA	72/6911
1987	Corey Pavin	341	Bermuda Dunes CC, Palm Springs, CA	72/6837
			Indian Wells CC, Indian Wells, CA	72/6478
			Indian Wells CC, Indian Wells, CA	72/6478
			Eldorado CC, Palm Springs, CA	72/6708
1988	Jay Haas	338	Bermuda Dunes CC, Palm Springs, CA	72/6837
			Indian Wells CC, Indian Wells, CA	72/6478
			La Quinta CC, La Quinta, CA	72/6911
			Palmer Course at PGA West, La Quinta, CA	72/6924

KEY * = Playoff   # = Amateur   ~ = Rain-curtailed

Year	Winner	Score	Location	Par/Yards
1989	*Steve Jones	343	Bermuda Dunes CC, Palm Springs, CA	72/6837
			Indian Wells CC, Indian Wells, CA	72/6478
			Eldorado CC, Palm Springs, CA	72/6708
			PGA West/Palmer Course, La Quinta, CA	72/6924
1990	Peter Jacobsen	339	PGA West/Palmer Course, La Quinta, CA	72/6924
			Bermuda Dunes CC, Palm Springs, CA	72/6927
			Indian Wells CC, Indian Wells, CA	72/6478
			Tamarisk CC, Palm Springs, CA	72/6875
1991	*Corey Pavin	331	PGA West/Palmer Course, La Quinta, CA	72/6924
			Bermuda Dunes CC, Palm Springs, CA	72/6927
			Indian Wells CC, Indian Wells, CA	72/6478
			La Quinta CC, La Quinta, CA	72/6911
1992	*John Cook	336	PGA West/Palmer Course, La Quinta, CA	72/6924
			Bermuda Dunes CC, Palm Springs, CA	72/6927
			Indian Wells CC, Indian Wells, CA	72/6478
			La Quinta CC, La Quinta, CA	72/6911
1993	Tom Kite	325	PGA West/Palmer Course, La Quinta, CA	72/6924
			Bermuda Dunes CC, Palm Springs, CA	72/6927
			Indian Wells CC, Indian Wells, CA	72/6478
			Tamarisk CC, La Quinta, CA	72/6881
1994	Scott Hoch	334	PGA West/Palmer Course, La Quinta, CA	72/6924
			Bermuda Dunes CC, Palm Springs, CA	72/6927
			Indian Wells CC, Indian Wells, CA	72/6478
			La Quinta CC, La Quinta, CA	72/6888

NISSAN OPEN

Year	Winner	Score	Location	Par/Yards

LOS ANGELES OPEN

Year	Winner	Score	Location	Par/Yards
1926	Harry Cooper	279	Los Angeles CC, Los Angeles, CA	71/6895 (North)
1927	Bobby Cruikshank	282	El Caballero CC, Los Angeles, CA	71/6830
1928	Mac Smith	284	Wilshire CC, Los Angeles, CA	71/6442
1929	Mac Smith	285	Riviera CC, Pacific Palisades, CA	71/7029
1930	Densmore Shute	296	Riviera CC, Pacific Palisades, CA	71/7029
1931	Ed Dudley	285	Wilshire CC, Los Angeles, CA	71/6442
1932	Mac Smith	281	Hillcrest CC, Los Angeles, CA	71/6911
1933	Craig Wood	281	Wilshire CC, Los Angeles, CA	71/6442
1934	Mac Smith	280	Los Angeles CC, Los Angeles, CA	71/6895 (North)
1935	*Vic Ghezzi	285	Los Angeles CC, Los Angeles, CA	71/6895 (North)
1936	Jimmy Hines	280	Los Angeles CC, Los Angeles, CA	71/6895 (North)
1937	Harry Cooper	274	Griffith Park, Los Angeles, CA	
			Wilson-72/6802, Harding-72/6488	
1938	Jimmy Thomson	273	Griffith Park, Los Angeles, CA	
			Wilson-72/6802, Harding-72/6488	
1939	Jimmy Demaret	274	Griffith Park, Los Angeles, CA	
			Wilson-72/6802, Harding-72/6488	
1940	Lawson Little	282	Los Angeles CC, Los Angeles, CA	71/6895 (North)
1941	Johnny Bulla	281	Riviera CC, Pacific Palisades, CA	71/7029
1942	*Ben Hogan	282	Hillcrest CC, Los Angeles, CA	71/6911
1943	No Tournament			
1944	Harold McSpaden	278	Wilshire CC, Los Angeles, CA	71/6442
1945	Sam Snead	283	Riviera CC, Pacific Palisades, CA	71/7029
1946	Byron Nelson	284	Riviera CC, Pacific Palisades, CA	71/7029
1947	Ben Hogan	280	Riviera CC, Pacific Palisades, CA	71/7029
1948	Ben Hogan	275	Riviera CC, Pacific Palisades, CA	71/7029
1949	Lloyd Mangrum	284	Riviera CC, Pacific Palisades, CA	71/7029
1950	*Sam Snead	280	Riviera CC, Pacific Palisades, CA	71/7029

KEY * = Playoff # = Amateur ~ = Rain-curtailed

Year	Winner	Score	Location	Par/Yards
1951	Lloyd Mangrum	280	Riviera CC, Pacific Palisades, CA	71/7029
1952	Tommy Bolt	289	Riviera CC, Pacific Palisades, CA	71/7029
1953	Lloyd Mangrum	280	Riviera CC, Pacific Palisades, CA	71/7029
1954	Fred Wampler	281	Fox Hills CC, Culver City, CA	N/A
1955	Gene Littler	276	Inglewood CC, Inglewood, CA	N/A
1956	Lloyd Mangrum	272	Rancho Municipal GC, Los Angeles, CA	71/6827
1957	Doug Ford	280	Rancho Municipal GC, Los Angeles, CA	71/6827
1958	Frank Stranahan	275	Rancho Municipal GC, Los Angeles, CA	71/6827
1959	Ken Venturi	278	Rancho Municipal GC, Los Angeles, CA	71/6827
1960	Dow Finsterwald	280	Rancho Municipal GC, Los Angeles, CA	71/6827
1961	Bob Goalby	275	Rancho Municipal GC, Los Angeles, CA	71/6827
1962	Phil Rodgers	268	Rancho Municipal GC, Los Angeles, CA	71/6827
1963	Arnold Palmer	274	Rancho Municipal GC, Los Angeles, CA	71/6827
1964	Paul Harney	280	Rancho Municipal GC, Los Angeles, CA	71/6827
1965	Paul Harney	276	Rancho Municipal GC, Los Angeles, CA	71/6827
1966	Arnold Palmer	273	Rancho Municipal GC, Los Angeles, CA	71/6827
1967	Arnold Palmer	269	Rancho Municipal GC, Los Angeles, CA	71/6827
1968	Billy Casper	274	Brookside GC, Pasadena, CA	71/7021
1969	*Charles Sifford	276	Rancho Municipal GC, Los Angeles, CA	71/6827
1970	*Billy Casper	276	Rancho Municipal GC. Los Angeles, CA	71/6827

GLEN CAMPBELL LOS ANGELES OPEN

Year	Winner	Score	Location	Par/Yards
1971	*Bob Lunn	274	Rancho Municipal GC, Los Angeles, CA	71/6827
1972	*George Archer	270	Rancho Municipal GC, Los Angeles, CA	71/6827
1973	Rod Funseth	276	Riviera CC, Pacific Palisades, CA	71/7029
1974	Dave Stockton	276	Riviera CC, Pacific Palisades, CA	71/7029
1975	Pat Fitzsimons	275	Riviera CC, Pacific Palisades, CA	71/7029
1976	Hale Irwin	272	Riviera CC, Pacific Palisades, CA	71/7029
1977	Tom Purtzer	273	Riviera CC, Pacific Palisades, CA	71/7029
1978	Gil Morgan	278	Riviera CC, Pacific Palisades, CA	71/7029
1979	Lanny Wadkins	276	Riviera CC, Pacific Palisades, CA	71/7029
1980	Tom Watson	276	Riviera CC, Pacific Palisades, CA	71/7029
1981	Johnny Miller	270	Riviera CC, Pacific Palisades, CA	71/7029
1982	*Tom Watson	271	Riviera CC, Pacific Palisades, CA	71/7029
1983	Gil Morgan	270	Rancho Municipal GC, Los Angeles, CA	71/6827

LOS ANGELES OPEN

1984	David Edwards	279	Riviera CC, Pacific Palisades, CA	71/7029
1985	Lanny Wadkins	264	Riviera CC, Pacific Palisades, CA	71/7029
1986	Doug Tewell	270	Riviera CC, Pacific Palisades, CA	71/7029

LOS ANGELES OPEN PRESENTED BY NISSAN

1987	*Tze-Chung Chen	275	Riviera CC, Pacific Palisades, CA	71/7029
1988	Chip Beck	267	Riviera CC, Pacific Palisades, CA	71/7029

NISSAN LOS ANGELES OPEN

1989	Mark Calcavecchia	272	Riviera CC, Pacific Palisades, CA	71/7029
1990	Fred Couples	266	Riviera CC, Pacific Palisades, CA	71/7029
1991	Ted Schulz	272	Riviera CC, Pacific Palisades, CA	71/7029
1992	*Fred Couples	269	Riviera CC, Pacific Palisades, CA	71/7029
1993	~Tom Kite	206	Riviera CC, Pacific Palisades, CA	71/7029
1994	Corey Pavin	271	Riviera CC, Pacific Palisades, CA	71/6946

DORAL-RYDER OPEN

Year	Winner	Score	Location	Par/Yards

DORAL CC OPEN INVITATIONAL

1962	Billy Casper	283	Doral CC (Blue), Miami, FL	72/6939
1963	Dan Sikes	283	Doral CC (Blue), Miami, FL	72/6939
1964	Billy Casper	277	Doral CC (Blue), Miami, FL	72/6939
1965	Doug Sanders	274	Doral CC (Blue), Miami, FL	72/6939

KEY * = Playoff # = Amateur ~ = Rain-curtailed

Past Winners of PGA TOUR Events *(cont'd.)*

Year	Winner	Score	Location	Par/Yards
1966	Phil Rodgers	278	Doral CC (Blue), Miami, FL	72/6939
1967	Doug Sanders	275	Doral CC (Blue), Miami, FL	72/6939
1968	Gardner Dickinson	275	Doral CC (Blue), Miami, FL	72/6939
1969	Tom Shaw	276	Doral CC (Blue), Miami, FL	72/6939
DORAL-EASTERN OPEN INVITATIONAL				
1970	Mike Hill	279	Doral CC (Blue), Miami, FL	72/6939
1971	J.C. Snead	275	Doral CC (Blue), Miami, FL	72/6939
1972	Jack Nicklaus	276	Doral CC (Blue), Miami, FL	72/6939
1973	Lee Trevino	276	Doral CC (Blue), Miami, FL	72/6939
1974	Brian Allin	272	Doral CC (Blue), Miami, FL	72/6939
1975	Jack Nicklaus	276	Doral CC (Blue), Miami, FL	72/6939
1976	Hubert Green	270	Doral CC (Blue), Miami, FL	72/6939
1977	Andy Bean	277	Doral CC (Blue), Miami, FL	72/6939
1978	Tom Weiskopf	272	Doral CC (Blue), Miami, FL	72/6939
1979	Mark McCumber	279	Doral CC (Blue), Miami, FL	72/6939
1980	*Raymond Floyd	279	Doral CC (Blue), Miami, FL	72/6939
1981	Raymond Floyd	273	Doral CC (Blue), Miami, FL	72/6939
1982	Andy Bean	278	Doral CC (Blue), Miami, FL	72/6939
1983	Gary Koch	271	Doral CC (Blue), Miami, FL	72/6939
1984	Tom Kite	272	Doral CC (Blue), Miami, FL	72/6939
1985	Mark McCumber	284	Doral CC (Blue), Miami, FL	72/6939
1986	*Andy Bean	276	Doral CC (Blue), Miami, FL	72/6939
DORAL-RYDER OPEN				
1987	Lanny Wadkins	277	Doral CC (Blue), Miami, FL	72/6939
1988	Ben Crenshaw	274	Doral CC (Blue), Miami, FL	72/6939
1989	Bill Glasson	275	Doral CC (Blue), Miami, FL	72/6939
1990	*Greg Norman	273	Doral CC (Blue), Miami, FL	72/6939
1991	*Rocco Mediate	276	Doral CC (Blue), Miami, FL	72/6939
1992	Raymond Floyd	271	Doral CC (Blue), Miami, FL	72/6939
1993	Greg Norman	265	Doral CC (Blue), Miami, FL	72/6939
1994	John Huston	274	Doral CC (Blue), Miami, FL	72/6939

HONDA CLASSIC

Year	Winner	Score	Location	Par/Yards
JACKIE GLEASON'S INVERRARY CLASSIC				
1972	Tom Weiskopf	278	Inverrary G&CC (East), Lauderhill, FL	72/7128
JACKIE GLEASON'S INVERRARY NATIONAL AIRLINES CLASSIC				
1973	Lee Trevino	279	Inverrary G&CC (East), Lauderhill, FL	72/7128
JACKIE GLEASON'S INVERRARY CLASSIC				
1974	Leonard Thompson	278	Inverrary G&CC (East), Lauderhill, FL	72/7128
1975	Bob Murphy	273	Inverrary G&CC (East), Lauderhill, FL	72/7128
1976	Hosted Tournament Players Championship			
1977	Jack Nicklaus	275	Inverrary G&CC (East), Lauderhill, FL	72/7128
1978	Jack Nicklaus	276	Inverrary G&CC (East), Lauderhill, FL	72/7128
1979	Larry Nelson	274	Inverrary G&CC (East), Lauderhill, FL	72/7128
1980	Johnny Miller	274	Inverrary G&CC (East), Lauderhill, FL	72/7128
AMERICAN MOTORS INVERRARY CLASSIC				
1981	Tom Kite	274	Inverrary G&CC (East), Lauderhill, FL	72/7128
HONDA INVERRARY CLASSIC				
1982	Hale Irwin	269	Inverrary G&CC (East), Lauderhill, FL	72/7128
1983	Johnny Miller	278	Inverrary G&CC (East), Lauderhill, FL	72/7128
HONDA CLASSIC				
1984	*Bruce Lietzke	280	TPC at Eagle Trace, Coral Springs, FL	72/7030
1985	*Curtis Strange	275	TPC at Eagle Trace, Coral Springs, FL	72/7030
1986	Kenny Knox	287	TPC at Eagle Trace, Coral Springs, FL	72/7030
1987	Mark Calcavecchia	279	TPC at Eagle Trace, Coral Springs, FL	72/7030
1988	Joey Sindelar	276	TPC at Eagle Trace, Coral Springs, FL	72/7030
1989	Blaine McCallister	266	TPC at Eagle Trace, Coral Springs, FL	72/7030
1990	John Huston	282	TPC at Eagle Trace, Coral Springs, FL	72/7030
1991	Steve Pate	279	TPC at Eagle Trace, Coral Springs, FL	72/7030
1992	*Corey Pavin	273	Weston Hills G&CC, Ft. Lauderdale, FL	72/7069
1993	~*Fred Couples	207	Weston Hills G&CC, Ft. Lauderdale, FL	72/7069
1994	Nick Price	276	Weston Hills G&CC, Ft. Lauderdale, FL	71/6964

KEY * = Playoff # = Amateur ~ = Rain-curtailed

THE NESTLE INVITATIONAL

Year	Winner	Score	Location	Par/Yards
FLORIDA CITRUS OPEN INVITATIONAL				
1966	Lionel Hebert	279	Rio Pinar CC, Orlando, FL	72/7012
1967	Julius Boros	274	Rio Pinar CC, Orlando, FL	72/7012
1968	Dan Sikes	274	Rio Pinar CC, Orlando, FL	72/7012
1969	Ken Still	278	Rio Pinar CC, Orlando, FL	72/7012
1970	Bob Lunn	271	Rio Pinar CC, Orlando, FL	72/7012
1971	Arnold Palmer	270	Rio Pinar CC, Orlando, FL	72/7012
1972	Jerry Heard	276	Rio Pinar CC, Orlando, FL	72/7012
1973	Brian Allin	265	Rio Pinar CC, Orlando, FL	72/7012
1974	Jerry Heard	273	Rio Pinar CC, Orlando, FL	72/7012
1975	Lee Trevino	276	Rio Pinar CC, Orlando, FL	72/7012
1976	*Hale Irwin	270	Rio Pinar CC, Orlando, FL	72/7012
1977	Gary Koch	274	Rio Pinar CC, Orlando, FL	72/7012
1978	Mac McLendon	271	Rio Pinar CC, Orlando, FL	72/7012
BAY HILL CITRUS CLASSIC				
1979	*Bob Byman	278	Bay Hill Club, Orlando, FL	71/7103
BAY HILL CLASSIC				
1980	Dave Eichelberger	279	Bay Hill Club, Orlando, FL	71/7103
1981	Andy Bean	266	Bay Hill Club, Orlando, FL	71/7103
1982	*Tom Kite	278	Bay Hill Club, Orlando, FL	71/7103
1983	*Mike Nicolette	283	Bay Hill Club, Orlando, FL	71/7103
1984	*Gary Koch	272	Bay Hill Club, Orlando, FL	71/7103
HERTZ BAY HILL CLASSIC				
1985	Fuzzy Zoeller	275	Bay Hill Club, Orlando, FL	71/7103
1986	~Dan Forsman	202	Bay Hill Club, Orlando, FL	71/7103
1987	Payne Stewart	264	Bay Hill Club, Orlando, FL	71/7103
1988	Paul Azinger	271	Bay Hill Club, Orlando, FL	71/7103
THE NESTLE INVITATIONAL				
1989	*Tom Kite	278	Bay Hill Club, Orlando, FL	71/7103
1990	Robert Gamez	274	Bay Hill Club, Orlando, FL	71/7103
1991	~Andrew Magee	203	Bay Hill Club, Orlando, FL	71/7103
1992	Fred Couples	269	Bay Hill Club, Orlando, FL	71/7103
1993	Ben Crenshaw	280	Bay Hill Club, Orlando, FL	71/7103
1994	Loren Roberts	275	Bay Hill Club, Orlando, FL	71/7114

THE PLAYERS CHAMPIONSHIP

Year	Winner	Score	Location	Par/Yards
TOURNAMENT PLAYERS CHAMPIONSHIP				
1974	Jack Nicklaus	272	Atlanta CC, Atlanta, GA	72/6883
1975	Al Geiberger	270	Colonial CC, Fort Worth, TX	70/7160
1976	Jack Nicklaus	269	Inverrary G&CC, Lauderhill, FL	72/7127
1977	Mark Hayes	289	Sawgrass, Ponte Vedra, FL	72/7174
1978	Jack Nicklaus	289	Sawgrass, Ponte Vedra, FL	72/7174
1979	Lanny Wadkins	283	Sawgrass, Ponte Vedra, FL	72/7174
1980	Lee Trevino	278	Sawgrass, Ponte Vedra, FL	72/7174
1981	*Raymond Floyd	285	Sawgrass, Ponte Vedra, FL	72/7174
1982	Jerry Pate	280	TPC at Sawgrass, Ponte Vedra, FL	72/6857
1983	Hal Sutton	283	TPC at Sawgrass, Ponte Vedra, FL	72/6857
1984	Fred Couples	277	TPC at Sawgrass, Ponte Vedra, FL	72/6857
1985	Calvin Peete	274	TPC at Sawgrass, Ponte Vedra, FL	72/6857
1986	John Mahaffey	275	TPC at Sawgrass, Ponte Vedra, FL	72/6857
1987	*Sandy Lyle	274	TPC at Sawgrass, Ponte Vedra, FL	72/6857
THE PLAYERS CHAMPIONSHIP				
1988	Mark McCumber	273	TPC at Sawgrass, Ponte Vedra, FL	72/6857
1989	Tom Kite	279	TPC at Sawgrass, Ponte Vedra, FL	72/6857
1990	Jodie Mudd	278	TPC at Sawgrass, Ponte Vedra, FL	72/6857
1991	Steve Elkington	276	TPC at Sawgrass, Ponte Vedra, FL	72/6857
1992	Davis Love III	273	TPC at Sawgrass, Ponte Vedra, FL	72/6857
1993	Nick Price	270	TPC at Sawgrass, Ponte Vedra, FL	72/6857

KEY * = Playoff   # = Amateur   ~ = Rain-curtailed

Year	Winner	Score	Location	Par/Yards
1994	Greg Norman	264	TPC at Sawgrass, Ponte Vedra, FL	72/6857

FREEPORT-MCMORAN CLASSIC

Year	Winner	Score	Location	Par/Yards
GREATER NEW ORLEANS OPEN INVITATIONAL				
1938	Harry Cooper	285	City Park GC, New Orleans, LA	72/6656
1939	Henry Picard	284	City Park GC, New Orleans, LA	72/6656
1940	Jimmy Demaret	286	City Park GC, New Orleans, LA	72/6656
1941	Henry Picard	276	City Park GC, New Orleans, LA	72/6656
1942	Lloyd Mangrum	281	City Park GC, New Orleans, LA	72/6656
1943	No Tournament			
1944	Sammy Byrd	285	City Park GC, New Orleans, LA	72/6656
1945	*Byron Nelson	284	City Park GC, New Orleans, LA	72/6656
1946	Byron Nelson	277	City Park GC, New Orleans, LA	72/6656
1947	No Tournament			
1948	Bob Hamilton	280	City Park GC. New Orleans, LA	72/6656
1949-				
1957	No Tournaments			
1958	*Billy Casper	278	City Park GC, New Orleans, LA	72/6656
1959	Bill Collins	280	City Park GC, New Orleans, LA	72/6656
1960	Dow Finsterwald	270	City Park GC, New Orleans, LA	72/6656
1961	Doug Sanders	272	City Park GC, New Orleans, LA	72/6656
1962	Bo Wininger	281	City Park GC, New Orleans, LA	72/6656
1963	Bo Wininger	279	Lakewood CC, New Orleans, LA	72/7080
1964	Mason Rudolph	283	Lakewood CC, New Orleans, LA	72/7080
1965	Dick Mayer	273	Lakewood CC, New Orleans, LA	72/7080
1966	Frank Beard	276	Lakewood CC, New Orleans, LA	72/7080
1967	George Knudson	277	Lakewood CC, New Orleans, LA	72/7080
1968	George Archer	271	Lakewood CC, New Orleans, LA	72/7080
1969	*Larry Hinson	275	Lakewood CC, New Orleans, LA	72/7080
1970	*Miller Barber	278	Lakewood CC, New Orleans, LA	72/7080
1971	Frank Beard	276	Lakewood CC, New Orleans, LA	72/7080
1972	Gary Player	279	Lakewood CC, New Orleans, LA	72/7080
1973	*Jack Nicklaus	280	Lakewood CC, New Orleans, LA	72/7080
1974	Lee Trevino	267	Lakewood CC, New Orleans, LA	72/7080
FIRST NBC NEW ORLEANS OPEN				
1975	Billy Casper	271	Lakewood CC, New Orleans, LA	72/7080
1976	Larry Ziegler	274	Lakewood CC, New Orleans, LA	72/7080
1977	Jim Simons	273	Lakewood CC, New Orleans, LA	72/7080
1978	Lon Hinkle	271	Lakewood CC, New Orleans, LA	72/7080
1979	Hubert Green	273	Lakewood CC, New Orleans, LA	72/7080
GREATER NEW ORLEANS OPEN				
1980	Tom Watson	273	Lakewood CC, New Orleans, LA	72/7080
USF&G NEW ORLEANS OPEN				
1981	Tom Watson	270	Lakewood CC, New Orleans, LA	72/7080
USF&G CLASSIC				
1982	~Scott Hoch	206	Lakewood CC, New Orleans, LA	72/7080
1983	Bill Rogers	274	Lakewood CC, New Orleans, LA	72/7080
1984	Bob Eastwood	272	Lakewood CC, New Orleans, LA	72/7080
1985	~Seve Ballesteros	205	Lakewood CC, New Orleans, LA	72/7080
1986	Calvin Peete	269	Lakewood CC, New Orleans, LA	72/7080
1987	Ben Crenshaw	268	Lakewood CC, New Orleans, LA	72/7080
1988	Chip Beck	262	Lakewood CC, New Orleans, LA	72/7080
1989	Tim Simpson	274	English Turn G&CC, New Orleans, LA	72/7106
1990	David Frost	276	English Turn G&CC, New Orleans, LA	72/7106
1991	*Ian Woosnam	275	English Turn G&CC, New Orleans, LA	72/7106
FREEPORT-MCMORAN CLASSIC				
1992	Chip Beck	276	English Turn G&CC, New Orleans, LA	72/7106
1993	Mike Standly	281	English Turn G&CC, New Orleans, LA	72/7106
1994	Ben Crenshaw	273	English Turn G&CC, New Orleans, LA	72/7106

KEY * = Playoff # = Amateur ~ = Rain-curtailed

MCI CLASSIC

Year	Winner	Score	Location	Par/Yards
HERITAGE CLASSIC				
1969	Arnold Palmer	283	Harbour Town GL, Hilton Head, SC	71/6657
1970	Bob Goalby	280	Harbour Town GL, Hilton Head, SC	71/6657
SEA PINES HERITAGE CLASSIC				
1971	Hale Irwin	279	Harbour Town GL, Hilton Head, SC	71/6657
1972	Johnny Miller	281	Ocean Course, Hilton Head, SC (first two rounds)	72/6600
			Harbour Town GL, Hilton Head, SC (second two rounds)	71/6657
1973	Hale Irwin	272	Harbour Town GL, Hilton Head, SC	71/6657
1974	Johnny Miller	276	Harbour Town GL, Hilton Head, SC	71/6657
1975	Jack Nicklaus	271	Harbour Town GL, Hilton Head, SC	71/6657
1976	Hubert Green	274	Harbour Town GL, Hilton Head, SC	71/6657
1977	Graham Marsh	273	Harbour Town GL, Hilton Head, SC	71/6657
1978	Hubert Green	277	Harbour Town GL, Hilton Head, SC	71/6657
1979	Tom Watson	270	Harbour Town GL, Hilton Head, SC	71/6657
1980	*Doug Tewell	280	Harbour Town GL, Hilton Head, SC	71/6657
1981	Bill Rogers	278	Harbour Town GL, Hilton Head, SC	71/6657
1982	*Tom Watson	280	Harbour Town GL, Hilton Head, SC	71/6657
1983	Fuzzy Zoeller	275	Harbour Town GL, Hilton Head, SC	71/6657
1984	Nick Faldo	270	Harbour Town GL, Hilton Head, SC	71/6657
1985	*Bernhard Langer	273	Harbour Town GL, Hilton Head, SC	71/6657
1986	Fuzzy Zoeller	276	Harbour Town GL, Hilton Head, SC	71/6657
MCI HERITAGE CLASSIC				
1987	Davis Love III	271	Harbour Town GL, Hilton Head, SC	71/6657
1988	Greg Norman	271	Harbour Town GL, Hilton Head, SC	71/6657
1989	Payne Stewart	268	Harbour Town GL, Hilton Head, SC	71/6657
1990	*Payne Stewart	276	Harbour Town GL, Hilton Head, SC	71/6657
1991	Davis Love III	271	Harbour Town GL, Hilton Head, SC	71/6657
1992	Davis Love III	269	Harbour Town GL, Hilton Head, SC	71/6657
1993	David Edwards	273	Harbour Town GL, Hilton Head, SC	71/6657
1994	Hale Irwin	266	Harbour Town GL, Hilton Head, SC	71/6657

KMART GREATER GREENSBORO OPEN

Year	Winner	Score	Location	Par/Yards
GREATER GREENSBORO OPEN				
1938	Sam Snead	272	Starmount Forest CC, Greensboro, NC	71/6630
			Sedgefield CC, Greensboro, NC	70/6680
1939	Ralph Guldahl	280	Starmount Forest CC, Greensboro, NC	71/6630
			Sedgefield CC, Greensboro, NC	70/6680
1940	Ben Hogan	270	Starmount Forest CC, Greensboro, NC	71/6630
			Sedgefield CC, Greensboro, NC	70/6680
1941	Byron Nelson	276	Starmount Forest CC, Greensboro, NC	71/6630
			Sedgefield CC, Greensboro, NC	70/6680
1942	Sam Byrd	279	Starmount Forest CC, Greensboro, NC	71/6630
1943-				
1944	No Tournaments			
1945	Byron Nelson	271	Starmount Forest CC, Greensboro, NC	71/6630
1946	Sam Snead	270	Sedgefield CC, Greensboro, NC	70/6680
1947	Vic Ghezzi	286	Starmount Forest CC, Greensboro, NC	71/6630
1948	Lloyd Mangrum	278	Sedgefield CC, Greensboro, NC	70/6680
1949	*Sam Snead	276	Starmount Forest CC, Greensboro, NC	71/6630
1950	Sam Snead	269	Sedgefield CC, Greensboro, NC	70/6680
1951	Art Doering	279	Starmount Forest CC, Greensboro, NC	71/6630
1952	Dave Douglas	277	Starmount Forest CC, Greensboro, NC	71/6630
1953	*Earl Stewart	275	Sedgefield CC, Greensboro, NC	70/6680
1954	*Doug Ford	283	Starmount Forest CC, Greensboro, NC	71/6630
1955	Sam Snead	273	Sedgefield CC, Greensboro, NC	70/6680
1956	*Sam Snead	279	Starmount Forest CC, Greensboro, NC	71/6630
1957	Stan Leonard	276	Sedgefield CC, Greensboro, NC	70/6680
1958	Bob Goalby	275	Starmount Forest CC, Greensboro, NC	71/6630

KEY * = Playoff # = Amateur ~ = Rain-curtailed

Year	Winner	Score	Location	Par/Yards
1959	Dow Finsterwald	278	Starmount Forest CC, Greensboro, NC	71/6630
1960	Sam Snead	270	Starmount Forest CC, Greensboro, NC	71/6630
1961	Mike Souchak	276	Sedgefield CC, Greensboro, NC	70/6680
1962	Billy Casper	275	Sedgefield CC, Greensboro, NC	70/6680
1963	Doug Sanders	270	Sedgefield CC, Greensboro, NC	70/6680
1964	*Julius Boros	277	Sedgefield CC, Greensboro, NC	70/6680
1965	Sam Snead	273	Sedgefield CC, Greensboro, NC	70/6680
1966	*Doug Sanders	276	Sedgefield CC, Greensboro, NC	70/6680
1967	George Archer	267	Sedgefield CC, Greensboro, NC	70/6680
1968	Billy Casper	267	Sedgefield CC, Greensboro, NC	70/6680
1969	*Gene Littler	274	Sedgefield CC, Greensboro, NC	70/6680
1970	Gary Player	271	Sedgefield CC, Greensboro, NC	71/7034
1971	*Bud Allin	275	Sedgefield CC, Greensboro, NC	71/7034
1972	*George Archer	272	Sedgefield CC, Greensboro, NC	71/7034
1973	Chi Chi Rodriguez	267	Sedgefield CC, Greensboro, NC	71/7012
1974	Bob Charles	270	Sedgefield CC, Greensboro, NC	71/7012
1975	Tom Weiskopf	275	Sedgefield CC, Greensboro, NC	71/6643
1976	Al Geiberger	268	Sedgefield CC, Greensboro, NC	71/6643
1977	Danny Edwards	276	Forest Oaks CC, Greensboro, NC	72/7075
1978	Seve Ballesteros	282	Forest Oaks CC, Greensboro, NC	72/6958
1979	Raymond Floyd	282	Forest Oaks CC, Greensboro, NC	72/6958
1980	Craig Stadler	275	Forest Oaks CC, Greensboro, NC	72/6958
1981	*Larry Nelson	281	Forest Oaks CC, Greensboro, NC	72/6984
1982	Danny Edwards	285	Forest Oaks CC, Greensboro, NC	72/6984
1983	Lanny Wadkins	275	Forest Oaks CC, Greensboro, NC	72/6984
1984	Andy Bean	280	Forest Oaks CC, Greensboro, NC	72/6984
1985	Joey Sindelar	285	Forest Oaks CC, Greensboro, NC	72/6984
1986	Sandy Lyle	275	Forest Oaks CC, Greensboro, NC	72/6984
1987	Scott Simpson	282	Forest Oaks CC, Greensboro, NC	72/6984

KMART GREATER GREENSBORO OPEN

Year	Winner	Score	Location	Par/Yards
1988	*Sandy Lyle	271	Forest Oaks CC, Greensboro, NC	72/6984
1989	Ken Green	277	Forest Oaks CC, Greensboro, NC	72/6984
1990	Steve Elkington	282	Forest Oaks CC, Greensboro, NC	72/6984
1991	*Mark Brooks	275	Forest Oaks CC, Greensboro, NC	72/6984
1992	Davis Love III	272	Forest Oaks CC, Greensboro, NC	72/6984
1993	*Rocco Mediate	281	Forest Oaks CC, Greensboro, NC	72/6984
1994	Mike Springer	275	Forest Oaks CC, Greensboro, NC	72/6984

SHELL HOUSTON OPEN

Year	Winner	Score	Location	Par/Yards
TOURNAMENT OF CHAMPIONS				
1946	Byron Nelson	274	River Oaks CC, Houston, TX	71/6588
1947	Bobby Locke	277	Memorial Park GC, Houston, TX	72/7421
1948	No Tournament			
1949	John Palmer	272	Pine Forest CC, Houston, TX	72/6510
HOUSTON OPEN				
1950	Cary Middlecoff	277	Brae Burn CC, Houston, TX	72/6725
1951	Marty Furgol	277	Memorial Park GC, Houston, TX	70/7212
1952	Jack Burke, Jr.	277	Memorial Park GC, Houston, TX	70/7212
1953	*Cary Middlecoff	283	Memorial Park GC, Houston, TX	70/7212
1954	Dave Douglas	277	Memorial Park GC, Houston, TX	70/7212
1955	Mike Souchak	273	Memorial Park GC, Houston, TX	70/7212
1956	Ted Kroll	277	Memorial Park GC, Houston, TX	70/7212
1957	Arnold Palmer	279	Memorial Park GC, Houston, TX	70/7212
1958	Ed Oliver	281	Memorial Park GC, Houston, TX	70/7212
HOUSTON CLASSIC				
1959	*Jack Burke, Jr.	277	Memorial Park GC, Houston, TX	70/7212
1960	*Bill Collins	280	Memorial Park GC, Houston, TX	70/7212
1961	*Jay Hebert	276	Memorial Park GC, Houston, TX	72/7122
1962	*Bobby Nichols	278	Memorial Park GC, Houston, TX	72/7201
1963	Bob Charles	268	Memorial Park GC, Houston, TX	72/7201
1964	Mike Souchak	278	Sharpstown CC, Houston, TX	71/7201
1965	Bobby Nichols	273	Sharpstown CC, Houston, TX	71/7201

KEY * = Playoff # = Amateur ~ = Rain-curtailed

Past Winners of PGA TOUR Events *(cont'd.)*

Year	Winner	Score	Location	Par/Yards
HOUSTON CHAMPION INTERNATIONAL				
1966	Arnold Palmer	275	Champions GC, Houston, TX	71/7166
1967	Frank Beard	274	Champions GC, Houston, TX	71/7166
1968	Roberto De Vicenzo	274	Champions GC, Houston, TX	71/7166
1969	Hosted U.S. Open			70/6967
1970	*Gibby Gilbert	282	Champions GC, Houston, TX	70/6967
1971	*Hubert Green	280	Champions GC, Houston, TX	70/6967
HOUSTON OPEN				
1972	Bruce Devlin	278	Westwood CC, Houston, TX	72/6998
1973	Bruce Crampton	277	Quail Valley GC, Houston, TX	72/6905
1974	Dave Hill	276	Quail Valley GC, Houston, TX	72/6905
1975	Bruce Crampton	273	Woodlands CC, The Woodlands, TX	72/6929
1976	Lee Elder	278	Woodlands CC, The Woodlands, TX	72/6997
1977	Gene Littler	276	Woodlands CC, The Woodlands, TX	72/6997
1978	Gary Player	270	Woodlands CC, The Woodlands, TX	72/6997
1979	Wayne Levi	268	Woodlands CC, The Woodlands, TX	71/6918
MICHELOB HOUSTON OPEN				
1980	*Curtis Strange	266	Woodlands CC, The Woodlands, TX	71/6918
1981	~Ron Streck	198	Woodlands CC, The Woodlands, TX	71/7071
1982	*Ed Sneed	275	Woodlands CC, The Woodlands, TX	71/7031
HOUSTON COCA-COLA OPEN				
1983	David Graham	275	Woodlands CC, The Woodlands, TX	71/7031
1984	Corey Pavin	274	Woodlands CC, The Woodlands, TX	71/7031
HOUSTON OPEN				
1985	Raymond Floyd	277	TPC at The Woodlands, The Woodlands, TX	72/7042
1986	*Curtis Strange	274	TPC at The Woodlands, The Woodlands, TX	72/7045
BIG I HOUSTON OPEN				
1987	*Jay Haas	276	TPC at The Woodlands, The Woodlands, TX	72/7045
INDEPENDENT INSURANCE AGENT OPEN				
1988	*Curtis Strange	270	TPC at The Woodlands, The Woodlands, TX	72/7042
1989	Mike Sullivan	280	TPC at The Woodlands, The Woodlands, TX	72/7042
1990	~*Tony Sills	204	TPC at The Woodlands, The Woodlands, TX	72/7042
1991	Fulton Allem	273	TPC at The Woodlands, The Woodlands, TX	72/7042
SHELL HOUSTON OPEN				
1992	Fred Funk	272	TPC at The Woodlands, The Woodlands, TX	72/7042
1993	~*Jim McGovern	199	TPC at The Woodlands, The Woodlands, TX	72/7042
1994	Mike Heinen	272	TPC at The Woodlands, The Woodlands, TX	72/7042

BELLSOUTH CLASSIC

Year	Winner	Score	Location	Par/Yards
ATLANTA CLASSIC				
1967	Bob Charles	282	Atlanta CC, Atlanta, GA	72/7007
1968	Bob Lunn	280	Atlanta CC, Atlanta, GA	72/7007
1969	*Bert Yancey	277	Atlanta CC, Atlanta, GA	72/7007
1970	Tommy Aaron	275	Atlanta CC, Atlanta, GA	72/7007
1971	*Gardner Dickinson	275	Atlanta CC, Atlanta, GA	72/7007
1972	Bob Lunn	275	Atlanta CC, Atlanta, GA	72/7007
1973	Jack Nicklaus	272	Atlanta CC, Atlanta, GA	72/7007
1974	Hosted TPC			
1975	Hale Irwin	271	Atlanta CC, Atlanta, GA	72/7007
1976	Hosted U.S. Open			
1977	Hale Irwin	273	Atlanta CC, Atlanta, GA	72/7007
1978	Jerry Heard	269	Atlanta CC, Atlanta, GA	72/7007
1979	Andy Bean	265	Atlanta CC, Atlanta, GA	72/7007
1980	Larry Nelson	270	Atlanta CC, Atlanta, GA	72/7007
1981	*Tom Watson	277	Atlanta CC, Atlanta, GA	72/7007
GEORGIA-PACIFIC ATLANTA GOLF CLASSIC				
1982	*Keith Fergus	273	Atlanta CC, Atlanta, GA	72/7007
1983	~*Calvin Peete	206	Atlanta CC, Atlanta, GA	72/7007
1984	Tom Kite	269	Atlanta CC, Atlanta, GA	72/7007
1985	*Wayne Levi	273	Atlanta CC, Atlanta, GA	72/7007
1986	Bob Tway	269	Atlanta CC, Atlanta, GA	72/7007
1987	Dave Barr	265	Atlanta CC, Atlanta, GA	72/7007

KEY * = Playoff # = Amateur ~ = Rain-curtailed A = Second tournament that year

Year	Winner	Score	Location	Par/Yards
1988	Larry Nelson	268	Atlanta CC, Atlanta, GA	72/7007
BELLSOUTH ATLANTA GOLF CLASSIC				
1989	*Scott Simpson	278	Atlanta CC, Atlanta, GA	72/7007
1990	Wayne Levi	275	Atlanta CC, Atlanta, GA	72/7007
1991	*Corey Pavin	272	Atlanta CC, Atlanta, GA	72/7007
BELLSOUTH CLASSIC				
1992	Tom Kite	272	Atlanta CC, Atlanta, GA	72/7007
1993	Nolan Henke	271	Atlanta CC, Atlanta, GA	72/7007
1994	John Daly	274	Atlanta CC, Marietta, GA	72/7007

GTE BYRON NELSON CLASSIC

Year	Winner	Score	Location	Par/Yards
DALLAS OPEN				
1944	Byron Nelson	276	Lakewood CC, Dallas, TX	N/A
1945	Sam Snead	276	Dallas CC, Dallas, TX	N/A
1946	Ben Hogan	284	Brook Hollow CC, Dallas, TX	N/A
1947-1955	No Tournaments			
1956	Don January	268	Preston Hollow CC, Dallas, TX	N/A
1956A	*Peter Thomson	267	Preston Hollow CC, Dallas, TX	N/A
1957	Sam Snead	264	Glen Lakes CC, Dallas, TX	N/A
1958	*Sam Snead	272	Oak Cliffs CC, Dallas, TX	71/6836
1959	Julius Boros	274	Oak Cliffs CC, Dallas, TX	71/6836
1960	*Johnny Pott	275	Oak Cliffs CC, Dallas, TX	71/6836
1961	Earl Stewart, Jr.	278	Oak Cliffs CC, Dallas, TX	71/6836
1962	Billy Maxwell	277	Oak Cliffs CC, Dallas, TX	71/6836
1963	No Tournament			
1964	Charles Coody	271	Oak Cliffs CC, Dallas, TX	71/6836
1965	No Tournament			
1966	Roberto De Vicenzo	276	Oak Cliffs CC, Dallas, TX	71/6836
1967	Bert Yancey	274	Oak Cliffs CC, Dallas, TX	71/6836
BYRON NELSON GOLF CLASSIC				
1968	Miller Barber	270	Preston Trail Golf Club, Dallas, TX	70/6993
1969	Bruce Devlin	277	Preston Trail Golf Club, Dallas, TX	70/6993
1970	*Jack Nicklaus	274	Preston Trail Golf Club, Dallas, TX	70/6993
1971	Jack Nicklaus	274	Preston Trail Golf Club, Dallas, TX	70/6993
1972	*Chi Chi Rodriquez	273	Preston Trail Golf Club, Dallas, TX	70/6993
1973	*Lanny Wadkins	277	Preston Trail Golf Club, Dallas, TX	70/6993
1974	Brian Allin	269	Preston Trail Golf Club, Dallas, TX	70/6993
1975	Tom Watson	269	Preston Trail Golf Club, Dallas, TX	70/6993
1976	Mark Hayes	273	Preston Trail Golf Club, Dallas, TX	70/6993
1977	Raymond Floyd	276	Preston Trail Golf Club, Dallas, TX	70/6993
1978	Tom Watson	272	Preston Trail Golf Club, Dallas, TX	70/6993
1979	*Tom Watson	275	Preston Trail Golf Club, Dallas, TX	70/6993
1980	Tom Watson	274	Preston Trail Golf Club, Dallas, TX	70/6993
1981	*Bruce Lietzke	281	Preston Trail Golf Club, Dallas, TX	70/6993
1982	Bob Gilder	266	Preston Trail Golf Club, Dallas, TX	70/6993
1983	Ben Crenshaw	273	Las Colinas Sports Club, Irving, TX	71/6982
1984	Craig Stadler	276	Las Colinas Sports Club, Irving, TX	71/6982
1985	*Bob Eastwood	272	Las Colinas Sports Club, Irving, TX	71/6982
1986	Andy Bean	269	TPC at Las Colinas, Irving, TX	70/6767
1987	*Fred Couples	266	TPC at Las Colinas, Irving, TX	70/6767
GTE BYRON NELSON GOLF CLASSIC				
1988	*Bruce Lietzke	271	TPC at Las Colinas, Irving, TX	70/6767
1989	*Jodie Mudd	265	TPC at Las Colinas, Irving, TX	70/6767
1990	~Payne Stewart	202	TPC at Las Colinas, Irving, TX	70/6767
1991	Nick Price	270	TPC at Las Colinas, Irving, TX	70/6767
1992	*~Billy Ray Brown	199	TPC at Las Colinas, Irving, TX	70/6850
1993	Scott Simpson	270	TPC at Las Colinas, Irving, TX	70/6850
1994	*~Neal Lancaster	132	TPC at Las Colinas, Irving, TX	70/6850
			Cottonwood Valley Course, Irving, TX	71/6862

KEY * = Playoff   # = Amateur   ~ = Rain-curtailed

BUICK CLASSIC

Year	Winner	Score	Location	Par/Yards
WESTCHESTER CLASSIC				
1967	Jack Nicklaus	272	Westchester CC, Harrison, NY	72/6573
1968	Julius Boros	272	Westchester CC, Harrison, NY	72/6648
1969	Frank Beard	275	Westchester CC, Harrison, NY	72/6677
1970	Bruce Crampton	273	Westchester CC, Harrison, NY	72/6700
1971	Arnold Palmer	270	Westchester CC, Harrison, NY	72/6700
1972	Jack Nicklaus	270	Westchester CC, Harrison, NY	72/6700
1973	*Bobby Nichols	272	Westchester CC, Harrison, NY	72/6614
1974	Johnny Miller	269	Westchester CC, Harrison, NY	72/6614
1975	*Gene Littler	271	Westchester CC, Harrison, NY	72/6614
AMERICAN EXPRESS WESTCHESTER CLASSIC				
1976	David Graham	272	Westchester CC, Harrison, NY	71/6603
1977	Andy North	272	Westchester CC, Harrison, NY	71/6603
1978	Lee Elder	274	Westchester CC, Harrison, NY	71/6603
MANUFACTURERS HANOVER WESTCHESTER CLASSIC				
1979	Jack Renner	277	Westchester CC, Harrison, NY	71/6603
1980	Curtis Strange	273	Westchester CC, Harrison, NY	71/6603
1981	Raymond Floyd	275	Westchester CC, Harrison, NY	71/6603
1982	Bob Gilder	261	Westchester CC, Harrison, NY	70/6329
1983	Seve Ballesteros	276	Westchester CC, Harrison, NY	71/6687
1984	Scott Simpson	269	Westchester CC, Harrison, NY	71/6687
1985	*Roger Maltbie	275	Westchester CC, Harrison, NY	71/6722
1986	Bob Tway	272	Westchester CC, Harrison, NY	71/6723
1987	*J.C. Snead	276	Westchester CC, Harrison, NY	71/6769
1988	*Seve Ballesteros	276	Westchester CC, Harrison, NY	71/6779
1989	*Wayne Grady	277	Westchester CC, Harrison, NY	71/6779
BUICK CLASSIC				
1990	Hale Irwin	269	Westchester CC, Harrison, NY	71/6779
1991	Billy Andrade	273	Westchester CC, Harrison, NY	71/6779
1992	David Frost	268	Westchester CC, Harrison, NY	71/6779
1993	*Vijay Singh	280	Westchester CC, Harrison, NY	71/6779
1994	Lee Janzen	268	Westchester CC, Harrison, NY	71/6779

COLONIAL

Year	Winner	Score	Location	Par/Yards
COLONIAL NATIONAL INVITATION TOURNAMENT				
1946	Ben Hogan	279	Colonial CC, Fort Worth, TX	70/7035
1947	Ben Hogan	279	Colonial CC, Fort Worth, TX	70/7035
1948	Clayton Heafner	272	Colonial CC, Fort Worth, TX	70/7035
1949	No Tournament			
1950	Sam Snead	277	Colonial CC, Fort Worth, TX	70/7035
1951	Cary Middlecoff	282	Colonial CC, Fort Worth, TX	70/7035
1952	Ben Hogan	279	Colonial CC, Fort Worth, TX	70/7035
1953	Ben Hogan	282	Colonial CC, Fort Worth, TX	70/7035
1954	Johnny Palmer	280	Colonial CC, Fort Worth, TX	70/7035
1955	Chandler Harper	276	Colonial CC, Fort Worth, TX	70/7035
1956	Mike Souchak	280	Colonial CC, Fort Worth, TX	70/7035
1957	Roberto De Vicenzo	284	Colonial CC, Fort Worth, TX	70/7021
1958	Tommy Bolt	282	Colonial CC, Fort Worth, TX	70/7021
1959	*Ben Hogan	285	Colonial CC, Fort Worth, TX	70/7021
1960	Julius Boros	280	Colonial CC, Fort Worth, TX	70/7021
1961	Doug Sanders	281	Colonial CC, Fort Worth, TX	70/7021
1962	*Arnold Palmer	281	Colonial CC, Fort Worth, TX	70/7021
1963	Julius Boros	279	Colonial CC, Fort Worth, TX	70/7021
1964	Billy Casper	279	Colonial CC, Fort Worth, TX	70/7021
1965	Bruce Crampton	276	Colonial CC, Fort Worth, TX	70/7021
1966	Bruce Devlin	280	Colonial CC, Fort Worth, TX	70/7021
1967	Dave Stockton	278	Colonial CC, Fort Worth, TX	70/7021
1968	Billy Casper	275	Colonial CC, Fort Worth, TX	70/7021
1969	Gardner Dickinson	278	Colonial CC, Fort Worth, TX	70/7142

KEY * = Playoff # = Amateur ~ = Rain-curtailed

Year	Winner	Score	Location	Par/Yards
1970	Homero Blancas	273	Colonial CC, Fort Worth, TX	70/7142
1971	Gene Littler	283	Colonial CC, Fort Worth, TX	70/7142
1972	Jerry Heard	275	Colonial CC, Fort Worth, TX	70/7142
1973	Tom Weiskopf	276	Colonial CC, Fort Worth, TX	70/7142
1974	Rod Curl	276	Colonial CC, Fort Worth, TX	70/7142
1975	Hosted TPC			
1976	Lee Trevino	273	Colonial CC, Fort Worth, TX	70/7142
1977	Ben Crenshaw	272	Colonial CC, Fort Worth, TX	70/7142
1978	Lee Trevino	268	Colonial CC, Fort Worth, TX	70/7142
1979	Al Geiberger	274	Colonial CC, Fort Worth, TX	70/7096
1980	Bruce Lietzke	271	Colonial CC, Fort Worth, TX	70/7096
1981	Fuzzy Zoeller	274	Colonial CC, Fort Worth, TX	70/7096
1982	Jack Nicklaus	273	Colonial CC, Fort Worth, TX	70/7096
1983	*Jim Colbert	278	Colonial CC, Fort Worth, TX	70/7096
1984	*Peter Jacobsen	270	Colonial CC, Fort Worth, TX	70/7096
1985	Corey Pavin	266	Colonial CC, Fort Worth, TX	70/7096
1986	*~Dan Pohl	205	Colonial CC, Fort Worth, TX	70/7096
1987	Keith Clearwater	266	Colonial CC, Fort Worth, TX	70/7096
1988	Lanny Wadkins	270	Colonial CC, Fort Worth, TX	70/7096

SOUTHWESTERN BELL COLONIAL

Year	Winner	Score	Location	Par/Yards
1989	Ian Baker-Finch	270	Colonial CC, Fort Worth, TX	70/7096
1990	Ben Crenshaw	272	Colonial CC, Fort Worth, TX	70/7096
1991	Tom Purtzer	267	Colonial CC, Fort Worth, TX	70/7096
1992	*Bruce Lietzke	267	Colonial CC, Fort Worth, TX	70/7096
1993	Fulton Allem	264	Colonial CC, Fort Worth, TX	70/7096
1994	*Nick Price	266	Colonial CC, Fort Worth, TX	70/7096

THE MEMORIAL TOURNAMENT

Year	Winner	Score	Location	Par/Yards
THE MEMORIAL TOURNAMENT				
1976	*Roger Maltbie	288	Muirfield Village GC, Dublin, OH	72/7027
1977	Jack Nicklaus	281	Muirfield Village GC, Dublin, OH	72/7101
1978	Jim Simons	284	Muirfield Village GC, Dublin, OH	72/7101
1979	Tom Watson	285	Muirfield Village GC, Dublin, OH	72/7101
1980	David Graham	280	Muirfield Village GC, Dublin, OH	72/7116
1981	Keith Fergus	284	Muirfield Village GC, Dublin, OH	72/7116
1982	Raymond Floyd	281	Muirfield Village GC, Dublin, OH	72/7116
1983	Hale Irwin	281	Muirfield Village GC, Dublin, OH	72/7116
1984	*Jack Nicklaus	280	Muirfield Village GC, Dublin, OH	72/7116
1985	Hale Irwin	281	Muirfield Village GC, Dublin, OH	72/7106
1986	Hal Sutton	271	Muirfield Village GC, Dublin, OH	72/7106
1987	Don Pooley	272	Muirfield Village GC, Dublin, OH	72/7104
1988	Curtis Strange	274	Muirfield Village GC, Dublin, OH	72/7104
1989	Bob Tway	277	Muirfield Village GC, Dublin, OH	72/7104
1990	~Greg Norman	216	Muirfield Village GC, Dublin, OH	72/7104
1991	*Kenny Perry	273	Muirfield Village GC, Dublin, OH	72/7104
1992	*David Edwards	273	Muirfield Village GC, Dublin, OH	72/7104
1993	Paul Azinger	274	Muirfield Village GC, Dublin, OH	72/7104
1994	Tom Lehman	268	Muirfield Village GC, Dublin, OH	72/7104

KEMPER OPEN

Year	Winner	Score	Location	Par/Yards
KEMPER OPEN				
1968	Arnold Palmer	276	Pleasant Valley CC, Sutton, MA	71/7205
1969	Dale Douglass	274	Quail Hollow CC, Charlotte, NC	72/7205
1970	Dick Lotz	278	Quail Hollow CC, Charlotte, NC	72/7205
1971	*Tom Weiskopf	277	Quail Hollow CC, Charlotte, NC	72/7205
1972	Doug Sanders	275	Quail Hollow CC, Charlotte, NC	72/7205
1973	Tom Weiskopf	271	Quail Hollow CC, Charlotte, NC	72/7205
1974	*Bob Menne	270	Quail Hollow CC, Charlotte, NC	72/7205
1975	Raymond Floyd	278	Quail Hollow CC, Charlotte, NC	72/7205

KEY * = Playoff # = Amateur ~ = Rain-curtailed

Year	Winner	Score	Location	Par/Yards
1976	Joe Inman	277	Quail Hollow CC, Charlotte, NC	72/7205
1977	Tom Weiskopf	277	Quail Hollow CC, Charlotte, NC	72/7205
1978	Andy Bean	273	Quail Hollow CC, Charlotte, NC	72/7205
1979	Jerry McGee	272	Quail Hollow CC, Charlotte, NC	72/7205
1980	John Mahaffey	275	Congressional CC, Bethesda, MD	72/7173
1981	Craig Stadler	270	Congressional CC, Bethesda, MD	72/7173
1982	Craig Stadler	275	Congressional CC, Bethesda, MD	72/7173
1983	*Fred Couples	287	Congressional CC, Bethesda, MD	72/7173
1984	Greg Norman	280	Congressional CC, Bethesda, MD	72/7173
1985	Bill Glasson	278	Congressional CC, Bethesda, MD	72/7173
1986	*Greg Norman	277	Congressional CC, Bethesda, MD	72/7173
1987	Tom Kite	270	TPC at Avenel, Potomac, MD	71/6864
1988	*Morris Hatalsky	274	TPC at Avenel, Potomac, MD	71/6864
1989	Tom Byrum	268	TPC at Avenel, Potomac, MD	71/6864
1990	Gil Morgan	274	TPC at Avenel, Potomac, MD	71/6864
1991	*Billy Andrade	263	TPC at Avenel, Potomac, MD	71/6864
1992	Bill Glasson	276	TPC at Avenel, Potomac, MD	71/6864
1993	Grant Waite	275	TPC at Avenel, Potomac, MD	71/6864
1994	Mark Brooks	271	TPC at Avenel, Potomac, MD	71/6864

CANON GREATER HARTFORD OPEN

Year	Winner	Score	Location	Par/Yards
INSURANCE CITY OPEN				
1952	Ted Kroll	273	Wethersfield CC, Hartford, CT	71/6568
1953	Bob Toski	269	Wethersfield CC, Hartford, CT	71/6568
1954	*Tommy Bolt	271	Wethersfield CC, Hartford, CT	71/6568
1955	Sam Snead	269	Wethersfield CC, Hartford, CT	71/6568
1956	*Arnold Palmer	274	Wethersfield CC, Hartford, CT	71/6568
1957	Gardner Dickinson	272	Wethersfield CC, Hartford, CT	71/6568
1958	Jack Burke, Jr.	268	Wethersfield CC, Hartford, CT	71/6568
1959	Gene Littler	272	Wethersfield CC, Hartford, CT	71/6568
1960	*Arnold Palmer	270	Wethersfield CC, Hartford, CT	71/6568
1961	*Billy Maxwell	271	Wethersfield CC, Hartford, CT	71/6568
1962	*Bob Goalby	271	Wethersfield CC, Hartford, CT	71/6568
1963	Billy Casper	271	Wethersfield CC, Hartford, CT	71/6568
1964	Ken Venturi	273	Wethersfield CC, Hartford, CT	71/6568
1965	*Billy Casper	274	Wethersfield CC, Hartford, CT	71/6568
1966	Art Wall	266	Wethersfield CC, Hartford, CT	71/6568
GREATER HARTFORD OPEN INVITATIONAL				
1967	Charlie. Sifford	272	Wethersfield CC, Hartford, CT	71/6568
1968	Billy Casper	266	Wethersfield CC, Hartford, CT	71/6568
1969	*Bob Lunn	268	Wethersfield CC, Hartford, CT	71/6568
1970	Bob Murphy	267	Wethersfield CC, Hartford, CT	71/6568
1971	*George Archer	268	Wethersfield CC, Hartford, CT	71/6568
1972	*Lee Trevino	269	Wethersfield CC, Hartford, CT	71/6568
SAMMY DAVIS JR. GREATER HARTFORD OPEN				
1973	Billy Casper	264	Wethersfield CC, Hartford, CT	71/6568
1974	Dave Stockton	268	Wethersfield CC, Hartford, CT	71/6568
1975	*Don Bies	267	Wethersfield CC, Hartford, CT	71/6568
1976	Rik Massengale	266	Wethersfield CC, Hartford, CT	71/6568
1977	Bill Kratzert	265	Wethersfield CC, Hartford, CT	71/6568
1978	Rod Funseth	264	Wethersfield CC, Hartford, CT	71/6568
1979	Jerry McGee	267	Wethersfield CC, Hartford, CT	71/6568
1980	*Howard Twitty	266	Wethersfield CC, Hartford, CT	71/6568
1981	Hubert Green	264	Wethersfield CC, Hartford, CT	71/6568
1982	Tim Norris	259	Wethersfield CC, Hartford, CT	71/6568
1983	Curtis Strange	268	Wethersfield CC, Hartford, CT	71/6568
1984	Peter Jacobsen	269	TPC of Connecticut, Cromwell, CT	71/6786
1985	*Phil Blackmar	271	TPC of Connecticut, Cromwell, CT	71/6786
CANON SAMMY DAVIS JR.GREATER HARTFORD OPEN				
1986	*Mac O'Grady	269	TPC of Connecticut, Cromwell, CT	71/6786

KEY * = Playoff # = Amateur ~ = Rain-curtailed

Year	Winner	Score	Location	Par/Yards
1987	Paul Azinger	269	TPC of Connecticut, Cromwell, CT	71/6786
1988	*Mark Brooks	269	TPC of Connecticut, Cromwell, CT	71/6786
CANON GREATER HARTFORD OPEN				
1989	Paul Azinger	267	TPC of Connecticut, Cromwell, CT	71/6786
1990	Wayne Levi	267	TPC of Connecticut, Cromwell, CT	70/6531
1991	*Billy Ray Brown	271	TPC at River Highlands, Cromwell, CT	70/6820
1992	Lanny Wadkins	274	TPC at River Highlands, Cromwell, CT	70/6820
1993	Nick Price	271	TPC at River Highlands, Cromwell, CT	70/6820
1994	David Frost	268	TPC at River Highlands, Cromwell, CT	70/6820

FEDEX ST. JUDE CLASSIC

Year	Winner	Score	Location	Par/Yards
MEMPHIS INVITATIONAL OPEN				
1958	Billy Maxwell	267	Colonial CC, Memphis, TN	70/6466
1959	*Don Whitt	272	Colonial CC, Memphis, TN	70/6466
1960	*Tommy Bolt	273	Colonial CC, Memphis, TN	70/6466
1961	Cary Middlecoff	266	Colonial CC, Memphis, TN	70/6466
1962	*Lionel Hebert	267	Colonial CC, Memphis, TN	70/6466
1963	*Tony Lema	270	Colonial CC, Memphis, TN	70/6466
1964	Mike Souchak	270	Colonial CC, Memphis, TN	70/6466
1965	*Jack Nicklaus	271	Colonial CC, Memphis, TN	70/6466
1966	Bert Yancey	265	Colonial CC, Memphis, TN	70/6466
1967	Dave Hill	272	Colonial CC, Memphis, TN	70/6466
1968	Bob Lunn	268	Colonial CC, Memphis, TN	70/6466
1969	Dave Hill	265	Colonial CC, Memphis, TN	70/6466
DANNY THOMAS MEMPHIS CLASSIC				
1970	Dave Hill	267	Colonial CC, Memphis, TN	70/6466
1971	Lee Trevino	268	Colonial CC, Memphis, TN	70/6466
1972	Lee Trevino	281	Colonial CC, Cordova, TN	S-72/6883
1973	Dave Hill	283	Colonial CC, Cordova, TN	S-72/7282
1974	Gary Player	273	Colonial CC, Cordova, TN	S-72/7282
1975	Gene Littler	270	Colonial CC, Cordova, TN	S-72/7282
1976	Gibby Gilbert	273	Colonial CC, Cordova, TN	S-72/7282
1977	Al Geiberger	273	Colonial CC, Cordova, TN	S-72/7282
1978	*Andy Bean	277	Colonial CC, Cordova, TN	S-72/7282
1979	*Gil Morgan	278	Colonial CC, Cordova, TN	S-72/7282
1980	Lee Trevino	272	Colonial CC, Cordova, TN	S-72/7282
1981	Jerry Pate	274	Colonial CC, Cordova, TN	S-72/7282
1982	Raymond Floyd	271	Colonial CC, Cordova, TN	S-72/7282
1983	Larry Mize	274	Colonial CC, Cordova, TN	S-72/7282
1984	Bob Eastwood	280	Colonial CC, Cordova, TN	S-72/7282
ST. JUDE MEMPHIS CLASSIC				
1985	*Hal Sutton	279	Colonial CC, Cordova, TN	S-72/7282
FEDERAL EXPRESS ST. JUDE CLASSIC				
1986	Mike Hulbert	280	Colonial CC, Cordova, TN	S-72/7282
1987	Curtis Strange	275	Colonial CC, Cordova, TN	S-72/7282
1988	Jodie Mudd	273	Colonial CC, Cordova, TN	S-72/7282
1989	John Mahaffey	272	TPC at Southwind, Germantown, TN	71/7006
1990	*Tom Kite	269	TPC at Southwind, Germantown, TN	71/7006
1991	Fred Couples	269	TPC at Southwind, Germantown, TN	71/7006
1992	Jay Haas	263	TPC at Southwind, Germantown, TN	71/7006
1993	Nick Price	266	TPC at Southwind, Germantown, TN	71/7006
1994	*Dicky Pride	267	TPC at Southwind, Germantown, TN	71/7006

MOTOROLA WESTERN OPEN

Year	Winner	Score	Location	Par/Yards
WESTERN OPEN				
1899	*Willie Smith	156	Glenview GC, Chicago, IL	72/6362
1900	No Tournament			
1901	Laurie Auchterlonie	160	Midlothian CC, Chicago, IL	71/6654
1902	Willie Anderson	299	Euclid Club, Cleveland, OH	N/A

KEY * = Playoff   # = Amateur   ~ = Rain-curtailed   A = Second tournament that year

Year	Winner	Score	Location	Par/Yards
1903	Alex Smith	318	Milwaukee CC, Milwaukee, WI	72/6867
1904	Willie Anderson	304	Kent CC, Grand Rapids, MI	71/6514
1905	Arthur Smith	278	Cincinnati GC, Cincinnati, OH	71/6231
1906	Alex Smith	306	Homewood CC, Chicago, IL	70/6311
1907	Robert Simpson	307	Hinsdale GC, Hinsdale, IL	71/6475
1908	Willie Anderson	299	Normancie GC, St. Louis, MO	71/6534
1909	Willie Anderson	288	Skokie CC, Chicago, IL	72/6913
1910	#Chick Evans, Jr.	6&5	Beverly CC, Chicago, IL	72/6754
1911	Robert Simpson	2&1	Kent CC, Grand Rapids, MI	71/6514
1912	Mac Smith	299	Idlewild CC, Chicago, IL	72/6754
1913	John McDermott	295	Memphis CC, Memphis, TN	70/6695
1914	Jim Barnes	293	Interlachen CC, Minneapolis, MN	73/6733
1915	Tom McNamara	304	Glen Oak CC, Chicago, IL	72/6503
1916	Walter Hagen	286	Blue Mound CC, Chicago, IL	N/A
1917	Jim Barnes	283	Westmoreland CC, Chicago, IL	72/6798
1918	No Tournament			
1919	Jim Barnes	283	Mayfield CC, Cleveland, OH	72/6609
1920	Jock Hutchinson	296	Olympia Fields CC, Chicago, IL	71/6749
1921	Walter Hagen	287	Oakwood Club, Cleveland, OH	71/6709
1922	Mike Brady	291	Oakland Hills CC, Detroit, MI	72/7052
1923	Jock Hutchinson	281	Colonial CC, Memphis, TN	70/7116
1924	Bill Mehlhorn	293	Calumet CC, Chicago, IL	72/6524
1925	Mac Smith	281	Youngstown CC, Youngstown, OH	71/6597
1926	Walter Hagen	279	Highland G&CC, Indianapolis, IN	70/6501
1927	Walter Hagen	281	Olympia Fields CC, Chicago, IL	71/6749
1928	Abe Espinosa	291	North Shore GC, Chicago, IL	72/7024
1929	Tommy Armour	273	Ozaukee CC, Milwaukee, WI	70/6553
1930	Gene Sarazen	278	Indianwood G&CC, Detroit, MI	N/A
1931	Ed Dudley	280	Miami Valley GC, Dayton, OH	71/6589
1932	Walter Hagen	287	Canterbury GC, Cleveland, OH	72/6877
1933	Mac Smith	282	Olympia Fields CC, Chicago, IL	71/6749
1934	*Harry Cooper	274	Country Club of Peoria, Peoria, IL	70/6068
1935	John Revolta	290	South Bend CC, South Bend, IN	71/6455
1936	Ralph Guldahl	274	Davenport CC, Davenport, IA	71/6458
1937	*Ralph Guldahl	288	Canterbury CC, Cleveland, OH	72/6877
1938	Ralph Guldahl	279	Westwood CC, St. Louis, MO	72/6785
1939	Byron Nelson	281	Medinah CC, Chicago, IL	71/7104
1940	*Jimmy Demaret	293	River Oaks CC, Houston, TX	72/6868
1941	Ed Oliver	275	Phoenix GC, Phoenix, AZ	71/6726
1942	Herman Barron	276	Phoenix GC, Phoenix, AZ	71/6726
1943-				
1945	No Tournaments			
1946	Ben Hogan	271	Sunset CC, St. Louis, MO	72/6323
1947	Johnny Palmer	270	Salt Lake City CC, Salt Lake City, UT	72/6891
1948	*Ben Hogan	281	Brookfield CC, Buffalo, NY	72/6813
1949	Sam Snead	268	Keller GC, St. Paul, MN	72/6542
1950	Sam Snead	282	Brentwood CC, Los Angeles, CA	72/6729
1951	Marty Furgol	270	Davenport CC, Davenport, IA	71/6450
1952	Lloyd Mangrum	274	Westwood CC, St. Louis, MO	72/6785
1953	Dutch Harrison	278	Bellerive CC, St. Louis, MO	71/7305
1954	*Lloyd Mangrum	277	Kenwood CC, Cincinnati, OH	72/6950
1955	Cary Middlecoff	272	Portland GC, Portland, OR	72/6564
1956	*Mike Fetchick	284	Presidio CC, San Francisco, CA	72/6488
1957	*Doug Ford	279	Plum Hollow GC, Detroit, MI	72/6854
1958	Doug Sanders	275	Red Run GC, Royal Oak, MI	72/6801
1959	Mike Souchak	272	Pittsburgh Field Club, Fox Chapel, PA	71/6586
1960	*Stan Leonard	278	Western G & CC, Detroit, MI	72/6808
1961	Arnold Palmer	271	Blythefield CC, Grand Rapids, MI	71/6730
1962	Jacky Cupit	281	Medinah CC, Medinah, IL	71/7014
1963	*Arnold Palmer	280	Beverly CC, Chicago, IL	71/6923
1964	Chi Chi Rodriguez	268	Tam O'Shanter CC, Niles, IL	71/6686
1965	Billy Casper	270	Tam O'Shanter CC, Niles, IL	71/6686
1966	Billy Casper	283	Medinah CC, Medinah, IL	71/7014
1967	Jack Nicklaus	274	Beverly CC, Chicago, IL	71/6923

KEY * = Playoff # = Amateur ~ = Rain-curtailed

Past Winners of PGA TOUR Events *(cont'd.)*

Year	Winner	Score	Location	Par/Yards
1968	Jack Nicklaus	273	Olympia Fields CC, Olympia Fields, IL	71/6749
1969	Billy Casper	276	Midlothia CC, Midlothia, IL	71/6654
1970	Hugh Royer	273	Beverly CC, Chicago, IL	71/6923
1971	Bruce Crampton	279	Olympia Fields CC, Olympia Fields, IL	71/6749
1972	Jim Jamieson	271	Sunset Ridge, Winnetka, IL	71/6716
1973	Billy Casper	272	Midlothian CC, Midlothian, IL	71/6654
1974	Tom Watson	287	Butler National GC, Oak Brook, IL	71/7002
1975	Hale Irwin	283	Butler National GC, Oak Brook, IL	71/7002
1976	Al Geiberger	288	Butler National GC, Oak Brook, IL	71/7002
1977	Tom Watson	283	Butler National GC, Oak Brook, IL	72/7097
1978	*Andy Bean	282	Butler National GC, Oak Brook, IL	72/7097
1979	*Larry Nelson	286	Butler National GC, Oak Brook, IL	72/7097
1980	Scott Simpson	281	Butler National GC, Oak Brook, IL	72/7097
1981	Ed Fiori	277	Butler National GC, Oak Brook, IL	72/7097
1982	Tom Weiskopf	276	Butler National GC, Oak Brook, IL	72/7097
1983	Mark McCumber	284	Butler National GC, Oak Brook, IL	72/7097
1984	*Tom Watson	280	Butler National GC, Oak Brook, IL	72/7097
1985	#Scott Verplank	279	Butler National GC, Oak Brook, IL	72/7097
1986	*Tom Kite	286	Butler National GC, Oak Brook, IL	72/7097

BEATRICE WESTERN OPEN

Year	Winner	Score	Location	Par/Yards
1987	~D. A. Weibring	207	Butler National GC, Oak Brook, IL**	72/6752

** Rain forced play to be held on nine holes of Butler National and nine holes at adjacent Oak Brook Village course.

Year	Winner	Score	Location	Par/Yards
1988	Jim Benepe	278	Butler National GC, Oak Brook, IL	72/7097
1989	*Mark McCumber	275	Butler National GC, Oak Brook, IL	72/7097

CENTEL WESTERN OPEN

Year	Winner	Score	Location	Par/Yards
1990	Wayne Levi	275	Butler National GC, Oak Brook, IL	72/7097
1991	Russ Cochran	275	Cog Hill CC (Dubsdread), Lemont, IL	72/7040
1992	Ben Crenshaw	276	Cog Hill CC (Dubsdread), Lemont, IL	72/7040

SPRINT WESTERN OPEN

Year	Winner	Score	Location	Par/Yards
1993	Nick Price	269	Cog Hill CC (Dubsdread), Lemont, IL	72/7040

MOTOROLA WESTERN OPEN

Year	Winner	Score	Location	Par/Yards
1994	Nick Price	277	Cog Hill CC (Dubsdread), Lemont, IL	72/7040

ANHEUSER-BUSCH GOLF CLASSIC

Year	Winner	Score	Location	Par/Yards

KAISER INTERNATIONAL OPEN INVITATIONAL

Year	Winner	Score	Location	Par/Yards
1968	Kermit Zarley	273	Silverado CC, Napa, CA	N-72/6849, S-71/6602
1969	~Miller Barber	135	Silverado CC, Napa, CA	N-72/6849, S-71/6602
1969A	*Jack Nicklaus	273	Silverado CC, Napa, CA	N-72/6849, S-71/6602
1970	*Ken Still	278	Silverado CC, Napa, CA	N-72/6849, S-71/6602
1971	Billy Casper	269	Silverado CC, Napa, CA	N-72/6849, S-71/6602
1972	George Knudson	271	Silverado CC, Napa, CA	N-72/6849, S-71/6602
1973	*Ed Sneed	275	Silverado CC, Napa, CA	N-72/6849, S-71/6602
1974	Johnny Miller	271	Silverado CC, Napa, CA	N-72/6849, S-71/6602
1975	Johnny Miller	272	Silverado CC, Napa, CA	N-72/6849, S-71/6602
1976	J. C. Snead	274	Silverado CC, Napa, CA	N-72/6849, S-71/6602

ANHEUSER-BUSCH GOLF CLASSIC

Year	Winner	Score	Location	Par/Yards
1977	Miller Barber	272	Silverado CC, Napa, CA	N-72/6849, S-71/6602
1978	Tom Watson	270	Silverado CC, Napa, CA	N-72/6849, S-71/6602
1979	John Fought	277	Silverado CC, Napa, CA	N-72/6849, S-72/6619
1980	Ben Crenshaw	272	Silverado CC, Napa, CA	N-72/6849, S-72/6619
1981	John Mahaffey	276	Kingsmill GC, Kingsmill, VA	71/6776
1982	~Calvin Peete	203	Kingsmill GC, Kingsmill, VA	71/6776
1983	Calvin Peete	276	Kingsmill GC, Kingsmill, VA	71/6776
1984	Ronnie Black	267	Kingsmill GC, Kingsmill, VA	71/6776
1985	*Mark Wiebe	273	Kingsmill GC, Kingsmill, VA	71/6776
1986	Fuzzy Zoeller	274	Kingsmill GC, Kingsmill, VA	71/6776
1987	Mark McCumber	267	Kingsmill GC, Kingsmill, VA	71/6776
1988	*Tom Sieckmann	270	Kingsmill GC, Kingsmill, VA	71/6776
1989	*Mike Donald	268	Kingsmill GC, Kingsmill, VA	71/6776
1990	Lanny Wadkins	266	Kingsmill GC, Kingsmill, VA	71/6776
1991	*Mike Hulbert	266	Kingsmill GC, Kingsmill, VA	71/6776

KEY * = Playoff # = Amateur ~ = Rain-curtailed

Year	Winner	Score	Location	Par/Yards
1992	David Peoples	271	Kingsmill GC, Kingsmill, VA	71/6776
1993	Jim Gallagher, Jr.	269	Kingsmill GC, Kingsmill, VA	71/6776
1994	Mark McCumber	267	Kingsmill GC, Kingsmill, VA	71/6776

DEPOSIT GUARANTY GOLF CLASSIC

Year	Winner	Score	Location	Par/Yards
MAGNOLIA STATE CLASSIC				
1968	*B.R. McLendon	269	Hattiesburg CC, Hattiesburg, MS	70/6280
1969	Larry Mowry	272	Hattiesburg CC, Hattiesburg, MS	70/6280
1970	Chris Blocker	271	Hattiesburg CC, Hattiesburg, MS	70/6280
1971	Roy Pace	270	Hattiesburg CC, Hattiesburg, MS	70/6280
1972	Mike Morley	269	Hattiesburg CC, Hattiesburg, MS	70/6280
1973	Dwight Nevil	268	Hattiesburg CC, Hattiesburg, MS	70/6280
1974	~Dwight Nevil	133	Hattiesburg CC, Hattiesburg, MS	70/6280
1975	Bob Wynn	270	Hattiesburg CC, Hattiesburg, MS	70/6280
1976	Dennis Meyer	271	Hattiesburg CC, Hattiesburg, MS	70/6280
1977	Mike McCullough	269	Hattiesburg CC, Hattiesburg, MS	70/6280
1978	Craig Stadler	268	Hattiesburg CC, Hattiesburg, MS	70/6280
1979	Bobby Walzel	272	Hattiesburg CC, Hattiesburg, MS	70/6280
1980	~*Roger Maltbie	65	Hattiesburg CC, Hattiesburg, MS	70/6280
1981	*Tom Jones	268	Hattiesburg CC, Hattiesburg, MS	70/6280
1982	Payne Stewart	270	Hattiesburg CC, Hattiesburg, MS	70/6280
1983	~Russ Cochran	203	Hattiesburg CC, Hattiesburg, MS	70/6280
1984	~*Lance Ten Broeck	201	Hattiesburg CC, Hattiesburg, MS	70/6280
1985	~*Jim Gallagher, Jr.	131	Hattiesburg CC, Hattiesburg, MS	70/6280
DEPOSIT GUARANTY CLASSIC				
1986	Dan Halldorson	263	Hattiesburg CC, Hattiesburg, MS	72/6594
1987	David Ogrin	267	Hattiesburg CC, Hattiesburg, MS	72/6594
1988	Frank Conner	267	Hattiesburg CC, Hattiesburg, MS	72/6594
1989	~*Jim Booros	199	Hattiesburg CC, Hattiesburg, MS	72/6594
1990	Gene Sauers	268	Hattiesburg CC, Hattiesburg, MS	72/6594
1991	*Larry Silveira	266	Hattiesburg CC, Hattiesburg, MS	72/6594
1992	Richard Zokol	267	Hattiesburg CC, Hattiesburg, MS	72/6594
1993	Greg Kraft	267	Hattiesburg CC, Hattiesburg, MS	72/6594
1994	~*Brian Henninger	135	Annandale GC, Jackson, MS	72/7157

Note: 1983-85 TPS Event

NEW ENGLAND CLASSIC

Year	Winner	Score	Location	Par/Yards
CARLING WORLD OPEN				
1965	Tony Lema	279	Pleasant Valley CC, Sutton, MA	71/7110
KEMPER OPEN				
1968	Arnold Palmer	276	Pleasant Valley CC, Sutton, MA	71/7110
AVCO GOLF CLASSIC				
1969	Tom Shaw	280	Pleasant Valley CC, Sutton, MA	71/7110
1970	Billy Casper	277	Pleasant Valley CC, Sutton, MA	71/7110
MASSACHUSETTS CLASSIC				
1971	Dave Stockton	275	Pleasant Valley CC, Sutton, MA	72/7241
USI CLASSIC				
1972	Bruce Devlin	275	Pleasant Valley CC, Sutton, MA	72/7241
1973	Lanny Wadkins	279	Pleasant Valley CC, Sutton, MA	72/7241
PLEASANT VALLEY CLASSIC				
1974	Victor Regalado	278	Pleasant Valley CC, Sutton, MA	71/7110
1975	Roger Maltbie	276	Pleasant Valley CC, Sutton, MA	71/7110
1976	Bud Allin	277	Pleasant Valley CC, Sutton, MA	71/7110
1977	Raymond Floyd	271	Pleasant Valley CC, Sutton, MA	71/7110
AMERICAN OPTICAL CLASSIC				
1978	John Mahaffey	270	Pleasant Valley CC, Sutton, MA	71/7110
1979	Lou Graham	275	Pleasant Valley CC, Sutton, MA	71/7110
PLEASANT VALLEY JIMMY FUND CLASSIC				
1980	*Wayne Levi	273	Pleasant Valley CC, Sutton, MA	71/7110
1981	Jack Renner	273	Pleasant Valley CC, Sutton, MA	71/7110

KEY * = Playoff # = Amateur ~ = Rain-curtailed

Past Winners of PGA TOUR Events *(cont'd.)*

Year	Winner	Score	Location	Par/Yards
BANK OF BOSTON CLASSIC				
1982	Bob Gilder	271	Pleasant Valley CC, Sutton, MA	71/7110
1983	Mark Lye	273	Pleasant Valley CC, Sutton, MA	71/7110
1984	George Archer	270	Pleasant Valley CC, Sutton, MA	71/7110
1985	George Burns	267	Pleasant Valley CC, Sutton, MA	71/7110
1986	*Gene Sauers	274	Pleasant Valley CC, Sutton, MA	71/7110
1987	~Sam Randolph	199	Pleasant Valley CC, Sutton, MA	71/7110
1988	Mark Calcavecchia	274	Pleasant Valley CC, Sutton, MA	71/7110
1989	Blaine McCallister	271	Pleasant Valley CC, Sutton, MA	71/7110
1990	Morris Hatalsky	275	Pleasant Valley CC, Sutton, MA	71/7110
NEW ENGLAND CLASSIC				
1991	*Bruce Fleisher	268	Pleasant Valley CC, Sutton, MA	71/7110
1992	Brad Faxon	268	Pleasant Valley CC, Sutton, MA	71/7110
1993	Paul Azinger	268	Pleasant Valley CC, Sutton, MA	71/7110
1994	Kenny Perry	268	Pleasant Valley CC, Sutton, MA	71/7110

BUICK OPEN

Year	Winner	Score	Location	Par/Yards
BUICK OPEN INVITATIONAL				
1958	Billy Casper	285	Warwick Hills CC, Grand Blanc, MI	72/7014
1959	Art Wall	282	Warwick Hills CC, Grand Blanc, MI	72/7014
1960	Mike Souchak	282	Warwick Hills CC, Grand Blanc, MI	72/7014
1961	Jack Burke, Jr.	284	Warwick Hills CC, Grand Blanc, MI	72/7014
1962	Bill Collins	284	Warwick Hills CC, Grand Blanc, MI	72/7014
1963	Julius Boros	274	Warwick Hills CC, Grand Blanc, MI	72/7014
1964	Tony Lema	277	Warwick Hills CC, Grand Blanc, MI	72/7014
1965	Tony Lema	280	Warwick Hills CC, Grand Blanc, MI	72/7014
1966	Phil Rodgers	284	Warwick Hills CC, Grand Blanc, MI	72/7014
1967	Julius Boros	283	Warwick Hills CC, Grand Blanc, MI	72/7014
1968	Tom Weiskopf	280	Warwick Hills CC, Grand Blanc, MI	72/7014
1969	Dave Hill	277	Warwick Hills CC, Grand Blanc, MI	72/7014
VERN PARSELL BUICK OPEN				
1972	Gary Groh	273	Flint Elks CC, Flint, MI	72/6902
LAKE MICHIGAN CLASSIC				
1973	(2T) Wilf Homenuik	215	Benton Harbor Elks CC, Benton Harbor, MI	71/6690
FLINT ELKS OPEN				
1974	(2T) Bryan Abbott	135	Flint Elks CC, Flint, MI	72/6902
1975	(2T) Spike Kelley	208	Flint Elks CC, Flint, MI	72/6902
1976	(2T) Ed Sabo	279	Flint Elks CC, Flint, MI	72/6902
1977	Bobby Cole	271	Flint Elks CC, Flint, MI	72/6902
BUICK GOODWRENCH OPEN				
1978	*Jack Newton	280	Warwick Hills CC, Grand Blanc, MI	72/7014
1979	*John Fought	280	Warwick Hills CC, Grand Blanc, MI	72/7014
1980	Peter Jacobsen	276	Warwick Hills CC, Grand Blanc, MI	72/7014
BUICK OPEN				
1981	*Hale Irwin	277	Warwick Hills CC, Grand Blanc, MI	72/7014
1982	Lanny Wadkins	273	Warwick Hills CC, Grand Blanc, MI	72/7014
1983	Wayne Levi	272	Warwick Hills CC, Grand Blanc, MI	72/7014
1984	Denis Watson	271	Warwick Hills CC, Grand Blanc, MI	72/7014
1985	Ken Green	268	Warwick Hills CC, Grand Blanc, MI	72/7014
1986	Ben Crenshaw	270	Warwick Hills CC, Grand Blanc, MI	72/7014
1987	Robert Wrenn	262	Warwick Hills CC, Grand Blanc, MI	72/7014
1988	Scott Verplank	268	Warwick Hills CC, Grand Blanc, MI	72/7014
1989	Leonard Thompson	273	Warwick Hills CC, Grand Blanc, MI	72/7014
1990	Chip Beck	272	Warwick Hills CC, Grand Blanc, MI	72/7014
1991	*Brad Faxon	271	Warwick Hills CC, Grand Blanc, MI	72/7014
1992	*Dan Forsman	276	Warwick Hills CC, Grand Blanc, MI	72/7014
1993	Larry Mize	272	Warwick Hills CC, Grand Blanc, MI	72/7014
1994	Fred Couples	270	Warwick Hills CC, Grand Blanc, MI	72/7014

KEY * = Playoff   # = Amateur   ~ = Rain-curtailed   2T = Second Tour

Past Winners of PGA TOUR Events (cont'd.)

THE SPRINT INTERNATIONAL

Year	Winner	Score	Location	Par/Yards
1986	Ken Green	Plus 12	Castle Pines GC, Castle Rock, CO	72/7503
1987	John Cook	Plus 11	Castle Pines GC, Castle Rock, CO	72/7503
1988	Joey Sindelar	Plus 17	Castle Pines GC, Castle Rock, CO	72/7503
1989	Greg Norman	Plus 13	Castle Pines GC, Castle Rock, CO	72/7503
1990	Davis Love III	Plus 14	Castle Pines GC, Castle Rock, CO	72/7503
1991	Jose Maria Olazabal	Plus 10	Castle Pines GC, Castle Rock, CO	72/7503
1992	Brad Faxon	Plus 14	Castle Pines GC, Castle Rock, CO	72/7503
1993	Phil Mickelson	Plus 45	Castle Pines GC, Castle Rock, CO	72/7503
THE SPRINT INTERNATIONAL				
1994	*Steve Lowery	Plus 35	Castle Pines GC, Castle Rock, CO	72/7503

(Note: Prior to 1993, winning score was for fourth round only. Beginning in 1993, winning score was total for four rounds)

NEC WORLD SERIES OF GOLF

Year	Winner	Score	Location	Par/Yards
WORLD SERIES OF GOLF				
1976	Jack Nicklaus	275	Firestone CC (South Course), Akron, OH	70/7149
1977	Lanny Wadkins	267	Firestone CC (South Course), Akron, OH	70/7149
1978	Gil Morgan	278	Firestone CC (South Course), Akron, OH	70/7149
1979	Lon Hinkle	272	Firestone CC (South Course), Akron, OH	70/7149
1980	Tom Watson	270	Firestone CC (South Course), Akron, OH	70/7149
1981	Bill Rogers	275	Firestone CC (South Course), Akron, OH	70/7149
1982	Craig Stadler	278	Firestone CC (South Course), Akron, OH	70/7149
1983	Nick Price	270	Firestone CC (South Course), Akron, OH	70/7149
NEC WORLD SERIES OF GOLF				
1984	Denis Watson	271	Firestone CC (South Course), Akron, OH	70/7149
1985	Roger Maltbie	268	Firestone CC (South Course), Akron, OH	70/7149
1986	Dan Pohl	277	Firestone CC (South Course), Akron, OH	70/7149
1987	Curtis Strange	275	Firestone CC (South Course), Akron, OH	70/7149
1988	Mike Reid	275	Firestone CC (South Course), Akron, OH	70/7149
1989	David Frost	276	Firestone CC (South Course), Akron, OH	70/7149
1990	Jose Maria Olazabal	262	Firestone CC (South Course), Akron, OH	70/7149
1991	Tom Purtzer	279	Firestone CC (South Course), Akron, OH	70/7149
1992	Craig Stadler	273	Firestone CC (South Course), Akron, OH	70/7149
1993	Fulton Allem	270	Firestone CC (South Course), Akron, OH	70/7149
1994	Jose Maria Olazabal	269	Firestone CC (North Course), Akron, OH	70/6918

GREATER MILWAUKEE OPEN

Year	Winner	Score	Location	Par/Yards
GREATER MILWAUKEE OPEN				
1968	Dave Stockton	275	Northshore CC, Mequon, WI	71/7075
1969	Ken Still	277	Northshore CC, Mequon, WI	71/7075
1970	Deane Beman	276	Northshore CC, Mequon, WI	71/7075
1971	Dave Eichelberger	270	Tripoli GC, Milwaukee, WI	71/6514
1972	Jim Colbert	271	Tripoli GC, Milwaukee, WI	71/6514
1973	Dave Stockton	276	Tuckaway CC, Franklin, WI	72/7030
1974	Ed Sneed	276	Tuckaway CC, Franklin, WI	72/7030
1975	Art Wall	271	Tuckaway CC, Franklin, WI	72/7030
1976	Dave Hill	270	Tuckaway CC, Franklin, WI	72/7030
1977	Dave Eichelberger	278	Tuckaway CC, Franklin, WI	72/7030
1978	*Lee Elder	275	Tuckaway CC, Franklin, WI	72/7030
1979	Calvin Peete	269	Tuckaway CC, Franklin, WI	72/7030
1980	Bill Kratzert	266	Tuckaway CC, Franklin, WI	72/7030
1981	Jay Haas	274	Tuckaway CC, Franklin, WI	72/7030
1982	Calvin Peete	274	Tuckaway CC, Franklin, WI	72/7030
1983	*Morris Hatalsky	275	Tuckaway CC, Franklin, WI	72/7030

KEY * = Playoff # = Amateur ~ = Rain-curtailed

Year	Winner	Score	Location	Par/Yards
1984	Mark O'Meara	272	Tuckaway CC, Franklin, WI	72/7030
1985	Jim Thorpe	274	Tuckaway CC, Franklin, WI	72/7030
1986	*Corey Pavin	272	Tuckaway CC, Franklin, WI	72/7030
1987	Gary Hallberg	269	Tuckaway CC, Franklin, WI	72/7030
1988	Ken Green	268	Tuckaway CC, Franklin, WI	72/7030
1989	Greg Norman	269	Tuckaway CC, Franklin, WI	72/7030
1990	*Jim Gallagher, Jr.	271	Tuckaway CC, Franklin, WI	72/7030
1991	Mark Brooks	270	Tuckaway CC, Franklin, WI	72/7030
1992	Richard Zokol	269	Tuckaway CC, Franklin, WI	72/7030
1993	*Billy Mayfair	270	Tuckaway CC, Franklin, WI	72/7030
1994	Mike Springer	268	Brown Deer Park GC, Milwaukee, WI	71/6716

BELL CANADIAN OPEN

Year	Winner	Score	Location	Par/Yards
1904	J. H. Oke	156	Royal Montreal GC, Montreal, Quebec	N/A
1905	George Cumming	148	Toronto GC, Toronto, Ontario	N/A
1906	Charles Murray	170	Royal Ottawa GC, Ottawa, Ontario	N/A
1907	Percy Barrett	306	Lambton GC, Toronto, Ontario	N/A
1908	Albert Murray	300	Royal Montreal GC, Montreal, Quebec	N/A
1909	Karl Keffer	309	Toronto GC, Toronto, Ontario	N/A
1910	Daniel Kenny	303	Lambton GC, Toronto, Ontario	70/N/A
1911	Charles Murray	314	Royal Ottawa GC, Ottawa, Ontario	N/A
1912	George Sargent	299	Rosedale GC, Toronto, Ontario	N/A
1913	Albert Murray	295	Royal Montreal GC, Montreal, Quebec	N/A
1914	Karl Keffer	300	Toronto GC, Toronto, Ontario	N/A
1915-1918	No Tournaments			
1919	J. Douglas Edgar	278	Hamilton GC, Hamilton, Ontario	N/A
1920	*J. Douglas Edgar	298	Rivermead GC, Ottawa, Ontario	N/A
1921	W. H. Trovinger	293	Toronto GC, Toronto, Ontario	N/A
1922	Al Watrous	303	Mt. Bruno GC, Montreal, Quebec	72/6643
1923	C. W. Hackney	295	Lakeview CG, Toronto, Ontario	N/A
1924	Leo Diegel	285	Mt. Bruno GC, Montreal, Quebec	72/6643
1925	Leo Diegel	295	Lambton GC, Toronto, Ontario	N/A
1926	Mac Smith	283	Royal Montreal GC, Montreal, Quebec	N/A
1927	Tommy Armour	288	Toronto GC, Toronto, Ontario	N/A
1928	Leo Diegel	282	Rosedale GC, Toronto, Ontario	N/A
1929	Leo Diegel	274	Kanawaki GC, Montreal, Quebec	N/A
1930	*Tommy Armour	273	Hamilton GC, Hamilton, Ontario	N/A
1931	*Walter Hagen	292	Mississauga G & CC, Toronto, Ontario	N/A
1932	Harry Cooper	290	Ottawa Hunt Club, Ottawa, Ontario	N/A
1933	Joe Kirkwood	282	Royal York CG, Toronto, Ontario	N/A
1934	Tommy Armour	287	Lakeview CG, Toronto, Ontario	N/A
1935	Gene Kunes	280	Summerlea GC, Montreal, Quebec	N/A
1936	Lawson Little	271	St. Andrews GC, Toronto, Ontario	70/N/A
1937	Harry Cooper	285	St. Andrews GC, Toronto, Ontario	70/N/A
1938	*Sam Snead	277	Mississauga G&CC, Toronto, Ontario	N/A
1939	Harold McSpaden	282	Riverside GC, St. John, New Brunswick	70/6231
1940	*Sam Snead	281	Scarborough G&CC, Toronto, Ontario	/6685
1941	Sam Snead	274	Lambton GC, Toronto, Ontario	70/N/A
1942	Craig Wood	275	Mississauga G&CC, Toronto, Ontario	N/A
1943-1944	No Tournaments			
1945	Byron Nelson	280	Thornhill GC, Toronto, Ontario	N/A
1946	*George Fazio	278	Beaconsfield GC, Montreal, Quebec	N/A
1947	Bobby Locke	268	Scarborough G&CC, Toronto, Ontario	N/A
1948	C. W. Congdon	280	Shaugnessy Heights GC, Vancouver, B.C.	N/A
1949	Dutch Harrison	271	St. Georges G&CC, Toronto, Ontario	N/A
1950	Jim Ferrier	271	Royal Montreal GC, Montreal, Quebec	N/A
1951	Jim Ferrier	273	Mississauga G & CC, Toronto, Ontario	N/A
1952	John Palmer	263	St. Charles CC, Winnipeg, Manitoba	N/A
1953	Dave Douglas	273	Scarborough G&CC, Toronto, Ontario	N/A
1954	Pat Fletcher	280	Point Grey GC, Vancouver, B.C.	N/A

KEY * = Playoff # = Amateur ~ = Rain-curtailed

Past Winners of PGA TOUR Events *(cont'd.)*

Year	Winner	Score	Location	Par/Yards
1955	Arnold Palmer	265	Weston GC, Toronto, Ontario	N/A
1956	#Doug Sanders	273	Beaconsfield GC, Montreal, Quebec	N/A
1957	George Bayer	271	Westmount G&CC, Kitchener, Ontario	N/A
1958	Wesley Ellis, Jr.	267	Mayfair G&CC, Edmonton, Alberta	N/A
1959	Doug Ford	276	Islesmere G&CC, Montreal, Quebec	N/A
1960	Art Wall, Jr.	269	St. Georges G&CC, Toronto, Ontario	N/A
1961	Jacky Cupit	270	Niakwa GC, Winnipeg, Manitoba	N/A
1962	Ted Kroll	278	Laval sue-le-Lac, Montreal, Quebec	N/A
1963	Doug Ford	280	Scarborough G&CC, Toronto, Ontario	N/A
1964	Kel Nagle	277	Pinegrove CC, St. Luc, Quebec	N/A
1965	Gene Littler	273	Mississauga G&CC, Toronto, Ontario	N/A
1966	Don Massengale	280	Shaughnessy G&CC, Toronto, Ontario	N/A
1967	*Billy Casper	279	Montreal Municipal GC, Montreal, Quebec	N/A
1968	Bob Charles	274	St. Georges G&CC, Toronto, Ontario	70/6792
1969	*Tommy Aaron	275	Pinegrove G&CC, St. Luc, Quebec	72/7076
1970	Kermit Zarley	279	London Hunt & CC, London, Ontario	72/7168
1971	*Lee Trevino	275	Richelieu Valley GC, Montreal, Quebec	72/6920
1972	Gay Brewer	275	Cherry Hill Club, Ridgeway, Ontario	71/6751
1973	Tom Weiskopf	278	Reichelieu Valley G&CC, Ste. Julie de Vercheres, Que.	72/6905
1974	Bobby Nichols	270	Mississaugua G&CC, Mississauga, Ontario	70/6788
1975	*Tom Weiskopf	274	Royal Montreal GC, Ile Bizard, Quebec	70/6628
1976	Jerry Pate	267	Essex G&CC,Windsor, Ontario.	70/6696
1977	Lee Trevino	280	Glen Abbey GC, Oakville, Ontario	72/7096
1978	Bruce Lietzke	283	Glen Abbey GC, Oakville, Ontario	71/7050
1979	Lee Trevino	281	Glen Abbey GC, Oakville, Ontario	71/7059
1980	Bob Gilder	274	Royal Montreal GC, Ile Bizard, Quebec	70/6628
1981	Peter Oosterhuis	280	Glen Abbey GC, Oakville, Ontario	71/7060
1982	Bruce Lietzke	277	Glen Abbey GC, Oakville, Ontario	71/7060
1983	*John Cook	277	Glen Abbey GC, Oakville, Ontario	71/7055
1984	Greg Norman	278	Glen Abbey GC, Oakville, Ontario	72/7102
1985	Curtis Strange	279	Glen Abbey GC, Oakville, Ontario	72/7102
1986	Bob Murphy	280	Glen Abbey GC, Oakville, Ontario	72/7102
1987	Curtis Strange	276	Glen Abbey GC, Oakville, Ontario	72/7102
1988	Ken Green	275	Glen Abbey GC, Oakville, Ontario	72/7102
1989	Steve Jones	271	Glen Abbey GC, Oakville, Ontario	72/7102
1990	Wayne Levi	278	Glen Abbey GC, Oakville, Ontario	72/7102
1991	Nick Price	273	Glen Abbey GC, Oakville, Ontario	72/7102
1992	*Greg Norman	280	Glen Abbey GC, Oakville, Ontario	72/7102
1993	David Frost	279	Glen Abbey GC, Oakville, Ontario	72/7102
BELL CANADIAN OPEN				
1994	Nick Price	275	Glen Abbey GC, Oakville, Ontario	72/7102

B. C. OPEN

Year	Winner	Score	Location	Par/Yards
BROOME COUNTY OPEN				
1971	*Claude Harmon, Jr.	69	En Joie GC, Endicott, NY	71/6966
B. C. OPEN				
1972	Bob Payne	136	En Joie GC, Endicott, NY	71/6966
1973	Hubert Green	266	En Joie GC, Endicott, NY	71/6966
1974	*Richie Karl	273	En Joie GC, Endicott, NY	71/6966
1975	Don Iverson	274	En Joie GC, Endicott, NY	71/6966
1976	Bob Wynn	271	En Joie GC, Endicott, NY	71/6966
1977	Gil Morgan	270	En Joie GC, Endicott, NY	71/6966
1978	Tom Kite	267	En Joie GC, Endicott, NY	71/6966
1979	Howard Twitty	270	En Joie GC, Endicott, NY	71/6966
1980	Don Pooley	271	En Joie GC, Endicott, NY	71/6966
1981	Jay Haas	270	En Joie GC, Endicott, NY	71/6966
1982	Calvin Peete	265	En Joie GC, Endicott, NY	71/6966
1983	Pat Lindsey	268	En Joie GC, Endicott, NY	71/6966
1984	Wayne Levi	275	En Joie GC, Endicott, NY	71/6966
1985	Joey Sindelar	274	En Joie GC, Endicott, NY	71/6966
1986	Rick Fehr	267	En Joie GC, Endicott, NY	71/6966

KEY * = Playoff # = Amateur ~ = Rain-curtailed

Year	Winner	Score	Location	Par/Yards
1987	Joey Sindelar	266	En Joie GC, Endicott, NY	71/6966
1988	Bill Glasson	268	En Joie GC, Endicott, NY	71/6966
1989	*Mike Hulbert	268	En Joie GC, Endicott, NY	71/6966
1990	Nolan Henke	268	En Joie GC, Endicott, NY	71/6966
1991	Fred Couples	269	En Joie GC, Endicott, NY	71/6966
1992	John Daly	266	En Joie GC, Endicott, NY	71/6966
1993	Blaine McCallister	271	En Joie GC, Endicott, NY	71/6966
1994	Mike Sullivan	266	En Joie GC, Endicott, NY	71/6966

QUAD CITIES OPEN

Year	Winner	Score	Location	Par/Yards
QUAD CITIES OPEN				
1972	Deane Beman	279	Crow Valley CC, Bettendorf, IA	71/6501
1973	Sam Adams	268	Crow Valley CC, Bettendorf, IA	71/6501
1974	Dave Stockton	271	Crow Valley CC, Bettendorf, IA	71/6501
ED MCMAHON-JAYCEES QUAD CITY OPEN				
1975	Roger Maltbie	275	Oakwood CC, Coal Valley, IL	70/6602
1976	John Lister	268	Oakwood CC, Coal Valley, IL	70/6602
1977	Mike Morley	267	Oakwood CC, Coal Valley, IL	70/6602
1978	Victor Regalado	269	Oakwood CC, Coal Valley, IL	70/6602
1979	D. A. Weibring	266	Oakwood CC, Coal Valley, IL	70/6602
QUAD CITIES OPEN				
1980	Scott Hoch	266	Oakwood CC, Coal Valley, IL	70/6602
1981	*Dave Barr	270	Oakwood CC, Coal Valley, IL	70/6602
MILLER HIGH-LIFE QUAD CITIES OPEN				
1982	Payne Stewart	268	Oakwood CC, Coal Valley, IL	70/6602
1983	*Danny Edwards	266	Oakwood CC, Coal Valley, IL	70/6602
1984	Scott Hoch	266	Oakwood CC, Coal Valley, IL	70/6602
LITE QUAD CITIES OPEN				
1985	Dan Forsman	267	Oakwood CC, Coal Valley, IL	70/6602
HARDEE'S GOLF CLASSIC				
1986	Mark Wiebe	268	Oakwood CC, Coal Valley, IL	70/6602
1987	Kenny Knox	265	Oakwood CC, Coal Valley, IL	70/6606
1988	Blaine McCallister	261	Oakwood CC, Coal Valley, IL	70/6606
1989	Curt Byrum	268	Oakwood CC, Coal Valley, IL	70/6606
1990	*Joey Sindelar	268	Oakwood CC, Coal Valley, IL	70/6606
1991	D. A. Weibring	267	Oakwood CC, Coal Valley, IL	70/6796
1992	David Frost	266	Oakwood CC, Coal Valley, IL	70/6796
1993	David Frost	259	Oakwood CC, Coal Valley, IL	70/6796
1994	Mark McCumber	265	Oakwood CC, Coal Valley, IL	70/6796

BUICK SOUTHERN OPEN

Year	Winner	Score	Location	Par/Yards
GREEN ISLAND OPEN INVITATIONAL				
1970	Mason Rudolph	274	Green Island CC, Columbus, GA	70/6791
SOUTHERN OPEN INVITATIONAL				
1971	Johnny Miller	267	Green Island CC, Columbus, GA	70/6791
1972	*DeWitt Weaver	276	Green Island CC, Columbus, GA	70/6791
1973	Gary Player	270	Green Island CC, Columbus, GA	70/6791
1974	Forrest Fezler	271	Green Island CC, Columbus, GA	70/6791
1975	Hubert Green	264	Green Island CC, Columbus, GA	70/6791
1976	Mac McClendon	274	Green Island CC, Columbus, GA	70/6791
1977	Jerry Pate	266	Green Island CC, Columbus, GA	70/6791
1978	Jerry Pate	269	Green Island CC, Columbus, GA	70/6791
1979	*Ed Fiori	274	Green Island CC, Columbus, GA	70/6791
1980	Mike Sullivan	269	Green Island CC, Columbus, GA	70/6791
1981	*J. C. Snead	271	Green Island CC, Columbus, GA	70/6791
1982	Bobby Clampett	266	Green Island CC, Columbus, GA	70/6791
1983	*Ronnie Black	271	Green Island CC, Columbus, GA	70/6791
1984	Hubert Green	265	Green Island CC, Columbus, GA	70/6791
1985	Tim Simpson	264	Green Island CC, Columbus, GA	70/6791
1986	Fred Wadsworth	269	Green Island CC, Columbus, GA	70/6791

KEY * = Playoff   # = Amateur   ~ = Rain-curtailed

Year	Winner	Score	Location	Par/Yards
1987	Ken Brown	266	Green Island CC, Columbus, GA	70/6791
1988	*David Frost	270	Green Island CC, Columbus, GA	70/6791
1989	Ted Schulz	266	Green Island CC, Columbus, GA	70/6791

BUICK SOUTHERN OPEN

Year	Winner	Score	Location	Par/Yards
1990	*Kenny Knox	265	Green Island CC, Columbus, GA	70/6791
1991	David Peoples	276	Callaway Gardens Resort, Pine Mountain, GA	72/7057
1992	~Gary Hallberg	206	Callaway Gardens Resort, Pine Mountain, GA	72/7057
1993	*John Inman	278	Callaway Gardens Resort, Pine Mountain, GA	72/7057
1994	~Steve Elkington	200	Callaway Gardens Resort, Pine Mountain, GA	72/7057

WALT DISNEY WORLD/OLDSMOBILE CLASSIC

WALT DISNEY WORLD OPEN INVITATIONAL

Year	Winner	Score	Location	Par/Yards
1971	Jack Nicklaus	273	Magnolia, Walt Disney World, Lake Buena Vista, FL	72/7190
1972	Jack Nicklaus	267	Palm, Walt Disney World, Lake Buena Vista, FL	72/6941
			Magnolia, Walt Disney World, Lake Buena Vista, FL	72/7190
1973	Jack Nicklaus	275	Palm, Walt Disney World, Lake Buena Vista, FL	72/6941
			Magnolia, Walt Disney World, Lake Buena Vista, FL	72/7190

WALT DISNEY WORLD NATIONAL TEAM CHAMPIONSHIP

Year	Winner	Score	Location	Par/Yards
1974	Hubert Green/ Mac McClendon	255	Palm, Walt Disney World, Lake Buena Vista, FL	72/6941
			Magnolia, Walt Disney World, Lake Buena Vista, FL	72/7190
1975	Jim Colbert/ Dean Refram	252	Palm, Walt Disney World, Lake Buena Vista, FL	72/6941
			Magnolia, Walt Disney World, Lake Buena Vista, FL	72/7190
1976	*Woody Blackburn/ Bill Kratzert	260	Palm, Walt Disney World, Lake Buena Vista, FL	72/6941
			Magnolia, Walt Disney World, Lake Buena Vista, FL	72/7190
1977	Gibby Gilbert/ Grier Jones	253	Palm, Walt Disney World, Lake Buena Vista, FL	72/6941
			Magnolia, Walt Disney World, Lake Buena Vista, FL	72/7190
1978	Wayne Levi/ Bob Mann	254	Palm, Walt Disney World, Lake Buena Vista, FL	72/6941
			Magnolia, Walt Disney World, Lake Buena Vista, FL	72/7190
1979	George Burns/ Ben Crenshaw	255	Palm, Walt Disney World, Lake Buena Vista, FL	72/6941
			Magnolia, Walt Disney World, Lake Buena Vista, FL	72/7190
1980	Danny Edwards/ Dave Edwards	253	Palm, Walt Disney World, Lake Buena Vista, FL	72/6941
			Magnolia, Walt Disney World, Lake Buena Vista, FL	72/7190
1981	Vance Heafner/ Mike Holland	275	Palm, Walt Disney World, Lake Buena Vista, FL	72/6941
			Magnolia, Walt Disney World, Lake Buena Vista, FL	72/7190

WALT DISNEY WORLD GOLF CLASSIC

Year	Winner	Score	Location	Par/Yards
1982	*Hal Sutton	269	Palm, Walt Disney World, Lake Buena Vista, FL	72/6941
			Magnolia, Walt Disney World, Lake Buena Vista, FL	72/7190
			Lake Buena Vista CC, Lake Buena Vista, FL	72/6706
1983	Payne Stewart	269	Palm, Walt Disney World, Lake Buena Vista, FL	72/6941
			Magnolia, Walt Disney World, Lake Buena Vista, FL	72/7190
			Lake Buena Vista CC, Lake Buena Vista, FL	72/6706
1984	Larry Nelson	266	Palm, Walt Disney World, Lake Buena Vista, FL	72/6941
			Magnolia, Walt Disney World, Lake Buena Vista, FL	72/7190
			Lake Buena Vista CC, Lake Buena Vista, FL	72/6706

WALT DISNEY WORLD OLDSMOBILE CLASSIC

Year	Winner	Score	Location	Par/Yards
1985	Lanny Wadkins	267	Palm, Walt Disney World, Lake Buena Vista, FL	72/6941
			Magnolia, Walt Disney World, Lake Buena Vista, FL	72/7190
			Lake Buena Vista CC, Lake Buena Vista, FL	72/6706
1986	*Ray Floyd	275	Palm, Walt Disney World, Lake Buena Vista, FL	72/6941
			Magnolia, Walt Disney World, Lake Buena Vista, FL	72/7190
			Lake Buena Vista CC, Lake Buena Vista, FL	72/6706
1987	Larry Nelson	268	Palm, Walt Disney World, Lake Buena Vista, FL	72/6941
			Magnolia, Walt Disney World, Lake Buena Vista, FL	72/7190
			Lake Buena Vista CC, Lake Buena Vista, FL	72/6706
1988	*Bob Lohr	263	Palm, Walt Disney World, Lake Buena Vista, FL	72/6941
			Magnolia, Walt Disney World, Lake Buena Vista, FL	72/7190
			Lake Buena Vista CC, Lake Buena Vista, FL	72/6706
1989	Tim Simpson	272	Palm, Walt Disney World, Lake Buena Vista, FL	72/6941
			Magnolia, Walt Disney World, Lake Buena Vista, FL	72/7190
			Lake Buena Vista CC, Lake Buena Vista, FL	72/6706

KEY * = Playoff   # = Amateur   ~ = Rain-curtailed

Year	Winner	Score	Location	Par/Yards
1990	Tim Simpson	264	Palm, Walt Disney World, Lake Buena Vista, FL	72/6941
			Magnolia, Walt Disney World, Lake Buena Vista, FL	72/7190
			Lake Buena Vista CC, Lake Buena Vista, FL	72/6706
1991	Mark O'Meara	267	Palm, Walt Disney World, Lake Buena Vista, FL	72/6941
			Magnolia, Walt Disney World, Lake Buena Vista, FL	72/7190
			Lake Buena Vista CC, Lake Buena Vista, FL	72/6706
1992	John Huston	262	Palm, Walt Disney World, Lake Buena Vista, FL	72/6941
			Magnolia, Walt Disney World, Lake Buena Vista, FL	72/7190
			Lake Buena Vista CC, Lake Buena Vista, FL	72/6706
1993	Jeff Maggert	265	Palm, Walt Disney World, Lake Buena Vista, FL	72/6941
			Magnolia, Walt Disney World, Lake Buena Vista, FL	72/7190
			Lake Buena Vista CC, Lake Buena Vista, FL	72/6706
1994	Rick Fehr	265	Palm, Walt Disney World, Lake Buena Vista, FL	72/6941
			Magnolia, Walt Disney World, Lake Buena Vista, FL	72/7190
			Lake Buena Vista CC, Lake Buena Vista, FL	72/6772

LAS VEGAS INVITATIONAL

Year	Winner	Score	Location	Par/Yards

PANASONIC LAS VEGAS PRO-CELEBRITY CLASSIC

Year	Winner	Score	Location	Par/Yards
1983	Fuzzy Zoeller	340	Las Vegas CC, Las Vegas, NV	72/7162
			Desert Inn CC, Las Vegas, NV	72/7111
			Dunes CC, Las Vegas, NV	72/7240
			Showboat CC, Las Vegas, NV	72/7045

PANASONIC LAS VEGAS INVITATIONAL

Year	Winner	Score	Location	Par/Yards
1984	Denis Watson	341	Las Vegas CC, Las Vegas, NV	72/7162
			Desert Inn CC, Las Vegas, NV	72/7111
			Showboat CC, Las Vegas, NV	72/7045
			Tropicana CC, Las Vegas, NV	71/6481
1985	Curtis Strange	338	Las Vegas CC, Las Vegas, NV	72/7162
			Desert Inn CC, Las Vegas, NV	72/7111
			Tropicana CC, Las Vegas, NV	71/6481
1986	Greg Norman	333	Las Vegas CC, Las Vegas, NV	72/7162
			Desert Inn CC, Las Vegas, NV	72/7111
			Spanish Trail G&CC, Las Vegas, NV	72/7088
1987	~Paul Azinger	271	Las Vegas CC, Las Vegas, NV	72/7162
			Desert Inn CC, Las Vegas, NV	72/7111
			Spanish Trail G&CC, Las Vegas, NV	72/7088
1988	~Gary Koch	274	Las Vegas CC, Las Vegas, NV	72/7162
			Desert Inn CC, Las Vegas, NV	72/7111
			Spanish Trail G&CC, Las Vegas, NV	72/7088

LAS VEGAS INVITATIONAL

Year	Winner	Score	Location	Par/Yards
1989	*Scott Hoch	336	Las Vegas CC, Las Vegas, NV	72/7162
			Desert Inn CC, Las Vegas, NV	72/7111
			Spanish Trail G&CC, Las Vegas, NV	72/7088
1990	*Bob Tway	334	Las Vegas CC, Las Vegas, NV	72/7162
			Desert Inn CC, Las Vegas, NV	72/7111
			Spanish Trail G&CC, Las Vegas, NV	72/7088
1991	*Andrew Magee	329	Las Vegas CC, Las Vegas, NV	72/7162
			Desert Inn CC, Las Vegas, NV	72/7111
			Sunrise GC, Las Vegas, NV	72/6914
1992	John Cook	334	Las Vegas CC, Las Vegas, NV	72/7162
			Desert Inn CC, Las Vegas, NV	72/7111
			TPC at Summerlin, Las Vegas, NV	72/7243
1993	Davis Love III	331	Las Vegas CC, Las Vegas, NV	72/7162
			Desert Inn CC, Las Vegas, NV	72/7111
			TPC at Summerlin, Las Vegas, NV	72/7243
1994	Bruce Lietzke	332	Las Vegas CC, Las Vegas, NV	72/7162
			Sahara CC, Las Vegas, NV	71/6815
			TPC at Summerlin, Las Vegas, NV	71/7111

KEY * = Playoff # = Amateur ~ = Rain-curtailed

TEXAS OPEN

Year	Winner	Score	Location	Par/Yards
1922	Bob MacDonald	281	Brackenridge Park GC, San Antonio, TX	71/6185
1923	Walter Hagen	279	Brackenridge Park GC, San Antonio, TX	71/6185
1924	Joe Kirkwood	279	Brackenridge Park GC, San Antonio, TX	71/6185
1925	Joe Turnesa	284	Brackenridge Park GC, San Antonio, TX	71/6185
1926	Mac Smith	288	Brackenridge Park GC, San Antonio, TX	71/6185
1927	Bobby Cruikshank	272	Willow Springs GC, San Antonio, TX	72/6930
1928	Bill Mehlhorn	297	Willow Springs GC, San Antonio, TX	72/6930
1929	Bill Mehlhorn	277	Brackenridge Park GC, San Antonio, TX	71/6185
1930	Denny Shute	277	Brackenridge Park GC, San Antonio, TX	71/6185
1931	Abe Espinosa	281	Brackenridge Park GC, San Antonio, TX	71/6185
1932	Clarence Clark	287	Brackenridge Park GC, San Antonio, TX	71/6185
1933	No Tournament			
1934	Wiffy Cox	283	Brackenridge Park GC, San Antonio, TX	71/6185
1935-1938	No Tournaments			
1939	Dutch Harrison	271	Brackenridge Park GC, San Antonio, TX	71/6185
1940	Byron Nelson	271	Brackenridge Park GC, San Antonio, TX	71/6185
1941	Lawson Little	273	Willow Springs GC, San Antonio, TX	72/6930
1942	*Chick Harbert	272	Willow Springs GC, San Antonio, TX	72/6930
1943	No Tournament			
1944	Johnny Revolta	273	Willow Springs GC, San Antonio, TX	72/6930
1945	Sam Byrd	268	Willow Springs GC, San Antonio, TX	72/6930
1946	Ben Hogan	264	Willow Springs GC, San Antonio, TX	72/6930
1947	Ed Oliver	265	Willow Springs GC, San Antonio, TX	72/6930
1948	Sam Snead	264	Willow Springs GC, San Antonio, TX	72/6930
1949	Dave Douglas	268	Willow Springs GC, San Antonio, TX	72/6930
1950	Sam Snead	265	Brackenridge Park GC, San Antonio, TX	71/6185
			Ft. Sam Houston GC, San Antonio, TX	72/6566
1951	*Dutch Harrison	265	Brackenridge Park GC, San Antonio, TX	71/6185
			Ft. Sam Houston GC, San Antonio, TX	72/6566
1952	Jack Burke, Jr.	260	Brackenridge Park GC, San Antonio, TX	71/6185
1953	Tony Holguin	264	Brackenridge Park GC, San Antonio, TX	71/6185
1954	Chandler Harper	259	Brackenridge Park GC, San Antonio, TX	71/6185
1955	Mike Souchak	257	Brackenridge Park GC, San Antonio, TX	71/6185
1956	Gene Littler	276	Ft. Sam Houston GC, San Antonio, TX	72/6566
1957	Jay Hebert	271	Brackenridge Park GC, San Antonio, TX	71/6185
1958	Bill Johnston	274	Brackenridge Park GC, San Antonio, TX	71/6185
1959	Wes Ellis	276	Brackenridge Park GC, San Antonio, TX	71/6185
1960	Arnold Palmer	276	Ft. Sam Houston GC, San Antonio, TX	72/6566
1961	Arnold Palmer	270	Oak Hills CC, San Antonio, TX	70/6576
1962	Arnold Palmer	273	Oak Hills CC, San Antonio, TX	70/6576
1963	Phil Rodgers	268	Oak Hills CC, San Antonio, TX	70/6576
1964	Bruce Crampton	273	Oak Hills CC, San Antonio, TX	70/6576
1965	Frank Beard	270	Oak Hills CC, San Antonio, TX	70/6576
1966	Harold Henning	272	Oak Hills CC, San Antonio, TX	70/6576
1967	Chi Chi Rodriquez	277	Pecan Valley CC, San Antonio, TX	71/7183
1968	No Tournament			
1969	*Deane Beman	274	Pecan Valley CC, San Antonio, TX	71/7183

SAN ANTONIO TEXAS OPEN

Year	Winner	Score	Location	Par/Yards
1970	Ron Cerrudo	273	Pecan Valley CC, San Antonio, TX	71/7183
1971	No Tournament			
1972	Mike Hill	273	Woodlake GC, San Antonio, TX	72/7143
1973	Ben Crenshaw	270	Woodlake GC, San Antonio, TX	71/6990
1974	Terry Diehl	269	Woodlake GC, San Antonio, TX	72/7143
1975	*Don January	275	Woodlake GC, San Antonio, TX	72/7143
1976	*Butch Baird	273	Woodlake GC, San Antonio, TX	72/7143
1977	Hale Irwin	266	Oak Hills CC, San Antonio, TX	70/6576
1978	Ron Streck	265	Oak Hills CC, San Antonio, TX	70/6576
1979	Lou Graham	268	Oak Hills CC, San Antonio, TX	70/6576
1980	Lee Trevino	265	Oak Hills CC, San Antonio, TX	70/6576

KEY * = Playoff # = Amateur ~ = Rain-curtailed

Past Winners of PGA TOUR Events *(cont'd.)*

Year	Winner	Score	Location	Par/Yards
TEXAS OPEN				
1981	*Bill Rogers	266	Oak Hills CC, San Antonio, TX	70/6576
1982	Jay Haas	262	Oak Hills CC, San Antonio, TX	70/6576
1983	Jim Colbert	261	Oak Hills CC, San Antonio, TX	70/6576
1984	Calvin Peete	266	Oak Hills CC, San Antonio, TX	70/6576
1985	*John Mahaffey	268	Oak Hills CC, San Antonio, TX	70/6576
VANTAGE CHAMPIONSHIP				
1986	~Ben Crenshaw	196	Oak Hills CC, San Antonio, TX	70/6576
TEXAS OPEN PRESENTED BY NABISCO				
1988	Corey Pavin	259	Oak Hills CC, San Antonio, TX	70/6576
1989	Donnie Hammond	258	Oak Hills CC, San Antonio, TX	70/6576
H-E-B TEXAS OPEN				
1990	Mark O'Meara	261	Oak Hills CC, San Antonio, TX	70/6576
1991	*Blaine McCallister	269	Oak Hills CC, San Antonio, TX	70/6576
1992	*Nick Price	263	Oak Hills CC, San Antonio, TX	71/6650
1993	*Jay Haas	263	Oak Hills CC, San Antonio, TX	71/6650
TEXAS OPEN				
1994	Bob Estes	265	Oak Hills CC, San Antonio, TX	71/6650

THE TOUR CHAMPIONSHIP

Year	Winner	Score	Location	Par/Yards
NABISCO CHAMPIONSHIPS OF GOLF				
1987	Tom Watson	268	Oak Hills CC, San Antonio, TX	70/6576
NABISCO GOLF CHAMPIONSHIPS				
1988	*Curtis Strange	279	Pebble Beach GL, Monterey Peninsula, CA	72/6815
NABISCO CHAMPIONSHIPS				
1989	*Tom Kite	276	Harbour Town GL, Hilton Head, SC	71/6657
1990	*Jodie Mudd	273	Champions GC, Houston, TX	71/7187
THE TOUR CHAMPIONSHIP				
1991	*Craig Stadler	279	Pinehurst No. 2, Pinehurst, NC	71/7005
1992	Paul Azinger	276	Pinehurst No. 2, Pinehurst, NC	71/7005
1993	Jim Gallagher, Jr.	277	The Olympic Club, San Francisco, CA	71/6812
1994	*Mark McCumber	274	The Olympic Club, San Francisco, CA	71/6812

LINCOLN-MERCURY KAPALUA INTERNATIONAL

Year	Winner	Score	Location	Par/Yards
KAPALUA INTERNATIONAL				
1983	Greg Norman	268	Bay Course, Kapalua GC, Kapalua, Maui, HI	71/6731
1984	Sandy Lyle	266	Bay Course, Kapalua GC, Kapalua, Maui, HI	71/6731
ISUZU KAPALUA INTERNATIONAL				
1985	Mark O'Meara	275	Bay Course, Kapalua GC, Kapalua, Maui, HI	72/6731
1986	Andy Bean	278	Bay Course, Kapalua GC, Kapalua, Maui, HI	72/6731
1987	Andy Bean	267	Bay Course, Kapalua GC, Kapalua, Maui, HI	72/6731
1988	Bob Gilder	266	Bay Course, Kapalua GC, Kapalua, Maui, HI	72/6731
1989	*Peter Jacobsen	270	Bay Course, Kapalua GC, Kapalua, Maui, HI	72/6731
1990	David Peoples	264	Bay Course, Kapalua GC, Kapalua, Maui, HI	71/6731
PING KAPALUA INTERNATIONAL				
1991	*Mike Hulbert	276	Plantation Course, Kapalua GC, Kapalua, Maui, HI	73/7263
LINCOLN-MERCURY KAPALUA INTERNATIONAL				
1992	Davis Love III	275	Plantation Course, Kapalua GC, Kapalua, Maui, HI	73/7263
			Bay Course, Kapalua GC, Kapalua, Maui, HI	71/6731
1993	Fred Couples	274	Plantation Course, Kapalua GC, Kapalua, Maui, HI	73/7263
			Bay Course, Kapalua GC, Kapalua, Maui, HI	71/6731
1994	Fred Couples	279	Plantation Course, Kapalua GC, Kapalua, Maui, HI	73/7263
			Bay Course, Kapalua GC, Kapalua, Maui, HI	71/6731

KEY * = Playoff # = Amateur ~ = Rain-curtailed

FRANKLIN FUNDS SHARK SHOOTOUT

Year	Winner	Score	Location	Par/Yards
RMCC INVITATIONAL				
1989	Curtis Strange/	190	Sherwood CC	72/7025
	Mark O'Meara		Thousand Oaks, CA	
1990	Ray Floyd/	182	Sherwood CC	72/7025
	Fred Couples		Thousand Oaks, CA	
SHARK SHOOTOUT BENEFITING RMCC				
1991	Tom Purtzer/	189	Sherwood CC	72/7025
	Lanny Wadkins		Thousand Oaks, CA	
FRANKLIN FUNDS SHARK SHOOT OUT				
1992	Davis Love III/	191	Sherwood CC	72/7025
	Tom Kite		Thousand Oaks, CA	
1993	Steve Elkington/	188	Sherwood CC	72/7025
	Ray Floyd		Thousand Oaks, CA	
1994	Fred Couples/	190	Sherwood CC	72/7025
	Brad Faxon		Thousand Oaks, CA	

SKINS GAME

Year	Winner	Winnings	Location	Par/Yards
1983	Gary Player	$170,000	Desert Highlands CC, Scottsdale, AZ	72/7100
1984	Jack Nicklaus	$240,000	Desert Highlands CC, Scottsdale, AZ	72/7100
1985	Fuzzy Zoeller	$255,000	Bear Creek CC, Murietta, CA	72/7024
1986	Fuzzy Zoeller	$370,000	TPC at PGA West, La Quinta, CA	72/7271
1987	Lee Trevino	$310,000	TPC at PGA West, La Quinta, CA	72/7271
1988	Ray Floyd	$290,000	TPC at PGA West, La Quinta, CA	72/7271
1989	Curtis Strange	$265,000	TPC at PGA West, La Quinta, CA	72/7271
1990	Curtis Strange	$225,000	TPC at PGA West, La Quinta, CA	72/7271
1991	Payne Stewart	$260,000	TPC at PGA West, La Quinta, CA	72/7271
1992	Payne Stewart	$220,000	Bighorn GC, Palm Desert, CA	72/6848
1993	Payne Stewart	$280,000	Bighorn GC, Palm Desert, CA	72/6848
1994	Tom Watson	$210,000	Bighorn GC, Palm Desert, CA	72/6848

JCPENNEY CLASSIC

Year	Winner	Score	Location	Par/Yards
HAIG & HAIG SCOTCH FOURSOME				
1960	*Jim Turnesa		Pinecrest Lake Club, Avon Park, FL	72/6449
	Gloria Armstrong	+139	Harder Hall, Sebring, FL	72/6300
1961	Dave Ragan		Pinecrest Lake Club, Avon Park, FL	72/6449
	Mickey Wright	272	Harder Hall, Sebring, FL	72/6300
1962	Mason Rudolph		Pinecrest Lake Club, Avon Park, FL	72/6449
	Kathy Whitworth	272	Harder Hall, Sebring, FL	72/6300
1963	Dave Ragan		Pinecrest Lake Club, Avon Park, FL	72/6449
	Mickey Wright	273	Harder Hall, Sebring, FL	72/6300
1964	Sam Snead		Pinecrest Lake Club, Avon Park, FL	72/6449
	Shirley Englehorn	272	Harder Hall, Sebring, FL	72/6300
1965	Gardner Dickinson			
	Ruth Jessen	281	La Costa CC, Encinitas, CA	72/6607
1966	Jack Rule			
	Sandra Spuzich	276	La Costa CC, Encinitas, CA	72/6607

PEPSI-COLA MIXED TEAM

Year	Winner	Score	Location	Par/Yards
1976	Chi Chi Rodriguez			
	JoAnn Washam	275	Doral CC, Miami, FL	72/6939
1977	Jerry Pate			
	Hollis Stacy	270	Bardmoor CC, Largo, FL	M-72/6957, W-72/6464

KEY * = Playoff # = Amateur ~ = Rain-curtailed

Past Winners of PGA TOUR Events (cont'd.)

Year	Winner	Score	Location	Par/Yards

JC PENNEY CLASSIC

Year	Winner	Score	Location	Par/Yards
1978	*Lon Hinkle Pat Bradley	267	Bardmoor CC, Largo, FL	M-72/6957, W-72/6464
1979	Dave Eichelberger Murle Breer	268	Bardmoor CC, Largo, FL	M-72/6957, W-72/6464
1980	Curtis Strange Nancy Lopez	268	Bardmoor CC, Largo, FL	M-72/6957, W-72/6464
1981	Tom Kite Beth Daniel	270	Bardmoor CC, Largo, FL	M-72/6957, W-72/6464
1982	John Mahaffey JoAnne Carner	268	Bardmoor CC, Largo, FL	M-72/6957, W-72/6464
1983	Fred Couples Jan Stephenson	264	Bardmoor CC, Largo, FL	M-72/6957, W-72/6464
1984	Mike Donald Vicki Alvarez	270	Bardmoor CC, Largo, FL	M-72/6957, W-72/6464
1985	Larry Rinker Laurie Rinker	267	Bardmoor CC, Largo, FL	M-72/6957, W-72/6464
1986	Tom Purtzer Juli Inkster	267	Bardmoor CC, Largo, FL	M-72/6957, W-72/6464
1987	Steve Jones Jane Crafter	268	Bardmoor CC, Largo, FL	M-72/6957, W-72/6464
1988	John Huston Amy Benz	269	Bardmoor CC, Largo, FL	M-72/6957, W-72/6464
1989	*Bill Glasson Pat Bradley	267	Bardmoor CC, Largo, FL	M-72/6957, W-72/6464
1990	Davis Love III Beth Daniel	266	Innisbrook Resort, Tarpon Springs, FL	M-71/7031, W-71/6400
1991	*Billy Andrade Kris Tschetter	266	Innisbrook Resort, Tarpon Springs, FL	M-71/7031, W-71/6400
1992	Dan Forsman Dottie Mochrie	264	Innisbrook Resort, Tarpon Springs, FL	M-71/7031, W-71/6400
1993	Mike Springer Melissa McNamara	265	Innisbrook Resort, Tarpon Springs, FL	M-71/7031, W-71/6400
1994	*Brad Bryant Marta Figueras-Dotti	262	Innisbrook Resort, Tarpon Springs, FL	M-71/7031, W-71/6400

KEY * = Playoff # = Amateur ~ = Rain-curtailed

THE PLAYERS CHAMPIONSHIP

Tournament Players Club at Sawgrass, Ponte Vedra, FL

YEAR	WINNER	SCORE	RUNNERUP	PLAYED AT
1974	Jack Nicklaus	272	J. C. Snead	Atlanta CC, Atlanta, GA
1975	Al Geiberger	270	Dave Stockton	Colonial CC, Fort Worth, TX
1976	Jack Nicklaus	269	J. C. Snead	Inverrary G&CC, Lauderhill, FL
1977	Mark Hayes	289	Mike McCullough	Sawgrass, Ponte Vedra, FL
1978	Jack Nicklaus	289	Lou Graham	Sawgrass, Ponte Vedra, FL
1979	Lanny Wadkins	283	Tom Watson	Sawgrass, Ponte Vedra, FL
1980	Lee Trevino	278	Ben Crenshaw	Sawgrass, Ponte Vedra, FL
1981	Ray Floyd*	285	Barry Jaeckel	Sawgrass, Ponte Vedra, FL
			Curtis Strange	
	*(Won playoff with par on first extra hole)			
1982	Jerry Pate	280	Scott Simpson	TPC at Sawgrass, Ponte Vedra, FL
			Brad Bryant	
1983	Hal Sutton	283	Bob Eastwood	TPC at Sawgrass, Ponte Vedra, FL
1984	Fred Couples	277	Lee Trevino	TPC at Sawgrass, Ponte Vedra, FL
1985	Calvin Peete	274	D. A. Weibring	TPC at Sawgrass, Ponte Vedra, FL
1986	John Mahaffey	275	Larry Mize	TPC at Sawgrass, Ponte Vedra, FL
1987	Sandy Lyle*	274	Jeff Sluman	TPC at Sawgrass, Ponte Vedra, FL
	*(Won playoff with par on third extra hole)			
1988	Mark McCumber	273	Mike Reid	TPC at Sawgrass, Ponte Vedra, FL
1989	Tom Kite	279	Chip Beck	TPC at Sawgrass, Ponte Vedra, FL
1990	Jodie Mudd	278	Mark Calcavecchia	TPC at Sawgrass, Ponte Vedra, FL
1991	Steve Elkington	276	Fuzzy Zoeller	TPC at Sawgrass, Ponte Vedra, FL
1992	Davis Love III	273	4 Tied at 277	TPC at Sawgrass, Ponte Vedra, FL
1993	Nick Price	270	Bernhard Langer	TPC at Sawgrass, Ponte Vedra, FL
1994	Greg Norman	264	Fuzzy Zoeller	TPC at Sawgrass, Ponte Vedra, FL

Eligibility Requirements for the 1995 PLAYERS Championship

The starting field for the 1995 PLAYERS Championship shall consist of the following players:

1) The top 125 PGA TOUR members from Final 1994 Official Money List.
2) All winners of PGA TOUR events awarding official money and official victory status in the preceding 12 months concluding with the Nestle Invitational.
3) Designated players.
4) Any foreign player meeting the requirements of a designated player, whether or not he is a PGA TOUR member.
5) Winners in the last 10 calendar years of THE PLAYERS Championship, Masters, U.S. Open, PGA Championship and NEC World Series of Golf.
6) British Open winners since 1990.
7) Six players, not otherwise eligible, designated by THE PLAYERS Championship Committee as "special selections."
8) To complete a field of 144 players, those players in order, not otherwise eligible, from the 1995 Official Money List, as of the completion of the Nestle Invitational.

Greg Norman's 24-under-par 264 bettered the previous tournament record by five strokes.

358

THE TOUR CHAMPIONSHIP

Each year the top-30 PGA TOUR members on the money list compete at the season-ending TOUR Championship. The 1995 TOUR Championship will be played at Southern Hills CC in Tulsa, OK.

YEAR	WINNER	SCORE	RUNNERUP	PLAYED AT
1987	Tom Watson	268	Chip Beck	Oak Hills CC, San Antonio, TX
1988	Curtis Strange*	279	Tom Kite	Pebble Beach GL, Pebble Beach, CA
	*(won playoff with birdie on second extra hole)			
1989	Tom Kite*	276	Payne Stewart	Harbour Town GL, Hilton Head, SC
	*(won playoff with par on second extra hole)			
1990	Jodie Mudd*	273	Billy Mayfair	Champions GC, Houston, TX
	*(won playoff with birdie on first extra hole)			
1991	Craig Stadler*	279	Russ Cochran	Pinehurst Resort & CC, Pinehurst, NC
	*(won playoff with birdie on second extra hole)			
1992	Paul Azinger	276	Corey Pavin	Pinehurst Resort & CC, Pinehurst, NC
			Lee Janzen	
1993	Jim Gallagher, Jr.	277	Greg Norman	The Olympic Club, San Francisco, CA
			David Frost	
			John Huston	
			Scott Simpson	
1994	Mark McCumber*	274	Fuzzy Zoeller	The Olympic Club, San Francisco, CA
	*(won playoff with birdie on first extra hole)			

Mark McCumber with the 1994 TOUR Championship trophy.

Firestone Country Club, South Course, Akron, OH

From 1962 through 1975, the World Series of Golf was played as a four-man, 36-hole exhibition. All monies won in the tournament were unofficial. The winners in those years (with winning totals in parentheses):

1962—Jack Nicklaus (135)	1967—Jack Nicklaus (144)	1972—Gary Player (142)
1963—Jack Nicklaus (140)	1968—Gary Player (143)	1973—Tom Weiskopf (137)
1964—Tony Lema (138)	1969—Orville Moody (141)	1974—Lee Trevino (139)
1965—Gary Player (139)	1970—Jack Nicklaus (136)	1975—Tom Watson (140)
1966—Gene Littler (143)	1971—Charles Coody (141)	

Jose Maria Olazabal won his second NEC World Series of Golf in 1994.

YEAR	WINNER	SCORE	RUNNERUP
1976	Jack Nicklaus	275	Hale Irwin
1977	Lanny Wadkins	267	Hale Irwin
			Tom Weiskopf
1978	Gil Morgan*	278	Hubert Green
*(Won playoff with par on first extra hole)			
1979	Lon Hinkle	272	Bill Rogers
			Larry Nelson
			Lee Trevino
1980	Tom Watson	270	Raymond Floyd
1981	Bill Rogers	275	Tom Kite
1982	Craig Stadler*	278	Raymond Floyd
*(Won playoff with par on fourth extra hole)			
1983	Nick Price	270	Jack Nicklaus
1984	Denis Watson	271	Bruce Lietzke
1985	Roger Maltbie	268	Denis Watson
1986	Dan Pohl	277	Lanny Wadkins
1987	Curtis Strange	275	Fulton Allem
1988	Mike Reid*	275	Tom Watson
*(Won playoff with par on first extra hole)			
1989	David Frost*	276	Ben Crenshaw
*(Won playoff with par on second extra hole)			
1990	Jose M. Olazabal	262	Lanny Wadkins
1991	Tom Purtzer*	279	Jim Gallagher Jr.
			Davis Love III
*(Won playoff with par on second extra hole)			
1992	Craig Stadler	273	Corey Pavin
1993	Fulton Allem	270	Nick Price, Jim Gallagher, Jr., Craig Stadler
1994	Jose M. Olazabal	269	Scott Hoch

Eligibility Requirements for the 1995 NEC World Series of Golf

1) The defending champion, Jose Maria Olazabal
2) Winner, 1995 PLAYERS Championship
3) Winner, 1995 PGA Championship
4) Winner, 1995 Masters Tournament
5) Winner, 1995 United States Open
6) Winner, 1995 British Open
7) Winner, 1994 PGA National Club Pro Championship
8) All winners of PGA TOUR co-sponsored events since the preceding year's WSOG.
9) Winners of the following overseas events:

PGA European Tour
a. Volvo European PGA Championship
b. Johnnie Walker World Championship
c. Scottish Open
d. Dunhill British Masters
e. Trophee Lancome
f. Volvo Masters
g. Mercedes German Masters
h. Toyota World Match Play
i. Carroll's Irish Open
j. GA European Open

PGA Tour of Japan
a. Visa Taiheyo Club Masters
b. Dunlop Phoenix
c. Bridgestone Open
d. Chunichi Crowns
e. Japan Open
f. ANA Sapporo Open
g. Casio World Open
h. ABC Lark Cup
i. Asahi Beer Golf Digest Open
j. Japan PGA Championship
k. Japan Series of Golf

Australasian PGA Tour
a. Pyramid Australian Masters
b. Australian Open
c. Greg Norman's Holden Classic
d. Ford Australian PGA Championship

South African Tour
a. Sun City $1,000,000 Challenge
b. FNB Players Championship
c. Lexington PGA Championship
d. South African Open

10) Individual winner, 1994 World Cup

THE MASTERS TOURNAMENT

Augusta National Golf Club, Augusta, Georgia

YEAR	WINNER	SCORE	RUNNERUP
1934	Horton Smith	284	Craig Wood
1935	*Gene Sarazen (144)	282	Craig Wood (149)
1936	Horton Smith	285	Harry Cooper
1937	Byron Nelson	283	Ralph Guldahl
1938	Henry Picard	285	Ralph Guldahl, Harry Cooper
1939	Ralph Guldahl	279	Sam Snead
1940	Jimmy Demaret	280	Lloyd Mangrum
1941	Craig Wood	280	Byron Nelson
1942	*Byron Nelson (69)	280	Ben Hogan (70)
1943	No Tournament—World War II		
1944	No Tournament—World War II		
1945	No Tournament—World War II		
1946	Herman Keiser	282	Ben Hogan
1947	Jimmy Demaret	281	Byron Nelson, Frank Stranahan
1948	Claude Harmon	279	Cary Middlecoff
1949	Sam Snead	282	Johnny Bulla, Lloyd Mangrum
1950	Jimmy Demaret	283	Jim Ferrier
1951	Ben Hogan	280	Skee Riegel
1952	Sam Snead	286	Jack Burke, Jr.
1953	Ben Hogan	274	Ed Oliver, Jr.
1954	*Sam Snead (70)	289	Ben Hogan (71)
1955	Cary Middlecoff	279	Ben Hogan
1956	Jack Burke, Jr.	289	Ken Venturi
1957	Doug Ford	282	Sam Snead
1958	Arnold Palmer	284	Doug Ford, Fred Hawkins
1959	Art Wall, Jr.	284	Cary Middlecoff
1960	Arnold Palmer	282	Ken Venturi
1961	Gary Player	280	Charles R. Coe, Arnold Palmer
1962	*Arnold Palmer (68)	280	Gary Player (71), Dow Finsterwald (77)
1963	Jack Nicklaus	286	Tony Lema
1964	Arnold Palmer	276	Dave Marr, Jack Nicklaus
1965	Jack Nicklaus	271	Arnold Palmer, Gary Player
1966	*Jack Nicklaus (70)	288	Tommy Jacobs (72), Gay Brewer, Jr. (78)
1967	Gay Brewer, Jr.	280	Bobby Nichols
1968	Bob Goalby	277	Roberto DeVicenzo
1969	George Archer	281	Billy Casper, George Knudson, Tom Weiskopf
1970	*Billy Casper (69)	279	Gene Littler (74)
1971	Charles Coody	279	Johnny Miller, Jack Nicklaus
1972	Jack Nicklaus	286	Bruce Crampton, Bobby Mitchell, Tom Weiskopf
1973	Tommy Aaron	283	J. C. Snead
1974	Gary Player	278	Tom Weiskopf, Dave Stockton
1975	Jack Nicklaus	276	Johnny Miller, Tom Weiskopf
1976	Ray Floyd	271	Ben Crenshaw
1977	Tom Watson	276	Jack Nicklaus
1978	Gary Player	277	Hubert Green, Rod Funseth, Tom Watson
1979	*Fuzzy Zoeller	280	Ed Sneed, Tom Watson
1980	Seve Ballesteros	275	Gibby Gilbert, Jack Newton
1981	Tom Watson	280	Johnny Miller, Jack Nicklaus
1982	*Craig Stadler	284	Dan Pohl
1983	Seve Ballesteros	280	Ben Crenshaw, Tom Kite
1984	Ben Crenshaw	277	Tom Watson
1985	Bernhard Langer	282	Curtis Strange, Seve Ballesteros, Ray Floyd
1986	Jack Nicklaus	279	Greg Norman, Tom Kite
1987	*Larry Mize	285	Seve Ballesteros, Greg Norman
1988	Sandy Lyle	281	Mark Calcavecchia
1989	*Nick Faldo	283	Scott Hoch
1990	*Nick Faldo	278	Ray Floyd
1991	Ian Woosnam	277	Jose Maria Olazabal
1992	Fred Couples	275	Ray Floyd
1993	Bernhard Langer	277	Chip Beck
1994	Jose Maria Olazabal	279	Tom Lehman

* WINNER IN PLAYOFF.

FIGURES IN PARENTHESES INDICATE SCORES.

UNITED STATES OPEN CHAMPIONSHIP

YEAR	WINNER	SCORE	RUNNERUP	PLAYED AT
1895	Horace Rawlins	173-36 Holes	Willie Dunn	Newport GC, Newport, RI
1896	James Foulis	152-36 Holes	Horace Rawlins	Shinnecock Hills GC, SouthHampton , NY
1897	Joe Lloyd	162-36 Holes	Willie Anderson	Chicago GC, Wheaton, IL
1898	Fred Herd	328-72 Holes	Alex Smith	Myopia Hunt Club, Hamilton, MA
1899	Willie Smith	315	George Low	Baltimore CC, Baltimore, MD
			Val Fitzjohn	
			W. H. Way	
1900	Harry Vardon	313	J. H. Taylor	Chicago GC, Wheaton, IL
1901	*Willie Anderson (85)	331	Alex Smith (86)	Myopia Hunt Club, Hamilton, MA
1902	Laurie Auchterlonie	307	Stewart Gardner	Garden City GC, Garden City, LI, NY
1903	*Willie Anderson (82)	307	David Brown (84)	Baltusrol GC, Short Hills, NY
1904	Willie Anderson	303	Gil Nicholls	Glen View Club, Golf, IL
1905	Willie Anderson	314	Alex Smith	Myopia Hunt Club, Hamilton, MA
1906	Alex Smith	295	Willie Smith	Onwentsia Club Lake Forest, IL
1907	Alex Ross	302	Gil Nicholls	Philadelphia Cricket Club, Chestnut Hill,PA
1908	*Fred McLeod (77)	322	Willie Smith (83)	Myopia Hunt Club, Hamilton, MA
1909	George Sargent	290	Tom McNamara	Englewood GC Englewood, NJ
1910	*Alex Smith (71)	298	John McDermott (75)	Philadelphia Cricket Club, Chestnut Hill, PA
			Macdonald Smith (77)	
1911	*John McDermott (80)	307	Mike Brady (82)	Chicago GC, Wheaton, IL.
			George Simpson (85)	
1912	John McDermott	294	Tom McNamara	CC of Buffalo, Buffalo, NY
1913	*Francis Ouimet (72)	304	Harry Vardon (77)	The Country Club, Brookline, MA
			Edward Ray (78)	
1914	Walter Hagen	290	Charles Evans, Jr.	Midlothian CC, Blue Island, IL
1915	Jerome Travers	297	Tom McNamara	Baltusrol GC, Short Hills, NJ
1916	Charles Evans, Jr.	286	Jock Hutchison	Minikahda Club, Minneapolis, MN
1917—1918 No Championships Played—World War I				
1919	*Walter Hagen (77)	301	Mike Brady (78)	Brae Burn CC, West Newton, MA
1920	Edward Ray	295	Harry Vardon	Inverness CC, Toledo, OH
			Jack Burke	
			Leo Diegel	
			Jock Hutchison	
1921	James M. Barnes	289	Walter Hagen	Columbia CC, Chevy Chase, MD
			Fred McLeod	
1922	Gene Sarazen	288	John L. Black	Skokie CC, Glencoe, IL
			Robert T. Jones, Jr.	
1923	*Robert. T. Jones, Jr. (76)	296	Bobby Cruickshank(78)	Inwood CC, Inwood, LI, NY
1924	Cyril Walker	297	Robert T. Jones, Jr.	Oakland Hills CC, Birmingham, MI
1925	*W. MacFarlane (147)	291	R. T. Jones, Jr. (148)	Worcester CC, Worcester, MA
1926	Robert T. Jones, Jr.	293	Joe Turnesa	Scioto CC, Columbus, OH
1927	*Tommy Armour (76)	301	Harry Cooper (79)	Oakmont CC, Oakmont, PA
1928	*Johnny Farrell (143)	294	R. T. Jones, Jr. (144)	Olympia Fields CC, Matteson, IL
1929	*Robert.T. Jones, Jr. (141)	294	Al Espinosa (164)	Winged Foot GC, Marmaroneck, NY
1930	Robert T. Jones, Jr.	287	Macdonald Smith	Interlachen CC, Hopkins, MN
1931	*Billy Burke (149-148)	292	George Von Elm (149-149)	Inverness Club, Toledo, OH
1932	Gene Sarazen	286	Phil Perkins	Fresh Meadows CC, Flushing, NY
			Bobby Cruickshank	
1933	Johnny Goodman	287	Ralph Guldahl	North Shore CC, Glenview, IL
1934	Olin Dutra	293	Gene Sarazen	Merion Cricket Club, Ardmore, PA
1935	Sam Parks, Jr.	299	Jimmy Thompson	Oakmont CC, Oakmont, PA
1936	Tony Manero	282	Harry Cooper	Baltusrol GC, Springfield, NJ
1937	Ralph Guldahl	281	Sam Snead	Oakland Hills CC, Birmingham, MI
1938	Ralph Guldahl	284	Dick Metz	Cherry Hills CC, Denver, CO
1939	*Byron Nelson (68-70)	284	Craig Wood (68-73)	Philadelphia CC, Philadelphia, PA
			Denny Shute (76)	
1940	*Lawson Little (70)	287	Gene Sarazen (73)	Canterbury GC, Cleveland, OH

* WINNER IN PLAYOFF   FIGURES IN PARENTHESES INDICATE SCORES

UNITED STATES OPEN CHAMPIONSHIP (CONT'D.)

YEAR	WINNER	SCORE	RUNNERUP	PLAYED AT
1941	Craig Wood	284	Denny Shute	Colonial Club, Fort Worth, TX
1942—1945 No Championships Played—World War II				
1946	*Lloyd Mangrum (72-72)	284	Vic Ghezzi (72-73) Byron Nelson (72-73)	Canterbury GC, Cleveland, OH
1947	*Lew Worsham (69)	282	Sam Snead (70)	St. Louis CC, Clayton, MO
1948	Ben Hogan	276	Jimmy Demaret	Riviera CC, Los Angeles, CA
1949	Cary Middlecoff	286	Sam Snead Clayton Heafner	Medinah CC, Medinah, IL
1950	*Ben Hogan (69)	287	Lloyd Mangrum (73) George Fazio (75)	Merion Golf Club, Ardmore, PA
1951	Ben Hogan	287	Clayton Heafner	Oakland Hills CC, Birmingham, MI
1952	Julius Boros	281	Ed Oliver	Northwood CC, Dallas, TX
1953	Ben Hogan	283	Sam Snead	Oakmont CC, Oakmont, PA
1954	Ed Furgol	284	Gene Littler	Baltusrol GC, Springfield, NJ
1955	*Jack Fleck (69)	287	Ben Hogan (72)	Olympic Club, San Francisco, CA
1956	Cary Middlecoff	281	Ben Hogan Julius Boros	Oak Hill CC, Rochester, NY
1957	*Dick Mayer (72)	282	Cary Middlecoff (79)	Inverness Club, Toledo, OH
1958	Tommy Bolt	283	Gary Player	Southern Hills CC, Tulsa, OK
1959	Billy Casper	282	Bob Rosburg	Winged Foot GC, Mamaroneck, NY
1960	Arnold Palmer	280	Jack Nicklaus	Cherry Hills CC, Denver, CO
1961	Gene Littler	281	Bob Goalby Doug Sanders	Oakland Hills CC, Birmingham, MI
1962	*Jack Nicklaus (71)	283	Arnold Palmer (74)	Oakmont CC, Oakmont PA
1963	*Julius Boros (70)	293	Jacky Cupit (73) Arnold Palmer (76)	The Country Club, Brookline, MA
1964	Ken Venturi	278	Tommy Jacobs	Congressional CC, Washington, DC
1965	*Gary Player (71)	282	Kel Nagle (74)	Bellerive CC, St Louis, MO
1966	*Billy Casper (69)	278	Arnold Palmer (73)	Olympic Club, San Francisco, CA
1967	Jack Nicklaus	275	Arnold Palmer	Baltusrol GC, Springfield, NJ
1968	Lee Trevino	275	Jack Nicklaus	Oak Hill CC, Rochester NY
1969	Orville Moody	281	Deane Beman Al Geiberger Bob Rosburg	Champions GC, Houston, TX
1970	Tony Jacklin	281	Dave Hill	Hazeltine GC, Chaska, MN
1971	*Lee Trevino (68)	280	Jack Nicklaus (71)	Merion Golf Club, Ardmore, PA
1972	Jack Nicklaus	290	Bruce Crampton	Pebble Beach GL, Pebble Beach, CA
1973	Johnny Miller	279	John Schlee	Oakmont CC, Oakmont, PA
1974	Hale Irwin	287	Forrest Fezler	Winged Foot GC, Mamaroneck, NY
1975	*Lou Graham (71)	287	John Mahaffey (73)	Medinah CC, Medinah, IL.
1976	Jerry Pate	277	Tom Weiskopf Al Geiberger	Atlanta Athletic Club, Duluth, GA
1977	Hubert Green	278	Lou Graham	Southern Hills CC, Tulsa, OK
1978	Andy North	285	Dave Stockton J. C. Snead	Cherry Hills CC, Denver, CO
1979	Hale Irwin	284	Gary Player Jerry Pate	Inverness Club, Toledo, OH
1980	Jack Nicklaus	272	Isao Aoki	Baltusrol GC, Springfield NJ
1981	David Graham	273	George Burns Bill Rogers	Merion GC, Ardmore, PA
1982	Tom Watson	282	Jack Nicklaus	Pebble Beach GL, Pebble Beach, CA
1983	Larry Nelson	280	Tom Watson	Oakmont CC, Oakmont, PA
1984	*Fuzzy Zoeller (67)	276	Greg Norman (75)	Winged Foot GC, Mamaroneck, NY
1985	Andy North	279	Dave Barr T.C. Chen Denis Watson	Oakland Hills CC, Birmingham, MI
1986	Ray Floyd	279	Lanny Wadkins Chip Beck	Shinnecock Hills GC, Southampton, NY
1987	Scott Simpson	277	Tom Watson	Olympic Club Lake Course, San Francisco,CA
1988	*Curtis Strange (71)	278	Nick Faldo (75)	The Country Club, Brookline, MA
1989	Curtis Strange	278	Chip Beck Mark McCumber Ian Woosnam	Oak Hill CC, Rochester, NY

* WINNER IN PLAYOFF   FIGURES IN PARENTHESES INDICATE SCORES

YEAR	WINNER	SCORE	RUNNERUP	PLAYED AT
1990	*Hale Irwin (74-3)	280	Mike Donald (74-4)	Medinah CC, Medinah, IL
1991	*Payne Stewart (75)	282	Scott Simpson (77)	Hazeltine National GC, Chaska, MN
1992	Tom Kite	285	Jeff Sluman	Pebble Beach GL, Pebble Beach, CA
1993	Lee Janzen	272	Payne Stewart	Baltusrol GC, Springfield, NJ
1994	*Ernie Els (74-4-4)	279	Loren Roberts (74-4-5)	Oakmont CC, Oakmont, PA
			Colin Montgomerie (78)	

THE BRITISH OPEN

1860	Willie Park	174	Tom Morris, Sr.	Prestwick, Scotland
	(The First Event Was Open Only To Professional Golfers)			
1861	Tom Morris, Sr.,	163	Willie Park	Prestwick, Scotland
	(The Second Annual Open Was Open To Amateurs Also)			
1862	Tom Morris, Sr.	163	Willie Park	Prestwick, Scotland
1863	Willie Park	168	Tom Morris Sr.	Prestwick, Scotland
1864	Tom Morris, Sr.	160	Andrew Strath	Prestwick, Scotland
1865	Andrew Strath	162	Willie Park	Prestwick, Scotland
1866	Willie Park	169	David Park	Prestwick, Scotland
1867	Tom Morris, Sr.	170	Willie Park	Prestwick, Scotland
1868	Tom Morris, Jr.	154	Tom Morris, Sr.	Prestwick, Scotland
1869	Tom Morris, Jr.	157	Tom Morris, Sr.	Prestwick, Scotland
1870	Tom Morris, Jr.	149	David Strath	Prestwick, Scotland
			Bob Kirk	
1871	No Championship Played			
1872	Tom Morris, Jr.	166	David Strath	Prestwick, Scotland
1873	Tom Kidd	179	Jamie Anderson	St. Andrews, Scotland
1874	Mungo Park	159	No Record	Musselburgh, Scotland
1875	Willie Park	166	Bob Martin	Prestwick, Scotland
1876	Bob Martin	176	David Strath	St. Andrews, Scotland
			(Tied, But Refused Playoff)	
1877	Jamie Anderson	160	R. Pringle	Musselburgh, Scotland
1878	Jamie Anderson	157	Robert Kirk	Prestwick, Scotland
1879	Jamie Anderson	169	A. Kirkaldy	St. Andrews, Scotland
			J. Allan	
1880	Robert Ferguson	162	No Record	Musselburgh, Scotland
1881	Robert Ferguson	170	Jamie Anderson	Prestwick, Scotland
1882	Robert Ferguson	171	Willie Fernie	St. Andrews, Scotland
1883	*Willie Fernie	159	Robert Ferguson	Musselburgh, Scotland
1884	Jack Simpson	160	D. Rolland	Prestwick, Scotland
			Willie Fernie	
1885	Bob Martin	171	Archie Simpson	St. Andrews, Scotland
1886	David Brown	157	Willie Campbell	Musselburgh, Scotland
1887	Willie Park, Jr.	161	Bob Martin	Prestwick, Scotland
1888	Jack Burns	171	B. Sayers	St. Andrews, Scotland
			D. Anderson	
1889	*Willie Park, Jr.	155 (158)	Andrew Kirkaldy (163)	Musselburgh, Scotland
1890	John Ball	164	Willie Fernie	Prestwick, Scotland
1891	Hugh Kirkaldy	166	Andrew Kirkaldy	St. Andrews, Scotland
			Willie Fernie	
	(Championship Extended From 36 to 72 Holes)			
1892	Harold H. Hilton	305	John Ball	Muirfield, Scotland
			H. Kirkaldy	
1893	William Auchterlonie	322	John E. Laidlay	Prestwick, Scotland
1894	John H. Taylor	326	Douglas Rolland	Royal St. George's, England
1895	John H. Taylor	322	Alexander Herd	St. Andrews, Scotland
1896	*Harry Vardon	316 (157)	John H. Taylor (161)	Muirfield, Scotland
1897	Harold H. Hilton	314	James Braid	Hoylake, England
1898	Harry Vardon	307	Willie Park, Jr.	Prestwick, Scotland
1899	Harry Vardon	310	Jack White	Royal St. George's, England
1900	John H. Taylor	309	Harry Vardon	St Andrews, Scotland

* WINNER IN PLAYOFF   FIGURES IN PARENTHESES INDICATE SCORES

YEAR	WINNER	SCORE	RUNNERUP	PLAYED AT
1901	James Braid	309	Harry Vardon	Muirfield, Scotland
1902	Alexander Herd	307	Harry Vardon	Hoylake, England
1903	Harry Vardon	300	Tom Vardon	Prestwick, Scotland
1904	Jack White	296	John H. Taylor	Royal St. George's, England
1905	James Braid	318	John H. Taylor	St. Andrews, Scotland
			Rolland Jones	
1906	James Braid	300	John H. Taylor	Muirfield, Scotland
1907	Arnaud Massy	312	John H. Taylor	Hoylake, England
1908	James Braid	291	Tom Ball	Prestwick, Scotland
1909	John H. Taylor	295	James Braid	Deal, England
			Tom Ball	
1910	James Braid	299	Alexander Herd	St. Andrews, Scotland
1911	Harry Vardon	303	Arnaud Massy	Royal St. George's, England
1912	Edward (Ted) Ray	295	Harry Vardon	Muirfield, Scotland
1913	John H. Taylor	304	Edward Ray	Hoylake, England
1914	Harry Vardon	306	John H. Taylor	Prestwick, Scotland
1915—1919 No Championships Played—World War I				
1920	George Duncan	303	Alexander Herd	Deal, England
1921	*Jock Hutchison	296 (150)	Roger Wethered (159)	St Andrews, Scotland
1922	Walter Hagen	300	George Duncan	Royal St. George's, England
			James M. Barnes	
1923	Arthur G. Havers	295	Walter Hagen	Troon, Scotland
1924	Walter Hagen	301	Ernest Whitcombe	Hoylake, England
1925	James M. Barnes	300	Archie Compston	Prestwick, Scotland
			Ted Ray	
1926	Robert T. Jones, Jr.	291	Al Watrous	Royal Lytham, England
1927	Robert T. Jones, Jr.	285	Aubrey Boomer	St. Andrews, Scotland
1928	Walter Hagen	292	Gene Sarazen	Royal St. George's, England
1929	Walter Hagen	292	Johnny Farrell	Muirfield, Scotland
1930	Robert T. Jones, Jr.	291	Macdonald Smith	Hoylake, England
			Leo Diegel	
1931	Tommy D. Armour	296	J. Jurado	Carnoustie, Scotland
1932	Gene Sarazen	283	Macdonald Smith	Prince's, England
1933	*Denny Shute (149)	292	Craig Wood (154)	St. Andrews, Scotland
1934	Henry Cotton	283	S. F. Brews	Royal St. George's, England
1935	Alfred Perry	283	Alfred Padgham	Muirfield, Scotland
1936	Alfred Padgham	287	J. Adams	Hoylake, England
1937	Henry Cotton	290	R. A. Whitcombe	Carnoustie, Scotland
1938	R. A. Whitcombe	295	James Adams	Royal St. George's, England
1939	Richard Burton	290	Johnny Bulla	St. Andrews, Scotland
1940—1945 No Championships Played—World War II				
1946	Sam Snead	290	Bobby Locke	St. Andrews, Scotland
			Johnny Bulla	
1947	Fred Daly	293	R. W. Horne	Hoylake, England
			Frank Stranahan	
1948	Henry Cotton	294	Fred Daly	Muirfield, Scotland
1949	*Bobby Locke	283(135)	Harry Bradshaw (147)	Royal St. George's, England
1950	Bobby Locke	279	Roberto DeVicenzo	Troon, Scotland
1951	Max Faulkner	285	A. Cerda	Portrush, Ireland
1952	Bobby Locke	287	Peter Thomson	Royal Lytham, England
1953	Ben Hogan	282	Frank Stranahan	Carnoustie, Scotland
			D. J. Rees	
			Peter Thomson	
			A. Cerda	
1954	Peter Thomson	283	S. S. Scott	Royal Birkdale, England
			Dai Rees	
			Bobby Locke	
1955	Peter Thomson	281	John Fallon	St. Andrews, Scotland
1956	Peter Thomson	286	Flory Van Donck	Hoylake, England
1957	Bobby Locke	279	Peter Thomson	St Andrews, Scotland
1958	*Peter Thomson	278(139)	Dave Thomas (143)	Royal Lytham, England

* WINNER IN PLAYOFF   FIGURES IN PARENTHESES INDICATE SCORES

THE BRITISH OPEN (CONT'D.)

YEAR	WINNER	SCORE	RUNNERUP	PLAYED AT
1959	Gary Player	284	Fred Bullock Flory Van Donck	Muirfield, Scotland
1960	Kel Nagle	278	Arnold Palmer	St. Andrews, Scotland
1961	Arnold Palmer	284	Dai Rees	Royal Birkdale, England
1962	Arnold Palmer	276	Kel Nagle	Troon, Scotland
1963	*Bob Charles	277(140)	Phil Rodgers (148)	Royal Lytham, England
1964	Tony Lema	279	Jack Nicklaus	St. Andrews, Scotland
1965	Peter Thomson	285	Brian Huggett Christy O'Connor	Southport, England
1966	Jack Nicklaus	282	Doug Sanders Dave Thomas	Muirfield, Scotland
1967	Roberto DeVicenzo	278	Jack Nicklaus	Hoylake, England
1968	Gary Player	289	Jack Nicklaus Bob Charles	Carnoustie, Scotland
1969	Tony Jacklin	280	Bob Charles	Royal Lytham, England
1970	*Jack Nicklaus	283 (72)	Doug Sanders (73)	St. Andrews, Scotland
1971	Lee Trevino	278	Lu Liang Huan	Royal Birkdale, England
1972	Lee Trevino	278	Jack Nicklaus	Muirfield, Scotland
1973	Tom Weiskopf	276	Johnny Miller	Troon, Scotland
1974	Gary Player	282	Peter Oosterhuis	Royal Lytham, England
1975	*Tom Watson	279 (71)	Jack Newton (72)	Carnoustie, Scotland
1976	Johnny Miller	279	Jack Nicklaus S. Ballesteros	Royal Birkdale, England
1977	Tom Watson	268	Jack Nicklaus	Turnberry, Scotland
1978	Jack Nicklaus	281	Ben Crenshaw Tom Kite Ray Floyd Simon Owen	St. Andrews, Scotland
1979	Seve Ballesteros	283	Ben Crenshaw Jack Nicklaus	Royal Lytham, England
1980	Tom Watson	271	Lee Trevino	Muirfield, Scotland
1981	Bill Rogers	276	Bernhard Langer	Royal St George's, England
1982	Tom Watson	284	Nick Price Peter Oosterhuis	Royal Troon, Scotland
1983	Tom Watson	275	Andy Bean	Royal Birkdale, England
1984	Seve Ballesteros	276	Tom Watson Bernhard Langer	St. Andrews, Scotland
1985	Sandy Lyle	282	Payne Stewart	Royal St. George's, England
1986	Greg Norman	280	Gordon Brand	Turnberry GL, Scotland
1987	Nick Faldo	279	Paul Azinger Rodger Davis	Muirfield, Gullane, Scotland
1988	Seve Ballesteros	273	Nick Price	Royal Lytham and St. Annes, St. Annes-On-The-Sea, England
1989	*Mark Calcavecchia	275	Wayne Grady Greg Norman	Royal Troon GC, Troon, Scotland
1990	Nick Faldo	270	Payne Stewart Mark McNulty	St. Andrews, Scotland
1991	Ian Baker-Finch	272	Mike Harwood	Royal Birkdale, England
1992	Nick Faldo	272	John Cook	Muirfield, Gullane, Scotland
1993	Greg Norman	267	Nick Faldo	Royal St. George's, England
1994	Nick Price	268	Jesper Parnevik	Turnberry GL, Scotland

PGA CHAMPIONSHIP

YEAR	WINNER	SCORE	RUNNERUP	PLAYED AT
1916	James M. Barnes	1 up	Jock Hutchison	Siwanoy CC, Bronxville, NY
1917—1918 No Championships Played—World War I				

* WINNER IN PLAYOFF

FIGURES IN PARENTHESES INDICATE SCORES

YEAR	WINNER	SCORE	RUNNERUP	PLAYED AT
1919	James M. Barnes	6 & 5	Fred McLeod	Engineers CC, Roslyn, LI, NY
1920	Jock Hutchison	1 up	J. Douglas Edgar	Flossmoor CC, Flossmoor, IL
1921	Walter Hagen	3 & 2	James M. Barnes	Inwood CC, Far Rockaway, NY
1922	Gene Sarazen	4 & 3	Emmet French	Oakmont CC, Oakmont, PA
1923	Gene Sarazen	1 up (38)	Walter Hagen	Pelham CC, Pelham N Y
1924	Walter Hagen	2 up	James M. Barnes	French Lick CC, French Lick, IN
1925	Walter Hagen	6 & 5	William Mehlhorn	Olympia Fields, Olympia Fields, IL
1926	Walter Hagen	5 & 3	Leo Diegel	Salisbury GC, Westbury, LI, NY
1927	Walter Hagen	1 up	Joe Turnesa	Cedar Crest C C, Dallas TX
1928	Leo Diegel	6 & 5	Al Espinosa	Five Farms CC Baltimore, MD
1929	Leo Diegel	6 & 4	Johnny Farrell	Hillcrest CC Los Angeles, CA
1930	Tommy Armour	1 up	Gene Sarazen	Fresh Meadow CC, Flushing, NY
1931	Tom Creavy	2 & 1	Denny Shute	Wannamoisett CC Rumford, RI
1932	Olin Dutra	4 & 3	Frank Walsh	Keller GC, St. Paul MN
1933	Gene Sarazen	5 & 4	Willie Goggin	Blue Mound CC, Milwaukee, WI
1934	Paul Runyan	1 up (38)	Craig Wood	Park CC, Williamsville NY
1935	Johnny Revolta	5 & 4	Tommy Armour	Twin Hills CC, Oklahoma City, OK
1936	Denny Shute	3 & 2	Jimmy Thomson	Pinehurst CC, Pinehurst NC
1937	Denny Shute	1 up (37)	Harold McSpaden	Pittsburgh Field Club, Aspinwall, PA
1938	Paul Runyan	8 & 7	Sam Snead	Shawnee CC, Shawnee-on-Delaware,
1939	Henry Picard	1 up (37)	Byron Nelson	Pomonok CC, Flushing LI, NY
1940	Byron Nelson	1 up	Sam Snead	Hershey CC, Hershey, PA
1941	Vic Ghezzi	1 up (38)	Byron Nelson	Cherry Hills CC Denver CO
1942	Sam Snead	2 & 1	Jim Turnesa	Seaview CC, Atlantic City, NJ
1943—No Championship Played—World War II				
1944	Bob Hamilton	1 up	Byron Nelson	Manito G & CC, Spokane WA
1945	Byron Nelson	4 & 3	Sam Byrd	Morraine CC, Dayton, OH
1946	Ben Hogan	6 & 4	Ed Oliver	Portland GC, Portland, OR
1947	Jim Ferrier	2 & 1	Chick Harbert	Plum Hollow CC, Detroit, MI
1948	Ben Hogan	7 & 6	Mike Turnesa	Norwood Hills CC St. Louis MO
1949	Sam Snead	3 & 2	Johnny Palmer	Hermitage CC, Richmond, VA
1950	Chandler Harper	4 & 3	Henry Williams, Jr.	Scioto CC, Columbus, OH
1951	Sam Snead	7 & 6	Walter Burkemo	Oakmont CC Oakmont PA
1952	Jim Turnesa	1 up	Chick Harbert	Big Spring CC, Louisvillie, KY
1953	Walter Burkemo	2 & 1	Felice Torza	Birmingham CC, Birmingham, MI
1954	Chick Harbert	4 & 3	Walter Burkemo	Keller GC, St. Paul, MN
1955	Doug Ford	4 & 3	Cary Middlecoff	Meadowbrook CC Detroit MI
1956	Jack Burke	3 & 2	Ted Kroll	Blue Hill CC, Boston, MA
1957	Lionel Hebert	2 & 1	Dow Finsterwald	Miami Valley CC, Dayton, OH
1958	Dow Finsterwald	276	Billy Casper	Llanerch CC, Havertown, PA
1959	Bob Rosburg	277	Jerry Barber	Minneapolis GC, St. Louis Park, MN
			Doug Sanders	
1960	Jay Hebert	281	Jim Ferrier	Firestone CC, Akron, OH
1961	*Jerry Barber (67)	277	Don January (68)	Olympia Fields CC, Olympia Fields, IL
1962	Gary Player	278	Bob Goalby	Aronomink GC, Newtown Square, PA
1963	Jack Nicklaus	279	Dave Ragan, Jr.	Dallas Athletic Club, Dallas, TX
1964	Bobby Nichols	271	Jack Nicklaus	Columbus CC, Columbus, OH
			Arnold Palmer	
1965	Dave Marr	280	Billy Casper	Laurel Valley CC, Ligonier, PA
			Jack Nicklaus	
1966	Al Geiberger	280	Dudley Wysong	Firestone CC Akron OH
1967	*Don January (69)	281	Don Massengale (71)	Columbine CC, Littleton, CO
1968	Julius Boros	281	Bob Charles	Pecan Valley CC, San Antonio, TX
			Arnold Palmer	
1969	Ray Floyd	276	Gary Player	NCR CC, Dayton, OH
1970	Dave Stockton	279	Arnold Palmer	Southern Hills CC, Tulsa, OK
			Bob Murphy	
1971	Jack Nicklaus	281	Billy Casper	PGA National GC, Palm Beach Gardens, FL
1972	Gary Player	281	Tommy Aaron	Oakland Hills CC, Birmingham, MI
			Jim Jamieson	

* WINNER IN PLAYOFF

FIGURES IN PARENTHESES INDICATE SCORES

PGA CHAMPIONSHIP (CONT'D.)

YEAR	WINNER	SCORE	RUNNERUP	PLAYED AT
1973	Jack Nicklaus	277	Bruce Crampton	Canterbury GC, Cleveland, OH
1974	Lee Trevino	276	Jack Nicklaus	Tanglewood GC, Winston-Salem, NC
1975	Jack Nicklaus	276	Bruce Crampton	Firestone CC, Akron OH
1976	Dave Stockton	281	Ray Floyd	Congressional CC, Bethesda, MD
			Don January	
1977	*Lanny Wadkins	282	Gene Littler	Pebble Beach GL, Pebble Beach, CA
1978	*John Mahaffey	276	Jerry Pate	Oakmont CC, Oakmont, PA
			Tom Watson	
1979	*David Graham	272	Ben Crenshaw	Oakland Hills CC, Birmingham, MI
1980	Jack Nicklaus	274	Andy Bean	Oak Hill CC, Rochester NY
1981	Larry Nelson	273	Fuzzy Zoeller	Atlanta Athletic Club, Duluth, GA
1982	Raymond Floyd	272	Lanny Wadkins	Southern Hills CC, Tulsa, OK
1983	Hal Sutton	274	Jack Nicklaus	Riviera CC, Pacific Palisades, CA
1984	Lee Trevino	273	Gary Player	Shoal Creek, Birmingham, AL
			Lanny Wadkins	
1985	Hubert Green	278	Lee Trevino	Cherry Hills CC, Denver CO
1986	Bob Tway	276	Greg Norman	Inverness Club, Toledo OH
1987	*Larry Nelson	287	Lanny Wadkins	PGA National, Palm Beach Gardens, FL
1988	Jeff Sluman	272	Paul Azinger	Oak Tree GC, Edmond, OK
1989	Payne Stewart	276	Mike Reid	Kemper Lakes GC, Hawthorn Woods, IL
1990	Wayne Grady	282	Fred Couples	Shoal Creek, Birmingham, AL
1991	John Daly	276	Bruce Lietzke	Crooked Stick GC, Carmel, IN
1992	Nick Price	278	John Cook	Bellerive CC, St. Louis, MO
			Jim Gallagher, Jr.	
			Gene Sauers	
			Nick Faldo	
1993	*Paul Azinger	272	Greg Norman	Inverness Club, Toledo, OH
1994	Nick Price	269	Corey Pavin	Southern Hills CC, Tulsa, OK

* WINNER IN PLAYOFF

FIGURES IN PARENTHESES INDICATE SCORES

THE PRESIDENTS CUP

The Presidents Cup Match, conceived as a means of giving some of the world's best (non-European) players an opportunity to compete in international team match play competition, is a biennial event played in non-Ryder Cup years.

The first Presidents Cup Match was contested September 16-18, 1994 at Robert Trent Jones Golf Club on Lake Manassas in Prince William County, VA. The United States Team, captained by Hale Irwin, defeated the International side of David Graham, 20-12. Irwin, who qualified as a player for his own squad, had as his non-playing co-captain Paul Azinger, who at that time was continuing his recovery from lymphoma.

Members of the U.S. team for the inaugural Presidents Cup were selected from rankings based on official money won from the end of the 1993 NEC World Series of Golf through the 1994 NEC World Series of Golf. International Team players were chosen on the basis of Sony World Rankings at the conclusion of the 1994 NEC World Series of Golf. International Teams will not include any players eligible for the European Ryder Cup team.

The rankings were used for selection of 10 members of each squad. Two captain's choices apiece rounded out the 12-man teams.

The Presidents Cup competition consists of 10 matches (five foursomes and five four-ball matches) each of the first two days. Each member of the two 12-man squads must play each day.

There are 12 singles matches involving all players on the final Sunday, all of which are to be played to conclusion. No singles matches will be halved, or tied. All matches are worth one point each, for a total of 32 points.

If, at any time, a Presidents Cup Match is deadlocked at the end of singles play, there is to be a sudden-death playoff between two players designated in advance by the respective captains.

As is the case with virtually all activity involving the PGA TOUR, charity is the ultimate winner at the Presidents Cup.

There is no purse for the players. Net revenues from the inaugural match were divided into 26 equal shares, which the players and captains designated for charities or golf-related projects of their choice. Contributions in their names were made through PGA TOUR Charities, Inc.

Former President Gerald R. Ford presided over the first Presidents Cup Match as Honorary Chairman. Members of the Presidents Cup Committee include, among others, representatives of the PGA Tour of Australasia, PGA of South Africa, Asia-Pacific Golf Confederation and the Royal and Ancient Golf Club of St. Andrews.

The next Presidents Cup competition will be staged in 1996, also at Robert Trent Jones GC.

Results of the 1994 Presidents Cup Match are on page 250

369

RYDER CUP MATCHES

The Ryder Cup Matches developed from a match played between representatives of the American and British Professional Golfers' Association in England in 1926. That unofficial match, incidentally, was won by the British 13½ to 1½.

Following this highly successful exhibition, Samuel A. Ryder, a wealthy British seed merchant, offered to donate a solid gold trophy bearing his name to be competed for in a series of matches between professionals of the two nations.

From the start of the series through the 1959 Ryder Cup matches, the competition was comprised of four foursome matches one day and eight singles matches the other day, each at 36 holes.

In 1961, the format was changed to provide for four 18-hole foursomes the morning of the first day and four more that afternoon, then for eight 18-hole singles the morning of the second day and eight more that afternoon. As in the past, one point was at stake in each match, so the total number of points was doubled.

In 1963, for the first time, a day of four-ball matches augmented the program to add new interest to the overall competition. This brought the total number of points to 32.

In 1977, the format was altered once again. This time there were five foursomes on the opening day, five four-ball matches on the second day, and ten singles matches on the final day. This reduced the total number of points to 20.

For 1979, eligibility for the Great Britain-Ireland side was expanded to include all British PGA/European TPD members who are residents of European nations.

The 1995 Ryder Cup Matches will be played September 21-24, 1995, at Oak Hill CC, Rochester, NY.

Year	Played at	Date	Result			
1927	Worcester Country Club, Worcester, MA	June 3-4	U.S.	9½	Britain	2½
1929	Moortown, England	May 26-27	Britain	7	U.S.	5
1931	Scioto Country Club, Columbus, OH	June 26-27	U.S.	9	Britain	3
1933	Southport & Ainsdale Courses, England	June 26-27	Britain	6½	U.S.	5½
1935	Ridgewood Country Club, Ridgewood, NJ	Sept. 28-29	U S.	9	Britain	3
1937	Southport & Ainsdale Courses, England	June 29-30	U.S.	8	Britain	4
	Ryder Cup Matches not held during World War II years.					
1947	Portland Golf Club, Portland, OR	Nov. 1-2	U.S.	11	Britain	1
1949	Ganton Golf Course, Scarborough, England	Sept 16-17	U.S.	7	Britain	5
1951	Pinehurst Country Club, Pinehurst, NC	Nov. 2-4	U.S.	9½	Britain	2½
1953	Wentworth, England	Oct. 2-3	U.S.	6½	Britain	5½
1955	Thunderbird Ranch and CC, Palm Springs, CA	Nov. 5-6	U.S.	8	Britain	4
1957	Lindrick Golf Club, Yorkshire, England	Oct. 4-5	Britain	7½	U.S	4½
1959	Eldorado Country Club, Palm Desert, CA	Nov. 6-7	U.S.	8½	Britain	3½
1961	Royal Lytham and St. Anne's Golf Club, St. Anne's-On-The-Sea, England	Oct. 13-14	U.S.	14½	Britain	9½
1963	East Lake Country Club, Atlanta, GA	Oct. 11-13	U.S.	23	Britain	9
1965	Royal Birkdale Golf Club, Southport, England	Oct. 7-9	U.S.	19½	Britain	12½
1967	Champions Golf Club, Houston, TX	Oct. 20-22	U.S.	23½	Britain	8½
1969	Royal Birkdale Golf Club, Southport, England	Sept.18-20	U.S.	16-Tie	Britain	16
1971	Old Warson Country Club, St. Louis, MO	Sept. 16-18	U S.	18½	Britain	13½
1973	Muirfield, Scotland	Sept. 20-22	U.S.	19	Britain	13
1975	Laurel Valley Golf Club, Ligonier, PA	Sept. 19-21	U.S.	21	Britain	11
1977	Royal Lytham and St. Anne's Golf Club, St. Anne's-On-The-Sea, England	Sept. 15-17	U S	12½	Britain	7½
1979	Greenbrier, White Sulphur Springs, WV	Sept. 13-15	U.S.	17	Europe	11
1981	Walton Heath Golf Club, Surrey, England	Sept. 18-20	U.S.	18½	Europe	9½
1983	PGA National GC, Palm Beach Gardens, FL	Oct. 14-16	U.S.	14½	Europe	13½
1985	The Belfry Golf Club Sutton, Coldfield, England	Sept. 13-15	Europe	16½	U.S.	11½
1987	Muirfield Village Golf Club, Dublin, OH	Sept. 24-27	Europe	15	U.S.	13
1989	The Belfry Golf Club, Sutton Coldfield, England	Sept. 22-24	U.S.	14-Tie	Europe	14
1991	The Ocean Course, Kiawah Island, SC	Sept. 26-29	U.S.	14½	Europe	13½
1993	The Belfry Golf Club, Sutton Coldfield, England	Sept. 24-26	U.S.	15	Europe	13

(The United States leads the series, 23-5-2.)

THE RYDER CUP

The 1995 U.S. Ryder Cup Team will be selected by way of Ryder Cup points earned from the beginning of 1994 through the 1995 PGA Championship. The top ten point-getters qualify for the 12-man team. Then the U.S. Captain will select the final two players to complete the team.

Points are awarded to the first ten positions in each PGA TOUR event on the following basis with points being weighted towards the 1995 season:

PGA Championship, U.S. Open, Masters Tournament and the British Open (1994/1995): 1st-225/300; 2nd-135/180; 3rd-120/160; 4th-105/140; 5th-90/120; 6th-75/100; 7th-60/80; 8th-45/60; 9th-30/40; 10th-15/20.

All other PGA TOUR events (1994/1995): 1st-75/150; 2nd-45/90; 3rd-40/80; 4th-35/70; 5th-30/60; 6th-25/50; 7th-2040; 8th-15/30; 9th-10/20; 10th-5/10.

If a player who is ineligible finishes in one of those positions, no points are awarded for that position. In order to be eligible, a player must be a U.S. citizen and a member of the PGA of America.

1993 MATCH RESULTS
FIRST DAY
Foursomes--United States 2, Europe 2
Lanny Wadkins/Corey Pavin (U.S.) def. Sam Torrance/Mark James, 4&3
Ian Woosnam/Bernhard Langer (Europe) def. Payne Stewart/Paul Azinger, 7&5
Tom Kite/Davis Love III (U.S.) def. Seve Ballesteros/Jose Maria Olazabal, 2&1
Nick Faldo/Colin Montgomerie (Europe) def. Raymond Floyd/Fred Couples, 4&3

Four-Ball--Europe 2 1/2, United States 1 1/2
Woosnam/Peter Baker (Europe) def. Jim Gallagher, Jr./Lee Janzen, 1 up
Wadkins/Pavin (U.S.) def. Langer/Barry Lane, 4&2
Azinger/Couples (U.S.) halved with Faldo/Montgomerie
Ballesteros/Olazabal (Europe) def. Kite/Love, 4&3

Totals: Europe 4 1/2, United States 3 1/2

SECOND DAY
Foursomes--Europe 3, United States 1
Faldo/Montgomerie (Europe) def. Wadkins/Pavin, 3&2
Woosnam/Langer (Europe) def. Azinger/Couples, 2&1
Floyd/Stewart (U.S.) def. Baker/Lane, 3&2
Ballesteros/Olazabal (Europe) def. Kite/Love, 2&1

Totals: Europe 7 1/2, United States 4 1/2

Four-Ball--United States 3, Europe 1
John Cook/Chip Beck (U.S.) def. Faldo/Montgomerie, 2 up
Pavin/Gallagher (U.S.) def. James/Constantino Rocca, 5&4
Woosnam/Baker (Europe) def. Azinger/Couples, 6&5
Floyd/Stewart (U.S.) def. Olazabal/Joakim Haeggman, 2&1

Totals: Europe 8 1/2, United States 7 1/2

THIRD DAY
Singles--United States 7 1/2, Europe 4 1/2
Couples (U.S.) halved with Woosnam
Beck (U.S.) def. Lane, 1 up
Montgomerie (Europe) def. Janzen, 1 up
Baker (Europe) def. Pavin, 2 up
Haeggman (Europe) def. Cook, 1 up
Wadkins (U.S) halved with Torrance
(Match not played by agreement. Torrance forced to withdraw due to injury. Each player awarded one-half point)
Stewart (U.S.) def. James, 3&2
Love (U.S.) def. Rocca, 1 up
Gallagher (U.S.) def. Ballesteros, 3&2
Floyd (U.S.) def. Olazabal, 2 up
Kite (U.S.) def. Langer, 5&3
Azinger (U.S.) halved with Faldo.

Totals: United States 15, Europe 13

WORLD CUP OF GOLF

YEAR	COUNTRY	WINNING TEAM MEMBERS	INDIVIDUAL MEDALIST
1953	Argentina	Antonio Cerda, Roberto de Vicenzo	Antonio Cerda, Argentina
1954	Australia	Peter Thomson, Kel Nagle	Stan Leonard, Canada
1955	United States	Chick Harbert, Ed Furgol	Ed Furgol, United States
1956	United States	Ben Hogan, Sam Snead	Sam Snead, United States
1957	Japan	Torakichi Nakamura, Koichi Ono	Torakichi Nakamura, Japan
1958	Ireland	Harry Bradshaw, Christy O'Connor	Angel Miguel, Spain
1959	Australia	Peter Thomson, Kel Nagle	Stan Leonard, Canada
1960	United States	Sam Snead, Arnold Palmer	Fleury Von Donck, Belgium
1961	United States	Sam Snead, Jimmy Demaret	Sam Snead, United States
1962	United States	Sam Snead Arnold Palmer	Roberto de Vicenzo, Argentina
1963	United States	Arnold Palmer, Jack Nicklaus	Jack Nicklaus, United States
1964	United States	Arnold Palmer, Jack Nicklaus	Jack Nicklaus, United States
1965	South Africa	Gary Player, Harold Henning	Gary Player, South Africa
1966	United States	Jack Nicklaus, Arnold Palmer	George Knudson, Canada
1967	United States	Jack Nicklaus, Arnold Palmer	Arnold Palmer, United States
1968	Canada	Al Balding, George Knudson	Al Balding, Canada
1969	United States	Orville Moody, Lee Trevino	Lee Trevino, United States
1970	Australia	Bruce Devlin, David Graham	Roberto de Vicenzo, Argentina
1971	United States	Jack Nicklaus, Lee Trevino	Jack Nicklaus, United States
1972	Taiwan	Hsieh Min Nan, Lu Liang Huan	Hsieh Min Nan, Taiwan
1973	United States	Jack Nicklaus, Johnny Miller	Johnny Miller, United States
1974	South Africa	Bobby Cole, Dale Hayes	Bobby Cole, South Africa
1975	United States	Johnny Miller, Lou Graham	Johnny Miller, United States
1976	Spain	Seve Ballesteros, Manuel Pinero	Ernesto Acosta, Mexico
1977	Spain	Seve Ballesteros, Antonio Garrido	Gary Player, South Africa
1978	United States	John Mahaffey, Andy North	John Mahaffey, United States
1979	United States	John Mahaffey, Hale Irwin	Hale Irwin, United States
1980	Canada	Dan Halldorson, Jim Nelford	Sandy Lyle, Scotland
1981	Not played		
1982	Spain	Manuel Pinero, Jose Maria Canizares	Manuel Pinero, Spain
1983	United States	Rex Caldwell, John Cook	Dave Barr, Canada
1984	Spain	Jose Maria Canizares, Jose Rivero	Jose Maria Canizares
1985	Canada	Dan Halldorson, Dave Barr	Howard Clark, England
1986	Not played		
1987	Wales	Ian Woosnam, David Llewellyn	Ian Woosnam, Wales
1988	United States	Ben Crenshaw, Mark McCumber	Ben Crenshaw, United States
1989	Australia	Wayne Grady, Peter Fowler	Peter Fowler, Australia
1990	Germany	Bernhard Langer, Torsten Gideon	Payne Stewart, United States
1991	Sweden	Anders Forsbrand, Per Ulrik Johansson	Ian Woosnam, Wales
1992	United States	Fred Couples, Davis Love III	Brett Ogle, Australia
1993	United States	Fred Couples, Davis Love III	Bernhard Langer, Germany
1994	United States	Fred Couples, Davis Love III	Fred Couples, United States

Andersen Consulting World Championship of Golf

On October 19, 1994, plans were announced for an international match-play competition designed to determine "the best professional golfer in the world," the Andersen Consulting World Championship of Golf. The competition will be conducted on courses in the United States, Japan, England and Spain throughout 1995, with the champion to be crowned Dec. 31 at Grayhawk Golf Club in Scottsdale, AZ.

The event is sanctioned by all five of the world's major tours -- the PGA TOUR, the PGA European Tour, the Japan PGA Tour, the PGA Tour of Australasia and the FNB Tour in South Africa.

Eight players from each of four regions -- the United States, Europe, Japan and "the Rest of the World" -- comprise the 32-man field. Seven players from each region were invited based on the Sony World Rankings as of December 31, 1994. The eighth competitor from each region is a sponsor's invitation.

The four regional champions will compete in 18-hole semifinals on Dec. 30 at Grayhawk. The highest ranked semifinalist, based on the Sony World Rankings, will face the lowest ranked semifinalist in this round. No. 2 will meet No. 3.

A 36-hole final on Dec. 31 will determine the "World Champion," who will earn $1 million from a total purse of $3.65 million. The runner-up will receive $500,000. The semifinal losers will compete in an 18-hole third-place match on Dec. 31, with the winner earning $350,000 and the loser $300,000.

The schedule for matches is as follows:

Date	Round	Site
March 3-4	Japan -- 1st Round	Golden Palm Golf Club Kagoshima, Japan
April 10-11	U.S. & Rest of World -- 1st Rounds	Reynolds Plantation (Great Waters Course) Lake Oconee, GA
May 22-23	Europe -- 1st Round	La Moraleja Golf Club Madrid, Spain
June 26	Japan Championship	Cypress Golf Club Osaka, Japan
July 24-25	Europe & Rest of World Championships	The Oxfordshire Golf Club Thame, England
July 31- Aug. 1	U.S. Championship	Blackwolf Run (River Course) Kohler, WI
Dec. 30-31	World Semifinals & Final	Grayhawk Golf Club Scottsdale, AZ

Fifty-two hours of U.S. television coverage and more than 30 hours of international telecasts of the event are scheduled. ESPN will provide same-day, prime-time coverage of early-round matches and will televise the semifinals. ABC will provide live coverage of the championship match, as well as a two-hour highlight package leading into it.

NCAA CHAMPIONS (SINCE 1949)

Year	Winner
1949	Harvie Ward, North Carolina
1950	Fred Wampler, Purdue
1951	Tom Nieporte, Ohio State
1952	Jim Vickers, Oklahoma
1953	Earl Moeller, Oklahoma State
1954	Hillman Robbins, Memphis State
1955	Joe Campbell, Purdue
1956	Rick Jones, Ohio State
1957	Rex Baxter Jr. Houston
1958	Phil Rodgers, Houston
1959	Dick Crawford, Houston
1960	Dick Crawford, Houston
1961	Jack Nicklaus, Ohio State
1962	Kermit Zarley, Houston
1963	R.H. Sikes, Arkansas
1964	Terry Small, San Jose State
1965	Marty Fleckman, Houston
1966	Bob Murphy, Florida
1967	Hale Irwin, Colorado
1968	Grier Jones, Oklahoma State
1969	Bob Clark, Los Angeles State
1970	John Mahaffey, Houston
1971	Ben Crenshaw, Texas
1972	Ben Crenshaw, Texas
	Tom Kite, Texas
1973	Ben Crenshaw, Texas
1974	Curtis Strange, Wake Forest
1975	Jay Haas, Wake Forest
1976	Scott Simpson, USC
1977	Scott Simpson, USC
1978	David Edwards, Oklahoma State
1979	Gary Hallberg, Wake Forest
1980	Jay Don Blake, Utah State
1981	Ron Commans, USC
1982	Billy Ray Brown, Houston
1983	Jim Carter, Anzona State
1984	John Inman, North Carolina
1985	Clark Burroughs, Ohio State
1986	Scott Verplank, Oklahoma State
1987	Brian Watts, Oklahoma State
1988	E.J. Pfister, Oklahoma State
1989	Phil Mickelson, Arizona State
1990	Phil Mickelson, Arizona State
1991	Warren Schutte, Nevada-Las Vegas
1992	Phil Mickelson, Arizona State
1993	Todd Demsey, Arizona State
1994	Justin Leonard, Texas

U.S. AMATEUR CHAMPIONS (SINCE 1949)

Year	Match Play
1949	Charles R. Coe
1950	Sam Urzetta
1951	Billy Maxwell
1952	Jack Westland
1953	Gene A. Littler
1954	Arnold Palmer
1955	E. Harvie Ward, Jr.
1956	E. Harvie Ward, Jr.
1957	Hillman Robbins, Jr.
1958	Charles R. Coe
1959	Jack W. Nicklaus
1960	Deane R. Beman
1961	Jack W. Nicklaus
1962	Labron E. Harris Jr.
1963	Deane R. Beman
1964	William C. Campbell

Stroke Play

1965	Robert J. Murphy	291
1966	Gary Cowan	285
1967	Robert B. Dickson	285
1968	Bruce Fleisher	284
1969	Steven N. Melnyk	286
1970	Lanny Wadkins	*279
1971	Gary Cowan	280
1972	Vinny Giles	285

Match Play

1973	Craig Stadler
1974	Jerry Pate
1975	Fred Ridley
1976	Bill Sander
1977	John Fought
1978	John Cook
1979	Mark O'Meara
1980	Hal Sutton
1981	Nathaniel Crosby
1982	Jay Sigel
1983	Jay Sigel
1984	Scott Verplank
1985	Sam Randolph
1986	Buddy Alexander
1987	Bill Mayfair
1988	Eric Meeks
1989	Chris Patton
1990	Phil Mickelson
1991	Mitch Voges
1992	Justin Leonard
1993	John Harris
1994	Tiger Woods

U.S. PUBLIC LINKS CHAMPIONS (SINCE 1949)

Year	Match Play
1949	Kenneth J. Towns
1950	Stanley Bielat
1951	Dave Stanley
1952	Omer L. Bogan
1953	Ted Richards, Jr.
1954	Gene Andrews
1955	Sam D. Kocsis
1956	James H. Buxbaum
1957	Don Essig, III
1958	Daniel D. Sikes, Jr.
1959	William A Wright
1960	Verne Callison
1961	Richard H. Sikes
1962	Richard H. Sikes
1963	Robert Lunn
1964	William McDonald
1965	Arne Dokka
1966	Lamont Kaser

Stroke Play

1967	Verne Callison	287
1968	Gene Towry	292
1969	J. M. Jackson	292
1970	Robert Risch	293
1971	Fred Haney	290
1972	Bob Allard	285
1973	Stan Stopa	294
1974	Chas. Barenaba	290

Match Play

1975	Randy Barenaba
1976	Eddie Mudd
1977	Jerry Vidovic
1978	Dean Prince
1979	Dennis Walsh
1980	Jodie Mudd
1981	Jodie Mudd
1982	Billy Tuten
1983	Billy Tuten
1984	Bill Malley
1985	Jim Sorenson
1986	Bill Mayfair
1987	Kevin Johnson
1988	Ralph Howe
1989	Tim Hobby
1990	Mike Combs
1991	David Berganio, Jr.
1992	Warren Schutte
1993	David Berganio, Jr.
1994	Guy Yamamoto

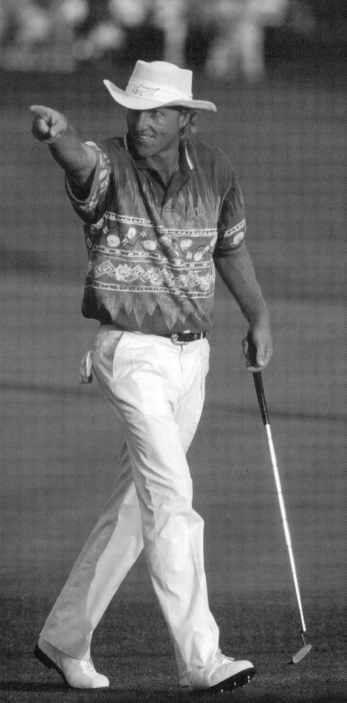

Greg Norman finished second on the 1994 money list with
$1,330,307, posting 11 top-10 finishes in 16 starts, including
a victory in THE PLAYERS Championship.

1994 PGA TOUR
PLAYER of the Year

TOURNAMENT HIGHLIGHTS:

- Won 1994 Honda Classic
- Won 1994 Southwestern Bell Colonial
- Won 1994 Motorola Western Open
- Won 1994 PGA Championship
- Won 1994 Bell Canadian Open
- *Also won the 1994 British Open*

- Earned $1,499,927, bettering his own record for single-season earnings.

- First player to earn $1 million in a season three consecutive years.

- First player to win British Open and PGA Championship titles in the same year since Walter Hagen in 1924.

NICK PRICE

PGA TOUR PLAYER OF THE YEAR	
1990	Wayne Levi
1991	Fred Couples
1992	Fred Couples
1993	Nick Price
1994	Nick Price

1994 PGA TOUR
ROOKIE of the Year

TOURNAMENT HIGHLIGHTS:

- Won U.S. Open in a playoff over Loren Roberts and Colin Montgomerie.

- U.S. Open title came the week after finishing runnerup to Lee Janzen in the Buick Classic.

- Also posted top-10 finishes at the Sprint International and the Masters Tournament.

- Set the PGA TOUR record for earnings by a rookie with $684,440.

ERNIE ELS

PGA TOUR ROOKIE OF THE YEAR	
1990	Robert Gamez
1991	John Daly
1992	Mark Carnevale
1993	Vijay Singh
1994	Ernie Els

Arnold Palmer Award

Awarded each year to the PGA TOUR's leading money winner.

1981	Tom Kite	$ 375,699	1988	Curtis Strange	$1,147,644
1982	Craig Stadler	$ 446,462	1989	Tom Kite	$1,395,278
1983	Hal Sutton	$ 426,668	1990	Greg Norman	$1,165,477
1984	Tom Watson	$ 476,260	1991	Corey Pavin	$ 979,430
1985	Curtis Strange	$ 542,321	1992	Fred Couples	$1,344,188
1986	Greg Norman	$ 653,296	1993	Nick Price	$1,478,557
1987	Curtis Strange	$ 925,941	1994	Nick Price	$1,499,927

Card Walker Award

The Card Walker Award is given annually by the PGA TOUR to the person or group who has made significant contributions to the support of Junior Golf.

1981	Mrs. Lou Smith
1982	Frank Emmet
1983	Jack Nicklaus
1984	Sally Carroll
1985	Don Padgett, Sr.
1986	Chi Chi Rodriguez
1987	James S. Kemper
1988	William V. Powers
1989	Selina Johnson
1990	Tucson Conquistadores
1991	American Junior Golf Association
1992	Bill Dickey
1993	Western Golf Association
1994	Fred Engh
1995	Ryder System, Inc.

PGA TOUR Charity of the Year Award

The PGA TOUR Charity of the Year Award was started in 1987. Charities are nominated by the American Golf Sponsors and voted on by the Tournament Policy Board.

1987	Egleston Hospital for Children	BellSouth Classic
1988	Siskin Memorial Foundation	Chattanooga Classic
1989	Bobby Benson Foundation	United Airlines Hawaiian Open
1990	Salesmanship Club	GTE Byron Nelson Classic
1991	Arrowhead Ranch for Boys	Hardee's Golf Classic
1992	United Health Services System	B.C. Open
1993	Chinquapin School	Shell Houston Open
1994	Louisiana Children's Research Center for Developing and Learning	Freeport-McMoRan Classic

Other Awards Won by PGA TOUR Golfers

Sporting News Man of the Year

1971	Lee Trevino

Sports Illustrated Sportsman of the Year

1960	Arnold Palmer
1964	Ken Venturi
1971	Lee Trevino
1978	Jack Nicklaus

Associated Press Male Athlete of the Year

1932	Gene Sarazen
1944	Byron Nelson
1945	Byron Nelson
1953	Ben Hogan
1971	Lee Trevino

VARDON TROPHY

The Vardon Trophy is awarded each year by the PGA of America to the PGA TOUR player who posts the season's best scoring average. The system was amended in 1988 to allow all TOUR members to compete for the prestigious award provided they have played in 60 rounds. The new system also uses an "adjusted" score for purposes of computing the scoring average. The adjusted score is computed based upon the average score of the field at each tournament. As a result, a player's adjusted score may be higher or lower than his actual score. For example, a player shoots 70 each day at a tournament while the field average was 73. His 280 total would then be adjusted to 268 since he actually played 12 shots better than the field did during the tournament. The Vardon Trophy is a bronze-colored plaque measuring 39" by 27".

Year	Winner	Average	Year	Winner	Average
1937	Harry Cooper	*500	1967	Arnold Palmer	70.18
1938	Sam Snead	520	1968	Billy Casper	69.82
1939	Byron Nelson	473	1969	Dave Hill	70.34
1940	Ben Hogan	423	1970	Lee Trevino	70.64
1941	Ben Hogan	494	1971	Lee Trevino	70.27
1942-			1972	Lee Trevino	70.89
1946	No Award-World War II		1973	Bruce Crampton	70.57
1947	Jimmy Demaret	69.90	1974	Lee Trevino	70.53
1948	Ben Hogan	69.30	1975	Bruce Crampton	70.51
1949	Sam Snead	69.37	1976	Don January	70.56
1950	Sam Snead	69.23	1977	Tom Watson	70.32
1951	Lloyd Mangrum	70.05	1978	Tom Watson	70.16
1952	Jack Burke	70.54	1979	Tom Watson	70.27
1953	Lloyd Mangrum	70.22	1980	Lee Trevino	69.73
1954	E. J. Harrison	70.41	1981	Tom Kite	69.80
1955	Sam Snead	69.86	1982	Tom Kite	70.21
1956	Cary Middlecoff	70.35	1983	Raymond Floyd	70.61
1957	Dow Finsterwald	70.30	1984	Calvin Peete	70.56
1958	Bob Rosburg	70.11	1985	Don Pooley	70.36
1959	Art Wall	70.35	1986	Scott Hoch	70.08
1960	Billy Casper	69.95	1987	Dan Pohl	70.25
1961	Arnold Palmer	69.85	1988	Chip Beck	69.46
1962	Arnold Palmer	70.27	1989	Greg Norman	69.49
1963	Billy Casper	70.58	1990	Greg Norman	69.10
1964	Arnold Palmer	70.01	1991	Fred Couples	69.59
1965	Billy Casper	70.85	1992	Fred Couples	69.38
1966	Billy Casper	70.27	1993	Nick Price	69.11
			1994	Greg Norman	68.81

*Point system used, 1937—'41.

PGA PLAYER OF THE YEAR AWARD

1948—Ben Hogan
1949—Sam Snead
1950—Ben Hogan
1951—Ben Hogan
1952—Julius Boros
1953—Ben Hogan
1954—Ed Furgol
1955—Doug Ford
1956—Jack Burke
1957—Dick Mayer
1958—Dow Finsterwald
1959—Art Wall
1960—Arnold Palmer
1961—Jerry Barber
1962—Arnold Palmer
1963—Julius Boros

1964—Ken Venturi
1965—Dave Marr
1966—Billy Casper
1967—Jack Nicklaus
1968—Not Awarded
1969—Orville Moody
1970—Billy Casper
1971—Lee Trevino
1972—Jack Nicklaus
1973—Jack Nicklaus
1974—Johnny Miller
1975—Jack Nicklaus
1976—Jack Nicklaus
1977—Tom Watson
1978—Tom Watson

1979—Tom Watson
1980—Tom Watson
1981—Bill Rogers
1982—Tom Watson
1983—Hal Sutton
1984—Tom Watson
1985—Lanny Wadkins
1986—Bob Tway
1987—Paul Azinger
1988—Curtis Strange
1989—Tom Kite
1990—Nick Faldo
1991—Corey Pavin
1992—Fred Couples
1993—Nick Price
1994—Nick Price

Each year the PGA of America honors the TOUR's leading player by presenting him with the PGA Player of the Year Award.

The award now is made on the basis of playing record for the year. Points are awarded on the following basis: 30 points to winner of Masters, U.S. Open, British Open, PGA Championship. 20 points to winner of THE PLAYERS Championship, NEC World Series of Golf. 10 points to winners of all other co-sponsored or approved events. Points also awarded to top 10 on the year's money list and top 10 on year's scoring average list (20 for first, 18 for second, 16 for third, etc. down to 2 for 10th).

PGA HALL OF FAME

Palm Beach Gardens, Florida

1940	Willie Anderson, Tommy Armour, Jim Barnes, Chick Evans, Walter Hagen, Bobby Jones, John McDermott, Francis Ouimet, Gene Sarazen, Alex Smith, Jerry Travers, Walter Travis.
1953	Ben Hogan, Byron Nelson, Sam Snead,
1954	Macdonald Smith
1955	Leo Diegel
1956	Craig Wood
1957	Denny Shute
1958	Horton Smith
1959	Harry Cooper, Jock Hutchison, Sr., Paul Runyan
1960	Mike Brady, Jimmy Demaret, Fred McLeod
1961	Johnny Farrell, Lawson Little, Henry Picard
1962	Dutch Harrison, Olin Dutra
1963	Ralph Guldahl, Johnny Revolta
1964	Lloyd Mangrum, Ed Dudley
1965	Vic Ghezzi
1966	Billy Burke
1967	Bobby Cruickshank
1968	Chick Harbert
1969	Chandler Harper
1974	Julius Boros, Cary Middlecoff
1975	Jack Burke, Jr., Doug Ford
1976	Babe Zaharias
1978	Patty Berg
1979	Roberto DeVicenzo
1980	Arnold Palmer
1982	Gene Littler, Billy Casper

PGA WORLD GOLF HALL OF FAME

Pinehurst, North Carolina

1974	Patty Berg, Walter Hagen, Ben Hogan, Robert T. Jones, Byron Nelson, Jack Nicklaus, Francis Ouimet, Arnold Palmer, Gary Player, Gene Sarazen, Sam Snead, Harry Vardon, Babe Zaharias
1975	Willie Anderson, Fred Corcoran, Joseph C. Dey, Chick Evans, Tom Morris, Jr., John H. Taylor, Glenna C. Vare, Joyce Wethered
1976	Tommy Armour, James Braid, Tom Morris Sr., Jerome Travers, Mickey Wright
1977	Bobby Locke, John Ball, Herb Graffis, Donald Ross
1978	Billy Casper, Harold Hilton, Dorothy Campbell, Herd Howe, Bing Crosby, Clifford Roberts
1979	Louise Suggs, Walter Travis
1980	Lawson Little, Henry Cotton
1981	Lee Trevino, Ralph Guldahl
1982	Julius Boros, Kathy Whitworth
1983	Bob Hope, Jimmy Demaret
1985	JoAnne Carner
1986	Cary Middlecoff
1987	Robert Trent Jones, Betsy Rawls
1988	Tom Watson, Peter Thomson, Bob Harlow
1989	Raymond Floyd, Nancy Lopez, Roberto De Vicenzo, Jim Barnes
1990	William C. Campbell, Paul Runyan, Gene Littler, Horton Smith
1992	Hale Irwin, Chi Chi Rodriguez, Richard Tufts, Harry Cooper

NOTE: Selected by the Golf Writers Association of America

Hale Irwin won his third MCI Heritage Classic
in 1994 and led the United States team to
victory in the inaugural Presidents Cup

PGA TOUR MARKETING PARTNERS

ANHEUSER-BUSCH

One of golf's most enduring corporate supporters, Anheuser-Busch, isone of the PGA TOUR's leading sponsors.

Through the years, Michelob, which is brewed by Anheuser-Busch, has sponsored thousands of local golf tournaments, a host of touring pros and a long list of professional tournaments.

Primary features of the Michelob/PGA TOUR relationship include Michelob as the "Official Sponsor of the PGA TOUR's 19th hole," a unique interactive display, and presenting sponsor for THE TOUR Championship, as well as media-driven national sweepstakes and extensive participation in ESPN's TOUR coverage.

In addition, O'Doul's TOUR program includes network television advertising, national point-of-sale promotions and tournament sampling opportunities.

O'Doul's is the official non-alcoholic beer of the PGA TOUR ans Senior PGA TOUR.

AT&T

AT&T has been the title sponsor of the AT&T Pebble Beach National Pro-Am since 1986. In addition to this successful sponsorship, AT&T has entered into an agreement as the "Official Telecommunications Company of the PGA TOUR and the Senior PGA TOUR." As part of this agreement, AT&T provides phones and video phones for player use in locker rooms at PGA TOUR and Senior PGA TOUR events. Players also are offered special rates on AT&T telecommunications equipment.

AT&T entertains its clients at PGA TOUR and Senior PGA TOUR events throughout the year, and is a major advertiser on PGA TOUR telecasts. Future involvement will include themed advertising and promotions.

BAYER ASPIRIN

Bayer Aspirin is the "Official Pain Reliever of the PGA TOUR and Senior PGA TOUR" and is provided to players via the Centinela Fitness Training Facilities. Bayer, a longtime industry leader for pain relief and prevention, conducts consumer sampling at a number of tournaments and advertises in such TOUR media products as *ON TOUR Magazine* and "Inside the Senior PGA TOUR."

BUICK

Buick Motor Division is a longtime marketing partner of the PGA TOUR. The relationship between the TOUR and Buick over the last 30 years has led to sponsorship of PGA TOUR tournaments across the country.

It all began with the Buick Open, now the PGA TOUR event with the longest continuing sponsorship. The tournament is played in Flint, Mich., Buick's "hometown." Each year, countless Buick employees use their vacation time to volunteer at the event, which they consider their own.

Buick's partnership with the PGA TOUR includes the sponsorship of four tournaments: the Buick Open (Flint, MI); Buick Southern Open (Callaway Gardens, GA); the Buick Invitational of California (San Diego, CA); and the Buick Classic (Rye, NY).

To enhance fans' awareness of Buick tournaments, the company has set up a nationwide sweepstakes that encourages fans to test drive and register to win a Buick. The company has said its golf-related promotions are the most successful it has ever run.

COCA-COLA

Coca-Cola is entering its fourth year of sponsorship as the "Official Soft Drink of the PGA TOUR." Coca-Cola Scoreboards will travel to 39 PGA TOUR tournaments in 1995, providing up-to-the-minute scores, weather warnings and other important information for golf fans.

The Coca-Cola classic Clinics, scheduled at 38 tournaments in 1995, provide an opportunity for children in the community to receive tips from PGA TOUR professionals. They also have a chance to win a "Coca-Cola classic Behind the Scenes VIP TOUR" of the tournament. The winner has an opportunity to meet some TOUR players and visit the media room, the Scoreboard trailer and the TV compound.

Coca-Cola utilizes its relationship with the PGA TOUR as an entertainment opportunity for its clients, as well as in promotional programs at retail. In 1995, 41 PGA TOUR tournaments will serve Coca-Cola products.

DELTA

Delta Air Lines is the "Official Airline of the PGA TOUR, Senior PGA TOUR and NIKE TOUR." Delta offers PGA TOUR players preferred rates on air travel and awards tournament winners with Frequent Flyer mileage. Delta is involved with over 65 tournaments on the three tours through advertising or hospitality.

Delta prints PGA TOUR, Senior PGA TOUR and NIKE TOUR schedules in its timetables and includes PGA TOUR stories in Sky Magazine. Delta rewards its most frequent flyers with Sweepstakes programs featuring a chance to win trips to TOUR events and pro-am spots.

IBM

In one of the most appropriate sports collaborations ever, IBM entered into an agreement with the PGA TOUR to develop the IBM Scoring System. This is an agreement which benefits everyone, from the players to the media to the television viewers to the spectators at each PGA TOUR event.

The IBM Scoring System is so fast that scoring updates are seen just seconds after a player completes a hole. Players and galleries on the course know where the field stands at all times. Remote computers keep fans informed at other locations, such as hospitality areas, host hotels, etc.

The PGA TOUR's agreement with IBM as the "Official Scoring System of the PGA TOUR" runs through 1998.

MERRILL LYNCH

Merrill Lynch sponsors the popular Merrill Lynch Shoot-Outs at PGA TOUR, Senior PGA TOUR and NIKE TOUR events. The 10-man, nine-hole elimination competitions culminate at year-end finals. The Shoot-Outs are crowd pleasers wherever they are played. ABC will televise the Shoot-Out Final for the PGA TOUR; ESPN will air the Senior PGA TOUR Shoot-Out final. Results from the 1994 Merrill Lynch Shoot-Out Series on the PGA TOUR can be found on page 389.

NATIONAL INTERRENT

National InterRent is the "Official Car Rental Company of the PGA TOUR and the Senior PGA TOUR." National offers TOUR players excellent rental car rates and other benefits, such as Emerald Club Membership. National also awards tournament winners on both tours with free use for a week of a full-size rental car in recognition of their achievements. National rental cars and vans are used at several PGA TOUR tournaments. The Emerald Club members benefit from the sponsorship through special offers outlined in Emerald Club newsletters.

ROYAL CARIBBEAN CRUISE LINE

Royal Caribbean is the "Official Cruise Line of the PGA TOUR." The company offers special Golf Ahoy! cruises along with special cruise rates for PGA TOUR members. In 1995, for the sixth consecutive year, the Royal Caribbean Classic will be played on Key Biscayne, FL as part of the Senior PGA TOUR.

SKYTEL

SkyTel, as the "Official Wireless Messaging Company of the PGA TOUR," supports the TOUR by providing SkyPagers for use in several areas of the TOUR. SkyTel also seeks to have pro-am guests and tournament volunteers use SkyPagers to help them communicate better throughout tournament week. SkyTel, whose products are targeted to the business traveler, is a natural partner when considering the nature of the TOUR's business.

Publications

BUSINESS WEEK

Once again in 1995, *Business Week* will publish two special supplements which deal exclusively with the PGA TOUR. In the spring, "The 1995 Senior TOUR Journal" will be published. "The Business of the PGA TOUR" will be published in midyear. *Business Week* also publishes *ON TOUR Magazine* for PGA TOUR Partners.

GOLF MAGAZINE

Golf Magazine covers events on the PGA TOUR in *TOUR Magazine*. This insert appears in the magazine's January issue and as a handout at most PGA TOUR events. *Golf Magazine* also produces a supplement which is distributed at NIKE TOUR events.

Leo McCullagh
Vice President,
Marketing

Tom Wade
Vice President,
Business Development

PGA TOUR PARTNERS

The PGA TOUR Partners Program, which Jack Nicklaus serves as chairman, gives golf fans an opportunity to become involved with the PGA TOUR, to learn more about the TOUR itself, its players, tournaments and benefitting charities.

The Partners Program, established in 1991, is designed to help golfers and golf fans get closer to the PGA TOUR. The program's objective is to make Partners feel like a valuable part of the TOUR, for the PGA TOUR is the people who support it. There were 87,000 Partnrs in 1994, an all-time high; the goal is 300,000 members within the next two years.

For an annual membership fee of $38, a Partner receives numerous benefits, including:

--The Official PGA TOUR Media Guide

--An annual subscription to ON TOUR Magazine

--A free ticket to the PGA TOUR event of his/her choice

--An opportunity to be part of the Partners Team Competition

The latter, according to the Partners themselves, is one of the most appreciated benefits. In the Team Competition, each Partner selects four players to represent him/her throughout the year. Money won by those players in each week's tournament determines the team's standing against all other Partners.

As a direct result, Partners around the country pore through their sports pages each Monday to see how their players did. The reason? The Partners Team Competition offers the chance to win a number of exciting prizes, with the Grand Prize being an all-expenses paid trip to THE TOUR Championship, replete with a berth in the Wednesday Pro-Am.

ON TOUR Magazine, rated as another particularly valuable benefit, is a monthly publication exclusively for Partners which goes behind the scenes of the PGA TOUR. It offers, among a wide variety of features, "up close and personal" articles about players, stories on the TOUR, golf tips, a monthly calendar of events, and items about "the real winners" (through charities supported by PGA TOUR events). The Partners Program, in fact, provides the funds the individual tournaments donate to charity through their own PGA TOUR Charity Team Competition.

PGA TOUR Partners Golf Classics allow Partners to travel to exciting golf destinations and play in TOUR-style tournaments on some of the finest resort courses: all in all, an excellent opportunity for Partners to play--at great value--courses the professionals play.

Research done in 1994 focused on how to improve the program. Among the suggestions: expand the Partners Classics to give members greater variety and more access to top courses.

Three tiers of membership also will be offered in 1995, and Senior PGA events will be included in the tournament pass aspect of the program. All of this is in keeping with improvements in customer service and fulfillment with new vendors.

The Partners Program is administered by the PGA TOUR Marketing Department under the direction of Tom Wade, Vice President, Consumer Marketing. Barry Hyde is Account Manager, Consumer Marketing.

For more information about the PGA TOUR Partners Program, the number to call is 1-800-545-9920.

MERRILL LYNCH SHOOT-OUT SERIES

A 10-man competition covering nine holes of play, the Merrill Lynch Shoot-Out Series, now in its eighth season, will be held at 18 different PGA TOUR events in 1995 with the weekly winners collecting $5,000 from the $15,100 purse.

What is a Shoot-Out? The format is easy to understand and a pleasure to watch. Ten players begin. On each hole, the player with the highest score is dropped from the field. If there is a tie, those players participate in a sudden-death playoff where a pitch shot, a chip or a long putt is executed to eliminate the player farthest from the hole.

Weekly Shoot-Outs: The 1995 Merrill Lynch Shoot-Out Series Competitions will be held on Tuesday of tournament week. The field for each Shoot-Out consists of that tournament's defending champion, the six leading money winners entered into that tournament and three sponsor selections.

Shoot-Out Championship: The field for the final competition consists of the top three money winners on the 1995 PGA TOUR Official Money List and seven sponsor selections. Ten players will vie for $500,000 in prize money, with $130,000 going to the winner. Corey Pavin won the title in 1994 at the Mid Ocean Club in Tucker's Town, Bermuda. The 1995 Merrill Lynch Shoot-Out Championship will return to the Mid Ocean Club.

1994 MERRILL LYNCH SHOOT-OUT WINNERS

AT&T Pebble Beach National Pro-Am	Chip Beck
Nissan Los Angeles Open	Chip Beck (2)
Bob Hope Chrysler Classic	Peter Jacobsen
THE PLAYERS Championship	Scott Hoch
Freeport-McMoRan Classic	Kirk Triplett
MCI Heritage Classic	Craig Stadler
Kmart Greater Greensboro Open	Mike Springer
Shell Houston Open	Andrew Magee
BellSouth Golf Classic	rained out
GTE Byron Nelson Golf Classic	Steve Lowery
Kemper Open	Duffy Waldorf
Federal Express St. Jude Classic	Jim Gallagher, Jr.
	Bill Glasson
	Scott Hoch (2)
	Curtis Strange
NEC World Series of Golf	Jeff Maggert
Greater Milwaukee Open	rained out
B.C. Open	Mike Heinen
Hardee's Golf Classic	John Huston
Walt Disney World/Oldsmobile Classic	Kenny Perry
Las Vegas Invitational	Steve Lowery (2)

1995 MERRILL LYNCH SHOOT-OUT SCHEDULE

AT&T Pebble Beach National Pro-Am	Jan.	31
Bob Hope Chrysler Classic	Feb.	14
Nissan Open	Feb.	21
THE PLAYERS Championship	Mar.	21
Freeport-McMoRan Classic	Mar.	28
MCI Classic	Apr.	11
Kmart Greater Greensboro Open	Apr.	18
Shell Houston Open	Apr.	25
BellSouth Classic	May	2
GTE Byron Nelson Classic	May	9
Kemper Open	June	6
FedEx St. Jude Classic	June	27
NEC World Series of Golf	Aug.	22
Greater Milwaukee Open	Aug.	29
B.C. Open	Sept.	12
Quad Cities Open	Sept.	19
Walt Disney World/Oldsmobile Classic	Oct.	3
Las Vegas Invitational	Oct.	10

CHAMPIONSHIP WINNERS

1987	Fuzzy Zoeller
1988	David Frost
1989	Chip Beck
1990	John Mahaffey
1991	Davis Love III
1992	Chip Beck
1993	Davis Love III
1994	Corey Pavin

1995 CHAMPIONSHIP PRIZE MONEY BREAKDOWN

1st	$130,000
2nd	80,000
3rd	55,000
4th	40,000
5th	35,000
6th	34,000
7th	33,000
8th	32,000
9th	31,000
10th	30,000

WEEKLY PRIZE MONEY BREAKDOWN

1st	$5,000
2nd	3,000
3rd	1,500
4th	1,100
5th	1,000
6th	900
7th	800
8th	700
9th	600
10th	500

CENTINELA FITNESS CENTER

The "Official Hospital of the PGA TOUR" since 1984, Centinela Hospital Medical Center in Inglewood, CA, again will sponsor the Centinela Hospital Fitness Center (CHFC) on TOUR in 1994.

One of the most popular innovations on the circuit, the CHFC is a mobile gymnasium that includes state-of-the-art exercise equipment, television, stereo, three treatment tables, various physical therapy modalities, and a full line of vitamins.

Staffed by qualified physical therapists, the CHFC travels to the vast majority of TOUR events across the country providing both rehabilitative and preventative care.

Through its first nine years on the TOUR, the Centinela Hospital Fitness Center has attracted the interest of virtually every player with at least 80 percent using the mobile unit on a regular basis. Housed in a 45-foot long trailer (expandable to 24' wide when parked), the Centinela Hospital Fitness Center enables TOUR pros to maintain peak levels of performance at absolutely no cost to the individual player.

According to Dr. Frank Jobe, Medical Director of the PGA TOUR and team physician to the Los Angeles Dodgers, "Centinela Hospital Medical Center provides each player with a personal physical conditioning program based on that individual's current level of conditioning." Dr. Jobe is assisted by Dr. Lewis Yocum, his associate and orthopedic consultant to the California Angels.

The CHFC has made its impact with many players finding the center and available technicians an invaluable aid to their success on the TOUR. In fact, many players have commented that they would have been unable to compete in some tournaments without the facility.

"If they had this setup several years ago," Fuzzy Zoeller said, "It might have saved me from having back surgery."

"If it wasn't for Centinela Hospital's Fitness Center," said Curtis Strange, "I wouldn't be here."

Centinela Hospital's Biomechanics Laboratory has done research and testing on professional golfers' swings and, based on the results, developed scientific exercise programs which are available through books and videotapes. These programs, designed by Dr. Jobe and Dr. Yocum, have helped countless golfers stretch their potential while minimizing their risk of injury. For more information, contact Centinela Hospital.

Bayer Aspirin supports the Centinela Hospital Fitness Training Centers by providing players with one of the leading pain-relievers on the market. Bayer also conducts consumer sampling at tournaments and explores new ways to provide better healthcare products for golfers.

The products contributed by each sponsor of the Centinela Hospital Fitness Training Centers have helped make the facility such a success that a similar Fitness Van was introduced on the Senior TOUR in late 1986.

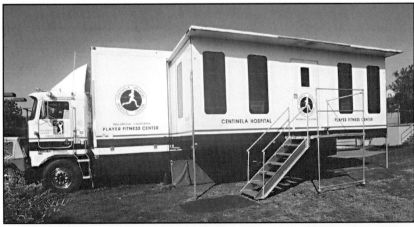

The Centinela Hospital Fitness Training Centers will be out on TOUR again in 1995.

PGA TOUR AND AGS DONATE RECORD $24.7 MILLION TO CHARITY IN 1994

PGA TOUR events produced a record contribution to charity of $24,701,631 in 1994.

"The announcement of a new charity record is a highlight of the season," said Commissioner Tim Finchem.

"This record is a tribute to our players, tournament sponsors and, of course the thousands of volunteers who make the PGA TOUR possible. This announcement is recognition of a lot of hard work and dedication."

Charity dollars raised by Senior PGA TOUR and NIKE TOUR events should push the PGA TOUR total for the year to more than $30 million.

The $24.7 million on the PGA TOUR tops the one-season record of $22.8 million raised for charity in 1993.

"The efforts put forth by all the volunteers and tournament sponsors continue to produce fantastic results, as evidenced by this new mark for charitable giving," said AGS President Tommy Wulff. "Hopefully, we will be able to build on these efforts and establish an even higher level in 1995."

Since the AGS began keeping records in 1977, contributions have increased each year except one. Charity dollars have grown significantly in this decade, with more than $109 million raised in the 1990s alone.

The overall contribution from PGA TOUR events now is in excess of $250 million since the first donation in 1938.

More than 900 charities benefit from PGA TOUR events across the United States and Canada.

A Brief History of TOUR Charitable Contributions

1938	First Contribution	$ 10,000	(Palm Beach Invitational)
1950	Contributions reach	$ 1,000,000	
1960	Contributions reach	$ 5,000,000	
1976	TOUR reaches	$10,000,000	
1977	AGS formed	$ 3,300,000	for year
1978		$ 4,300,000	"
1979	$20 million overall	$ 4,400,000	"
1980		$ 4,500,000	"
1981	$30 million overall	$ 6,800,000	"
1982		$ 7,200,000	"
1983		$ 7,800,000	"
1984	$50 million overall	$ 9,400,000	"
1985		$11,300,000	"
1986		$16,100,000	"
1987	$100 million overall	$17,600,000	"
1988	$125 million overall	$18,390,000	"
1989	$145 million overall	$19,779,000	"
1990	$165 million overall	$20,191,000	"
1991	$185 million overall	$19,534,000	"
1992	$200 million overall	$22,223,055	"
1993	$230 million overall	$22,752,137	"
1994	$250 million overall	$24,701,631	"

CHARITY is the leading winner on the **PGA TOUR**

FINAL 1994 PGA TOUR CHARITY TEAM COMPETITION STANDINGS

TOURNAMENT NAME	TOURNAMENT TOTAL	TOURNAMENT BONUS
1. WALT DISNEY WORLD/OLDSMOBILE CLASSIC	2,473,697	$100,000
2. BUICK OPEN	1,894,015	75,000
3. TOUR CHAMPIONSHIP	1,802,850	50,000
4. MOTOROLA WESTERN OPEN	1,794,418	40,000
5. THE PLAYERS CHAMPIONSHIP	1,747,060	35,000
6. UNITED AIRLINES HAWAIIAN OPEN	1,739,296	30,800
7. GTE BYRON NELSON CLASSIC	1,630,595	28,000
8. SOUTHWESTERN BELL COLONIAL	1,510,570	27,000
9. CANON GREATER HARTFORD OPEN	1,399,615	26,000
10. BUICK SOUTHERN OPEN	1,389,804	25,000
11. DEPOSIT GUARANTY GOLF CLASSIC	1,374,448	17,600
12. THE MEMORIAL TOURNAMENT	1,369,387	17,600
13. LINCOLN/MERCURY KAPALUA INTERNATIONAL	1,309,631	17,600
14. TEXAS OPEN	1,301,783	17,600
15. NEC WORLD SERIES OF GOLF	1,272,583	17,600
16. PHOENIX OPEN	1,252,240	17,600
17. BELL CANADIAN OPEN	1,208,779	17,600
18. AT&T PEBBLE BEACH NATIONAL PRO-AM	1,203,775	17,600
19. NISSAN LOS ANGELES OPEN	1,069,774	17,600
20. BELLSOUTH CLASSIC	1,035,779	17,600
21. MERCEDES CHAMPIONSHIPS	1,027,667	17,600
22. BUICK CLASSIC	1,017,445	17,600
23. NEW ENGLAND CLASSIC	955,321	17,600
24. BUICK INVITATIONAL OF CALIFORNIA	934,374	17,600
25. GREATER MILWAUKEE OPEN	913,949	17,600
26. ANHEUSER-BUSCH GOLF CLASSIC	901,874	17,600
27. B.C. OPEN	900,352	17,600
28. HONDA CLASSIC	897,224	17,600
29. HARDEE'S CLASSIC	887,628	17,600
30. THE SPRINT INTERNATIONAL	884,493	17,600
31. NORTHERN TELECOM OPEN	881,880	17,600
32. KMART GREATER GREENSBORO OPEN	873,953	17,600
33. SHELL HOUSTON OPEN	838,656	17,600
34. KEMPER OPEN	826,425	17,600
35. BOB HOPE CHRYSLER CLASSIC	824,235	17,600
36. FREEPORT-MCMORAN CLASSIC	749,565	17,600
37. FEDERAL EXPRESS ST. JUDE CLASSIC	719,651	17,600
38. JCPENNEY CLASSIC	681,423	17,600
39. MCI HERITAGE GOLF CLASSIC	670,557	17,600
40. NESTLE INVITATIONAL	618,771	17,600
41. LAS VEGAS INVITATIONAL	440,666	17,600
42. DORAL-RYDER OPEN	313,188	17,600
	Total	$1,000,000

1995 PGA TOUR CHARITY TEAM COMPETITION DRAFT

1. MERCEDES CHAMPIONSHIPS
1. Greg Norman
2. Duffy Waldorf
3. D.A. Weibring
4. Bart Bryant

2. LAS VEGAS INVITATIONAL
1. Fred Couples
2. Peter Jacobsen
3. Tom Purtzer
4. Tom Sieckmann

3. JCPENNEY CLASSIC
1. Nick Price
2. Chris DiMarco
3. Neal Lancaster
4. Jerry Haas

4. SPRINT INTERNATIONAL
1. Phil Mickelson
2. Ian Baker-Finch
3. Rocco Mediate
4. Richard Zokol

5. NISSAN OPEN
1. Ernie Els
2. Fulton Allem
3. Donnie Hammond
4. Harry Taylor

6. NEC WORLD SERIES OF GOLF
1. Corey Pavin
2. Clark Dennis
3. Scott Verplank
4. Bruce Fleisher

7. DEPOSIT GUARANTY GOLF CLASSIC
1. Nick Faldo
2. Brian Henninger
3. Mike Standly
4. Dick Mast

8. NESTLE INVITATIONAL
1. Scott Hoch
2. Dicky Pride
3. David Duval
4. Jerry Pate

9. MCI CLASSIC
1. Davis Love III
2. Mike Hulbert
3. Pat Bates
4. Ronnie Black

10. FEDEX ST. JUDE CLASSIC
1. Loren Roberts
2. Russ Cochran
3. Chris Perry
4. Jodie Mudd

11. KMART GREATER GREENSBORO OPEN
1. Fuzzy Zoeller
2. Guy Boros
3. David Feherty
4. TBA

12. BUICK CLASSIC
1. David Frost
2. Dave Stockton, Jr.
3. Greg Kraft
4. Mark Wiebe

13. TEXAS OPEN
1. Tom Kite
2. Gil Morgan
3. David Ogrin
4. David Peoples

14. BUICK INVITATIONAL OF CALIFORNIA
1. Tom Lehman
2. Fred Funk
3. Ted Tryba
4. Steve Brodie

15. LINCOLN-MERCURY KAPALUA INTERNATIONAL
1. Bob Estes
2. Nolan Henke
3. Bob Lohr
4. Marco Dawson

16. QUAD CITIES OPEN
1. Mark McCumber
2. Keith Clearwater
3. Paul Goydos
4. Robert Wrenn

17. BELLSOUTH CLASSIC
1. Payne Stewart
2. Jim McGovern
3. Michael Bradley
4. Yoshinori Mizumaki

18. GREATER MILWAUKEE OPEN
1. Jim Gallagher, Jr.
2. Dan Forsman
3. Brandell Chamblee
4. John Inman

19. BOB HOPE CHRYSLER CLASSIC
1. Steve Elkington
2. Dave Barr
3. Mike Sullivan
4. Keith Fergus

20. BELL CANADIAN OPEN
1. Mark Calcavecchia
2. Jesper Parnevik
3. Robin Freeman
4. Tray Tyner

21. AT&T PEBBLE BEACH NATIONAL PRO-AM
1. Mike Springer
2. Scott Simpson
3. Wayne Levi
4. Tim Loustalot

22. MEMORIAL TOURNAMENT
1. Hale Irwin
2. Brett Ogle
3. Gene Sauers
4. Raymond Floyd

23. NEW ENGLAND CLASSIC
1. Brad Faxon
2. Lennie Clements
3. Dennis Paulson
4. Mike Donald

24. SHELL HOUSTON OPEN
1. Jeff Maggert
2. John Daly
3. Lanny Wadkins
4. Don Pooley

25. B.C. OPEN
1. Paul Azinger
2. Mark McNulty
3. Billy Mayfair
4. Joel Edwards

26. NORTHERN TELECOM OPEN
1. Bill Glasson
2. Jim Furyk
3. Joey Sindelar
4. John Adams

27. HONDA CLASSIC
1. Jay Haas
2. Steve Pate
3. Gary Hallberg
4. John Morse

28. DORAL-RYDER OPEN
1. John Huston
2. Robert Gamez
3. Scott Gump
4. Paul Stankowski

29. ANHEUSER-BUSCH GOLF CLASSIC
1. Curtis Strange
2. Tom Watson
3. Dillard Pruitt
4. Ken Green

30. KEMPER OPEN
1. Hal Sutton
2. Jay Don Blake
3. Brian Kamm
4. Eduardo Romero

31. PHOENIX OPEN
1. Andrew Magee
2. Larry Mize
3. Jim Carter
4. Bob Burns

32. FREEPORT-MCMORAN CLASSIC
1. Ben Crenshaw
2. Mike Heinen
3. Steve Jones
4. Emlyn Aubrey

33. BUICK SOUTHERN OPEN
1. Steve Lowery
2. Steve Rintoul
3. Bobby Wadkins
4. Jim Thorpe

34. CANON GREATER HARTFORD OPEN
1. Lee Janzen
2. Jeff Sluman
3. Tommy Armour III
4. Kelly Gibson

35. COLONIAL
1. Mark Brooks
2. Bruce Lietzke
3. Mike Reid
4. Wayne Grady

36. GTE BYRON NELSON CLASSIC
1. Kenny Perry
2. Justin Leonard
3. Mark Carnevale
4. Curt Byrum

37. UNITED AIRLINES HAWAIIAN OPEN
1. Brad Bryant
2. Kirk Triplett
3. Bob Gilder
4. Ed Humenik

38. THE PLAYERS CHAMPIONSHIP
1. Rick Fehr
2. Blaine McCallister
3. Skip Kendall
4. Tim Simpson

39. MOTOROLA WESTERN OPEN
1. Chip Beck
2. Billy Andrade
3. Grant Waite
4. Dudley Hart

40. THE TOUR CHAMPIONSHIP
1. David Edwards
2. Glen Day
3. Doug Tewell
4. Woody Austin

41. BUICK OPEN
1. Vijay Singh
2. Craig Stadler
3. Jay Delsing
4. Howard Twitty

42. WALT DISNEY WORLD/ OLDSMOBILE CLASSIC
1. John Cook
2. Mark O'Meara
3. Brian Claar
4. Bob Tway

43. FRANKLIN FUNDS SHARK SHOOTOUT
1. Craig Parry
2. Steve Stricker
3. John Wilson
4. Joe Ozaki

TOURNAMENT PLAYERS CLUBS

An original concept of the PGA TOUR, Tournament Players Clubs have gone from a dream to a network that now encompasses 14 courses in 10 states and, with the addition of International TPCs, three foreign countries.

It was the TOUR's view that the spectator had been left out in golf course design throughout the years. When it came time for the PGA TOUR to build its own course, the opportunity presented itself to design a course that not only challenged the players but also allowed spectators to see the action as never before.

It's called "Stadium Golf"-- and once you've viewed a tournament on a Stadium Golf Course, you'll understand why the network has grown in such a short period of time.

Spectator mounds abound that afford fans unrestricted views, whether on tee shots, fairway shots or on the greens. In fact, the 18th hole at the original TPC at Sawgrass can accommodate crowds of some 30,000 people--all with a clear view of the action. You won't see any periscopes at an event on a Tournament Players Club golf course.

The network began in 1980 with the TPC at Sawgrass, which annually is host to THE PLAYERS Championship, and quickly grew into the present number of 14. All TPCs are designed to play host PGA TOUR or Senior PGA TOUR events, and to date the clubs have been designed by some of the top architects in the business--Pete Dye, Arnold Palmer, Arthur Hills, Jay Morrish, Bob Von Hagge and Jack Nicklaus, to name just a few.

In addition, one of the things that adds a bit of spice to all TPCs is that a PGA TOUR player (or, in some cases, two) is assigned to serve as consultant to the designer. To date, Ed Sneed, Tom Weiskopf, Fuzzy Zoeller, Hubert Green, Craig Stadler, Ben Crenshaw, Al Geiberger and Chi Chi Rodriguez have been among those lending their expertise to the TPC Network.

In reality a nationwide country club, a premium membership at one TPC affords the member a chance to play at any of the other clubs across the country and an opportunity to view the greatest players in the world in action on his own course once a year.

Since the Tournament Players Club at Sawgrass opened, the TPC Network has now truly become "the best set of clubs in America."

Vernon Kelly
President, PGA TOUR
Golf Course Properties

Joe Walser
Chief Operating Officer,
PGA TOUR Golf
Course Properties

Pete Davison
Vice President, PGA
TOUR Golf Course
Properties

Mike Bodney
Director of
International Affairs

Cal Roth
National Director of
Superintendents

Chris Wilkerson
Director of Real Estate,
PGA TOUR Golf
Course Properties

Mike Diffenderffer
National Director of
Membership/
Marketing

Chris Gray
Design Administrator,
Design Services, Inc.

TPC Network

Club	Architect	Consultant	Host
1. **TPC at Sawgrass** Ponte Vedra, FL	Pete Dye	--	THE PLAYERS Championship
2. **TPC at Eagle Trace** Coral Springs, FL	Arthur Hills	--	--
3. **TPC at River Highlands** Cromwell, CT	Pete Dye/ Robert Weed	Howard Twitty/ Roger Maltbie	Canon Greater Hartford Open
4. **TPC at Prestancia** Sarasota, FL	Ron Garl	Mike Souchak	
5. **TPC at Avenel** Potomac, MD	Ault, Clark & Associates	Ed Sneed	Kemper Open
6. **TPC of Scottsdale** Scottsdale, AZ	Jay Morrish/ Tom Weiskopf	Jim Colbert/ Howard Twitty	Phoenix Open
7. **TPC at Piper Glen** Charlotte, NC	Arnold Palmer	--	PaineWebber Invitational
8. **TPC at Southwind** Memphis, TN	Ron Prichard	Hubert Green/ Fuzzy Zoeller	FedEx St. Jude Classic
9. **TPC of Michigan** Dearborn, MI	Jack Nicklaus	--	FORD SENIOR PLAYERS Championship
10. **TPC of Tampa Bay** Tampa, FL	Robert Weed	Chi Chi Rodriguez	GTE Suncoast Classic
11. **TPC at Summerlin** Las Vegas, NV	Robert Weed	Fuzzy Zoeller	Las Vegas Invitational & Las Vegas Senior Classic

Tournament Players Courses (Licensed Facilities)

Club	Architect	Consultant	Host
1. **TPC at The Woodlands** The Woodlands, TX	Bob Von Hagge	--	Shell Houston Open
2. **TPC at Las Colinas** Irving, TX	Jay Morrish	Ben Crenshaw/ Byron Nelson	GTE Byron Nelson Classic
3. **TPC at PGA West** La Quinta, CA	Pete Dye	--	--

Future TPCs-(Announced, Planned or Under Construction)

Club	Architect	Consultant	Host
TPC at Heron Bay Coral Springs, FL	Mark McCumber	--	Honda Classic
TPC at Snoqualmie Ridge King County, WA	Jack Nicklaus		TBA
TPC at Summerlin (Resort Course) Las Vegas, NV	Robert Weed	Raymond Floyd	--

International TPCs

ITPC of Batoh
Tochigi Prefecture, Japan

ITPC of Mito
Ibaraki Prefecture, Japan

ITPC Mission Hills
Shenzhen, China

ITPC Mission Hills
Kanchanaburi, Thailand

ITPC Mission Hills
Khao Yai, Thailand

PGA TOUR PRODUCTIONS

PGA TOUR Productions is the television and video production company of the PGA TOUR.

Most fans know PGA TOUR Productions by its award-winning "Inside the PGA TOUR" and "Inside the Senior PGA TOUR" programs which are broadcast each week on ESPN. "Inside the PGA TOUR" celebrated its 10th anniversary in 1994.

Productions is a diverse company delivering a wide range of services and talents to an international clientele. Their film capacity has expanded to include production of the TOUR'S PSA campaign, as well as commercials and travel pieces. Additional programming includes made for TV events such as the Merrill Lynch Shoot-Out and United Van Lines Aces Championship, as well as tournament and pro-am highlight programs, corporate promotional and sales videos and home videos.

PGA TOUR Productions also serves its worldwide clientele by producing, in conjunction with the networks, international live telecasts of PGA TOUR events.

Along with the latest in television and communication technology, PGA TOUR Productions houses the world's most extensive library of golf footage. In the near future, PGA TOUR Productions will move its headquarters to the World Golf Village complex that will be located in St. Johns County, FL.

The PGA TOUR Productions van covers TOUR events across the country.

FINANCE AND LEGAL

Ed Moorhouse
Executive Vice President/
General Counsel

Charles L. Zink
Executive Vice President/
Chief Financial Officer,
PGA TOUR

Helen Atter
Vice President/
Human Resources

Jeanne Lightcap
Controller
PGA TOUR, Inc.

Andrea King
Treasury Manager

Linda Altman
Director/
Human Resources

Jim Triola
Associate General Counsel

Jerry Hawks
Director/
Information Services

Steve Winsor
Director of Finances/
PGA TOUR
Golf Course Properties

WORLD GOLF VILLAGE

Florida's First Coast, home of the PGA TOUR since 1979, will soon welcome one of the most exciting projects in the history of the game of golf: the World Golf Village.

Situated on Interstate 95 in St. Johns County, just 22 miles south of Jacksonville and eight miles northwest of St. Augustine, the World Golf Village will offer year-round golf and resort facilities, not to mention the new 75,000 square-foot Golf Hall of Fame. Additional amenities will include a major hotel and conference center, a clubhouse and 36 holes of golf, a PGA TOUR Golf Academy, the new home for PGA TOUR Productions, and a sports medicine branch of

Ruffin Beckwith
Executive
Director

the Mayo Clinic. The first phase of the Village is scheduled to open in late 1996.

The exhibits in the new Golf Hall of Fame are being designed by Ralph Applebaum Associates of New York, which has received considerable acclaim for creating the exhibits at the United States Memorial Holocaust Museum. Their work is being overseen by an Advisory Board including representatives of all the major golf organizations, among them the PGA TOUR, LPGA, PGA of America, USGA, Augusta National, Royal & Ancient, National Golf Foundation and the PGA Tours of Europe, South Africa and Australasia.

"This endeavor represents the first time that all the major entities in the game have united behind a project of this magnitude," says World Golf Village Executive Director Ruffin Beckwith. "We believe it is destined to become something very special for the game of golf, for its great players, and for all its fans and supporters."

The Hall of Fame itself will combine traditional exhibits on the history of the game with a new generation of interactive and technology based exhibits. "The philosophy behind the design is to make the experience appealing to kids as well as adults, and novices as well as avid golfers," says Beckwith. "Hopefully every visitor will leave the facility feeling they have been entertained as well as enlightened."

The World Golf Village is part of a 6,300-acre development called St. Johns, which will also include 7,200 residences and more than six million square feet of office, commercial and industrial space.

INTERNATIONAL GOLF MUSEUM AND HALL OF FAME

MEDIA REGULATIONS

GENERAL REGULATIONS

The following regulations are to be followed by *all* members of the media:

1. An armband is necessary to walk inside the gallery ropes. Remain not more than an arm's length from the ropes, so as to blend into the gallery and appear to be a part of the gallery at all times.
2. Players are not to be distracted during play. Do not interview players or ask them to pose for photographs during their rounds.
3. Do not interview players or ask them to pose for photographs during their practice sessions before a round, except by prior arrangement with the player.
4. If an interview is to be conducted in the practice areas, either the range or the putting green, it must be done by prior arrangement with the player, up against the ropes and not in the middle of the areas where it could be distracting to other players.
5. Do not disturb players at their 18th green and/or scoring tent until after they have checked, signed and returned their scorecards. Media are not allowed in the scoring tent.

WORKING PRESS REGULATIONS

To avoid embarrassment to you and distraction to the contestants:

1. Do not walk or stand in playing areas.
2, Follow directions of marshals and other officials.
3. Do not interview during play. The leading players each day -- and others requested -- will be interviewed following their rounds in the Press Room interview area.

TAPE RECORDER REGULATIONS

1. All tape recorder work should be done in the proximity of the Press Room and/or clubhouse.
2. Tape recorders are not permitted in the locker room.
3. Tape recorders are not permitted within the playing area of the golf course unless written permission has been granted from PGA TOUR.

WEATHER DELAY GUIDELINES

1. During weather delay situations, no one other than players and essential staff will be permitted in the locker room. This means the media are not permitted in the locker room in such situations. However, whenever possible, arrangements will be made to provide players for interviews during such situations.
2. Fully accredited members of the news media will be welcome in the locker room at all other times to carry out their assigned duties. (Note: Cameras and tape recorders are not permitted in the locker room.)

PHOTOGRAPHY REGULATIONS

Photo credentials will be issued only to personnel on assignment from recognized and accredited publications or news services. Requests for credentials must be made by the appropriate news agency, not by the photographer.

Photographic likenesses of PGA TOUR, Senior PGA TOUR and NIKE TOUR players may be used only for legitimate newspaper and magazine coverage of the events in which they are competing.

Commercial exploitation of these likenesses without written consent of the players and PGA TOUR is prohibited.

A limited number of photo armbands (or photo bibs), which permit the wearer access inside the gallery ropes, may be issued. Photographers and photographic assistants who do not have armbands or bibs must stay outside the gallery ropes. Photographic assistants will not be issued armbands.

Cameras may be used only by accredited media representatives who have been assigned photo credentials, and such use is subject to the following conditions:

1. Photographers with photo armbands must stay within one arm's length of the ropes at all times. Photographers without armbands are not permitted inside the ropes at any time.
2. The use of golf carts is prohibited at all times.
3. Photographers must not position themselves in the line of play. If requested to move by a player, his caddie or an official, the photographer will do so without delay or discussion.
4. No photograph shall be taken until a player has completed his stroke.
5. Players should not be asked to pose during a round.
6. Noise-free equipment must be used at all times.
7. Cameras are not permitted in the scoring tent or in the locker rooms.

The Photographer shall indemnify, defend and hold the Tournament and the PGA TOUR and their respective officers, agents, representatives, successors and assigns harmless from and against any and all expenses, lawsuits, damages, costs and liabilities (including reasonable attorney's fees and expenses) incurred by, arising from, or in connection with (1) the unauthorized use of photographs taken by the Photographer, whether such unauthorized use is by the Photographer, the company designating the Photographer to use the credential on its behalf, or some third party to whom the photographs are distributed: (2) any injuries resulting from acts or omissions by the Photographer or some third party to whom the Photographer directly or indirectly distributed the material; (3) any cameras, wires, cables or other equipment brought to the premises by the Photographer, or (4) the use of any photographs of any matter other than coverage of the Tournament.

PRIZE MONEY DISTRIBUTION CHARTS

PRO-AM CHARTS

$5,000 — Individual & team

POSITION	PRIZE
1	$500
2	400
3	350
4	300
5	250
6	200
7	155
8	130
9	115
10	100

$7,500 — Individual & team

POSITION	PRIZE
1	$750
2	600
3	525
4	450
5	375
6	300
7	225
8	200
9	175
10	150

$10,000 — Individual & team

POSITION	PRIZE
1	$1,000
2	800
3	700
4	600
5	500
6	400
7	310
8	260
9	230
10	200

POSITION	$700,000 PRIZE	$900,000 PRIZE	$1,000,000 PRIZE	$1,100,000 PRIZE	$1,200,000 PRIZE
1	$126,000	$162,000	$180,000	$198,000	$216,000
2	75,600	97,200	108,000	118,800	129,600
3	47,600	61,200	68,000	74,800	81,600
4	33,600	43,200	48,000	52,800	57,600
5	28,000	36,000	40,000	44,000	48,000
6	25,200	32,400	36,000	39,600	43,200
7	23,450	30,150	33,500	36,850	40,200
8	21,700	27,900	31,000	34,100	37,200
9	20,300	26,100	29,000	31,900	34,800
10	18,900	24,300	27,000	29,700	32,400
11	17,500	22,500	25,000	27,500	30,000
12	16,100	20,700	23,000	25,300	27,600
13	14,700	18,900	21,000	23,100	25,200
14	13,300	17,100	19,000	20,900	22,800
15	12,600	16,200	18,000	19,800	21,600
16	11,900	15,300	17,000	18,700	20,400
17	11,200	14,400	16,000	17,600	19,200
18	10,500	13,500	15,000	16,500	18,000
19	9,800	12,600	14,000	15,400	16,800
20	9,100	11,700	13,000	14,300	15,600
21	8,400	10,800	12,000	13,200	14,400
22	7,840	10,080	11,200	12,320	13,440
23	7,280	9,360	10,400	11,440	12,480
24	6,720	8,640	9,600	10,560	11,520
25	6,160	7,920	8,800	9,680	10,560
26	5,600	7,200	8,000	8,800	9,600
27	5,390	6,930	7,700	8,470	9,240
28	5,180	6,660	7,400	8,140	8,880
29	4,970	6,390	7,100	7,810	8,520
30	4,760	6,120	6,800	7,480	8,160
31	4,550	5,850	6,500	7,150	7,800
32	4,340	5,580	6,200	6,820	7,440
33	4,130	5,310	5,900	6,490	7,080
34	3,955	5,085	5,650	6,215	6,780
35	3,780	4,860	5,400	5,940	6,480
36	3,605	4,635	5,150	5,665	6,180
37	3,430	4,410	4,900	5,390	5,880
38	3,290	4,230	4,700	5,170	5,640
39	3,150	4,050	4,500	4,950	5,400
40	3,010	3,870	4,300	4,730	5,160
41	2,870	3,690	4,100	4,510	4,920
42	2,730	3,510	3,900	4,290	4,680
43	2,590	3,330	3,700	4,070	4,440
44	2,450	3,150	3,500	3,850	4,200
45	2,310	2,970	3,300	3,630	3,960
46	2,170	2,790	3,100	3,410	3,720
47	2,030	2,610	2,900	3,190	3,480
48	1,918	2,466	2,740	3,014	3,288
49	1,820	2,340	2,600	2,816	3,120
50	1,764	2,268	2,520	2,772	3,024
51	1,722	2,214	2,460	2,706	2,952
52	1,680	2,160	2,400	2,640	2,880
53	1,652	2,124	2,360	2,596	2,832
54	1,624	2,088	2,320	2,552	2,784
55	1,610	2,070	2,300	2,530	2,760
56	1,596	2,052	2,280	2,508	2,736
57	1,582	2,034	2,260	2,486	2,712
58	1,568	2,016	2,240	2,464	2,688
59	1,554	1,998	2,220	2,442	2,664
60	1,540	1,980	2,200	2,420	2,640
61	1,526	1,962	2,180	2,398	2,616
62	1,512	1,944	2,160	2,376	2,592
63	1,498	1,926	2,140	2,354	2,568
64	1,484	1,908	2,120	2,332	2,544
65	1,470	1,890	2,100	2,310	2,520
66	1,456	1,872	2,080	2,288	2,495
67	1,442	1,854	2,060	2,266	2,472
68	1,428	1,836	2,040	2,244	2,448
69	1,414	1,818	2,020	2,222	2,424
70	1,400	1,800	2,000	2,200	2,400

PRIZE MONEY DISTRIBUTION CHARTS

POSITION	$1,250,000 PRIZE	$1,300,000 PRIZE	$1,400,000 PRIZE	$1,500,000 PRIZE	$1,700,000 PRIZE	$2,500,000 PRIZE
1	$225,000	$234,000	$252,000	$270,000	$306,000	$450,000
2	35,000	140,400	151,200	162,000	183,600	270,000
3	85,000	88,400	95,200	102,000	115,600	170,000
4	60,000	62,400	67,200	72,000	81,600	120,000
5	50,000	52,000	56,000	60,000	68,000	100,000
6	45,000	46,800	50,400	54,000	61,200	90,000
7	41,875	43,550	46,900	50,250	56,950	83,750
8	38,750	40,300	43,400	46,500	52,700	77,500
9	36,250	37,700	40,600	43,500	49,300	72,500
10	33,750	35,100	37,800	40,500	45,900	67,500
11	31,250	32,500	35,000	37,500	42,500	62,500
12	28,750	29,900	32,200	34,500	39,100	57,500
13	26,250	27,300	29,400	31,500	35,700	52,500
14	23,750	24,700	26,600	28,500	32,300	47,500
15	22,500	23,400	25,200	27,000	30,600	45,000
16	21,250	22,100	23,800	25,500	28,900	42,500
17	20,000	20,800	22,400	24,000	27,200	40,000
18	18,750	19,500	21,000	22,500	25,500	37,500
19	17,500	18,200	19,600	21,000	23,800	35,000
20	16,250	16,900	18,200	19,500	22,100	32,500
21	15,000	15,600	16,800	18,000	20,400	30,000
22	14,000	14,560	15,680	16,800	19,040	28,000
23	13,000	13,520	14,560	15,600	17,680	26,000
24	12,000	12,480	13,440	14,400	16,320	24,000
25	11,000	11,440	12,320	13,200	14,960	22,000
26	10,000	10,400	11,200	12,000	13,600	20,000
27	9,625	10,010	10,785	11,550	13,090	19,250
28	9,250	9,620	10,360	11,100	12,580	18,500
29	8,875	9,230	9,940	10,650	12,070	17,750
30	8,500	8,840	9,520	10,200	11,560	17,000
31	8,125	8,450	9,100	9,750	11,050	16,250
32	7,750	8,060	8,680	9,300	10,540	15,500
33	7,375	7,670	8,260	8,850	10,030	14,750
34	7,065	7,345	7,910	8,475	9,605	14,125
35	6,750	7,020	7,560	8,100	9,180	13,500
36	6,435	6,695	7,210	7,725	8,755	12,875
37	6,125	6,370	6,860	7,350	8,330	12,250
38	5,875	6,110	6,580	7,050	7,990	11,750
39	5,625	5,850	6,300	6,750	7,650	11,250
40	5,375	5,590	6,020	6,450	7,310	10,750
41	5,125	5,330	5,740	6,150	6,970	10,250
42	4,875	5,070	5,460	5,850	6,630	9,750
43	4,625	4,810	5,180	5,550	6,290	9,250
44	4,375	4,550	4,900	5,250	5,950	8,750
45	4,125	4,290	4,620	4,950	5,610	8,250
46	3,875	4,030	4,340	4,650	5,270	7,750
47	3,625	3,770	4,060	4,350	4,930	7,250
48	3,425	3,562	3,836	4,110	4,658	6,850
49	3,250	3,380	3,640	3,900	4,420	6,500
50	3,150	3,276	3,528	3,780	4,284	6,300
51	3,075	3,198	3,444	3,690	4,182	6,150
52	3,000	3,120	3,360	3,600	4,080	6,000
53	2,950	3,068	3,304	3,540	4,012	5,900
54	2,900	3,016	3,248	3,480	3,944	5,800
55	2,875	2,990	3,220	3,450	3,910	5,750
56	2,850	2,964	3,192	3,420	3,876	5,700
57	2,825	2,938	3,164	3,390	3,842	5,650
58	2,800	2,912	3,136	3,360	3,808	5,600
59	2,775	2,886	3,108	3,330	3,774	5,550
60	2,750	2,860	3,080	3,300	3,740	5,500
61	2,725	2,834	3,052	3,270	3,706	5,450
62	2,700	2,808	3,024	3,240	3,672	5,400
63	2,675	2,782	2,996	3,210	3,638	5,350
64	2,650	2,756	2,968	3,180	3,604	5,300
65	2,625	2,730	2,940	3,150	3,570	5,250
66	2,600	2,704	2,912	3,120	3,536	5,200
67	2,575	2,678	2,884	3,090	3,502	5,150
68	2,550	2,652	2,856	3,060	3,468	5,100
69	2,525	2,626	2,828	3,030	3,434	5,050
70	2,500	2,600	2,800	3,000	3,400	5,000

SONY RANKING

Originally formulated in 1986, and approved by the PGA TOUR's Tournament Policy Board since 1990, the Sony Ranking is a computerized system which provides a reference source to the relative performances of the world's leading professional golfers.

The Sony Ranking is issued every Monday, following the completion of the previous week's tournaments from around the world. The official events from all the world's golf tours are taken into account. Points are awarded according to the players' finishing positions and the number and ranking of the players in the respective tournament fields.

The Masters Tournament, United States Open, British Open, PGA Championship and THE PLAYERS Championship are rated separately to reflect the higher quality of the events and the stronger fields participating.

The Sony Ranking is based on a three-year "rolling" period weighted in favor of the more recent results. Points accumulated in the most recent 52-week period are multiplied by four, points earned over the previous 52-week period are doubled and points from the first 52-week period are simply added to the total.

Each player is then ranked according to his average points per tournament, which is determined by dividing his total number of points by the number of tournaments he has played over that three-year period. There is a minimum requirement of 20 tournaments for each 52-week period.

For example, if a player were in 32 tournaments in the most recent 52 weeks, 15 tournaments in the previous 52 weeks, and eight tournaments in the first 52 weeks, his divisor would be 72 (32 plus 20 plus 20). A player who was in 32 tournaments in each of the three 52-week periods would have a divisor of 96 (32 plus 32 plus 32).

The winners of the Masters, U.S. Open, British Open and PGA Championship are awarded 50 points (x4) and the winner of THE PLAYERS Championship is awarded 40 points (x4), which also is the most points possible to be earned from winning any other tournament in the world. The winner of a tournament with a strong field probably would receive approximately 25-30 points (x4).

Minimum points for the winners of official tour events have been set at six points for Asia and South Africa, eight points for Australia/New Zealand and Japan, and 10 points for Europe and the PGA TOUR. In addition, the PGA Championship in Europe has a minimum of 32 points (x4) for the winner, and the Open Championships of Australia and Japan have a minimum of 16 points (x4) for the winner.

Points are reduced proportionally for tournaments curtailed for 36 or 54 holes because of inclement weather or other reasons.

The Sony Ranking Advisory Committee, and an international panel which includes a representative from the PGA TOUR, meets periodically to review and monitor the Sony Ranking system in order to recommend refinements or modifications for the consideration of the Championship Committee of the Royal and Ancient Golf Club of St. Andrews, the sanctioning body of the Sony Ranking.

The Sony Ranking is available each week at PGA TOUR sites. The top 20 as of Dec. 5, 1994, follows.

POS.	PLAYER	AVERAGE	POS.	PLAYER	AVERAGE
1.	Nick Price	21.39	11.	David Frost	10.07
2.	Greg Norman	20.22	12.	Fuzzy Zoeller	9.75
3.	Bernhard Langer	15.99	13.	Tom Kite	9.19
4.	Nick Faldo	15.62	14.	Vijay Singh	8.93
5.	Jose M. Olazabal	15.24	15.	Seve Ballesteros	8.81
6.	Fred Couples	14.16	16.	Mark McNulty	8.76
7.	Ernie Els	14.16	17.	Tom Lehman	8.42
8.	Colin Montgomerie	12.30	18.	Ian Woosnam	8.37
9.	Corey Pavin	10.99	19.	Phil Mickelson	7.51
10.	Masashi Ozaki	10.76	20.	Loren Roberts	7.46

COMPLETE SCHEDULES

1995	PGA TOUR	SENIOR PGA TOUR	NIKE TOUR
Jan. 5-8	Mercedes Championships	Open	Open
12-15	United Airlines Hawaiian Open	Senior Tournament of Champions	Open
19-22	Northern Telecom Open	Open	Open
26-29	Phoenix Open	+Senior Skins Game	Open
Feb. 2-5	AT&T Pebble Beach National Pro-Am	Royal Caribbean Classic	Open
9-12	Buick Invitational of California	The IntelliNet Challenge	Open
16-19	Bob Hope Chrysler Classic	GTE Suncoast Classic	Open
23-26	Nissan Open	+Chrysler Cup	NIKE San Jose Open
March 2-5	Doral-Ryder Open	FHP Health Care Classic	NIKE Inland Empire Open
9-12	Honda Classic	SBC Dominion Seniors/+Senior Slam	Open
16-19	Nestle Invitational	Toshiba Senior Classic	NIKE Monterrey Open
23-26	THE PLAYERS Championship	+American Express Grandslam	NIKE Louisiana Open
30-2	Freeport-McMoRan Classic	The Tradition	NIKE Pensacola Classic
April 6-9	*The Masters	Open	NIKE Mississippi Gulf Coast Classic
13-16	MCI Classic	*PGA Seniors Championship	NIKE Tallahassee Classic
20-23	Kmart Greater Greensboro Open	+Liberty Mutual Legends of Golf	NIKE Shreveport Open
27-30	Shell Houston Open	Las Vegas Senior Classic	NIKE Alabama Classic
May 4-7	BellSouth Classic	PaineWebber Invitational	NIKE South Carolina Classic
11-14	GTE Byron Nelson Classic	Cadillac NFL Golf Classic	NIKE Central Georgia Open
18-21	Buick Classic	Bell Atlantic Classic	NIKE Knoxville Open
25-28	Colonial	Quicksilver Classic	NIKE Greater Greenville Classic
June 1-4	Memorial Tournament	Bruno's Memorial Classic	NIKE Dominion Open
8-11	Kemper Open	BellSouth Senior Classic at Opryland	NIKE Miami Valley Open
15-18	*U.S. Open	Dallas Reunion Pro-Am	NIKE Cleveland Open
22-25	Canon Greater Hartford Open	Nationwide Championship	NIKE Carolina Classic
29-2	FedEx St. Jude Classic	*U.S. Senior Open	NIKE Philadelphia Open
July 6-9	Motorola Western Open	Kroger Senior Classic	Open
13-16	Anheuser-Busch Golf Classic	FORD SENIOR PLAYERS Championship	NIKE Buffalo Classic
20-23	Deposit Guaranty Golf Classic / *British Open	First of America Classic	NIKE Gateway Classic
27-30	The New England Classic	Ameritech Senior Open	NIKE Wichita Open
Aug. 3-6	Buick Open	VFW Senior Championship	NIKE Dakota Dunes Open
10-13	*PGA Championship	Burnet Senior Classic	NIKE Ozarks Open
17-20	The Sprint International	Northville Long Island Classic	NIKE Permian Basin Open
24-27	NEC World Series of Golf	Bank of Boston Senior Golf Classic	NIKE Texarkana Open
31-3	Greater Milwaukee Open	Franklin Quest Championship	Open
Sept. 7-10	Bell Canadian Open	GTE Northwest Classic	NIKE Utah Classic (54 holes)
14-17	B.C. Open	Brickyard Crossing Championship	NIKE Tri-Cities Open (54 holes)
21-24	Quad Cities Open /+*The Ryder Cup	Bank One Classic	NIKE Boise Open (54 holes)
28-1	Buick Southern Open	Vantage Championship	NIKE Sonoma County Open
Oct. 5-8	Walt Disney World/Oldsmobile Classic	The Transamerica	Open
12-15	Las Vegas Invitational	Raley's Senior Gold Rush	Open
19-22	Texas Open	Ralphs Senior Classic	NIKE TOUR Championship
26-29	THE TOUR Championship	Hyatt Regency Maui Kaanapali Classic	
Nov. 2-5	+Lincoln-Mercury Kapalua International	Emerald Coast Classic	
9-12	+The World Cup of Golf	SENIOR TOUR Championship	
16-19	+Franklin Funds Shark Shootout	Open	
23-26	+The Skins Game	Open	
Dec. 30-3	+JCPenney Classic	Open	
7-10	+Diners Club Matches	+*Diners Club Matches	
30-31	+Andersen Consulting WCOG		

* non-PGA TOUR co-sponsored events + Unofficial Event

405

INDEX